The Development of Ethics, Volume III

The Development of Ethics

A Historical and Critical Study

Volume III: From Kant to Rawls

TERENCE IRWIN

OXFORD

UNIVERSITY PRESS

OXFORD

UNIVERSITY PRESS

Great Clarendon Street, Oxford OX2 6DP

Oxford University Press is a department of the University of Oxford.
It furthers the University's objective of excellence in research, scholarship,
and education by publishing worldwide in

Oxford New York

Auckland Cape Town Dar es Salaam Hong Kong Karachi
Kuala Lumpur Madrid Melbourne Mexico City Nairobi
New Delhi Shanghai Taipei Toronto

With offices in

Argentina Austria Brazil Chile Czech Republic France Greece
Guatemala Hungary Italy Japan Poland Portugal Singapore
South Korea Switzerland Thailand Turkey Ukraine Vietnam

Oxford is a registered trade mark of Oxford University Press
in the UK and in certain other countries

Published in the United States
by Oxford University Press Inc., New York

British Library Cataloguing in Publication Data

Data available

Library of Congress Cataloging in Publication Data

Data available

Typeset by Laserwords Private Limited, Chennai, India
Printed in Great Britain
on acid-free paper by
CPI Antony Rowe, Chippenham, Wiltshire

ISBN 978–0–19–957178–9

1 3 5 7 9 10 8 6 4 2

PREFATORY NOTE

This is the third of three volumes. The division into volumes is not meant to be thematically significant, and so the third volume simply begins where the second left off. The numeration of the sections continues from the second volume. References to §§1–422 and to §§423–893 refer to the first two volumes. The preface, dedication, and introduction to the first volume belong equally to the other two. In particular, the introduction explains the aims, scope, and limits of the book. The bibliography at the end of this volume lists the works cited in all three volumes.

All three volumes have benefited from the careful copy-editing of Virginia Williams. Among the helpful comments and advice by readers for the Press, I can gratefully acknowledge by name the remarks of Thomas Hurka, David McNaughton, and Allen Wood.

Faculty of Philosophy
University of Oxford
July, 2009

SUMMARY CONTENTS

CONTENTS

Contents

ABBREVIATIONS

This list includes only the most frequently used abbreviations, and those that might puzzle a reader. I have tried to cite primary texts from sources that will be fairly readily available.

Greek and Latin texts appearing in the OCT, BT, and Loeb series are listed with a reference to the relevant series, but without further details.

I have mentioned only a few of the available translations and editions.

Acronyms are normally used for the titles of books, journals, and collections. Short titles are used for articles and essays.

Page references include 'p.' only in cases where it might avoid ambiguity.

A page number with a letter (e.g., 'Reid, *EAP* 755 H') usually indicates the relevant edition.

Ac. = Cicero, *Academica*
ACPQ = *American Catholic Philosophical Quarterly*
AJP = *Australasian Journal of Philosophy*
AP = *Ancient Philosophy*
APQ = *American Philosophical Quarterly*
Aquinas, *in EN* (etc.) = Aquinas' commentaries on Aristotle and on Biblical books.
Arr. = Epicurus, ed. Arrighetti
Articles, see English Articles
AV = Bible (1611)
BCP = *Book of Common Prayer*
BF = Aquinas, Blackfriars edn.
BT = Bibliotheca Teubneriana. Greek and Latin texts
BT = Bibliotheca Teubneriana. Greek and Latin texts. Leipzig: Teubner (later Stuttgart: Teubner and Stuttgart: K. G. Saur)
CAG = Commentaria in Aristotelem Graeca
CD = Augustine, *De Civitate Dei*
Cic. = Cicero
CSEL = *Corpus Scriptorum Ecclesiasticorum Latinorum*
CT = Cambridge Translation of Kant (CUP)
CUAP = Catholic University of America Press (Washington, DC)
CUP = Cambridge University Press (Cambridge, London, New York)
CW = *Collected Works*
D or Denz. = Denziger, *Enchiridion Symbolorum*
DK = Diels-Kranz, *Fragmente der Vorsokratiker*
DL = Diogenes Laertius
DM = Suarez, *Disputationes Metaphysicae*

DTC = *Dictionnaire de Théologie Catholique*

E = *Ethics*

EK = Poseidonius, *Fragments*, ed. Edelstein and Kidd

EN = Aristotle, *Ethica Nicomachea (Nicomachean Ethics)*

ET = English Translation

F. = Cicero, *De Finibus*

Fat. = Alexander, *De Fato*, or Cicero, *De Fato*

Fin. = Cicero, *De Finibus*

FS = *Franciscan Studies*

G = Kant, *Grundlegung (Groundwork)*

H = Hutton, edn. of Cudworth; or Hoadly, edn. of Clarke; or Hamilton, edn. of Reid

HJ = *Historical Journal*

HPQ = *History of Philosophy Quarterly*

HS = *Hume Studies*

HUP = Harvard University Press (Cambridge, Mass.)

IPM (or *I*) = Hume, *Inquiry concerning the Principles of Morals*

JHI = *Journal of the History of Ideas*

JHP = *Journal of the History of Philosophy*

JP = *Journal of Philosophy*

KS = *Kant-Studien*

L = Aquinas, Leonine edn.

L = Hobbes, *Leviathan*

Leg. = Suarez, *De Legibus*

Loeb = Loeb Classical Library (Cambridge MA: Harvard University Press, and London: Heinemann)

LS = Long and Sedley, *The Hellenistic Philosophers*

LXX, see Bible, Septuaginta

M = Aquinas, Marietti edns.

M = Sextus Empiricus, *Adversus Mathematicos*

M = *Mind*

Mal. = Aquinas, *De Malo*

MdS = Kant, *Metaphysik der Sitten*

ME = Sidgwick, *Methods of Ethics*

NP = Plutarch, *Non posse suaviter vivere secundum Epicurum*

NRSV, see Bible. New Revised Standard Version

OCT Oxford Classical Texts (Scriptorum Classicorum Bibliotheca Oxoniensis). Greek and Latin texts (OUP)

Off. = Cicero, *De Officiis*

OO = *Opera Omnia,* various authors

OO = Scotus, *Opera Omnia*, ed. Wadding

OP = Scotus, *Opera Philosophica*

OSAP = *Oxford Studies in Ancient Philosophy*

OT = Ockham, *Opera Theologica*

OUP = Oxford University Press, including Clarendon Press (Oxford, London, New York)

P = Aquinas, Parma edn.

P = Sextus Empiricus, *Pyrrhoneae Hypotyposes*

PAS = *Proceedings of the Aristotelian Society*

PBA = *Proceedings of the British Academy*

PBACAP = *Proceedings of the Boston Area Colloquium in Ancient Philosophy*

PG = *Patrologiae Graecae Cursus Completus*, ed. Migne. Greek texts of early Christian writers

Phil. = *Philosophy*

PHP = Galen, *De Placitis Hippocratis et Platonis*

Phr. = *Phronesis*

PhS = *Philosophical Studies*

PL = *Patrologiae Latinae Cursus Completus*, ed. Migne. Latin texts of early Christian writers

Plu. = Plutarch

PPA = *Philosophy and Public Affairs*

PQ = *Philosophical Quarterly*

PR = *Philosophical Review*

PS = *Political Studies*

PUP = Princeton University Press (Princeton)

QM = Scotus, *Quaestiones . . . in Metaphysica*

R = Raphael, ed., *British Moralists* (cited by section)

RIP = *Revue Internationale de Philosophie*

RKP = Routledge; or Routledge and Kegan Paul (London)

RM = Raphael and Macfie (see Smith, *TMS*)

RM = *Review of Metaphysics*

RTAM = *Recherches de théologie ancienne et médiévale*

SB = Selby-Bigge, ed., *British Moralists* (cited by section)

Sent = *Sententiae* or *Scriptum super Sententiis* (various authors)

SG = Aquinas, *Summa Contra Gentiles*

SJP = *Southern Journal of Philosophy*

SPAS = *Proceedings of the Aristotelian Society, Supplementary Volume*

SR = Plutarch, *De Stoicorum Repugnantiis*

SR = *Socraticorum Reliquiae*, ed. Giannantoni

ST = Aquinas, *Summa Theologiae*

Stob. = Stobaeus

SVF = *Stoicorum Veterum Fragmenta*, ed. von Arnim

Sx = Sextus Empiricus

T = Hume, *Treatise of Human Nature*

TD = Cicero, *Tusculan Disputations*

TDNT = *Theological Dictionary of the New Testament*, ed. Kittel

U = Usener, *Epicurea*

UBS, see *Greek New Testament*

UCP = University of California Press (Berkeley and Los Angeles)

V = Scotus, *Opera Omnia*, Vatican edn.
Ver = Aquinas, *De Veritate*
VM = Plutarch, *De Virtute Morali*
Vulg., see Bible
W = *Duns Scotus on the Will and Morality*, ed. Wolter

66

KANT: PRACTICAL LAWS

894. Strategy in Theoretical and Practical Philosophy

Kant's attitude to rationalist intuitionism and sentimentalism in ethics may be compared with his attitude to rationalism and empiricism in metaphysics and epistemology. In the *First Critique*, he agrees with rationalists against empiricists in believing that there are true non-empirical principles in addition to the truths grasped by experience. But he does not simply assert that these are innate principles, or that they are grasped by rational intuition.[1] He argues that they are true and non-empirical. In his view, we must recognize their truth and their non-empirical character if we admit any empirical knowledge, or even admit some basic truths about self-consciousness. If he is right, we must reject empiricism if we believe some elementary truths that an empiricist must believe. Kant tries to do something similar in his moral philosophy. He wants to display the rational necessity of the moral point of view, to those who accept moral judgments, or even any plausible conception of rational agency.

He argues, therefore, in two different directions, which he calls 'regressive' (or 'analytic') and 'progressive' (or 'synthetic').[2] The regressive method argues from common-sense convictions about morality and moral reasons, to an account of the sort of agent and the sort of will that can be moved by such reasons. The progressive method begins from claims about rational agency—the sorts of agents that we take ourselves to be, and the sorts of reasons that concern us. It argues from these claims to an account of the practical principles that we have reason to accept. These two different directions of argument should agree in their conclusions. On the one hand, the kind of agent who is presupposed by morality ought to be one whom we can reasonably believe to exist. On the other hand, the principles that a rational agent has reason to accept ought to include recognizably moral principles.

---

[1] Kant criticizes innatism at *KrV* B167–8. I follow convention in citing Kant by the pages of the Akademie edition, or (for *KrV*) the pages of the original German editions. Most English versions, including CT, give the relevant page numbers in the margins. My quotations mostly follow Beck or CT.

[2] The *G* argues in the first direction, *KpV* in the second. See Beck, *CKCPR* 52. The two directions of argument are clearly marked in §5 and §6 of *KpV*, ch. 1, 28–9. Problem 1 is: Granted something about morality, find the sort of will that is determined by it alone. Problem 2 is: Granted a free will, find the law that alone is competent to determine it necessarily.

The two central concepts that Kant relies on are those of morality and of freedom, which he connects closely with rational agency. Through the moral law we discover the principles that move a will if there is any free will; but we still need some further argument to show that the kind of free will postulated by the moral law is possible.[3]

We might reasonably compare Kant's two directions of argument with those that Aristotle distinguishes; one begins from what is 'more knowable to us' and proceeds towards the principles that are 'more knowable by nature'.[4] The principles are 'more knowable by nature' because they capture the real explanatory and justificatory relations between the ordinary convictions we begin with and the less accessible truths that underlie these convictions. A progressive argument setting out from the principles known 'by nature' ought not to take the truth of our moral convictions for granted, but ought to justify our conviction of their truth by further principles. In the *First Critique*, Kant distinguishes a question of fact from a question of right (quid iuris), and takes the second question to require an answer giving a 'deduction' that constitutes a justification.[5] Similar questions seem to be relevant to morality. We find an 'apparent contradiction between the mechanism of nature and freedom' (*KpV* 97). If we could go no further, we would have to conclude that our moral convictions lead us to believe something that we have good reason to reject.

In Kant's view, however, the conception of freedom we reach through morality is also reasonable in its own right, and therefore supports the rationality of our moral beliefs. To this extent he offers a 'deduction' for practical reason. He claims that our moral beliefs are the foundation of our belief in freedom, and our belief in freedom is the foundation of our moral beliefs. These two claims are consistent, and indeed support each other, if they refer to different types of foundation. We will need to return to these questions in our examination of Kant's claims about freedom.

895. Kant and Rationalism

The successes and failures of ethical rationalism help to clarify Kant's argument. Price and Reid object to the sentimentalist account of moral judgments. They argue that our common understanding of moral judgments treats them as rational judgments, and not as reports or expressions of our feelings of approval. But they do not explain as clearly what is rational about moral judgments, or how their rationality can be shown.[6]

The rationalists fail us partly because they rely so strongly on intuition. The bare claim that basic moral principles are rational intuitions does not answer doubts about whether morality has a rational basis. We might reasonably hope for some account of the rational aspect of moral principles. This hope might turn out to be misguided. Perhaps we must accept some rational intuitions without further defence; why should we be less willing to accept them in ethics than elsewhere? Price and Reid give this answer to critics of intuitions. To assess this answer, we need to face two epistemological issues: (1) Should we appeal to

---

[3] *KpV* 4–5, quoted in §939.   [4] See §67. Paton, *CI* 29, compares Aristotle and Kant.
[5] See *KrV* A84/B116. *KpV* 46–50 marks an apparent disanalogy with practical reason.
[6] See Hutcheson's reply to Burnet, §655.

intuition as a source of our knowledge of basic principles? (2) Is it especially plausible or implausible to appeal to it in ethics?

Kant's *First Critique* offers an alternative to intuition as the source of our knowledge of basic principles. Instead of simply asserting that (e.g.) events are connected by causal relations, he argues that this connexion is necessary for the possibility of experience. Our experience and its presuppositions make it reasonable, in Kant's view, to accept principles that rationalists simply present to us without defence or explanation. It is worth seeing whether Kant offers a similar alternative to intuitionism in ethics.

Not all intuitionists, or sympathizers with intuitionism, simply appeal to intuition. Butler and Reid argue that self-love is a rational principle because it expresses my conception of myself as a whole temporally extended agent. Their account of the rationality of the moral point of view is less satisfactory; Butler sketches an argument for the rationality of conscience, claiming that conscience expresses our nature as rational agents in relation to other rational agents. We might reasonably expect a defender of the rationalist position to develop Butler's argument.

An intuitionist might argue that these arguments do not avoid intuitionism; perhaps they simply explain why we must accept the basic intuitions that we accept. Alternatively, one might argue that in offering these arguments to explain our alleged intuitions, we really show that they are not intuitions after all. Intuitions fit a foundationalist epistemology; for they neither require nor allow further justification. In trying to connect the prudential or the moral outlook with further facts about agency, we seem to offer a holist defence of prudence or morality. We need to consider these epistemological issues to grasp the relation between Kantian and intuitionist conceptions of moral principles.

896. Kant and Sentimentalism

Some of Kant's objections to sentimentalism are closely related to those already raised by the rationalists. Balguy attacks Hutcheson's position on the ground that 'virtue appears in it to be of an arbitrary and positive nature; as entirely depending upon instincts, that might originally have been otherwise'.[7] Kant agrees with the form of argument (derived from Cudworth) that evaluates specific theories about the nature of moral properties by comparing them with our views about the immutability of morality. Hutcheson agrees with Cudworth and Balguy in believing that moral properties are not arbitrary and positive, but have a firmer basis in nature; hence he tries to show that his sentimentalism does not introduce an unwelcome degree of mutability. Hume takes a different view of the rationalist objection about mutability. He believes that rationalists are right to allege that the mutability that they criticize follows from the truth of a sentimentalist view, but he denies that this constitutes an objection to sentimentalism; sentimentalists, in his view, must simply acknowledge the sort of mutability that the rationalists allege against them.[8]

In the *First Critique*, Kant argues that Hume's opponents have failed to learn from him. They have been content to assert that Hume is wrong about causation, but they have not

---

[7] Quoted in §660.   [8] Cf. Hume, §785.

tried to show where he is wrong, and what we can learn from him about the status of the principles that he questions. The fruitful and stimulating influence of Hume's sceptical questions has not been adequately appreciated.[9]

Sentimentalism raises parallel questions in moral philosophy.[10] One might argue that the degree of mutability implied by sentimentalist theories clashes with our ordinary moral convictions. But this answer does not refute Hume. He might be persuaded that it clashes with them more than he allows in his own works. But he might answer that ordinary views are mistaken, because the facts about moral sentiments imply the mutability that he recognizes. Kant does not discuss the sceptical tendency of Hume's theory. This may be partly because Hume does not regard himself as a sceptic about morality, and partly because Kant knows of sentimentalism mainly through Hutcheson's non-sceptical presentation of it.[11] But it is worth seeing how far Kant recognizes or answers the sceptical tendencies that Balguy and Price see in sentimentalism. He should show that sentimentalism gives an inadequate account of our moral judgments, and that we have reason to treat our moral judgments as true rather than adopt the sceptical attitude that follows from sentimentalism.

Sentimentalism, as Hutcheson and Hume conceive it, is not simply an account of moral judgment and moral properties. It is also an account of practical reason in general, and of the features, or alleged features, of the world that we grasp in practical reasoning. Sentimentalist claims about reason and passion apply no less to prudential than to moral thinking. To grasp the extent of Kant's disagreement with sentimentalists, we need to consider whether he rejects their account of practical reason and motivation in general, or only their account of moral reason and motivation. A similar question can be raised about the *First Critique*. We might at first sight suppose that Kant simply criticizes the empiricists' view of a priori knowledge, and leaves their view of empirical knowledge untouched; but the progress of the argument shows that he attacks the empiricist conception of empirical knowledge as well. Though Kant does not formulate the issue in exactly parallel terms in his moral philosophy, similar questions may be raised.

897. Kant and Naturalism

If Kant rejects both the ungrounded intuitions of Clarke and Price and the mutability resulting from sentimentalism, we might expect him to consider the position that we have called 'traditional naturalism'. Though Butler and Reid are sympathetic to some aspects of rationalist intuitionism, their position, in contrast to Clarke's and Price's, is not entirely

---

[9] See *KrV* B19–20; *Prol.* 258–9.

[10] Kant knows Hume's *Inquiries*, and probably some of the *Treatise*. But in his ethics, in contrast to *KrV*, he does not show acquaintance with specific claims and arguments of Hume's. The British moralist he refers to most often is Hutcheson; and so we can use his views on Hutcheson to infer his views on Hume. There is no reason to believe that he was acquainted with Butler's *Sermons*, or with Balguy and Price. See Beck, *CKCPR* 41n, 101. On Kant and Hutcheson see Schneewind, *IA* 501–2. Warda, *IKB* 45–56, lists among Kant's books German translations of works of Hutcheson and the Latin version of Cudworth's *TIS*. Kant also possessed copies of Aristotle, of Cicero's *De Officiis*, and of Seneca.

[11] Kant might not get a radically different impression of sentimentalism if he knew Hume mainly through the *Second Inquiry*. On Kant's relation to British moralists see Schilpp, *KPE* 31–3, 47–54, 60–1, 75–7; Ward, *DKVE*, ch. 3. Henrich, 'Hutcheson', discusses the different stages of Kant's engagement with Hutcheson.

intuitionist. They try to connect an account of morality with an account of human nature. Butler tries to defend conscience through an account of human nature that recognizes the role of superior principles. In appealing to human nature, Butler follows a traditional strategy for explaining and defending the moral point of view. The doctrine of the ancient moralists is maintained by Aquinas and Suarez in their identification of moral rightness with fitness to rational nature. This is the position that Butler defends in his normative naturalism.[12]

Kant returns, in one respect, to traditional naturalism. He rejects the immediacy of rightness, as Clarke tries to explain it. In his view, right action is fitting for a rational agent; we cannot see the rightness of an action by inspecting the action in itself, but we must see it in relation to the rational agent who does the action. In recognizing this relational and contextual aspect of rightness, Kant is closer to Butler and to Suarez than to Clarke.

On another point, however, he abandons naturalism. He argues that we cannot explain or defend morality through an account of human nature; naturalism tries to rest morality on 'anthropology' (G 389, 410). His explicit objections, however, are not aimed directly at traditional naturalism, but at Humean naturalism. He does not discuss the normative version of naturalism that the Greek moralists, Aquinas, and Butler all accept. Perhaps he agrees with Wollaston and Hume who, despite their sharp disagreements on the nature of morality, agree that a normative conception of nature has no role in an account of morality. Butler argues convincingly that Wollaston's objections do not refute traditional normative naturalism; and Hume's further objections to Butler and his predecessors are not compelling. We might reasonably ask, then, whether Kant has better reasons than Hume's or Wollaston's.

We may be able to grasp his attitude to traditional naturalism from his discussion of Leibniz and Wolff. He takes their position to be a form of perfectionism, and though he criticizes them, he does not accuse them of resting morality on mere anthropology. They are partly inspired by traditional naturalism, but they develop it in distinctive ways. We may ask whether Kant's criticisms apply to special features of their position or can be generalized so as to apply to the Aristotelian views elaborated by Aquinas and Suarez. If his objections do not refute traditional naturalism, is it a serious rival to Kant's position? Or are the two positions compatible?[13]

Whatever Kant says, it is not always clear that he rejects normative naturalism. Sometimes he simply seems to replace fitness to rational nature with fitness to rational beings. He seems to disagree, therefore, with traditional naturalism only in denying that the rational aspect of rational beings is a feature of their nature. We may wonder whether he is entitled to draw the line between the natural and the non-natural where he does. Clarification of these issues should make it easier to see where disputes arise between Kant and traditional naturalism, and whether his answer to them is better than a traditional naturalist answer.

898. Meta-Ethical Consequences of Kant's Strategy

In the Analytic of the *First Critique*, Kant defends the 'objective validity' of our claims to knowledge of an objective world, against sceptics who argue that our assumptions about

---

[12] On normative naturalism see §716.   [13] On Leibniz see §588. On perfectionism see §§937, 992.

objectivity are unjustified. Kant argues that the truth of these assumptions is necessary for the possibility of experience; for any possible experience must include the relevant belief in objects, cause and effect, and so on.

This form of argument is closely connected with Kant's claim that knowledge is limited to appearances, and does not extend to things in themselves. This transcendental idealist claim means at least that we cannot claim any knowledge of things that goes beyond appropriate inferences (as Kant understands them) from our sense-experience, and that we cannot know about aspects of things that are unconnected (as Kant understands 'connexion') with our sense-experience.[14] These are epistemological constraints on the sorts of facts and properties we can know. But does Kant also intend these constraints to limit the kind of thing we can know? Does he intend to confine our knowledge to what consists in or is constructed from our appearances (understood as states of consciousness) and to deny us any knowledge of things or properties that exist independently of our experiencing them? If he intends this further limit, his answer to scepticism may well appear to concede a crucial part of the sceptic's position.

Kant's moral theory raises a similar question. Clarke and Price affirm the objectivity of moral properties, whereas Hutcheson and Hume deny it. The rationalists' commitment to objectivity seems to require an unacceptable form of intuitionism. Apart from our alleged moral convictions, it may seem difficult to believe that eternal fitnesses are real features of the world, and difficult to see how we can know such things; the kinds of properties that the rationalists introduce seem to be unconnected with any properties that we recognize on other grounds. If rationalists tell us that this is simply how things are, that moral properties are sui generis, and that we know them by intuition, we may be dissatisfied. We may look for some holist argument that would give us some further reason for believing in objective moral properties accessible to rational judgment.[15]

Kant's conception of the basis of our moral knowledge raises a question about whether he means to defend objectivity or to replace it. He argues that we have a priori knowledge of moral properties; our knowledge rests on necessary features of rational and moral agents. We might say (perhaps exaggerating the parallel with the *First Critique*) that some moral facts are necessary for the possibility of our experience of ourselves as moral agents.[16] But then we might ask whether these necessary features of our experience tell us about objective moral facts, or simply about our experience. The question about Kant's realism or anti-realism in the *First Critique* returns when we consider his practical philosophy.

This comparison with the *First Critique* needs to consider the differences that Kant sees between theoretical and practical philosophy. Since moral beliefs are not suitably connected to our empirical knowledge, they cannot be about appearances; hence, if they are true about anything, they must be true about things in themselves. But in that case must they not give us knowledge of things in themselves, contrary to the *First Critique*?

Our views about the meta-ethical implications of Kant's views depend on specific claims about his ethical arguments, and on more general claims about the connexion between

---

[14] For the principle that what causally explains a phenomenon is a phenomenon see *KrV* A376.
[15] Cf. Rawls, *LHMP* 75, 83 and §992.
[16] Kant does not use 'experience' in this way for moral awareness.

his practical philosophy and the rest of his philosophical position. Some of the main interpretative issues can best be decided when we have discussed Kant's views on freedom.

899. Normative Consequences

Kant agrees with Butler, Price, and Reid in accepting a rationalist account of the nature and basis of morality, even though he does not rely on intuitionism to support rationalism. He agrees with their view that rationalism conflicts with utilitarianism. Hutcheson and Hume believe that their sentimentalism supports a utilitarian normative theory, though, as we have seen, their belief is open to question.[17]

Not everyone, however, agrees with these links between meta-ethical and normative theses. Balguy, for instance, is a rationalist and somewhat sympathetic to utilitarianism, anticipating Sidgwick's rationalist argument for utilitarianism.[18] Sidgwick takes Kantian principles to support utilitarianism, though he recognizes that Kant is not a utilitarian. In Sidgwick's view, Kant shows that a moral principle must embody a universal law acceptable to all rational beings. Sidgwick believes that the principle of utility uniquely satisfies Kant's condition. He sets out from a Kantian contrast between the form and the matter of a moral principle.[19] This contrast, as Sidgwick understands it, separates the truths that define a moral principle from those that state the content of the principle. Since Kant distinguishes form from matter, we might infer that his main task, if he sticks consistently to his own distinction, is a conceptual inquiry into the nature of moral principles.

Some unfriendly critics, including Hegel and Schopenhauer, have assumed this interpretation of Kant, but some friendly critics have also accepted it, following Sidgwick's example. Some twentieth-century moral philosophers look to Kant as an inspiration for a strictly formal characterization of moral judgments as prescriptive and universalizable.[20] Perhaps Kant describes the moral point of view at a very general level that is neutral between different normative views. Whatever we think about his own normative views, he may still be right in his formal description of morality.

One prominent modern development of Kant's position takes a quite different view about the normative implications of his conception of morality.[21] In Rawls's view, Kant provides the basis for a viable non-utilitarian theory of morality. Rawls agrees, against Sidgwick, with Kant's estimate of the importance of his position. Kant believes that his account of the basis of morality frees rationalist and non-utilitarian positions from the intuitionism of Price and Reid. For the earlier rationalists, ultimate normative principles are irreducibly plural. We are supposed to see the rightness of basic principles of justice, equity, beneficence, and so on,

---

[17] On sentimentalism and utilitarianism see §644.

[18] See Sidgwick, *ME* xvii. Despite his remarks on benevolence, Balguy rejects utilitarianism; see §664.

[19] On form and matter see §901.

[20] See Hare, *SOE* 159–62. Singer, *GE*, ch. 8–9, offers a clear defence of the formula of Universal Law and a reply to some objections and misunderstandings. On the categorical imperative of consistency see Lewis, *AKV* 481, discussed in §1321.

[21] 'To be avoided at all costs is the idea that Kant's doctrine simply provides the general, or formal, elements for a utilitarian (or indeed for any other) theory.' (Rawls, *TJ* [1] 251. At [2] 221 Rawls says more moderately: 'Especially to be avoided is the idea that Kant's doctrine provides at best only the general . . .')

and to see that these principles cannot be subordinated or reduced to any general utilitarian principle. Kant tries to do better.

He argues that, once we understand the nature of morality, and in particular its relation to practical reason, we need not appeal to intuition in order to support basic normative principles. We can see that the rational basis for morality is non-utilitarian; for once we see that a genuinely moral principle must appeal to practical reason rather than sentiment, we can infer enough about its content to reject utilitarianism. Instead of recognizing a number of ultimate principles relying on intuitions without further explanation, we unify these principles by showing that they all express the implications of the basic point that a moral principle must appeal to practical reason.

Is Kant right about the coherence of his position? Both his meta-ethical rationalism and his non-utilitarian normative theory raise doubts and objections; and even if both of these aspects of his position are reasonable, Kant's view about their connexion might be wrong. To see how a Kantian view might reply, we may consider Kant's argument for rationalism and the further conclusions he draws from it.

900. Kant's Tasks

In the *First Critique*, Kant tries to prove that every subject of experience must accept specific synthetic and a priori truths that require belief in an objective world. The parallel task in the *Second Critique* is to prove that every rational agent has reason to accept certain 'practical laws', principles that are valid for the will of every rational being.

Kant contrasts a practical law with a mere maxim. My maxim in doing a particular action is (approximately) my reason for acting as I do. The maxim on which I do this action gives the description under which I choose to do it. If, for instance, I brush my teeth, my maxim is (normally) keeping my teeth clean. We might capture the maxim by saying that I brush my teeth to keep them clean, or that what I am doing in brushing my teeth is keeping my teeth clean (rather than wearing out the brush or exercising my arm).[22] A mere maxim, unrelated to any practical law, appeals to a motive that may be present in different rational beings to different degrees. A practical law, by contrast, rests on some ground that applies to rational beings as such.[23]

Kant sets out to prove three claims: (1) A practical law is a principle with a certain form. (2) There are principles with this form, and hence there are practical laws. (3) Moral principles rest on them. These three claims are distinct. We might agree that Kant has a coherent conception of what a practical law would have to be like, but deny that any

[22] As Kant says, 421n, the maxim is the 'subjective principle of acting'. On maxims see §§902, 915; O'Neill, *CR* 83–9.

[23] 'But for reason to be legislative, it is required that reason need presuppose only itself, because the rule is objectively and universally valid only when it holds without any contingent, subjective conditions that differentiate one rational being from another.' (*KpV* 20–1) Kant's different remarks on maxims and laws seem to reflect some confusion. Sometimes he suggests that a maxim is a subjective principle and a law is an objective principle that we may or may not incorporate in our subjective principle; the law provides a justifying reason that becomes a motivating reason when it is incorporated in our maxim. See G 421n. In this sense both hypothetical and categorical imperatives should give practical laws. But Kant also (in *KpV*) seems to say that all laws are a priori, and the hypothetical imperative is a mere maxim. Perhaps he confuses different ways something can be subjective.

principles satisfy this conception. Again, we might agree that some principles are practical laws, but deny that moral principles are among them—either because moral principles are too specific to be practical laws, though they fall under them, or because they are outside the area of practical laws.

In trying to describe the outlook and presuppositions of the moral point of view, Kant revives an argument of Balguy's against sentimentalism. From a sentimentalist point of view, there are no practical laws; the implicit outlook of morality, therefore, is inconsistent with the meta-ethical view that moral judgments are based on sentiments, rather than on pure practical reason. Balguy argues against sentimentalism on this point, maintaining that since moral judgments are corrigible and non-arbitrary, a sentimentalist analysis must be wrong. We need to see whether Kant adds something to Balguy's argument.

Kant fulfils his first task by arguing that no material practical principles are laws (KpV 22), and that a law contains the determining grounds of the will (27). The only such law is the one that requires us to act on a maxim that could be a principle establishing universal law (30). In drawing a corollary from this 'fundamental law of practical reason', Kant fulfils his second and third tasks at once. He asserts that 'pure reason is practical of itself alone, and it gives (to man) a universal law, which we call *the moral law*' (31).

He does not argue separately that moral principles are practical laws; he explicates his conception of practical laws by reference to assumptions about morality. Suppose that you consider the maxim of denying that a deposit has been made when no one can prove the contrary, and you ask whether this maxim could be a universal law (27). Kant assumes that this question concerns the moral acceptability of the maxim. Similarly, in arguing that a free will must be determined by a pure and unconditional practical law, he appeals to our recognition of our ability to do what we regard as morally obligatory, apart from the comparative strength of our various desires (30). Our awareness of moral obligation is awareness of a practical law.[24]

Some questions are clearer if we separate Kant's conception of practical laws from his argument to show that we are subject to practical laws, and from his argument to show that moral principles are practical laws. It is sometimes difficult to separate these points, because he normally illustrates the character of practical laws with examples of moral principles and moral reasoning. Still, we need to decide what practical laws must be like if there are any before we ask which principles meet our conditions for practical laws. Moral principles are distinct from principles that might aim at my own good or at the contemplation of truth and beauty for their own sake; but we should not assume in advance that neither prudential nor aesthetic principles (for instance) are practical laws. To see whether all and only moral laws are practical laws, we will first to try to keep the discussion at a more abstract level than Kant's, to see what a practical law is supposed to be, before trying to decide which principles, if any, are practical laws.

This division between Kant's general claims about practical laws and his specific claims about moral laws helps us to understand both Kant and his critics. Kant may have a plausible conception of a practical law, and may show that there are practical laws, but we may still

---

[24] '. . . we can become aware of pure practical laws in the same way we become aware of pure theoretical principles, by attending to the necessity with which reason prescribes them to us and to the setting aside of all empirical conditions, which reason directs.' (KpV 30)

wonder whether he has identified the right ones. In particular, we may wonder whether all and only practical laws are also moral laws. Some people who have agreed with Kant in recognizing practical laws have taken one's own good to be the ultimate source of all practical laws; others have taken one's own good and morality to be distinct sources of practical laws. Unless we distinguish Kant's general claims about practical laws from his specific claims about moral laws, we cannot decide whether we should agree with him, or with those who recognize different practical laws, or with those who recognize no practical laws.

Kant claims that principles are practical laws if they rely on some condition that is 'recognized as objective, i.e., as valid for the will of every rational being' (*KpV* 19). He does not mean that all rational agents recognize them as valid. He treats them as justifying reasons, not as exciting reasons, for all rational agents. In his view, not all justifying reasons rest on the desires of the agents for whom they are justifying reasons. Some reasons rest on facts about agents that they may not recognize or care about. Practical laws are valid for the will of every rational being, because of facts about rational beings, not primarily because of what rational beings recognize or desire.

901. Form and Matter

Practical principles are laws if they 'contain the determining grounds of the will because of their form and not because of their matter' (*KpV* 27, g48). The matter of a practical principle is 'the object of the will'. Every practical principle has an object whose role determines the character of the principle. If the object is also the determining ground of the will, the principle is not a practical law. In a practical law, the form of the principle, abstracted from the object, gives the determining ground. A purely formal justifying reason distinguishes practical laws from those justifying reasons that depend on some further feature of a specific kind of rational agent.[25]

Kant distinguishes (1) the objective ground of self-determination—the end (Zweck), which is also the ground of determination (Bewegungsgrund) of the action—from (2) the subjective ground of desire (Begehren)—the incentive (or 'spring', Triebfeder) that causes me to do the action (G 427).[26] If someone wants to eat an apple, the eating of the apple is the objective ground; it is the intentional object, or state of affairs represented as desirable. Kant uses 'objective' in the Scholastic sense, referring to the object of thought.[27] The objective ground need not be an existing object, and need not be valid for all rational agents. It is objective simply because it is a represented state of affairs, rather than an attitude the agent

---

[25] 'This object either is the determining ground of the will or it is not. If it is, the rule of the will is subject to an empirical condition (to the relation of the determining representation [Vorstellung] to the feeling of pleasure or displeasure), and therefore is not a practical law. If all material of a law, i.e., every object of the will (as its determining ground), is abstracted from it, nothing remains except the mere *form* of giving universal law.' (*KpV* 27) On Hegel's criticism of Kant's appeal to form see §1026.

[26] This contrast between 'objective' and 'subjective' may mislead. Paton's suggestion (*CI* 167n) that 'objective' may be a slip for 'subjective' is misguided, but shows that he sees that something needs to be explained. Cf. Beck, *CKCPR* 90–1. On objective ends see §902.

[27] See Suarez, §438.

takes to it. The 'incentive' is the agent's desire for the object. In order to act, the agent needs both the objective ground and the subjective ground—both a representation of the state of affairs aimed at and a desire to realize it.[28]

An agent's purpose or object cannot belong to a practical law, because Kant has a narrow conception of purposes and objects. In his view, they are all the products of empirical desires and impulses, and therefore are empirical objects of the will. These empirical objects may vary from one agent to another (whether or not they actually vary). If they were the basis of moral principles, the reasons given by moral principles would also vary according to the different desires of different agents. These empirical objects could not support practical laws.

This conclusion might still allow an object of desire to be the basis of practical laws. 'Object of desire' might refer either to what a given agent desires or to what is desirable for, or ought to be desired by, this sort of agent. If something is desirable for all rational agents as such, whether or not they desire it, it could be the basis, for all Kant has said so far, of practical laws. Kant has not shown that there can be no such object of desire; and therefore he has not shown that no object of desire could be a basis for practical laws.

Kant assumes that practical laws must be known a priori, but he gives no distinct argument for this claim. He refers to 'the necessity which is conceived in every law, an objective necessity arising from a priori grounds' (KpV 26), and remarks that 'practical laws . . . must have an objective and not just subjective necessity, and . . . must be known a priori by reason instead of by experience' (KpV 26). They must be known a priori because they apply to rational agents as rational.[29] Practical laws are derived from the 'universal concept of a rational being generally' (G 412); we can understand them without reference to mere empirical facts about human beings.

902. Practical Laws and Objective Ends

Kant connects practical laws with objective, as opposed to subjective, ends. Subjective ends rest on (beruhen auf) incentives, whereas objective ends have to do with (ankommen auf) grounds of determination that hold good for every rational being (G 427).[30] We have subjective ends in so far as some things become desirable to us because we already desire

---

[28] For this reason 'motive' (used by Gregor in G 427) does not seem to be a good rendering of 'Bewegungsgrund'. In KpV, 21 Beck renders the closely connected term 'Bestimmungsgrund' (cf. 'self-determination', Selbstbestimmung, in our passage) as 'determining ground' (followed by Gregor), which would be better here. For we often use 'motive' as Kant uses 'incentive' here, not for the object of our desire. And so 'ground of determination' is preferable.

[29] See KpV 20–1, quoted above.

[30] Kant's terminology is confusing. Subjective and objective ends are two types of 'objective grounds of determination', according to his classification of grounds of determination. To see what he has in mind, it is important (see note above on G 427) not to translate 'Bewegungsgrund' by 'motive', if we give 'motive' its normal sense in contemporary English. Though subjective ends 'rest on' incentives, they are not themselves incentives ('motives' in the normal sense in contemporary English), but the states of affairs we aim at. This distinction between the ground of determination and the incentive helps to explain why Kant uses 'ankommen auf' rather than 'beruhen auf' for objective ends. Objective ends do not depend on grounds of determination; they are grounds of determination, as he has said above. Probably, then, 'ankommen auf' means 'have to do with' (as in the phrase 'es kommt mir nicht darauf an'; 'it's nothing to do with me'). He does not mean that objective ends depend on something else, or that they depend on 'motives' (as we would normally understand them).

them; this is the only way, according to Hume, in which an end can become desirable to us. In these cases, we can distinguish the desire or 'spring' (incentive) from the desirable state of affairs, and the desire is prior. With objective ends, the relation between the desire and the desirable object is reversed. Our having a justifying reason to aim at this end does not depend on our already desiring it; on the contrary, it is because we recognize some justifying reason to aim at this end that we come to desire it.

Not all objective ends apply to all rational agents as such. If there are ends that certain kinds of rational beings have reason to pursue, not all objective ends (i.e., those in which the reason is antecedent to the desire) are valid for every rational being in the sense Kant has in mind. Perhaps, for instance, agents who have some considerable degree of artistic, musical, or athletic talent have some reason (not necessarily overriding) to develop it, irrespective of what they may already desire. This external reason is an appropriate basis of action for some, but not all, rational agents.

Kant's belief in an objective end explains why he speaks of an end in itself. An end 'in itself' is to be contrasted with something's being an end 'for me'; 'for me' refers to me with the sorts of incentive I happen to have. If an end is objective, I have reason to pursue the object because it is worth pursuing, not because I already have the relevant sort of desire.[31] An objective end is therefore a limiting condition of everyone's freedom of action (G 430–1). Our freedom of action is the freedom to pursue the subjective ends we may have; the objective end limits, but does not supersede, the pursuit of subjective ends.

The same contrast between an objective and a subjective end appears in the distinction between absolute value and value relative to some other end (G 428). Absolute value is not relative to our desires and incentives. If the value of two subjective ends depends on incentives, it is reasonable to trade the end we want less for the end we want more. But if something is an objective end, it is not appropriately traded for something we desire more.

Kant's contrast between price and dignity (G 434–5) draws the same distinctions. Whatever has a price has relative value; its price is what it would take for me to give it up in favour of some other goal. Something of absolute value cannot have that sort of price. Kant assumes that price is fixed by degree of antecedent desire; I find the price of x when I find some y such that I want y more than I want x and I would have to give up y in order to keep x. Objective ends do not have this sort of price, since their value is not fixed by the strength of the desire that I happen to have for them; and so they have a different kind of value from the value attached to things with a price.

903. Practical Laws and Categorical Imperatives

The basis of Kant's division between practical laws and maxims, and between objective and subjective ends, is also the basis of his division between categorical and hypothetical imperatives. This division rests on the relation of different imperatives to empirical motives and inclinations. A hypothetical imperative results from justifying reasons that rest on some

[31] Cf. Balguy, §658.

particular empirical desire or impulse. A categorical imperative relies on justifying reasons that are independent of empirical desires.[32]

When Kant speaks of imperatives, he refers to laws as they apply to agents who have motives that potentially conflict with practical reason. Practical laws move purely rational agents without being imperatives, but they are imperatives in agents who have potentially conflicting sources of motivation.[33] Kant normally discusses agents for whom practical laws are imperatives, since all human agents belong to this class. But his claims about reasons and about moral goodness do not require the potential internal conflict that is needed for imperatives.[34]

Hypothetical imperatives depend on an antecedent inclination. This inclination may be actual, not merely possible. 'Since you want x, you ought to do y' is a hypothetical imperative no less than 'If you want x, you ought to do y' is.[35] The relevant inclination may even be unavoidable. The desire for happiness is universal and necessary for human beings with our specific mental and physical characteristics, but it results in hypothetical imperatives (G 417). A practical law is based on a reason that is independent of the agent's desires and inclinations.

How many practical laws are there? Kant has clear reasons to deny that technical imperatives, concerned with the satisfaction of particular empirical desires, are practical laws. His reasons for dismissing pragmatic imperatives, derived from happiness, need closer examination.

904. Happiness and Desire

The objections to principles based on happiness rest on objections to all 'practical principles which presuppose an object (material) of the faculty of desire as the determining ground of the will'. In Kant's view, no such principle can be the basis of moral principles (KpV 21). The 'material of the faculty of desire' is an object whose reality is desired. If the desire for the object precedes any practical rule, the principle is empirical. In such cases, pleasure presents an end for the practical rule to achieve. The practical rule, therefore, is merely empirical, because we cannot know a priori whether or not we will gain pleasure.[36]

---

[32] 'Now tell someone that he ought never to make a deceitful promise; this is a rule which concerns only his will regardless of whether any purposes the human being may have can be achieved by it or not. The bare (blosse) volition is to be completely determined a priori by this rule. If, now, it is found that this rule is practically right, it is a law, because it is a categorical imperative.' (KpV 21)

[33] 'In practical cognition, . . . the principles that one makes for oneself are not yet laws by which one is inexorably bound, because reason, in practice, has to do with a subject and especially with its faculty of desire, the special character of which may occasion various adjustments in the rule . . . This rule, . . . is an imperative for a being whose reason is not the sole determinant of the will. It is a rule indicated by "ought", which expresses the objective necessitation of the act and signifies that, if reason completely determined the will, the action would without exception take place according to the rule.' (KpV 20)

[34] See also G 439; MdS 223, discussed in §988.

[35] '. . . whatever is necessary merely in order to attain some arbitrary (beliebigen) purpose can be regarded as itself contingent, and we can always be rid of the precept if we give up the purpose.' (G 420)

[36] '. . . the determining ground of choice (Willkür) is the representation of an object and its relation to the subject, whereby the faculty of desire is determined to the realization of it [sc. the object]. Such a relation to the subject is called pleasure in the reality of an object, and it must be presupposed as the condition of the possibility of the determination of choice.' (KpV 21)

After claiming that material practical principles aim at pleasure, Kant claims that they all belong under 'the general principle of self-love or one's own happiness' (22). He identifies pleasure with the 'sensation of agreeableness' produced by the achievement of some objects of desire.[37] He accepts a hedonist account of happiness, identifying happiness with the awareness of durable and uninterrupted pleasure.

Some of Kant's remarks, however, suggest a non-hedonist conception of happiness. Knowledge of happiness rests on 'mere data of experience' (*KpV* 36), and it is difficult to find the elements of happiness (*G* 417–18).[38] This difficulty would not arise if happiness consisted entirely in the pleasure resulting from the satisfaction of desire; for in that case the only constituent element of happiness would be pleasure, and the difficulty would lie not in identifying the elements of happiness, but in finding the means to happiness. Perhaps, however, we should take Kant to be speaking inexactly in suggesting that the elements of happiness itself are difficult to find. He may simply mean that it is difficult to discover what gives us pleasure.[39]

A hedonist analysis of desire supports Kant's claim that no principle based on the agent's highest good can be a practical law.[40] If this analysis is right, his criticism of happiness is cogent. If practical rules are prescriptions for achieving happiness, they depend on the agent's feelings of pleasure.

905. Inclinations and Reasons

This explanation of the difference between categorical and hypothetical imperatives suggests that hypothetical imperatives rest ultimately on a desire for pleasure. This particular feature of Kant's position, however, is not necessary for his main contrast between the two types of imperatives.[41]

The contrast is marked by two different types of judgment of value, which are more sharply separated (Kant supposes) in German than in Greek and Latin. The Latin 'bonum' and 'malum' cover both judgments about weal and woe ('Wohl' and 'Weh') and judgments about the strictly good and evil ('Gut' and 'Böse') (*KpV* 59–60). For instance, 'whoever submits to a surgical operation feels it without doubt as an ill (übel), but by reason he and everyone else describe it as a good' (61).[42]

---

[37] '. . . a rational being's consciousness of the agreeableness of life which without interruption accompanies his whole existence is happiness, and to make this the supreme ground for the determination of choice (Willkür) is the principle of self-love.' (*KpV* 22) At 124 Kant gives a similar account of happiness.

[38] In the correction at *KU* 200 (printed by Beck as a footnote to *G* 415), Kant says that imperatives based on happiness depend on 'a determination of what constitutes the end itself (happiness)'.

[39] '. . . where one places his happiness is a question of the particular feeling of pleasure or displeasure in each man, and even of the differences in needs occasioned by changes of feeling in one and the same man.' (*KpV* 25)

[40] 'If the concept of the good is not to be derived from an antecedent practical law, but rather is to serve as the ground of the latter, it can only be the concept of something whose existence promises pleasure and thus determines the causality of the subject (i.e. the faculty of desire) to produce it.' (*KpV* 58)

[41] See Beck, *CKCPR* 101–2. Reath, 'Hedonism', denies that Kant holds the hedonist views that I have attributed to him. See also Allison, *KTF* 103.

[42] He mentions Poseidonius suffering from the gout, who said that however annoying (molestum) the pain might be, he would never agree that it was bad (malum). As Kant understands this, Poseidonius says that pain is an ill (übel) but not strictly bad (böse) (*KpV* 60). Kant explains: 'for the pain did not in the least diminish the worth of his person, but

The strictly good is the good recognized by reason, in contrast to the pleasant. A judgment about our welfare is not about the strictly good, because reason is not simply a device for finding means to the satisfaction of inclination (61–2; cf. G 395). The value we attach to reason is not exhausted by its effectiveness in securing the ends pursued by inclination; indeed, we recognize that it is not always very effective in this instrumental role. The contrast between judgments of weal and judgments of strict goodness is the contrast between good assessed by reference to effectiveness in satisfying inclination (in the short or the long term) and good assessed by reason independently of inclination. That is why principles prescribing what is to be done to secure our happiness cannot be judgments about strict goodness.

If happiness consists in the satisfaction of our inclinations (or most of them, or those we care most about, or a consistent set of them), judgments about what is required for happiness refer to the goodness that depends on inclination, and hence refer to weal rather than to strict goodness. In Kant's view, the necessity of our pursuing happiness is a necessity of the human condition, not of practical reason, so that it depends on empirical facts about the strength of our inclinations.[43]

The appeal to happiness, therefore, supports justifying reasons that appeal to inclinations. The fact that I can buy an air ticket to London more cheaply if I book tomorrow than if I book the next day is a reason for me to book tomorrow only if I want to go to London and I want to save money. Hence 'You ought to book tomorrow' is a hypothetical imperative of the sort that Kant calls a counsel rather than a command (G 418). Imperatives based on happiness manifest our predisposition to humanity; the self-love that aims at happiness 'is rooted in a reason which is indeed practical, but only as subservient to other incentives'. Only the predisposition to personality, involving the capacity for respect for the moral law as in itself a sufficient incentive of the will, is really 'rooted in reason practical of itself, i.e., in reason legislating unconditionally' (Rel. 28).

906. The Status of Hypothetical Imperatives

Kant's treatment of reasons of self-interest is not completely clear. We need to distinguish three possible places for reason in prudential deliberation: (1) Given that you want x, reason tells you that y is a means to x. (2) Reason tells you that it is reasonable to pursue y, given that you want x and y is a means to x. (3) Reason tells you that it is reasonable to pursue y, given that x is good for you, and y is a means to x.

The first of these claims expresses Hume's position. The second claim goes beyond Hume, since reason tells you something that it is reasonable to do, irrespective of whether you want

only the worth of his condition. A single lie of which he was conscious would have had to strike down his pride, but pain served only as an occasion for raising it when he was conscious that he had not made himself liable to it by a wrong action and thereby deserving of punishment.' (60)

[43] 'There is one end, however, which we may presuppose as actual in all rational beings, so far as imperatives apply to them, i.e., so far as they are dependent beings; there is one purpose not only which they all *can* have but which we can presuppose that they all *do* have by a necessity of nature. This purpose is happiness. The hypothetical imperative which represents the practical necessity of action as means to the promotion of happiness is an assertorical imperative. We may not expound it as merely necessary to an uncertain and a merely possible purpose, but as necessary to a purpose which we can a priori and with assurance assume for everyone because it belongs to his essence.' (G 415)

to or not; this is to pursue some means to an end you want. According to Hume, the second claim is false; it is just a psychological fact that the desire for the end results in the desire for the means. One might argue, however, that this is not a purely psychological fact, and that it involves the application of a superior principle (as Butler supposes).[44]

One might wonder whether we could consistently affirm the second claim, asserting that it is reasonable to pursue means to our ends, without the third claim, asserting that it is reasonable to care about our good. To explain why we have a reason (not necessarily overriding) to pursue a means to some end of ours, we might say that it depends on thinking of our end as our own, as belonging to us, as agents with interests and concerns extending over time; and so it depends on its being reasonable to be concerned for ourselves as such agents. But if we go this far to explain the rationality of pursuing a means to our end, must we not agree that it is reasonable to choose, not merely some means, but efficient means to our ends, and that it is reasonable to have some concern for oneself as a whole?

Kant accepts at least the first, Humean, claim. He rejects the third claim, since he rejects categorical imperatives of prudence. One might be inclined to ascribe the second claim to him.[45] He seems to suppose it is rational to pursue means to our ends, and that we do not need a further inclination in order to make this rational. If, however, we cannot plausibly accept the second claim without the third, Kant's position is unstable. Though he is fairly clear about the sort of reason provided by a hypothetical imperative, he is less clear about the rationality of following hypothetical imperatives.

He normally takes a hypothetical imperative to rest on the sort of reason that Hume allows, appealing to some antecedent desire and preference. A categorical imperative, by contrast, rests on the sort of justifying reason that Hume does not allow, independent of any antecedent desire and preference. Hence, a categorical imperative 'represents an action as objectively necessary in itself, without reference to another end' (G 414). It 'declares an action to be of itself objectively necessary without reference to any purpose, i.e. without any other end' (G 415).

A categorical imperative is independent of any purpose that is given by some prior preference. It must present external justifying reasons that are reasons for all rational agents as such, not because some rational agents have the particular aims and needs that human beings have. Such reasons do not cease to be reasons simply because human inclinations change. If we care less about our happiness today than we did yesterday, such a fluctuation of inclination makes different hypothetical imperatives apply to us, but it does not change the practical laws that apply to us as rational agents.

907. Self-Interest as a Source of Self-Love and Self-Conceit

Kant has shown that happiness, as he understands it, does not support categorical imperatives or practical laws, as he understands them. But to see whether his argument also shows that

---

[44] Sidgwick, *ME* 37, raises a question about what Kant actually means in his discussion of hypothetical imperatives. His question is explored further by Prior, *LBE* 37–41.

[45] For further discussion see Hill, 'Hypothetical'; Korsgaard, 'Instrumental'.

happiness, correctly understood, cannot be a source of practical laws, we must compare Kant's conception of happiness with the conception that we find in traditional naturalist eudaemonism. His case against happiness does not apply directly to the traditional conception of happiness, as we find it in Aristotle and Aquinas. For they do not take happiness to consist simply in pleasure; hence Kant's arguments that rest on claims about pleasure do not show that happiness cannot be the source of practical laws.

The eudaemonist position would still be open to Kant's criticisms, however, if our reason for pursuing happiness and its components depended wholly on our inclination towards them. Kant claims that this is our only reason to pursue happiness, and that it is a mistake to attach any further importance to happiness. He believes we are prone to such a mistake; we tend to make the maxims of the pathologically determinable self into 'the first and originally valid' claims.[46] In doing this, we mistakenly suppose that we need no further reason apart from inclination in order to have a good reason to act on our inclinations.

This mistake underlies the attitude of 'self-love', which treats 'the subjective determining grounds of one's choice' as 'objective determining grounds of the will'. Self-love exaggerates its importance even more when it 'makes itself legislative and makes itself into the unconditioned practical principle'; this exaggerated attitude is 'self-conceit'. Self-love and self-conceit differ in that self-love regards one's own interest as an objective determining ground, without claiming that it is the supreme determining ground, whereas self-conceit claims supremacy for one's own interest in contrast to any other motive (73).[47] In both attitudes, the rational will accepts maxims that aim at the satisfaction of inclination, on the false assumption that these maxims give us an objective determining ground. An objective determining ground would give us good reason, apart from our inclinations, to promote our own happiness. If happiness does not give us an objective determining ground, it does not give us external reasons—considerations that constitute good reasons for action, independently of the inclinations of the subject. This conception of happiness requires the Humean conception of hypothetical imperatives, even though Kant himself does not unambiguously endorse this conception.[48]

908. External Reasons and Universal Laws

Kant's treatment of happiness makes it especially clear why we need to distinguish two features of categorical imperatives: (1) Kant's broader account of a categorical imperative takes every non-hypothetical imperative to be categorical. (2) His narrower conception restricts categorical imperatives to those that rely on reasons that are equally reasons for all rational agents as such.

---

[46] 'We find now, however, our nature as sensuous beings so characterized that the material of the faculty of desire (objects of the inclination, whether of hope or fear) first presses upon us; and we find our pathologically determinable self, although by its maxims it is wholly incapable of giving universal law, nonetheless—as though it constituted our whole self—striving from the start to make its claims primarily and originally valid. This propensity to make oneself, in accordance with the subjective determining grounds of one's choice (Willkür), into the objective determining ground of the will (Wille) in general one can call self-love (Selbstliebe), which, if self-love makes itself legislative and makes itself into the unconditioned practical principle can be called self-conceit (Eigendünkel).' (KpV 74) See Engstrom, 'Concept', 758.

[47] On self-conceit and the moral law see §966.   [48] On external reasons see §268.

17

These two criteria for a categorical imperative are equivalent only if we accept some controversial features of Kant's view of external reasons. In his view, all non-moral reasons are internal reasons, so that the only external reasons are moral reasons applying to all rational agents as such. But we might reasonably suppose that some of them meet the broader, but not the narrower, criterion for being categorical. Some imperatives apply to some rational agents and not to others, but not because of different preferences. These imperatives might include: (a) People with musical talent ought to develop it. (b) After that serious illness, you ought to take it easy for a while. These imperatives seem to rest on external reasons, independent of any prior preference of the agent; and so, by this test, they are not hypothetical, but categorical. But they seem to apply to some agents and not to others, not to all rational agents as such.

One might reply that these imperatives based on external reasons may really apply to all rational agents. Perhaps all rational agents as such have reason, if they have musical talent, to develop it. This 'conditional' categorical imperative is different from a hypothetical imperative, because the condition it includes does not involve the agent's desires. The fact that all imperatives based on external reasons apply to all rational agents in this sense may make it easier for Kant to believe that his narrower conception of a categorical imperative includes all non-hypothetical imperatives.

Kant's conception of a categorical imperative, however, normally requires not this conditional universality, but unconditional universality; he takes a categorical imperative to rest on an external reason that applies unconditionally (i.e., without essentially referring to any conditions distinguishing one rational agent from another) to all rational agents as such. His claims about the features of a categorical imperative apply to unconditionally universal categorical imperatives.

909. Happiness and the Highest Good

If we restrict ourselves to these unconditionally universal categorical imperatives, is Kant right to suppose that we cannot find them in traditional naturalism? His answer to this question will be clearer in the light of some of his remarks about the ancient moralists. Complications in these remarks raise questions about his arguments about categorical imperatives.

If we render 'eudaimonia' by 'happiness', we might suppose that Kant's remarks about happiness also apply to eudaimonia. But if we supposed this, we would be misled. For Kant's predominant concept of happiness treats it as a collection of pleasures, but he recognizes that the ancient concept of eudaimonia is not essentially hedonist. And so he uses 'highest good', not 'happiness', to refer to eudaimonia. Since he notices that the Greeks disagree about the place of pleasure in eudaimonia, he represents this disagreement as a dispute about the place of happiness in the highest good.

Given this distinction between happiness and the highest good, the ancient moralists do not believe that happiness, without qualification, is the highest good.[49] Since they give virtue

[49] 'The ancients realized that mere happiness could not be the one highest good. For if all men might obtain this happiness without distinction of just and unjust, then there would indeed be happiness, but no worthiness of it, and if

a special place in the highest good, they do not say that the highest good is nothing more than happiness.[50] The Epicurean view comes closest to identifying the highest good with happiness, since it treats virtue simply as a means to happiness. The Stoics deny that the highest good is happiness.[51] When they say that virtue is identical to the highest good, they mean (according to Kant) that happiness results from virtue.[52]

But though Kant sees that the ancients regard the highest good, rather than happiness, as the ultimate end, he still believes that they subordinate practical reason to inclination. In his view, the appeal to the highest good is an appeal to an object of inclination that can yield only hypothetical imperatives.[53] Hence the ancients introduce the 'heteronomy' of practical reason, because they do not allow practical reason to follow its own laws, but they make it subservient to inclination.[54]

the latter is included, than that is the highest good.' (LE 247) Kant takes this claim to be consistent with his account of the Epicurean position because Epicurus wants to give virtue a special connexion to happiness; though it is not part of happiness, it is an indispensable means to it. Sullivan, KMT 364n12, suggests that Kant criticizes the Stoics for claiming that to be conscious of one's virtue is happiness or eudaimonia.

[50] Kant considers two accounts, the Epicurean and the Stoic of the nature of the highest good: '... so far as the definition of the concept of the highest good is concerned, they followed one and the same method, since neither held virtue and happiness to be two different elements of the highest good ... The Epicurean said: To be conscious of one's maxim leading to happiness is virtue. The Stoic said: To be conscious of one's virtue is happiness. To the former, prudence amounted to morality; to the latter, who chose a higher term for virtue, morality alone was true wisdom.' (KpV 111) 'Epicurus' doctrine was that the highest good was happiness and that well-doing was but a means to happiness. ... Zeno taught that the highest good is to be found only in morality, in merit (and thus in well-doing), and that happiness is a consequence of morality. Whoever conducts himself well is happy.' (LE 248)

[51] The ancients are also discussed in the lectures of Kant that underlie the various notes printed in KGS xxvii 1. See 101 (Powolski's notes: the primacy of the question about the nature of the summum bonum); 104 (the Stoics on happiness); 248–50 (Collins's notes: the Stoics on the priority of virtue to happiness). Kant's views are similar to those in LE.

[52] 'The concept of virtue, according to the Epicureans, lay already in the maxim of furthering one's own happiness; the feeling of happiness, for the Stoic, was, on the contrary, already contained in the consciousness of his virtue.' (KpV 112) Kant seeks to correct the shared error of the two Greek views: 'Whatever is contained in another concept, however, is the same as one of its parts, but not the same as the whole, and two wholes can, moreover, be specifically different from each other though they consist of the same content, if their parts are combined in different ways. The Stoic asserted virtue to be the whole highest good, and happiness was only the consciousness of this possession as belonging to the state of the subject. The Epicurean stated that happiness was the whole highest good and that virtue was only the form of the maxim for seeking to obtain it, namely in the rational use of means to it.' (KpV 112) Kant might cite some support in some Stoic sources for his claims about happiness. In some places Stoics speak of eudaimonia as a 'good flow' (eurhoia) of life, and sometimes seem to identify this 'good flow' with a subjective condition of the agent. If one focuses on these passages to the exclusion of other remarks about eudaimonia and virtue, one might come out with something like Kant's view. See §182 on the Stoics; §800 (Smith's interpretation). If one turned from these passages to the sources in which the Stoics are said to identify the summum bonum with virtue, and one noticed the difference between virtue and a consequence of virtue, one might reasonably come to the conclusion that the Stoics regard eudaimonia as a consequence of the summum bonum rather than as the summum bonum itself. Hegel's criticism of Stoic views on virtue and happiness; §1026.

[53] Hence he takes all the ancients to commit the errors that he ascribes to the position that he calls eudaemonist.

[54] '... [Previous philosophers] sought an object of the will in order to make it into the material and the ground of a law (which would then not be the immediately determining ground of the will, but only mediated by that object referred to the feeling of pleasure or displeasure); instead, they should have looked first for a law which immediately determined the will a priori and only then sought the object suitable to it. Whether they placed this object of pleasure, which was to deliver the supreme concept of the good, in happiness, or in perfection, or in the moral law, or in the will of God—their fundamental principle was always heteronomy, and they came inevitably to empirical conditions for a moral law.' (KpV 64) (Editors follow Hartenstein in emending the first occurrence of 'moral law' to 'moral feeling'.) None of the Greek moralists escapes this criticism: 'The ancients openly revealed this error in that they devoted their ethical investigations entirely to the definition of the concept of the highest good and thereby posited an object which they intended subsequently to make the determining ground of the will in the moral law.' (KpV 64)

910. Are There Practical Laws of Prudence?

Is Kant right to claim that the highest good, as the ancients understand it, can yield only hypothetical imperatives? Let us suppose for the moment that the ancients regard the highest good egoistically, as one's own good. In claiming that this yields only hypothetical imperatives, Kant denies that there are any categorical imperatives of prudence. His denial rests on the assumption that one's good is happiness (as Kant understands it), or some other object of inclination. In that case, one's own good is not an 'objective determining ground' that one has a reason to pursue apart from the strength of one's own desire.

We might, however, doubt Kant's assumptions. One's own good does not seem to provide only internal reasons based on antecedent inclination. We seem to have reason to pursue our own good even if we do not care enough about it; the very fact that something would promote my welfare seems to make it reasonable for me to do it, whether or not I care about my welfare, and whether or not I regard this as an element of my welfare. People seem to be open to criticism for acting unreasonably if they harm themselves, whether or not they care about this. Sometimes we criticize them in the light of what they usually care about, or would care about if they stopped to think. But this is not always the basis of our criticism. Even if further reflexion would not free them from foolish inclinations that are bad for them, they would still be open to rational criticism.

This conception of a person's good is characteristic of traditional naturalism. Aquinas claims that we have external reasons both for pursuing our conception of our good and for pursuing one conception of our good rather than another. Though we all desire our own good, our desire does not provide our reason for pursuing our ultimate good. We ought to pursue our ultimate good, correctly conceived, because of our nature as rational agents, not because we have some more specific desire. Aquinas recognizes this aspect of the good in his claim that we aim at perfection rather than the mere satisfaction of desire.

A similar external conception of reasons underlies the conception of one's good in Suarez, Butler, and Reid. Butler calls self-love a superior principle because the reasons it gives refer not to the strength of my inclinations, but to the sort of agent that I am; hence they accord with my nature. In Butler's view, then, my reason for pursuing my own happiness justifies my inclination to do it, not the other way round. Reid explains that superior principles reflect our conception of our good on the whole, which results from our conception of ourselves as the temporally extended agents whose good is to be considered. Once we recognize that we are temporally extended agents, we see that we have interests that we cannot achieve by simply following the stronger current impulse; and so we discover that in our own interest we ought to follow principles that rely on authority rather than mere strength.[55]

According to this conception, the fact that restoration of my health, say, would be good for me is by itself a justifying reason for me to restore my health, whether or not I want health or anything to which my health might be a means. If I begin to want health, I do not make it reasonable for me to care about it; I now want something that was reasonable for

---

[55] Reid; §832.

me to care about even before I wanted it.[56] Similarly, if I stop wanting to be healthy, I do not make it unreasonable to care about it; rather, I cease to want what it is still reasonable for me to want. My own good, therefore, fits Kant's conception of an objective end. Kant's rejection of this conclusion relies on his questionable views about external reasons of prudence.

This discussion of prudence allows us to see more exactly where Kant rejects the naturalist position that is most fully stated by Aquinas, but most familiar to Kant through Leibniz. Kant's separation of practical laws from inclination-based maxims matches Aquinas' division between the desires that belong to the will and those that belong to the passions. Aquinas agrees that practical reason is capable of finding ends that apply to us independently of antecedent non-rational inclinations, and that we are capable of acting on them. But he holds, contrary to Kant, that one's own good is a source of practical laws, as Kant conceives them. Kant rejects this view because he identifies one's good with the satisfaction of inclination.

If, then, there are practical laws of prudence, eudaemonist naturalism does not make practical reason heteronomous; for it does not subordinate practical reason to non-rational inclination. On this issue, Kant is less rationalist than eudaemonist naturalists are.

911. Practical Laws: A Dilemma for Kant

How much does it matter whether Kant is right or wrong about practical laws of prudence? One might argue that if he is wrong, all that follows is that there are more practical laws than he recognizes. Since his main question is about whether there are practical laws of morality, we might think that the question about practical laws of prudence is peripheral. To see that this is not so, we should compare Kant's position with the naturalist view and with an anti-rationalist view.

Hutcheson and Hume attack belief in any external reasons. In Hume's view, Butler's conception of a superior principle rests on failure to notice that the rationality of prudence depends on the strength of one's inclination towards one's longer-term good. Butler is mistaken, in Hume's view, in supposing that superior principles do not depend on inclination. According to Hume, agents who act in accord with their informed preferences are immune to criticism for irrationality. Hence the view that a person's good is the source of justifying reasons independent of an agent's desires presupposes a false view of justifying reasons. If Kant agrees with Hume on all these points about justifying reasons, he has a good reason to reject categorical imperatives of prudence.

But he does not endorse Hume's general objections to external justifying reasons. He believes that moral imperatives give external reasons. He assumes that agents deserve criticism for acting against reason, whatever their inclinations may have been, if they violate principles of morality. If they did not deserve it, the imperative of morality would not be categorical.

Kant relies on our intuitive judgment that moral imperatives are categorical; we do not suppose that our moral reasons go away if we lose the inclinations that favour the

---

[56] I use 'rational' and 'reasonable' without distinction, following Butler and Reid. Kant uses the single word 'vernünftig', which Rawls prefers to render by 'rational and reasonable'. Cf. Rawls, 'Themes', 87–8, *LHMP* 164–5; Engstrom, 'Concept', 753n10; Scanlon, *WWOEO* 25–30.

morally right course of action. But he tries to undermine our intuitive belief in prudential categorical imperatives. If he succeeded, he would cast doubt on the possibility of external justifying reasons. Such doubts would spread to moral imperatives. For he relies on the intuitive judgment that rational agents are sometimes open to moral criticism, however their inclinations may vary. From a sentimentalist point of view, this intuitive judgment is false, but we can explain (causally and psychologically) why it appears to be true. But Kant accepts the intuitive judgment; for he appeals to the various moral attitudes and judgments connected with belief in external moral reasons.

If Kant argues in this way, he cannot fairly ignore parallel arguments for external prudential reasons. There must be some external reasons, if there are practical laws. If there are no practical laws, Kant's whole argument collapses, and there are no categorical imperatives of morality. Hence, his objection to external prudential reasons ought to be more specific than a general Humean objection to external reasons.

We might defend Kant by arguing that moral reasons are external, whereas prudential reasons are purely internal and dependent on the agent's desires. But what would explain this difference between prudence and morality? Belief in external prudential reasons rests on claims about our nature and what is suitable for it. If Kant, following Hume, denies that such claims support external reasons, he undermines his claims about categorical imperatives, which apply to rational agents because they are rational agents, not because of some further desire. Doubts about prudential external reasons, therefore, seem to spread to moral external reasons. Since Kant accepts moral external reasons, he ought to accept prudential external reasons.

Kant might modify his position by conceding that prudential reasons are external, and therefore independent of inclination, but still denying that they apply to all rational agents as such; for some external reasons depend not on desires, but on facts about some people and not others. Might Kant argue, then, that external prudential reasons do not hold for all rational agents as such? Perhaps naturalist theories appeal to human nature, and so do not apply to rational agents as such.

This conception of an appeal to nature does not fit Aquinas. In his view, the appeal to nature is not simply an appeal to empirical facts about what people want; nor are moral principles simply means of satisfying these wants. His account of human nature is an account of the essential rational agency in agents who also have non-rational desires. He takes the pursuit of happiness to be necessary for rational agents, because it is a feature of rational agency. The virtues that specify the correct conception of happiness are aspects of rational agency. Suarez expresses this general view in treating the right as what fits rational nature.[57] Similarly, Butler appeals to nature to show that we are agents guided by superior principles; self-love is natural because it expresses our nature as rational agents, not because of special properties of human beings.

On this point, traditional eudaemonism differs from Hume's appeal to human nature. Hume appeals to specifically human needs, impulses, and sentiments that do not support practical laws. This result does not bother Hume, since he does not believe there are any practical laws.

[57] Suarez on fitting rational nature; §438.

We might doubt the claim of traditional eudaemonism to rely on truths about rational agents as such, if we doubt whether there are any sufficiently determinate truths. Kant, however, does not share this general doubt, since he believes that truths about rational agents as such support practical laws in morality. He assumes that the case for prudential practical laws is weaker than the case for moral practical laws.

His assumption is open to question. The best defence of his objections to prudential practical laws appeals to general Humean doubts about external reasons. If we do not share these doubts, it is difficult to reject prudential laws. But if we share Humean doubts about external reasons, we undermine Kant's case for moral practical laws.

So far we have examined Kant's views about practical laws without considering his reasons for believing that these laws are moral principles. The examination shows that he has reasonable arguments for recognizing practical laws, but that they do not support exactly the conclusions he draws from them. He supposes that his arguments expose errors in eudaemonism, because it makes all practical reason heteronomous. But he does not evidently refute a eudaemonist case for practical laws of prudence.

KANT: FROM PRACTICAL LAWS TO MORALITY

912. The Good Will

So far we have discussed Kant's claims about practical laws and categorical imperatives as general claims about practical reason, not as specific claims about morality. He defends claims about external reasons that we might accept without believing that all and only moral principles are practical laws. The next stage in a clear presentation of Kant's position ought to show how moral principles are practical laws.

Kant offers two sorts of arguments for this conclusion about moral principles: (1) Our views about morality, reasons, praise, and blame imply that moral principles are practical laws. (2) We can see (without relying on the truth of our moral views) that moral principles are practical laws. It is more difficult to defend the second claim than to defend the first. We may begin, therefore, with the description of our moral beliefs that Kant takes to support his first claim.

In the *Groundwork*, he begins by claiming that the good will is the only sort of good that we can regard as good 'without limitation' (G 393).[1] Some things are good only for their consequences, and these lack unconditional goodness.[2] Some things, in particular some traits of character, 'are not only good in a number of aspects, but seem actually to constitute a part of the *inner* worth of the person'. Kant comments that the ancients esteemed them unconditionally; he does not reject this unconditional esteem. These goods lack unlimited goodness, because they become bad if they are not controlled by a good will (394). A good will, by contrast, does not become bad when it fails to achieve some good that we value from some non-moral point of view.

Though Kant contrasts his view on traits of character with the view of the ancients, some of their views on the virtues support and clarify his claims about the good will. Plato, Aristotle, and the Stoics agree that if a trait of character can be misused, it is not a genuine

---

[1] He does not mean that a good will is the only thing that has non-consequential (and in that sense 'intrinsic') goodness; he means that we take moral goodness to mark the limit of the goodness of other things. See §§902, 921.

[2] 'haben keinen inneren unbedingten Wert', 394.

virtue.[3] They notice that if the common conception of bravery were right, bravery would be good in some circumstances but bad in others; they infer that the common conception of bravery and of the other virtues of character is mistaken.[4] Since each virtue must be responsive to the requirements of the other virtues, the objections to bravery, as commonly conceived, do not apply to the virtue of bravery. This traditional doctrine of the virtues, shared by the ancient moralists, is re-affirmed in the claim of Augustine and Aquinas that virtue is 'the good use of free will'.[5]

The traditional doctrine that Kant endorses here treats the moral virtues as expressing a critical point of view on other goods. We need some basis for regulating our use of other goods, since we recognize that in some cases their unregulated use can lead to bad results. The point of view from which we recognize the bad results of bad use of other goods is the point of view from which we recognize the supreme principles of practical reason. The Platonic, Aristotelian, and Stoic tradition, accepted by Aquinas, takes this point of view to be our view of the ultimate end. Kant rejects this eudaemonist interpretation of the supreme principles of practical reason. We have already seen some of his reasons. Since his disagreement with the ancients about misuse actually points out a crucial area of agreement, we may find that he differs from traditional eudaemonism less than we might suppose from his explicit remarks. We will return to this question later.[6]

Since the goodness recognized in moral evaluation is not subordinate to any other sort of goodness, it is unconditionally good. It cannot depend on the actual achievement of results external to morality; for if it did depend on them, it would simply be another resource for acquiring further goods. Hence the goodness recognized from the moral point of view consists at least partly in moral virtue itself. As the ancient moralists claim, moral virtue is to be chosen for its own sake as a non-instrumental good that is not subordinate to other goods. Kant captures this point by claiming that the unlimited goodness recognized from the moral point of view consists in the good will.[7] This goodness is an object of moral praise apart from its results. The Stoic acknowledged that gout was an evil (übel), but saw that it was not morally bad (böse).[8] In avoiding anything morally bad, he avoided justified moral blame.

Once he has identified the will that is open to praise and blame from the moral point of view, Kant asks what makes it praiseworthy and blameworthy. Since wills differ from one another in their maxims, we need to find the maxim that makes one sort of agent

---

[3] Virtue requires the right use of resources, but mere possession of resources does not guarantee their right use (Plato, *Euthd.* 280de). Aristotle suggests that liability to misuse is 'a common feature of all goods, except virtue' (*Rhet.* 1355b4–5). The Stoics rely on the same point in order to explain their use of 'good': 'What can be used both well or badly is not good; but wealth and health can be used both well and badly; hence wealth and health are not goods' (Diogenes Laertius vii 103). Only the virtuous person knows the correct use of these assets, and that is why 'the good person is the one for whom the natural goods are good' (Aristotle, *EE* 1248b26–7); only the good person uses assets correctly.

[4] See Plato, *Meno*, 87–8.   [5] See Aquinas, §284.   [6] Eudaemonism; §§970–1.

[7] '. . . if anything is, or is taken to be, good altogether (schlechthin) (and from every point of view and without further condition), it could not be a thing, but only the maxim of the will, and therewith the acting person himself as a good or bad man.' (*KpV* 60)

[8] See §905.

morally praiseworthy.[9] If we consider what we praise and blame agents for, and under what conditions we limit our praise and blame, we can see what sort of reason a moral principle gives an agent.

913. Praise, Blame, and Morality

By treating the morally good will as an object of praise, Kant introduces the aspects of morality that make moral imperatives categorical. He implicitly distinguishes three different, but connected roles of morality: (1) Persons are moral agents; they guide their actions by moral principles. (2) They are moral beneficiaries; their interests are considered in moral principles. (3) They are moral subjects; moral principles apply to them, and we evaluate their actions morally.

If we are related to morality in any one of these ways, must we be related to it in the other two ways as well? Not all beneficiaries of morality, and not all moral subjects, guide their actions by morality. Nor, apparently, need all beneficiaries be moral subjects; animals, children, or people with severe mental handicaps might be exceptions.[10] Still, the three classes defined by these three relations to morality overlap considerably.

This overlap does not seem coincidental. If some people were moral subjects, but different people were agents and beneficiaries, some people would be evaluated, praised, and blamed, by moral criteria, even though morality had nothing in it for them. We would be criticizing them for other people's benefit, not for their own benefit. This situation, however, violates a commonly shared assumption about morality. Though we do not assume that we must ourselves benefit from every action required by morality, we do not assume that we are required to conform to morality and evaluated in the light of it, simply because other people find it convenient, apart from any reason of our own, to impose these requirements on us. We are inclined to assume that moral principles are those that every moral subject has a reason to accept.

If we are moral subjects open to moral evaluation, we are responsible agents. Praise or blame, consideration as morally good or bad, is not appropriate for creatures with a non-rational will (arbitrium brutum), but requires a free will with practical freedom.[11] We assume that responsible agents are open to moral evaluation. If our assumption is right, every responsible agent has reason to be a moral agent. Kant believes that every rational agent has a reason to follow the principles that support justified praise and blame; the principles that a critic can reasonably apply are also those that an agent can reasonably follow.

In asserting this connexion between what is reasonable for a critic and what is reasonable for the agent criticized, Kant separates justified praise or blame from the other favourable or unfavourable attitudes we might take to other people's actions. We can certainly wish that

---

[9] '. . . the concept of a will which is to be esteemed as good in itself without reference to anything further . . . [which] in the estimation of the total worth of our actions . . . always takes first place, and is the condition of everything else.' (G 397)

[10] I am abstracting from Kant's actual views on animals. See MdS 443.

[11] On the animal will and the free will see §942.

someone had acted more in the public interest or in our interest, and we can even try to induce someone to do this by threats, offers, and so on. But if we wish that someone would act differently, we do not necessarily assume that he has a sufficient reason to do what we wish he would do. Justified blame is different, and if we treat an agent as responsible, we rely on this difference. If we blame agents for violating some principle, we assume that they could reasonably have been expected to follow it, and therefore had some justifying reason for following it. They need not have been aware of the reason they had, but none the less, Kant assumes, it was available to them.

If Kant is right about this, and if a responsible agent is open to this sort of praise and blame, justifying reasons for accepting moral principles are good reasons for every responsible agent. If Kant is wrong, it seems unfair and arbitrary to blame an agent for violating moral principles.

If praise and blame presuppose this conception of moral principles, but we reject this conception, our conception of morality does not support praise and blame. To see whether praise and blame fit our conception of morality, we may consider Kant's argument to show that our conception includes the appropriate view of moral justifying reasons.

Kant's concern with the principles supporting justified praise and blame guides his inquiry into the goodness of a morally good agent. Many different kinds of goodness can be attributed to agents, as well as to other things, but only some kinds of goodness should be expected of agents from the moral point of view. These are the appropriate objects of praise; and so Kant looks for the goodness of the morally good agent by considering the sort of goodness that is open to praise. He needs to show that this goodness consists in being guided by principles that all rational agents have reason to accept.

914. Acting from Duty

Kant claims that from the moral point of view we praise those who act 'from duty': they do what is morally required because it is morally required, not because of some distinct inclination. They recognize what is morally required, and they believe that its being morally required is a sufficient reason for doing the action, no matter what else may be said for or against it. If they are right to believe this, morality gives us justifying reasons independent of non-moral aims and desires.

Kant distinguishes three types of people: (a) those who do what is morally required, but for some purely instrumental reason; (b) those who do it because of some direct inclination to the action that is (in fact) in accordance with duty; (c) those who do it because it is morally required, and therefore act 'from duty' (G 397). He isolates the moral motive by a thought-experiment, constructing cases where other motives oppose it.[12] If we imagine such

---

[12] He compares this comparison of different cases with an experiment: '[The philosopher], almost like the chemist, . . . can at any time arrange an experiment with the practical reason of any man, in order to distinguish the moral (pure) determining ground from the empirical; he does so when he adds the moral law (as a determining ground) to the empirically affected will (e.g. to the will of a person who would like to tell a lie so that he could thereby gain something). . . . if a man who is otherwise honest (or who this one time puts himself only in thought in the place

cases, we can see why the moral motive must move a morally good agent independently of all other motives. Kant illustrates this point from a person who is not philanthropic by nature, but benefits others because it is required by morality.[13]

Kant does not mean, however, that in someone who acts from duty the moral motive opposes all others.[14] Opposition is a part of the experiment intended to reveal the distinctness of the moral motive; it is not a requirement for a morally good will. The heuristic role of the examples does not imply that the moral motive is always opposed to other motives.[15]

This account of acting from duty is meant to show we appropriately praise and blame moral agents quite generally, without restricting our praise and blame to a particular subset of rational agents. If Kant is right, the morally praiseworthy motive does not require any feeling or sentiment that might not belong to all rational agents. The justifying reasons provided by morality are not subordinate to reasons that have a non-moral source. Kant rejects Hume's view that I have a justifying reason to do x if and only if I have a prior desire (independent of reasons for doing x) to do y, and doing x is a means to doing y.

Kant believes that (1) you are justified in blaming me for failure to do x only if I have a justifying reason for doing x. If he accepted (2) Hume's view that justifying reasons presuppose desires, he would have to conclude that (3) you justifiably blame me for not doing x only if I already desire some object to which doing x is a means. If, then, Hume's view about reasons were correct, the extent of justified blame would be drastically curtailed. Kant avoids the unwelcome conclusion in (3) by rejecting the Humean claim about justifying reasons in (2).

Hume might accept this argument, if he believes that everyone has some share in the sentiment of humanity; the conclusion in (3) should not be unwelcome, because it does not curtail the extent of justified blame. But this is not a completely satisfactory answer. Even if everyone has some of the appropriate sentiment, different people have it to different degrees, and so people who have less of it should be less subject to praise and blame for acting rightly or wrongly. It is an unwelcome result if we become less blameworthy by becoming more callous.

An alternative that might be open to Hume is the denial of (1); he might reject Kant's assumption that justified blame requires the people who are blamed to have a justifying reason for not doing what they do. Sometimes Hume denies that praise and blame presuppose that an action is voluntary; this is his objection to the divines. He has equally good reason to deny that they presuppose any justifying reason. Since praise and blame are

---

of an honest man) is confronted with the moral law, by which he recognizes the worthlessness of the liar, his practical reason, in its judgment of what ought to be done, immediately forsakes the advantage, combines with that which maintains in him respect for his own person (truthfulness), and the advantage is easily weighed by anyone after it is separated and washed of any particle of reason (which is wholly on the side of duty).' (*KpV* 92–3) In *G*, Kant conducts the sort of experiment that he describes in the comparison with a chemist.

   [13] '. . . it is just here that the worth of the character is brought out, which is morally and incomparably the highest of all: he is beneficent not from inclination but from duty.' (*G* 398–9)

   [14] 'Thus [one's own advantage] can enter into combination with reason in still other cases, though not in any case where it could be opposed to the moral law, for reason never forsakes this but rather combines most closely with it. But this distinction of the principle of happiness from that of morality is not for this reason an opposition between them, and pure practical reason does not require that we should renounce the claims to happiness; it requires only that we take no account of them whenever duty is in question.' (*KpV* 93)

   [15] Cf. Balguy on the principle of subtraction, §669. Further discussion; §§928, 1045.

passions, they are not internally connected to evaluative beliefs about the people and actions that are subject to blame. This response to Kant relies on some of Hume's controversial claims about passions and sentiments.

Against Hume, Kant appeals to our judgments of moral worth in order to show that we regard agents as open to praise and blame, from the moral point of view, irrespective of their other desires. We do not suppose that moral worth consists in acting on some feeling that explains our conviction that we have a reason to do what is morally required. We assume that agents who lack a philanthropic impulse can still see that they have reason, from the moral point of view, to benefit others. If they benefit others for this reason, they deserve praise, and their action has moral worth. If they do not benefit others for this reason, they deserve blame, and their action lacks moral worth. In praising and blaming, we assume that agents have a justifying reason to do what morality requires, even if no antecedent desire induces them to attend to the demands of morality. If some antecedent sentiment or desire underlies reasons for acting morally, someone who lacks the sentiment has no reason for acting morally. Moreover, if I lose or weaken the sentiment, I lose, to the same degree, my reason for acting morally. These are consequences of Hutcheson's and Hume's sentimentalism.[16]

According to Kant, the sentimentalist view reverses the proper connexion between moral reasons and moral sentiments. Sometimes the loss of a sentiment or inclination deprives me of all the reason I had; if, for instance, I lose my taste for jazz, I also lose my reason to buy jazz records. But someone who lacks the relevant sentiment in favour of morality has reason to acquire the sentiment, because he has reason to act morally.[17] Similarly, someone who loses a pro-moral sentiment still has reason to act morally.

It is difficult, in any case, for sentimentalists to identify the appropriate pro-moral sentiment. They cannot say that it is the sentiment evoked by the conviction that we have moral reason to do this action. It must be a sentiment that is independent of such convictions, if it is to be the source of justifying reasons. Hutcheson suggests benevolence and the approval of benevolence. Hume suggests the sentiment of humanity. But it does not seem obvious that the action we think morally justified will also excite this sort of sentiment.[18] Kant points out that sometimes the morally right action not only fails to excite our benevolence, but actually repels us, because our normal sympathetic feelings have been extinguished or diverted. He argues that these facts about our feelings do not cancel the moral obligation. We are therefore sometimes justified in praising and blaming people independently of the strength of their inclination to care about morality; we think our blame is appropriate for agents who lack pro-moral feelings.

But if our blame is appropriate, then (i) the agents must be responsible for their actions, and so capable of modifying them in the light of blame, and (ii) there must be some good reason for them to modify their actions. Kant accepts the second claim because he believes that, contrary to Hume, justified praise and blame are different from expressions of our preferences or our invitations to other people to do what we would prefer them to do. If

---

[16] For Hutcheson's reply to this sort of objection see §659.
[17] Kant would have to qualify this claim, given his view about the involuntariness of sentiments; but he can still accept it in some form. See §929.
[18] Hume recognizes this possibility; see §765.

the blame is really justified, some principles make it reasonable for the agents themselves to agree with us about what they should do.

915. The Scope of Moral Reasons

If Kant is right in these claims about moral evaluation, moral reasons, praise, and blame, they apply to all rational agents, irrespective of other motives and desires, and the facts about praise and blame support his view about the nature of moral reasons. He infers: 'An action performed from duty does not have its moral worth in the purpose to be achieved through it but in the maxim by which it is determined' (G 399). Kant claims that this point has emerged from the previous discussion of acting from duty in contrast to acting in accordance with duty. His distinction between purpose and maxim is intended to correspond to the distinction between object and formal principle.[19]

If our purpose is irrelevant to the moral worth of our action, 'purpose' should have a narrow sense, confined to purposes derived from antecedent inclination. Since a particular agent's inclination is irrelevant to morality, a purpose that depends on inclination is also irrelevant to morality. An action is morally right not because it aims at some purpose to which we are already inclined, but because of a principle that has some distinctively moral character yet to be explained. If my action is to express a moral principle, it has some specific purpose; if we act from duty we give money (e.g.) in order to relieve someone's need, not to enhance our own reputation. But in this case the moral principle we act on determines the purpose, not the other way round.

Kant insists that in acting from duty the will must be determined by the form and not the matter of its maxims.[20] The contrast between form and matter relies on the contrast between empirical desires and reasons that apply to rational agents as such. Kant does not mean to contrast form with content; the distinctive feature of moral principles is not purely 'formal', in the familiar sense referring to grammatical or logical form in contrast to content.[21] Kant means that no particular purpose resting on inclination implies that an action is done from duty; for such a purpose presupposes that the agent already desires the end. The agent's maxim should have the characteristic, not yet explained, of a genuine moral principle.

Kant's objection to empirical objects of desire is summed up in his claim that we have no antecedent feeling tending to morality.[22] If moral reasons relied on antecedent feeling, they would not support our praise and blame of rational agents as such. If they do not rely on antecedent feelings, they are justifying reasons because of their form, as Kant understands 'form'. We do not yet know how much moral content belongs to reasons that apply to rational agents as such.

---

[19] 'Its moral value, therefore, does not depend on the realization of the object of the action but merely on the principle of volition by which the action is done, without any regard to the objects of the faculty of desire.' (G 399–400)

[20] See Wolff, AR 71–7; Beck, CKCPR 71–2.

[21] Kant's views on some related points about form in the *First Critique* are discussed by Pippin, KTF. See e.g., 90, on 'categorial' v. purely 'logical' formality. See also Beck, CKCPR 96.

[22] 'In the subject there is no antecedent feeling tending to morality; that is impossible, because all feeling is sensuous, and the incentives of the moral disposition must be free from every sensuous condition.' (KpV 75)

916. The A Priori Character of Moral Principles

Kant has claimed that moral principles give justifying reasons to all agents who can fairly be praised or blamed from the moral point of view. To be such agents we need only be rational agents, whatever our particular needs or desires or sentiments apart from rational agency. Moreover, if I am appropriately praised and blamed, I have reason to act morally. If, then, I am simply a rational agent, I have reason to act morally. Moral principles apply to rational agents as such, not because of some further inclination, desire, or need.

Kant's claim about moral reasons opposes Hume. In Hume's view, we would have no reason to value equality or fairness in treatment if we did not face moderate scarcity that (in his view) makes just arrangements advantageous to everyone.[23] Kant, however, maintains that some principles about fairness and equality are rationally compelling, whatever our needs or external circumstances may be, in so far as we are rational agents. Different kinds of treatment are appropriate for rational agents with different particular needs and in different external circumstances. The principles applying to rational agents as such identify common features that justify these different kinds of treatment.

Moral principles are therefore knowable a priori. Since they apply to rational agents as such, not to rational agents with some feature that is inessential to being a rational agent, they give justifying reasons to rational agents, irrespective of empirical features. For the same reasons, they are categorical imperatives; for they apply to rational agents, not to rational agents with some further inclination that gives them reason to accept moral principles.

Kant has now argued for a connexion between practical laws and morality. Our conception of moral praise and blame presupposes that moral reasons are based on practical laws. Moral praise and blame rest on the appropriate moral principles only if these moral principles are practical laws, giving reasons to rational agents as such, irrespective of the specific desires and inclinations of individuals.

Kant sees that this argument does not prove that there are any practical laws or categorical imperatives. It proves at most that if we are right about the proper extent of praise and blame, there are categorical imperatives.[24] It does not follow that anything satisfies the conditions for a categorical imperative. We might, indeed, use Kant's argument to draw a nihilist conclusion about morality.[25] If all true moral principles are categorical imperatives, but there are no moral categorical imperatives, there are no true moral principles. In that case, we might return to sentimentalism, not as an account of morality, but as an account of the outlook that we might substitute for morality, once we see that nothing satisfies our conditions for moral principles.

To forestall this reaction, and to prove that there are moral categorical imperatives, Kant needs to argue in three stages: (1) He should indicate what a moral categorical imperative will say, if there is any such thing. Hence he should find a plausible supreme principle of

---

[23] Hume on pre-conditions for justice; §769.
[24] Once we have shown that we regard moral imperatives as categorical, we must still 'investigate purely a priori the possibility of a categorical imperative' (G 419). We can show that 'if duty is a concept which is to have significance and actual legislation for our actions, it can be expressed only in categorical imperatives, not at all in hypothetical ones' (424f).
[25] This is Mackie's view about categorical imperatives. See §§606, 1374.

morality. (2) He should show that this principle is not simply a hypothetical imperative, because it does not give us a justifying reason by appeal to some antecedent non-moral preference. (3) He should show that it is a categorical imperative. For this purpose, it is not enough to show that it is not a hypothetical imperative; we must also have some reason to accept it independently of whatever else we happen to desire. This reason has to be equally good for every agent who is an appropriate object of justified praise and blame.[26]

These three stages are connected. For at the third stage we might not find the principles demanded by the first stage. In that case, we might abandon our initial conception of a supreme moral principle, or we might conclude that we cannot justify morality by appeal to a categorical imperative.

Kant discusses the first two stages in *Groundwork*, Chapter 2. He presents six different formulations of the categorical imperative, to show that he has found a credible account of the supreme principle of morality, and that this principle is not a hypothetical imperative. If we accept this part of the argument, we can consider the third stage, where Kant introduces his doctrine of freedom.

917. The Idea and the Formulae of the Categorical Imperative

If moral principles must be categorical imperatives, but there are no moral categorical imperatives, there are no moral principles. To avoid this nihilist conclusion, Kant argues that there are categorical imperatives that commit us to the acceptance of principles with enough moral content to be supreme moral principles.

We grasp the 'idea' or 'concept' of a categorical imperative if we see that we take some imperatives to be independent of particular empirical inclinations, and to depend only on the essential features of rational agency. To grasp the concept of a hypothetical imperative is not to grasp the specific principles that are hypothetical imperatives. In the case of the categorical imperative, however, Kant asks 'whether perhaps the mere concept of a categorical imperative may not also supply us with the formula containing the proposition that can alone be a categorical imperative' (G 420).

His answer to this question is Yes; for consideration of the concept of a categorical imperative yields a statement of the one categorical imperative. Since the concept of a categorical imperative is the concept of a law for all rational agents, the one categorical imperative is the principle that requires acting in accord with a universal law for all rational agents.[27] This Formula of Universal Law, therefore, satisfies the concept of a categorical imperative.

---

[26] See Foot, 'System'. To show that not all imperatives satisfying (2) also satisfy (3), she suggests that principles of etiquette are non-hypothetical imperatives. It is not clear that she is right about this. They are not overtly hypothetical, since they do not say 'If you want to avoid offending your host, you ought not to eat your peas with a knife'; they are simply principles about what you ought to do. But the hypothetical character of an imperative is determined by the reason that it rests on, not by its explicit expression; if we apply this test, we may argue that imperatives of etiquette are hypothetical or (when they embody moral principles requiring respect and consideration for others) categorical.

[27] '. . . since, besides the law, the imperative contains only the necessity that the maxim should accord with this law, while the law contains no condition to which it is limited, their remains nothing but the universality of a law as such with which the maxim of the action should conform.' (G 420)

According to Kant, the universal law 'contains no condition to which it is limited'. He relies on his original claim that the good will is the only unlimited good.[28] It is good without limitation, because it expresses the moral point of view from which we see the limits on other goods; hence moral imperatives rest on reasons that are not limited by non-moral preferences. When Kant denies that the moral law is limited by any condition, he means that it does not depend on some agent's having some particular antecedent preference giving her a specific purpose. Hence, any categorical imperative must rely on some reason that is independent of antecedent preferences. Since this reason is equally good for all rational agents, irrespective of their preferences, it is a universal law for all rational agents.

Kant's inference about categorical imperatives is open to question, for reasons we have already noticed. If we allow external reasons that do not depend on an agent's preference, we may recognize such reasons that depend on special features of particular agents, apart from their desires. Kant overlooks the possibility of imperatives based on such reasons. To support his conclusion about moral reasons, we must add the further premiss that moral reasons do not depend on peculiarities of some rational agents as opposed to others, any more than they depend on the preferences of particular rational agents. The arguments he offers for the universality of moral reasons support this further premiss.

If a moral reason is a universal law for all rational agents, does this tell us anything about what is morally acceptable? Kant tries to show that it does. He considers an agent's reason for doing some specific action; this is the maxim of the action. If the reason is unacceptable to rational agents as such, action on this maxim is morally unacceptable. We are to sort out those reasons that seem acceptable only from the point of view of a particular preference; these would be rejected from the point of view of rational agents as such.

This test is useful only if we can say what is or is not unacceptable to rational agents as such. It is relatively easy to say that some courses of action do not appeal to rational agents as such. If some rational agents lack our particular tastes in music, listening to that music will not appeal to them. But that does not make it wrong to listen to the music that we like and others dislike. We need to defend the stronger claim that rational agents as such do not simply lack these particular preferences, but reject them.

To justify his claim that rational agents as such reject some maxims and endorse others, Kant expounds the categorical imperative in six different formulae (from G 421).[29] Sometimes he suggests that the first formula, requiring us to act on a maxim that we can will to be a universal law, is the canonical statement of the categorical imperative (e.g., KpV 30–1). To understand this formula, however, we need the other formulae. Kant claims that they 'are fundamentally only so many formulae of the very same law, and each of them unites the others in itself' (G 436). The first formula provides 'the rigorous method' (G 436–7); 'but if one wishes to gain a hearing for the moral law, it is very useful to bring one and the same

---

[28] 'Limited' in 420 renders 'eingeschränkt'. Cf. 'ohne Einschränkung', 393.

[29] The six formulae are: Formula 1 (421); the formula of universal law. Formula 2; the universal law of nature (421). Formula 3; the end in itself (the Formula of Humanity, 429). Formula 4; universal legislation by every rational being (431). Formula 5; the kingdom of ends (438). Formula 6; autonomy (440). Kant speaks of three formulae (G 436) because he regards Formulae 1–2 and Formulae 4–6 as different expressions of (respectively) Formula 1 and Formula 3, treating Formula 3 as the second formulation. This list of formulae is adapted from Paton, CI 129.

action under the three stated principles and thus, so far as possible, to bring it nearer to intuition' (G 437).

The later formulae, therefore, ought to explain the first formula. Kant may be mistaken; some of his claims about the first formula may conflict with an interpretation that relies on the later formulae. But if some question arises about the interpretation of the first formula, we ought at least to consider Kant's instructions for interpreting it, and so we ought to turn to the later formulae.

918. Universal Law

Since Kant uses the concept of a categorical imperative to determine the goodness of an agent's will, he must connect it with the agent's maxim, and so with the reason that the agent acts on. Hence he formulates the categorical imperative with reference to a maxim: 'Act only according to the maxim by which you can at the same time will that it should become a universal law' (G 421).[30]

To decide whether a maxim 'can' be willed to be a universal law or 'can' become a universal law, Kant asks whether its becoming a universal law would involve some sort of contradiction. But the nature of the contradiction is not clear. Kant offers an example of deceitful promising. Someone moved by self-love acts on the maxim, 'When I believe myself to be in need of money, I will borrow money and promise to repay it, although I know I shall never do so'. This maxim could not become a universal law, because the universalized maxim would involve a contradiction. If the maxim were treated as a universal law, everyone would know that everyone made promises on this assumption. Knowing this, people would be unwilling to accept promises; and so the whole practice of promising, on which the deceitful promisor relies, would collapse. Since the deceitful promisor's maxim both presupposes promises and (if universalized) undermines promises, the universalized maxim contains a contradiction.[31]

This example suggests what Kant has in mind in speaking of a contradiction in willing. He does not intend a purely logical interpretation; for contradiction in willing does not require the acceptance of inconsistent propositions. It would be inconsistent to say both 'I will make a promise' and 'No one will make a promise', but it is consistent to make a promise on a maxim that would, if universalized, make it difficult or impossible to make promises.

Perhaps, then, Kant has in mind a practical contradiction; I will a particular action, but also will the existence of conditions that make it difficult to perform the action, so that my policy is self-defeating even if it is consistent. In that case, Kant might be describing the adoption of policies that would be self-defeating if they were universalized; he suggests that these are the ones that are morally unacceptable.

---

[30] He does not always present this formula with a reference to what the agent can will. Sometimes the formula just says: 'So act that the maxim of your will could always hold at the same time as a maxim establishing universal law' (*KpV* 30), or 'Act so that the maxim of your action can become a universal law' (*MdS* 389).

[31] 'For the universality of a law which says that anyone who believes himself to be in need could promise what he pleased with the intention of not fulfilling it would make the promise itself and the end to be accomplished by it impossible; no one would believe what was promised to him but would only laugh at any such assertion as vain pretence.' (G 422)

This sort of contradiction, however, does not make a policy irrational, and so it does not seem obvious that the avoidance of such contradiction is a universal law for rational agents. Even if the universalization of my maxim would be self-defeating, the maxim need not be self-defeating. If it is most improbable that everyone will act on my maxim, why should I, as a rational agent, reject it?

One might argue that Kant intends simply to propose a test of moral acceptability, so that a maxim is to be rejected if its universalization is self-defeating. He does not mean (on this view) that acting on the maxim is irrational in any further sense. This way of understanding Kant's test faces two objections: (1) It is not clear why the avoidance of these morally unacceptable maxims is a categorical imperative, since it is not clear why all rational agents have a reason to avoid them. (2) It is not even clear that all policies that would be self-defeating if universalized are morally wrong. If I like to walk in a deserted place, the fact that it would not be deserted if other people knew about it does not make my current preference wrong.

These objections ignore one feature of Kant's example. If I walk where other people do not walk, I am (we may suppose) not taking any unfair advantage of them. But in making a promise I do not intend to keep, I take unfair advantage of people's general willingness to keep rules that I do not want to keep. The fact that promise-breakers make an unjustified and unfair exception for themselves is exposed by the self-defeating character of the maxim when it is universalized.

This answer may deal with some apparent counter-examples, but it does not vindicate Kant's appeal to universal law and to contradiction. It shows that these tests will pick out some morally wrong actions only if we supplement them with some appeal to fairness. If the Formula of Universal Law includes the supplement, it is not obviously a categorical imperative; for it is not obvious that the supplement provides a reason for all rational agents as such.

From a sentimentalist point of view, the supplement that introduces fairness shows that Kant needs to rely on some sentiment favouring fairness. In that case, the 'contradiction in willing' consists in a contradiction between the initial maxim and the universal principle plus the appropriate sentiment. The supposed categorical imperative collapses, therefore, into a hypothetical imperative: if we care about fairness, we cannot consistently accept the maxim allowing false promises.

If this answer to Kant is right, he cannot derive a categorical imperative with the moral content that he wants. If the Formula of Universal Law could not be violated without inconsistent willing ('Let there be promises and let there be no promises'), it would be a categorical imperative, but it would lack the appropriate moral content.[32] Moral content apparently cannot be derived from rational agency alone, but must come from an empirical motive—in this case, from some sentiment favouring fairness.

But even if we were to supplement Kant's formula with a sentiment favouring fairness, we would not have found the supreme principle of morality. For some maxims are open to moral objection, even if they can be willed consistently with a sentiment of fairness. For instance, I can avoid taking unfair advantage of everyone else, if I forgo my own legitimate

---

[32] See Sidgwick's discussion, ME 385–6.

demands. If I do not care about being humiliated, then the universal law of humiliating people does not seem to introduce any contradiction into my willing, since it does not seem to involve any conflict with fairness.

And so either the Formula of Universal Law is open to cogent objections, or we should interpret it differently.

919. Rational Wills and Universal Law

Kant offers an interpretation of his formula that responds to these objections. He examines a maxim that neither defeats itself when universalized nor takes unfair advantage of other people, but still—in his view—violates the Formula of Universal Law. He considers a 'maxim of independence'—the maxim of someone who does not want to help other people. Kant argues that this maxim is unacceptable, because we 'cannot will' its universalization, which leaves everyone free to refuse to help others if they feel like refusing.[33]

What does Kant mean by saying that we 'cannot will' the universalization of the maxim of independence? He admits that the universal law of independence is consistent; it is not self-defeating in the way that a universal law of deceitful promises would be. Nor does the universal law of independence seem to conflict with the desires of all actual people. Even if we cannot give up wanting other people to help us, we might surely want their help less than we want other things, so that we could consistently accept a universal law of independence. And even if a universal law of independence were psychologically impossible for actual people, this would not help Kant in the search for a categorical imperative that gives a reason to all rational agents.

Nor does Kant appeal to self-centred egoistic calculation of one's own interest. Even if he appealed to the effect of the universalized maxim on my hypothetical interests (i.e., those I would have in the situation where the maxim would be universally accepted), the outlook of the Formula would not be egoistic. From a self-centred point of view, I have no reason to be concerned with hypothetical consequences for my interest unless these are also likely. If I consider the impact of a universal law on everyone's interest, I am not concerned simply with my own interest.

Nor does Kant consider total utility. He does not ask whether the total consequences of the universal law of independence would be worse than the consequences of some other universal law. He simply asks us to consider whether we 'can will' the universal law.

To see what Kant means in speaking of what we can will, we should consider a further example that applies the Formula of Universal Law. He discusses a 'lazy maxim' of someone who does not want to be bothered about developing his talents. This person has no objection to the universal law of laziness, allowing all rational agents to neglect the development of

---

[33] 'Now although it is possible that a universal law of nature according to that maxim could exist, it is nevertheless impossible to will that such a principle should hold everywhere as a law of nature. For a will which resolved this would conflict with itself, since instances can often arise in which he would need the love and sympathy of others, and in which he would have robbed himself, by such a law of nature springing from his own will, of all hope of the aid he desires.' (G 423)

their talents. But Kant claims that we 'cannot will' the universal law of laziness.[34] He argues that, as rational beings, we necessarily will the development of our talents. By this he does not mean that all actual rational beings want to develop their talents. He means that refusal to develop talents reflects an empirical preference that would be rejected by a rational agent who is guided by the outlook of rational agents as such.

An assumption about the outlook of rational beings as such, and hence about what we can will 'as' rational beings, also explains Kant's objection to the maxim of independence. He maintains that I cannot will universal neglect of other people's needs, because rational agents cannot will neglect of their needs. This claim is false if it means that particular rational agents cannot have the empirical inclinations that make them willing to accept other people's neglect. Kant avoids this objection if he means that such willing is inconsistent with what a rational being as such chooses.

In rejecting the maxims of independence and laziness, Kant distinguishes his categorical imperative from the Golden Rule. We might have thought that the Formula of Universal Law, in the example of false promising, expresses the Golden Rule, prohibiting us from endorsing actions that we would not want to allow other people to do to us. Kant, however, dismisses the Golden Rule as 'trivial'.[35] In distinguishing his principle from the Golden Rule, he denies that fairness of the sort that is consistent with the maxims of independence and laziness adequately captures the categorical imperative. When he asks what someone 'can will' or what 'can be' a universal law, he answers from the point of view of a rational agent as such. Though particular rational agents may put up with all sorts of universal laws, only some of these are laws that rational agents, as such, can will.

Kant believes that this formulation of the categorical imperative can be derived from the concept of a categorical imperative. Such an imperative must rest on reasons that are independent of any antecedent preferences or inclinations; hence it must rest on the considerations that are reasons for rational agents as such, apart from their empirical preferences.[36] Any practical law must be a law for all rational agents as such; and so any maxim that conforms to a practical law must be a maxim that we can will, from the point of view of rational agents as such, to be a universal law.

Even if this explanation of the categorical imperative captures Kant's meaning, we may find it unsatisfying. We are tempted to suppose that his examples allow us to apply the categorical imperative in a simple test of the rightness or wrongness of maxims. But if we have understood the Formula of Universal Law correctly, its application depends on further assumptions. It refers to what a rational agent as such wills and chooses, and Kant has told us nothing about what that is. If we took the formula to prescribe consistent action,

---

[34] 'But he cannot possibly will that this should become a universal law of nature or that it should be implanted in us by a natural instinct. For, as a rational being, he necessarily wills that all his faculties should be developed, inasmuch as they are given to him for all sorts of possible purposes.' (G 423)

[35] 'For it is merely derived from our principle, although with several limitations. It cannot be a universal law, for it contains the ground neither of duties to oneself nor of duties of love towards others (for many a man would gladly consent that others should not benefit him, if only he might be excused from benefiting them). Nor, finally, does it contain the ground of strict duties towards others, for the criminal would on this ground be able to dispute with the judges who punish him; and so on.' (G 430n) Kant attaches this comment to the second formula of the categorical imperative; but, since he takes the formulae to be equivalent, it also shows how he understands the first formula. Contrast Leibniz's appeal to the Golden Rule, §589.

[36] Kant's inference is open to question, for the reason mentioned in §908.

self-interested action, or action aiming at the best total consequences, we would at least know what actions the categorical imperative prescribes. If, on the contrary, Kant's formula refers to what rational beings as such can will, it needs further explanation.

This consequence suggests that we have found the right interpretation of the Formula of Universal Law. For Kant believes that the later formulae of the categorical imperative help to explain this first formula. If the first formula refers to what a rational agent as such can will, he is right to direct us towards the later formulae, since they seem to offer some explanation.

920. The Formula of Humanity

To explain the Formula of Universal Law, Kant introduces a second formula of the categorical imperative, the 'Formula of Humanity', which requires us to treat persons as ends in themselves. He reaches the conception of an end in itself by introducing the idea of an objective end that is an end for all rational agents. The only objective end is humanity. Hence the only categorical imperative is the one that prescribes treatment of persons as objective ends, and hence as ends in themselves.[37]

Kant re-examines the examples that illustrate the Formula of Universal Law, and argues that in each case the prohibited maxim violates the Formula of Humanity, because it treats people as means to some further end, and not as ends in themselves (G 429). Suicide just for the sake of avoiding distress undervalues the rational aspect of persons, and treats them purely as subjects of pleasure and pain. The categorical imperative goes beyond mere reciprocity and so excludes the rejection of mutual aid (in the third example). It is not simply the Golden Rule (G 430n). Since rational beings want concern for rational beings to be reciprocated, they reject complete subordination of rational beings to one person's interests.[38]

In Kant's treatment of the third and fourth examples, the Formula of Humanity is needed to explicate the previous formulae. If the previous formulae (Universal Law and Law of Nature) prescribe merely consistent willing, they do not exclude maxims that Kant wants to exclude.[39] If, however, the categorical imperative requires non-instrumental concern for the interests and aims of rational beings in their own right, it excludes consistent policies that subordinate the interests and aims of some rational beings to the subjective ends of anyone. The Formula of Humanity expresses this aspect of the categorical imperative. In the *Metaphysics of Morals*, Kant uses this formula to explain duties to oneself and others; it demands respect both for one's own humanity and for the humanity of others.[40]

The Formula of Humanity seems to conflict with utilitarianism. The conception of persons as ends in themselves supports Butler's claim that it is wrong to treat individuals

---

[37] 'Supposing, however, that there were something whose existence has in itself an absolute worth, something which, being an end in itself, could be a source of definite laws; then in this and this alone would lie the source of a possible categorical imperative, i.e., of a practical law. Now I say: man and generally any rational being exists as an end in himself, not merely as a means to be arbitrarily used by this or that will, but in all his actions, whether they concern himself or other rational beings, he must be always regarded at the same time as an end.' (G 428)

[38] This consideration may not prohibit false promising in all circumstances.

[39] Hegelian criticism on this point; §§1021, 1224.   [40] See Wood, Intro. to Kant, *PP*, CT xxxi–xxxii.

in whatever way will promote the public good, without reference to what they intended to do or are responsible for having done. If we simply consider the public good, we give a secondary place to treatment of persons in accordance with what they decide and choose, and a primary place to the results for some larger end. This policy faces Kant's objections, since the utilitarian principle regards the welfare and harm of persons simply from the point of view of its effectiveness in promoting some sort of total welfare.[41]

In Kant's view, the Formula of Humanity is equivalent to the Formula of Universal Law. The claims in the Formula of Universal Law about non-contradictory willing need to be explained by an account of what a rational agent as such can will; rational agents as such will the treatment of rational agents as ends in themselves. The demand for treatment of rational agents as ends in themselves has enough moral content to show that Kant's formulation of the categorical imperative gives some moral guidance.

Many readers agree that Kant's demand that persons be treated as ends in themselves captures an important aspect of morality. Among these, many agree that the implications of his demand expose a basic flaw in utilitarianism. But many fewer agree with his claims about the formula. In particular, many doubt whether it meets Kant's conditions for being a categorical imperative. For similar reasons, many doubt whether it is equivalent to the Formula of Universal Law, as Kant claims. While the Formula of Humanity may express a fundamental moral intuition, it cannot (according to these doubts) be derived from Kant's general claims about reasons that are valid for all rational agents.

To see whether these doubts are reasonable, we should consider Kant's explanation of the Formula of Humanity, and especially his conception of an objective end. He believes that his account of a rational will and of a practical law justifies his claims about the objective end, and that from this he can derive his claims about ends in themselves and the moral consequences that support his claims about permissible maxims.

921. Rational Beings as Objective Ends

Kant argues that if moral principles express a categorical imperative, they must rest on an objective end. As we have seen, his separation of objective from subjective ends separates those ends that give reasons only on the basis of an antecedent desire from the ends that give reasons independent of desires. But this minimal conception of an objective end does not yet show that objective ends must be ends for all rational agents as such.[42] Without some rather controversial assumptions about the nature of ends, the independence of an end from antecedent inclination is only a necessary condition for being suitable for all rational agents as such. Kant wants to show that the objective end relevant to morality is an end for all rational agents as such.

---

[41] This might not be a conclusive objection to the utilitarian principle, however. If utilitarians could show that every rational being, as such, has overriding reason to be concerned for the maximization of utility above all else, then they could argue that the utilitarian principle succeeds in treating persons as ends. Sidgwick offers a defence of utilitarianism along these lines.

[42] See §902 on objective ends.

The objective end for rational beings must impose a limit on the pursuit of subjective ends. Kant might intend either of two claims: (1) The objective end is a source of value distinct from the inclination-dependent value of subjective ends. Since, therefore, it claims some of our attention, it claims to limit the attention we give to subjective ends. (2) It claims priority over subjective ends; its demands come before the demands of subjective ends, and determine the degree to which we ought to pursue subjective ends.

To see the difference between the two kinds of limit, suppose that Kant used to keep one dog, and then acquired a second. Since the second dog needs his attention no less than the first one did, it limits the attention he can give the first dog; but he has no reason to believe that caring for it takes precedence over caring for the first dog, or that the needs of the second dog should limit his care for the first. Even if the second dog could eat all the dog food that Kant bought for both dogs, it should not be given all the food.

An objective end for all rational agents imposes both kinds of limit on the pursuit of subjective ends. It is 'the supreme limiting condition of every man's freedom of action' (G 431). It provides a 'supreme practical principle' (428), so that its demands specify the legitimate degree of satisfaction of our other ends. Returning to his initial contrast between the unlimited goodness of the good will and the limited goodness of other goods, Kant claims that the unlimited goodness prescribes the limits for the pursuit of the limited goods.

If all value were the result of antecedent desire, and hence of subjective ends, there would be no supreme practical principle (according to Kant) for reason. If there is such a principle, something must be an end in itself. This end is an object of respect, not appraised simply from the point of view of our inclinations.

An objective end is an object of respect, not an end to be achieved. This apparently paradoxical claim is intelligible if we consider different influences on goal-directed action. We may speak in general of the end of our action as the state of affairs whose properties guide us in choosing what to do. The end we seek to achieve obviously satisfies this description; if we want to achieve an end that includes having a wall painted red, we try to get red paint. Things that are not ends we aim to achieve may also guide our choices. Suppose we want to renovate a building, while preserving its original character. The character of the building—the height of the ceilings, the size of the rooms, and so on—constrains the changes we can make in the course of renovation. The original character is not something we try to achieve, since it is already there. But we respect it, if we attribute to it some value that determines the permissible ends we try to achieve and the means we adopt. It is part of the total end that we seek to achieve, since we do not achieve our aims unless we respect the original character of the building; but it is not itself something that we achieve.

This example may suggest how morality requires an objective end. The example is not perfectly analogous; for the end that is an object of respect in relation to our plans for renovation may result from inclination. Kant requires an objective end that is an object of respect in relation to every end resulting from inclination. For morality evaluates and criticizes preference-based reasons. It gives us good reasons to act, independently of any antecedent preferences or feelings; these reasons tell us which of our antecedent preferences and feelings we can legitimately act on. Since the objective end has this limiting function, Kant calls it a 'supreme limiting condition on the pursuit of subjective ends' (G 430f).

922. The Objective End and the Formula of Humanity

What, then, is the objective end that is the basis of a categorical imperative for all rational agents? To identify it, Kant returns to his initial remarks about the good will. In our conception of a good will we distinguish two kinds of end: (a) an end to be achieved (ein zu bewirkender Zweck), and (b) a self-sufficient or independent end (selbständiger Zweck). We abstract from every end to be achieved, and we are left with an independent end. The only independent end is 'the subject of all possible ends themselves, because this at the same time is the subject of a possible absolutely good will; for this sort of will cannot without contradiction be subordinated to any other object (Gegenstand)' (G 437).

The subject of all possible ends is a person, who is not merely a means to be arbitrarily used (zum beliebigen Gebrauche) for this or that will (Wille) (G 428). Since persons are not to be used simply as means, they 'limit all choice' (alle Willkür einschränkt)[43] by considerations about rational beings. This objective end for all rational agents is not simply a rival to subjective ends; it also prescribes the legitimate extent of their pursuit. Kant believes he has found the right sort of end by identifying rational agents as objective ends and ends in themselves; their rational agency includes a limit on the pursuit of subjective ends.

Kant's argument is rather brief and elliptical. It sets out from the value we attach to a good will apart from its results, and concludes that we treat a rational agent as an objective end. A fuller statement of his argument might be this:

1. Suppose that we did not value the rational will as an end in itself, deserving respect in its own right apart from any result it tends to achieve.
2. In that case, we would value it in relation to some end to be achieved.
3. In that case, it would have purely instrumental value, and we would have no reason to value it in circumstances where it was ineffective.
4. But we have reason to value the good will irrespective of whether or not it is effective.
5. So we must regard it as an end in itself—something that we respect as a limit on the pursuit of other ends.

Kant appeals (in (4)) to the fact that we value the good will in itself, apart from its instrumental value; he infers that we regard the rational will as an end in itself. Why does his claim about the good will support his claim about the rational will?

The answer depends on Kant's account of what we value in a good will. If a good will were distinct from a rational will, respect for a good will would not imply respect for a rational will, even if only rational wills could be good wills. Kant argues, however, that the good will is good because it responds to the reasons that are good reasons for every rational agent as such, irrespective of any particular empirical inclinations. Hence the good will is a rational will functioning purely as such; and hence, if the rational will being thoroughly rational deserves respect, the rational will itself deserves respect.

A different argument for the same conclusion sets out from the premiss that we recognize a categorical imperative, and proceeds as follows:

1. To accept a categorical imperative is to be guided by a principle appealing to rational agents as such, over principles that appeal to subjective ends.

---

[43] Cf. 431: 'einschränkende Bedingung der Freiehit der Handlungen'.

2.   To be guided by a principle appealing to rational agents as such is to give practical priority to rational agency over subjective ends, so that we act on the requirements of rational agency before fulfilling the demands of any subjective ends.

3.   In giving such priority to rational agency, we treat rational agency as an objective end.

4.   Hence, in accepting a categorical imperative, we treat rational agents, as such, as objective ends, that is, as ends in themselves.[44]

The most important claim is the second. Kant means that when we commit ourselves to a categorical imperative, we accept the claims of rational agency over the claims of subjective ends; the prior considerations are those that matter from the point of view of rational agency, not from the point of view of this or that particular rational agent. It is reasonable to recognize this priority if and only if we value acting on the claims of rational agency over the claims of subjective ends. If we take this attitude, we imply that rational agents, as such, are not subordinate to any subjective end.

Kant's point could also be defended by a negative argument. If we thought that rational agency is to be valued only in so far as it promotes subjective ends, we would not accept any categorical imperative. Since, however, we do (Kant assumes) accept a categorical imperative, we must attribute to rational agency, and hence to rational agents as such, some value apart from their promotion of subjective ends.

This feature of the moral law tells us something more about unacceptable maxims. If a maxim satisfies some subjective end, and if this is the only justification that can be given for treating a rational agent in a particular way, this does not show that the maxim is acceptable from the moral point of view.

This conclusion may appear to give the wrong criterion for an unacceptable maxim. If A would enjoy doing x, is that not normally a good reason for A to do x, even though A's enjoyment is a purely subjective end? Kant must reply that other questions arise about whether doing x is justified. If A's doing x threatens B's life, A's enjoyment of x does not justify A in doing x. If, then, there is no moral objection to A's doing x, the satisfaction of A's subjective end is not a sufficient justification; A's doing x is justified only if we can give appropriate answers to the various questions that arise about the impact of the action on others.

We may express this point in Kantian terms by complicating our previous description of the maxim of one's action. If I swim just for enjoyment, we might say that my maxim is 'I'm doing something I enjoy' or 'I'm doing it because I enjoy it', and that it is a morally acceptable maxim; surely there is nothing wrong with swimming just for fun? In Kant's view, however, this is not the maxim of a person with a good will, since it is not a morally acceptable maxim. If we act on an acceptable maxim, we are responsive to possible moral objections, even if the objections do not arise in this particular case. These moral conditions must be presupposed as the background in which a morally good agent pursues enjoyment. Hence a subjective end alone does not yield a morally acceptable maxim.

Kant's point is plausible if he does not mean that people with a good will must always be thinking about the bearing of morality on each of their actions. He is right to point out that we assume that a morally good person responds to moral considerations if they arise. Even

---

[44] Korsgaard, 'Humanity', takes the argument to claim that we create value by choosing ends (see 122–3).

if moral objections do not arise in a particular case, we suppose that some aspect of good people's attitude to their actions expresses their willingness to do something else if morality were to require it. Hence the maxim that they could will to be a universal law is not (e.g.) 'Do what you enjoy', but 'Do what you enjoy in the right circumstances', where the right circumstances are those in which no moral objection arises.

To express Kant's point about subjective ends, we might say that an acceptable maxim must include, or implicitly refer to, conditions that would justify the particular action. The relevant justification includes satisfactory answers to the questions that can be asked about the effects of x on rational agents. Given this conception of a maxim, it follows that if we can justify this action only by reference to some subjective end, our maxim is morally unacceptable.

923. How Can We Treat Rational Beings as Ends in Themselves?

To see what maxims are acceptable to rational agents as such, we need to see how to treat a rational agent as an end. One can take this attitude to oneself and to others. It is helpful to see how far the attitude is similar or different in the two cases, and why one might suppose that it is rationally necessary.

Kant claims that 'man necessarily thinks of his own existence in this way; thus far it is a subjective principle of human actions' (G 429). Later remarks suggest that we treat ourselves as ends in so far as we set ends for ourselves.[45] Setting ends for oneself is a distinguishing mark of a rational agent, and it somehow commits us to regarding ourselves as ends. What is the connexion?

If setting ends for oneself is distinctive of rational agents, it is not simply pursuing an end, or aiming at an end, since non-rational animals can do that. 'Setting ends' should refer to some rational and deliberate act of choosing an end; this act is peculiar to rational choosers. To set an end for myself, therefore, is not the same as pursuing an end. It differs in two respects: (1) I set an end and do not simply pursue it. (2) I set it for myself. What do these conditions imply?

Rational agents who set ends do not act on arbitrary choices. According to Aquinas, rational agents grasp 'the character of the end' (ratio finis);[46] they see what is good about this end in relation to the other ends that they see reason to pursue. If Kant has something similar in mind, he is right to claim that setting an end requires a distinctively rational capacity. His second condition, that one sets the end for oneself, also seems to follow Aquinas. In Aquinas'

---

[45] 'Rational nature is distinguished from the rest of nature by the fact that it sets itself an end. This end would be the matter of every good will. But in the idea of an absolutely good will—good without any limiting condition (of attaining this or that end)—complete abstraction must be made from every end to be effected (since that would make every will only relatively good). And so the end must here be conceived, not as an end to be effected, but as an independently existing end. Hence it must be conceived only negatively, i.e., as an end which must never be acted against and therefore as one which in all willing must never be estimated merely as means but always at the same time as an end. Now this end can be nothing but the subject of all possible ends themselves, because this subject is at the same time the subject of a possible absolutely good will; for such a will cannot without contradiction be subordinated to any other object.' (G 437)

[46] Aquinas, *ST* 1–2 q6 a2. See §243.

view, we choose ends as goods in relation to the ultimate good for ourselves. Kant seems to agree that when I set an end as an end for myself, I choose it with myself in mind. To have myself in mind in choosing an end is to rely on some conception of myself and my other ends. A particular end deserves to be chosen not simply because I find it appealing in its own right, but because it fits appropriately with my conception of myself and my other ends.

Kant's point recalls not only Aquinas' views on happiness, but also Butler's and Reid's account of self-love. My attitude to my ends as a whole explains the limits I think it reasonable to impose on the pursuit of any particular end. I do not want to pursue any particular end to a degree that conflicts with the structure of ends that I attribute to myself; and so I attach greater value to myself than I do to any single end just as such. Part of my reason for wanting to satisfy my hunger is the discomfort caused by hunger; but part of the reason comes from my thought about how that benefits me. I think of myself as consisting of something more than this particular feeling of discomfort.

Kant seems to intend the same conception of choice by a rational agent, when he introduces the duty to aim at one's own perfection.[47] If I am a rational agent, I propose an end with myself in mind, and hence in the light of some conception of myself. If I regard myself as a limit on the pursuit of other ends, I rely on a conception of myself that I value as a guide to the choice of other ends. If I value myself, I must also (Kant assumes) value my abilities, and hence seek to realize them. Hence the capacity to set ends for myself supports the demand for cultivation of one's talents.

This argument for development of one's capacities as a rational agent recalls still another aspect of Aquinas' description of rational agency. In Aquinas' view, our pursuit of happiness includes a desire for perfection.[48] He refers to perfection to make it clear that the rational pursuit of one's final good does not simply involve the adjustment of some of our desires to others, but also requires some conception of the aspects of oneself that are worth realizing. This conception is one's idea of perfection. Kant agrees; for he believes that setting ends for oneself implies valuing oneself as a rational agent, and hence valuing one's rational agency and its development.

Given this conception of setting an end for oneself, Kant believes that rational agency implies treating oneself, as a rational agent, as an end in itself. In choosing ends with myself in mind, I treat myself as a limiting condition on the pursuit of particular ends. Kant does not imply that my simple choice makes one end more valuable than another, so that the value of particular ends is entirely the product of choice. On the contrary, the reference to choosing 'for myself' suggests that it is the character of my self that determines whether one or another choice is correct. My grounds for pursuing one or another end to this or that degree rest partly on its being an end for me; the traits, characteristics, and ends that

---

[47] 'The capacity to propose an end to oneself is the characteristic of humanity (as distinguished from animality. The rational will is therefore bound up with the end of humanity in our own person, as is also, consequently, the duty to deserve well of humanity by means of culture in general, and to acquire or promote the capacity of carrying out all sorts of ends, as far as this capacity is to be found in man. This is to say that cultivating the crude predispositions of one's nature is a duty, since thus the animal is first raised to man; therefore, it is a duty in itself.' (MdS 392) Kant offers a similar argument at G 430 to explain why the categorical imperative requires the cultivation of one's own talents and capacities.

[48] Aquinas on perfection; §274.

constitute me are a condition that limits the pursuit of this end. Hence rational agents necessarily regard themselves individually as ends. We can therefore defend Kant's claims about treating oneself as an end by reflexion on the character of prudential thought in a rational agent.

In moral choice, one treats oneself as an end not only in relation to one's own desires, but also in relation to other people's. This treatment reflects an individual's self-respect—a demand for non-instrumental consideration by other people. Such a demand is supported by one's attitude to oneself in relation to one's particular passions. In both cases, I value myself above any particular end to be achieved, and I attach this value to myself as a rational agent. It would be unreasonable to suppose that I am a limiting condition for my own subjective ends, but not for other people's subjective ends; why should the mere fact that they are other people's ends rather than mine make it reasonable for me to subordinate myself to them? Kant argues that respect for myself as a rational agent also commits me to respect for rational agents, and hence commits me to the treatment of rational agents as ends in themselves.

924. Humanity v. Personality

Respect for myself and others as beings with dignity supports some of the duties that Kant discusses in the *Metaphysics of Morals*. His discussion of servility partly clarifies and partly complicates his position. He argues that servility conflicts with the dignity and absolute inner worth of persons that makes them objects of respect as ends in themselves. He now suggests that the simple capacity to set ends for themselves does not make them ends in themselves; this status comes only from their morally practical reason.[49] Here Kant seems to contradict his account in the *Groundwork* of the sources of human dignity.

In other places, too, he distinguishes humanity from personality, claiming that the moral law reveals personality as something that 'elevates man above himself as a part of the world of sense' (*KpV* 86). The demand for persons to be treated as ends in themselves 'rests on the personality of these beings, whereby alone they are ends in themselves' (87).[50]

---

[49] 'A human being in the system of nature (homo phaenomenon, animal rationale) is a being of little significance, and, along with the other animals, as products of the earth, has an ordinary value (pretium vulgare). Even the fact that he excels these in having understanding and can set ends for himself still gives him only an external value for his usefulness (pretium usus)... But a human being considered as a person, i.e., as the subject of a morally practical reason, is raised above all price. For as such (homo noumenon) he is not to be valued merely as a means to the ends of other people, or even to his own ends, but as an end in himself. This is to say, he possesses a dignity (an absolute inner worth) by which he exacts (abnötigt) respect for himself from all other rational beings in the world, can measure himself against each member of his species, and can value himself on a footing of equality with them.' (*MdS* 434–5)

[50] 'It can be nothing less than what raises a human being above himself (as a part of the world of sense), a power that connects him with an order of things that only the understanding can think, and that at the same time has under it the whole sensible world, and with it the empirically determinable existence of human beings in time, and the whole of all ends (which whole alone suits such unconditional practical laws as the moral). This is nothing else than personality, that is, freedom and independence of the mechanism of the whole of nature, yet, regarded also as a faculty of a being which is subject to special laws, namely, pure practical laws given by his own reason; so that the person as belonging to the sensible world is subject to his own personality in so far as he at the same time belongs to the intelligible world. It is then not to be wondered at that a human being, as belonging to both worlds, must regard his own nature in reference to its second and highest vocation, only with reverence, and its laws with the highest respect.' (*KpV* 86)

Kant contrasts man as phenomenon and man as noumenon, and suggests that personality belongs to the noumenal self, in contrast to the mere humanity that makes us capable of setting ends.

In the *Religion*, Kant develops his contrast between humanity and personality most extensively. Humanity involves our conception of ourselves as having interests and as having practical reason as a means to achieving them. The predisposition to humanity 'is based on practical reason, but a reason thereby subservient to other incentives' (*Rel.* 26–7). The conception of personality, however, 'is rooted in reason which is practical of itself, that is, reason which dictates laws unconditionally'.[51]

In this passage, Kant does not speak of setting ends for oneself, or of the phenomenal versus the noumenal self. He distinguishes humanity from personality by alluding to different roles of practical reason. His allusions reveal some of the obscurity that we have previously noticed in his discussions of practical reason, prudence, and morality. He alludes to four functions of practical reason: (1) It is purely instrumental, finding means to a end given by inclination. (2) It aims at maximization, at what satisfies the 'greatest sum' of inclinations. (3) It prescribes ends without reliance on inclination. (4) In the moral law, it guides us independently of any other incentive.

It is not clear, however, how Kant takes these four functions to be related. Does he, for instance, take the maximizing function to be an instance of the instrumental function of practical reason? This question takes us back to an obscurity that we noticed in his treatment of the hypothetical imperative. In speaking of the rationality of maximizing, we might have two different claims in mind: (a) Given that I want to maximize the satisfaction of my inclinations, it is rational for me to find ways to do it. (b) It is rational for me to find ways to maximize the satisfaction of my inclinations. The two claims have different implications if I happen not to care about maximizing the satisfaction of my inclinations. The first claim implies that I have no reason to find ways to maximize, but the second claim implies that it is still rational for me to maximize, even though I do not care about it. If practical reason aims at maximization irrespective of my inclinations about it, it is not purely instrumental to inclination. Hence the second function of practical reason does not seem to be simply an instance of the first function.

Kant is equally obscure about the relation between the third and the fourth functions. His only example of the third function is moral practical reason. Does he believe, therefore, that this is the only case in which practical reason can present ends independently of inclinations? It would not be surprising if he believed this, given his assumption that prudence is not a source of categorical imperatives. But if he had been clearer about the difference between

---

[51] 'For from the fact that a being has reason does not at all follow that, by the mere representation of representing its maxims as suited to universal legislation, this reason contains a faculty of determining choice (Willkür) unconditionally, and hence to be practical on its own; at least, not so far as we can see. The most rational being of this world might still need certain incentives, coming to him from the objects of inclination, to determine his choice. He might apply the most rational reflexion to these objects—about what concerns the greatest sum of incentives as well as the means for attaining the goal determined through them—without thereby suspecting the possibility of such a thing as the absolutely imperative moral law which announces itself to be itself an incentive, and, indeed, the highest incentive. If this law were not given in ourselves, no amount of subtle reasoning on our part would produce it or win our choice over to it. Yet this law is the only law that makes us conscious of the independence of our choice from determination by all other incentives ([i.e., makes us conscious] of our freedom) and thereby also of the accountability of all actions.' (*Rel.* 26n)

the first and the second functions of practical reason, he could not so easily have assumed that the only non-instrumental function is found in morality.

But even though Kant does not clearly distinguish these different functions of practical reason, we need to distinguish them, so that we can see the source of the dignity of rational agents. The *Religion* suggests a possible reconciliation of the apparently conflicting claims in the *Groundwork* and in the *Doctrine of Virtue* about whether the capacity to set ends for oneself is the source of dignity. If 'setting ends for oneself' refers to subordinate ends that are instrumental to ends given by inclination, Kant has a good reason to deny that this is a source of dignity; for in pursuing such ends, we do not attribute any special value to ourselves. But we might take 'setting ends for oneself' more narrowly, so that Kant agrees with Aquinas about the rational pursuit of ends. In that case, setting ends for oneself is a source of dignity; for we choose ends rationally as suitable ends for ourselves as rational agents with certain capacities. When Kant claims we are objective ends because we set ends for ourselves, we may take 'setting ends for ourselves' in the narrower and more demanding sense. When he denies that setting ends for ourselves implies dignity, he takes 'setting ends' to refer to a purely instrumental choice of subordinate ends.

Kant's claims about practical reason and dignity help to clarify a further question about humanity and personality. Does he believe that the non-instrumental role of practical reason is the source of dignity in its own right? Or is moral reason the source of dignity, and does Kant treat non-instrumental practical reason as the source of dignity only because it coincides with moral reason?

He has good reason to take non-instrumental practical reason itself to be the source of dignity. For he connects morality with a categorical imperative that appeals to rational agents as such. If our attitude to moral practical reason includes an element that cannot be justified by appeal to rational agency as such, he defeats his argument about morality. If dignity belongs to moral agents for some reason unconnected with rational agency, moral imperatives do not seem to be categorical imperatives. If, then, Kant attributes dignity exclusively to moral agency, he faces this damaging consequence. He ought to take practical reason itself to be the source of dignity, so that moral agency is a source of dignity because it is rational agency.

925.   The End-in-Itself and the Categorical Imperative

In so far as we recognize ourselves as ends, we attribute dignity to ourselves, and therefore we respect ourselves as more than a means to the satisfaction of desires—our own or other people's. It would be unreasonable to recognize ourselves as limits on our inclinations but not as limits on other people's inclinations. To recognize ourselves as limits is to show self-respect. If A believes that B's desires matter more than A's, A is willing to sacrifice A and to be exploited in ways that A would reject if A had more self-respect. In respecting ourselves as ends, we refuse to regard ourselves as purely instrumental to satisfying the desires of others.

Morality, as Kant presents it, generalizes this attitude to ourselves so that we take it impartially towards all rational agents. Failure to respect another person as an end would result in too much concern about our own desires in relation to other people's desires. Both in regarding ourselves as mere instruments for other people's desires and in regarding them as mere instruments for our own desires, we fail to respect persons in relation to subjective ends.

If I respect myself as a rational agent, I have some concern for the rational aims I form in my own interest; even though I could be a rational agent without these particular aims, they are valuable for me as a rational agent partly because I have chosen them. Hence if we value a person's rational agency, we ought to regard a person's rational aims and interests as themselves deserving respect, not to be exploited in someone else's interest. If we see grounds for respecting persons as rational agents, we ought also to respect their interests, and refuse to subordinate their interests to other people's interests. This connexion between respect for persons as ends and concern for the interests of persons is the source of moral content in the Formula of Humanity.

Morality is concerned with the interests of persons, and especially with the impact of actions, states of character, and so on, on the interests of persons. If we conceive these interests as simply the satisfaction of inclinations, apart from their relation to the person whose interests they are, we will endorse a utilitarian conception of the morally appropriate end, and suppose that we promote a person's interest by satisfying inclinations. Kant, however, believes that rational agents care about their own interest because they are agents with a specific identity and specific aims apart from any particular collection of inclinations. The agents who have the aims, as opposed to the aims themselves, deserve respect.

This account of interests and respect gives us a further reason to believe that Kant takes rational agency itself, rather than moral goodness, to be the source of dignity. If the only aspect of rational agents that has dignity is their moral goodness, why should respect for this require respect for their interests? Could I not recognize that A is a morally good person and deserves respect for her moral goodness, without supposing that A deserves any particular attention to her aims and interests? In Kant's view, the respect we owe to a person requires some respect for her aims and interests. If I ascribe dignity to myself, I expect to have my own interests, not simply my moral aims, considered for my sake. That is why he advises: 'Be no man's lackey.—Do not let others tread with impunity on your rights' (MdS 436).[52]

If persons are treated as ends, some moral limits are imposed on the permissible treatment of them; it follows that they have moral rights to be treated one way rather than another. Can we express this point by sticking to rights and entitlements without reference to interests and welfare? The introduction of interests and welfare may appear to introduce the empirical elements that Kant seeks to exclude from the basic principles of morality.

This objection to welfare goes too far. If we exclude it altogether from our understanding of Kant's principles, we exclude not only empirical elements, but teleological elements in general, from basic moral principles. Kant does not exclude teleology, however. He relies on it in his interpretation of the formulae of the categorical imperative. The Formula of the Law of Nature speaks of a system of nature in which different actions and agents fulfil the ends appropriate for them. Consideration of which maxims we can will to be universal laws requires us to refer to the needs of the people involved.[53] Kant rejects a conception

[52] On servility see §967. [53] See Rawls, *LHMP* 173–4.

of the good that is entirely independent of morality, but he accepts a conception that is appropriately influenced by moral considerations.[54] To respect people as ends is to consider their interests appropriately.

It would be difficult, in any case, to explain obligations and rights satisfactorily without some appeal to the interests of the right-holders.[55] Though we might try to explain rights and duties reciprocally, our explanation will be rather thin or rather dogmatic if we do not connect it to interests. If we want to go beyond the bare claim that people have rights to be treated in ways in which other people are morally obliged to treat them, and that we are obliged to respect their rights, we have to give some further content to obligations or to rights or to both. It is unsatisfactory simply to present a list of duties or rights without further explanation; for we may want to defend one list of alleged rights over another. A suitable defence appeals to the welfare or good or interests or needs of the right-holder; a reason for believing that an alleged right is harmful to the right-holder would also be a reason for believing it is not a genuine right. It is therefore reasonable to examine the implications of the Formula of Humanity by considering its impact on the interests of those affected. The introduction of interests at this stage does not make Kant a utilitarian.

As Kant promised, the Formula of Humanity helps to explain the Formula of Universal Law. In particular, it explains what is meant in speaking of what one can or cannot will as a rational being. One wills as a rational being on the basis of justifying reasons that apply to rational agents as such. Kant argues that any such reasons treat rational agents as ends. If, then, there is a categorical imperative, it prescribes treatment of rational agents as ends. This argument does not prove that there is a categorical imperative; for the reasons we take to be valid for rational agents as such may not really be valid for them. The moral point of view asserts the validity of these reasons; but to show that these reasons are valid, we need some further argument that does not simply take the moral point of view for granted. The further argument comes from the connexion between morality and freedom.

---

[54] See §971 on the object of practical reason.
[55] Some connexions and distinctions between interests and rights are discussed by Kamm, *IE*, ch. 8.

68

KANT: SOME OBJECTIONS AND REPLIES

926. 'Spurious Principles of Morality'

From the summary account of the supreme principle of morality that we have considered, we can see some points of comparison between Kant's view and the main views that he opposes. He claims to have presented the true account of morality that embodies the autonomy of the will, whereas the heteronomy of the will is the source of all the spurious principles that he rejects.[1] To evaluate this claim properly, we need to examine Kant's account of freedom and autonomy. But even before we discuss his attempt to connect morality with freedom and the rational will, we can see part of his case for preferring his account of morality over others. If we can see the strong and weak points in this case, we can see how much it matters whether he succeeds in his efforts to connect morality with freedom.

If Kant succeeds in the parts of his argument that we have considered so far, he has given an account of the moral point of view, though he has not justified it. In his view, morality claims to present categorical imperatives, and we can support this claim by further argument about freedom. If his attempt to support morality fails, we might decide (1) that there are no categorical imperatives, because there are no reasons that apply to rational beings as such, or (2) that there are no categorical imperatives of morality, even though there are non-moral categorical imperatives, or (3) that we cannot give any compelling non-moral reason for accepting or rejecting categorical imperatives of morality. In the first and second cases, Kant's account of morality supports a nihilist or a sceptical conclusion about morality. In the third case, our conclusion is more complicated. Kant speaks as though we can find some further reason for believing in categorical imperatives beyond the fact that morality requires us to believe in them, though it is not always clear what the further reason is.[2] But if there is no further reason to be found, we have to decide whether the fact that morality says there is a categorical imperative is a good enough reason by itself for believing in this categorical imperative.

---

[1] See G 441. For discussion of autonomy and heteronomy see §§984–7.   [2] The fact of reason; §939.

If, then, we abstract from Kant's further argument for the moment, we can examine his reasons for believing that his account of the principle of morality gives a better description of the moral point of view than other theories can give. We can approach this question from two directions. We should consider Kant's analysis of the defects in other views. But we should also consider the apparent defects in his view, as they appear to other theorists or to common sense. Many critics have argued that a Kantian conception of morality is inadequate or one-sided when it is measured by plausible intuitive views about right actions and good characters.

In examining objections to Kant, we often have to separate two questions: (1) Do Kant's remarks about different aspects of morality express a one-sided or distorted view? (2) Does his theory commit him to such a view? We may give different answers to these two questions, and they may make Kant's theory seem more or less plausible. If his theory commits him to mistaken views that he does not notice, we have good reason to doubt the theory. But if he expresses mistaken views that do not follow from the basic principles of his theory, we may find his theory plausible even if we reject his views on this or that particular topic.

One familiar case in which we need to separate these two questions is his treatment of lying. He is famous, or notorious, for arguing that one ought not to lie, even to a murderer in pursuit of his victim.[3] Kant believes that this rigid prohibition on lying can be justified by appeal to the categorical imperative. But the justification must include other steps besides the mere formula of the categorical imperative, and we might find reasons to reject some of these steps. If the steps we reject are not essential elements in Kant's conception of morality, doubts about his views on lying need not spread to his whole account of morality.

Admittedly, this way of defending Kant may be too easy. If our agreement is confined to very general principles, the plausible elements in his position may not be enough to constitute a theory of morality. In that case, we will have to revert to the view of critics who claim that he offers only a schematic account of the structure of a moral theory, without any plausible intermediate principles that might allow us to understand its implications for action. But if we can separate a reasonable Kantian theory from some of Kant's own specific moral doctrines, we may be able to avoid misplaced criticisms of the theory.

927. The Errors of Sentimentalism

Kant believes a sentimentalist account of morality and of practical reason is inadequate, because it treats moral imperatives as though they were hypothetical. His exposition of the good will and its relation to the categorical imperative is an implicit attack on the sentimentalist analysis of morality. If all rational agents are properly open to justified praise and blame, moral principles must state good reasons for all rational agents, whether or not particular rational agents happen to care about them. He assumes that justified praise and blame require some systematic connexion between the observer's (or critic's) and the agent's point of view, and he argues that the sentimentalist account of this relation is inadequate. Praise and blame are still justified, and hence (in his view) the same justifying reason is

---

[3] See Kant, 'Supposed right'.

present, even if the agent lacks the feelings that appeal to the moral sense. The morally good will, therefore, must recognize reasons that do not depend on antecedent desires.

The rationalists use the 'Euthyphro argument' against sentimentalism in ways that anticipate Kant. Balguy explains why Hutcheson is wrong to identify praiseworthiness with a tendency to provoke a particular sort of reaction; since an action rightly tends to provoke the reaction because it is praiseworthy, its praiseworthiness cannot be identified with the tendency.[4] For related reasons, Butler believes that sentimentalism about justifying reasons fails to recognize that conscience is a superior principle, relying on authority rather than strength. To recognize conscience as a superior principle is to recognize that morality tells us not what we ought to approve of in the light of inclinations we have, but what sorts of inclinations we ought to have and ought to approve of by attending to their merits.

Kant agrees that moral reasons do not primarily appeal to existing sentiments, but show us what sentiments are appropriate. Hence an appeal to a moral sense misconceives the nature of moral reasons.[5] If the moral sense approves of moral goodness, it recognizes that specific sentiments are appropriate, irrespective of any sentiments that we may already have. We could not recognize this if we did not already approve and disapprove of the relevant actions (etc.) on moral grounds.[6] Hence moral reasons neither consist in nor depend on the reactions of a moral sense; a genuine moral sense would recognize that any reasons that depended on its reactions would not be moral reasons. An attempt to make moral reasons depend on the reactions of the moral sense would be viciously circular. The moral sense theory has to presuppose rational grounds for morally right action, and so cannot reasonably substitute the moral sense for the rational grasp of these grounds.

Hutcheson and Hume might be unmoved by this objection to the moral sense. Kant assumes that it requires a specific reaction to which a specific intentional object is essential; moral approval is not really moral unless it is directed at something we believe to be right or wrong in advance of our reacting to it in this way.[7] His account of approval is similar to Butler's account of resentment, which rests on the belief that something is wrong in advance of our resenting it. Hutcheson does not explicitly discuss this conception of approval, but Hume explicitly rejects it; he regards the connexion between a passion and its object as purely contingent and causal. According to a sentimentalist view, awareness of benevolence arouses the specific feeling of approval that belongs to the moral sense. The relation is causal and discovered empirically. We recognize the relevant sort of approval by its introspectible quality, and we notice that this feeling results from awareness of benevolence or utility.[8] Kant's objection seems to be misdirected.

This reply to Kant, however, may simply reveal a more basic objection to the sentimentalist account of approval. If moral approval is only contingently connected with actions that deserve moral praise and blame, the same feeling may be aroused by different objects,

---

⁴ Balguy and Hutcheson; §660.   ⁵ KpV 38, MdS 376.

⁶ 'One must already value the importance of what we call duty, the authority (Ansehen; Beck renders "respect") for the moral law, and the immediate worth which a person obtains in his own eyes through obedience to it, in order to feel satisfaction in the consciousness of his conformity to law or the bitter remorse whic accompanies his awareness that he has transgressed it. Therefore this satisfaction or spiritual unrest cannt be felt prior to the cognition of obligation, nor can it be made the basis of the latter. One must be at leasthalfway honest even to be able to have a representation of these feelings.' (KpV 38)

⁷ Cf. Ross's objection to emotivism, FE 32–40, discussed in §1326.   ⁸ Hume; §§732, 761. Hutcheson; §644.

perhaps by those that we take to be harmful to all those affected by them, or those that give pleasure to the agent and extreme pain to the victim. If morally right actions are defined as those that arouse the peculiar feeling of approval, morally right actions are liable to change in accordance with changes in our feeling of approval. Hence this conception of moral approval revives the objection about mutability. If sentimentalists reject Kant's claim that moral approval presupposes a prior belief in rightness, they force themselves into worse difficulties about approval.

Moreover, if the moral sense does not rest on some prior belief about the rightness of the action being approved of, it does not seem to give the right sort of justifying reason; for it seems to give a reason for action only in proportion to the strength of the sentiments connected with it. In approving of an action I do not imply (in the sentimentalist view) that it deserves the approval of anyone else, or that anything in it deserves approval apart from my favourable feeling. A purely sentimentalist account that avoids Kant's allegation of circularity makes moral reasons a matter of comparative strength.[9] Since it does not attribute to the moral sense any judgment that the action deserves a favourable reaction, it cannot offer other people a reason for approving the action if they do not already share our own reaction to it.[10] A moral judgment, however, professes to 'judge validly . . . for other men', since it claims to offer reasons for other people, apart from what they may happen to want or to feel.

Hume and Smith try to answer this objection by appealing to the inter-personal character of the moral sense or moral sentiments. Instead of treating moral approval as simply our own reaction to an action or person, we may connect it to the reactions of most people, or of an impartial spectator. Hence we might take our moral judgment to predict the approval of the spectator, and regard our moral sentiments as the result of our collective efforts to adjust our own reactions to those of the spectator. This conception of moral approval explains why we expect all our audience to concur with us, as Hume puts it.[11]

The inter-personal aspects of the moral sentiments, however, do not completely answer Kant's demand for a point of view that 'judges validly for others'. A prediction that other people, or the impartial spectator, will react in this way does not give me a reason for caring about whether I react this way, and it does not presume that I judge validly for the other people who will react in the same way as I react. An impartial spectator captures the moral point of view only if he reacts in the way that one ought to react to a right or wrong action; the fact about how he ought to react is presupposed in treating him as a moral standard.

From the sentimentalist point of view, the reactions of the impartial spectator give me or anyone else a reason to approve or disapprove of an action only to the extent that we care

---

[9] 'But the concept of duty cannot be derived from it [sc. a feeling of satisfaction], for we would have to presuppose a feeling for law as such and regard as an object of sensation what can only be thought by reason. If this did not end up in the flattest contradiction, it would destroy every concept of duty and fill its place with a merely mechanical play of refined inclinations, sometimes contending with the coarser.' (*KpV* 38–9) The apodosis of the last sentence ('it would destroy . . .') describes the result of accepting the sentimentalist reply that we have just described.

[10] '. . . the appeal to the principle of moral feeling is superficial, since men who cannot think believe that they will be helped out by feeling, even when the question is solely one of universal law. They do so even thoug feelings naturally differ from one another by an infinity of degrees, so that feelings are not capable of providing a uniform measure of good and evil; furthermore, they do so even though one man cannot by his feeling judge validly at all for others.' (*G* 442)

[11] See Hume, *IPM* 9.6, discussed in §766.

about adjusting our reactions to his reactions. But we care about this to different degrees, and the moral judgment, as sentimentalists understand it, does not say that I have a reason to care more than I do; it depends on how much I already care. Even if everyone has the desires presupposed by moral judgment and criticism, people have them to different degrees. Hence, if reasons depend on the strength of the relevant desires, moral criticism cannot offer reasons to other people apart from the strength of specific desires. Since we believe that moral criticism offers such reasons, sentimentalism cannot be true if we are right about moral criticism.

These objections do not refute sentimentalism, but they suggest, as some of Balguy's criticisms suggest, that the sentimentalists should declare themselves to be moral sceptics or nihilists, instead of claiming to offer an account of the nature of moral judgments and reasons. Kant's claim that moral reasons apply to rational agents irrespective of the strength of their particular inclinations is not a peculiarly Kantian claim. It also rests on plausible intuitive judgments about morality. The sentimentalist account makes it difficult to see how moral judgments can give us reasons to change the strength of our sentiments, since the sentimentalist makes them dependent on the antecedent strength of these sentiments. Kant is justified in believing that if we discovered that there are no moral reasons of the sort he described, we would have to deny that there are true moral judgments. The sentiments that Hume and Smith describe might be the closest that we could come to moral judgments, but they fall far short of being moral judgments.

928. Morality and Non-Rational Motives

But even if we are inclined to prefer this part of Kant's account of morality over a sentimentalist account, we may hesitate to endorse his account as a whole. For we may still sympathize with sentimentalism. Morality seems to have indispensable non-rational elements that do not fit into Kant's account of moral reasons and moral motivation. Some familiar aspects of our moral attitudes do not seem to be concerned with rational agents as such. If Kant's exclusive focus on rational agency leaves out these aspects of morality, his approach appears to be misguided. To see whether he can answer this objection, we should consider some of his views on the non-rational aspects of morality.

We may object to his initial claims about moral praise and blame. His claim that moral worth belongs to the rational will alone relies on our intuitive judgments about what is praiseworthy and blameworthy. But his appeal to these judgments seems one-sided; he seems to claim that non-rational motives, sentiments, and reactions are either irrelevant or antagonistic to moral worth, whereas common moral views seem to connect people's moral worth with their sentiments. As Hume points out, our reaction to people's sentiments seems to be a significant part of our idea of personal merit.

How far does Kant disagree on this point? One argument for thinking he disagrees completely may be derived from his description of acting from duty. He explains the difference between acting from duty and acting on other motives by considering someone who does what is morally required when he has to struggle against his other motives and emotions.[12] According to some readers, he means that moral worth belongs to acting on moral reasons against all other motives, so that non-rational motives favouring morality are not simply irrelevant to a good person's moral character, but necessarily opposed to it. On this view, sentiments favourable to morality not only do not belong to moral worth, but actually exclude it.

We might take this view if we measured virtue by quantity of effort, so that the measure of our moral worth is the amount of effort we exert in doing the morally right action. In that case, the stronger the inclination I overcome, the more moral worth my action has. Balguy seems to take this view about the worth of an action.[13]

When Kant discusses the moral motive and inclination, he does not endorse this quantitative view. Admittedly, he sometimes speaks as though we have all our other ends, motives, and concerns on one side and the moral motive on the other, so that the normal situation is conflict. Hence he remarks that the idea of personality 'strikes down our self-conceit' (KpV 87). Are we to suppose that the morally good person always feels humiliation and conflict?

If Kant were committed to this, something would be wrong with his account of morality. For conflicting and antagonistic motives do not seem to be essential to moral goodness. If we must struggle to conform to morality, in ordinary circumstances that include no special danger or temptation, we need further moral education. It is even stranger to suggest that we would make ourselves worse if we kept our moral outlook firmly fixed on the right aims, and reconciled our inclinations with our moral outlook. The quantitative view implies that maximum moral worth requires our inclinations to be almost strong enough to overcome the moral motive, so that our moral worth would be less if the moral motive could overcome with any less effort. This view of moral worth treats it as a sort of athletic achievement, as though morally good agents were like weight-lifters who have to lift an especially heavy weight to win a contest.

Kant does not endorse this extreme view about quantity of effort. He argues that the morally good person's moral motive must be strong enough to motivate her, even if she were acting in the face of strong conflicting motives. But it may be strong enough to do this even if the strong conflicting motives are absent. Kant mentions cases of actual conflict for illustrative purposes; these cases show the sort of motive that is needed for moral worth. They provide a sign of moral worth, but they need not be the only cases in which someone's action proceeds from a good will and has moral worth.[14] Kant does not suggest that the degree of actual conflict determines moral worth.

A further argument to show why the concurrence of moral and non-moral motives would reduce moral worth might rely on a 'subtractive' view of moral worth. According to this view, the goodness of one's will is measured by the proportion of one's actual motivation for the action that is purely moral. If, then, part of one's motivation comes from inclination, this is so much subtracted from the moral worth of the action.[15]

[12] See §914. Kant's position is helpfully discussed and clarified by Henson, 'Worth', and Herman. 'Valu',
[13] Balguy; §669.
[14] On overcoming as a sign of moral worth see Aquinas, ST 2–2 q27 a7.
[15] Ross, RG 170–3, FE 305, ascribes this subtractive view to Kant, and rejects it. He explains the differece between Kant's supposed view and his own view: 'Kant is really assuming that all similar actions have n equal total intensity of

This subtractive view differs from the 'quantity of effort' view in cases where someone acts on the moral motive and has no non-moral motives either for or against the same action. Though the quantity of effort involved would be less than what would be needed in the case of conflicting motives, the proportion of motivation that is moral would be the same as in cases of conflict. In cases of conflict, the subtractive view gives the same answers as the quantitative view.

The implications of the subtractive view for moral education are less extreme than those of the quantitative view, but are still open to question. The subtractive view does not imply that the elimination of conflicting motives reduces someone's moral worth, but it still implies that any non-moral motive co-operating with the moral motive reduces moral worth. Moral training, therefore, should try to remove conflicting motives; it should not encourage co-operating motives.

We have no good reason to ascribe this view to Kant. His examples of conflict do not imply that co-operating non-moral motives reduce moral worth. He says only that their presence is not necessary for a good person's moral motive. He holds neither the quantitative nor the subtractive view about moral worth, and so he does not face the objections that arise from these views.

929. Kant and Aristotle on Non-Rational Motives

Still, even if Kant does not maintain that sentiments favouring morality exclude or reduce moral worth, he seems to maintain that they are irrelevant to moral worth, so that it makes no difference to the moral worth of one's action whether one's feelings favour it or not. His view may be explained by his tendency to treat non-rational motives as essentially egoistic, concerned with my own pleasure and happiness. Hence he objects that theorists who try to connect the morally good will with a certain sort of feeling thereby make it a desire for one's own happiness (*KpV* 22–6 , G 442). This conception of non-rational motives rests on Kant's version of psychological hedonism about desires.

Sometimes he also suggests that feelings are not voluntary enough to be relevant to moral worth. He contrasts practical with pathological love, and argues that only practical love can be morally required (G 399). Moreover, he argues, a given feeling is not a necessary feature of a rational agent, but varies in degree in different people, and perhaps is absent in some people.

These claims suggest why Kant might think inclinations are irrelevant to moral worth. But if he thinks so, his view is open to question. If he believes some morally good people might none the less always be deeply reluctant to do the morally right thing, he disagrees sharply with common sense. People who always have to strain to overcome their selfish

motivation, so that by the extent to which any other motive is effective, the sensef duty must be less effective than it would have been if acting alone. We, on the other hand, are suggesting that the sense of duty may be present with equal intensity and effectiveness whether another motive is or i not effective. . . . he is assuming that the motivation is always exactly enough to produce the doing of the given ct, while we are suggesting that there may be some to spare, so that in a man who does an act, e.g., from nse of duty + love, the sense of duty may yet be strong enough to have secured the doing of the act from alone . . .' (*RG* 171–2)

impulses and to do something for other people's benefit, no matter how little effort it may cost them, seem to be open to moral criticism. If we are terribly conscientious in respecting rational agents, but do not care about them beyond that, something seems to be missing in our attitude to them.[16]

If non-rational motives matter to morality, but they are entirely non-voluntary and contingent, Kant is wrong about morality, and Hume is right to maintain that the difference between non-voluntary conditions are relevant to the moral evaluation of agents and characters. If Hume is right, good moral characters belong only to agents with certain kinds of feelings and sentiments, contrary to Kant's claims about the universality of moral principles and moral worth.

But we need not agree with Kant's view that if voluntariness is relevant to moral worth, non-rational motives are irrelevant. If a good person does not suffer from permanent conflict between her moral principles and her emotions, perhaps Kant is wrong to claim that emotions are not appropriately voluntary. We can modify emotions in the light of our moral beliefs. Though we cannot modify them all at once on demand, we can take steps to modify them over time. And so we might expect morally good agents to adapt their emotions to their moral principles.

The view that emotions can be adapted to rational principles underlies Aristotelian views of moral education. Aristotle and Aquinas give emotions a place in moral goodness. In their view, agents who fail to make their emotions conform to their good will fail to reconcile their thoughts and actions with the requirements of morality; hence they ignore an opportunity that a morally good person would not ignore. This view that the emotions are a 'subject' (as Aquinas puts it) of moral goodness agrees with Kant's claim that moral goodness must be voluntary, praiseworthy, and therefore in the control of the good will.[17] It differs from Kant in taking a more plausible view about the voluntary character of the emotions.

In that case, Kant's refusal to allow any place in moral goodness for the emotions does not result from his basic principles, but from an assumption about the emotions that we can abandon without rejecting all the rest of his position. If we believe emotions are adaptable, we have good reason, from a Kantian point of view, to require morally good people to do what they can to adapt their emotions to the good will. The difference between the Kantian and the Aristotelian view is not a basic difference between two attitudes to moral goodness.[18]

This reconciliation of the Kantian and the Aristotelian views overlooks one complication. Aristotle argues that the training of the emotions must begin in early childhood, when we cannot yet act on the rational motives that move the virtuous agent. He reminds us that if

---

[16] Park, SA 61, quotes Coleridge, (L iv 791–2): 'I reject Kant's stoic principle, as false, unnatural, and even moral, where . . . he treats the affections as indifferent . . . in ethics, and would persuade us that a man who dsliking, and without any feeling of love for, virtue yet acted virtuously, because and only because it was his duy, is more worthy of our esteem, than the man whose affections were aidant to, and congruous with, his conscnce.' Coleridge revives a criticism of Kant by Schiller, discussed by Reiner, DI 29–51.

[17] Aquinas on the passions as a subject of virtue; §284.

[18] Korsgaard, 'Duty', 219–27, compares and contrasts Aristotle and Kant on the relation of moral virtue to emtion. She concludes (227) that the points of contrast do not constitute a difference in the basic ethical outloos. Relevant questions are discussed by Sherman, MNV, esp. chs. 1, 4, 7–8.

this early training is neglected, adults are seriously handicapped in trying to reach virtue. If virtue depends on early training, and hence on conditions that are not up to us, virtue itself may appear not to be up to us, and hence not to be praiseworthy. This conclusion conflicts with Kant's guiding assumption about the good will.

This argument, however, does not show that the Aristotelian conception of virtue is basically opposed to the Kantian conception of the good will. For the conclusion that virtue is not up to us and is not praiseworthy conflicts with Aristotle and to Aquinas no less than with Kant. They all agree with Hume's 'divines'.[19] Aristotle assumes that upbringing is not so coercive that it normally rules out becoming virtuous, and so he holds that it is up to us to be virtuous. If he were proved wrong on this point, he would have to hold that we can be praised and blamed for the part of virtue that is up to us; we would be praiseworthy for doing what we can do to acquire virtue in the circumstances resulting from our upbringing. This answer would agree with Kant's conception of the agent who does the best that can be done with the provisions of a 'step-motherly nature' (G 394).

We would be entitled to mark a sharp contrast between Aristotle and Kant on the place of the emotions in moral virtue if each accepted an extreme claim, so that (i) Kant believed that emotions have no part in virtue, and (ii) Aristotle believed that virtue requires the right emotions, even when they are not up to us. Neither Kant nor Aristotle, however, accepts the extreme claim; acceptance of it would cause serious difficulties for the rest of their positions. A reasonable assumption about the adaptability of emotions reconciles the Kantian and the Aristotelian positions.

930. The Positive Role of Non-Rational Motives

Some further reflexion on the proper place of emotions in virtue supports Kant's claims about the primacy of the good will. For while emotions and sentiments help us to reach the right moral conclusions, they may also mislead us. Even though A may be worse off than B, and may need and deserve my help more, I may sympathize with B more readily than with A. Perhaps B is suffering from an illness I have suffered from and A is suffering from something quite different, so that it is easier for me to imagine how B feels than how A feels. In such cases, the range of our sympathy may distort our moral concern. Sometimes we try to think carefully about what other people are suffering so that their situation will engage our sympathy. Efforts to correct sympathy suggest that sympathy does not fix the proper scope of moral concern.[20]

These features of sympathy suggest that unaided emotions are not good guides for moral concern. Hume admits this to some extent; for he maintains the sympathy that approves of moral guidance is not untrained sympathy, but the sympathy that has been shaped and educated through the influence of society. But this answer does not meet the original difficulty about misguided sympathy. If we are influenced by the sympathy of other people, but this also lacks rational guidance, the result will not be appropriate sympathy. Reflexion on the modification of emotions favours a Kantian over a Humean position.

[19] Hume on the 'divines'; §776.   [20] On the limitations of sympathy see §798.

Still, Kant's position would be defective if he could not explain why we are right to attach importance to the right emotional reactions. We normally suppose they will help us if they are turned in the right direction. Sometimes, indeed, we may discover that they are more reliable than our rational deliberation in finding the right answer; it may be easier to deceive ourselves by rational argument than to modify our emotional reactions to behaviour that we have tried to persuade ourselves is not really bad.

These views about the role of the emotions raise difficulties for Kant's position, if he maintains that we are always obliged to act conscientiously, by applying the formulae of the categorical imperative and acting on our conception of what they require. He sometimes speaks as though all we need to do is to ask ourselves whether we can will the maxim of our action to be a universal law, and to act on the answer to our question.[21] He has to say that the considerations that move a good will are accessible to all rational agents as such; how then could a good will be influenced by specific emotional reactions? It seems especially difficult to see how it could be influenced by them when they are contrary to the conclusion we reach by asking Kant's question about making our maxim a universal law.

But if this is Kant's position, it faces objections. Some people act steadily and scrupulously, and to this extent conscientiously, but on deplorable principles. Some of them might have some trace of decency left in their emotional reactions, if (for instance) they cannot help feeling some revulsion at the cruelty that they regard as morally required. Does Kant give such people the wrong advice?[22]

To see where Kant stands on this question, we need to divide it into two questions, one about objective rightness and the other about subjective rightness.[23] In Aquinas' terms, the first is about what makes the will good and conscience correct, and the second is about whether an erring conscience binds. Aquinas answers that the goodness of the will depends on the object willed (*ST* 1–2 q19 a2), but none the less an erring conscience binds (q19 a5); though the will is not good when it follows an erring conscience, it would be worse if it acted against the erring conscience (q19 a6).

Kant's answers to the first question are sometimes over-simplified, since he sometimes suggests it is easy to apply the categorical imperative. His formulations of the categorical imperative show that his theory conflicts with his simple answer. Though the principle of morality is accessible to all rational agents without any special empirical knowledge or non-rational reactions, recognition of the action that correctly applies the principle in particular cases may not be equally easy. When Kant sets out different principles in the *Doctrine of Virtue*, he appends 'casuistical questions' that illustrate some of the difficulties that arise in applying these principles to specific cases. Though he is notorious for his rigid prohibition of lying, he recognizes some cases where it is not easy to distinguish a 'white lie' or socially expected untruth from a morally significant lie.[24] The correct application of principles apparently relies on empirical knowledge and on well-trained emotions.

We can see this in the Formula of Humanity. Treating people as ends in themselves requires respect for them as rational agents. This respect sometimes requires us to promote

---

[21] Cf. G 403, KpV 28. [22] Bennett, 'Conscience', raises this objection to conscientious action on a bad morality.

[23] See Ross, FE, ch. 7, who discusses Prichard, 'Ignorance'.

[24] See MdS 431; the servant is responsible for the consequences of obeying the order to say that his maste is 'not at home'.

someone's interest or to meet someone's need. To find the action that actually promotes interests or meets needs, we may need some empirical information; morality may not require us to possess this information, but it requires us to do what can reasonably be expected of us to acquire it. Similarly, respect for rational agents may require consideration for their aims and their reactions; we may not know how to show such consideration if we do not understand them, and hence morality may require us to try to understand them. Kant is therefore right to raise casuistical questions. His formulation and explanation of the categorical imperative should lead us to expect them.

These facts about the application of the categorical imperative also help to answer the question about subjective rightness. Kant need not claim that we ought to trust our rational judgment against our emotions in every case of perplexity, if our rational judgment has been formed simply by finding some answer to the question about universal law. His theory gives him no reason to suppose that everyone's rational judgments are appropriately formed. If I do not consider any of the questions that ought to be asked in this situation in order to apply the categorical imperative, Kant gives me no special reason to trust the judgment that results from deliberation about what to do here and now; for this judgment may be hasty, superficial, or self-serving. In many cases, a rational judgment should recognize that (for instance) it is easy to deceive myself in cases like this one and I ought to pay some attention to my feelings of reluctance or revulsion. Kant does not imply that I ought always to follow my deliberative judgment, however I have formed it.

But he is committed to a controversial claim about subjective rightness. If we have made a reasonable and honest effort to apply the categorical imperative, we are obliged, in Kant's view, to act on the conclusion of our rational reflexion, even against our feelings of reluctance. The subjectively right action may conflict with the tendency of moral feeling and non-rational reactions that give us the objectively right answer in this particular case. Some critics might infer that Kant's position on subjective rightness must be mistaken.

But we ought not to be so easily convinced. Admittedly, the subjectively right answer, by Kant's criterion, will sometimes be objectively wrong. But we have no more reliable alternative. We may also be misled if we trust our emotions in cases where they conflict with the results of our careful and considered deliberative efforts. In many such cases, reflective agents will be subjectively and objectively right to reject the tendency of their recalcitrant emotions. The mere fact that emotions sometimes lead to the objectively right action is not a good enough reason for trusting them.

We can illustrate this point through one of the examples often used against Kant, the case of the 'conscientious Nazi' who overcomes his reluctance to kill innocent Jews because he believes it to be his duty.[25] This case offers a counter-example to Kant only if two conditions are satisfied: (1) The Nazi's conviction about his duty is the result of an honest and impartial examination of the source of the conviction. (2) He has good reason, which he ought to have seen, to trust his reluctance. Let us suppose (contrary to historical fact) that the Nazi satisfies the first condition. He still might not satisfy the second condition. If he reasonably believes that he is reluctant only because he cannot stand the sight of blood, he might recall that he was right to overcome this reluctance in order to help injured people to safety; hence

---

[25] See Geach, V 8–9.

he might reasonably conclude that his reluctance is irrational, and should not persuade him to act against his presumed conscientious convictions. The mere fact that his squeamishness at the sight of blood would lead to the objectively right action in this case does not show that he would have been subjectively right to follow it.

If, on the contrary, he would have been subjectively right to follow his emotion, it is difficult to see a sharp conflict with following one's conscience. For any justification we might give for following the recalcitrant emotions would have to say why they are likely to be reliable in certain cases; but any such likelihood is already considered by a reflective rational agent forming a rational judgment. If the 'conscientious Nazi' has failed to consider his reasons for trusting his emotional reactions, he fails to meet the first condition mentioned above; for his judgment does not rest on honest and impartial examination. Hence he is not really 'conscientious' in the way that would create a counter-example to Kant.

Kant believes, therefore, as Aquinas does, that an erring conscience binds; but an erring conscience is different from hasty, careless, or self-serving moral judgment. We ought not to ignore aspects of moral judgment that depend on emotions, non-rational reactions, and grasp of specific features of particular situations. Kant exaggerates the ease, simplicity, and purely procedural character of moral judgments. But his theory not only allows, but actually requires, attention to the non-rational aspects of moral judgment.

We need not, therefore, reject Kant's arguments against sentimentalism in order to reach a fair estimate of the place of non-rational motives in moral worth and character. We may reasonably accept his views about the rational character of the moral motive and the nature of moral reasons, while still maintaining that in a morally good person the rational motives moving us to act from duty should be supported by appropriate non-rational motives. The most plausible version of Kant's position requires a good person to integrate the moral motive with the other motives and tendencies that form a character.

931. Objections to Rationalism

Kant's statement of the supreme principle of morality makes clear his opposition to the sentimentalism of Hutcheson and Hume. It is more difficult to see the bearing of his argument on the rationalism of Clarke and Price. In fact we might reasonably take him to defend a version of rationalism. It would be surprising, however, if this were true, since the *First Critique* opposes rationalism no less than empiricism. Is Kant more sympathetic to rationalism in his moral theory?

Clarke and Price do not simply argue that reason rather than sentiment is the basis of moral judgment, moral reasons, and moral motivation. They are also intuitionists, since they claim that moral first principles can be known independently of any inferential justification. Intuitionism does not imply pluralism, but it goes naturally with it. If we treat the principle of benevolence as the only self-evident principle, we are utilitarians; but Price points out that it seems equally plausible to treat principles of justice and fidelity in the same way. If we thought that the supreme principle is the one that formulates the right balance between the claims of justice, fidelity, benevolence, and the other 'heads of virtue', it would be more difficult to give an intuitionist account of this principle. On the contrary, it would be plausible to argue that the first principle is inferentially justified, by its role in adjusting the claims of the different heads of virtue.[26] Price's position, therefore, seems to make intuitionism more plausible by combining it with pluralism. To see whether Kant has a good case against rationalism, we may consider his attitude to intuitionism and pluralism.

Does he believe that moral imperatives rest on fundamental intuitions? His argument does not simply try to uncover a series of fundamental moral principles that the good will simply accepts without further defence or explanation. He does not suggest that fundamental principles express 'fitnesses' that are intrinsically necessary, in the way that mathematical truths are, according to Clarke. In general, Kant is hostile to appeals to self-evidence; he objects that the mere claim of self-evidence does not allow us to discriminate between mutually contradictory claimants to this title. This objection seems especially pertinent to allegedly self-evident moral principles that are in fact often contested.[27] In contrast to intuitionist appeals to self-evidence, Kant argues that categorical imperatives are true and necessary because of their relation to rational agency, not because of some intrinsic necessity.

Kant does not complete this argument against rationalist intuitionism in his exposition of the categorical imperative as the supreme principle of morality. But if he can complete it, he may avoid appeal to intuitions. For if we can show that a principle relies on reasons that apply to rational agents as such, we connect moral principles with principles of rational agency. If these principles are intuitively known and prior to moral principles, Kant is an intuitionist not about moral principles, but about principles of rational agency. If they are not intuitively known, but are prior to moral principles, and rely on some inferential justification, Kant is not an intuitionist about practical principles, but a holist. If neither moral principles nor rational principles are prior, but they are known through each other, Kant is still a holist, though the circle of justification is smaller.

Since Kant opposes intuitionism about moral principles, he believes that if he cannot connect morality to freedom and rational agency in ways that vindicate his claims about categorical imperatives, the only alternative is scepticism or nihilism about morality. But we may not be inclined to draw this drastic conclusion. Even if we cannot defend moral principles by appeal to distinct principles of reason, why should they not stand on their own feet without external support? We might concede to Kant that morality would be in a rationally stronger position if its principles could be shown to be principles of practical reason, but we might still treat intuitionism as a second-best that is preferable to scepticism or nihilism.[28]

We might give a different account of how moral principles could 'stand on their own feet' without appeal to a strong version of intuitionism. In arguing for his account of the moral motive and the supreme principle of morality, Kant proceeds first 'from common rational to philosophic moral cognition', and then 'from popular moral philosophy to

---

[26] Price; §823. See further §§1171, 1292, 1412.

[27] See *KrV* A233/B285–6: '. . . if we were to allow that synthetic propositions, no matter how evident they mighte, could claim unconditional acceptance without any deduction, merely on their own claim, then all critiqu of the understanding would be lost, and since there is no lack of audacious pretensions that common beliefoes not refuse (which is, however, no credential), our understanding would therefore be open to every delusin, without being able to deny its approval to those axioms that, though unjustifiable, demand to be admitd as actual axioms in the very same confident tone.' Paton, *CI* 28–9, comments on this passage.

[28] Cf. Plato's *deuteros plous*, *Phaedo* 99cd.

metaphysics of morals'.[29] He proceeds from reflexion on examples in common moral judgment to discover the relevant general principles.[30] He argues that in our advance towards the metaphysics of morals, we should not rely wholly on examples, but should look for the general principles, even if we cannot at once embody them in clear examples.[31] If we succeed in this task, we give a systematic account of the principles underlying common moral judgments. Why not claim that success in this task gives us an inferential justification for the principles that we have reached? If we are right to claim this, we avoid intuitionism about the principles, provided that the moral judgments we begin with are initially credible.

This is a description of the 'analytic' or 'regressive' method that Kant follows in the *Groundwork*. He does not believe it is completely satisfactory. In the *Second Critique*, he follows a 'synthetic' or 'progressive' method that begins from the higher principles and derives the lower from them. One might suppose that this method commits him to intuitionism. Aristotle contrasts argument from what is better-known 'to us', leading us to the principles, and argument from what is better-known 'by nature'. He sometimes uses this contrast to distinguish dialectical argument, starting from common beliefs, and demonstrative argument, proceeding from principles that ultimately rest on self-evident principles.[32]

If Kant follows this aspect of Aristotle, his progressive method relies on intuitionist foundationalism. But he avoids appeals to intuition of moral first principles if he relies on principles about practical reason. These are not grasped by intuition, if they are principles presupposed by acknowledged facts about practical reason. In that case, Kant's progressive method relies on some appeal outside morality to practical reason. Whether it relies on intuitionism about principles of practical reason depends on the status he assigns to these principles.

These reflexions suggest why Kant seeks to avoid intuitionism, and why, none the less, an intuitionist might be willing to co-opt part of Kant's argument. At any rate, we might reasonably doubt whether claims to moral knowledge would be as groundless as Kant thinks they would be if his progressive argument failed.

It is even less clear whether Kant is justified in his rejection of intuitionist pluralism about moral principles. One might suppose that his argument reduces the various fundamental intuitions of Clarke and Price to the single principle of the categorical imperative in its various formulations. But even if the Formula of Humanity expresses the categorical imperative of morality, and it has some practical content, it does not seem to offer us a supreme principle parallel to the utilitarian principle. If the utilitarian principle is right, we do not need 'heads of virtue' without any rule of priority. But if Kant is right, we do not yet know that treating persons as ends will replace heads of virtue that may conflict. One might argue that some aspects of intrinsic concern for rational beings require impartial benevolence, others require

---

[29] These are the titles of the first two sections of G.   [30] On common rational cognition see Wood, *KET* 19–20.

[31] '. . . in order to advance by natural steps . . . from a popular philosophy, which goes no further than it can by groping with the help of examples, to metaphysics (which no longer lets itself be held back by anything empiral and, since it must measure out the whole sum of rational cognition of this kind, goes if need be all the way t ideas, where examples themselves fail us), we must follow and present distinctly the practical faculty of reaso, from its general rules of determination to the point where the concept of duty arises from it.' (G 412)

[32] Aristotle; §67.

impartial justice, and still others require special ties to particular individuals. If we do not know that treatment of persons as ends gives priority to one of these heads of virtue rather than the others, we retain Price's pluralism.

For these reasons, it is more difficult to compare Kant with rationalism than with sentimentalism. His regressive analysis of morality opposes sentimentalism, and, as far as it goes, agrees with rationalism. His disagreements with rationalism depend on doctrines that he does not defend in his regressive analysis. The comparison with rationalist intuitionism draws our attention to questions about both the foundations and the applications of Kant's account of morality. Until we examine these aspects of his position, we may suspend judgment about how far he avoids intuitionism.

932. Action and Virtue

Kant and the rationalist intuitionists seem to share one important presupposition in their approach to morality. Butler and Price object to utilitarianism and support pluralism by mentioning actions that would be wrong even if they maximized utility. When Kant formulates the supreme principle of morality, he represents it as a law that tells us how to act. They seem to agree, therefore, in a law-based, action-directed approach to morality. The appeal to law and the orientation towards action seem to explain each other. If we think of laws and imperatives, we think of commands to act; and if we are looking for a morality that guides action, we look for rules or principles that tell us what to do. This law-based and action-oriented outlook is often taken to be characteristic of modern as opposed to ancient moral outlooks.[33]

If we consider sentimentalism with this contrast in mind, it seems to go in the 'ancient' direction. Hutcheson takes the moral sense to approve of benevolence, a state of the agent. Hume presents an account of the different virtues that form our conception of 'personal merit'.[34] On this point, we may want to connect Hume with Aristotle and Cicero (whom Hume often cites), and contrast him with Kant, who seems to revive a conception of morality as 'the whole duty of man'.[35]

We have already found good reasons, however, to question any sharp contrast between a 'virtue-based' and a 'law-based' conception of morality, especially if this contrast is identified with the contrast between orientation towards states of character and orientation towards actions. Reflexion on Aquinas shows us especially clearly how an account of natural law may support an account of morality that is fundamentally about the virtues; the 'action' required by the highest principles of natural law is the formation of one's outlook and character through the different virtues. Aquinas does not intend his introduction of natural law to shift the emphasis of his moral theory from virtues to actions or from the internal to the external.[36] We need not assume, therefore, that Kant is different from Aquinas on this

---

[33] Sidgwick and the 'jural' conception; §456. Cf. Schneewind, IA 286–8.

[34] '. . . that complication of mental qualities, which form what, in common life, we call personal merit: we shall cnsider every attribute of the mind, which renders a man an object either of esteem or affection, or of hatredand contempt . . .' (Hume, IPM 1.10)

[35] On Hume's reference to the book with this title see §723.   [36] Aquinas on natural law and the virtues; §315.

point. We need to look more closely to see whether his emphasis on laws and imperatives is intended to relegate character and virtue to a secondary place.

In looking more closely, we need to recall questions about the role of non-rational motives and tendencies. The virtues are important, in Aquinas' view, partly because they integrate the passions with the will. Kant does not entirely share this view, because he sometimes doubts whether the passions are voluntary.[37] If we discount these doubts, questions still remain about the role of the virtues: (1) Does Kant agree with those who emphasize the virtues because they take states of a person to be non-instrumentally valuable, and not simply valuable for the results that they produce? This is Aristotle's and Aquinas' view about the virtues, in contrast to Hume's. (2) Does he agree with those who take virtues to be necessary even for right action, because the range of right actions cannot be completely specified without appeal to the judgment of the virtuous person?

Some answer the first question by claiming that Kant's theory is action-centred and rule-centred, whereas an Aristotelian theory is person-centred.[38] If this claim means that Kant's concern with goodness of persons is only secondary to, or derived from, his concern with the rightness of actions and of rules guiding actions, the claim is false. For Kant begins the *Groundwork* with an inquiry into the good will, and he continues by trying to describe the motives and principles that define a good will. Similarly, in the *Second Critique*, he seeks to distinguish the free and autonomous will from the heteronomous will.

The view that Kant is primarily concerned with actions and rules assumes that the categorical imperative, in its Formula of Universal Law, is meant to provide an effective method for identifying a right action. This view of the formula can claim support from some of Kant's remarks, but it does not fit most of them. He does not take the main aim of a moral theory to be the identification of right actions; he tries to find the good will.

A further contrast between Aristotle and Kant rests on the view that Aristotle is a 'virtue theorist', not only in the obvious sense that he attaches moral importance to virtues and not simply to actions, but in the narrower sense that he assigns some metaphysical or epistemological or explanatory priority to virtues over actions. One might express this claim about priority by saying that an action is virtuous because it is the action a virtuous person would do, and the converse is not true.[39]

If this is what it takes to be a virtue theorist, neither Kant nor Aristotle nor Aquinas is a virtue theorist. To describe the actions characteristic of the different virtues, Aristotle refers to the human good; he does not suggest that, for instance, facing danger for the sake of a good cause is brave simply because it is what a brave person would choose. On the contrary, the brave person chooses this sort of action because it promotes the common good of his community. Similarly, Aquinas believes that the natural law prescribes the actions belonging to all the virtues; conformity to the natural law, which in turn prescribes the pursuit of the human good, makes them virtuous actions. Kant's failure to be a virtue theorist (in the sense just described) does not distinguish him from the most prominent moralists who have given a central place to the virtues.

---

[37] Sherman, *MNV*, chs. 2, 4, discusses these questions further.
[38] Some relevant questions are discussed by Blum, *FAM*, ch. 1; Sherman, *MNV*, chs. 6–8; Hursthouse, *OVE*, hs. 4, 6–7.
[39] On different versions of virtue theory see §112.

933. Duty, Law, and Virtue

To see the place that Kant finds for virtue and the virtues, we may begin with his introduction of different types of duties. In offering examples of the application of the formulae of the categorical imperative, he divides duties into those owed to oneself and to others, and into 'perfect' and 'imperfect' duties. This latter division, discussed more fully in the *Metaphysics of Morals,* underlies the division between the spheres of law and of virtue.

Virtue enters the discussion because of the specific role of ends in virtues. In the *Second Critique* (ch. 2), Kant argues that practical reason aims at a certain kind of end, though he insists that this end is not prior to the moral law. In the *Doctrine of Virtue,* he appeals to this feature of practical reason to distinguish principles of law (or 'right', Recht) from principles of virtue (Tugend). It is not so clear how he distinguishes them, since he seems to rely on a number of non-equivalent contrasts. If we survey these contrasts, we may be able to clarify his conception of virtue.

The doctrine of law prescribes certain actions that the state must compel citizens to do if the state is to follow the prescriptions of the categorical imperative. These actions are required so that the freedom of each agent can co-exist with the freedom of every other agent according to a universal law (*MdS* 381). The state enforces only what is 'possible'. By 'possible', Kant usually seems to mean 'physically possible'. He suggests, for instance (218), that while the state can compel me to act, it cannot compel me to act from a certain motive.

This point does not show why the state should not encourage me to act from a certain motive, since encouragement is physically possible. Kant gives a different reason to show why the use of compulsion to produce virtue is not possible (382); being virtuous depends on the free choice of a maxim and an end, in some sense that excludes external compulsion. Here the impossibility seems to be logical. Kant seems to mean that no one can compel me to change my motives freely.

Sometimes the law prescribes actions and the virtuous will does the very same actions from the right motive—because they are morally required and not because they are legally prescribed. Someone might conform to the law for fear of punishment or because it is good for business.[40] The virtuous person, however, accepts the moral duties imposed by law because they are moral duties. She would not steal her neighbour's property (an action forbidden by law) even if she could steal it with impunity and no one would find out.

In these cases, principles of virtue prescribe distinctively virtuous 'actions' that include a reference to the 'interests' underlying them. Since the law prescribes actions without reference to the agent's intention, these actions do not fall under the prescriptions of law. Kant speaks of 'inner legislation', which may not prescribe different behaviour, but demands 'actions' that include an appropriate motive:[41] Virtuous people differ from those who merely conform to the moral law, because they take a different attitude to the same behaviour.

But virtuous people also aim at ends that go beyond the moral demands of law. Since they accept the categorical imperative as their principle, they acknowledge ends that are also duties. Acceptance of the moral law for its own sake requires the acceptance of ethical

---

[40] Cf. the honest trader discussed in G 397.

[41] 'Thus it is an external duty to keep the promises made in a contract; but the command to do this merely becaue it is a duty, without regard for any other incentive, belongs only to *inner* legislation.' (*MdS* 220)

ends; there could not even be a categorical imperative unless there were objective ends (*MdS* 384).[42] Recognition of an objective end is the basis for the virtuous person's fulfilment of duties of law as well as duties of virtue; but only specific duties of virtue correspond to specific obligatory ends.[43]

The obligatory ends aim at our own perfection and the happiness of others. We form these ends if we accept the categorical imperative, and so treat rational beings as ends. We might wonder why we should not aim at the happiness and perfection of rational beings impartially, but Kant argues (*MdS* 385) that we cannot treat our own happiness or the perfection of others as obligatory ends.

He claims that I cannot take my own happiness as an obligatory end, because I aim at it anyhow. But he also admits that I may not always aim at my happiness, and that I may care more about it at some times than at other times (*G* 399). In that case—even if we accept Kant's views about the conditions for obligation[44]—he should allow that I am obliged to care about my happiness to the appropriate degree on the appropriate occasions.

His argument to show that the perfection of others cannot be an obligatory end is also questionable. Even though he is right to claim that I cannot, strictly speaking, achieve the perfection of others, ought I not to try to promote it? It is equally true that I cannot achieve the happiness of others, but none the less he believes their happiness is an obligatory end for me. Perhaps he means that, strictly speaking, promoting their happiness is an obligatory end; but, in that case, he ought also to say that aiming at their perfection is an obligatory end for me.

In some cases, Kant believes that virtue prescribes actions that are not prescribed by the moral law to the non-virtuous person. But virtue does not add more duties of the same kind to duties of law. It prescribes 'duties of wide obligation', whereas law prescribes duties of narrow obligation (389). The law enjoins respect for other people's property and lives without exception. It does not allow me to choose to leave one person alive rather than another, but it requires all the actions of the relevant type. Virtue, however, allows us some freedom to choose which of the actions that fall under a rule we will do.[45] In enjoining charity, virtue does not require me to do every possible act of charity that might be open to me. Virtue prescribes an appropriate maxim (391) and an appropriate end to aim at, but it does not necessarily prescribe a given particular action that falls under the maxim. It therefore does not specify any definitely required actions that could be enjoined rigorously by the law.

So far we have found three divisions between law and virtue: (1) Law prescribes actions that we 'can' be compelled to perform, but virtue prescribes actions that cannot be compelled. (2) Law prescribes actions only, but virtue also prescribes motives and ends.

---

[42] 'But among these ends there must be some that are also (i.e., by their concept) duties.—For were there no suh ends, then all ends would hold for practical reason only as means to other ends; and since there can be noction without an end, a *categorical* imperative would be impossible.' (*MdS* 385)

[43] '. . . reverence for law as such does not yet establish an end as a duty, and only such an end is a duty of virtueHence there is only one obligation of virtue (Tugendverpflichtigung), whereas there are many duties of virtuefor there are indeed many objects which it is our duty to have as ends, but only one virtuous disposition, the sujective determining ground to fulfil our duty.' (*MdS* 411) In the previous sentence, Kant distinguishes the generl Tugendverpflichtigung as 'obligatio ethica' from a specific Tugendpflicht as 'officium ethicum, i.e. officiu virtutis'.

[44] On laws, imperatives, and obligation see §903.   [45] Cf. Aquinas, *ST* 2–2 q31 a2 ad1.

(3) Law prescribes duties of narrow obligation, but virtue prescribes duties of wide obligation. To these Kant adds a fourth division: (4) Law prescribes what is simply required, but virtue prescribes what is supererogatory or meritorious. Hence failure to follow the prescriptions of virtue is proof not of demerit (a minus quantity), but only of lack of merit (zero), 'unless the agent makes it his principle not to submit to these duties' (389).

It is difficult to see how Kant takes these four divisions between law and virtue to be connected. It is not obvious that they coincide. The connexion of the fourth division with the other three is especially obscure. Kant may suggest that since virtue prescribes duties of wide obligation, it is more meritorious to fulfil a duty of virtue than to fulfil a duty of law. But if he means this, his view is open to question. For it is no more difficult or praiseworthy to do some small act of charity than to fulfil one's obligation to serve in the armed forces in wartime.

Nor do the first and third divisions coincide. If duties of virtue are duties of wide obligation, perhaps law cannot compel us to perform any particular action prescribed by virtue.[46] But it can still compel us disjunctively. A law might compel us to give at least 1 per cent of our income to at least one of the charities on a list of registered charities; such compulsion would be neither logically nor physically impossible. Though Kant is right to distinguish observance of law from virtue, he is not so clearly right to suggest (if indeed he means to suggest) that they always involve duties of different types.[47]

While each of Kant's divisions might be legitimate for different purposes, the one that is most relevant for separating conformity to law from virtue is the one that relies on an appropriate end. A virtue essentially involves specific states of character and motivation that are not simply tendencies to specific sorts of action. The notion of an obligatory end captures the central features of a virtue, as the Aristotelian outlook conceives it: (1) It includes one's aiming at a certain end and acting for the sake of the end, not simply a tendency to act a specific way. (2) Aristotle identifies the end of virtuous action with the fine, which he also identifies with the right (deon); he seeks to distinguish it from other goods that one might aim at as non-instrumental ends.[48] Kant captures this feature of the fine and the right, by saying that the end aimed at by the virtuous person is the one that we have a duty to aim at.

If virtue requires us to aim at certain characteristic ends, it also imposes duties of wide obligation and supererogatory duties. Aiming at an end does not give us precise guidance about what to do in every specific situation, and it goes beyond the types of actions that can reasonably be demanded as matters of strict obligation. If we take the obligatory end to be the basic description of virtue, the other features that Kant ascribes to duties of virtue are intelligible. He is wrong to suppose that they are confined to duties of virtue, but right to suppose that they are characteristic of it.

Kant's doctrine of virtue and obligatory ends shows how misleading it is to contrast him with a virtue theorist, if Aristotle and Aquinas are paradigms of virtue theorists. Kant has

[46] Cf. Aquinas, ST 2–2 q32 a5: '... since it is not possible for one individual to help all to have some necessity, not all necessity obliges us to the precept, but only that without which the one who suffers the necessity cannot be sustained. For in that case the words of Ambrose apply, "Feed the one who is dying of hunger: if you have not fed him, you have killed him".'

[47] Leibniz's view of justice as the charity of the wise may therefore be preferable to Kant's separation of justice from charity. See §589.

[48] Aristotle on virtue and the fine; §116.

quite a bit to say about morality and the good will that these virtue theorists do not say. But he still makes the virtues central in the character of a person with a good will. He resists some claims that have been maintained by some advocates of the virtues; he does not affirm that actions are virtuous only because they are chosen by a virtuous person, or that the rightness of an action consists in its being seen as right by a virtuous person. But these more extreme views about the importance of the virtues are neither plausible in themselves nor held by Aristotle or Aquinas.[49]

934. Objections to Traditional Naturalism

Discussion of Kant's treatment of virtue introduces a broader comparison with the Aristotelian tradition. So far we have compared his views with Aristotelian views without considering the foundation of Aristotelian virtues. Aristotle takes the virtues to fulfil the human function and to perfect human nature in achieving the agent's own good. Both Aristotle and Aquinas are naturalists and eudaemonists. Butler is a non-eudaemonist naturalist.

Kant does not distinguish these versions of 'traditional' naturalism from the Humean naturalism that he rejects. Though he rejects traditional naturalism, he does not confront it directly, on the basis of a correct understanding. We have to gather his views from his criticisms of Leibnizian perfectionism, and from his various remarks on eudaemonism and on the Greek moralists.

Kant's objections to naturalism rest on contestable assumptions: (1) Naturalism takes facts about nature to be prior to facts about morality, and takes the truth of moral principles to depend on their correspondence to prior truths about nature. Kant believes that moral principles are fundamental in a way that is obscured by naturalism. (2) Facts about nature are facts about actual human beings as they are; they are empirical facts unsuitable for the support of moral principles. An appeal to human nature introduces an empirical element into the grounds of moral obligation. If these grounds are empirical, they lie in circumstances that do not belong to the rational will as such. Hence an appeal to human nature cannot acknowledge that grounds of moral obligation belong essentially to the rational will.[50] (3) Facts about nature are facts about what human beings actually want and how they react, and so they make the truth of moral principles depend on facts about human desires and sentiments.

These are features of the conception of human nature that underlies the ethical theories of Hobbes, Hutcheson, and Hume. Kant's reasons for avoiding arguments from nature are similar to Clarke's, Balguy's, and Price's reasons. The rationalists agree that (to use Cudworth's terms) moral facts are immutable in relation to facts about human sentiments

---

[49] Schneewind, 'Misfortunes', 58–61, discusses Kant's treatment of virtue.

[50] 'Everyone must admit that a law, if it is to hold morally, i.e., as a ground of obligation, must imply absolte necessity; that the command "Thou shalt not lie" does not apply to human beings only as if other rationl beings had no need to observe it. The same is true of all other moral laws properly so called. The groun of obligation here, therefore, must not be sought in human nature, or in the circumstances in which a huma being is placed, but sought a priori solely in the concepts of pure reason.' (G 389) 'However, it never occur to the authors to ask whether the principles of morality are, after all, to be sought at all in acquaintance with hman nature (which we can derive only from experience).' (G 410)

or desires. Hutcheson argues that sentimentalism allows immutability, but Hume embraces mutability. Kant shares the rationalist view that to make moral facts depend on facts about desires is to misunderstand how they give reasons.

One might argue that Aquinas' first principle of natural law exposes him to Kant's objections. When Aquinas claims that we necessarily pursue a final good, to be identified with happiness, he might appear to appeal to empirical features, as Kant understands them, of human beings. Though Kant agrees that all human beings pursue happiness,[51] he believes that this sort of universality makes happiness a source of merely empirical principles, and hence a source of heteronomous willing. A rational will that treats happiness as its first principle derives its law from something external, and therefore does not act autonomously.[52]

This objection overlooks Aquinas' view that one's ultimate good one is not an empirical end.[53] The first principle of natural law prescribes the pursuit of good and the avoidance of evil, because rational agents necessarily pursue their ultimate good. Aquinas does not refer to empirical peculiarities of human mental states. On the contrary, he describes essential properties of rational agents. A rational human will observes the natural law not because of some empirical feature of human agents, but simply because of its rational agency. This form of naturalism, therefore, does not make moral principles inappropriately empirical or inappropriately dependent on actual desires and sentiments.[54]

It is harder to say whether Aquinas' naturalism makes the relevant facts about human nature prior to moral facts, and whether such a claim about priority would be mistaken. He introduces the ultimate end, identified with happiness, without explicit reference to morality; we are expected to recognize that rational agents pursue happiness as their ultimate end even before we agree that they have good reason to follow moral principles. To this extent happiness is theoretically prior to morality. But what is wrong with that sort of theoretical priority? We might well sympathize with Kant's objections to a theory that fixed the content of happiness independently of morality and then relegated morality to the status of an instrumental means to happiness. But neither Aristotle nor Aquinas accepts a theory of that sort.[55]

We should not, therefore, immediately endorse Kant's rejection of appeals to human nature, even if we accept his objections to the specific naturalist doctrines he discusses. His objections require him to depart from traditional arguments from human nature only if he correctly describes and evaluates the traditional arguments. Both his description and his evaluation are open to question.

935. The Final Good and Moral Rightness

These reasons for doubt about Kant's objections to traditional naturalism also apply to his objections to those accounts of the basis of morality that rely on a prior conception of

---

[51] See G 415, quoted in §905.   [52] See Korsgaard, 'Freedom', 165–7.   [53] On Aquinas see §272.

[54] This description of Aquinas' position runs the necessary and the a priori together in ways that would need o be defended by fuller discussion.

[55] On Aristotle see §96. On Aquinas see §320. On appeals to human nature see §§77–81, 1400.

the good. In his view, such accounts make moral agency heteronomous, since they treat moral principles as hypothetical imperatives. They imply that we have sufficient reason to act on a moral principle only if we are strongly enough inclined to pursue the end that we would promote by acting on the principle. Hence we cannot accept happiness as a basis for morality, once we recognize that the principles of morality are independent of inclination.

The attempt of 'hedonists' and 'eudaemonists' to ground moral judgment in pleasure or happiness is futile, in Kant's view, because 'moral happiness' is a kind of pleasure that we enjoy only if we recognize some reason to follow moral requirements apart from the expected pleasure.[56] Eudaemonists agree with sentimentalists in supposing that appeal to a special feeling gives a ground for moral judgment. But Kant believes they face a dilemma: (1) They may agree with Kant's view that the relevant pleasure in morality depends on recognition of the rational grounds of rightness that explain our pleasure in it. In that case, any attempt to ground moral judgment or motivation in a special pleasure involves a vicious circle. (2) Alternatively, they may try to understand the relevant pleasure so that it does not presuppose independent acceptance of morality, but grounds morality on mere inclination.[57] In that case, eudaemonists endorse 'the euthanasia of all morals', because they appeal to happiness as an inclination that is prior to moral imperatives.[58] Their view implies that in following moral principles we act heteronomously, because the rational will does not follow its own law, but simply follows a hypothetical imperative aiming at the satisfaction of inclination.[59]

To show that eudaemonists cannot give a satisfactory account of morality, Kant relies on two objections: (a) Since the subordination of morality to the good reduces morality to a means to happiness, it conflicts with the demand that we choose morality for its own sake. (b) Since imperatives of happiness are merely hypothetical, the subordination of morality to happiness treats moral imperatives as merely hypothetical. These two objections need to be considered, to see whether they affect all plausible versions of eudaemonism.

[56] 'After it has all these explanations that the principle of duty is derived from pure reason, one may well wondr how the principle could again be traced back to a doctrine of happiness (Glückseligkeitslehre), though in suc a way that a certain *moral* happiness that does not rest on empirical causes is conceived as the end—a sort o happiness that is a self-contradictory nonentity (Unding), For when a thoughtful human being has overcme temptations to vice and is conscious of having done his often bitter duty, he finds himself in a condiion that one can well call happiness, a condition of contentment and peace of soul in which virtue is its own rward.—Now the eudaemonist says: this delight, this happiness, is really his motive for acting virtuously.' (*MdS*377) '. . . he must find himself bound (verbunden) to do his duty before thinking, and without thinking, of the fat that happiness will be the consequence of his observance of duty. The eudaemonist's aetiology involvs him in a circle; he can hope to be happy (or inwardly blissful) only if he is conscious of his observance of dut, but he can be moved to the observance of duty only if he foresees that he will make himself happy by it.' (*MS* 378)

[57] 'But there is also a contradiction in this subtle reasoning. For, on the one hand, he ought to observe his duty without first asking what effect this will have on his happiness, and so on a moral ground; but, on the other and, he can recognize something as his duty only if he can count on gaining happiness through it, and so in accrdance with a pathological principle, which is the direct opposite of the former [sc. the moral ground].' (*MdS*378)

[58] 'Pleasure that must precede one's observance of the law in order for one to act in conformity with the law ispathological and one's conduct follows the order of nature; but pleasure that must be preceded by the law inorder to be felt is in the moral order.—If this distinction is not observed, if *eudaemonism* (the principle of happiness) is set up as the basic principle instead of *eleutheronomy* (the principle of the freedom of internal lawgiving), the consequence is the *euthanasia* (easy death) of all morals.' (*MdS* 378)

[59] 'For one sees from the Analytic that when we assume any object, under the name of good, as the determining ground of the will prior to the moral law, and then derive the supreme practical principle from it, this alays produces heteronomy and pushes aside the moral principle.' (*KpV* 109)

The second objection fails, if we recognize categorical imperatives of prudence. If there are external prudential reasons, eudaemonism does not subordinate practical reason to inclination. According to the eudaemonist, I have a reason to pursue happiness not because I desire it, but because it is my ultimate good. Kant believes that in judgments of strict goodness 'a principle of reason is thought of as already the determining ground of the will without reference to possible objects of the faculty of the desire' (KpV 62). He believes that only moral judgments are judgments of strict goodness, but eudaemonists believe that principles derived from one's own good meet the appropriate condition.[60]

Kant does not consider this interpretation of the Stoic doctrine that pain is not an evil. He interprets 'evil' as 'morally evil', but he does not consider a prudential interpretation. The Stoics believe that virtue is self-sufficient for happiness;[61] since, therefore, pain does not remove virtue, it does not remove happiness, and therefore is not prudentially evil. Stoic doctrine does not support Kant's claim that judgments of strict goodness are judgments about moral rightness.

Kant's second objection, therefore, does not defeat eudaemonist doctrines that treat prudential imperatives as categorical. Hence he has not shown that eudaemonism necessarily subordinates practical reason to inclination. If morality is subordinate only to the summum bonum, and the summum bonum provides external reasons, morality is not subordinate to inclination. The priority of the good to the morally right does not subordinate morality to inclination.

This answer to Kant's second objection does not answer his first objection. If we believe that prudential imperatives are categorical, but we still treat morality as simply an instrumental means to happiness, we violate Kant's demand that we act on moral requirements for their own sake and not simply as a means. But Aristotle and Aquinas are not open to this objection, Neither of them regards morality simply as an instrumental means to be chosen only for the sake of happiness; they both regard morality as a non-instrumental good to be chosen as a part of happiness.

936. Differences Among the Ancients

These replies to Kant's criticism of eudaemonist naturalism gain some support from his discussion of the ancient moralists. Though he sometimes takes both the Epicureans and the Stoics to commit the eudaemonist error, he sometimes attributes the error to the Epicureans, but not to the Stoics. In his view, the Epicureans subordinate morality to happiness, but the Stoics do not.[62] Since the Stoics make virtue their supreme practical principle, they do not

---

[60] On strict goodness see §905.   [61] Stoics; §181.

[62] 'The Epicureans had indeed raised a wholly false principle of morality, i.e., that of happiness, into the supree one, and for law had substituted a maxim of arbitrary (beliebigen) choice of each according to his inclination. But they proceeded consistently enough, in that they degraded their highest good in proportion to the baseness of their principle and expected no greater happiness than that which could be attained through huma prudence.' (KpV 126) 'The Stoics . . . had chosen their supreme practical principle, virtue, quite correctly as the condition of the highest good. . . . they refused to accept the second component of the highest good, i.e., happiness, as a special object of human desire. Rather, they made their sage like a god in the conscousness of the excellence of his person, wholly independent of nature (as regards his own contentment) . . . Ths they really left out of the highest good the second element (one's own happiness),

subordinate it to any higher principle. On the contrary, they make virtue too dominant in happiness, since they identify happiness with the contentment that results from awareness of acting virtuously.[63]

Kant acknowledges, therefore, that one can argue from the highest good without giving the wrong account of morality. Though the Stoics 'devoted their ethical investigations entirely to the definition of the concept of the highest good' (*KpV* 64), they still make virtue the supreme practical principle. It is difficult to reconcile this remark with Kant's claim that the ancient moralists subordinate the moral law to some prior object of inclination, and thereby make action on moral motives heteronomous (*KpV* 64).

Moreover, acknowledgment of the supremacy of virtue is not peculiar to the Stoics among ancient moralists. Aristotle (whom Kant does not mention) also accepts the supremacy of virtue over other practical principles; in his view, the requirements of virtue are to be chosen over every possible combination of other components of eudaimonia.[64] Kant objects that the Stoics mistakenly overlook the non-moral components of the highest good.[65] This objection does not affect Aristotle and Aquinas, who affirm the supremacy of morality, but also recognize non-moral components of the good. Even if we agree with Kant's view that the Stoics do not appropriately distinguish virtue from happiness, we should not suppose that this criticism applies to all ancient moralists who reject the subordination of virtue to non-moral goods.

Kant's position is puzzling, then, because he argues both that (1) the ancients all fail to make morality their supreme practical principle and that (2) the Stoics make it their supreme practical principle. It is easier to defend his second claim; for the Stoics believe that moral considerations always take precedence over any other practical considerations. But Kant's first claim might be modified so as to fit the Stoic position; for the Stoic appeal to the highest good implies that in some way a conception of the non-morally good is prior to a conception of the moral law. In one respect, therefore, virtue is not the supreme practical principle; for, in the Stoic view, we ought to be guided by virtue only because it is necessary and sufficient for achieving the highest good. The Stoics have a consistent position because they believe that virtue is not subordinate to any end that is distinct from it. Kant does not attribute this view to the Stoics. Similarly, Reid, as we have seen, argues both that the ancients, being eudaemonists, cannot make room for the non-mercenary choice of morality for its own sake and that the Stoics take the appropriate attitude to morality.[66] Neither Reid nor Kant seems to have formed a stable view about the implications of eudaemonism.

Kant recognizes one central element in Stoic ethics.[67] The Stoics recognize a sharp distinction between the value to be attached to virtue and the good will and the value to be attached to other so-called goods, which they regard as preferred indifferents. In their

since they placed the hihest good only in acting and in contentment with one's own personal worth, including it in the conscousness of moral character.' (*KpV* 126–7)

[63] Kant expresses the same view of the Stoics in the places where he expresses approval of their moral ideal s 'the most correct (richtigste) pure ideal of ethics', though he criticizes it as being not correct for human nature. See his note in *GS* xix 106, no. 6607 (cited by Düsing, 'Problem', 10). He raises a similar objection whene says in his lectures (Collins's notes) that Zeno 'setzte die Glückseligkeit in den Werth und gab der Tugend keine Triebfeder', *LE* 250.

[64] Plato defends this view in the main argument of the *Republic*. See §§51–2.

[65] Kant's criticism of the Stoics overlooks preferred indifferents. See §182.

[66] Reid; §855.   [67] Reich, 'Greek II', 446–8, discusses Kant's debt to Cicero's *Off.*

view, it is always rational to choose the virtuous course of action apart from one's prospects for gaining the preferred indifferents. Moreover, they agree with Kant's view that morality embodies a common and impartial point of view that is appropriately shared between rational agents. The Stoics, however, argue that virtue achieves happiness; that is why they accept the supremacy of virtue. Kant rejects this eudaemonist claim, on the ground that it subordinates morality to inclination. His claims about the Stoics undermine his objection.

Kant's objections to naturalist eudaemonism would be sound if he were right to claim that all non-moral justifying reasons depend on inclination. If there are no categorical imperatives of prudence, the subordination of morality to the highest good in fact requires—even if the ancients did not see this—the subordination of morality to inclination. But since Kant does not always think the Stoics are open to this objection, he casts doubt on his view of justifying reasons. Since we have already seen grounds for doubting these claims, we have reason to doubt Kant's objections to naturalist eudaemonism.

The form of a naturalist eudaemonist argument, therefore, does not conflict with Kant's claims about morality and autonomy or about the categorical status of moral principles. If morality is a constituent of an end that is the object of a categorical imperative, morality is itself the object of a categorical imperative.

937. Naturalism, Eudaemonism, and Perfectionism

Apart from these direct criticisms of eudaemonism, Kant also objects to Leibnizian perfectionism. Since this doctrine incorporates some elements of traditional naturalism, Kant's objections also help to clarify his attitude to naturalism.[68] He argues that perfectionism agrees with sentimentalism in so far as it relies on an end that is an empirical object of the rational will. If Leibniz's conception of perfection is non-moral—'the fitness or adequacy of a thing for all sorts of ends' (*KpV* 41), it does not seem to give a reason to all rational wills. It seems to give a reason only to rational wills that happen to take some antecedent interest in non-moral perfection. Hence perfectionism reduces morality to a system of hypothetical imperatives.

Leibniz's claims about perfection are not clear on the point on which Kant attacks him. But one might argue, in Leibniz's defence, that his idea of perfection is not this purely non-moral idea that Kant ascribes to him. It might be taken to include moral perfection as well. But if that is what Leibniz means, his view faces another of Kant's objections to sentimentalism. For if we believe moral perfection gives us a reason for acting one way or another, we have already seen a reason to care about morality; hence perfectionism assumes what it seeks to prove. This is a version of an argument that Kant uses against a 'refined' version of eudaemonism.

A defence of naturalism against Kant's objections might reasonably concede one point. When Scholastic naturalism, following Aristotle, recognizes the right (the honestum) as the distinctively moral good, it does not try to subordinate the right to some non-moral good to which it is instrumental. But it does not necessarily commit itself to an unhelpful circle.

---

[68] Leibniz; §588. Cf. Rawls, *LHMP* 228–30, 235–7.

When Suarez claims that the right is what is suitable to rational nature, he offers some argument to show that the moral good expresses an aspect of rational agents that would not be expressed if we were concerned only for the useful and the pleasant. Similarly, when Butler argues that it is natural to act on conscience, he appeals to a conception of nature that connects it with acting on superior principles. The claim that morality expresses and fits our rational nature does not make morality instrumental to some end wholly external to it; but it contributes something to an account of why morality is worth choosing for a rational agent.

This account of morality seems quite close to Kant's position. He objects to intuitionist rationalism because it simply asserts the truth of moral principles without showing why they are true. In his view, we ought to show they are true by showing that they are practical laws that rational agents have reason to accept. Traditional naturalists try to show this by arguing that the right is what is suitable to rational nature. To see whether Kant disagrees with traditional naturalism on this point, we need to look more closely at the connexions he sees between morality and rational agency.

938. The Significance of Naturalism for Kant's Argument

This examination of Kant's objections to naturalist eudaemonism is useful not only for the sake of a more accurate comparison between his position and traditional naturalism, but also because it shows that his main objections rely on assumptions that create serious difficulties for his own position. We have already noticed that his rejection of categorical imperatives of prudence raises a difficulty for him. Sentimentalism gives us a reason to reject prudential categorical imperatives; Hume expresses most clearly the view that belief in external reasons is unintelligible, because it ascribes functions to practical reason that we know it cannot have. Kant cannot accept this reason for rejecting categorical imperatives of prudence, since it would not allow categorical imperatives of morality. But unless we reject external reasons altogether, it is difficult to see how we can reject them for prudence; they seem no less plausible for prudence than for morality.

Moreover, the acceptance of categorical imperatives of prudence helps Kant to explain how rational agents have dignity and therefore deserve respect. Rational agency, not just moral agency, deserves respect. If respect is attached to a rational agent's relation to rationally chosen ends chosen for the sake of the agent herself, it is easier to explain why the moral principles relying on respect for rational agents require respect for the self-regarding interests of rational agents, and not simply respect for the capacity of moral agents for morality. If this is the right account of Kant's position, he would weaken his position if he were right to reject eudaemonism and traditional naturalism. If his claims about morality are right, his claims about prudential rational agency are wrong.

This argument to show that Kant needs traditional naturalism has overlooked one apparently important further disagreement. Even if Kant were persuaded to allow categorical imperatives of prudence, his objections to eudaemonist naturalism would not be completely answered. For eudaemonism is a teleological outlook that makes one's pursuit of a final good supreme. Even if we do not subordinate morality to the good by making it purely causal and instrumental, the structure of a eudaemonist outlook subordinates morality in some way; otherwise the claim about the supremacy of the final good is false. If Kant has a good reason to reject the type of subordination that follows from the teleological aspect of eudaemonism, he has a good reason to reject eudaemonist naturalism. His claim that eudaemonism makes moral imperatives hypothetical does not seem to be a good reason. To see whether he has a better reason, we need to look more closely at his views about the relation between morality and the final good. But even if these views give him a good reason to reject eudaemonist naturalism, they do not necessarily give a good reason to reject the non-eudaemonist naturalism of Butler.

We have found, therefore, that Kant need not and should not reject traditional naturalism for the reasons that he gives. If these were good reasons, they would undermine his position as well as the naturalist position. It is not yet clear whether this conclusion counts against Kant's moral theory in itself, or simply against his view about its relation to other theories. We can return to this question once we have considered the connexions that Kant traces between freedom, autonomy, morality, and rational agency.

KANT: FREEDOM

939. How can Freedom Justify Morality? The Fact of Reason

Kant has argued that if there is a categorical imperative of morality, it has the features he ascribes to it in the different formulations of the categorical imperative. He does not claim to have shown thereby that there is a categorical imperative, or that it is a supreme principle of morality, or that it requires the treatment of persons as ends. He still needs to prove both (1) that there is a categorical imperative, giving a reason to all rational agents as such, irrespective of their particular empirical motives and inclinations, and (2) that this is the principle of morality.

To see whether Kant offers a further defence of these two claims about morality, we need to examine his claims about freedom. He claims that the reality of freedom is necessarily connected with the reality of the moral law; but the nature of the connexion is not always clear. We know freedom through our awareness of the moral law, and if we were not aware of the moral law, we would not be entitled to assume that we are free; hence the moral law is our way of knowing (ratio cognoscendi) freedom. But the reality of the moral law (its ratio essendi) consists in freedom; we are obliged by the moral law because we are free.[1]

This division between the ratio cognoscendi and the ratio essendi allows the ratio essendi to be relevant to knowledge and justification. Kant's division corresponds to his two methods of argument, regressive and progressive. The regressive argument proceeding through our moral convictions leads us to the conviction that we are free. The progressive argument, beginning from our freedom, justifies us in believing that there is a categorical imperative, and hence that there are true moral principles.[2] That is why Kant suggests that the belief in freedom plays some justifying role. In the *Groundwork*, he observes that, even if common moral beliefs presuppose a categorical imperative, there may be no such thing. To vindicate

---

[1] 'To avoid having anyone imagine that there is an inconsistency when I now call freedom the condition of the moral law and later in the treatise assert that the moral law is the only condition under which freedom can be known, I will only remind the reader that, though freedom is certainly the ratio essendi of the moral law, the latter is the ratio cognoscendi of freedom. For had not the moral law already been distinctly thought in our reason, we would never have been justified in assuming anything like freedom, even though it is not self-contradictory. But if there were no freedom, the moral law would never have been encountered in us.' (*KpV* 4n)

[2] See §894.

belief in a categorical imperative, we must also have good reason to believe that we are free. Once we recognize we are free, we will see that we have reason to follow the moral law, and so we will recognize it as a categorical imperative.

If the progressive argument gives us the ratio essendi, it begins from a principle that is better-known 'by nature', because it gives the true explanation of the purported facts about morality that we recognize in our moral convictions. Hence Kant should show us that claims about freedom rest on some basis that is distinct from the moral convictions we begin from, and that shows how those moral convictions are correct.

Some of Kant's remarks, however, may appear to deny this justificatory role of freedom. He asserts that our consciousness of the moral law is a basic 'fact of reason'.[3] We have no independent access to freedom apart from our moral convictions, nor can we find a deduction of the moral law parallel to the deduction of the categories.[4] On the contrary, the moral law has to serve as a 'principle of the deduction of freedom' (48). Whereas the moral law itself needs no justification, it proves the reality of freedom.[5] Do these claims mean that we cannot hope to defend our moral convictions by appeal to anything further? If so, Kant seems to agree with rationalist intuitionism on one basic question. But if this is his view, why is he so reserved about the arguments in the first two chapters of the *Groundwork*? He warns us that they do not show that there is a categorical imperative, but only what it would have to be like if there is one? Does the *Second Critique* abandon that reservation?

One might argue that the further argument one needs to support our awareness of the moral law is simply an argument to show that freedom is possible, in so far as it does not contradict our other reasonable beliefs about the world. Kant believes that we need to go far enough into metaphysics to settle this question about possibility. But if that is all we can settle, it seems a weak basis for asserting that there is a categorical imperative. For even if we are free, we still need some argument to show that we must recognize reasons that apply to all rational agents as such.

To see what the fact of reason does and does not settle, we need to say more precisely what the fact is. Two possibilities are these: (a) A weaker fact: we are aware of principles that present themselves as categorical imperatives. (b) A stronger fact: we are subject to a categorical imperative of morality. The weaker fact presents a plausible claim about what we have discovered in the regressive argument. If Kant has succeeded in this argument, he has shown that our moral convictions represent moral principles as categorical imperatives;

---

[3] 'Consciousness of this fundamental law may be called a fact of reason, because one cannot reason it out from antecedent data of reason, for example, the consciousness of freedom (since this is not antecedently given to us) and because it instead forces itself upon us of itself as a synthetic a priori proposition that is not based on any intuition, either pure or empirical, although it would be analytic if the freedom of the will were presupposed; but for this, as a positive concept, an intellectual intuition would be required, which certainly cannot be assumed here.' (*KpV* 31) Cf. 'a fact absolutely inexplicable from any data of the sensible world' (43); '. . . the moral law is given, as it were, as a fact of pure reason of which we are a priori conscious and which is apodictically certain . . .' (47)

[4] 'But I cannot take such a course in the deduction of the moral law. For the moral law is not concerned with cognition of the constitution of objects that may be given to reason from elsewhere . . .'. (46)

[5] '. . . the moral principle . . . serves as the principle of the deduction of . . . the faculty of freedom, of which the moral law, which itself has no need of justifying grounds, proves not only the possibility but the reality in beings who cognize this law as binding upon them. . . . This kind of credential of the moral law—that it is itself laid down as a principle of the deduction of freedom as a causality of pure reason—is fully sufficient in place of any a priori justification . . .' (47–8)

but it is a further question whether our moral convictions are right in representing them this way. In the *Groundwork*, Kant recognizes this further question. If the fact of reason that Kant has in mind is the weaker fact, his remarks in the *Second Critique* do not rule out an examination of the further question. If, however, the relevant fact is the stronger fact, Kant does not leave room for a further question about whether the moral law really is a categorical imperative. Since Kant does not commit himself to affirming the stronger fact as a fact of reason needing no further defence, we may reasonably suppose that he affirms only the weaker fact, and see whether he has an argument to answer the further question that arises from the weaker fact.

We can now sketch the argument that Kant may reasonably intend: (1) We are conscious of a moral law. (2) If we are conscious of a moral law, we are free. (3) We are free. (4) If we are free, we have reason to recognize the moral law as a categorical imperative. If we are right to suppose that the fact of reason that Kant has in mind is the weaker fact, he maintains only (1) at the outset. We need metaphysics to show that freedom is possible, so that we can affirm, on the basis of (1) and (2), that we are free, without any contradiction between theoretical and practical reason. But if we accept (3), we still leave (4) open. The weaker fact of reason that Kant recognizes (in (1)) does not answer every question about justification. An answer to (4) might settle a question that rationalist intuitionism leaves unanswered. We may be convinced that we have rational certainty about some basic moral principles; but why should we trust that conviction? The rationalist answer that we have no choice may be true, but it does not tell us what is rational about our trust in moral convictions.[6]

940. Free Will, Practical Law, and Moral Law

The sketch of the argument linking freedom with morality points to some of the questions that need to be asked. Kant claims that if the will is free, we need to find the law 'that alone is competent to determine it necessarily' (29). To determine a free will, as such, we need a determining ground that is formal rather than material; for the matter of a maxim depends on empirical desires that do not belong to a free will as such (29).

This claim may puzzle us. Why should Kant suppose that a free will as such must be determinable, and therefore determinable purely formally?[7] We might suppose that the free will as such is not determinable at all; in order to be determined one way or another, does it not need some empirical motive that does not belong essentially to the free will? The moral law answers this question by asserting that the free will as such is determinable, but we still might want some reason for agreeing with the moral law on this point. When Kant claims that 'freedom and unconditional practical law reciprocally imply each other' (29), we might agree, if he means only that a free will is determinable as such if and only if it is moved by

[6] Reid on scepticism; §844. On Kant's predecessors in moral philosophy see (on Leibniz and perfectionism) §597; Henrich, 'Ethik'; Schneewind, Intro. to Kant, *LE* xviii–xxiii (on Baumgarten).
[7] 'Since the matter of a practical law . . . can never be given otherwise than empirically, whereas a free will, as independent of empirical conditions . . . must nevertheless be determinable, a free will must find a determining ground in the law but independently of the matter of the law.' (29)

unconditional practical law, but we might still doubt whether a free will is determinable as such.

Our previous discussion of practical laws and moral laws raises a further question about Kant's claims. When he says that freedom and unconditional practical law imply each other, he means to identify the practical law with a universal law, which he identifies with the moral law.[8] But if we agree with his claim that the free will as such acts on practical laws, we need not yet agree that practical laws include moral laws. We need an argument from freedom first to practical law, but then to moral law.

These questions show us that Kant's fact of reason neither answers nor excludes further questions of justification. He claims only that we are aware of moral principles that claim to be categorical imperatives; he does not yet claim that we know that this claim is correct. It is worth our while to ask whether he gives further reasons, proceeding from principles about free agency, to believe in moral categorical imperatives.

To see what sort of argument Kant can offer, we should set out from the weaker fact of reason, that we are aware of principles that present themselves as categorical imperatives. We can then ask whether this awareness of ostensible categorical imperatives reveals freedom to us. This question should be clearer if we consider the different types of freedom that he might have in mind; for different types of freedom might have different roles in an account of morality.

Kant's claims about freedom lead him into some controversial metaphysical claims. In his view, freedom and morality require acceptance of his version of indeterminism about free will, relying on his division between the phenomenal and the noumenal world. In his view, the moral will is the noumenal will, operating outside ordinary empirically observable causal relations. We need to consider the relevance of these metaphysical views about freedom and determinism to Kant's moral theory.

941. What does the Moral Law Reveal?

Kant argues that our awareness of the moral law reveals a certain capacity to us. He contrasts two cases: (1) A choice between gratifying my allegedly overwhelming lust and staying alive. (2) A choice between inventing a false charge against an innocent person and staying alive. In the first case, Kant assumes that the fear of death would be strong enough to overcome even 'overwhelming' lust. To answer the suggestion that I might endanger my life for the sake of a more immediate satisfaction, Kant assumes that the threat of death is just as imminent as the prospect of the immediate satisfaction. In this case, one chooses to stay alive by frustrating one's lust, because one desire is stronger than the other. But in the second case, the fear of death does not necessarily overcome the opposed motive, and the eventual choice—whichever it is—is not simply the result of the comparative strength of one's desires.[9]

---

[8] These further steps are taken in §7 and its corollary (30–3).

[9] 'Whether he would or not [refuse to invent the false charge] he perhaps will not venture to say; but that it would be possible for him he would certainly admit without hesitation. He judges, therefore, that he can do something because he is conscious that he ought, and he recognizes that he is free—a fact which, without the moral law, would have remained unknown to him.' (*KpV* 30)

The second case is different from the first because we recognize reasons that are independent of the strength of our desires and we act on these reasons. If we see strong reasons for refusing to do x, these count against our satisfying our strong desire to do x, and count differently from the way in which our strong desire to do something incompatible with x would count. Even if we act on our strongest desire, the explanation is still different from the explanation of the first case; our views about good and bad reasons affect the comparative strength of our desires, and do not simply reflect it. I recognize a capacity to act on something other than the comparative strength of desires, since I recognize a capacity to act on rational principles.[10]

For the purposes of this argument, I need not believe that the moral law actually presents me with a categorical imperative. Nor need I agree that it is ever rational to try to change my strongest occurrent desire by reflexion. Kant claims only that I recognize a capacity to modify my strongest desire. He relies, therefore, only on the weak fact of reason.

942. Practical Reason and Practical Freedom

The capacity that is revealed by the claims of morality is the type of freedom that Kant calls 'practical' freedom, the will's independence of necessitation by 'sensuous' or 'empirical' impulses. This practical freedom distinguishes the rational will from the purely animal will (arbitrium brutum, MdS 212; KrV A534/B562).[11] In the animal will, choice and action result from the strongest desire, but in the free will, rational reflexion affects my choice apart from the initial strength of my desires. This conception of practical freedom agrees with Butler's and Reid's conception of rational agency. The rational agent is not determined simply by the 'animal strength' (as Reid calls it) of impulses, but is capable of acting on considerations of comparative value.[12]

Kant compares practical reason with theoretical understanding. They are similar in so far as they are both rational capacities, to be contrasted with the senses (in the theoretical case) and with sensory impulses (in the practical case). They are different in so far as one is concerned with rational prediction of the world and the other with rationally changing the world.

The understanding is the 'faculty of rules' (KrV A126). I think of one perception as a good reason for expecting another, and I do not regard the tendency to think of the second as simply a product of association. This is the basis of an objection to Hume's account of our knowledge of causal laws. In practical reason also, I apply rules and norms. In both theoretical and practical cases, I recognize these rules and laws as aspects of myself as a single subject; I am a single subject in so far as I use a single set of rules and norms to respond to varied and transitory experiences or impulses.

My awareness of my practical freedom, therefore, gives me self-knowledge that in some ways is similar to the self-knowledge that Kant describes in his account of the

---

[10] Kant's main point does not presuppose that the rational judgment is always capable of overriding the strong contrary desire (so that reason is never 'bound', as Aquinas puts it; see §253). He only needs to say that sometimes we are free to override strong desires by reasons.
[11] CT renders 'Willkür' by 'power of choice'.   [12] Reid; see §841.

understanding.[13] Through understanding, I am aware of myself as more than a series of episodes of consciousness; I also recognize myself as a continuing self, forming them into judgments under concepts and forming expectations on this basis. In practical reason also, I recognize unity and rational activity. I recognize myself as something more than a series of impulses, since I have aims and interests that continue over time and form my attitude to particular impulses. Reflexion, unity, and continuity are common to the types of self-consciousness we achieve through understanding and reason.

Practical reason differs from understanding in so far as I am not simply aware of something going on, but I also recognize myself as active in changing things and bringing them into existence. I do not simply suppose that the actual occurrence of A is a good reason for predicting B; I suppose that my thought of A is a good reason for bringing A about, whether or not I actually predict that I will do A. Hence my attitude is more than awareness of causal laws relating events. In using practical reason to reflect on our impulses, we do not look at possible actions simply as events in a purely causal order; we look at them in a normative order. This normative order is expressed by the practical use of 'ought'. We do not simply report or register events. In our judgments about what ought to be done, we express our view about how it would be reasonable for things to be.[14]

Practical freedom is therefore a source of self-knowledge. My conception of myself is partly expressed in the aims, interests, and values that guide my examination of particular impulses. This conception is similar to theoretical self-consciousness in certain ways, since it includes awareness of reasons, and not simply awareness of tendencies to expect. But it differs from theoretical self-consciousness, since it also involves changing things in accordance with rules and reasons.

In appealing to practical freedom to mark a division between the free will (arbitrium) and the animal will, Kant follows Aquinas' division between will (voluntas) and passion. Aquinas believes that we have free will (liberum arbitrium) because we have a will (voluntas)—rational desire that is formed by response to reasons, not on the strength of passions, and is therefore not coerced by sensory impulses. Kant agrees with this connexion between freedom and rational will.

Kant's position conflicts with one argument for the compatibility of freedom and determinism. To insist on the division between rational will and passion is to reject the simple compatibilism of Hobbes and Hume. They reject the division between will and passion, and therefore reject the possibility of freedom from coercion by sensuous impulses; hence they reduce freedom to internal causation. According to Kant, practical freedom requires not only internal causation, but also rational causation. Aquinas' conception of the will and free choice expresses this demand for rational causation.

---

[13] 'A human being, however, who otherwise knows all the rest of nature solely through the senses, knows himself also through bare apperception; and this, indeed, in acts and inner determinations which cannot at all be accounted impressions of the senses. He is thus to himself, in one part phenomenon, but in another part, namely in regard to certain faculties, he is a merely intelligible object, because the actions of this object cannot at all be ascribed to the receptivity of sensibility. We entitle these faculties understanding and reason.' (*KrV* A546–7/B574–5)

[14] ' "Ought" expresses a kind of necessity and of connexion with grounds which is found nowhere else in the whole of nature. The understanding can know in nature only what is, what has been or what will be. It is impossible that something in it ought to be other than what in all these time-relations it actually is . . . The "ought" expresses a possible action the ground of which cannot be anything but a mere concept.' (*KrV* A547/B575)

Aquinas' position, however, allows practical freedom to co-exist with causal determinism. If Kant agreed on this point, he could assert practical freedom without taking any particular position on the truth of determinism. Since Kant believes he has compelling theoretical reasons to accept determinism for appearances—the subject-matter of scientific theories—he has a good reason to welcome a compatibilist account of freedom.

943. Negative and Positive Freedom

Sometimes Kant elaborates his view of freedom by distinguishing the will as the power of election, the Willkür (arbitrium), from the will as rational will, the Wille (voluntas).[15] The elective will and the rational will are the same appetitive power,[16] but they have different properties. The Wille is neither free nor unfree (MdS 226), whereas the Willkür is free, by not being necessitated by sensuous impulses. The Willkür initiates action, and is the source of maxims that guide action, whereas the Wille is the source of practical laws.

This division may be clarified through Aquinas' discussion of freewill and rational will. When we act freely, we act on our will, but the will is not related in the same way to all free actions. Though the will is never necessitated by the passions, it may be influenced by them, so that our deliberation is affected by the apparent goods presented by the passions. In such cases, we act on our election or on consent by the will, but the will is not self-determining in the same way as when it deliberates without the influence of the passions.

This is Kant's view of the relation between Wille and Willkür. When we act freely, we act on a maxim that is accepted by the Wille. But the Wille may accept a maxim for different reasons; it either acts on its own initiative or accepts the suggestions of sensuous impulses. These different attitudes of the Wille determine the character of the Willkür, which determines our action. Whatever attitude the Wille takes, we act freely; and this is the freedom that is revealed by our awareness of the moral law.

The different attitudes of the rational will towards the suggestions of sensuous impulses underlie the two different types of freedom that Kant calls 'negative' and 'positive'. We are negatively free in so far as nothing coerces the Willkür; we are positively free in so far as we are determined by the legislation of the Wille giving itself the law.[17] Negative freedom is the freedom of responsibility, but positive freedom is the freedom of the good will. When

---

[15] Beck, CKCPR 177n, cites evidence to show that Kant and Wolff intend 'Willkür' to render 'arbitrium' and 'Wille' to render 'voluntas'. See also Allison, KTF, ch. 7.

[16] 'The Wille is therefore the appetitive power regarded not so much (as the Willkür is) in relation to the action, but rather in relation to the ground determining the Willkür to the action. The Wille itself has, properly speaking, no determining ground, but in so far as it [sc. reason] can determine the Willkür, it is practical reason itself.' (MdS 213) 'The freedom of the Willkür is this independence from sensuous impulse in the determination of the Willkür. This is the negative concept of freedom. The positive concept of freedom is that of the power of pure reason to be of itself practical. But pure reason can be practical only if the maxim of every action is subjected to the condition that it qualifies as a universal law.' (MdS 213–14)

[17] Kant also introduces a negative and a positive conception of freedom at G 446. But here these seem to be two ways of conceiving the same condition, rather than two distinct conditions; at least Kant does not insist on their distinctness as sharply as he needs to. For more discussion of Willkür and Wille see Silber, 'Ethical', xciv–cvi.

we are negatively but not positively free, our Wille is heteronomous, and so is the resulting Willkür.[18] When we are positively free, we are autonomous; 'autonomy of the Wille is that property of it, by which it is to itself (independently of any property of objects of volition) a law' (G 440). Heteronomy results if the Wille 'goes outside itself and seeks the law in the property of any of its objects' (441). In this case, 'the Wille does not give itself the law, but the object through its relation to the Wille gives the law to it'.

The contrast between heteronomy and autonomy supports Kant's criticism of mistaken moral theories and of mistaken moral attitudes.[19] If non-Kantian theories about practical reason were correct, our willing would be necessarily heteronomous, since these theories claim that practical reason can only find ways to fulfil some aim given to it from outside. These theories do not recognize the possibility of autonomy. We can adopt a heteronomous outlook by restricting our practical reason to the subordinate role that, according to mistaken moral theories, is its only possible role. The theories are mistaken because they do not recognize that even heteronomous agents are capable of autonomy, and hence not necessarily heteronomous.

The division between negative and positive freedom helps Kant to avoid a misunderstanding that might result from his tendency to identify morality with freedom. Since he believes that acting on the moral law results from motivation by reason rather than by sensuous impulses, we might infer that if we are motivated by sensuous impulses contrary to reason, we are not free but compelled; in that case, our desires or urges are 'overwhelming' or 'uncontrollable'. When Kant says that heteronomy involves the dependence of the rational will on sensuous impulses, so that it gives only hypothetical imperatives, we might infer that the rational will is overcome and subjected.

But he rejects this inference. The acceptance of an evil maxim results from the exercise of free will. Heteronomous agents have negative freedom, the freedom of responsibility. Their rational will is not compelled to accept maxims that have some other source than the rational will itself, and even when it has accepted them, it is still capable of giving itself the law. Hence, our permanent negative freedom is a permanent capacity for autonomy. The difference between heteronomy and autonomy does not consist in the difference between compulsion and free acceptance, but in the source of the principles that we freely accept.

We become evil, therefore, not by being overcome by an evil principle, but by freely incorporating such a principle in our maxim.[20] Hence an evil disposition 'must have been adopted by free choice (Willkür)' (Rel. 25). Evil does not belong to a person's sensuous,

---

[18] 'The sole principle of morality consists in independence from all material of the law (i.e. a desired object) and in the accompanying determination of Willkür by the mere form of giving universal law which a maxim must be capable of having. That independence, however, is freedom in the negative sense; this lawgiving by pure and, as such, practical reason in its own right (diese eigene Gesetzgebung) is freedom in the positive sense.' (KpV 33)

[19] A rational will (Wille) is heteronomous if it does not give itself for the law, so that the matter of volition is a determining ground of the Wille. See KpV 36, 39, 41. It is difficult to reconcile this view with G, ch. 3, but it fits KpV and MdS. See Allison, KTF 94–106. Contrast Hill, DPR 84–5, who believes that all normal adults are autonomous, and that heteronomy is a condition conceived by mistaken theorists, not an actual condition of some agents.

[20] '...freedom of the Willkür has the characteristic, entirely peculiar to it, that it cannot be determined to action through any incentive except so far as the human being has incorporated it into his maxim (has made it into a universal rule for himself, according to which he wills to conduct himself); only thus can an incentive, whatever it may be, co-exist with the absolute spontaneity of the Willkür (of freedom).' (Rel. 23–4)

non-rational nature (*Rel. 35*).We become evil only because we accept the demands of this non-rational nature and incorporate them into our maxim as the overriding principle.[21]

944. Degrees of Autonomy and Heteronomy

When Kant denies that vice results from compulsion, he raises a further question. If we become evil because our rational will incorporates an evil principle into its maxim, how does the rational will do this? Indeed, how can it do this, if it is a rational will? Kant suggests (*Rel. 36*) that if we had no sensuous impulses, the will would accept the moral law, but since we have these impulses, we have a potential rival to the guidance of the moral law. Why do we choose one guide rather than the other?

Kant may seem to have no acceptable solution. Our mistaken choice, incorporating the satisfaction of sensuous impulses in our maxim as the overriding aim, cannot simply result from non-rational compulsion. But if it is an action of the rational will, why are we any less positively free by following sensuous impulses than by accepting the moral law? We can see how we are positively free, to the extent that we exercise our capacity to choose between maxims. But if the choice of evil is a rational choice by the rational will, why does the rational will not give itself the law in choosing evil? Positive freedom seems to have no special connexion with morality.

This difficulty for Kant is similar to the one that Aristotle and Aquinas face in trying to do justice to the rationality of vice. They believe that the vicious person is not overcome by passion; he elects his perverse end, and so reaches it by some sort of deliberation about the final good.[22] The virtuous person reaches his correct end by deliberation about the final good. How, then, can the virtuous person be guided by reason in some way that distinguishes him from the vicious person? Aristotelian deliberation raises the difficulties that arise for Kantian incorporation into a maxim; in both cases, we find it hard to maintain a special connexion between moral virtue and guidance by practical reason.

We may understand the Aristotelian and Kantian position better if we recognize that sometimes it is open to us to criticize or to evaluate our inclinations, but we decide not to bother. Often this is sensible; we might, for instance, be trying to choose between two films that we might go to, and we might conceive some aversion to one of them (perhaps the title or subject sounds unappealing, even though we have read favourable reviews). In such a case we could deliberate more fully, but it might be a waste of time. Sometimes, however, it is appropriate to examine our initial impulses and aversions. If we do not like stepping on cracks in the footpath, that may be a harmless aversion; but if we cannot bear the thought of travelling by air, that may be a severe handicap, and perhaps we ought to try to overcome it.

According to Kant, we are guided by an evil maxim in cases where we realize that we could subject some end to further rational scrutiny, but we decide it is not worth our while.

---

[21] 'Hence the difference between a good man and one who is evil cannot lie in the difference between the incentives which they adopt into their maxim (not in the content of the maxim), but rather must depend on subordination (the form of the maxim), i.e., which of the two incentives he makes the condition of the other.' (*Rel. 36*)

[22] Aristotle and Aquinas; §§105, 298.

We exercise practical reason to some extent, in choosing between some inclinations; but we do not exercise it on ultimate ends. We do not recognize, until we think about it, that practical reason has any function at this level. If we believe that reason does not support any ultimate end over any other, we recognize no rational ground for incorporating the moral law into our maxim. According to this view about ends, some people favour morality without a further rational ground and others do not. We come to understand the falsity of this view once we see that we can make the rational choices that would not be open to us if ends were a matter of mere inclination.

In this claim about vice, Kant agrees with Aristotle and Aquinas. They also see that we would distort the voluntary and rational aspects of vice if we supposed that it results from simply being moved by the wrong motives. If it is genuine vice, vicious people are moved freely and rationally. They cannot, however, differ from virtuous people only in having reached the wrong answers. Kant accepts the Aristotelian view that vicious people act on the assumption that something like Hume's account of the capacity of practical reason is true. They see the possibility of attempting non-instrumental practical reasoning, but they think the attempt is futile, since they see no prospect of answering questions about ends by practical reason.

In Kant's view, autonomy is peculiar to the will that is guided by the categorical imperative. All other accounts of moral principles imply that heteronomy of choice is inevitable, rather than a misuse of the rational will.[23] Since we are all capable of autonomy, and hence of being guided by practical reason independently of 'pathological law', we are capable of autonomy even when we act heteronomously. Even in heteronomous agents the rational will is not determined by empirical impulses in a way that prevents choice about whether or not to act on them.

945. Autonomy, Prudence, and Morality

This discussion of negative and positive freedom allows us a more precise answer to our initial question about what the moral law reveals about freedom. If we begin from the weaker interpretation of the fact of reason, we recognize moral principles that present themselves as categorical imperatives. We are capable of considering whether to act on these principles. Hence we are capable of considering whether to act on categorical imperatives. The moral law reveals to us our negative freedom, and hence our capacity for positive freedom; it shows us that we are capable of thinking about maxims that result from the outlook of practical reason and not from the strength of desires. Kant's example of the fear of death recalls Butler's argument to demonstrate the absurdity of supposing that we do not act on superior principles.[24] It illustrates Butler's distinction between power and authority, which Reid calls 'animal strength' and 'rational strength'. In my awareness of a moral requirement,

---

[23] 'If, therefore, the material of volition, which cannot be other than an object of desire which is connected to the law, comes into the practical law *as a condition of its possibility*, there results heteronomy of Wiilkür, namely dependence on the natural law of following some impulse or inclination, and the Wille does not give itself the law but only the prescription for reasonable obedience to pathological law.' (*KpV* 33)

[24] Butler, *Sermons*, ii 17. See §685.

I see that I am not confined to choices that simply register the comparative strength of my desires.

From this it does not follow that we are capable of acting on categorical imperatives; for it may still turn out that there are no categorical imperatives. Even if we are capable of thinking about practical laws, we may be unable to act on them, because we may be unable to find any when we look for them. We may agree that we could get beyond a purely Humean outlook if we could find external reasons that apply to rational agents as such; but unless we can find some such reasons, we cannot act on them.

Do Kant's reflexions about freedom give us any reason to believe that there are external reasons? We may approach this question by asking whether Kant is right to claim that only the moral law reveals freedom to us. His claim brings us back to our previous discussion of practical laws and categorical imperatives. We found that Kant has a reasonable argument for practical laws that do not depend on inclination but apply to rational agents as such. But we found that he has no good reason to claim that only moral principles are practical laws and categorical imperatives. If we agree with Aquinas, Butler, and Reid, we will also believe in categorical imperatives of prudence.

This point bears on Kant's claim that the moral law reveals freedom to us. His claim does not apply exclusively to morality. We have equally good reason to believe that rational self-love reveals freedom. Kant does not agree, because he treats the desire for happiness as a purely 'pathological' (i.e., sensuous, non-rational) desire that is similar to a Humean passion. But if we doubt his conception of self-love, we may apply his claim about the moral law and freedom more widely. The practical freedom revealed by morality is the capacity to be guided by practical reason that does not incorporate ends derived from inclination into its maxim. A will that is guided by practical reason in this way is guided by practical laws and categorical imperatives. That is why Kant claims that the autonomous will is the will guided by categorical imperatives. If categorical imperatives are not restricted to moral principles, prudence as well as morality reveals to us the possibility of autonomy.

Kant's claims about categorical imperatives, autonomy, and freedom will not appear reasonable to everyone. From Hutcheson's and Hume's point of view, they rest on exaggerated claims about the capacity of practical reason, and on a mistaken view about the connexion between free will and practical reason. But these objections to Kant's view are equally objections to Aquinas' view, and to the general position that we have called traditional naturalism. Kant's claims about practical reason, and especially his claim that it provides justifying and motivating reasons independent of inclination, agree with Aquinas.

Kant's argument from morality, rather than prudence, to practical freedom is open to doubt. He relies on our ability to follow moral principles against inclinations. Butler and Reid argue that we are capable of acting on rational appreciation of our own good, contrary to our inclinations. In Kant's view, Butler and Reid are mistaken, for the reasons that Hume gives. But if we reject their view of prudence, why should we accept Kant's view of morality? The apparent ability that supports Kant's distinction between moral reason and non-moral inclination is very similar to the apparent ability that supports Butler and Reid on power and authority. Butler relies on this apparent ability in order to explain his conception of a superior principle in general. If Kant disagrees with Butler and Reid, he seems to undermine his own position too. We have already pointed out that Kant's agreement with Hume about prudence and with Butler about morality leaves him a less stable position than either Butler's or Hume's. The same is true of his claims about freedom.

If Kant agreed with Aquinas and Butler about the range of practical reason, would he make his claims about morality easier or more difficult to defend? He would help his position, in so far as he would strengthen his case for practical laws. For Aquinas and Butler implicitly attribute the characteristics of autonomy and independence of inclination to prudential as well as to moral motivation. If Kant rejects prudential imperatives independent of inclination, he undermines his own claims about moral imperatives.

946. Why Should We Be Autonomous?

Why should we even take this point of view of practical reason evaluating ends? An answer to this question will also help us to see whether we find anything when we take this point of view.

Moral agents may act on rational reflexion to different degrees. Why should they exercise this capacity rather than leaving it unexercised? Butler answers that action on rational self-love is natural, in so far as it expresses myself; for I am a whole person, not just a series of episodes and impulses. In acting on rational reflexion, I express myself as a person and a rational agent; and since that is what I essentially am, I thereby express myself. This argument supports Kant's claim that we should actualize the capacity we have, as negatively free agents, to act on reason rather than strength of impulses. In actualizing this capacity, we achieve positive freedom.

Positive freedom and autonomy, so understood, admit of degrees. I have some degree of positive freedom in so far as I decide to resist, say, anger or frustration, in the light of the other ends I accept (if, for instance, my anger will damage my prospects with someone I want to impress or conciliate). Butler recognizes this feature of positive freedom; we are 'a law unto ourselves' by having and acting on a superior rational principle that regulates our particular passions.[25] But Kant recognizes that such a degree of autonomy may co-exist with a high degree of heteronomy. Even though I adjust particular passions to the rest of my ends, I may still take those particular ends to be outside rational deliberation and reflexion. In this case, my choice (Willkür) and the underlying will (Wille) are heteronomous, though I have not lost the capacity for autonomy. We are more autonomous if we apply rational deliberation and reflexion to the choice of ends that we pursue.

Butler assumes that a superior principle has this function. He maintains, for instance, that we have reason to pursue the public good for its own sake, following the rational principle of benevolence, even though this principle is not innate, or instinctive, or a natural product of human development, as the passion of benevolence is. The actions prescribed by the rational principle are not means to satisfy the natural passion of benevolence, since they involve people and situations that do not engage the natural passion. Nor, however, are

---

[25] *Sermons*, ii 9. See §681.

they unrelated to the natural passion. Reflexion on the rationally appropriate object for my benevolent passions shows me that benevolence is appropriate in some cases where I have no antecedent passion. I may see, for instance, that it is arbitrary to distinguish cases where I help someone I already know from cases where I refuse to help someone in equal need just because I do not already know them. I adopt new ends, and do not merely discover new means to the ends I already had. Reid sees that the criticism and adoption of ends is a hallmark of practical reason.[26]

In such a case, we exercise autonomy, as Kant understands it, to a higher degree than if we simply take ends for granted, and pursue them without rational examination, as a result of inclination. If we examine and reflect on our ultimate ends in the same way, we will not act on hypothetical imperatives, dependent on some unquestioned inclination; we will act on categorical imperatives, determined by reason at the highest level.

So far we have found a defence of Kant's conception of autonomy, but no defence of his claim that autonomy requires morality. If we agree that we are capable of autonomy and of acting on categorical imperatives, why should we agree that if we fully realize this capacity, we act on moral imperatives?

947. Morality and Personality

In Kant's view, the moral law reveals not only freedom, but also 'personality', something that 'elevates a human being above himself as a part of the world of sense' (*KpV* 86). Since personality is closely connected to freedom, we might find that the relation of morality to personality supports Kant's claims about morality and freedom. Alternatively, we might find that the connexion between morality and personality offers a defence of the basis of morality that avoids the apparent weaknesses in his claims about freedom.

Personality is important in Kant's claims about the Formula of Humanity.[27] The right of persons to be treated as ends in themselves 'rests on the personality of these beings, whereby alone they are ends in themselves' (*KpV* 87). Personality is to be distinguished from mere 'humanity' (*Rel.* 26), because it 'is rooted in reason which is practical of itself, that is, reason which dictates laws unconditionally'. This is why the origin of the sense of duty is personality.[28] The idea of personality awakens the respect that is appropriate for ends in themselves.

Kant is justified in claiming that the moral law uniquely reveals personality, if personality implies the capacity to be moved by the moral law. When the *Groundwork* explains how personality makes people ends in themselves, it identifies personality not simply with the capacity to be moved by the moral law, but, more broadly, with the capacity to be moved by practical reason that is not subordinate to inclination. Personality, so understood, is the same capacity as practical freedom.

---

[26] Reid on reason and ends; §837.   [27] Personality; §924.

[28] '... the freedom and independence from the mechanism of the whole of nature, yet at the same time regarded as a capacity of a being subject to special laws (pure practical laws given by his own reason), so that the person as belonging to the world of sense is subject to his own personality in so far as he at the same time belongs to the intelligible world.' (*KpV* 87)

Since Kant thinks practical reason moves us independently of inclination only when we act on the moral law, he believes that the capacity to act on the moral law is the only one that satisfies the criterion for personality. But if prudential reasoning also satisfies the criterion for personality, we have no reason to believe that only the moral law reveals personality, or that the personality it reveals is only the capacity for morality.

Kant suggests that prudence belongs to humanity rather than to personality, because prudential practical reason is subservient to other incentives (*Rel.* 27). He is right to say this, if a Humean account of prudence is right. But such an account does not fit prudence as Butler and Reid understand it. Kant treats as distinctive features of morality features of practical reason that Butler and Reid attribute to self-love as well as to morality. Their position, expressed in Kantian terms, claims that self-love presents us with categorical imperatives, and therefore reveals personality, not merely humanity, to us. If they are right, Kant loses his support for the claim that morality uniquely reveals personality.

His discussion of prudence is incomplete, since he offers a purely hedonistic account of self-love, and does not examine the case that can be made for treating imperatives of self-love as categorical. Recognition of the claims of self-love tends to support Kant's claim that the autonomous condition is valuable, but tends to undermine the prospect of finding any special defence of morality by appeal to autonomy.

It is difficult, therefore, to accept Kant's claim that in the moral law we discover practical freedom or personality that 'without the moral law would have remained unknown' to us.[29] In our discussion of practical laws, categorical imperatives, morality, freedom, and personality, we have traced the consequences of Kant's narrow conception of practical reason, and we have found reasons to prefer the broader conception of Aquinas, Butler, and Reid. His claim about the role of morality in revealing freedom is open to question.

Rejection of this argument does not, however, require the rejection of connexions between morality and freedom that support morality. The reasons we can give for valuing the outlook of self-love may also give us reasons for valuing the outlook of morality. We might seek to show that the outlook of morality manifests autonomy to the highest degree. If the proper expansion of rational reflexion and autonomy through my different ends leads to the moral outlook, morality and full autonomy coincide, even though not every degree of positive freedom manifests morality.

Butler has something like this in mind about conscience. For he maintains that conscience finds what is most in accordance with my nature, and so presumably relies on the fullest reflexion about how my different aims and capacities should be related and expressed. But Butler does not explain why the result of this full reflexion coincides with the requirements of morality. Can Kant do any better?

948. From Practical Freedom to Transcendental Freedom

Before we try to answer this question, we need to return to our earlier question about the sort of freedom we discover through the moral law. What we have said so far may seem

---

[29] *KpV* 30, quoted in §941.

to do less than justice to Kant. For we have supposed that the moral law reveals practical freedom, and on that basis we have found reason to doubt his claim that the moral law uniquely reveals freedom. But he also claims that the moral law reveals our freedom by revealing our independence from the mechanism of nature.[30] We might reasonably take him to refer to his doctrine that the moral will is noumenal, and hence not subject to the deterministic laws that apply to nature. In his view, practical freedom implies transcendental freedom—the ability to act spontaneously, on one's own initiative, and not because one is determined by past events. Transcendental freedom and spontaneity are incompatible with determinism. Kant infers that our awareness of our own agency requires us to believe in the falsity of determinism.

Kant's conception of practical freedom gives us no reason to introduce transcendental freedom. He rejects the simple compatibilism of Hobbes and Hume that makes internal causation sufficient for freedom. Kant argues that freedom also requires the capacity for being moved by practical laws, and hence by reasons that are independent of the strength of our desires. We have found no reason so far to believe that this capacity presupposes the falsity of determinism.

Kant, however, believes that if we allow practical freedom, we must reject compatibilism.[31] He might believe this for either of two reasons: (1) Perhaps practical freedom, as we have understood it so far, is incompatible with determinism. (2) Perhaps our description of practical freedom so far is inadequate, because Kant attributes further features to it beyond those we have discussed, and argues that these further features require indeterminism.

Each of these arguments raises some difficulties for Kant. Even if the first argument succeeds, it does not help his claim that morality uniquely reveals practical freedom. For if we have correctly explained practical freedom, it belongs to prudence as well as to morality; if it requires indeterminism, then prudence as well as morality requires indeterminism, and we have not yet discovered any special connexion between morality and freedom. The second argument might be more helpful to Kant, if the additional features of practical freedom do not belong to prudence, but belong to morality.

We should therefore consider the connexions that Kant affirms between practical freedom, morality, and indeterminism. We especially need to see whether his views about freedom reflect the demands of his moral theory, or depend on his non-moral doctrines. In the first case, any doubts that arise about his account of freedom may spread to parts of his moral theory. In the second case, objections to his treatment of freedom may not affect his moral philosophy in particular.

Kant connects practical freedom with transcendental freedom by this argument:

1. If we are practically free, we are not coerced by sensuous impulses.
2. If we are not coerced, we can do otherwise than we do.
3. If determinism is true, we cannot do otherwise than we do.
4. And so if determinism is true, we lack practical freedom.

---

[30] *KpV* 86–7, quoted in §947.
[31] Kant's attitude to compatibilism is discussed by Wood, 'Compatibilism'; Allison, *KTF*, ch. 2.

This argument for incompatibilism, claiming that if we are determined, we are forced to do what we do and we lack the ability required by practical freedom, goes back to Epicurus and Alexander. Some aspects of it influence Bramhall, Price, and Reid.[32]

Kant relies especially on claims about the past and the laws of nature. If we assume the necessity of the laws of nature, we can go back to the distant past and (if we know enough) trace a series of sufficient conditions in which the earlier is sufficient for its successor.[33] Hence, everything that happens now has been determined in the distant past, and therefore everything is necessitated by the distant past, so that nothing else can happen.[34] If nothing else can happen, how can we do anything different from what we do, and how can we be responsible for our actions? Determinism seems to cancel responsibility.

Kant dismisses any compatibilist defence of freedom. The attempt to explain freedom as an ordinary psychological property does not reckon with the fact that if past conditions determine my action, my action is not free.[35] To suppose that we can get round this incompatibilist argument by distinguishing internal from external causation is a 'wretched subterfuge' (KpV 96). In Kant's view, this supposed freedom 'would in essence be no better than the freedom of a turnspit which when once wound up also carries out its motions of itself' (97).

The relevant feature of practical freedom seems to be its connexion with ought-judgments, and with responsibility, praise, and blame. But these features do not help Kant's claim that morality uniquely reveals practical freedom. For they seem to belong to prudence no less than to morality. We often say that people ought to take more care of their health, for their own sakes; and, as Butler remarks, failures of prudence are 'faulty and blameable' (D 6).[36] If we take these features of prudence at face value, they reveal the truth of indeterminism no less than morality reveals it. Kant might argue that they are not to be taken at face value; but then he revives the question we have already raised, about whether he undermines his case about morality by questioning the categorical status of prudential reasons. In that case, indeterminism does not help Kant to show that morality uniquely reveals freedom.

---

[32] See §§147, 172, 475, 809, 833.

[33] 'Obviously, if all causality in the sensible world were bare nature, every event would be determined by another in time, in accordance with necessary laws, and hence—since appearances, in so far as they determine the Willkür, would have to render every action necessary as their natural consequence—the abolition of transcendental freedom would also simultaneously eliminate all practical freedom.' (KrV A534/B562) '...if we could investigate all the appearances of his Willkür down to their basis, there would not be found a single human action that we could not predict with certainty, and recognize as necessary given its antecedent conditions.' (A549–50/B577–8)

[34] 'Since the past is no longer in my power, every action which I perform is necessary because of determining grounds that are not in my power. This means that at the time I act I am never free...For at every point of time I still stand under the necessity of being determined to act by what is not in my power...' (KpV 94–5)

[35] 'There are many who believe they can nevertheless explain this freedom with empirical principles, just as they can explain other natural abilities. They regard it as a psychological property, the explanation of which turns solely upon a more exact investigation of the nature of the soul and of the incentives of the Wille, and not as the transcendental predicate of the causality of a being which belongs to the world of sense; but it is the latter that really counts.' (KpV 94)

[36] In the rest of this section, Butler explains why we are less inclined to blame failures of prudence than to blame failures in other-regarding morality. Cf. Aquinas, ST 1–2 q100 a5 and §313.

949. Objections to Kant's Argument

Whether the argument for indeterminism applies only to morality or also to prudence, it is open to question. Kant relies on assumptions common to many incompatibilists. In particular, he relies on two claims:

(1) If we have the ability to do not-x, and are in a position to exercise it, it is possible for us to do not-x.

(2) The relevant sort of possibility is the one that is excluded if the past and the laws of nature determine that we will do x.

Examination of these two claims raises some questions about Kant's argument.

The first claim expresses a disputable view of the relation between ability and possibility. Against Kant, we might argue that responsibility and freedom require an ability to do otherwise that is present even in circumstances that make it impossible to do what we are able to do. Even if we grant that the past and the laws of nature make it necessary for me to do x, and make it impossible for me to do not-x in the same circumstances, we might argue that this impossibility does not interfere with the crucial ability to do not-x. If, then, we grant (2), we might reasonably reject (1).

Alternatively, we might grant that ability to do otherwise implies some sort of possibility (thereby granting (1)), but still argue that it is possible for me to exercise my ability now if nothing in my internal states or the external conditions actually prevents me from doing x. The mere fact that I am causally determined to do not-x does not (according to this view) imply that I am prevented from doing x. In that case, compatibilists have no reason to accept both of Kant's assumptions about ability and possibility in (1) and (2).

He may also beg the question in asserting (2). Alternative possibilities fit into a deterministic world only if they involve a difference in the past or in the laws of nature:

(3) If I can do not-x, even though I am determined to do x, it is possible for me to act so that the past or the laws of nature would have been different from what they were.

One interpretation of (3) would be this:

(4) If it is possible for me to act so that the past or the laws of nature would have been different from what they were, it is possible for me to change the past or the laws of nature.

If it is open to me to change the past or the laws of nature in the way in which I change the future, backward causation is possible. If, however, backward causation is impossible, and (4) is true, alternative possibilities cannot be present in a deterministic world.

We need not, however, agree that (4) follows from (3); not every case of acting so that the past would be different from what it was involves backward causation. If the British Parliament were to abolish the monarchy during the reign of Elizabeth II, it would make George VI the last king of England. If, however, a king succeeds Elizabeth II, and then the monarchy is abolished, Parliament will make George VI the penultimate king of England. It is easy to change these facts about the past, because they are 'soft' facts, logical consequences of choosing one or another future action; such changes do not require backward causation.[37]

Compatibilists who accept (1) must accept (3), but soft facts raise a doubt about (4). Compatibilists who believe in alternative possibilities believe that it is possible for me to act in such a way that the past would be different from how it was. But this possibility does not require backward causation, if the relevant possibility rests on soft facts that are compatible with determinism. A compatibilist requires only the possibility of making the past different that follows from the existence of soft facts about the past. An argument that relies on (4), therefore, does not refute compatibilism.

We have tried to spell out the assumptions underlying Kant's argument against the 'wretched subterfuge' of compatibilism. For all that we have said, the argument may be sound; but it does not seem dialectically effective against compatibilists, since they have plausible grounds for doubting some of the premises. Kant does not show why they are wrong to combine the necessity that belongs to the past and the laws of nature with the ability and possibility that belong to practical freedom and responsibility. It is not clear that the necessity of the past and of the laws of nature excludes the possibility needed for the specific ability to do otherwise that is necessary for practical freedom. Hence practical freedom does not seem to require transcendental freedom.

A different, though not entirely separate, defence of Kant's argument for indeterminism may be constructed from some aspects of voluntarism. He sets out, as the mediaeval voluntarists do, from a contrast between being compelled by the strength of one's desires and freely choosing on the basis of reasons.[38] An intellectualist such as Aquinas identifies this contrast with the contrast between being moved by one's rational conception of the good and being moved by non-rational appetite. Kant, however, following other voluntarists, supposes that any sort of causal determination implies the compulsion that excludes free choice. Hence he rejects the intellectualist solution.

It is difficult, however, to be convinced by this argument from voluntarism to indeterminism unless we are already sympathetic to incompatibilism. For intellectualists can explain our conviction that rational agency involves free choice rather than compulsion by one's desires; their explanation fits Kant's description of practical freedom. In recognizing positive freedom, he affirms that we are more completely free when we are guided by practical reason. This corresponds to Scotus' view that freedom is especially embodied in the affection for justice.[39]

We have a reason to be dissatisfied with an intellectualist account of practical freedom if we believe that we are free to reject practical reason as well as passion. Intellectualism denies us this freedom, because it claims that if we act against practical reason, we are either ignorant or compelled by passion. This voluntarist conception of freedom is at least part of Scotus' view; Ockham defends it more single-mindedly. But it does not fit Kant's position so well; for he identifies the rational will with practical reason, and identifies positive freedom with determination by the rational will. Hence it would be difficult for him to rely on a voluntarist argument for indeterminism.

---

[37] Hard and soft facts are explained and discussed by Adams, ' "Hard" fact?'; Fischer, 'Foreknowledge', and Hoffman and Rosenkrantz, 'Hard and soft facts'.

[38] Voluntarism and reasons; §§390–1.   [39] Scotus; §368.

A voluntarist conception of freedom asserts that the will is influenced, but not determined, by both reason and passion; its freedom consists in its not necessarily agreeing with either of them. If Kant understands freedom in this way, he ought to assert that the free will is subject to influences, but not to determination, from rational and non-rational motives. To see whether he conceives the free will in this way, we need to take account of some special features of his indeterminism.

950. Phenomena and Noumena

Kant's incompatibilism raises some difficulties for him, since he also believes in the truth of determinism, and indeed believes that our knowledge of nature implies determinism. He seems to be committed to the rejection of freedom. Our practical reason and our knowledge of nature, therefore, seem to give us contradictory answers about the truth of determinism. If the contradiction is genuine, we must reconsider our views about practical freedom or about our knowledge of nature.

Kant, however, denies that our knowledge of nature contradicts our views about practical freedom. He suggests that our practical beliefs are true of things in themselves, whereas our claims about nature are true of appearances (*KpV* 42). Since our beliefs about freedom are not knowledge, they do not conflict with the doctrine that our knowledge is limited to appearances.

If practical beliefs are about things in themselves, our knowledge of nature still allows Kant to claim that responsible actions are undetermined. But this result should not be his only reason for taking practical beliefs to be about things in themselves; if it were his only reason, he could fairly be accused of simply tailoring his conception of practical beliefs to fit indeterminism. In fact he has further reasons for taking practical beliefs, including those about morally good and bad responsible actions, to be about noumena.

To show that moral features of actions are noumenal, and hence belong to things in themselves rather than to appearances, it is not enough to show that they cannot be directly observed in the way that colours or sounds can be; for something may be an appearance without being an object of the senses. In the *First Critique*, Kant distinguishes appearances from observables. He argues that the distinction between secondary and primary qualities does not correspond to his distinction between appearances and things in themselves,[40] because the former distinction applies only to observables, whereas some unobservable aspects of things belong to appearances, not to things in themselves.[41] Appearances include

---

[40] 'The above remark is intended only to guard anyone from supposing that the ideality of space as here asserted can be illustrated by examples so altogether insufficient as colours, tastes, etc. For these cannot rightly be regarded as properties of things, but simply as changes in the subject, changes which may, indeed, be different in different people.' (*KrV* A29/B45)

[41] For evidence of this extended conception of appearances see *KrV* B279: 'Whether this or that supposed experience is not purely imaginary, must be ascertained from its special determinations, and through its coherence with the criteria of all real experience'. Whether x is an appearance or not depends on whether it is 'coherent' with my appearances—whether I have to recognize x in an adequate explanation of my appearances. As he says in A376, 'Whatever is connected with a perception according to empirical laws is actual'. Similarly, at A495/B523 he explains belief in the past by reference to '. . . the possibility of extending the chain of experience from the present perception back to the conditions that determine this perception in respect of time'.

everything that is recognized by common sense or empirical science; elementary particles, forces, events in the distant past, are all appearances without being observable. Empirical motives are not observable either, but they are appearances because they explain observable actions.

When Kant claims that noumenal events are undetermined, he does not mean that they are extra events beyond those that are part of the phenomenal order. The most plausible interpretation of transcendental idealism implies that appearances and things in themselves are the same things, under different aspects.[42] Things in themselves are not different things from appearances, but the same things in different aspects. Things as appearances are things in so far as they have properties knowable in experience; the same things as things in themselves are things in so far as they do not have properties knowable in experience. Kant says, for instance, that an appearance has two sides, one of which treats the object in itself; the same object that appears to us also has properties that do not appear to us (A38/B55). When he distinguishes the object as appearance from the object in itself, he assumes that he is speaking of the same object in both cases (B69).[43]

951. The Noumenal and the Practical

If we apply this understanding of transcendental idealism to freedom and determinism, Kant claims that my choice is an event about which we can say two things:[44] (1) It has properties that make it part of the phenomenal order, conforming to deterministic laws of nature. (2) It also has properties that make it an undetermined state of my rational self, and these properties are relevant to freedom and responsibility.

It follows at least that our judgments about reasons for action and about responsibility are not ordinary empirical causal judgments. They do not simply describe or predict some connexion between cause and effect, and they do not report the results of our

[42] On this question about the interpretation of transcendental idealism see Langton, *KH*, esp. chs. 4–6; Allison *KTI*, esp. chs. 2–3. Van Cleve, *PK*, chs. 1, 10, offers a good defence of the less plausible view.

[43] His explanation of 'in themselves' suggests the same view: 'How things may be in themselves (without regard to the representations through which they affect us) is entirely beyond our cognitive sphere' (A190/B235). Things in themselves are things apart from how they appear to us. Kant refers to the doctrine of the noumenon in the negative sense; 'that is, of things which the understanding must think without this reference to our mode of intuition, therefore not merely as appearances, but as things in themselves' (B307). To speak of a thing in itself is not to speak of a different thing, but simply to speak of a thing without speaking of how it appears to us. See also A251: 'The sensibility and its field, that of the appearances, is itself limited by the understanding, in that it does not deal with things in themselves, but only with the mode in which, owing to our subjective constitution, things appear'. Things, not things in themselves, are said to appear to us, because things in themselves do not—as such—appear to us, though the things that are (also) things in themselves do appear to us. And so this passage implies that the same things can be called both appearances and things in themselves.

At A249–50 Kant considers the counterfactual possibility of our knowing things without reference to the senses. In that case, we would not know them simply as they appear, but in the actual circumstances, he implies, we do know these very same things as they appear. He does not mean, then, that there are things that we do not know. He means that there are some properties of things that we do not know. He does not imply that the properties that appear to us are any less objective than the properties that do not appear to us.

[44] This is an over-simplified claim about the implications of Kant's position. A more careful statement would allow for the possibility of one event constituting a second, or the second supervening on the first. These ways of conceiving the relation between the two events do not affect the main questions that arise about Kant's conception of freedom.

self-observation. When I assert that x is a reason for doing y, I think of x as a justifying reason; I set out to guide my behaviour, not simply to observe a particular causal force operating on me. Similarly, when I recognize that x was my reason for doing y, I think of x as an exciting reason that seemed to justify (to some degree) my doing y. Hence my judgments about reasons include a timeless element. If I judge that x is a reason for y, I do not mean that x precedes y and causes it; I mean that if x holds, it is to some degree reasonable to do y.

The ordinary conception of causation, therefore, does not capture the relation between the reason and the action. In Kant's view, the 'causation' that is relevant here is not the sort that holds between earlier and later events, but the 'unschematized' concept that he identifies with 'ground and consequent', displayed in conditionals.[45] In this case, we assert that the truth of the antecedent gives a reason for asserting the consequent. In the case of practical reason, we say that the antecedent gives a reason for bringing the consequent about.

The phenomenal world is the area of empirical knowledge. Knowledge of phenomena is a part of our theoretical understanding of the sensible world, and it is the basis for predictions, hypotheses, and further extensions of our empirical knowledge. In Kant's view, however, practical beliefs, including moral beliefs and assessments of merit and responsibility, are not part of our empirical knowledge; to learn more about morality is not to add further predictions about how aspects of the sensible world are likely to behave. We might be inclined to accept this claim about the non-predictive character of practical judgment if we consider deliberation and intention. These are not primarily predictions about what we will do; they guide us in the light of our assessment of the situation, and they are not falsified by the mere non-occurrence of what we decide or intend to do. Similarly, holding someone responsible for what he has done seems to be different from simply claiming that he has stood in a specific causal relation.[46]

Some moral judgments, however, include causal, explanatory, and predictive elements, and so cast doubt on Kant's claims. If I hold you responsible for a malicious or careless action, on the ground that you broke my window, I imply that you broke a window; if I discover that you never threw anything at the window, but a strong wind broke it, my judgment of responsibility is false. Similarly, my claim that someone is honest commits me to predictions; I believe, for instance, that if he is offered a small bribe to give false testimony in a murder case, he will probably refuse the bribe. Moral and other practical judgments may help to extend our empirical knowledge.

But even if practical judgments are not entirely separable from empirical knowledge, Kant may still be right to argue that they do not primarily constitute empirical knowledge, and therefore are not about appearances. Moral judgments are those we make about ourselves and the world on the assumption that we are rational agents, not as inquirers into the world. For this reason, we may agree with Kant's claim that moral judgments are not about appearances, and that therefore the properties that are essential to moral judgments are not phenomenal properties.

[45] See *KrV* A144/B183.
[46] Hart and Hampshire, 'Decision', explore some contrasts between 'two possible kinds of certainty about one's future actions—inductive certainty and certainty based upon reasons, which is decision' (4).

If Kant is right about this, and about the basis of determinism, we have no reason to assume that moral properties are essentially involved in deterministic laws. For the determinist assumption, in his view, is required for knowledge of a single objective sensible world. It is part of the outlook of empirical knowledge, and so it cannot be transferred to the practical point of view from the point of view of empirical inquiry.

It does not follow, however, that moral properties are phenomenally undetermined. To refrain from claiming that they are always phenomenally determined is a negative thesis that falls short of Kant's indeterminist thesis. He does not simply claim that in giving reasons for actions, we do not think of reason and action as simply linked by ordinary empirical causation. He also claims that we believe that they are related by some sort of non-empirical causation, and believe that they are not related by empirical causation. In his view, we positively deny that our choices and actions belong to any empirical causal series. But this denial does not follow from the observation that the practical point of view is distinct from the point of view of empirical causal inquiry. His thesis about the undetermined character of our choices and actions presupposes incompatibilism; but he has not shown that this is a presupposition of the practical point of view. Kant's argument for incompatibilism is open to question.

952. Kant's Solution

Kant's various claims about determinism and freedom threaten to make his position incoherent. He believes that every event that is an undetermined, free choice of mine is also phenomenally determined (since phenomena and noumena are the same things). It follows that the 'empirical character' (as Kant calls it) of every such event is determined (*KrV* A539–41/B567–9; A551/B579). Since the phenomenal character of previous events is sufficient for the phenomenal character of this event, the noumenal character of previous events cannot make the phenomenal character of any event different from what it would have been if the phenomenal character of previous events had been the same and the noumenal character different. The noumenal character of an event cannot make any difference to its phenomenal character, since noumenal causation would be outside the series of phenomenal causes that determine the phenomenal character. The aspect of choice that makes us responsible for our actions cannot, therefore, affect the phenomenal character of our choices or actions.

We may doubt these claims, if we return to Kant's initial remarks on the difference between a free will and a purely animal will. We initially suppose that we are not coerced by sensuous impulses, because our rational reflexion makes some difference to what we actually do, and hence to phenomenal events—going to a film as opposed to staying at home. But if phenomenal events, apart from the noumenal aspect of my choice, determine my doing something with the phenomenal character of going to the film, the noumenal aspect of my choice does not give me much freedom to determine my action.[47] If this aspect

---

[47] See Kant's hesitations at *KrV* A551n/B579n.

does not affect the phenomenal character of actions, it does not seem to make us responsible for the phenomenal character of actions.

But this is a surprising result, given our initial conception of practical freedom and responsibility. For we are normally held responsible for murder, theft, or (in the case of good actions) acting bravely in battle, making a sensible decision, or devising a successful strategy. All these descriptions refer both to our choices and aims and to the phenomenal character of the actions caused and explained (we assume) by these choices and aims. If, then, the moral motive explains observable actions, it must also be an appearance, according to Kant's conception of appearances. Kant seems to discuss the wills of agents whose actions, including their phenomenal character, are explained by their acceptance of the moral law. States of a morally good or bad will, therefore, seem to be appearances.

Kant creates these difficulties because he does not accept compatibilism far enough to justify his transcendental idealist solution. He accepts some degree of compatibilism: our claims about responsibility have to be compatible with phenomenal causal determinism, so that the causality we exercise in free and responsible action cannot violate phenomenal determinism. Incompatibilists, however, may fairly reply that Kant's position implies that no phenomenally determined action can be free. They can even quote Kant against himself. For he rejects compatibilism on the ground that if agents are determined to act by past events, and hence by events no longer in their power, they are not free (*KpV* 95).

We do not answer the incompatibilist objection if we insist that the noumenal aspect of an event is not temporal. If the noumenal aspect belongs to an event that is also phenomenal, and the event, qua phenomenal, is causally determined by a past phenomenal event, the event with the noumenal aspect is also causally determined by that past phenomenal event. Kant saves indeterminism at the noumenal level by making it inert at the phenomenal level, and hence making the free and responsible aspects of our rational choices irrelevant to the phenomenal events that we bring about. This result conflicts with the intuitive beliefs about agency that Kant seeks to preserve and defend.

Since Kant accepts phenomenal determinism, he has a reason to reject the incompatibilist argument. Acceptance of compatibilism would undermine one of his reasons for believing that judgments about agency and freedom require transcendental idealism, but it would not remove all his reasons. Whatever he believes about determinism and compatibilism, he has good reasons for claiming that practical judgments are not ordinary empirical causal judgments. His position would be more plausible, however, if he acknowledged that judgments about reasons for action imply some judgments about phenomenal causation (so that, for instance, if I decide to stay at home rather than go out, I believe that some phenomenal mental act of mine will bring about one phenomenal effect rather than another). He ought to retain his beliefs about practical freedom and deny that it implies transcendental freedom.

It is worth our while to examine these details of Kant's claims about freedom, even though they take us beyond Kant's moral theory and into his metaphysics, because our conclusions help us towards an estimate of Kant's views on practical freedom. If his conception of practical freedom required transcendental freedom, it would depart from the conceptions of freedom that rest on a division between will and passion; moreover, it would make Kant's whole position incoherent, given his acceptance of phenomenal determinism. But his views on practical freedom do not lead to these conclusions.

In saying this, we need not decide dogmatically in favour of compatibilism against incompatibilism. If we abstract from this dispute about free will, Kant's views on practical freedom do not mark any sharp disagreement with the conception that Aquinas accepts and Hume rejects. His use of transcendental idealism to explain the difference between judgments about practical freedom and ordinary causal judgments is an important innovation; but it should be understood and evaluated apart from his claims about noumenal indeterminism.

953. Does Morality Require Noumenal Freedom?

Kant appeals to transcendental idealism not only to explain the freedom of responsibility, but also to explain the distinctive character of moral motivation. He argues that since the moral will is determined by the form and not by the matter of a maxim, it is determined by reason, hence not by the senses, hence not by appearances, hence not by past events.[48]

This argument from non-sensory motivation to non-phenomenal motivation, and thence to indeterminism, is dubious. As we have seen, the world of appearances is the world that we know through sensory experience, plus whatever explains that experience; the mere fact that something is not an object of sensory experience does not imply that it is non-phenomenal. We should therefore ask: Does Kant believe that the moral motive contributes to the explanation of our experience?

The beginning of the *Groundwork* suggests that the moral motive explains some phenomenal actions. People who act from duty act fairly in cases where the shrewd shopkeeper would not, and they do this precisely because have a good will. We normally suppose that this 'because' is causal. If our alleged belief in the truth of the moral law exerted no causal influence on our actions, we would normally regard this as a reason for denying that we have a morally good will. Similarly, if we act from a good will, belief that this action is morally required (apart from any further advantages) causally influences our phenomenal action. According to Kant, therefore, the moral motive must be part of the phenomenal, and hence deterministic, series of causes and effects. Hence common moral beliefs require the moral motive to be phenomenal.

This point is not affected by Kant's view that it is often difficult to tell whether we act on the moral motive or not (G 407; R 75). He suggests that the possible concurrence of moral and non-moral motives, and our tendency to deceive ourselves about our motives, raise doubts about whether we really have a good will or not. Even if Kant is right about the difficulty of knowing people's motives, the moral motive is relevant to the explanation of phenomena. For what we find difficult to decide is the degree to which the moral motive

---

[48] 'Since the mere form of a law can be represented only by reason and is consequently not an object of the senses and therefore does not belong among appearances, the representation of this form as the determining ground of the Wille is distinct from all determining grounds of events in nature according to the law of causality, because these grounds must themselves be appearances.' (*KpV* 28)

influences our phenomenal actions. If the moral motive could not explain phenomena, it would not be difficult to know whether we act on the moral motive or not; it would be certain that we do not and cannot.[49]

We may suppose that Kant can support his claim that the moral motive is non-sensible and noumenal, by arguing that all and only non-moral motives are 'empirical' (*KpV* 21), that they rely on subjective rather than objective principles (26), and that reason exhibits the moral law as 'a ground of determination which is completely independent of and not to be outweighed by any sensuous condition' (30).

This argument relies on Kant's different claims about sensuous impulses and empirical motives: (1) Every motive except the moral motive rests on the desire for happiness, and 'the lower faculty of desire' (*KpV* 22), and so ultimately on feelings of pleasure rather than on any rational principle. (2) Every motive except the moral motive is empirical. For non-moral motives do not belong to human beings qua rational agents; they belong to us as beings with this or that taste or interest, or (in the case of more widely shared desires) as beings with these needs or interests distinct from those belonging to rational beings as such. Hence only the moral motive is a priori. (3) Empirical motives are those that can appear in empirical causal laws, and therefore belong to the phenomenal world.[50]

Since Kant tends not to distinguish these three claims about non-moral motives, he is not clear about the extent to which considered moral judgments support his indeterminism. In support of the first claim, he argues, reasonably, that morality assumes our capacity to be motivated by reason rather than passion (contrary to Hume). The second claim is also defensible; morality requires us to be capable of acting on an a priori motive (i.e., one that belongs to rational agents as such), and hence, in one sense, on a non-empirical motive. The third claim, however, does not follow from the first two. The sense in which the first two claims treat the moral motive as non-empirical does not imply that it is non-phenomenal.[51]

Kant may be fortunate to have no cogent argument for his claims that the moral motive is the only noumenal motive and that action on the moral motive is the only action that is not determined by past events. For a cogent argument for these claims would create further difficulties. The argument that contrasts the 'moral' and 'non-moral' motive contrasts the motive of the morally good person with other motives. We refer to these other motives in our practical judgments and assessments about responsible agents, and so we consider them from the practical point of view. Hence, according to Kant, they are all noumenal motives and all undetermined. In acting on them, we exercise our practical freedom. But practical freedom (according to Kant) requires transcendental freedom. Hence, all responsible agents are phenomenally undetermined whenever they act responsibly. Since, according to common sense and to Kant, we can act responsibly even if we fail to act on the moral motive, our action on non-moral motives is sometimes undetermined. Hence the freedom of responsibility requires the sources of all responsible actions to be noumenal.

---

[49] Wolff, *AR* 66–8, argues that, in Kant's view, we cannot in principle act on the moral motive (in the causal sense of 'act on' that I am considering here).

[50] Schopenhauer and Kant on empirical motives; §1059.

[51] Cf. Hegel, *PS* §622. Hegel's discussion of this aspect of Kant; §1024.

This conclusion conflicts with Kant's claim that only the moral motive is 'non-empirical' and therefore noumenal. That claim implies that everyone except the person with a morally good will acts on empirical motives, and that only action that proceeds from a good will is free action. But this claim about the extent of freedom raises questions about the freedom of responsibility.[52] If action on a good will is the only undetermined action, and all action from 'empirical' motives is phenomenally determined, agents who act on morally good wills are the only responsible agents. But Kant rejects this conclusion.

954. An Unsuccessful Defence of Freedom and Morality

These claims about the character of the good will suggest that Kant sometimes confuses the freedom of responsibility with the freedom of the good will. He seems to confuse them in an argument that he offers in the *Groundwork* for connecting freedom and morality. The faults in this argument help to explain some of the complications that he introduces into his account of freedom in other works.

At the end of Chapter 2 in the *Groundwork*, Kant faces the question he has postponed throughout his account of the supreme principle of morality, about whether there is a categorical imperative. Reflexion on morality shows that morality assumes there is a categorical imperative, and that it tells us what this alleged categorical imperative says. But a categorical imperative must give a reason to all rational beings as such—no matter what their specific desires or impulses may be. Is there any such thing?

Kant believes that an answer this question needs to explain the connexion between morality and freedom of the will. He accepts two claims: (1) Awareness of the moral law reveals freedom to us. By being aware of moral obligation, we become aware that we are free in a way that we would not otherwise have recognized. (2) Because we are free, the moral law is a categorical imperative for us. When we understand what freedom consists in, we see that it makes us the sorts of agents who have reason, irrespective of our particular desires, to follow the moral law.[53]

The simplest exposition of Kant's argument appears in the *Groundwork*, Chapter 3. The major difficulty arises at the very beginning. Kant first defines freedom as independence of alien causes.[54] He argues that 'freedom must be presupposed as a property of the will of all rational beings' (447). But then he also describes it as determination by laws that are the will's own laws, and hence imply autonomy. If freedom is to be identified with autonomy, all rational beings are autonomous; but this is not what Kant wants to prove.[55] If the autonomous will is the will of the morally good person, and if the autonomous will is the free will, the only people with free wills are morally good people.

Kant faces a dilemma. If he believes we are responsible for morally bad action, freedom is required for praise and blame; but if freedom is autonomy, good and bad people are equally

---

[52] See Sidgwick, *ME*, Appendix on Kant, discussed by Wood, 'Compatibilism'.
[53] Ratio cognoscendi and ratio essendi; §939.
[54] 'The will is a kind of causality belonging to living beings in so far as they are rational; freedom would be the property of this causality that makes it effective independent of any determination by alien causes.' (G 446)
[55] On this argument see Allison, *KTF*, ch. 12.

autonomous. Alternatively, if only morally good people are autonomous, and freedom is autonomy, bad people are not responsible for their actions. Kant rejects both consequences, but it is difficult to see how he can avoid them, if he takes freedom to require both independence of alien causes and autonomy.

955. Negative and Positive Freedom v. Indeterminism

It would be unfair to reject Kant's attempt to connect freedom with noumenal causation because of these objections to the argument in the *Groundwork*. For we have seen that in the *Second Critique* and later works he distinguishes the freedom of responsibility from the freedom of moral autonomy. His division between negative and positive freedom separates the negatively free and responsible heteronomous agent from the positively free agent who has realized the capacity for autonomy that is present in all negatively free agents. But does this division make it easier or harder to defend Kant's claims about indeterminism and noumenal causation?

The division between the two types of freedom requires us to decide which type should be connected with noumenal causation and with indeterminism. Kant's arguments against compatibilism apply to the freedom of responsibility. Unless we take negative freedom to require indeterminism, we give up all Kant's reasons for believing that responsibility requires indeterminism. Hence we have a strong Kantian reason for claiming that negative freedom is incompatible with determinism. But indeterminism does not come in degrees; hence positive freedom does not involve less determination than negative freedom involves; they are equally phenomenally undetermined.

This conclusion casts doubt on Kant's attempt to identify the contrast between the moral motive and empirical motives with the contrast between phenomenal determination and noumenal causation. He affirms a special connexion between noumenal causation and the 'non-sensuous' moral motivation of the autonomous good will. But if noumenal causation is necessary for negative freedom, it does not distinguish the actions of morally good agents from the actions of other free agents. The connexion that Kant affirms between the non-sensuous, the non-empirical, the non-phenomenal, and the undetermined is difficult to accept.

Kant's improvements in his account of freedom raise questions, therefore, about transcendental and practical freedom. Either transcendental freedom explains nothing about responsibility, or it explains nothing about moral motivation. We keep more of Kant's position if we keep the link between transcendental freedom and responsibility, but abandon any link with moral motivation. We can retain his argument against compatibilism if we say that transcendental freedom is needed for negative freedom, but the difference between negative and positive freedom is unconnected with transcendental freedom.

But if we go this far, we leave Kant with an unstable position. For if we admit that we can explain positive freedom without indeterminism, we invite a similar explanation of negative freedom. Negative freedom is the capacity for positive freedom; the rational will is capable of acting either on its own law or on a principle derived from inclination. This capacity seems to be explicable by reference to the agent's deliberative capacities, without reference to undetermined causation. In that case, Kant does not need to reject a compatibilist account of freedom.

956. Transcendental Idealism v. Voluntarism

Our discussion of the noumenal will raises a further question about the compatibility of indeterminism with transcendental idealism. Though Kant believes that transcendental idealism reconciles the truth of indeterminism with the truth of phenomenal determinism, the reconciliation is not easy. Sometimes he claims that only the moral motive allows free action, so that the moral law is the only ground of determination that can determine a free will (*KpV* 29). If the will is free, it cannot be determined by any empirical condition, and so it must be determined by the form rather than the matter of a maxim, so that 'freedom and unconditional practical law reciprocally imply each other'.

This view of the free will is relevant to a question that arises for a voluntarist defence of indeterminism. It is difficult to see how, in a voluntarist view, the will is rational. It is even more difficult to see how the Kantian noumenal will is rational. For it is not only undetermined by any sort of rational consideration, but it cannot even be influenced—as a voluntarist who is not a transcendental idealist might claim—by any such consideration; for influence requires phenomenal causation, and hence temporal relations that are excluded for the noumenal will.

In reply, we might distinguish determination by prior events from the determination that is part of rationality. As Aquinas explains, God's knowledge does not rest on a process of reasoning in which previous events causally determine later ones so as to lead God to the right conclusions; for God does not think or act in time at all.[56] Still, God's beliefs are necessitated, and therefore determined, by the truth, since it is not possible for p to be true and for God not to know p. Moreover God believes p because it is true, and it is false that p is true because God believes it. God does not have a choice about whether to believe what is true or to will what a benevolent agent would will; but this lack of choice does not make God any less free.[57] Kant might argue, then, that the freedom of the noumenal will consists in freedom from determination by previous events, but not in freedom from the rational determination that Aquinas attributes to God's non-temporal agency. If he says this, he can explain how the noumenal will chooses rationally and is determined—though non-temporally—by rational considerations.

This, however, is not a completely satisfactory answer. Voluntarist concerns about freedom raise doubts about whether God is really free, if he is determined in the way Aquinas allows; this is why Ockham doubts whether Aquinas has given good reasons for thinking God is free. Kant's conception of the free will that necessarily follows a purely formal practical law is rather similar to Aquinas' account of God's freedom, in so far as it implicitly rejects the incompatibilist view that freedom requires the possibility of choosing otherwise. Even though the free will is not determined by previous events, it seems to be determined by rational considerations.

---

[56] See Aquinas, *ST* 1a q19 a5.   [57] Ockham and Aquinas on divine freedom; §396.

If Kant shares voluntarist concerns about freedom, he should apply them to non-temporal agency. Hence he should deny that the noumenal will is essentially rational, and so accept more of the voluntarist account of freedom than he explicitly endorses. In that case, the free will may act on one or another motive, but there is no reason to suppose that it must act on just one sort of motive. Given Kant's account of practical freedom, it is difficult to see why the free will must act on a moral motive rather than a sensuous motive; since neither of them determines it, it should be free to act on either. This objection to Kant suggests that there is no special reason to connect the moral will with freedom.

Our examination of Kant's views on freedom has shown, therefore, that the aspects of transcendental idealism that involve indeterminism are not necessary for his moral philosophy. At most, they are necessary—if incompatibilism is correct—for the freedom of responsibility. When Kant appeals to transcendental idealism to explain the distinctive character of the moral motive, he introduces confusion into his position. Fortunately, he shows us how to remove this confusion, through his explanation of negative and positive freedom. This explanation suggests that, despite Kant's claims about the noumenal will and the moral will, we should try to understand positive freedom without appeal to indeterminism.

KANT: FROM FREEDOM TO MORALITY

957. Does Autonomy Require Morality?

We have seen that not all of Kant's views on freedom depend on his acceptance of incompatibilism or on the aspects of noumenal causation that involve indeterminism. He is right to claim that his conception of freedom is not the simple compatibilist conception of Hobbes and Hume; he does not identify practical freedom with the causation of our actions by our thoughts and desires. In his view, freedom is independence of non-rational desire in our choice and motivation. The source of this independence is our capacity to act on practical reason apart from non-rational motives.

All responsible agents are negatively free; if they act on non-rational motives, they act on their acceptance of them, and are not simply coerced by them, as they would be if they had purely animal desires. But they are not all positively free, because they do not all recognize that there are rational grounds for accepting one sort of motive rather than another, and so they do not all act on the basis of rational conviction about what they ought to do. In people who simply accept their non-rational motives, the will does not give itself the law, because its principles are not derived from practical reason, but are simply maxims for the pursuit of non-rational aims. In Aquinas' terms, all rational agents consent to actions and motives, but only some agents act on practical reason about ends. These agents are autonomous.

What sort of consideration guides autonomous agents? Kant believes that since they act on practical laws, not on mere maxims, they act on moral categorical imperatives. So far, however, we have found no good reason to believe that autonomy is peculiar to morality, as opposed to prudence. Freedom does not seem to be uniquely revealed by morality, since we can also act on non-moral superior principles. Kant's questionable analysis of prudence affects his claims about morality and freedom.

The same question arises about Kant's claim that the morally bad person lacks a degree of positive freedom that is present in the good person. If positive freedom consists in being moved by practical laws rather than inclination in our choice of ends, why is it not consistent with moral evil? Perhaps refusal to consider ends in the light of practical reason is one source of vice, but is it the only one? If prudential reason is non-instrumental and autonomous, why could someone not exercise it flawlessly, so that he is guided by rational will apart from inclination, but still reject morality?

In claiming that a vicious person must have rejected practical reasoning about ends, Kant implies that if we engage fully in practical reasoning about ends, we will accept the moral law; failure to accept it must be traced to some fault in practical reason. If he explains vice in this way, Kant answers our previous objection that he ignores the traditional naturalist belief in autonomous prudential reason. For he can consistently recognize autonomous prudential reasoning, but still argue that we limit autonomous reasoning if we confine it to prudence; if we exercise practical reason fully, he believes, we will accept morality.[1]

958. Mutual Respect and the Predisposition to Personality

To see how the argument we have discussed helps us to understand Kant's position, we may return to his distinction between humanity and personality (*Rel.* 26).[2] Earlier we raised doubts about his assumption that only the moral point of view captures the predisposition to personality in which practical reason guides us non-instrumentally. His assumption is unjustified because it overlooks prudential categorical imperatives. But he may still be right to claim that the non-instrumental use of practical reason commits us to morality, whether or not we see this.

He argues that from the point of view of humanity, we regard other people as rivals, because our self-love moves us to 'acquire worth in the opinion of others'. We treat other people as means to our ends and so regard them as potential associates or rivals. This is the outlook that Rousseau attributes to inflamed amour propre, which pursues respect for oneself by competition with others.[3]

The point of view of mere humanity invites other people to look at me in the same way, simply as a potential associate or rival who may or may not fit in with their aims. If I do not value practical reason for its own sake, I value it only as a means to the satisfaction of other ends. If I regard rational agency as purely instrumental, I have no reason to attribute non-instrumental value to myself, and no reason to regard myself as an end. But I have a reason, based on inclination, to induce other people to ascribe instrumental value to me; for if they value me, they help me to advance my interests. I gain more from you if you value you me more highly than you value others. Hence I have reason to compete with others. In Kant's view, a Humean attitude to myself results in a Hobbesian attitude to others.

---

[1] Kosch, *FRKSK*, ch. 2, argues that Kant's conception of freedom and autonomy leaves him unable to explain the morally evil will, understood as the will that deliberately rejects the moral law. Hence she argues that Kant is not entitled to recognize moral responsibility without autonomy. The account of responsibility suggested here does not satisfy Kosch, because she does not allow any appeal to ignorance or negligence to figure in an explanation of immorality that one is responsible for; she takes an appeal to ignorance to undermine a claim of responsibility. We may be more inclined to think that responsibility is explained by a form of ignorance if we consider Aquinas' explanation of evil; see § 262.

[2] Humanity and personality; § 924. The dispositions to humanity and personality are discussed by Herman, 'Training', esp. 261–3.

[3] Rousseau and Kant; § 893.

Is this suggestion unfair to Hume? We might argue that Hume has implicitly refuted Kant's attempt to connect mere humanity with rivalry and competition; for he distinguishes the 'language of self-love' in which someone 'denominates another his enemy, his rival', and so on, from the language in which someone 'expresses sentiments in which he expects all his audience are to concur with him' (*IPM* 9.1). The second language expresses the outlook of humanity, and claims agreement from others.[4] If I have the appropriate sympathetic sentiments, I can take a co-operative rather than a competitive attitude to others, even though I do not ascribe non-instrumental value to myself. Hence the outlook of humanity seems to do what Kant thinks only the outlook of personality can do; it eliminates the rivalry and competition that belong to the outlook of self-love.

Kant might reasonably have modified his description of the predisposition to humanity, in order to acknowledge Hume's claims about the point of view of humanity. But this modification would not undermine the main contrast that concerns him. For, according to Hume, the point of view of humanity does not express the point of view of reason any more or less than self-love or any particular passion expresses it. Whether I take a competitive or a sympathetic attitude to others depends on my predominant inclination. Practical reason is purely instrumental, and does nothing by itself to resist the tendency to competition and conflict. I have no reason, therefore, to suppose I am entitled to any sort of treatment from others because of what I am in my own right; I can claim an entitlement only on the basis of sentiments I share with others.

The Humean outlook of humanity, therefore, implies lack of self-respect. Self-respect, as Kant understands it, involves the belief that I deserve certain kinds of treatment simply by being a person, apart from the strength of this or that sentiment either in me or in other people.

But even if the predisposition to personality includes self-respect, based on the recognition of non-instrumental value in oneself, does this aspect of personality lead to morality? Why should it lead to any special attitude to others? Even if we remove one source of rivalry and competition, how does respect for oneself lead us to treat others as ends?

959. Practical Reason and the Harmony of Ends

To clarify Kant's claim that the outlook of personality leads to mutual respect rather than competition, we may consider another of his initially questionable claims about reason. He argues that concern for one's own happiness cannot provide the basis of a universal practical law, because concern for one's happiness introduces competition, whereas a practical law introduces harmony. The fact that A wants A's welfare and B wants B's may often lead to conflict, which would not result from a genuine practical law.[5] Kant believes that the

---

[4] Hume on the outlook of humanity; § 763.

[5] 'Though elsewhere natural laws make everything harmonious, if one here attributed the universality of law to this maxim, there would be the extreme opposite of harmony, the worst conflict, and the complete annihilation of the maxim itself and its purpose. For the Wille of all has not got one and the same object, but each person has his own (his own welfare), which, to be sure, can accidentally agree with the purposes of others who are pursuing their own, but is far from sufficing for a law because the occasional exceptions which one is permitted to make are endless and cannot be definitely comprehended in a universal rule.' (*KpV* 28)

pursuit of happiness as one's supreme end belongs to the point of view of humanity, which is essentially competitive; harmony between rational agents results from the outlook of personality, which is the outlook of practical reason not subordinate to inclination.

This argument is not convincing by itself. Why must practical laws introduce the sort of harmony that Kant has in mind? Kant argues that natural laws introduce harmony, so that practical laws should do the same. But the parallel does not seem helpful; for the harmony in natural laws does not exclude two agents from acting against each other's interests or aims. We may not want conflict between rational agents; but why is this a demand of practical reason itself? And even if we answer this question, we need further argument to show that the demand can be satisfied by practical laws that are independent of inclination.

Kant expresses the same conviction about practical reason and harmony, in the two 'social' formulations of the categorical imperative. The first of these identifies the categorical imperative with the law that results from the will of every rational being legislating universal law (G 432). The second identifies it with the law for a 'kingdom of ends' (G 433). In both cases, in contrast to the first two formulae, Kant explicitly assumes co-ordination between the wills of rational agents, so that the will of any rational being, willing as a rational being, agrees with the will of all rational beings, willing as rational beings.

It is not clear how this conclusion emerges from claims about practical laws. Kant has a reasonable argument to show that agents who act on practical laws also have self-respect, because they ascribe non-instrumental value to themselves and to their rational agency. Despite Kant's views on prudence, it is reasonable to agree with Butler and Reid in recognizing that these rational agents act on categorical imperatives of prudence. But a further question arises about the appropriate attitude for practical reason to take in the face of other people who also act on such imperatives.

Aristotle and Aquinas answer this question through an account of happiness that shows our grounds for concern about the good of others for their own sake. Butler is dissatisfied with this conception of the relation of practical reason to morality. In his view, consideration of human nature, as a system guided by practical reason, shows that conscience is superior to rational self-love. Kant's position is similar to Butler's; he believes that if we consider practical reason and practical laws independently of the good for a rational agent, we can see that other people are to be treated as ends.

960. Treating Persons as Ends: What Needs to be Proved

In revealing personality to us, the moral law also reveals that persons are ends in themselves because of their personality (KpV 87). Kant means not only that I recognize myself as an end, but also that this attitude commits me to a certain attitude to others. But what is the relevant attitude to others? Two attitudes need to be distinguished:

(1) Each person has reason to agree that if S is a person, S has reason to regard S as an end in itself.

(2) If S is a person, S has reason to regard every person as an end in itself.

Kant needs (2) if his argument supports a morally significant conclusion. But (2) does not follow from (1).

We can see the difficulty that arises for Kant if we consider parallel claims about a person's interest. If I think I have reason to consider my own interest as a rational being (a person), two further attitudes may be distinguished:

(3)   Each person has reason to agree that if S is a person, S has reason to consider S's interest.
(4)   If S is a person, S has reason to consider every person's interest.

One might agree that if I think I have reason to consider my own interest, I am committed to (3); but (4) does not follow from (3), and further argument is needed to show that a rationally self-interested agent is committed to (4). Similarly, if Kant assumes without argument that (2) follows from (1), he fails to connect autonomy with morality. He still needs to show that S's conception of S as an end commits S to regarding other persons as ends in themselves for S and for everyone else.

Kant would secure the conclusion he needs if he could prove that my recognition of myself as an end requires the recognition of other selves who are equally ends both for themselves and for me. Fichte supposes that this strong connexion between recognition of oneself as an end and recognition of others as ends can be proved, but his argument is neither easily comprehensible nor immediately persuasive.[6]

Since Kant does not clearly state what he needs to prove, he does not argue in detail for the crucial elements in his position. But his views suggest arguments that might reasonably be called Kantian. We can perhaps form a clearer idea of his claims and their significance if we try to present these arguments in more detail. They are distinct but connected arguments for convergent conclusions.

961.   First Argument from Freedom to Morality: Respect for Oneself and for Others

Kant claims that every person regards himself as an objective end in relation to his desires. The self that I regard as an objective end is my rational nature, in contrast to my particular desires. The continuous and persistent element in me is not this or that desire, but a pattern of rational choice among my desires. Concern for ourselves is more than concern for simply satisfying the desires that we happen to have; it also involves concern for the desires we will have in the future, and concern for the ways we might or might not act to form this or that future desire. In this case, we have some concern for a person and a rational agent that is distinct from our concern to satisfy this or that particular desire or even to satisfy all our desires.

I act on my concern for myself as a whole in so far as I act (in Butler's terms) on a superior principle. If I had no practical rational capacities, and did not modify my other desires through rational planning, I could still form desires and discover that I have satisfied this or that desire. But to satisfy a desire, and even to be pleased by this satisfaction, is not to value

---

[6] See Fichte, *FNR* § 4, 39–45; *SE* 207–10. Fichte concludes: 'It can thus be proven strictly a priori that a rational being does not become rational in an isolated state, but that at least *one* individual outside it must be assumed, another individual who elevates this being to freedom'. Fichte's claims are discussed by Wood, 'Principle' and 'Right'; Neuhouser, *FTS*, ch. 4; Ameriks, 'Foundation'. Some connected arguments in Hegel are discussed by Wallace, *HPRFG*; see, e.g., 39–44.

it. In finding the satisfaction of a desire valuable, rather than simply pleasant, I take some attitude that connects the desire and its object to my other rational choices and pursuits. Something appears valuable to me, as a particular agent with relatively stable concerns, in so far as I connect it with my rational aims and their objects, and hence with my rational agency. I regard myself as a rational agent, and I take my rational agency to constrain the appropriate pursuit of my various subjective ends. I therefore regard my rational agency as an objective end and an object of respect.

Though prudential agency presupposes some degree of self-respect, this self-respect does not always guide everyone. We criticize people for lack of self-respect in their treatment of themselves, even without reference to other people. If, for instance, I am completely indifferent or reckless about my health, or if I neglect my longer-term aims simply for the sake of some appetite for a trivial immediate satisfaction, I seem to lack respect for myself. In such cases, I am willing to exploit and to subordinate myself to some impulse that I admit is not worth satisfying at the expense of myself. In these cases, then, self-respect is appropriate for a rational agent, apart from any moral obligation. Each of us has reason to maintain the self-respect that precludes 'self-exploitation', the subordination of myself to any particular impulse.

But my own impulses are not the only possible source of exploitation and subordination; threats of subordination may also come from other people's desires. If I have reason to maintain self-respect against threats of exploitation that come from my impulses, I have reason to maintain it against all threats of exploitation, not only against those that come from myself. I therefore have reason to resist threats of exploitation coming from other people as well as from my impulses.

To resist threats of exploitation coming from others, we might simply assert our preferences against their preferences, and try to impose our preferences by force. Alternatively, we might try to find preferences that we share with other people. But both of these approaches to others would be, to some degree, self-defeating; for they would make rational agents treat each other simply on the basis of their preferences, and so would subordinate everyone's rational agency to their preferences. If I respect myself by protecting my rational agency against intra-personal subordination and self-exploitation, I ought not to undermine this respect by allowing my own preferences or other people's to dominate my rational agency in guiding inter-personal relations.

I therefore have some reason to try to find a rational basis, not simply a preference-based reason, for mutual respect for rational agency. I can find this rational basis if I recognize that what I respect in myself is not a peculiarity of my rational agency, as opposed to someone else's; it is the rational agency that I find in me. Since other people have the same reason for self-respect that I have, we all have reason to respect rational agency. I can therefore put forward a reason-based case, not simply a preference-based case, to other people for respecting rational agency. I have good reason, in order to support my own self-respect, to avoid inter-personal exploitation directed against me; I can give a good reason to other people if I appeal to the reasonableness of avoiding inter-personal exploitation. To avoid inter-personal exploitation is to recognize rational agents as ends in themselves.

Hence the self-respecting attitude that is displayed in rational prudence gives us good reason to accept the attitude of respect for rational agents as ends in themselves. If we think we deserve nothing from other people, because no particular sort of treatment is due to us as persons, we lack self-respect and proper concern for ourselves. We imply that there is no reason why other people owe us a special kind of treatment as rational agents, apart from their purposes and sentiments. If we think this, it is not clear why a person should suppose he has any reason to treat himself in any special way because he is a rational agent. But then we seem to undermine our basis for taking prudence seriously too. This may explain Kant's claim that our awareness of the moral law is closely connected with our awareness of ourselves as persons.

We have reached this conclusion by exploring the implications of respect for oneself as an end. Kant takes this sort of self-respect to belong to rational agents generally. We have now found some support for the social formulae of the categorical imperative, referring to everyone's legislation and to legislation for a kingdom of ends. These formulae imply that a categorical imperative expresses the will of every rational being, because it appeals to reasons that are equally good reasons for every rational agent. Since every rational agent regards himself as an object of respect, in so far as he acts on superior principles, every rational being has a reason to regard every rational being as an object of respect for every rational being. Hence, every rational being legislating universal law will legislate a law that includes the Formula of Humanity. Since this law expresses every person's demand to be treated as an end, it is an imperative that everyone can reasonably accept; it is reached from a point of view that legitimately appeals equally to everyone. And since the principles that everyone has reason to accept treat everyone as an end, the rational agents who accept these principles constitute a kingdom of ends.

962. Second Argument from Freedom to Morality: Non-Egocentric Reasons

In trying to understand Kant's reasons for believing that morality fully expresses personality, we have begun from an egocentric attitude of respect for oneself, and argued that this commits us to acceptance of principles of mutual respect. A different attempt to articulate his views might challenge the legitimacy of the egocentric starting point.

Kant's claims about morality rely on the cogency of non-egocentric reasons.[7] The moral point of view rests on the principle that rational agents are ends for rational agents, so that I respond to reasons that are reasons for rational agents in general, not simply reasons for me. When I regard myself as an end, some essential part of this attitude must be independent of my belief that the person whom I regard as an end is myself.

We might compare ownership of something that is valuable whether or not I own it.[8] I might take an egocentric attitude to a Rembrandt I own; I might be pleased that I own it, and might want to protect and restore it for the same reason that I would want to protect

---

[7] Non-egocentric reasons are not necessarily the same as 'impersonal', or 'agent-neutral', or 'objective' reasons, as other people understand them. Some further argument beyond the recognition of non-egocentric reasons is needed to show that these reasons are not 'agent-relative'. Rational agents as such might, for instance, approve of special concern for one's own family or one's own benefactors, or the person to whom one has made a promise, which all involve agent-relative reasons (according to one conception). See also §§ 1016, 1203, 1273.

[8] Egocentric and non-egocentric reasons are discussed by Perry, 'Importance', esp. 77–83.

and polish my furniture, because it is my possession. I would not see the same reason for polishing someone else's furniture, or for taking a piece of equally good furniture off a scrap-heap and trying to restore it. But I might also have a further attitude to the Rembrandt; I might value it as a painting, apart from the fact that I own it. In that case, I would regard myself as having a reason to protect and restore the painting just because it is a Rembrandt, not because it is mine. I would also have that sort of reason to try to repair and to restore a Rembrandt that I found on a scrap-heap, even if I could not expect to profit by it. If I own a Rembrandt, my actual attitude to it will be a combination of egocentric attitudes that depend on my relation to it and attitudes that depend on its nature apart from my relation to it.

Can Kant find the same combination of attitudes in one's attitude to oneself as an end? Do I rationally value my rational agency in relation to my desires because of something about me in particular, and about my particular relation to rational agency? Or have I reason to take this attitude to rational agency in general, either in me or in someone else.

If prudence is a source of practical laws, I have external reasons, applying to every other rational agent, for concern about my own welfare. One might argue that I am committed to allowing non-egocentric reasons, if I recognize reasons applying to all rational agents. But in what sense is this true? We might distinguish two principles: (1) S has reason to respect S as a rational agent—whoever S is. (2) S has reason to respect every rational agent. In order to prove anything relevant to morality, Kant needs (2) rather than (1). But treating prudence as a source of practical laws seems to justify only (1). This is the difficulty that we have already encountered in trying to see how Kant can reach a principle requiring universal respect.

Perhaps, however, the objection is not decisive. We might ask, on Kant's behalf, how (1) could be reasonable if (2) is not. How could I have a reason to respect myself as a rational agent unless being a rational agent is itself worthy of my respect? If it is worthy of my respect, it must be worthy of my respect in any rational agent. Hence I am committed to an attitude of unrestricted respect, parallel to an unrestricted concern to preserve Rembrandts.

We might maintain this conclusion while acknowledging that I have special reasons to respect myself as a rational agent, since I am in a special relation to myself, and can do some things for myself that I cannot do for others. But the fact that I am in this special relation does not show that my reasons for respecting my own rational agency apply only to myself and do not extend to other people.

If this claim about non-egocentric reasons is correct, it suggests that our previous argument from respect for oneself to respect for others conceded too much to an egocentric starting point. For we conceded that it is reasonable to respect myself without initially respecting rational agents in general. According to the present argument, the egocentric starting point is not independently reasonable; its reasonableness depends on the reasonableness of the non-egocentric principle.

963. Significance of the Argument about Non-Egocentric Reasons

Kant seems to presuppose this claim about non-egocentric reasons. This is why (we might argue) he claims that the standpoint of practical reason is the standpoint of universal law for all rational agents, and that this standpoint prescribes universal respect, not simply respect for each agent by the agent. This presupposition may also help to explain why Kant does not present an argument from prudence to morality. We are likely to think we need such an argument if we accept the legitimacy of an egocentric starting point; but if Kant does not take egocentric prudence to be independently reasonable, he will see no need to present an argument that starts from an egocentric conception of prudence.

The argument about non-egocentric reasons does not reveal any incoherence in a Humean view about practical reason. For we have a basis for introducing non-egocentric reasons only if we assume that there are practical laws prescribing self-concern. Hume does not accept this assumption. In his view, the basis for self-concern is inclination. I have no external reason for concern for myself, rather than indifference towards myself, and no reason for efficient rather than inefficient pursuit of my ends; any reason I have is an internal reason that rests on my having further non-rational inclinations. This is Hume's position, but it is a far more extreme position than most people sympathetic to 'Humean' views are willing to maintain, and it rests on Hume's least cogent arguments about practical reason.[9] Kant's position compares favourably with the Humean position that one needs to maintain to avoid the force of Kant's argument.

In emphasizing the importance of non-egocentric reasons, Kant does not try to introduce a type of reason that has no intuitive grip on us. On the contrary, he simply emphasizes a point of view that is entrenched in our view of ourselves and of other people. We expect to be treated according to non-egocentric reasons, even though we do not always recognize this. Both Clarke and Reid[10] point out that, however little we seem to care about morality in guiding our own actions, we often appeal to it in assessing other people and in making claims on them. We do not give up our view that we have been treated unfairly or that we have just cause for resentment or gratitude towards another person. In taking these attitudes, we do not simply express our preference about how we would like people to treat us; we also express some view about how it is reasonable to expect people to treat each other.

Perhaps a consistent opponent could abandon these non-egocentric interpersonal attitudes as well. If it is indeed inconsistent to take these attitudes to other people while refusing to take them to ourselves, why should we not make our position consistent by forgoing any non-egocentric claim on other people? Kant strengthens Clarke's and Reid's answer to this question, by arguing that if we fail to look at ourselves from an impartial point of view, we have to abandon our belief in external reasons and settle for a Humean view of practical reason.

Though a reasonable case can be made for supposing that Kant means to reject the independent rationality of egocentric reasons, we need not be convinced by this case. For we have seen that he also has an argument from self-respect to respect for others that does not rely on this claim about egocentric reasons. This is a sensible strategy; the two lines of argument are complementary. Whether or not we accept the independent rationality of egocentric reasons, Kant has an argument to offer from practical freedom to morality.

The questions about non-egocentric reasons complicate further the relation between Kant's position and traditional eudaemonism and naturalism. On the one hand, we have

---

[9] Hume v. 'Humean' views; § 736.　　[10] Clarke on appeals to fairness; § 621. Cf. Reid, § 857.

found that Kant's argument gains support from categorical imperatives of prudence, whereas his Humean attitude towards prudence undermines the account of self-concern that supports him on the necessity of non-egocentric reasons. On the other hand, if Kant is right to insist on non-egocentric reasons, he exposes a weakness, or at least a gap, in traditional eudaemonism. Both Aristotle and Aquinas speak as though egocentric reasons are basic, and so intelligible without reference to anything more basic. But if Kant is right, the status that eudaemonists assign to egocentric reasons is unjustifiable unless it rests on the recognition of some non-egocentric reasons for valuing rational agency as such, in abstraction from the fact that it is mine in particular.[11]

Traditional eudaemonists do not deny the reality of non-egocentric reasons, but they do not recognize the importance of such reasons in their own position.[12] Some of Kant's claims and arguments suggest that non-egocentric reasons are fundamental, and therefore we need to take account of them in the first steps of our moral theory. We should not, for instance, follow Aristotle and Aquinas in postponing questions about the interests of others until we have gone some way towards working out our conception of the ultimate good; for even before we have worked this out, we already know that other rational agents count because non-egocentric reasons count.[13]

964. Third Argument from Freedom to Morality: Extension of Practical Reason

Kant's claims about the co-ordinating and harmonizing functions of practical reason support a further line of argument, distinct from the previous two, for his claim that practical reason is more completely realized in a moral system of mutual respect than in inter-personal relations guided only by inclinations—whether these are Hobbesian competitive inclinations or Humean inclinations of humanity.

In recognizing that I am practically free, I recognize myself as a rational agent. In acting on reasonable self-love, I apply practical reason to my various non-rational impulses; I do not subordinate one non-rational impulse to another, but I direct my non-rational impulses in the light of principles that tell me what is worth desiring, not simply what I desire. If I take this view about myself, I want to extend the scope of rational agency in relation to my other desires; I do not want them to be completely unresponsive to rational considerations, or completely inflexible in relation to other aims and desires. I do not necessarily want every aspect of my aims and motives to be determined by rational reflexion—indeed, it might well be irrational and self-defeating to try to do this; but I want to exercise rational agency in my life as a whole.

If one takes such an attitude to oneself, it would be unreasonable not to want to take it in relation to other people as well. To treat others as responsible agents, and hence as proper objects of the attitudes appropriate to responsible agents, is to include them, to

---

[11] Scotus' objections to the basic status of egocentric reasons; § 368.
[12] On egocentric and non-egocentric reasons in Aristotle see § 128. Contrast Whiting, 'Nicomachean'. On the Stoics see § 194. On Aquinas see §§ 335–6.
[13] Further discussion; § 1245 on Green.

some extent, within the scope of one's own rational agency. For the attitudes appropriate to responsible agents involve the use of reasons and evaluative attitudes, rather than simple force or manipulation. To express gratitude or resentment to another person we have to recognize something that gives us a ground for being grateful or resentful, and we expect the other to grasp that ground for our attitude as a reason for reconsidering his own action. We exercise theoretical reason in so far as we argue with others. We exercise practical reason in so far as we interact with others on the basis of shared assumptions about responsibility. Someone who regards herself as an end has some reason to regard other rational agents as responsible agents, entitled in their own right to the treatment proper to responsible agents.

If Kant is entitled to this conclusion, he has shown something important for his purposes. For he has shown that my attitude to myself as a rational agent commits me to a certain attitude to rational agents as such, and to valuing myself as a rational agent on grounds that commit me to attaching the same value to rational agents in general. If I demand respect from others, I extend my policy of guiding my choices and actions by practical reason. If I did not demand respect from others, I would be choosing to regard my treatment by others as an area that falls outside the scope of rational regulation and evaluation of desires. And so it seems reasonable for me to demand respect for myself as an end on the ground that I am a rational agent.

In Kant's view, practical reason is not simply a way of achieving the ends that appeal to us independently of reason. It is also a way of regulating our pursuit of other ends through rational principles; as Kant says, an objective end imposes a limit on the pursuit of other ends.[14] Concern for myself as a rational agent makes it reasonable for me to demand respect for myself as a rational agent, and this demand requires me to treat other people as objects of respect as well. When we take this point of view, we regard other people as equals, in so far as they have the features that make it reasonable for me to claim some sort of respect. The moral law reveals personality in so far as it expresses a view of persons as equals and participants, rather than as rivals or instruments.

If I do not recognize principles demanding mutual respect, I imply that practical reason fails in regulating and guiding our treatment of each other. If I rely on force in asserting my preferences and trying to get someone else to follow them, I cannot claim to be giving him any reason to follow them. If I appeal instead to his antecedent preferences to show that they make it reasonable to go along with my preferences, my approach to him depends on what he happens to prefer. If he alters his preferences so that they no longer fit in so easily with mine, I cannot appeal to some principle that he shares with me to show that he ought not to have altered them.

If, then, I take relations with others to be simply guided by our preferences, I do not try to regulate these relations by rational principles. Once I agree, however, that as a rational agent I have reason to want rational principles to guide this aspect of my life, I need moral principles, as Kant conceives them, giving us a basis for evaluating each other on common principles, not simply under the influence of similar inclinations.

In attributing this argument to Kant, we connect his position with the Aristotelian argument for friendship. Aristotle understands the co-operative elements of friendship as

---

[14] Objective ends as limits; § 921.

the extension of practical reason and deliberation to inter-personal relations.[15] Aquinas expresses this point in terms even closer to Kant's; one kind of friendship is an expression of intellectual love, applied to the aspects of our lives that include co-operation with others.[16] Intellectual love consists of the aims that are formed by practical reason and election rather than by instrumental reasoning about the satisfaction of antecedent preferences. Aquinas argues that our impulse to live in society results from intellectual love, and so not only from the sorts of desires that either Hobbes or Hume recognizes. Kant develops this argument by claiming that the extension of practical reason to interaction with others requires acceptance of principles that prescribe mutual respect for persons as ends.

This point of similarity between the Kantian and the Aristotelian position is especially significant in the light of the various contrasts between the two positions. Despite these contrasts, the two positions share the view that moral principles are basically the complete expression of practical reason. To understand the demands of morality, in their view, we ought not to consider primarily the compromises that we have to make because of the collision of our Hobbesian preferences with other people's preferences, nor the Humean sentiments of sympathy and fellow-feeling that we share, but our common aim of directing our lives by practical reason. We achieve this aim through a system of principles prescribing mutual respect.

965. Treating Persons as Ends and the Basis of Morality

Kant believes that respect for oneself requires one to recognize that rational agents appropriately demand some kind of treatment from other rational agents. To recognize the legitimacy of this demand is to agree that rational agents deserve some kind of respect in their own right. In so far as they deserve such respect in their own right, they are ends in themselves.

If we treat others as responsible agents, praising and blaming them for their voluntary actions, we treat them as ends in themselves. If I treat you as responsible, I treat your past actions and choices as the basis for how I treat you in the present and future; they restrain me from treating you in ways that I might otherwise prefer.[17] No matter how much I might want to harm you for something you have done, and no matter how useful it might be for other people if I did it, the discovery that you did it out of non-culpable ignorance prohibits me from doing what I might otherwise have done to you.

If I expect this sort of treatment for myself because I am a rational agent, not because I am the particular agent I am, I assume that it is reasonable for every rational agent to take this attitude to every rational agent. The reasons supporting the treatment of rational agents—as such and apart from their usefulness to other people's purposes—as responsible agents imply that they are ends in themselves.

If we acknowledge that someone's being a rational agent makes it appropriate to treat her in certain ways, irrespective of other people's aims, we acknowledge that she has some rights

---

[15] Aristotle on the extension of practical reason; § 125.   [16] Aquinas on friendship and the basis of justice; §§ 336–7.
[17] This aspect of responsibility is briefly and clearly explained by Hart, PR 17–24.

that do not depend on people's purposes. Hence the claim to treatment as a responsible agent rests on a more general claim about the value of rational agents apart from their usefulness to other people's purposes. But what does this general claim imply? We might treat people as rational and responsible agents in praising, blaming, and punishing them, but treat them as means in every other respect. Why would this policy be unreasonable?

If we recognize someone as a rational and responsible agent, we regard their aims and concerns as counting for something independently of what suits us. For in treating them as responsible, we guide our treatment of them by reference to their choices and decisions, not simply by what we would prefer to do to them. In constraining our treatment of them in these ways, we allow them greater freedom to act in accordance with their own aims and plans; for we assure them that they can avoid certain kinds of treatment by others if they choose in the appropriate ways. It would be unreasonable to treat people in this way if we attached no non-instrumental value to their acting on their own choices. If, then, we respect a rational being apart from his instrumental usefulness, we have reason for concern about his desires, interests, and aims, apart from their usefulness to other people; the fact that these are important to a particular person gives other people a reason to care about them, apart from their usefulness to these other people.

Some aspects of Kant's theory may make this point harder to see. For, in his view, these particular desires and aims belong to the sensuous, non-moral, non-rational self; and therefore, we might think, Kant can hardly value them from the moral point of view. But this is a mistaken inference from Kant's separation between the moral and the non-moral aspects of a person. A rational agent has some rational conception of his own good, and rationally cares about that. In so far as particular desires are accepted in his rational conception of his good, they deserve his rational concern. If the argument about respect works, his desires deserve respect by others. Though the fact that I want something may not be morally significant in itself, the fact that it is part of my concern as a rational agent makes it morally significant. If a rational agent has a legitimate concern with her particular contingent aims (those that belong to her as the particular human being she is, not simply a rational agent), her aims are suitable objects of respect and concern for others.

We have now explored some arguments from positive freedom to morality, to show that if we recognize ourselves as positively free, we have reason to treat persons as ends in themselves. These arguments expand some of Kant's views about the connexion between treating oneself as an end and treating others as ends. If he shows that these two attitudes are connected in the way that he claims, he supports his claim that moral principles are categorical imperatives, and do not simply present themselves as categorical imperatives. In recognizing the fact of reason, we recognize that we are negatively free rational agents, but we need to reflect further on rational agency to see that we have reasons to treat rational agents as ends.

Though Kant accepts this connexion between treating oneself as an end and treating others as ends, he explores it less fully than its importance would warrant. Part of the reason for his relatively brief treatment is his restrictive conception of categorical imperatives. By confining them to moral imperatives and leaving prudence to hypothetical imperatives, he supports his claim that the moral law uniquely reveals freedom. But this support is costly; for it weakens his case for the claim that the moral law expresses a categorical imperative. Once we see that categorical imperatives extend beyond morality, we see that Kant has a stronger case for claiming that rational agents as such have reason to accept moral imperatives.

966. The Effect of the Moral Law on the Non-Moral Self

If this defence of Kant's position is plausible, he has a reason to agree with Butler in recognizing practical laws of prudence. We can confirm this suggestion if we consider some of his claims about the effect of the moral motive on the non-moral self. In 'The Incentives of Pure Practical Reason' (*KpV*, ch. 3) he examines the relation of moral motivation to other motives. Moral reason, in his view, is a sufficient motive by itself, independently of all non-moral inclinations. The result of this operation of moral reason is respect for the moral law. This feeling of respect belongs to the non-moral aspects of the self, and it seems to be a favourable feeling, encouraging us to act on the moral law. But Kant hesitates to say that the moral law appeals to, or attracts, the non-moral self. The feeling of respect is supposed to explain why the non-moral self takes an interest in following morality, but it does not refer to any non-moral desire to support morality.

Kant suggests that non-moral inclinations can all be assigned to self-love and the desire for the agent's happiness; and this desire (in his view) conflicts with the moral motive. When the non-moral self is confronted with the moral law, and finds itself conforming to it, it is frustrated and its self-conceit is struck down. Self-conceit is the attitude that treats one's own inclinations as an ultimate determining ground for one's action, and so the moral law humiliates us by showing that we are not the only people who matter.[18] Until we recognize the moral law, we incline towards inordinate self-love; and so we find it unwelcome to be reminded of our real importance.[19]

So far, then, following the moral law apparently increases frustration and suffering within the self. Kant recognizes this, observing that motivation by the moral law results in a feeling of pain. He claims that respect for the law is not the incentive to morality, and that there is no antecedent feeling tending to morality. Hence moral reasons are not subordinate to non-moral feelings and inclinations. On the contrary, the moral law produces a feeling of frustration and humiliation in the non-moral self.

But how is this pain connected with respect? If we see that the moral law overrides our other desires, should we not (from the non-moral point of view) regard our moral motive as simply an unfortunate compulsive desire that we would be better off without? Kant answers that the moral law also produces a favourable attitude that removes resistance to the law; this is the feeling of respect.[20] A mere feeling of humiliation could hardly have this effect; it would produce hostility and resistance. Kant, however, believes that a favourable feeling results from following the moral law. Why is this so?

He distinguishes respect from the attitudes that result from recognizing something as powerful, dangerous, formidable, or even admirable; he assumes that respect includes a

---

[18] On self-conceit see § 907.   [19] Inordinate self-love and superbia; § 365.

[20] '...for this law there is no feeling, but, as it removes a resistance, this dislodgement of an obstacle is, in the judgment of reason, equally esteemed as a positive assistance to its causality. Therefore this feeling can also be called a feeling of respect for the moral law; on both grounds it can be called a moral feeling.' (*KpV* 75)

favourable feeling distinct from admiration. It includes, but it is not exhausted by, the aesthetic attitude that Kant describes in his discussion of the sublime.[21] Respect for some person S is connected with a favourable attitude to S's moral character, resting on the belief that S's own efforts as a rational agent have produced this result. The soul of the moral agent 'believes itself to be elevated in proportion as it sees the holy law elevated over it and its frail nature'. This sense of elevation is difficult to understand if the non-moral soul regards the moral motive as wholly alien and unwelcome. How can it be converted, so that it wants to contemplate the law and cares about the development of other people's moral characters?

Kant argues that when we follow the moral law, we feel displeasure because our inclinations are frustrated, but still we feel some kind of 'self-approbation with reference to pure practical reason', because we recognize we are acting on a practical law that is appropriate for us as persons.[22] Recognition of the moral law as expressing a conception of personality explains our respect for the law; this respect is the favourable attitude of the non-moral self towards the law. Hence the conception of myself as a personality moved by practical reason apart from inclination must somehow appeal to my non-moral self.

My non-moral self, therefore, cannot be just a bundle of sensuous impulses that are humiliated by confrontation with the moral law. The law reveals something that can interest and concern me, from the point of the view of the non-moral self. The relevant sort of interest is more intelligible if we recognize the morally good will as the actualization of the capacity for rational reflexion that we already recognize as an appropriate expression of our nature as rational agents.

This account of respect for the moral law supports our claim that Kant needs the conception of practical reason that he explicitly repudiates. According to his explicit view, non-moral practical reasoning is purely instrumental; if we abstract from our acceptance of the moral law, we simply regard ourselves from the point of view of mere 'humanity'. From this 'Humean' point of view, the moral law, as Kant understands it, cannot provide a source of self-approbation; it must appear to reflect empty pretensions of reason. Kant's explicit view, therefore, does not show how the non-moral self could find a source of self-approbation in the moral law. If, however, he recognizes non-moral categorical imperatives, and if he is right to claim that the moral law embodies a categorical imperative, the non-moral self has reason to respect the moral law; for the non-moral self is already guided by categorical imperatives.

This explanation of respect for the moral law presupposes that the non-moral self regards the moral law as embodying a categorical imperative, constituting reasons for rational agents as such. If respect is well founded, the non-moral self is correct in taking this view of the moral law. Kant's strongest claim, that the moral law alone reveals positive freedom and personality, is too strong, even for Kant's own purposes; hence it does not appropriately connect rational agency with morality. A better argument would show that rational agency is incompletely realized in prudence, but more completely realized in morality. This is

---

[21] Kant discusses the sublime in *KU* § 25–6.

[22] '. . . for one knows himself to be determined thereto solely by the law and without any [sensuous] interest; he becomes conscious of an altogether different interest which is subjectively produced by the law and which is purely practical and free. Our taking this interest in an action of duty is not advised by an inclination, but reason through the practical law absolutely commands it and also actually produces it.' (*KpV* 81)

Butler's conclusion about self-love and conscience. Though Kant does not accept Butler's conception of prudential practical reason, Butler's conception suggests a Kantian argument about practical reason and morality that supports Butler's conclusion.

Consideration of the non-moral self suggests a further modification of Kant's explicit position. The non-moral self includes not only prudence in contrast to morality, but also the passions and emotions in contrast to will and reason. If Kant's account of respect requires integration between the moral and prudential aspects of the self, it also requires integration between the rational and non-rational aspects of the self. We have noticed that Kant makes this task more difficult for himself than it needs to be, because of his views about the non-voluntary character of the emotions. If he allowed that they can co-operate with reason and will, his account of respect would be more plausible; for it would be clearer how the rest of the self could favour the moral law. In this case also, the central elements of Kant's position warrant a modification of some of his views.

967. Some Moral Implications

If Kant has justified a demand for rational agents to be treated as ends, not simply with reference to their usefulness to other people, Kantian arguments support a constraint on the content of acceptable moral principles.

Kant insists on the moral principles appropriate for self-respecting persons. Self-respect is distinct from love or esteem for ourselves. It includes the conviction that we have some value that justifies the treatment of us with due consideration for our interests and aims. Some people's self-respect might rest on their belief in their own brilliant achievements or on their belief in their usefulness to others; and if we want to encourage self-respect in others, we might sometimes want to convince them of their success or their usefulness. Such beliefs might be a legitimate source not only of self-esteem (involving pride in one's achievements) but also of self-respect (involving a conviction of one's value).[23] But someone who depended entirely on these sources for self-respect would lack some appropriate degree of self-respect. For if we thought we became worthless if we no longer could claim the same successes or the same usefulness to others, we would no longer expect anything for ourselves, and would see no reason to object to any sort of bad treatment by others. If we say that someone's self-respect has been undermined by failure or uselessness, however, we do not mean that such a person has no appropriate basis for self-respect. We would admire someone all the more if they kept their self-respect and the belief in their own worth even in these adverse conditions.[24]

Kantian ethics requires the treatment of persons as ends, and so expresses what self-respecting persons might reasonably demand from themselves and from one another. A self-respecting person does not believe that his rights, entitlements, and justified claims on others or on himself depend on his being so useful to others that concern for his interests increases the total good. Hence a moral principle acceptable to a self-respecting person will

---

[23] Different types of self-respect are discussed by Hill, 'Servility', and his further thoughts, 'Self-respect'.
[24] Contrast Nietzsche's criticism of self-respect independent of achievement; § 1097.

not prescribe the treatment of persons simply as means to the ends of other people; for such treatment fails to guarantee what a self-respecting person reasonably demands. We can use some of our beliefs and assumptions about self-respect to see what sort of value Kant means to capture in his formulation of the categorical imperative.

Kant's views about the respect that one owes to oneself and others underlie his affirmation of duties to oneself. Reasons for respecting rational agents impartially apply to oneself as well as to others; hence we cannot consistently believe we are obliged to treat others as they deserve, but free to let ourselves be treated however we please.[25] The rejection of servility (*MdS* 434–5) rests on the claim that 'a human being regarded as a *person*, that is, as the subject of a morally practical reason, is exalted above any price'.[26] When we attach the right value to ourselves, we must pursue our ends 'not in a servile spirit, as if [we] were asking a favour'; we must not treat as a favour what we ought to expect as our due.

To see what Kant's demands might imply, it is worth reverting to some of the questions raised in our discussion of Butler and utilitarianism, about the role of the public interest and benevolence in explaining the basis of all or some moral principles.[27] If concern for the public interest involves simply the consideration of the total benefit, it sacrifices the interests of individual people to the total good. If general benevolence implies this sort of maximizing concern for the public interest, Kant has a reasonable objection to it, if he is right to demand the treatment of persons as ends.

Kant, then, should agree with Butler, Price, and Reid in their criticisms of the view that morality rests on considerations of utility and the public interest. His three predecessors register the fact that some of our ordinary conception of morality does not fit the utilitarian reconstruction. They do not, however, try to trace anti-utilitarian beliefs to more basic principles; Price maintains there are no such principles. They fail, therefore, to explain why opposition to utilitarian reconstruction is not simply irrational, or the product of mistaken assumptions that we would reject if they were made explicit. Price, in turn, might throw this challenge back at the utilitarian. Do we not need some intuition of the rightness of the utilitarian principle? Why should we not recognize several intuitively certain principles, rather than just one?

We might help to resolve this dispute if we could find some rational basis for accepting utilitarian or non-utilitarian principles, so that they do not rest simply on unsupported intuition. Kant offers an argument of this form. Since rational agents essentially value the point of view of personality, and morality most fully expresses the point of view of personality, it most fully expresses the point of view that rational agents essentially value. If we connect morality with personality, we see that the most plausible basic moral principles reject utilitarian benevolence. Viable non-utilitarian principles restrict the application of utilitarian reasoning.

Kant's position supports non-utilitarian principles that treat persons as ends. To retain utilitarian principles on a Kantian basis, we would have to show that some practical law, binding on rational agents as such, prescribes the maximization of utility. If we could show this, we would face a potential conflict in our practical laws, since one practical law would

---

[25] Aquinas explains duties to oneself similarly; § 313.   [26] Quoted in full in § 924.
[27] Butler and utilitarianism; §§ 698–700.

reject utilitarianism and another would embrace it, and we would (so far) have no basis for taking one to be prior to the other. Kant, however, does not consider this possibility, since he does not believe that any practical law prescribes utilitarianism. Questions about conflict and priority arise from Sidgwick's argument to show that the principle of utility is a categorical imperative.[28]

Kant believes that Butler's distinction between power and authority applies to relations between people as well as to relations between the desires of an individual. Within an individual, this distinction is expressed in the Platonic view that it is possible to achieve psychic justice by treating different desires fairly, not simply by registering their comparative strength. Between persons, the particular principles are different, but, in Kant's view, the same outlook is expressed. Kant extends and supports Butler's claims about conscience, by arguing that the proper attitude of practical reason is the outlook of personality, which involves the treatment of persons as ends.

These arguments from self-respect to respect for rational agents support Kant's claim that the outlook of personality, recognizing practical laws, is also committed to the outlook of morality. His conception of personality is inadequate, since he does not recognize prudential practical laws. But this flaw in his conception does not undermine his claims about morality. On the contrary, a clearer understanding of prudential practical laws helps to explain the connexion between personality and morality. A reasonable account of prudential practical laws commits us to respect for others as well as ourselves.

We may therefore doubt Kant's claim that the predisposition to personality is realized only in moral reasons; but we may still agree that this predisposition is realized only in agents who are committed (whether they recognize it or not) to the acceptance of mutual respect. This is a reason to agree that the moral law fully realizes the predisposition to personality.[29]

---

[28] Sidgwick on the priority of the utilitarian principle; §§ 1198–9.
[29] On full realization cf. Rawls, *TJ* 254–5/224–5.

71

KANT: MORALITY
AND THE GOOD

968. Autonomy and Kantian Morality

We have now examined Kant's argument to show that practical laws must include moral principles, and that we are not completely guided by practical laws until we follow moral principles that prescribe the treatment of persons as ends. In following these practical laws, we achieve positive freedom. If we are to be autonomous, acting on principles that are the laws of the rational will itself and are not derived from outside, we must follow the categorical imperative of morality.

This conclusion supports Kant's opposition to systems of morality that make the supreme moral principles hypothetical imperatives. We have already considered his reasons for believing that such principles do not adequately capture our convictions about the nature of moral principles.[1] We can now add a further objection: a moral system that does not rest on moral categorical imperatives does not realize the freedom of the rational will. If we seek to realize freedom, so that we act on our practical reason rather than on non-rational incentives, we must reject the heteronomy of will that is the source of all 'spurious principles of morality' (G 441).

To see whether Kant is right to reject all non-Kantian moral systems by appeal to autonomy, we may return to our comparison between his position and the eudaemonist naturalism of Aquinas. We have found that Kant's conception of the difference between himself and the naturalist position rests on doubtful assumptions about naturalism. Indeed, some of his claims about self-respect and freedom are better supported by eudaemonist principles than by his own views about practical reason. With all this in mind, we can turn to questions about autonomy.

Here as elsewhere, it is sometimes easier if we speak of 'eudaemonism' and 'naturalism' interchangeably, to refer to the position of Aquinas, which includes both eudaemonism and naturalism. The two doctrines need to be distinguished if we are discussing Butler and Reid, who are naturalists but not eudaemonists. Since many of the same issues arise about the two

---

[1] Spurious principles make moral principles into hypothetical imperatives; §927.

doctrines in relation to Kant's arguments, we can usefully treat them together. Sometimes, however, we need to be more careful; for we may find reasons that would justify Kant in agreeing with Butler and Reid without going beyond them to eudaemonism.

969. Is Naturalism Compatible with Autonomy?

Kant follows Rousseau in claiming that we are free by giving ourselves the law.[2] He recalls a long tradition connecting self-legislation with morality. Self-legislation has a firm place in the traditional view that connects it with awareness of the natural law. When Aquinas explains how self-legislation is a mark of worth (dignitas), he refers to the contrast between following one's own guidance and following the guidance of another.[3]

Kant believes that traditional naturalism offers an inadequate conception of autonomy. He would be right to believe that it cannot allow autonomy if he were right to believe that it appeals to empirical features of human nature. But we have found that Aquinas does not appeal primarily to empirical features of human beings; his basic principles rest on essential features of a rational will. On this point, Kant has no reason to deny that Aquinas also tries to formulate Kantian practical laws.[4]

Still, we might object that Aquinas violates Kant's demands on self-legislation. For if the will follows the natural law, and is guided by an ultimate good, simply in so far as it is a rational will, perhaps the will does not freely give itself the law, but finds that it has no alternative but to accept the law. In that case, the connexion between self-legislation and freedom is lost, and naturalism excludes autonomy, if autonomy requires freely giving oneself the law.

To see whether this is a genuine conflict between Kant's claims about freedom and Aquinas' naturalism, we should return to Aquinas' views on the connexion between natural law and the freedom of the will. In his view, it is essential to the rationality and freedom of rational agents that the will necessarily pursues an ultimate end and freely chooses the means to it (1a q60 a2; 1a q82 a1–2; 1–2 q10 a1–2). Human intellect directs itself to some things, and in doing so presents ends to itself, but its pursuit of the ultimate end arises from nature, so that it cannot fail to will the ultimate end. The will is free in so far as it can deliberate about means towards this ultimate end and can elect on the basis of deliberation. Our pursuit of the ultimate end gives us control of our actions.[5]

If Aquinas is right to connect will, freedom, the ultimate good, and the natural law in these ways, he shows that in binding the will to pursuit of the ultimate good, he does not remove freedom and autonomy. He believes that these connexions show how the will is free in its pursuit of specific conceptions of the good. Is this position open to reasonable Kantian objections?

Someone might reject Aquinas' claim that our freedom depends on our pursuing something necessarily. But Kant cannot reasonably endorse this objection to Aquinas, since

---

[2] Beck, *CKCPR* 200, cites Rousseau, *SC* i 8, quoted in §889.

[3] See Aquinas, *ad Rom.* §217, quoted in §301. Butler exploits this connexion between natural law and legislation for oneself; see §681.

[4] On eudaemonism and practical laws see §910.   [5] Aquinas on freedom and the ultimate end; §266.

he also believes that the will is free because of something that it does necessarily. Whether we follow the moral law or some sensuous motive, we are not simply compelled by one of the other principle; we must incorporate a particular incentive in our maxim.[6] We do not freely choose to perform or to omit this act of incorporation, but we exercise our freedom in performing it. This necessary action of the will corresponds to the necessary action of the will in choosing means to an ultimate end (as Aquinas conceives it).

Kant's conception of a holy will also agrees with Aquinas' view of freedom based on necessity. A holy will is free and autonomous, but it is not free to reject the moral law, since the moral law simply states the requirements of practical reason, which necessarily move a holy will.[7] Even a limited will such as the human will is necessarily moved to some extent by practical law, though other incentives also influence it. This necessary element in its motivation does not reduce its freedom. Kant has no reason, therefore, to reject Aquinas' claim that freedom requires acceptance of some first principle.

Even if we allow that freedom may be based on necessity, we may object to Aquinas' view that freedom involves determination by reason independent of our pre-existent desires. But such an objection is not open to Kant, who also insists that freedom requires independence of any end given by non-rational desire. He acknowledges, just as Aquinas does, external reasons that do not depend on antecedent desires. He agrees with Aquinas in connecting freedom with determination by reason, as opposed to non-rational desire.

A Kantian point of view equally supports some of Aquinas' claims about natural law. The precepts of natural law are supposed to describe the content of morality. But the first principle of natural law, about the pursuit of good, seems to describe the form of a system of morality, not its content. We have to deliberate about how to fulfil the requirements of natural law before we find practical content, and Aquinas needs to provide an appropriate basis for such deliberation. Similarly, Kant needs to argue from the purely formal fact that a rational will necessarily follows law to the more specific conclusion that it has reason to follow principles with the moral content that Kant assigns to the categorical imperative. Both Aquinas and Kant begin with a purely formal account of a rational will, and both claim that this purely formal starting point is a reasonable basis for the discovery of more specific moral requirements.

These aspects of traditional naturalist doctrine, therefore, do not separate Kant's position from naturalism.

970. The Errors of Eudaemonism about the Role of the Highest Good

But even if traditional naturalism does not deny the autonomy of the rational will, it may still give the wrong place to the highest good. In arguing for the rational necessity of morality as a basic principle of practical reason, Kant believes he opposes the theorists who take the highest good to be the basis of practical principles and derive moral principles from it. In his view, such theorists have things the wrong way round, since our conception of the highest

---

[6] See *Rel.* 24, quoted in §943.
[7] On the holy will, and the difference between practical laws and imperatives, see §§903, 988.

good should be derived from our account of morality. He agrees with Greek and mediaeval moralists in believing that a complete account of the moral life includes an account of the highest good; but he believes we can see the proper place of the good only if we recognize the priority of the moral law. Kant's criticisms of the illegitimate use, as he supposes, of appeals to the highest good in Greek moralists may help us to see some questions that arise in his own treatment of it.[8]

His criticism rests partly on his rejection of categorical imperatives of prudence.[9] Since he does not acknowledge that he rejects the traditional naturalist position on this point, he assumes that naturalists share his views about happiness and prudence. Since he believes that imperatives of prudence are purely hypothetical because they are based on inclination, he believes that any subordination of morality to prudence also subordinates morality to inclination. Since he assumes that the naturalists agree with him in regarding imperatives of prudence as hypothetical, he infers that they subordinate morality to inclination. Kant's view of the implications of naturalism conflicts with the intentions of naturalists; for they believe that prudential imperatives are categorical, and so they do not believe that if morality is subordinate to prudence, it is subordinate to inclination.

Kant's assumption that eudaemonism subordinates morality to inclination gives him a reason to argue that eudaemonists have the wrong account of the relation of the right to the good. This reason collapses if eudaemonists do not subordinate morality to inclination.

We might, then, try to modify Kant's position so as to preserve its main point. Even if we grant that eudaemonists do not intend to subordinate morality to inclination, we may still argue that in fact they subordinate it, since they are wrong to believe that prudential imperatives are categorical. But this modification does not make Kant's position easier to defend; for, as we have seen, it is difficult to be convinced by his Humean conception of prudential imperatives without being convinced by a Humean conception of moral imperatives too. A defender of Kant might be well advised, therefore, to abandon the objection that eudaemonists subordinate morality to inclination.

But even if the eudaemonist subordination of morality to the good does not imply its subordination to inclination, it may still be open to objection. We should now try to see whether Kant has a plausible objection that rests on a true conception of the eudaemonist position.

971. Kant v. Eudaemonism: The Priority of the Right to the Good[10]

In treating the highest good as prior to virtue, eudaemonists insist that practical reason at every stage is constrained by the holistic formal constraints imposed by the highest good. If

---

[8] This aspect of Kant is helpfully discussed by Engstrom, 'Concept' and 'Happiness'.   [9] Prudence; §910.

[10] Larmore, *MM* 26–34, discusses Kant's views on the right and the good, with reference to the issues raised by Pistorius (whom Kant alludes to at *KpV* 8). According to Larmore, Kant's basic objection to making the good fundamental is his belief that the good varies between different people according to their preferences and that any idea of the good is subject to reasonable disagreement. Larmore (12) takes such diversity and disagreement about the good to be a primary source of modern moral philosophy

moral principles are to emerge from the essential concerns of a rational will, they must be part of a system of aims that meet the holistic constraints. The role of the holistic constraints is clear in Aristotle's appeals to the criteria of completeness and self-sufficiency, and in Aquinas' appeal to the criterion of perfection. These constraints, as Aristotle and Aquinas understand them, also introduce naturalism into eudaemonism, since they involve reference to the fulfilment of human nature and capacities as a whole.

Kant would have a clear reason for disagreeing with eudaemonism on this point if he were an intuitionist about moral principles. If he maintained that we are immediately, non-inferentially, justified in believing that true moral principles are categorical imperatives, he could reasonably reject any attempt to relate them to holistic formal constraints. Kant, however, is not an intuitionist; in his view, we can reasonably ask whether moral principles are really categorical imperatives, and the 'fact of reason' does not make this question unnecessary or inappropriate. Some argument is needed to show that moral principles are practical laws, resting on reasons that apply to rational agents as such. Eudaemonists are not mistaken simply because they try to connect morality with reasons that apply to rational agents as such.

One might argue, however, that they are mistaken in claiming that the relevant connexions are of the sort that eudaemonists assert. According to Aristotle and Aquinas, moral principles are practical laws for rational agents because they have the right place among ends that a rational agent pursues towards his own good. This argument may be criticized because it rests on holist and egocentric assumptions. It rests on holist assumptions because it assumes that in order to see that moral principles are practical laws we have to see what other practical laws there are, and how morality fits in with them. It rests on egocentric assumptions because it assumes that the relevant system of practical laws aims at the agent's own good.

Questions about the legitimacy of the eudaemonist constraints are relevant to Kant's discussion of the priority of the moral law to one's account of the good. He claims to have shown that nothing prior to the moral law is the unconditioned good, and therefore nothing prior to it ought to be a sufficient determining ground of the will.[11] His claim is open to question if it rests only on the claims about the highest good that we have already discussed. Kant sometimes assumes that if we treat the good as prior to the moral law, we make morality simply a means to pleasure (*KpV* 58–9, 63). The eudaemonist view need not subordinate morality as simply an instrumental means to some further good.

Kant has a better objection to eudaemonism, however, if moral reasons are independent of beliefs about the good. In that case, eudaemonists are wrong to proceed as Aristotle and Aquinas proceed, by setting out formal criteria for the good and then arguing that moral principles and virtues meet these criteria. If we can settle the rational cogency of moral principles without fitting them to these criteria, Kant has a reasonable objection to the eudaemonist procedure.

---

[11] 'In the preceding chapter [sc. ch. 2, on the object of practical reason] we have seen that anything which presents itself as an object of the will prior to the moral law is excluded from the determining grounds of the will called the unconditionally good by that moral law itself as the supreme condition of practical reason, and that the mere practical form, which consists in the fitness of maxims for giving universal law, first determines what is good in itself and absolutely and grounds the maxims of a pure will, which alone is good in every respect.' (*KpV* 74)

Do Kant's arguments from freedom to morality refute eudaemonism? We have found that his argument attributes a more basic status to non-egocentric reasons than eudaemonists characteristically attribute to them. In his view, we do not need to show that the various ends of a rational agent require non-instrumental concern for others; we find that simply valuing oneself as a rational agent requires acceptance of non-egocentric reasons that require us to regard rational agents as ends.

Perhaps we might briefly capture the difference between Kant and eudaemonism by saying that they differ about how far we need a rational grasp of the appropriate non-moral ends if we are to grasp moral reasons. According to Aristotle, we need to see that we are rational agents who seek to realize our nature as a whole, both its rational and its non-rational side, in deliberation about our overall good; then we can see that we need the kind of friendship that treats another person as another self. Aquinas argues in the same way, by considering the aspects of human nature that make social life appropriate for us. Kant introduces impartial and non-egocentric reason at an earlier stage, through reflexion on what we are committed to if we value ourselves as rational agents. This reflexion does not require the extensive reflexion on human nature and reasonable goals that is needed for the Aristotelian argument.

Kant introduces moral reasons at a basic stage of practical reflexion by asking what is presupposed by our conception of ourselves as rational agents. This question is not alien to Aquinas; his claims about perfection and about intellectual love support Kant's conclusions about treating rational agents as ends. But Aquinas does not make these conclusions explicit and central in his moral argument as Kant does.[12] If Kant is right this far, he has an argument to show that we can reasonably accept moral principles without subordinating them to principles related to self-love.

This is not only the claim that moral deliberation does not explicitly rest on self-love; Aristotle and Aquinas agree with that claim, since they insulate deliberation about the *kalon* and the honestum from other considerations about happiness.[13] Kant has also argued for the stronger claim that in explaining why we have reason to engage in moral deliberation, we need only appeal to basic features of rational agency, rather than to relatively specific features of the human good.

This is equally an argument to support Kant's claim that the good is not prior to the right. If the moral point of view reflects basic features of rational agency, its status does not depend on a prior conception of the different components of the good. On the contrary, a correct conception of the components of the good depends on a grasp of the principles of morality.

972. Kant v. Eudaemonism: Holism and Justification

Kant's argument, however, does not show that eudaemonist reasoning has no legitimate place in the understanding and justification of morality. His defence of the priority of the right shows that we have good reason to take morality seriously, apart from our views about the composition of the good. But it does not tell us how seriously we ought to take

---

[12] Aquinas on perfection and intellectual love; §§336–7.   [13] Aristotle on the fine; §§106–7, 116–17. Aquinas; §334.

morality. Even if we agree that the moral law expresses a categorical imperative, we may still doubt Kant's further claim that the moral law is the supreme practical law. We may still ask why we should take moral considerations seriously in relation to other things that we have reason to take seriously. This is Butler's question about the supremacy of conscience; even if we agree that conscience is natural because it expresses a superior principle, we still need to know how it is related to other superior principles.[14]

Kant's argument for the priority of the right does not exclude a holist answer to this question. A holist answer is especially plausible if we agree with Butler and Reid in regarding prudence, no less than morality, as a genuine expression of practical reason. Their view makes it reasonable to ask how the two points of view are related. When we raise this question, a eudaemonist argument for according rational authority to the non-eudaemonist point of view of morality seems quite appropriate. For it explains how the moral point of view fits with other aspects of our rational agency.

Kant needs such an explanation. He could dispense with it only if he could plausibly maintain that all our non-moral aims and concerns are purely sensuous and empirical, and have no rational standing in relation to morality. But if he maintained this, he would undermine his views about the source of human dignity and self-respect. His account of how an individual regards himself as an end implies that I can regard myself as an end in relation to my non-rational desires, even without reference to morality. The feature of rational agents that makes them sources of dignity is their setting ends for themselves; they do this if they act on reasonable self-love. Kant has a reason, therefore, to agree that non-moral practical aims may express the outlook of practical reason, and hence may be a source of dignity.

Kant has a good reason, therefore, to recognize non-moral rational aims that support non-hypothetical imperatives. We may reasonably ask how much we ought to care about these aims in relation to morality. The fact that moral considerations present themselves without explicit reference to our other rational aims does not mean that practical reason need not ask about their relation to these other aims. Once we see that we face this question, we may see the point of the arguments that lead Aristotle and Aquinas to their formal criteria of the highest good; they argue that virtue fits these criteria because it fits appropriately with our other rational aims. Kant leaves unanswered a central question about the rational status of the moral point of view. We find an answer if we turn to eudaemonism.

Perhaps, however, a holist argument need not be eudaemonist. We might believe in a duality of practical reason, as Scotus and Butler do.[15] Reasons directed to one's own good are egocentric, but moral reasons are non-egocentric. If non-egocentric reasons are as basic as egocentric reasons, why should a rational reconciliation of them take the egocentric view? Should it not take a third point of view that stands outside the egocentric and the moral point of view?

The difficulty of finding a third point of view persuades Sidgwick that a duality of practical reason is a dualism—two superior principles, neither of which can be shown to be superior to the other.[16] For what third point of view could fix the relative importance of the egocentric and the moral point of view? If we cannot find it, must we not admit that we cannot settle the

---

[14] Butler on the natural character of conscience; §§705–8.
[15] Scotus and Butler on the duality of practical reason; §§368, 708.   [16] Sidgwick's dualism; §1201.

relative importance of moral and egocentric reasons? Kant avoids this question by denying that egocentric reasons can yield practical law. If we do not take this drastic approach to egocentric reasons, Scotus' and Butler's position seems to lead to unwelcome results. And so both eudaemonism and dualism seem to raise serious doubts.

But perhaps this conclusion is premature. We may not need a supreme principle above egocentric and moral reasons. To defend the moral point of view by appeal to happiness, we do not need to assert that the egocentric view is prior to morality. We simply need to say that it is a legitimate point of view from which we can consider the significance of the moral point of view. It is equally legitimate to consider the significance of the egocentric point of view within the moral point of view. If our appraisal of morality by reference to happiness and of happiness by reference to morality results in the endorsement of each point of view by the other, we have a good reason for affirming the legitimacy of each point of view, and a reason for regulating each point of view by reference to the other.

We need not agree, then, that if prudence and morality are both sources of practical laws, we can decide their relative importance only by finding a third point of view that is superior to both of them. Instead of looking for the elusive third point of view, we can consider their relative importance by examining each by appeal to the other. This procedure supports the eudaemonist approach that tries to fit morality into a reasonable account of the composition of the good.

One might argue, as Sidgwick does, that it is naively optimistic to suppose that this examination of morality from the point of view of happiness will vindicate morality. But to decide this question we need to understand happiness. Butler, Sidgwick, and Kant, for different reasons, incline to a hedonist and subjectivist account of the human good that makes it difficult to see how one can find a plausible place for the moral point of view as a primary element of the good; judged by this standard, Butler may appear too optimistic when he affirms the harmony of self-love and conscience. But this is not the Aristotelian eudaemonist account of happiness. The Aristotelian view offers a better prospect of a successful defence of morality by reference to the agent's good. We have seen that Butler's conception of happiness weakens his defence of the harmony of self-love and conscience. A similar conception of happiness turns Kant against eudaemonist and holist defences of morality.

Kant's over-simple conception of happiness betrays itself in his view of what eudaemonists can say about the connexion between morality and happiness. He recognizes only two options: (a) If they maintain that virtue achieves the highest good, they simply repeat the claim that morality is the supreme practical principle and they do not add any argument to it. (b) If they maintain that virtue achieves happiness, they subordinate morality to pleasure and inclination.

But these are not the only options. Neither of them captures Aristotelian arguments that try to connect virtue with happiness. These arguments rely on the formal criteria for happiness. Traditional naturalism claims that the virtues meet these criteria, because they realize human nature both in their own right and by co-ordinating and organizing non-moral goods. To argue that virtue is a component of happiness is not a trivial task, and so the conclusion that it meets these criteria is not a trivial conclusion. Such an argument to show that virtue is suitably related to the non-moral components of the human good requires some examination of the specific requirements of the different virtues of character.

If Kant had been more sympathetic to the Aristotelian appeal to the highest good, he might also have agreed that the Aristotelian arguments about virtue and happiness raise questions that he ought to answer. The eudaemonist arguments are relevant to morality as Kant understands it.

973. How Traditional Naturalism Might Support Kant

This conclusion on eudaemonism also suggests how Kant's position is related to naturalism. He treats naturalism as the position of Hobbes and Hutcheson. But this is not the only version of naturalism, and Kant's objections to Hobbes and Hutcheson do not affect the traditional naturalism accepted by Greek moralists, Aquinas, and Butler. These traditional naturalists, except Butler, are also eudaemonists. If, then, Kant has not shown that eudaemonist defences of morality are inappropriate, neither has he shown that naturalist defences are inappropriate.

If we agree with Butler, and accept naturalism without eudaemonism, we still rely on a form of argument that Kant rejects. Butler's defence of conscience relies on his defence of prudence as an aspect of rational agency; conscience is natural because it is a superior principle expressing the same nature that prudence also expresses. When we see that rational self-love expresses our rational agency, guiding us by considerations of authority rather than strength, we can see that conscience does the same sort of thing, by allowing us a systematic way of guiding our relations with others by authority rather than strength. Hume marks this connexion between prudence and conscience, by arguing, against Butler, that neither is rational.

Kant accepts a Humean conception of prudence, but his account of morality relies on Butler's marks of a superior principle. He explains, better than Butler does, how moral principles are superior, but he rejects any parallel argument for self-love. Kant's acceptance of one half of Butler without the other weakens his position.

If we accept the parallel argument, we strengthen the argument to show that morality expresses freedom. If morality expressed some kind of freedom that would not rationally concern us if we did not already care about morality, the connexion between freedom and morality would not support morality. The connexion provides a defence, however, if morality reveals the same thing that self-love also reveals. If Kant is right about morality, and Butler is right about self-love, Kant provides a stronger defence than Butler provides for the natural character of conscience.

These considerations show that Kant has a reason to accept Butler's naturalism. Do they also show that he has a reason to accept eudaemonism? Our answer depends on whether we agree with the argument to show that Butler's naturalism needs eudaemonist holism to vindicate the supremacy of conscience. Once we see how holist arguments support the supremacy of morality, we can see why both Butler and Kant have a good reason to rely on a eudaemonist defence of morality.

This argument to show that Kant is closer than he recognizes to traditional naturalism is relevant to later developments and later criticisms of Kantian ethics. Hegel criticizes Kantian morality for its radical dualism, expressed in the sharp division between the non-moral and the moral self; Bradley develops this objection to Kant.[17] In Hegel's view, any suggestion of a connexion between morality and happiness—in the conception of the highest good, for instance—is a sign of Kant's confusion, perhaps even of his dishonesty. Hegel infers that Kant should not try to derive morality from purely rational principles. We have some reason to question Hegel's argument if we take Kant's arguments to support Butler's position. In that case, Kant may be right to connect the moral point of view with rational non-moral principles.

A similar objection to Kant leads Schopenhauer in a direction quite opposite to Hegel's.[18] He also rejects any tendencies in Kant towards eudaemonism, and argues that a defence of Kant's position should emphasize the purely formal role of reason in morality, the absolute opposition between morality and self-interest, and the absolutely transcendent and non-empirical character of Kant's claims about freedom. If we favour a reconciliation of Kant with Butler and with naturalism more generally, we will not agree with Schopenhauer's selection of Kantian doctrines to accept and to discard.

Hegel's and Schopenhauer's criticisms all assume that Kant is mistaken to concede anything to eudaemonist or naturalist views. Against them, one might argue that Kant ought to accept eudaemonism and naturalism, precisely in order to maintain his central claims about morality. His objections to eudaemonism and naturalism rest on failure to distinguish the traditional naturalist position (as we have described it) from the naturalism of Hobbes and Hume and the specific version of naturalist perfectionism that he finds in Leibniz.[19] The appropriate relation between Kant and traditional naturalism is mutual support, not mutual antagonism.

974. Elements of the Highest Good

In examining Kant's objections to eudaemonism, we have suggested that Kant underestimates the case for holism about the relation of morality to other elements of the good. This suggestion needs to be reconsidered in the light of the positive role that he sees for an account of the highest good. Though he disagrees with the eudaemonist position, he agrees with it in taking the highest good to be important for morality. He therefore offers an account of the highest good. Some have criticized him for doing this, but we have seen reasons to reject such criticisms.[20] We should therefore look sympathetically on his attempt to make some room for appeals to the highest good.

A comparison between traditional eudaemonism and Kant's position on the highest good supports two conclusions: (1) Kant is sympathetic to some of the holist arguments of traditional eudaemonism, and so we ought not to take him to oppose such arguments altogether. His criticisms of eudaemonism suggest a simpler position than we find in his account of the good. (2) But his account suffers from some of the over-simplifications that we have found in his criticisms of eudaemonism. If he had given a more sympathetic account

---

[17] Hegel on Kantian dualism; §1022. Bradley; §1225.   [18] Schopenhauer on Kant; §1053.
[19] Leibniz's perfectionism; §§588–9. Kant's criticism; §937.
[20] Hegel's and Schopenhauer's objections; §§1024, 1053. Wood, *KMR*, chs. 2–3, defends Kant convincingly. See also Engstrom, 'Concept', and Silber, 'Importance'.

of traditional eudaemonist views on the relation of the moral virtues to the final good, he would be able to apply some of these views to his own position, and would therefore have made his position more plausible.

In 'The Dialectic of Pure Practical Reason' (*KpV*, Book ii), Kant argues that appeal to an ultimate good is legitimate. It does not provide an object to motivate the moral will, but it provides the moral will with an object to aim at. In order to make a particular moral decision, I need not, and should not, consider what good I will achieve by my moral action; if I insist on an answer to that question, I am not really moved by the moral law. Still, Kant argues, it is reasonable for me to ask what result I can expect from my observance of the law; a conception of the highest good answers this question (*Rel.* 4–6). Here, then, he endorses one aspect of the holism of traditional eudaemonism about the relation of morality to other goods.

In Kant's view, the highest good has two elements: (1) Virtue is the supreme good, or supreme condition of the highest good. It is supreme because it is indispensable for any highest good that a morally good person would rationally choose. It is not subject to bargaining, trading, or balancing, with any other elements of the good. (2) The 'residual' good (as we may call it) is added to the supreme good, resulting in the perfect or complete good (bonum consummatum), which Kant normally refers to when he speaks of the highest good (*KpV* 110).

His description of the complete good expresses an over-simplified conception of happiness and the ultimate good. Kant's hedonistic conception of happiness misleads him about the composition of the residual good. For he sometimes takes the appropriate question to be: 'How can virtue finally be attached to maximum pleasure?' As we have seen, the contribution of the virtues to non-moral goods is more complex than this. Both Kant and the eudaemonist need to say how the results of morality ought to be combined with the various non-moral goods that a rational agent appropriately seeks.

This question arises even if we accept Kant's view—shared with traditional eudaemonism—that morality is not simply a device for securing non-moral ends. Even if it is not subordinate to them, we may raise the holist question about the co-ordination of morality with other rational aims. Kant does not suggest that morality rejects the pursuit of non-moral goods. It is reasonable, therefore, to find some place for the pursuit of other goods within the life guided by morality. And so the highest good contains the residual good as well as the good achieved by morality alone. If there are other non-moral non-instrumental goods besides pleasure, the aim of morality will not simply be (as Kant thinks) to ensure that maximum pleasure and contentment are annexed to virtue, but also to find the proper place for non-moral goods in the life guided by morality.

A correct conception of the highest good should include the ends to be achieved by morality, plus the non-moral non-instrumental goods, in some systematic order. Kant insists that no such conception of the highest good is needed in order to move us to do what the moral law requires (*Rel.* 4); the end is not the ground, but the consequence, of the maxims adopted by the morally good person. Without the conception of the highest good, we can know how we should act, but not 'whither'; we can achieve no 'satisfaction', since the moral law arouses respect, but only a good inspires love. If we cannot fulfil our natural need to conceive a final end, our failure is a hindrance to our moral decisions (*Rel.* 5–6).

In the light of this claim about the good, we should either revise or re-interpret Kant's claim that the good will is moved by maxims that follow the moral law, not by any desire for an end (*MdS* 381–4). This claim is plausible if 'end' means in this context 'any end chosen antecedently to morality'. But it is implausible if it means that no end pursued by virtuous people produces a desire that affects their will. For it seems difficult for Kant to deny that such an end produces a motive. In his view, the moral law itself generates aims that give a further purpose to actions that are guided by respect for the law. These aims apparently both move the will of a virtuous person and ought to move it.

When Kant claims that the will is moved by the moral law alone, and not by a desire for an end, he seems to ignore ends that we pursue because we accept the moral law. He would be right to claim that the good will finds the moral law a sufficient motive for action; if it did not, the aims that result from acceptance from the moral law would not move it. But if it is moved by the moral law, it must also be moved by the ends whose achievement constitutes the highest good. This is a more plausible role to ascribe to the highest good than the role that Kant ascribes to it. It is also the role of the highest good in traditional eudaemonism.

We have good reason, therefore, to accept Kant's view that the highest good has a legitimate and necessary role in an account of morality. His position is open to doubt not because he introduces the highest good, but because he allows it such a limited role. His view reflects the questionable aspects of his criticisms of eudaemonism. A fair estimate of eudaemonism, and especially of its holist aspect, allows us both to maintain Kant's claims about the non-instrumental and basic status of morality and to allow holist argument about the relation between morality and non-moral elements of the good.

975. The Antinomy of Practical Reason

If we are persuaded that a Kantian theory of morality legitimately appeals to the highest good, we should also be able to appraise fairly Kant's argument from morality to the existence of God. This argument rests on the practical role of the highest good; for he claims that an adequate conception of the highest good, including the harmony of morality and happiness, must include the existence of God and the reality of an afterlife. He agrees with Aquinas in supposing that a complete conception of the total end that we aim at in morally virtuous action requires an idea of God, and of an afterlife in which the aims and hopes of the moral virtues are realized.

We cannot reasonably dismiss this argument on the ground that a conception of the highest good is irrelevant to morality. Nor can we reply that it does not matter whether our conception of the highest good is achievable. In both the Aristotelian and the Kantian conception, the highest good is an end to be aimed at; it guides actions directed towards its achievement. It is not simply an ideal that affects our imagination, but a goal that guides our action more directly. Kant claims that if we are justified in treating the highest good as a source of goals and aims, we must justifiably believe it can be achieved, and therefore we must be justified in believing that God exists.

This conclusion commits Kant to positive assertions about the existence of God that might surprise us in the light of the *First Critique*, where he rejects all 'theoretical' proofs of the existence of God. He believes his position is consistent, because the belief in God resting on the moral argument asserts the existence of God only from a practical point of view. He needs to explain, therefore, why the practical point of view supports a belief that lacks any theoretical proof. To understand his explanation, we need to understand what difference it makes that we assert a claim from a practical point of view. We have already found that Kant's defence of claims about freedom from a practical point of view raises some difficulties; in particular, it is difficult to accept his claim that practical assertions make no theoretical difference to our assertions about the world we know through experience. We need to see whether similar difficulties arise for his claims about the existence of God.

One question arises from the distinction in the *First Critique* between the constitutive and the regulative use of ideas. Though Kant rejects the Cosmological Argument for the existence of God, which argues from the observed effects in the world to the existence of a first cause (A603/B631–A614/B642), he does not reject all the assumptions that underlie the Cosmological Argument. He endorses the search for connected explanations of the sort that the Cosmological Argument offers. The conception of unity and connexion is an 'idea of reason'.[21] If we act as if everything had a single connected explanation that we are trying to find, we will not abandon the search for connected explanations, and so we will probably find more of them. But—in Kant's view—this attitude does not license us to suppose that there really is any total connected explanation, or any transcendent being who might provide this explanation.

One might, therefore express one of his objections to the Cosmological Argument, and to the arguments of rational theology in general, by saying that they mistake a regulative for a constitutive use of these ideas. Keeping this in mind, we may reasonably ask whether facts about morality justify a constitutive, rather than a purely regulative, use of the idea of God. At first sight, a purely regulative use seems to fit morality quite well. How could morality require belief in the existence of God, as opposed to the mere tendency or willingness to act as if God exists?

In the *Second Critique*, however, Kant argues that morality is committed to belief in God. To explain the nature of this commitment, and to distinguish it from a claim that would require theoretical proof, he presents an antinomy that is meant to correspond to the Antinomy of Pure Reason in the *First Critique* (KpV 113). It seems to us that the connexion between virtue and happiness is necessary (because morality demands it), but also impossible (given what we know about the world). We seem to contradict ourselves if we confine ourselves only to the course of the world we know; but if we introduce a non-sensible world, our claims are consistent. We resolve the antinomy by saying that virtue and happiness cannot be combined in this world, but can be combined in an afterlife.

Does the moral point of view force us into the apparent contradiction that needs to be resolved by an afterlife? Kant's argument is this:

1. The moral law requires us to pursue the highest good.
2. The realization of the highest good requires the union of virtue and happiness (i.e., requires that those who are virtuous, and therefore worthy of being happy, should be happy).

[21] On the ideas of reason see *KrV* A619/B647, and at length A642–68/B670–96.

3. The moral law would not be justified in prescribing this pursuit unless the highest good could be realized.
4. But the highest good cannot be realized in this life.
5. But the prescription of the moral law is justified.
6. Therefore the highest good can be realized in an afterlife.

Since this argument raises questions that are important not only for Kant's views about morality and theology, but for his views about the role of the highest good in morality, we should examine the premisses.

976. Why Must We Aim at the Highest Good?

Should we accept Kant's first premiss? We might use some of his own claims against him; perhaps the moral law requires only the fulfilment of the requirements of the categorical imperative for their own sake, and so does not require us to pursue the highest good. Kant agrees that virtuous agents do not make their observance of morality depend on the belief that it is beneficial for them. Still, they are justifiably concerned about whether the moral law achieves its goal of promoting the legitimate ends of rational agents. These ends include the happiness of others (an obligatory end for virtue) and one's own happiness (a legitimate end for everyone); hence we want to know whether morality will achieve the happiness that it aims at. If we are committed to morality, we do not need a conception of its end in order to stick to that commitment. But it is legitimate for us to form a conception of what we hope to achieve by morality, in order to see whether the various demands of morality constitute a reasonable goal for us.[22] This is the role of the highest good in offering a holist justification for the primacy of morality among our rational aims.

Kant insists that pursuit of the highest good does not conflict with his previous account of the moral motive, since fear or hope does not replace respect for the law as the virtuous person's motive. We are not entitled to reject the moral law, even if we cannot assure ourselves of the reality of God.[23] The highest good cannot be necessary for the justification of the moral law, because it neither constitutes nor replaces our fundamental reason for accepting the moral law. I still have a sufficient reason to follow the moral law even if I do not ask any further question about the final result of following the moral law.[24]

Nonetheless, the pursuit of the highest good is indispensable in the moral life.[25] Those who deny that the highest good can be realized must abandon the purpose that is characteristic

[22] 'So morality really has no need of an end for right conduct. On the contrary, the law that contains the formal condition of the use of freedom in general suffices to it. Yet an end proceeds from morality just the same; for it cannot possibly be a matter of indifference to reason how to answer the question, "What is then the result of this right conduct of ours?" nor to what we are to direct our doings or non-doings, even granted this is not fully in our control, at least as something with which they are to harmonize.' (Rel. 4–5)

[23] The mistaken view says: '. . . it is as necessary to assume the Being of God as to recognize the validity of the moral law, and consequently he who cannot convince himself of the first can judge himself free of the obligations of the second.' (KU 450–1)

[24] 'But although for its own sake morality needs no representation of an end which must precede the determining of the will, it is quite possible that it is necessarily related to such an end, taken not as the ground but as the [sum of] inevitable consequences of maxims adopted as conformable to that end.' (Rel. 4)

[25] 'The goal (Zweck), then, which this well-intentioned person had and ought to have before him in his conformity to the moral law, he must certainly give up as impossible. Or else, if he wishes to remain dependent on the call of his

of the virtuous person. Without this purpose, we cannot say how observance of morality fits our other reasonable aims; though we still recognize that it is reasonable in itself, we are less strongly committed to it than we would be if we saw how it fits our other reasonable aims. We have a further reason and motive for observing the moral law if we grasp its contribution to the highest good. Conversely, if we doubt whether we really promote the highest good by observing the moral law, we lose a reason and motive that we would we have if we had no such doubts.

Kant makes two claims: (1) We can observe the moral law for morally right reasons without having any conception of the highest good. (2) We are required to form purposes that include a conception of the highest good. Both claims are legitimate, in the light of Kant's views about morality and the highest good. In the first claim, he affirms that our conception of the right is not dependent on a prior and independent conception of the composition of the good. In the second claim, he affirms that morality ought to shape our conception of the good, without being its only component. Hence we ought to aim at a good that includes both moral and non-moral components.

If this is Kant's view, he is right to say that a conception of the highest good is needed, because questions about the relation between morality and other rational considerations are reasonable and legitimate questions. If we could find no reasonable answer to them, or if our answer were unfavourable to morality, would that conclusion not legitimately weaken our commitment to morality? Kant is right to say that we would not be justified in abandoning morality; for we would still (if the rest of his argument is right) have good reason to regard it as a necessary commitment of self-respecting rational agents. But if we could not co-ordinate it at all with our other rational aims, we would lose a reason for taking morality seriously that we would have if we could fit it into a conception of the highest good.

At this point, we ought to reconsider our conclusions about Kant's reactions to eudae-monism. We found that he is unsympathetic to the holist aspects of the eudaemonist view of morality. But his views on the highest good show that he is sometimes sympathetic to holist arguments about morality. We therefore ought to revise our previous judgment on Kant's attitude to eudaemonism, since on one important issue he is closer to eudaemonism than we might have gathered from his explicit criticisms of it. If Kant had recognized this feature of his position in his explicit criticisms of eudaemonism, he would have done more justice to the eudaemonist outlook.

977. Why Must We Be Able to Achieve the Highest Good?

Kant has a good case, therefore, for believing that if we take morality seriously, we must form a conception of the highest good that shows us the impact of morality on our other rational aims. But he assumes that we are justified in aiming at this end—at the union of

moral internal vocation and not to weaken the respect (Achtung) by which the moral law immediately inspires him to obedience, by assuming the nothingness of the single, ideal, final goal (Endzweck) adequate to its high demand (which cannot be brought about without damage to the moral disposition), he must assume the being of a moral author of the world, i.e., of God, from a practical point of view, i.e., in order to form a concept of at least the possibility of the final goal that is prescribed to him by morality—which he very well can do, since it is at least not self-contradictory.' (KU 452–3)

virtue and happiness—only if it can be fully realized. His assumption is open to question. Admittedly, the moral law would be wasting our time if we could do nothing to realize its prescriptions and aims. But this seems only to show that we need a reasonable prospect of some success in achieving its ends. Does it follow that the highest good must be realizable to a degree that is impossible in this life?

The difficulty in Kant's position becomes clear when we look at some of his claims about the connexion between the pursuit of morality and the pursuit of the highest good. He has a good reason to claim that in morality we make the highest good our object and aim, since we try to realize various parts or aspects of it. But he also supposes that we must believe the highest good to be possible.[26] Why must we believe this?

I can reasonably aim at an end that is not wholly in my power, provided that I believe some aspect of it is in my power. Each person engaged in some collective action may aim at some end that will be achieved only if they all do their part; it is not futile for individuals to take this as their aim, provided that each of them can do something towards it. This is what individuals do when they serve in a disciplined army, or play in a team, or take part in a political demonstration, or vote in an election. Similarly, we might agree that morality requires us to make the highest good the final object of our conduct, because this is our guiding aim. But we still might doubt whether we must be assured of success in that final object; we need only be assured that we can do something towards success.

To understand Kant's concern with success, we ought to recall the social aspect of his conception of moral effort and aspiration. This aspect is present and indispensable, though not always prominent, in his main ethical works. In the *Groundwork*, one formulation of the categorical imperative involves a 'kingdom' or 'realm' of ends (G 433–4). This is a social system in which rational beings systematically treat one another as ends and live according to principles that involve this attitude. This system has two roles: (1) The actual conduct required by morality is—in certain respects—the conduct that would be generally accepted if such an ideal community came into existence. (2) The aim of morality in the conduct it requires is to make this ideal community actual.

These two roles may conflict, as they sometimes do in revolutionary movements that engage in war and repression for the sake of a future social order that will abolish war and repression. Kant rejects such strategies, if they involve the use of particular people simply as means to secure the ideal in which people will all be treated as ends.

To see that Kant conceives of morality as involving this sort of aspiration and striving towards an ideal community, we may turn to 'Theory and Practice' and 'Perpetual Peace'. Perpetual peace is the end that morality aims at as its ideal. Kant expresses similar aspirations in an essay closely related to 'Perpetual Peace', the 'Idea for a universal history from a cosmopolitan point of view'. The idea of such a universal history treats human history as progress—though not uniform progress—towards the kingdom of ends in which people,

---

[26] 'Nevertheless, in the practical task of pure reason, i.e., in the necessary endeavour after the highest good, such a connexion is postulated as necessary: we *should* seek to further the highest good (which therefore must be at least possible).' (*KpV* 124–5) 'But here again everything remains disinterested and based only on duty, without being based on fear or hope as incentives, which, if they became principles, would destroy the entire moral worth of the actions. The moral law commands us to make the highest possible good in a world the final object of all our conduct. This I cannot hope to effect except through the agreement of my will with that of a holy and beneficent author of the world.' (129–30)

both within a society and in the relations of one society to another, treat each other with the respect they deserve as ends.

The social and historical aspects of morality and its aspirations may seem to conflict with Kant's insistence that we must be able to achieve the highest good. His idea of a universal history is not an unbiased account of the actual course of history, but a point of view on history that may help us to realize the aims of morality. Similarly, we might form an idea of the kingdom of God on earth not as an actual or probable social order but as an ideal and inspiration for moral practice. Might we not think of the realization of the highest good in this way, as a utopian ideal that we do not expect to be realized? This attitude to it seems quite close to the regulative use of an idea. If that is our only use of the idea of the highest good, we do not commit ourselves to the beliefs that create the antinomy of practical reason.

Kant might reasonably reject this 'utopian' interpretation of the highest good. A utopian ideal that we pursue without regard to its practicability may mislead us no less than it inspires us. If the utopian conditions that prescribe a particular course of action are too different from the actual or probable historical conditions, our doing what would be required in a utopia may be morally disastrous in actual conditions. The application of utopian ideals to actual circumstances requires some further views about how we can approach the utopian circumstances, and how we can adapt the utopian ideals to probable historical conditions. We therefore need to combine our ideals with some views about probable historical conditions. If we are really required to try to realize the highest good, we cannot treat it simply as a utopian ideal that might (if we are lucky) inspire us or (if we are unlucky) mislead us.

For this reason, Kant denies that his idea of a universal history is simply a myth or romance.[27] It would be simply a romance if it rested on no reasonable belief in the direction of history. But if we can see a possible direction in history, we can recognize it as an expression of God's wisdom.[28]

978. Morality, History, and God

It may seem unwise to appeal to Kant's claims about history in order to justify his claims about God and immortality. For if we find that our moralized idea of history corresponds to the actual direction of history, have we not found a purely natural basis for supposing that the aims of morality are achievable, without recourse to an afterlife? One might suppose that pessimism about history is needed for belief in an afterlife, and that optimism undermines the belief. Similarly, if we find historical grounds for our idea of history, do we not also make any idea of a providential God superfluous?

---

[27] 'It is strange and apparently silly to wish to write a history in accordance with an Idea of how the course of the world must be if it is to lead to certain rational ends. It seems that with such an Idea only a romance could be written. Nevertheless, if one may assume that Nature, even in the play of human freedom, works not without plan or purpose, this Idea could still be of use.' (*IUH* 29)

[28] 'Such a justification of nature—or better, of Providence—is no unimportant reason for choosing a standpoint toward world history. For what is the good of esteeming the majesty and wisdom of Creation in the realm of brute nature and of recommending that we contemplate it, if that part of the great stage of supreme wisdom which contains the purpose of all the others—the history of mankind—must remain an unceasing reproach to it? If we are forced to turn our eyes from it in disgust, doubting that we can ever find a perfectly rational purpose in it, and hoping for that only in another world?' (*IUH* 30)

This attempt to separate Kant's views about history from his claims about God is too simple. The point of view from which one forms the idea of a universal history with a particular direction and goal is not the point of view of empirical historians; Kant does not seek to compete with them.[29] It is a point of view based on morality. From this point of view, we can form a conception of the natural end of natural capacities, and of how natural capacities can be directed to the use of reason (*IUH* 18–19). Moral theory tells us how human beings should be related to one another in a 'perfect civic constitution' (24). But historical experience, trial, and error are needed to devise institutions and mechanisms that embody such a constitution. Morality, therefore, forms in us the expectations that guide us in looking for tendencies and directions in history.

These expectations are closely related to those that guide us in believing in God and immortality. In both cases, we are looking for some reason to believe that the conception of the good that we form on the basis of morality is achievable. But why, we might wonder, should our expectations be directed to history as well as to the afterlife? Would it not be enough to believe in a morally satisfactory afterlife and to regard history as a tale told by an idiot?

Kant answers this question by asserting that if human history is part of the story of creation, and if the creation is the work of a supremely good creator, it should not be a complete chaos. If we had to treat it as a complete chaos, we would face an objection to our belief in God as supremely good creator. We would have to think of many of the tasks and aims required by morality as merely devices to test our moral wills, similar to athletic contests designed to test strength and ability; just as someone's running a four-minute mile has no further value beyond the proof of someone's athletic ability, so also working to achieve a better future would have no value beyond the proof of someone's good will.

This is not how Kant conceives the good person's attitude to the aims of morality. Since morality requires us to adopt certain ends, it requires us to attribute value to the achievement of these ends. If some of these ends are to be achieved in history, but history is chaotic, we would be adopting ends that it is pointless to adopt. If, then, morality gives us reason to suppose that it is not pointless to adopt certain ends, it justifies us in taking a providential view of history as well.

This providential view of history would be naive and useless if it were simply optimistic. Kant recognizes that a realistic view of history does not make the moralistic interpretation seem obviously correct; that is why it has to rest on a moral rather than an empirical point of view. Human progress towards a perfect civic constitution depends on combinations of motives and forces that also tend to retard and to reverse this progress. Competitiveness and unsociability lead to the development of rational capacities; their development in turn leads to the development of a moral outlook to which the competitive outlook is antagonistic.[30] The outlook of humanity is both a necessary preliminary to the outlook of personality and a threat to it.[31] If we did not accept the moral law and we did not believe that its aims are

---

[29] 'That I would want to displace the work of practising empirical historians with this Idea of world history, which is to some extent based upon an a priori principle, would be a misinterpretation of my intention.' (*IUH* 30)

[30] 'The means employed by Nature to bring about the development of all the capacities of men is their antagonism in society, so far as this is, in the end, the cause of a lawful order among men.' (*IUH* 20)

[31] See *Rel.* 26–7, and discussion in §§924, 958. Marx on history: §1042.

achievable, we would not see the signs of progress towards their achievement in history, since the means to their achievement also tend to impede them.

These questions about realizing the highest good bring us back to Kant's questions about belief in God. Such questions would not arise if the aims and aspirations we acquire through morality were easy to fulfil. If, for instance, we already lived in a kingdom of ends, only two centuries after Kant formed the idea, his moral argument for the existence of God would not be very powerful. A well-informed empirical survey of the course of history would vindicate belief in the achievability of the end required by morality; this belief would rest on an easy inference (we might grant) from the plain evidence of history. For instance, even if we do not believe in historical laws, we might think it reasonable to rely on the general rule that a sudden economic decline tends to produce social unrest. If the belief in the achievability of the moral ideal rested on general rules and assumptions that are as immediately plausible as this one, we would not be tempted to accept the premises of Kant's antinomy.

It is not so easy to avoid the antinomy. One might argue that, from our empirical knowledge of human history, the achievement of a kingdom of ends seems an uphill process, and at times even a Sisyphean process. One might well ask whether it is reasonable to have these aspirations towards the realization of the kingdom of ends. If the achieving of the highest good has to be empirically plausible in order to be a reasonable ideal, it seems to fail that test. Perhaps, then, we should avoid Kant's antinomy by denying that the highest good must be achievable. Should we reject this aspiration as a misleading form of utopian ideal, and simply do what morality requires of us without being moved by hopes of achieving a better world?

Kant certainly recognizes this possibility, which we might call 'despairing morality'. On the one hand—as the sorts of beings we are—we are required to treat persons as ends. But on the other hand, the aspirations that inevitably result from this attitude must be abandoned as hopelessly optimistic, according to despairing morality. Kant suggests that if we have reason to believe in a God who will eventually bring about the kingdom of God that is also the kingdom of ends, we need not settle for despairing morality. We can instead have morality with reasonable hope and expectation.

The role that Kant sees for belief in the achievability of the kingdom of God illustrates the principle that 'Faith is the substance of things hoped for'.[32] Belief that goes beyond the limits of what would otherwise seem empirically plausible gives substance to hopes, because it transforms hopes that would otherwise be mere wishful optimism into potentially reasonable expectations. They are potentially reasonable because they rest on a view of the universe and history that makes such expectations reasonable, if it is itself reasonable.[33]

If Kant conceives the role of the highest good in this way, he is right to distinguish it from a utopian ideal. If he is to show that despairing morality is not the most we can expect, he needs to show that the beliefs that transform wishful thinking into reasonable expectation are reasonable. If these beliefs include belief in God, they introduce questions about the

---

[32] *Heb.* 11:1. 'Substance' is the AV's rendering of *hupostasis* (Vulg. 'substantia'). Other versions, including NRSV, follow Luther in preferring 'assurance', but *TDNT* viii 586, argues effectively in favour of 'substance'.

[33] This might be part of a reply to the objection that Kant's belief in God is based on wishful thinking. This objection was known to Kant from Wizenmann's criticism in 'Kant', 122–30, discussed by Beiser, *FR* 120–1.

existence of God. Faith gives substance to hopes not by imagining a God, but by believing that God exists.[34]

979. The Highest Good and the Existence of God

If belief in the realization of the highest good has this role in morality, have we a good reason to believe in God, on that account? Does the fact that the existence of God would make the final purpose of morality realizable give us a reason to believe in God?

The considerations that Kant mentions are relevant to belief in God. If he is right, the aspirations arising from our essential nature as rational beings lead us to a belief in a God who will eventually realize the highest good. If we trust these aspirations, we will believe in such a God. But should we trust them?

We would have a clear reason for trusting them if we had a general reason for believing that our deep-seated aspirations cannot be ultimately pointless or frustrated; in that case, the fact that we have these moral aspirations would be a reason for believing that they will ultimately be successful. But if we have this general reason for believing that these aspirations are not pointless, we would have a general reason for believing that in this respect the world is rationally and teleologically ordered to reasonable goals. This would be a reason, not resting solely on morality, for belief in God.

This reflexion on morality leads us back to the physico-theological argument that Kant discusses in the *First Critique*, arguing from the order of the world to the existence of a creator (A620/B648–A630/B658). Moral aspiration rests on something more than wishful thinking, if we have some reason, apart from morality, for believing that the universe is not entirely purposeless. But such a reason would have to come from the sorts of considerations that go into the physico-theological argument.[35]

If moral aspiration without belief in God would lead to despair, someone who takes morality seriously, and understands it as Kant does, has a good reason to try to find out whether there is any good reason for believing in the right sort of God. A good reason for believing in such a God ought to be welcome to someone who cares about morality.

Kant, therefore, has good reason to claim that some aspects of morality are connected with questions about the existence of God, and that such questions appropriately arise from thinking about morality. But these claims fall short of a cogent argument from moral premises to the existence of God. His claim that morality by itself provides an argument for the existence of God is controversial. Why should we not regard a belief in God on the basis of morality as wishful thinking with no claim to truth?

980. Practical Faith

Kant agrees that belief in the existence of God would be wishful thinking if it were simply based on inclination—on wanting to believe that something we would like to be true is

---

[34] Kant's views on the highest good and on moral faith are carefully discussed by Hare, *MG*, ch. 2–3.
[35] At *KrV* A633/B660 Kant tries to separate 'physico-theology' from 'moral theology', which is 'a conviction of the existence of a supreme being—a conviction which bases itself on moral laws'.

indeed true. Even if we could induce belief in ourselves as a result of this inclination, such a belief would have no reasonable claim to truth. But he denies that this is our position with the moral law and the highest good.[36] Since we have reason to believe that the basic principles of morality are true, and that they require belief that the highest good can be realized, we have good reason to believe that the highest good is realizable.

Kant's account of this need of reason makes it clear that he takes the demands of morality to give a reason for belief in the existence of God, not simply for acting as if God existed. Similarly, he takes them to give a sufficient reason for belief in the reality of freedom, not simply for acting as if we were free. In defending 'the right of pure reason to an extension in its practical use which is not possible to it in its speculative use' (KpV 51), Kant maintains that the practical use of pure reason gives us sufficient grounds for restricted claims about objective reality.

Kant must reject the 'as if' interpretation of these practically based beliefs; for he supposes that our beliefs in God, freedom, and immortality would be open to serious doubt if they clearly conflicted with our theoretical beliefs. If we were not making claims about objective reality, we would not make claims that might appear to conflict with our theoretical knowledge; for there is no apparent conflict between acting as if p were true and knowing that p is false, whereas Kant supposes that our morally based beliefs about God might appear to conflict with our other beliefs about the objective world. This question would not arise for Kant if he did not take claims about God and freedom to be claims about objective reality, and therefore to be capable of conflicting with our theoretical knowledge of objective reality.

Kant argues that morally based belief in God and immortality does not conflict with our theoretical knowledge; for though our theoretical knowledge does not support this belief in God, it does not refute it either. If our morally based belief in God and freedom were intended to contribute to our theoretical knowledge, it would have to conform to the principles that underlie our theoretical knowledge, and hence it would have to conform to the a priori principles that underlie our knowledge of the phenomenal world—with the principle of universal causation, for instance. But its failure to conform to these principles does not matter, if it is not meant to advance our theoretical knowledge. We would misunderstand these a priori principles if we did not recognize that they are justified only with reference to the phenomenal world that we know through the senses.

In contrast to our theoretical knowledge, our morally based beliefs in God and freedom are purely 'practical' beliefs. By this Kant does not mean that they are beliefs about our practice rather than about the world; for the reasons we have seen, he takes them to affirm truths about a reality external to our beliefs and practice. They are purely practical in so far as they arise from practical reason and their function is to guide moral practice. They are not intended to suggest hypotheses or principles that will advance our understanding of the phenomenal world.[37] Hence they are not rivals to our theoretical knowledge.

---

[36] 'Here we have to do, however, with a need of reason arising from an objective determining ground of the will, i.e., the moral law, which is necessarily binding on every rational being, and, therefore justifies him a priori in presupposing suitable conditions in nature and makes them inseparable from the complete practical use of reason.' (KpV 144)

[37] 'This objective reality, however, is of only practical application, since it has not the slightest effect in enlarging theoretical knowledge of these objects as insight into their nature by pure reason. As we shall find in the sequel, these

We have already noticed some difficulties in claiming that moral beliefs do not extend our empirical knowledge at all. If we believe someone is an autonomous agent moved by the free and rational will, we have reason to predict that she will act differently in the phenomenal world from how a different sort of person would act in the same circumstances. Similarly, if we believe in a God who unites virtue with happiness, it is difficult to see how we could fail to believe that God is benevolent and omnipotent. Such a God might reasonably be expected to act in such a way that the phenomenal world is different from how it would otherwise be.

If moral beliefs have empirical implications, including implications for our causal beliefs, they must be capable of interacting with our theoretical beliefs to reach conclusions that are not clearly excluded by our other theoretical beliefs. If our empirical psychology implied that beliefs and desires have no causal and explanatory role in actions, then either we would have to abandon our practical beliefs about morality, or else we would have to revise our empirical psychology. Our practical and theoretical beliefs could not reasonably co-exist. Similarly, if we believed that the actual world has properties incompatible with its being the work of a benevolent creator, we could not retain this belief together with a practical belief in God. The fact that one belief is practical and one theoretical does not remove the possibility of conflict. Kant over-simplifies the issues, therefore, if he believes that he avoids any possibility of such conflicts by introducing practical belief and separating it from theoretical knowledge.

This point, however, does not undermine Kant's claim that our belief in God and freedom is not to be regarded as part of our total theory of empirical reality; it is not open to objection, for instance, simply because it fails to combine fruitfully with our other theories of the empirical world. Though it is reasonable to expect practical beliefs to be consistent with theoretical knowledge, this expectation is much weaker than the requirement that we impose in demanding system or unification in our theories of the empirical world.[38]

We ought not, therefore, to reject the theological consequences of morality simply because they include beliefs about causation that are unwarranted by the rest of our view of the world; for practical beliefs are not to be evaluated by the standards that apply to our empirical knowledge. We would be right to object to a theory in chemistry if it assumed that matter is composed in ways that have no basis in anything discoverable by physics; and we would be right to object to applied economics if it assumed that people think and choose in ways that are entirely unsupported by anything we can discover in empirical psychology. According to Kant, we ought not to object to a similar degree of discontinuity between our moral beliefs and our theoretical beliefs.

In claiming that we are entitled to isolate—in the specific sense just described—our moral beliefs and their consequences from our empirical theories, Kant makes it clear how much weight he rests on these moral beliefs. He does not assume, as Hume does, that if

---

categories have reference only to beings as intelligences, and in them only to the relation of the reason to the will, and consequently only to the practical; further than that they pretend to no knowledge of them.' (*KpV* 56–7)

[38] On unity in theoretical reason see *KrV* A645/B673: 'If we survey the cognitions of our understanding in their entire range, then we find that what reason quite uniquely prescribes and seeks to bring about concerning it is the systematic in cognition, i.e., the interconnexion based on one principle. . . . this idea postulates complete unity of the understanding's cognition, through which this cognition comes to be . . . a system interconnected in accordance with necessary laws.'

they are not explicable within the psychology and metaphysics that has been established independently of moral beliefs, they must be illusory. He claims for them, as the intuitionists do, some independent weight in arguing for claims about the nature of reality. He differs from the intuitionists in denying that our moral beliefs give us knowledge of truths that provide fundamental principles for our theoretical knowledge of empirical reality. But his limitation of these beliefs to practical purposes does not remove the strong metaphysical claim that Hume rejects. This part of Kant's moral philosophy shows how seriously he takes his claim to have marked the limits of theoretical knowledge in order to make room for practical belief.[39]

[39] See *KrV* B xxix–xxx: 'Thus I cannot even assume God, freedom, and immortality for the sake of the necessary practical use of my reason unless I simultaneously deprive speculative reason of its pretensions to extravagant insights . . . Thus I had to deny knowledge, in order to make room for belief (Glaube).' Chignell, 'Belief', explores Kant's views on Glaube.

KANT: META-ETHICAL
QUESTIONS

981. Some Meta-Ethical Implications of Kant's Normative
Theory

After examining the connexions between Kant's moral philosophy and his metaphysics, in discussing his views on freedom and God, we may turn to his metaphysics of morals in a narrower sense; does he take moral principles to correspond to facts about reality independent of the moral beliefs of rational agents? We have already given some reasons, explicitly or implicitly, for attributing this realist view to Kant, but we need to examine these reasons more closely.

The questions that arise here renew a theme that we have pursued through the chapters on Kant, about the relations between his views and traditional eudaemonism and naturalism. We have noticed some important differences, especially on the relation of the moral law to the good. But we have also noticed that some differences are less clear than they may appear to be at first sight. Though Kant rejects naturalism and eudaemonism, his reasons depend partly on his questionable account of these views.

Contrary to Kant, Aristotelian eudaemonism does not reduce moral principles to hypothetical imperatives; nor does the naturalist position set out by Aquinas and Butler derive morality from empirical features of human beings. Kant's objections to attempts to found moral theory on facts about human nature do not affect traditional naturalism. Aquinas derives an account of morality from human nature, but he does not rely on empirical facts about human beings; he appeals to facts about the nature of rational agents as such. When Butler argues from facts about human nature to moral conclusions, he does not try to derive normative conclusions from entirely non-normative facts about human nature; he accepts normative naturalism. Kant, therefore, seems to accept traditional naturalism on the very points on which he claims to reject it; for he also seems to rely on facts about the nature of rational agents as such.

Butler's meta-ethical position is a form of traditional naturalism because it includes Suarez's central claim that the morally right is what is suitable (conveniens) to rational nature. Suarez correctly attributes this position to Aquinas.[1] In accepting this form of naturalism, Butler affirms the objectivity of moral properties and moral truths. The relevant facts about human nature are not primarily facts about our beliefs, or our reactions of approval or disapproval. Actions are not right or wrong, according to Butler, because they are approved or disapproved by conscience. On the contrary, we are right to attend to our conscience because it is a superior principle that recognizes natural action.

If we have correctly described Kant's position, we may reasonably expect that he will agree with traditional naturalism (though not with his conception of it). He regards moral facts as facts about autonomous wills in rational agents, and about what is appropriate for these wills. If this is his view, he accepts normative naturalism and objectivism.

We reach the same conclusion if we consider Kant's disagreements with intuitionist versions of objectivism. Clarke and Price claim that moral truths correspond to eternal fitnesses that depend only on the nature of various actions (benefit, gratitude, injustice, punishment) in abstraction from any facts about the nature of the agents involved. The relevant fitnesses have to be known non-inferentially because no further fact is the basis for moral fitness and rightness. Kant does not rest his claims about morality on claims about fitness known by intuition, because he denies that an appeal to intuition can show that moral principles are categorical imperatives. To answer this further question, we need to appeal to the relation between moral principles and rational agency. Since this is the aspect of human nature that concerns traditional naturalism, Kant accepts a naturalist conception of moral properties.

He therefore holds a realist account of moral properties together with a holist account of moral knowledge and justification. The relevant facts are facts about rational agency as such; we know them by relating our moral beliefs to our beliefs about rational agency. If we believe that holism about justification is incompatible with realism, we may be unwilling to attribute both holism and realism to Kant. But it is not clear that Kant sees any conflict between holist epistemology and realist metaphysics.

Some critics, however, deny that Kant is a moral realist, and therefore deny that he agrees in substance with traditional naturalism on this point. In their view, Kant is right to assert that he differs from traditional naturalism; his assertions do not result simply from his misinterpretation of the naturalist position. Even if our account of the naturalist position is right, it still differs (according to these critics) from Kant's position on the metaphysics of moral properties, because Kant rejects naturalist realism. Is this a plausible view of Kant?

982. Naturalism v. Transcendental Idealism

The first argument against an objectivist interpretation of Kant appeals to transcendental idealism. The claim that Kant agrees with traditional naturalism may well appear too simple, because it overlooks distinctive elements in Kant's metaphysical position. In his view, moral truths cannot be truths about nature. The knowledge of nature is empirical knowledge,

---

[1] Suarez and Aquinas; §439.

derived from the senses, subject to the schematized categories. It is subject to deterministic laws, and therefore does not acknowledge freedom.

Kant rejects the views of Aristotle and Aquinas about the relation of ethics to natural science and to metaphysics. They believe that a single account of nature and causation underlies claims about inanimate and animate nature, and that the account of the soul that suits psychology fits ethics as well. But in Kant's view, knowledge of nature must be separated from any claims about God and human freedom.[2]

In moral theory, Kant's conviction about the separateness of moral knowledge rests especially on his belief in determinism for phenomenal nature and in indeterminism for free human action. We have seen, however, that it does not rest entirely on this belief. His views about the aims of practical beliefs also give him reasons for believing that they should not be treated as part of our theoretical knowledge of the phenomenal world.

We may sum up our earlier discussion of Kant's separation of moral knowledge from knowledge of nature in this way: (1) In so far as his views rest on his beliefs about determinism and indeterminism, they are open to question. Both his reasons for accepting phenomenal determinism and his reasons for insisting on indeterminism in free action are inadequate. He is not justified, on these grounds, in claiming that moral truths are about noumena. (2) In so far as they rest on beliefs about the difference between practical and theoretical knowledge, Kant's claims about moral truth and noumena are defensible. But this defence of his position does not justify his indeterminism.[3]

We might, however, doubt whether our earlier discussion gave the best account of transcendental idealism. Whatever we say about the theoretical functions of this doctrine, we might argue that its role in moral philosophy is to emancipate the practical point of view from claims about the objective world. Perhaps Kant does not intend his claims about morality to describe objective facts about a reality independent of the beliefs of moral agents. One might emphasize Kant's claim that moral beliefs are practical, and one might infer that they express a point of view we take for practical purposes, not a source of true beliefs about any independent reality. Kant gives some support to this way of understanding the place of moral beliefs within his transcendental idealism. In the *Groundwork*, he maintains that 'every being which cannot act in any way other than under the idea of freedom is for this very reason free from a practical point of view' (G 448). Perhaps moral theory tells us the ideas under which we must act, without giving us reason to believe in any moral reality that is not constituted by our moral beliefs.

We may defend this interpretation of transcendental idealism as an account of what Kant really means, or is trying to say, rather than an account of what he says. Perhaps Kant's actual statement of his doctrine is his misleading way of recognizing that moral principles, and the associated claims about God and freedom, are not objective truths. According to this reconstruction of Kant, phenomenal reality is the whole of objective reality, and his attempt to connect moral truths to noumenal reality is an imperfect recognition of the conclusion he ought to draw—that nothing in the objective world corresponds to moral truths. We will be more convinced that this is the right way to reconstruct Kant's position if we believe

---

[2] Hence Hegel speaks of the 'indifference' of nature from the point of view of Kantian morality. See PS §600, quoted in §1020.

[3] Practical knowledge and transcendental idealism; §951.

that his conception of noumena is incoherent, or does not leave room for his views about morality.

We might, then, take Kant's transcendental idealism to support an anti-realist conception of moral facts. Hume supposes that our moral beliefs tell us about our sentiments. Kant (we might say) supposes that they tell us about our practical point of view and not about our sentiments, but agrees with Hume in denying that they tell us about any external facts.[4]

This reconstruction of Kant rests on two assumptions: (1) He is right to claim that the phenomenal world described by empirical science leaves no room for moral truths. (2) His attempt to describe a noumenal reality that moral truths are about is hopelessly flawed. Each assumption is doubtful. Kant's claim that the practical point of view describes a noumenal reality is not all unreasonable. He does not take noumenal reality to introduce a new set of objects or events that have no place in the phenomenal world; he takes noumenal properties to belong to objects and events that are also phenomenal. The noumenal properties are those that we have reason to ascribe to objects, but not because they extend the theoretical knowledge we gain from natural science. If this is a reasonable defence of some aspects of transcendental idealism, it casts doubt on an anti-realist reconstruction of Kant's position.

Moreover, it is difficult to see how Kant could have thought that transcendental idealism explains the character of moral truths if he did not suppose that they are truths about some objective reality. He distinguishes phenomena from noumena because (among other things) he wants to make room for belief by restricting knowledge (*KrV* B xxx). If our moral beliefs did not claim to be about objective reality, and if Kant did not accept this claim, he would have no reason to introduce objective noumenal properties. If moral claims made no claim to objectivity, they would need nothing more than the phenomenal properties that are grasped by the natural sciences; for no further objective properties would be needed to make them true. Kant does not suggest that the conception of the world that is required by empirical science excludes the possibility of objective truths that do not fit into the principles underlying empirical science. On the contrary, the objective truth of moral claims requires objective properties; Kant identifies the appropriate properties by distinguishing phenomena from noumena.

983. Knowledge and Passivity

A different sort of reason for attributing anti-realism to Kant in his practical philosophy emerges from consideration of the preconditions for realism in his theoretical philosophy. We know about an objective world in so far as we are passive in relation to it. We are passive in so far as our knowledge depends on our 'receptivity', on sensory intuition. The role of intuition explains why we do not construct the natural world that we know through empirical science; our construction (it may be said) is confined to the principles through

---

[4] Korsgaard, *SN* 29, contrasts the Kantian constructivist view, treating autonomy as the source of normativity, with realism. O'Neill, *CR* 60–1 gives a non-realist account of transcendental idealism in *G*, ch. 3. Hill, *DPR* 83–4, also rejects a realist interpretation. Korsgaard, 'Freedom', 185, argues that difficulties about freedom and transcendental idealism arise from a misunderstanding of Kant's division between the theoretical and the practical point of view.

which we organize the material provided by sense. But (we might argue) when we are not constrained by the sensory material, we are not passive in relation to any objective reality, and so we have no knowledge of any objective state of affairs.

This is not Kant's conclusion, however, since he recognizes objective facts about things in themselves. Does his view betray the incoherence of his claims about things in themselves? If it does not, we need to reconsider his claims about knowledge, objectivity, and passivity.

A certain kind of passivity is necessary for objectivity. Since objective facts are as they are apart from anyone's acts of believing or imagining, our being aware of them involves some passivity; we recognize them and discover them, but we do not bring them into existence. This form of passivity, however, is not the same as our receptivity to sensory data. Sensory receptivity is the means of meeting the demand for passivity in the case of our knowledge of an objective physical world. Since we are passive through sensory receptivity, we are capable of passive awareness of objective facts, so that we do not construct the sensible world. Kant takes sensory receptivity seriously enough to claim that the limits of sensory receptivity are also the limits of our scientific knowledge. We are not purely passive, however, in relation to sensory data. Kant also believes that the understanding is the 'lawgiver' of nature, because we must grasp, and present to ourselves, the laws that allow us to understand the sensory data as data about an objective world.[5]

The passivity required by recognition of objective facts is not the same as receptivity to sensory data. Nor does Kant identify the two. He claims that receptivity is necessary for scientific knowledge; hence he claims to limit knowledge in order to make room for belief about things in themselves. This belief is not creation, construction, or imagination; it recognizes facts independent of us, and in that respect it is passive, even though our recognition of these facts cannot be the basis of a body of scientific knowledge, and cannot support the extension of our scientific knowledge.

This account of Kant's position may appear to overlook a major objection. We might suppose that passivity is required for knowledge of objective facts because we accept a causal conception of knowledge; we believe that we know some independent fact or property because the fact or property enters a causal relation with us. But according to Kant, casual relations hold between phenomenal events in time. If, therefore, noumenal events are outside laws that relate phenomenal events, must they not also be unknowable?

Two points may help to answer this objection: (1) Kant does not take all causation to be phenomenal; he believes that noumena can stand in the relation of ground and consequent without temporal priority and succession. Hence relations between noumena and cognitive subjects include the passive element that is necessary for the causal aspect of knowledge. (2) Though noumena are not related to us by phenomenal causal laws, they are not noumenal events outside the phenomenal causal framework. On the contrary, we have seen that noumenal properties belong to things that also have phenomenal properties with which we have phenomenal causal interaction. Even if we take phenomenal causation to be necessary for the passivity that belongs to knowledge, we may hold that noumena satisfy

---

[5] We need not assume in this case, any more than in the practical case, that the understanding is the author (auctor, Urheber) of the law of nature. See §987.

this necessary condition. The sort of relation that Kant has in mind is relatively familiar. We causally interact with a painting because it is coloured, but its properties qua coloured are not the only ones we know about or appreciate; we might also recognize it as one of Turner's most daring late works. To recognize this about it, we do not need to be causally affected by its audacity or its lateness; we recognize these properties as a result of interaction with its colours and shapes, which our 'lawgiving' understanding recognizes as signs of audacity and lateness.

If this is the right way to understand knowledge and passivity, we cannot reasonably appeal to Kant's theoretical philosophy and general metaphysics to support an anti-realist interpretation of his moral philosophy. He does not intend practical philosophy to exclude the passivity of recognition, or to substitute the activity of invention or construction.

984. Conditions for Autonomy: Law and Nature

A further argument for denying that Kant holds an objectivist view of moral facts requires us to return to his account of autonomy, and specifically to his claim that the autonomous will 'gives itself the law' or that the will acts on its 'own' law, rather than on some law that is 'external' to it. Our interpretation of his position turns on our understanding of 'own' and 'external' in such claims.

One understanding conflicts with objectivism; it claims that the will's own law must be a law that it creates, but does not discover in some prior fact. This conception of self-legislation and nature may appear to mark a crucial point of disagreement between Kant and naturalist views about being a 'law to oneself'. Aquinas recognizes that a free human will is not moved exclusively by external forces, or by passions that it cannot control; free agents move themselves through their conception of the good and through the principles formed by deliberation about the good. They therefore act on a law within them rather than outside them. If this is all it takes to be autonomous, Kant has no good reason for denying that Aristotelian naturalism ensures the autonomy of the will; naturalism does not subordinate the rational will to inclination. But if Kant insists that autonomy requires the creation of one's own law, he rejects naturalism.

Among the readers who understand Kant in this way are some modern Thomists.[6] In their view, Kant makes a mistake in supposing that the will is free to create its own law. If he were right, there would be no external fact about morality for us to discover, and we would not bound by any law that has an authority apart from what we choose to give it. The

---

[6] 'Kant, it is clear, does not see the sublimity of good-in-itself, which, though it is also delightful, is desired primarily for its own sake. Kant thinks that the human will, in order to be truly rational, moral, and free, must be its own law, otherwise it falls into slavery. Thus the human will is autonomous, independent of any higher and extrinsic law. Individual man, then, is to judge whether his own activity is or is not the standard of universal legislation. Individual reason is the supreme arbiter of good and evil. Individual will, as first cause, imposes obligation on itself.' (Garrigou-Lagrange, B 22–3) Cronin says something similar, also from a Thomist point of view, about the difference between Aquinas and Kant: 'This doctrine of St Thomas, that the moral order of the human act is set up in the act by human reason, is to be carefully distinguished from the Kantian theory of the autonomy of reason—the theory, namely, that the moral law springs from our own reason. According to St Thomas, reason sets up in the human act the right order, but in doing so it follows laws that spring not from reason itself, but from nature. According to Kant, reason not only directs the act, but also creates the laws according to which the act should be directed.' (SE i 2n)

modern Thomists demand some external authority. It might be found in natural facts, which do not require an act of legislation. Alternatively, it might be found in divine commands, which involve an act of legislation. According to the first view, moral requirements depend on non-legislative natural facts, and Kant is wrong to suppose that they depend on an act of legislation. According to the second view, Kant is right to suppose that they depend on an act of legislation, but wrong to suppose that they can be created by one's own act of legislation.[7] The first view reflects the naturalism of Suarez; the second reflects the voluntarism of Pufendorf.

Others who believe that Kant rejects objectivism are 'modern Kantians' who believe he is right to reject it.[8] In their view, Kant sees that any belief in 'discovery' in this area conflicts with the freedom of the will; if the will had to conform to some independent moral facts, it would not be giving itself its own law, and so it would not be autonomous. From this point of view, Kant appears to belong to the voluntarist tradition, replacing the legislative will of God with the legislative will of the individual rational agent.

985. Aspects and Degrees of Autonomy

Would Kant be right to claim that freedom and morality require us to create our own law?[9] We might defend such a claim by appealing to familiar points about freedom and autonomy, as many people might understand them. If we suppose that Kant tries to do justice to these familiar points, we might be still more inclined to attribute the creative, anti-objectivist view of autonomy to him.

To begin with, free agency seems to be connected with rational agency. If we do not simply act on our impulses, but have selves distinct from our impulses, we act freely in engaging ourselves. We do not engage ourselves simply by forming higher-order desires about our first-order desires, and acting on the higher-order desires; for our higher-order desires may be no less irrational and no more expressive of ourselves than our lower-order desires.[10] We might argue that we act freely and express ourselves, in so far as we act on our reasoned evaluations of our actions and desires. This conception of freedom underlies Kant's view of practical freedom as independence from sensory impulses.

But we may suppose that rationality and independence from sensory impulse are insufficient for the practical freedom that matters to us, because they do not recognize the distinctive role of freedom in agency. If we act on theoretical reason, we do not depend on sensory impulses; we correct them in the light of our rational beliefs about the world, and act on our corrected outlook. But free agency does not seem to consist simply in this

---

[7] See Rickaby, *MP*, ch. 6, and Cathrein, *PM*, ch. 5, both quoted in §603.

[8] See Korsgaard, 'Duty', 228–9: 'There are two elements to Kant's notion of heteronomy: (a) the law is not the will's own law, but rather is given to it from outside, and (b) the will therefore can be bound by that law only through an inclination or an interest, which renders the imperative to follow the law hypothetical. ... But I think that the real essence of heteronomy lies in its first element: the problem with the eudaimonistic principle is that it is not the will's *own* law. ... Only the categorical imperative, which *describes* the activity of a free will as such (a free will chooses a maxim it regards as a law) is the will's *own* law.' Cf. Rawls, discussed in §993.

[9] Cf. Hare on freedom and reason; §1325.

[10] This objection applies to an account of freedom that relies on higher-order desires. See §684 on Frankfurt, 'Freedom'.

guidance by reason; we are not free in the exercise of theoretical reason, since we are constrained by the facts and standards relevant to theoretical knowledge. Free agency, then, seems to require something more than the sort of guidance that is available to theoretical reason.

We may suppose we come closer to free and autonomous agency if we consider the freedom of the creative artist. This type of freedom does not consist in the guidance of rational norms; on the contrary, the relevant norms do not require the production of one sort of work rather than another. The artist is free to create without being constrained by rational norms. This conception of creative freedom is too simple, and it would be misleading if it were applied directly to morality. But it suggests why we might believe Kant is right to connect freedom, autonomy, and creation. We have practical freedom and autonomy, on this view, only if we are not externally constrained, by force, or sensory impulse, or rational norms, to choose one way or the other. Since rational norms based on facts about objective reality would constitute an external authority, autonomous agents cannot be constrained by such norms. Kant captures this thought about practical freedom if he believes that free and autonomous agents must create their own law, and do not simply recognize that they are a law to themselves.

986. Autonomy and Independent Judgment

The belief that autonomy requires freedom from external authority may appear to underlie Kant's view that the development of autonomy involves making up one's own mind about what to believe and how to act. The critical examination of reason in the *First Critique* is intended to fulfil the legitimate demands of contemporary society in an 'age of criticism'. A critical age expects thorough criticism of accepted beliefs and institutions through 'free and public examination' by reason.[11] Kant describes the critical attitude in his essay 'What is enlightenment?' Enlightened people free themselves from 'minority' and 'immaturity' through their critical reason. Immature people cannot use their own understanding without direction from another (WE 35), whereas mature and independent thinkers 'disseminate the spirit of a rational valuing of one's own worth and of the calling of each individual to think for himself' (36).

If the result of the free and public use of reason is our acceptance of a principle that we have examined, we may claim to be autonomous in relation to that principle. We have not simply accepted it on authority; we have also come to accept it for reasons of our own. Hence we ourselves give the law, since we do not simply take over a law given by someone else. And we give our own law, since it is a law that we accept for our own reasons, not because we accept it uncritically from someone else.

What does it mean to refuse to take over a law from an external source? This might be interpreted so as to be compatible with objectivism. According to this interpretation, the

---

[11] 'Our age is the genuine age of criticism, to which everything must submit. Religion through its holiness and legislation through its majesty commonly seek to exempt themselves from it. But in this way they excite a just suspicion against themselves, and cannot lay claim to that unfeigned respect that reason grants only to that which has been able to withstand its free and public examination.' (*KrV* Axi)

autonomous attitude rests on our own judgment about the facts, or about who is a reliable authority on the facts; we try to free ourselves of influences that would interfere with our judging as accurately as we can about the facts, and so we try to avoid being influenced by pretensions to external authority that might interfere with this judgment.

But is this all that Kant means when he describes enlightened people who think for themselves? One might argue that this is only partial emancipation from external authority. We cannot be thinking for ourselves (one might argue) if we are bound to conform to external facts and standards; we are autonomous only if we create our own standards to guide our action.[12]

Kant's remarks about enlightenment do not assert that autonomy precludes reliance on external facts and standards. But we might argue that he accepts this view of autonomy, because nothing less than freedom from external standards achieves the sort of independence that he describes. Hence (on this view) his doctrine of self-legislation completely fulfils the demand for independence.[13]

If this is indeed Kant's conception of autonomy, he rejects traditional naturalism on a point that we have so far overlooked. For Aquinas implies that the will does not select its objects simply by willing. It does not select the final good at all; it selects subordinate objects by discovering their connexion with the final good, and it is guided in that discovery by external reasons. We might argue that this element of externality marks the crucial way in which the will does not give itself the law, but relies on something external to it.[14]

To distinguish Kant's position from the traditional naturalist position on this issue, we may distinguish the will's having its own law from the will's giving the law to itself. So far we have spoken as though Kant's demand for autonomy could be met as long as the will has its own law, and does not simply devise means for satisfying inclinations independent of it. But this condition does not give the will any choice about what its own law is to be. We might suppose that Kant's conception of autonomy requires the law of the will to result from the choice of the will.[15]

---

[12] One might draw this conclusion from Godwin's advocacy of private judgment in *EPJ* ii 5: 'Man is a being who can never be an object of just approbation, any further than he is independent. He must consult his own reason, draw his own conclusions, and conscientiously conform himself to his ideas of propriety. . . . it is necessary, that every man should stand by himself, and rest upon his own understanding.' (169). But he does not clearly apply his anarchism to external facts and standards.

[13] Pinkard, *GI*, ch. 2, attributes a constructivist interpretation of autonomy to Kant: 'The moral order . . . is an ideal, communally instituted order; not a natural or created order; and it is the reciprocity involved in each autonomous agent legislating for himself and others that is to be considered as that which "institutes" the law . . .' (34) This description would be compatible with an objectivist conception of the law if the 'moral order' were simply the order constituted by persons who observe moral principles. But then it would be trivial that such an order does not exist by nature or creation. Kant's position, as Pinkard understands it, is non-trivial if the 'moral order' is constituted by the moral law itself. Later he takes Kant to maintain that 'we are subject only to those norms for which we can regard ourselves as the author' (108).

[14] According to Darwall, *BMIO* 279, Butler also takes autonomy to conflict with externality. Contrast §720.

[15] See Schneewind, 'Autonomy', 316: 'Suppose that a kind of state of affairs is intrinsically good because of the nature of that state of affairs. Then the goodness occurs independently of the will of any finite moral agent, and if she must will to pursue it, she is not self-legislating. Suppose the goodness of states of affairs comes from some standard. Then the standard is either the outcome of someone's will—say God's—or it is self-subsistent and eternal. In either case conformity to it is not autonomy. Conformity would be what Kant calls heteronomy.' The view that Schneewind contrasts with Kant's view is not the view I have ascribed to Aquinas and Suarez. They do not think the relevant standard comes from God's will or is self-subsistent; in their view, it comes from facts about human nature. At 315 Schneewind seems to impose less extreme anti-objectivist conditions for self-legislation.

To decide whether Kant connects autonomy and anti-objectivism about morality in these ways, we should try to decide whether he rejects objectivism, and whether he takes self-legislation to imply that the will creates its own law. If he accepts both objectivism and the creative conception of self-legislation, his position is inconsistent. But he holds a consistent view if he accepts anti-objectivism plus creative self-legislation, or if he accepts objectivism plus self-legislation without creation.

987. The Author of the Law v. the Author of the Obligation

In Kant's view, an autonomous will does not 'go outside itself' to seek the law that will determine it 'in the property of any of its objects' (G 440–1). Hence the law that determines the will is the law proper to the will, and not introduced from any object of inclination. This aspect of autonomy does not preclude objectivity, if the law proper to the will is the law recognized by reason. But Kant also claims that we are autonomous only in so far as the will legislates for itself, or 'gives' itself the law.[16] In his discussion of the categorical imperative, he often speaks of rational agents giving themselves the law, and of being legislators in a kingdom of ends. This reference to legislation may appear to preclude objectivity; for if the will actually makes the law, apparently it cannot have been the law without the will's having chosen to make it the law. What, then, does Kant mean by saying that the will legislates for itself?[17]

He clarifies his claim about legislation, by distinguishing the legislator from the author of a law.[18] A morally practical law contains a categorical imperative. The legislator is the author of the obligation in accordance with this law, but not necessarily the author of the law. The author of the law decides what the content of the law is to be, by formulating an appropriate principle; the legislator accepts that principle and makes it the law. Legislators may also be authors of laws; if they are, these laws are positive and arbitrary.[19] When legislators are not authors of laws, they may be authorized to accept or to reject proposed laws that the author of the law presents. In this case, the author of the law fixes its content, and the legislator is the author of the obligation.

In 'Use', 66, Schneewind contrasts Kant with Butler: 'The defining feature of an autonomous agent, in Kant's view, is its ability to guide its own action by the choice of a will that is such that whatever it wills is good simply because it is willed by it. The point is not that the autonomous will unerringly hones in on what is independently and antecedently good, as Butler's conscience does. The point is rather that when something is chosen or pursued by such a will, that very fact makes the object of the will good. An agent so guided is not led by anything outside himself.' Schneewind goes on to compare and contrast Kant with Pufendorf.

[16] '. . . this legislation of its own by pure and thus practical reason is freedom in the positive sense.' (KpV 33)

[17] Reath discusses many relevant issues helpfully in 'Moral law', and 'Realm'. At some places, he seems to suggest that one gives the law to oneself simply in so far as the law is the law of the will. See 'Moral law', 456: 'The fundamental law regulating moral deliberation is a principle derived from the nature of rational volition; it is thus the law which the rational will gives to itself.' In that case, the will need not choose what the content of the law will be.

[18] 'A law (a morally-practical one) is a proposition which contains a categorical imperative (a command). He who commands (imperans) through a law is the lawgiver (legislator). He is the author (auctor) of the obligation (Verbindlichkeit) in accordance with the law, but he is not always the author of the law. If he were so, the law would be positive (contingent) and arbitrary (willkürlich).' (MdS 227)

[19] Rousseau draws a somewhat analogous contrast between the legislator (corresponding to Kant's 'author of the law') and the person or body who adopts the laws for a given state. See Rousseau, SC ii 7 (ed. Grimsley, 30).

This distinction between the author and the legislator clarifies Kant's claims about autonomy. When he claims that autonomy consists in the will's giving itself the law, he means that the will imposes the obligation of the law; it does not decide what the moral law is to be, but only chooses whether or not to accept it. This is all that follows from the fact that the will is the legislator. Being the legislator does not preclude being the author of the law, but Kant gives good reason to deny that the will is the author of the moral law; for a law that has an author is positive and arbitrary. When we think of God as the supreme legislator, we do not make God the author of the moral law. Nor is God the author of a law that God imposes on himself. By the same token, moral agents cannot be authors of any law that is a categorical imperative; for if they were the authors, the law would be 'positive and arbitrary' and so could not be a categorical imperative.

Kant does not always seem to observe this important distinction between the legislator and the author of a law. In the *Groundwork*, he suggests that the will both legislates universal law and is the author of the law.[20] If 'author of the law' is taken in the strict sense explained in the *Metaphysics of Morals*, Kant implies that rational agents decide on the content of the law, and that therefore the law is 'positive and arbitrary'. Probably, however, he is simply using 'author' loosely in this passage of the *Groundwork*, so that he does not distinguish the author of the law from the legislator who is the author of the obligation. The rest of his discussion of autonomy and the categorical imperative supports this suggestion; he speaks of rational wills only as legislators, and does not suggest that they choose the content of the law. Probably, then, he does not mean to affirm in the *Groundwork* the claim about authorship of the law that he denies in the *Metaphysics of Morals*.

So far, then, we might reasonably take Kant to say that we are autonomous in so far as we are the authors of the obligation of the moral law. Though we do not decide what the principles of morality are to be, we decide whether or not to impose them on ourselves. He does not suggest, therefore, that we create the law that we impose on ourselves.

988. Laws, Imperatives, and Legislation

We need to complicate our account of Kant's view, however, if we return to his views on wills and laws, to see how it affects his views about autonomy and the moral law.[21] The complication arises from his division between holy wills and finite human wills. Moral law, as practical law, belongs to all rational wills, but a holy will does not conceive the practical law as an imperative, or as prescribing a duty; imperatives and duty belong only to wills that have motives that do not essentially conform to practical reason.[22] Since Kant believes a holy will is autonomous, he cannot consistently believe that autonomy requires the imposition

---

[20] 'The will is thus not merely subject to the law, but is subject to the law in such a way that it must be regarded also as legislating for itself and only on this account as being subject to the law (of which it can regard itself as the author).' (G 431)

[21] Laws v. imperatives; §903.

[22] 'That will whose maxims are necessarily in accord with the laws of autonomy is a holy, or absolutely good, will. The dependence of a will which is not absolutely good upon the principle of autonomy (i.e., moral necessitation) is obligation, which cannot therefore be applied to a holy will. The objective necessity of an action from obligation is called duty.' (G 439)

of an obligation on oneself. A holy will is guided autonomously by its own law without any imperative, obligation, or duty; for it observes a practical law without constraint.[23] Practical laws reveal practical necessities, but they are not necessarily imperatives. They are imperatives, and introduce an 'ought', only in finite rational agents whose practical reason does not necessarily determine their will.[24] A holy will does not conceive the practical law as an imperative, or as prescribing a duty.

Imperatives and duty, therefore, belong only to wills that have motives that do not essentially conform to practical reason.[25] Kant's discussion of the formulae of the categorical imperative is really about the supreme practical law, which is an imperative only in finite rational agents. Whenever he speaks of a law introducing a categorical imperative, we have to limit this claim to finite rational agents who are not purely rational.

For most purposes, it does not matter that Kant discusses categorical imperatives rather than practical laws; for he is legitimately interested in the relation between the moral law and finite rational agents. But for some purposes, it is useful to be more precise about what he means. It is especially useful in discussions of autonomy. Kant believes a holy will is autonomous; its lack of incentives that might cause it to deviate from the moral law is not a reason for denying it positive freedom and autonomy. But it does not impose imperatives,

---

[23] 'A categorical imperative, because it asserts an obligation with respect to certain actions, is a morally practical law. But since obligation involves not only practical necessity (Notwendigkeit) (which law in general asserts), but also necessitation (Nötigung), a categorical imperative is a law that either commands or prohibits . . .' (MdS 223) The second sentence explains the first. Strictly speaking, it is not because an imperative asserts an obligation that it is a practical law, but because obligation includes necessity, and practical law asserts necessity. Hence categorical imperatives are a proper subset of practical laws. See also G 439 (quoted above).

[24] See KpV 20, quoted in §903.

[25] 'If reason infallibly determines the will, then the actions of such a being which are recognized as objectively necessary are subjectively necessary also, i.e., the will is a faculty to choose that only which reason independent of inclination recognizes as practically necessary, i.e., as good. But if reason of itself does not sufficiently determine the will, if the latter is subject also to subjective conditions (particular incentives) which do not always coincide with the objective conditions; in a word, if the will does not in itself completely accord with reason (which is actually the case with human beings), then the actions which objectively are recognized as necessary are subjectively contingent, and the determination of such a will according to objective laws is necessitation, that is to say, the relation of the objective laws to a will that is not thoroughly good is conceived as the determination of the will of a rational being by principles of reason indeed, but principles which the will from its nature does not of necessity follow. The conception of an objective principle, in so far as it is obligatory for a will, is called a command (of reason), and the formula of the command is called an imperative. All imperatives are expressed by an ought, and thereby indicate the relation of an objective law of reason to a will that from its subjective constitution is not necessarily determined by it (a necessitation). They say that something would be good to do or to forbear, but they say it to a will which does not always do a thing because it is conceived to be good to do it.' (G 412–13) 'Now this principle of morality, . . . includes the Infinite Being as the supreme intelligence. [In finite beings], . . . the moral law is an imperative that commands categorically, because the law is unconditional; the relation of such a will to this law is dependence under the name of obligation, which signifies a necessitation to an action, though only by reason and its objective law; and this action is called duty, because a choice subject to pathological affections (though not determined by them, and, therefore, still free), implies a wish that arises from subjective causes and therefore may often be opposed to the pure objective determining principle; whence it requires the moral necessitation of a resistance of the practical reason, which may be called an internal but intellectual, constraint. In the most self-sufficient intelligence choice (Willkür) is rightly conceived as incapable of any maxim which could not at the same time be objectively a law; and the notion of holiness, which on that account belongs to it, places it, not indeed *above all practical laws, but* above all practically restrictive laws, and consequently above obligation and duty. This holiness of will is, however, a practical idea, which must necessarily serve as a type to which finite rational beings can only approximate indefinitely, and which the pure moral law, which is itself on this account called holy, constantly and rightly holds before their eyes.' (KpV 32–4. CT omits the words in italics above) 'An imperative differs from a practical law in that a law indeed represents an action as necessary but takes no account of whether this action already inheres by an inner necessity in the acting subject (as in a holy being) or whether it is contingent (as in the human being); for where the former is the case there is no imperative.' (MdS 222)

obligations, or duties on itself; for these are relevant only to finite rational agents. Hence the imposition of imperatives and so on is not necessary for autonomy.

But if that is so, how is autonomy connected to legislation by the will? According to Kant, the legislator is not the author of the law, but the author of the obligation of the law. But holy wills are not under obligations; hence they are not legislators. Kant's account of a holy will prevents him from taking self-legislation to be necessary for autonomy. A holy will, therefore, follows the moral law without any legislation, since legislation introduces obligation. The moral law is an imperative only in relation to an imperfect will. In an imperfect will, a legislator commands and is the author of an obligation; but a holy will is not subject to commands or obligations. Since legislation imposes obligation, a holy will does not legislate for itself, because it does not impose obligation on itself.

We should therefore question Kant's account of autonomy as self-legislation. Though he distinguishes holy wills from the imperfect wills of human beings, and therefore distinguishes practical laws from categorical imperatives, his discussion of autonomy does not observe these distinctions. Given his views about holy wills, autonomy does not consist in self-legislation; holy wills are autonomous without any legislation by themselves or for themselves.

989. Autonomy Without Legislation?

If we apply Kant's view of autonomy to holy wills, we have to say that self-legislation is needed for autonomy in finite rational agents, but not for autonomy in holy wills. As finite rational agents, we have to accept the moral law that holy wills accept, and we have to choose it over potentially conflicting motives. In doing this, we legislate for ourselves, in so far as we impose the obligation of the moral law on ourselves. But this cannot be what makes holy wills autonomous? Can we say more exactly what their autonomy consists in?

Kant's statement of his position is sometimes obscure, because he speaks of legislation in cases where there seems to be no obligation and therefore no law. Pure reason legislates for human beings; but Kant also suggests that the 'universality of the lawgiving' makes the principle of morality a law for all rational beings, and hence not only for human beings who are subject to obligation, but also for holy wills that are not subject to obligation.[26] If 'universal lawgiving' applies to them, we must understand 'lawgiving' so that, contrary to Kant's explicit account, it does not involve obligation and imperatives.[27]

Can we understand a type of lawgiving that does not impose an obligation, because it does not confront any potentially opposed motives? Kant suggests that the universality of

---

[26] 'Pure reason is of itself alone practical, and gives (to the human being) a universal law, which we call the moral law. ... Now this principle of morality, just on account of the universality of the lawgiving that makes it the formal supreme determining ground of the will regardless of all subjective differences, reason declares (erklärt) to be at the same time a law for all rational beings in so far as they have a will, i.e., faculty of determining their causality through the conception of a rule, and consequently in so far as they are competent to determine their actions according to principles and thus to act according to practical principles a priori, since these alone have the necessity that reason demands in a principle. It is thus not limited to human beings, but extends to all finite beings having reason and will; indeed it includes the Infinite Being as the supreme intelligence. In the former case, however, the law has the form of an imperative.' (KpV 32)

[27] Gregor, n ad G 403 (in CT), raises some related questions about lawgiving.

the lawgiving by practical reason makes the moral law applicable to all rational agents. The role of practical reason is to 'declare' this moral law. A declaration is different from an imperative because it does not include the imposition of any obligation; hence Kant can consistently claim that practical reason declares the law even in agents who are not subject to obligation. The type of lawgiving that is open to these agents is declaration to themselves of the moral law that they follow without obligation. Autonomy for these agents, therefore, is declaration of one's own law to oneself; that is the aspect of legislation for oneself that is open to holy wills.

If a holy will is autonomous in so far as it declares to itself a law that is not taken from any object outside the rational will, it does not create this law by its declaration. Kant has good reason to deny that the existence of the law depends on its declaration by practical reason. He denies that our legislating the moral law makes us authors of the law; he has equally good reason to deny that our declaration of the law makes us authors of it. The content of the law and its appropriateness for rational beings are independent of the declaration by practical reason. Kant does not suggest that it is the act of declaration that makes the law a law for rational agents.

A remark about natural law shows that Kant at least sometimes recognizes this implication of his position.[28] He argues that positive laws—those that exist only because of acts of legislation—presuppose a natural non-positive law that provides the ground of the authority of the legislator. Reason recognizes this natural law as obligatory independently of any act of legislation. As it stands, this claim does not cover holy wills that are not subject to obligation, but we can easily adapt it. In holy wills, reason recognizes natural law as being law and as being necessary (though not as obligatory).

Kant's remark about natural law explains why he has no reason to treat the moral law as the product of legislation. For if we were to claim that practical reason makes the moral law a law because of its act of declaring the law, we would make the moral law a special kind of positive law. We would then have to postulate a further moral law that authorizes practical reason to legislate. This further moral law could not itself be made law by some act of practical reason. Practical reason, therefore, can declare a moral law only by recognizing some law that exists apart from acts of declaration.

Kantian autonomy, therefore, does not depend on our acknowledging only those laws that are made laws by our own acts of legislating or declaration. On the contrary, autonomy requires us to recognize at least one practical law that is a law apart from any act of legislation or declaration.

From this discussion, we can extract an account of autonomy that observes the distinctions that Kant sometimes draws and sometimes blurs: (1) Taken generally, so as to apply to all rational agents, autonomy consists in the recognition of the moral law as the universal law for all rational agents. (2) In its specific application to finite rational agents, autonomy consists in the legislation that consists in making the moral law obligatory for us. In the second case,

---

[28] 'Those external laws whose obligation can be recognized a priori by reason even without external legislation are natural laws; those, on the other hand, which without actual external legislation do not oblige (and so without it would not be laws) are called positive laws. Hence it is possible to conceive of an external legislation which contains only positive laws; but then it would have to be preceded by a natural law that would ground the authority of the legislator (i.e., his authorization to obligate others by his mere choice (Willkür).' (MdS 224)

but not the first, rational agents are legislators, as authors of obligation. In neither case are they authors of the law itself; they do not decide the content of the moral law.

990. Kant's View of Disputes About Natural Law

Kant's remark on natural and positive law helps us to understand his position in the dispute between naturalists and voluntarists about natural law and morality. If he had claimed that autonomy requires us to create our own moral law, he would be a voluntarist in this dispute. But since this is not his view of autonomy, he is closer to naturalism.

Naturalists and voluntarists disagree about the relation of moral rightness to laws, obligations, and commands. Their different views mark disagreements about the possibility of 'intrinsic' morality, as Suarez conceives it—rightness and wrongness that follow from the existence of human beings, without reference to any further choice, will, command, or legislation. One version of a naturalist view, held probably by Aquinas and certainly by Vasquez, takes rightness to imply law and obligation, but not to imply commands. Hence it recognizes intrinsic moral rightness, and takes it to imply natural law. The voluntarist doctrine of Pufendorf takes moral rightness to imply law, obligation, and commands. Hence it denies intrinsic moral rightness. The intermediate position of Suarez separates moral rightness and duty (debitum) from law, obligation, and commands. Hence it recognizes intrinsic moral rightness without natural law.[29]

Kant's claims about law and obligation separate his position, at least verbally, from all of these positions. He agrees with voluntarists against naturalists in so far as he connects the moral 'ought' with obligations and imperatives. But he agrees with naturalists in accepting moral rightness and law without imperatives. He seems to accept a strange position, therefore, since he seems to allow the possibility of moral principles that include no moral 'ought'.

But his position is less strange if we take account of his claim that 'ought' implies actual or possible reluctance because of conflicting motives. This account of 'ought' distinguishes Kant's use from the use of 'ought' or 'due' (debere, debitum) by Aquinas and Suarez, who do not take 'ought' to imply reluctance. If, then, we state Kant's position in the terms used by Aquinas and Suarez, he believes that moral oughts (debita) and requirements exist without acts of legislation. Given Aquinas' broad use of 'command' (rejected by Suarez), we would express Kant's position in Aquinas' terms by saying that he recognizes moral law, moral oughts, and moral commands, without acts of legislation.[30]

Kant's division between a holy will and a finite rational will draws some of the distinctions that Suarez draws, but in different terms. In recognizing moral law without obligation, Kant presents his own version of a doctrine of intrinsic rightness. He agrees with Suarez that moral principles present intrinsic rightness apart from obligations and command, but he supposes, contrary to Suarez, that they also present law. In Kant's view, commands and acts

---

[29] The use of 'without' over-simplifies Suarez's position, as we see from *Leg*. ii 5.5; ii 6.11 (both passages quoted in §441).

[30] Aquinas on imperium; §§257, 306.

of binding are relevant to limited rational agents, who are also subject to other incentives and so have to be instructed and urged to follow the moral law. But commands and acts of binding are unnecessary for the existence of the moral law, which is the law for all rational wills, whether wholly rational or subject to non-rational impulses.

The distinction between the author of the law and the author of the obligation agrees in substance, though not in vocabulary, with Suarez. Voluntarists about natural law claim that God not only commands observance of the natural law, but also decides on the content of the law. In Kantian terms, voluntarists claim that God is both author of the obligation, as legislator, and author of the law itself; this is Pufendorf's view. Naturalists argue that, though God commands observance of the natural law, God does not decide on its content; its content is fixed by intrinsic morality, apart from divine commands. In Kant's terms, naturalists claim that God is the author of obligation for finite rational beings, but not the author of the law. This is not how Suarez expresses the naturalist view, since he disagrees with Kant's claim that law can exist without acts of legislation; but the distinction that he draws agrees with Kant on the existence of non-legislative intrinsic morality.

Kant's view on the relation of God's legislative will to the moral law agrees with naturalism. He accepts God as legislator, and hence as author of the obligation of the law. But he denies that God is the author of the law.[31] God does not decide on the content of the moral law.[32] The natural law is not the product of God's legislative will, but captures the intrinsic morality that is prior to any legislative will.

It is difficult to compare Kant's position with voluntarist and naturalist views on natural law, intrinsic morality, and divine commands. Kant's vocabulary creates part of the difficulty. Given his conception of law and obligation, he sometimes appears to contradict the substance of naturalist claims when in fact he does not. Moreover, he is not always clear about how autonomy is related to legislation; his identification of autonomy with self-legislation takes no account of the difference between the holy will and the finite will. Because of these complications, we need to be careful in comparing Kant's views with

[31] 'The law which obliges (verbindet) us a priori and unconditionally through our own reason can also be expressed as proceeding from the will of a supreme lawgiver, i.e. of one who has only rights and no duties (accordingly, from the Divine Will). But this only signifies the idea of a moral being whose will is law for all, without his being conceived as the author of the law.' (*MdS* 227)

[32] Wood, *KET* 161, takes this passage to show that the rational will must be the author of the moral law: 'He distinguishes the *legislator* of a law, the one who issues a command and may attach positive or negative sanctions to it, from the law's author, the one whose will imposes the obligation to obey it. In these terms Kant has no objection to regarding God's will as the legislator of the moral law, but thinks only the rational will of the person obligated can be its author.' The passage, however, offers no support for 'but thinks only . . .'. If Wood were correct, it would imply that the law by which we are obliged is 'positive and arbitrary'. As further evidence of Kant's holding the view he ascribes to him, Wood cites two other passages: (1) *G* 448: 'Reason must regard itself as the author (Urheberin) of its principles, independently of alien influences.' It is not clear that being the author of its principles implies being the author of the moral law that its principles embody. (2) *Rel.* 99: 'But neither can ethical laws be thought of as proceeding *originally* merely from the will of this superior (as statutes that would not be binding without his prior sanction), for then they would not be ethical laws, and the duty commensurate to them would not be a free virtue, but an entirely enforceable legal duty. Therefore only such a one can be thought of as the supreme lawgiver of an ethical community, with respect to whom all *true duties*, hence also the ethical, must be represented as *at the same time* his commands.' This passage says nothing about the will of the person obliged being the author of the law. On the contrary, it suggests that ethical laws do not proceed from anyone's will. Kant's remark about the supreme lawgiver suggests that something's already being a true duty is presupposed by its being one of his commands.

naturalist and voluntarist views. But a careful comparison brings out the basic agreement with naturalism.

If we take account of all this, Kant does not differ substantially from Aquinas about autonomy, and does not imply that autonomy requires us to create our own moral law. Aquinas, therefore, does not preclude Kantian autonomy by recognizing a law that applies to us independently of our choosing to apply it to ourselves. This sort of externality cannot preclude autonomy, since Kant regards practical laws as external to our choices in just the same way. For Aquinas, as for Butler (*Sermon*, iii 5), the natural law is the 'law of our nature'. It is part of our nature that we are agents who choose autonomously, and this fact about our nature determines the moral principles that apply to us.[33]

On this issue about autonomy, Kant holds an objectivist position. Nothing suggests that, on this point, he disagrees with the objectivism of traditional naturalism. His disagreements with traditional naturalism rest on the assumption that naturalist claims are empirical. If this assumption is mistaken, Kant has no reason to disagree with the actual view of traditional naturalists on meta-ethical issues. His views about autonomy do not introduce any disagreement.

991. Autonomy Without Construction

If we take Kant to combine belief in the value of autonomy with belief in objective moral properties, do we underestimate his commitment to those aspects of autonomy that reflect the demand for enlightenment?[34] This explicit commitment distinguishes him from earlier naturalists about morality and natural law. Does he, or should he, interpret his commitment as an objection to moral objectivism?

He does not seem to take enlightenment to exclude acceptance of intrinsic morality. Enlightened individuals do not assume uncritically that something is the moral law. They act on their individual rational understanding that a principle with this content is the universal law for rational beings, and hence they act on their individual reason. If they are finite rational agents, they must act on this rational understanding by assenting to the moral law and seeking to conform their other impulses to its demands. But, if they recognize objective moral properties, they use their enlightened rational understanding to discover the moral law, and not to create it.

If this is Kant's view of autonomy, he believes that autonomy requires us to act on our own rational understanding, but not that it requires us to act on principles that are the product of our own will. We exercise autonomy (as a non-Kantian might describe it) in relation to objective theoretical truths if we make our minds up for ourselves about whether they, or the authorities that present them to us, seem to be supported by the appropriate

---

[33] Green's discussion of autonomy (*LK* §125) draws a helpful distinction between the law's being imposed by oneself and its being created by oneself. See §1241.

[34] See Wood, in *PP* xxii: 'The principle of autonomy is also a principle of *enlightenment*, because it locates the source of moral legislation in the reason of human individuals who think for themselves, locating the ultimate criterion of morality in "the moral judgment of every human being in so far as he makes the effort to think [the moral law] clearly" (A807/B835).'

reasons. Kantian practical autonomy is similar. Practical principles are not (in Kant's view) part of our theoretical knowledge of the world, but that does not introduce a basically different kind of autonomy. In both the theoretical and the practical cases, we act on our own reasoned judgments in recognizing the relevant reasons.

In our initial discussion of autonomy, we defended the view that autonomy requires creation, by suggesting that an artist who does not try to conform to objective facts is more autonomous than a scientist who tries to conform to them. Kant, however, might dispute this suggestion. He might reasonably argue that the autonomy of the artist who is not constrained by objective facts is really a lower degree of autonomy than the autonomy of the scientist or the moral agent who is constrained by the facts. If autonomy requires control by our rational judgment rather than by external influences, the artist's freedom reduces his autonomy. If we are free of constraint by objective facts, we follow our own inclinations and impulses. In doing so, we are influenced by inclinations external to our own practical reason, and to that extent we are less autonomous. Given this conception of autonomy, Kant has a good reason to claim that full autonomy in moral judgment requires choice that is guided by objective moral facts and properties.

992. Heteronomy and the Spurious Principles of Morality

To evaluate this account of Kant's views on autonomy, we may review his objections to the spurious sources of morality. He believes that they lead to heteronomy because in some way they lead us outside the rational will, and seek the law in a property of the possible objects of the will (G 441).[35] If the objects of the will include everything that exists independently of a rational will, the demand for autonomy excludes all forms of objectivism.

But this is too simple an account of Kant's conception of an object of the will, in these contexts. He treats the object as part of the matter of volition, in contrast to the form; this matter is an empirical condition.[36] The object of a volition is an empirical feature of it, because it distinguishes one volition from another, and so is not a necessary feature of all volition.

Moral principles that depend on the matter of volitions give us the wrong sort of reason for following morality. Since they depend on possible objects of volition that are not required for all rational agents, they give us a reason only if we have the appropriate antecedent motive. We have seen how this criticism applies to a sentimentalist position. In Kant's view, an appeal to the moral sense either is useless or gets the issues the wrong way round. His attack on sentimentalism shows that 'going outside' the rational will need not be taken to refer to objective moral properties. We go outside the rational will in appealing to other sorts of incentives that are not essential to a rational will; he does not say that we go 'outside' it if we introduce an objective reality that guides the will.

---

[35] In this case 'the matter of volition, which can be nothing other than the object of a desire that is connected with the law, enters into the practical law as a condition of its possibility' (*KpV* 33).

[36] Hence 'a practical precept that brings with it a material (hence empirical) condition must never be reckoned a practical law' (*KpV* 34).

It is more difficult, however, to see how rationalist intuitionism and Leibnizian perfectionism introduce heteronomy, if we take Kant's objections to be compatible with objectivism. These do not seem to be anti-rationalist positions, and hence Kant cannot object to them on the ground that they appeal to non-rational motives. Moreover, they seem to be objectivist positions, since both of them claim that we grasp true moral principles by grasping some fact external to the beliefs and wills of rational agents. The intuitionist claims that moral principles describe special moral facts that cannot be further analysed or explained, whereas the perfectionist claims that the relevant facts are facts about perfection. If Kant rejects both of these positions, does he reject the objectivism that they share?

We need not draw this conclusion if we recall our previous account of Kant's objections to these positions. He believes that they go outside the rational will because they do not show that moral principles rest on reasons that are reasons for rational agents as such. If we simply appeal to unanalysable moral facts, we have not yet shown that moral principles express practical laws, and so we have not shown that they rest on reasons that apply to rational beings as such; hence we may not be able to find reasons unless we go 'outside' the rational will to other incentives. We might suppose that perfectionists answer this objection by appealing to more than a bare assertion that moral principles express categorical imperatives; for they claim that true moral principles are those that describe facts about perfection. But Kant is dissatisfied with this further feature that perfectionists ascribe to moral principles. In his view, a purely metaphysical and non-normative conception of perfection fails to identify the right sort of reason, and hence will give reasons only on the basis of incentives that are external to a rational will.

Whether or not this criticism of rationalist intuitionism and perfectionism is justified, it does not require the rejection of all forms of objectivism. Kant believes he can do better than the heteronomous views not because he abandons any appeal to objective facts, but because he appeals to the right sort of objective fact. His refusal to go 'outside' the rational will does not imply any denial of objective moral principles that are true independently of any acts of will. When he speaks of principles or objects that are external to the will, he means that they are only contingently connected to the will.

This is a familiar conception of the internal. Examples of 'internal relations' or 'internal connexions' are easy to find in functional contexts. A sausage-making machine is internally related to sausages; it would not be what it is unless it were appropriately related to that product, but the sausage may none the less be made and exist without the machine. More controversially, we might consider the relation of senses to their objects. Colour is not externally related to sight, because (let us suppose) sight is essentially the sense that is aware of colour. Hence it is not a contingent fact that we see colours as opposed to sounds. None the less, colours are external to sight, if they exist independently of it and are not the creation of sight. Rational thought and the Principle of Non-Contradiction may be internally related in the same way. The fact that this principle is in some way a 'law of thought' does not make it a law about thought, or a law that depends on thought. One might say that the dependence goes the other way; an activity is not rational thought unless it refrains from simultaneously denying every property that it affirms of a given subject. In these cases, x's being internal to y does not make x dependent on y.

In Aquinas' view, the good is internally related to the will in the same way. The will essentially aims at the final good, and so the connexion between will and good is not contingent. Still, the final good is not the creation of the will, but is an independent object for the will to aim at. If Kant intends such a connexion between the rational will and the moral law, he believes that a rational will is not the sort of will it is unless the sorts of reasons that are provided by the moral law are reasons for it.

He argues for this sort of connexion in claiming that if we regard our rational nature as an end, we have overriding reason to treat rational agents as ends in themselves. The rational will grasps the reasons that correspond to facts that are external to it, but it does not, in Kant's terms, go 'outside' the rational will to find the relevant principles and reasons. This aspect of Kant's position is objectivist, and agrees with Aquinas' view that certain reasons and principles are internal to the rational will. Though he disagrees with Aquinas about what these reasons and principles are, he agrees that they correspond to facts about human rational agency.

While Kant disagrees on some points with rationalist intuitionism, perfectionism, and traditional naturalist eudaemonism, he agrees with them on questions about objectivity. His views on autonomy give us no reason to retract our previous conclusions about the points on which he agrees with naturalism.

993. Kantian Constructivism

In the light of this discussion of Kant's views on autonomy, we can usefully consider Rawls's argument to show that Kant is committed to 'constructivism'.[37] Rawls uses this term to refer to the metaphysical claim that moral truth is constituted by a correct constructive procedure whose correctness does not depend on its reaching true results. In Rawls's view, Kant accepts this metaphysical constructivism because autonomy precludes the recognition of any objective moral truths independent of how rational agents view themselves.[38] Moral principles depend on what Rawls calls 'our conception of ourselves as reasonable and rational persons'.

We can understand the constructivist elements of Rawls's account of Kant if we consider rules that are derived from shared practices. An account of the rules of a deliberative assembly may record the practice that has grown up over time. The members of the assembly must accept this practice, but they need not have made any deliberate decision that these are to

---

[37] This position is the 'moral constructivism' that Rawls ascribes to Kant at *PL* 99–101. Ameriks, *IKC*, ch.11, *KFA* 72–4, raises reasonable doubts about constructivist and other non-realist interpretations of Kant.

[38] '. . . it suffices for heteronomy that first principles obtain in virtue of relations among objects the nature of which is not affected or determined by our conception of ourselves as reasonable and rational persons (as possessing the powers of practical reason), and of the public role of moral principles in a society of such persons. Of particular importance is the conception of persons as reasonable and rational, and, therefore, as free and equal, and the basic units of agency and responsibility. Kant's idea of autonomy implies that there exists no moral order prior to and independent of these conceptions that is to determine the form of the procedure that specifies the content of first principles of right and justice among free and equal persons. Heteronomy obtains not only when these first principles are fixed by the special psychological constitution of human nature, as in Hume, but also when they are fixed by an order of universals, or of moral values grasped by rational intuition, as in Plato's realm of forms or in Leibniz's hierarchy of perfections'. (Rawls, 'Themes', 512. Cf. 'Constructivism', 345–6; *LHMP* 236, with clarifications at 72, 229)

be the rules. If the practice of the assembly changes, again without any further deliberate decision, these rules will no longer be correct; the actual shared practice of the assembly decides the correctness or incorrectness of any account of its rules.

Though this is not a complete parallel to the relation between practical reason and moral law that Rawls has in mind, it helps to identify some features of a constructivist view. We must be able to describe the relevant activities of practical reason without essential reference to the truth of the moral law or to belief in the moral law; if either of these is introduced, we no longer have the sort of independence that a constructivist view requires. It would not be plausible, for instance, to claim that scientific laws are constituted by our scientific activities, if we refer to those scientific activities that presuppose the truth of these laws; on the contrary, such activities are themselves legitimate only if the relevant laws are true.[39] The activities of practical reason that determine the truth of moral principles cannot themselves depend on acceptance of the truth of moral principles.

This constructivist doctrine needs to be distinguished from a constructive method.[40] This method proceeds on the assumption that we will reach morally correct results by following a certain procedure; by tracing the results of this procedure we construct the correct moral principles. Rawls quite reasonably ascribes this method to Kant in speaking of 'the categorical imperative procedure'. Instead of simply asserting (say) the Principle of Utility or Price's different 'heads of virtue', we examine proposed courses of action and moral rules by comparing them with the formulae of the categorical imperative. This procedure for testing proposed principles allows us to construct correct rules and principles. But we may follow this procedure and still hold that it corresponds to objective facts about reasons for rational agents as such. Hence it does not require metaphysical constructivism.

Rawls holds that Kant accepts metaphysical constructivism because moral principles depend on our activity of conceiving ourselves as rational and reasonable persons.[41] Our conceiving ourselves in this way makes it reasonable to follow a particular procedure of practical reasoning. This procedure is not correct because it achieves some specific conclusion. The reverse is true: moral principles are correct because they are the product of the procedure that we follow when we think of ourselves as reasonable and rational.

[39] On Rawls's position see §1442.

[40] O'Neill, CR 188n, explains 'constructivist' in this way: 'I use the term to cover approaches that seek to justify ethical principles by reference to an account of agency and rationality, without relying on claims about desires or preferences'. It is not clear, without further argument, whether a 'constructivist' in this sense must be a metaphysical constructivist (in the sense that excludes moral realism). Similarly, Hill, DPR 231, identifies Kantian constructivism with Rawls's use of the original position: 'The choosers are not seen as seeking to *discover* a moral order, Platonic, natural, or divine, which exists independently of their reasoned choices; rather, we are to view principles as justifiable by virtue of their being what persons with the specified values would choose in the defined situation.' This description of a constructivist method does not endorse a constructivist metaphysics. Even if people in the original position are not conceived as metaphysical realists about morality, the constructive method involving the original position may still be correct because it matches moral truths, as a metaphysical realist understands them.

[41] 'In contrast with rational intuitionism, constitutive autonomy says that the so-called independent order of values does not constitute itself but is constituted by the activity, actual or ideal, of practical (human) reason itself. I believe this, or something like it, is Kant's view.' (Rawls, PL 99.) 'Rational intuitionism says: the procedure is correct because following it correctly usually gives the correct (independently given) result. Constructivism says: the result is correct because it issues from the correct reasonable and rational procedure correctly followed.' (LHMP 242)

994. Does Autonomy Require Construction?

To support this interpretation, Rawls appeals to Kant's claims about heteronomous principles of morality (G 441). If, as Rawls asserts, the principles Kant regards as spurious include all non-constructivist accounts of morality, Kant implies that autonomy requires construction. Rawls believes that, in Kant's view, heteronomy results from treating moral principles as external to the activity of practical reasoning.

This diagnosis of the error of heteronomous systems is similar to the diagnosis that we have offered on Kant's behalf. Rawls notices that Kant rejects systems of morality that do not give the appropriate place to rational agency, and therefore go outside the rational will. But Rawls's diagnosis differs from our diagnosis in the way it appeals to rational agency. According to Rawls, moral principles are true because of facts about how we conceive ourselves and how we act; our choosing to regard ourselves a certain way and our choosing to act in accordance with this conception make the principles true. But according to the diagnosis we have accepted, Kant believes that moral principles depend on facts about rational agency; we would still be rational agents even if we did not choose to conceive ourselves or to act in particular ways, and moral principles would apply to us simply because we are rational agents. This objectivist view makes moral principles depend on facts about rational agents, whereas a constructivist view makes them depend on how agents conceive themselves and on what agents choose to do.

Rawls's constructivist interpretation of Kant is therefore open to question. For we have found no reason to believe that Kant's claims about autonomy require moral principles to depend on activities of rational agents. On the contrary, Kant seems to make autonomy depend on facts about rational agents. Hence we have no reason to suppose that all objectivist accounts of moral facts violate the requirements of autonomy.

This statement of the difference between a constructivist and an objectivist interpretation may still be obscure. For, we might ask, how can we capture facts about rational agents as such without including facts about the activities of rational agents? If we must include facts about rational activities, and these are among the facts from which we derive moral principles, do constructivist and objectivist views collapse into each other?

Rawls's constructivist claims raise a genuine issue about Kant if the rational activities that Rawls has in mind are in some way optional, so that rational agents might or might not choose to engage in them. In that case, the truth of the relevant moral principles depends on whether or not we undertake the relevant optional activities. If, however, the activities are essential features of rational agents, the moral principles derived from them are objective, since their truth is not constituted by our believing or choosing, as opposed to objective facts.

Rawls does not say that the rational activities he speaks of are optional. But these are the sorts of activities that he introduces in his account of a constructivist view. If he refers to optional activities, his constructivist interpretation of Kant offers a clear alternative to an objectivist interpretation of the derivation of moral principles from rational agency. But once we see the alternatives, we see that we have no reason to ascribe a constructivist view to Kant.

995. Objections to a Constructivist Account of Autonomy

The discussion of Rawls so far may suggest that his account and an objectivist account are equally plausible interpretations of Kant's position. Can we decide between them?

Arguments to show that Kant rejects voluntarism do not immediately show that he rejects constructivism. Kant objects to voluntarism on the ground that it would make us the authors of the moral law, and therefore would make the moral law positive and arbitrary; any genuine law rests on a natural law 'providing the ground of the authority of the legislator' (MdS 224).[42] Constructivism, however, does not make us authors of the moral law; it differs from voluntarism in so far as it dispenses with any explicit commands and acts of legislation. Moral principles might depend on, and be constituted by, 'the activity of practical reason itself' (as Rawls puts it)[43] without our actually being their authors. Even if we do not decide and legislate that some specific principles rather than others are to be principles of morality, our rational activities make them the principles.

None the less, the main point of Kant's argument is relevant to constructivism no less than to voluntarism. For if the moral law were constituted by our activities of practical reason, it would apparently be a 'positive and arbitrary' law, as Kant conceives it. Kant claims that we face a vicious regress of justification unless we can appeal beyond positive and arbitrary laws to a natural law that is not established by legislation. He could reasonably raise the same objection if we tried to derive moral principles from activities of practical reason. If the derived moral principles are correct, we are morally justified in following them. But if we are justified in following the principles, must we not be justified in engaging in the activities from which we derive the principles? If we try to justify our engaging in these activities by reference to a second set of principles, and do not derive these from rational activities, we abandon constructivism. If, however, we say that the second set of principles is derived from a second set of rational activities, we can ask how the second set of rational activities is justified. Either we face a vicious regress or we accept a justifying principle that does not introduce further activities needing justification. Eventually, then, we need to introduce a natural law that does not derive from a further rational activity.

This argument adapts Kant's argument to show that the moral law cannot have a positive and arbitrary basis. If we can adapt his argument in this way, we show that we cannot avoid his objections to a legislative view by substituting constitution or construction for legislation. For we can still legitimately ask for the moral credentials of the constituted or constructed principles, and our answer has to recognize principles that are not derived by any construction.

A constructivist might reject the premises that introduce a regress, and claim that the constituting activities are neither morally right nor morally wrong, so that no question arises about their justification. In that case, constructivism is open to Kant's arguments about heteronomy. For if we do not show that the relevant activities are morally right, we do not show that every rational agent, as such, has a reason to engage in them, and so they do not

---

[42] Quoted more fully in §989.   [43] See §994.

rest on categorical imperatives.[44] In that case, we have a reason to engage in them only if we have some inclination that does not give a reason for every rational agent. If we act on the basis of such an inclination, we act heteronomously, because our will does not act on its own law.

Constructivists might be well advised at this point to reject Kant's demand for a categorical imperative, and to argue that we need not give reasons that apply to rational agents as such. But if that is the reply they choose, they undermine a constructivist interpretation of Kant. For if constructivists have to reject the demand for categorical imperatives, and have to deny that any reasons apply to rational agents as such, they reject not only Kant's conception of autonomy but also the basis of his moral theory. Though a constructivist argument relying on the activities of practical reason initially appears to offer a plausible interpretation of Kant, further examination shows that it is incompatible with his view.

For these reasons, Kant's conception of autonomy not only does not require constructivism, but positively excludes it. A constructivist account of moral principles implies that we act on them heteronomously; hence it must introduce one of the spurious principles of morality. The arguments for objectivism that we have considered rule out constructivism as well as voluntarism.

996. A Constructivist Revision of Kant?

Even if Kant does not accept a constructivist account of autonomy, we might raise about autonomy the question that we previously raised about transcendental idealism. We might grant that so-called 'Kantian constructivism' is not Kantian in the sense of being Kant's actual position. But we might take Kant's actual position to be a step towards a quasi-Kantian constructivist position that (according to this view) is the best way to understand his main insight. Should Kant have said, even if he does not say, that any will that does not create its own law by its choices is thereby lacking autonomy, because it takes its law from something outside its choices? This position leads us back to the claim that autonomy requires freedom from external control. The argument from autonomy to constructivism rests on the assumption that externality to one's choices implies the sort of externality that compromises autonomy.[45]

If we claim that a free will must give itself the law by creating it without reference to any external standard, we imply that the will cannot be free if it is essentially related, in the way Aquinas suggests, to the good. But this feature of Aquinas' account does not deny freedom to the will. We cannot reasonably expect the will to be free to be something other than what it essentially is; neither Aquinas nor Kant attributes this sort of freedom to the will. Aquinas' view of the respect in which the will is not free allows him to explain how the will is free; it is guided by rational deliberation independent of non-rational desire, in choosing morality

---

[44] This argument ignores the possibility of prudential categorical imperatives, which are not relevant to the discussion of Rawls's constructivism.

[45] Olafson, PP, ch. 3, traces Kant's influence on voluntarist, and hence on existentialist, conceptions of autonomy. See §1359.

over other conceptions of the good. The fact that the will responds to goods that are good independently of its choosing them does not make the will any less free.

A quasi-Kantian constructivist might reply that we are not free in the pursuit of a good unless its goodness is the creation of our will. In that case, contrary to Aquinas' view, autonomy requires creation. But this quasi-Kantian view rests on a doubtful assumption about autonomy. When Kant complains that the views of his opponents make the will heteronomous, he gives us a reason to prefer his view to their views. Heteronomy is to be avoided if autonomous agents accept a law that is a law for rational wills as such. But it is not clear that heteronomy is to be avoided if it simply implies that the will does not create the content of the law it accepts.

The claim that autonomy requires creation reflects a voluntarist conception of freedom that may reasonably be attributed to Scotus.[46] If we must agree with this voluntarist conception before we can accept the quasi-Kantian claims about autonomy, these claims about autonomy lose some of their plausibility; for a voluntarist account of freedom faces severe difficulties of its own.

We might try a different defence of quasi-Kantian constructivism. We might concede that Aquinas satisfies reasonable conditions for autonomy, and that his position would be worth considering if he could show that the will essentially pursues a final good of the sort that he describes, and that morality can be derived from the final good in the way he suggests. But if he cannot show either of these things, his position is merely a logically possible way of connecting morality and autonomy, not a position that we ought to take seriously. In that case, quasi-Kantian objections damage any naturalist position that is worth taking seriously. Facts about autonomy, therefore, taken together with the falsity of naturalism, imply that value is the creation of the will. Quasi-Kantian constructivism is therefore correct, if it says that all other moral systems worth taking seriously imply heteronomy of the will.

Our view about this defence of quasi-Kantian constructivism will depend on our estimate of Aquinas' and Butler's position. We may be doubtful about such a position if we are doubtful about its claim that there are objective facts about what is suitable for rational agents. Suarez recognizes such facts in speaking of 'fitness (convenientia) to rational nature'.[47] Though the reference to rational nature distinguishes such facts from Clarke's eternal fitnesses, the claim that facts about fitnesses, as opposed to other facts about rational nature, could be objective may seem unwarranted.

Our reason for objection to such facts might be either metaphysical or epistemological. (1) According to the metaphysical objection, normative facts, described by an ineliminable normative term such as 'fitness', cannot be part of objective reality. (2) According to the epistemological objection, we have no sufficient basis for believing that anything is fitting for rational nature, in itself and apart from our choices and preferences, and so we have no basis for believing that there are any facts about such fitness.

The metaphysical objection will convince us only if we agree with something like Hume's view that moral facts are not facts in the object; but that view rests on weak arguments and on doubtful assumptions about acceptable descriptions of objective reality. From Kant's point of view, the most plausible arguments against objective normative facts show only that

---

[46] Scotus on freedom; §§366–7.   [47] Suarez on fitness; §438.

they are not facts about the phenomenal world. Even if we do not endorse transcendental idealism as a whole, we may agree with Kant's view that an argument for excluding moral facts from the world as described by empirical science is not a good argument for excluding them from objective reality altogether.

The epistemological argument is more difficult to answer decisively, since it is always open to an anti-realist to express doubts about any claim to say what is appropriate for a rational agent. But many such claims are initially plausible, and underlie many of our intuitive judgments about prudence as well as morality. Kant argues that anyone who regards herself as an end has a reason to regard others as ends too.[48] It is difficult to resist the force of such arguments unless we are convinced that there cannot be normative facts of the relevant sort; and then we seem to revert to the metaphysical argument that has already been challenged.

This is rather a short way with arguments that seek to show that constructivism is the only tenable position for anyone who seeks to take Kant's insights seriously within a post-mediaeval scientific world-view. But these points suggest why quasi-Kantian constructivism is not Kantian. Nothing about Kant in particular makes a constructivist position seem reasonable or casts any special doubt on the view that there are normative facts about objective reality. Quasi-Kantian constructivism is not especially Kantian. On the contrary, it tries to combine some Kantian normative claims with a metaphysical and epistemological position that rests on some of the least plausible Humean doctrines.

---

[48] See §961.

73

HEGEL: HISTORY AND THEORY

---

997. Ethics and the History of Ethics

Hegel believes that the study of history is central in morality and moral philosophy, just as it is central in the history of thought and of philosophy as a whole.[1] The history of thought is an account of how we understand and make explicit what we had inarticulately grasped all along. We need to reflect on the stages of the history of thought.[2] If we impatiently try to grasp the product without the process that produced it, we will miss the whole point; for we cannot grasp the product separately from the process.[3] We might suppose that once we have corrected our various false and one-sided views, or the outlooks of earlier stages in the history of thought, we can forget about them, and stick to our corrected version. Hegel, however, argues that we have no rational basis for our present view independently of the views that it corrects; to grasp its correctness, we need to consider it in comparison with the views that it corrects.

Why does Hegel believe that philosophical understanding needs this historical and developmental aspect? We might think of historical reflexion as a way of arguing for a particular theory. If we take this view, we reject a particular version of foundationalism. For an extreme foundationalist, the basic principles are self-evident; we can see that they

---

[1] 'Science sets forth this formative process in all its detail and necessity, exposing the mature configuration of everything which has already been reduced to a moment and property of Spirit. The goal is Spirit's insight into what knowing is. Impatience demands the impossible, to wit, the attainment of the end without the means. But the *length* of the path has to be endured, for one thing, each moment is necessary; and further, each moment has to be *lingered* over, because each is itself a complete individual shape, and one is only viewed in absolute perspective when its determinateness is regarded as a concrete whole, or the whole is regarded as uniquely qualified by that determination.' (*PS* §29) As far as possible I cite Hegel by sections. If necessary, I cite pages of translations or of *Werke*.

[2] 'For the real issue is not exhausted by stating it as an aim, but by carrying it out, nor is the result the actual whole, but rather the result together with the process through which it came about. The aim by itself is a lifeless universal, just as the guiding tendency is a mere drive that as yet lacks an actual existence; and the bare result is the corpse which has left the guiding tendency behind it.' (*PS* §3).

[3] 'It [sc. philosophy] is the process which begets and traverses its own moments, and this whole movement constitutes what is positive and its truth. This truth therefore includes the negative also, what would be called the false, if it could be regarded as something from which one might abstract. The evanescent itself must, on the contrary, be regarded as essential, not as something fixed, cut off from the True, and left lying who knows where outside it, any more than the truth is to be regarded as something on the other side, positive and dead. Appearance is the arising and passing away that does not itself arise and pass away, but is "in itself", and constitutes the actuality and the movement of the life of truth.' (*PS* §47).

are true without reference to their inferential relations to any other beliefs, and we ought to build our theory on them. Clarke, Price, and Reid accept this sort of foundationalism. Hegel rejects it, and infers that philosophical argument must recognize some forms of circular argument as legitimate.[4]

According to Hegel's principles, we should treat our starting point as relative and provisional, prior (as Aristotle says) 'to us', but not prior 'by nature'. We begin from apparently reasonable beliefs, to see what can be said in criticism of them. To identify reasonable criticisms, we apply some conception of what is reasonable. But this conception itself is not immune from criticism; we seek to show that it is reasonable in the light of our most basic principles, which we must arrive at by arguing from assumptions that themselves appear reasonable in the light of those principles. We cannot set out from an ultimate principle that is guaranteed to be true. Instead, we assume that the area of thought we are trying to understand is implicitly rational, and we try to make its rationality explicit, by considering reasonable objections and answers to them.[5]

In making these claims about method and justification, Hegel recognizes that, if we reject foundationalism, we need a conception of justification that relies on the inferential relations of moral principles to our other beliefs. We will make a good case for our moral principles if we can show that they do better than any other principles would do in making sense of the beliefs that we take to be reasonable. We might show this if we could show that our preferred principles carry out this task better than any other principles that have been proposed. We give a reason for preferring our preferred principles if we show that they carry out the task proposed for them, and that other principles fail, even by their own standards of adequacy, to do what they set out to do.

This conception of justification is 'dialectical', in so far as Hegel's method agrees with the method of Platonic and Aristotelian dialectic. This dialectical approach to justification is not inherently historical; it may be confined to views that seem currently reasonable. We may argue more convincingly, however, if we apply dialectical method to theories of the past as well as the present. If we simply try to defend our position against contemporaries, we run the risk of relying on assumptions that are commonly accepted now, in our social and cultural environment, but would not seem plausible in a different environment. We strengthen our position if we can show that our preferred principles make sense of the moral beliefs of people in different environments.

Even foundationalists allow this sort of appeal to history. We noticed that Reid appeals to the Greek moralists to show that our convictions about the difference between duty and

---

[4] 'Philosophy forms a circle . . . It has a beginning, an immediate factor (for it must somehow make a start), something unproved which is not a result. But the terminus a quo of philosophy is simply relative, since it must appear in another terminus as a terminus ad quem. Philosophy is a sequence which does not hang in the air; it does not begin immediately; on the contrary, it circles back into itself.' (PR §2A) Knox and Wood cite similar remarks in PM, Intro. §13–15, where Hegel also discusses the relation of philosophy to the history of philosophy, and in SL, Bk. i ('With what must the science begin?'), 67–78. Quotations from PR are taken from or based on Knox or Nisbet.

[5] '. . . you might raise here the question why we do not begin at the highest point, i.e. with the concretely true. The answer is that it is precisely the truth in the form of a result that we are looking for, and for this purpose it is essential to start by grasping the abstract concept itself. What is actual, the shape in which the concept is embodied (die Gestalt des Begriffes), is for us therefore the subsequent thing and the sequel, even if it were itself first in the actual world. Our progress is that whereby the abstract forms reveal themselves not as self-subsistent but as false.' (PR §32A).

interest are intuitive and fundamental. He answers a possible objection to our apparent intuitions by arguing that they are not simply the product of one historically limited form of moral consciousness. But we may well suspect that this historical argument threatens to undermine foundationalism; Reid relies on a dialectical argument whose justifying role seems to conflict with foundationalism.[6]

These dialectical aspects of justification give an epistemological defence of Hegel's historical reflexions. They say nothing about the metaphysical status of the truths that we claim to discover by such reflexions. We may hold that the truths we discover are objective, not constituted by anyone's beliefs or by success in carrying out any specific intellectual task. We may reasonably look for such truths by historical and dialectical reflexion if we have some reason for believing that such reflexion gives us the best prospect of finding objective truths.

The modest epistemological conception of the historical aspects of dialectical argument does not fit Hegel's position. He seems to accept the further metaphysical claim that the truth and adequacy of a philosophical theory consist only in its ability to embrace and reconcile the historically available outlooks. In that case, we do not need some further reason for believing that dialectical reflexion leads us closer to the truth; truth is constituted by the result of dialectical reflexion.

This metaphysical interpretation of dialectical reflexion commits Hegel to a form of constructivism that does not follow from a dialectical account of justification. It is reasonable to attribute a constructivist position to him, since he does not seem to admit the possibility of any further question about the truth of a position that results from dialectical reflexion. But, whether or not he endorses this view, we need not accept it if we endorse his historical and dialectical method of argument. The method raises metaphysical questions, but we need not give Hegel's answers.

998. Normative Theory and Critical Morality

To form a fuller picture of Hegel's view of moral theories and their justification, we must take account of his surprisingly hostile attitude to one recognized function of moral theory. According to critical moralists, philosophical theory starts from and appeals to common-sense moral beliefs, but it is not limited by them. In their view, a systematic theory of morality can explain, criticize, and improve the moral beliefs we started from. This normative and critical aspect of moral theory is most obvious in utilitarianism, but it is not confined to utilitarian moralists. Philosophical critics of ordinary morality claim to have compared it with principles that are closer to the truth than the assumptions of ordinary morality; and so they need some justifying reason for paying attention to the theory over ordinary morality.

In Hegel's view, these normative and critical pretensions of moral philosophy are groundless. The true principles are discovered and recognized as true only when the institutions and practices they depend on have already come into being; hence we must be

---

[6] Reid's appeal to the ancient moralists; §855. Sidgwick on dialectical argument; §§1181–2.

deceived if we suppose that we can rely on true principles to criticize or to reform existing practice.[7]

Hegel's rejection of critical morality does not follow from his account of dialectical reflexion. Even if an adequate theory must be defended as the reasonable outcome of the historical development of theories, these theories need not have been fully embodied in the practices of any society.[8] But if Hegel also assumes that the best theory at any time is the one that is embodied in the practice of its time, his anti-critical position is intelligible. We may be able to criticize the feudal system from the point of view of the industrial revolution, but we cannot criticize it from its own point of view. If moral theories are tied to some underlying practice, it is pointless to try to criticize a society by appeal to the theory that it embodies.

This attempt to match theories with underlying societies may seem to leave some room for critical morality. For why, we might ask Hegel, must the best theory at any time be completely embodied in the practice of contemporary society? If it is largely, but incompletely, embodied, criticism is still possible, if it is confined to pointing out the incomplete embodiment. If, for instance, the best defence of capitalism were a libertarian defence, a libertarian might legitimately criticize a capitalist society that does not abolish censorship, restrictions on pornography, or protections against exploitation, that conflict with thoroughly libertarian principles. This would not be fundamental criticism, but it would not be negligible or pointless. Hegel's position is too extreme if it is meant to rule out this non-fundamental criticism.

999. Critical Morality and Comprehension of the Actual

But how far does Hegel really reject critical morality? To avoid misunderstanding, we need to interpret his remarks about the possibility of criticism in connexion with his claims about the actual and the rational.[9] He claims that philosophy is the comprehension of the present and the actual (Wirklich). Here he rejects the position of philosophers who seek to go beyond the present and the actual to some external standpoint from which one constructs an ideal or a prescription for how things ought to be. If we desert the strictly philosophical

---

[7] 'One word more about giving instruction as to what the world ought to be. Philosophy in any case always comes on the scene too late to give it. As the thought of the world, it appears only when actuality is already there cut and dried after its process of formation has been completed. The teaching of the concept, which is also history's inescapable lesson, is that it is only when actuality is mature that the ideal first appears over against the real and that the ideal apprehends the same real world in its substance and builds it up for itself into the shape of an intellectual realm. . . . The owl of Minerva spreads its wings only with the falling of the dusk.' (PR, Pref. = Knox 13) Wood, HET 232–4, discusses the point of this remark.

[8] I take the phrase 'critical morality' from Hart, LLM 20: '. . . I would revive the terminology much favoured by the utilitarians of the past century, which distinguished "positive morality", the morality actually accepted and shared by a given social group, from the general moral principles used in the criticism of actual social institutions including positive morality. We may call such general principles "critical morality". . .'

[9] 'It is this very relation of philosophy to actuality which is the subject of misunderstandings, and I accordingly come back to my earlier observation that, since philosophy is explanation of the rational, it is for that very reason the comprehension of the present and the actual, not the setting up of a world beyond which exists God knows where—or rather, of which we can very well say that we know where it exists, namely in the errors of a one-sided and empty ratiocination.' (PR, Pref. = Nisbet 20).

task of comprehending our own time, we simply abandon ourselves to idle and arbitrary constructions of imagination.[10]

'The actual', however, does not refer to the institutions or practices that currently exist, but to their Aristotelian actuality (*energeia, entelecheia*), the fulfilment of their capacities.[11] From this point of view, we describe a sapling by reference to the apple tree that will (in appropriate circumstances) be its actuality. The mature apple tree bearing fruit will be both existent and also actual, because it fully expresses its essence.[12] But not every sapling will grow to the actuality that realizes its capacities, and not every apple tree realizes its actuality. If a tree has grown in poor soil, or has suffered from disease, it is a defective tree that does not fulfil the nature of an apple tree. In Hegel's terms, it exists, but is not actual.

If, then, we confine philosophy to the comprehension of the actual, we do not confine it to the comprehension of the existent.[13] An accurate exposition of the actuality of existing practices will have to make clear their present imperfections. Hence, if the present situation is imperfect, it may not be a reliable guide to the actuality.[14]

If Hegel allows this distance between existing practices and their actuality, does he cast doubt on his rejection of fundamental criticism? To find the 'actuality' of an existing practice, must we not examine it in the light of external principles? Hegel recognizes that some critical standards underlie judgments about actuality. If, for instance, we say that someone who is (from one point of view) clearly a poet is none the less not a 'real' or 'genuine' poet, we rely on some assumptions, not on mere generalizations from existing poets, about what a poet ought to do.[15] Similarly, must we not rely on critical moral principles to identify the actuality of moral practices? We cannot find the actuality of moral practices simply by considering how they are likely to develop. They might develop in better or worse ways, and to identify the better line of development, one must appeal to correct moral principles.

---

[10] 'As a philosophical composition, it [sc. this treatise] must distance itself as far as possible from the obligation (sollen) to construct a state as it ought (soll) to be; such instruction as it may contain cannot be aimed at instructing the state on how it ought to be, but rather at showing how the state, as the ethical universe, should be recognized . . . each individual is in any case a child of his time; thus philosophy too is its own time comprehended in thoughts. It is just as foolish to imagine that any philosophy can transcend its contemporary world as that an individual can overleap his own time or leap over Rhodes. If his theory does indeed transcend his own time, if it builds itself a world as it ought to be, then he certainly has an existence, but only within his opinions—a pliant medium in which the imagination can construct anything it pleases.' (PR, Pref. 21–2, Nisbet).

[11] Hegel explains his position by reference to Aristotle: '. . . although actuality certainly is the principle of the Aristotelian philosophy, it is not the vulgar actuality of what is immediately at hand, but the idea as actuality. . . . Aristotle calls the Platonic idea a mere *dunamis*, and establishes in opposition to Plato that the idea, which both equally recognize to be the only truth, is essentially to be viewed as an *energeia*, in other words, as the inward which is quite to the fore, or as the unity of inner and outer, or as actuality, in the emphatic sense here given to the word.' (Logic §142 = Wallace 202).

[12] See Logic §6 = Wallace 10 (quoted below). Cf. Wood, HET 10.

[13] 'For what is actual is rational. One must, however, know, distinguish what is in fact rational. In common life all is actual, but there is a difference between the world of appearance and actuality. The actual has also an external existence, which displays arbitrariness and contingency, like a tree, a horse, a plant, which in nature come into existence. What is on the surface in the moral sphere, men's action, involves much that is evil, and might in many ways be better. Once one recognizes the substance, one must penetrate beneath the surface. Men will ever be wicked and depraved, but this is not the Idea.' (LHP. ii 95–6 H&S = Werke xix, 110–11) Tr. by Wood, HET 10.

[14] See Neuhouser, FHST 257.

[15] 'So far is actuality [die Wirklichkeit], as distinguished from mere appearance, and primarily presenting a unity of inward and outward, from being in contrariety with reason, that it is rather thoroughly reasonable, and everything which is not reasonable must on that very ground cease to be held actual. The same view may be traced in the usages of educated speech, which declines to give the name of real [or "actual"; wirklichen] poet or real statesman to a poet or a statesman who can do nothing really meritorious or reasonable.' (Enc. Logic §142 = Wallace 201).

From Hegel's point of view, this supposedly Hegelian defence of fundamental moral criticism may appear naive. He sometimes suggests that criticism and 'oughts' miss the essential point; a purely critical approach to an existing practice or system suggests wrongly that philosophers should occupy themselves with the imperfections of existing practices. Imperfections can be taken for granted, but the philosopher should concentrate on the quite different task of expounding the actuality that is imperfectly embodied in existing practices.[16] Plato's *Republic*, as Hegel interprets it, confirms this view. For it is no mere utopia, but a clear expression of the ethical views underlying Greek society.[17] Even the Cynics were not as out of step as they might seem, since the form of their protest against Athenian life was itself determined by the forms of Athenian life (§195A).

It is difficult to evaluate this claim about Plato. It is true that his ideal state has many of the characteristic features of a Greek city, and that Plato himself regards it as the only true city (*Republic*, 422e). But how are we to decide whether Hegel is right to claim that Plato embodies Greek ethical life? He modifies the moral and political practices and outlooks of his contemporaries in accordance with his own moral and political principles. Nor is he the only philosopher to do this. Plato, Aristotle, and Zeno, among others, have different conceptions of the right direction of development for the Greek city. Each of them might be taken to present an account of its actuality. Zeno's account requires the most radical change, Plato somewhat less, and Aristotle less still; but each describes a moral and social order quite different from any Greek city that he knew. How are we to decide who captures the actuality of Greek ethical life?

One might answer that the best embodiment of Greek ethical life is the one that revises and reconstructs contemporary practice in accord with true moral and political principles. In that case, we ought to prefer Plato's embodiment over Aristotle's, if and only if Plato's principles are truer than Aristotle's or Zeno's. This answer, however, takes us back to appeals to the 'ought to be' of the sort that Hegel repudiates. His views about actuality seem to introduce the moralistic prescriptions that he tries to avoid.

In the case of Greek moral and political theory, it is difficult to see how Hegel's claims about actuality could rule out critical morality. Socrates, Plato, and the Stoics seem to criticize quite sharply some of the central moral assumptions of their time; Socrates' rejection of retaliation, Plato's feminism, and the Stoic doctrine that only the fine is good, seem to be

---

[16] 'When understanding turns this "ought" against trivial external and transitory objects, against social regulations or conditions, which very likely possess a great relative importance for a certain time and special circles, it may often be right. In such a case the intelligent observer may meet much that fails to satisfy the general requirements of right; for who is not acute enough to see a great deal in his own surroundings which is really far from being as it ought to be? But such acuteness is mistaken in the conceit that, when it examines these objects and pronounces what they ought to be, it is dealing with questions of philosophic science. The object of philosophy is the Idea: and the Idea is not so impotent as merely to have a right or an obligation to exist without actually existing. The object of philosophy is an actuality of which those objects, social regulations and conditions, are only the superficial outside.' (*Logic* §6 = Wallace 10).

[17] '. . . even Plato's *Republic*, which passes proverbially as an empty ideal, is in essence nothing but an interpretation of the nature of Greek ethical life.' (*PR*, Pref.) '. . . Plato has in fact represented Greek Ethical life (Sittlichkeit) according to its substantial mode, for it is the Greek state-life which constitutes the true content of the Platonic Republic. Plato is not the man to dabble in abstract theories and principles; his truth-loving mind has recognized and represented the truth, and this could not be anything else than the truth of the world he lived in, the truth of this *one* spirit which lived in him as well as in Greece. No man can overleap his time, the spirit of his time is his spirit also; but the point at issue is, to recognize that spirit by its content.' (*LHP* iii 96 H&S = Brown219 = *Werke*, xix 111).

doctrines that are far out of step with their time. The same might be said of early Christianity in its cultural context.

Hegel recognizes some of these points. He acknowledges that Socrates was out of step with his time, because he expressed the point of view of the individual conscience claiming its right to be heard.[18] Socrates anticipates the fuller expression of the individual conscience that results from the rise of Christianity.[19] He reflects an inadequacy in contemporary society; indeed Hegel even claims (with no historical basis) that Athenian democracy had fallen into ruin in Socrates' time.[20] But it is not clear how Hegel identifies this inadequacy unless he relies on moral principles that (on his own account) Socrates' contemporaries did not acknowledge. If we reply that Socrates was closer to the actuality of Athenian society, we seem to rely on standards external to Athenian society. Indeed, we seem to rely on critical morality.

It is difficult, then, to find any plausible Hegelian reason for denying the possibility or legitimacy of critical morality. Moreover, Hegel does not always seem to deny its possibility, since his account of Socrates assumes such a possibility.

1000. Historical and Analytic Approaches to Morality

Though Hegel looks at ethics in the light of history, he does not always have the same sort of historical and social framework in mind. Different sorts of frameworks seem to have different roles in his arguments.

In the *Phenomenology*, different ethical outlooks belong to different historical periods and to successive forms of society. The attitude of Ethical life belongs to Greek history and society. In this stage of historical development the individual is expected to follow the social rules and customs, and no further ethical or moral (in our normal sense) questions are raised. The focus of attention is the life of the state, and the ethical rules are designed for its benefit. The modern world is influenced by Christianity, especially Protestant Christianity, anticipated by Socrates. Hence it takes genuinely moral action to depend on the agent's conscientious attitude to his actions. According to this view, an action is not legitimate simply because it is required by social norms; it must also be approved as right by the individual's conscience relying on its own norms. This point of view is characteristic of what Hegel calls 'Morality'; it is systematically expressed by Kant, but it also underlies the attitudes discussed in the *Phenomenology* under the heads of 'Conscience' and 'The Beautiful Soul'.

In the *Philosophy of Right*, by contrast, different outlooks do not seem to form a historical sequence, because they are connected with different institutions in a single society. The family, Civil Society, and the State correspond to three different aspects of a modern

---

[18] 'As one of the commoner features of history (e.g., in Socrates, the Stoics, and others), the tendency to look deeper into oneself and to know and determine from within oneself what is right and good appears in ages when what is recognized as right and good in contemporary manners cannot satisfy the will of better men.' (*PR* §138) Cf. 279, 166A; *LHP* i 397 H&S.

[19] See also *PR* §§62, 124, 185, 270A.

[20] 'Only in ages where the actual world is a hollow, spiritless, and unsettled existence may the individual be permitted to flee from actuality and retreat into his inner life. Socrates made his appearance at the time when Athenian democracy had fallen into ruin.' (*PR* §138).

European society, as Hegel understands it. His division appears to be analytical and synchronic, and does not seem to describe any historical succession. His description of each outlook without reference to the others abstracts from the whole moral and social structure of a contemporary society. Hence, for instance, a civil servant by his profession takes the universal attitude of the State; a company director in his professional role takes the attitude of a member of Civil Society; and when each of them goes home in the evening, he looks at his private life from the ethical point of view proper to the family. Ethical life as a whole includes these different elements; and we understand it partly by understanding the elements, their conflicts, and the resolutions of these conflicts in Ethical life.

Hegel suggests that the moral questions arising in one of these social contexts are not necessarily those that arise in another. In relations between the State and accused criminals, we may take procedural fairness and separation of the roles of judge and prosecutor to be very important. But we may not take them to be equally important in relations between close friends or members of a family. In families and friendships, sympathy and affection may be needed to resolve disputes in the right way; but they are not relevant in the same way to disputes between the State and individual citizens.

Yet another analytical division of moral outlooks treats them as distinguishable, though perhaps inseparable, aspects of a single society, not necessarily assigned (as in the previous division) to different sub-groups or institutions in a society. In the *Philosophy of Right*, Abstract Right and Morality seem to be two aspects of a society. Abstract Right, including law and positive morality are features of every State; reflexion on them provokes the attitude of Morality asserting its claims in opposition to the merely external demands of Abstract Right. The external provisions of Abstract Right are reconciled with the internal outlook of Morality in the conditions of Ethical life, including Family, Civil Society, and State.[21]

Abstract Right, Morality, and Ethical life do not, on this view, form a historical succession. Nor do they belong to different institutions in a given society. On the contrary, they are different aspects of one society; Abstract Right and Morality perform their proper roles without exaggeration or one-sidedness when they are guided by the Ethical Life of the State.

If we think of these three outlooks as aspects of a single normative structure, we will not be tempted to think of them as historically successive, but we will suppose that these three outlooks will be characteristic, to some degree, of every State. This view of their relation seems to conflict with the view that primitive Ethical life and the subsequent Morality are characteristic of two different historical stages that result in a higher Ethical life.

We can also understand different phases of morality more psychologically, so that they reveal different phases of the alienated and divided self. The unity of Greek Ethical life is broken by the individual's awareness of his own aims and aspirations, and his recognition

---

[21] 'The sphere of right and that of morality cannot exist independently; they must have the ethical life as their support and foundation. For right lacks the moment of subjectivity, which in turn belongs solely to morality, so that neither of the two moments has any independent actuality. Only the infinite, the Idea, is actual. Right exists only as a branch of a whole, or as a climbing plant attached to a tree which has firm roots in and for itself.' (*PR* §141A).

that they do not always coincide with the demands of his society. Moreover, his recognition of conflict is not simply the result of the demands imposed by his society. His conception of himself and his aims may also be fragmented by other political, religious, and moral influences. The Roman Empire, the mediaeval Christian world, and the early modern Civil Society all frustrate some of a person's reasonable aspirations. In reaction to this frustration, people reject, explicitly or implicitly, this form of life and thought. The Roman Empire treats a person as a purely legal entity without political initiative. The mediaeval world speaks to his religious aspirations, but makes him an exile in this world, unable to identify himself with his present life and society. We can understand later outlooks as revolts, perhaps unconscious, against the one-sided aspects of a given society.

The two major moral theories discussed by Hegel are open to the same sort of objection. Utilitarianism, embodied especially in Civil Society, treats people as pleasure-seeking atoms, and regards their ethical and social relations as instruments of pleasure, neglecting other ends that people might pursue for their own sake. It therefore ignores the aspects of a person that do not take a purely instrumental attitude to action. On the other side, Kant's defence of the moral side of persons over-compensates for the errors of the utilitarian outlook; for he values only the moral will following universal principles, and he rejects other desires for being merely 'sensuous' and opposed to morality. The correct system will correct the errors that cause this internal division of the self.

A further option for comparing and evaluating different moral outlooks is acknowledged only implicitly by Hegel. Instead of connecting different outlooks with successive societies or with complementary features of one society, we might think of them as conflicting and competing interpretations of one society—either defending it or criticizing it or both. Aristotelian and Stoic ethics represent, according to Hegel, successive phases of Greek ethical thinking, but different people also accepted them at the same time, as different ways of understanding contemporary ethical views. In modern societies, utilitarianism and Kantian ethics seem to express different ways of understanding contemporary moral beliefs and aspirations. Each of the conflicting theories seems to offer rival accounts and revisions of the same ethical phenomena. Green and Bradley both assess utilitarian and Kantian theory to compare their degrees of adequacy and inadequacy. Hegel does not compare them in exactly the same way; but his general views seem to imply that such a comparison is legitimate.

These different standards of comparison for moral theories sometimes make it difficult to examine Hegel's judgments on them, since he may be asking different questions about them in different places. Sometimes his objections to a particular view that concerns him do not—whether he realizes this or not—directly affect the larger outlook to which this view belongs. This possibility is relevant to his discussion of Kant. Hegel may be right to say that Kant contains the point of view of Morality, which interests Hegel as a phase in a development that he seeks to exhibit. But if Morality is not the whole of Kant's outlook, Hegel's objections to Morality may not undermine Kant's position as a whole. To identify the point of view of Morality we may need to abstract from certain features of Kant's actual position; while this abstraction may be legitimate, given Hegel's purpose in a specific discussion, it may not be fair to Kant's position.

1001. Hegel and Idealist Moral Philosophy

Hegel's views develop some of the early discussion of Kant's moral philosophy.[22] They influence later idealist moral philosophy, and in particular the views of Green and Bradley. These later idealists are not slavish followers of Hegel; even if they were, they would not have found in Hegel an unambiguous guide to moral philosophy. They construct an idealist moral theory that has no clear source in Hegel himself. To see what they draw from Hegel, what they add, and what they elaborate, we should compare them with Hegel himself. It may turn out that we are wrong to treat them as genuinely Hegelian moralists;[23] but we can decide this question only after considering what Hegel has to say, and what it would take to make someone a genuinely Hegelian moralist.

The only moral theory that Hegel discusses at length is Kant's theory; and he does not even discuss Kant purely from the point of view of a moral philosopher. He does not examine the rationalist, sentimentalist, and utilitarian views that form the background for Kant's theory. Green and Bradley partly eliminate this shortcoming in Hegel. Green applies Hegelian views specifically to the arguments and disputes in moral philosophy that occupy Kant and his predecessors. Bradley continues this approach by arguing against Sidgwick and Mill. Green tries to focus Hegelian views on the problems that are defined by Hobbes, Butler, Hume, and Kant; and in doing so he allows us to make some idealist views more precise.

This difference between Hegel and later idealists is not simply the result of Hegel's silence or negligence. It is difficult to identify Hegel's comments on the proper concerns of moral philosophy partly because he believes that moral philosophy is not a distinct discipline. He does not take it to be concerned with questions that can be separated from those of metaphysics, political theory, or cultural history. In his view, moral theories are not formed by reflexion on human nature, or human sentiments, or rational wills, in abstraction from particular social and cultural circumstances. Nor should we try to evaluate them by appeal to non-historical rational standards that are appropriate for all moral theories. It is not clear how extreme a position Hegel maintains about the connexion between moral theory and social frameworks, or what would follow from it; but it is not surprising if his views make him disinclined to pursue moral theory in the way that most previous moral philosophers pursue it.

On this issue, the later idealists seem less extreme than Hegel. They address the arguments and claims of previous moralists, and put forward their own views by appeal to the considerations that are recognized as relevant to moral philosophy. One might argue that they miss the essential point in Hegel's approach to ethics. Alternatively, perhaps they separate the more reasonable from the less reasonable aspects of his approach.

1002. The Will and Freedom

After we have taken notice of the historical dimension of Hegel's inquiry, and of the difference between his outlook and the moral theories of his predecessors, we may be

---

[22] On Hegel's reaction to defenders and critics of Kant see Ameriks, *KFA*, ch. 7.
[23] Wood, *HET* 44, expresses doubt about whether the British idealists are really Hegelian.

surprised by the familiarity of his starting point. Though his argument leads him through cultural and historical reflexions that are foreign to Aquinas, Butler, and Kant, he begins where they do. He claims that the main subject of the philosophy of right is the will and its freedom.[24] Since we necessarily conceive the will as free, our preliminary analysis should identify the freedom that is the origin of right.[25] But this preliminary analysis does not give us an account of freedom as 'actual'; such an account requires us to grasp the world of mind 'brought forth out of itself'.

Our preliminary analysis of the will and its freedom does not offer a full account of right. Still, we must set out from a conception that is clear and definite enough to allow some ways of making freedom actual and to exclude others. Green and Bradley agree with Hegel in offering a preliminary analysis as a guide to their later argument. That is why they regard true morality as the realization of the self that we implicitly grasp in recognizing ourselves as agents.

According to Hegel's analysis, the determinate element in the will is its awareness of a specific intentional object of its desire, and the indeterminate element is the will's awareness of itself.[26] If we are to realize the capacities of the will, we must want something in particular that gives a determinate content to our willing. But we are aware of something more than this particular object.[27] Though I want this specific object, I also want it for myself, and I want it because it is a concern of my will, which is to be distinguished from the particular desire for this object.[28] In a normal act of willing and choosing I am aware of myself as 'standing above' my impulses, and as having 'put myself' into them, or (equivalently) as having put them into my ego. It is up to me whether or not to put myself into them; in that respect I am, as Aquinas puts it, 'in control' (dominus) of my actions.[29]

What is the difference between the self and the particular objects of desire? If I consider my particular desires, I find 'a medley and multiplicity of impulses, each of which is merely "my

---

[24] 'The basis of right is, in general, mind; its precise place and point of origin is the will. The will is free, so that freedom is both the substance of right and its goal, while the system of right is the realm of freedom made actual, the world of mind brought forth out of itself like a second nature.' (PR §4).

[25] 'Freedom, I mean is just as fundamental a character of the will as weight is of bodies. If we say matter is "heavy", we might mean that this predicate is only contingent; but it is nothing of the kind, for nothing in matter is without weight. Matter is rather weight itself. Heaviness constitutes the body and is the body. The same is the case with freedom and the will, since the free entity is the will. Will without freedom is an empty word, while freedom is actual only as will, as subject.' (PR §4A).

[26] 'The will contains (a) the element of pure indeterminacy or that pure reflexion of the ego into itself which involves the dissipation of every restriction and every content either immediately presented by nature, by needs, desires, and impulses, or given and determined by any means whatever. This is the unrestricted infinity of absolute abstraction or universality, the pure thought of oneself.' (PR §5) '(b) At the same time, the ego is also the transition from undifferentiated indeterminacy to the differentiation, determination, and positing of a determinacy as a content and object. Now further, this content may either be given by nature or engendered by the concept of mind. Through this positing of itself as something determinate, the ego steps in principle into determinate existence.' (§6).

[27] 'The ego determines itself in so far as it is the relating of negativity to itself. As this self-relation, it is indifferent to this determinacy; it knows it as something which is its own, something which is only ideal, a mere possibility by which it is not constrained and in which it is confined only because it has put itself into it.—This is the freedom of the will...' (PR §7).

[28] 'An animal has impulses, desires, inclinations, but it has no will and must obey its impulse, if nothing external deters it. Man, however, the wholly undetermined, stands above his impulses and may make them his own, put them in himself as his own. An impulse is something natural, but to put it into my ego depends on my will which thus cannot fall back on the plea that the impulse has its basis in nature.' (PR §11A).

[29] Aquinas on control of one's actions; §243.

desire" but exists alongside other desires which are likewise all "mine". . . .' (PR §12). I cannot take myself to consist wholly in this particular desire, since I recognize that I now have, have had, will have, and might have other desires that equally belong, or have belonged, or will belong, or might belong, to me. And so I must recognize that I persist through changes in my desires, and that the concerns of my persisting self are not the same as those that occupy me in this particular desire. Here Hegel states the conception of a temporally extended self that underlies Butler's and Reid's views on self-love.

However, the mere awareness of a self that persists through a sequence of desires is not all that Hegel has in mind. If this were all we could say about our conception of ourselves, the self and the will would be nothing more than a sequence of desires, and hence (as Hume puts it) nothing more than a bundle of perceptions.[30] Hegel, however, adds a further point that Butler and Reid recognize in their discussion of rational self-love. I do not simply recognize a sequence of desires as mine; I also recognize that it is also to some extent up to me which desires will be mine. I 'put myself' into some specific desires rather than others because I take them to be suitably related to other desires that I attribute to myself. If I make a desire my own or 'put myself' into a desire, I do not only recognize that I have it, but I also favour it as appropriate for myself.

Why might we, or why should we, favour or accept one desire or another? The minimal attitude would be to favour every single desire as it happens to come along. But Hegel rejects this attitude. A self that takes a present-centred attitude is self-destructive, because it fails to recognize its equal reality in the future, and fails to apply the reasons derived from its future reality to its present choice.[31] Hegel's criticism of this attitude assumes that an ineliminable reason for my approving of a present desire is my conception of it as mine. If that is my reason, I have no reason to refuse to consider other desires that I also recognize as mine even though they are not present.[32]

One might argue that we can regulate desires without appeal to any standard that is external to them. Perhaps we can regulate the satisfaction of any given desire simply by reference to its implications for the satisfaction of my other desires. This regulative principle frees me from exclusive preoccupation with each desire as it comes along, and it seems to suggest a possible 'hierarchy' of desires. But it does not seem to give me clear directions for modifying my desires; for consideration of their implications makes us aware of many different sorts of implications for other desires, and many different possible courses of action that favour one or another desire. Until we form a view about what considerations and implications matter, we have no standard for deciding which desires to favour. Hegel believes, therefore, that a mere hierarchy of desires is a waste of time.[33] If we simply compare impulses with each other, and do not apply any standard external to them, we will reach no satisfactory principle for ordering them.

---

[30] Hume on the self; §730.

[31] 'Now if I neglect all the others and put myself in one of them by itself, I find myself under a restriction which destroys me, since just by so doing I have surrendered my universality, which is a system of all impulses.' (PR §17A).

[32] Reid on prudence and the self; §§839–40.

[33] 'But it is just as little help to make a mere hierarchy of impulses—a device to which the Understanding usually resorts—since no criterion for so ordering them is available here, and therefore the demand for such a hierarchy runs out in the tedium of generalities.' (PR §17A).

The first external standard that Hegel considers is a conception of maximum satisfaction of desires over time.[34] In thinking about happiness, 'the thinker is not content with the momentary but requires happiness in a whole' (§20A), and so we apply a standard external to a particular impulse. As Hegel conceives happiness, however, it still involves simply 'universal pleasure', and its content 'lies in everyone's subjectivity and feeling' (§20A). And so it cannot apply any standard that is external to the satisfaction of particular impulses.

Happiness is insufficiently universal, because 'there is still not present in it any genuine unity of form and content' (§20A). In saying that the universality of the will is insufficiently recognized, Hegel means that we do not adequately recognize the difference between the rational will and the particular content that is suggested for it by particular impulses. When we reflect on our will and the rational self that we express in it, we see (according to Hegel) that we are not simply to be identified with our desires, even with some collection of them. We also have the capacity to form, criticize, and reject desires.[35] We have a satisfactory content for the will only when the content reflects these further rational capacities in the appropriate way.

1003. The Free Will and its Objects

The separation of non-rational impulses from the independent, critical outlook of the rational will may lead us to a false conclusion. If we suppose that any definite content for our will is a limitation of its freedom, we will identify the free element in choice and action with the self-conscious rational element, and the unfree element with the content. This attitude, however, is self-defeating. For if we take the extreme view that any determinate content limits the freedom and self-expression of the rational will, we frustrate our aim of expressing our free and rational will in the appropriate sort of choice and action; for the extreme view implies that no choice or action can appropriately express the free will.

Hegel's views about freedom reflect an intellectualist as opposed to a voluntarist conception.[36] He does not suggest that the relevant sort of freedom requires the truth of indeterminism. In fact, he rejects the indeterminist analysis of freedom by suggesting that it identifies freedom with arbitrariness (§15) and chance (§15A). This is a standard intellectualist objection; voluntarism makes the allegedly rational will the opposite of what it is supposed to be, because it makes the will subject to some sort of chance that is the opposite of rational determination.

Hegel believes that a voluntarist error about freedom is the source of Kant's conception of the free and rational will. Kant accepts one aspect of the intellectualist conception of

---

[34] 'When reflexion is brought to bear on impulses, they are imaged, estimated, compared with one another, with their means of satisfaction and their consequences, etc., and with a sum of satisfaction (i.e. with happiness).' (PR §20).

[35] 'As immanent and so positive, the determinations of the immediate will are good; thus man is said to be by nature good. But, in so far as these determinations are natural and thus are in general opposed to freedom and the concept of mind, and hence negative, they must be uprooted, and so man is said to be by nature evil.' (PR §18) 'As mind, man is a free substance which is in the position of not allowing itself to be determined by natural impulse. When man's condition is immediate and mentally undeveloped, he is in a situation in which he ought not to be and from which he must free himself.' (§18A).

[36] On intellectualism, rationalism, and voluntarism see Aquinas, §§258–9; Hobbes, §470; Hutcheson, §637.

the will, in so far as he connects freedom with reason (in contrast to Hobbes and Hume); but he also accepts one aspect of voluntarism, in so far as he connects freedom with absence of determination. This combination of intellectualist and voluntarist elements in Kant produces an incoherent account of free and rational choice. According to Hegel, 'In every philosophy of reflexion, like Kant's, . . . freedom is nothing but this empty self-activity' (§15). The expression of freedom requires the right particular content for our choice (the intellectualist view), but determination by any particular content is the negation of freedom (the voluntarist view); and so the free and rational will lacks the content that is necessary for it to express itself. This is Hegel's diagnosis of the error in Kant's conception of freedom; and if we attend to the aspects of Kant's theory that rely on indeterminism, we must recognize the justice of some of Hegel's objections.

Kant's identification of the rational will with the will guided by universal principles, but free of any specific end or aim, presupposes a false conception of the relation of the individual and the particular to reason and will. Hegel criticizes Kant's account of right as 'the restriction which makes it possible for my freedom or self-will to co-exist with the self-will of each and all according to a universal law' (§29).[37] This account suggests falsely that the universal and the rational is necessarily a restriction on the individual. Hegel attributes the same error to Rousseau.[38] He is not entirely fair to Kant and Rousseau, but he raises an important issue about dualism. Their position, in his view, presupposes a sharp division between the individual's private, self-seeking aims unaffected by practical reason, and the universal, rational point of view that restricts the possible satisfactions of particular inclinations, but does not change the character of the inclinations.

In opposition to the dualism of Kant and Rousseau, Hegel aims at an account of the will that displays a third aspect besides unrestricted universality and determinate particularity (§§5–6). The third aspect is the unity of the first two, 'particularity reflected into itself and so brought back to universality, i.e., . . . individuality' (§7). The unity of the will 'is individuality, not individuality in its immediacy as a unit, our first idea of individuality, but individuality in accordance with its concept' (§7).[39] The concept contains an aspect of potentiality that needs to be actualized.[40]

These claims about the possible unification of the two aspects of the will rest on a controversial assumption about the possible scope of practical reason. Hegel's claims might provoke a Humean reaction. We might admit that rational agents display a universal and

---

[37] Cf. and contrast Kant, *MdS* 230.

[38] 'The definition of right which I have quoted involves that way of looking at the matter, especially popular since Rousseau, according to which what is fundamental, substantive, and primary is supposed to be the will of a single person in his own private self-will, not the absolute or rational will, and mind as a particular individual, not mind as it is in its truth. Once this principle is adopted, of course the rational can come on the scene only as a restriction on the type of freedom which this principle involves, and so also not as something immanently rational but only as an external abstract universal.' (*PR* §29).

[39] Cf. *Enc. Logic* §§163–5 = Wallace 291–7. Here Hegel acknowledges Rousseau more generously: 'The distinction . . . between what is merely in common (bloss Geminschaftlichen) and what is truly universal (wahrhaft Allgemeinen) is strikingly expressed by Rousseau in his famous "Contrat Social" when he says that the laws of a state must spring from the universal will (volonté générale), but need not on that account be the will of all (volonté de tous). Rousseau would have made a sounder contribution towards a theory of the state if he had always kept this distinction in sight.' (§163).

[40] 'Now what exists purely implicitly in this way does not yet exist in its actuality. Man is implicitly rational, but he must also become explicitly so by struggling to create himself, not only by going forth from himself but also by building himself up within.' (*PR* §10A).

rational element in their choice, in addition to the purely determinate and particular element found in non-rational animals. We are capable of explicit instrumental reasoning about our desires and their satisfaction, and we modify our desires as a result of this reasoning. The questions raised by instrumental reasoning are universal, in the sense that they are not specific to this or that person's initial inclinations. But they do not constrain anyone's inclinations very much. We unite the universal and the particular aspects of the will in so far as our inclinations are affected by our instrumental causal judgments.

If something more than this uninteresting result is to emerge from Hegel's claims about unification, Hume must be wrong. Kant must be wrong also. Against Hume, Kant believes that the universal side of the will supports something more than instrumental reasoning; it yields the categorical imperative of morality. But, in Hegel's view, this does not inform the content of inclinations; it simply restrains them and opposes them. If Hegel is right and unification goes beyond Hume and Kant, the universal side of the will must inform the particular inclinations. If we can express freedom and rationality in the content of some choices rather than others, the right choices have some content that differs from the content of the wrong choices, in so far as it appropriately expresses the free and rational will. The task of a theory is to say what this content is.

1004. Content for the Free Will

The free and rational will that fully expresses itself is not unreflectively satisfied with the content that is offered to it by non-rational impulses or by its social environment. An unreflective will cannot assert the critical outlook that is essential to the rational will, and its rationality remains merely implicit and potential ('in itself'), not explicit ('for itself').[41] However, the will ought not to rest content with merely asserting its difference from the initial impulses; that is the sterile Kantian terminus. It must be able to identify itself with some particular content; but it must have something better than the unreflective basis that it began from.

We do not satisfy Hegel's demands if we simply choose, by an arbitrary act of will, to identify ourselves with some particular content.[42] That would be only one step further than Kantian arbitrariness. In such a case, the rational will would not treat any particular inclination as especially appropriate for itself, and so it would have no reason to endorse one rather than another. In Hegel's view, we must discover the appropriate content for the rational will, since we cannot simply stipulate it by an act of endorsement. We can discover whether this or that inclination gives the appropriate content for the will only if we understand the rational self better.[43]

Hegel's suggestion is not completely original. Butler and Reid connect self-love with one's conception of oneself and with the difference between strength and authority. Their

---

[41] On being for itself see PM §398.   [42] This might be understood as an existentialist reaction to Kant. See §1343.

[43] 'Underlying the demand for the *purification of the drives* is the general idea that they should be freed from the *form* of their immediate natural determinacy and from the subjectivity and contingency of their content, and restored to their substantial essence. The truth behind this indeterminate demand is that the drives should become the rational system of the will's determination; to grasp them thus in terms of the concept is the content of the science of right.' (PR §19).

conception of self-love returns to the conception that Aquinas explains in his account of the ultimate end. To guide our actions by a true conception of the ultimate end is to form and to execute our desires in accordance with some view of the perfection and fulfilment of our nature and capacities as rational agents.

This introduction of perfection, fulfilment, and realization of capacities recalls Aristotle's claims about happiness and the human function. We might suppose, then, that the eudaemonist outlook of Greek ethics will satisfy Hegel's demand for a unification of the universal and the particular. It seems to give a fairly clear idea of how rational reflexion can change the content of specific inclinations; and this idea is clarified further by the detailed accounts of the different virtues of character.

To see whether this is the sort of unification that Hegel has in mind, we must ask two questions. First, does he believe that Aristotelian eudaemonism fulfils his demands? Secondly, if he does not think so, is he right? We might find either that he is too easily satisfied with Aristotelian eudaemonism and that it does not satisfy his criteria, or that he is unreasonably dissatisfied with it, because he does not recognize that it satisfies his criteria.

1005. Classical Greek Ethics

Our questions about possible ways of satisfying Hegel's demand for the unification of particular and universal in the will lead naturally into a discussion of his views on Greek ethics. Though this discussion takes us away from the order of topics in the *Philosophy of Right*, it will raise some helpful questions about the later stages of his argument. Hegel is interested in 'Greek ethics' both in the broad sense that includes the moral practices and reflexions known to us through Greek history and culture and in the narrow sense that includes the efforts of Greek philosophers to give a theoretical account of morality.

Hegel sees a connexion between the two sorts of 'ethics' he discusses. He tries to understand Greek moral theory as the rational expression of the outlook that he finds embodied in Greek society and culture. Greek philosophers recognize different moral phenomena from those we recognize, and it is natural to suppose that they are influenced by the moral phenomena that they find around them. In recognizing this fact, Hegel is a pioneer in a contextual approach to Greek ethics (and to the history of thought more generally) that tries to avoid anachronistic questions. Such an approach tries to distinguish the questions asked by the thinkers we study from the questions that strike us as natural.[44]

In Hegel's view, Greek society and the Greek moral outlook express an un-self-conscious form of Ethical life. Citizens identify themselves, their interests, and their values, with the way of life of their community. This identification is not self-conscious, because individuals lack a definite conception of themselves as something distinct from their socially imposed roles. Hence they cannot suppose they have freely accepted their social roles as suitable to them; for they have never conceived the self that can freely accept something. The difference

---

[44] Some Hegelian views of Greek ethics are discussed by White, *ICGE*.

between customs, social demands, and freely accepted roles has not become explicit for them. In the light of Hegel's analysis of the will, we can see that this sort of Ethical life inadequately expresses the freedom of the will.

Hegel believes Greek moral philosophy is inadequate in the same way. He regards Plato's *Republic* as 'an interpretation of the nature of Greek ethical life' (PR, Pref., p. 10). The very accuracy of its interpretation implies that it shares the limitations of the Greek moral outlook.[45] Plato sees 'subjective freedom' simply as the capricious rejection of moral reason and order, and so he tries to regulate his ideal state on principles that prescribe the maximum integration of individuals with their social roles and give only very limited scope to the operation of purely personal preference.[46] Plato cannot give the appropriate place to the subjective freedom of individuals who are conscious of themselves as free, because he has not seen the real nature of subjective freedom. In particular, he has not seen the difference between freedom and the mere satisfaction of impulse or caprice.[47]

When Hegel claims that Greek ethics does not consider the claims of subjective freedom, he does not mean simply that it gives too little attention to the demands and claims of the individual. He also intends the stronger claim that it does not consider these demands and claims as having any possible significance against the demands of the community, or as liable to conflict with the community. The demands that go unrecognized in Greek society and Greek ethics are asserted by the Christian consciousness, especially in its Protestant form, especially in its Lutheran form, as Hegel interprets it.

1006. Moral Theory and Classical Greek Society

This claim about Greek society and Greek ethics is difficult to reconcile with the character of Achilles in the *Iliad*, or Ajax in Sophocles' play, or Pericles' Funeral Speech, or Socrates' refusal to submit to an order to give up philosophy, or Thrasymachus' account of justice.

---

[45] 'In his *Republic*, Plato displays the substance of ethical life in its ideal beauty and truth; but he could only cope with the principle of self-subsistent particularity, which in its day had forced its way into Greek ethical life, by setting up in opposition to it his purely substantial state . . . The principle of the self-subsistent inherently infinite personality of the individual, the principle of subjective freedom, is denied its right in the purely substantial form which Plato gave to mind in its actuality. This principle dawned in an inward form in the Christian religion and in an external form (and therefore in one linked with abstract universality) in the Roman world. It is historically subsequent to the Greek world, and the philosophic reflexion which descends to its depth is likewise subsequent to the substantial Idea of Greek philosophy.' (PR §185) On Christianity, cf. PM §482: 'Whole continents, Africa and the East, have never had this Idea [sc. "the abstract concept of full-blown liberty"], and are without it still. The Greeks and Romans, Plato and Aristotle, even the Stoics, did not have it. . . . It was through Christianity that this Idea came into the world.' On the different types of freedom see Inwood's note in Hegel, PM, ad loc.

[46] '. . . it might seem that universal ends would be more readily attainable if the universal absorbed the strength of the particulars in the way described, for instance, in Plato's *Republic*. But this, too, is only an illusion, since both universal and particular turn into one another and exist only for and by means of one another. If I further my ends, I further the ends of the universal, and this in turn furthers my end.' (§184A) 'In Plato's state, subjective freedom does not count because people have their occupations assigned to them by the Guardians. In many oriental states, this assignment is determined by birth. But subjective freedom, which must be respected, demands that individuals should have free choice in this matter.' (§261A) Hegel is wrong about the *Republic*. The rulers assign citizens only to classes, and hence to types of occupation. They do not decide whether someone is to be a weaver as opposed to a tanner.

[47] Hegel's view of Plato's *Republic* and of its relation to Greek societies is well described and criticized by Inwood, 'Sittlichkeit'.

These examples can hardly be described without attributing to some Greeks clear recognition of the possibilities that Hegel takes to be closed to them.

Hegel's judgment about Greek society seems to rely on his view of the *Republic*, or, more precisely, his view of the ideal state described in the *Republic*, and on his assumption that Plato simply articulates the common presuppositions of Greek or Athenian society. His argument does not seem to proceed in the right order. We might expect him to justify his claim that the Platonic ideal state articulates the common presuppositions of Athenian society; a justification would apparently require a rather detailed study of Athens in Plato's time, and a detailed comparison with the Platonic ideal state. The results of such a study and comparison would probably not support Hegel's claim.

Hegel dispenses with this detailed study because he is already convinced by his claim about the Platonic ideal state, and so believes it is reasonable to read features of Athenian society off features of the Platonic state. This procedure has the disadvantage of leaving us without any reason to believe his claim about the ideal state. Perhaps he would defend this claim by relying on the general thesis that moral and political philosophers can only articulate the common presuppositions of their society. But we may well doubt this general thesis, if we find that it does not fit particular works of moral and political philosophy, including the *Republic*.

We have good reason to doubt Hegel's claim about the *Republic*. It seems to fit neither Plato's intentions nor the content of the dialogue. If Hegel were right about Plato, it would be strange that Plato says most people implicitly agree with the view that Glaucon and Adeimantus offer to explain Thrasymachus' position.[48] For if Plato is right about the view of most people, they find it quite easy to distinguish the interest of the individual from the interest of the community, and they see quite a plausible case for subordinating the interest of the community to one's own interest. Plato tries to show, as Aristotle does, that the interest of the individual requires pursuit of the good of the community for its own sake. But he does not suggest that this connexion between individual and community is an obvious point that everyone takes for granted. On the contrary, he thinks it is worth arguing for, because he thinks most people do not recognize this point. The Platonic ideal state takes extraordinary and unfamiliar measures to make the connexion between individual and collective interest clear to its citizens. Plato takes these measures to be necessary because the connexion is not clear to most people in non-ideal states.

If we are to reject Hegel's view that Plato articulates the presuppositions of his society, we may still agree that Plato captures the spirit of the Greek city in some sense in which he does not capture the spirit of other types of political and social organization. The shared concerns, common aspirations, and sense of solidarity that he expects in the ideal city of the *Republic* are intelligible idealizations of a Greek city, not of the Persian Empire or of feudal England. In this respect, Plato might be taken to have grasped the 'actuality' of the Greek city. But Plato also takes some central elements of fourth-century BC Athenian democracy to be deeply misguided, and therefore discards them from the ideal state. These discarded elements help us to state an alternative conception of the actuality of the Greek city. This alternative conception includes the elements of subjective freedom that Plato rejects.

---

[48] See Plato, *Rep.* 363e–364b.

Hegel recognizes that some conception of subjective freedom was present in the Greek city; that was why Plato struggled to eliminate it from the ideal city. But this fact casts doubt on the claim that Plato captures the spirit of the Greek city. It would have been worth his while to compare Aristotle's political principles with Plato's. The comparison would show that Aristotle is far more favourable than Plato is to subjective freedom, though he remains critical of it (*Pol.* 1317a40–b17). Why should we suppose that Plato captures the Greek spirit better than Aristotle captures it? A good answer to this question would require some comparison of Plato and Aristotle with Athenian politics and society, as far as we know about them. A comparison is likely to show that Aristotle comes closer than Plato comes to capturing the importance of subjective freedom in fourth-century Athens.

We have good grounds, therefore, for rejecting Hegel's claims about subjective freedom. Still, they may contain or suggest claims that are either true or worth considering. It is true, for instance, that Plato and Aristotle do not understand the division between self-love and morality as Butler and Kant understand it, and that they do not give to the rights and claims of individuals the place that Kant gives to them. These points of disagreement may well be connected. We might plausibly claim that the Greek moralists do not take the potentially conflicting interests and demands of individuals to be as important as modern moralists take them to be. And we might claim that this difference is connected to differences between Athens in the fourth century BC and Europe in the 18th century AD.

But, however we explain such differences between Greek and modern moralists, we can hardly accept Hegel's explanation. Plato and Aristotle are well aware of the view that individual interests diverge from those of the community, and that morality is needed to restrain the pursuit of individual interest; but they reject the arguments that support such a view. The differences between them and modern moral theorists rest on philosophical disagreements. Hegel's broad historical and cultural claims are unhelpful for this purpose.

1007. Later Antiquity

Not all the moral philosophy of antiquity appears to Hegel to express the outlook of the city-state. He agrees with those who affirm a sharp division between Classical and Hellenistic Greek society and culture.[49] Hence Stoicism seems to him to be distinctively Hellenistic and Roman, in so far as it assumes a quite different social and political situation from the situation familiar to Plato. Stoicism is the philosophy of a universal empire in which individuals, having lost their ties with a particular community, think of themselves as isolated victims in a system that is too large for them. They react to their surroundings by declaring independence from them, and they identify the isolated individual, in abstraction from any specific community or concern, as the only bearer of absolute value.[50]

---

[49] On the Hellenistic world see §161.

[50] 'Self-will is the freedom which entrenches itself in some particularity and is still in bondage, while Stoicism is the freedom which always comes directly out of bondage and returns to the pure universality of thought. As a universal

This abstract character of Stoicism makes it liable to pass into Scepticism. The Sceptic notices that all the Stoics have left when they attribute absolute value to the isolated individual is an empty abstraction, because we cannot reasonably ascribe value to individuals apart from specific aims and social roles. If neither the social roles available in the world nor the individuals who fulfil them have any genuine value, neither individuals nor the world deserve to be taken seriously (*PS* §202).

Hegel's treatment of Stoicism obscures the continuity of Stoic ethics with earlier Greek moral philosophy.[51] Contrary to his division, Hellenistic ethics, and Hellenistic philosophy generally, is not a new intellectual outlook replacing the outlook that belongs to the 'world of the polis'; it is simply a further stage in the discussion of themes already familiar in earlier Greek philosophy. If we recognize that Stoic ethics and Platonic and Aristotelian ethics express the same general theoretical position, we can no longer maintain so easily that the basic character of Greek ethics expresses the character of the Classical Greek city. Hegel can maintain his claim about the connexion between Greek ethics and the Classical city only because he separates Stoicism from earlier Greek philosophy as the philosophy of the universal empire rather than the independent city. But the theoretical character of Stoicism does not support this separation.

Hegel's views about the decline of the Classical city-state and the connexion between Stoicism and the post-Classical Greco-Roman world may even have encouraged the view that Stoicism represents a decline from Plato and Aristotle, corresponding to the decline in social and political life. In both cases, his claims about decline are open to question. Even if he were right about social and political decline, the inference about philosophical decline would be unwarranted. We have no reason to agree that the Stoics manifest any decline from Plato and Aristotle. They are not philosophical pioneers, as Plato and Aristotle are. But their philosophical understanding of morality is not at all inferior to that of Plato and Aristotle.

This favourable view of Stoicism is prevalent among modern moralists up to the 19th century. Seventeenth and 18th century moralists take the Stoics to be no less important, and often more important, than Plato and Aristotle. In so far as Hegel reflects and encourages the view that the Stoics are post-Classical, and therefore inferior, he contributes to the unreasonable under-valuation of Stoicism among many 19th and 20th century readers. His social and political explanation of Greek moral thought, and his views about post-Classical decline, seriously distort the impressive continuity of Greek moral philosophy.

1008. Ancient and Mediaeval

According to Hegel, the Middle Ages are even further than the Roman Empire is from the world of the Greek cities. The characteristic outlook of the Middle Ages is the 'unhappy

---

form of the World-Spirit, Stoicism could only appear on the scene in a time of universal fear and bondage, but also a time of universal culture which had raised itself to the level of thought.' (*PS* §199).

[51] In *LHP* ii 275 (Brown) Hegel mentions that Stoic ethics treats questions in earlier Greek ethics: '. . . what came to the fore at this time was the ancient issue of the harmony of virtue (morality) with happiness'. Unfortunately, these lectures do not discuss any earlier treatments of this ancient issue.

consciousness', which regards itself as an alien in this world and renounces it in favour of another world. Though this consciousness tries to identify itself with the unchangeable being of the other world, it cannot really eliminate the changeable being that belongs to it in this world, and so it suffers permanent conflict between them (*PS* §208). Neither the ethical outlook of the Greek city nor that of Stoicism or Scepticism can fit the divided consciousness of the Middle Ages, whose characteristic product is the monastic outlook.

In this case also, Hegel's divisions obscure the continuity that we discover from a more careful study of the history of ethics. On the one hand, the characteristics of the 'unhappy consciousness' correspond quite closely to some of Plato's *Phaedo*, and they are prominent in later Platonism. On the other hand, Hegel's historical divisions do not prepare us for the fact that mediaeval writers continue Greek ethics, both Aristotelian and (as transmitted by Patristic sources) Stoic. Moral theories do not seem to reflect the social and cultural transformations that Hegel invokes to explain the development of philosophical thought.

This observation may appear too simple to refute Hegel. We might, for instance, concede on his behalf that Aquinas' ethical theory has the outward appearance of an Aristotelian theory. But we may still hold that he is right to affirm that the spirit of Aquinas' philosophy is essentially different, because of the historical, cultural, and theological differences that separate Aristotle from Aquinas. We ought not to be misled, according to a Hegelian point of view, by outward similarities that conceal the essential differences.

The assumption that Hegel must be right has influenced the study of mediaeval philosophy, including moral philosophy. It is one source of the widespread tendency to believe that Aquinas must have misunderstood or distorted Aristotle. But in fact Aquinas understands Aristotle's moral philosophy quite well, and a student of Aristotelian ethics can learn from Aquinas' discussion of the issues that arise for Aristotle. We do not find the discontinuity that we ought to expect if Hegel's approach to the history of philosophy were correct. We find that some important aspects of Aquinas' position are understood better as developments of the Aristotelian position, rather than as transformations of it into the world of the 'unhappy consciousness'.

These reflexions on Hegel's attitude to ancient and mediaeval ethics suggest a further question about his views on modern theories too. Just as he supposes that the Middle Ages must be sharply distinct, philosophically as well as culturally, from the Greek cities and from the pagan Roman Empire, he also supposes that the distinctive features of modern thought must correspond to something distinctive about the modern world and modern culture. Hence he places Kantian Morality firmly in the context of the Enlightenment and the French Revolution. This may be a misleading approach to Kant; perhaps Hegel exaggerates the discontinuity between Kant and his predecessors.

1009. Hegel's Criticism of Eudaemonism

Now that we have expressed some doubts about Hegel's approach to the history of moral philosophy, and especially to his claims about its connexion to be broader history of thought and society, we should try to support these doubts by a more detailed discussion of some of his specific claims. It is useful to consider his evaluation of the eudaemonist element in Greek ethics.

We have found reasons to believe that Greek eudaemonism fits into the outlook of Butler, Reid, and Kant, and that these philosophers reject the eudaemonism of Aristotle and Aquinas because they misunderstand it. On this point, modern moral philosophy does not really depart from earlier outlooks as sharply as modern moral philosophers suppose. But if Hegel is right, these attempts to question the appearance of sharp divisions in the history of ethics are misguided. He believes that Greek theories cannot express the modern moral consciousness because they omit some essential aspect of morality, as we now conceive it. In particular, he believes that Greek eudaemonism has been discarded, and should be discarded, by the modern outlook. Is he right to believe this?

His verdict on Greek moral philosophy rests on a more general objection to eudaemonism. He uses 'eudaemonism', as Kant does,[52] for a view that relies on happiness as the ultimate end. Indeed, he takes eudaemonism to be a prevalent moral outlook among Kant's predecessors.[53] Hegel's concept of happiness is similar to Kant's, and he takes the eudaemonists to be concerned with happiness, as Kant understands it.[54] Solon and Croesus, for instance, discuss the question about who is the happiest of human beings by simply considering different people's success in achieving and retaining the actual objects of human pursuit. We find what happiness is simply by listing the ends that people pursue for their own sakes. In so far as different people pursue different ends, happiness is also different. Though Hegel often criticizes Kant, he believes Kant marks a decisive advance over the eudaemonism of Greek ethics.[55]

1010. Eudaemonism v. Freedom

The eudaemonist outlook, as Hegel understands it, belongs to an early stage of moral progress because it does not take proper account of human freedom.[56] If we identify the

---

[52] See Kant's use of 'eudaemonism', §935.

[53] 'To estimate rightly what we owe to Kant in the matter, we ought to set before our minds the form of practical philosophy and in particular of "moral philosophy" which prevailed in his time. It may be generally described as a system of Eudaemonism, which, when asked what man's chief end ought to be, replied Happiness. And by happiness Eudaemonism understood the satisfaction of the private appetites, wishes, and wants of the man, thus raising the contingent and particular into a principle for the will and its actualization.' (Logic §54).

[54] '. . . before Kant, morality as eudaemonism was based on the determination of happiness. . . . Eudaemonism signifies happiness as a condition of the whole of life; it sets up a totality of enjoyment which is a universal and a rule for individual enjoyment, in that it does not allow it to give way to what is momentary, but restrains desires and sets a universal standard before one's eyes. . . . The stage of reflexion that we reach in happiness stands midway between mere desire and the other extreme, which is right as right and duty as duty. In happiness, the individual enjoyment has disappeared; the form of universality is there, but the universal does not yet come forth on its own account . . .' (LHP i 162–3 H&S).

[55] '. . . the will is not here as it is in its immediacy; on the contrary, this content now belongs to a will reflected into itself and so is elevated to become a universal end, the end of welfare or happiness; this happens at the level of the thinking which does not yet apprehend the will in its freedom but reflects on its content as on one natural and given—the level, for example of the time of Croesus and Solon.' (PR §123) '. . . as happiness has its sole affirmative contents in the springs of action, it is on them that the decision turns, and it is the subjective feeling and good pleasure which must have the casting vote as to where happiness is to be placed.' (PM §479) On happiness cf. PM §478–80.

[56] 'Since the specifications of happiness are given, they are not true specifications of freedom, because freedom is not genuinely free in its own eyes except in the good, i.e. except when it is its own end. Consequently we may raise the

ultimate end of rational choice with pleasure or with satisfaction of desire, we overlook the universal side of the will, because we overlook the capacity of the rational will to criticize and modify the ends presented to it by particular desires (PR §20).

Hegel believes that this objection undermines eudaemonism in general, because eudaemonists simply derive their conception of the ultimate end for rational agents from the objects of actual desires that are independent of rational agency. The desire for pleasure is a clear case of such a desire, if we draw no distinction between different objects of pleasure. The conception of the end as the satisfaction of the desires we already have removes any critical or constructive role for practical reason in the formation of the ultimate end. We can see why Hegel believes that this sort of practical thought 'happens at the level of the thinking which does not yet apprehend the will in its freedom but reflects on its content as on one natural and given' (PR §123).

This criticism of eudaemonist views about the role of practical reason also applies to morality. Hegel rejects the eudaemonist view that a conception of happiness as the final end should constrain the content of morality. The eudaemonist, according to Hegel, prescribes a determinate end as the proper end of rational pursuit independently of our moral choices and principles. This view treats moral principles as hypothetical imperatives aiming at ends that they cannot evaluate or criticize. Hegel rejects this view because he agrees with Kant in believing that morality does not simply formulate principles for achieving ends that we value independently of morality, but affects our conception of the ends worth pursuing.

Hegel's attack on eudaemonism is more effective than Kant's in so far as he avoids Kant's assumption that eudaemonists must be egoists in some objectionable sense. Hegel does not complain that eudaemonism reduces morality to the sort of self-love that precludes unselfish action. He sees that Kant's objection to the reduction of moral principles to hypothetical imperatives is independent of objections to a narrow form of egoism. Hence he comes closer to identifying the main issues than Butler, Price, or Reid ever comes.

This criticism of eudaemonism seems to be connected with Hegel's objection that Greek ethics does not allow the proper role to subjective freedom.[57] For subjective freedom is more than mere caprice or preference; it rests on critical practical reason. An essential stage in the developing self-awareness of our free will is our recognition that the ends presented to us by something external to our practical reason are not beyond our choice and decision; it is up to us to criticize and evaluate them. Eudaemonism, however, treats ends as though they were independent of practical reason. We should not be surprised at this, if we follow Hegel. For Greek moral philosophy, in his view, never allows a critical and reflective role to practical reason. Hence it identifies subjective freedom with mere irrational whims and preferences. If practical reason has no critical role, it is legitimate to treat our ends as eudaemonism treats them.

If, on the contrary, we recognize that moral principles are not merely hypothetical imperatives, we must already have recognized the critical functions of practical reason. And

---

question whether a man has the right to set before himself ends not freely chosen but resting solely on the fact that the subject is a living being. The fact that a man is a living being, however, is not fortuitous, but in conformity with reason, and to that extent he has a right to make his needs his end. ... It is only the raising of the given to something self-created which yields the higher orbit of the good . . .' (PR §123A).

[57] Cf. Wood, *HET* 57.

if we have recognized these, we must recognize that subjective freedom expresses critical practical reason, and therefore deserves respect. Though Greek eudaemonism and Greek neglect of subjective freedom may seem to be two independent errors, Hegel suggests that they are really products of the same more basic error—failure to recognize the critical functions of practical reason.

1011. Doubts about Hegel on Eudaemonism

This criticism is effective against hedonism and against any form of eudaemonism that identifies happiness with the satisfaction of desires, whatever the desires may be. We may call this a 'conative' conception of happiness. But this is not the only possible version of eudaemonism; nor does it seem to be the version that Plato, or Aristotle, and the Stoics accept. In Aristotle's view, for instance, the end for a rational agent is what fulfils the agent's nature as a rational agent, not simply what satisfies the actual desires of a particular agent. Our desires are open to criticism in the light of our account of what suits the nature of a rational agent. This account is reached by deliberation and practical reason; and the beliefs that lead to the conclusions of this deliberation include moral beliefs.

The view that eudaemonism implies the uncritical acceptance of ends external to practical reason does not fit Platonic and Aristotelian eudaemonism. It is even clearer that it does not fit the Stoic conception of the good, or the account of the ultimate end that Aquinas offers to clarify the Aristotelian view. In both the Stoics and Aquinas, it is clear that practical reason and deliberation reach a conception of the end after examining and revising the ostensible goods that might strike us as suitable candidates for being the end. Hegel's assumption of discontinuity in the history of ethics leads him to overlook an objection to his judgment on eudaemonism. Since he assumes that Greek ethics undervalues practical reason and subjective freedom, he does not see that Greek eudaemonism departs from his description of eudaemonism. Even if he were right about Plato or Aristotle, he would still be wrong about the Stoics and Aquinas. But he does not examine these different versions of eudaemonism.

1012. Defences of Hegel on Eudaemonism

Ought we, then, to conclude that Hegel's line of criticism lacks all force against the versions of eudaemonism that are accepted by Aristotle and Aquinas? So far we have simply taken these eudaemonist views at face value. We have taken them to claim that they do not take for granted any specification of the ultimate end that is beyond the scope of critical practical reason. Moreover, we have supposed that this claim is correct. But we may still doubt whether such a eudaemonist view can attribute any significant content to eudaimonia unless it relies on the sort of content that provokes Hegel's objections.

To see how Hegel's objections might apply, we may offer Aristotelian eudaemonism a dilemma. (1) Though Aristotle (we may concede) rejects a purely conative conception of happiness that would constrain practical reason by reference to desires and impulses that are independent of it, he retains a conception of human nature that seems to play the same constraining role. But we miss Kant's insight about the role of morality if we suppose that natural philosophy or metaphysics can form a conception of human nature that determines the ultimate end for morality. If we suppose that we can fix an end for practical reason and morality that is independent of them, we retain a mistaken assumption of the conative conception of happiness. (2) Eudaemonists may reply that we cannot discover the relevant end without reference to morality, and it is not imposed externally on morality as a source of hypothetical imperatives. But in that case, we may wonder what is left of eudaemonism; what is the point of an appeal to happiness if we can give it no content independent of morality? In this case, we seem to be conceding the force of Hegel's criticism; for we seem to have identified no clear eudaemonist position with any real interest for morality.

This dilemmatic criticism of eudaemonism tries to express the widespread suspicion that if some version of eudaemonism avoids unreasonable restrictions of the scope of morality in fixing ends, it will be empty. In Sidgwick's view, any such version will be a mere form of words; it can accommodate any moral theory, but has no distinctive theoretical significance.[58] If this is true, eudaemonists do not avoid Hegel's criticism by adopting a normative conception of happiness in place of a conative conception.

The eudaemonist ought to reply that the two horns of the supposed dilemma are not mutually exclusive, and that, when they are properly understood, neither horn is as bad as it seems. Eudaemonism and naturalism need not treat moral principles as hypothetical imperatives. Whereas hypothetical imperatives are subordinate to inclinations,[59] traditional naturalism claims that imperatives of happiness give reasons to rational agents as such, not to agents with certain specific inclinations or needs, so that they are categorical rather than hypothetical imperatives. Even if moral imperatives are subordinate to imperatives of happiness, they need not be hypothetical.

Hegel's criticism of eudaemonism assumes that eudaemonists must be naturalists, in the purely psychological sense, so that they take moral principles to be derivable from an empirical description of human desires and inclinations. Hobbes, Hutcheson, and Hume are purely psychological naturalists, but this is not the traditional naturalist position that Butler defends. Traditional naturalism rests on claims about human nature and what is appropriate to it that are not purely psychological claims, but rest on a conception of the human good that is irreducible to claims about inclinations. This fact about traditional naturalism leaves it open to suspicion of being un-empirical and unscientific. But if it is open to this suspicion, it is not open to Hegel's objection, which would apply only to purely psychological naturalism.

Traditional eudaemonism must subordinate morality to some further end, but it need not derive moral principles from principles that entirely lack moral content. If some normative judgments are needed to reach the right conception of happiness, these may include moral judgments. If we allow moral judgments to determine the right judgments about the content of the ultimate end, we will accept the second horn of Hegel's dilemma.

---

[58] Cf. Sidgwick's criticism of eudaemonism, §1164.   [59] Kant on hypothetical imperatives; §906.

The second horn, like the first, is not as bad as Hegel makes it seem; for he may be wrong to claim that it makes eudaemonism empty. To see the line of defence open to a eudaemonist, we ought to distinguish two eudaemonist claims: (1) A conception of happiness provides an independent basis for morality; we can know what is morally right by reference to our knowledge about happiness, and this knowledge about happiness does not presuppose knowledge about morality. Hence a conception of happiness is epistemologically prior to the true moral principles. (2) Happiness imposes some constraints on morality. Not all our beliefs about happiness are moral beliefs; and our moral beliefs must be appropriately connected to our other beliefs about happiness.[60]

The difference between the second eudaemonist claim and the first rests on the difference between holism and foundationalism. The second claim does not try to rest morality on a wholly non-moral foundation. Hegel seems to attack belief in a non-moral foundation; he claims that eudaemonism exaggerates the role of necessity and underestimates the role of reason in forming a conception of the ultimate end. But rejection of a non-moral foundation does not remove all constraints on the content of morality. If one conception of morality prevented us from achieving the non-moral components of happiness, while another conception allowed us to achieve them, we would have a reason for preferring the second conception of morality over the first. If this is a legitimate role for eudaemonism to play in appraising different conceptions of morality, acceptance of the second horn of Hegel's dilemma does not reduce eudaemonism to emptiness or triviality.

It is not obvious that we ought to expect morality to satisfy the holist constraint that emerges from the second role of happiness. But Hegel has not shown that anything is wrong with this appeal to happiness. Moreover, unless we accept some holist constraint, it will be difficult to sympathize with the later stages of Hegel's argument about the higher forms of the moral consciousness.

1013. Eudaemonism in Hegel's Argument

Hegel's criticisms, therefore, overlook the difference between a conative and a normative conception of happiness, and the difference between a foundationalist and a holist conception of the relation between morality and happiness. His criticisms of crude eudaemonism do not apply to the traditional naturalist eudaemonism maintained by Aristotle and Aquinas, and defended by Butler.

This objection to Hegel gains some force from the development of his position. For his account of enlightened Ethical life seems to rest on holist eudaemonist assumptions; this is how Green and Bradley understand him.[61] If they are right, he accepts some version of eudaemonism that is close to the Aristotelian version. In that case, he ought not to claim that he has refuted eudaemonism, or even Greek eudaemonism, as an undeveloped form

---

[60] On the ambitions of eudaemonism see §§81, 113, 1402.

[61] Wood, *HET* 31, argues that in Hegel's view self-actualization is not the end or goal of the self; it 'is not to begin with an end with a specifiable content to which such a self directs its efforts', because 'the content of this "self-actualization" cannot be specified independently of these actions and ends'. Since similar things could be said about eudaimonia, as Aristotle conceives it, these features of Hegel's position are consistent with eudaemonism.

of the moral consciousness. The version of eudaemonism that he criticizes may indeed fail to recognize the claims of morality; but it is not the version that is characteristic of Greek moral philosophy.

Our discussion of Hegel's criticism of Greek ethics suggests that his historical perspective on moral theories may distract him from some of his philosophically significant reflexions. His criticism of eudaemonism is influenced by his views about the character of Greek society and his conviction that moral theories embody the outlook of the society in which they are formed. This historical claim seems to offer the prospect of illumination, since it claims to explain the historical succession of moral theories. In Hegel's view, an earlier theory is not discarded because of some real or supposed philosophical error, but because it does not fit its social environment. But our discussion of eudaemonism shows that Hegel does not provide the illumination he promises, because his analysis of the eudaemonist position is philosophically inadequate.

But even if his analysis is open to question, it still deserves consideration. It suggests that eudaemonism is not self-sufficient as an account of morality. If we accepted it in its foundationalist version, a correct conception of happiness would allow us to read off a correct conception of morality. But if we do not accept this foundationalist version, we may have to admit that the nature of morality cannot be established from purely non-moral eudaemonist considerations. And if this is true, it gives us a reason for considering accounts of the nature of morality that do not attempt to derive it from eudaemonist considerations.

If Hegel raises a reasonable question about eudaemonism, his question also shows how eudaemonism might naturally fit into his argument. In his view, the preliminary understanding of the freedom of the will, and of its particular and universal elements, should be a starting point for ethical argument. As we noticed earlier, a version of eudaemonism is one way of stating the constraints imposed by a free will. Hence Aquinas understands his account of the ultimate end to describe the object that a free will, as free, necessarily pursues. If Hegel had shown that such an account is useless, he would also have undermined his own strategy.

Green and Bradley seem to grasp what Hegel could have said, but does not say, about eudaemonism. For they return to a eudaemonist starting point, in so far as they treat the ultimate good as the necessary object of the free will. They suggest that different ethical theories may be assessed by their degree of success in meeting the constraints imposed by the formal account of the ultimate good.

Though this is not Hegel's method, it is still Hegelian. It is the most plausible element in Hegel's discussion of Greek ethics. Green and Bradley follow Hegel's non-historical analysis of the free will and its objects, and they see that this analysis may be used to support a version of eudaemonism. Hegel does not take account of this version in his criticism of eudaemonism, and if he had taken account of it, he would have had to modify his objections to eudaemonism. Here his historical argument seems to obscure points that he recognizes in his more analytic, non-historical argument in moral psychology. His discussion seems to contain the outline of a reasonable basis for the examination of other moral theories. We can test this suggestion against his account of modern moral theories.

74

HEGEL: MORALITY AND BEYOND

1014. Hedonism

We have seen how Hegel's views on eudaemonism help us to understand his judgment on Greek ethics. It is more difficult to describe his views on the modern moral theories of the 17th and 18th centuries. His discussion of Kant would be easier to evaluate if we could consider other theories that try to give an account of Morality. But Hegel is not interested in the history of modern moral philosophy before Kant.

We can raise some relevant questions, however, if we examine his treatment of utilitarianism, with the help of his idealist successors. Both Bradley and Green treat hedonist utilitarianism as a one-sided conception of the good and the right that can usefully be contrasted with Kant. According to Bradley, both utilitarianism and Kantian ethics fail to give a correct account of the self in its relation to morality. For him, the right account is contained in a version of eudaemonism. The same sort of contrast is clear in Green, though Green's version is more explicitly sympathetic to Kant. Both Bradley and Green depart from Hegel, who offers no extended treatment of utilitarianism that would allow a clear comparison and contrast with Kant. They depart from Hegel partly because they have access to a utilitarian theory worked fully by Bentham, Mill, and Sidgwick.

Still, we can gather some of Hegel's views about utilitarianism from remarks in the *Phenomenology*. The section on 'Pleasure and Necessity' (§§360–6) considers hedonism as a stage in the development of self-consciousness and the free will's understanding of itself. His discussion of hedonism also applies to some aspects of utilitarianism.

In an inexplicit stage of Ethical life, the individual does not recognize himself as even having the capacity to deviate from his current social role, and so he raises no objection to the place assigned to him in the current social order (*PS* §352). But Hegel does not regard this as the final goal of historical or ethical development. From the perspective of the *Philosophy of Right*, we can see that unconscious and unquestioning identification of oneself with a given social order does not adequately embody the freedom of the rational will. The proper goal for a free will must be a condition in which we recognize our freedom and recognize that this particular moral and social order is the right one for a free will. Hence the primitive unity of the unconscious Ethical order has to be broken by the individual's recognition of his distinctness from the role he has been assigned to, and from the outlook and aims he has acquired from his social role.

The assertion of oneself as a conscious subject distinct from other subjects, and from social aims, expectations, and institutions, leads to the acceptance of pleasure as an end. If I try to define my end independently of other people and the social order they have created, it seems plausible to define it simply as a feature of my own consciousness. Whatever my other evaluative beliefs may be, whatever successes or failures I meet in action, something that I can take to be worth my while to aim at in all circumstances is an obviously desirable feature of my own consciousness. One obvious candidate for this role is my own pleasure.

This way of understanding hedonism makes it the counterpart of empiricism about knowledge. Empiricism seeks a foundation for knowledge in states that are accessible to us as subjects, distinct from any other beliefs, or theories, or assumptions about causal relations to the external world. It involves a certain kind of self-assertion, since it demands a foundation for knowledge that depends on states of myself as distinct from anything else.[1] Hume argues that this empiricist demand leads to scepticism about the external world and about the persistent self. But he does not raise any parallel objection to hedonism as the basis of beliefs about value.[2] We might understand Hegel as applying Hume's criticism to action as well as knowledge, so that he extends the sceptical criticism of empiricism to its practical application in hedonism.

The hedonistic outlook takes happiness as its overriding and exclusive goal.[3] The hedonist looks at other things, including other people (whom Hegel considers here), simply as means to his own gratification. But he does not confine this instrumental attitude to other people; he also treats himself purely instrumentally, in so far as he recognizes nothing valuable about himself except as a means to securing states of gratification.[4] This aspect of hedonism may explain Hegel's claim that the hedonist outlook involves a transition into 'a lifeless necessity' (*PS* §365). All values and practical principles are transformed into technical maxims for maximizing pleasure. If we make pleasure alone our ultimate end, we conceive all the aspects of ourselves apart from our hedonistic consciousness as merely instrumental to our hedonistic consciousness.

Hegel suggests that, even though hedonism expresses the assertion of one's own individuality against other people and the external world in general, it also implies a loss of individuality. Perhaps he means that if I simply identify my end as pleasure, I also think of myself 'abstractly'; what I value about myself is no different from what any other hedonist subject values about himself. From the ethical point of view, I regard both myself and other subjects as bare subjects of pleasure.

The hedonist outlook, therefore, does not simply alter our conception of the world and of other people's relation to us. It also alters our conception of ourselves. Hegel does not

---

[1] Hegel discusses the immediacy of sense-certainty at *PS* §§100–5.

[2] Hume and scepticism: §§722–3. Hume on pleasure: §782.

[3] 'It does not so much make its own happiness as straightway take it and enjoy it. The shadowy existence of science, laws, and principles, which alone stand between it and its own reality, vanishes like a lifeless mist which cannot compare with the certainty of its own reality. It takes hold of life much as a ripe fruit is plucked, which readily offers itself to the hand that takes it.' (*PS* §361)

[4] 'The pleasure enjoyed has indeed the positive significance that self-consciousness has become objective *to itself*; but equally it has the negative one of having reduced *itself* to a moment.' (§363)

simply argue, as non-hedonists often do, that we have desires and aims that are irreducible to our desire for pleasure. If non-hedonic desires and aims are not essential to us, a failure to recognize them does not imply a misconception of the self. But Hegel believes that non-hedonic aims are essential to us, so that if we ignore them, we form a false conception of ourselves. This is the mistake that hedonists make. Since they take happiness for granted as our ultimate end, they do not recognize that we are rational agents who can detach ourselves from the particular impulses and feelings that we may happen to have. Hedonists neglect this fact about us, and so they believe that value can be reduced to some state that does not essentially involve practical reason.

1015. Hedonism and Utility

These remarks apply to the hedonist conception of the good. Hegel also comments on the appeal to utility as a standard for right action.[5] He connects the idea of utility with the outlook of enlightenment (PS §§574–81). The enlightened attitude abandons any appeal to the supernatural, and hence to any divine moral law (§486). In its effort to make the world comprehensible, it simplifies its conception of the physical world; hence Descartes conceives the world as mere extension, while allowing some place for thought as a distinct substance (§578). In practical terms, the enlightened attitude reduces different practical attitudes to one basic attitude that appraises external objects for their utility (§583). The enlightened consciousness thinks of things as primarily useful to itself, and so conceives them as subordinate to itself. Enlightened people do not, for instance, see themselves as primarily parts of some larger system or institution that has goals outside human purposes. On the contrary, they take their own purposes to be primary, since they conceive external things as primarily instrumental to their purposes.

In Hegel's view, the utilitarian attitude is enlightened because it promotes and manifests the advance of self-consciousness. We affirm our own aims and needs as distinct from the functions that may be ascribed to us as slaves, tenants, retainers, officials, husbands, wives, and so on. We no longer regard ourselves as instrumental to the maintenance of institutions and communities, but we now regard them as instrumental to our aims and needs. This sort of self-affirmation is a necessary stage in expression of 'subjective freedom', as Hegel conceives it in the Philosophy of Right; and it is a distinct step beyond taking a hedonist attitude to my own good. I might be a hedonist about my own good without thinking that my own good is terribly important in relation to other social goals; but the utilitarian attitude treats the satisfaction of needs and desires as the goal to which everything else is subordinated.

Bentham's attitude to the law illustrates Hegel's point. Bentham's utilitarianism makes him indifferent to every argument for or against a law or a social policy apart from its contribution to utility. In his view, the individual interests of the people affected are the only standard relevant for evaluation. From this point of view, each person's actions are purely instrumental. But Bentham also believes that each individual pursues her own pleasure as

---

[5] His comments apply directly to egoistic rather than universalistic hedonism, but they suggest an analysis of the universalistic doctrine too.

ultimate end. He therefore has no plausible account of why an individual should take overall utility as her own end; he abandons Paley's theistic account, but has nothing to replace it.[6]

Hegel believes that the utilitarian attitude reflects genuine enlightenment, but also that it is incompletely developed self-consciousness, because it still thinks of external objects as purely external and separate from the agent.[7] The objects are separated from the agent because of their instrumental character. Since they are purely instrumental to our satisfaction, which is defined in terms independent of them, they do not enter essentially into our conception of ourselves. According to Bentham, pushpin is as good as poetry as long as it provides the same quantity of pleasure. Hence it is not essential to me or to my ends that I play pushpin or read poetry, and my changing from one activity to the other makes no essential difference to me and to my ends. The only activity that is essential to me is the one that these other two activities are instrumental to. For reasons that still need to be considered, Hegel thinks this sort of external, instrumental attitude to external objects is a mark of an incompletely developed consciousness.

1016. Hedonism and Practical Reason

Hegel connects the enlightened, utilitarian outlook with the general will described by Rousseau.[8] Each utilitarian will recognizes the others as indistinguishable from itself in its aims, and, in this sense, thinks of itself as a general will, agreeing with the aims of every other will.

We may doubt whether this conception of generality captures Rousseau's conception of the general will. For though both you and I satisfy the general description of a subject that aims at its own utility, that is no reason—as Kant points out—to suppose that we will agree on any more determinate description of any action that we should both perform.[9] What promotes my utility may conflict with what promotes yours; hence, the self-directed will of each of us will not be a general will prescribing courses of action that we can all agree on. Hence Hegel seems not to have found any interesting connexion between utilitarianism and Rousseau.

His failure is not surprising; for we would expect any plausible account of Rousseau to include something like Kantian Morality. Rousseau seeks to distinguish the specific impulses that rely on natural inclination from the wider view that arises from practical reason. This wider view results from reflexion on one's freedom in relation both to one's specific impulses and to other people. Hegel recognizes this aspect of Rousseau, in the *Philosophy of Right*;

---

[6] Bentham; §§1107–8. Paley; §879.

[7] 'Consciousness has found its Notion in Utility. But it [sc. the notion] is partly still an *object*, and partly, for that very reason, still an *End* to be attained, which consciousness does not find itself to possess immediately. Utility is still a predicate of the object, not itself a subject or the immediate and sole *actuality* of the object.' (PS §582)

[8] 'Spirit thus comes before us as absolute freedom. It is self-consciousness which grasps the fact that its certainty of itself is the essence of all the spiritual "masses", or spheres, of the real as well as the supersensible world, or conversely, that essence and actuality are consciousness's knowledge of itself. It is conscious of its pure personality and therein of all spiritual reality, and all reality is solely spiritual; the world is for it simply its own will, and this is a general will.' (PS §584)

[9] Kant comments on the conflict that may result from agreement on the principle of happiness, at KpV 28 (his example of Francis I and Charles V agreeing that each of them wanted Milan for himself).

there he rightly connects Rousseau's conception of the general will with the Kantian dualism of practical reason and inclination.[10] This treatment of Rousseau is plausible, within Hegel's general assumptions; but it conflicts with the role he is given in the *Phenomenology*.

If we reject Hegel's unsatisfactorily vague attempt to connect hedonist and utilitarian generality with Rousseau's general will, we might try to connect each person's pursuit of his own maximum pleasure with everyone's pursuit of maximum total pleasure. Perhaps Hegel believes that if I regard my own pleasure as my ultimate self-regarding end, I necessarily will regard, or rationally ought to regard, maximum overall pleasure as my overall end, or as the appropriate end for morality. Bentham assumes this psychological or rational connexion. Mill defends the transition from one's own happiness to overall happiness. Sidgwick, in contrast to Bentham and Mill, sharply distinguishes the psychological from the rational connexion, in order to reject the psychological connexion and to defend the rational connexion.

We might take the rational connexion to depend on the purely instrumental status that the hedonist assigns to the self. Sidgwick might be taken to argue that if I aim at maximum pleasure for myself, I am really aiming to maximize pleasure, because there is nothing special about myself. The hedonist, we might argue on Hegel's behalf, simply treats himself as one place where pleasure can be maximized; hence he is already committed to maximizing overall pleasure. If this argument is defensible, it might be taken both to explain and to vindicate Hegel's claim that hedonism involves the negation of individuality, treating oneself as simply one subject of pleasure who differs in no practically relevant way from other subjects of pleasure.

These arguments may be taken to show that the consistent hedonist has no special concern for himself, in contrast to other subjects of pleasure. But this conclusion does not entirely vindicate Hegel's attempt to show that the hedonist outlook leads to a general will, as Rousseau conceives it. Sidgwick and Mill believe both that (i) there is no rationally relevant difference between my own overall good and the general good, and that (ii) I am rationally justified in pursuing my own overall good. We may accept the first claim without the second, if we deny that there is anything especially rational about the pursuit of my own overall good. We may argue, for instance, that it is not irrational to stop at a shorter-term good.[11] Or we may follow Hume and deny that any question of rationality arises in pursuing my overall good; if most people pursue it, that is a contingent fact about them, not a fact about practical reason.

Mill and Sidgwick, then, do not directly vindicate Hegel's move from the pursuit of utility for oneself to the recognition and acceptance of the general will. The arguments that might be offered to defend such a move depend on a role for practical reason that Hegel has not yet introduced into his argument. Whatever may be true historically, hedonism seems logically separable from the recognition of critical reason that is independent of inclination. The hedonist outlook seems to be committed to nothing more than an instrumental role for practical reason, and hence it takes no account of an essential aspect of the freedom of the rational will.

---

[10] Rousseau and Kant; §§892–3.
[11] Parfit, *RP* 117–20, introduces a 'present aim theory'. See also Sidgwick, §1193.

1017. Utilitarianism and Civil Society

In the *Philosophy of Right*, Hegel does not discuss utilitarianism as explicitly as he discusses it in these passages of the *Phenomenology*. But he seems to ascribe to Civil Society a moral outlook close to utilitarianism, as he understands it.[12] We will have to consider later the ways in which Civil Society belongs or does not belong to Ethical life; but, for the moment, we can confine ourselves to the aspects that throw light on Hegel's attitude to utilitarianism.

He describes Civil Society as intermediate (even if not temporally intermediate) between the Family and the State (*PR* §182A).[13] Hegel conceives the individuals who constitute Civil Society as self-seeking hedonists.[14] He thinks unrestrained self-seeking is self-destructive, because he assumes that if an individual does what he wants for its own sake, without consideration of its bad instrumental effects resulting from its effects on other people, he will care only about his own selfish gratification. Hegel would have no reason for this assumption unless he supposed that the agents are selfish hedonists. If, for instance, I cared about the good of my friends for the friends' own sake, the bad instrumental effects for me of treating my friends badly would not be my only reason for treating my friends well. Since Hegel does not consider this possibility, he seems to assume that the characteristic outlook of Civil Society is selfish hedonism.

Civil Society comes into being, then, when people find that their selfish ends require some restraint through mutual coordination and cooperation (§183).[15] This selfish attitude to other individuals is characteristic of Civil Society, and to this extent the solidarity of primitive Ethical life is lost.[16] The need for cooperation, however, tends to produce less selfish attitudes. These less selfish attitudes help to form the outlook characteristic of the State, and so they create a more stable environment for the pursuit of one's selfish aims.

Multiplication of needs and desires is both cause and effect of Civil Society. To this extent, it is similar to the 'swollen city' that replaces the 'city of pigs' in Plato's *Republic*.[17] As desires grow, we need other people, in steadily more extensive and complex relations to us, to satisfy our desires; and when we form these relations, we increase our desires (§§194, 199). If, for instance, I have fewer potatoes than I want, I may try to buy them from you; but when I notice that you also offer bananas for sale, I may form a desire for bananas; and if I have wine to offer you in return for your potatoes, I may cause you to want my wine.

Hence we reveal only part of the truth about Civil Society if we think of people entering Civil Society, as Hobbes and Locke conceive it, in order to satisfy needs that they would have had anyhow. This is only part of the truth, because we form expanded needs and

---

[12] Wood, *HET* 239–41, discusses the role of Civil Society in the ethical formation of individuals.

[13] 'Moreover, the creation of civil society is the achievement of the modern world which has for the first time given all determinations of the Idea their due. If the state is presented as a unity of different persons, as a unity which is only a partnership, then what is really meant is only civil society.' (*PR* §182A)

[14] 'Particularity in itself given free rein in every direction to satisfy its needs, accidental caprices, and subjective desires, destroys itself and its substantive concept in this process of gratification.' (*PR* §185)

[15] 'Individuals in their capacity as burghers in this state are private persons whose end is their own interest. This end is *mediated* through the universal which thus *appears* as a *means* to its realization.' (§187)

[16] 'The ethical life is split into extremes and lost . . . Reality here is externality, the decomposing of the concept, the self-subsistence of its moments which have now won their freedom and their determinate existence. Though in civil society universal and particular have fallen apart, both are still reciprocally bound together and conditioned.' (§184A)

[17] See Plato, *Rep.* 372e–373a.

desires as a result of the interdependent existence characteristic of Civil Society (§§191–2). Desires can arise either from the existence of the social environment without any deliberate effort by other people, or from conscious influence by others who stand to profit by the multiplication of my desires (§191A).

The attitude characteristic of Civil Society tries to coordinate the self-seeking desires of egoistic hedonists. It need not be utilitarian in the specific sense advocated by utilitarian moralists; for the best way to coordinate individual hedonists may not be the pursuit of maximum total pleasure. Hegel does not discuss the version of utilitarianism that has been most widely accepted as a moral theory.

His conception of the moral outlook characteristic of Civil Society seems to be closer to the position of Hobbes or Hume. Its members do not care about the good of other people for the other people's own sake—or, at any rate, this attitude does not extend far enough to support the moral requirements imposed by Civil Society. A strictly instrumental outlook is the basis for the universal aspects of civil society.[18] The characteristic form of moral restraint rests on a mutual agreement that each person can recognize to be in his own interest because of his dependence on others.

Hegel attributes belief in such a mutual agreement to Rousseau.[19] In his view, Rousseau regards the social contract as an agreement between individuals seeking to satisfy their various self-seeking desires. These desires form the outlook of their 'arbitrary wills'. Their consent to the contract is the work of co-ordinated arbitrary wills, because self-seeking individuals believe that the contract will promote the satisfaction of our self-seeking desires.

This is an unreasonable interpretation of Rousseau. It is not Hegel's only view; we have seen that Hegel sometimes attributes a quite different view to Rousseau that fits much better with Rousseau's main claims. It is particularly difficult to accept Hegel's suggestion that Rousseau takes consent to the contract to come from an individual's calculation of self-interest. The will that consents to the contract is the rational will that takes a point of view separate from that of the self-seeking individual will. Hegel seems to believe that all social contract theories imply the sort of role for the self-seeking arbitrary will that we find in Hobbes, and that therefore any appeal to a social contract is simply a device for co-ordinating the various self-seeking desires of particular arbitrary wills. This claim about contract theories fits neither Rousseau nor Kant.

Nor does it seem to fit utilitarianism. Hegel's remarks about selfish individuals do not seem to apply to universalistic hedonism, as the English utilitarians understand it; for neither the self-seeking individuals he describes nor the principles they agree on will be concerned with maximizing total pleasure. Hegel's remarks fit Hobbes much better than they fit utilitarianism. He does not seem to distinguish the limited benevolence of Hobbesian individuals from the universal benevolence required by utilitarianism.

---

[18] 'This unity [sc. of particular and universal] is present not as freedom but as necessity, since it is by compulsion that the particular rises to the form of universality and seeks and gains its stability in that form.' (PR §186)

[19] 'Unfortunately, . . . he takes the will only in a determinate form as the individual will, and he regards the universal will not as the absolutely rational element in the will, but only as a "general" will which proceeds out of this individual will as out of a conscious will. The result is that he reduces the union of individuals in the state to a contract, and therefore to something based on their arbitrary wills, their opinion, and their capriciously given express consent.' (§258)

His remarks are relevant, however, to the foundations of utilitarianism. For both Sidgwick and Mill accept prudential hedonism, identifying one's own good with one's own maximum pleasure. Hegel suggests that it is difficult to maintain this doctrine without also accepting a Hobbesian contractarian view of ethics. Hence he implicitly challenges the later utilitarians to explain why the limited benevolence expressed by Hobbesian principles is not rationally preferable to the unlimited benevolence advocated by Hutcheson, Sidgwick, and Mill. The conflict between the Hobbesian contractarian view and the universalist utilitarian view is especially clear in Hume's discussion of justice and utility.[20] Hegel's remarks implicitly suggest that prudential hedonism supports Hobbesian morality better than it supports universalistic hedonism.

Both prudential and universalistic hedonism maintain that all non-hedonic values are ultimately reducible to hedonic value, and so they make all action instrumental, since an action is not itself an episode of pleasure, but a proximate or remote means to pleasure. As Hegel remarks, they make most of one's life, especially the part concerned with the good of others, a matter of necessity, because everything except pleasure has only instrumental value. The view that we care only about maximum pleasure, irrespective of any other features of the end, also implies that we are formless subjects, defined simply by our capacity for experiencing pleasure. If we took other aspects of ourselves to be essential to us—if, for instance, we regarded ourselves as essentially having a life with some structure of aims and fulfilments—this structure constrains any plausible conception of the ultimate end. This objection to hedonism, and hence to utilitarianism, is pressed more explicitly and more vigorously by Green and Bradley.

1018. From Abstract Right to Kantian Morality

In contrast to his rather brief and scattered remarks on utilitarianism, Hegel's discussion of Kant is quite elaborate; but it is still scattered and unsystematic. Kant is discussed in several different contexts, and introduced as one side of several different Hegelian contrasts. These different remarks make it hard to grasp Hegel's general view.

The context for the introduction of Morality in the *Philosophy of Right* is Abstract Right, which expresses the outlook of positive law. Abstract Right recognizes individual persons as the subjects to whom the law applies. They are capable of obeying or disobeying the law, and if they disobey, they are liable to punishment. But they are conceived as wholly external to the law, in so far as nothing essential to them involves their accepting this particular law.[21] The demands of the law have no necessary connexion with the outlook and values of the individual persons themselves. The law recognizes particular persons as subject to the law, and capable of observing or breaking it, but it does not assume anything further about their aims or motives.

Since the law does not assume anything about individuals, apart from their capacity to keep or to break the law, it does not demand anything from them beyond the bare keeping

---

[20] Hume on justice and utility; §§770–1.
[21] 'In formal right . . . there is no question of particular interests, of my advantage or my welfare, any more than there is of the particular motive behind my volition, of insight and intention.' (*PR* §37)

of the different provisions of the law.[22] The same principle of abstract right is expressed in the imperative: 'Be a person and respect others as persons' (§36).

This form of expression sounds rather like one of Kant's formulations of the categorical imperative, which ought to belong to Morality rather than to Abstract Right. Hegel, however, does not intend the principle as a maxim (in Kant's sense) that subjects are to accept in guiding their actions. He means that this is the content and tendency of the various prescriptions of Abstract Right; the maxim that guides the subject in observing the law is indifferent from the point of view of the law.

Provision for property and its protection allow expression to personality within the framework of Abstract Right; 'property is the first embodiment of freedom and so is in itself a substantive end' (§45). To have property is to be protected in the free use of certain assets, and so the property-holder comes to recognize himself as a free agent who is not constrained by the laws in all of his deliberate choices and actions.

The other aspect of freedom that emerges within Abstract Right results from the operations of a system of punishment. Questions about punishment provoke the questions that lead us to the Moral point of view. Punishment is the infliction of harm in return for harm; and so it may appear to be an action of the same sort as the action that provoked it, the expression of one will in conflict with another.[23] Punishment claims to be more than the infliction of harm in return for harm in so far as it claims to be just; and in so far as it is just, it gives the victim a reason not to retaliate further. But how does the claim of justice give the victim a reason not to retaliate? Hegel suggests that it must appeal to something that the offender himself can recognize as giving a reason for obedience, and hence to some universal principle.[24] A will that claims to impose just punishment, therefore, claims to will the universal, and to that extent has adopted the point of view of Morality. In so far as we take this point of view, we claim not simply to be asserting our preference against someone else's, but to appeal to a more universal standard that the other person has some reason to take seriously.

Hegel is right to connect the Kantian outlook especially with contexts in which we evaluate other people. Kant takes praise and blame to be justified if and only if they appeal to principles that the recipient can reasonably be expected to endorse; and since all rational agents are appropriate recipients of praise and blame, moral principles must rest on reasons that all agents have reason to endorse. Hegel sees this important element in the Kantian position when he connects Morality with questions about the fairness of moral appraisal. He recognizes that Kantian Morality advances beyond Abstract Right, and he believes that a developed Ethical system should preserve this advance.

---

[22] 'The unconditional commands of abstract right are restricted, once again because of its abstractness, to the negative: "Do not infringe personality and what personality entails". The result is that there are only prohibitions in the sphere of right . . .' (§38)

[23] 'But in its form it is an act of a subjective will which can place its infinity in every act of transgression and whose justification, therefore, is in all cases contingent, while to the other party too it appears as only particular. Hence revenge, because it is a positive action of a particular will, becomes a new transgression; as thus contradictory in character, it falls into an infinite progression and descends from one generation to another ad infinitum.' (§102)

[24] 'The demand that this contradiction, which is present here in the manner in which wrong is annulled, be resolved like contradictions in the case of other types of wrong . . . is the demand for a justice freed from subjective interest and a subjective form and no longer contingent on might, i.e. it is the demand for justice not as revenge but as punishment. Fundamentally, this implies the demand for a will which, though particular and subjective, yet wills the universal as such.' (§103)

1019. Morality within Abstract Right?

In this development from Abstract Right to Morality, we might suppose that a system of Abstract right without any Moral content is gradually rejected in favour of one that has Moral content, once we recognize the inadequacy of a system of punishment that does not appeal to norms that demand acceptance from the persons who are subject to them. But it is doubtful whether we can consistently understand Hegel to be speaking of such a process. If we did not regard persons as free agents capable of guiding their actions by moral principles, it is difficult to see why our legal system could embody a practice of punishment at all. If Abstract Right were really as indifferent to motives and inner states as Hegel suggests it is, it might have a system of penalties and sanctions that might discourage people from violating the rules, but these penalties and sanctions would not amount to punishment. Punishment seems to require blameworthy actions; and the capacity for blameworthy action seems to presuppose some capacity to follow moral principles. Similarly, why would a system of Abstract Right protect property unless we attached some importance to agents acting on their own initiative and for their own reasons? But how could we attach importance to this if we did not regard agents as free and did not regard their freedom as something worth protecting and extending?

These comments on Abstract Right may not constitute an objection to Hegel. He may intend the 'inner' reference of property and punishment to be a feature of any system of Abstract Right, so that, despite appearances, any system that meets his conditions for Abstract Right will also satisfy inner conditions that belong to Morality. Or he may intend his description of the system of Abstract Right to abstract from the inner aspects of any actual legal system that would satisfy the description. In that case, he describes only the external conditions of Abstract Right without claiming that they are sufficient by themselves. But he does not make it clear whether his separation of Abstract Right from morality is simply an expository device.

This question may matter for our view of Hegel's account of Kantian Morality. So far we have shown not that Abstract Right implies Morality, but only that it implies a more generic and less precise conception of morality. Still, morality is closely connected to Kantian Morality; for Kant's account of morality claims to present the presuppositions of ordinary views about morality, especially as they are embodied in claims about responsibility. If we could show that some of Kant's distinctive doctrines can be defended as presuppositions of ordinary morality, we would have a reason for doubting Hegel's charge that they express a one-sided exaggeration.

1020. Kant and Enlightenment

In the *Phenomenology*, Kantian ethics appears in a different context, after Enlightenment and its dissolution into Absolute Freedom and Terror; Kantian Morality represents the view of 'Spirit that is certain of itself' (*PS* §596). Morality is different from the unreflective attitude of primitive Ethical consciousness (§597); for it does not simply accept the obligations and roles that are prescribed for it by its social environment. To this extent it shares the outlook of Enlightenment. As we have seen, Hegel connects Enlightenment with a broadly hedonist and utilitarian outlook. The enlightened individual looks at himself and others from an egocentric point of view that separates him from the demands of society. He breaks away, therefore, from the naive identification of oneself with society that is characteristic of primitive Ethical life. He rejects any divine source for moral principles, and equally rejects any source in the nature of reality outside human preferences. Hegel seems to regard the Enlightened attitude as a rejection of Butler as well as of theocentric morality.

Kantian Morality rejects some aspects of the merely Enlightened attitude. It is not simply self-assertive in opposition to society, as the attitude of Enlightenment is. The Moral person goes a step further; instead of looking at himself as a mere individual, he thinks of himself as expressing a universal point of view. The universality comes from the idea of duty expressed in universal Moral principles that do not depend on his individual caprice but are valid for every moral agent. Morality gives us an impartial, rational point of view for evaluating the demands and expectations imposed by other people. It therefore, fulfils the demand for impartial criticism that Kant takes to be the hallmark of the enlightened attitude.[25]

The idea of universality also belongs to the Enlightenment as Hegel conceives it. But he connects with an individualist outlook that is absent from Kant's conception of the enlightened attitude. Hegel suggests that in asserting ourselves against primitive Ethical life, which ties us to our specific social roles, we come to see ourselves as bare individuals to whom anything beyond our pursuit of pleasure is non-essential. But this pure subjectivity leads us only to reject one after another possible content for our ends. Hegel connects this attitude with the uncontrollable destructiveness that he attributes to the French Revolution (*PS* §§590–1). At this point, we recognize that we share the practical reason that we use to pursue our ends. If the ends we pursue lead us to no satisfaction, we turn instead to the means we have used, and make them into our supreme principle (§594).

This may be what Hegel means in saying that absolute freedom looks for truth within the subject.[26] He suggests that utilitarian and Kantian morality agree in the pursuit of universality. The two outlooks share the ambition of formulating a comprehensive moral theory on the basis of perfectly general facts about persons. This shared ambition distinguishes them from the Ethical outlook. Everyone, according to the utilitarian, is a rational pleasure-seeker, and so ought to accept utilitarianism. Everyone, according to the Kantian, is a rational agent, and so ought to accept the categorical imperative.

The search for a self-contained Moral will is evident in the sharp division that the Moral outlook marks between Morality and nature.[27] Hegel believes the Moral point of view

---

[25] See Kant's essay 'Enlightenment'. He refers to the same attitude at *KrV* A xii. See §986.

[26] 'Just as the realm of the real world passes over into the realm of faith and insight, so does absolute freedom leave its self-destroying reality and pass over into another land of self-conscious Spirit where, in this unreal world, freedom has the value of truth.' (*PS* §595)

[27] 'From this determination is developed a moral view of the world which consists in the relation between the absoluteness of morality and the absoluteness of Nature. This relation is based, on the one hand, on the complete *indifference* and independence of Nature towards moral purposes and activity, and, on the other hand, on the consciousness of duty alone as the essential fact, and of Nature as completely devoid of independence and essential being. The moral view of the world contains the development of the moments which are present in this relation of such completely conflicting presuppositions.' (*PS* §600)

involves conflicting attitudes to nature because it demands some necessary connexion between morality and happiness. He seems to assume that Kantian moral theory abandons the traditional appeal to nature as a source of norms and principles.

It is difficult to say whether Hegel means to divorce Morality from the aspects of nature that are external to human beings as rational agents, or to divorce it from everything external to acts of will and choice. The difference between these two claims is extremely important, as we have seen, for the understanding of Kant's position and its relation to the traditional naturalism of Butler.[28] The second position commits Morality to some version of anti-realism and constructivism, since it assigns a constitutive role to choices and to acts of will. This view may be close to what Hegel intends, since he seems to separate nature from acts of the moral consciousness, and to regard these as constitutive of moral truth. If this is what he means, he believes that Kant rejects any basis for moral principles outside acts of will and choice. We have seen why this constructivist interpretation does not fit Kant's views about the relation between moral truths and facts about objective reality.

Do these differences between Hegel's ways of introducing Kantian Morality matter for his presentation of it? The connexion with Enlightenment in the *Phenomenology* perhaps offers a more complex account of the reaction to Abstract Right than we can gather from the *Philosophy of Right* alone. Self-assertion is one aspect of the self-discovery of the individual in relation to Abstract Right, but it does not lead immediately to the recognition of a Moral principle governing one's relation to a legal system; Morality emerges from the discovery of the futility of the merely Enlightened attitude. The Enlightened attitude seems to fit Civil Society, as the *Philosophy of Right* understands it. From this point of view, as we have already seen in discussing utility, Civil Society seems to be a predecessor of Kantian Morality, rather than a stage of the Ethical life that succeeds Morality. In these ways, the order of the *Phenomenology* makes some connexions clear that the *Philosophy of Right* tends to obscure.

1021. The Emptiness of Kantian Morality

Hegel believes that the Moral point of view is necessary for a true conception of freedom. It asserts that an agent's motives and aims should affect judgments about the agent, and that we ought to judge actions in accordance with a universal law applying to rational agents, not merely a specific law applying to this or that group of agents. A free will appeals justifiably and appropriately to reason and universality. According to Hegel, Ethical life ought to retain and to respect the legitimate demands of the Moral point of view. It is relevant, therefore, to see what these demands amount to, and how Ethical life satisfies them.[29]

None the less, according to Hegel, Kantian Morality is inadequate. Some of his criticisms have become familiar objections to Kant. In some cases, they raise questions about the proper interpretation of Kant's position. Once these questions are answered, further questions arise about the soundness of Hegel's objections.

---

[28] On nature see Butler, §682; Kant, §990.
[29] Hegel's criticism of Kant is sympathetically discussed by Westphal, 'Context', 250–4.

Both sorts of questions arise from Hegel's objection that Morality is empty.[30] He rests this objection partly on the assumption that the categorical imperative is simply a demand for consistency, and can neither support nor proscribe any one internally consistent policy rather than another. If we begin by assuming the existence of property and the preservation of human life, we can proscribe theft and murder as contradictory to these initial principles.[31] But equally, if we assume that there should be no property, we can proscribe actions that establish and preserve property as contradictory to our original principles.

Hegel's objection is not merely epistemological. He does not simply mean that Kant has to go beyond the good will for knowledge of the specific principle that is to be consistently followed. He also attacks the attitude that Kant attributes to the good will. Since Kant advocates duty for duty's sake, and since (in Hegel's view) he finds the principle of duty in mere consistency, Kant advocates consistency for consistency's sake.

One reaction to Kantian Morality, so understood, is the outlook that Hegel attributes to 'Conscience' (PS §§632–71).[32] Conscience avoids the difficulty that seems to arise for followers of Morality who acknowledge that Morality is empty. If Morality cannot prohibit any consistent course of action as immoral, it must apparently allow all sorts of conflicting courses of action as morally acceptable. If we suppose that morality ought to prescribe some definite courses of action and ought to prohibit others as immoral for everyone in such and such circumstances, we will be dissatisfied by the emptiness of Morality. We avoid this dissatisfaction, however, if we do not require morality to prescribe universal principles with any definite content. Conscience takes this way out, maintaining that whatever satisfies one's sincere conscience is thereby right.[33] The aspects of morality that seem to conflict with the emptiness of the categorical imperative just disappear.

Kantian Morality rejects this subjectivist attitude that Conscience takes to moral rightness. But it has no satisfactory account of objective moral rightness. Hence it offers no way out of the attitude of Conscience. Though Conscience does not endorse the Kantian categorical imperative, someone who begins from the Kantian position easily lapses into the outlook of Conscience.

To demonstrate that the categorical imperative can provide no account of the content of morality, Hegel claims that it commits Kant to a contradiction.[34] He seems to intend two objections: (1) The very fact that the categorical imperative needs to be specified with some

[30] Hegel's objection to the emptiness and formalism of Kantian Morality is discussed fully by Sedgwick, 'Content', and 'Subjective idealism'.

[31] 'It is to a principle of that kind alone, therefore, that an action can be related either by correspondence or contradiction. But if duty is to be willed simply for duty's sake and not for the sake of some content, it is only a formal identity whose nature it is to exclude all content and specification.' (PR §135; cf. 135A)

[32] Wood, HET, ch. 10, discusses Hegel on conscience.

[33] 'This content at the same time counts as a moral essentiality or as duty. For pure duty, as was found when testing laws, is utterly indifferent to any content and tolerates any content. Here it has, at the same time, the essential form of being-for-self, and this form of individual conviction is nothing else but consciousness of the emptiness of pure duty and of the fact that pure duty is only a moment, that its substantiality is a predicate which has its subject in the individual, whose caprice gives it its content and can associate every content with this form and attach its conscientiousness to the content.' (PS §644)

[34] 'But though the good is the universal of will—a will determined in itself—and thus including in it particularity—still so far as this particularity is in the first instance still abstract, there is no principle at hand to determine it. Such determination therefore starts up also outside that universal; and as heteronomy or determinance of a will which is free and has rights of its own, there awakes here the deepest contradiction. ... In consequence of the indeterminate determinism of the good, there are always several sorts of goods and many kinds of duties, the variety of which is a dialectic of one against

more determinate description of obligatory actions in determinate circumstances contradicts Kant's claims about the moral status of the categorical imperative. (2) Even if we allow Kant to specify the categorical imperative in some way, he cannot specify it satisfactorily; for, since duties conflict, he will have to say that incompatible actions are both required and prohibited by the categorical imperative. Hence, in any case in which we face a conflict of duties, we cannot do what the categorical imperative requires of us.

Hegel's criticisms would be formidable if he had interpreted Kant correctly. But Kant does not take the formulae of the categorical imperative to require mere consistency. Nor does he say anything that implies that, as Hegel's first objection assumes, all specific maxims introduce heteronomy. Hegel may misinterpret Kant here because he believes (as we will see) that Kant takes the primacy of the moral motive to require that we act from no other motive whenever we observe duty for duty's sake.

The second objection assumes that the categorical imperative is meant to be the basis of every genuine prima facie obligation, so that if we recognize a conflict of duties, we must recognize that the categorical imperative gives us conflicting instructions. But this is not Kant's view of the role of the categorical imperative. In his view, there can be conflicting grounds of obligation, but a ground of obligation does not necessarily specify a type of action required by the categorical imperative. The action required by the categorical imperative is the obligatory action that we discover by finding the stronger ground of obligation. Kant expresses this view by saying that grounds of obligation can conflict, but obligations cannot.[35]

Hegel's two objections are reasonable, in so far as they mark some of the complications that arise in the application of the categorical imperative. It is misleading of Kant to suggest that someone who simply applies the formula of universal law can be sure of avoiding culpable error.[36] But Kant does not always over-simplify his position in this way. He sometimes recognizes that we cannot apply the formulations of the categorical imperative directly to actions without intermediate principles, and that discovery of the intermediate principles requires more than the intention to follow the categorical imperative.

This answer does not help Kant if Hegel is right to say that the categorical imperative prescribes only consistency in action and allows no further content. But this treatment of the formula of universal law ignores Kant's claim that all the formulae of the categorical imperative are equivalent. He is not concerned with what we 'can' will in the sense that we can consistently will it, but with what we 'can' will if our maxims conform to the principles that are appropriate for rational agents. He argues that the principles appropriate for rational agents are those that treat rational agents as ends in themselves.

Hegel might argue either (i) that Kant fails to show that it is appropriate for rational agents to treat rational agents as ends,[37] or (ii) that he fails to show that the demand to treat rational agents as ends is definite enough to give the appropriate content to moral principles, or both (i) and (ii). We have found that Kant can be defended on (i). When we consider (ii), we need to ask Hegel how specific a maxim we ought to expect from a moral theory.

another and brings them into collision. At the same time because good is one, they ought to stand in harmony; and yet each of them, though it is a particular duty, is as good and as duty absolute.' (PM §508)

[35] On grounds of obligation see Kant, *MdS* 224.   [36] See Kant, *G* 403.

[37] Wood, *HET* 163–9, defends some of Hegel's criticisms from this point of view. He also (156) rightly emphasizes the importance of the Formula of Humanity in giving some content to the categorical imperative.

On this second point, Hegel seems to demand rather a lot. In the *Phenomenology*, he argues that since the requirements to speak the truth and to love one's neighbour as oneself need to be qualified and interpreted in various ways to prevent misunderstanding and mistaken application, they really have no definite content.[38] Hence, he infers, even if Kant intends the categorical imperative to favour some definite maxims beyond consistency, he cannot find anything definite enough.

This objection overlooks the fact that a principle can be practically relevant and useful even if it does not interpret itself, or if it needs to be used with other principles and with the appropriate empirical information. If a principle is indefinite or lacks content unless it meets Hegel's exacting test, the Kantian categorical imperative is indefinite and lacks content; but his test seems to be too exacting, since many useful and applicable principles fail it.

We may concede, for instance, that respecting persons as ends requires respect for their interests; and so, if we intend to respect persons effectively, we must know something about what their interests are in particular situations. This sort of knowledge may be empirically difficult to find in some situations; and in some situations, the difficulty may not be merely empirical, but may reflect some normative dispute about a person's genuine interests. Mere acceptance of the Kantian principle will not allow us to answer or avoid all these questions; but why should that be an objection to the Kantian principle? It would be an objection only if the Kantian principle made no moral difference; but the difficulties that Hegel raises do not prove that.

Nor does Kant consistently believe that the categorical imperative must be sufficient, together with uncontroversial empirical information, to give an answer to every request for guidance in a particular situation.[39] Something like this conception of the role of moral principles underlies Sidgwick's defence of the Principle of Utility;[40] but we have no reason to attribute such a view to Kant. Kant recognizes 'casuistical questions' about virtue, and he does not seem to assume that they can be solved simply be applying the categorical imperative with the right empirical information.[41] Perhaps Hegel generalizes rashly from Kant's examples of the application of the categorical imperative.[42]

This defence of Kant might seem to play directly into Hegel's hands. For if we admit these limitations on the relevance of the categorical imperative to particular situations, do we not strengthen some of Hegel's objections to Morality as an empty and inadequate guide to practice? If Hegel were simply out to deflate exaggerated claims on behalf of Morality, this would be a fair point in his support. But it does not follow that Kantian Morality is mistaken in principle. While we may not want to use the categorical imperative as the only

---

[38] 'All that is left, then, for the making of a law is the mere form of universality, or, in fact, the tautology of consciousness which stands over against the content, and the knowledge, not of an *existing* or a real content, but only of the essence or self-identity of a content. The ethical nature, therefore, is not itself simply as such a content, but only a standard for deciding whether a content is capable of being a law or not, i.e. whether it is or is not self-contradictory. Reason as the giver of laws is reduced to a Reason which merely critically examines them.' (*PS* §§427–8)

[39] One might however, defend Hegel by reference to places where Kant seems to suggest that, even if one is 'inexperienced in the course of the world, incapable of being prepared for whatever might come to pass in it', simply asking oneself whether one's action fits the Formula of Universal Law is a sure way to avoid wrong action. See *G* 403. This passage, however, discusses only how one's volition may be morally good; it does not suggest that whatever particular action one decides on as a result of applying the categorical imperative will be the right action.

[40] Sidgwick's demand; §1177.   [41] Kant on casuistical questions; *MdS* 423 and often thereafter.

[42] See Kant, *G*, ch. 2.

moral principle that is relevant to moral education or moral decisions, we may still think it is important. If Kant is right, it captures the feature of the moral point of view that makes it reasonable for a rational agent. Moreover, if Kant is right, the demand for treatment of persons as ends has an important practical consequence; for it seems to rule out a utilitarian position.

1022. Kantian Dualism and the Examination of Motives

Hegel suggests a second line of criticism of Kant that is developed by later idealists. Instead of complaining that Morality is empty, he asserts that it involves an unacceptable dualism. This dualism arises from Kant's distinction between the rational, moral self and the sensuous, empirical, non-moral self. Hegel thinks this distinction is necessary and legitimate, if we are to progress beyond the outlook of Abstract Right; we must recognize the claims of universal reason in order to see why our moral expectations of each other do not simply express preferences. Kant, however, treats this distinction as a sharp separation; the point of view of Morality attributes moral value to the rational will, not to the sensuous self. Kant thereby makes the Moral attitude incoherent, because he is wrong about the relation between form (purely rational) and content (merely sensory).

Hegel believes that this conflict in Kant is the result of a deplorable tendency that he shares with other people. We are wrong, in his view, to inquire into the motives of actions that would seem quite admirable if we avoided any such inquiry.[43] It would be better to stick to our original admiration than to allow this morbid curiosity about motives. Hegel suggests that this preoccupation with motives is a distinctive feature of 'modern' history, when people have become concerned with an agent's subjective attitude to actions.[44] Kant's insistence on the moral motive is the extreme manifestation of the unhealthy modern obsession with motives.

Hegel's claim about the modern attitude is open to question, whether he contrasts modern with ancient, or mediaeval, or pre-19th century. The distinction between the rightness of the action and the goodness of the agent's motive is central in Platonic, Aristotelian, and Stoic ethics. The examination of motives is characteristic of Christian moral theology, and in particular of casuistry. Hegel himself recognizes and denounces the preoccupation of casuistry with motives and intentions (§140); and so perhaps he takes the 'modern' age to go back at least to the 17th century. But if he is willing to go back this far, he ought to recognize that questions about motives have a much longer history. His historical claim suggests that inquiry into motives is a sign of excessive and one-sided preoccupation with subjectivity.

This objection to Kant is one manifestation of a Hegel's general and repeated antagonism to concern with motives and intentions. He argues that such a concern implies that we

---

[43] 'Abstract reflexion, however, fixes this moment in its distinction from and opposition to the universal and so produces a view of morality as nothing but a bitter, unending, struggle against satisfaction, as the command: "Do with abhorrence what duty enjoins". It is just this type of ratiocination which adduces that familiar psychological view of history which understands how to belittle and disparage all great deeds and great men . . .' (PR §124)

[44] 'It is a striking modern innovation to inquire continually about the motives of men's actions. Formerly, the question was simply: "Is he an honest man? Does he do his duty" Nowadays we insist on looking to men's hearts and so we presuppose a gulf between the objectivity of actions and their inner side, the subjective motives.' (PR §121A)

do not take actions and achievements seriously, because we attach moral value to nothing except mental states. Hence the person we admire is the 'knight of virtue' who does not really care about succeeding in his aims, provided that he has enough opportunities for displaying his virtue.[45] The virtuous person, therefore, turns out to be like someone who does not want poverty to be eradicated, because he wants the opportunity to display charity to beggars, or does not want struggles for justice to succeed, because then there would be no need to struggle for justice. This criticism recalls Adam Smith's allegation that the Stoics care about virtuous actions not because they care about their expected consequences, but simply because they are displays of virtue.[46]

These objections rest on misunderstanding both of the Stoics and of Kant. Even if, as Kant believes, only the good will is good without limitation, it is not the only proper object of concern or interest or effort. Since the categorical imperative requires us to treat rational agents as ends in themselves, it requires some respect for the interests of rational agents; and so success in promoting the interests of rational agents must matter. It does not cease to matter simply because something else also matters.

Hegel might be right to suggest that if motives are the only thing that matter, it is too easy to justify everything. If I count as acting from a good motive as long as I say the right sort of thing to myself, and if this is enough to excuse my action, it becomes too easy to act rightly.[47] But Kant does not commit himself to any such view about good motives. Hegel's indiscriminate suspicion of concern with the moral value of mental states is questionable. Indeed, it may threaten his own account of Ethical life.[48]

1023. Is Kantian Dualism Incoherent?

But even if some concern with mental states is morally acceptable, the particular mental states that concern Kant raise a particular difficulty. In Hegel's view, Kant assumes that if I have any concurrent non-moral motive favouring the morally right action, I cannot be acting from duty. Since we would never pick one action rather than another unless we had some non-moral motive favouring it, every action that we choose to do requires some concurrent non-moral motive, and so lacks moral worth. The more we care about something other than acting from duty, the further our action must be from having any moral worth.[49]

Kant is even worse off than this criticism might suggest. For his account of rational action ensures that we can never act on the moral motive, as he understands it. According to

---

[45] 'Virtue is not merely like the combatant who, in the conflict, is only concerned with keeping his sword bright, but it has even started the fight in order to preserve the weapons. And not only can it not use its own weapons, it must also preserve intact those of the enemy and protect them against its own attack, for all are noble parts of the good, on behalf of which it went into the battle.' (PS §386; cf. 405, 408, 415)

[46] Smith on the Stoics; §800.

[47] Similarly, Anscombe attacks the misuse of a doctrine of double effect as 'a marvellous way . . . of making any action seem lawful. You only had to "direct your attention" in a suitable way. In practice, this means making a little speech to yourself: "What I mean to be doing is . . ." ' ('War', 59)

[48] Wood, HET 148–53, defends Hegel's criticism of Kant on motives. It is not clear that he finally attributes a consistent position to Hegel.

[49] On mixed motives and moral worth see Balguy (§669); Kant (§928); Schopenhauer (§1045).

Hegel, Kant believes: (1) The morally good person does duty for duty's sake. (2) If I do x for duty's sake, then I cannot do x for some other motive besides the fact that I recognize x as my duty. (3) But my principle of doing duty for duty's sake cannot be fulfilled unless I do some determinate action for duty's sake; my principle has to have some content. (4) I find some content only if my action appeals to some non-moral motive of mine. (5) But if the action appeals to some non-moral motive, I do not do it for the sake of duty.

This argument shows that, according to Kant as Hegel understands him, I can never do my duty for duty's sake. For in order to do my duty I must do some determinate action; but every determinate action appeals to some non-moral motive. It follows that I cannot do any action for the sake of duty.

Hegel is not the only reader who has taken Kant to claim that any concurrent non-moral motive prevents that purity of motive that is necessary for the good will. But he goes further than other critics go, because he maintains that Kant's account of the moral motive and of rational action ensures that we can never act on the pure motive that morality demands. Is he right to attribute the extreme demand for purity to Kant?

In the argument that we have constructed on Hegel's behalf, the most controversial step is (2) If I do x for duty's sake, then I cannot do x for some other motive besides the recognition of x as my duty. But Kant does not commit himself to (2). He requires the moral motive to be supreme in the virtuous agent, so that it will, if necessary, override conflicting non-moral motives; and he requires it to be sufficient to move agents to do the right action, so that they would not refuse to do the right action if other motives were absent or favoured a different action. But these demands are not the extreme demand for purity that Hegel ascribes to Kant.

Even if the argument about purity does not apply to Kant, it is still worth considering the sense in which the moral motive depends on non-moral motives for a maxim, and how far this sort of dependence might affect the claim that the moral motive must be sufficient for the right action. Kant need not agree that the categorical imperative is as empty as Hegel thinks it is; and so he need not agree that some non-moral motive is needed if the agent is to have a definite maxim. In some cases, however, we might say that an action becomes morally obligatory if and only if I have some non-moral motive; perhaps, for instance, I am obliged to do something for a friend that I would not be obliged to do if my attitude to the friendship changed.

To take account of these cases, we need to say that, in a morally good agent, the awareness of the morally relevant considerations is sufficient for motivation, apart from any other motives of the agent. In this case, the fact that I have a friendly attitude to another person may oblige me (let us suppose) to lend him my car if he wants it and I can easily do without it; the existence of a non-moral motive is a morally relevant consideration, and I take proper account of it if I recognize it as a necessary condition for a moral obligation to do this action. Even in this case, we ought not to accept Hegel's view that Kant must assume a role for non-moral motives that conflicts with the demand for purity. Hegel's errors about the emptiness of the categorical imperative reinforce his errors about the demand for purity of motives.

1024. Purpose and Success in Kantian Morality

The objections about emptiness and about duality imply that Kant's moral demands cannot be satisfied; if Hegel is right, we can never achieve morally worthy action. Another line of criticism suggests that if we could satisfy Kant's moral demands, we would raise further difficulties for Kant's theory.

Kant believes that morality and happiness are not reconciled in this life. Though morality is the supreme condition of worthiness to be happy, it is neither necessary nor sufficient for being happy. Hence the harmony of morality and happiness must be postponed to the afterlife. That is why we need a Postulate of Practical Reason to support a metaphysical belief required by morality.

But do Kant's claims about morality justify his claim that we cannot achieve both morality and happiness in this life?[50] Hegel believes that Kant's claims about morality actually undermine his belief that morality and happiness are separated in this life. For someone who succeeds in doing morally right action, as Kant conceives it, achieves harmony between morality and purpose; this harmony results in pleasure, satisfaction, and happiness. But if that is so, the morally good person achieves happiness in this life. Hence Kant is wrong to claim that we must postulate the harmony of morality and happiness only in another world.

Kant need not accept this argument, however, if he has a reasonable conception of success and happiness. For the sort of success and pleasure we gain from doing a morally worthy action is not the only sort of success and pleasure that matters to us as rational agents with non-moral aims and preferences. The part of our happiness that is secured by moral success is not the whole of our happiness. And so, if we are entitled to assume that the whole of our happiness must be achievable, we have a good reason for postulating its achievement in another life.

But if we admit, on Kant's behalf that non-moral purposes and needs are relevant and important to morality, we leave him open to Hegel's next criticism. If we seek to realize a highest good that goes beyond morality, 'consciousness is not in earnest with morality at all' (PS §620). For Morality requires a conflict between moral and non-moral motives, but if the highest good is achieved, this conflict is abolished.[51] Morality requires nature to be opposed to it, but its end is the reconciliation of morality and nature in the highest good.[52] Since the

---

[50] '...the performance of the action is a fact of which consciousness is aware, it is the *presence* of the unity of actuality and purpose, and because, in the accomplished deed, consciousness knows itself to be actualized as this particular consciousness, or beholds existence returned into itself—and enjoyment consists in this—there is also contained in the actuality of the moral purpose that form of actuality which is called enjoyment and happiness. Action, therefore, in fact directly fulfils what was asserted could not take place, what was supposed to be merely a postulate, merely a beyond.' (PS §618)

[51] 'Morality is the "in-itself", the merely *implicit* element; if it is to be *actual*, the final purpose of the world cannot be fulfilled; rather the moral consciousness must exist on its own account and find itself confronted by a Nature *opposed* to it.' (PS §622)

[52] '...the consummation of this progress has to be projected into a future infinitely remote; for if it actually came about, this would do away with the moral consciousness. For morality is only moral consciousness as negative essence, for whose pure duty sensuousness has only a negative significance, is only not in conformity with duty. But, in that harmony, morality qua consciousness, i.e. its actuality, vanishes, just as in the moral consciousness, or in the actuality of morality, the harmony vanishes. The consummation, therefore, cannot be attained, but is to be thought of merely as an absolute task, i.e. one which simply remains a task.' (PS §603) 'In the assumption that the highest good is what essentially matters, there is admitted a situation in which moral action is superfluous, and does not take place at all. The postulate of

fulfilment of the purpose that Morality claims to pursue would be the abolition of Morality, Morality cannot seriously pursue this purpose. If the Moral will could have its way, it would abolish all sensuous motives; but if it did that, it would have nothing left to oppose, and so would have put itself out of existence.[53]

Hegel's claim that Morality requires conflict between moral and non-moral motives is difficult to reconcile with Kant's distinction between a will subject to duty and a holy will.[54] We are not aware of something as duty in opposition to sensuous impulse unless we have impulses that tend to conflict with the moral law. But the holy will still observes the moral law for its own sake. The transformation of a dutiful will into a holy will would raise no difficulties for Morality. Similarly, success in achieving the end of Morality does not abolish the Moral outlook.

This reply does not cope with all of Hegel's objections. For he suggests that the Moral will needs sensuous motives not only as opponents but also as instruments for making it effective. Hence, in Hegel's view, the success of the Moral will would make the Moral will ineffective. This objection identifies a difficulty that results from Kant's confusing and confused claims about 'empirical' or 'sensuous' motives. Sometimes he seems to oppose them to the moral motive, but sometimes he seems to identify them with phenomenal in contrast to noumenal motives. If he intends the second contrast, he is committed to the view that the moral motive can be effective in the phenomenal world only through the mediation of empirical (i.e., phenomenal) causes, and Hegel is right to say that the abolition of these motives would imply the ineffectiveness of the moral will.[55]

In this case, then, Hegel seems to have a fair objection, but it is not clear that it touches the centre of Kant's position. For Kant is open to Hegel's objection in so far as he is confused about the nature of empirical motives. If we can state his views so as to free them from this confusion, we also overcome Hegel's objection. We have good reason, independently of Hegel's objections, to believe that Kant's account of empirical motives needs to be revised. A reasonable revision of this account leaves Kant's main claims about the moral will undamaged, and removes the basis of Hegel's criticism.

However, even the suggestion that morality does not necessarily result in happiness, and that happiness has to be an external result, appears to Hegel to betray some duplicity in our attitude to Morality. He suggests that the argument to show that morality does not necessarily yield happiness rests on the alleged observation that morally good people do not in fact achieve happiness. But the only people we have access to are imperfectly virtuous people, since no one can completely get rid of sensuous motives. Hence the evidence for the observational claim about virtue and happiness is drawn from people who are admitted to be imperfectly virtuous; how then can it show that perfect virtue does not necessarily result

---

the harmony of morality and reality—a harmony posited by the Notion of moral action, which implies bringing the two into agreement—is expressed from this point of view, too, in the form: "Because moral action is the absolute purpose, the absolute purpose is, that there should be no such thing as moral action." ' (§620)

[53] 'Moral self-consciousness asserts that its purpose is pure, is independent of inclinations and impulses, which implies that it has eliminated within itself sensuous purposes. But this alleged elimination of the element of sense it dissembles again. It acts, brings its purpose into actual existence, and the self-conscious sense-nature which is supposed to be eliminated is precisely this middle term or mediating element between pure consciousness and actual existence—it is the instrument or organ of the former for its realization, and what is called impulse, inclination.' (§622)

[54] Kant on the holy will; §§903, 969, 988.   [55] Kant on the sensuous and the empirical; §953.

in happiness? Since the argument about virtue and happiness is based on imperfect virtue, it is worthless.[56]

Kant's argument depends on a conception of happiness as completely external to morality; hence Hegel speaks of 'happiness as such without reference to morality'. Failure to recognize this externality, according to Kant, is the mistake of the Stoics.[57] Hegel replies that the Stoics may not have been so badly mistaken, because the content of happiness should not be determined only in ways that exclude morality. This objection to Kant is reasonable. It is difficult, however, to reconcile it with Hegel's own treatment of 'eudaemonism', and with his belief that all pre-Kantian moral systems are eudaemonist. His view of eudaemonism seemed to rest on the assumption that happiness is wholly external to morality, but this is the assumption that Hegel attributes to Kant and takes to be mistaken.

But even if Hegel is right to claim that happiness is not wholly external to virtue, he has not shown that Kant's problem about virtue and happiness disappears. For even if virtue and virtuous action are a part of happiness, they may not be the whole of it. If happiness has other aspects, we can ask whether virtue guarantees them. If it does not guarantee them, we can still ask, as Kant does, whether the moral point of view somehow requires us to believe that virtue will eventually secure them. Hegel's observations about virtue and happiness do not dissolve Kant's problem. Nor does Hegel show that it is unreasonable to believe that morality does not completely achieve the aims it sets itself. We therefore have reason to dispute his view that the right Ethical order should reject any doubts about the complete success of morality. Hegel supposes that these doubts reflect an error of the Moral point of view, but we may maintain that they reflect an appropriately modest approach to morality and its success.

1025. The Truth in Kantian Morality

These replies to Hegel's criticisms of Kant may in turn be criticized for missing Hegel's main point. For his main aim is not to understand the views on morality that can be found in Kant's writings. He treats Kant as an example of the Moral outlook, which Hegel regards as a necessary, though one-sided, stage in the development in the self-understanding of the moral consciousness. It is not surprising, therefore, that he does not attend to the aspects of Kant that do not fit very well into the picture of Morality. From a Hegelian point of view, the aspects of Kant that are not open to Hegel's criticism of Morality are those aspects that do not fit the Moral outlook that is central in Kant's position. Their presence in Kant only shows that Kant's position is not consistently Moral, and hence they do not cast any doubt on the criticism of Morality.

We miss the point, therefore, if we try to answer Hegel's objections to Morality by trying to construct a revised Kantian Moral system that avoids these objections. For, in his view,

---

[56] 'Since, then, it is not moral perfection that is taken seriously, but rather the intermediate state, i.e. as just argued, non-morality, we thus return, from another aspect, to the content of the first postulate: viz. we cannot understand how happiness is to be demanded for this moral consciousness on the ground of its worthiness. It is aware of its imperfection, and cannot, therefore, in point of fact demand happiness as a desert, as something of which it is worthy. It can only ask for happiness to be granted as a free act of grace, i.e. it can only ask for happiness as such, as something existing in and for itself . . . Here, then, non-morality declares just what it is—that it is not concerned about morality, but solely about happiness as such without reference to morality.' (PS §624)

[57] Kant on the Stoics; §§937–8.

we ought not to conclude that Kant is wrong to make Morality empty. On the contrary, we ought to recognize that Morality is, in one important sense, essentially empty, and that therefore it cannot be expected to yield definite moral principles.

An approximate analogy with Morality, as Hegel understands it, would be playing a game in the right spirit. We might suppose that playing a game consisted wholly in conformity to the rules of the game; and the rules do not normally say anything about the appropriate attitude of the player. If we look upon the game simply as a pattern of action defined by the analogue to Abstract Right, we can conform to the rules whether or not we are trying to win, or trying to do our best, or trying to keep to the rules whether the referee sees us or not. The referee, as the enforcer of Abstract Right, does not care what the players think about their playing, as long as they keep to the rules.

To introduce the analogue to Morality into a game, we would have to insist that the game requires—even if the rule book does not mention—appropriate attitudes in the players. It will not work as it is supposed to unless the players co-operate with others on their team, do their best to win within the rules, and so on. To take these attitudes is to take the view of the ideal participant presupposed by the game; there would not be much point in going through the motions unless the players came reasonably close to this view. Similarly, then, the point of view of morality is the point of view of the ideal participant in social life within the constraints of Abstract Right.

This comparison with a game suggests why Hegel believes that Morality is essentially empty, and that Kant tries to do the wrong thing with it. We would be making a parallel mistake about a game if we said that all there is to playing a game is acting in the right spirit, with the right intentions, and so on. We would misunderstand games if we supposed that from reflexion on these attitudes we could compile a rule book that would replace the rule books of soccer, rugby, baseball, and so on. For there is no distinct game that we can play simply by acting in the right spirit and without playing some particular game. The general rules for being an ideal participant do not tell us enough to guide us in picking up a bat, kicking or throwing a ball, passing forwards or backwards, and so on.

Though the Morality of a game is empty, it is not pointless. On the contrary, it captures an essential aspect of the ideal participant. Partisans of Morality are mistaken only if they suppose that we can somehow derive the rules of rugby from the rules of ideal participation, or that we can pronounce in favour of rugby rather than soccer by appeal to these more general rules. The rules of rugby and soccer are not special cases of general rules for playing a game; on the contrary, we follow the general rules only if we already know what we must do to play soccer or rugby.

Given this conception of Morality, we cannot derive specific content from the categorical imperative, and from connected principles about treating rational beings as ends. The attempt to reach definite moral rules from Morality betrays a basic error about the essential emptiness of Morality. In Hegel's view, Kantian arguments cannot tell us what we are to do, but only how, in what spirit, we are to do it. To seek to derive any more content from Kantian principles is to try to conjure verbs out of adverbs.[58]

---

[58] One might try to connect the attitude that Hegel criticizes in Morality with the Puritan attitude to morality explored by Taylor, *SS* 211–18.

1026. The Value of Hegel's Criticism of Kant

Still, even when we take account of Hegel's aims, we may fairly object to some of his criticisms of Kant. For he ignores features of Kant that tend to show that the Moral point of view is neither empty nor practically useless. His attack on Morality is part of a general attack on critical normative theory; and he does not consider the aspects of Kant that might make the critical ambitions of moral theory seem less misguided. Hence he interprets the categorical imperative as a requirement of mere consistency, because he thinks this is all we can expect from very general theories of morality. He assumes that Kant intends an extreme demand for purity of motive, because he thinks inquiry into motives is bound to distort moral evaluation.

In general, Kantian Morality is a target for Hegel's hostility to theories that examine and criticize received moral beliefs and assumptions according to some general principles. He thinks this comparison of what is with what ought to be is an idle exercise; and his interpretation of Kant certainly makes the exercise seem idle. But in so far as the interpretation involves misunderstanding or incomplete representation of Kant's position, the criticism of Morality is less convincing.

Hegel's criticisms of Kantian formalism should not be ignored, however. For even if we think Kant can be defended and that Hegel misinterprets him, the misinterpretations are not without excuse. It is not difficult to suppose that Kant intends the categorical imperative to be purely formal in the sense that Hegel assumes. He sometimes seems to be trying to derive important moral consequences from a mere requirement of non-contradiction. In so far as Hegel points out some of the consequences of this interpretation of Kant, he gives us a good reason for reconsidering any tendency to suppose that this is what Kant means.

Reconsideration shows that Kant's conception of morality as 'formal' does not mean what Hegel takes it to mean.[59] The form of a maxim is not purely logical, and hence it is not purely formal in the sense Hegel intends; it contains the features of a maxim that provide reasons for rational agents as such. Kant needs to show that there are such reasons. If we accept his claims about autonomy and respect for persons as ends, we need to explain how these principles can be justified by reference to pure practical reason. The appeal to practical reason should mark the distinctive difference that Kant sees between his theory and sentimentalist theories. Hegel's criticism draws attention to one side of Kant that leads Kant into serious difficulties; it should therefore also draw our attention to the aspects of Kant that need to be emphasized and developed to avoid these difficulties.

If Kant needs to be revised in order to avoid Hegel's criticisms of Kantian formalism, some of Hegel's objections to Kantian dualism are legitimate. Kant needs to take a more sympathetic attitude than he takes to eudaemonism. To explain how rational agents regard themselves as ends, Kant needs to follow Butler and to recognize self-love as a rational principle. To explain why the moral law can be expected to arouse respect, Kant should attribute more shared concerns to the moral and the non-moral selves. To explain how

---

[59] Kant on form and matter; §901.

morality expresses freedom, Kant needs to agree that guidance by rational self-love also expresses freedom.[60]

It is not surprising that Hegel does not consider such a revision of Kant. For we have seen that his attitude to eudaemonism is rather similar to Kant's. He identifies it with an attitude to morality that does not recognize the critical role of practical reason in relation to our other ends. Since Hegel does not recognize the more complex conception of happiness that predominates in Aristotle and Aquinas, he fails to see the role of eudaemonism in defending the main Kantian claims.

This role of eudaemonism in defending Kant helps us to understand the conclusions of Green's critique of Kant. Though Green accepts many Hegelian criticisms, he does not abandon Kant's main views. Instead, he believes that Kant's main views are reconcilable with Aristotle's, and that when they are reconciled with Aristotle's views, they also incorporate sound idealist criticisms of Kant.

We may well suspect that Green's attempt to reconcile Aristotle, Kant, Butler, and Hegel is the product of wishful thinking and vagueness. But this suspicion is not clearly justified. After comparing Kant with Hegel's criticisms, we have seen that there is room for a Kantian defence that abandons some of Kant's hostility to eudaemonism. From this point of view, the reconciling project that appeals to Green appears more reasonable and realistic than it may initially seem.

If Green is right, Hegel's criticism of Kant performs a more complicated dialectical role than the one Hegel intends for it. He believes he has shown that Kant's Moral system is a one-sided and limited view of morality that needs to be transcended. In fact, he may have put forward a one-sided interpretation of Kant that shows the need for a re-interpretation of Kant that avoids the tendencies that are open to Hegelian criticism.

Are these two conclusions really very different, however? We might suppose that Hegel's rejection of Kant includes acceptance of enough Kantian elements so that from someone else's point of view it might count as a version of Kantian ethics. Alternatively, we might say that Green's alleged version of Kantian ethics contains so many non-Kantian elements that it is really only a Kantian shell. We may be able to make up our minds on these questions if we examine Hegel's view of the further development of the moral consciousness. Eventually we should compare his view with Green's attempt to revise and reconstruct Kantian ethics.[61]

1027. Primitive Ethical Life

Ethical life overcomes the one-sided outlooks of Abstract Right and Morality.[62] We might, therefore, suppose that, since it incorporates the truth in the Moral outlook, it is self-consciously guided by rational principle. Hegel, however, mentions Antigone as representing

---

[60] Kant and naturalism; §§969–73. Hegel's criticism of this aspect of Kantian dualism is helpfully discussed by Sedgwick, 'Metaphysics', 314–21.

[61] Taylor, *H*, ch. 14, esp. 370–4, discusses Hegel's attempt to improve on the empty formalism that he ascribes to Kant.

[62] 'The right and the moral cannot exist independently; they must have the ethical as their support and foundation, for the right lacks the moment of subjectivity, while morality in turn possesses that moment alone, and consequently both the right and the moral lack actuality by themselves.' (*PR* §141A)

un-self-conscious Ethical life (§144A); and in the *Phenomenology*, un-self-conscious Ethical life seems to be a stage of development that precedes Moral life. It is characteristic of classical Greece, in which the individual does not recognize himself as having aims and principles that might in principle be distinct from those of his society.[63]

Hegel recognizes, however, that this is not a satisfactory description of Ethical life.[64] Without Morality, self-consciousness cannot freely identify its rational demands with the demands of its social environment; for it has not yet noticed that any question can reasonably raised, and hence has not noticed that this form of society answers it.

In the argument of the *Philosophy of Right*, the role of Ethical Life is equally difficult to grasp. The unconscious Ethical life (as described in the *Phenomenology*) cannot be the reconciliation of the purely 'objective' outlook of positive law and abstract Right with the self-conscious demand for universality and rationality that is found in Morality. On the contrary, it seems to be more primitive than Morality. Hence Hegel sometimes distinguishes primitive Ethical life from the conscious Ethical life that incorporates the legitimate demands of Morality.[65]

Different forms of Ethical life succeed Abstract Right and Morality. These forms are the Family, Civil Society, and the State. It seems surprising that these should be called forms of Ethical life. For the Family and Civil Society mark (in Hegel's view) different stages of development towards the State, but they do not seem to be different forms of Ethical life, if Ethical life is conceived as a stage of development higher than Morality.

Hegel seems to admit this point about the Family. The form of Ethical life that is embodied in the Family is not self-sufficient; it raises questions that are partly answered only in the larger community of Civil Society. Moreover, self-conscious universal reason seems to have no necessary role in the Family. If the Family has a place in Ethical life, it must be because we conceive Ethical life as the primitive reconciliation of self and society that results from failure to notice the possible distinction between them.

It is not clear whether Hegel recognizes all this, since he offers a general description of Ethical life (*PR* §§141–57) before he describes the Family and Civil Society. In Ethical life, institutions and practices are superior to, but not alien to, the individual.[66] The duties assigned to me by my social role appear to me to be a limit on my freedom only if I conceive myself as something different from, or additional to, a parent or a child (in the case of Family life); but in Ethical life, I have no such distinct conception of myself and my interests.[67]

---

[63] See *PS* §§348, 352, 360, 441, 462.

[64] 'But from this happy state of having realized its essential character and of living in it, self-consciousness, which at first is Spirit only immediately and in principle, has withdrawn, or else has not yet realized it; for both may equally be said.' (*PS* §353)

[65] '... the objective will, being without the infinite form of self-consciousness, is the will absorbed in its object or condition, whatever the content of these may be; it is the will of the child, the ethical will, also the will of the slave, the superstitious man, etc.' (*PR* §26). See Knox's note. Wood, *HET* 205–6, 217–18, discusses Hegel's different conceptions of Ethical life.

[66] 'The ethical substance and its laws and powers are on the one hand an object over against the subject, and from his point of view they are—"are" in the highest sense of self-subsistent being.' (*PR* §146) 'On the other hand, they are not something alien to the subject. On the contrary, his spirit bears witness to them as to its own essence, the essence in which he has a feeling of his selfhood, and in which he lives as in his own element which is not distinguished from himself.' (§147)

[67] 'The bond of duty can appear as a restriction only on indeterminate subjectivity or abstract freedom, and on the impulses either of the natural will or of the moral will which determines its indeterminate good arbitrarily. The truth is, however, that in duty the individual finds his liberation; first, liberation from dependence on mere natural impulse and

Hence individuals now have no reason to reject or criticize their station and its duties.[68] Since they have no basis for criticism of the existing order, Ethical life eliminates the dualism of the Moral point of view.[69]

This general description, however, fits neither the Family nor Civil Society. The Family seems to require nothing more than primitive Ethical life, which does not satisfy the general description of Ethical life. Moreover, Hegel suggests that Civil Society weakens Ethical life, since it undermines the unconscious Ethical life of the Family.[70] Civil Society forces me to think of myself not just in one network of social relations—as a member of this particular family—but also as a 'concrete person', an individual with preferences, needs, and abilities, interacting with others whom I conceive in the same way.

In this economic system, universality, as Hegel says, is the basic principle; we live within a single system of supply, demand, and other economic arrangements within which I seek to satisfy my needs through interaction with others who look at me in the same way. Hegel also seems to believe, following Adam Smith, that each person's pursuit of satisfaction for individual needs and preferences results in greater benefit to everyone than would result from some explicit concern with everyone's interest. This alleged universal rationality of economic activity guided by laissez-faire principles illustrates what Hegel means in saying that the universal underlies the individualistic appearance.

We noticed earlier that it might seem plausible to connect Civil Society with the appeal of utilitarianism, which does not fit very easily into Hegel's account either of Abstract Right or of Morality. It might also seem plausible to connect Civil Society with the outlook of Kantian

from that depression which as a particular subject he cannot escape in his moral reflections on what ought to be and what might be . . .' (PR §149)

[68] 'When virtue displays itself solely as the individual's simple conformity with the duties of the station to which he belongs it is rectitude. In an *ethical* community, it is easy to say what man must do, what are the duties he has to fulfil in order to be virtuous: he has imply to follow the well-known and explicit rules of his own situation. . . . But from the standpoint of *morality*, rectitude often seems to be something comparatively inferior, something beyond which still higher demands must be made on oneself and others, because the craving to be something special is not satisfied with what is absolute and universal; it finds consciousness of peculiarity only in what is exceptional.' (§150)

[69] 'That is to say, the self-will of the individual has vanished together with his private conscience which had claimed independence and opposed itself to the ethical substance . . . He knows that his own dignity and the whole stability of his particular ends are grounded in this same universal, and it is therein that he actually attains them.' (§152)

[70] 'This gives us, to use abstract language in the first place, the determination of particularity which is related to universality but in such a way that universality is its basic principle, though still only as inward principle; for that reason the universal merely shows in the particular as its form. Hence this relation of reflection prima facie portrays the disappearance of ethical life or, since this life as the essence necessarily shows itself, this relation constitutes the world of ethical appearance—civil society.' (§181) 'Here ethical life is split into its extremes and lost; the immediate unity of the family has fallen apart into a plurality. Reality here is externality, the decomposing of the concept, the self-subsistence of its moments which have now one their freedom and their determinate existence.' (§184A) The difficulty of separating Hegel's two conceptions of Ethical life becomes clear in another of his descriptions of the progress from Morality to Ethical life: 'Morality and formal right are two abstract moments whose truth is ethical life alone. Hence ethical life is the unity of the will in its concept with the will of the individual, i.e. of the subject. Its first embodiment is again something natural, whose form is love and feeling—the family. Here the individual has transcended his shyness of personality and finds himself and his consciousness of himself in a whole. At the next stage, however, we see substantial unity disappearing along with ethical life proper; the family falls asunder and its members relate themselves to each other as self-subsistent, since their only bond of connexion is reciprocal need. This stage—civil society—has often been looked upon as the state, but the state is first present at the third stage, the stage of ethical life and the stage of mind in which the prodigious unification of self-subsistent individuality with universal substantiality has been achieved.' (PR §33A) The first sentence suggests that the Ethical life Hegel will describe is the one that unifies Abstract Right and Morality. But the rest of the passage does not bear out this suggestion. The Family and Civil Society do not seem to embody something higher than Morality, but something lower that requires completion by Morality.

Morality, treating Morality (as many have treated it) as the product of the individualism that is expressed in the economic conception of Civil Society. We might think of Morality as an attempt to find the moral principles that are suitable for individuals as such, if individuals are conceived as the purely economic units that are recognized in Civil Society. On this view, it is natural to think of one's own interest as purely private, and of the universal point of view of morality as an outlook that is entirely separate from self-interest. We have seen, and Hegel sees, that the Kantian dualism between morality and self-interest partly depends on a narrow conception of self-interest; and such a conception might seem to fit Civil Society.

Hegel, however, forgoes this opportunity to connect Civil Society with Morality; he treats it as a stage of Ethical life instead. Presumably he thinks it is a form of Ethical life, rather than the negation of Ethical life, because it involves some sort of harmony between particular and universal. Individuals see themselves both as members of a family and of other smaller groups and as economic units related to other economic units in the universal system of the economy and the institutions that support economic interaction. But this still does not seem similar to Ethical life in the Family. Individuals in Civil Society distinguish their conception of themselves from their social roles, whereas the hallmark of Ethical life in the family was individuals' complete identification of themselves and their interests with their socially defined roles.

Perhaps Hegel thinks Civil Society must be an aspect of Ethical life because it comes between the Family and the State and both of these are forms of Ethical life. But this is not a good reason. The Family and the State correspond to two distinct types of Ethical life; the Family embodies primitive Ethical life, whereas the State embodies conscious Ethical life. Civil Society meets the conditions for neither type of Ethical life. Why should we not we pass from one type of Ethical life to another through something that is not a type of Ethical life?

1028. Conscious Ethical Life

We might defend Hegel's different remarks on Ethical life, by arguing that in some ways primitive Ethical life anticipates conscious Ethical life. This defence, however, is rather weak. Primitive Ethical life anticipates only one part of conscious Ethical life—the acceptance by individuals of their social roles. It does not anticipate the other crucial feature of conscious Ethical life—the acceptance by universal, critical, moral reason of one's social role. This second feature of conscious Ethical life requires two intermediate stages that are not part of, but hostile to, primitive Ethical life.

Perhaps, then, we should confine Hegel's claims about Ethical life and Morality to conscious Ethical life. If we do not try to show that the Family and Civil Society embody a higher form of freedom than we find in Morality, we will take the only higher form of freedom to be the State; for the State restores the unity of Ethical life that was disrupted by the individualistic tendencies of Civil Society.[71] Civil Society may be understood as

---

[71] 'Actually, therefore, the state as such is not so much the result as the beginning. It is within the state that the family is first developed into civil society, and it is the Idea of the state itself which disrupts itself into these two moments.' (§256)

the product of an incomplete idea of the State.[72] The State is the more comprehensive community that does justice to the claims of the Family and of Civil Society.

The State presupposes Civil Society, because it assigns the proper place to the claims of both primitive Ethical life and critical individualism. The State returns to the Ethical outlook of the Family in so far as it is another community that defines individuals' conception of themselves. Just as at the first Ethical level I do not see myself as a self distinct from my role in the family, so also at the higher Ethical level I do not see myself as a self distinct from the State.[73]

The State, however, also incorporates an element of Civil Society that was absent from the primitive Ethical life of the Family. Though the State is external to the Family and to Civil Society, it is not wholly external.[74] The mature citizen of the State is not like someone living a primitive Ethical life. In primitive Ethical life, the individual has no conception of himself as distinct from the expectations of others. The mature citizen, by contrast, attributes distinct needs and aims to himself, and acknowledges the State as protector of his rights. He does not think of himself, as the member of Civil Society does, simply as an individual with private needs and interests, and so he does not evaluate the State simply by its contribution to these private ends. But he recognizes himself as an individual with distinct needs, claims, and rights. He identifies his aims with those of the State because he sees that the State protects his needs and rights.

In saying that this is characteristic of the State, Hegel means more precisely that it is characteristic of the modern State.[75] Respect for subjectivity was not characteristic of antiquity, because ancient states manifested the unquestioning, unreflective Ethical life that belongs to the Family.[76] In the modern State, individuals identify their interests and concerns with those of the State, not because they never contemplate doing anything else, but because they have some rational basis for their judgment that the State deserves this sort of allegiance.

---

[72] 'Civil society is the [stage of] difference which intervenes between the family and the state, even if its formation follows later in time than that of the state, because, as [the stage of] difference, it presupposes the state; to subsist itself, it must have the state before its eyes as something self-subsistent. Moreover, the creation of civil society is the achievement of the modern world which has for the first time given all determinations of the idea their due. If the state is represented as a unity of different persons, as a unit which is only a partnership, then what is really meant is only civil society.' (§182A)

[73] 'If the state is confused with civil society, and if its specific end is laid down as the security and protection of property and personal freedom, then the interest of the individuals as such becomes the ultimate end of their association, and it follows that membership of the state is something optional. But the state's relation to the individual is quite different from this. Since the state is mind objectified, it is only as one of its members that the individual himself has objectivity, genuine individuality, and an ethical life.' (§258)

[74] 'On the other hand, however, it is the end immanent within them, and its strength lies in the unity of its own universal end and aim with the particular interest of individuals, in the fact that individuals have duties to the state in proportion as they have rights against it.' (§261)

[75] 'The essence of the modern state is that the universal be bound up with the complete freedom of its particular members and with private well-being, that thus the interests of family and civil society must concentrate themselves on the state, although the universal end cannot be advanced without the personal knowledge and will of its particular members, whose own rights must be maintained. Thus the universal must be furthered, but subjectivity on the other hand must attain its full and living development. It is only when both these moments subsist in their strength that the state can be regarded as articulated and genuinely organized.' (§260A)

[76] 'In the state everything depends on the unity of universal and particular. In the states of antiquity, the subjective end simply coincided with the state's will. In modern times, however, we make claims for private judgment, private willing, and private conscience.' (§261A)

We have already questioned Hegel's view about the deep contrast between ancient and modern states in their attitude to subjectivity.[77] But his questionable view does not affect his account of why the Ethical life of the State satisfies the legitimate demands of Morality. The primitive form of Ethical life is deficient from the Moral point of view, because the individual in primitive Ethical life does not assert the claims of self-conscious universal reason as a standard for evaluating positive law and Abstract Right. In the later form of Ethical life, however, individuals have formed reasonable expectations about what is rightly due to them and demanded from them as rational individuals, and have found that the State meets their expectations.

1029. Subjective and Objective Elements of Ethical Life

Let us suppose, then, that the form of Ethical life embodied in the State is the form that has the best prospect of justifying Hegel's claim to have overcome the one-sidedness of Morality. How far does it justify his claim?

We may doubt whether this is a plausible claim about the State in general. It fits, at most, the states of the modern world as opposed to the states of antiquity; and the reasons that lead Hegel to exclude antiquity should also lead him to exclude some of the states in the modern world. Not every society that maintains some social and legal framework recognizing the Family and Civil Society seems to guarantee the sorts of individual rights that Hegel takes to be necessary for the harmony of Ethical life.

This doubt is most pressing if we consider the implications of Hegel's claims that (i) Civil Society depends on the State, and (ii) some people conceive the State as though it were merely Civil Society (§182A). In this situation, he seems to grant that a State really exists (because of (i)), but its citizens have not formed the correct conception of the State (because of (ii)). If they have not formed the correct conception of the State, they do not understand how to reconcile universal aims with individual rights. In that case, not all States reconcile universal aims with individual rights; and so not all States achieve the highest form of Ethical life.

We might defend Hegel on this point by arguing that States whose citizens have the wrong conception of the State have really reconciled universal aims with individual rights, but the citizens do not realize this; in that case, they live an Ethical life without believing that they do. This option, however, is difficult to make plausible. As Hegel understands the Ethical life of modern States, it is conscious Ethical life, in which we recognize that the legitimate demands of Morality are satisfied in social roles. These roles are not simply instrumental to our other needs, but are aspects of our self-realization as free agents. It is difficult to see how all this could be true of us if we do not believe that our actual state does this for us. While our conception of ourselves and our moral principles are not exhausted by our conscious beliefs, it is difficult to believe that, if we hold the views of those who identify the State with Civil Society, our view of ourselves can still recognize the State as realizing us in an Ethical life.

---

[77] Ancient states; §§1105–6.

Apparently, then, Hegel would be wise to claim that only a proper subset of States (as he conceives them) achieve complete Ethical life. How, then, are we to distinguish those that achieve it from those that do not? Would it be enough if they contained some specific legal provisions different from those of States that lack Ethical life? This does not seem sufficient, without the appropriate convictions shared by individual citizens; for Hegel believes that Ethical life essentially includes the appropriate conception of myself and my rights and interests in relation to the State.

If Ethical life requires these attitudes in individuals, does it allow these attitudes to be mistaken? Might citizens be deceived in believing that they live in a community that reconciles universal aims with particular rights? If they are deceived, do they none the less live an Ethical form of life? Or do they achieve Ethical life only if the State actually does what they believe it does?

Hegel neither asks these questions clearly nor offers any unambiguous answer. But he might reasonably affirm that citizens living an Ethical life have true beliefs about how they are related to the State. If we mistakenly identify Civil Society with the State, and we convince ourselves that all the demands of Morality are met within Civil Society, we are mistaken. We have not achieved the Ethical life of a State until the institutions of the State reconcile universal and particular. If the belief that a Civil Society reconciles them is mistaken, Ethical life has an objective component that distinguishes it from life in Civil Society. There must be some normative objection to a state that takes its functions to be only those that are recognized by laissez-faire economists.

1030. The Place of Critical Morality in Ethical Life

If this is the right view of Ethical life, what normative standards ought we to apply to see whether a State is doing what it ought to do? This seems to be a reasonable question, in the light of Hegel's claims about the State. But his attack on Morality makes it difficult to see how he can suppose it is a reasonable question. For he objects to Morality partly because it compares what is with what ought to be; it criticizes actual moral practices by reference to an external standard that is supposedly derived from the universal demands of reason. The use of moral principles to judge or criticize existing moral practices seems to Hegel to be misguided and futile. It is surprising, therefore, that his claims about Ethical life force us to ask questions that he has dismissed as typical errors of Morality.

Hegel's account of Ethical life makes it easier to see why he thinks critical moral thinking is impossible. He rejects the attitude to a State that underlies a social contract theory (§258), because he thinks it implies a mistaken and limited conception of the self. A contractarian theory assumes that we can justify the State by deriving it from a choice that people outside the State can make on the basis of interests and needs that they recognize outside the State. Even if we treat the contract as an analytical device for making clear the prudential or moral basis of the State rather than as a historical account, we assume that the self contemplating the institutions of the State from outside is entitled to judge the institutions of the State.

This assumption is present in Hobbes's version of a social contract theory. Hegel objects to Rousseau's conception of the general will in the same way, and takes Kant's use of the social contract to be similar to Rousseau's.[78] In fact, however, Kant and Rousseau differ from Hobbes on an important point. Kant does not assess the State by reference to the prudential judgments of people outside the State. He assesses it by moral imperatives that are taken to be equally valid outside and inside the State. Hence the basis for the foundation of the State is a moral imperative to enter into a 'rightful' condition that guarantees what morally ought to be guaranteed to individuals.[79]

Hegel argues that a social contract theory relies on an over-simplified conception of the self and its interests. Perhaps the self-interest of individuals is a reasonable basis for judging the moral legitimacy of a State; but what I identify as my self-interest depends on how I conceive myself. How I conceive myself depends on the forms of life in which I participate and in which I form my conception of what matters to me. If I conceive myself as a member of a group, I may come to care about my ends as a member of that group; and then these ends are as much a part of my self-interest as would be the ends I would form if I were not a member of this group. If, then, we are appealing to self-interest, we have no right to exclude the interests that a person forms through membership in a group. If we appeal to a distinction between moral and purely sensuous motives, we should recognize that not all self-interested motives are purely sensuous or non-rational or non-moral. I may come to care about my aims as a member of this group on rational and moral grounds—because, for instance, I come to admire the type of life that is embodied in members of this group—but they are still, in one important sense, self-interested aims. And so they do not fit into either side of the Kantian division between the moral and the self-interested.

These remarks about the possible content of our conception of ourselves and our interests raise a reasonable question about both sentimentalism and rationalism. Hobbes, Butler, and Kant agree that self-interest consists in the satisfaction of desires for selfish pleasure. Even Reid, who rejects a simple hedonist account of self-interest still draws a sharper contrast between self-interest and the moral motive than his theory seems to justify.[80] Hegel is right to argue that this excessively narrow conception of self-interest distorts the conception of morality and its relation to self-interest in all these philosophers.

We might say that he rejects the narrow conception of self-interest that is present in his modern predecessors, and replaces it with something closer to the conception that is characteristic of Greek and mediaeval eudaemonism, as it is found in Plato, Aristotle, the Stoics, and Aquinas. But this is not how Hegel sees it. For he criticizes eudaemonism for many of the errors that he sees in crude hedonism; he supposes that eudaemonists take a rational agent's ends as given by nature, and do not recognize that they are open to rational choice and reflexion. His views on the proper conception of the self and self-interest do not seem very far from the eudaemonist views that Hobbes abandons. If Hegel's position differs from older forms of eudaemonism, it seems to differ primarily in his emphasis on the role of free, rational, moral judgment in forming agents' conceptions of themselves.

Hegel's attack on crude conceptions of the self and self-interest does not seem to justify his rejection of critical moral theory. Though social attachments and concerns legitimately alter our conception of our self-interest, not everything we might come to identify with our

---

[78] Rousseau and Kant; §§891, 893. Neuhouser, *FHST* 204–28, discusses the relation between Hegel and Rousseau.
[79] Kant discusses the moral basis for the formation of a state at *MdS* 312.
[80] Self-interest and selfish pleasure: §689 (Butler); 854–5 (Reid); 904 (Kant).

interest is really in our interest. In some societies, people may be taught and accustomed to conceive their aims and interests in ways that are bad for them and contrary to their real interest. Hegel should agree that this is possible in pre-modern societies and in modern societies that rest on a conception of the State that confuses it with Civil Society. If this is true, the demand that the State should promote the interests of its citizens is not an empty demand. The fact that self-interest has some social component does not show our interest is simply the fulfilment of the conception we have formed of ourselves and our interests in this particular State.

For similar reasons, we need not agree with Hegel's apparent suggestion that a true conception of self-interest and its relation to morality excludes any critical role for morality. Even if moral considerations are not wholly separate from considerations derived from one's conception of oneself, the two sorts of considerations are distinguishable. Morality need not automatically endorse the aims that we form in a particular sort of social environment.

In some ways, it is a good thing for Hegel that his arguments against critical moral theory are unsuccessful. For some of his claims about the State and Ethical life require a more definite critical and normative role for moral theory than he elsewhere allows. But the recognition of a critical function for moral theory raises difficulties that Hegel would escape if he consistently maintained his opposition to critical moral theory. His silences are intelligible, given his hostility to critical moral theory; he does not expect a moralist to be able to apply external standards to decide whether the practices and institutions of a particular community are morally acceptable or not. But the silences also raise a difficulty for Hegel's view that not all States fully embody Ethical life. He needs to raise the normative and critical questions that he elsewhere dismisses.

Perhaps Hegel has not made some decisions that he needs to make about Ethical life. External criticism is out of place if the point of conscious Ethical life is to recapture the unquestioning unity of primitive Ethical life. According to this view, conscious Ethical life does not apply different standards from those applied in primitive Ethical life, but simply applies consciously those that primitive Ethical life applies unconsciously. Morality simply shows that primitive Ethical life, consciously accepted, satisfies the legitimate demands of universal reason. This is the contribution that we expect from Morality if we agree with Hegel's conception of it as simply acting 'in the right spirit', parallel to playing a game in the right spirit. Modern social and political life calls for one's identification of one's own aims, as those of a free and rational agent, with the aims of one's State. Proper citizens are not those who simply conform to the rules, as though mere Abstract Right were involved; nor are they those who simply treat the State as a means to the satisfaction of some pre-social needs and inclinations. They find that the life of the State itself deserves their conscientious acceptance as something to be chosen for its own sake and not simply for its consequences. This conception of Ethical Life and of Morality supports the rejection of external criticism. Hegel believes that Morality cannot tell us why one Ethical system is better than another; it simply tells us the spirit in which we ought to accept Ethical life.

But this position does not seem to fit everything Hegel says about the State. For he seems to believe that the State includes some of the ways in which Civil Society differs from primitive Ethical life. It recognizes individuals as sources of distinct demands, and protects their rights, freedoms, and property. Though we do not conceive ourselves simply as members of Civil Society, our conception of ourselves includes some of the features that belong to us as members of Civil Society. Some States go further than others in endorsing or revising the outlook of Civil Society. A decision about which States are better seems to require some judgment about different ways of organizing a State. Such judgments seem to introduce external criticism of the sort that Hegel rejects.

Instead of treating conscious Ethical life as the conscious acceptance of one's role in a State, one might treat it as the acceptance, on Moral grounds, of a specific form of State and of one's role in it. This outlook presupposes the possibility of discriminating States that satisfy the demands of Morality from those that do not, and so it presupposes critical morality. Though this view of Ethical life makes some of Hegel's views more intelligible, it does not fit his attacks on Morality. He maintains that Morality is empty, and cannot discriminate one State from another. If we can have good moral grounds for rejecting one State and accepting another, it is difficult to see where these grounds can come from if not from Morality. For if they give us a basis for moral discrimination between States, they cannot simply rest on claims about human needs and inclinations; these are an inadequate basis for claims that express our freedom as rational agents. The only appropriate claims are those that express the demands of rational and free agents as such; but these are the demands that Kant seeks to capture in the moral law. Apparently, then, Morality cannot be open to all of Hegel's objections.[81]

1031. Hegel and His Successors

Examination of Hegel's discussion of different moral theories confirms our earlier suggestion that Hegel does not seem to have a consistent position, and that someone who wants a consistent 'Hegelian' position must reject some central elements in Hegel's position. The choice between the 'moralist' and the 'anti-moralist' (or 'Marxist') approaches faces us again when we consider Hegel's claims about Ethical life and consider what he needs to support these claims.

One reasonable reaction to Hegel's claims would be to look for a clearer account of the appropriate moral constraints on Ethical life. We would expect that such an account would do justice to Kantian moral theory and to the important elements of morality that are left out of Kant. This is the sort of account that Green tries to present. He sketches a normative argument in enough detail to sharpen the question about whether idealist ethics has any reasonable normative content. Green claims to find normative content. For he believes he can support many of the institutions of liberal democracy on a non-utilitarian basis, and that he has reasons to advocate reforms that a utilitarian would not advocate.[82]

The opposite reaction to Hegel would be to take seriously his claims about the impossibility of critical moral theory, and to conclude that the emptiness of his account of Ethical life is

---

[81] Some of these questions about Morality and Ethical life are connected with Carritt's criticisms of Hegel in 'Sittlichkeit'. Though his claim that Hegel confuses political propaganda with philosophical analysis is too simple, he is right to argue that some of Hegel's criticisms of Kant turn out to be questionable in the light of Hegel's views about conscious Ethical life.

[82] Green on the common good; §1248.

predictable. On this view, Hegel's distinction between the State and Civil Society does not really rest on any further normative standard that the State has to satisfy. To speak of the Hegelian State, on this view, is simply to speak of Civil Society from the internal point of view of people who persuade themselves that the specific interests served by Civil Society are the rationally satisfactory reconciliation of morality and self-interest.

If this is the right conclusion, the fact that people take this Ethical point of view shows something about what they can convince themselves of, but shows nothing about the conformity of the State to some independent moral standard. Those who accept the outlook of a particular State have good reason to accept the Ethical point of view on it.[83] But for those who reject the interests served by a particular State, the possibility of taking an Ethical point of view towards the State is no reason for changing their mind, since the Ethical point of view has no independent rational weight.

From the moralist's point of view, Hegel makes an important contribution to moral philosophy. His discussion makes it clear, for instance, why the outlook of Greek ethics has been insufficiently appreciated, even by Hegel himself. From the anti-moralist's point of view, Hegel shows that the conception of moral philosophy shared by most of his predecessors rests on an error about the force of moral arguments.

A different, but related, conclusion that one might draw from reflexion on Hegel is that moral philosophy ought to be absorbed in social and political philosophy. Hegel discusses questions about morality in his work on political theory, and in a social and political context. In contrast to Aristotle, Aquinas, Hobbes, Hume, and Kant, he does not defend moral principles as a foundation for the social and political order that embodies them. In his view, different moral outlooks may appear to be epiphenomena of different social and political structures, and moral reflexion may appear to apply only to the specific structure to which it belongs. The comparative treatment of different societies and ages is not moral reflexion or evaluation. From a Hegelian point of view, moral evaluation of different societies, from a point of view that professes to stand outside any of them, may appear to be misguided and illusory.

This impression that Hegelian moral philosophy is subordinate to social and political theory is not completely accurate. We have noticed that Hegel begins, as Aquinas does, with an account of the free will and its aims. Different sections of PR reveal the different degrees to which different social structures and forms of thought realize the aims of the free will. This progress would not be relevant to moral philosophy if Hegel had not begun with a correct account of the free will and if he did not show that moral evaluation fundamentally concerns the demands of the free will. His argument, so understood, proceeds from basic moral principles that both Aquinas and Kant accept. These principles are not simply those that are appropriate for a given form of society. On the contrary, we need to rely on them if we are to understand the development of different forms of society, and especially to understand how far this development constitutes progress or regress in the realization of freedom.

If we concentrate on the role of freedom, the view of morality and moral theory that we form is not the view that results from Hegel's remarks about Morality and moral criticism.

---

[83] This criticism may be applied to Bradley's account of my station and its duties. See §§1226–7.

233

Even though *PR* may (to put it crudely) appear to be a work of political theory rather than a work of moral philosophy, this appearance is misleading. Its underlying principles rely on recognizable arguments in moral philosophy. Once we see this, we may doubt whether the restricted role that Hegel sometimes seems to allow to moral argument is consistent with the fundamental role that he must recognize for it in his own position.

75

MARX AND IDEALIST MORAL THEORY

1032. Reactions to Hegel

A reasonably full discussion of Marx's views on social theory would go far beyond moral philosophy. Indeed, moral philosophy might not be very prominent in a full exposition of his views, since he does not discuss questions in moral theory at length. The views he expresses are often implicit rather than explicit, and even when they are explicit, they are often assertions rather than conclusions of theoretical argument. Moreover, a full discussion would have to take account of questions about the relation between Marx's earlier works, in which the Hegelian influence is more evident, and his later works. The development of Marx's thought, and the importance or unimportance of Hegelian philosophical assumptions in different stages of his thought, are controversial topics that are quite relevant to his views on questions about morality.

Still, a brief and fragmentary treatment of Marx may be useful as a sequel to our discussion of Hegel, and as a preparation (however little this would have pleased Marx) for our discussion of Green and Bradley. In our discussion of Hegel on Ethical life, we noticed that he seems not to hold a clear view about the critical role of the Ethical outlook. On the one hand, he believes that the Ethical outlook incorporates what is true in Morality, and that it constitutes the full expression of the free will. It does not seem obvious that all states meet these conditions, and we might expect the Ethical outlook to show us which states do not meet it, and where they fall short of it. On the other hand, Hegel attacks efforts to criticize a particular society by appeal to standards external to it. While he believes it is legitimate to appeal to the actuality in order to show that an existing society falls short of it, he believes that criticism that tries to take a position outside the actuality of this or that society is necessarily baseless.

Whether or not these two aspects of Hegel amount to a contradiction, they represent conflicting tendencies that invite development in different directions. One might study these different directions in Hegelians after Hegel. We will simply take Marx as an influential example of one reaction to Hegel. Instead of exploring other reactions among earlier Hegelians, we will examine the reactions that are more directly relevant to moral philosophy, in Green and Bradley.

1033. Difficulties in Hegel's View of the State

In the 'Critique of Hegel's Philosophy of the State', Marx examines some sections of PR in detail. One relevant part of his discussion concerns Hegel's conception of the State in relation to his views on Civil Society. Though he does not directly criticize Hegel's conception of Ethical life, his remarks may reasonably be connected with the questions about Ethical life that we have already raised.

Marx attends to the gap between Civil Society and the State, as Hegel conceives them. In many ways, they seem to be antagonistic. Civil Society contains individuals who take a selfish view of their individual interests, and act co-operatively only in so far as they see some benefit to themselves individually from the co-operation. This is the Hobbesian attitude that Hegel claims to find even in Rousseau's conception of the social contract. In contrast to this attitude, the State is supposed to embody Ethical life. Within the State, the individual does not separate his interest from the good of the community, because he includes the aims of the community in his own aims, and does not regard himself as an individual with interests separate from those of other individuals.

In Marx's view, Hegel does not explain how these sharply opposed outlooks can co-exist within a single society that is a State, but contains a Civil Society within it. We might try to answer, on Hegel's behalf, that the different outlooks belong to different people in the society. The owners and workers in different commercial enterprises might be taken to belong to Civil Society, and the politicians and civil servants might be taken to embody the outlook of the State. The State includes Civil Society, but extends beyond it; the institutions of the State provide the framework within which Civil Society carries on its business.

This attempt to allocate the functions of Civil Society and State to different individuals and institutions within a society does not seem completely satisfactory. For we might wonder how a single community can be formed from the two apparently opposed outlooks of Civil Society and State. If the Ethical outlook of the State is imposed on Civil Society, it seems to include obligations that, from the point of view of Civil Society, are rationally unjustified, since they do not necessarily promote the interests of individuals who take the Hobbesian outlook of Civil Society. We would expect a particular society that includes Civil Society and State to include tensions and conflicts that Hegel does not recognize.

Hegel's view seems to face an even more serious objection. For we have spoken as though there are some individuals who take the point of view of Civil Society and others who uphold the outlook of the State. But it cannot be quite as simple as this. For each citizen of a society is expected to take the Ethical point of view, and hence to share the outlook of the State. How are they to do this, if they are also owners or workers in a business, and hence members of Civil Society? The tensions between the two points of view do not seem to be confined to tensions between individuals; they also seem to arise within an individual. If the Hegelian citizen is both a member of Civil Society, when he goes to work and draws his wages or dividend, and a member of the State when he votes and reflects on his civic obligations, how is he to resolve this tension? Even if Ethical life resolves tensions between the outlooks that it supersedes, it seems to co-exist with an outlook that creates further tensions.

Marx sees this feature of Hegel's position when he remarks that Civil Society and State turn out to be two hostile armies, and that individuals have to choose between the two outlooks.[1] Marx agrees with Hegel's view that the outlook reflected in the social contract and in the American and French declarations of rights is basically selfish, and that this is the outlook of Civil Society.[2] If the Ethical life of the Hegelian State reaches a higher level than the Hobbesian outlook of Civil Society, Hegel owes an explanation of how the tension between the two outlooks is to be resolved.

In Marx's view, Hegel conceals this difficulty from himself by simply treating the State as an organism that includes Family and Civil Society as aspects. They perform their functions within the life of the State, and represent different elements within the Ethical life of the State as a whole. But Marx objects that Hegel has simply helped himself to this idea of the State as an organism whose functions belong to Family and Civil Society.[3] An organism has parts that perform some function that harmonizes with the functions of other parts in the characteristic activity of the whole. But when Hegel takes a modern society containing families, businesses, owners, and workers, and claims that this is an organism whose functions are Family and Civil Society, he assumes what he ought to prove.

Does Hegel assume what Marx takes him to assume? We might try to defend him by claiming that his organic conception of the State is not meant to describe the empirical character of existing states, but to describe a community that actual states may approach to different degrees. Marx is mistaken, then, if he believes that Hegel offers a purely descriptive account of existing modern societies.

But this defence does not extricate Hegel from the main difficulty. For we may now ask whether Ethical life, as Hegel conceives it, is even possible. If we assumed that Ethical life can be found in, say, 19th century France or Germany, we could easily show that it is possible; for we could point to historical examples. But if we do not assume that Ethical life is found in these historical examples, we have not shown how the Ethical outlook can co-exist with Civil Society, and even include it. We seem to return to the objection that Ethical life contains tensions that threaten its existence.

1034. Marx's Answer to Difficulties in Hegel

We might try to reply to Marx's objections by finding a more detailed account of Ethical life. Once we do this, we can see what conditions Civil Society has to satisfy if it is to be an

---

[1] 'The identity Hegel has set up between civil society and the state is the identity of two hostile armies, where any soldier has the "chance" to join the "enemy" through "desertion". Thus does Hegel correctly describe the existing empirical situation.' ('Critique of Hegel', 190, on Hegel, PR §297)

[2] 'The rights of man as such are distinguished from the rights of the citizen. Who is this man distinguished from the citizen? None other than the member of civil society. . . . Let us note first of all that the so-called rights of man . . . are only the rights of the member of civil society, that is, of egoistic man, man separated from other men and from the community.' ('Jewish', 235)

[3] 'It is a great step forward to view the political state as an organism, to view the diversity of powers no longer as an [in]organic, but as a living and rational distinction.' ('Hegel', 160 on §269)

aspect of Ethical life. We might then conclude that the description of Civil Society needs to the modified so that a revised Civil Society can perform functions that belong to Ethical life and do not conflict with it.

We noticed, however, that Hegel has a reason to oppose this approach to Ethical life. If the approach works, it vindicates the possibility of external moral criticism of existing societies. Since Hegel believes that such moral criticism is misguided and futile, he might intelligibly reject the suggestion that an account of Ethical life can be used to criticize Civil Society. If Civil Society is embodied in an existing society, Ethical criticism seems to do what Hegel says it cannot do.

Whether or not this argument accurately represents Hegel's attitude to external criticism, it captures the point of Marx's response to Hegel's claims about State and Civil Society. Though Marx sometimes speaks of the Hegelian State and Civil Society as hostile armies, he also argues that their apparent hostility is misleading, because their outlooks are not as distinct as Hegel makes them appear. Though the Ethical outlook of the State represents itself as superior to Civil Society, as a whole of which Civil Society is a proper part, in fact Ethical life simply represents the point of view of Civil Society as supreme. On the one hand, Hegel defines the State in opposition to Civil Society.[4] On the other hand, it has nothing to add to the outlook of Civil Society.[5]

This view of the Hegelian State does not make it identical to Civil Society. For Civil Society is simply an aggregate of companies and workers interacting with each other. It does not contain within itself the resources to safeguard its own activities. For that purpose, it needs the organs of government, law, police, courts, and so on. These organs of government take a broader point of view than any individual corporation takes. An individual owner or worker thinks of his competitive position in relation to others in the same position, whereas the government does not take this point of view, but takes a more universal point of view that embraces all the members of civil society. In so far as it provides conditions for the safe pursuit of the competition, it is not itself a competitor. Civil Society needs a State to sustain it, but the sort of State it needs is the one that endorses the competitive outlook within the bounds that are needed to keep the competition going.[6]

This analysis shows how Marx's criticism of the political theory of the Enlightenment applies to Hegel as well. He agrees with Hegel in treating the Enlightenment point of view as the outlook of 'egoistic man' (YM 235); this is Hegel's account of the presuppositions of Rousseau's social contract. Marx notices that Hegel finds the same outlook in Civil Society.[7] But since the Hegelian State does not really introduce an outlook distinct from that of Civil Society, it simply endorses the egoistic outlook that Hegel attributes to the theory of the

---

[4] 'Thus the antithesis of state and society is fixed. The state does not reside in but outside civil society.' ('Hegel', 189 on §297)

[5] 'The corporations are the materialism of bureaucracy, and bureaucracy is the spiritualism of the corporation.' ('Hegel', 184 on §297)

[6] 'The corporation is the attempt of civil society to become the state; but bureaucracy is the state which in actuality has become civil society.' ('Hegel', 185 on §297)

[7] In commenting on §289, Marx emphasizes Hegel's description of Civil Society as 'the battleground of the individual interests of each against all'. He represents this as 'the definition of civil society as bellum omnium contra omnes' ('Hegel', 179).

Enlightenment. Though the Hegelian State appears to advance beyond the egoism of the Enlightenment, it does not really advance beyond it.

In Marx's view, Hegel is open to criticism for failing to notice that he does not escape the egoistic outlook of Civil Society. But he is not to be criticized for his failure to engage in moral criticism of Civil Society. Marx agrees with Hegelian doubts about the pretensions of critical morality. In his view, we should not be surprised at the failure of the State to advance beyond Civil Society. We should only be surprised at Hegel's failure to draw this failure to our attention.

1035. Marx's Rejection of Moral Criticism

Marx applies this Hegelian lesson about the impotence of critical morality not only to Hegel on Ethical life, but also to his own treatment of capitalism. For he sometimes claims that he forgoes any criticism of capitalism that might rely on moral principles. In particular, he rejects the criticism that the exploitative elements in capitalism make it unjust. In his view, the rules of property, labour, and wages under capitalism are not unjust.

Why does he reject moral criticism of capitalism? He does not rely on any explicit analysis of morality that would correspond to Hegel's account of Morality and Ethical life. But reflexion on Hegel might suggest different reasons for believing that moral criticism is misplaced: (1) Perhaps Marx assumes that moral principles have to be roughly what Kant says they are—abstract and universal, but with enough content to support critical judgments on actions and institutions. If he doubts whether there are any such principles, he may conclude that we have no moral basis for either vindication or criticism of any actual or possible form of economic or social life. (2) If we take a more selective attitude to Kant, we may suppose that there are true, abstract, universal moral principles, just as Kant supposed. But we might infer that any principles satisfying these conditions will lack critical content. Hence every economic and social system will conform to them. This attitude to Kant reflects Hegel's criticism of the emptiness of Morality. (3) Kantian moral principles are really not abstract and universal, but are simply an abstract-sounding formulation of the underlying assumptions of capitalist society, just as Aristotle's claims about men, women, and slaves (for instance) are claims about the Greek society he was familiar with represented as universal features of human nature. Since moral principles are simply a reflexion of capitalist society, the practices of capitalist society are, as their apologists claim, perfectly just and right, and are not open to moral criticism.

Though all these accounts of moral principles lead to the conclusion that external moral criticism of capitalism, or of some other social and economic order, is misguided, their implications are different. According to the first view, institutions are neither morally right nor morally wrong, since moral principles cannot be found to give answers on this point. According to the second view, capitalism (e.g.) is right, and every consistent alternative economic and social order is also right. Overthrowing capitalism and replacing it with socialism would replace one just order with another. According to the third view, capitalism is right, and alternative orders are wrong, because the moral point of view is parochial, resting on the capitalist order. If, then, we seek to replace the capitalist economic order with one that will remove the insecurity and dependence characteristic of capitalist economic cycles, these alternative institutions and practices will be unjust, if they violate the basic assumptions of capitalist society.

Most of Marx's comments on morality seem to reflect the second or the third view, but it is sometimes difficult to tell which view he has in mind. He does not confine himself to saying that capitalism and its institutions are not unjust; he also allows that private property and freedom of contract are just. It is less clear whether he thinks a socialist order would also be just. If he does, he believes that moral evaluation is useless for comparing different social orders, though not necessarily useless within a particular order.

The best reason for attributing the third view to Marx may be found in his comments on the outlook of the Enlightenment and the French Revolution. He takes the Revolution to be inspired by the moral and political principles underlying the social contract. Marx analyses the rights of man, in contrast to the rights of citizens, and concludes that the rights of man are really the rights of the member of civil society, the 'egoistic man, man separated from other men and from the community' (YM 235).[8] His reason for interpreting the rights of man in this way appears in his comments on liberty. The permission to act in ways that do not harm others rests on some sharp separation between one's own interests and the interests of others, and it requires some acknowledged legal basis for determining what does and does not harm others.[9]

Marx seems to assume, then, that if we recognize rights belonging to an individual person that limit the permissible ways in which other people may treat him, we recognize the rights of 'egoistic man'. He observes that the institutions connected with property recognize such a right, since they allow the owner of the property to dispose of it as he pleases, within specified limits, without reference to the wishes or demands of other people. This feature of property reflects a general feature of many rights, that they protect someone from interference from others, even on occasions when interference might be better for the right-holder or for everyone. In this respect, Marx is right to claim that the recognition of rights protects egoistic man. He would have equally good reason to claim that any moral system that recognizes rights also protects egoistic man. His claim fits not only moral positions, such as Butler's or Price's or Kant's, that recognize basic principles conferring rights on individuals, but also indirect utilitarian positions, such as Hobbes's or Berkeley's, that assign a derivative place to rights.

Marx's objection, therefore, applies perhaps not to all moral outlooks, but at least to the many different types of moral outlooks that uphold and protect individual rights. His objection that they protect 'egoistic man' is simply a hostile expression of Butler's observation that morality does justice to self-love and does not require complete sacrifice of one's own interest for the interest of others. If Marx consistently maintains his

---

[8] Context quoted in §1033.
[9] 'Liberty is thus the right to do and perform anything that does not harm others. The limits within which each can act without harming others is determined by law just as the boundary between two fields is marked by a stake. This is the liberty of man viewed as an isolated monad, withdrawn into himself.' 'The practical application of the right of liberty is the right of private property . . . the right to enjoy and dispose of one's own possessions as one wills, without regard for other men and independently of society. It is the right of self-interest.' ('Jewish', 235–6)

objection to an outlook that protects egoistic man, he opposes one central and widely acknowledged element of morality. To this extent, he may reasonably be called an opponent of morality.

In so far as morality protects egoistic man, Marx wants to abolish morality, since he wants to abolish the social order that protects egoistic man. Capitalism is organized around the protection of egoistic man, in so far as it protects private property. A socialist order will abolish private property, and therefore will abandon the principle of protecting egoistic man. Marx's objection to property is simply an instance of his general objection to institutions and principles that give permission to individuals to pursue their own desires and interests without regard to the interests of others. Hence a social order that rejects any such permission should have nothing to do with the protection of rights that are protected by most systems of morality.

1036. The Replacement of Morality?

If Marx regards the capitalist order as just, and rejects moral criticism of it, why does he believe that it should be replaced by a socialist order? He does not simply express his desire for it to be replaced, and he does not confine himself to the prediction that it will be replaced. He also seems to believe that the world will in some way be better if socialism replaces capitalism. In what respect will it be better, and why should this fact about it persuade us that it ought to replace capitalism?

Marx sometimes displays some impatience with this sort of question. He represents himself as a social scientist whose concern is to understand the existing order and the social forces that will result in the collapse of the existing order and the rise of the new order. If he correctly identifies these forces and describes how they will work, he has completed his task as a social scientist, and it is up to us to decide whether we want to accept the new order or to struggle vainly against it. If Marx understands his role in this way, he has no need to take a moral position, and in particular he has no need to denounce capitalism as immoral or to make a moral case for socialism.

It is difficult to suppose, however, that Marx views himself primarily as a purely predictive social scientist. He also advocates revolutionary action to overthrow the capitalist order. He believes that such action should be based on knowledge of present conditions and well-informed predictions of the future. Attempts to replace capitalism with socialism in unfavourable conditions are misguided and foolish, because they have no prospect of success without the appropriate economic and social developments. Still, someone who considers whether or not to engage in revolutionary activity in favourable conditions apparently has a choice about whether to do it or not. How, in Marx's view, would it be reasonable to decide what to do?

Apparently we cannot answer this question by deciding that the capitalist order is unjust and that it ought to be replaced by a just order. If Marx holds the view of morality that is implied in his remarks about egoistic man, capitalism is not unjust, in so far as it protects private property. If we try to replace it with an order that abolishes private property, we try to abolish a just order and to replace it with an unjust order. More generally, if we try to replace a social order that protects rights with an order that recognizes no rights for egoistic man, we violate principles of morality.[10]

If we have no moral reason for revolutionary activity, what other sort of reason is available? If we will ourselves benefit from the social changes resulting from successful revolution, we have a self-interested reason to try to bring the changes about, if no one else will do it. But it is not clear that everyone who considers revolutionary activity will gain by it; Marx, for instance, does not seem to stand to gain anything by it. He can hardly claim to replace moral reasons with purely prudential reasons.

It would be strange, in any case, if Marx were to suggest that only self-interested reasons should be invoked. For his objection to moral systems that protect rights is that they protect 'egoistic man'. This is an objection only if egoistic man leaves out something important. If egoistic reasons are the only ones that we can reasonably rely on, it is difficult to see what is wrong with the protection of egoistic man. We might reasonably expect Marx to appeal to motives and reasons that do not move a purely egoistic individual.

It may be too restrictive, however, to confine ourselves to moral reasons and self-interested reasons, as though these were the only ones that Marx could appeal to. We might argue, for instance, that an immediate sympathetic reaction to someone's sufferings is neither egoistic nor strictly moral, but still gives us a good reason to act. Or again, we might be moved by an ideal that conforms to some impartial standard that is not necessarily a moral standard. Aesthetic ideals are obvious examples, but they need not be the only ideals that are relevant. Perhaps Marx can appeal to some impartial non-moral ideal that will support revolutionary action.[11]

To see what sort of ideal he might appeal to, we need to see what he objects to in capitalism, and what might be different under socialism. If we know what he wants to get rid of, we may be able to see why one might have reason to get rid of it.

1037. The Evils of Capitalism

Some of Marx's comments on capitalism are fairly easy to understand without any elaborate theoretical background. He often remarks that it forces many people into poverty, or destitution, or back-breaking work for long hours. It does not improve most people's prospects in life, but leaves them stuck in a cycle of poverty and dependence. Readers of Marx's description of the conditions of the working class do not need to reflect very elaborately in order to see that if the description is true, it is an indictment of capitalism.

A natural reaction to this description would be sympathy with the condition of the workers and some form of anger at the situation that produces this condition. This combination of attitudes normally results in some desire to change the situation so as to relieve the condition that provokes the sympathy. Will this series of non-moral attitudes produce non-moral reasons that explain and justify remedial and, if necessary, revolutionary action?

We might raise a question about the character of the anger that results from sympathy aroused by deprivation. Does this anger constitute indignation, an attitude that presupposes

---

[10] See Plamenatz, *KMPM* 311–13.   [11] Marx on morality; Wood, *KM*, ch. 9–10.

some responsibility for the deprivation? If so, we seem to need some basis for indignation at capitalists who profit by the deprivation of the workers. But we seem to lack any basis for indignation until we also believe that the capitalists are acting wrongly and taking more than they are entitled to take. Even if they are acting perfectly justly, as far as the rules of the system go, the system itself seems to be unjust, and the agents within it seem to act unjustly, if they really arouse our indignation. If this is so, Marx's rejection of moral criticism of capitalism seems to conflict with his view about the appropriate attitude to it.

This objection to Marx's anti-moralism may be too hasty. Anger need not include indignation at any agent who is supposed to be responsible for the bad condition that arouses our anger. We may witness a natural disaster and be angry enough about it to want to do something; but we need not be angry at anyone, if we think it could not have been avoided. Admittedly, perhaps our distress in such a case does not really count as anger; but if we say that, we need not suppose that anger is necessary for sympathy to lead us to remedial action. Alternatively, we may say that the anger is directed at the agents who are not doing something that they could do to remedy the situation. Even if people who know of a natural disaster are not responsible for the disaster itself (e.g., an earthquake), they may still be objects of anger if they do not do what it is appropriate to do for the relief of the sufferings caused by the disaster.

Would either of these ways of explaining responses to deprivation support Marx's anti-moralism? The first explanation tries to do without any reaction connected to anger, and to connect sympathy directly with remedial action. But this does not seem adequate. For we might notice that someone is suffering, and sympathize with their suffering, but still not try to do anything about it. If, for instance, we learn that someone is having their tooth extracted to prevent further pain and infection, we would conclude that it is better not to intervene. Alternatively, we might notice that we cannot relieve this person's suffering without making things worse for some equally undeserving person, and so we might regret the situation without thinking we ought to do anything to change it. This second possibility is especially relevant to the questions about capitalism; for defenders of this system might argue that the deprivation suffered by the worst-off cannot be reduced without making things much worse for everyone. The cogency of this defence seems to be relevant to a decision about whether we should try to change the situation that results in the deprivation. Apparently, then, we cannot reasonably translate sympathy into remedial action until we satisfy ourselves that the remedial action would not be open to decisive moral objections.

The second explanation, referring to anger at those who permit the deprivation and do nothing about it, also seems unsatisfactory by itself. For we need to know what reasons can be offered for permitting the deprivation. If they are morally cogent reasons, we seem to have a good argument against remedial action. If, then, we are to answer any such argument, we apparently need a strong enough moral case for the remedial action.

Marx might answer that this appeal to moral considerations would cripple revolutionary action. For it seems easy to think of moral objections to revolutionary action; it may involve violence, harm to innocent people, expropriation of people who are legally entitled to their property, civil war, restrictions on civil and political liberty, and so on. The moral case against revolution may seem to be overwhelming. On this point, we might agree with

Hobbes, even if not exactly for his reasons. If we none the less think revolution is sometimes appropriate, must we not be appealing to non-moral considerations?

This argument does not show that revolutionary action can do without an appeal to moral considerations. If we admit that the moral case against killing this innocent person is decisive, but we believe that someone would benefit considerably from her death, we do not yet seem to have given a good reason to kill her. Moreover, revolutionaries do not seem to be in this position of admitting that the moral case against them is decisive. On the contrary, they often argue or assume that the suffering imposed by capitalism is so severe that the removal of this suffering justifies the violation of rights. They do not seem to compare moral rights with non-moral goods; they seem to urge the precedence of one sort of right over another.

But even if we can understand revolutionary arguments in these moral terms, should we suppose that this is the best way to understand them? Perhaps Marxian revolutionaries might argue in this way if they are addressing people who are used to taking moral considerations to be overriding. But might they not dispense with this form of argument, and state their case in the non-moral terms that Marx seems to favour? Perhaps we might use Hobbes to support Marx here. If we think of different social orders and their partisans as being in a state of nature in relation to one another, we may argue that the appropriate standards for guiding and justifying their action are non-moral. In this war of all against all, different sides prosecute their aims with all the resources they can use, but they are not constrained by moral considerations, since morality does not apply to this sort of situation. In order to begin this sort of revolution, we must act immorally, from Hobbes's point of view, since we must disturb a stable commonwealth. But once we have successfully begun a revolution, moral principles no longer apply to us.

If we are justified in using this Hobbesian argument in Marx's support, we need to agree with Hobbes's view that morality does not apply outside the commonwealth.[12] But this view is cogently criticized by Suarez, Cudworth, and Clarke, who argue that war alters, but does not cancel, the demands of morality.[13] If they are right, Marxian revolutionaries might say that their actions are morally wrong, rather than beyond morality. Alternatively, they might argue that the moral considerations appropriate to this situation justify their action. Those who recognize moral principles applying to war agree that they justify actions that would not be justified in other circumstances. To see whether a similar argument fits Marx, we need to ask what sorts of moral principles are appropriate to the situation he envisages. Once we identify these principles, we can see whether he relies on them or rejects them.

1038. Capitalism and Human Nature

We have noticed that some of Marx's objections to capitalism are relatively non-theoretical. It does not take much theoretical background to recognize that he thinks it is bad to cause poverty, dependence, and deprivation. But if we consider only these objections, we overlook the theoretical principles that he relies on.

---

[12] Hobbes on the state of nature; §§489–90.   [13] Criticism of Hobbes on morality in the state of nature; §§624–9.

He objects to capitalism on the basis of an Aristotelian conception of human beings as essentially rational and social. Society is appropriate for human beings in so far as it allows them to develop their rational and social capacities. Capitalism contributes to this development, because it frees people from the narrow sphere of activity that ties them to villages, guilds, and other groups that prescribe a limited range of tasks and roles. In so far as people enter urban, industrial society, they can associate with more people, join unions, improve their situation in life, and so on. Moreover, industrial production and the use of steam, gas, and electricity relieve people from some of the burden of manual labour, and allow them to spend more of their time on something beyond the struggle for survival. As Aristotle says, they release us from the demands of necessity.[14]

But this side of capitalism carries a high cost. Workers have to work long hours in unhealthy conditions. Economic cycles make their livelihood insecure. The division of labour confines them to routine tasks without any intrinsic interest or opportunity for enjoyment or pride in their work. They are stuck in a subordinate status, and they have no opportunity to influence the conditions in which they work and live. Even if they have votes, the choices open to them offer no prospect of an improvement in their conditions.

In Marx's view, these are different ways in which capitalism violates human nature. The violation consists in the imposition of conditions that prevent or impede the realization of the essential human capacities, and hence prevent or impede the achievement of the human good. He expresses this point by saying that a human being is a 'species being' with a determinate nature constituted by rational and social capacities.[15] We can discover the right social order by considering what will realize the essential human capacities. On this point, Marx returns to the Aristotelian conception of human nature and political society.

This Aristotelian outlook explains Marx's hostility to the conception of rights that he attributes to Rousseau, the French Revolution, and the social contract. He interprets the social contract, as Hegel does, as the result of an exclusively self-confined conception of one's own good. According to this view, we make an agreement with other people in order to protect our self-confined interest, and this is the only reason for any concern with the good of others. Understood this way, the outlook of the social contract protects egoistic man, because it relies on this conception of human nature and human interests. It conflicts with the Aristotelian conception that takes social concerns to be part of the human good, not an unwelcome necessity that has to be borne for the sake of its instrumental benefits.

The opposition between the egoistic assumptions of the social contract and the Aristotelian emphasis on the social aspects of human nature is familiar from Hegel's contrast between Civil Society and State. In the Ethical life of the State, we do not regard the State as simply an instrument for the protection of egoistic man; citizens think of their social life as citizens

---

[14] Aristotle on necessity; *Pol.* 1326b26–32, 1332a7–27.

[15] Marx explains 'species being' by reference to freedom and self-determination: 'Conscious life activity distinguishes man immediately from the life activity of the animal. Only thereby is he a species being. Or rather, he is only a conscious being—that is, his own life is an object for him—since he is a species being. Only on that account is his activity free activity. Alienated labour reverses the relationship in that man, since he is a conscious being, makes his life activity, his *essence*, only a means for his *existence*.' ('Manuscripts' (Alienated Labour), 294) Plamenatz, *KMPM*, ch. 3, and Wood, *KM*, ch. 2, discuss Marx's conception of species-being.

as part of their good, and not simply as a means to it. Marx's Aristotelian view, however, supports his objections to Hegel's attempt to reconcile the outlook of Civil Society with the outlook of the State. Hegel supposes that the same people can consistently take the point of view of Civil Society and the point of view of citizens of the State. He might be entitled to say this if the two points of view were simply distinct. But the conflict between the two points of view casts doubt on his attempted reconciliation. If we look closely at the capitalist system, we see that it prevents us from realizing our social nature. Once we see that, we cannot be satisfied with the Hegelian co-existence of Civil Society with the State. Given the character of Civil Society under capitalism, the Hegelian State is empty pretension.

According to Marx, we can achieve the outlook of Hegelian Ethical life only by getting rid of Civil Society with its capitalist forms of oppression, and replacing it eventually with communist society. We need not examine his account of communist society in detail. It is enough to notice that he intends it to embody the Aristotelian conception of the human essence and the human good. It will not entirely remove the contrast between the realm of necessity and the realm of freedom. But the realm of necessity will no longer dominate our lives. On the one hand, we will have more control over the organization and aims of the system of production and distribution. On the other hand, we will have to devote less of our lives to the realm of necessity. Marx expects, correctly, that advances in production will make labour easier and less exhausting. His further expectation that people will take advantage of this change to expand the area of freedom in their lives has not yet been fulfilled. But in any case he does not expect changes in the conditions of production to make the whole difference. He also expects people in communist society to take more control over their lives, and to recognize that their activities as a whole realize their capacities as rational beings, and so are worthwhile for themselves, not simply as means to some distinct state of enjoyment.

It is not always clear how far Marx thinks a true conception of one's own good will result in different forms of activity, or in different attitudes to the same form of activity. In some places, he seems to argue that since the division of labour under capitalism prevents people from finding self-realization and satisfaction in their work, full communist society will abolish the division of labour. It will allow the same person to hunt in the morning, paint in the afternoon, and write poetry in the evening.[16] To the objection that this aim of realizing all human capacities is unrealistic and unreasonable, Marx and Engels reply that full communist society will release new human capacities and open new possibilities for their fulfilment.

---

[16] 'And finally, the division of labour offers us the first example of how, as long as man remains in natural society, that is, as long as a cleavage exists between the particular and the common interest, as long, therefore, as activity is not voluntarily, but naturally, divided, man's own deed becomes an alien power opposed to him, which enslaves him instead of being controlled by him. For as soon as the distribution of labour comes into being, each man has a particular, exclusive sphere of activity, which is forced upon him and from which he cannot escape. He is a hunter, a fisherman, a herdsman, or a critical critic, and must remain so if he does not want to lose his means of livelihood; while in communist society, where nobody has one exclusive sphere of activity but each can become accomplished in any branch he wishes, society regulates the general production and thus makes it possible for me to do one thing today and another tomorrow, to hunt in the morning, fish in the afternoon, rear cattle in the evening, criticize after dinner, just as I have a mind, without ever becoming hunter, fisherman, herdsman or critic.' (Marx and Engels, *GI* 53 (Part 1, on 'Private property and communism'), discussed in §125) On Marx's conception of full communist society see Plamenatz, *KMPM* 273–6.

We may doubt, however, whether the realization of human capacities needs the abolition of the division of labour. The social aspects of human self-realization should allow individuals to find their individual self-realization in their contribution to social activities. A division of labour under capitalism does not allow this sort of self-realization, because the relevant social activities are undertaken only as means to secure necessities. But when we value social activities for their own sakes, and value our individual activities as contributions to them, we need not insist on a wide expansion of our individual activities. Someone who plays a violin in an orchestra only to earn a living may not find his self-realization in contributing to the collective project of playing a symphony. But a musician who cares about musical performance for its own sake values the realization of his capacities as a violinist in contributing to the playing of the whole symphony. It would be foolish to insist that he can realize himself as a musician only if he is a one-man orchestra. Similarly, we need not make unrealistic demands for abolition of the division of labour if we are to understand how a different kind of society might achieve the realization of rational and social nature. And if we are doubtful about Marx's goal of self-realization because we think it demands an unrealistic attitude to the division of labour, we can at least reduce that doubt by reflexion on human social nature.

1039. The Moral Status of Marx's Criticism

This sketch of Marx's Aristotelian conception of rational and social nature is relevant to our previous question about whether his revolutionary critique of capitalism should be taken to express a moral point of view or not.

He clearly rejects one way of stating a moral objection; he does not argue that the oppressed classes under capitalism have fundamental human rights that are violated by the capitalist system. If he argued in this way, he would simply be claiming that more is due to egoistic man than the Enlightenment has recognized. While this sort of argument has appealed to liberals in the 19th century and later, it is not Marx's argument.

If Marx does not offer this sort of moral argument, we might infer, and he seems to infer, that he does not offer a moral argument at all. Perhaps we should accept a Hobbesian interpretation that treats the struggle between oppressors and oppressed as a war that involves a clash of wills and desires, but is not subject to moral evaluation. According to this view, the aim of overthrowing capitalism gives the victims of capitalism a purely internal reason to overthrow it. For those who care about developing their rational and social capacities, capitalism is not the best way to do it, and so there is a conflict of desires and aims between supporters and opponents of capitalism. But, on this view, there is no reason, apart from their current aims and desires, for the oppressed victims of capitalism to adopt the desire to develop their rational and social capacities.

Marx's conception of rational and social nature does not seem to offer a merely internal reason, however. Since he offers an account of human nature, rather than simply of human aims, he appeals to facts that go beyond particular people's actual aspirations. He sees that their actual aims may be moulded and distorted by the dominant social order, and so he does not treat actual aims as appropriate guides to action. We can see that people's aims become distorted, rather than simply altered, only if we can compare actual aims with appropriate aims. To find appropriate aims for people who suffer from distorted aims, Marx sets out his account of rational and social nature. The realization of rational and social capacities fixes the end that should guide criticism, reform, and revolution. He therefore offers external reasons to support his critique of capitalism.

For whom, then, are these reasons external reasons? Should we take Marx to assert that there are external reasons for the victims of capitalism to want to realize their human capacities, but there are no such reasons for the oppressors to realize their human capacities? If that is what he means, his advice is addressed to the oppressed, not to the oppressors. But it is difficult to see how the external reasons he offers could be limited in this way. For his appeal to the realization of human capacities seems to identify reasons that are reasons for every human being. How, then, could they not be reasons for the oppressors as well? If they are reasons for everyone, everyone has the same reasons to want to realize their own human nature.

If Marx appeals to universal external reasons that are equally reasons for everyone, he comes close to offering a moral argument. But he does not necessarily come close enough to count as a moralist. For we may recognize reasons that are universal, in so far as they make the same end reasonable for everyone, without thereby recognizing that we have reason to pursue or to promote this end on behalf of other people. If I have external reasons to take care of my health, and you have the same external reasons to take care of your health, it does not follow that I have good reason to take care of your health. If my concern for my health and your concern for your health require limited resources that we have to compete for, the recognition of universal external reasons does not seem to justify me in leaving something for you, or to justify you in leaving something for me. We noticed in our discussion of Kant that something more is needed to justify the move from a universal reason to impartial concern. If Marx believes that nothing can justify this move to impartial concern, he has a reason to claim that his appeal to universal external reasons does not constitute a moral argument against capitalism.

But he may none the less provide a plausible basis for a moral argument. Marx does not seem to confine himself to arguments that will make the oppressed more inclined to assert themselves by acting to achieve their good. He also offers arguments that will make the oppressed more inclined to recognize their dignity, so that they will not simply assert their aims and desires, but will also be more inclined to demand what they are entitled to. In so far as they recognize that their legitimate aims are not confined to those that are formed in them by the prevailing social order, but should be formed by a true conception of their good, they recognize that they deserve more than they have been given and that their legitimate aspirations deserve to be recognized and fulfilled. In so far as people recognize external reasons that require them, as Kant puts it, to treat themselves as ends, they see reasons to demand recognition for themselves as ends, and hence to demand recognition for persons as ends.

On this basis, we may reasonably regard a true conception of the human good as Aristotle and Aquinas regard it, so that it becomes a basis for moral criticism of existing societies, and a basis for an argument about justice, resting on a conception of justice as giving what is appropriate to each person. Part of the point of understanding the claim in this way is to make it clear that we assert that this is a reason for the oppressors to remove the oppression, whether or not they recognize the reason.

1040. Marx's Vindication of Morality

Marx's claims about human nature, therefore, constitute an argument for the moral justifiability of the demands of the oppressed. By offering this argument, Marx implicitly refutes the views of morality that would exclude justified moral criticism of capitalism. Kantian moral principles are not so empty that they cannot justify any criticism of any social order; in fact they justify criticism of capitalism. Nor are they so parochial that they make it fruitless to deny that capitalism is just; on the contrary, Marx presents a plausible case to show that it is not just. The demand to realize one's nature as a rational and social being seems the sort of demand that one could reasonably put forward in a kingdom of ends as a proper subject for universal legislation. If Marx endorses these reasons for thinking moral criticism of capitalism unjustified, he undermines his case by explaining how it is justified.

If this is an appropriate basis for Marx's criticism of capitalism, it also shows how far he is right and wrong in separating himself from the Enlightenment appeal to fundamental rights and to a social contract. He is correct to object that appeals to a contract and to basic rights offer protection to egoistic man, if the underlying conception of human nature is basically selfish. But if we accept Marx's more traditional conception of human nature, we may recognize rights and agreements that do not rely on a basically selfish condition. If we take justice and rights to involve giving people what is due to them and appropriate for them, justice requires what is appropriate for rational and social nature, and basic rights should reflect this basic requirement of justice. Since facts about rational and social nature include facts about the self-confined elements of one's good, a correct conception of rights will include some protection for egoistic man. If Marx means to claim that any protection for egoistic man is incompatible with a correct view of human nature, he does not seem to see all the implications of his own view. Though he is justified in claiming that the French Revolution does not recognize all the rights that deserve recognition, he is not justified in claiming that it is radically wrong in its view of the relevant rights.

Marx himself may not have seen that his description of the effects of capitalism and his conception of rational and social nature support a moral critique of capitalism. Historically, his failure to see this is quite important. Later Marxists are sometimes reluctant to present an explicitly moral argument, even though they present a detailed indictment of capitalism and advocate its overthrow. They represent socialist demands as essentially antagonistic to the moral outlook of the oppressors, and have been suspicious of the 'moralizing' tendency that tries to represent socialist demands as a reasonable interpretation of moral principles common to oppressors and oppressed.[17] A sceptical attitude towards morality, on the ground

---

[17] A sharp rejection of any moralizing interpretation of socialist demands appears in Trotsky's 'Morals'. One section (19–20) argues against the recognition of 'moral precepts obligatory upon all', on the ground that when one tries to give them any determinate content, it turns out that 'the norms of "obligatory" morality are in reality filled with

that it is essentially a device of the oppressors, might reasonably be expected to result in decreased reluctance to violate widely accepted moral principles.

Marx's attitude to his different arguments, however, is not their most relevant philosophical aspect. His different claims about morality and capitalist oppression are important because they appear to justify one inference from Hegel's remarks on morality and ethical life, but they really justify another. We distinguished an 'anti-moralist' and a 'moralist' view of critical moral theory. The anti-moralist view emphasizes Hegel's hostile remarks about any attempt by moral theorists at fundamental criticism of existing practices or institutions. From this point of view, it is not surprising that Hegel has not much to tell us about how to evaluate particular states and their institutions from the standpoint of a critical theory of the right form of Ethical life. Since Marx declares his opposition to prevailing institutions, the anti-moralist Hegelian view assures him that morality cannot support him. The moralist view, by contrast, seeks to find ways of filling in the aspects of critical moral theory that Hegel leaves out in his account of Ethical life; from this point of view, reflexion on the inadequacies of Kantian Morality, taken by itself, helps us to find better principles that will allow us to identify the best form of Ethical life. The moralist may reasonably regard Marx's claims about the realization of rational and social nature as a sketch of the appropriate sort of critical moral theory.

Marx's explicit intentions correspond most closely to the anti-moralist reaction to Hegel. But we have seen how his actual account of capitalist oppression really undermines the anti-moralist reaction and supports the moralist reaction. We have not tried to show that his claims about human nature are all true, or that they justify the objections he raises against capitalism. But if the arguments and considerations that he presents are at least reasonable and relevant, he shows what a critical moral theory might be like.

1041. Aristotelian and Kantian Theories

The considerations that Marx appeals to in his account of rational and social nature are not especially novel. Quite the reverse: in appealing to the nature of human beings as rational and social, he goes back to a traditional Aristotelian line of argument, maintained by Suarez, Grotius, Leibniz, and Butler, and abandoned by Hume and Kant. The claims that underlie this argument have often been dismissed as the products of outdated science, or as merely culturally determined preferences pretending to be universal norms. Among the critics who are especially prone to unmask the pretensions of culturally determined preferences, Marxists have often been quite prominent. When Marx incorporates claims about human nature in his attack on capitalism, he offers—again implicitly—a powerful reply to such objections. For the features of human nature he appeals to do not seem especially controversial; nor does it seem very controversial that expression of them is a central aspect of the human

---

class, that is, antagonistic content' (20). The bourgeoisie imposes its moral views on the exploited masses through these obligatory norms; 'The appeal to abstract norms is not a disinterested philosophical mistake but a necessary element in the mechanics of class deception' (20). Trotsky reacts against the attempt to formulate a socialist moral ideal by Kautsky, *EMCH*.

good; nor does it seem completely strained to argue that capitalism does not allow the degree of expression of them that would be desirable.

To say that these appeals to human nature do not seem especially controversial is not to deny that someone might dispute them; but (as Aristotle remarks) it will not be easy for those who dispute them to find anything more plausible to rely on. Indeed, it will not be easy for these critics to avoid implicit reliance on these same appeals to features of human nature. This is especially clear when we consider Nietzsche's critique of morality.

If we take Marx to support a Kantian conception of morality by appeal to claims about human nature, we can reasonably take him to support a particular method of reconciling Kantian with Aristotelian moral theory. A Kantian theory, requiring morality to consist of categorical imperatives, binding on all rational agents as such, makes rather stringent demands on the sorts of considerations that could be mentioned in a categorical imperative. Kant believes, for reasons that we have considered and found inadequate, that appeal to human nature is not an appropriate consideration. Reflexion on Marx's criticisms of capitalism suggests that an appeal to human nature as rational and social is an appropriate consideration to support a categorical imperative; we might even suggest that it is the only appropriate consideration.

This assessment of Marx's place in the clarification of a Hegelian approach to moral theory suggests that it is reasonable to combine Kantian with Aristotelian principles. Marx himself, not being interested in moral theory and its history for their own sakes, does not explore the possibility of this combination. But Green takes up the suggestion, in ignorance (as far as we know) of Marx. The fact that a similar suggestion emerges from Marx, setting out from significantly different presuppositions and with significantly different aims, may reasonably create some presumption in favour of Green's approach.

1042. Marx, Kant, and History

Marx is one of the Hegelians who try to develop Kant's 'idea for a universal history' into a more definite theory of historical development. Marx's distinctive contribution is his attempt to explain historical change through closer attention to social and economic changes. He shares Kant's emphasis on the progressive implications of unintended consequences. According to Kant, human beings are competitive, and their competition forms the outlook of 'humanity' as opposed to 'personality'.[18] But the competition also develops rational capacities, and helps us to recognize human beings as rational agents who deserve something in their own right. To take this point of view on human beings is to accept the outlook of personality, which restricts the purely competitive impulses of humanity. Similarly, Marx regards capitalism as a step towards freedom, not because it embodies freedom, and not because capitalists aim at freedom, but because capitalist modes of production and the resulting social order tend to create the conditions in which freedom can be realized.

Marx's view of historical development might be taken to describe laws of historical change from which one can predict the future social order. If we understand his view in

---

[18] Kant on history; §978.

this way, we might take it to replace the Kantian idea, which is sharply distinct from an empirical, predictive, theory. Perhaps, then, Marx refutes Kant's view that the aspirations of morality can only be embodied in faith and hope and cannot claim the status of empirical knowledge. For similar reasons, we might claim that Marxian views of history undermine Kant's argument for believing that morality needs belief in God in order to support the necessary faith and hope.

This interpretation of Marx's theory of history might be offered in support of an anti-moralist account of Marx's critique of capitalism. If we understand what will happen, the rational attitude is to adapt ourselves to it, whether or not we want it to happen. Whether it ought to happen or not may seem beside the point, if it is going to happen in any case irrespective of our efforts. The appropriate role for practical reason is to prepare for what will happen, and to ignore pointless questions about what ought to be the case.

If we take this to be the point of Marx's theory of historical change, he seems to be open to two objections: (1) We may well doubt whether he gives good reason to believe that he describes an inevitable process that operates independently of individual or collective choices by individuals and societies. The history of the 19th and 20th centuries may be taken to strengthen these doubts. (2) Even if we thought he had identified an inevitable process, we would not have made moral evaluation relevant. If I knew that an earthquake would happen in London in July 2050, my moral judgments would make some difference to my choices; I would tend to support the evacuation of London before that date rather than increased immigration into London. Similarly, if I thought the future society projected by Marx would be morally worse than the present order, I would have a reason to do all I could to delay it, or to try to mitigate its effects.

But, whatever Marx may have intended, we need not interpret his views on historical change in ways that leave him open to these objections. Instead of taking them to replace Kant, we may take them to offer some support to Kantian aspirations. If Marx is right, the aim of creating a society guided by the outlook of personality is not a purely utopian dream; on the contrary, economic and social developments may promote the development of such a society even when they currently conflict with it. Advanced capitalism offers better prospects, in Marx's view, for the emergence of full communist society than the feudal system or the Ancien Régime would have offered. We need the moral point of view to recognize these prospects and to see how they might be exploited. That is why Kantian morality allows us to discover the progressive elements in history, without ignoring the elements that impede progress.

From this point of view, therefore, a selective and critical use of Marx may support the outlook of Kantian moral faith. Though Marx would no doubt have denounced Kantian faith as moralistic obfuscation of the sort that he deplores, it may be the right basis for the absorption of those elements of Marx's position that deserve to be absorbed in a historically informed moral theory.

76

SCHOPENHAUER

1043. Schopenhauer and Kant

Schopenhauer's attitude to morality is most strongly influenced by Kant. He does not discuss any of Kant's predecessors in any detail. He has more to say about Kant's successors, but he believes they are misguided; he disagrees both with previous attempts to develop Kant's general position and with Hegel's attempt to treat problems of moral theory historically.[1] He believes he knows which parts of Kant's philosophy are genuine insights, and which parts are errors that need to be discarded. He attacks Kant's rationalist conception of morality, and argues that morality is based on the feeling of compassion, not on rational principle. Here he seems close to the view of Hutcheson and (in some places) Hume.

Schopenhauer agrees with Kant, however, and disagrees with the sentimentalists, in believing that morality has a metaphysical basis, and that our moral attitudes make us aware of the metaphysical truths that underlie them. As Kant says, morality provides the ratio sciendi of the metaphysical facts, and the metaphysical facts provide the ratio essendi of morality. Schopenhauer believes that the primacy of compassion in morality makes us aware of the basic metaphysical fact discovered by transcendental idealism; the basis for individuating and distinguishing persons is purely phenomenal, and is not a feature of things in themselves. Morality, understood in this way, accustoms us to looking at ourselves as things in themselves.

From the noumenal point of view, will is the only reality, and there are no distinct individual wills. Critics of Kant often reproach him for assuming that there must be a plurality of things in themselves, and that they correspond one-to-one to phenomenal things. This assumption about correspondence matters to Kant's conception of free will and morality. Schopenhauer rejects the assumption, and claims that the moral consciousness refutes our ordinary belief in distinct persons.

Some of Schopenhauer's arguments are internal to the moral point of view. He tries to show that Kantian moral theory leaves out facts that we can appreciate from the point of view of ordinary morality. Here he takes the standpoint of the first two chapters of Kant's

---

[1] '...no more here than in the previous books shall we relate histories and give them out as philosophy' (WR iv §53 = P i 273). I cite WR by book and section or by chapters (of the 'Supplements' in vol. ii), with the volume and page of Payne's translation (marked 'P'). I cite BM by section number, followed by the page of Payne's translation.

Groundwork, and claims to follow Kant's 'analytic method'.[2] His argument against Kant and in favour of compassion as the basis of morality does not seem to depend on Schopenhauer's metaphysics. But his other arguments rely on metaphysical claims, not on an appeal to ordinary morality.

He accepts some central elements of Kant's theory, as he understands them. Hence morality is to be sharply distinguished from self-interest. It is Kant's great merit to have 'purged ethics of all eudaemonism' (*BM* §3, 49), since he denies that morality is a means to one's own happiness. A motive that gives moral worth to an action or an agent must be entirely separate from self-interested motives. Kant also sees that practical reason yields only the form of a maxim, not its content. The a priori examination of morality, from the point of view of pure practical reason, describes only the formal features of a moral principle.

But because Schopenhauer agrees with Kant on these points, he argues against a further Kantian claim about morality. Kant is a rationalist, in so far as he thinks morality has to be distinguished not only from self-interest, but also from action on any non-rational impulse, emotion, or sentiment. But Schopenhauer believes that morality rests on a certain sort of sentiment, and specifically on compassion. According to Kant, the reasons that ought to convince us to divorce morality from self-interest ought also to persuade us to divorce it from sentiments and feelings. Since Schopenhauer disagrees with Kant on this point, he should reject Kant's view about the nature of sentiments and their relation to morality, or about why one ought not to appeal to self-interest.

We have found reasons to believe that Kant's case for rationalism is stronger than his case against eudaemonism, and that he does not take adequate account of the possibility of rationalism combined with eudaemonism. Schopenhauer, however, draws exactly the opposite conclusion about where Kant is right and where he is wrong.

Schopenhauer's criticism of Kant deserves consideration whether or not he convinces us of his alternative. If he is right about what is needed to restore consistency to Kant's position, and if we agree with his evaluation of the position that he regards as authentically Kantian, then Kant's moral philosophy faces serious objections. If we agree with Schopenhauer in believing that Kant's actual views contain inconsistencies or conflicts, but we do not agree with Schopenhauer's conception of the authentically Kantian position, we have some reason to look for a different way to revise Kant's position.

1044. Eudaemonism

Schopenhauer agrees with Kant's rejection of eudaemonism. He follows Hegel in ascribing eudaemonism to most of Kant's predecessors (*BM* §3, 49). But he takes Plato to reject it, because Plato argues that virtue is to be chosen for its own sake.[3] Plato is the only ancient moralist to reject eudaemonism. Lutheran theology also embodies a conception of wholly unselfish virtue, since Luther denies that good works are a means to salvation and treats

---

[2] *BM*, Pref. to 1st edn., 10–11.
[3] Schopenhauer on Plato; §58 (quoting *WR* iv Appx = i 524). Cf. *WR* i §16 = P i 86; ch. 16 = P ii 150.

them simply as an accompaniment of faith, 'which therefore appears quite gratuitously and of its own accord' (*WR* iv Appx = P i 524).[4]

Schopenhauer's description of Plato's *Republic* throws some light on his assumptions. He does not discuss Plato's clearly stated intention to defend virtue by showing that it promotes the agent's happiness; he attends to Plato's intention to prove that virtue is to be chosen for its own sake. He refuses to attribute both intentions to Plato, because he thinks the two are inconsistent. It is surprising, however, that he singles out Plato among Greek moralists; for the claim that he attributes to Plato, that virtue is to be chosen for its own sake, is accepted no less emphatically by Aristotle and the Stoics. Schopenhauer does not say much about Aristotle, but he argues that the Stoics are eudaemonists, on the ground that they conceive happiness as tranquillity and freedom from unsatisfied desire, and regard virtue as simply a means to this end.[5]

In drawing this sharp contrast between the Platonic and the Stoic position, Schopenhauer seems not to consider the view that virtue is to be valued for its own sake as a good in itself, and therefore as a component of happiness. He therefore misunderstands the relation between Plato's view and the Aristotelian and Stoic views. Aristotle and the Stoics agree with Plato that virtue is to be chosen for its own sake, and Plato agrees with them that a defence of virtue should connect it with the agent's happiness.

Schopenhauer seems not to recognize this position on virtue and happiness, and seems not to notice that some moralists have actually held it. In his view, evidence of valuing virtue for its own sake is evidence of rejection of eudaemonism, and evidence of eudaemonism is evidence of valuing virtue only as a means. In suggesting that the Stoics regard virtue simply as a means to tranquillity, he exploits one line of thought that is to be found in Stoic sources;[6] but he overlooks the fact that the Stoics agree with Plato in valuing virtue for its own sake. His one-sided interpretation of the Stoics supports his one-sided view of Plato, and causes him to overlook the degree of agreement between the Platonic and the Stoic position.

If some eudaemonist positions recognize the non-instrumental and dominant value of virtue, how does this affect the cogency of Schopenhauer's objections to eudaemonism? Are his objections plausible only to the extent that he attacks an instrumentalist version of eudaemonism? Normally he rejects egoism on the ground that it implies a mercenary attitude that treats virtue simply as a means to some selfish advantage. The form of egoism that is open to this charge conceives the agent's good in purely selfish terms, not including the good of any other person. If this is Schopenhauer's charge, non-instrumental eudaemonism seems to avoid it. Though self-interested action, as such, is not morally admirable, self-interest does not exclude an action from being morally admirable. In some circumstances, indeed, the pursuit of one's own interest may be morally required, for reasons emphasized by Butler and

---

[4] Schopenhauer cites (but without a precise reference) Luther, 'On the Freedom of a Christian' (see C ii 1–28 = *Works*, xxxi 333–77 (which is less definite than Schopenhauer suggests). Luther on self-love; §§416–17.

[5] 'For the Stoic ethics is originally and essentially not a doctrine of virtue, but merely a guide to the rational life, whose end and aim is happiness through peace of mind. Virtuous conduct appears in it, so to speak, only by accident, as means, not as end. Therefore the Stoic ethics is by its whole nature and point of view fundamentally different from the ethical systems that insist directly on virtue, such as the doctrines of the Vedas, of Plato, of Christianity, and of Kant. The aim of Stoic ethics is happiness . . .' (*WR* i §16 = P i 86)

[6] On tranquillity in Stoic ethics, and on mistaken conclusions drawn from it, see §182.

Price.[7] So far, then, Schopenhauer's objections do not seem to show that non-instrumentalist eudaemonism involves an objectionable form of selfishness.

Some of his objections, however, are more directly relevant to non-instrumentalist eudaemonism. For, according to his conception, virtue seems to preclude any non-instrumentalist eudaemonist outlook. He seems to object to all forms of self-interest if they constitute any part of our motive for being virtuous; any virtue based in any way on self-interest is not genuine moral virtue.[8] But this condition for virtue needs further argument, which Schopenhauer does not offer. He does not explain why objections to selfish egoism are objections to egoism in general; hence he does not explain his rejection of Greek eudaemonism as a foundation for morality.

In rejecting egoism altogether, Schopenhauer seems to go beyond common morality. We might change our minds about people's character if we realize that their apparently virtuous actions were really aiming only at some selfish advantage for them; but should we change our minds if we simply believe that they care about the virtuous action for its own sake and regard it as part of their own happiness? Schopenhauer needs some further argument against this role for self-interest in virtue.

1045. Moral Motivation

Schopenhauer would have a stronger case for his extreme anti-egoism if he could defend his implicit view of moral motivation. He assumes, as others have assumed, that an action has a fixed quantity of motivation that can be taken up either by the moral motive or by some other motive.[9] If we have a litre jug, we have it filled purely with wine if it is filled with wine and nothing else. If we fill it with half a litre of wine and half a litre of bleach, we have adulterated the wine, and someone who wants to buy a litre of wine has been cheated if he buys the mixture we have produced. If this is the right way to think of motivation, we would be justified in complaining that a moral motive combined with non-moral motives has been adulterated and is not present in the pure and genuine form we expected.

A different sort of demand seems reasonable, however, if we conceive motivation as involving sufficiency for a given task or a given demand. If an aircraft is required to reach London from New York in eight hours even in an 80 km/h headwind, its engines need to be powerful enough to carry the plane at the appropriate speed even against the wind. Similarly, if a rugby player is training as a place kicker, she needs to be able to kick the ball over the posts from some distance, even allowing for unfavourable winds. If the aircraft travels in a tailwind, it may travel no faster than an inferior aircraft would travel (if the inferior aircraft runs at full power, and the better aircraft runs below full power). Similarly, the good place kicker in favourable winds may do no better than an inferior kicker would do.

---

[7] On the requirement to take care of one's own interest see §§703–4 (Butler); §807 (Price); §920 (Kant on duties to oneself).

[8] 'For I repeat that all virtue in any way practised for the sake of a reward is based on a prudent far-seeing egoism.' (WR iv Appx. = P i 524) The distinctive feature of actions that have moral worth is 'the exclusion of that class of motives whereby all human actions are otherwise prompted, namely, those of self-interest in the widest sense of the term.' (BM §15, 139)

[9] On motivation and subtraction in Kant see §§914, 928. On Balguy and Silvester see §669.

If we conceive moral motives as relative to demands or tasks in this way, mixture does not seem to be objectionable in itself. If the moral motive is sufficient to ensure the right action, even in the face of 'headwinds' from other motives, we need not accuse a person of lacking this motive simply because she acts with the aid of 'tailwinds' from other motives. The moral motive and the non-moral motives need not compete with each other in a zero-sum contest to be 'the' motive of the action.

Schopenhauer, however, assumes that the 'competitive' picture fits moral motivation. He therefore assumes a 'principle of subtraction', so that the more motivation is taken up by non-moral motives, the more is subtracted from the moral worth of the action.[10] He prefers this picture over a non-competitive picture that replaces the principle of subtraction with a principle of sufficiency.

We need some reason, therefore, to prefer the principle of subtraction over the principle of sufficiency. Perhaps the ground or point of moral evaluation makes it reasonable to evaluate people and their actions by reference to the principle of subtraction. But Schopenhauer does not explicitly contrast the two principles, and does not explain his preference for the principle of subtraction. Hence it is difficult to see what he has in mind. More generally, it is difficult to see how any reasonable claims about the point of moral evaluation might justify the principle of subtraction.

The principle of sufficiency, however, fits some reasonable assumptions about moral evaluation. We may reasonably want to identify people whose moral convictions are firm enough to move them even in cases where they face some opposition from other motives. It is reasonable to distinguish these people from those who care about morality, but only enough to follow it when other motives make it easy for them. Since we want to distinguish these two types of people, we sometimes attend to circumstances in which the moral motive faces opposition, in order to decide whether a person has a morally good will. But we need not insist that actions have moral worth only if they are done in just those circumstances, or that people are virtuous only if they act in circumstances where the moral motive faces opposition.

If our account of the moral motive relies on the principle of subtraction, it rejects any contribution from non-moral motives. A further condition would require the actual presence of conflicting non-moral motives. We might argue that the moral motive demonstrates its sufficiency only if moves us against actual non-moral motives. This view is sometimes attributed to Kant. Schopenhauer neither endorses nor rejects it. But one might argue that his defence of the principle of subtraction commits him to the claim about conflicting motives too. If we can know that we act from the moral motive only if we have no other motive favouring an action, we reject any counterfactual criterion for the moral motive. According to a counterfactual criterion, we act from the moral motive in so far as we would still act from it if we had conflicting motives. If we reject this counterfactual criterion, we should also reject a counterfactual account of how the moral motive is sufficient to override motives that might conflict with it. Hence we should say that the moral motive is sufficient for action, only in so far as it overrides actual motives that conflict with it.

---

[10] Mandeville exploits this implication of the principle of subtraction, to cast doubt on the existence of virtuous characters; see §§633, 635, 669.

But ought we to require morally good people to suffer the permanent conflict of motives that is implied by the demand for actual conflict? The contrary view seems more reasonable. However much we emphasize the importance of acting from the moral motive, it is reasonable to want other motives to co-operate with it. For even if they are strictly unnecessary, they may be helpful; they make us readier to recognize the requirements of morality and more vigorous in carrying them out.[11] We may, therefore, reasonably favour the principle of sufficiency. Schopenhauer has no good reason for insisting on the principle of subtraction, either on Kant's behalf or on his own.

1046. Duty and Inclination

Schopenhauer's attitude to the principle of subtraction becomes more puzzling if we turn to his discussion of Kant on duty and inclination. He endorses Schiller's satire on Kant (*BM* 66), and therefore attributes the principle of subtraction to Kant. But he does not justify this attribution. Though he points out that Kant sometimes condemns inclinations more strongly than he should, he fails to show that in the crucial passage Kant commits himself to Schiller's version of him. Kant accepts the principle of sufficiency rather than the principle of subtraction.

Schopenhauer rejects the account of moral motivation, based on the principle of subtraction, that he erroneously attributes to Kant, He argues that Kant is wrong to condemn (as Schopenhauer supposes) anyone in whom inclination and the sense of duty coincide in recommending the same action. He believes, therefore, that the principle of subtraction gives the wrong results, and would give the wrong results even if Kant were right to believe that the moral motive is purely rational.

This is surprising, because Schopenhauer's critique of egoism appears to rely on the principle of subtraction. He argues that the genuine moral motive excludes any admixture of self-interested motivation. On this view, people who identify their own good partly with acting on moral motives are condemned, and so all forms of eudaemonism are condemned. Schopenhauer makes this clear in his own discussion of the actions to which we attribute real moral worth.[12] We might take some of his remarks simply to insist that in a morally good person self-interested motives cannot be necessary for a morally right action; if this is all he means, he simply demands a moral motive that is sufficient for the action. But this is not all he says; he also insists that self-interested motives cannot make any contribution—even it is unnecessary for the action. Schopenhauer's conception of moral worth seems to agree with Kant, as Schiller understands him, except that Schopenhauer substitutes compassion for the sense of duty, and self-interested motives for inclinations.

[11] See Price on the help given by passions, §817.

[12] 'We find that their characteristic feature is the exclusion of that class of motives whereby all human actions are otherwise prompted, namely, those of *self-interest* in the widest sense of the term. If a self-interested motive is the only one, its discovery entirely destroys the moral worth of an action; and if such a motive acts as an accessory, the moral worth of the action is reduced by its discovery. The absence of all egoistic motivation is, therefore, *the criterion of an action of moral worth.*' (*BM* §15, 139–40)

1047. Egoism and Morality

Schopenhauer sees that self-interest enters some areas of what we normally regard as morality. These areas involve agreements for mutual advantage, and hence include the distributive questions that are characteristic of justice. In such cases, we are neither required to abandon all consideration of our own advantage so that we can sacrifice ourselves to others nor licensed to consider the advantage of others simply as means to our own advantage.

Schopenhauer, however, does not treat these apparent areas of morality as a counter-example to his claim that morality excludes egoism. Instead, he infers that they are not really areas of morality. In his view, Glaucon (in *Republic*, ii) and Hobbes give the right account of the origin of the state and of the principles of justice and right that guide it (*WR* iv §62 = P i 343). Most of the actions connected with justice, fairness, and honesty can be traced to self-interest and the desire for a good reputation (*BM* §13, 122). He suggests that cases of 'disinterested philanthropy' and of 'entirely voluntary justice' are rare.[13] The presence of any element of self-interest in our motives for doing an action implies that the action is outside the area of morality.

If Schopenhauer is right, he proves that many practices we ordinarily count as parts of morality really are not parts of it at all. For many 'moral' (as we suppose) practices and institutions benefit the participants, and the benefit matters to them. To explain why people make and keep promises, it is relevant to mention that they believe this practice is mutually advantageous. We would look at it quite differently if we supposed that it would never be in our interest to be able to rely on someone else's promise, and that we would always be required to fulfil burdensome promises without ever benefiting from our fidelity. We might well think morality was asking too much of us if we would never benefit from it.

It does not follow, however, that the actions prescribed by such practices and rules are really not moral, but rest entirely on self-interested motives. Schopenhauer is impressed by the reasons Hobbes gives to show that each member of a collection of purely self-interested individuals might find it to be in his individual interest to participate in setting up institutions that restrain the individual pursuit of self-interest, so that everyone can be protected against aggression by others. But Schopenhauer does not discuss the difficulty of securing stable compliance with the rules of such institutions. Even though it is good for me if a stable practice of promising exists, it is not necessarily in my interest to keep my own promises, since I can often see obvious benefits in breaking them. Schopenhauer cites the benefits of having a good name and being generally regarded as trustworthy. But even if these matter to me to some extent, it is not obvious why they should matter to me most, if I am purely self-interested. The mere fact that I gain some benefit from fulfilling the requirements of justice, honesty, or fidelity does not explain why I fulfil them, if I stand to benefit more by doing something else.

Some recognized areas of morality, therefore, often involve the sacrifice, or possible sacrifice, of my maximum advantage for the sake of some mutual advantage that does not

---

[13] '. . . the surprise, the deep emotion, and the high respect with which we welcome them are clear evidence that they belong to the things we do not expect, and are rare exceptions.' (*BM* §13, 126)

maximize the advantage of any of the parties benefited. Readiness to accept this sort of sacrifice cannot be explained by appeal to purely self-interested motives. Moreover, even if we could secure the compliance of purely self-interested agents to some practices involving contracts and promises for mutual advantage, people who are not purely self-interested will accept more contracts and promises, and will adhere to them more reliably, even when the consequences of violating them are not so disadvantageous to them individually.[14]

Rules of justice do not require renunciation of concern for one's own interest, but they require impartiality between the interests of different people. Schopenhauer does not take this impartial attitude to be a part of morality, and so he does not believe that just actions resulting from this attitude belong to genuine justice. He therefore overlooks an important area of morality that is neither wholly altruistic nor wholly explained by self-interest. In many cases, the fact that an action or policy secures my interest is relevant to my acceptance of it, but my acceptance of it does not rest on purely selfish considerations. Principles whose observance is beneficial to everyone, but less beneficial to me than their violation would be, seem to be moral principles. In assuming that selfish concerns adequately explain our acceptance of such principles, Schopenhauer both overlooks difficulties that arise for a Hobbesian view and overlooks an area that throws light on the point of moral principles. On this issue about egoism, then, Schopenhauer goes further than Kant. But in doing so, he misses the role of morality in explaining adherence to practices that promote mutual advantage. His demand for pure altruism as a basis for genuine morality is questionable.

He may have been tempted to set aside this whole (broadly speaking) 'political' area of morality because he believes that a state can only control actions, and cannot control motives. He infers that it cannot legitimately be concerned about whether citizens are virtuous; it can prescribe only the sorts of actions that an enlightened selfish egoist might endorse.

These claims about actions and motives do not support Schopenhauer's conclusion. We may concede that the state cannot directly influence anything except external behaviour. But it may still be concerned about motives. A state might reasonably ask whether most citizens will obey rules of justice only out of fear of punishment; for if this were everyone's only motive, the state's apparatus of coercion would have to be far more extensive than we expect it to be in most states. The sorts of communities that we are familiar with depend on citizens who have something more than a purely selfish reason for observing rules of justice. Motives and characters, therefore, are vitally important for legislators to consider, even if legislation does not alter them directly. If legislators want to spend less on police, judges, tax inspectors, and prisons, they should want citizens to have some moral, and not purely self-interested, concern for justice and fidelity.

Moreover, even if these attitudes were outside the competence of legislators, they would matter to citizens, educators, moral philosophers, and anyone else who wanted the state to spend less on the apparatus of coercion. Schopenhauer's dismissal of this area of morality distorts his understanding of the areas of morality that he recognizes.

Schopenhauer's attitude to self-interest and morality may be understood as an extreme version of Luther's doctrine of 'civil righteousness', which may in turn be understood as

---

[14] See Gauthier, 'Advantage'; *MBA*, ch. 6.

an extreme version of Augustine's doctrine of earthly peace. One might take Augustine to claim that earthly peace requires outer action rather than inner will and intention, and that therefore it does not require genuine virtue. Similarly, Luther takes civil righteousness to involve outer action, rather than the inner reform of motives that is necessary for genuine virtue.[15] If it involves only outer action, it does not involve any modification of naturally selfish motives. This interpretation of Luther is mistaken, though Luther is partly responsible for the mistake. When he speaks of the outer and the inner, he does not contrast behaviour with intention; he contrasts the sorts of motives that natural human beings are capable of with those that require divine grace. Hence he does not mean that civil society rests on mere conformity of behaviour among self-seeking individuals rather than on any genuinely moral concern. Schopenhauer, however, relies on the mistaken interpretation of Luther, and takes the further unjustified step of excluding civil righteousness from morality. His contrast between the Hobbesian outlook of the social contract and the area of genuine morality is misleading about both areas. On the one hand, he overlooks the relevance of non-Hobbesian moral concern to social morality. On the other hand, he exaggerates the role of compassion in individual morality.

1048. Laws and Imperatives in Kant

Once he has distinguished the proper concerns of morality from all questions that involve any element of self-interest, Schopenhauer attacks Kant for conceiving moral principles as laws and as imperatives. His criticisms point out the basic error that he alleges in Kant's conception of morality. For he traces back Kant's concern with imperatives and laws to a search for an a priori foundation of morality. Kant's philosophical panacea is his belief in the a priori basis of knowledge. He thinks that he can find an a priori basis for moral knowledge as well as for empirical knowledge of the world; that is why the principles of morality cannot depend on any empirical facts about human nature or human motivation.[16]

According to Schopenhauer, if Kant had understood his discovery of the synthetic a priori, he would have seen how misguided it would be to look for synthetic a priori moral principles. For synthetic a priori knowledge informs us only about our strictly subjective point of view, and in this sense tells us only about appearances, not about any reality existing independently of our states of consciousness (BM §6, 64–5). Similarly, if we accept this subjectivist version of transcendental idealism, synthetic a priori moral principles would only tell us how we look at moral phenomena, and could not tell us which moral principles are objectively correct. Kant, however, wants to find objectively correct a priori principles, and believes he can reach moral principles that are synthetic, a priori, and objective. To find them, he begins from ordinary moral principles and removes their empirical features. He is mistaken, because removal of these features also removes the features that make

---

[15] Augustine; §§228, 231, 234. Luther; §417.

[16] 'Directly tied up with the *imperative form* of ethics . . . is a favourite notion of Kant that is indeed excusable but not acceptable. We sometimes see a doctor who has applied a remedy with brilliant success henceforth prescribe it for almost all diseases; I liken Kant to such a man.' (BM §6, 61)

them intelligible; we are left with unintelligible formulae, not with genuine a priori moral principles.

This mistaken procedure underlies Kant's claims about law and imperatives. He holds an 'imperative' conception of morality, supposing that morality is concerned with 'laws as regards what ought to happen, even though it may never happen' (*BM* §4, 52). Our initial, non-Kantian, understanding of moral principles may treat them, in legal contexts, as expressing laws and commands; and, in a theological context, as expressing divine laws and commands. Schopenhauer claims that the 'real and original meaning' of 'law' is limited to civil law. If, then, Kant thinks of a law without any human legislator, his idea is intelligible only in so far as he thinks of a divine legislator with power to reward or punish.[17]

But Kant does not notice this condition for the intelligibility of claims about a moral law. On the contrary, he introduces an alleged law that is independent of any legislator and any rewards or punishments, human or divine. But when he tries to describe this supposed moral 'law', he really deprives the notion of a law of any sense. Though he rejects a conception of morality that identifies it with human or divine laws or commands, he retains the notion of law and command, and removes the empirical sanction that makes the action-guiding character of law intelligible.[18]

Kant's error becomes clear if we try to explain this action-guiding character of laws and commands. Actual human beings act on laws and imperatives because they are connected with specific rewards and punishments. But Kant argues that these rewards and punishments are not a satisfactory basis for genuine moral principles, because they are relevant only to actual human beings with the desires and needs that are familiar to us. He infers that genuine moral principles must rest on laws and imperatives that do not depend on any empirical sanction or motive. Schopenhauer agrees with Kant that the obligatory force of ordinary human and divine laws depends on motives that are inappropriate for morality. But he does not infer that there is some a priori moral law whose obligatory force depends on no empirical motive. On the contrary, he infers that imperatives and obligations do not belong to morality. Kant tries to reject motivation by reward and punishment, but only replaces it with its metaphysical shadow. The moral 'law' is, according to Schopenhauer, clearly modelled on the divine law that it is supposed to replace; and it is intelligible only to the extent that we transfer to it aspects of the system of reward and punishment that we are told to exclude.

This criticism assumes that references to laws and obligations are intelligible only in a context of legislative acts, reward, and punishment. But this conception of law is not beyond dispute. It does not fit the view of natural law that we find in Aquinas and in the naturalist tradition opposed by Suarez. It is closer to the conception that Suarez defends, followed by Hobbes, Cumberland, Locke, and Pufendorf. Kant appeals to a naturalist conception of

[17] 'In the centuries of Christianity, philosophical ethics has generally taken its form unconsciously from the theological. Now as theological ethics is essentially *dictatorial*, the philosophical has also appeared in the form of precept and moral obligation, in all innocence and without suspecting that for this, first another sanction is necessary.' (*BM* §4, 54)

[18] 'Every ought is thus necessarily conditioned by punishment or reward; consequently, to use Kant's language, it is essentially and inevitably hypothetical, and never categorical, as he asserts. But if these conditions are thought away, the concept of ought or obligation is left without any meaning.' (§4, 55) Schopenhauer's criticism of Kant's supposedly 'legal' and 'imperative' conception of morality is sympathetically discussed by Cartwright, 'Morality', 254–63.

natural law, in claiming that there must be some natural law underlying every law that has an author.[19]

But even if we agree with Suarez and the others who believe that commands and legislators are necessary for law in the strict sense, does that do any serious damage to Kant's position? What does he lose if he appeals to 'law' in the broader sense recognized by Aquinas, Vasquez, and Hooker, as a rule and norm for actions, and claims simply that the principles of morality are rules of this sort? Nothing essential in his characterization of practical laws, in contrast to mere maxims,[20] seems to be lost if they are identified with practical principles, as Suarez, Clarke, and Price (for instance) understand them.

We can strengthen this defence of Kant by noticing a feature of his account of laws that Schopenhauer overlooks. Kant does not take practical principles to be essentially imperatives. A holy will is guided by practical laws that are not imperatives; these laws become imperatives only in our wills, which include tendencies that might oppose the moral law. Non-imperative practical laws are action-guiding principles for rational agents even if no other tendencies oppose them. Schopenhauer takes no account of Kant's reasons for believing that practical laws are not essentially imperatives.

Nor does his emphasis on commands apply directly to Kant's description of an imperative. The imperatives that Kant considers are principles revealing reasons for action; when we express these as ought-judgments, we imply that there is some principle giving us a reason to act, but the reason need not rest on any act of legislation. When Kant speaks of imperatives, he is not thinking of a command issued by some authoritative commander external to the agent. The counsels and maxims of craft and prudence are expressed in hypothetical imperatives, but they do not require any metaphysical shadow of an external commander. The mere fact that moral principles are described as imperatives does not imply that they imply some shadow of a commander.

Kant, therefore, does not treat moral principles as imperatives in any sense that presupposes commands and commanders. He maintains only that they are action-guiding principles. If Schopenhauer believes that the relevant sorts of action-guiding principles must express commands in the literal sense, he commits himself to a controversial thesis about the connexion between these action-guiding principles and commands.

In Schopenhauer's support, we might argue that Kant needs some parallel to positive laws, if he is to convince us that we have some inescapable obligation to obey moral laws and imperatives; for in the case of these alleged imperatives, we find no intelligible source of the obligation such as we find for hypothetical imperatives. If this objection is sound, Kant gives us no good reason to believe in a source of obligation that is independent of the agent's actual desires.

In reply to such an objection, Kant maintains that we assume—from the point of view of ordinary morality—that there is some source of obligation that is independent of actual desires. If we assumed that all imperatives are hypothetical, we would not suppose that people have any moral reason to be guided by moral principles if they lack the relevant sorts of desires; in that case, we would have to withdraw any moral objections to their behaviour once we discovered that they lack the relevant desires. But in fact we do not withdraw

---

[19] Kant on natural law; §987.   [20] Kant on practical laws; §900.

these objections; on the contrary, we are likely (in some conditions) to object even more if someone lacks the appropriate desires and reactions.

This line of argument is not peculiar to Kant; Burnet mentions it as part of his criticism of Hutcheson's appeal to the moral sense.[21] But Kant exploits it effectively; it gives a reason for believing that ordinary forms of evaluation presuppose the sort of non-hypothetical imperative that he describes. The presupposition may still be false; but it tends to support Kant's position, and it does not rely on the misapplied legal analogy that Schopenhauer attacks.

Schopenhauer might reply that every reason requires some antecedent motive. Hypothetical ought-judgments rest on some reason that we already have because we have some further desire or aim. A Kantian categorical imperative is misconceived, therefore, because it relies on no pre-existing motive, and therefore overlooks the fact that all reasons, both exciting and justifying,[22] depend on some antecedent motive.

This assumption about reasons is open to question. We often speak as though people have good justifying reasons to do something that they are not inclined to do and that is not instrumental to anything that they have an overriding inclination for. When Kant says that moral imperatives are categorical, he means—among other things—that they rely on a justifying reason with no antecedent desire. If Schopenhauer simply asserts that there can be no such justifying reason, he relies on a conception of justifying reasons that does not even seem to fit non-moral reasons. If Kant is right about justifying reasons, morality may give us good justifying reasons, even if we will not be moved to do anything until we form some desire.

Kant also maintains, however, that moral reasons can constitute exciting reasons without antecedent desires. Common sense seems to support him on this point too. If we are convinced that by indulging our jealous impulses without thought for their effects we are ruining our lives, we may try to act differently. If we act on the conviction that we are ruining our lives, we will form a desire to promote our future welfare rather than the satisfaction of our impulses with more immediate objects. But it is not obvious that this desire explains our action, or that it is prior to our acting on our rational conviction. In Reid's view, for instance, the fact that we have a stronger desire does not explain our action, if strength of desire is understood as 'animal' rather than 'rational' strength.[23] If our acting on the overriding desire for our happiness is simply the result of our recognizing that we are jeopardizing our happiness and that we ought not to, Kant has a reason to believe in exciting reasons that do not depend on antecedent desires.

These arguments do not show that there must be a moral categorical imperative. But they give reasons for doubting Schopenhauer's claim that the idea of a categorical imperative is misconceived. He misunderstands the role of commands and imperatives in Kant's account of moral principles. His assumptions about justification and motivation do not seem to fit either non-moral or moral reasons.

1049. The Character of the Categorical Imperative

Schopenhauer rejects a mistaken interpretation—as he supposes—of Kant's argument for the supreme principle of morality and of the sense in which it is a priori (*BM* §6, 61–5).

---

[21] Burnet on Hutcheson; §659.   [22] Justifying and exciting reasons; §639.   [23] Reid on types of strength; §841.

According to this mistaken interpretation, Kant finds the supreme moral principle by reflexion on the moral consciousness. But if Kant argued this way, he would rely on 'experience'—on facts about human moral consciousness—to establish his principle, which would therefore not be a priori (62). If we understand the moral law as a fact of consciousness, we make it empirical.[24] This misinterpretation that appeals to the moral consciousness derives some support from Kant's reliance on a 'fact of pure reason' (BM §6, 77).[25] But if Kant really intends to appeal to the moral consciousness, he contradicts himself.

In Schopenhauer's view, many readers fail to recognize contradictions in Kant. They do not see, for instance, that the alterations Kant introduced in the second edition of the First Critique made it 'an incoherent and self-contradictory book' (BM §6, 72). Schopenhauer is unmoved by the objection that if his 'accurate' interpretation makes Kant seem so incoherent, we ought to look for an interpretation that attributes a more consistent position to Kant.

Schopenhauer's interpretation appeals to one of Kant's explanations of the categorical imperative. According to Kant, we should look for the categorical imperative by attending to the form, not the content, of a moral principle; and this procedure shows that the only categorical imperative is the principle of conformity to a universal law (BM §6, 73; cf. Kant, G 420). Schopenhauer argues that this principle is 'purely formal' in a very strong sense, so that Kant defines a moral principle as something that conforms to some universal law or other. This conformity to a universal law requires some sort of consistency or non-contradiction. But if the categorical imperative prescribes only non-contradiction, it cannot justify any specific set of consistent moral principles over any other.

This account of the categorical imperative results from Kant's attempt to derive the categorical imperative from the concept of pure practical reason itself. The only principle that could be derived from pure reason for all possible rational beings is, according to Schopenhauer, the principle of non-contradiction (§6, 63). And so the categorical imperative consists wholly in non-contradictory willing of a law for all possible rational beings (§6, 75). Kant's formulation of the categorical imperative does not rely on the moral beliefs of the ordinary moral consciousness, or on substantive principles or standards that we implicitly accept. He derives the categorical imperative from the concept of pure practical reason, understood as non-contradiction. Schopenhauer believes that the categorical imperative derived by this procedure is empty and useless. But he thinks that only his interpretation explains why Kant regards the principle as a priori.

He is right to insist that Kant does not suppose that whatever ordinary morality accepts as its supreme principle must be a categorical imperative. To show that a principle is a categorical imperative, we must show that it gives reasons for all rational agents to follow it, irrespective of their particular desires and inclinations; such a conclusion does not follow from the mere fact that ordinary morality rests on the principle. Still, facts about the moral consciousness are relevant. Kant may reasonably appeal to them to show that he has found basic principles of the metaphysics of morals, not of the metaphysics of something else. If the principles that give reasons for all rational agents were irrelevant to ordinary moral principles, why should we believe that they are foundations of the metaphysics of morals?

---

[24] '... the basis of such an imperative would be *anthropological* through *experience*, albeit inner experience, and would therefore be *empirical*.' (BM §6, 71)

[25] Cf. Kant, *KpV* 47, discussed in §939.

An appeal to the common moral consciousness shows (according to Kant) that we believe there are categorical imperatives with a specific content; Kant has the further task of saying whether we are right in our beliefs. This role for the common moral consciousness is clear enough in the structure and argument of the first two chapters of the *Groundwork*.

Schopenhauer does not consider this line of argument. In his view, the principle Kant reaches by appeal to the principle of non-contradiction lacks any sort of content that would explain how it gives the right reason for any determinate moral actions. This is the price that Kant has to pay for a principle that is genuinely a priori.

1050. Kant and Rationalism

For Schopenhauer, Kant's argument illustrates the mistake of trying to identify the morally good and right with the rational. The only strictly rational element in morality is non-contradiction, though Kant confusedly believes that he can derive more moral content from this rational element.[26] In over-estimating the force of an appeal to reason, Kant introduces a new mistake into moral philosophy.

This historical claim implies that Schopenhauer forgets or ignores the rationalist tradition that is as old as moral philosophy. His historical claim is not an isolated aberration, however. He maintains this claim elsewhere too (*PP* ii §114, 209), and tries to justify it (*WR* iv Appx. = P i 517–22). He mentions Aristotle's claim that the moral virtues belong to the non-rational part of the soul, but he does not mention what the Stoics or Socrates think about this claim; nor does he mention the role of right reason in Aristotle's account of moral virtue.

Moreover, his claim about Kant and rationalism is difficult to reconcile with his other views. For he mentions and accepts the identification of practical reason with prudence (518), and attributes to the Stoics the general aim of deriving the virtues from prudence. He therefore implies that Stoics take virtue to be an expression of practical reason. Though they do not take Kant's view of what reason requires, they agree with him in connecting moral virtue with reason.

Schopenhauer's attack on Kant, therefore, seems to lead him astray. It causes him to ignore the extent to which Kant's rationalism has clear historical precedents, not only in Greek and mediaeval ethics, but in Cudworth, Clarke, and the other modern rationalists. He traces Kant's conception of reason to Descartes and his successors, as though Kant's predecessors had all confined discussions of reason to metaphysical and epistemological contexts. He ignores the clear historical sources in moral philosophy for Kantian moral rationalism.

Schopenhauer believes that Kant's appeal to practical reason leads him only to the principle of non-contradiction, and that something else is needed for definite moral principles. This criticism reminds us of Hegel's objection to the emptiness of the categorical imperative.[27]

---

[26] 'Hence it never occurred to anyone *prior* to Kant to identify just, virtuous, and noble conduct with *reasonable* or *rational*, but the two have been clearly distinguished and kept apart.' (*BM* §6, 83)

[27] Hegel on the categorical imperative; §1021.

In Hegel's view, Kant's formula gives us different results depending on the sorts of institutions—for example, property or no property—that we take for granted. And so we might expect Schopenhauer to agree with Hegel on this point.

1051. Self-Interest and the Formula of Universal Law

Schopenhauer's interpretation, however, departs from Hegel's. He argues that Kant can provide content for the categorical imperative, and therefore can provide the determinate answers that he offers in his examples of the first formula of the categorical imperative.[28] But Kant can do this only because he tacitly presupposes the truth of egoism and so interprets the question 'What can you will to be a universal law?' as 'What universal law do you think will be most advantageous for you?'.[29] Schopenhauer applies this interpretation to Kant's two examples illustrating duties to others. It does not cover the two that illustrate duties to oneself; but that does not matter. For Schopenhauer believes there are no duties to oneself, and so we need not fit them into an account of the categorical imperative.

Even if Schopenhauer's explication of Kant's question about a universal law were right, it would not show that Kant accepts egoism. For even if I decide what I can will to be a universal law by deciding which law would be most beneficial to me if it were observed, it does not follow that I am motivated by self-interest if I act on such a law. My acting on such a law shows that I am motivated by self-interest only if I believe that the law is universally observed. Kant, therefore, must be appealing to something other than self-interest if he thinks I have some reason to obey a maxim conforming to the universal law, even if Schopenhauer correctly describes my basis for evaluating the universal law.

But in any case Schopenhauer's interpretation is open to doubt. Kant assumes that rational agents have good reason to be concerned about their own interest (in the example about mutual aid) and about the fulfilment of their aims (in the example about keeping a promise). But he does not argue that a universal law about mutual aid will be most advantageous to me; he argues that my legitimate and rational concern for my own interest will be safeguarded by the observance of this universal law and violated if the law is not observed. I am asked to appraise the relevant universal laws by reference not to my own interest, but to each person's interest. Schopenhauer is right, then, to say that self-interest has an important role in Kant's argument, but he does not describe that role correctly.

To understand Kant, we need to distinguish two claims: (1) In applying the categorical imperative, we need to assume that each person has some egoistic motives—that is,

---

[28] Schopenhauer does not seem to distinguish the Formula of Universal Law from the Formula of the Law of Nature, which is the formula that Kant actually claims to apply. See §925.

[29] 'My being able to will is the hinge on which the given order or instruction turns. But what *can* I really will, and what not? To determine what I can will in the above respect, I obviously again need a regulation . . . Now where is this regulation to be sought? Certainly nowhere but in my egoism.' (*BM* §7, 89)

that each person cares to some degree about their own interest. (2) Kant's different moral principles—that is, the different examples of the application of the categorical imperative—are reached by egoistic reasoning.

To see the different implications of these claims, we may consider Kant's fourth example, about mutual aid. Kant imagines an individualist who does not want to help other people, and so is willing to accept the maxim of no one helping others. If this maxim becomes a universal law, the individualist cannot count on help from other people. Since this is supposed to be an unacceptable result, Kant appeals to what rational self-interest would approve in the hypothetical situation where the individualist's maxim is universal law and there is no mutual aid. But he neither shows nor tries to show that an egoist must accept the principle of mutual aid. Whether an egoist accepts it or not depends on whether the hypothetical situation described is at all likely. One might reasonably answer that is quite unlikely. It seems unrealistic, from a self-interested point of view, to assert that we must choose between a world in which everyone helps everyone else and a world in which no one helps anyone else. Egoism, therefore, would not lead rationally to acceptance of the principle of mutual aid. This point can be generalized: if we are willing to do in actual conditions what an egoist would do in unlikely counterfactual conditions, we do not show ourselves to be egoists.[30]

Schopenhauer is mistaken, therefore, to claim that Kant's categorical imperative turns into a hypothetical imperative (*BM* §7, 91). He suggests that Kant's examples rest on far-sighted self-interested calculation; but in fact they rest on calculation about unlikely counterfactual circumstances, which is not egoistic calculation at all. If I am an egoist, I seek to maximize my interest in expected future circumstances, not in unlikely counterfactual circumstances. If I am moved by my calculation of my hypothetical interest in the unlikely counterfactual circumstances envisaged by Kant, I try to ensure that moral principles do not benefit some people at the expense of others simply because that inequality satisfies some desire of one person or of many persons.

If I am willing to follow principles that secure this equal treatment of people's interests, I am neither simply an egoist nor a wholly self-sacrificing altruist; I consider the interests of others equally with my own. Once we see the point of view that Kant appeals to, we may ask how he can show that this impartial regard for the interests of rational agents constitutes a categorical imperative. Here we raise genuine difficulties, not the imaginary difficulties that Schopenhauer raises.

Schopenhauer's account results partly from his expulsion of all considerations of self-interest from morality. He endorses a Hobbesian account of the basis of political obligation and of principles of justice, because he assumes that any consideration of self-interest introduces Hobbesian egoism. Hence he believes that any principles recognizing the legitimacy of self-interest belong to Hobbesian self-interest and fall outside morality. He does not recognize that my acceptance of the moral legitimacy of my own and other people's self-interest is different from a Hobbesian strategic bargain to refrain from aggression against

---

[30] The Original Position described by Rawls illustrates this point; see §1417.

others as the best means to secure myself from aggression. His treatment of this area of morality makes it difficult for him to understand Kant.

1052. The Formula of Humanity

But even if Schopenhauer is wrong in his claim that Kant appeals to egoistic motives in applying the Formula of Universal Law, he may still be right to argue that Kant provides no intelligible reason for accepting principles that satisfy the categorical imperative. This is his objection to the Formula of Humanity, which recognizes rational beings as ends in themselves (BM §8, 94–9). In his view, the concept of an end essentially involves being an end for someone's purpose, so that the idea of being an unconditioned end, an end for no one's purpose, is simply self-contradictory. It is a metaphysical shell of the concept Kant is trying to escape. It is similar to the idea of a law with no empirical sanction attached, in that the exclusion of an empirical element makes the resulting concept incoherent.

This criticism invites a defence that also answers Schopenhauer's attack on Kant's treatment of obligations and imperatives. Kant explains the notion of an end-in-itself by separating it from 'subjective ends'. To see whether he has an intelligible conception, we ought to see not whether it is natural to call this an end, but whether it is an intelligible conception that does the work Kant intends. Kant seeks to distinguish an objective end—something to be respected because of its non-instrumental value—from a subjective end—something to be achieved in action. An end-in-itself is an objective end because it is a limit that must be respected in the pursuit of subjective ends. Kant has good reason to believe that common morality recognizes an objective end. If Schopenhauer believes that such a conception is unintelligible, he has to say that the only things that have non-instrumental value are states of affairs to be achieved. This claim about the limits of non-instrumental value seems less plausible than Kant's conception of an objective end.

Kant's Formula of Humanity prohibits the treatment of persons as mere means. Schopenhauer agrees with this prohibition. Kant has 'distinguished egoism and its opposite by an extremely characteristic feature' (§8, 99). According to Schopenhauer, the attitude that treats people as mere means is an egoistic attitude, Kant might well agree with him, since Kant has the unfortunate tendency to treat all motives based on inclination as egoistic. The Formula of Humanity, however, is not simply an attack on egoism, since it exposes an important moral error that is not confined to egoism.[31] We can still treat other people simply as means if we are quite non-egoistically committed to some cause that does not essentially involve the welfare of persons (the preservation of ancient trees, the rule of the saints), and even if it involves the welfare of people (if, e.g., we sacrifice the welfare of some people as a means to the welfare of others we take to be more important). This exploitative attitude to persons need not be egoistic. Similarly, Kant's rejection of the exploitative attitude does not merely rule out egoism. His demand for treatment of persons as ends extends further than Schopenhauer recognizes.

---

[31] The Formula of Humanity may not even exclude egoism, if versions of eudaemonism that ascribe non-instrumental value to the good of others are forms of egoism. See §§970–1.

Schopenhauer's praise of Kant for recognizing the difference between morality and egoism both misinterprets Kant and casts doubt on Schopenhauer's conception of the moral point of view. For Schopenhauer tends to identify the moral outlook with altruism, just as he identifies the immoral outlook with egoism. The Formula of Humanity shows why morality is more complex than altruism.

1053. Kant's Egoism and the Highest Good

After discussing the categorical imperative, Schopenhauer argues that Kant makes a further fatal concession to egoism. Though he professes to reject any egoistic basis for morality, Kant introduces an egoistic basis by postulating happiness in a future life as a reward for virtue (BM §4, 55; WR iv Appx. = P i 524).[32] Kant is inconsistent because he now prescribes virtuous action for the sake of post-mortem rewards, and hence (Schopenhauer infers) not simply for its own sake. Kant's postulate shows that the supposedly unconditioned moral law is really just a metaphysical shell of a divine command supported by rewards and punishments; for Kant eventually appeals to these rewards and punishments.[33]

Whether or not Kant's postulate is reasonable, it does not conflict, as Schopenhauer suggests it does, with his account of the moral motive. The postulate is not intended to show why we are rationally justified in acting on the moral motive; for Kant supposes that he has answered that question. His answer, however, has left open further questions. If we accept Kant's account of the moral motive, and we agree that we are rationally justified in acting on it, we can still ask what the consequences will be for us and for the future state of the world. We may have sufficient reason to accept morality even if we regard the consequences as unknowable, or even to some extent bad. But we have a further reason if we believe that it promotes some desirable result for ourselves and for the future of the world.

Kant's postulates and his account of the tendency of world history provide answers to these questions. If they are good answers, they give us further good reasons for caring about morality in connexion with other rational aims. But they do not cancel the reasons that emerge from his arguments about the moral motive and the categorical imperative.

Kant is inconsistent in his views about morality and the highest good only if he maintains that pursuit of the highest good excludes the practice of morality for its own sake. He might maintain that practice of morality for its own sake is inconsistent with its practice for some further end. Again, he might apply the principle of subtraction to the moral motive, so that acting on the moral motive excludes any kind of self-interested motive. But in fact he regards morality as part of the highest (consummate) good; this view is close to the eudaemonism of Aristotle and Aquinas. His account of the place of morality in the highest good may provoke objections to his other claims about the status of happiness, but it does not conflict with the practice of morality for itself. Nor do Kant's remarks about the moral worth of actions rely on the principle of subtraction. On the contrary, they rest only on the principle

---

[32] Hegel presents a similar criticism of Kant's appeal to happiness; see §1024.

[33] 'In that self-mystification I should liken Kant to a man at a ball, who all evening has been carrying on a love affair with a masked beauty in the vain hope of making a conquest, when at last she throws off her mask and reveals herself as his wife.' (BM §8, 103)

of sufficiency. According to this principle, the presence of a non-moral motive concentrated on those aspects of the highest good that lie outside morality does not exclude moral worth.

Since he attributes the principle of subtraction to Kant, Schopenhauer assumes that Kant demands a moral motive that is not combined with any self-regarding motive. Hence he infers that Kant contradicts himself by introducing the postulates. But this is a contradiction in Kant only if Kant believes Schopenhauer's strong claim about motivation. We have seen, however, that Kant does not believe it. Nor does Schopenhauer show why Kant ought to believe it.

Schopenhauer's attack on eudaemonism and on Kantian ethics rests on his objections to self-regarding motives in morality. The result of his reliance on these objections suggests that the complete exclusion of self-regarding motives makes the moral point of view incomprehensible. The effect of Schopenhauer's critique of Kant is to separate the genuinely Kantian elements (as Schopenhauer understands them) from the naturalist and eudaemonist views of Butler, Leibniz, and the Aristotelian tradition. We have given reasons for believing that we ought to try to reconcile Kant with this tradition; if these are good reasons, Schopenhauer goes in the wrong direction. The implausibility of his account of morality is a further reason for believing that one ought to avoid his approach to Kant.[34]

1054. Sources of Egoism

Schopenhauer's view about the basis of genuine moral motivation arises partly out of his views about egoism. He believes that the epistemological priority of the egocentric point of view underlies the practical priority of the egoistic point of view. The epistemological egocentric doubts the independent reality of other people and their states of mind, whereas the practical egoist denies that the states of other people matter in their own right. To overcome egoism, therefore, we must overcome the effects of epistemological egocentrism.[35]

Schopenhauer's suggestion is difficult to accept. The selfish manipulation of other people can hardly dispense with the belief in their independent reality, or with the belief that their reactions matter as much to them as mine do to me. If I want to offer some reward to other people to get them to co-operate in my selfish purposes, I will be unable to find the best inducement if I simply consider inducements that would please me. I have to think about what would please them, on the assumption that what pleases them will matter as much to them as what pleases me matters to me. An egoist who denies the independent reality of other people, or does not notice how they differ from himself, will not manipulate them successfully.

The same is true of disinterested malice, which Schopenhauer takes to be a non-egoistic motive contrary to morality (BM §14, 134–6). Cruelty would be clumsy and unsuccessful if cruel people did not have a clear sense of what makes other people suffer and of how

---

[34] Kant, naturalism, and eudaemonism; see §§972–3.

[35] 'There is even a comic side to seeing innumerable individuals of whom each regards himself alone as *real*, at any rate from a practical point of view, and all others to a certain extent as mere phantoms. This is due ultimately to the fact that everyone is given to himself *directly*, but the rest are given to him only *indirectly* through their representation in his head; and the directness asserts its right.' (BM §14, 132)

much they will suffer. The serpent manipulated Eve and Adam because he understood what mattered to them. Similarly, diabolical cruelty and spite depend on an acute sense of what matters to other people and of how much it matters. If this is true of cruelty, it seems no less true of selfishness. Schopenhauer's claims about the epistemological sources of egoism seem to conflict with obvious facts.

In a less literal sense, Schopenhauer may be right to suggest that selfish people do not recognize the reality of other people. If they fully understood the implications of the existence of other people with thoughts and feelings similar to their own, perhaps they would see the irrationality of selfishness. But this conclusion needs some further argument beyond the one given by Schopenhauer; the relevant 'implications' need to be explored more fully.[36]

The claim about epistemological egocentricity determines the character of Schopenhauer's solution. But it does so in a peculiar way. We might expect him to say that in order to transcend the egocentric outlook, I must recognize that other people are not just phantoms. To recognize this, I must take the objective point of view from which I can see that each individual is equally real. If my reason for caring only about the person who is myself is my belief that this is the only person who really exists, I cure this condition by recognizing that others are as real as myself. Since they are not parts of my consciousness, I ought to recognize them as distinct centres of consciousness; and to this extent I ought to recognize the separateness of persons.

But this is not Schopenhauer's solution. He does not take the recognition of a plurality of equally real persons to be the cure for egoism.

1055. The Relevance of Compassion

Schopenhauer's reply to egoism and defence of morality begin from the assumption that an action with moral worth is one in which 'the ultimate motive for doing or omitting to do a thing is precisely and exclusively centred in the *weal and woe of someone else*' (BM §16, 143). This attitude is needed to secure acceptance of the fundamental principle of morality, which is: 'Harm no one; rather, help everyone as much as you can' (§7, 92). We accept this principle, according to Schopenhauer, because of compassion.

Even apart from his claim about compassion, Schopenhauer's basic principle is open to question, in both its negative and its positive aspects. 'Harm no one' is not exactly right, since we sometimes have to harm some people in order to avoid harm to others. 'Help everyone as much as you can' seems to demand an extreme degree of self-sacrifice; if I could help everyone else a little by harming myself very severely, Schopenhauer's principle seems to require me to impose that severe harm on myself. If Schopenhauer replies that helping everyone else is not helping everyone, and that we should do only what helps everyone by

---

[36] With Schopenhauer's attempt to connect solipsism and egoism, cf. Nagel, PA, ch. 11. Nagel does not reach Schopenhauer's extreme conclusion that denies the existence of distinct persons. Against such a view he remarks: 'To identify with one's future self is not to hold the absurd view that present and future stages of one's life are identical. One need only identify the present as one time among others all of which are contained in a single life. And what corresponds to this in the interpersonal case is not an identification of oneself with other persons or with all persons, but rather a conception of oneself as simply a person among others, all of whom are included in a single world.' (99–100)

making everyone better off, he seems to raise the first objection again; for a small harm to myself might sometimes be justified by a large benefit to others. Schopenhauer's principles disagree with Kant's Formula of Humanity, which limits both self-sacrifice and self-interest.

Schopenhauer believes that morality is possible just in case the welfare and harm of another person can be 'directly my motive' (§16, 143), just as my own welfare and harm are directly my motive for acting on my own behalf.[37] To explain how this is possible, Schopenhauer introduces identification with the other. The direct motivation that is characteristic of genuine compassion, and hence the basis of all morality, requires the rejection of any distinction between the other person and myself.[38]

Morality, therefore, does not rest on a belief in the reality of other persons distinct from oneself. On the contrary, Schopenhauer takes it to rest on the belief that other people are just as real as I am because they are identical to me. The crucial failure of the egoist is not his failure to recognize other real people who are distinct from him and no less real than he is. He is mistaken because he does not see that these supposedly other people are as real as himself because they are identical to himself. Compassion, therefore, requires the recognition of the unreality of the supposed differences between different people.

This conclusion needs to be qualified, because Schopenhauer also affirms that compassion does not require the denial of the distinction between persons. He rejects the account of compassion offered by Cassina, because it denies the evident fact that when we feel compassion for others, we recognize that we are different from them.[39] On this point, Schopenhauer improves on Hume and Smith; he sees that simply feeling a sympathetic pain as a result of another's pain does not explain why we should want to do something to relieve the other person's pain rather than our own.[40] None the less he also believes that compassion implies some rejection of a distinction between persons.[41] The genuinely moral outlook assumes that different people do not constitute distinct realities.[42]

These different remarks are consistent. Schopenhauer rejects Cassina's view because it falsely implies that I imagine myself (the ordinary phenomenal person) feeling the pain that the other person suffers, as though the pain were not really the other person's but belonged

[37] The other person's benefit and harm move me directly and immediately, 'that is to say, in exactly the same way in which it [sc. my will] is usually moved only by my own weal and woe' (BM §16, 143).

[38] 'But this necessarily presupposes that, in the case of his *woe* as such, I suffer directly with him, I feel *his* woe just as I ordinarily feel only my own; and, likewise, I directly desire his weal in the same way I otherwise desire only my own. But this requires that I am in some way *identified with him*, in other words, that this entire *difference* between me and everyone else, which is the very basis of my egoism, is eliminated, to a certain extent at least.' (BM §16, 143–4)

[39] 'His [sc. Cassina's] view is that compassion arises from an instantaneous deception of the imagination, since we put ourselves in the position of the sufferer, and have the idea that we are suffering *his* pains in our person. This is by no means the case; on the contrary, at every moment we remain clearly conscious that *he* is the sufferer, not *we*; and it is precisely in *his* person, not in ours, that we feel the suffering, to our grief and sorrow. We suffer *with* him and hence *in* him; we feel his pain as *his*, and do not imagine that it is ours.' (BM §16, 147)

[40] See Smith, §790; Price on Hutcheson, §810.

[41] '...I...*feel it with him, feel it as my own*, and yet not *within me*, but *in another person* .... But this presupposes that to a certain extent I have identified myself with the other man, and in consequence the barrier between the ego and non-ego is for the moment abolished .... I share the suffering *in him*, in spite of the fact that his skin does not enclose my nerves. Only in this way can *his* woe, *his* distress, become a motive *for me* ...' (BM §18, 165–6)

[42] 'Accordingly, if plurality and separateness belong only to the *phenomenon*, and if it is one and the same essence that manifests itself in all living things, then that conception that abolishes the difference between ego and non-ego is not erroneous; but on the contrary, the opposite conception must be. ... Accordingly, it would be the metaphysical basis of ethics and consist in *one* individual's again recognizing in *another* his own self, his own true nature.' (BM §22, 209)

to me (as phenomenal person). This might happen sometimes, but Schopenhauer argues that it is not a satisfactory basis for a moral attitude. For if my taking the pain seriously results from the illusion that it is my own, why should it cause me to seek to benefit the other rather than myself? If the other is hungry, and I care about his hunger because of the illusion that it is my hunger, why should I get food for the other rather than for myself? In order to benefit the other I must be free of the illusion that the pain is my own, and once I am free of the illusion, I can no longer (according to this theory) be expected to take the pain seriously.

Schopenhauer sees, therefore, that the beliefs underlying the desire to help another person cannot be in conflict with the beliefs underlying my tendency to feel compassion for the other. He correctly infers that the fact that the pain belongs to another person must somehow be recognized within the attitude that causes me to be concerned about the other's pain.

The compassionate person's recognition of the reality of other phenomenal persons is consistent with the claim that compassion somehow rejects distinctions between persons. To reconcile them, we must distinguish a person as a sequence of phenomenal conscious states (the 'phenomenal self') from the real self that underlies this phenomenal sequence (the 'underlying self'). Compassionate people recognize the distinction between phenomenal selves; if I am compassionate, I do not falsely imagine that the pains of another phenomenal self really belong to my phenomenal self. Still, I really identify myself with the other; I feel compassion in my phenomenal self for the sufferings expressed in another phenomenal self because I recognize that the two phenomenal selves are really expressions of one and the same underlying self. Schopenhauer's view differs from Cassina's in so far as it requires me to recognize the phenomenal reality and ultimate unreality of both my own distinct self and the other person's.

This metaphysical attitude underlying compassion overcomes the egoistic outlook. If I am an egoist, I think that my phenomenal self manifests the only real self there is. I do not think of other phenomenal selves as having the same relation to a real self that my phenomenal self has; for I suppose that my phenomenal self manifests a real self, but other phenomenal selves are only constructs of my phenomenal self, and so have a more indirect relation to any real self than my phenomenal self has. In feeling compassion for others I do not take this egoistic view. Instead, I recognize that their phenomenal selves are as directly related to a real self as my phenomenal self is, and that the self they are related to is the very same self as the self that my phenomenal self is related to.

Schopenhauer's position reveals some uncertainty about the exact source of egoism. He seeks to characterize the egoist attitude in two ways: (1) I care only about my phenomenal self because it manifests the only real self and other phenomenal selves do not manifest real selves in the same way. (2) I care only about my phenomenal self because it is the only one that manifests the real self that is me. The first egoist attitude is not intrinsically self-regarding; it intrinsically cares equally about however many real selves there may be, and confines its concern to myself only because of the belief that I am the only real self. I overcome this attitude by recognizing that there are other real selves; I need not prove that the other selves are really me. The second attitude, however, is intrinsically self-regarding; it is unmoved by the recognition of other real selves, since it assumes that there is always some special reason for concern about myself. The second attitude takes the self-referential attitude to be basic and ultimately reasonable, whereas the first attitude does not assume this.

Sidgwick distinguishes the two forms of egoism,[43] but Schopenhauer does not seem to distinguish them, and it is not clear which he has in mind at each stage. He seems to have the first form in mind when he accuses the egoist of not fully recognizing the reality of other people. He refutes this version of egoism if he shows that other people are just as real as I am. But in claiming that the moral attitude requires the rejection of distinctions between real selves, he seems to have the second egoist attitude in mind. If that is his view, he ought not to say that the egoist fails to recognize the reality of other people.

Moreover, he turns out not to disagree fundamentally with egoism. The egoist is wrong in thinking that his phenomenal self is the only one that manifests a real underlying self. But he does not discover that there are other real selves he should care about; all he discovers is that there are other phenomenal selves manifesting the real self that also underlies his phenomenal self. On this view, he is concerned with one and the same real self whether he is being selfish or compassionate. Schopenhauer does not challenge the view that it is ultimately reasonable to be concerned only about the real self underlying my phenomenal self and about no other real selves. He simply argues that other phenomenal selves should be included in my concern for this one real self.

Schopenhauer's account of egoism raises some difficult questions. The most plausible form of selfish egoism seems to recognize the reality of other people; for this recognition seems to underlie many forms of manipulation and abuse. And so it is most plausible to construe the egoist as saying that even though there are other real selves, he has a special reason for being concerned only about himself. We need not agree that exclusively egoistic concern is ultimately reasonable; but Schopenhauer's arguments fail to show why it is not, since all the metaphysical discoveries he describes are compatible with acceptance of the ultimate reasonableness of self-referential egoism. He might point out that his metaphysical views make it less practically important to refute egoism, since in fact there is only one real self that we need to bother about; but this conclusion is much weaker than the one that he defends. Despite his attacks on egoism, Schopenhauer agrees with the egoist claim that it is ultimately reasonable to care only about the real self that is identical to me, and not ultimately reasonable to care about any real selves that are not identical to me.

1056. The Importance of Compassion

Schopenhauer's metaphysical account of compassion achieves its goals only if he shows that this attitude is a plausible basis for morality. Kant cannot expect us to believe that his formulations of the categorical imperative are the basic principle of morality, if he cannot show that their implications are morally acceptable. It is fair to apply the same test to Schopenhauer.

Let us take for granted the existence of compassion as he describes it, a feeling involving direct concern to relieve the suffering of another. This attitude is relevant to morality.

---

[43] Sidgwick; §1200.

We may even agree that this feeling is an essential aspect of the character of any morally good person, because we may not even be capable of moral concern if we are incapable of compassion. If we are to benefit others and to avoid harming them, we must know how they feel, since how they feel makes a significant difference to their welfare. In many cases, knowing how someone is feeling is a result of compassion for them—not the other way round. If we know that A's friend has died, we might approach A in a 'neutral' frame of mind, without any concern for A, and wonder whether A feels any grief about it. We might not be able to notice any signs of grief. If, however, we feel compassion towards A because of this loss, we may be able to notice evidence of grief that we would have overlooked if we had been looking at A in a more 'neutral' frame of mind.

For this reason, we might agree with Schopenhauer's view that compassion is necessary for morality. If we lacked it, we would have no access to many facts that are relevant to morality. We might therefore agree that compassion is one of the foundations of morality, because morality is partly founded on, and developed from, a capacity for compassion.

But if Schopenhauer appeals to compassion, it is difficult for him to explain those moral obligations that do not seem to respond to some awareness of suffering in another person. In some cases, we seem to be able to benefit another person who is not suffering any serious relevant deprivation. If the benefit is significant and the cost to ourselves very slight, we seem to have a moral reason to confer the benefit. Schopenhauer agrees, since he recognizes positive obligations of aid, not simply negative obligations to refrain from harm.

Still, he also insists on a strong asymmetry between pain and pleasure as a reason for action. Only pain expresses a genuine need to which we cannot remain indifferent (BM §16, 146). On this view, the positive obligation to help must be limited to the obligation to relieve perceived suffering. It does not require us to confer benefits that do not relieve any previous perceived suffering.

Even if we focus on the prevention or removal of harm, this restriction on positive duties faces some difficulties. Schopenhauer's emphasis on the phenomenology of compassion leaves us with a question about cases in which victims are harmed, but do not know it, or they positively welcome some treatment that harms them, and so do not suffer in the way that (according to Schopenhauer) evokes a compassionate response. Apparently, we have no moral reason, as far as compassion goes, to prevent or to remove this harm.

Might we reply, on Schopenhauer's behalf, that compassion should result from awareness of harms to other people, and not simply from awareness of their sufferings? If we say this, the relevant sort of 'compassion' seems to be different from what he has in mind. For he seems to understand compassion as my transferring to another person's sufferings the attitude I take to my own sufferings. Since I have no attitude to harms to myself that I am unaware of, I seem to have nothing to transfer to others who suffer harms they are unaware of.

Even if we set aside this objection, and restrict ourselves to cases in which we are aware of other people's awareness of their suffering, Schopenhauer seems to provide an inadequate basis for the right attitudes. For compassion is often restricted in morally irrelevant or misleading ways. We may feel more strongly about people we know better, or people whose sufferings intrude themselves on us more strongly, or people whose sufferings we find it easy to imagine; and our degree of compassion may be affected, in one direction or the other, by the sorts of troubles we suffer. But we might doubt whether these degrees ought to determine our degree of moral concern without any further regulation. The fact that, for instance, we find it easier to feel compassion for someone with the same racial, or social, or educational background as ourselves does not show that such a person deserves more of our moral concern. Perhaps, indeed, we should even be especially concerned for the interests of people for whom we find it difficult to feel compassion.

Schopenhauer tries to answer this objection, by insisting that when he refers to compassion, he does not mean the degree of compassion that particular people actually feel. He suggests (§20, 192) that we can increase people's insight by causing them to alter their sympathies in the light of further information; we may take account of the remoter consequences of our actions for other people, and so we may care about people's sufferings more than we originally did.[44]

Perhaps, then, we might take Schopenhauer to hold that the basis of morality is not our actual compassionate feelings but our educated compassion. What sort of education is relevant? Why does he believe that such education will result in a 'more logical expression' of goodness of character? If our actual feelings of compassion are the basis of morality, wider or narrower compassion is neither better nor worse; two people with different extents of compassion are morally equally good or bad in so far as they act on their feelings of compassion.

Even if we can explain why more extensive sympathy is more 'logical', we face a further difficulty. The effect of further information may be different on different people's sympathies, so that even if we all have our compassion extended, different people may have it extended in different ways. These differences do not seem to affect what is morally right or wrong. An appeal to a 'normal' observer may not help; for we may find that, statistically speaking, normal people find it difficult to extend their compassion in morally desirable ways.

Perhaps Schopenhauer could appeal to an 'ideal' observer's compassionate reactions. In that case, he would follow Smith's response to similar difficulties.[45] He would also face the questions that arise for Smith. What makes an observer ideal? We seem to rely on our views about what is morally important in order to determine the appropriate occasions for compassion and the appropriate degree of compassion on different occasions. Hence an account of the ideal observer seems to depend on an account of what is morally important, and cannot be the basis for it. Hence we do not seem to rely on compassion to discover the basis of morality. Nor does people's actual compassion seem to explain why we have good reason to care about morality.

Schopenhauer, therefore, seems to face a dilemma. If he relies on actual or educated or normal compassion, he does not provide an adequate basis for morality. But if he relies on idealized compassion, he does not really treat compassion as the basis of morality.

---

[44] 'Through an increase in insight, through instruction concerning the circumstances of life, and thus by enlightening the mind, even goodness of character can be brought to a more logical expression of its true nature. This happens, for examples, when the remoter consequences that our action has for others are pointed out to us, such as the sufferings which come to them indirectly and only in the course of time, and which arise from this or that action that we did not consider to be so bad.' (*BM* §20, 194)

[45] Smith on the impartial spectator; §798.

These objections have assumed only that compassion sometimes falls short of the morally right answer. Further objections arise in cases where it seems to give the wrong answer.[46] We may concede, waiving previous objections on this point, that a compassionate person will have no positive desire to violate the rights of other people, and that a compassionate person will not be both unjust and malicious. But none of this shows that a compassionate person will not sometimes have a mistaken desire to violate a principle of justice. If A's sufferings happen to move me more than B's, but A and B are equally deserving of aid, I may be moved to help A and to neglect B. In this case, I will be treating B unfairly. Schopenhauer's principles do not ensure that equally deserving people will be treated fairly and impartially. Kant's principles are intended to secure the impartiality that Kant takes to be central to morality.

If this is a reasonable conclusion about Schopenhauer's position, it also supports Kant's claim that moral principles have to be categorical imperatives. In Kant's view, we can appeal to moral principles to criticize any empirical principles or motives that may be suggested as the basis for morality. He argues, for instance, that morality cannot be subordinate to our desire for our own happiness, since this desire can lead us to act contrary to morality, and make us liable to legitimate moral criticism. This form of argument against empirical principles also applies to Schopenhauer. Compassion is open to moral criticism that seems to rely on a Kantian conception of morality. This gives some reason to agree with Kant that moral principles cannot be purely hypothetical—subordinate to some antecedent aim or motive.

1057. Compassion and Metaphysics

Perhaps Schopenhauer could answer these objections about the inappropriate restriction of compassion, if he appealed to his metaphysical claims. In his view, compassion is possible because it rests on the inexplicit recognition that there is no genuine distinction between real selves; the strength of our compassionate feelings helps to assure us about this metaphysical fact. But this is not the only basis for the metaphysical claim; if it were, we might say that morality rests on a metaphysical illusion (as many people have said, for instance, about the connexion between morality and freedom). Schopenhauer thinks there is no metaphysical illusion, because the outlook of compassion agrees with the independent arguments derived from transcendental idealism, as he interprets it.

The Kantian Critical Philosophy (he thinks) assures us that spatio-temporal distinctions and causal relations are parts of the phenomenal world, and therefore are simply aspects of our own consciousness, not of any independent reality. Schopenhauer sees that if we believe this, we should also doubt the assumption, never questioned by Kant, that phenomenal

---

[46] Schopenhauer mentions and dismisses one apparent case of this sort: 'Whoever is inspired with it [sc. compassion] will assuredly injure no one, will wrong no one, will encroach on no one's rights; on the contrary, he will be lenient and patient with everyone, will forgive everyone, will help everyone as much as he can, and all his actions will bear the stamp of justice, philanthropy, and loving-kindness. On the other hand, if we attempt to say, "This man is virtuous but knows no compassion", or, "He is an unjust and malicious man yet he is very compassionate", the contradiction is obvious.' (BM §19, 172)

selves correspond one-to-one with things in themselves. If our ways of distinguishing persons seem unavoidably spatio-temporal, we have no noumenal basis for recognizing a plurality of selves. Schopenhauer infers that just one noumenal will underlies the many phenomenal wills.

If we accept this conclusion, we can perhaps escape the idiosyncrasies of ordinary compassion; for we can appeal to Schopenhauer's argument against the second form of egoism. My initial reason for caring about my phenomenal self commits me to equal concern for all other phenomenal selves, once I see that they all manifest the one real self; restriction of concern rests on the false assumption that other phenomenal selves do not express a real self in the same way as I do. If, then, I am equally concerned for every aspect of my real self, I should be equally concerned for every other phenomenal self, since all of them belong to the same real self. While we may take ordinary compassion as a symptom of this impartial concern for the one real self, we do not need it to justify the impartial concern; that is justified by concern for myself combined with Schopenhauer's metaphysics.[47]

This view removes some of the difficulties that arise from reliance on compassion, but it casts doubt on the rest of Schopenhauer's argument. For if the metaphysical argument is accepted, the appeal to compassion seems misleading. Compassion does not seem to be the basis of genuine morality. On the contrary, we appreciate the strictly limited value of compassion once we understand its metaphysical basis. Schopenhauer seems to have inconsistent views about whether compassion is fundamental in morality.

Might we defend Schopenhauer on this point by allowing him to appeal to Kant's division between an analytic and a synthetic method?[48] Compassion might be basic within the analytic method; it is the aspect of the ordinary moral outlook that we can use (according to Schopenhauer) to understand the moral distinctions that we draw. The metaphysics of persons and wills might be basic within the synthetic method; it is the fundamental fact that we grasp to some degree in the exercise of compassion. If we still follow Kant's division, we might say that compassion is the ratio sciendi of the basic metaphysical fact about persons, which is the ratio essendi of the morality of compassion.

This Kantian division might help Schopenhauer to answer the objection that he gives two inconsistent accounts of the basis of morality. But it does not seem to give a complete answer. If we claim to approach the same body of principles by two methods, we need to show that the two methods give harmonious results. It would be a serious objection to Kant if facts about freedom did not support morality in the way he claims they do. Similarly, if the metaphysics of persons makes compassion unimportant in morality, Schopenhauer's two methods do not give harmonious results. We seem to be faced with a choice between the principles that result from each method.

But even if Schopenhauer were persuaded to bring his account of morality into line with his metaphysical argument, he would not have removed all his difficulties. For he seems to require inconsistent attitudes to belief in one real self. On the one hand, we are supposed to take it literally and to attribute overriding moral significance to it. According to Schopenhauer's metaphysics, I and the other person are really one and the same underlying

---

[47] Schopenhauer's claims about compassion and metaphysics are discussed by Atwell, *SHC* 115–23.
[48] Kant on the analytic ad synthetic (regressive and progressive) methods; §939.

self that is expressed in our two phenomenal selves; that is why I care directly about the other person's sufferings in the way I care about my own. The distinction between phenomenal selves, therefore, is morally irrelevant. On the other hand, Schopenhauer assumes that the result of my compassion for the other person will be a desire to help the other person, not a desire to help myself rather than the other. Why should this be so? If the difference between phenomenal selves has no moral significance, why should it be relevant to questions about distribution of benefit?

If Schopenhauer's view allows this question to arise, it raises difficulties that also arise for utilitarianism. Utilitarians do not deny the reality of phenomenal selves, but they maintain that the difference between them is irrelevant to certain kinds of moral decisions; and so the utilitarian policy seeks to maximize the total pleasure, irrespective of who gets it (except in so far as this is relevant to increasing the total). Schopenhauer does not advocate the maximization of pleasure, since he thinks morality is concerned with removing pain rather than with increasing pleasure; but he seems to face the question that the utilitarian faces, about why we are required to keep promises to the people we have made them to, instead of deciding what course of action maximizes total utility. The question for Schopenhauer is: if two phenomenal selves express one and the same real self, why is it important to direct our actions to benefiting one phenomenal self rather than another?

To answer this question, Schopenhauer needs some account of why the difference between phenomenal selves matters from the point of view of distribution, but does not matter from the point of view of compassion. If I regard your pain as an immediate reason for my action, just as my own pain is, why should I not regard your pain as a reason to benefit myself, since the same real self is involved in each case? The obvious answer is that your pain harms you, and it harms me only because it harms you. But how can Schopenhauer give this obvious answer, after he has argued that compassion exposes the illusory character of the distinction we tend to draw, from the phenomenal point of view, between our two selves? It seems that the illusion has to overcome us before we can respond appropriately to the harms that arouse compassion.

Does Schopenhauer exaggerate, then, in his claim that the appearance of distinct selves is illusory? Should we emphasize his insistence on the compassionate person's awareness of distinct phenomenal selves? If we do, we raise equally severe difficulties. For we now lose his explanation of how compassion is possible, and of why ordinary compassion should be corrected to remove its capricious (from the impartial moral point of view) discriminations between people. We also lose the connexion between morality and metaphysics, which is meant to assure us that the moral point of view does not rest on illusion.

1058. Metaphysical Objections to Morality

Schopenhauer's views on compassion, therefore, seem to provide an unsatisfactory basis for morality, whether or not we take the underlying metaphysical claims seriously. But he might still have given the right account of morality. For we might argue that moral principles and attitudes both presuppose the identification of real selves accepted by Schopenhauer, and presuppose the distinctness of persons that is needed to explain distribution of benefits. If these presuppositions conflict, morality rests on inconsistent presuppositions.[49] Schopenhauer's arguments, then, seem to constitute a fundamental objection to the moral point of view. Though this is not his conclusion, it would be an important conclusion, if he had given cogent arguments for it.

Do his arguments justify this conclusion? Some grounds for doubt remain: (1) Compassion does not have the central and basic role in morality that Schopenhauer assigns to it. (2) It does not require the strong denial of distinct real selves. (3) Even if we suppose there are no distinct selves, some distributive questions may be answerable. For there may be intra-personal principles of distribution, and these may turn out to give adequate answers to questions about distribution between (as we supposed before we realized that there is only one real self) different selves.[50]

These three objections are independent and consistent. Each of them seems to give a reasonable answer to the sceptical doubts about morality that might be raised as a result of reflexion on Schopenhauer's account of it.

1059. Criticisms of Kant on Freedom

Some of Schopenhauer's further objections to Kantian morality attend to the Formula of Autonomy. These objections encourage a comparison of his views on freedom with Kant's. His discussion of autonomy revives his previous objection about Kant's search for the a priori. Once again, Kant offers an a priori shell that abstracts from a concept with too much empirical content for Kant's purpose; but the shell contains too little to be intelligible. In this case, the initial concept is choice on the basis of interest or inclination. Kant's abstraction results in an alleged concept of choice that is not based on any interest at all. Schopenhauer protests that this shell is unintelligible, not a genuine concept; since every motive requires an interest, Kant's alleged concept of choice without any interest really introduces choice without a motive, which is not a genuine choice.[51] Since Kant himself does not intend to be describing a choice without a motive, he describes something he must recognize as unintelligible.

It is doubtful, however, whether every sort of motive would be an 'interest' in the sense that Kant intends. He seeks to distinguish action caused by some inclination antecedent to the moral motive from action caused by the moral motive independently of any previous inclination. The first sort of action is heteronomous and the second autonomous. The 'interest' he has in mind is an inclination that is independent of motivation by the moral law. He has no reason to concede that all motivation rests on some antecedent interest of this sort. He might well agree with the weaker claim that all motivation includes some interest

---

[49] Someone might draw this conclusion from some of Parfit's arguments in *RP*. Parfit does not draw it, because he believes the correct account of persons is consistent with a utilitarian moral theory.

[50] On intra-personal principles see §705, on Butler; §1195, on Sidgwick.

[51] '...in point of fact, it means nothing less than a willing *without motive* and hence an effect without a cause. Interest and motive are convertible terms; does not interest mean *quod mea interest*, that which is of importance to me? And is this not generally everything that stirs and moves my will? Consequently, what else is an interest but the influence or operation of a motive on the will? Therefore whenever a *motive* moves it, the will has an *interest*....' (*BM* §8, 99)

in the action; but if the interest is created by, and is not antecedent to, the moral motive, we act on the moral motive rather than on the interest.[52]

This reply introduces Kant's views about 'empirical' motives, which raise further difficulties for him. He speaks of empirical motives in two ways: (1) He often contrasts the moral motive with empirical motives, and he identifies action on inclination with action on empirical motives. These depend on particular desires of particular human beings that are inessential to their being rational agents. (2) But he also speaks of empirical motives in discussions of transcendental idealism. Here 'empirical' seems to mean 'phenomenal', and refers to all those motives that play a causal role in the spatio-temporal phenomenal order. Since Kant believes that free actions at the noumenal level are always identical to phenomenally determined actions, he must agree that a true account of the phenomenal, empirical motives of every action is available in principle.[53]

If these two uses of 'empirical' are not distinguished, Kant has to say that every action has an empirical motive, and that since every empirical motive depends on inclination, every action is determined by inclination, so that there cannot be any action determined by a moral, non-empirical motive independently of inclination.[54] If Kant is forced to accept this conclusion, he comes close to the position that Schopenhauer attributes to him (though not exactly for Schopenhauer's reasons). Schopenhauer's criticism, therefore, exposes a difficulty in Kant's position.

To remove this difficulty, Kant must allow that the moral motive has some distinct phenomenal expression. Hence it must be non-empirical in one sense, since it is essential to a rational agent, in contrast to empirical motives. But it must be empirical in another sense, because it is phenomenal. But if he allows that, he cannot also argue that the autonomy and freedom characteristic of morality is the same as, or especially closely connected with, the freedom that consists in noumenal causality. For moral freedom must show itself at the phenomenal level in some distinctive sort of phenomenal cause, whereas noumenal freedom belongs to moral and immoral actions alike and has no distinctive phenomenal expression.

Kant needs to explain the freedom characteristic of morality and to distinguish it from the non-phenomenal causation postulated by transcendental idealism. He offers some explanation in his remarks on freedom and autonomy, especially in the *Religion* and in the *Metaphysics of Morals*.[55] This is a revision of the position that Kant accepts when he identifies moral freedom with strictly noumenal freedom. The revision implies that transcendental idealism alone does not give a satisfactory account of freedom. Kant begins from the simple and plausible assumption that moral virtues and vices are praiseworthy and blameworthy; that praiseworthiness and blameworthiness presuppose that agents are free to acquire virtues and to avoid vices, and free to act virtuously and avoid acting viciously; and that therefore moral virtue must result from the exercise of the free will. He goes further, however; for he believes that virtue realizes freedom in a way that distinguishes it from vice. To explain

---

[52] On Kant's rejection of any antecedent motive explaining the moral motive see §§927, 937.

[53] On this explanation of transcendental idealism see §950. Kant on empirical motives; §953.

[54] We might try to draw some support from Kant's remarks about the difficulty of knowing what motive one has acted on, and about the pervasiveness of empirical motives. But these remarks do not really support the view that every action is phenomenally caused by an empirical motive. See §953.

[55] Kant on freedom and autonomy; §943.

this distinctive connexion of virtue with freedom, Kant has to distinguish the freedom of autonomy from the freedom of responsibility, and therefore has to distinguish autonomy from noumenal causation.

1060. Morality and Freedom

This suggested revision of Kant's doctrine of freedom, suggested by his views on autonomy, differs from Schopenhauer's attitude to Kant; for we have tried to retain Kant's view that freedom involves a distinctive kind of causation of ordinary phenomenal actions. We have found that the identification of autonomy with noumenal causation does not fit the division between empirical and non-empirical motives that is required by Kant's account of morality. To make Kant's position reasonable, we have to allow that moral motivation is present at the phenomenal as well as the noumenal level.

Schopenhauer, by contrast, accepts transcendental idealism, as he understands it, and agrees with Kant's claim that freedom of the will is present at the noumenal, not the phenomenal, level. He sticks to this claim far more rigorously than Kant does; and in doing so he unintentionally suggests good reasons for Kant to abandon it. For Kant believes that whether we have a free or an unfree will makes some phenomenal difference; the free will (with the appropriate sort of freedom) expresses itself in autonomous action guided by the moral motive, whereas the unfree will expresses itself in heteronomous action guided by inclination.

In Schopenhauer's view, however, all action at the phenomenal level is equally unfree. He argues that our empirical characters are fixed and beyond our control; any apparent development or change in them is simply a result of the same character meeting different circumstances. He even supports his claim by appealing to Aristotle's remarks about the natural virtues (FW iv 57–8). Our tendency to reject his view results from our belief in liberty of indifference, which he blames on Judaism (PP ii §119, 238). He accepts the incompatibilist claim that if determinism is true, we cannot have the sort of control over our character that is necessary for responsibility.

Still, Schopenhauer believes that we are in some way responsible for our characters, and indeed that they are all we can be responsible for. We cannot be responsible for particular actions, since they are the inevitable result of our empirical characters, which are out of our control. We can only 'play our part' more or less coherently and harmoniously; but presumably whether or not we do this is also fixed independently of our control. Freedom and responsibility enter at the noumenal level, where it is not inevitable for us to be the sorts of people we are.

What sort of freedom enters at the noumenal level? Schopenhauer speaks as though he agrees with Plato's myths of reincarnation and the choice of lives (cf. PP ii §116, 227): we can properly regard ourselves as responsible for being the sorts of people we are, despite the fact that there is no particular time at which we chose to be one sort of person rather than another. But it is not clear how similar Schopenhauer's picture is to the picture presented in stories of reincarnation. If those stories are taken literally, they imply a choice of character before our lifetime. If they are taken metaphorically, they might be taken to suggest that we make ourselves by our choices in the course of our lifetime even if not by any particular choice. In either case, they seem to assume that it is the same person who both chooses and is responsible for being that sort of person.[56] The stories assume that the choosing self and the responsible self are the same self, and that this particular self is distinct from all other choosing and responsible selves. But it is not clear that Schopenhauer accepts these assumptions.

In his view, the will is free at the noumenal level because it is not causally determined by previous events; causal relations belong to spatio-temporal, and hence phenomenal, events. Hence the will in itself is undetermined; and so if absence of determination is sufficient for freedom, the will in itself is free. Moreover, if freedom is sufficient for responsibility, we are responsible for the real selves of which our phenomenal selves and empirical characters are expressions.

Some differences between Schopenhauer's and Kant's versions of transcendental idealism are relevant here. First, Kant relies on noumenal causality to show that the phenomenal character results from noumenal choice, so that we are responsible for it. Responsibility seems to involve the right sort of causal relation to the action or character we are responsible for; and Kant tries to secure that by appealing to noumenal causality. Schopenhauer does not attribute this role to noumenal causality. He believes the will in itself underlies the phenomenal character, but he does not suggest that particular actions of a person's noumenal will form distinctive features of the same person's phenomenal character. In departing from Kant on this point, Schopenhauer may appear to grasp some of the implications of transcendental idealism better than Kant grasps them.

But his view has a disadvantage. For if noumenal causation does not form the empirical character, we seem to have no adequate basis for responsibility. Absence of determination is relevant to responsibility only if the undetermined states are appropriately connected to the states or actions that we are responsible for. The right sort of connexion must lead to responsibility for the empirical character, since only that sort of responsibility can explain our actually holding people responsible for anything. But Schopenhauer does not seem to have found the right sort of connexion.[57]

A further and related difficulty for morality arises from his view that real noumenal selves are not distinct. Noumenal reality excludes time and causal determination by previous events, and so allows no one-to-one correspondence between noumenal wills and phenomenal characters. Perhaps Schopenhauer is right about one implication of transcendental idealism. But his negative argument against distinctness of noumenal wills does not show that there is only one noumenal will; it only shows that we cannot say how many there are. This agnostic view falls short of what Schopenhauer needs for his account of compassion; for that account seems to presuppose that my phenomenal self and the other person's phenomenal self manifest the same real self.

---

[56] This claim about persistence need not be a feature of all conceptions of reincarnation. See, e.g., Collins, *SP* 188–91 on Buddhist views. But these views are even less suitable for Schopenhauer's claims about freedom than the Platonic conception is.

[57] Janaway, *SWSP*, chs. 3, 9, discusses Kant and Schopenhauer on determinism and freedom, taking an unsympathetic view of Kant.

Given this conclusion about individuation and his claims about noumenal freedom, can Schopenhauer say anything useful about responsibility? If A's empirical character is good and B's is bad, and if responsibility is to be attributed to a noumenal self, which noumenal self is responsible for each character? We have no reason to believe that distinct noumenal selves are responsible for A's empirical character, B's empirical character, and every other empirical character. We seem to have no basis for holding A responsible for A's empirical character, given that the underlying noumenal self may be no more praiseworthy for A's empirical character than blameworthy for B's empirical character.

If we are to take Schopenhauer's metaphysics as seriously as we must take it in order to support his account of the basis of morality, he seems to leave no worthwhile connexion between character, responsibility, and freedom. He would apparently be more consistent if he rejected attitudes connected with responsibility and freedom, since he gives them no tenable metaphysical basis.

1061. Implications of Schopenhauer's Views

Here also, then, Schopenhauer's arguments seem to undermine morality in ways that he does not intend.[58] We saw that his arguments might be used to show that morality both denies and requires the distinctness of persons. And we have just seen that a correct metaphysical position leaves no room for any belief in responsibility or free will of the sort relevant to morality. A sceptical attitude to morality seems to be the only reasonable conclusion.

We may recoil from this conclusion to take refuge in the apparently less metaphysical side of Schopenhauer's attitude to morality. In so far as he attacks Kant and defends compassion as the basis of morality, he rejects a rationalistic conception of morality as a set of abstract principles that deserve to be recognized as binding by all enlightened rational agents. Instead of this rationalistic conception, he finds the central elements of morality in our reactions to particular human needs and feelings in particular situations. The right reactions and responses, as opposed to principles allegedly derived from pure reason, turn out to be essential for any genuine moral goodness.

This rejection of rationalism and abstraction in morality may attract those who think Kant takes the wrong direction.[59] But Schopenhauer unintentionally exposes weaknesses in his attitude to morality. Compassion alone provides no satisfactory basis for morality, since it needs to be regulated by other considerations that cannot be reduced to compassion. Schopenhauer's account of the metaphysical basis of morality offers grounds for the morally appropriate regulation of compassion. But the grounds that it offers seem to undermine morality. This conclusion suggests that he has found the wrong sort of metaphysical basis for morality. He may none the less be right to suppose that some sort of metaphysical basis

---

[58] Perhaps Nietzsche sees and exploits the undermining tendency of Schopenhauer's argument. See §1103. Cf. Janaway, *SWSP* 245.

[59] Some of Schopenhauer's reasons for rejecting rationalism and abstraction are similar to those offered by Taylor, *GE*, ch. 15 (an account of compassion that is sympathetic to Schopenhauer), and Blum, *FAM*, ch. 5 (agreement and disagreement with Schopenhauer; see 8, 85).

is needed. Some metaphysical basis may provide the sort of regulation that compassion and other emotions and sentiments need if they are to be morally reliable.

If Schopenhauer's reform and revision of Kant raise some doubts, we may conclude that he is too ready to abandon the aspects of Kant that he rejects. On some points, his disputes with Kant rest on misunderstanding. We have good reason to reject his account of Kant's views on the moral motive, on the place of self-interest in morality, and on the purely formal character of the categorical imperative. In these cases, we may reasonably conclude that Kant's actual position is better than Schopenhauer takes it to be. His criticisms of Kant on freedom, however, suggest a different conclusion. He is right to say that Kant's claims about noumenal causation, freedom, and the empirical self create a serious conflict in Kant's position and that some revision is needed. When we see the results of revising Kant in the way that Schopenhauer recommends, we have good reason to try a different sort of revision. In this case also, we can learn from Schopenhauer's argument even if we do not accept his conclusions.

KIERKEGAARD

1062. Different Conceptions of the Moral Point of View

In *Either-Or* Kierkegaard tries to capture an essential feature of the moral outlook. By this he means not the outlook of someone who accepts and follows the correct moral system or principles or virtues, but the outlook of someone who thinks it is worth looking for the correct moral system (etc.). Such people may not have grasped what is morally right, but they are the people who take questions about what is morally right or wrong, good or evil, to be practically important. Kierkegaard calls this outlook the 'ethical' outlook. He contrasts it with a non-moral attitude to one's life that he calls the 'aesthetic' outlook. If we understand and accept the ethical outlook, we may not have found what is morally right, but at least we think it important for the conduct of our lives to find out what is right. From the aesthetic point of view, questions about moral rightness are purely theoretical questions that we do not regard as having any practical bearing on our lives.

To grasp Kierkegaard's contrast between the aesthetic and the ethical, we may compare it with some other ways of trying to capture the essential features of the moral outlook. His contrast does not seem to match any of these descriptions of the moral point of view, and we will find it useful to bear these descriptions in mind in looking for the distinctive features of his description.

According to Plato, Aristotle, and Aquinas, the moral point of view results from living by reason rather than passion. The application of practical reason to one's life is the systematic pursuit of one's ultimate good, and the enlightened pursuit of one's own good reveals the goodness of the moral virtues. Practical reason is exercised in prudence, reflecting on one's own good; and this reflexion reveals the importance of morality.

Hobbes believes that this eudaemonist conception of the moral point of view is wrong to connect morality with practical reason. For he does not identify prudence with practical reason. Prudence simply involves instrumental reasoning directed to the satisfaction of our predominant desire. Morality is connected with prudential reason not because prudential reason forms our ends in life, but simply because instrumental reasoning about our passions endorses the moral virtues.

Hume agrees with this Hobbesian view on reason and passion, but disagrees about the way in which morality emerges from it. He believes, with Hobbes's opponents, that morality is not simply instrumental to the satisfaction of the passions that Hobbes considers—the passions that are summed up in the desire for peace. He believes that the moral outlook requires the predominance of specific passions and sentiments that distinguish it from prudence. The person to whom morality matters is the one whose sympathetic and benevolent sentiments are strong enough to influence choices and actions.

Kant returns partly, but only partly, to the identification of the moral with the rational outlook. He follows Hobbes and Hume in believing that the prudential outlook is not distinctively rational. But he agrees with the traditional eudaemonist view that the moral outlook belongs to practical reason guiding our choice of ends. Hence he combines a Hobbesian analysis of prudence with a rationalist conception of morality, and severs the Aristotelian connexion between prudential and moral practical reason.

These are only some of the main possibilities for trying to identify the point of view of morality. But they will give us a start in trying to see what Kierkegaard is trying to do.

1063. Morality and Reason

Kierkegaard's description of the ethical does not initially appear to be closely aligned with any of the conceptions we have mentioned. He neither identifies it with Aristotelian or Kantian practical reason nor requires Humean sympathy and benevolence. But he relies on another Kantian contrast, between freedom and necessity. Ethical agents choose freely, and take responsibility for their lives, in contrast to aesthetic agents, who fail to affirm their freedom.

This description of Kierkegaard's position recalls a question about Kant. Does Kierkegaard claim that aesthetic agents are not free until they take the ethical point of view? Or are they are free all along, so that when they take the ethical point of view, they recognize, but do not acquire, their freedom? To say that ethical agents 'affirm' their freedom might be taken to make either of these claims. Perhaps Kierkegaard intends something like Kant's contrast between negative and positive freedom.

Kierkegaard's contrast between the aesthetic and the ethical point of view warns us against a possible over-simplification. If we identify the moral outlook with the outlook of practical reason, we misrepresent the amoral agent as irrational, a creature of whim, passion, and impulse without any definite aim in life. It is easy to reach this conclusion if we distinguish the moral from the non-moral by distinguishing (as Aristotle puts it) living in accordance with reason from living in accordance with passion (*pathos, EN* 1169a5–6). Plato and Aristotle try not to present the vicious agent as grossly irrational; they try to represent the degree of control by practical reason that can be found in an intemperate, cowardly, and unjust person's life. But one might still object that they do not do justice to the possibility of a coherent, well-planned, and apparently satisfying life without the moral outlook.

Realistic consideration of the amoral agent may encourage doubts not only about the Platonic and Aristotle treatment of morality as rational prudence, but also about the general rationalist aim, shared by, among others, Cudworth, Clarke, Price, Reid, and Kant, of identifying morality with the rational outlook. Once we recognize the possibility of rational amorality, we may infer that morality has to be understood as Hume understands it, by reference to specific sentiments and aims that are independent of practical reason.

We should be able to learn something about rationalist and anti-rationalist attitudes to the moral point of view, if we consider Kierkegaard's account of the aesthetic outlook. For he tries to present a form of non-moral life in appropriate detail, through the reflexions of a self-conscious agent who plans his actions rationally with reference to his characteristic ends. If we examine this outlook and see how it differs from an ethical outlook, we may be able to see whether rationalism about morality depends on failure to appreciate the possibilities of practical reason without morality.

In calling this amoral outlook 'aesthetic', Kierkegaard separates it both from the mere satisfaction of appetites and impulses and from the imposition of moral imperatives. The objects of my aesthetic admiration do not seem to be forced on me by my biological needs, basic impulses, or social environment.[1] They are not like the sorts of desires that press Hobbesian agents to form a commonwealth. They are desires that result from some degree of reflexion. That is why the presentation of a seducer requires some representation of his reflexion and deliberation.[2] Nor, however, are they chosen on principle, or required by any rule or law. Objects and aims to which I take an aesthetic attitude just appeal to me and attract me, irrespective of any obligation to prefer them.

Kierkegaard's examination of the aesthetic conveys his judgment on philosophers who tend to assimilate moral to aesthetic judgment. Both Hutcheson and Hume notice the disinterested character of aesthetic judgment, and take this to provide a parallel to moral judgment. Kant partly agrees, in treating the awareness of beauty as a preparation for the recognition of moral value. Kierkegaard does not necessarily disagree with these comparisons between aesthetic and moral judgment. But he suggests that they may mislead us, if they encourage us to attend to the points of similarity between the two attitudes and to overlook their differences. The aesthetic attitude is in some ways disinterested and impartial; but this form of appreciation does not take us all the way to morality.

1064. The Imperative Aspect of Morality

To show how the aesthetic outlook differs from the ethical, Kierkegaard connects the aesthetic with attraction and inclination, and the ethical with requirement. Here he recalls Sidgwick's division between the attractive outlook of ancient ethics and the imperative outlook of modern ethics.[3] He suggests that the imperative character of one's aims and principles takes us beyond the purely aesthetic attitude. If Kierkegaard is right, he seems to support the criticism of Greek ethics for its purely attractive outlook. If our choices are guided by consideration of the beneficial and the fine (beautiful, *kalon*), we seem to overlook

---

[1] This is why Don Giovanni does not take the aesthetic attitude; *EO* i 97.

[2] 'To be a seducer always takes a certain reflexion and consciousness, and as soon as this is present, it can be appropriate to speak of craftiness and machinations and subtle wiles. Don Giovanni lacks this consciousness. . . . A seducer, therefore, ought to possess a power that Don Giovanni does not have; . . . the power of words.' (*EO* i 98–9)

[3] Attractive v. imperative; §456.

a distinctive feature of moral principles. Sidgwick speaks of duty and of imperatives in order to capture this element of morality.

We may take two different views, however, about what is missing in a purely attractive conception of the ends of action: (1) We may object that they leave out the required and compulsory character of morality. If we adopt an end simply by being attracted to it, we need not suppose we are required to adopt it, or that it is a necessary end for a rational agent; we would still be equally rational agents if we were unmoved by this end. (2) We may object that a purely attractive conception of ends leaves out the role of legislation and imposition. The acceptance of a purely attractive end is simply a relation between the end and ourselves. Imposition, however, requires a third party; the commander or legislator imposes his will on us, and this is the distinctive feature of moral principles.

These two views about what is missing in a purely attractive conception of ends result in two different views about the character of moral principles. According to the first view, it is not so obvious that a teleological conception of morality, such as we find in the Greek moralists, is purely attractive. For if we recognize that we have no rational alternative to the acceptance of a particular end, we no longer hold that ends all depend on attractiveness, but we recognize that some ends deserve to attract us. If we take that view, it is the deservingness, not the simple fact of attraction, that makes them appropriate ends for us. According to the second view of morality, however, morality requires imposition; rational necessity alone is not enough. The difference between these two ways of understanding the non-attractive aspect of morality underlies some of the disputes between naturalism and voluntarism that we have discussed. Kierkegaard's contrast between the aesthetic and the ethical may show where he stands on these disputes.

1065. Freedom and the Ethical Outlook

Whichever view we take about the non-attractive character of morality, it seems paradoxical to claim that the ethical is the area of freedom. For we might suppose that in introducing imperatives and laws, we reduce freedom. This seems a reasonable complaint whether we think of rational necessity or of imposition by a legislator. Whether rational considerations themselves or other people's demands are the source of the relevant compulsion, morality seems to involve some sort of compulsion, and therefore seems to reduce freedom, and not to increase it.

This is the complaint of the aesthetic outlook against the principles imposed by ethics. Kierkegaard illustrates the contrast between the two outlooks by discussing two different attitudes to marriage. The aesthetic agent avoids it because it restricts his freedom; Kierkegaard illustrates the aesthetic life through his description of Don Juan and his 'Diary of a Seducer'. He illustrates the ethical life through Judge William's defence of marriage. We need not agree that either speaker is entirely right about marriage in order to see why this is an appropriate example. From Johannes' aesthetic point of view, engagement and marriage take all the fun away and make everything boring because they introduce the ethical.[4] It seems to illustrate the imposition of compulsion, conformity to social expectations, prescribed forms of sentiment and behaviour. It therefore seems to remove personal choice, spontaneity, and freedom to change one's mind. Even though it begins, supposedly, with an expression of individual inclination and preference, it suppresses these aspects of individuality in the interest of social demands and expectations.

The aesthetic critique of the ethical, therefore, does not simply say that aesthetic agents have more fun, but adds that they are genuinely free agents. Judge William's defence of the ethical tries to answer this defence of the aesthetic outlook.

The contrast between these two outlooks is illuminating, whether or not it entirely captures the moral outlook. We might agree that the ethical outlook differs from the aesthetic in the ways that Kierkegaard describes, but we might still not agree that the ethical outlook is sufficient for morality. Perhaps morality incorporates an ethical outlook, but needs something more as well. We ought to separate questions about the reasonableness of an ethical outlook from questions about its connexion with morality.

1066. The Aesthetic Outlook

The examples of people guided by an aesthetic outlook are unattractive in ways that might seem irrelevant to an accurate description of the aesthetic point of view. The 'Diary of a Seducer' presents a cold-blooded character who tries to ingratiate himself with others, and tries to make himself agreeable to them, but simply for his own self-centred ends. He wins their trust, and then betrays it, as part of his strategy for enjoying himself at their expense.

Johannes (the seducer) is openly selfish. He wants to win Cordelia's trust and affection in order to seduce her, and he cares about doing this for his own sake only. He does not wish her harm, but he is not concerned about the effects of his plans on her, except in so far as they affect him. The ends he pursues in his treatment of other people are ends that simply appeal to him. In these respects, he treats people as means to his own ends, not as ends in themselves.

We might object that Kierkegaard presents the aesthetic point of view in an inappropriately unfavourable light. Could we not follow our inclinations, but have less selfish inclinations than Johannes has? If his inclinations included benevolent attitudes to others, or even to a restricted group of others, he would not deceive Cordelia, or Cordelia's other lover who trusts Johannes, or her aunt whose confidence and trust he wins. Could we not be aesthetic, but altruistic?

This is how the sentimentalist moralist replies to the Aristotelian criticism of vice as gratification of one's non-rational part.[5] Someone who conforms to the theory of Hutcheson and Hume seems to form an outlook that Kierkegaard regards as aesthetic. The aesthetic agent does not form his ends in life because he has some rational conviction that they matter,

---

[4] 'The ethical is just as boring in scholarship as in life. . . . Under the aesthetic sky, everything is buoyant, beautiful, transient; when ethics arrives on the scene, everything becomes harsh, angular, infinitely *langweiligt*.' (*EO* i 367)

[5] Aristotle on vice: §111.

and so he does not act on the view that reason requires these ends rather than those. Could we not be attached to the interests of others, and in general to the concerns of morality, without any conviction that they matter, but simply because they appeal to us? This is the attitude that we will form if we are convinced by the sentimentalist view that there is no justifying reason to be given in favour of pursuing one end rather than another.

1067. Differences between Kierkegaard and Hume

We may have overlooked a significant difference between the Humean agent and Kierkegaard's aesthetic agent. For it seems unfair to suggest that Humean agents do not think it matters whether they have the ends that they have. They care about having these ends rather than others. In so far as they care about the needs and interests of others, they also approve of benevolence and kindness; they want to have these traits themselves and approve of the same traits in others.

It is not clear that this sort of approval is part of Kierkegaard's aesthetic agents. Johannes feels like being a seducer for the sake of conquest, but he does not seem to care whether he or other people have this inclination. He does not seem to care about whether he remains a seducer, or turns from being a seducer to being a sadist, or to being a philanthropist. He does not seem to look with any special disapproval on a future radical change in his ends. On the contrary, he seems to pass from one end to another, as he feels inclined at a particular time. He does not do this so quickly that his life is chaotic or episodic. But he does not suggest that he would be ruined if he changed into a radically different sort of person.

One might suggest, then, that Johannes and the Humean agent differ in so far as Johannes does not care about whether he and other people have these ends or others. But this suggestion does not seem quite right. If Johannes neither approved nor disapproved of his ends, how could he carry out his longer-term aims? In the course of trying to win Cordelia's confidence, he might have suddenly become tired of the effort that his various devices and strategies require of him. If he is to stick to his strategy of seduction, he needs to act on some preference for his particular long-term pursuit over the short-term attraction or obstacle that threatens to divert him now. He must therefore approve of his longer-term end over the particular short-term attraction or obstacle. That is why Johannes deliberates about different strategies that would make him one or another sort of seducer, and decides which sort of seducer he wants to be.[6]

Here the aesthetic agent can appeal to Hume's remarks about the possibility of prudence.[7] If he pursues the means to his longer-term goals, he can be said to care about these goals; he has a stronger inclination towards them than towards the short-term goals that might get in their way. That is why Hume thinks he can explain, within his own views on reason and passion, the sorts of actions that other people take to result from practical reason. So far, then, we have no reason to say that the Humean moral agent differs from the aesthetic agent in his attitude to his ends.

---

[6] '. . . I desire nothing that in the strictest sense is not freedom's gift. Let vulgar seducers use such means. What do they gain anyway? . . . I am an aesthete, an eroticist, who has grasped the nature and the point of love . . .' (*EO* i 367–8)

[7] Hume on prudence; §738.

But perhaps what we have said suggests where we should look for the relevant difference. While the seducer approves his longer-term goals over his short-term goals, it is not clear that he cares about having the particular longer-term goals he has over others that he might have formed. Though he prefers being a seducer over pursuing a short-term satisfaction, he does not approve of being a seducer over being an athlete or a philanthropist. On this point, the Humean moral agent might claim to be different. The aesthetic agent seems to be superficial in so far as he does not care what sort of person he is. According to the Humean moralist, we miss the importance of other ends if we believe it is all right to make them depend on what attracts us, or what we incline to, from time to time. The aesthetic agent may be accused of treating all his ends as though they were no more important than his taste in food, or even his taste in music, which he regards himself as perfectly free to change on the basis of how they appeal to him. Not all of one's ends, we might say, are mere tastes, but the aesthetic agent takes a superficial view of ends by trying to reduce them all to mere tastes.

The Humean answer to the apparent superficiality of the aesthetic agent is to deny that all one's ends are mere tastes or inclinations. Some ends and concerns stand out from others because they are supported by further attitudes of approval and disapproval. Hume argues that our moral sentiments are stable because they are the objects of our own approval. When we look at them and their formation, we approve of how we got them and we approve of their persistence; hence we take action to avoid any tendency to weaken or abandon them.[8] Our commitment to morality is deeper than our current inclinations and tastes; it is supported by the further attitudes directed to these inclinations and tastes, in so far as they concern morality.

1068. Similarities between Kierkegaard and Hume

On this basis, then, we might argue that Kierkegaard's aesthetic agent does not match a Humean moral agent. If the argument is sound, objections to the aesthetic outlook may not be objections to the Humean account of the moral agent. To see whether the argument is sound, we need to see how deep a difference between the Humean agent and Kierkegaard's aesthetic agent emerges from our discussion.

The extent of the difference partly depends on Hume's conception of approval. As Hume conceives it, approval is a second-order attitude, consisting in a favourable feeling towards a first-order inclination, but not directly towards an action based on that first-order inclination. In recognizing such attitudes, Hume does not depart from his general conception of approval as a sentiment; it is a specific feeling, distinguishable by its introspectible character. It is a contingent fact that some instances of this feeling take other feelings as their objects.

Does Hume's conception of approval directed towards one's own sentiments mark a basic difference between a Humean agent and Kierkegaard's aesthetic agent? We suggested, on Hume's behalf, that the aesthetic agent is rather superficially attached to his aims, and that he is himself a rather superficial person. If he thinks that nothing beyond his current

---

[8] Hume on self-approval; §780.

inclination towards being a seducer warrants him in being a seducer rather than an athlete, we may say that he lacks the appropriate attitude of commitment that Humean moral agents take towards their character. He does not recognize his character as an appropriate object of commitment, but his aims are simply the results of his transitory inclinations. Humean attitudes of commitment introduce a more stable attachment and a broader concern than a mere inclination would give him.

Attitudes of commitment may be expected to make it harder to give up a specific end. If we are attached to that end not only by a first-order inclination to it but also by a higher-order commitment to the first-order inclination, we have to lose two attitudes rather than one; a momentary lapse in our first-order inclination may be counteracted by the higher-order commitment tending to restore the first-order inclination. Higher-order commitments do not necessarily come and go with first-order inclinations; they may persist when first-order inclinations are transitory.

But if attitudes of commitment are simply expressions of approval, they are simply higher-order inclinations that consist in my approval of my being the sort of person who approves the sorts of things I characteristically approve of. To overcome the superficiality of the aesthetic life based on inclination, Hume supports one's choice of life with a higher-order inclination. But why should the introduction of higher-order inclinations makes a vital difference? They cannot be counted on to be any more stable than first-order inclinations. If we can change our first-order inclinations on a whim, and we see nothing wrong with this, why should the same not be true of higher-order inclinations? The aesthetic attitude to our ends seems to apply to higher-order inclinations and ends.[9]

We might even expect some people's higher-order attitudes to make their characters less stable. Even during the time that their first-order inclinations are stable, fluctuations in their higher-order inclinations may change their outlook. Indeed, we might expect this to result from the aesthetic attitude. If the aesthetic agent includes himself and his character in his aesthetic attitude, we would expect his character to be among the things that change as his whims and tastes vary.

Moreover, we might doubt whether an aesthetic agent would be better if his choice of a way of life and character were supported by higher-order attitudes. Admittedly, if these attitudes are relatively stable, and directed towards better ends, they will improve him; this is the result that Hume expects in someone who approves of his own moral sentiments. But if they are unstable, and tend to disapprove of his better first-order sentiments, they will have a bad effect on his character.[10] He may, for instance, have kind impulses, but disapprove of them as a mark of weakness and effeminacy, which he finds unappealing. In that case, the operation of his second-order sentiments will make him worse than he otherwise would have been.

The conclusion of this argument is simple. If we are dissatisfied with aesthetic agency and its treatment of ends as the products of inclination and taste, we do not remove the sources of our dissatisfaction if we simply add inclinations of a higher order. The mere fact

---

[9] Frankfurt discusses the role of higher-order volitions in 'Identification', esp. 166–9. See also Hutcheson and Butler on conscience, §715.

[10] This point underlies the objections directed at Kant on the basis of the examples of Huckleberry Finn and the conscientious Nazi. See §930.

that they are of a higher order does not make them essentially different in the relevant respects.[11]

1069. An Objection to Hume

Kierkegaard does not discuss this question about the aesthetic agent. Johannes' higher-order attitudes are not prominent in the description of his character, and from a Humean point of view we might think this is his crucial failing. Hence we might identify the aesthetic attitude with the outlook of unreflective lower-order inclination. But mere attention to higher-order attitudes does not seem to make a decisive difference. Johannes would not cease to be a basically aesthetic agent if he were guided by his higher-order attitudes. If we decide that a purely aesthetic attitude to one's basic aims and commitments is open to objection, we will also have reason to object to a Humean account of moral character; for the Humean character is similar to the aesthetic agent in the relevant respects.

It is not entirely illegitimate, therefore, of Kierkegaard to present the aesthetic attitude through the rather unattractive example of Johannes. His concentration on this example may be misleading, however. It would be illegitimate of Kierkegaard to insinuate that anyone who takes an aesthetic attitude will necessarily take the calculating and manipulative attitude that Johannes takes to other people. His account would be easier to apply to more cases if he had shown that we can find the same basic attitude in people with kind and generous sentiments, such as Kant's 'philanthropist'.[12] The essential features of the aesthetic agent can be found in people whose character we might welcome and admire in some respects. The outlook that Kierkegaard attributes to the aesthetic agent is the one that Kant criticizes in people who care about morality only because they have unselfish and benevolent attitudes.

If the aesthetic attitude were found only in selfish and manipulative people such as Johannes, it would not be especially useful for Kierkegaard's purposes. Such a narrow conception of the aesthetic attitude seems to leave many options open before we ever come to the ethical outlook. Hence it would not be clear why we should regard the choice between the aesthetic and the ethical as an 'either-or' choice. Kierkegaard's picture of the aesthetic outlook raises wider questions if this outlook is present in people who seem more attractive than Johannes. Hume's description of the moral sentiments and of higher-order approval allows us to see that the aesthetic attitude is present even here.

The Humean moral agent is an aesthetic agent because Hume believes that we have no better reason to be a philanthropist than to be a seducer. If one's philanthropic inclinations and tastes were to change, one would have no reason not to be a seducer. What we have a reason to do depends on the tastes we already have, and we cannot have a reason to acquire one taste rather than another, except in so far as it fits better with our current tastes. Kierkegaard's example shows that, from the Humean point of view, the seducer's outlook is no less reasonable than the philanthropist's.

---

[11] Perhaps this objection might also be used against Blackburn's non-cognitivist account of higher-order attitudes. See §1369. One might argue that attitudes resting on no further reasons provide an insufficient basis for a non-aesthetic principle.

[12] Kant's philanthropist; G 397, discussed in §914.

We might think this is a boring conclusion, and not really an objection to Hume, since it simply reminds us that, according to the sentimentalist view, justifying reasons cannot support one end rather than another. To say that the seducer is not unreasonable is not to say that we have no reason to disapprove of him. On the contrary, if our sentiments are closer to the philanthropist's, we have good reason, in the light of these sentiments, to approve of the philanthropist and to approve of philanthropic motives and actions in ourselves.

Still, even if Kierkegaard's point is basically familiar, his development of it in his specific example of the seducer is worthwhile. For it makes clear why we might be reluctant to agree that the seducer differs from better people simply in his tastes and inclinations. We also tend to suppose that he is mistaken in fixing his ends by his inclinations and tastes. According to Hume, this tendency to reject the seducer's way of choosing his ends is misguided. It is not a sign of the seducer's superficial and thoughtless attitude to his aims and concerns; it is the way in which we all choose our ends, and we have no alternative. Kierkegaard's discussion of the aesthetic outlook gives us reasons to explore outlooks that do not treat ends as matters of inclination.

1070. The Aesthetic Attitude v. Rational Prudence

This conclusion from Kierkegaard's discussion may be criticized for an inappropriately rationalist bias. We have treated it as support for Kant. But Kierkegaard does not seem to look at it this way. Though he takes the aesthetic agent to regard his ends as matters of inclination, he does not contrast inclination with practical reason. He may not believe that the Kantian reaction is the only viable reaction. To settle his view on this question, we need to look more closely at his account of the ethical outlook, to see whether he accepts anything like Kantian rationalism.

We may usefully begin by considering rational prudence in Kierkegaard's picture of the aesthetic outlook. Butler recognizes reasonable self-love as a superior principle that does not yet incorporate the demands of conscience. How are we to understand the aesthetic agent? Does Kierkegaard ascribe rational self-love to him?

Rational prudence is relevant to questions about the deliberations of the aesthetic agent because it introduces considerations of authority as well as strength.[13] When self-love is involved, we recognize reasons for preferring one action over another that do not depend simply on the strength of our desire for the option that we choose. Sometimes, indeed, we may recognize that we have better reason to choose one option, but a stronger desire for another. But Kierkegaard's description of the aesthetic agent seems to omit this difference between authority and strength. Johannes seems to decide what to do according to his predominant aims, which are fixed by the comparative strength of his desires.

If this is true of the aesthetic agent, he seems to be open to criticism from Butler's point of view, for not recognizing an important fact about himself and his agency. But, if Butler's account of rational self-love is right, it should be present in the choices of the aesthetic agent. Butler does not believe that some human beings lack rational self-love and need to be taught

---

[13] Butler on authority and strength; §§683–4.

to acquire it. If it were possible to lack superior principles and live a human life, the ancient Sceptics would be right in supposing we could live a human life without evaluative beliefs. Butler, however, believes it is an absurdity to think of human beings without this superior principle. The aesthetic agent must be implicitly guided to some degree by rational self-love, even if he does not explicitly recognize considerations of authority as distinct from strength. Where might we find choices that implicitly rely on rational self-love?

In Butler's view, rational self-love affects choices about one's future, since they involve reference to one's continuing self and its interests. To form these judgments I think about myself as a whole, not simply about the desires that are currently strongest, and I think about what is best for this self, consisting of more than my current desires. Johannes has to recognize such a self, since he plans quite elaborately in ways that will form his future desires in the longer term as well as the short term. One might say, from Butler's point of view, that Johannes conceives himself as a seducer. He does not simply go off in pursuit of his latest inclination. His inclinations form a plan that he accepts as an outlook for himself.

Just as Kierkegaard does not make it clear how higher-order desires are related to aesthetic agency, he does not make it clear how the aesthetic agent chooses for his future self. But he seems to agree implicitly with Butler; for he takes the aesthetic agent to plan consciously for his future self and to regard this conscious planning as the right way to conduct his life. Agents who were impervious to consequences for their future selves would not think of themselves as (e.g.) seducers, and would not plan for themselves under this conception. In this respect at least, the aesthetic agent is not entirely a creature of inclination.

1071. The Differences between the Aesthetic and the Ethical Outlook

Kierkegaard mentions differences between the ethical and the aesthetic agent, but he does not say whether the different conditions he mentions are logically or psychologically distinct, or are different manifestations of the same basic difference. The simplest way to capture the main difference emerges from the initial description of the aesthetic outlook. The aesthetic agent chooses his actions by acting on the ends that appeal to him, and so acts on ends that are objects of inclination. The ethical agent acts on ends that seem to him to matter.

Kierkegaard's description of the ethical outlook follows a traditional conception of practical reason. According to Aquinas, rational desire does not aim simply at the achievement of my ultimate end, understood simply as the ordered satisfaction of the ends I happen to pursue. It also includes the pursuit of one's own perfection; among the ends that one might pursue for their own sake, the rational agent selects those that are worth pursuing from the point of view of one's own perfection. The objects of our desires are not to be pursued uncritically; we ask whether our ultimate ends are the appropriate ones for agents with our nature. Aquinas believes that everyone takes this critical attitude to their ends to some extent, and that enlightened agents differ from others in acting on a thoroughly critical attitude to their ends.

Why should we raise this question about our ends? We might think that the aesthetic agent can get on quite well without it, and that he has no reason to take the further step that the ethical agent takes. But according to Kierkegaard, the aesthetic attitude leads to the condition he calls 'despair' (ii 212, 215). In this condition I give up hope, but in doing so, I make a choice that gets me into the area of the ethical life. To see why this is so, we need to examine the sources of despair more closely.[14]

Despair is not simply the condition we are in when we recognize that we are tired of pursuing one of our aesthetically chosen ends, and therefore recognize that the pursuit of this end will no longer satisfy us. We might say that we now despair of being satisfied by pursuing this end. But such despair does not take us outside the aesthetic life. For if I recognize that my old goals no longer satisfy me, I may simply predict that I will find something else. If I 'despair' of clothes in last year's fashion, I may not give up following the latest fashions; I may buy clothes in this year's fashion.

What more, then, does Kierkegaard see in despair than simply getting tired of the things that one previously enjoyed? A broader sort of despair would consist in recognizing that the pursuit of this sort of life will never satisfy my self. This sort of life is always liable to fluctuation of aims, since my particular ends are kept in place by nothing more than transitory inclination. Kierkegaard suggests that reflexion on my aesthetic life will show me that its particular form of mutability cannot satisfy my self.[15]

If aesthetic agents are to be convinced on this point, they must be able to grasp Kierkegaard's conception of a self, and see why such a self cannot be satisfied by an aesthetic life.[16] At this point, it is relevant to return to our questions about Butler on reasonable self-love. When we see how reasonable self-love enters the aesthetic agent's life, we will perhaps see why aesthetic agency cannot satisfy the sort of self that he attributes to himself.

The most basic level at which we can raise Butler's question is the aesthetic agent's choice of a way of life. He is not completely immersed in his particular inclinations, but he is able to distinguish himself from them, so that, as Kierkegaard puts it, he hovers above himself.[17] He sees that he will still exist when he has got tired of this aim and turned to another. Indeed, each of his aims is purely accidental to him; none of them is more central to him than any of the others, since they are all liable to be abandoned with a change in his whims, tastes, or inclinations. Some aims are deeper than others only because the relevant inclinations are less likely to change.

One aspect of the aesthetic agent's choice, however, does not seem to be a matter of inclination. He plans his actions and strategies for his life. He does not simply plan the ways of satisfying this or that desire; he also plans the orderly satisfaction of his desire so as to achieve the degree of satisfaction corresponding to the strength of his desire for different aims. He chooses to try to plan for his life rather than for specific desires as they come.

---

[14] Some relevant questions about the aesthetic outlook are explored by Kosch, *FRKSK*, ch. 5.

[15] Hence Judge William warns against a superficial attitude to despair: 'The person who despairs about something in particular runs the risk that his despair will not be authentic and deep, that it is an illusion, a distress over the particular. . . . If the despairing person errs and thinks that the trouble is somewhere in the multiplicity outside himself, then his despair is not authentic, and it will lead him to hate the world and not love it . . .' (*EO* ii 208)

[16] Kierkegarad's claims about despair and the self are discussed by Rudd, *KLE*, ch.3, esp. 79–93. The attempt to attribute an argument to Kierkegaard is criticized by MacIntyre, 'Once more', 343–7.

[17] 'You constantly hover above yourself, but the higher atmosphere . . . into which you are vaporized, is the nothing of despair . . .' (*EO* ii 198) 'You hover above your self, and what you see down below you is a multiplicity of moods and conditions that you make use of in order to find interesting contacts with life.' (199)

Could he reasonably treat this choice as the result of an inclination? If he did, a further question would arise, about why he should follow this inclination to choose for his life as a whole. But how could he answer that question without considering what he should choose? And if he considers what he himself should choose for himself, he recognizes himself as an agent for whom things matter beyond his specific transitory inclinations.

This argument does not show that it is inevitable for us to choose for our lives as a whole. We might change into agents, or quasi-agents, who do not raise these questions. Such agents are not Kierkegaard's aesthetic agents. His aesthetic agents recognize themselves as continuing selves for whom it is appropriate to ask about what they ought to do, and not simply what they are inclined to do. Once they recognize that this question is appropriate for their lives as a whole, they cannot reasonably deny that it may apply to the evaluation of particular ends.

1072. Aesthetic Agency and Despair

We can now see why the aesthetic agent is liable to despair. This is not because purely aesthetic agency inevitably results in frustration or dissatisfaction, but because aesthetic agency in human beings presupposes some basis of non-aesthetic agency. Since we regard ourselves as continuing selves, and think it right, irrespective of the strength of our desires, to plan for our continuing selves, we can also see—though we may not see—that a purely aesthetic attitude to ourselves cannot satisfy us. If we treat our ends as matters of mere inclination, we do not ask the questions that, as continuing agents, we recognize as legitimate, about whether we have reason to pursue this end rather than another. The aesthetic outlook does not fit the self that adopts it.

Kierkegaard is justified, therefore, in saying that the aesthetic agent hovers above himself. In one way he is not detached from his particular ends. He chooses them for himself, and he does not pursue them half-heartedly. But he recognizes them as external to himself, in so far as they are objects of inclination that are purely accidental to him. He would be less detached from his ends if he could regard them as appropriate for him, as the sort of agent he is. He would have engaged himself in a specific end if he had accepted it as appropriate for him, the sort of end that he ought to choose irrespective of the strength of his inclinations. But, since he does not accept his ends on this basis, he remains 'outside' them.

The aesthetic agent still thinks of himself as a particular self who stays 'outside' his inclinations. He recognizes that he is the same person who will also be the subject of his future inclinations, and on this basis he decides what to do. Neither his present nor his future inclination is essential to him. The common feature of the present and the future self is the rational planner who considers himself as the owner of each inclination. The self to be satisfied is this rational planner, and so it is appropriate to find the aims—if there are any—that are appropriate for him as a rational planner.

When we introduce questions about what is appropriate for a certain sort of self, we enter the area of good and evil. Kierkegaard argues that the central feature of the ethical outlook is not that it chooses the good rather than the evil, but that it recognizes good and evil as features to be considered in a choice. If we recognize good and evil, we recognize the merits of different courses of action, not only the strength of our inclination towards one or another of them. This is another way of expressing the basic claim that the ethical agent believes that it matters whether he pursues one or another end.

If, then, despair reflects recognition of the inadequacy of aesthetic agency, it inspires a choice of oneself. This is not a choice of different particular ends, but recognition of good and evil as the basis for choice among ends.[18] If we recognize this sort of self, we choose it in its 'eternal validity'.[19] In one way, we choose to be this sort of self rather than an aesthetic self. But in another way, we do not choose to be something we were not; for only a self that was not purely aesthetic all along could discover that a purely aesthetic outlook was inadequate for it.[20] We affirm that we are the sort of self we have always been, and we choose to act in ways that are appropriate for this sort of self.

To say that something matters non-aesthetically is not necessarily to admit that it is a question for practical reason. The alternative is to try to capture the thought that something matters by introducing Humean second-order attitudes and sentiments. But we have seen that this alternative move is not satisfactory; it simply introduces more of the same inclinations that leave out the crucial idea of what matters. The relevant idea of what matters is the idea of comparative merits or grounds for choosing one or another option. To capture these comparative merits we need to introduce grounds for rational choice. For rational choice, in contrast to inclination, is choice that is grounded in the merits of different options. The aesthetic agent must recognize himself as the sort of subject who reasonably asks for such grounds.

1073. Freedom

Ethical agents differ from aesthetic agents in affirming their free will.[21] Kierkegaard's conception of freedom can usefully be compared with Hegel's. In Hegel's view, ethical development aims at the condition in which the free will wills itself as free.[22] We do not have to wait until the final stage of ethical maturity before we acquire a free will. On the contrary, we have a free will all along, but we do not affirm its freedom in relation to the various desires and aims that provide its content. At one stage, we do not separate the will from our various impulses at all. At the second stage, we think of it as Kant (allegedly) does, as entirely empty of real content. At the mature stage, we recognize that it is free because it orders our various aims and impulses in a rational system.

---

[18] 'Through this choice, I actually do not choose between good and evil, but I choose the good; but when I choose the good, I choose eo ipso the choice between good and evil. The original choice is forever present in every succeeding choice.' (EO ii 219)

[19] 'And in despairing a person chooses again . . . He chooses himself, not in his immediacy, not as this accidental individual, but he chooses himself in his eternal validity.' (EO ii 211) 'When a person has truly chosen despair, he has truly chosen what despair chooses: himself in his eternal validity.' (213)

[20] 'He chooses himself—not in the finite sense, ... —but in the absolute sense, and yet he does choose himself and not someone else. The self that he chooses in this way is infinitely concrete, for it is he himself, and yet it is absolutely different from his former self, for he has chosen it absolutely. This self has not existed before, because it came into existence through the choice, and yet it has existed, for it was indeed "himself".' (EO ii 215)

[21] 'But what is this self of mine? . . . It is the most abstract of all, and yet in itself it is also the most concrete of all—it is freedom.' (ii 214)

[22] Hegel on freedom; §1003.

Kierkegaard agrees with this Hegelian conception of freedom, in so far as he regards aesthetic agents as free, but denies that they recognize or affirm their freedom. Recognition and affirmation belong to the ethical outlook. Aesthetic agents belong neither to Hegel's first stage of 'immediate' ethical life, in which individuals raise no questions about the traditional moral outlook in which they have been brought up, nor to the stage of Kantian 'Morality'. The seducer sees that he can choose options that depart from the behaviour required by common ethical life, and even more from its spirit. But he does not adopt the outlook of purely rational Morality. He resembles the Moral outlook, however, in detaching himself not only from common ethical life, but also from the various ends that result from his inclinations at various times. He does not take any of these ends to be any more essential to him than the ends of common ethical life. While we might say that he regards himself as 'empty', he does not explicitly regard himself as essentially rational.

According to Kierkegaard, these facts about aesthetic agents show that they do not recognize the freedom that belongs to their will. We might be surprised at this claim that the adoption of the ethical outlook is necessary for the affirmation of freedom. For the aesthetic agent may appear to be genuinely free and to affirm his freedom, since he sees that he is not necessarily committed to any of his first-order ends.[23] The ethical agent, by contrast, recognizes some actions as required, and he is subject to principles that impose necessity on him. Why is he not less free than the aesthetic agent?

Kierkegaard answers this objection with an account of freedom derived from Rousseau, Kant, and Hegel, though he goes into less detail. He claims that the ethical agent has a type of freedom that is preferable to the aesthetic agent's condition. Though the aesthetic agent keeps his distance from his particular inclinations, in recognizing his distinctness from them, he does not recognize his capacity to choose to follow or to reject one or another inclination. The ethical agent, however, both recognizes and exercises this power of choice. Hence the ethical self actualizes a type of freedom that the aesthetic person fails to exercise.[24]

To make this claim plausible, Kierkegaard needs to rely on a conception of freedom as independence of one's passions and impulses. A creature with no free will would have no choice about whether to follow a particular desire or impulse. The aesthetic agent recognizes that he is not simply a creature of impulse, since he 'hovers above' his particular inclinations. But he treats himself as the recipient, rather than the agent, of his inclinations; they just come over him, remain, or go away, independently of his choices. The ethical agent, however, has a genuine choice about his inclinations, and uses this power of choice.[25]

---

[23] 'When an individual considers himself aesthetically, . . . his soul is like soil out of which grow all sorts of herbs, all with equal claim to flourish; his self consists of this multiplicity, and he has no self that is higher than this. . . . he will perceive that it is impossible for everything to flourish equally. Then he will choose . . . From this you see what aesthetic development signifies; it is a development just like that of a plant, and although the individual becomes, he becomes that which he immediately is.' (*EO* ii 225)

[24] 'Someone who views the personality ethically has at once an absolute difference: namely, the difference between good and evil. And if he finds more of evil in him than of good, this still does not mean that it is the evil that is to advance; but it means that it is the evil that is to recede and the good that is to advance. When the individual develops ethically, he becomes that which he becomes, for even when he lets the aesthetic within him (which means something different from what it means for one who lives only aesthetically) have its validity, it is nevertheless dethroned.' (*EO* ii 225–6)

[25] 'The aesthetic . . . is that in a person whereby he immediately is the person he is; the ethical is that whereby a person becomes what he becomes. This by no means says that the person who lives aesthetically does not develop, but he develops with necessity, not in freedom . . .' (*EO* ii 225)

As we have seen, we do not introduce an appropriate power of choice simply by saying that the ethical agent endorses or rejects a particular first-order end, if this endorsement or rejection is itself simply a further inclination. Resort to a higher-order inclination does not necessarily replace inclination with genuine choice. Freedom requires the exercise of will rather than inclination at this higher order.

What is the exercise of will in relation to inclinations? Voluntarists and intellectualists give different answers.[26] According to the voluntarist, free agents are like aesthetic agents in not being determined by reasons, but different in not being determined by inclinations; free agents are determined by nothing external to the act of will itself. According to the rationalist, free agents are determined by reasons rather than by inclinations; this is the crucial difference between free agents and aesthetic agents.

If Kierkegaard accepts the voluntarist account of freedom, he returns to the position of Scotus and Ockham, and he anticipates the 20th-century existentialists who are preoccupied with radical freedom.[27] According to this view, ethical agents are free because they not only choose which inclinations to follow in the light of considerations that they take to be important, but they also choose which considerations to count as important. This second choice is not based on further considerations.

It is difficult to explain, however, the difference between this radically free agent and the agent who simply has a higher-order inclination that endorses lower-order inclinations. Radically free agents are supposed to commit themselves to first-order ends, instead of simply being inclined towards them. How is a commitment of the will to be distinguished from an inclination? If we go through all the reasons for accepting one first-order end over another, and then simply endorse one of them, without being guided by better reasons, we do not seem to have made any progress beyond the aesthetic person's inclination. If ethical agents differ from aesthetic agents because their ends matter to them, we do not seem to have captured how and why the ends matter if we refer to radical freedom.

These objections to a voluntarist account of ethical agency make an intellectualist account more plausible. This is the sort of account that Rousseau and Kant offer. They take the rational will to be guided by the appropriate reasons, which require acceptance of a moral law, which the will does not choose to make the moral law. Hence ethical agents escape the aesthetic outlook because they see reasons for endorsing one or another inclination, and they act on the reasons that they see. Their freedom does not consist in choosing to count these reasons as good or bad.

According to a voluntarist, this account of freedom is open to objection because it simply replaces one type of determination by another, and so gets us no closer to freedom. The intellectualist replies that determination by the reasons for an action is no more a lack of freedom than determination by the reasons for believing is a lack of freedom. We are no less free agents because we try to find out the truth in order to match our beliefs to it. We would not increase our freedom if we could habituate ourselves to ignore reasons for taking something to be true, so that we would not find ourselves compelled to believe it. If there are genuine reasons for believing one thing rather than another, a rational agent tries to find these reasons, and to be guided by them. The same is true of rational action. Rational agents

[26] Voluntarism v. intellectualism; §§269, 389–91.   [27] Radical freedom; §1343.

try to find the best reasons for acting one way or another, so that they can be determined by these reasons.

Kierkegaard does not discuss the merits of the voluntarist and the rationalist explanation of freedom. But we have given some reasons for believing that he would be better off if he accepted the rationalist explanation. He tries to capture the ethical agent's conviction that it matters to have some ends rather than others. A voluntarist explanation allows ethical agents to assert that their ends matter, but not to show why they matter. If we examine Kierkegaard's other claims about the ethical agent, we can perhaps find his explicit or implicit views about voluntarism.

1074. The Ethical Outlook and Objectivity

The aesthetic agent objects to the ethical life because it represses individuality. The aesthetic criticism of marriage illustrates the objection to the boring and rigid aspects of the ethical. Though marriage is supposed to begin with attraction and preference between individuals, it submerges this individuality in the conventional duties and expectations imposed on married people. It seems to force people into a specific social mould that they may tire of sooner or later. But even if they tire of it, ethical life requires them to stick to their initial commitment. These features may be more obvious in some forms of marriage than in others, but compulsion and social pressure are characteristic of many forms of ethical life, and seem to be open to similar criticism from the point of view of freedom and individuality.

Judge William rejects this reason for believing that ethical agents sacrifice freedom for ethical constraint. He answers that the ethical agent prefers the institution of marriage, and does not sacrifice genuine freedom. Marriage is 'objective' in a Hegelian sense, in so far as it is part of ethical life.[28] As Hegel understands the objective, it exists independently of the agent's preferences and desires, in so far as it is embodied in the actual institutions of society. But how is this sort of objectivity relevant to an agent's freedom? It might well appear to support the aesthetic objection to the ethical life.

One might also connect objectivity with truth; true beliefs match objective facts that are not simply constituted by our beliefs and preferences. This conception of objectivity is relevant to freedom, if we accept a rationalist account of freedom. If we are free in so far as we act on rational will rather than inclination, and if rational will acts on the merits of different courses of action rather than on our non-rational inclination towards them, freedom requires us to act on the merits of different options. A rational will, formed by practical reason, evaluates inclinations by rational standards. These standards are objective, in so far as they are not constituted by our initial inclinations, beliefs, and desire; hence practical reason tries to discover the merits of different actions in the light of these standards. In this way, a free will is guided by objective standards.

---

[28] 'The self that is the objective is not only a personal self, but a social, a civic self. ... He transfers himself from personal to civic life, from this to personal life. Personal life as such was an isolation, and therefore imperfect, but when he turns back into his personality through the civic life, the personal life appears in a higher form.' (*EO* ii 262–3) Kierkegaard and Hegelian ethical life; Hannay, *K* 59; Stewart, *KRHR* 228–9.

Ethical agents, therefore, do not give up their freedom. Admittedly, they act against their inclination, or rather against their pre-rational inclination; but they are no less free. On the contrary, they are free in so far as they act on rational standards that correct and modify one's initial inclinations. 'Submission'—as the aesthetic agent regards it—to objective standards does not reduce freedom.

This connexion between freedom and objectivity supports part of the ethical reply to the aesthetic point of view. It does not support Judge William's contention that he achieves freedom in the 'objective' institution of marriage. For though marriage is objective in the Hegelian sense, existing outside the agent's beliefs and preferences, in the structure of society, it is not thereby objective in the sense that is relevant to freedom. Not every social institution necessarily conforms to the appropriate standards of objective correctness and truth, and so not every social institution necessarily realizes the freedom that requires objective correctness. The Roman institution of augury was objective, in being part of Roman society, but it did not conform to any objective truths connecting the behaviour of birds with future events. Similarly, slavery was objective, since it was embodied in the institutions of some societies, but it was not objectively correct.

Once we see how Judge William's Hegelian conception of objectivity differs from the conception that is relevant to freedom, we may doubt his claim that duty does not involve any constraint that reduces freedom (ii 150).[29] He argues that ethical life does not consist in a series of discrete duties. A superficial view takes different duties to involve different constraints that restrict one's freedom in these various ways. But if we recognize the ethical life as a life of duty (in the singular) rather than a mere series of duties, we take it to express freedom. This conception of ethical life as a single socially embodied way of life may exaggerate the coherent and systematic character of duties and obligations in many societies. But even if it is correct, we might doubt whether its unity makes it an expression of freedom. Kierkegaard seems to rely too heavily on the Hegelian conception of objectivity.

He would be on stronger ground if he could argue that the life of duty expresses freedom because it follows principles that are objectively correct and because practical reason recognizes them as objectively correct. If it recognizes the objectively correct principles, practical reason is working correctly, and if we follow it, we determine our choices entirely by practical reason without distortion by non-rational inclination. In so far as freedom consists in following reason, we achieve freedom by following objectively correct principles.

If, therefore, Kierkegaard takes freedom to rest on objectivity, he has a good reason to accept a Kantian rather than a Hegelian conception of the objective character of the ethical life. Kant believes that the moral law expresses the requirements of practical reason, and hence of free agency. This argument for connecting freedom with practical reason, and practical reason with morality, is indispensable for Kierkegaard's purposes, if he is right to believe that the ethical life expresses freedom.

---

[29] Judge William discusses the alleged conflict between duty and the spontaneity of love: 'For me, duty is not one climate, love another, but for me duty makes love the true temperate climate, and for me love makes duty the true temperate climate, and this unity is perfection.' (ii 147)

1075. Does Ethical Agency Require Morality?

Judge William has a reasonable case for his claim that freedom requires something more than the aesthetic outlook, and that it requires an objective outlook, if 'objective' is understood in the way we have suggested. We might say, then, that the ethical life expresses freedom because it rests on the rational conviction that some ends matter more than others and are not simply objects of inclination. But this is not all that Judge William assumes about the ethical life. He also believes that it is a moral life, because freedom requires us to accept a social 'station' and its duties (as Bradley understands them).[30] The station and its duties embody a moral outlook because they are formed by consideration of the rights and welfare of others and of the community, not simply by one's conception of one's own good. Hegel distinguishes the Ethical life from the outlook of Morality, which he ascribes to Kant. But the Ethical life rests on moral principles (in the broader, non-Hegelian sense of 'moral'). Kierkegaard also assumes that ethical life requires morality, and that morality requires stations and their duties.

He seems to assume that aesthetic agency does not allow the moral point of view, and that ethical agency requires morality. But neither assumption seems obviously true. On the one hand, Humean agents are aesthetic agents, but they care about morality; hence they seem to show that aesthetic agency is compatible with concern for morality. On the other hand, some agents might adopt an ethical point of view, in so far as they are guided by correct reason, as it appears to them, but see no reason to accept the constraints of morality in particular.

We have found some reasons, however, for believing that Humean agency does not really reconcile aesthetic agency with the moral outlook. Admittedly, it allows aesthetic agents to care about the subject-matter of morality, and to maintain their attachment to their moral sentiments through higher-order attitudes. But it is not so clear that this attachment to (for instance) the good of others is sufficient for taking the moral point of view. Kant argues plausibly that the sentimental philanthropist misses a vital point about moral requirements if he thinks his reason for observing them depends on his having the appropriate inclination. If Kant is right to argue that the moral point of view requires the recognition of reasons that remain reasons whether or not I have the appropriate inclinations, the aesthetic agent cannot take the moral point of view. Though Kierkegaard makes the aesthetic point of view appear more opposed to morality than it really is, by picking the seducer as his example, he is not basically unfair to the aesthetic agent.

If he is right to claim that the aesthetic agent cannot take the moral outlook, is he also right to claim that ethical agency requires morality? Kierkegaard simply takes it for granted that the ethical agent takes the principles of practical reason to include the principles of morality. Kant gives us some reasons for believing that Kierkegaard is correct on this point, but Kierkegaard does not seem to add anything to Kant's arguments. If the ethical point of view requires objectivity (in the sense we have described), it recognizes that the status of other people in relation to myself depends on facts about them and about me, and not simply on my inclinations, selfish or unselfish, in relation to them. But why should the

---

[30] Bradley on my station and its duties; §§1226–7.

ethical agent not conclude that other people matter only as means to one's own ends, or that one is allowed to treat them as one feels inclined?

Kierkegaard might appeal to the Kantian claim that once we see that the status of other people depends on facts about them, we cannot reasonably avoid treating them as our moral equals. If I consider the basis of my claims on others, and recognize that they depend on facts about me, I see that I deserve certain kinds of treatment from myself and from others by being a rational and responsible agent. I must, therefore, recognize that other rational and responsible agents have similar claims on others, including claims on me.

This Kantian argument is not Kierkegaard's explicit argument. But unless he relies on it, it is difficult to see how he could be entitled to assume that the ethical outlook is also the moral outlook, involving obligations to other people independently of their instrumental benefit to oneself.

1076. How Are We Free to Choose Ourselves?

This discussion of connexions between freedom, objectivity, and morality, may answer our previous question, about Kierkegaard's explanation of freedom. A voluntarist explanation commits him to a radical choice of one's character and actions, independently of any consideration of the merits of one or another choice, whereas a rationalist explanation commits him to determination by reasons. If we have given the right account of his views on objectivity and morality, he has good reason to accept a rationalist view of freedom. In that case, he does not really anticipate existentialist claims about radical freedom and choice; he accepts the views of Rousseau, Kant, and Hegel, connecting freedom, reason, and morality.

One may ask whether this rationalist explanation fits the remarks by Kierkegaard that sound most like anticipations of an existentialist view of freedom. He claims that in an ethical life we 'choose ourselves' and 'take responsibility' for ourselves (218, 220). If he means that it is entirely up to us, irrespective of any considerations for or against, to choose to be one or another sort of person, he attributes radical freedom to us. But we need not take his claims in this way. In choosing myself, I need not take myself to be free to choose to produce a self of any sort. I choose to be a self to whom things matter, and a self who is subject to my choice.

In choosing myself, I choose to be a 'definite individual' (255). If I am an aesthetic agent, I do not choose to be a definite individual. The definite individual I am appears to me to be a product of inclination, and I hold myself outside all the particular inclinations that constitute my ends. But if I am an ethical agent, I recognize some of my characteristics as more central to myself than others. These are the ones that I recognize as worth developing and retaining, and so I do not 'hover above' these as the aesthetic agent hovers above all his ends. As an agent for whom things matter, I accept some ends rather than others, and choose myself as an agent with these ends.

This is why Kierkegaard claims that the ethical agent sees 'tasks' and even sees himself as a task.[31] A task is a matter for rational deliberation and action. The aesthetic agent has tasks

---

[31] 'The person who has ethically chosen and found himself possesses himself defined in his entire concretion. . . . Here he then possesses himself as a task in such a way that it is chiefly to order, shape temper, inflame, control . . . here the

designed to forward the particular ends he has acquired by inclination; but since he does not regard these ends themselves as matters for deliberation, he does not include them among his tasks. The ethical agent, however, regards it as a task for rational deliberation and choice to fix the ends that he will pursue, and hence to form the sort of person he will become. Hence the area of tasks open to deliberation will be wider in his life than in the aesthetic agent's life.

If I regard my ends as tasks for rational deliberation, I also 'take responsibility' for myself.[32] This would be an unreasonable attitude if it meant that I at once take myself to be responsible for every aspect of myself, however it has been acquired. Why should I suppose that I am responsible for traits that I have inherited or have acquired in childhood before I was responsible for everything? But it is a more reasonable attitude if I assume responsibility, in the sense in which someone might become responsible for a company that has been in other hands. In becoming responsible and assuming responsibility, I acknowledge that I will be responsible for the future developments that I initiate; I cannot blame all of these on the previous managers of the company. This is the sort of responsibility that ethical agents assume in taking the ethical point of view. They do not take themselves to be immediately responsible for the selves they have become, but they acknowledge that they are now responsible for future development by choosing the ends to pursue.

Kierkegaard claims that in taking the ethical point of view, I affirm myself as I am. This claim suggests that he does not have radical freedom in mind, since radical freedom includes the freedom to choose to be any sort of self at all. One might indeed suppose that if I am required to affirm myself as I am, my freedom is unduly limited. But we need not take affirmation to imply acceptance of every feature of myself as I am.[33] If I am to take an ethical point of view, I have to assume responsibility for something. If I undertake to assume responsibility for some future self when it has reached some ideal condition that I am unwilling to try to develop in it, I can never get started; I procrastinate as Augustine did when he prayed for charity and continence, but not yet. Agents who refuse to affirm themselves as they are postpone indefinitely the time when they will take responsibility for forming and modifying themselves.

The claim that ethical agents take responsibility for themselves does not mean that aesthetic agents are not responsible for themselves. Kierkegaard means that aesthetic agents do not acknowledge their actual responsibility for themselves. Since they hover above themselves, they assume they are constituted by ends that come through inclination. In placing ends outside rational deliberation, they disclaim responsibility for them. They are wrong, since they are responsible for the results of their negligence in failing to do what they are capable of doing. They are capable of rational choice about the ends that they treat as objects of inclination.

---

objective for his activity is himself, but nevertheless not arbitrarily determined, for he possesses himself as a task that has been assigned him, even though it became his by his own choosing.' (*EO* ii 262)

[32] 'The individual, then, becomes conscious as this specific individual with these capacities, these inclinations, these drives, these passions, influenced by this specific social milieu, as this specific product of a specific environment. But as he becomes aware of all this, he takes upon himself responsibility for it all.' (*EO* ii 251)

[33] 'The ethical individual knows himself, but this knowing is not simply contemplation . . . It is a collecting of oneself, and this is why I have with afterthought used the expression "to choose oneself" instead of "to know oneself".' (*EO* ii 258)

Kierkegaard's apparently voluntarist remarks, therefore, do not support a voluntarist account of the freedom that belongs to the ethical outlook.

1077. How Kantian is Kierkegaard?

Our account of Kierkegaard's view of the ethical life appeals to Kantian rationalism about freedom and morality. We have gone beyond his actual words, and perhaps beyond his intentions. His emphasis on freedom and choice and the starkness of the 'either-or' appears to disagree with Kant. Perhaps he means that the ethical life ultimately rests on commitment and decision rather than on rational insight. We may lose this essential feature of Kierkegaard's position if we resort to the sort of rational insight that underlies Kantian ethics and the earlier traditional of ethical rationalism.

But we have found that a defence of the ethical outlook, as Kierkegaard describes it, seems to need Kantian rationalism.[34] We cannot simply assert that for the ethical agent ends and goals matter in a way in which they do not matter for the aesthetic agent. We also need to explain how they matter, and how the commitment of the ethical agent differs from the inclination of the aesthetic agent. If we say that it involves a commitment of the will rather than inclination, we need to say what is needed for the will to be involved. A plausible way to clarify appeals to commitment and to the will relies on rational standards and rational deliberation. In relying on such standards, we go back from Kierkegaard to Kant.

The reasons for preferring an intellectualist explanation of Kierkegaard's conception of the ethical life go back beyond Kant. They recall the reasons for preferring an intellectualist over a voluntarist conception of the will in the first place. The question we have raised for Kierkegaard is basically the question of how a voluntarist can plausibly distinguish acting on will from acting on passion. If the necessary distinctions require us to return to an intellectualist conception of the will, the voluntarist conception cannot explain itself satisfactorily.

And so, whether or not Kierkegaard would welcome an interpretation that draws heavily on Kant to emphasize the rational aspects of the ethical life, the best defence of his conception of ethical agency seems to rely on Kantian rationalism about will and morality.[35]

1078. Rejection of Pagan Virtue

So far we have traced a Kantian element in Kierkegaard's account of the ethical in contrast to the aesthetic. But he also believes that, from the Christian point of view, the ethical

---

[34] Schrader, 'Duty', compares Kierkegaard with Kant.

[35] If the best arguments for the superiority of the ethical over the aesthetic outlook rely on this intellectualist account of free and rational choice, this conclusion is relevant to Kierkegaard's later attack on the ethical way of life. According to Kosch, *FRKSK* 169–74, Kierkegaard rejects the ethical outlook because it cannot acknowledge genuine responsibility for evil. Kosch argues (see §957) that this objection succeeds against Kant's account of moral evil. If Kierkegaard's account of the ethical outlook is the one I have described, his criticism would be justified if and only if he were right to suppose that an intellectualist account of choice precludes responsibility.

is unsatisfactory, and that it leads to a 'teleological suspension of the ethical' (FT 54–67). This suspension of the ethical leads to the outlook of Christianity. While we may speak of the 'morality' of Christianity, in so far as we refer to the aspects of Christian life that cover the actions usually included in ethics or morality, we should not think of it as a Christian version of, or supplement to, ethics, but as the Christian replacement of the ethical outlook.

Kierkegaard's attitude may be contrasted with two other attitudes to Christian morality: (1) Clarke and Balguy minimize the distance between Christian morality and the rational outlook we learn from moral philosophy. Waterland protests against their view in his defence of 'positive' duties, as distinct from purely 'moral' duties. Kant's conception of Christian theology as a sort of historical presentation of rational morality may be taken to maintain the position of Clarke and Balguy.[36] (2) Aquinas does not regard Christian morality as a mere republication of rational morality. Nor, however, does he suppose that it abandons the outlook of rational morality. The virtues that result from the infusion of the Holy Spirit are not available to agents who have only the help of natural reason, and they are not limited by the ends of the acquired moral virtues. But these infused virtues are not entirely separate from the acquired moral virtues; Aquinas claims that they perfect the acquired moral virtues.[37]

Kierkegaard's view is closer to the (supposedly) Augustinian view that is revived by Luther, Baius, and Jansen. According to this view, Christian virtues are to be separated from rational moral virtues because they are directed towards a different end. If we examine ordinary moral virtues from the appropriate supernatural end, they turn out to be simply 'splendid vices'. We have found reasons to deny that Augustine holds this extreme view.[38] But whether or not he holds it, the opponents of pagan virtue whom we have mentioned take themselves to maintain an Augustinian position. Kierkegaard follows them; indeed he refers with approval to the view that pagan virtues are simply splendid vices.[39]

Kierkegaard does not simply repeat the Augustinian view of pagan virtue. He extends it to include the Kantian conception of morality and the Hegelian conception of the Ethical.[40] He believes that both these outlooks are opposed to the outlook of faith, and that therefore the outlook of faith has to suspend them. It suspends them teleologically, because the end of faith is opposed to the end of the moral point of view.

1079. Inadequate Accounts of Faith

Kierkegaard explains the outlook of faith by rejecting two accounts that would make it readily intelligible at the price of obscuring its most important and disturbing characteristics.

---

[36] Balguy and Clarke; §672. Waterland's criticism; §869. [37] Aquinas on infused virtues; §354.

[38] Augustine on pagan virtue; §§228–34.

[39] 'But if passionate preference is essentially another form of self-love, then one sees here again the truth in the saying of the venerable fathers: "that the virtues of paganism are glittering vices".' (WL 53) The editor refers to Lactantius, Div. Inst. vi 9, which does not contain the expression.

[40] In FT, Kierkegaard normally has the Hegelian view of the Ethical in mind. But his main objections apply equally to the Kantian conception of morality. Hence I will speak indifferently of the moral and the ethical.

These two accounts identify faith with (respectively) the aesthetic and the ethical outlook, as these are described in *Either/Or*.

We misunderstand faith, as Christianity understands it, if we identify it with what is sometimes called 'simple faith'.[41] This is an 'immediate' attitude in the sense in which sensory experience is immediate. It is an unquestioning tendency to believe that does not pause to consider objections or alternatives or reasons. Though one might admire simple faith, and though it might persist in the face of temptation and difficulty, the simple believer does not form this attitude on the basis of rational reflexion. Kierkegaard refers to the advice of Jesus to count the cost of faith before we commit ourselves to it.[42] An unquestioning tendency to believe does not reflect enough to count the cost of faith. Hence simple believers do not believe in the face of difficulties or objections, in so far as they have not considered obstacles to faith in adopting their faith. We might find ourselves liking someone without reflexion, and we might continue to like them despite all the unattractive features we discover in them. But our persistence in our unreflective liking does not mean that we have decided that the unattractive features do not make it reasonable to avoid them; our persistent liking may simply be impervious to such questions. That is the attitude of simple belief that has never counted the cost.

If we identify faith with the ethical outlook, or with an aspect of it, we can be said to have counted the cost to some degree. For we find that it is justified, or at least not rejected, by a rational outlook that is defined by universal moral principles. This view might be accepted by Clarke and Balguy; in their view, faith is justified by the fact that it moves us to believe moral truths that can be demonstrated by natural reason. Though faith may precede rational demonstration, it is needed only as long as we lack the demonstration that can eventually be found. One might take Kant's conception of religion within the limits of reason to maintain a similar view about the role of faith.

One might argue that Aquinas agrees with this view, not entirely, but to an extent that exposes him to Kierkegaard's criticism. He does not believe that Christian faith simply anticipates the conclusions of natural reason, but he believes that it remains within the principles of rational morality. This is his answer to the difficulties about dispensations. In his view, Abraham does not violate the principles of natural law in being ready to kill Isaac; he has simply been guided by God to act on principles that are more complex than we might have thought. We might have thought that morality could never have required a father to be ready to kill his innocent son if the son's life constituted no threat to anyone else's life or well-being. But the case of Abraham shows us that we cannot endorse this principle; we have to add another clause that recognizes God's right of life and death. Abraham needs faith to believe that God is giving him this command, and to believe that God will avert the death of Isaac. But the rational morality that Abraham already accepts assures him that if he believes these things about God, it is morally right to obey.

---

[41] 'Precisely because resignation is antecedent, faith is no aesthetic emotion, but something far higher; it is not the spontaneous inclination of the heart but the paradox of existence.' (*FT* 47)

[42] *FT* 72, referring to *Luke* 14:28: 'For which of you, desiring to build a tower, does not first sit down and count the cost, whether he has enough to complete it?'

In the case of Abraham, as explained by Aquinas, some aspects of the ethical are suspended, in so far as the generalizations we normally rely on have to be modified to fit a particular case. This does not mean that ethical principles are altogether suspended; for we modify our normal generalizations in the light of higher principles that allow us to state more complex generalizations. Kierkegaard regards tragic choices as examples of suspension of the ethical within the ethical. We can both recognize that Agamemnon faced a tragic choice and maintain that he did the right thing; for we can recognize the extreme moral cost of his action, which would normally rule it out altogether, and still believe that in these specific circumstances, he was right, all things considered, to sacrifice Iphigeneia.[43]

This understanding of tragic dilemmas assumes that the agent does either the right thing or the wrong thing, all things considered. If we suppose instead that in some cases both actions are equally right and wrong, or that we cannot tell which is right and which is wrong, we do not affect Kierkegaard's point. For in all these cases, ethical principles still determine our judgment about the agent's situation and action.

We might wonder whether Kierkegaard's case would be affected if we introduced a type, or alleged type, of tragic choice that he does not examine. Sometimes people claim that they are violating moral principles for the sake of some worthwhile, but non-moral end. Machiavelli takes this attitude to the safety of the state. Marx takes it towards revolutionary activity. Artists might offer a similar defence for the pursuit of art at the expense of moral obligations. If we reject the attempt to incorporate all these ends within morality, the pursuit of them represents a teleological suspension of the ethical for the sake of an end outside morality.

In such cases, we may none the less claim that the pursuit of these ends is rationally worthwhile and appropriate, either for everyone or for the situation of these particular people. Revolutionaries need (as we might say) some faith that their individual assassinations will not be senseless violence, but will be part of a successful movement. Artists need some faith that they are good enough artists to produce work that will in some way justify their violation of moral obligations. But though they may need to rely on these insecure or hazardous assumptions, the aims and ideals they pursue are recognized as worthwhile from the moral point of view. If morality recognizes its own limits, it gives way to ideals that it endorses. From this point of view, Kierkegaard might still claim that the ethical is not wholly suspended; for it recognizes a legitimate case for its suspension.

According to Aquinas' explanation, those who violate normal moral requirements because of their faith might be regarded as being tragic heroes, if they face the kind of choice that Abraham faced. Even if we do not share their beliefs about what God requires of them, we can see that their attitude is morally legitimate, in the light of those beliefs. Faith may complicate ethical requirements, and it may even show that morality has to recognize ideals that take precedence over morality; but it does not fall outside the range of moral understanding and justification.

---

[43] 'The tragic hero is still within the ethical. He allows an expression of the ethical to have its *telos*, in a higher expression of the ethical; he scales down the ethical relation between father and son or daughter and father to a feeling that has its dialectic in its relation to the idea of moral conduct. Here there can be no question of a teleological suspension of the ethical itself.' (*FT* 59)

1080. Why Faith Suspends the Ethical

This reconciliation of faith with the moral point of view contains the main mistake that Kierkegaard identifies in other accounts of faith. The reconciliation fails to count the cost of faith accurately; for it does not see that faith has to go further in its suspension of the moral point of view.[44]

If we treat Abraham as a tragic hero, we overlook the features of his situation that separate his choice from morality. According to Kierkegaard, Abraham's duties, from the moral point of view, are his duties as a husband and a father.[45] From the moral point of view, then, it is clear that he violates his duties. We cannot offer for him the ethical defence we could offer for Agamemnon, Jephthah, or Brutus, who could claim they had to sacrifice the life of their child for the sake of the community (FT 57–9). The story of Abraham includes no higher ethical end that embraces the suspension of some ethical principles to observe others. That is why Abraham is not a tragic hero.[46]

Abraham's faith does not consist simply in a belief that does not rest on ordinary empirical evidence; Aquinas' description allows him faith of that sort, in so far as it presents him as believing that God is giving him a specific instruction. According to Kierkegaard, Abraham's faith goes beyond this purely factual belief, on two points: (1) He believes that what God instructs him to do is completely wrong from the ethical point of view, without any defence from a broader universal point of view (the non-moral principles mentioned earlier). (2) But he does not simply resign himself to the loss that will apparently result from obeying the divine command. He continues to hope for the outcome that his intended action will apparently prevent; for he still hopes unreasonably that Isaac will not die.

The first feature of Abraham separates him from tragic heroes; they can find the ethical defence that is entirely denied to Abraham. The second feature separates him from those who might simply renounce their ordinary goals when faith seems to require them to act in ways that are bound to frustrate these goals. Renunciation leads to 'infinite resignation', which is the last stage before faith, but is not yet faith (FT 46). Infinite resignation ceases to hope for the goods that we can no longer reasonably hope for once we understand the divine instructions. Faith, however, still hopes for them even when the hope has been shown to be unreasonable; for it still trusts God.[47] This is how Abraham hoped 'against hope'.[48]

---

[44] The relation between faith and morality in FT is discussed by Green, 'Developing'.

[45] 'In ethical terms, Abraham's relation to Isaac is quite simply this: the father shall love the son more than himself. But within its own confines the ethical has various gradations. We shall see whether this story contains any higher expression for the ethical life that can ethically explain his behaviour, can ethically justify his suspending the ethical obligation to the son, but without moving beyond the teleology of the ethical.' (FT 57)

[46] 'By his act he [sc. Abraham] transgressed the ethical altogether and had a higher telos outside it, in relation to which he suspended it. For I certainly would like to know how Abraham's act can be related to the universal, whether any point of contract between what Abraham did and the universal can be found other than that Abraham transgressed it.' (FT 59)

[47] 'By faith Abraham did not renounce Isaac, but by faith Abraham received Isaac. By virtue of resignation, that rich young man should have given away everything; but if he had done so, then the knight of faith would have said to him: By virtue of the absurd, you will get every penny back again—believe it!' (FT 49) The second sentence alludes to *Matthew* 19:16–22, and the last sentence alludes to 19:29. Kierkegaard introduced this passage on the rich young man at 28.

[48] 'In hope he [Abraham] believed against hope that he should become the father of many nations: as he had been told . . .' (*Romans* 4:18)

These two features of Abraham's faith mark two aspects of absurdity in his outlook. He recognizes he is being told to do something absurd, because it is unjustifiable from the ethical point of view. Moreover, he admits that he hopes for something that he cannot rationally hope for. He cannot justify or excuse his action by pointing to some feature of his situation that would bring it under a general ethical principle. Any such principle would allow an appeal to the universal; but faith moves the individual to reject the universal in favour of the absurd.[49]

Once we accurately count the cost of faith, and once we see how it commits us to acceptance of the absurd, we can see how misguided it would be to treat Abraham as a tragic hero who had to make a difficult moral choice. Tragic heroes have a far easier task; for they can make an ethical case for their action, on the basis of universal principles that can convince a rational person that what they did was right or permissible. Those who act on faith acknowledge that they have to renounce all appeal to universal ethical principles. From the ethical point of view, Abraham is simply a murderer. This is why faith demands a complete teleological suspension of the ethical.[50]

1081. Morality in the Light of Faith

The outlook of faith does not simply demand an occasional suspension of the ethical in especially difficult circumstances, as though we could accept the ordinary ethical outlook almost all of the time. Faith does not reject ordinary moral duties and obligations, but it explains them differently, by appeal to different basic principles.

Kierkegaard explains his view of the relation of God to morality, by contrast with a view that he rejects, on the ground that it makes a reference to God idle. We might hold that God is in some way the source of all moral duties, in so far as God necessarily knows all moral truths and necessarily wills that human beings act in accordance with them. But in another way, according to this view, God is not the source of moral duties; for divine wisdom simply grasps completely the moral principles that are available to natural reason. We do not need to refer to God in order to discover these principles or to have some reason for following them. God endorses and enjoins what we believe to be right on a purely rational basis.[51]

We can grasp Kierkegaard's main point without reference to the specifically Hegelian view that he has in mind. We may usefully return to the different views that we discussed earlier on fundamental morality and the natural law. In the view of a naturalist Christian philosopher such as Aquinas and Suarez, God is the source of morality as creator and

---

[49] 'But if the ethical is teleologically suspended in this manner, how does this single individual in whom it is suspended exist? He exists as the single individual in contrast to the universal. . . . the paradox is that he as single individual places himself in an absolute relation to the absolute. Is he justified? Again, his justification is the paradoxical, for if he is, then he is justified not by virtue of being something universal but by virtue of being the single individual.' (FT 61–2)

[50] 'The story of Abraham contains, then, a teleological suspension of the ethical. As the single individual he becomes higher than the universal. This is the paradox, which cannot be mediated. . . . If this is not Abraham's situation, then Abraham is not even a tragic hero, but a murderer.' (FT 66)

[51] 'The ethical is the universal, and as such it is also the divine. Thus it is proper to say that every duty is essentially duty to God, but if no more can be said than this, then it is also said that I actually have no duty to God. The duty becomes a duty by being traced back to God, but in the duty itself I do not enter into relation to God.' (68)

teacher; if there were no God, there would be no human beings with a nature for which morality is suitable. But the content of morality is not the product of God's legislative will, and we need not refer to God's legislative will to explain why something is our duty. In these respects, a naturalist account of morality is open to Kierkegaard's objection that it makes God idle.[52] But a voluntarist account is also open to this objection. Even if voluntarists maintain that without the divine legislative will we would have no moral duties or obligations, they do not normally maintain that divine commands have no further rational basis. Pufendorf, for instance, believes that God commands observance of principles that prescribe what is appropriate for rational nature, and that we can know what these principles are without reference to God.

A more strongly voluntarist position might come closer to Kierkegaard. Ockham admits that God might command what is inappropriate for rational nature, by the exercise of divine unqualified power. God might even lay down a moral principle that we could not observe, if God were to command us to hate God. But though such things are within the scope of God's unqualified power, they are ruled out by God's exercise of ordered power. In relation to God's ordered power, we are not actually required to act in ways that are inappropriate for rational nature. Hence we can still maintain that God requires us to act in ways that we can see to be reasonable without reference to God. Even this Ockhamist view, therefore, does not escape Kierkegaard's objection that it makes God an invisible vanishing point.[53]

In opposition to all these views, Kierkegaard maintains that the outlook of faith recognizes an 'absolute' duty to God. His use of 'absolute' may be gathered by contrast. Kierkegaard believes that if God is simply the source (in one of the ways discussed above) of a duty to love my neighbour, my duty to God is not absolute; for my immediate duty is to my neighbour. In such a case, God may instruct me to do what I owe to my neighbour; but what I owe, I owe to my neighbour directly.[54] My neighbour's needs and situation give me a compelling reason to do something for him. God confirms that this is a compelling reason.

If, then, I have an absolute duty to God, two features distinguish it from a duty to my neighbour that is derived from God: (1) I owe the duty directly to God, not to my neighbour. (2) I cannot explain why I owe it by reference to features of the situation that would make it appropriate to do what I am obliged to do. These two features explain each other; for if there were something about my neighbour's situation that made the action appropriate, I would owe it to my neighbour whatever God might or might not tell me, and so I would not owe it directly to God.

We can discern this absolute duty to God only from the point of view of faith. For, given the second feature of absolute duty, I cannot discover such a duty by reflexion on what it would be reasonable to do in this situation. Hence an absolute duty to God must require something that is absurd from the moral point of view, and hence it must require a

---

[52] On Kierkegaard's attitude to naturalist Christian moral philosophy, see Rudd, *KLE* 143–54.

[53] 'The whole existence of the human race rounds itself off as a perfect, self-contained sphere; and then the ethical is that which limits and fills at one and the same time. God comes to be an invisible vanishing point, an impotent thought; his power is only in the ethical, which fills all of existence.' (*FT* 68)

[54] 'For example, it is a duty to love one's neighbour. It is a duty by its being traced back to God, but in the duty I enter into relation not to God but to the neighbour I love.' (*FT* 68)

suspension of the ethical. It is a duty I could not have discovered by reflexion on the morally relevant features of the situation, and hence it does not reduce God to an invisible vanishing point in determining my conduct.

Faith does not demand the recognition of absolute duty to God only on special occasions. On the contrary, it transforms one's attitude to the ethical by placing it on a different basis. God does not abrogate the requirements of morality; if Abraham were indifferent to them, no faith would be involved in his obedience to God, and his attitude would be similar to the aesthetic 'simple faith' that is to be distinguished from real faith. Faith accepts the ethical within limits, but it reinterprets ethical requirements in the light of absolute duty to God.[55]

1082. The Errors in Pagan Virtue

Now that we have seen why Kierkegaard requires a teleological suspension of the ethical, and why he takes absolute duty to God as the foundation of the ethical, we can form a clearer view of the faults that he sees in pagan virtue, and in the ethical outlook as a whole.

Kierkegaard's defence of the Augustinian view is similar at some points to the argument that Augustine uses to explain what is wrong with pagan virtue: (1) Whether or not someone is virtuous is determined not by their actions but by the end they aim at in their actions. (2) Christians are moved by the love of God and their aim is supernatural happiness. (3) Pagans are moved by self-love and their aim is earthly happiness. (4) Pagans have no virtues, but only vices.

Kierkegaard does not entirely agree with this argument against pagan virtue. Augustine accepts the eudaemonist aspects of pagan Greek ethics, and so he agrees that Christians aim at happiness; he disagrees with pagan moral theory only in saying that the happiness they aim at is supernatural. If Augustine were right about this, he would make faith, as Kierkegaard understands it, irrelevant. For while it may take faith to believe a promise of supernatural happiness, it is not unreasonable to do what is needed to achieve supernatural happiness, if we think we have reliable beliefs about what is needed. This is not how Kierkegaard understands Abraham. If Abraham had been told to sacrifice Isaac for the sake of supernatural happiness, his situation might have been tragic, but his choice (assuming he had a reliable belief about what he had been told to do and about its consequences) would be reasonable. Kierkegaard, however, supposes that Abraham is simply told to sacrifice Isaac, with no further promise about the results. Hence he cannot accept the view of Augustine and Aquinas that Christians ought to act for the sake of supernatural happiness.

Some later Christian moralists reject this eudaemonist view that Augustine and Aquinas share with pagan moral theory. Scotus argues that the affection for justice is separate from

---

[55] '. . . there is an absolute duty to God, for in this relationship of duty the individual relates himself as the single individual absolutely to the absolute. In this connexion, to say that it is a duty to love God means something different from the above; for if this duty is absolute, then the ethical is reduced to the relative. From this it does not follow that the ethical should be invalidated; rather, the ethical receives a completely different expression, a paradoxical expression, such as, for example, that love to God may bring the knight of faith to give his love to the neighbour—an expression opposite to that which, ethically speaking, is duty.' (FT 70)

the desire for one's happiness, natural or supernatural. The most extreme version of the anti-eudaemonist view is accepted by the Quietists, who insist that the love of God should be entirely disinterested, and that any intrusion of self-love is vicious. Both Bossuet and Butler reject this extreme opposition to self-love, and deny that it is authentically Christian.[56] Kierkegaard, however, is closer to the Quietist position.

Still, the Quietists do not seem to take the selfless love of God to be absurd. In so far as it is an instance of disinterested love of the good and admirable, it seems to be defensible from the moral point of view, even it is directed at a different sort of object from those that directly concern morality. Kierkegaard goes beyond the Quietists in so far as he claims that the outlook of faith is ethically indefensible.

Once we eliminate the eudaemonist elements from Augustine's position, we may be ready to endorse his exclusive and exhaustive division of motives; we act either from cupidity or from charity.[57] If we take this view, we suppose that only Christian love, a self-forgetful love centred on God, is capable of a genuinely unselfish outlook, and that all other supposed virtues are really more or less disguised forms of selfishness. This description of Christian love seems to fit Kierkegaard's conception of an absolute duty to God.

If this contrast between Christian morality and the ethical outlook is correct, the ethical outlook admits its defeat. For it expects the virtuous agent to act unselfishly, and admits that the right action is no proof of moral worth if it is the result of selfish motives. If, then, we have to admit that actions resulting from anything other than the self-forgetful love of God are all selfish, because this is the only genuinely unselfish motive, we have to admit that no one's actions have moral worth without the love of God.

One might well suppose that Kant is exposed to this argument. For he sometimes denies moral worth to action based on non-moral motives, on the ground that it is merely selfish. He seems to suppose that the only unselfish action is action that is done for the sake of duty, on the basis of respect for the moral law. If we find either that action on this motive is also selfish, we have to admit that it has no moral worth. In that case, the motives that Kant takes to be characteristic of the morally good person cannot confer moral worth on actions.

Kierkegaard presents his analysis of motivation, and especially of the dichotomy of cupidity and charity, in *The Works of Love*. He argues that only Christian love, centred on the love of God and on absolute duty to God, can satisfy the demand of the ethical outlook for unselfish concern with others. If the ethical outlook tries to manage with the motives that are available to it from its unaided resources, it cannot escape the selfish outlook that it condemns. Only Christian love fulfils the command to love one's neighbour as oneself.

1083. Selfish Conceptions of Love

Kierkegaard rejects the conceptions of love that, in his view, reduce it to a selfish attitude. He rejects, as Luther does, the interpretation of the command to love one's neighbour that includes a command to love oneself. According to the view he rejects, we need to grasp

---

[56] Quietism; §§611, 717, 864.   [57] 'aut cupiditate aut caritate.' See §230.

what deserves love in ourselves in order to see that the same thing is to be loved in our neighbours. But Kierkegaard believes that this attitude betrays the basic mistake that we make about love from the ethical point of view. The command to love neighbours 'as ourselves' is not meant to endorse self-love, but only to make sure that we do not fall short in our love of neighbours.[58] Christian love reforms self-love, and does not entirely abolish it, but it does not begin by affirming the legitimacy of self-love.[59]

According to the view that Kierkegaard rejects, we might affirm the appropriateness of self-love by identifying the features of ourselves that deserve love because they are in some way attractive or valuable. We extend our love to other people in so far as we recognize in them the features that deserve love in ourselves. Kierkegaard believes that this view misunderstands the basis of Christian love. Admiration, esteem, and valuing are out of place in love of one's neighbour. Since pagan views of friendship rely on these attitudes, they assimilate friendship to selfish attitudes, and miss the point of Christian love.[60] The command to love is not a command to admire or to esteem all of one's neighbours.

Kierkegaard especially opposes any account of Christian love that relies on Aristotle's conception of the friend as another self. He believes that this conception gives priority to self-love, and thereby distorts the character of the love that should extend to everyone equally.[61] Since the pagan attitude takes love to be based on admiration, no pagan has been able to conceive the possibility of genuine love for one's neighbour.[62]

Once we see that pagan love is all based on preference, we can also see the distinctions that matter to pagan moralists—and especially the distinction between appetitive love and amicable love (amor concupiscentiae v. amor amicitiae).[63] According to Aquinas, amicable love is love of persons for their own sakes, and Christian charity is a form of amicable love. The difference between the two kinds of love is that appetitive love is based on previous desire, whereas amicable love is based on the recognition of value in the other person that

---

[58] 'Is it possible for anyone to misunderstand this, as if it were Christianity's intention to proclaim self-love as a prescriptive right? Indeed, on the contrary, it is Christianity's intention to wrest self-love away from human beings.' (WL 17)

[59] 'When the Law's *as yourself* has wrested from you the self-love that Christianity sadly enough must presuppose to be in every human being, then you have actually learned to love yourself. The Law is therefore: You shall love yourself in the same way as you love your neighbour when you love him as yourself.' (WL 22–3)

[60] 'Christianity has misgivings about erotic love and friendship simply because preferential love in passion or passionate preference is actually another form of self-love. Paganism has never dreamed of this. Because paganism has never had an inkling of self-denial's love for the neighbour, whom one *shall* love, it divided love this way: self-love is abhorrent because it is love of self, but erotic love and friendship, which are passionate preferential love, are love. But Christianity, which has made manifest what love is, divides otherwise: self-love and passionate preferential love are essentially the same, but love for the neighbour—that is love.' (WL 53)

[61] '...passionate preferential love is another form of self-love, also...self-denial's love, in contrast loves the neighbour, whom one *shall* love. Just as self-love selfishly embraces this one and only *self* that makes it self-love, so also...friendship's passionate preference encircles the one and only friend. For this reason, the beloved and the friend are called, remarkably and profoundly, to be sure, the other self, the other I—since the neighbour is the other you, or quite, precisely, the third party of equality. The other self, the other I. But where does self-love reside. It resides in the I, in the self. Would not self-love then also start loving the other I, the other self?' (WL 53)

[62] 'Moreover, just as self-love in the strictest sense has been designation as self-deification, so also erotic love and friendship...are idol-worship. Ultimately, love for God is the decisive factor; from this originates love for the neighbour—but paganism had no inkling of this. It left out God, made erotic love and friendship into love, and abhorred self-love. But the Christian love commandment commands loving God above all else, and then loving the neighbour.' (WL 57)

[63] Aquinas on amicable love; §336. Kierkegaard's criticism of non-Christian forms of love is discussed by Hannay, *K* 243–62.

forms the basis for desire. In Kierkegaard's view, however, this distinction is unimportant; it does not show that amicable love is not selfish.

But why should we agree with Kierkegaard's view that love based on the recognition of value in another person is really selfish? His argument may be this: (1) If A loves B for some valuable property in B, A loves B because A is attracted to B. (2) If A loves B because A is attracted to B, A loves B because of something in B that is attractive to A. (3) If A loves B because of something that is attractive to A, A loves B selfishly. This way of representing love that is based on value supports Kierkegaard's claim that it is basically no different in the relevant respects from appetitive love. In both cases, A is moved by what A finds attractive, and B has to have some attractive property before B is an object of any interest to A.

This objection to amicable love explains why Kierkegaard attaches such importance to the imperative form of the command to love one's neighbour. But its imperative form needs to be correctly understood. Some commands simply draw our attention to something that we will recognize as deserving our attention. If you say 'Look at that view', you may be simply drawing my attention to a view that I would not want to miss. This is a naturalist explanation of divine commands; according to such a view, God draws our attention to considerations that we ought to recognize as important apart from any command. But this is not the sort of imperative that Kierkegaard has in mind. In his view, the command to love does not draw our attention to anything in another person that deserves to be loved. This type of command does not point out something that we had antecedent reason to value, but tells us to act independently of any antecedent convictions about value.

Love, therefore, has to be primarily love to God. If a command draws our attention to something valuable, we may continue to attend to that valuable object even if the command is withdrawn or we have forgotten about it. But if the command is independent of any value recognized in the object, our attention to the object depends on the command. To obey such a command, we have to rely on an absolute duty to God. This absolute duty requires us to love what we might otherwise see no reason to love.

But why do we need to accept this command-based love in order to avoid the selfish outlook? We might reasonably object to Kierkegaard's attempt to reduce amicable love to a selfish attitude. A selfish person is not concerned about the good of another for the other's own sake, but only in so far as the other satisfies some previous desire for some self-confined end. The fact that we learn to find some feature of an object attractive because we recognize something valuable about it does not transform my attitude into a selfish attitude. Even if we initially recognize the valuable feature in ourselves, and recognize it in the friend as in another self, it does not follow that our attitude is essentially selfish. Kierkegaard has no good reason to claim that a pagan is incapable of unselfish love.

The failure of this argument also undermines Kierkegaard's argument to show that the ethical outlook imposes standards that it cannot meet from its own resources. For he does not show that the ethical outlook demands a form of unselfishness that it cannot achieve. If the ethical outlook prescribes concern for persons for their own sakes, it seems to be able, for all Kierkegaard has shown, to achieve that concern.

Perhaps Kierkegaard does not mean that the recognition of value in another person results in purely instrumental concern, and so results in a selfish attitude. Perhaps he means that love that is based on recognition of value is essentially selfish for that very reason. He might say that if I love only because I recognize something valuable or attractive in the other person, I am acting only to gratify myself. But this argument proves too much. For it seems to rely on the expanded notion of selfishness that makes every action for the sake of satisfying a desire a selfish action. We have no reason to believe that all 'selfish' actions of this sort are open to objection. When Kierkegaard describes the pagan outlook as selfish, he means to criticize it, and he means us to understand and to accept his criticism from the ethical point of view we already accept. He does not simply intend the trivial point that this outlook is different from the Christian outlook, as he conceives it. If, then, we understand his claims about selfishness to refer to selfishness as the ethical outlook understands it, we have no reason to accept his criticism.

1084. Universal Love

But if we reject Kierkegaard's charge of selfishness against the pagan outlook, we do not answer all his objections. For the ethical outlook, especially in its Kantian form, does not simply prescribe unselfish concern. It prescribes this concern for other people without distinction; that is the point on which it accepts the command to love one's neighbour as oneself. Kantian ethics agrees with the expansive interpretation of 'neighbour' in the Gospels, and so it takes moral requirements to extend to everyone.[64] According to Kant, the command requires 'practical' rather than 'pathological' love (*KpV* 83). It is not based on any antecedent liking for other people, and it does not try to subordinate love of others to love of oneself.[65] Kierkegaard agrees with this demand, but he argues that we cannot satisfy it until we base it on our absolute duty to God.[66]

Even if the pagan ethical outlook allows unselfish concern, it does not follow that it allows such concern for everyone. In fact, we may well appear to have raised a doubt about universal concern in our defence of unselfishness. For if we suppose that concern is based on recognition of valuable properties in persons, we apparently have to acknowledge that concern is selective; for different people have the relevant properties to different degrees. But if we acknowledge the requirement to love one's neighbour, understood as every other person, we cannot base this concern on valuable properties. We have to understand the basis of the obligation as the command, not as the valuable property to which the command draws our attention.[67] Christian love is not the extension of amicable love to everyone,

---

[64] 'At a distance everyone recognizes the neighbour, and yet it is impossible to see him at a distance; if you do not see him so close at hand that before God you unconditionally see him in every human being, you do not see him at all.' (*WL* 79–80)

[65] According to Kant, the command is: 'Love God above all and your neighbour as yourself'. It is opposed to 'the principle of one's own happiness, which some would make the supreme principle of morality'. This principle says: 'Love yourself above all, but God and your neighbour for your own sake'. The command of the moral law 'requires respect for a law that commands love and does not leave it to one's discretionary choice to make this one's principle' (*KpV* 83).

[66] Kant and Kierkegaard are compared by Martens, 'Love'.

[67] '. . . when we speak about conscientiously loving wife and friend, we usually mean loving in a divisive way, or, what amounts to the same thing, loving them so preferentially in the sense of an alliance that one has nothing at all to do with other human beings. But in the Christian sense that kind of conscientiousness is simply a lack of conscientiousness. . . . it is God who by himself and by means of the middle term "neighbour" checks on whether the love for wife and friend is conscientious. In other words, only then is your love a matter of conscience.' (*WL* 142)

but an entirely different kind of attitude that is based on absolute duty. It does not have to discover anything valuable about other people, since it is not based on any recognition of value.[68]

Clear recognition of the command as the basis of the obligation helps us to achieve greater clarity about other people.[69] If we recognized a universal obligation but took it to be based in valuable properties, we would be tempted to imagine good qualities in other people, and to ignore their obvious bad qualities; for recognition of the facts might undermine our moral commitment. Kierkegaard argues that if we accept the command of universal love, we can recognize the facts about other people, and in particular we can acknowledge how people differ.[70] Since universal love is based exclusively on a command and not on any claim about the appropriateness of the object, variations in its different objects cast no doubt on its universality.[71]

Since Christian love is unconditional and groundless (according to the voluntarist interpretation just described), it avoids a dispute that inevitably arises from the ethical point of view. If concern for others has to rest on some valuable property, what property is suitable? And can we be sure that it belongs equally to everyone who is an appropriate object of concern? We seem to face further disputes about these questions. Only the universal command-based requirement of love avoids these disputes.[72]

We might use this point to answer Nietzsche's attack on the Christian outlook. He believes that the Christian command of universal love is a basis for fictions and self-deception about other people. Since we have to love everyone equally, we have to pretend that everyone is equally lovable, equally deserving of love; and so we have to deny or ignore the obvious facts about differences between people. Our attempts to deny the facts lead us to undervalue the genuinely valuable traits that are present in some people and not in others. Kierkegaard denies that Christian love engages in this sort of fiction or illusion. We would have to agree with Nietzsche's charge if we supposed that the command to love is based on value. But once we see that the command is independent of value, we do not need to imagine uniform value to support universal and equal love.

Kierkegaard's treatment of Christian love, therefore, is an extended exposition of the voluntarism that Luther sets out briefly in his claim that divine love does not find but creates its object of love.[73] The frank affirmation of a voluntarist account of Christian love overcomes the limitations of the ethical point of view. Since the ethical outlook assumes

[68] '...Christianity is not related as a more explicit definition pertaining to what in paganism and in general has been called love but is a fundamental change. Christianity has not come into the world to teach this or that change in how you are to love your wife and your friend in particular, but to teach how you are to love all human beings universally-humanly.' (WL 142–3)

[69] The role of a divine command in Kierkegaard's account of the obligation to love is discussed by Quinn, 'Christian', 352–61.

[70] 'Christianity, then, does not want to take away the dissimilarity, neither of high rank nor of lowliness. But, on the other hand, there is no temporal dissimilarity, neither the lowest nor the most acceptable in the eyes of the world, with which Christianity sides in partiality.' (WL 71)

[71] 'To love the neighbour is, while remaining in the earthly dissimilarity allotted to one, essentially to will to exist equally for unconditionally every human being.' (83–4)

[72] 'Only when all of us, each one separately, receive our orders at one place . . . and then each one separately unconditionally obeys the same orders, only then are there substance and purpose and truth and actuality in existence.' (WL 117)

[73] Luther; §412.

intellectualism, in so far as it takes love to rest on the qualities of the object, it cannot justify the universal and unconditional concern for others that it demands.

1085. Questions about Kierkegaard's Voluntarism

One may doubt, however, whether Kierkegaard avoids the difficulties that affect voluntarism in other situations. If the requirement of universal love rests entirely on a divine command, what is the basis for obedience to the divine command? If Kierkegaard agrees that Christian love of other people is love of them for God's sake and because of our love of God, he needs to say why we should love God and why we should pay attention to the commands of God. Since he agrees with Augustine's view that love of God is the basis of the appropriate form of self-love, he can hardly avoid this question about love for God.[74]

If we say that our love for God is our response to God's unconditional love of us, that does not entirely answer the question. For if we do not think God was acting rightly, we might be pleased that he created us and loved us, but that does not give us sufficient reason to do what God tells us to do. A simple response to God's having done something good for us is no basis for taking God's commands as a guide to morality. Apparently, then, we have to love God because of something about God that deserves love.

Could we say, then, that only God deserves to be loved, and that other people are to be loved only because God commands it and not because of anything valuable about them? We can understand this attitude in some cases. Perhaps our friend has asked us to take care of a particularly ugly painting because he has left it with us for safe keeping. If he had not asked us, we might be pleased to get it off our hands, but we treat it as we would treat something that we valued in its own right, only because he has asked us. If he told us he had turned against the painting, we would get rid of it. Does Kierkegaard mean that this is the attitude we should take to other people?

This is not how Aquinas and others interpret the idea of loving people for God's sake. In their view, our love for God makes us attend to something that is worth loving in other people. Though God has created rocks, and though we might admire them as parts of God's creation, God does not tell us to love rocks for God's sake. We love other people for God's sake because we recognize that God has created them in the divine image, so that we find in them some image of the valuable qualities that we find in God. According to this view, we could not love God appropriately unless we loved the creatures made in God's image because of their valuable qualities. If, then, we love God for God's valuable properties, we have to love other people for their valuable properties as well.

If Kierkegaard's solution to the problem that he has set himself is too simple, we may ask whether the problem is as severe as he thinks it is. When Kant claims that rational agents as such are ends in themselves, he identifies a valuable property in them that is also the property that Aquinas identifies with the image of God in human beings.[75] When Kant

---

[74] 'To love God is to love oneself truly; to help another person to love God is to love another person; to be helped by another person to love God is to be loved.' (*WL* 107)

[75] Aquinas, *ST* 1–2 prol. See §239.

speaks of practical as opposed to pathological love for our neighbour, we should not take him to agree with Kierkegaard's view that love of our neighbour is simply commanded, apart from any valuable property in our neighbour. Kant identifies the feature of other human beings that is the appropriate object of amicable love.[76]

On this basis, we can reasonably reject Kierkegaard's attempt to show that Christian morality requires the rejection or suspension of the ethical point of view, and that Christian love requires an attitude that cannot be explained or justified within the ethical point of view. We found earlier that he sees some of the central points in the Kantian point of view, in his contrast between the ethical and the aesthetic outlooks. We have good reason to follow him from the aesthetic to the ethical, and good reason to refuse to take the further step that takes us beyond the ethical to the specifically Christian.

Disagreement with Kierkegaard on this point does not commit us to rejection of his view that the Christian outlook contributes something distinctive to morality. We may agree that the distinctive elements in the Christian outlook are centrally connected with Christian love. He suggests that if we love people for God's sake, we are not deterred by disappointment in actual people, and we do not have to pretend that people will not disappoint us. Since we recognize other people as proper objects of love for God's sake, their imperfections, real or imagined, will not dissuade us from the requirement of love.[77]

When we see other people in their relation to God, some things may become clear about them that would not be clear if we did not see them in this relation. In this respect, we may expect Christian love to make a difference to morality. But we do not have to abandon Kantian ethics, or reject the view of Christian love as the perfection of the ethical outlook. Examination of Kierkegaard supports the conclusion that Aquinas' account of charity fits a Kantian account of the supreme principle of morality. Kant's claims about practical love are most plausible if we take the reference to love seriously, and explain it by reference to Aquinas' conception of amicable love. This conclusion might be surprising to Kant, but it suggests once again that the naturalist outlook and the Kantian outlook are complementary rather than opposed.

1086. Is Christian Love Absurd?

One might object that this attempt to connect the Christian conception of love with the ethical outlook misses Kierkegaard's main point, and that we see this point only if we connect *The Works of Love* with *Fear and Trembling* in the right way. The attempt to find some reasonable basis for universal love may appear to overlook Kierkegaard's view that it essentially has no reasonable basis. If it relies on a pure command, its basis is faith, which requires a suspension of the ethical. The command to love one's neighbour does not, or does not obviously, require us to violate ethical principles as obviously as Abraham had

---

[76] Some themes connected with this Kantian claim are explored in Velleman's illuminating paper, 'Love'.

[77] 'Christ's love for Peter was boundless in this way: in loving Peter he accomplished loving the person one sees. He did not say, "Peter must first change and become another person before I can love him again." No, he said exactly the opposite, "Peter is Peter, and I love him. My love, if anything, will help him to become another person."... However much and in whatever way a person is changed, he still is not changed in such a way that he becomes invisible.' (172)

to violate them in being ready to kill Isaac. But this command is based on overriding and unconditional love for God, and this requires the sort of violation that was demanded of Abraham.

The demand for universal love, therefore, is based on the absurd. If we find that Kierkegaard has no rational basis for the outlook that underlies universal love, this is exactly the point he wants us to grasp about faith. Faith requires the teleological suspension of the ethical in favour of aims that go beyond the ethical. Moreover, the ethical points towards its own teleological suspension; for we cannot reach the unselfish attitude of rational morality until we derive it from the unconditional love of God, which requires the suspension of the ethical.

But this is not a wholly satisfactory answer on behalf of Kierkegaard. For it leaves out his assumption that we admire the faith of Abraham and the universal love that is based on faith in God and love of God. This assumption needs some defence. Why should we not find Abraham's faith wholly unappealing and deplorable? We might think he is moved simply by some sort of awe at God's power. If it were fear of punishment by God, it would be at least intelligible, even though it would be selfish. But if it is directed to God in a wholly self-forgetful way, we might think it is analogous to one's attitude to the sublime, as Kant describes it.[78] We might be capable of some disinterested appreciation of Niagara Falls, if we contemplate it when we are in no danger from it. Perhaps we could understand the love of God on this pattern. But if we did, we might well infer that it is not necessarily a morally desirable attitude. It would be foolish to be so fascinated by a quasi-aesthetic admiration for a very powerful person that we always wanted to do what he told us, no matter what he said. If that is how we understood Kierkegaard's view of the love of God, he would not have achieved his main aims.

Kierkegaard does not take this attitude to Abraham. *Fear and Trembling* takes the point of view of someone who finds Abraham difficult to understand, and in some ways appalling, but also finds him admirable.[79] We should recognize him as someone who is willing to suspend the ethical for the sake of something higher. But if he suspended the ethical simply out of fascination with the power or incomprehensibility of God, it is not clear how he could be aiming at something higher, or how we could acknowledge that he aims at something higher. If we could see nothing in God, as Abraham conceives God, that would deserve the allegiance of someone who already recognizes the claims of the ethical, why should we admire him, or suppose that he aims at something higher than the merely ethical? The same point is still clearer in the case of the command of universal love. Kierkegaard represents universal love as an admirable attitude because it achieves the unselfish love of all human beings that the ethical point of view demands, but cannot produce. But if this love of human beings is simply the product of an absolute duty to God, and if we do not recognize God as an appropriate object of love, we might doubt whether it is admirable from the ethical point of view. While we may find it difficult to believe what Abraham believes, we should not be repelled by his acting as he does on the basis of what he believes. We should see that even

---

[78] Kant on respect for the moral law; §966.

[79] '. . . although Abraham arouses my admiration, he also appals me. . . . the person who gives up the universal in order to grasp something even higher that is not the universal—what does he do? . . . One cannot weep over Abraham. One approaches him with a *horror religiosus*, as Israel approached Mount Sinai.' (*FT* 60–1)

if faith requires us to go beyond, or even against, the requirements of the ethical outlook, it none the less fulfils some recognizable requirement or ideal of morality.

On this point, then, Kierkegaard would be wise to agree with Aquinas' claim that grace completes nature.[80] His position is stronger if he does not emancipate himself from the ethical as far as he thinks he should. His view that faith suspends the ethical for the sake of the absurd opposes Kant's view that we should compare even divine perfection with our antecedent moral ideal before we accept it as a guide to action (G 408–9). Kant's view is too simple, if it assumes that a moral ideal cannot be appropriately modified in the light of beliefs about God. But Kierkegaard cannot reasonably reject Kant's view completely. For it is difficult to admire someone who recognizes an absolute duty to God, as Kierkegaard conceives it. The knight of faith seems to need some reason to believe that God deserves his trust and loyalty. To show that he has such a reason is to appeal again to the ethical outlook. Kierkegaard's exploration of faith and its demands helps to show why the ethical outlook should not be suspended.

---

[80] 'For since grace does not abolish (tollat) nature, but completes it, it is necessary that natural reason serves (subserviat) faith, just as the natural inclination of the will serves (obsequitur) charity.' (Aquinas, *ST* 1a q1 a8 ad2)

78

NIETZSCHE

1087. The Criticism of Morality

Nietzsche believes that previous theorists have been asking the wrong question about morality. They have looked for the rational foundation of morality, on the assumption that morality could safely be taken as 'given', and beyond question.[1] They have therefore overlooked some questions about morality that throw an unfamiliar and subversive light on the issues that they choose to discuss.

Many readers of Nietzsche might agree with this summary of his approach to morality. But it is more difficult to find any more precise account of his subversive questions, or of what he takes them to show. Questions of interpretation are difficult to settle, partly because of the non-argumentative character of the texts, and partly because they depend on views about aspects of Nietzsche's philosophy outside moral philosophy. The questions include these: (1) What does Nietzsche mean by 'morality' when he attacks morality? (2) Does he advocate the replacement of 'morality', as he understands it, with a different moral outlook, or with a non-moral outlook? (3) Does he advocate anything? (4) Do his doubts about 'morality' express doubts about one attempt to state a rational evaluative outlook, or about the possibility of rational evaluation in general? Or do they reflect his broader sceptical doubts?

Answers to these questions might support different possible conclusions: (a) Nietzsche defends an 'Aristotelian' as opposed to a 'Kantian' ethical outlook. (b) He advocates a psychological and social approach to morality as a natural science. (c) He opposes morality and supports non-moral values. (d) He is a nihilist, or sceptic, or relativist about moral and non-moral values. If we believe that Nietzsche intends to present a consistent position on these questions, we might try to find his predominant outlook; then we might either explain other passages so that they fit it, or dismiss them as aberrations, misleading statements, or exaggerations. But if we doubt whether we should even look for a consistent position, we may be less inclined to explain away apparent conflicts.

---

[1] 'With a stiff seriousness that inspires laughter, all our philosophers demanded something far more exalted, presumptuous, and solemn from themselves as soon as they approached the study of morality: they wanted to supply a *rational foundation* for morality—and every philosopher so far has believed that he has provided such a foundation. Morality itself, however, was accepted as "given".' (*BGE* 186) As far as possible, I have cited Nietzsche's works by the original section numbers.

We can grasp some aspects of Nietzsche's discussions of morality and moral theory without resolving these questions. Different interpretations rest on arguments that might readily appear to support nihilist, subjectivist, sceptical, or Aristotelian conclusions about morality and other values. Whether or not Nietzsche draws these conclusions, it is useful to ask how one might support them from the material he provides.[2]

1088. Against Moral Facts

According to Nietzsche, philosophers who look for a rational foundation of 'morality' assume that they can speak of morality as a single uniform outlook. They accept this unjustified assumption because they are ignorant of the various moral outlooks found in different societies.[3] To avoid the naive assumption of uniformity, we need a 'typology of morals', so that we do not thoughtlessly endorse the particular moral outlook that is most familiar to us.[4] Philosophers who study other moral outlooks too little are too ready to assume that their own outlook is justified.[5] Not only have they tried to justify too narrow a range of moral practices (because they have considered too few moral outlooks), but they have even failed to justify the narrow range they have considered.

Why should one's failure to consider other moral outlooks discredit one's attempt to find the rational foundation of morality? The mere fact that I have not considered all possible moral outlooks does not show that I have failed to justify the one I have considered. For the mere fact that (let us suppose) astronomers do not consider all the observations of the planets reported before 1500 would not show that they have not found a plausible theory of the movements of the planets; they might have some good reason for disregarding the earlier observations.

Nietzsche assumes that this is not the right way to look at other moral outlooks. Once we consider them, we should see that our task of finding the rational foundation of morality includes the task of showing why one moral outlook is rationally preferable to others. This is a more difficult task than simply finding principles that seem acceptable to an adherent of the moral outlook under discussion. If we need a rational foundation that will seem correct to adherents of different moral outlooks, we may have to give different arguments. Even if

---

[2] Different assessments of Nietzsche's ethical position are offered by Schacht, *N*, chs. 6–7; Geuss, 'Genealogy' and 'Morality'; Leiter, *NM*.

[3] 'One should own up in all strictness to what is still necessary here for a long time to come, to what alone is justified, so far: to collect material, to conceptualize and arrange a vast realm of subtle feelings of value and differences of value . . . all to prepare a *typology* of morals.' (*BGE* 186)

[4] 'Just because our moral philosophers knew the facts of morality only very approximately in arbitrary extracts or in accidental epitomes—for example, as the morality of their environment, their class, their church, the spirit of their time, their climate and part of the world—just because they were poorly informed and not even very curious about different peoples, times, and past ages—they never laid their eyes on the real problems of morality; for these emerge only when we compare *many* moralities.' (*BGE* 186)

[5] 'In all "science of morals" so far one thing was *lacking*, strange as it may sound: the problem of morality itself: what was lacking was any suspicion that there was something problematic here. What the philosophers called "a rational foundation for morality" and tried to supply was, seen in the right light, merely a scholarly variation of the common *faith* in the prevalent morality; a new means of *expression* for this faith; and thus just another fact within a particular morality; indeed, in the last analysis a kind of denial that this morality might ever be considered problematic—certainly the very opposite of an examination, analysis, questioning, and vivisection of this very faith.' (*BGE* 186)

we do not agree that we need to convince everyone, we ought to explain why we need not convince adherents of this or that moral outlook.

Once we understand the task of finding a rational foundation for morality, we will be less confident of success. Nietzsche believes that study of other moral outlooks will raise doubts about the correctness of our outlook, and that these doubts will subvert our attempted justification. Attempts to find a rational foundation for morality have failed, and can be expected to fail. Moral philosophy is a spurious science 'whose ultimate masters still talk like children and little old women' (BGE 186). Schopenhauer, for instance, sets out to be a tough-minded critic of accepted assumptions; but he cannot escape the sentimental illusions that underlie belief in the justifiability of morality. His claims about compassion show that he is still a victim of these illusions.[6]

In denying that morality has a rational foundation, Nietzsche denies that it is universally or generally reasonable to accept moral principles. We need to add 'or generally' to indicate that Nietzsche's opponent need not be concerned about exceptional human beings (living on desert islands, exceptionally strong and resourceful, severely mentally disordered etc.) who turn out to have no reason to accept morality. Nietzsche does not rest his case on exceptions of this sort. He also means to deny that most people with ordinary human characteristics in ordinary circumstances have reason to accept morality. His denial that it is universally or generally reasonable to accept morality is consistent with the admission that it is reasonable for some people. Certain kinds of aims, preferences, biases, and so on may make it reasonable—relative to these specific aims, preferences, and so on, which are not characteristic of human beings as such—to prefer morality. Nietzsche denies that reasons to accept morality extend beyond these specific aims and preferences.

He denies any rational foundation of morality by asserting that there are no moral facts. Since there are no moral facts, moral judgment is an illusion, and morality is a misinterpretation of certain phenomena.[7] Moralists, therefore, cannot discover truths that are not wholly constituted by the preferences of believers and inquirers. In this respect, moral beliefs differ from beliefs about the physical world (as we ordinarily understand them, before we consider the implications of Nietzsche's views).

Nietzsche assumes that if there are no moral facts, moral judgments are an 'illusion', and cannot be literally true. He therefore accepts a realist account of our moral concepts.[8] In his view, we cannot find a rational foundation for morality unless we show that our judgments are literally true because they describe some objective reality. He does not discuss

---

[6] 'The difficulty of providing a rational foundation for the principle cited [sc. Schopenhauer's principle of morality] may indeed be great—as is well known, Schopenhauer did not succeed either—and whoever has once felt deeply how insipidly false and sentimental this principle is in a world whose essence is will to power, may allow himself to be reminded that Schopenhauer, though a pessimist, really—played the flute.' (BGE 186) Nietzsche's critique of Schopenhauer is discussed by Janaway, BS, esp. ch. 3.

[7] 'My demand upon the philosopher is known, that he take his stand beyond good and evil and leave the illusion of moral judgment beneath himself. This demand follows from an insight which I was the first to formulate, that there are altogether no moral facts. Moral judgments agree with religious ones in believing in realities which are no realities. Morality is merely an interpretation of certain phenomena—more precisely, a misinterpretation. . . . Moral judgments are therefore never to be taken literally: so understood, they always contain mere absurdity. Semeiotically, however, they remain invaluable: they reveal, at least for those who know, the most valuable realities of culture and inwardness which did not know enough to "understand" themselves. Morality is mere sign language, mere symptomatology: one must know what it is all about to be able to profit from it.' (TI vii 1 = PN 501)

[8] Hence he holds an 'error theory', as Mackie understands it. See §1372.

a sentimentalist and anti-objectivist meta-ethical position, such as Hutcheson's or Hume's. Hume agrees with Nietzsche in denying that morality has a rational foundation, but he does not infer that moral judgment is an illusion. In Hume's view, the inference from the denial of moral facts to the illusory character of moral judgment rests on a misguided meta-ethical assumption. In the 20th century, many have accepted this Humean response to realism and nihilism.[9]

How should a Nietzschean react to this Humean response? Perhaps it captures what Nietzsche really means. If we do not assume that moral judgment is worthwhile only on some realist basis, we see that a sentimentalist meta-ethics still allows us to take moral judgment seriously in our actions and attitudes. Even if we agree with Nietzsche that there are no moral facts, and that morality has no rational foundations, we might still think and act in morally appropriate ways.

Alternatively, perhaps the Humean response simply tries to evade the radical implications of Nietzsche's critique of moral judgment and moral philosophy. He is scornful of those who reject Christianity but maintain the moral outlook that is based on it.[10] Should he be equally scornful of the Humean effort to disregard the unsettling implications of our discovery that there are no moral facts? We need to look more closely at the implications of our discovery that moral judgments are illusory, and what he thinks we should do about this discovery. Should the discovery lead us to reject morality? Hume answers No, but Nietzsche may not agree with him.

The historical study of morality, as Nietzsche understands it, not only exposes the psychological and social forces that move us to search for a rational foundation, but also explains why our search is hopeless. Cultural and historical study reveals the variety of moral practices and so exposes 'the real problem of morality' (*BGE* 186) that undermines attempts at justification. Moral beliefs develop in response to beliefs and emotions that have no systematic connexion with any moral facts. Similarly, the forces that sustain moral beliefs are not systematically connected with moral facts. We have no reason, therefore, to believe in any moral facts.[11]

Historical study itself does not refute a moral theory.[12] But it may help us to see that we should not take the claims of a moral theory at face value. If we find a theory that claims to

---

[9] Non-cognitivism and nihilism; §§1314, 1371, 1380.

[10] 'They are rid of the Christian God and now believe all the more firmly that they must cling to Christian morality. That is an English consistency; we do not wish to hold it against little moralistic females à la Eliot. In England one must rehabilitate oneself after every little emancipation from theology by showing in a veritably awe-inspiring manner what a moral fanatic one is . . . When one gives up the Christian faith, one pulls the right to Christian morality out from under one's feet. . . . When the English actually believe that they know "intuitively" what is good and evil, when they therefore suppose that they no longer require Christianity as the guarantee of morality, we merely witness the *effects* of the domination of the Christian value judgment . . .' (*TI* ix 5 = *PN* 515f–6)

Sartre criticizes in similar terms 'a certain kind of secular ethics which would like to abolish God with the least possible expense . . . In other words—and this, I believe, is the tendency of everything called reformism in France—nothing will be changed if God does not exist.' ('Humanism', 40). Heidegger suggests that Sartre does not completely free himself of this attitude; see §1343.

[11] On the nature and aims of genealogy, see Geuss, 'Genealogy'.

[12] 'The inquiry into the *origin of our evaluations* and tables of the good is in absolutely no way identical with a critique of them, as is so often believed: even though the insight into some *pudenda origo* certainly brings with it a *feeling* of diminution in value of the thing that originated thus and prepares the way to a critical mood and attitude towards it.' (*WP* 254) Cf. Schacht, *N* 352–4.

justify our current moral outlook, we may agree that we have discovered the appropriate moral facts. But the different theories that fit incompatible moral outlooks cannot all reveal moral facts (if moral facts cannot be inconsistent). Once we doubt whether moral theories fit facts, we may be inclined to treat them as the products and symptoms of different emotions and attitudes.[13] If we study a moral philosopher's views, we should look for the unacknowledged desires and impulses that underlie the position that the philosopher takes to be rationally justifiable. Schopenhauer's examination of these aspects of Kant demolishes the rational pretensions of Kant's position.[14]

1089. Moral and Non-Moral Values

These remarks suggest that Nietzsche is a nihilist about moral properties. He believes that there are no moral facts, and that moral judgments reveal the emotions of the judge, but no facts about the object of judgment.

Many nihilists have argued that they are still entitled to make moral judgments and to act on them. Nihilism only rules out the defence of one's own moral outlook by appeal to its fitting the moral facts better. We need not be surprised, therefore, if we find that Nietzsche puts forward his own moral convictions, in opposition to the 'modern' outlook that he attributes to Christianity, the French Revolution, and Kant. If morality does not fit any moral facts, his own moral outlook does not fit any moral facts either. But he is free to express his preference for his own outlook, as long as he does not claim it is objectively preferable to the modern outlook.

Is this Nietzsche's position? We might suppose that he does not take modern morality and his own evaluative outlook to be equally unjustified by facts. For he sometimes seems to suggest that modern morality rests on illusion and that we ought to replace it by an outlook that is based on a less misguided view of human beings and their place in the world. Perhaps he uses 'morality' only to refer to the specific outlook of modern morality, and he proposes some form of non-moral evaluative outlook that rests on the relevant non-moral facts.[15]

But how would an objectively correct non-moral evaluative outlook fit into Nietzsche's general view? His arguments to show that moral judgments express affect and emotion seem to apply to more than moral judgments. To show that no moral judgments are objectively

---

[13] 'Even apart from the value of such claims as "there is a categorical imperative in us", one can still always ask: what does such a claim tell us about the man who makes it? There are moralities which are meant to justify their creator before others. Other moralities are meant to calm him and lead him to be satisfied with himself. . . . In short, moralities are also merely a *sign language of the affects*.' (*BGE* 187) 'What is the meaning of the act of evaluation itself? Does it point back or down to another, metaphysical world? (As Kant still believed, who belongs *before* the great historical movement.) . . . moral evaluation is an exegesis, a way of interpreting. The exegesis itself is a symptom of certain physiological conditions, likewise of a particular spiritual level of prevalent judgments. Who interprets?—Our affects.' (*WP* 254)

[14] See Schopenhauer, §1048. Nietzsche agrees with his analysis of categorical imperatives: 'It was in *this* sphere, then, the sphere of legal obligation, that the moral conceptual world of "guilt", "conscience", "duty", "sacredness of duty" had its origins . . . And might one not add that, fundamentally, this world has never since lost a certain odour of blood and torture? (Not even in old Kant; the categorical imperative smells of cruelty.)' (*GM* ii 6)

[15] See Clark, 'Immoralism', 17, citing *BGE* 32.

correct, he remarks that people and societies with different emotions and prejudices reach different moral judgments. This argument can easily be extended to non-moral evaluative judgments, since they seem to vary no less than moral judgments do, and the same explanations of the variation seem no less plausible. Hence Nietzsche's argument seems to rule out objectively correct non-moral evaluations.

This conclusion may be premature. Perhaps he means that morality rests on false claims about the nature of reality, whereas justified non-moral evaluations rest on true claims about reality. In that case, he should not rely on the argument from variation in emotions and moral judgments; rather, he needs to show that certain claims about reality are false and that morality relies essentially on these claims.

This question about the interpretation of Nietzsche's arguments against morality leads us into the more general question about the relation between the negative and the positive side of Nietzsche's outlook. Do his sweeping attacks on morality leave him room for his positive evaluative claims?

1090. Why a Historical Approach?

Nietzsche believes that his historical approach to morality exposes the central error underlying the belief in moral facts. He contrasts his approach with the work of British writers on the origins of the moral sentiments, who trace the formation of moral feelings to psychological mechanisms of association (GM i 1–2).[16] In contrast to these investigators, he examines the actual history of moral conceptions and outlooks, rather than postulated psychological or biological mechanisms.

These other students of the origins of morality assume a fixed human nature and fixed human desires, in abstraction from specific historical and cultural circumstances. This is the philosopher's 'Egypticist' neglect of history.[17] If Nietzsche improves on these other students of the origins of morality, his history must have some reasonable claim to be true; the historical details should not simply be illustrations of some favoured theories about morality, as they are in the British writers.

Nietzsche also separates himself from other investigators of the origin of morality in so far as he takes an explicitly critical attitude to morality. Smith, Hartley, and Hume do not suggest that their investigations of the origins of morality expose embarrassing aspects of morality that shake our confidence in it. They speak as though their psychological investigations will leave all or most of morality as it is. Nietzsche, however, expects his investigations to raise serious questions about morality and about our attitude to it.

Perhaps this is not a fair criticism of his predecessors. Hobbes, for instance, seems to take questions about the justification of morality quite seriously; he tries to show that the

---

[16] In particular he acknowledges the inquiries of Paul Rée, who presented a Darwinian account of the growth of morality (GM, Pref. 4).

[17] 'You ask me which of the philosophers' traits are actually idiosyncrasies? For example, their lack of historical sense, their hatred of the very idea of becoming, their Egypticism. They think that they show their *respect* for a subject when they de-historicize it, *sub specie aeternitatis*—when they turn it into a mummy. All that philosophers have handled for thousands of years have been concept-mummies; nothing real escaped their grasp alive.' (*TI* iii 1)

rational egoists he describes have a good reason to take moral principles seriously. But Nietzsche might reply that Hobbes's psychology is unrealistic, and that he does not press his critical questions very far. We might agree with Hobbes's view that morality plays some role in maintaining social stability; but Hobbes does not ask whether the cost of maintaining social stability by relying on our conventional morality is too high a price to pay. Nietzsche considers the costs as well as the benefits of morality, and does not take it for granted that the benefits outweigh the costs.

Sometimes he questions the assumption that moral principles are superior to all others. He thereby contests a view expressed by Butler and Kant. But he also seems to doubt the more moderate claim that morality is a good thing. We might agree that moral principles are not supreme, and that in some circumstances we have good reason to violate them in favour of other values, but we might still take them quite seriously and believe that they normally ought to carry weight. Nietzsche casts doubt on even this reserved commitment to morality.[18]

Study of the actual history of morals, as opposed to the imaginary psychology of morality, casts doubt on morality, because it exposes the psychic sources of moral attitudes, and the psychic cost of maintaining them. The moral outlook belongs to inferior people who are disappointed in the struggle for the worthwhile achievements of human life and who find their compensation in denying the value of the achievements that are beyond them. Morality begins as the revenge of the frustrated, and only the attitudes of the frustrated sustain morality. All alleged rational justifications manifest the non-rational attitudes that underlie the formation of a moral outlook.

Nietzsche's argument relies on three main claims: (1) The relevant parts of his history of morals are plausible. If his history seems false, it does not raise justified doubts about the value of morality. A fictional genealogy of morals would not by itself justify suspicion. Nietzsche intends his genealogy to show that we are easily misled into believing our moral outlook has some objective support, because our emotional commitments to it are so powerful and tenacious. A purely fictional process of formation does not explain the actual power and tenacity of our moral commitments. (2) No good reasons support and sustain morality. The historical argument alone does not justify this conclusion, even if the history is true. (3) The people who form moral attitudes are inferior people, moved by bad emotions. If we thought that the people prone to form moral attitudes are good, and that their emotions direct them towards the truth, we would have no reason to agree that history discredits morality.

1091. The Social Origin of Morals

Though Nietzsche repudiates any attempt to trace morality to a social contract, either in Hobbes's or in Hume's version, some of his remarks are not very different from

---

[18] 'Let us articulate this *new demand*: we need a critique of moral values, *the value of these values themselves must first be called into question*—and for that there is needed a knowledge of the conditions and circumstances in which they grew, under which they evolved and changed (morality as consequence, as symptom, as mask; as tartufferie, as illness, as misunderstanding; but also morality as cause, as remedy, as stimulant, as restraint, as poison), a knowledge of a kind that has never yet existed or even been desired.' (*GM*, Pref. 6)

their explanation of the basis of morality. Social morality begins in the 'taming' of the aggressive instincts of the human animal, and in making human beings capable of living in a 'herd'. At this primitive stage, good and bad actions are judged merely by their consequences (*BGE* 32). Morality as we know it develops with the rise of interest in intentions and will.

At the primitive stage, the love of one's neighbour has not developed and does not influence moral attitudes.[19] In these conditions, people fear one another's aggressive tendencies, and the community rests on 'fear of the neighbour', resulting in rules that tend to restrain aggression. The formation of societies that conform to rules of mutual non-aggression follows after primitive bargaining between individuals of roughly equal power.[20]

Nietzsche's story is coherent only if the attitudes characteristic of bargains and agreements are independent of any social morality. Since he claims that social morality results from these commercial relations, it should be possible for these relations to exist without moral attitudes. To defend his story, he might appeal to primitive 'agreements' such as Hume's tacit convention about rowing a boat. But these pre-moral situations do not explain how we might form the mutual confidence needed for agreements to defer payments. Nor do they explain how a sense of shame, guilt, or obligation could be present to support such agreements if it had not been formed by some prior conception of moral demands. Nietzsche seems to presuppose the attitudes that he tries to explain.

Moreover, his remarks about primitive social relations suggest different processes of development: (1) He assumes primitive collectivism, in which I have no sense of my own individual interest as something distinct from that of the 'herd'. (2) But his discussion of primitive agreements assumes primitive individualism, and hence distinct individual interests that we want a society to protect. These two stories seem inconsistent, since they rely on opposite assumptions on what should be taken for granted and what needs to be historically explained.

Though Nietzsche's remarks on social morality are brief, they are worth comparing with his fuller account of master morality and slave morality. For he does not suppose that all moral principles rest on the outlooks of masters and slaves. Some of them rest on the needs of any human society. Though Nietzsche admits this, he may not always see the consequences of his admission. If, for instance, he suggests that a particular moral principle is the product of slave morality, we may ask whether this is the only or the best possible explanation, and whether the same attitude could be justified by appeal to the minimal social morality needed for human society.

---

[19] 'As long as the utility reigning in moral value judgments is solely the utility of the herd, as long as one considers only the preservation of the community, and immorality is sought exactly and exclusively in what seems dangerous to the survival of the community—there can be no morality of "neighbour love".' (*BGE* 201)

[20] 'Buying and selling, together with their psychological appurtenances, are older even than the beginnings of any kind of social forms of organization and alliances: it was rather out of the most rudimentary form of personal legal rights that the budding sense of exchange, contract, guilt, right, obligation, settlement first *transferred* itself to the coarsest and most elementary social complexes . . . Justice on this elementary level is the good will among parties of approximately equal power to come to terms with one another, to reach an "understanding" by means of a settlement—and to *compel* parties of lesser power to reach a settlement among themselves.—' (*GM* ii 8) In 'equal power', Nietzsche recalls Thucydides i 77, v 105. Cf. *HATH* i 92 (in *GM*, tr. Kaufmann, 168).

1092. Master Morality

Master morality and slave morality are two basic types. Nietzsche does not assume that the moral outlook of every person or every society conforms to just one of his two types, or that actual rulers will observe one type of morality and actual subjects another. The moral outlook of a society or person includes different attitudes with these different social and psychological sources.[21]

This genealogy is intended to replace the unhistorical explanations offered by the British associationists, who have got things back to front.[22] They are wrong to assume that the point of view of the recipient determines goodness. On the contrary, the powerful people determine the patterns of evaluation in their society.[23] Since they are not calculators of utility, morality does not arise from calculations of utility.[24]

The etymology and history of moral terms support this claim about the origin of moral evaluations. Since the terms used to pick out goodness and related properties originally refer to the 'nobility' displayed by the ruling class, moral distinctions reflect the desire of the ruling class to distinguish their characteristics from those of the subject class.[25] This is why the original objects of moral evaluation are people, not actions.[26] The different characteristics of the rulers and the ruled are the original objects of moral evaluation.

Nietzsche points out that evaluative terms used by aristocratic Greeks and Germans to praise their aristocratic traits were later used to express moral evaluation. In Homer and

---

[21] '...I finally discovered two basic types and one basic difference. There are *master morality* and *slave morality*—I add immediately that in all the higher and more mixed cultures there also appear attempts at mediation between these two moralities, and yet more often the interpenetration and mutual misunderstanding of both, and at times they occur directly alongside each other—even in the same human being, within a *single* soul. The moral discrimination of values has originated either among a ruling group whose consciousness of its difference from the ruled group is accompanied by delight—or among the ruled, the slaves and dependents of every degree.' (*BGE* 260)

[22] 'As is the hallowed custom with philosophers, the thinking of all of them is *by nature* unhistorical ... "Originally"—so they decree—"one approved unegoistic actions and called them good from the point of view of those to whom they were done, that is to say, those to whom they were *useful*; later one *forgot* how the approval originated, and simply because unegoistic actions were always *habitually* praised as good, one also felt them to be good—as if they were something good in themselves."' (*GM* i 2) Though Nietzsche makes fun of the British tendency to invoke forgetfulness, he also invokes it in his account of justice. See *HATH* i 92 = GM, ed. Kaufmann, 168.

[23] '...that is to say, the noble, powerful, high-stationed and high-minded, who felt and established themselves and their actions as good, that is, of the first rank, in contradistinction to all the low, low-minded, common and plebeian ... The viewpoint of utility is as remote and inappropriate as it possibly could be in face of such a burning eruption of the highest rank-ordering, rank-defining value judgments; for here feeling has attained the antithesis of that low degree of warmth which any calculating prudence, any calculus of utility, presupposes ...' (*GM* i 2)

[24] Why should we agree with Nietzsche's claim that the ruling class determines the original patterns of moral evaluation in a society? We might take his claim to be trivially true; for we might say that if a class does not determine something as important as the patterns of evaluation in a society, it does not determine everything important, and therefore it is not really the ruling class. This is not a very useful suggestion, however. If it were true, then it would be self-contradictory to claim that a ruling class has accepted the language, or religion, or culture, of the class it rules. Nietzsche's position is more interesting if he means that the ruling class, as established by criteria independently of the source of moral evaluations in a given society, is also the source of moral evaluations in that society.

[25] 'The signpost to the *right* road was for me the question: what was the real etymological significance of the designation for "good" coined in the various languages? I found they all led back to the same *conceptual transformation*—that everywhere "noble", "aristocratic" in the social sense, is the basic concept from which "good" in the sense of "with aristocratic soul", "noble", "with a soul of a high order", "with a privileged soul", necessarily developed.' (*GM* i 4)

[26] 'It is obvious that moral designations were everywhere first applied to *human beings* and only later, derivatively, to actions. Therefore it is a gross mistake when historians of morality start from such questions as: why was the compassionate act praised? The noble type of man experiences *itself* as determining values ... Everything it knows as part of itself it honours; such a morality is self-glorification.' (*BGE* 260) Cf. *HATH* i 45 = GM, tr. Kaufmann, 167.

other early Greek poems,[27] 'good' and 'bad' (*agathos* and *kakos*) often refer to people of higher and lower birth and social rank. In calling Achilles 'good', Homer does not mean that he is just or trustworthy or benevolent.

Nietzsche recognizes that evaluative terms can change their reference without changing their sense. In both Homeric Greek and (say) New Testament or Patristic Greek, '*agathos*' refers to the person who best fulfils the standards that are properly applied to a human being, and to someone who is 'good for' the proper goals of a human being. But between Homer and St Paul, views about the relevant standards and goals have changed. This example suggests how a term might retain the same sense, but develop from a non-moral to a moral use and reference.[28]

Does this sort of historical development show that the origin of morality lies in the self-admiration of the ruling class? Nietzsche does not prove his point if he simply shows that '*agathos*' and related terms, later used for moral evaluation, were originally applied to the qualities expected to characterize the ruling class. He also needs to show that the members of the ruling class did not use any terms, either these terms or others, to convey the sort of moral evaluation that expresses recognition of the interests of others or of the community.

Closer study of Homeric values does not support all of Nietzsche's position.[29] Some of Homer's characters regard total disregard for the interests of others as inappropriate for a hero, even though the hero who displays such disregard does not cease to be *agathos*. Though violations of justice (for instance) do not remove someone's title to be *agathos*, they are still disapproved of and liable to punishment by human beings or gods. Homeric agents do not always take moral evaluations to be superior to other sorts of evaluations; Achilles and Hector, for instance, are more concerned to display their strength and bravery than to fulfil obligations to others.[30] But the fact that moral attitudes do not always determine people's behaviour does not show that people regard them as unimportant.

This is not merely a point of pedantic historical detail. Nietzsche needs to show that other-regarding considerations are a later growth and that they do not belong to the origins of morality in the evaluations of the ruling class.[31] His case is undermined if other-regarding morality is also present in the outlook of the ruling class.

It is not surprising that we find other-regarding morality in Homer, or that we find it more prominently in the *Odyssey* than in the *Iliad*. Homeric society cannot do without rules and practices that promote the interests of the society and its members, and restrain the selfish

---

[27] He mentions Theognis at *GM* i 5.

[28] ' "Good" is what one calls those who do what is moral as if they did it by nature . . . whatever may be moral in this sense . . . He is called good because he is good "for something"; but because benevolence, pity, and that sort of thing have always been felt to be, through many changes in mores, "good for something" and useful, it has come to pass that now the benevolent and helpful are pre-eminently considered "good". . . . Harming the neighbour has been felt to be pre-eminently harmful in all the moral laws of different ages, until now the word "evil" is associated primarily with the deliberate harming of the neighbour.' (*HATH* i 96 = *GM*, K, p.169)

[29] Studies of Homer that emphasize aspects omitted by Nietzsche include Long, 'Morals'; Lloyd-Jones, *JZ*, ch. 1; Griffin, *HLD*, ch. 5.

[30] Hence Achilles stays out of the battle and allows Patroclus to be killed. Hector insists on fighting Achilles even though he endangers the city by risking death at Achilles' hands.

[31] Adkins's account of Homeric ethics, *MR*, ch. 3, agrees with Nietzsche's picture in so far as it attributes to the upper class in Homeric society an outlook rather similar to Nietzsche's master morality. But Adkins departs from Nietzsche in so far as he offers a functionalist explanation of the outlook of the ruling class. Adkins argues that their status relies on an implicit agreement between rulers and ruled, in support of which he cites *Iliad*, xii 310–21.

pursuits of individual members. The same is true of many societies that have any reasonable prospect of survival and stability. Homeric agents are well aware of this; they often cite the interests of the expedition (on the Greek side) or the city (on the Trojan side, or in Ithaca) as a reason for a particular course of action, and they take such interests to have a claim on the attention of an individual.

Nietzsche traces the origins of co-operative morality to the needs of society. But this feature of morality disappears in his contrast between master morality and slave morality. As Nietzsche conceives slave morality, it is characteristic of people who are ruled by others. But even individual members of the master class have to be ruled by others, and have to follow rules designed to ensure co-operation, if they are to remain a tolerable society at all. The danger to heroic society of the one-sided cultivation of heroic, unco-operative values is clear in the behaviour of Agamemnon and Achilles. If moral attitudes result from the demands of co-operation, this origin does not undermine the legitimacy of other-regarding morality.

Nietzsche sometimes acknowledges the role of co-operative attitudes in the moral outlook of the masters. He suggests that master morality reflects the rulers' conception of themselves and of their difference from their subjects. They look on their subjects with contempt and pity rather than hatred; hatred would involve taking inferior people more seriously than they deserve (GM i 10). They distinguish relations with their peers from relations with their inferiors. In dealing with each other, mutual consideration and respect restrain them, but in dealing with their inferiors they throw off these restraints.[32]

Since superior people inevitably express their superiority in this way, they have no choice about this, and they cannot fail to express themselves in the way that is natural to them.[33] It is an illusion to suppose that the agents' choice is the product of a will that makes them free to choose differently. When we speak of the 'subject' of an action, we wrongly suppose that something behind the motive of the action controls the operation of the motive.

Nietzsche's claims about superior people seem to conflict. If these people exercise strength 'expressing itself as strength', and are not free to choose not to do this, they are likely to exercise it against their peers, who provide the best trial of strength. The Homeric poems provide many examples of such self-assertion. But Nietzsche suggests that on the whole they leave their peers alone if they recognize them as members of the same society. How do they restrain themselves towards their peers, if they are not free to choose not to exercise their strength?

The motives that Nietzsche mentions—respect, self-control, custom, loyalty, and friendship—are unlikely to restrain an irresistible urge to express one's strength. For the most

---

[32] '... the same men who are held so sternly in check *inter pares* by custom, respect, usage, gratitude, and even more by mutual suspicion and jealousy, and who on the other hand in their relations with one another show themselves so resourceful in consideration, self-control, delicacy, loyalty, pride, and friendship—once they go outside, where the strange, the *stranger* is found, they are not much better than uncaged beasts of prey. There they savour a freedom from all social constraints, they compensate themselves in the wilderness for the tension engendered by protracted confinement and enclosure within the peace of society, they *go back* to the innocent conscience of the beast of prey, as triumphant monsters who perhaps emerge from a disgusting procession of murder, arson, rape, and torture, exhilarated and undisturbed of soul, as if it were no more than a students' prank....' (GM i 11)

[33] 'To demand of strength that it should *not* express itself as strength, that it should *not* be a desire to overcome, a desire to throw down, a desire to become master, a thirst for enemies and resistances and triumphs, is just as absurd as to demand of weakness that it should express itself as strength.' (GM i 13)

striking expression of strength might well be its expression against one's friends or allies; this is how it seems to Achilles. But if everyone were like Achilles, there would be no heroic society, since no stable co-operative relations could be formed. In order to form them, superior people must be able to restrain their strength from expressing itself as strength. If they can restrain it in this area, why can they not restrain it in relation to their inferiors? Nietzsche speaks as though resentment at cruelty by superiors to inferiors is as pointless as resentment directed against wild animals would be, since superior people are no more capable of failing to express their nature than wild animals are. But he cannot consistently accept the implications of this claim.

What is admirable about the aristocrats who manifest master morality? Nietzsche suggests that attempts to restrain the aggressive traits of these superior people cause the regression of humanity, because these people embody some human ideal.[34] But what is this ideal? If they are rulers, then they are superior in whatever features are necessary for them to rule; but these may not be features that constitute human superiority in general. Stentor the herald needed a loud voice to do his job, but this did not make him a superior human being. The aggressive traits of Nietzsche's superior people might evoke the kind of aesthetic admiration that might be appropriate (let us assume) for destructive wild beasts or natural phenomena; but why should we admire these traits as part of ideal human nature?

We might admire other features of the Homeric hero's outlook; perhaps his pride and self-esteem, or his loyalty to his friends, or his willingness to risk what is less important for the sake of what is more important. But these seem to be separable from aggressiveness. Unless they are inseparable from the aggressive aspects of a hero, restraint of aggressiveness need not cause the regression of humanity.

1093. Slave Morality

Even if Nietzsche's account of master morality gives us no reason to admire its distinctively aggressive aspects, his criticism of slave morality might be correct. Perhaps master morality simply fulfils the impulses and desires of people in a superior social position. There may be nothing admirable about this, except from the point of view of people in such a position. But if a similar social and psychological explanation can be given for every moral outlook, perhaps none of them, including our own, deserves admiration from an external point of view. If this is Nietzsche's position, his attitude to slave morality denies any objectively correct moral outlook and so expresses a nihilist view rather than an objectivist view that judges slave morality against the correct moral outlook.

Slave morality results from the same social situation that produces master morality. Both moral outlooks start from the same 'superior' ideal. In the view of superior people, this is a genuine ideal; the good person is the one who conforms to it, and the bad person is the

---

[34] 'These bearers of the oppressive instincts that thirst for reprisals, the descendants of every kind of European and non-European slavery, and especially of the entire pre-Aryan populace—they represent the *regression* of mankind! . . . One may be quite justified in continuing to fear the blond beast at the core of all noble races, and in being on one's guard against it; but who would not a hundred times sooner fear where one can also admire than *not* fear but be permanently condemned to the repellent sight of the ill-constituted, dwarfed, atrophied, and poisoned?' (*GM* i 11)

unfortunate creature who cannot approach it. From the point of view of slave morality, however, the supposedly good person is evil, and the good person is the one who avoids the features of the evil person.[35] Slave morality, then, arises from opposition; it lives as a parasite on master morality by resenting the superior person conceived by master morality.

The primary source of slave morality is hatred arising from fear. The inferior person looks on the superior person as a threat, and fears his aggressiveness.[36] In deploring and prohibiting the aggressiveness of superior people, slave morality expresses the preferences of inferior people as though they were independently legitimate. Inferior people convince themselves that the ideal of master morality is not legitimate, and that the goals of the superior person are not worthwhile.

This expression of hatred and revenge against superior people is especially characteristic of the Jews.[37] The Jewish attitude denies that the superior people have any valuable aims and achievements. If inferior people convince themselves that superior people are not only acting badly, but failing to achieve anything worthwhile by their bad actions, they can add contempt to hatred. To compensate for recognized inadequacies, they persuade themselves that only weak people can achieve anything valuable;[38] they are justly praised for being the way they are, whereas the superior people are justly blamed for doing what they do and being what they are.

Inferior people none the less suffer from self-hatred. However much they cultivate contempt for the strong, they cannot ignore their own weakness and inadequacy, and they hate themselves for these failures. Their self-hatred produces their sense of sin, guilt, and inadequacy; but they mitigate these effects of self-hatred by constructing their inverted conception of human excellence, their 'manufactured ideals' (GM i 14).

The reactions of inferior people may appear no less reasonable than the actions of superior people. Superior people (according to Nietzsche) necessarily express their aggressive nature in their choices and actions; inferior people do the same. It would be as unreasonable to expect the inferior people not to develop slave morality as it would be to expect the superior people not to exert their strength. Both moral systems are expressions of the desires, wishes, and emotions of their manufacturers. Neither side seems open to any justified moral objection from some point of view external to both.

This account of the development of moral beliefs and outlooks supports Nietzsche's claim that there are no moral facts. Both superior and inferior people falsely represent their own preferences, derived from their social status and circumstances, as an objective standard of

---

[35] '... "the enemy" as the man of *ressentiment* conceives him—and here precisely is his deed, his creation: he has conceived "the evil enemy", "*the Evil One*", and this in fact is his basic concept, from which he then evolves, as an afterthought and pendant, a "good one"—himself!' (GM i 10)

[36] '... he who knows these "good men" only as enemies knows only *evil enemies*.' (GM i 11)

[37] 'It was the Jews who, with awe-inspiring consistency, dared to invert the aristocratic value-equation (good = noble = powerful = beautiful = happy = beloved of God) and to hang on to this inversion with their teeth, the teeth of the most abysmal hatred (the hatred of impotence), saying "the wretched alone are the good; the poor, impotent, lowly alone are the good; the suffering, deprived, sick, ugly alone are pious, alone are blessed by God..."' (GM i 7)

[38] '... this ... really amounts to no more than: "we weak ones are, after all, weak; it would be good if we did nothing *for which we are not strong enough*"; but this dry matter of fact, this prudence of the lowest order ... has, thanks to the counterfeit and self-deception of impotence, clad itself in the ostentatious garb of the virtue of quiet, calm, resignation, just as if the weakness of the weak—that is to say, their *essence*, their effects, their sole ineluctable, irremovable reality—were a voluntary achievement, willed, chosen, a *deed*, a *meritorious* act.' (GM i 13)

values. This is a moral 'misinterpretation' of reality. It asserts that we have some reason for preferring the outlook of the master or the slave apart from our own particular circumstances and preferences. But if we see that each outlook simply devises some allegedly objective standard that endorses its own preferences, we can see through the misinterpretations.

This account explains why slave morality is 'sign language' and 'symptomatology', but it does not explain why Nietzsche supposes it is inferior to master morality. He assumes that slave morality has to pretend that the values of master morality are evil, and he assumes that master morality grasps the true human values that are inverted by the hatred and resentment of the inferior people. But why not say instead that each morality is merely a symptomatology, and that neither expresses true human values? Perhaps slave morality invents the Jewish and Christian God to support its passive and resigned values, whereas master morality invents the Homeric or Norse gods to support its values. Each system seems to project its preferences on to reality no less than the other does.

Sometimes Nietzsche seems to imply that he occupies a position outside the two 'interpretations' that he describes, and that from this position he endorses one over the other. But his approach to morality appears to disallow such a third position.

1094. The Hellenic Outlook in the Culture of the Sophists

So far we have found that Nietzsche's historical account of morality supports his nihilist conclusion that morality is simply a mistaken attempt to present subjective needs, desires, and emotions as objective requirements imposed by moral facts. But some historical complications raise questions about this argument for the rejection of moral facts. If the truth of his historical account is relevant, in the ways we have seen, to his philosophical position, some questions about his historical claims are relevant. Though our pursuit of these historical questions will require some digression from Nietzsche's examination of morality, it will eventually throw some light on his philosophical views as well.

In the picture so far, the Greeks provide one historical source for master morality. The Jews, with the Christians treated as honorary Jews, are the historical source for slave morality.[39] For illustrations of the Greek view, Nietzsche turns to Homer, Hesiod, Theognis, and Pericles (as reported by Thucydides) (GM i 11). He relies on two main sources for the ethical outlook of Classical Greece, which is also the traditional ethical outlook found in Homer. His first source is the history of Thucydides, especially the 'realistic' (as opposed to 'moralistic') outlook that is expressed there.[40] His

---

[39] Cf. Machiavelli's contrast between pagan and Christian outlooks, §403.

[40] 'My recreation, my preference, my *cure* from all Platonism has always been Thucydides. Thucydides and, perhaps, Machiavelli's *Principe* are most closely related to myself by the unconditional will not to gull oneself and to see reason in *reality*—not in "reason", still less in "morality". . . . With him the culture of the Sophists, by which I mean the culture of the realists, reaches its perfect expression—this inestimable movement amid the moralistic and idealistic swindle set loose on all sides by the Socratic schools. Greek philosophy: the decadence of the Greek instinct. Thucydides: the great sum, the last revelation of that strong, severe, hard factuality, which was instinctive with the older Hellenes. In the end, it is *courage* in the face of reality that distinguishes a man like Thucydides from Plato: Plato is a coward before reality, consequently he flees into the ideal; Thucydides has control of *himself*, consequently he also maintains control of things.' (TI x 2 = PN 558–9)

second source is the 'culture of the sophists', and especially its immoralism, relativism, and nihilism.[41] This outlook is continuous with the master morality that we find in Homer.

Nietzsche's conception of the genuinely Hellenic spirit reflects his view of the 'culture of the sophists' and of its connexion with Thucydides.[42] He assumes that the sophists constitute a unified intellectual movement, with a distinctive philosophical outlook including immoralism, relativism, and nihilism. He connects the sophists with immoralism, because he includes the views of Callicles (in Plato's *Gorgias*) and Thrasymachus (in the *Republic*) among the sources for the sophistic position.[43] These Platonic characters are immoralists in so far as they attack a moral position that asserts the priority of social morality over self-assertion.

The social morality attacked by Plato's Callicles involves the principles and expectations characteristic of the virtues of justice and temperance.[44] These two virtues go together; temperance involves self-control and self-restraint in the pursuit of one's own power and pleasure, while justice requires this self-restraint for the good of others and for the common good of some community. If we think temperance is misguided, we will think the same about justice. Social morality takes the principles of temperance and justice to impose justified limits on one's self-assertion—the pursuit of one's own self-centred power, advantage, and pleasure.

Callicles takes an immoralist attitude to the requirements of social morality, because he believes these requirements have no legitimate rational claim on anyone who can violate them with impunity. These moral principles are simply the product of convention and agreement, and have nothing more to be said in their favour. Hence, the rational person who sees an opportunity to advance his self-centred interest asserts himself without regard for conventional justice. This outlook is the 'audacious realism and immoralism' of the Greeks.[45]

[41] 'It is a very remarkable moment: the Sophists verge upon the first *critique of morality*, the first *insight* into morality:—they juxtapose the multiplicity (the geographical relativity) of the moral value judgments:—they let it be known that every morality can be dialectically justified; i.e. they divine that all attempts to give reasons for morality are necessarily *sophistical*—a proposition later proved on the grand scale by the ancient philosophers, from Plato onwards (down to Kant):—they postulate the first truth that a "morality-in-itself", a "good-in-itself" do not exist, that it is a swindle to talk of "truth" in this field.' (*WP* 428)

[42] On Nietzsche and the sophists, see Nestle, 'Philosophie', esp. 571. Nestle suggests that Nietzsche first approved, and then rejected, Grote's defence of the sophists. The passages he quotes suggest only that Nietzsche later rejected just one aspect of Grote's defence. Brobjer, 'Disinterest', discusses the changes in Nietzsche's views towards the sophists. The evidence that he presents undermines his claim that Nietzsche is 'disinterested' (i.e., uninterested) in the sophists.

[43] Plato, *Gorg.* 483b–484c; *Rep.* 343b. On Nietzsche and Callicles, see Dodds, *G*, Appendix.

[44] See esp. Plato, *Gorg.* 483bc.

[45] 'The magnificent physical suppleness, the audacious realism and immoralism which distinguished the Hellene constituted a *need*, not "nature". It only resulted, it was not there from the start. And with festivals and the arts they also aimed at nothing other than to feel *on top*, to *show* themselves on top. These are means of glorifying oneself, and in certain cases, of inspiring fear of oneself. How could one possibly judge the Greeks by their philosophers, as the Germans have done, and use the Philistine moralism of the Socratic schools as a clue to what was basically Hellenic! After all, the philosophers are the decadents of Greek culture, the counter-movement to the ancient, noble taste (to the agonistic instinct, to the *polis*, to the value of race, to true authority of descent). The Socratic virtues were preached because the Greeks had lost them: excitable, timid, fickle comedians, every one of them, they had a few reasons too many for having morals preached to them.' (*TI* x 3 = *PN* 559–60)

This is Thucydides' view.[46] Considerations of justice are irrelevant to situations in which considerations of superior force and self-interest are taken to be overriding. Disregard for recognized principles of justice is appropriate, even inevitable.[47] This outlook in Thucydides seems similar to the outlook of Plato's Callicles. Since Nietzsche takes Callicles to express distinctively sophistic views, he also takes the immoralism in Thucydides to represent the culture of the sophists.

Nietzsche regards the immoralism of Thucydides as genuinely Hellenic because it recalls Homer. Homeric characters seem to choose self-assertion over the demands of self-control and restraint for the common good. Paris's abduction of Helen, Agamemnon's insult to Achilles, Achilles' withdrawal from the battle, Patroclus' refusal to withdraw, Hector's refusal to withdraw, all involve some act of self-assertion that rejects the demands or needs of others. This self-assertion expresses the attitude that Callicles describes as 'bravery' or 'manliness'.[48] Callicles prefers self-assertive bravery over justice and temperance, and the Homeric heroes seem to agree with him. Nietzsche seems to agree with him too, since he prefers the master morality of Homer to the degenerate outlook of Plato and Aristotle.

One might argue that, contrary to our earlier suggestions, the demands of social morality do not enter Homeric morality. For when these Homeric characters engage in acts of self-assertion that violate the expectations of social morality, they are not deprived of the moral admiration that belongs to them for their character and actions. Achilles remains the best of the Greeks; Paris is still accepted among the best of the Trojans; when Hector puts the safety of the city second to his desire not to appear cowardly, he is not condemned for his decision. Some of the attitudes of blame and condemnation that we would normally attach to violations of social morality are not attached to Homeric characters when they violate social morality.

One might say the same about (for instance) Ajax in Sophocles' play, and about Alcibiades in Thucydides' history. Their actions, and other people's attitude to their actions, tend to support Nietzsche's view that traditional Greek ethics is immoralist. Plato's target, as presented by Callicles, is the Homeric outlook that values self-assertion over the demands of social morality. Since Nietzsche takes the outlook of Callicles to be the sophistic outlook, he identifies the culture of the sophists with the 'hard factuality' of Thucydides and with the traditional Hellenic outlook.

The second component of the culture of the sophists is relativism. The most obvious source of this component is Protagoras. Protagoras was a sophist, and we may grant, for present purposes, that he maintained some version of relativism.[49] Nietzsche, therefore, includes both immoralism and relativism in the culture of the sophists. Thucydides is the

---

[46] Nietzsche identifies Thucydides' outlook with the outlook expressed in some of the speeches that the historian puts in the mouth of participants in his history. He comments on Thucydides v 89: 'The Sophists are no more than realists: they formulate the values and practices common to everyone on the level of values—they possess the courage of all strong spirits to *know* their own immorality—Do you suppose perchance that these little Greek free cities, which from rage and envy would have liked to devour each other, were ever guided by philanthropic and righteous principles? Does one reproach Thucydides for the words he put into the mouths of the Athenian ambassadors when they negotiated with the Melians on the question of destruction or submission?' (WP 429)

[47] This attitude is not confined to inter-state relations. Some episodes—most notably, the revolution in Corcyra—suggest that some individuals also adopt this attitude in relations among individuals and groups within a state. See Thucydides iii 81–5.

[48] *andreia: Gorg.* 492a2.   [49] Plato, *Tht.* 152a, 166d, 167c. Protagorean relativism; §133.

'perfect expression' not only of the culture of the sophists, but also of the 'severe, hard, factuality' characteristic of the older Hellenes. Hence relativism and immoralism manifest the old Hellenic spirit.

The third component of the culture of the sophists is the nihilist claim that there is no 'morality-in-itself', and that it is a swindle to talk of truth in this area. Callicles and Protagoras argue that some moral principles are simply a matter of convention, and do not hold 'by nature'. This contrast between nature and convention is sometimes understood as a contrast between beliefs that correspond to an external reality and beliefs that do not. Hence someone who maintains that principles of justice hold only by convention may be taken to accept the nihilist view that nothing is really just or unjust, but things merely appear so. Nietzsche attributes this nihilist view to the sophists, and hence to the genuine Hellenic spirit.[50]

1095. The Un-Hellenic Outlook of Socrates and Plato

According to Nietzsche, this genuinely Hellenic outlook is sharply opposed to, and superior to, the moral outlook of Socrates and Plato, which is a symptom of degeneration.[51] The Socratic and Platonic outlook includes three basic errors: (1) Rationalism: Virtue is identified with a rational agent's well-being, because it is supremely rational, reflecting the primacy of reason over instinct (WP 434).[52] (2) Objectivism and the rejection of relativism:[53] Since (in the

[50] 'The appearance of the Greek philosophers from Socrates onwards is a symptom of decadence; the anti-Hellenic instincts come to the top—The "Sophist" is still completely Hellenic—including Anaxagoras, Democritus, the great Ionians—but as a transitional form. The polis loses its faith in the uniqueness of its culture, in its right to rule over every other polis.—One exchanges cultures, i.e., "the gods"—one thereby loses faith in the sole prerogative of the deus autochthonus. Good and evil of differing origin are mingled; the boundary between good and evil is blurred—This is the "Sophist"—' (WP 427)

[51] 'In the age of Socrates, among men of fatigued instincts, among the conservatives of ancient Athens who let themselves go—"toward happiness", as they said; toward pleasure, as they acted—and who all the while still mouthed the ancient pompous words to which their lives no longer gave them any right, Irony may have been required for greatness of soul, that Socratic sarcastic assurance of the old physician and plebeian who cut ruthlessly into his own flesh, as he did into the flesh and heart of the "noble", with a look that said clearly enough: "Don't dissemble in front of me! Here—we are equal."' (BGE 212)

[52] 'I try to understand from what partial and idiosyncratic states the Socratic problem derives: his equalization of reason = virtue = happiness. It was with this absurdity of a doctrine of identity that he fascinated: the philosophers of antiquity never again freed themselves from this fascination.' (WP 432) 'Consider the consequences of the Socratic maxims; "Virtue is knowledge; man sins only from ignorance; he who is virtuous is happy." In these three basic forms of optimism lies the death of tragedy. For now the virtuous hero must be a dialectician; now there must be a necessary, visible, connection between virtue and knowledge, faith and morality...' (BT 14) Elsewhere Nietzsche complicates his claim about Socratic rationalism: 'Socrates himself, to be sure... had initially sided with reason; and in fact, what did he do his life long, but laugh at the awkward incapacity of noble Athenians who, like all noble men, were men of instinct and never could give sufficient information about the reasons for their actions? In the end, however, privately and secretly, he laughed at himself too... This was the real falseness of the great ironic, so rich in secrets; he got his conscience to be satisfied with a kind of self-trickery: at bottom, he had seen through the irrational element in moral judgment.' (BGE 191)

[53] 'Positing proofs as the presupposition for personal excellence in virtue signified nothing less than the disintegration of Greek instincts. They are themselves types of disintegration, all these great "virtuous men" and word-spinners. In praxi, this means that moral judgments are torn from their conditionality, in which they have grown and alone possess any meaning, from their Greek and Greek-political ground and soil, to be denaturalized under the pretence of sublimation. The great concepts "good" and "just" are severed from the presuppositions to which they belong and, as liberated "ideas", become objects of dialectic. One looks for truth in them, one takes them for entities, or signs of entities: one invents a world where they are at home, where they originate—In summa: the mischief has already reached

Socratic view) true moral principles are provable matters of knowledge, not simply matters of instinct, they must grasp some objective fact that is independent of the preferences of particular people; hence they must correspond to some distinct reality apart from the norms, preferences, or prejudices of any individual or society. (3) Moralism: Socrates and Plato defend the legitimacy and rationality of social morality against the self-assertive outlook of immoralism. They defend the objective correctness of their claims about social morality.

Nietzsche describes Plato's outlook as a 'denaturalization' of morality.[54] This aspect of Plato makes him a forerunner of some of the unattractive features of Christianity, and makes his outlook alien to the traditional Hellenic outlook.[55] The Socratic moral outlook is to blame for the death of tragedy, because Socrates insists on rational defence and justification.[56] Sometimes, however, Nietzsche suggests that Socrates simply exposed ways in which his contemporaries had already degenerated, and was not himself responsible for the degeneration.[57]

Nietzsche also suggests that Socrates did not really intend to expose the imperfections in particular people's moral outlook; he intended to expose the irrationality of the moral outlook itself. He represents an early stage of the problem of instinct versus reason in moral thinking. His interrogations, on this view, do not expose any genuine fault or symptom of degeneration in his aristocratic interlocutors. They had no reason to be ashamed of their failure to give the sort of explicit defence that Socrates asked for; Socrates saw that no such defence of morality was either needed or available.

The content of Socrates' moral teaching strikes Nietzsche as plebeian. Socrates' eudae-monism and intellectualism (the claim that virtue is simply the knowledge of what promotes happiness, and that vice is cured by removing ignorance) is a utilitarian doctrine.[58] If Nietzsche believes that this doctrine betrays Socrates' plebeian origins, he assumes that the authentic representatives of traditional Greek master morality do not accept it. He does not ask whether the sophists, whom he represents as authentically Greek thinkers, accept any of the utilitarian doctrine that he deplores in Socrates.

its climax in Plato . . . In short, the consequence of the denaturalization of moral values was the creation of a degenerate type of man—"the good man", "the happy man", "the wise man".—Socrates represents a moment of the profoundest perversity in the history of values.' (WP 430)

[54] 'The place of origin of the notion of "another world": the philosopher who invents a world of reason, where reason and the logical functions are adequate: this is the origin of the "true" world; the religious man, who invents a "divine world"; this is the origin of the "denaturalized, anti-natural" world; the moral man, who invents a "free world": this is the origin of the "good, perfect, just, holy" world. . . . General insight: it is the instinct of life-weariness, and not that of life, which has created the "other world". Consequence: philosophy, religion, and morality are *symptoms of decadence*.' (WP 586) Cf. TI iii–iv = PN 479, 485.

[55] See TI x 3 = PN 559–60, quoted above in §1094.

[56] 'Consider the consequences of the Socratic maxims; "Virtue is knowledge; man sins only from ignorance; he who is virtuous is happy". In these three basic forms of optimism lies the death of tragedy. For now the virtuous hero must be a dialectician; now there must be a necessary, visible, connection between virtue and knowledge, faith and morality . . .' (BT 14)

[57] See BGE 212, quoted above.

[58] 'This type of inference smells of the *rabble* that sees nothing in bad actions but the unpleasant consequences and really judges "it is *stupid* to do what is bad", while "good" is taken without further ado to be identical with "useful and agreeable". In the case of every moral utilitarianism one may immediately infer the same original and follow one's nose; one will rarely go astray. Plato did everything he could in order to read something refined and noble into the proposition of his teacher—above all, himself.' (BGE 130)

The Socratic moral outlook is not only plebeian and utilitarian, but also typically rationalist.[59] In following Socrates, Plato attacks everything genuinely Hellenic (*WP* 435); he is a victim of the decadence that he tries to overcome. Whereas the sophists are genuinely Hellenic, Socrates and Plato betray this tradition.[60]

None of these attacks on Socratic and Platonic morality accuses Socrates or Plato of advocating slave morality. Nietzsche might be taken to suggest this accusation in his remark that they are not Greeks but 'Jews, or I know not what'.[61] He also regards Plato as a forerunner of some of the unattractive and degenerate features of Christianity.[62] But he does not connect his criticism of the non-Hellenic and 'Jewish' elements in Plato with the sources of slave morality.

On the contrary, he attacks Socrates and Plato primarily for their rationalism.[63] He argues that their search for moral knowledge leads to a misguided form of objectivism, and hence to the Platonic Theory of Forms. But he does not say much about the content of Greek philosophical ethics. Socrates, Plato, Aristotle, Epicurus, the Stoics all agree that virtue plays a decisive role in happiness, and on this point they seem to oppose the attitude that is characteristic of Greek tragedies. Sophocles' presentation of the sufferings of Ajax or Oedipus does not encourage the belief that if we retain virtue, we retain the crucial component of happiness.[64]

While Nietzsche recognizes that Greek moralists follow Socrates in seeing a close connexion between virtue and happiness, he does not explore their reasons for believing in it. All of these philosophers reject a conventional assumption about the importance of success and external goods in determining one's welfare. They all believe that, no matter what misfortunes happen to just people, they are still better off than unjust people. These doctrines fit Nietzsche's description of slave morality. Slave morality seeks some compensation for failure by turning to the goods that are available to the unsuccessful.

---

[59] 'I try to understand from what partial and idiosyncratic states the Socratic problem derives: his equalization of reason = virtue = happiness. It was with this absurdity of a doctrine of identity that he fascinated: the philosophers of antiquity never again freed themselves from this fascination.' (*WP* 432)

[60] In *PTAG* §2, Nietzsche allows Socrates to be genuinely Greek: 'With Plato, something entirely new has its beginning. Or it might be said with equal justice, from Plato on there is something essentially amiss with philosophers when one compares them to that "republic of creative minds" from Thales to Socrates.' (34) Plato was less genuinely Greek: '. . . beginning with Plato, philosophers became exiles, conspiring against their fatherland' (35).

[61] 'The Sophists were Greeks: when Socrates and Plato took up the cause of virtue and justice, they were *Jews*, or I know not what. Grote's tactics in defence of the Sophists are false: he wants to raise them to the rank of men of honour and ensigns of morality—but it was their honour not to indulge in any swindle with big words and virtues . . .' (*WP* 429)

[62] 'Two decadence movements and extremes run side by side; (a) sensual, charmingly wicked decadence, loving art and show, and (b) gloomy religio-moral pathos, Stoic self-hardening, Platonic slander of the senses, preparation of the soil for Christianity.' (*WP* 427) 'In the end, my mistrust of Plato goes deep: he represents such an aberration from all the basic instincts of the Hellene, is so moralistic, so pre-existently Christian. . . . We have paid dearly for the fact that the Athenian got his schooling from the Egyptians (or from the Jews in Egypt?). In that great calamity, Christianity, Plato represents that ambiguity and fascination, called an "ideal", which made it possible for the noblest spirits of antiquity to misunderstand themselves and to set foot on the bridge leading to the cross.' (*TI* x 2 = *PN* 558) Plato's 'invention of the pure spirit and the good as such' was 'the worst, most durable, and most dangerous of all errors so far', and in fighting against it we fight against Christianity as well, since 'Christianity is Platonism "for the people"' (*BGE*, Pref.)

[63] See *WP* 430, quoted above.

[64] Undeserved suffering and reversals of fortune are especially characteristic of Euripides. This explains why Aristotle regards Euripides as in some respects 'the most tragic' of poets (*Poetics* 1453a27–30). Nietzsche does not discuss this aspect of Euripides; instead he claims that Euripides fought 'the death-struggle of tragedy', *BT* 11. Cf. Silk and Stern, *NT* 230–2.

Though it might be natural for Nietzsche to say this, he does not say it. Some of his remarks about 'other-worldliness' suggest a similarity between slave morality and Socratic-Platonic 'denaturalization'. But though these errors are similar, they are distinct. The philosopher's futile search for knowledge and objectivity leads to the belief in a cognitively satisfactory 'other world'. The moral person's disappointment with the course of the world leads to the belief in another world that rectifies this disappointment. The philosophical and the moral error are different.

If Nietzsche does not accuse the Greek moral philosophers of endorsing slave morality, does this matter? We might say it is simply an oversight, and that Nietzsche would have no reason not to endorse the accusation. Perhaps, however, it is not so easy for him to agree that slave morality appears in the theories of the Greek moralists as well as in the Jewish and Christian Scriptures. For he argues that slave morality is the product of the resentment and anger of the subject classes aware of their own inferiority. This explanation does not fit the moral outlook of the Greek philosophers.

1096. Immoralism and Traditional Morality

We have now described the development of Hellenic and non-Hellenic outlooks in the history of Greek moral thinking. Nietzsche takes this development to be philosophically significant, because it displays the errors that underlie the characteristic outlook of moral philosophy. The misguided search for rationality and objective knowledge in morality encourages the belief in a spurious moral reality. These errors are still prevalent in modern moral philosophy. Nietzsche contrasts the Platonic moral and philosophical outlook with the sounder outlook of earlier Greek thought.

How plausible is this account of earlier Greek thought? If it is largely fictitious, it does not explain the alleged errors of the Platonic outlook. If we can find elements of the Platonic outlook in earlier Greek thought, we cannot attribute them wholly to errors by Plato.

Nietzsche's composite picture of sophistic culture raises some relevant doubts. He ascribes a single philosophical position to the sophists, as though they were a philosophical school. This position includes Callicles' immoralism, because Nietzsche assumes that Callicles represents sophistic views. Plato, however, does not present Callicles as a sophist, and we have no other evidence to confirm Nietzsche's assumption about Callicles.

If we confine ourselves to attested sophists, Nietzsche's composite picture is still open to objections. The sophists did not form a philosophical school, and did not share a specific philosophical outlook, any more than 'the professors' or 'the intellectuals' of later times share a definite position.[65]

We have no reason, then, to ascribe a unified position, including both relativism and immoralism, to the sophists in general. Callicles the immoralist is neither a relativist nor a sophist. Protagoras the relativist and sophist is not an immoralist. We have no reason to

---

[65] Grote, *HG*, ch. 67, argues effectively against the composite picture of the sophists as a single philosophical school. In his early work 'Vorplatonischen', Nietzsche seems to accept Grote's view (he describes it, but does not discuss it at length). The passages quoted above reflect Nietzsche's later view of the sophists as a school with the 'Hellenic' (pre-Platonic) spirit.

believe that any sophist, let alone all sophists, accepted both immoralism and relativism. Hence we have no reason to believe that Thucydides belongs to the culture of the sophists, or that he is both a relativist and an immoralist. For similar reasons, facts about the sophists do not support Nietzsche's claim that relativism and immoralism are characteristic of the traditional Hellenic outlook.

These objections do not refute Nietzsche's conclusions, but only show that they need better support. Even if he is wrong about the culture of the sophists, he might be right to claim that traditional Hellenic values embrace both immoralism and relativism. If he is right on this point, he is also right—whatever we say about the sophists—to claim that Socrates and Plato represent a sharp break from the traditional Greek outlook.

Some Homeric examples support Nietzsche's claim that the traditional Hellenic outlook is immoralist, because it values self-assertion above the claims of social morality. But these examples, taken in isolation, give a misleading and one-sided picture of the Homeric outlook as a whole. For this outlook treats social morality as a source of legitimate expectations, and it regards people as having made mistakes when they violate social morality. The Trojans who condone Paris's violation of the normal standards of hospitality are punished with him. Agamemnon eventually recognizes he was mistaken to assert himself against Achilles. When Achilles cannot restrain his anger even against the corpse of Hector, he is said to behave like a beast rather than a human being, because he has 'destroyed mercy'.[66] His attitude contrasts sharply with the attitude of Odysseus, who prohibits rejoicing over his dead enemies.[67]

These examples suggest that Homeric people recognize some requirements of social morality and disapprove of violations, even though they find it difficult to go beyond disapproval of the actions to any reduced esteem of a heroic agent. The Homeric moral outlook displays conflict, or at least indecision. The persistence of this indecision helps to explain some of the debates that are familiar in fifth-century Greek literature.

Within the 'hard factuality' that Nietzsche claims to find in Thucydides' history, social morality matters, even in relations between cities. The Athenians first voted in anger to punish the Mytileneans for their revolt against Athens by killing all the adult males and enslaving the women and children. But they thought better of it; their previous decision seemed 'savage', and they decided it would be a grave matter to kill not only the people responsible for the revolt, but the whole city. This second view was the one that prevailed. The Athenians' revulsion from their first decision is not explained simply by pity, but also by beliefs about justice; they refused to kill the innocent with the guilty.[68]

If the social morality of temperance and justice is part of traditional Greek ethics, Nietzsche is wrong to ascribe to traditional Hellenic culture the immoralism that he attributes to the culture of the sophists.

1097. Relativism, Nihilism, and Traditional Morality

Similarly, Nietzsche regards the relativism of Protagoras as both the sophistic position and as the traditional Hellenic position. Protagoras claims that moral qualities and political norms

---

[66] Homer, *Iliad*, xxiv 3–44.   [67] *Odyssey*, xxii 407–12.   [68] See Thucydides, iii 36.

are simply matters of convention that are right only in so far as they are conventionally established in a particular place. According to this view, there is no reason why one ought, for instance, to show hospitality to strangers beyond the fact that this is the convention in a particular place.

This, however, is not the traditional Greek view. As we can see from the presentation of the Cyclopes in the *Odyssey*, the people who violate the norm of hospitality are not living a proper human life at all; they are 'wild, and not just'; they do not simply have a different convention from the one Odysseus is used to.[69] Homer's implicit assumptions about morality conflict with the acceptance of Protagorean relativism.[70]

Nietzsche takes the traditional Greek outlook to be both immoralist and relativist. But immoralism and relativism are incompatible. The immoralist position recognizes some non-relative values, because it claims that one has good reason, whatever the conventions may be, to pursue one's own interest even if it conflicts with conventional morality. An immoralist who appealed to Protagorean relativism would be confused. Neither Protagoras nor Callicles nor Plato seems to connect the two positions.

Nietzsche, however, assumes that the different views of different sophists (counting Callicles as a sophist) are parts of one sophistic position. Since some sophists are relativists and some are immoralists, he assumes that this single sophistic position is both relativist and immoralist. Since Plato is against both positions, and Nietzsche is against Plato, Nietzsche defends both positions, without seeing that they are inconsistent.

The third component of Nietzsche's picture of the Hellenic outlook is nihilism. If he takes it to be a reasonable conclusion from Protagoras' arguments for relativism, he does not notice that nihilism and relativism about morality are incompatible. Moral relativists maintain that we can reject objective moral facts without rejecting moral facts and truths, because moral truths are relative to the outlook of a particular group, society, or convention, and do not correspond to any further objective facts. Protagoras seeks to vindicate, not to reject, the possibility of moral truths; he believes there are truths about justice because there are truths relative to Athenian conventions, Persian conventions, and so on.[71] If he were a nihilist, he would deny that there are moral facts and truths at all.

Why does Nietzsche not remark that the three components of the Hellenic culture of the sophists—immoralism, relativism, and nihilism—are inconsistent? We can perhaps explain his silence by recalling an obscurity in his arguments to show that moral judgments simply reflect different people's affects, and to show that there are no moral facts. These arguments might be taken to support immoralist or relativist or nihilist conclusions.

Sometimes Nietzsche suggests that slave morality is worse than master morality because the aspects of human nature that it appeals to are inferior aspects that ought not to be encouraged. This conclusion appears to favour immoralism; he connects modern morality with slave morality, and prefers the outlook that appeals to values opposed to slave morality. He maintains some non-relative non-moral practical principles; for he endorses an immoralist

---

[69] See *Odyssey*, ix 105–76.

[70] Homer's assumption also underlies the story told by Protagoras in Plato, *Protagoras* 322cd, that makes justice and 'the political craft' essential to being human.

[71] Protagoras; see §133.

attitude to social morality, and he appears to take his endorsement of immoralism to rest on non-relative practical principles.

Against this conclusion, however, we might argue that master morality no less than slave morality seems to reflect the desires and emotions of the people who maintain it. When Nietzsche concludes that there are no moral facts, he seems to rely on his arguments to show that moral judgments tell us about the attitudes of the judges, and not about any facts in the world. He seems to draw a nihilist conclusion that tells no less against the evaluative outlooks that he favours than against those he rejects.

An alternative to this nihilist conclusion might be a relativist interpretation of the claim about moral facts. Instead of the unqualified claim that there are no moral facts of any sort, the relativist may infer that there are moral facts and truths relative to the outlook of slave morality and different facts and truths relative to the outlook of master morality. This position would prohibit us from saying that either set of moral judgments is simply false; they would be true, as Protagoras argues, relative to their different outlooks.

A reader may find it difficult to decide whether Nietzsche is an immoralist, a nihilist, or a relativist; different passages seem to support one or another view. If he has not clearly decided between these views, it is not surprising that he attributes them all to the culture of the sophists.

His account of the sophists blurs a relevant question: Do any of the sophists accept nihilism? Those who accept a division between the natural and the conventional, and deny that anything is just or unjust by nature, might seem to be the most plausible candidates for being nihilists. But Protagoras' position suggests that they intend to avoid nihilism, not to embrace it; for they take facts about relative rightness to show that some things are right, not to show that nothing is right. To find the nihilist conclusion entertained, though not asserted, we have to turn to the Greek Sceptics.[72] Nietzsche does not discuss them, because he is concerned with Classical, and especially pre-Platonic, Greek culture.

1098. The Rise of Social Morality

We have found some reason to question reject Nietzsche's belief that the history of Greek moral thinking is sharply discontinuous, and that moralism and objectivism are un-Hellenic positions introduced by Socrates and Plato. This conclusion suggests a further question: Would an alternative to Nietzsche's version of history suggest a better account of morality?

Nietzsche takes the immoralists to embody the genuine Hellenic spirit. He ought to find it surprising, therefore, that they argue as though they need to refute the assumption that social morality is in some way prior to self-assertion against others. The immoralists attack the view that the requirements of justice and temperance impose rational limits on the pursuit of self-assertive aims. If they bother to attack this view, it may well have been fairly widespread among their contemporaries; Callicles, for instance, takes it to be a common view among 'the many', not a paradoxical Socratic view. We have found that Homeric

---

[72] Brobjer, 'Disinterest', 10–16, discusses, and perhaps exaggerates, the influence of Brochard's SG (published in 1887) on Nietzsche.

characters do not characteristically ascribe this priority to social morality, even though many of them give some weight to the needs and expectations of others. If this is the right account of Homer, many of Socrates' and Plato's contemporaries seem to reject this aspect of the traditional outlook.

The historian who is interested, as Nietzsche is, in finding the social and psychological origin of moral outlooks, might reasonably look for some historical understanding of this apparent change in moral outlook among the Greeks. Nietzsche, however, does not consider this question, since he does not recognize it. When he talks about the values of the Greek city, he primarily has in mind aristocratic values and respect for the claims of blood and descent. In fact he describes the Greek city as an 'aristocratic commonwealth' (*BGE* 262). His allusions to the history of Classical Greece do not emphasize the events and movements that made Athens less of an aristocratic commonwealth. In the modern world, he thinks, democracy is a natural companion of slave morality. He makes no similar claim about the ancient world.[73]

Though Greek democracy was different in many ways from modern democratic movements, it had some of the features that Nietzsche notices and deplores in modern democracy. It involved 'equal law' for rich and poor alike, and 'equal speaking' on political questions.[74] Plato's Callicles argues that principles prohibiting aggression are invented by the weak people who are aware of their own inferiority and have conspired against the strong. The morality that Socrates defends is the morality that Callicles denounces as the defence erected by the weak. The views described by Callicles, Thrasymachus, and Glaucon might have encouraged Nietzsche to attribute slave morality to the Greeks.

But this is not his view. He gives the Greeks (and to some extent the Nordic tribes) the credit for master morality, and gives the Jews the discredit for slave morality. The Jews, followed by the Christians, invented a world in which the resentment of the inferior people would be gratified and their aspirations would be rewarded. If this invention of another world were reasonable, slave morality would itself be reasonable. For those who believe in this illusory picture of the world, slave morality is subjectively reasonable. In order to make slave morality subjectively reasonable, we have to accept this picture of a world that ensures eventual success for the people who are failures by any worldly standard.

Greek social morality, however, includes some of the characteristic features of slave morality, as Nietzsche understands it. If slave morality emerges in Greek history, it raises a difficulty for Nietzsche. For it seems to have appealed to people who knew nothing of the Jewish and Christian beliefs that support it. Slave morality, therefore, does not need the support of metaphysical and religious beliefs.

But is Nietzsche right at least in his claim that slave morality arises from the resentment of inferior people? The Greek example casts some doubt on this claim too. Some concern

---

[73] Nietzsche's account of the pre-Platonic philosophers in *PTAG* says very little about their interest in justice, cosmic and human. In § 7, he warns against a moralizing interpretation or criticism of Heracleitus: 'Who could possibly demand from such a philosopher an ethic with its necessary imperatives "thou shalt", or, worse yet, accuse Heracleitus of lacking such!' (63). He criticizes the Stoics for their reinterpretation, 'dragging down his basically aesthetic perception of cosmic play to signify a vulgar consideration for the world's useful ends, especially those which benefit the human race. His physics became in their hands a crude optimism . . .' (65)

[74] On 'equal law' (*isonomia*), see Herodotus iii 80.1; on equal speaking (*isêgoria*) see v 78. On characteristics of democracy cf. Thucydides vi 39.

for social morality is quite traditional and long-established in Greek thinking. According to Callicles, the superior person rejects social morality as a mere reflexion of the interests of inferior people. This picture of the superior person is quite similar to Nietzsche's, but it distorts the traditional Greek aristocratic outlook.

One might, indeed, go further and point out that democracy in Athens (and probably in other Greek cities too) would not have worked unless its outlook had been widely accepted among the many aristocrats, such as Cleisthenes, Themistocles, and Pericles, who took a leading part in political life.[75] On these grounds, one might say that the growth of 'democratic' values is not an upsurge in slave morality, so that Nietzsche is right to be silent about slave morality in his account of Greece.

But such a defence of Nietzsche raises a more general doubt about his argument. For if we can explain some features of slave morality through a gradual growth from principles of master morality, we need not derive slave morality from the resentment of inferior people. Hence we cast doubt on Nietzsche's whole historical and psychological explanation of slave morality.

A further difficulty arises for Nietzsche if he admits this agreement between Jewish slave morality and the moral outlook supported by the Greek moral philosophers. Both Jewish and Greek social morality maintain the primacy of the moral virtues, including other-regarding justice, over any of the external goods that would have to be secured at the cost of the moral virtues. If this 'un-Hellenic' outlook is the product of resentment by the masses, why did the attitude of the masses appeal to the Greek philosophers, who do not usually seem especially sympathetic to the masses? Nietzsche suggests that Plato was deceived by the plebeian Socrates;[76] but this does not explain why Aristotle, Epicurus, and the Stoics were deceived in the same way.

He also suggests a different explanation of the Greek philosophical outlook, independent of any speculations about resentment by the masses. He argues that the characteristic errors of Greek moral philosophy are the product of a craving for objectivity and generality. Greek philosophers are not content to regard morality as a sign-language of the affects. They want to prove that justice, say, is objectively better, apart from whether it satisfies the impulses of this particular social group. Hence they have to construct an account of human nature in the abstract, apart from the impulses of particular human beings, to prove that justice is good for an abstract human being, apart from its effects on these particular people with their particular impulses in these particular circumstances. Hence these philosophers try to 'denaturalize'; they try to separate the grounds and justification of morality from the preferences, desires, and historical circumstances in which we find a particular moral outlook accepted.

A craving for objectivity might explain the Greek philosophers' rejection of relativism and nihilism and their acceptance of objectivism. It might also help to explain their acceptance of moralism over immoralism. If we consider what is reasonable for abstract human beings—for human beings from whom we abstract their superior or inferior position in a

---

[75] This role for aristocratic leaders in a democracy is mentioned by the hostile commentator on Athenian democracy known as the 'Old Oligarch', [Xenophon], *Ath. Pol.* 1.3. He makes a Nietzschean remark about the attitude of the poor to musical and gymnastic contests at 1.13.

[76] See *BGE* 212, quoted in §1095.

particular society—we are more likely to recognize some primary place for social morality. A rough explanation of the priority of social morality over self-assertion might point out that the appropriate demands of respect and concern for the interests of others also protect one's self-assertion against the interference of others, and shape the ways one asserts oneself so as to reduce interference with others. If we consider what is reasonable for anyone, and take no account of our actual capacity to impose our will on others, we can see some point in the priority of these provisions of social morality.[77]

In that case, the craving for objectivity seems to explain the rise of social morality without any appeal to masters and slaves.[78] Hence, some features of modern morality apparently do not need to be explained as the products of slavish resentment and Christianity.

1099. Objectivism and Traditional Morality

Suppose, then, that the craving for objectivity might explain both objectivism and moralism. Is this an irrational craving? If it is the source of objectivism and moralism, does it tend to discredit them?

We may come to doubt Nietzsche's view if we follow his lead in attending to Greek political history and experience. One effect—and perhaps one cause—of social and political struggle in the Greek cities was the demand for some argument and justification to support a particular political arrangement.[79] If we regard forms of government and social organization as open to deliberate control and modification, we may try to modify them on the basis of principles that are not merely the creation of a government or a society. If we try to decide whether one social organization is better than another, a rational decision cannot simply appeal to principles or norms that are legitimate only in relation to the old society or the new one. The appropriate principles should transcend both the old and the new, so that they can help us to evaluate them.

This simple demand is deeply embedded in Greek political literature of the fifth century.[80] This demand raises a reasonable question about the rational basis of social and political organization. Athenians who favoured democracy could not appeal to the traditional assumptions underlying social and political life; for these were the assumptions that democracy and equal laws undermined. To free themselves from the influence of custom and convention (nomos), they had to appeal to critical principles that would support a challenge to traditional assumptions.[81] This is a reasonable basis for the search for objective principles. In this light, we can understand the connexion between Socrates' critical attitude

---

[77] This sort of abstraction is elaborately developed in Rawls's Original Position. See §1414.

[78] This argument does not imply that no one can be both an objectivist and an immoralist. It says only that if one has the urge to abstract and to 'denaturalize', one might reasonably be both an objectivist and a moralist. Nietzsche is right, therefore, to suggest that it is not accidental that Plato is both an objectivist and a moralist.

[79] Herodotus iii 80–1 expresses this demand in a rather paradoxical form. He claims to report a debate among leading Persians who argue about whether they should adopt one or another of the forms of government found in Greek cities. They appeal to the moral and political principles underlying each form of government.

[80] See, e.g., Euripides, Supplices 399–455.

[81] Athenian reformers, therefore, would not have been able to defend their position cogently if they had used only the sorts of arguments that Rawls in PL attributes to 'political' philosophy. See §1442.

to tradition and his search for objective principles. He relies on the outlook that produced a major change in Greek political life.[82]

In Nietzsche's view, the desire for argument, rational justification, and objectivity results from the fear of relativity.[83] Hence Plato's ideal city replaces the real city; this is an example of the denaturalization that Nietzsche attributes to the craving for objectivity.[84] Since there is no objectivity in the moralities of the actual world, the philosopher has to devise some other reality to which our moral beliefs may be taken to correspond.

But reflexion on Greek political history casts doubt on Nietzsche's claim that the authentic Hellenic spirit is satisfied with relativity, and that the pursuit of objectivity is the result of some misguided philosophical dream divorced from the social and political context that gives moral concepts and principles their significance. The demand for objectivity and non-relativity is a reasonable presupposition of the rational assessment of social and political institutions and practices. The rational assessment of social and political institutions and practices is a central element in the authentic Hellenic spirit, if anything is.

1100. For and Against Nietzsche

Nietzsche's genealogical account of slave morality suggests that he may overlook an important connexion between Greek political history and Greek moral thought. To understand why Plato's contemporaries believe that the requirements of morality are prior to the demands of self-assertion, we should attend, as Callicles does, to the growth of democratic sentiment. The growth of democracy encouraged the view that the welfare of all one's fellow-citizens mattered in the formulation of moral and political principles. One could not expect to have one's position generally accepted if one represented it simply as a means to the welfare of one particular group. The principles of justice specify who counts, and whose interests are to be considered, in a decision about what to do. In a literal sense, democracy allowed more people's views to count, because their votes were counted.

This outlook pervades the un-democratic moral and political theory of Plato. The ideal constitution in the *Republic* is not a democracy. But it takes for granted the democratic principle that the interests and welfare of all the citizens count equally in the design of the ideal city and in the principles of justice that underlie this design. The influence of this democratic principle on Plato is all the more conspicuous because he does not try to justify it. Still less does he acknowledge his debt to democratic thinking; his account of the democratic outlook never mentions the basic assumption about justice.

---

[82] Hence Grote claims that both the sophists and Socrates engaged in the rational critique of inherited, traditional, moral assumptions—the complex of attitudes that Grote ascribes to 'King Nomos': 'It is against this ancient, established belief, passing for knowledge—communicated by unconscious contagion without any rational process . . . whereby King Nomos governs—that the general mission of Socrates is directed' (Grote, *POCS* i 424).

[83] 'The "philosopher", on the other hand, is the *reaction*: he desires the *old* virtue. He sees the grounds of decay in the decay of institutions, he desires *old* institutions;—he sees the decay in the decay of authority: he seeks new authorities (travels abroad, into foreign literatures, into exotic religions—); he desires the ideal *polis* after the concept "*polis*" has had its day (approximately as the Jews held firm as a "people" after they had fallen into slavery). They are interested in all tyrants: they want to restore virtue by *force majeure*.' (*WP* 427)

[84] *WP* 430 quoted in §1095.

Nietzsche's genealogical approach, therefore, helps us to highlight one central element in the moral outlook of the Greek philosophers. But we need not infer that morality is simply a product of the revolt of the inferior people, with no claim to truth or objectivity beyond their prejudices and resentments. On the contrary, one might argue that the growth of democratic sentiment made it clear that it is arbitrary and unjustified to restrict one's concern to oneself and to people of the same social status, since there are other people who are equally capable of co-operating in common aims and who have a similar claim to consideration.

This basis for a defence of the objectivity of moral principles opposes the nihilist conclusion that Nietzsche draws from his description of slave morality. We may benefit from his advice to trace some aspects of morality to some of their historical embodiments. But we need not endorse his conclusions. His philosophical preconceptions obscure some aspects of the story and distort other aspects. Once we free ourselves of his philosophical preconceptions, and adopt a more open mind towards the possibility of moral objectivity, we may understand Greek political history better than he understands it.

Nietzsche sometimes suggests that careful study of the historical evidence will explode moralists' pretensions to objectivity. It is useful, therefore, to see that closer study of part of his historical case, the part drawn from Greek history, warrants some doubt about his suggestion. Believers in moral facts need not fear Nietzsche's appeal to history.

1101. The Survival of Slave Morality

Nietzsche's genealogy of morals is important for his critique of morality. He believes that the modern morality prevalent among his contemporaries is a hangover from slave morality, and that once we see this, we are more likely to abandon modern morality. But if his genealogy does not fit the history of Greek moral thought, we can also question his claim that the genealogy of modern morality raises doubts about its credibility.

The connexion between modern morality and slave morality is indirect. It is mediated by Christianity, the most complete expression of the Jewish myth that was constructed to satisfy the longings of inferior people. Slave morality makes sense if it is really commanded by the God who redeems sinners, is pleased by meekness, pity, and self-sacrificing love, and will reward them with eternal happiness. The desire to find some vindication for the slavish outlook is part of the reason for the influence of the Jewish spirit in its Christian form. And Nietzsche believes the moral consequences of Christian influence continue to affect modern society. The Renaissance revived the Classical spirit (as Nietzsche understands it), but the Reformation, the Counter-Reformation, and the French Revolution were Jewish reactions.[85] Napoleon tried to overcome the Jewish spirit.

In the modern world, the Jewish spirit is present in movements for democracy and equality, in the praise of unselfishness and pity, in the desire to avoid suffering and inflicting

---

[85] 'With the French Revolution Judaea once again triumphed over the classical ideal, and this time in an even more profound and decisive sense: the last political noblesse in Europe . . . collapsed beneath the popular instincts of ressentiment.' (GM i 16)

pain, in concern for the rights of women, and in similar signs of degeneracy.[86] This egalitarian and universal outlook is the product of the Christian outlook that arose from the resentment of the inferior people.

Nietzsche supposes, however, both that Christianity is false and that his enlightened contemporaries generally believe it to be false. Now he faces the unwelcome fact that most people have not given up belief in modern morality with belief in Christianity. Nietzsche thinks they are mistaken; for he believes that if God is dead, everything is permitted.

Christian dogma is not the only psychological support of modern morality. Since modern morality is the heir to slave morality, it satisfies the same impulses of self-hatred, revenge, resentment, and so on that slave morality satisfied earlier. The modern world contains many inferior people who help modern morality to propagate itself. Its acceptance produces more and more of the inferior, unhealthy people who are subject to the emotions that find satisfaction in slave morality. Nietzsche ought not to be surprised, then, to find that modern morality is more tenacious than the Christian dogma that gives it metaphysical and moral support.

He believes none the less that modern morality is rational only if Christianity is true. Once we abandon Christianity, we have no good reason to care about modern morality.[87] Though our moral convictions may appear self-evident to us, this does not make them reasonable apart from Christian dogma. It may simply show that we take Christian assumptions for granted. If we once identify their source and recognize that they have no other rational basis to sustain them, we will not take them for granted any longer.

Since he tries to refute those who accept Christian morality without Christianity, Nietzsche assumes that believers in modern morality hold their beliefs in a certain spirit—a spirit similar to the one that he ascribes to believers in traditional Greek morality. If we did not care about how our moral feelings arise or about whether they are reasonable, we would not care if we discovered that they are Jewish and Christian remnants. Nietzsche believes that this is not our attitude to our moral feelings; if we hold them as genuinely moral feelings, we hold them in the belief that they rest on something more than our preferences, tastes, or desires.[88] That is why he expects us to be moved by the discovery that they have no rational basis beyond the untenable theological basis.

1102. Genealogy and Justification

If this is how Nietzsche argues against modern morality, he raises a further question. How is his historical and psychological account connected with his objections to modern

---

[86] '*Morality in Europe today is herd animal morality*. . . . Indeed, with the help of a religion which indulged and flattered the most sublime herd-animal desires, we have reached the point where we find even in political and social institutions an ever more visible expression of this morality: the *democratic* movement is the heir of the Christian movement.' (*BGE* 202) 'In no age has the weaker sex been treated with as much respect by men as in ours: that belongs to the democratic inclination and basic taste, just like disrespectfulness for old age. No wonder that this respect is immediately abused.' (*BGE* 239) Shklar, *OV*, ch. 1, discusses with some sympathy the trend that Nietzsche attacks: 'It seems to me that liberal and humane people . . . would, if they were asked to rank the vices, put cruelty first' (44). She discusses Nietzsche at 40–2. Rorty cites her view with approval, *CIS* xv, 146n, and develops this view in chs. 7–8.

[87] Cf. the comment on George Eliot (*TI* ix 5, quoted in §1088).

[88] Nietzsche agrees with Taylor's view in 'Agency' (mentioned in §259) that moral judgments express 'strong evaluations'.

morality? He acknowledges that the genealogical facts (assuming that they are facts) that he presents do not exclude a rational justification of morality. We might also be able to describe the historical, social, and psychological conditions that encourage the growth of scientific inquiry. We might find, for instance, that the competitive aspects of Greek society encouraged independent speculation and inquiry, and that Greek religion, Christian interest in the Bible, and Protestant theology have at different times encouraged scientific interest. We might even discover a pattern suggested by Hephaestus the lame blacksmith; perhaps people who have been disappointed or expect to be disappointed in more 'active' careers tend to take up scientific studies. It would not be obvious, however, that these facts give us good reason to reject the results of modern scientific inquiry; we suppose that it is reasonable apart from these facts about origins.

Is morality any different? Perhaps Nietzsche holds a general relativist or anti-objectivist position that extends his conclusion to science; but genealogical facts alone would not support global relativism or nihilism. If he maintains global relativism or nihilism, Nietzsche needs a general philosophical argument against the possibility of justifying claims to knowledge of objective facts. His arguments support neither a global attack on objectivity nor a local attack on moral objectivity.

Perhaps he just takes for granted the failure of any attempts at justification of morality that have been proposed, and infers that no rational justification is available. But if that is his view, his genealogical inquiry does not settle questions about the justification of morality. It could at most suggest that we need not keep looking for a rational justification of morality, because we can explain its tenacity without assuming its truth. Perhaps Nietzsche believes that Schopenhauer has discredited any Kantian form of justification for morality, and perhaps he assumes that we will abandon the search for justification. But it might be rash either to agree with Schopenhauer or to suppose that a Kantian justification is the only sort worth looking for.

Even if we agreed with Nietzsche in rejecting a Kantian justification for morality, we might not infer that we can give no reasonable grounds for retaining morality after the rejection of Christianity. A Kantian justification, showing that morality rests on grounds that all rational agents have good reason to accept, would answer Nietzsche; but perhaps something weaker would also answer him. Suppose, for instance, that something like Hume's or Hutcheson's view rather than Kant's is true, and that moral principles and attitudes are reasonable not for all rational agents whatever their empirical character or circumstances, but for creatures with desires, inclinations, emotions, needs, interests, and limitations such as ours. This sort of justification may not capture everything that is important and justifiable about morality, but it seems easier to find than a Kantian justification would be. If we could find this limited, Humean justification, would that answer Nietzsche's attempts to undermine the point of view of modern morality?

To show why this might answer Nietzsche, we should recall a difficulty in his position that we noticed earlier.[89] He suggests that the co-operative and other-regarding elements of morality belong to slave morality, and therefore result from resentment. But he also agrees that some co-operative attitudes are essential, or highly desirable, for the stability of any

---

[89] See §§1091–3.

society that embodies any tolerable relations between its members. We do not need any complicated moralizing reasons to see why we might prefer to trust other people rather than coerce them by force or threats. Nietzsche's examples suggest that some obvious features of human society make the co-operative and other-regarding aspects of morality reasonable and appropriate. We can understand these elements without the influence of Christian remnants.

Nietzsche has two sorts of answers to this defence of morality: (1) He can appeal to his general view that morality is simply the sign-language of the affects, and so corresponds to no reality. (2) He can argue that morality has bad effects that should move us to abandon it. He seems to offer both of these replies. We need to examine them both separately and together, to see whether he can consistently accept both positions.[90]

1103. The Subjectivist Critique of Morality

Nietzsche sometimes seems to suggest that the study of actual moral outlooks shows why they cannot claim objective justification. History shows that a moral outlook is the product of particular historical and social conditions and of the desires, impulses, and ideals of a particular social group. An attempt to show that a moral system is rational and justified tries to detach it from the particular aims and impulses that give it its life, and so is bound to fail.

This is why Nietzsche rejects the attempt of philosophers to 'denaturalize' morality. He takes this attempt to be the primary error of the Greek philosophers; anyone who attempts to show that it is rational for human beings in general to care about morality would be making the same error. We might be able to show that it is rational for human beings with these specific impulses to care about morality; Nietzsche explains how this is so in his account of slave morality. But the attempt to abstract from specific aims and impulses and to say what is justified for human beings in general commits the error of denaturalization.

This is a more general form of argument than the attempt to undermine modern morality by appealing to its sources in slave morality and Christianity; for now Nietzsche seeks to explain why any attempt by modern morality to escape from its origins would be misguided. No moral outlook, in Nietzsche's view, can claim any justification that does not depend on the point of view that provides its origin.

Such an argument, however, does not show that every attempt at justification must fail. If Nietzsche has some reason for believing that every attempt at separating a moral outlook from its origin must fail, he still needs some further argument to undermine every attempt at a general justification of morality. For if some needs, aims, and limitations belong to human beings in all or most circumstances, it may be possible and reasonable to abstract from the aims and desires of a particular social group or psychological type. Nietzsche's arguments do not show that every attempt to justify modern morality for human beings in general is bound to fail.

---

[90] Foot, 'Immoralism', argues plausibly that Nietzsche means to reject morality not only in a narrow sense, but also in the broad sense of principles that are concerned impartially with the welfare of persons. The different ways in which Nietzsche does and does not reject morality are explored by Clark, 'Immoralism'.

Suppose, however, that we were convinced by Nietzsche's arguments to show that modern morality is simply an erroneous projection of certain desires on to objective reality. Those arguments also apply to every other moral system—and, more generally, to every system of values. Hence, his view must also be true of master morality or of any other evaluative judgments that he seems to accept in the course of his denunciation of slave morality. He gives no reason for us to suppose that master morality is any less a distortion and misinterpretation of reality than slave morality is. Master morality claims that there is something really right, apart from the preference of the superior people, in their claim to superiority; but there is no reason to suppose that this claim about rightness is anything more than a projection of preferences on to reality.[91]

If, then, we see the implications of Nietzsche's argument, we must apply them to his critique of slave morality. For someone with Nietzsche's preferences, the objections to slave morality may well seem reasonable and justified; but we need not take them seriously if we do not begin by sharing Nietzsche's preference for the type of human being whose development is incompatible with the general acceptance of modern morality. And so we must treat all the evaluative judgments expressed in the course of his genealogical argument as projections of his own preferences.

Can we still argue, though, that the genealogical argument itself is rationally convincing, once its evaluative aspects are put to one side? We might consider offering a genealogical argument, not as a way of attacking slave morality by exposing the deplorable impulses that underlie it, but simply as an argument to undermine any objectivist illusions about any moral outlook—master morality, slave morality, Nietzsche's own moral outlook. Even if the evaluative remarks in Nietzsche's books merely represent his own preferences, the historical and psychological argument itself might seem to have a claim to objective truth and justification.

To draw such a distinction, however, would be to cling to a belief in objectivity that Nietzsche has tried to explode. For he does not believe in any independent area of facts that can be understood without the influence of distorting evaluations. He believes we have no access to facts independent of interpretation, no interpretation independent of evaluation, and no evaluation that does not impose a purely subjective perspective on the facts. This must apply to Nietzsche's historical and psychological inquiries.[92] Hence we should not understand his conclusions about the origins of morality as truths that we have good reason to accept whatever our initial preferences; we should regard them, no less than any other conclusions, as the product of unjustifiable preferences.

It is easy to argue that Nietzsche's historical account of morality is the product of his own evaluative outlook. If we were to analyse his outlook in the way he analyses slave morality and Christianity, we might say that he fears the egalitarian tendencies of modern morality because they threaten privilege and status; that is why he wants to discredit

---

[91] Nehamas, *NLL*, chs. 2 and 7, might be taken to attribute this conclusion to Nietzsche.

[92] One might connect Nietzsche's attitude in *GM* with his remark on one approach to history: 'Occasionally, however, the same life which needs forgetfulness demands the temporary destruction of the forgetfulness; then it is to become clear how unjust is the existence of some thing, a privilege, a caste, a dynasty for examples, how much this thing deserves destruction. Then its past is considered critically, then one puts the knife to the roots, then one cruelly treads all pieties under foot. It is always a dangerous process, namely dangerous for life itself: and men or ages which serve life in this manner of judging and annihilating a past are always dangerous and endangered men and ages.' (*ADHL* §3, p. 22)

modern morality. Since his attitude is fear and hatred rather than reasoned dissent, he wants to undermine modern morality without taking the trouble to examine its rational supports.

No doubt this would be an unfair attack on Nietzsche's own approach to morality. His defenders might fairly argue that if we dismiss his genealogical account as simply the product of his own prejudice and hatred, we will miss much that is true and illuminating. This is a reasonable defence. But we can reasonably accept such a defence only if we reject Nietzsche's general position about facts, interpretations, and values, and we recognize that his arguments do not undermine modern morality. Subjectivists undermine their own position, if they state it generally enough; Nietzsche undermines himself in this way. If he maintained a consistent subjectivist position, he could not claim to give any reasons for people to change their minds if they do not share Nietzsche's initial preferences.

Some of Nietzsche's ostensibly subjectivist remarks are part of his attack on the Kantian concept, as he construes it, of the thing-in-itself. Are his subjectivist remarks limited to an attack on the specifically Kantian conception of objectivity? Or do they attack all belief in objectivity, and do they reflect the conviction that such belief is committed to the extravagances of the Kantian position?

Many have supposed, rightly or wrongly, that one can reject the Kantian thing-in-itself without rejecting robust claims about objectivity. If, for instance, one takes Kant to believe that things-in-themselves do not stand in causal relations, one might quite reasonably believe that there are objective things that stand in causal relations independently of our belief that they stand in causal relations; this belief is not a belief in things-in-themselves, since these are not causally related. We ought not, therefore, to leap from Nietzsche's rejection of the Kantian position to the conclusion that he rejects objectivity altogether.

Still, even if we are cautious in our attitude to Nietzsche's remarks, it is difficult to deny that he takes the flaws in the Kantian conception of a thing-in-itself to raise objections against any belief—not specifically Kantian—in objectivity. After rejecting the Kantian conception (*WP* 558), he seems to reject the existence of things distinct from subjectivity and interpretation.[93]

1104. An Objectivist Critique of Morality

Since subjectivism raises serious difficulties for Nietzsche, it is worth asking how much of his criticism of modern morality is plausible without his subjectivism. Many aspects of his position that appeal to many readers are independent of his broader epistemological and metaphysical position. If we set aside arguments that rest on the impossibility of justifying morality, we can still see some reasons for taking some of Nietzsche's objections to modern morality seriously.

---

[93] 'That things possess a constitution in themselves, quite apart from interpretation and subjectivity, is a quite idle hypothesis: it presupposes that interpretation and subjectivity are not essential, that a thing freed from all relationships would still be a thing.' (*WP* 560) Different views about the implications of Nietzsche's rejection of things in themselves are defended by Schacht, *N* 99–115, 140–69, 187–99; Nehamas, *NLL*, ch. 2; Leiter, *NM* 13–21. These questions about Nietzsche are prominent in Heidegger's discussion; see §1360.

He urges us to consider the costs of morality, and in particular the sorts of activities and traits of character that have to be sacrificed if we follow the requirements of morality. He suggests that sometimes we have to sacrifice results that we ought to regard as more valuable than the goods we secure by following morality.

How serious an objection is this to the moral point of view? We can imagine that on some occasions a trivial violation of morality might lead to some enormous non-moral good. Suppose, for instance, that Michelangelo was able to paint the Sistine ceiling only because he stole his paintbrushes from a shop when he was too poor to pay for them. In this case, we might believe a trivial infraction of a moral rule is reasonable in the light of the enormous gains. If we believe this, we do not necessarily deny the supreme value of morality. Perhaps morality is self-limiting. It need not impose the observance of its smallest provisions in all circumstances; and it may make provision for the achievement of some non-moral goods.[94] In any case an occasional infraction of this sort would be consistent with a degree of commitment to morality beyond anything that Nietzsche endorses.

His more serious criticism alleges that morality discourages the growth of traits and personalities that ought to be encouraged. He objects especially to democratic and egalitarian tendencies in modern morality. Whereas Mill tries to avoid the bad effects of these tendencies by advocating the protection of individuality and of experiments in living, Nietzsche believes that modern morality should be abandoned.[95]

Why does he believe it has these bad effects? Sometimes he seems to suggest that the very tendency to feel sympathy and pity for human suffering is degenerate and disgusting, and that the tendency of morality to impose limits on human self-expression is a reason for suspicion. But he does not show that the tendency to feel sympathy is by itself deplorable or that we lose anything valuable if we restrain our enjoyment of cruelty.[96]

His more plausible criticism notices that modern morality assumes that everyone has equal moral value and therefore regards everyone as a holder of equal moral rights. Hence it tends to be hostile to any grading of people in order of achievement or merit. And since the moral outlook attaches supreme value to morality, and regards moral success as equally open to everyone, it rejects any evaluation that attaches importance to success that are not open equally to everyone. Nietzsche suggests that when people grow up in this atmosphere of morality, they will care most about avoiding suffering, their own and other people's, and will tend to envy those who excel them in any human achievement. If everyone is subject to these pressures, the level of achievement in valuable non-moral activities will decline.

The danger arising from morality, then, is not simply that Michelangelo might have to violate moral rules in order to go on with his painting. The real danger is that a Michelangelo brought up in the democratic atmosphere of modern morality would not even want to excel as a painter at all. He would be a conformist who would avoid any painful exertion leading

---

[94] This conception of morality is opposed to the rigorist position that Lecky attacks at *HEM* i 111–12.

[95] See Mill, §1133.

[96] On the feeling of pity, see Nussbaum, 'Pity', who emphasizes similarities between Nietzsche and Stoicism. Nietzsche's objections are not confined to emotions—the sorts of things that the Stoics regard as *pathê*. They also apply to rational concern for people's undeserved misfortunes—the attitude that the Stoics substitute for non-rational emotion. On Stoic views, §191.

to an achievement that might expose him to the envy of people who have been brought up in modern morality.

Nietzsche's objections describe one possible side-effect of a moral outlook that is exclusively attached to the values of morality. A moral fanatic might react in the way Nietzsche describes. Moreover, the tendencies that Nietzsche takes to underlie slave morality might also encourage moral fanaticism. At this point, his genealogy supports his account of the expected effects of the moral point of view.

But why ought the moral point of view to be blamed for the effects of fanatical attachment to it? If Nietzsche's genealogical account is not the whole truth about the nature and justification of modern morality, the results of fanatical attachment to morality may not reveal any fault in morality. For the moral point of view need not recommend fanatical and one-sided attachment to morality.

We might believe that the moral point of view recommends fanaticism, if we were confused about the sense in which it takes moral values to be supreme. Supremacy might be taken to imply that moral values are so much more important than anything else that on every occasion we ought to try to realize moral value in preference to any other value. If, then, Michelangelo ever had a choice between painting the Sistine ceiling and helping in a soup kitchen (or going shopping for his elderly neighbour, etc.), he should always have made the second choice. If moral values are supreme in this sense, we must always, in every situation, evaluate other people primarily by moral standards.

We need not, however, take this fanatical and exclusive view of the supremacy of moral values. A different claim about supremacy is suggested by Kant's explanation of the end-in-itself as the supreme limiting condition on the pursuit of other ends.[97] According to this claim, a moral principle specifies limits within which it is reasonable to pursue other ends, and it prohibits the pursuit of other ends when they interfere with the appropriate sort of respect for human beings as rational agents.

This conception of morality still contains an egalitarian aspect that is unwelcome to Nietzsche. But it does not imply exclusive or fanatical attachment to morality. Even if morality imposes demands that limit the pursuit of other ends, it need not prevent us from caring about other things, or from pursuing them in preference to moral pursuits on the appropriate occasions. The view that morality imposes limits does not imply that it is infinitely demanding or that it always takes precedence over every other kind of assessment. It allows us to give first prize in a race to the winner, but it prohibits us from giving a prize to the winner and shooting the losers or leaving them to starve.

Indeed, if we examine the human excellences that Nietzsche has in mind, we may want morality to limit other pursuits. For if desirable human traits are various, we cannot expect the same person to cultivate them all. If Nietzsche values artistic creativity and adventurous, innovative, thinking, he can hardly expect that even all forms of desirable intellectual and emotional growth will be found in the same person. The point is even clearer if we consider athletic or executive abilities and talents, to say nothing of those that essentially involve relations with other people.

---

[97] Kant on persons as ends; §921.

If, then, we recognize different types of achievement, we need to ask which of them should take priority in our treatment of people. If any one dimension of excellence takes priority, the cultivation of that dimension of excellence in a particular society threatens those who have less of it, and each dimension seems to struggle for supremacy over the others.

Our initial doubt about Nietzsche's account of master morality seems to apply again here. Nietzsche does not ask how the sorts of values that he describes in enthusiastic but unspecific terms could ever be cultivated or protected in any realistic social context. But if we ask this question, we notice the diversity of achievements that might reasonably be encouraged and rewarded. If we want to protect this diversity, we can see a role for the impartial, egalitarian morality that Nietzsche repudiates.[98]

Despite Nietzsche's disdain for the superficial English utilitarians, Mill's account of the importance of liberty seems to face Nietzsche's questions more constructively than Nietzsche faces them.[99] Mill sees that the development of human talents requires protection for liberty, and requires some moral basis for the protection of liberty. Whether or not utilitarianism is the right moral basis for the protection of liberty, Mill sees the relevance of morality to Nietzsche's questions. Nietzsche's enthusiasm for non-moral values gives him a good reason to support morality.

This might still be a weak case for morality, if Nietzsche had shown that the cultivation of superior (as he supposes) human traits and accomplishments prevents the development of moral attitudes. This would not simply be a conflict in the sorts of actions required by the different outlooks, but a conflict between the traits demanded by morality and the traits demanded by non-moral aims. Even if it would be desirable to cultivate both moral traits and the superior traits, we could not do both, and would have to choose between them.

But Nietzsche's arguments on this point are weaker than his arguments against moral fanaticism. For the cultivation of the egalitarian attitude required for morality does not seem to conflict with the desire to excel in non-moral areas or with the appreciation of people who excel in these areas. Someone who thought there was a conflict would misunderstand the egalitarian aspect of morality. Nietzsche shows at most that moral fanaticism conflicts with the development of higher human talents. His objections overlook the difference between moral fanaticism and the attachment to morality that morality demands.

Nietzsche may have been misled, then, by his genealogy. He does not argue that modern morality rests entirely on the psychological and historical basis he has exposed. For he assumes that the only outlook that could sustain modern morality is the envious, resentful, outlook that he attributes to slave morality. If these (alleged) genealogical facts are not the whole truth about our moral attitudes, Nietzsche's objections to the effects of morality on other values lose force.

1105. Reasonable Aspects of Nietzsche's Criticism

Even if we reject Nietzsche's argument against modern morality and the supremacy of the moral point of view, we ought to notice some instructive points in his criticisms. For even if

---

[98] Cf. Rawls on the diversity of goods, §1436.   [99] Mill on liberty; §1133.

they do not damage the most reasonable conception of morality, they may cast reasonable doubt on some initially plausible views of morality.

Objections to moral fanaticism may suggest some dangers in the separation of morality from self-interest, self-realization, and the other goods that are prominent in eudaemonist conceptions of morality. If we accept Kant's or Schopenhauer's divorce between moral considerations and the claims of self-interest, it is easier to be convinced by Nietzsche's suggestion that the moral point of view ignores the value of non-moral goods. If we understand morality as an indispensable aspect of the life that realizes human nature as a whole, Nietzsche's objections appear less plausible. While anti-eudaemonism about morality plays into Nietzsche's hands, recognition of the connexions between morality and other goods both makes eudaemonism seem more plausible and helps to answer Nietzsche's criticisms.

The defences of morality that we have explored do not preclude conflicts between morality and other values; nor do they show that it could never be reasonable to reject morality for the sake of other goods. It is easier to believe, on Kantian or Hume grounds, that morality is a justifiable and necessary feature of any tolerable human life and human society than to believe that it always overrides every other good. Bradley, for instance, argues that a sound conception of morality recognizes conflicts between morality and higher non-moral goods.[100]

A refutation of Nietzsche does not rule out such conflicts. But they do not justify general scepticism or nihilism about morality. Even if the sort of conflict he describes is possible, the area of such conflict is narrower than he suggests, and it need not undermine commitment to morality.

1106. The Value of Nietzsche's Questions

Even if we do not accept Nietzsche's arguments or conclusions about the nature and value of modern morality, we might believe that his questions and his approach are important and useful. He claims that he takes a more external and critical attitude to morality than his predecessors have taken. He does not take it to be a forgone conclusion that morality is reasonable and justified. He exposes it to the same external criticism that one might apply to any other system of values and rules, and he suggests why one might reasonably doubt whether morality is immune to criticism.

His criticism relies on his psychological and historical genealogy. A genealogical analysis might be true for some aspects of morality, even if it does not fit morality as a whole. The historical and psychological sources of some moral practices and sentiments might explain our tenacity in accepting them. Indeed, the role that morality has played and (in the view of its defenders) ought to play in the lives of individuals and societies makes it probable that some aspects of modern morality will be open to genealogical criticism. We expect moral principles to guide people's lives, and not only their conscious, deliberate, reflective actions. Hence moral principles need to rely on powerful and tenacious sentiments and

---

[100] See Bradley, §1233.

reactions. In some situations, these sentiments may include those that Nietzsche attributes to slave morality. This result should neither surprise nor embarrass a defender of morality. Moreover, if some moral principles are connected with strong and tenacious sentiments, the sentiments may sometimes determine our moral beliefs, even when they outrun their moral justification; for emotions and sentiments may not conform exactly to moral requirements.

Any psychologically and historically plausible account of how morality is taught, passed between generations, and applied to the institutions and structure of a society, has to assume the sorts of psychological mechanisms that leave some moral sentiments open to a Nietzschean genealogical explanation and criticism. But such criticism does not undermine morality. On the contrary, if we see why it may be appropriate in particular cases, we may be less inclined to believe that morality as a whole can be undermined by genealogical argument.

Nietzsche's attempt to take an external point of view towards morality raises questions for any followers. He tries to reject the evaluations of modern morality without rejecting evaluation. His genealogical analysis might be taken to anticipate a historical, anthropological, or psychological analysis of morality from the detached value-free position of observers who look at morality simply as a natural and social phenomenon for study. From this point of view, we might regret that Nietzsche combines his scientific style of analysis with an attack on morality, since he confuses two tasks that ought to be separated.

He raises a difficulty for himself by attempting to undermine modern morality and to advocate other values. For his genealogical critique of morality seems to prove either too little or too much. It proves too little if he does not undermine the possibility of a justification that rests on something other than the psychological and historical sources of morality. It proves too much if he claims to show that morality is necessarily an interpretation of reality with no claim to correspond to reality as it objectively is. For it is not clear how his argument for this conclusion could avoid undermining all evaluative outlooks, including his own.

Some of Nietzsche's criticisms of morality appeal to objectively correct non-moral values, but his criticism of morality seems to allow no such values. A similar difficulty faces Marx, whose genealogy derives morality from the structure of capitalist production. He refrains from moral criticism of morality, but he also seems to leave himself no room for any evaluative criticism beyond the expression of his subjective preferences.

'Scientific' students of morality do not face exactly this dilemma. If they admit that their historical and psychological studies do not necessarily rule out the possibility of rational justification, they may regard Nietzsche's genealogy as a fruitful line of inquiry into morality. If, however, they follow Nietzsche in his rejection of objective values, they have to rely on some distinction between facts and values. Anthropological students of morality have often taken this view.[101]

---

[101] Westermarck, *ER*, chs. 1–2 presents an argument against objective values through a series of brisk objections to different moral theories. He sets out anthropological evidence for the same conclusion at more length in *ODMI*. He agrees with Nietzsche in believing that moral judgments cannot be 'objectively valid' because 'the predicates of all moral judgments, all moral concepts, are ultimately based on emotions, and . . . no objectivity can come from an emotion' (*ER* 60). His attempt to use anthropology against objectivism is contested by Campbell, 'Intuition', and Macbeath, *EL*, esp. ch. 14.

If we claim to be guided by Nietzschean insights on this point, we have to consider the implications of his subjectivism about values. Nietzsche is willing to extend his argument to ostensibly factual disciplines in general; and it may be difficult to accept his position about values and to resist its application to factual inquiries. His arguments and speculations anticipate a long debate about the proper aims of the empirical study of morality and society. He may be thought to have given a powerful stimulus to such study; but he also suggests questions that might be raised about it.

MILL: EARLIER UTILITARIANISM AND ITS CRITICS

1107. Mill, Bentham, and their Predecessors

The most influential and most widely read defence of utilitarianism is Mill's short book *Utilitarianism*, published in 1861. This book is the result of Mill's reflexions on utilitarianism over the previous thirty years.[1] His reflexions make clear his views of the significant developments in controversy about utilitarianism from Bentham onwards. Since the developments explain some features of Mill's statement of utilitarianism, it is useful to survey them before turning to *Utilitarianism* itself. We should look at these developments through Mill's eyes, since his conception of the history of utilitarianism influences his view of what needs to be done. But we should also ask whether he is right about the main philosophical issues involved, and about the merits of the different sides.

Mill agrees with Whewell in tracing the origin of Bentham's utilitarianism to the theological voluntarism of Paley.[2] Whewell discusses theological voluntarism at length, not only because of its influence in contemporary Cambridge moral philosophy, but also because it illustrates the poor state of moral philosophy in England at the end of the 18th century. He applies this judgment not only to theological voluntarist utilitarians such as Paley, but also to the non-theological utilitarianism of Bentham and Godwin. Mill agrees with Whewell's low opinion of theological voluntarism, but he does not agree with Whewell in counting utilitarianism among Paley's errors. He believes that non-theological utilitarianism has turned in the right direction.

---

[1] 'Remarks on Bentham' and 'Blakey' were both published in 1833.

[2] Schneewind, 'Voluntarism', points to Cumberland and Leibniz as sources for utilitarianism, though he recognizes that Leibniz is not a utilitarian. In his view, utilitarianism is originally part of a reply to voluntarism. On Cumberland see §535. I would be more inclined to say that utilitarians and non-utilitarians are found on both sides of the division between voluntarists and naturalists (including rationalists among naturalists for this purpose).

1108. Whewell on Voluntarism and Utilitarianism

According to Whewell, Bentham changes two points in theological utilitarianism: (1) He criticizes standing assumptions about which actions and rules actually maximize utility. (2) He removes the theological element, and so eliminates any reference to divine commands and to divine rewards and punishments. Mill agrees on both points about Bentham.

Bentham is partly right, in Whewell's view, to make the first change. The earlier utilitarians were wrong to take it for granted that conventional morality and established political and social institutions maximized utility. Since they did not develop a systematic account of utility, they did not argue in detail that a specific rule or institution would maximize it.

Bentham's second change, however, leaves a gap in utilitarianism. For the utilitarian faces two questions that allow theological answers: (1) What makes it true that the principles of morality are those that maximize utility? The theological voluntarist answers this metaphysical question by arguing that moral principles express divine commands, and that God, in virtue of his ordered power, commands rules that maximize utility. On this view, moral principles are not essentially those that promote utility. But what is the right non-theological answer to the metaphysical question? Sentimentalists, no less than voluntarists, take morality to be contingently connected with utility, so that true moral principles promote utility only because of the contingent fact that the moral sense approves of utility. If utilitarians do not accept either the voluntarist or the sentimentalist answer, and seek some closer connexion between morality and utility, they need to explain it. (2) What reason have we to observe principles that maximize utility? The theological voluntarist says we have reason to secure the rewards and avoid the punishments that are attached to the observance and violation of God's commands. What is the alternative reason?

These questions expose significant gaps in Bentham's theory. He does not pursue the meta-ethical inquiries that might answer the first question. Moreover, while he believes that morality should aim at the greatest total happiness, he assumes that each person aims at his own happiness; hence he suggests no motivational basis for any attachment to utilitarianism in its own right. Godwin tries to answer these questions; he moves from a rationalist and realist answer to a sentimentalist answer.

Whewell attacks the theological voluntarists' attitude to morality, and especially to the aims and motives of morally virtuous people. When they suggest that only self-interest, narrowly conceived as self-confined pleasure or means to it, can provide a motive or reason for doing something to benefit another, their suggestion is psychologically incredible and morally indefensible. Whewell's objections to these views still stand even though utilitarians abandon theological voluntarism.

Reid expresses the same view, in his comparison of the British theological voluntarists with the French 'Epicureans' (as he describes them). He notices that these two opposed schools agree on some doctrines in the psychology and metaphysics of morals (egoism and voluntarism) and in normative ethics (utilitarianism).[3] Perhaps Reid refers to Scottish

---

[3] 'From what I learn, the French writers have all become rank Epicureans . . . Were it not that extremes sometimes meet, I should think it strange to see your atheist and your high-shod divine contending who should give the blackest representation of human nature. The atheist acts the more consistent part; for surely, such representations tend more to promote atheism than to promote religion.' (Reid, quoted by Kames, *EPMNR* 116).

Calvinists who—like the opponents of Doddridge and Grove—reject accounts of morality relying on natural reason. But his comment applies equally to the English theological voluntarists.

One might argue that the incredible psychological assumptions make voluntarism and French Epicureanism harmless, because such theories will not stop people acting from other motives than calculation of self-confined interest. This reassuring conclusion, however, is open to doubt. For a selfish theory of motives and reasons may discourage the formation and extension of unselfish motives, and may encourage the view that morally desirable motives cannot be distinguished from purely selfish motives. Butler attacks these bad results of the selfish theory. The popularity of theological utilitarianism justifies his complaints.

Mill tries to fill the gaps in non-theological utilitarianism, by answering the questions in meta-ethics and moral psychology that Bentham ignores. Sidgwick is dissatisfied with Mill's answers, and tries a different answer to Whewell's questions. Mill's and Sidgwick's answers should help us to decide whether a utilitarian theory becomes more or less plausible without the theological assumptions of Berkeley or Hutcheson or Paley.

1109. Mill's Version of the History of Utilitarianism

Though Mill agrees with Whewell in tracing Bentham's utilitarianism back to its sources in theological voluntarism, he disagrees about the place of utilitarianism in 18th-century moral philosophy. In contrast to Whewell, Mill agrees with the voluntarists' assumption that the identification of morality with divine commands is the appropriate position for a Christian philosopher to defend. In his view, theological voluntarist utilitarianism was the accepted view among theologically orthodox moralists in the 18th century, and they turned away from utilitarianism only when they saw that it could be used against the established institutions from which they benefited.[4] Mill suggests that the consensus of earlier moral philosophy supports utilitarianism, and that philosophers changed their mind only because they saw the radical political conclusions that more recent utilitarians derived from their outlook.

Throughout his life Mill rejects theological voluntarism. One of his earliest publications in moral philosophy is his critical discussion of Blakey's voluntarism, and in his later work

---

[4] 'The generalities of his [sc. Bentham's] philosophy itself have little or no novelty: to ascribe any to the doctrine that general utility is the foundation of morality, would imply great ignorance of the history of philosophy, of general literature, and of Bentham's own writings. He derived the idea, as he says himself, from Helvetius; and it was the doctrine no less, of the religious philosophers of that age, prior to Reid and Beattie. . . . It was by mere accident that this opinion became connected to Bentham with his peculiar method.' ('Bentham' = $CW \times 87$) 'During the greater part of the eighteenth century, the received opinions in religion and ethics were chiefly attacked, as by Shaftesbury and even by Hume, on the grounds of instinctive feelings of virtue, and the theory of a moral sense or taste. As a consequence of this, the defenders of established opinion, both lay and clerical, commonly professed utilitarianism. . . . This series of writers attained its culmination in Paley . . . But a change ensued, and the utilitarian doctrine, which had been the favourite theory of the defenders of orthodoxy, began to be used by its assailants. In the hands of the French philosophers, and in those of Godwin and of Bentham . . . a moral philosophy founded on utility led to many conclusions very unacceptable to the orthodox. . . . Utility was now abjured as a deadly heresy, and the doctrine of a priori or self-evident morality, an end in itself, independent of all consequences, became the orthodox theory. . . . the defenders of orthodoxy were insensibly led to seek their system where it exists in the most elaborate shape—in the German metaphysicians.' ('Whewell' = $CW \times 170$)

he still opposes it as a perversion of morality.[5] On this point, he takes himself to oppose the consensus of orthodox Christian philosophers. But he believes that his utilitarianism simply continues the consensus of the orthodox.

Some of the omissions in Mill's historical sketch make it misleading. Some especially relevant facts that Mill does not mention are these: (1) He assumes that utilitarians and believers in a moral sense form two opposed schools, and he does not say that Hutcheson and Hume accept both a moral sense and utilitarianism.[6] (2) Some rationalists—notably Balguy—are also sympathetic to utilitarianism, contrary to Mill's suggestion that one must choose between utilitarianism and 'a priori or self-evident morality'. (3) Butler is an important orthodox Christian philosopher, whom the 'moral-sense school' recognizes as an authority, but who rejects utilitarianism.[7] (4) Clarke and Price are both rationalists, and both (in the respects that concern Mill) orthodox Christian thinkers. Neither is a utilitarian, and neither believes in a moral sense. Price argues at length against both utilitarianism and sentimentalism. (5) Mill recognizes that Reid is an orthodox Christian moralist who rejects utilitarianism. But Mill's social and political explanation of opposition to utilitarianism does not fit Reid, who criticized utilitarianism before the political upheavals of 1789 and later. Many of Reid's arguments follow Price and Butler. (6) The suggestion that critics of the moral sense were utilitarians and political conservatives hardly fits Price. In Burke's view, Price's rationalism is the pernicious view of a priori philosophers of abstract rights, who want to introduce French philosophy and French revolutionary practice into England.[8]

---

[5] Mill and voluntarism; §1140.

[6] An especially striking example of failure to grasp the compatibility of utilitarianism with belief in a moral sense is offered by James Mill, who attacks Mackintosh's claim that Paley was wrong to see any conflict between belief in a moral sense and utilitarianism: 'There is not one of the theories of morals of which Sir James has a tolerable comprehension. The affirmation of a moral sense is an affirmation with respect to the act, as well as with respect to the mind of the person who thinks of the act. And its affirmation with respect to the act is a positive denial of the doctrine of utility. It affirms that moral distinctions need a particular faculty to discern them. Utility and its elements, however, need no particular faculty to discern them; the common feelings, and common understanding suffice. Paley, therefore, was right in considering the affirmation of a moral sense as inconsistent with the position that utility is the moral quality of actions.' (James Mill, FM 11) This claim about the moral sense ignores the role of the moral sense in approval, and it fails to explain how Hutcheson and Hume could be utilitarians. But it may help to explain J.S. Mill's strange classification of moral theories.

[7] 'Hear Bishop Butler, the oracle of the moral-sense school...' ('Sedgwick' = CW x 64) This connexion between Butler and the moral-sense school may reflect James Mill's tediously polemical treatment of Mackintosh. Mackintosh praises Butler, and James Mill castigates both the views that Mackintosh attributes to Butler and the views of Butler himself. He complains that Mackintosh does not justify his praise of Butler: '...if there be only two questions in ethical philosophy, viz., what is the moral faculty, and what the moral quality in actions; and if Butler has answered neither; what has he done? And where is the sense of Sir James's panegyrics, upon a man who has done nothing?...That which he [sc. Butler] attempted, we have seen that he did nothing towards accomplishing.' (FM 75)

[8] Price's political views; §822. On Burke and Price see Thomas, HM, ch. 15, esp. 328–9: 'Price was not prepared to identify respect for the moral order with reverence for established institutions, neither was he prepared to find that all our prejudices are imbued with practical wisdom. But above all he would not allow that the principles which should inspire political judgment were wholly embodied in existing institutions or that the criteria of rationality in politics are wholly contained within actual practice.' Burke, RRF 19 responds to Price's sermon, 'On the love of one's country', which he describes as a revolutionary revival of 17th-century Puritanism: 'I looked on that sermon as the public declaration of a man much connected with literary caballers and intriguing philosophers; with political theologians and theological politicians, both at home and abroad. I know they set him up as a sort of oracle; because, with the best intentions in the world, he naturally philippizes, and chants his prophetic song in exact unison with their designs.' Burke comments sceptically on Price's appeal to rights: 'These metaphysic rights entering into common life, like rays of light which pierce into a dense medium, are, by the laws of nature, refracted from their straight line. Indeed in the gross and complicated mass of human passions and concerns, the primitive rights of men undergo such a variety of refractions and reflections, that it becomes absurd to talk of them as if they continued in the simplicity of their original direction.' (61)

But Price's arguments for political reform do not persuade utilitarians. On the contrary, Bentham's attitude to Price's arguments is similar to Burke's; he regards Price's arguments from rationalist moral realism to political liberalism as worthless applications of a discredited metaphysics. His thoughtless dismissal of Price may have contributed to Mill's neglect of Price's political theory.[9]

Mill's account of the previous century in moral philosophy, therefore, finds no appropriate place for Clarke, Balguy, Butler, or Price. It distorts the philosophical debates and options recognized among his predecessors. It exaggerates the degree of consensus in favour of utilitarianism. Whewell claims to continue the argument of Butler and Price, but Mill simply excludes them from his historical generalizations.

The claim that theological utilitarianism was the predominant 18th-century English view also seems to influence Mill's judgment that Christian philosophers have been obscure or unconcerned about the relation between divine commands and moral rightness. He implies that Paley's conception of morality as essentially divine commands was simply the prevalent contemporary view that a Christian thinker would not have thought to question.[10] At first, Mill confines his claim to 'most English thinkers' of the period. But to explain their alleged unwillingness to raise the question about morality and the divine will, he maintains that no Christian of that age would have raised the question. This generalization ignores the rejection of theological voluntarism about morality by Cudworth, Clarke, Balguy, Butler, Hutcheson, and Price—not to mention the arguments of Suarez, Grotius, and Leibniz. The position that Mill thinks Christians of the previous century would not have questioned is the position that many Christian thinkers attributed to Hobbes in order to repudiate it.

Mill's treatment of Paley as the typical English Christian moralist of his century is so mistaken that it needs some special explanation. Perhaps Mill is misled by his conviction that utilitarianism is the only rational option for a philosopher who is not prejudiced by the desire to defend the Christian establishment and the social and political establishment that is inter-dependent with it. Previous philosophers have recognized the truth of utilitarianism within the theological voluntarist framework they took for granted, and now they have no reason to hold on to the theological framework against utilitarianism.

Mill's historical sketch results from the conviction that he shares with Bentham, that no reasonable and unprejudiced thinker can reject utilitarianism. Because of this conviction, Bentham does not argue in detail against other positions; he contents himself with mockery of them.[11] Mill shares Bentham's conviction, but he expresses the same conviction in more

---

[9] On the attitude of Bentham and his followers to Price's moral and political views, see Miller, *DCG* 373–99. At 393–5, he discusses Lind, *TLDP*, begun in collaboration with Bentham. Lind attacks Price's conception of liberty as something more than the absence of external interference; he sees in Price's political doctrines the same metaphysical outlook that Bentham dismisses so quickly. He often refers favourably to Bentham, and cites him (16–17) for the purely negative account of freedom that Lind maintains against Price. He addresses Price: 'The truth is, Sir, you set out with a capital mistake. It is a capital mistake to suppose liberty to be anything positive . . .' (14)

[10] 'In the minds of most English thinkers down to the middle of the last century, the idea of duty, and that of obedience to God, were so indissolubly united, as to be inseparable even in thought: and when we consider how in those days religious motives and ideas stood in the front of all speculations, it is not wonderful that religion should have been thought to constitute the "essence" of all obligations to which it annexed its "sanction". To have inquired, Why am I bound to obey God's will? would, to a Christian of that age, have appeared irreverent.' ('Sedgwick' = *CW* x 53)

[11] See the passage from Bentham, *PML* 2.14 = p. 25, that Mill quotes at length with qualified approval, in 'Bentham' = *CW* x 85–6, and 'Whewell' = *CW* x 177–8. 'The various systems that have been formed concerning the standard of

conciliatory terms. Instead of mocking other views, he takes it for granted that the rational and progressive elements in other outlooks agree with the utilitarian position. Hence his history of earlier moral philosophy takes no serious account of efforts to develop a rational and progressive account of morality that diverges from utilitarianism.

1110. Bentham's Contributions

Bentham is neither original nor unusual in accepting utilitarianism. Indeed, in Mill's view, Bentham is not a significant moral philosopher. He is a utilitarian pioneer because of his jurisprudence, his practical ethics, and his political theory, not in his reflexions on the principles of moral philosophy. Bentham argues that if we consider the effects of existing institutions from a utilitarian point of view, and we do not simply assume that their mere existence justifies them, we can see that they often have worse effects than some alternative institutions would have. This comparison of effects often gives a reason for trying to reform existing institutions. The effects in question involve benefits and harms to people whose interests seem obviously relevant to the justification of the institutions.

Bentham goes beyond the older utilitarians because he asks these new questions. Paley uses hedonistic utilitarianism to explain what is good about existing rules and institutions, whereas Bentham uses it to test and to criticize them. According to Mill, Bentham's relentless utilitarian examination of existing institutions is his great advance in utilitarian thinking.

The fact that Paley and Bentham draw opposite practical conclusions from similar philosophical premises might make us wonder whether utilitarianism is an important part of Bentham's position. To show that it is, one might argue that Bentham applies the utilitarian criterion honestly, without the prejudices that warp Paley's judgments. According to this argument, the utilitarian principle, together with an unprejudiced view of the relevant empirical information, supports Bentham's conclusions. Hence Bentham shows that the

right and wrong, may all be reduced to the principle of sympathy and antipathy. One account may serve for all of them. They consist, all of them, in so many contrivances for avoiding the obligation of appealing to any external standard, and for prevailing upon the reader to accept of the author's sentiment or opinion as a reason for itself. . . . 1. One man (Lord Shaftesbury, Hutchinson, Hume, etc.) says, he has a thing made on purpose to tell him what is right and what is wrong, and that it is called a moral sense; and then he goes to work at his ease, and says, such a thing is right, and such a thing is wrong—why? "because my moral sense tells me it is." 2. Another man (Dr Beattie) comes and alters the phrase; leaving out moral and putting in common in the room of it. He then tells you, that his common sense teaches him what is right and wrong, as much as the other's moral sense did: . . . the sense of those, whose sense is not the same as the author's, being struck out of the account as not worth taking. . . . 3. Another man (Dr Price) comes, and says, that as to a moral sense indeed, he cannot find that he has any such thing; that, however, he has an understanding which will do quite as well. This understanding, he says, is the standard of right and wrong: it tells him so and so. All good and wise men understand as he does: if other men's understandings differ in any point from his, so much the worse for them; it is a sure sign they are either defective or corrupt.

4. Another man says, that there is an eternal and immutable rule of right; that that rule of right dictates so and so; and then he begins giving you his sentiments upon anything that comes uppermost; and these sentiments (you are to take for granted) are so many branches of the eternal rule of right. 5. Another man (Dr Clark), or perhaps the same man (it's no matter), says, that there are certain practices conformable, and others repugnant, to the fitness of things; and then he tells you, at his leisure, what practices are conformable and what repugnant; just as he happens to like a practice or dislike it. 6. A great multitude of people are continually talking of the law of nature . . . 7. Instead of the phrase, Law of Nature, you have sometimes, Law of Reason, Right Reason, Natural Justice, Natural Equity, Good Order. Any of these will do equally well. . . . On most occasions, however, it will be better to say *utility; utility* is clearer, as referring more explicitly to pain and pleasure.'

utilitarian standard is important and practically applicable, and that it leads to radical political and legal conclusions.

Alternatively, one might argue that the utilitarian principle supports Bentham no more than it supports Paley. To reach Bentham's conclusions, perhaps we must not only free ourselves from Paley's prejudiced view of the relevant empirical information, but also appeal to moral principles that are independent of the utilitarian principle.[12] In that case, the dispute between Bentham and Paley is not simply empirical, but also moral.

Our view on these questions about Paley and Bentham will help to decide whether sympathy with Bentham's practical conclusions should incline us to his utilitarianism. Mill seems to suppose that Bentham traces the empirical consequences of the principle of utility. But he qualifies this view. The qualifications appear in his earlier works, and it will be relevant to consider whether they fit his position in *Utilitarianism*.

1111. Is the Principle of Utility Practically Unimportant?

In some places, Mill argues that our basic moral principle does not matter very much for most practical purposes. In his early review of Blakey, he attacks theological voluntarism, but suggests that other disputes about basic principles are less important than they are sometimes taken to be.[13] Bentham's utilitarianism is not very important for his practical conclusions; it is more important to agree on the more specific principles that Bacon calls 'intermediate axioms' ('Bentham', 111).[14]

Appeal to the principle of utility is often both unnecessary and unwise, because it may mislead us about the consequences that are most relevant to the evaluation of an action. If we try to apply the principle directly, we will tend to confine ourselves to the most obvious consequences of individual actions, which may not be the most important consequences.[15]

---

[12] Stephen describes different sides of Bentham in terms somewhat similar to Mill's: 'The relation, indeed, of Bentham's ethical doctrines to Paley's may be expressed by saying that Bentham is Paley without a belief in hell-fire. But Bentham, in another sense, is Paley plus a profound faith in himself, and an equally profound respect for realities. ... Bentham transformed the doctrine of utility from the sphere of speculation into that of immediate legislation.' (*ET* ii 125) Stephen's reference to 'realities' and to a 'transformation' of the doctrine of utility does not make it clear how far a doctrine of utility, as Bentham understands utility, actually supports Bentham's political and legislative views.

[13] 'But with regard to most of the other conflicting opinions respecting the primary grounds of moral obligation, it appears to us that a degree of importance is often attached to them, more than commensurate to the influence they really exercise for good or for evil. ... The real character of any man's ethical system depends not on his first and fundamental principle, which is of necessity so general as to be rarely susceptible of an immediate application to practice; but upon the nature of those secondary and intermediate maxims, vera illa et media axiomata, in which, as Bacon observes, real wisdom resides.' ('Blakey' = *CW* x 29)

[14] '... while, under proper explanations, we entirely agree with Bentham in his principle, we do not hold with him that all right thinking on the details of morals depends on its express assertion. We think utility, or happiness, much too complex and indefinite an end to be sought except through the medium of various secondary ends, concerning which there may be, and often is, agreement among persons who differ in their ultimate standard; and about which there does in fact prevail a much greater unanimity among thinking persons, than might be supposed from their diametrical divergence on the great questions of moral metaphysics.' ('Bentham' = *CW* x 110)

[15] '... the attempt to make the bearings of actions upon their ultimate end more evident than they can be made by referring them to the intermediate ends, and to estimate their value by a direct reference to human happiness, generally terminates in attaching most importance, not to those effects which are really the greatest, but to those which can most easily be pointed to and individually identified.' ('Bentham', 111) 'Without such middle principles, an universal principle, either in science or morals, serves for little but a thesaurus of commonplaces for the discussion of questions, instead of a means of deciding them.' ('Whewell', 173)

Though Bentham supposed that the principle of utility was the basis for discovery of practical principles, Mill disagrees, since he believes happiness is 'too complex and indefinite' (110).

According to this judgment on Bentham, Mill seems to concede that either Paley's or Bentham's view might equally be inferred from the principle of utility, but he prefers Bentham's view because Bentham grasps the appropriate intermediate principles. Without these principles, we cannot find the consequences that matter most in application of the principle of utility. While the principle of utility is worth arguing about, as a principle for systematizing moral thought (111), it is not the most important aspect of Bentham's position. Mill seems to suggest that Bentham could easily have accepted the same intermediate axioms on a non-utilitarian basis, without reducing the practical value of his thought.

This is only one side of Mill's view, however. He also asserts that we need the principle of utility to resolve conflicts between intermediate principles.[16] Though we tend to exaggerate the frequency of these conflicts, they arise, and we need a first principle to resolve them. This practical role presupposes a clear grasp of the content and the implications of the first principle without reliance on secondary principles.[17]

The principle of utility resolves conflicts between secondary principles because it is their basis. Bentham deduces his secondary principles from utility. Paley treats utility as a mere device for justifying existing practices, but Bentham uses it as an effective means of moral criticism.[18] Theological moralists such as Adam Sedgwick unfairly dismiss utilitarianism by attacking Paley's version of it, but they do not see that Bentham shows how utilitarianism can make a practical difference.[19] Mill defends this practical role for the utilitarian principle in his discussion of Whewell (1852). He alters his earlier essay on Bentham (1838) to acknowledge this role.

Does Mill adequately revise his earlier views about the practical unimportance of the principle of utility in Bentham's position? In both earlier and later essays, he takes secondary principles to be important. In the later essay, he claims that Bentham has deduced them

[16] 'It is when two or more of these secondary principles conflict, that a direct appeal to some first principle becomes necessary; and then commences the practical importance of the utilitarian controversy; which is, in other respects, a question of arrangement and logical subordination rather than of practice; important principally in a purely scientific point of view, for the sake of the systematic unity and coherency of ethical philosophy.' ('Bentham', 111) Here Mill alters his previous opinion. Instead of the passage up to 'a question of arrangement', the first version of his essay reads simply, 'We consider, therefore the utilitarian controversy as . . .' (111 n); it is a theoretical issue without practical significance (even though Bentham thought it had practical significance). The alteration appeared in the reprint of 'Bentham' in *DD* (1st edn., 1859).

[17] 'When disputes arise as to any of the secondary maxims, they can be decided, it is true, only by an appeal to first principles; but the necessity of this appeal may be avoided far oftener than is commonly believed; it is surprising how few, in comparison, of the disputed questions of practical morals, require for their determination any premises but such as are common to all philosophic sects.' ('Blakey', 29)

[18] 'With him, the first use to be made of his ultimate principle, was to erect on it, as a foundation, secondary or middle principles, capable of serving as premises for a body of ethical doctrine not derived from existing opinions, but fitted to be their test. . . . he was the first who, keeping clear of the direct and indirect influences of all doctrines inconsistent with it, deduced a set of subordinate generalities from utility alone, and by these consistently tested all particular questions. This great service, previously to which a scientific doctrine of ethics on the foundation of utility was impossible, has been performed by Bentham . . .' ('Whewell', 173) 'Utility, as a standard, is capable of being carried out singly and consistently; a moralist can deduce from it his whole system of ethics, without calling to his assistance any foreign principle. It is not so with one who relies on moral intuitions . . .' (194)

[19] See 'Sedgwick' = *CW* × 52–3.

from the principle of utility without any 'foreign' principle. If this claim about deduction is right, how can the utilitarian principle be practically unimportant?[20]

One might argue, from Mill's earlier point of view, that the principle of utility leads Bentham to accept secondary principles that one might also reasonably accept on non-utilitarian grounds. But, by Mill's admission, it does not lead Bentham to agree with Paley about practical consequences. Must it not lead him, then, to disagree with Paley about secondary principles? What, then, becomes of Mill's claim that secondary principles are generally agreed between utilitarians and non-utilitarians? Should we suppose that Paley is an isolated exception and that most people agree with Bentham's secondary principles? If they do, is it not a remarkable coincidence that utilitarians and non-utilitarians agree on practical principles, disagreeing only on whether they are primary or secondary? Such a coincidence needs some explanation.

1112. How is the Principle of Utility Practically Important?

Mill's most plausible explanation of the usefulness of the utilitarian principle assumes that non-utilitarians implicitly approach utilitarianism. He believes that 'thinking persons' (110) agree on secondary principles, because their moral reasoning appeals to consequences, no matter what their moral theory may be. According to Mill, worthwhile moral reasoning is teleological and consequentialist.[21] He even suggests that it is utilitarian, whatever a theorist may say about moral principles.[22] Mill refers to Kant to illustrate this point (U1.4). He says the same about Whewell. In his view, utilitarians agree with others on many secondary principles, but also improve ordinary moral thinking; they apply systematically and explicitly the consequentialist standard that thinking persons already apply unsystematically and implicitly.

But this defence of the utilitarian principle still seems to conflict with Mill's remarks on Bentham. If thinking persons all rely on utility, and if Bentham systematically deduces his practical recommendations from the principle of utility, the principle is practically important. How, then, can we appreciate Bentham's practical recommendations without attention to the principle of utility or to Bentham's understanding of it? Mill urges that happiness is 'much too complex and indefinite an end' to be pursued except through secondary ends

---

[20] Mill's reflexions on Bentham are discussed by Berger, *HJF*, ch. 3.

[21] 'Whether happiness be or be not the end to which morality be referred—that it be referred to an *end* of some sort, and not left to the dominion of vague feeling or inexplicable internal conviction, that it be made a matter of reason and calculation, and not merely of sentiment, is essential to the very idea of moral philosophy; is, in fact, what renders argument or discussion on moral questions possible. That the morality of actions depends on the consequences which they tend to produce, is the doctrine of rational persons of all schools; that the good or evil of those consequences is measured solely by pleasure or pain, is all of the doctrine of the school of utility, which is peculiar to it.' ('Bentham' = *CW* x 111)

[22] '. . . as men's sentiments, both of favour and of aversion, are greatly influenced by what they suppose to be the effects of things upon their happiness, the principle of utility, or as Bentham latterly called it, the greatest happiness principle, has had a large share in forming the moral doctrines even of those who most scornfully reject its authority. Nor is there any school of thought which refuses to admit that the influence of actions on happiness is a most material and even predominant consideration in many of the details of morals, however unwilling to acknowledge it as the fundamental principle of morality, and the source of moral obligation.' (*U* 1.4)

(110). But it cannot be too complex and indefinite to allow the discovery of secondary ends; for Mill claims that it allows the deduction of secondary ends without reliance on any foreign principle.

A defender of Bentham might argue that Bentham has a true grasp of the principle of utility and its implications, and that he exhibits these implications in the secondary principles he favours. Mill, however, suggests that Bentham does not offer a reliable account of the content of the principle of utility.[23] Bentham's explicit consequentialism is the most important part of his method. In being explicit, it differs from the consequentialism that is practised by all thinking persons when they think seriously about morality. According to Mill, Bentham also has some true views about the character of utility. But Mill does not wholly endorse Bentham's conception of utility. He attaches greater value to Bentham's explicit consequentialism than to his interpretation of utility or to his view of all its implications. Bentham's conception of utility is true as far as it goes, but it is incomplete, so that his practical recommendations include only some of the implications of the principle of utility.

Mill's measured and qualified praise of Bentham opposes the critics who take Bentham both to be basically misguided and to state utilitarianism accurately. He accepts, to some degree, some of the objections to Bentham, but he denies that the errors of Bentham—or of Paley—are inevitable utilitarian errors.

Bentham does not share Mill's views about the degree of consensus on secondary principles. He supposes that direct appeal to the principle of utility allows us to criticize common moral maxims, and to find the actions that maximize utility. Mill agrees with Bentham in so far as Bentham applies the principle of utility to laws and institutions, and Mill believes we will support Bentham's recommendations if we reason from generally accepted secondary principles. But he does not discuss all the places where Bentham seems to depart from accepted secondary principles. If Bentham is wrong in these places, Mill needs to say whether Bentham is wrong about the interpretation of the principle of utility, or about the implications of the principle (as he interprets it) for practice.

1113. Objections to Bentham

In these ways, Mill tries to isolate the real importance of Bentham's views from Bentham's formulation of utilitarianism. He objects to Bentham's utilitarianism most forcefully in his early, anonymous, essay 'Remarks on Bentham's Philosophy' (*CW* x 5–18), which he never reprinted. He later came to believe that the negative aspects of his early essays on Bentham had been unfortunate at the time, because they had tended to discredit Bentham before the salutary elements in his position had been appreciated.[24] His comments on the later

---

[23] 'In so far as Bentham's adoption of the principle of utility induced him to fix his attention upon the consequences of actions as the consideration determining their morality, so far he was indisputably in the right path, though to go far in it without wandering, there was needed a greater knowledge of the formation of character, and of the consequences of actions upon the agent's own frame of mind, than Bentham possessed.' ('Bentham', 111–12)

[24] 'The substance of this criticism [sc. in the essay 'Bentham'] I still think perfectly just; but I have sometimes doubted whether it was right to publish it at that time. I have often felt that Bentham's philosophy, as an instrument of progress, has been to some extent discredited before it had done its work, and that to lend a hand towards lowering its reputation was doing more harm than service to improvement. Now, however, when a counter-action appears to

essay 'Bentham' (1838) apply equally to the earlier 'Remarks' (1833), whose anonymity encouraged frankness.[25]

Mill points out that Bentham neither argues for the principle of utility nor defends it against other moral principles; he does not go into these questions, which Mill calls 'metaphysical' issues about the foundations of morality ('Remarks', 5). Bentham accepts questionable parts of Paley's account of moral properties, and does not ask what account needs to be given to replace Paley's theological voluntarism. Mill, following many others, attacks a theological voluntarist account of moral properties on the ground that they reduce such claims as 'What God wills is right' to boring tautologies such as 'What God wills is what God wills' ('Blakey', 27). Mill does not use this familiar argument explicitly against Paley, but he sees that Paley holds the theological voluntarist view ('Sedgwick', 53–4) that Mill attacks. Mill's criticisms assume that the theological voluntarist offers an account of moral concepts; though this assumption is not true of all voluntarist theories, it is true of Paley's theory.

On this point, Bentham follows Paley, except that he substitutes maximum pleasure for the will of God. Hence, he not only defends pure quantitative hedonism as an account of value, but also claims that it also provides an account of moral concepts. In his view, the meaning of 'good' and 'ought' are to be given in hedonist terms. Indeed, he sometimes advocates the replacement of 'ought' and related terms by commands and predictions about production of pleasure.[26]

These claims seem to damage Bentham's position. If we assert that it is right or good to promote pleasure and reduce suffering, we do not seem to say that the promotion of pleasure promotes pleasure. Bentham seems to make his main moral position unintelligible when he analyses the concept of rightness as tendency to promote pleasure. Whewell urges this criticism against Bentham no less than against Paley.[27]

But even if Bentham is wrong to treat hedonism as a correct account of moral concepts, he might still be right to maintain a hedonist account of moral properties, or of good-making or right-making properties.[28] To defend hedonist and utilitarian answers to these questions, we might claim that the concept of the right imposes constraints on rightness that are best satisfied by maximum utility. But this claim requires argument that Bentham does not provide. This aspect of Bentham illustrates Mill's objection that Bentham does not argue appropriately for the principle of utility. Surprisingly, however, Mill does not attack this aspect of Bentham's meta-ethics, even though Whewell points out the parallel with an aspect of theological voluntarism that Mill attacks.

Though Mill overlooks this question about meta-ethics, he raises legitimate questions about Bentham's moral epistemology. He argues that Bentham has been unfair to believers in a moral sense, both 'the Reid and Stewart school' and 'the German metaphysicians'. These opponents argue that moral judgments distinct from judgments about utility are no

---

be setting in towards what is good in Benthamism, I can look with more satisfaction on this criticism of its defects...' (*Autobiography* = *CW* i, 152–3)

[25] Though he tells some of his correspondents that he is the author of the essay, he tells one of them: 'It is not, and must not be, known to be mine' (to Nichol, 14–10–34 = *CW* xii 236; cf. 152, 172). See 'Textual introduction' to *CW* x, p. cxvii.

[26] Whewell, *LHMPE* 227 quoting Bentham, *Deontology*, i 31–2 (Bowring) = 250–1 (Goldworth).

[27] Whewell, *LHMPE* 208–9.   [28] See Sidgwick, §1155; Ross, §1282.

less natural than utilitarian judgments.[29] Bentham asserts that all non-utilitarian standards are simply a cloak for one's own prejudices. But he needs some argument to show that this is true of the other standards, and not true of the principle of utility. We need some reason to prefer the utilitarian principle over other contenders.

Mill especially objects to Bentham's view of the consequences that we should consider in the evaluation of actions. Bentham considers only the 'specific consequences'—the causal results for the agent or for others that can be traced to this or that particular action. He does not attend sufficiently, according to Mill, to consequences that are not peculiar to a particular action, but result from the cumulative effect of that action combined with other actions of the same type.

Among these non-specific consequences, Mill especially emphasizes effects of actions on the character of agents.[30] If A would rather watch this television programme than help B, but C has nothing better to do tonight than help B, one might argue that it is better, on utilitarian grounds, if C helps B than if A helps B. But A's readiness to prefer his own amusement over helping another person may tend—if the same pattern is repeated often enough—to produce a callous and selfish outlook in A, and (if enough people imitate A) in others. Consideration of cumulative consequences not assignable to particular actions complicates the assessment of consequences, but it is indispensable for a just estimate of overall utility.

1114. Bentham on Pleasure and Motivation

According to Mill, Bentham's conception of human motives is as limited as his judgment of consequences. Bentham does not (in Mill's view) deny the possibility of unselfish desires, but he believes that selfish motives always predominate over unselfish.[31] Individuals, therefore, will reliably act in ways that maximize happiness only if artificial sanctions make the same actions promote both one's own happiness and universal happiness. Bentham, James Mill, and George Grote[32] all accept this conclusion. The younger Mill rejects it as a serious mistake that utilitarians, of all people, ought to avoid.[33] He believes it is self-defeating for utilitarians

---

[29] 'The answer of such persons to Mr Bentham would be . . . that . . . our moral sentiments . . . are as much part of the original constitution of man's nature as the desire of happiness and the fear of suffering: That those sentiments do not indeed attach themselves to the same action under all circumstances, but neither do they, in attaching themselves to actions, follow the law of utility, but certain other general laws, which are the same in all mankind naturally. . . . No proof indeed can be given that we ought to abide by these laws; but neither can any proof be given, that we ought to regulate our conduct by utility. All that can be said is, that the pursuit of happiness is natural to us; and so, it is contended, is the reverence for, and the inclination to square our actions by, certain general laws of morality.' ('Bentham' = CW × 6)

[30] 'It is not considered (at least, not habitually considered), whether the act or habit in question, though not in itself necessarily pernicious, may not form part of a *character* essentially pernicious, or at least essentially deficient in some quality eminently conducive to the "greatest happiness".' ('Remarks on Bentham'= CW × 8)

[31] Bentham's views on the connexion between individual and universal happiness, and on duty and interest, are discussed in more detail by Lyons, *IG*, esp. ch. 4, and by Harrison, *B*, chs. 5–7. Harrison discusses Lyons at 267–71.

[32] James Mill, *FM*, section 4, objects to Mackintosh's attack on Bentham and on himself for their neglect of unselfish motives, but he does not oppose Bentham on the point on which J. S. Mill opposes him. Grote takes a similar view in *FES*, Essay 4.

[33] 'It is difficult to form the conception of a tendency more inconsistent with all rational hope of good for the human species, than that which must be impressed by such doctrines, upon any mind in which they find acceptance. . . . No

to deny the influence of motives whose influence is a prerequisite for any significant progress towards the end that utilitarians pursue.

Bentham not only underestimates the significance of unselfish motives, but also fails to appreciate their character.[34] Hence he overlooks the aspect of morality that consists in 'self-education; the training, by the human being himself, of his affections and will' (98). Bentham's limited view reflects his general attitude to human aims and aspirations. He not only supposes that people are moved predominantly by the selfish pursuit of their own pleasure, but he also has a narrow view of the possible sources of pleasure and of their value.[35] He attends exclusively to the moral aspect of actions, and their contribution to utility, but he neglects their possible appeal to our aesthetic and sympathetic sentiments apart from their utility. His indifference to these features of actions helps to explain his indifference to the exercise of the imagination in poetry (113).[36]

Mill seems to agree with critics who believe that Bentham attaches insufficient value to the sorts of pursuits and values that Mill mentions. One might reply on Bentham's behalf that the charge is groundless; if these things give people pleasure, that pleasure will be counted in the calculation of the consequences of actions. When Bentham says that 'quantity of pleasure being equal, push-pin is as good as poetry',[37] he equally concedes that, quantity of pleasure being equal, poetry is as good as pushpin. If he has indeed neglected the fact that people enjoy contemplating certain kinds of admirable or amiable characters, the neglected enjoyment simply needs to be added to the hedonic consequences of the relevant actions or practices.

Many of the critics whom Mill has in mind reject this utilitarian answer. In their view, hedonic calculation does not capture the value of the things Bentham neglects. It is misleading to suggest that Bentham makes the moral point of view supreme. He makes the hedonic view supreme and regards moral value, no less than aesthetic or sympathetic features of actions and people, as purely instrumental. One might suppose that this is his basic error. To say that poetry is as good as pushpin only because it produces the same quantity of pleasure appears to miss some aspect of its value that escapes the hedonist.

Mill does not endorse this criticism of Bentham, and he could not consistently both endorse it and accept Bentham's basic principles. Though the essay on Bentham goes as far as Mill ever goes in suggesting that the utilitarian controversy is unimportant for

---

man's individual share of any public good which he can hope to realize by his efforts, is an equivalent for the sacrifice of his ease, and of the personal objects which he might attain by another course of conduct. The balance can be turned in favour of virtuous exertion, only by the interest of *feeling* or that of *conscience*—those "social interests", the necessary subordination of which to self-regarding is so lightly assumed.' ('Remarks on Bentham' = CW × 15)

[34] 'Man is never recognized by him as a being capable of pursuing spiritual perfection as an end; of desiring, for its own sake, the conformity of his own character to his standard of excellence, without hope of good or fear of evil from other source than his own consciousness.' ('Bentham', 95)

[35] 'He is chargeable also with another error, which it would be improper to pass over, because nothing has tended more to place him in opposition to the common feelings of mankind, and to give to his philosophy that cold, mechanical, and ungenial air which characterizes the popular idea of a Benthamite. This error, or rather one-sidedness, belongs to him not as a utilitarian, but as a moralist by profession, and is common with almost all professed moralists, whether religious or philosophical; it is that of treating the *moral* view of actions and characters . . . as if it were the sole one . . . Every human action has three aspects: its moral aspect, or that of its right and wrong; its aesthetic aspect, or that of its beauty; its sympathetic aspect, or that of its loveableness.' ('Bentham', 112)

[36] On the relation of these criticisms of Bentham to *On Liberty* see §1134.

[37] Mill quotes this (from Bentham, *RR*, 253) at 'Bentham', 113.

most practical purposes, Mill affirms that 'under proper explanation' he entirely agrees with Bentham about the truth of the utilitarian principle (110). His criticisms of Bentham, therefore, seem to confront him with a dilemma. (1) If he agrees with the principle of utility, the criticisms of Bentham's philistinism seem to require only an empirical adjustment in hedonic calculations. (2) If he agrees with the critics in believing that there are non-hedonic values, he should not accept Bentham's principle of utility.

The essay on Bentham suggests that Mill accepts the first horn of the dilemma. If so, his criticisms do not seem to affect Bentham's system, even if they make a significant empirical difference to utilitarian calculations. If this is a fair judgment on the essay, Mill does not discuss, and does not even identify, one major point on which 'the common feelings of mankind' find Bentham's utilitarianism incredible.

1115. Godwin's Extreme Utilitarianism[38]

Our survey of utilitarianism before Mill ought to include Godwin as well as Bentham. Godwin deserves attention because, in contrast to Bentham, he defends, and does not simply assume, a utilitarian moral theory. Moreover, he goes well beyond Bentham in his opposition to Paley. And so when Mill refers to earlier utilitarianism and to misinterpretations of it, he might reasonably have considered Godwin's version as well as Bentham's. It is worth asking how far the misinterpretations that Mill complains of misinterpret Godwin's position, and how far Mill's defence of utilitarianism applies to Godwin.

Mill mentions Godwin only once, and does not discuss him at all. His silence is not wholly surprising, since Godwin had faded from public attention after the initial notoriety resulting from his *Enquiry concerning Political Justice* (first edition, 1793) and from his political activities.[39] His main work is long, digressive, and wide-ranging, but deals only briefly with the most basic and most controversial moral principles.

As Mill notices in his one brief reference to him, Godwin agrees with Bentham in turning away from the conservative indirect utilitarianism of Paley ('Whewell', 170). He goes further than Bentham in drawing radical political and social conclusions. He rejects the arguments of Locke and (more recently) Price for determining the right form of government by appeal to the rights that a government should protect. The principle of utility, as he interprets it, undermines the foundations of government altogether; hence the political justice that rests on a utilitarian foundation requires an anarchist conclusion.

Godwin reaches these conclusions by being a direct utilitarian.[40] Utilitarianism is no less familiar in English moral philosophy than in 18th-century French writers, but Godwin draws

---

[38] On Godwin and his critics, see Schneewind, *SEVMP* 134–40; Monro, *GMP*, chs. 1, 7. References are to book, chapter, and pages of Priestley's edn.

[39] Schneewind, *SEVMP* 144–7, describes contemporary reactions to Godwin. In 1812, Shelley was surprised to discover that Godwin was still alive. In 1825, Hazlitt says that Godwin 'is to all ordinary intents and purposes dead and buried' (*SA* 19).

[40] Philp, *GPJ* 81–9 argues that Godwin is not a utilitarian, but a perfectionist. He under-emphasizes the evidence of Godwin's acceptance of utilitarianism. He is right to claim that Godwin both accepts some perfectionist principles and fails to explain how they affect his commitment to utilitarianism. This obscurity about the relation of perfectionism to utilitarianism is not peculiar to Godwin; we can also find it in other utilitarian perfectionists, including Mill and Rashdall. See §1209.

conclusions from it that are antagonistic to his English predecessors.[41] He argues that the principle of utility requires the strictest attention to one's estimate of the overall effect of one's actions on the general happiness.[42] Given the priority of utility, rights are not justified moral limits on the pursuit of utility. Godwin does not discuss the arguments of Butler and Price for moral limits on the principle of utility, or the arguments of Berkeley and Hutcheson for indirect utilitarianism, though he must have been familiar with these arguments.[43] He simply assumes that the moral point of view is the utilitarian point of view, and that we must take the utilitarian point of view in individual actions and decisions.

All virtues are subordinate to the principle of utility, and a virtuous person is one who is moved by explicit and exclusive reference to utility. Justice, therefore, cannot impose morally legitimate restrictions on utility, and just laws cannot impede the pursuit of utility.[44] We can have no conflicting obligations, and utility cannot override other genuine obligations. No obligation conflicts with utility, because the principle of utility is both the supreme principle and the only principle of morality. All other supposed principles are either false or simply means to the promotion of utility; in either case, they can never conflict with the clear demands of utility in a particular case.

The virtue that directs us towards the maximization of utility is justice. Godwin rejects Hutcheson's view that the sentiment of benevolence approves of maximizing utility. He does not follow Balguy and Butler in appealing to a rational principle of benevolence; he follows Hume in denying that benevolence underlies the pursuit of utility. In his view, benevolent instincts should be subordinate to justice, and hence to utility.[45] Since the principle of utility is the only rationally justifiable principle, regulation by justice is the same as regulation by the principle of utility.

Godwin accepts the implications of his direct utilitarianism, by rejecting any obligations that seem to rest on a non-utilitarian basis. In his view, one ought to save the life of a great benefactor of humanity over one's own life, or the life of one's parent or child.[46] This principle excludes all obligations that depend on past actions by others without reference to utility. The 'great benefactor' is someone who can be expected to confer great benefits

---

[41] Philp, *GPJ*, chs. 1–2, emphasizes connexions between Godwin and earlier English moral philosophy, but he does not emphasize the prominence of utilitarianism in earlier English writers. As Mill notices, acceptance of utilitarianism is not by itself a French innovation.

[42] 'Morality is nothing else but that system which teaches us to contribute upon all occasions, to the extent of our power, to the well-being and happiness of every intellectual and sensitive existence. But there is no action of our lives which does not in some way affect that happiness. ... If then every one of our actions fall within the province of morals, it follows that we have no rights in relation to the selecting them.' (Godwin, *EPJ* ii 5, 159)

[43] Godwin refers to Butler in iv 10, 422n (on disinterested benevolence), and to Price in viii 7 Appx., 503n (a remark made by Price in conversation). Philp, *GPJ*, ch. 7 argues that that the revisions in the second edition of *EPJ* show more sympathy to indirect utilitarianism, and are more influenced by sentimentalism.

[44] 'The fable of Procrustes presents us with a faint shadow of the perpetual effort of law. ... It was in the contemplation of this system of jurisprudence that the strange maxim was invented that "strict justice would often prove the highest injustice". ... If, on the contrary, justice be a result flowing from the contemplation of all the circumstances of each individual case, if only the criterion of justice be general utility, the inevitable consequence is that, the more we have of justice, the more we shall have of truth, virtue, and happiness.' (*EPJ* vii 8, 403–4)

[45] 'There is no ingredient that so essentially contributes to a virtuous character as a sense of justice. Philanthropy, as contradistinguished to justice, is rather an unreflective feeling than a rational principle. ... But justice measures by one unalterable standard the claims of all, weighs their opposite pretensions, and seeks to diffuse happiness, because happiness is the fit and proper condition of a conscious being.' (iv 5 Appx., 312–13)

[46] 'Thus every view of the subject brings us back to the consideration of my neighbour's moral worth, and his importance to the general weal, as the only standard to determine the treatment to which he is entitled.' (ii 2, 129)

on humanity in the future; the fact that someone has conferred great benefits in the past is relevant only in so far as it supports the expectation of future benefits.

The consistent application of the utilitarian criterion requires large departures from common-sense principles. Gratitude cannot create an obligation distinct from utility (ii 2). Promises always need to be reconsidered from the point of view of utility.[47] On utilitarian grounds, Godwin denies that my having made a promise creates a strong presumption in favour of keeping it. Whether I should keep it or not depends wholly on my views about the balance of utility when the time comes to keep it.

Common sense regards retrospective considerations, involving guilt, innocence, intention, and responsibility, as constraints on punishment. In requiring the state to restrict the deliberate infliction of harm to punishment, except in extreme cases, we impose these retrospective limits on the pursuit of utility. Butler recognizes these limits among the non-utilitarian principles that express our attachment to justice. Godwin, however, rejects any such restraints on utilitarian calculation in determining the distribution of harm.[48] Since the principle of utility is the only non-derivative moral principle, we should not follow Butler or Price in recognizing moral principles that ought to limit the pursuit of utility.

1116. Godwin's Defence of Utilitarianism

Why should we believe Godwin's claim about the status of the principle of utility, as opposed to Price's belief in a number of ultimate principles or 'heads' of virtue? Though Godwin is familiar with Butler and Price, he does not argue with them on this basic question about ultimate moral principles. But we can gather some of what he assumes about the status of the principle of utility.

Godwin's view of the rational character of the utilitarian principle emerges from his account of how we learn to follow it. He believes that we come to care about universal pleasure because we have been accustomed to associate it with pleasure to ourselves, through the operations of reward and punishment. Because we are so strongly encouraged to act in ways that promote the pleasure of others, we come to find such action a source of pleasure in itself, even apart from the rewards and punishments that were attached to it.[49] In the same way, a miser has come to love money for its own sake, apart from the prospect

---

[47] 'The adherence to promises therefore, as well as their employment in the first instance, must be decided by the general criterion, and maintained only so far as, upon a comprehensive view, it shall be found productive of a balance of happiness.' (iii 3, 209)

[48] 'It is right that I should inflict suffering, in every case where it can be clearly shown that such infliction will produce an overbalance of good. But this infliction bears no reference to the mere innocence or guilt of the person upon whom it is made. An innocent man is the proper subject of it, if it tend to good. . . . The only sense of the word punishment that can be supposed to be compatible with the principles of the present work is that of pain inflicted on a person convicted of past injurious action for the purpose of preventing future mischief.' (vii 1, 327) Monro, *GMP* 147, suggests that Godwin's discussion of punishment in vii 1–2 inconsistently combines an exclusive commitment to utilitarianism with non-utilitarian considerations of fairness.

[49] 'But it is the nature of the passions speedily to convert what were at first means into ends. The avaricious man forgets the utility of money which first incited him to pursue it, fixes his passion upon the money itself and counts his gold, without having in his mind any idea but that of seeing and handling it. Something of this sort happens very early in the history of every passion.' (iv 10, 425)

of further benefits that initially moved him to accumulate money. This psychological story follows Hartley's associationism.[50] It explains why, if we are taught to act in ways that promote utility, we come to take pleasure in promoting utility without reference to pleasant consequences for ourselves. But it does not answer an opponent who claims that we are trained to follow other principles besides the principle of utility. Godwin's genetic account says nothing in favour of utilitarianism in contrast to other accounts of morality.

The comparison with the miser exposes a point that the associationist story does not explain. Though it explains how we might come to be attached to the principle of utility in the way that the miser is attached to money, apart from any further benefit to ourselves, it does not explain why we should believe in anything more than a non-rational attachment to virtue. We do not suppose that a miser sees some ultimate reason to accumulate wealth for its own sake; and the associationist story would not explain why he formed that attitude if he did. The parallel between the virtuous person and the miser appeals to those who believe that no questions of reasonableness arise when ultimate ends are concerned. But if we think some ends are more reasonable than others, we may want to say more about the virtuous person than we can say about the miser.[51]

We might expect that Godwin would be content with the anti-rationalist view that sees no significant difference between the miser's and the virtuous person's attachment to their ends; for he endorses Hume's views about the role of reason and passion.[52] But he is not a consistent anti-rationalist, and hence he is not satisfied with the associationist story. For he believes that rational reflexion confirms the unselfish utilitarian outlook; it is an intuition of reason that arises from an impartial point of view.[53] Though the associationist story explains how we can take the impartial point of view, it does not explain why we approve of it rationally. Godwin appeals to the impartial spectator, as Hume and Smith do, but he interprets the impartial outlook in the light of Price's rationalist view of first principles.[54] The impartial standpoint, he argues, allows us to assess our absolute value;

[50] Hartley; §871.

[51] See Bradley on Mill, §1216. Locke, FR 174, discusses Godwin on benevolence. At 177, he cites EPJ i 11, 447–8, for Godwin's doctrine of quality of pleasure.

[52] See the account of voluntary action at EPJ i 5, 57–8. Godwin concludes that 'passion is not to be conquered by reason, but by bringing some other passion into contention with it' (i 5, 80). Some of the unclarity in Godwin's position appears in his 'Summary', Part vi (Priestley i, p. xxvi): 'Reason is not an independent principle, and has no tendency to excite us to action; in a practical view, it is merely a comparison and balancing of different feelings. Reason, though it cannot excite us to action, is calculated to regulate our conduct, according to the comparative worth it ascribes to different excitement.' A minimal sense of 'regulate' and 'worth' is needed to make the second sentence consistent with the first. Locke, FR 144, lists features of the first edition of EPJ that Godwin later regarded as errors: Stoicism (i.e., opposition to hedonism), rationalism (in opposition to Hume on reason and passion), and the condemnation of private affections. See also Priestley, 'Introduction', 12–13, 90–5.

[53] 'When once we have entered into so auspicious a path as that of disinterestedness, reflexion confirms our choice, in a sense in which it never can confirm any of the factitious passions we have named. We find by observation that we are surrounded by beings of the same nature with ourselves. . . . We are able in imagination to go out of ourselves, and become impartial spectators of the system of which we are a part. We can then make an estimate of our intrinsic and absolute value; and detect the imposition of that self-regard which would represent our own existence as of as much value as that of all the world beside.' (iv 10, 427)

[54] The connexions between Godwin and Price are stressed by Priestley, 'Introduction', 8n; and Philp, GPJ, chs. 1–2 (in a more general discussion of Godwin and Dissenting thought). Nonetheless, Monro, GMP 36, maintains justifiably that 'actually he wavered between the two schools of thought; and in the end he is closer to Hutcheson or Hume than to Clarke or Price'.

then we see that only a distorted point of view gives a special place to ourselves. Once we set aside sources of unreasonable bias, and take the point of view of a perfect intelligence, we see that we have no good reason for discriminating in our own favour.[55] Since a perfect intelligence has no prejudice in our favour, it shows us that everyone's pleasure matters equally,

This impartial outlook also takes a maximizing point of view. Godwin's first illustration of disinterested motivation is one person's willingness 'to sacrifice his own existence to that of twenty others' (iv 10, 381 K). He treats a life sacrificed to preserve lives as an instance of the general principle of sacrificing some people's pleasure to maximize the total pleasure. Perhaps he assumes that a maximizing principle is obviously reasonable because prudential hedonism is true. One might suppose that if one applies maximizing hedonism to one's own case, and then one agrees that impartial reason sees nothing special about oneself, one will include everyone's pleasures and pains in the same maximizing calculation.[56]

Godwin, therefore, seems to offer a rationalist and objectivist account of the connexion between morality and utility. Theological voluntarists take the connexion to be contingent, mediated by the will of God. Sentimentalists also take it to be contingent, mediated by the approval of the moral sense. But Godwin seems to follow Clarke and Price in taking moral principles to embody objective facts grasped by reason. He takes these facts to be facts about utility. In this combination of rationalism, objectivism, and utilitarianism, Godwin anticipates Sidgwick—though he later accepts a more sentimentalist explanation of the truth of utilitarianism.[57]

Since Godwin believes that reason endorses the utilitarian attitude, and since he takes a virtuous person to be moved by the correct rational principle, he infers that the virtuous person in every action aims to maximize utility. He therefore rejects the indirect utilitarianism of Paley, and the 'hidden hand' explanation that Smith offers to show how action on non-utilitarian principles promotes the general happiness.[58]

Similarly, he rejects the egoist arguments of theological utilitarians who attribute utilitarian motives only to God, and take human beings to be moved only by self interest. He offers two sorts of argument against Paley's combination of theological voluntarism, egoism, and utilitarianism. First, he suggests that the prospect of rewards and punishments after death will probably not restrain many people who would be seriously tempted to act viciously.[59] Secondly, he argues that Paley's appeal to rewards and punishments is morally

[55] 'The delusion being thus sapped, we can, from time to time at least, fall back in idea into our proper post, and cultivate those views and affections which must be most familiar to the most perfect intelligence.' (EPJ iv 10, 427–8)

[56] Monro, GMP 46, suggests that Godwin accepts this parallel between prudential and utilitarian maximization.

[57] See Philp, GPJ 202–7.

[58] 'In this sense, we may admire the system of the universe, where public utility results from each man's contempt of that utility . . . But we can think with little complacence of the individuals of whom this universe is composed. . . . The system of disinterested benevolence proves to us that it is possible to be virtuous, and not merely to talk of virtue; that all which has been said by philosophers and moralists respecting impartial justice is not an unmeaning rant. . . . An idea like this . . . gives us reason to expect that, as men collectively advance in science and useful institution, they will proceed more and more to consolidate their private judgment, and their individual will, with abstract justice, and the unmixed approbation of general happiness.' (iv 10, 436–7)

[59] 'The respect I shall obtain, and the happiness I shall enjoy, for the remainder of my life are topics of which I feel the entire comprehension. I understand the value of ease, liberty, and knowledge, to myself, and my fellow men. I perceive that these things, and a certain conduct intending them, are connected, in the visible system of the world, and not by any supernatural and unusual interposition.' (v 15, 127)

inappropriate.[60] Godwin agrees with Butler in believing that the reaction against 'enthusiasm' goes too far when it rejects any appeal to motives distinct from self-interest.[61]

1117. Objections to Godwin

Godwin's work provoked a compact reply in a pamphlet by Thomas Green. While many critics deplored Godwin's moral conclusions, Green does most to try to identify the philosophical errors that lead to them.[62] In his view, utilitarianism is a fairly recent account of the basis of morality. It is not part of ancient moral philosophy, nor is it found in the 'earlier publicists' (i.e., natural law theorists), or in Shaftesbury, Clarke, or Wollaston (*Examination*, 17–18). But once it was introduced, it convinced both French radicals and English divines (20), though they drew opposite conclusions from it. Green mentions Helvetius as an example of a French radical and Paley as a representative English utilitarian (21). He mentions John Brown as Paley's source. He does not mention Cumberland and Berkeley as earlier sources of utilitarianism, and, though he mentions Hume as a utilitarian, he does not mention Hutcheson. He tends, as Mill does, to contrast moral sense theories with utilitarianism.

Though Green opposes the practical implications of utilitarianism, he concedes that utility is the final cause of the moral virtues. He denies that it is their efficient cause.[63] In Green's view, we neither can nor should form our moral sentiments on the basis of beliefs about utility, even though the result of all the virtues that we form in various non-utilitarian ways is the promotion of utility.

Green's view that the moral agent should not be explicitly guided by utility agrees with Berkeley and with the position entertained by Butler. But he does not seem to recognize the significance of his concession on final causation. If we believe on theological grounds that the goal of our moral sentiments is maximum happiness, we assume that utilitarian

---

[60] 'Great mischief, in this respect, has probably been done by those moralists who think only of stimulating men to good deeds by considerations of frigid prudence and mercenary self-interest . . . This has been too much the case with the teachers of religion, even those of them who are most eager in their hostility to religious enthusiasm.' (iv 10, 438)

[61] Locke, FR 137, discusses some contemporary novels that refer or allude, favourably or unfavourably, to Godwin. In Opie's *Adeline Mowbray*, the young woman adopts a utilitarian attitude of opposition to legal marriage. Her lover Glenmurray (= Godwin) first violates the principles set out in his utilitarian treatise, by fighting a duel so that Adeline will not be ashamed of him. Then he wants to marry Adeline, to avoid harming her reputation, Adeline is angry at him for abandoning his philosophy, which he still believes to be correct. [Adeline]: 'Then, if you still are convinced your theory is good, why let your practice be bad? It is incumbent on you to act up to the principles that you profess, in order to give them their proper weight in society—else you give the lie to your own declarations.' [Glenmurray]: 'But it is better for me to do that, than for you to be the sacrifice to my reputation?' 'I, replied Adeline, am entirely out of the question: you are to be governed by no other law but your desire to promote general utility, and are not to think at all of the interest of an individual.' 'How can I do so, when the individual is dearer to me than all the world beside?, cried Glenmurray passionately.' (vol. 1, ch. 10, 186–7) The utilitarian Glenmurray wants to violate his principles for the sake of another individual (just as he fights a duel for her), whereas Adeline wants to be a strict utilitarian, and quotes Glenmurray's principles back to him (ch. 6, 96–9).

[62] Schneewind, *SEVMP* 144–9, discusses Green and other critics of Godwin.

[63] '[This axiom] takes for granted that because the end of virtue is the general good (as it undoubtedly is, and of every other principle moulded into the composition of physical and moral nature) that it is its tendency to this end which determines us to distinguish it as virtue; that because the final cause of moral distinctions is utility, that utility must be its proximate cause also; . . .' (Green, *Exam.* 24)

benevolence is God's overriding moral characteristic. In that case, we might look for some evidence to show that we are forming the sentiments that are appropriate for the goal of virtue. If we reject the search for such evidence, on the ground that we know too little about the actual effects of our virtues, we seem to cast doubt on the belief that a benevolent God has given us our actual moral sentiments in order to maximize utility. But if we seek some reason to believe that we form the sentiments that maximize utility, it seems reasonable to appeal to utility in deciding what sentiments we ought to form. The position that Green maintains against Godwin is unstable.

Green accepts utility as the final cause of the virtues without any close consideration of the content of the utilitarian principle. According to Godwin, utilitarianism aims at the maximization of pleasure, irrespective of its distribution among different people, so that the infliction of pain on some or most people can be justified by an increase in total pleasure. Other utilitarians are less emphatic about utilitarian indifference to distribution of pleasure and pain. But Hutcheson already notices the maximizing aspects of utilitarianism, and these aspects are among the targets of Butler's remarks about the conflict between justice and utility.

Once this aspect of utilitarianism is clear, it is less clear why a benevolent God should be a utilitarian. If we appeal, as Cumberland does, to the common good of human beings, we can see why we might ascribe this aim to God; but an appeal to the common good is not clearly an appeal to utilitarian maximization. Green does not mention utilitarian indifference to distribution, and does not say why he believes the utilitarian end, so understood, is the final cause of the virtues.

Utilitarian indifference to distribution does not escape the notice of all critics, however. Hazlitt's attack on Bentham highlights utilitarian reasons for inflicting severe pain on some people simply to increase the pleasure of others. Utilitarians, according to Hazlitt, justify the suffering of slaves in the sugar plantations by reference to the pleasure of tea-drinkers.[64] Even if Hazlitt's specific criticism is unfair, it raises a legitimate question. Hazlitt observes that the utilitarian good is not necessarily good for everyone, and that it makes moral decisions depend on a type of calculation that does not seem characteristic of morality.

Hazlitt, however, infers illicitly that morality does not involve reasoning at all, and that the utilitarian error consists in treating it as a matter of reason rather than sentiment.[65] This is also Green's objection to Godwin. He accuses Godwin of accepting rationalism about first principles; against this he defends the sentimentalism of Hume (*Examination*, 56). He

---

[64] 'It has been made a plea (half jest, half earnest) for the horrors of war, that they promote trade and manufacturers. It has been said, as a set-off for the atrocities practised upon the negro slaves in the West Indies, that without their blood and sweat, so many millions of people could not have sugar to sweeten their tea. Fires and murders have been argued to be beneficial, as they serve to fill the newspapers, and for a subject to talk of—this is a sort of sophistry that it might be difficult to disprove on the bare scheme of contingent utility; but on the ground that we have stated, it must pass for mere irony. What the proportion between the good and the evil will really be found in any of the supposed cases, may be a question to the understanding; but to the imagination and the heart, that is, to the natural feelings of mankind, it admits none.' (Hazlitt, *SA* 10) See also 'Imagination', 49–50: '. . . with respect to the atrocities committed in the slave-trade, it could not be set up as a doubtful pleas in their favour, that the actual and intolerable sufferings inflicted on the individuals were compensated by certain advantages in a commercial and political point of view—in a moral sense they *cannot* be compensated. They hurt the public mind; they harden and wear the natural feelings.' Hazlitt attacks utilitarians further, though with less interesting argument, in 'Reform' (where he accuses them of being secular Scottish Calvinists). Park, *HSA*, ch. 2, discusses Hazlitt's criticism of Bentham.

[65] See Hazlitt, 'Imagination', 49.

endorses Smith's view that the moral sentiments are non-utilitarian in themselves, but their general acceptance promotes utility (56).

On the practical side of utilitarianism, Green accuses Paley of taking too much for granted. Paley assumes both that indirect utilitarianism is true and that it endorses the rules of common-sense morality (37). If we are to accept Paley's combination of theological voluntarism with utilitarianism, we need some reason to believe that the rules God imposes on us are those that maximize utility. However ignorant we may be of overall utility, we cannot be so ignorant that we have no idea of what maximizes utility; for in that case we would have no idea whether observance of the rules that God imposes will maximize utility. But once we ask what course of action maximizes utility, we may well doubt whether we should choose the rules recommended by Paley. Even if we can see that it is useful to have Paley's rules and to follow them most of the time, we may still believe that utilitarian calculation will sometimes favour breaking the rules. Godwin seems to present a more plausible utilitarian position.

1118. Godwin as an Alternative to Bentham

Godwin, therefore, presents a version of utilitarianism that is distinct both from the indirect version familiar from Paley and other 18th-century writers and from Bentham's version. Indirect utilitarians do not try to prove that the virtuous person is moved by the rational appreciation of the principle of benevolence. Godwin's identification of virtue with rational utilitarian benevolence is closest to Balguy's position, though Balguy is not a direct utilitarian. Godwin differs from Bentham in so far as he treats the principle of utility as a principle of rational motivation. Bentham and James Mill seem to accept the associationist view that Godwin rejects; nor do they suggest that the utilitarian principle conflicts with common-sense morality in the ways that Godwin describes.

Godwin cannot be accused, as Paley can be, of using the principle of utility to support the common moral assumptions and prejudices of his day. His version of utilitarianism, therefore, deserves Mill's attention, because it tries to put utilitarianism into practice without shrinking from its radical implications. We should recall it when we consider Mill's claims that utilitarianism has been misinterpreted, and Mill's various defences of the position that he regards as utilitarian.

If Godwin is right about the implications of the principle of utility, he casts doubt on parts of Mill's defence of Bentham. Sometimes Mill suggests that agreement on the principle of utility is not very important for moral and social practice, and that agreement on secondary principles is more important. He suggests that Bentham is important not because he is a utilitarian, but because he has discovered secondary principles that enlightened non-utilitarians will accept. These claims do not fit Godwin's utilitarianism. For Godwin derives all his moral principles from direct reflexion on the principle of utility; to see whether he is right about the secondary principles, it seems all-important to decide whether he is right about the principle of utility and about the derivation of these maxims. Nor do enlightened people readily accept the secondary principles that Godwin derives from the principle of utility.

How is this disagreement between Godwin and Mill to be explained? Mill might argue in different ways: (1) Godwin is wrong in his interpretation of the principle of utility; he has the wrong idea of maximum pleasure. (2) He rests his secondary principles on mistaken empirical beliefs; for observance of rules about (for instance) fidelity to promises, and about punishment rather than infliction of harm on the innocent, maximizes utility.

If Mill agrees with Godwin's rejection of Paley's conservative utilitarianism, he should not simply assume that utilitarianism agrees with common-sense secondary principles; the agreement needs to be demonstrated in particular cases. In *Utilitarianism*, Mill takes up this task that he neglects in his earlier defences of utilitarianism.

1119. Whewell's Principles

Mill's selective defence of Bentham is worth comparing not only with Godwin's version of utilitarianism, but also with non-utilitarian positions. His main defences of Bentham appear in his essays on non-utilitarian moralists—Blakey, Sedgwick, and Whewell. Whewell is by far the most significant of the three. Unlike Blakey and Sedgwick, he is not a theological voluntarist. Hence he agrees with Mill in looking for a rational foundation of morality apart from divine commands. Since Mill argues in defence of Bentham that we have no rational alternative to the use of the utilitarian criterion, his criticisms of Whewell are important to his main purpose. To see how good a case Mill presents against Whewell, we should sketch the relevant features of Whewell's position.[66]

One of Whewell's earlier works is a series of sermons that consciously imitate Butler's sermons in content and purpose.[67] He argues on philosophical and theological grounds for a Butlerian view of conscience and morality, and against the influence of Paley. Butler does not offer a complete system, but gives us an indication of where to start. Whewell looks forward to a 'system of morality' in the future. He appeals to Plato and the Stoics to show that ancient moralists support 'independent morality', because they take conscience to recognize moral rightness that is independent of the means to pleasure. This is the view of conscience that St Paul presupposes in his remarks on conscience and the moral law. When Plato argues that the just person is happiest, he takes the just person to regard moral goodness as worth choosing for its own sake.[68]

Whewell argues, then, that the ancients support the conception of independent morality that he traces through earlier British moralists. He asks whether Christianity supersedes independent morality because it treats the pursuit of divine rewards as the basis for morality (OFM 39). He answers that theocentric moralists should not take obedience to be independent of one's view about the moral character of God. The relevant sort of obedience to God results from the love of God's goodness, not simply from fear of God's power or from

[66] Whewell is helpfully discussed by Schneewind, *SEVMP* 101–17, and by Donagan, 'Elements'.

[67] Whewell, *OFM*.

[68] '...it cannot but be clear that he who thus promulgates such a conclusion endeavours to teach us that moral good and evil are, for their own sakes alone and without reference to ulterior regards, to be sought and to be shunned.' (Whewell, *OFM* 25)

the hope of reward.[69] Paley ignores this aspect of Christian morality, because he rejects the distinctive outlook and motive of moral conscience and treats pleasure as the basis of morality (61). The most serious error results from Paley's combination of a hedonistic account of the basis of virtue with a purely quantitative account of the difference among pleasures.[70] If he had said that the pleasures of virtue are superior because of their object, he would not have failed so completely to grasp the character of morality.

Whewell believes that his criticisms of Paley apply to Bentham, once the theological aspect is removed. In his preface to Mackintosh's *Dissertation on the Progress of Ethical Philosophy*, he argues that we need to recognize independent morality in order to capture our concepts of right, duty, and ought.[71] Bentham is right to suppose that if we reject independent morality, 'ought' should be banished from the vocabulary of morals.[72]

As well as writing his Butlerian sermons on human nature, Whewell recommends Butler's approach and doctrines. His edition of Butler's three sermons on human nature appeared in 1848. In his view, Butler provides a useful 'addition or correction to other works' (p. ix).[73] He means in particular that Butler corrects Paley and Bentham. Similarly, in order to disseminate older accounts of independent morality, Whewell published editions of Grotius on the law of war and peace, and of Sanderson on the obligation of conscience (as well as a series of translations of Plato).[74] He accepts Butler's arguments about nature, and rejects Paley's dismissal of such arguments (*PMP* i 6) as 'the usual declamations'.[75] To express his general outlook on morality, he invokes the naturalism of Butler and Grotius.[76]

---

[69] 'Thus the opinion which makes the goodness of our actions depend upon their being done in obedience to the divine will is consistent with itself, and in harmony with the belief of pious minds, only when we combine it with the conviction that in God are all justice and truth, righteousness and holiness. And thus, such an opinion does not negative, but on the contrary implies, that we have already ideas of those moral perfections which we thus ascribe to our almighty governor.' (*OFM* 43)

[70] 'To teach either of these things—either that virtue is the pursuit of pleasure, or that all pleasures, according to their amount, alike deserve our attention—would indeed be to delude our hearers and to forget ourselves. But what if we should have insisted at the same time on both these maxims? How then should we judge ourselves? This would surely seem as if we had exercised a perverse and obstinate ingenuity, in order that morality might have no escape from the debasing influence of our system.' (*OFM* 61–2)

[71] 'Right, duty, what we ought to do, are not expressed to the satisfaction of any one by any phraseology borrowed from the consideration of consequences.' (Whewell, Preface to Mackintosh, xxiv)

[72] Whewell cites Bentham, *Deontology*. See §1113 above. He comments on Bentham's use of 'deontology': 'But the term Deontology expresses moral science (and expresses it well) precisely because it signifies the science of duty, and contains no reference to utility. It is a term well chosen to describe a system of ethics founded on any other than Mr Bentham's principle. Mackintosh, who held that *to deon*—what men ought to do—was the fundamental notion of morality, might very properly have termed the science deontology. The system of which Mr Bentham is the representative—that of those who make morality dependent on the production of happiness, has long been designated in Germany by the term Eudemonism, derived from the Greek word for happiness (eudaimonia). If we were to adopt this term we should have to oppose the deontological to the eudemonist school . . .' (Preface, xxviii)

[73] Whewell mentions that this was why Butler had been added to the reading list in one Cambridge college around 1833.

[74] See Grotius, *JBP*; Sanderson, OC; Whewell, *PDER*.   [75] Whewell, Preface to Butler's Sermons, p. x

[76] 'We might answer, with Bishop Butler, that according to us, virtue is a course of action conformable to the whole constitution of human nature . . . man, being a creature constituted of desires, affections, reason, conscience, the rule of his being is, to act conformably to the relations of these elements; so that reason shall control desire and affections, and conscience shall indefinitely exalt the views of reason: or otherwise, thus; that man, (besides being an animal,) is an intellectual, moral, religious, and spiritual creature; and must be governed by rules derived from these characters. Such views are not new or unfamiliar. They are, for instance, the principles on which Grotius proceeds in his treatise De Iure Belli et Pacis, except that he dwells especially upon the attribute social . . .' (*EM* ix)

This is the general outlook that Whewell tries to articulate in his *Elements of Morality*. This large book contains long, elaborate, and not invariably fascinating, discussions of particular moral and legal rules and duties. Its treatment of basic theoretical issues is brief, dogmatic, and (to put it mildly) often enthymematic. But Whewell's position is clear enough to suggest a reasonable alternative to utilitarianism.

He argues that the basic elements of human nature, in its social relations, require some basic virtues, and that the demands of these virtues can be articulated in a system of rules, rights, duties, and institutions. Most of the book is devoted to the details of the system. It does not say much to explain how the general claims about aspects of human nature sustain the principles that justify the detailed system of rules.

According to Whewell's summary of his argument (*LSM* 77–91), he understands 'right' (in the singular) as the supreme reason for action. The supreme rule of human action is the one to which right action conforms, and when they conform to it, people have their rights. Each has a right to his own person, property, family, and place among fellows. The source of these rights is the endeavour to balance and to control the main springs of action. These springs include desires for bodily safety and well-being; for possession; for family society; for civil society; and for mutual understanding (a need rather than a desire; 86). The appropriate regulation of these desires results both in jural commands and in corresponding moral precepts about motives. The precepts correspond to five cardinal virtues: benevolence, justice, truth, purity, and order.

This scheme for the derivation of the basic moral requirements is similar, as Whewell recognizes, to the Platonic argument for finding the cardinal virtues by examining the different elements in the soul. He argues that his scheme of derivation yields definite enough results for the purposes of systematic morality.[77] Like Plato and Butler, Whewell believes that the 'due regulation' comes from the control exercised by practical reason in guiding the different basic impulses common to human beings.

This general scheme justifies virtues concerned with property (for the use of external objects), self-control (for the regulation of desires), and justice. Since society and community require some mutual regard and concern, benevolence is a basic virtue. This is not essentially confined to members of a particular society, but extends to all human beings in the form of 'love of mankind' or humanity.[78] Following Grotius and Barbeyrac, Whewell sees the basis of universal concern for humanity in Greek and Roman views about 'love of humanity' (*philanthrôpia*) and 'conciliation' (*oikeiôsis*).[79] From the point of view of humanity, we can

---

[77] '. . . we have certain definite ideas of such virtues which necessarily arise in our minds, when we consider the constitution of human nature, with its various elements and faculties, as subject to a supreme and universal rule . . . the measure of each virtue is to be found in a due regulation of that part of the constitution of man to which that virtue specially relates . . .'(*EM* 8) 'Without some provision for the tranquil gratification of these desires, society is disturbed, unbalanced, painful; we may even say, intolerable. We cannot conceive a condition of such privation to be the genuine condition of social man. The habitual gratification of the principal desires . . . must be a part of the order of the society. There must be rules which direct the course and limits of such gratification. Such rules are necessary for the peace, and even for the existence, of society.' (45)

[78] '. . . a universal benevolence towards all men, as partakers of the same common human nature with ourselves, is a part of the supreme law of human being.' (*EM* 224; cf. 72)

[79] See Grotius, discussed in §466.

see what is wrong with slavery; the institution depends on the false assumption that slaves do not share a common humanity with their masters.[80]

If the basic principles derived from the requirements of human nature are to guide action in detail, they must be embodied in social expectations, constituting rights and obligations. Hence 'right' (the noun) and 'obligation' have a different reference from 'right' (the adjective) and 'ought'; the latter pair refer to the principles, derived from the needs of human nature, that may be more or less successfully embodied in actual rights and obligations.[81] Rights, therefore, may not perfectly embody the requirements of the right.[82] We cannot have a precise idea of what the principles of right require of us until these principles inform a specific conception of 'my station and its duties' (as Bradley later expresses it).[83] But this conception is not infallible; it may need to be corrected by reference to the principles of right that we have tried to embody in specific rights.

This contrast between rights and the right separates the eternal and immutable aspects of morality from the mutable.[84] The basic principles of morality depend only on the basic needs of human beings. But they are definite enough, in Whewell's view, to constitute critical principles that support some concrete conceptions of specific rights.

1120. Mill on Whewell's 'Vicious Circles'

Mill's discussion of Whewell is harsh, and Whewell gives as good as he gets in the replies appended to the fourth edition of *Elements*.[85] Mill attacks Whewell's argument to show that the errors of Bentham and Paley are inseparable from the utilitarian outlook. As in his earlier essays on Bentham, Mill believes that the essential utilitarian position can be separated from

---

[80] '[A slave] is thus divested of his moral nature, which is contrary to the great Principle we have already laid down; that all men are moral beings;—a principle which . . . is one of the universal truths of morality, whether it be taken as a principle of justice or of humanity.' (*EM* 232)

[81] '. . . in order that moral rules may exist, there must also be abstract conceptions, including the principal objects of human desire and affection; which abstract conceptions must be realities, vested in particular persons as attributes or possessions, according to rules subordinate to the supreme rule of human action. . . . in order that moral rules may exist, men must have Rights.' (*EM* 50)

[82] 'Hence the two words may often be properly opposed. We may say that a poor man has no Right to relief, but it is right he should have it. A rich man has a Right to destroy the harvest of his fields, but to do so would not be right.' (54) 'My obligation is to give another man his Right; my duty is to do what is right. Hence duty is a wider term than obligation, exactly as right, the adjective, is wider than right, the substantive.' (54)

[83] See Bradley, §1226.

[84] 'The conceptions of the fundamental rights of men are universal, and flow necessarily from the moral nature of man; the definitions of these rights are diverse, and are determined by the laws of each state.' (*EM* 59)

[85] Martineau, *Essays*, chs. 9–10, also reviews Whewell quite severely. At 378, he comments on the ignorance of the history of modern philosophy among Oxford and Cambridge philosophers; 'They apply Greek or mediaeval doctrine directly to the exposure of existing fallacies and the correction of existing opinion. They leap down from Aristotle to Bentham, from Plato to Coleridge, with the fewest possible resting-places between. With the exception of Hooker, Locke, Butler and Paley (an exception far from constant), the series of great writers who have formed the modes of speculative thought in Protestant Europe is but little known to them. Hence they rarely appear at home in the province of modern philosophy; . . . and betray how difficult is the transition, for a mind trained in the schools of Athens and Rome, to the work of the Christian moralist and the Anglican ecclesiastic.' (378) This narrowness explains the inferiority of Oxford and Cambridge philosophy to Scottish philosophy (379). Martineau's comment does not do justice to Whewell's important work on the history of moral philosophy.

Bentham's specific articulation of it. While Bentham is open to criticism on some points, the essential utilitarian position should be defended because it offers the only hope of moral progress.

Mill believes utilitarianism partly because he believes that no non-utilitarian theory defended by the 'intuitive school' (U1.3) has any plausible moral content of its own. Non-utilitarian theories acquire whatever plausible content they may have by borrowing from utilitarianism. Whewell's theory illustrates this point; for it offers nothing of theoretical interest, but simply arranges common opinions in an obfuscating framework.[86] Whewell deserves attention only because he attacks utilitarianism and claims to get on better without it.[87]

Mill maintains two distinct points: (1) All objections to utilitarianism are mistaken. (2) All alleged alternatives to utilitarianism are futile. A proof of one point without the other would not achieve Mill's main aims. If he carried the first point but not the second, he would have to recognize a number of tenable ethical positions, and would not have vindicated utilitarianism over the others. If he carried the second point without the first, he would not have ruled out a sceptical position towards moral theories.

But though the two points are distinct, they are connected. For one might naturally suppose that if we can see the objections to utilitarianism, we may find a starting point for the construction of an alternative. If our non-utilitarian intuitive convictions are not utterly chaotic, we may reasonably try to articulate them by presenting an alternative theory that strengthens our objections to utilitarianism. Mill, therefore, needs to show that opponents of utilitarianism fail on both points.

In his view, Whewell's positive theory is practically empty, because his basic principles move in a circle, and so lack the informative content that we need.[88] Mill speaks as though a theory would be refuted if its explanation of its fundamental concepts were circular. This is a questionable assumption, however, since circular explanations may still be informative. Mill does not explain what would be wrong with recognizing a circle in explanation or justification.

His criticism is more plausible when he attacks Whewell for proceeding in small and non-explanatory circles. He identifies three of them, called 'vicious circle the first' and so on (187–9). But the allegation of vicious circularity rests on a misunderstanding of Whewell's position.[89] Whewell's claims about right and rights suggest to Mill that Whewell tries to explain each through the other. In fact, however, Whewell takes the general conception

---

[86] '. . . it can scarcely be counted as anything more than one of the thousand waves on the sea of commonplace, affording nothing to invite or to reward a separate examination.' (Mill, 'Whewell', 169) Whewell replies to Mill (to whom he refers only as 'an objector') in the Supplement to the 4th edn. of *EM*, ch. 2 (580–98).

[87] '. . . assaults on the only methods of philosophizing from which any improvement in ethical opinions can be looked for, ought to be repelled. And in doing this it is necessary to extend our comments to some of Dr Whewell's substantive opinions also. When he argues in condemnation of . . . utility, or tendency to happiness, as the principle or test of morality, it is material to examine how he gets on without it; how he fares in the attempt to construct a theory of morals on any other basis.' (169)

[88] 'Dr Whewell has failed in what it was impossible to succeed in. Every attempt to dress up an appeal to intuition in the forms of reasoning, must break down in the same manner. The system must, from the condition of the case, revolve in a circle. If morality is not to gravitate to any end, but to hang self-balanced in space, it is useless attempting to suspend one point of it upon another point.' ('Whewell', 190)

[89] Whewell points out Mill's misunderstanding at *EM* 582.

of the right, derived from general claims about human nature, to be prior to specific conceptions of rights. These conceptions try—adequately or inadequately—to embody the principles of right in specific practices.

One might criticize Whewell for saying too little about how one derives the different principles of right from the general requirements of human nature. But Mill does not argue the task of derivation is so hopeless that Whewell's attempt is futile. On the contrary, he claims that Whewell's derivation is plausible because it implicitly relies on utilitarianism. To see why Mill takes this view of Whewell, and to see whether it is the right view, we need to introduce some of Whewell's claims about happiness.

1121. Whewell on Happiness and Pleasure

Whewell's conception of happiness is intended to support two of his criticisms of utilitarianism: (1) It is wrong to conceive happiness as pleasure, or as the maximization of overall pleasure. (2) Once we conceive happiness correctly, we can see that it is the wrong sort of thing to appeal to in deciding what actions are right or wrong; properly understood, it is too indefinite to be a basis for morality, and it must acquire some of its content from morality.

He maintains a comprehensive conception of happiness, similar in certain respects to Reid's conception.[90] Sidgwick believes that this conception deviates from the common use of the word 'happiness', and is too indefinite for use in moral theory.[91] Though Whewell does not refer to Aristotle, his conception is Aristotelian.[92]

Whewell argues that because happiness is comprehensive, it must include the end of morality as a constituent end. Since happiness is the ultimate end of all action, every worthwhile end must be included in it somehow, and so the end of morality must be included. We should try to reconcile morality with the other ends that constitute the ultimate end, so that we reconcile morality with happiness.[93] In demanding this harmony between virtue and happiness, Whewell follows Kant; he also follows him in supposing that we must ultimately appeal to religion to assure us of this harmony.

---

[90] '. . . happiness is the object of human action in its most general form, as including all other objects and approved by the reason. As pleasure is the aim of mere desire, and interest the aim of prudence, happiness is conceived as necessarily an ultimate object of action.' (*EM* 241)

[91] See Sidgwick, §1164.

[92] *LSM* 130–6, has a fuller discussion of happiness. Whewell sums it up: 'Happiness, then, which is the object of the supreme rule, must be the supreme object of human action. And if in our notion of happiness . . . we include . . . that it is sought as the supreme object of action, the expressions which I have noted, that duty and virtue are means to happiness as an end, though not such expressions as we should have chosen, are admissible; for, inasmuch as duty and virtue are conformable to the supreme rule, they must be means to the supreme object. Happiness, then, is the supreme or ultimate object of human action, including all other objects. . . . In our system we allow that happiness is the ultimate end of human action . . . But we make no use of this declaration. It does not enter at all into the reasoning by which our rules are established.' (131–2) To show that happiness cannot be the basis of morality, Whewell cites Paley. He argues, as in *EM*, that Paley's account of happiness does no work in the rest of his book (134).

[93] '. . . Since happiness is necessarily the supreme object of our desires, and duty the supreme rule of our actions, there can be no harmony in our being, except our happiness coincide with our duty. That which we contemplate as the ultimate and universal object of desire, must be identical with that which we contemplate as the ultimate and supreme guide of our intentions. As moral beings, our happiness must be found in our moral progress, and in the consequences of our moral progress; we must be happy by being virtuous.' (*EM* 241)

This position would have been clearer if Whewell had clearly insisted that, according to this view of happiness, virtue is to be chosen for its own sake. Mill misunderstands him, and supposes that he cannot consistently defend virtue as a non-instrumental good.[94] Mill believes he is better off than Whewell on this point, but we may not share his confidence. His account of how we can pursue virtue for its own sake anticipates his discussion in *Utilitarianism*, and involves the same ambiguities and difficulties.[95]

Mill's objection to Whewell rests on a conception of happiness that Whewell rejects. Since Mill identifies happiness with pleasure, he thinks of it as a quantity of which we can find a lot or a little; hence we can find happiness in virtue if we simply find some pleasure in it. This conception of happiness is inconsistent with the conception of it as a whole containing heterogeneous parts, which Mill also relies on. It is also inconsistent with Whewell's conception of happiness. Since Whewell thinks of happiness as a whole composed of heterogeneous parts, he does not think we find happiness simply by finding some part of it. Hence, if virtue is choiceworthy for its own sake, all that follows is that it is a part of happiness, not that it is happiness. Hence Mill is wrong to allege that Whewell's claims about happiness conflict with recognizing that virtue is choiceworthy for its own sake.

The holistic conception of happiness makes it difficult to argue that some prior conception of happiness, understood independently of virtue, shows us whether one or another action is virtuous. Whewell avoids this argument, and instead argues in the reverse direction, that happiness contains moral elements. The promotion of other people's happiness is not the same as making them pleased or contented, and is sometimes even inconsistent with it.[96] Utilitarianism, therefore, seems to conflict with the promotion of happiness, and especially with its moral component. If we take utilitarianism seriously and confine ourselves to hedonic consequences, it appears to give us immoral advice. If we take happiness seriously, as Whewell understands it, it does not so clearly suggest immoral advice; but we must understand its content partly by reference to moral principles that the utilitarian mistakenly tries to derive entirely from happiness. Mill does not give a satisfactory answer to this aspect of Whewell's criticism.[97] He leaves a gap that he later tries to fill in *Utilitarianism*.

---

[94] 'To this we should have nothing to object, if by identification was meant that what we desire unselfishly must first, by a mental process, become an actual part of what we seek as our own happiness; that the good of others becomes our pleasure because we have learnt to find pleasure in it; this is, we think, the true philosophical account of the matter. But we do not understand this to be Dr Whewell's meaning; . . . he says that religion alone can assure us of the identity of happiness with duty. . . . Now, if the happiness connected with duty were the happiness we find *in* our duty, self-consciousness would give us a full account of this, without religion. The happiness, therefore, which Dr Whewell means, must consist, not in the thing itself, but in a reward appended to it . . .' ('Whewell', 184n)

[95] Mill on virtue and happiness; §1132.

[96] 'We ought not to wish the slave to be contented in his slavery. . . . On the contrary, we ought to wish that he should both desire and have liberty, in order that he may enter upon that course of moral agency, and moral progress, which is the only proper occupation of his human faculties.' (*EM* 242) A related objection to hedonistic utilitarianism must have been familiar to Mill from Lytton Bulwer (see *CW* x, App. C): 'In the dark ages, (said once to me the wittiest writer of the day, and one who has perhaps done more to familiarize Bentham's general doctrines to the public than any other individual,) in the dark ages, it would have been for the greatest happiness of the greatest number to burn the witches; it must have made the greatest number (all credulous of wizardry,) very uncomfortable to refuse their request for so reasonable a conflagration; their *happiness* demanded a bonfire of old women.' (*CW* x 502)

[97] Mill notices that Whewell takes happiness to include moral elements ('Whewell', 180). But his reply to this objection to utilitarianism discusses one of Whewell's less cogent arguments (183–5). He does not discuss Whewell's example of the slave or the example of burning witches.

1122. Whewell's Objections to Utilitarian Calculation

Opponents of utilitarianism argue that the hedonic consequences of actions are too uncertain to allow any definite practical conclusion. Mill takes this to be an unfair and unreasonable criticism. It assumes, in his view, that a utilitarian principle would be feasible only for omniscient agents. Such a demand for omniscience imposes an unreasonable burden on utilitarianism that we would not normally impose on principles intended to guide deliberation. We do not normally take deliberation to be worthwhile only if we are omniscient. In many areas—including prudential reasoning—we proceed on the basis of a reasonable estimate of consequences. Why not do this in moral reasoning ('Whewell', 180)?

Whewell answers that he does not object to utilitarian reasoning simply because it is uncertain. Sometimes the outcome of hedonic calculation is so obscure that we cannot have reasonable utilitarian grounds for believing that an action recommended by an accepted secondary principle is right. A flattering lie obviously gives some immediate pleasure, whereas the long-term pains it causes are either very uncertain, or probably too small to counterbalance the short-term pleasure. Should we not, then, endorse it on utilitarian grounds?

In reply, Mill concedes that individual vicious actions might indeed create a balance of pleasure, considered in isolation. Still, when we consider the types of actions of which they are instances, we can easily see that the balance of pain outweighs any pleasure. Mill takes the murder of a cruel person as an example.[98] Whewell seems to reply that he is not considering a general permission, but a particular violation of an accepted rule.[99] Mill answers that this is irrelevant.[100] Once we attend to the class and to the rule, the utilitarian position, Mill supposes, is easy to defend.

Mill might be introducing indirect utilitarianism here, but it is not clear what he means. He seems not to separate two arguments: (1) This particular murder will cause people to commit murders when they judge it expedient, and they will do this so often that the rule will not be reliably observed. (2) If we allowed people to act on their judgments of expediency, the overall balance of pain would be greater than it would be if we required them to follow a general rule against murder.[101]

The first argument is weak; it is not likely that all murders of the sort Mill describes would be so widely imitated that they would have this effect. If, for instance, a particular murder is not generally known to be a murder, it cannot set the bad example that is needed for his argument. The second argument is stronger, but its prediction about pleasure and pain needs to be tested by an enormously complicated assessment of consequences. In particular, it needs to be tested by a comparison of the effects of the unqualified rule that Mill favours

---

[98] 'Were such a man to be assassinated, the balance of traceable consequences would be greatly in favour of the act. The counter-consideration, on the principle of utility, is, that unless persons were punished for killing, and taught not to kill: that if it were thought allowable for any one to put to death at pleasure any human being whom he believes that the world would be well rid of, nobody's life would be safe.' ('Whewell', 181–2).

[99] The passage Mill quotes on 182 is not very clear.

[100] 'If one person may break through the rule on his own judgment, the same liberty cannot be refused to others; and since no one could rely on the rule's being observed, the rule would cease to exist'. ('Whewell', 182)

[101] As Mill notices (182), common sense recognizes some permissible homicides; these are not in dispute between him and Whewell.

with the effects of a qualified rule that would allow the sorts of exceptions that he mentions. It is not clear that the hedonic balance favours the unqualified rule against murder, or even favours indirect utilitarianism at all.

Mill fails, therefore, to disarm the argument about uncertainty. His resort to indirect utilitarianism makes the truth of common-sense rules depend on the results of an extremely complex calculation. We have to compare the effects of having a rule with the effects of having no rule. And then we have to compare the effects of an unqualified rule with the effects of different qualified rules with different exceptions.

Godwin's more extreme utilitarianism exposes the weakness of Mill's argument against Whewell. Godwin rejects the indirect utilitarianism of Hutcheson, Hume, and Paley, and treats secondary principles as mere rules of thumb, to be abandoned in particular cases where they do not maximize utility. To refute Godwin, Mill needs to show that hedonic calculation favours the treatment of common-sense secondary principles as more than mere rules of thumb. But his answer to Whewell does not try to show this. As Whewell remarks, it is difficult to show that impartial calculation of the pleasures and pains on each side supports the rules that Mill and common sense accept (*EM* 244, 601). Mill tries to justify these rules as 'secondary maxims' subordinate to the principle of utility, but he does not show that utilitarian calculation supports them.

1123. Which Consequences?

Mill is impatient with objections that rely on the difficulty of utilitarian calculation. In his view, we do not take these difficulties seriously in practice. Even if we cannot calculate utility completely or certainly, we get on quite well on the basis of reasonable estimates of utility. If we could not make such estimates, ordinary moral reasoning would be impossible. But we assume in our practice that practically useful calculations of utilitarian consequences are possible, and our assumption is borne out in practice. Hence all attempts to embarrass utilitarians with the difficulty of utilitarian calculation are debating tactics that we do not take seriously in practice.

This answer is reasonable if recognized secondary principles are based on utilitarian calculation. But Whewell denies this assumption (*EM* 245, 603). He observes that Paley's defence of specific rules does not rely on the sorts of consequences that would be relevant if Paley's hedonistic conception of happiness were correct. The same observation undermines Mill's argument to show that agreement on recognized secondary principles implies agreement on the possibility of practically useful hedonic calculations.

Mill's argument relies on the correct assumption that common-sense maxims can often be defended by appeal to consequences. The fact that broader permission to murder would make life, mutual trust, and property less secure is relevant to common-sense morality. Mill infers that the utilitarian is entitled to cite these bad consequences to support a utilitarian argument for a prohibition on murder. That is why he supposes that practical agreement on secondary principles does not require agreement on first principles.

But he is too quick to assume that the utilitarian is entitled to appeal to the bad consequences of permission to murder. His assumption is fair only if the bad consequences are bad hedonic consequences. But it is not clear that these are the consequences that common sense considers. For common sense probably does not bother to consider whether the increased pleasure resulting from a more qualified prohibition on murder would outweigh the bad consequences of broader permission to murder; it assumes that these bad consequences are decisive. If some kind of murder—say, revenge—gave extreme pleasure to the avenger, and if common sense cared primarily about hedonic consequences, it ought to be a serious question for common sense whether to allow murder for the sake of revenge by means that cause relatively slight pain to the victim. But common sense does not seem disposed to consider these hedonic consequences; indeed, it probably has no view on what the hedonic consequences of modifying its rule on murder would be.

If common sense is not committed to hedonism, it can consistently ignore these questions of hedonic calculation. But utilitarianism cannot consistently ignore them, since it takes a hedonist view about which consequences are relevant and why they are relevant. Hence Mill is not entitled to suppose that utilitarians should endorse the accepted secondary principle prohibiting murder, or to suppose that the general acceptance of this secondary principle proves the practical value and usefulness of utilitarian calculation.

Mill gives us no good reason to suppose that if some common-sense secondary principles rely on some estimates of some consequences, they rely on a utilitarian estimate of hedonic consequences, and therefore show that utilitarian calculation is feasible. Common sense relies on some assumptions about which consequences are relevant. Mill does not demonstrate that it takes all hedonic consequences to be relevant. Hence common-sense secondary principles do not show that calculation of hedonic consequences is possible and desirable.

1124. Whose Pleasures?

According to Whewell, the consequences that matter most to a utilitarian do not matter most to common sense. According to Bentham, the principle of utility extends to all sentient beings, not just to human beings, because all sentient beings are capable of pleasure and pain. Whewell objects that Bentham's principle obliges us to maximize the pleasure of non-rational animals.[102] Mill tries to turn Whewell's argument against him, by arguing that Bentham's humane attitude to the suffering of animals was simply ahead of its time, and that it has been vindicated by 'laws enacted nearly fifty years afterwards against cruelty to animals'. Bentham's attitude vindicates Mill's claim that utilitarianism articulates the implications of common sense.[103] Mill's eloquent defence of Bentham on cruelty to animals has been confirmed by the development of common-sense morality since 1850.

---

[102] Mill quotes Whewell: 'The morality which depends upon the increase of pleasure alone, would make it our duty to increase the pleasure of pigs or of geese rather than that of men, if we were sure that the pleasures we could give them were greater than the pleasures of men. . . . It is not only not an obvious, but to most persons not a tolerable doctrine, that we may sacrifice the happiness of men provided that we can in that way produce an overplus of pleasure to cats, dogs, and hogs.' ('Whewell', 186)

[103] 'Granted that any practice causes more pain to animals than it gives pleasure to man; is that practice moral or immoral? And if, exactly in proportion as human beings raise their heads out of the slough of selfishness, they do not with one voice answer "immoral", let the morality of the principle of utility be for ever condemned.' ('Whewell', 187)

But though Mill is right to urge this point, Whewell correctly replies that it does not answer all his objections to Bentham (*EM* 592–5). For the counter-intuitive aspect of Bentham's position that Whewell mentions is not the relief of animal pain, but the increase of animal pleasure. Bentham refers to the capacity of animals for feeling pain, as though we would accept utilitarianism if we were to agree that a non-rational animal's capacity for pain justifies us in protecting it from wanton torture.[104] But, as Whewell remarks, rejection of the wanton torture of animals is not the same as acceptance of a duty to maximize their pleasure. Hence, rejection of the duty to maximize the pleasure of sentient beings does not constitute acceptance of wanton torture.

To make his objection more vivid, Whewell might have said that the utilitarian is required to inflict excruciating pain on human beings in order to maintain a large population of rats who gain pleasure from the behaviour that causes the pain. Even if the pain of a particular person is greater than the pleasure gained by a particular rat, a large enough increase in the population of rats will ensure a surplus of pleasure.[105] Mill's answer to Whewell does not include an argument for increasing the pleasure of rats.[106] But if he embraces the reduction of animal suffering on utilitarian grounds, he needs to explain why he is not committed to the increase of animal pleasure.

In this case also, Mill seems to rely on common-sense maxims more than he is entitled to. Utilitarians may have educated common sense to be more attentive to the avoidance of unnecessary suffering to animals. But it does not follow that common sense proceeds on utilitarian grounds. Common sense, for instance, does not attach equal moral weight to the reduction of animal pain and the increase of animal pleasure. This would be irrational if common sense were implicitly utilitarian; but Mill has not yet shown that common sense is implicitly utilitarian.

1125. Whewell's Alleged Utilitarianism

Mill's answers to Whewell on utilitarian calculation and on the pleasures of sentient creatures assume that any consideration of consequences constitutes utilitarian calculation. The same assumption underlies Mill's claim that when Whewell tries to give specific moral content to his principles, he appeals to utility.

Whewell derives his basic virtues from the demands of human nature, and especially from what we need to ensure the co-ordinated satisfaction of our basic needs in our actual circumstances. Hence he sometimes argues that unless we recognize a specific virtue, rule, or practice, we will not be able to satisfy the relevant basic needs. Mill takes such an argument to appeal to utility. He infers that Whewell's naturalism has no moral content of its own,

---

[104] 'It may come one day to be recognized that the number of the legs, the villosity of the skin, or the termination of the os sacrum, are reasons insufficient for abandoning a sensitive being to the caprice of a tormentor. . . . The question is not, can they reason? nor, can they speak? but, can they suffer?' (Bentham, *PML* 17.4) Quoted by Whewell, *LHMPE* 224, and by Mill, 'Whewell', 185–6.

[105] Cf. Sidgwick's discussion of population, §1197.

[106] Singer, *AL* 8–25, defends Bentham. He also argues from the capacity of animals to feel pain rather than from their capacity for pleasure. His utilitarian argument is criticized by Regan, *CAR*, ch. 6. Carruthers criticizes Singer's assumptions about equality (but again with reference to pain rather than pleasure), *AI* 67–8.

because the secondary principles that he professes to derive from it are really derived from the principle of utility.[107]

This assessment of Whewell's argument is fair only if an appeal to the consequences of actions for any aspect of human welfare is an appeal to the principle of utility. But Mill does not defend this claim, and Whewell rejects it for good reasons. Whewell and Mill differ on at least three points: (1) Whewell does not conceive happiness as equivalent to pleasure. (2) He does not claim that the promotion of happiness is the basis of morality, even though he agrees that morality promotes happiness (*EM* 582). Since he believes that happiness includes moral elements (583), he does not treat the relation of morality to happiness as purely instrumental, and he does not assume that we can know the constitution of happiness independently of our moral beliefs. (3) He does not accept Mill's demand for maximization of pleasure.

Mill would be right to claim that Whewell implicitly appeals to utility, if Whewell's appeals to happiness and welfare were inconsistent with these three differences, and required the truth of utilitarianism. But Mill says nothing to support such a claim.

The discussion of Whewell is relevant to broader questions about the attitude of utilitarians to common sense. Mill takes over Bentham's assumption that any appeal to consequences, and especially to welfare and happiness, is an appeal to utility. Bentham assumes this because he believes that everyone implicitly accepts the principle of utility most of the time.[108] Perhaps he assumes, as Mill assumes about Whewell, that whenever we reason about consequences for human welfare, we rely on the principle of utility. A similar assumption may explain Bain's claim that no one really disputes utilitarianism, because no one disputes the importance of pursuing human welfare.[109]

We can agree with utilitarians on this point only if we have forgotten their account of the principle of utility. The three points on which Whewell disagrees with Mill about the morally appropriate consequences are three points on which the utilitarian doctrine departs from the common-sense assumption that consequences for human welfare are often important in deciding whether an action is right.

If Mill replies that Whewell's account of morality and happiness is still utilitarian, even though it disagrees with Mill on the three points we mentioned, he abandons his usual explication of the principle of utility. He also needs to abandon his claim that the principle of utility can be used, without reference to any 'foreign' principle, to deduce a body of secondary principles ('Whewell', 173, 194); for Whewell's claim that happiness has moral

---

[107] 'We now hear of the peace and comfort of society; of making man's life tolerable; of the satisfaction and gratification of human beings; of preventing a disturbed and painful state of society. This is utility—this is pleasure and pain. When real reasons are wanted, the repudiated happiness-principle is always the resource.' ('Whewell', 192) 'Though Dr Whewell will not recognize the promotion of happiness as the ultimate principle, he deduces his secondary principles from it, and supports his propositions by utilitarian reasons as far as they will go.' (193)

[108] 'Not that there ever is or ever has been that human creature breathing, however stupid or perverse, who has not on many, perhaps on most occasions of his life, deferred to it. By the natural constitution of the human frame, on most occasions of their lives men in general embrace this principle, without thinking of it: if not for the ordering of their own actions, yet for the trying of their own actions, as well as those of other men.' (Bentham, *PML* 1.12) 'Let him settle with himself, whether he would wish to discard this principle altogether; if so, let him consider what it is that all his reasonings (in matters of politics especially) can amount to? If he would, let him settle with himself, whether he would judge and act without any principle, or whether there is any other he would judge and act by?' (1.14)

[109] Bain is quoted in §1175.

elements introduces a 'foreign' element into the constitution of happiness that cannot be deduced simply from the balance of pleasure and pain. Since Mill's account of utilitarianism is not elastic enough to accommodate Whewell, Whewell's appeals to welfare are not tacit appeals to the principle of utility.

Mill's assumption that Whewell relies on utility reflects the attitude to utilitarianism that also leads him to suppose that recognized secondary principles embody traditional experience about how to maximize utility. Recognized secondary principles are concerned, at least in part, with consequences of actions and policies; but it does not follow that, as Mill supposes, they are concerned with utility. Mill overlooks the ways in which utilitarianism deviates from recognized secondary principles, if it follows his advice to deduce secondary principles from the principle of utility.

This conclusion about Mill's dispute with Whewell indicates some of the weaknesses of Mill's qualified defence of Bentham's utilitarianism. Sometimes he suggests that the principle of utility is practically unimportant, and that we need not accept Bentham's over-simple view of human welfare. But if this suggestion were correct, Mill would simply endorse the common view that consequences for welfare sometimes matter. Since he claims to go beyond common sense, he needs to rely on the principle of utility. But until he sets out the implications of the principle, he has not shown that common-sense secondary principles vindicate the practical usefulness of appeals to utility. On the one hand, Mill sees that the unqualified hedonism of Bentham's outlook may raise justifiable suspicion. On the other hand, he is unwilling to abandon the principle of utility as a basis for the criticism and reform of common-sense moral principles.

To answer such doubts, it would be reasonable for Mill to offer an account of the principle of utility and of its implications for the evaluation of secondary principles. He offers this account in *Utilitarianism*. We should now be able to approach this work with some idea of the questions that we might reasonably expect it to answer.

MILL: A REVISED VERSION
OF UTILITARIANISM

1126. A New Defence of Utilitarianism

If we approach Mill's *Utilitarianism* in the light of his earlier essays, its strategy is easier to understand, and some relevant questions emerge. Mill may have begun work on it around the time of his essay on Whewell.[1] In that essay, Mill tries a new defence of utilitarianism. In his view, Whewell's criticisms of Paley and Bentham do not damage the basic utilitarian position.[2] Though Mill dissociates himself from Paley, he defends Bentham, on the ground that Whewell's criticisms attack Bentham's strong points, but overlook Bentham's real weaknesses (174). He offers an indirect utilitarian defence of Bentham's appeal to utility as the test of rightness, and he supports Bentham's view on the pleasures of animals against Whewell. He alludes to Bentham's philistinism and disregard of character (173–4), but this criticism does not take Mill far from Bentham's principles.

Mill conceives *Utilitarianism* as an independent statement of a distinct version of utilitarianism. He designs it as a short book, to reach more readers.[3] He does not intend a systematic treatise on utilitarianism, or another reply to specific criticisms, similar to his discussion of Sedgwick and Whewell. His main purpose is to argue for the principle of utility as the first principle in ethics. But his first task, which takes up most of the book, is to explain the utilitarian position, and therefore to correct the misunderstandings that underlie irrelevant criticisms.

Mill believes that utilitarianism gets a bad name because people are wrong about its implications.[4] He does not directly challenge the hedonist psychology and sentimentalist

---

[1] *CW* x, p. cxxiii, quotes from Mill's letters and from Harriet Taylor to show that Mill was working on an essay on justice and an essay on utility between 1850 and 1858. The essay on Whewell appeared in 1852.

[2] 'It would be quite open to a defender of the principle of utility, to refuse encumbering himself with a defence of either of these authors. The principle is not bound up with what they have said in its behalf, nor with the degree of felicity which they may have shown in applying it.' ('Whewell', 173)

[3] 'But small books are so much more read than large ones that it is an advantage when one's matter will go into a small space.' (*CW* x, p. cxxiv, n21 (to Bain, 14-11-59))

[4] 'I believe that the very imperfect notion ordinarily formed of its meaning is the chief obstacle which impedes its reception, and that, could it be cleared even from only the grosser misconceptions, the question would be greatly simplified and a large proportion of its difficulties removed.' (Mill, *U* 1.6) *U* is cited by chapter and paragraph.

moral epistemology of earlier utilitarianism; nor does he emphasize or defend them. In his view, critics have misunderstood the theoretical basis of utilitarian normative claims, which does not depend on controversial doctrines in psychology and epistemology.

How has utilitarianism been misunderstood? In the essay on Whewell, Mill's defence of Bentham is vigorous but qualified. He maintains that Bentham derived some correct secondary principles from the principle of utility. But he does not suggest that a defender of utilitarianism has to defend all the conclusions that Bentham claims to derive from it. Similarly, in *Utilitarianism*, Mill does not say whether he means that (1) people have misunderstood the utilitarianism of Bentham and James Mill, or that (2) their version of utilitarianism is not the best version. The first claim involves a defence of Bentham, such as Mill offers in his earlier critical essays. But if he intends the second claim rather than the first, his defence of utilitarianism may not defend Bentham; on the contrary, it may concede the justice of some criticisms of Bentham.

John Grote argues that Mill does not decide between these two claims, and that his failure to decide undermines his claim to be defending utilitarianism.[5] Grote's objection presents a reasonable question that we ought to keep in mind in trying to understand the significance of Mill's claims. We ought to see how much of the earlier defence of Bentham still stands, given Mill's interpretation of utilitarianism.

1127. Utilitarianism and Quality of Pleasure

Mill reaffirms the utilitarian 'theory of life' as a hedonist theory of value.[6] He contrasts different types of desirable things. If he sticks to a hedonist conception of the end, things that are desirable for their 'inherent' pleasure should be those that cause pleasure by themselves, and those that are desirable as 'means' should be those that cause pleasure because they produce some effect that causes pleasure. Hence both types of desirable thing should, strictly speaking, be means to pleasure. Cooking is a means to producing dinner, whereas eating dinner does not need to produce any further effect beyond the effect of eating in order to produce pleasure, but (if we have cooked it well) produces pleasure by itself.

Mill asks whether his hedonist theory of value represents human nature 'in a degrading light' (2.4). He replies that hedonism does not imply that equal value is to be attached to moral, intellectual, and sensory pleasures.[7] The earlier hedonist writers have given a

---

[5] '...in meeting the objections, which he does with qualification, he gives us on the one hand a reassertion of old utilitarian doctrines; on the other, new (and professedly utilitarian) doctrines of his own. That he does the latter he to a certain extent avows, to that extent admitting the force of the objections made. ...he really does it to a much greater extent than he avows, and...his *neo-utilitarianism*, as I have called it, is something very different from that to which the objections were made.' (Grote, *EUP* 15)

[6] '...pleasure, and freedom from pain, are the only things desirable as ends; and...all desirable things (which are as numerous in the utilitarian as in any other scheme) are desirable either for the pleasure inherent in themselves, or as means to the promotion of pleasure and the prevention of pain.' (Mill, *U* 2.2)

[7] 'Human beings have faculties more elevated than the animal appetites, and when once made conscious of them, do not regard anything as happiness which does not include their gratification. ...there is no known Epicurean theory of life which does not assign to the pleasures of the intellect, of the feelings and imagination, and of the moral sentiments, a much higher value as pleasures than to those of mere sensation. It must be admitted, however, that utilitarian writers in general have placed the superiority of mental over bodily pleasures chiefly in the greater permanency, safety, uncostliness, etc., of the former—that is, in their circumstantial advantages rather than in their intrinsic nature.' (2.4)

misleading impression because they have considered the 'circumstantial advantages' rather than the 'intrinsic nature' of certain pleasures. What does this contrast mean? We might connect it with the contrast between things 'desirable for pleasure inherent in themselves' and 'means to the promotion of pleasure' (2.2). Perhaps Mill means that hedonists should have said, but have not said, that, for instance, intellectual activities themselves, even apart from being cheap, durable, safe, and so on, produce more pleasure than we get from eating and drinking.

A hedonist might hesitate to assert this about intellectual activities, because it does not seem true for everyone. Some people enjoy mathematics more than they enjoy lying on the beach; other people have the reverse preference. From a hedonist point of view, leaving circumstantial advantages to one side, we have no reason to prefer one sort of pleasure over the other. Hence the claim that one activity produces greater pleasure is apparently a false empirical claim.

Does Mill believe that this sort of hedonism represents human nature in a 'degrading light'? It does not advocate lying on the beach over mathematics, and it does not deny that mathematics is a source of pleasure; hence it does not deny that distinctively human activities are sources of pleasure. To this extent, it says nothing degrading. It makes the rationality of my choice between pushpin and poetry depend, as Bentham says, on how much pleasure I get from each of them.

An opponent of hedonism might believe that this conception of value is degrading, because it implies that quantity of pleasure is the only basis for choosing between different activities, and that we have no other ground for preferring distinctively human activities. According to this opponent, the hedonist theory is 'degrading' because it claims, as Mill says, that 'pleasure and freedom from pain are the only things desirable as ends'. This hedonist doctrine is Bentham's position. It is inevitably 'degrading' in the specific sense just described. But why should a hedonist not reply that it does not matter whether a theory is 'degrading' in this way?

In Mill's view, previous utilitarians have not said all they could say to show that their view is not 'degrading'. They could and should have pointed out that a hedonist theory of value allows us to count the quality of pleasure as an aspect of its value distinct from its quantity.[8] Judgments about quality are not to be resolved into judgments about quantity, because they mark a distinct dimension of value that may diverge from quantity.[9] Hence we may truly judge that one type of pleasure is to be preferred to another, even though the inferior type of pleasure is a larger quantity of pleasure.[10] In Mill's view, the recognition of qualitative

[8] '...but they might have taken the other, and, as it may be called, higher ground, with entire consistency. It is quite compatible with the principle of utility to recognize the fact, that some kinds of pleasure are more desirable and more valuable than others. It would be absurd that while, in estimating all other things, quality is considered as well as quantity, the estimation of pleasures should be supposed to depend on quantity alone.' (2.4)

[9] Mill's doctrine of qualities of pleasure is defended by Edwards, PP. In ch. 5, he discusses the relation of this doctrine to hedonism.

[10] 'If I am asked, what I mean by difference of quality in pleasures, or what makes one pleasure more valuable than another, merely as a pleasure, except its being greater in amount, there is but one possible answer. Of two pleasures, if there be one to which all or almost all who have experience of both give a decided preference, irrespective of any feeling of moral obligation to prefer it, that is the more desirable pleasure. ... we are justified in ascribing to the preferred enjoyment a superiority in quality, so far outweighing quantity as to render it, in comparison, of small account.' (Mill, U 2.5)

differences among pleasures does not undermine the utilitarian position, but strengthens it. For it allows the utilitarian to acknowledge the differences of non-instrumental value that seem to matter in the choices of informed and reflective agents who decide between different pleasures.

1128. Difficulties about Quality of Pleasure

These claims about quality of pleasure raise questions: (1) Does Mill explain the distinction between quality and quantity satisfactorily? (2) Does he introduce a plausible distinction? (3) If we accept the distinction, do we endorse or reject utilitarianism?

It is difficult to defend Mill on the first question. For he seems to offer two inconsistent characterizations of quality in pleasure: (a) He says that by 'higher quality' he means that if all or most of those who have experience of two pleasures prefer the second to the first, the second pleasure is of higher quality. (b) He says that if competent judges of the two pleasures prefer the second, the second is of higher quality.[11]

The first conception of quality is inadequate. It does not distinguish quality from quantity, since it does not rule out the possibility that my preference for one pleasure over another might be based on quantity. More important, it offers a test for quality that gives surprising results. If anyone who has had the slightest experience of an intellectual and a sensory pleasure finds one preferable to the other, their preference counts, according to condition (a), in deciding whether one pleasure or the other is higher. By this test, intellectual pleasures will be lower if most people have only a little experience of them, but on this slim experiential basis prefer sensory pleasures.

It is reasonable for Mill to prefer the second conception of quality over the first. He suggests that competent judges are those who are capable of appreciating higher pleasures, because they have had their higher faculties developed. Such people will sometimes prefer lower pleasures, if their capacity for the higher pleasures is impaired (2.7), but these variations in their preferences do not affect the quality of pleasures. Higher pleasures are identifiable independently of the choices of people with a certain kind of experience; they are the pleasures involved in exercising the higher faculties. Judges are competent if they have exercised their higher faculties, and therefore may be presumed to be better authorities on which pleasures are worth choosing.

In the view of some critics, Mill is wrong to introduce this distinction of quality among pleasures, because he simply treats his own preferences among pleasures as an index of quality. In their view, he ought to say that, since some people get more pleasure in intellectual pleasures than in sensory pleasures, a utilitarian social theorist ought to provide for the pursuit of both sorts of pleasures. This point does not require any dogmatic claim about the superiority of one pleasure over another.[12] It is compatible with Bentham's remark on pushpin and poetry.

---

[11] John Grote criticizes Mill for his wavering between these two accounts of higher quality, *EUP* 47–51. As Grote puts it, Mill sometimes treats the views of the experienced as testimony (as in the first conception of quality), and sometimes as opinion (as in the second conception).

[12] See Stephen, *EU* iii, 304–8.

Mill is not satisfied by this attempt to fit different types of pleasure into the utilitarian scheme. He argues, as Aristotle does, that our preference for rational activities does not rest simply on a belief that we enjoy them more than other things. We would not exchange a life of rational activity for a greater quantity of pleasure in some non-rational condition. Our preference for the rational activity rests on the conviction that it is better, irrespective of how much pleasure we get out of it.[13]

This conviction about greater value influences our conception of the character of our happiness. We regard the activities and conditions that we value for themselves as parts of our happiness.[14] Mill introduces his conception of happiness as having parts, and so prepares for his later explanation of happiness (Chapter 4).

Mill's implicitly Aristotelian convictions about value show why one might reasonably deny that rational preference for one activity over than another rests entirely on beliefs about hedonic consequences. The rational preference for an activity explains why we prefer pleasure taken in that activity; it is a higher pleasure, because it is taken in that preferable activity.

1129. Does Mill Abandon Utilitarianism?

But though we might agree with Mill's convictions about value, we might doubt whether they are consistent with utilitarianism.[15] They do not seem to fit the view that 'pleasure and the absence of pain are the only things desirable as ends' (2.2). John Grote points out the conflict with utilitarianism. If some pleasures are of higher quality than others, they are desirable as ends because of their higher quality; but in that case their desirability does not consist wholly in their pleasantness.[16] Earlier utilitarians were right, given their commitment to a hedonist account of value, to dismiss as mere 'declamations' the considerations that Mill adduces to support his doctrine of quality of pleasure.[17]

---

[13] 'Few human creatures would consent to be changed into any of the lower animals, for a promise of the fullest allowance of a beast's pleasures; no intelligent human being would consent to be a fool, no instructed person would be an ignoramus, no person of feeling and conscience would be selfish and base, even though they should be persuaded that the fool, the dunce, or the rascal is better satisfied with his lot than they are with theirs.' (Mill, U 2.6) Cf. Aristotle, EN 1174a1–4. Mill does not mention Aristotle.

[14] '. . . a sense of dignity . . . is so essential a part of the happiness of those in whom it is strong, that nothing which conflicts with it could be, otherwise than momentarily, an object of desire to them. Whoever supposes that this preference takes place at a sacrifice of happiness—that the superior being, in anything like equal circumstances, is not happier than the inferior—confounds the two very different ideas of happiness, and content.' (2.6)

[15] Questions about the consistency of qualitative hedonism are discussed by Crisp, MU, ch. 2.

[16] 'A consistent utilitarian can scarcely hold the difference of quality in pleasures in any sense: for if they differ, otherwise than in what, speaking largely, may be called quantity, they are not mutually comparable, and in determining as to the preferability of one pleasure to another, we must then be guided by some considerations not contained in the idea or experience of the pleasure itself.' (Grote, EUP 52)

[17] Grote, EUP 19n appositely quotes a passage from Paley: '. . . I will omit the usual declamation on the dignity and capacity of our nature; the superiority of the soul to the body, of the rational to the animal part of our constitution; upon the worthiness, refinement, and delicacy, of some satisfactions, or the meanness, grossness and sensuality of others: because I hope that pleasures differ in nothing but in continuance and intensity: from a just computation of which, confirmed by what we observe of the apparent cheerfulness, tranquillity, and contentment, of men of different tastes, tempers, stations, and pursuits, every question concerning human happiness must receive its decision.' (Paley, MPP i 6) Grote comments that 'Mr Mill's papers would have come, with the older utilitarians, under the head of "declamation"'. He adds further evidence from Bentham.

Recognition of qualitative differences in pleasures is consistent with the letter of Mill's formulation of utilitarianism, if the formulation means only that (i) an event (state of affairs, etc.) is desirable as an end only if it is a pleasure, rather than (ii) the only property that makes an event (etc.) desirable is an end is its pleasantness. The first interpretation allows higher pleasures to be higher, and therefore desirable, because of something other than their pleasantness, but the second interpretation rules out this possibility.

It would be unreasonable to ascribe the first interpretation to Mill, if we relied only on this passage about pleasure and pain as ends. Since he claims to capture the utilitarian position, he ought to accept the second interpretation; for the first interpretation yields a position that is not distinctive of utilitarianism. Since many non-utilitarians accept the claim expressed in the first interpretation, it does not match Mill's purpose. But once we read the discussion of quality of pleasure, the first interpretation seems to give a more plausible account of Mill's intention; for, in contrast to the second interpretation, it does not introduce a clear conflict between the doctrine of higher pleasures and the utilitarian doctrine. It may not be accidental that Mill formulates the utilitarian position ambiguously. His formulation may conceal from him the conflict between his doctrine of qualities of pleasure and the utilitarian position that he tries to defend. But his critics notice the conflict.[18] They object that it is misleading of him to speak of 'utilitarianism' if he intends the pluralist theory of non-instrumental value that underlies his doctrine of higher pleasures.

1130. Quality of Pleasure and the Standard of Morality

Mill concludes this discussion of higher pleasures by assuring readers that his doctrine is 'part of a perfectly just conception of utility or happiness' (2.9). He asserts, however, that it makes no difference to the utilitarian standard of morality, because the cultivation of noble character benefits others, and thereby increases utility, whether or not it is good for the individual. The utilitarian, therefore, would have to cultivate the traits of character that (according to Mill) yield higher pleasures to their possessors, even if they actually gave no pleasure to their possessors; for they are indisputable means to the pleasure of others.[19]

This does not show that the doctrine of higher pleasures makes no difference to utilitarian morality. For the doctrine also affects a utilitarian view about which pleasures should be maximized. Mill gives us no reason to believe that all sources of higher pleasures will be as useful as nobility of character is. If there are higher pleasures, they must be included in the utilitarian ultimate end. Mill acknowledges this in a reformulation of the utilitarian principle.[20] In his view, the utilitarian should pursue the maximum quantity of pleasure

---

[18] Critics of Mill on higher pleasures: see Schneewind, *SEVMP* 186n. For Sidgwick's criticism see §1163.

[19] '. . . for that standard is not the agent's own greatest happiness, but the greatest amount of happiness altogether; and if it may possibly be doubted whether a noble character is always the happier for its nobleness, there can be no doubt that it makes other people happier, and that the world in general is immensely a gainer by it.' (Mill, *U* 2.9)

[20] 'According to the Greatest Happiness Principle, as above explained, the ultimate end, with reference to and for the sake of which all other things are desirable (whether we are considering our own good or that of other people), is an existence exempt as far as possible from pain, and as rich as possible in enjoyments, both in point of quantity and quality; . . . This, being, according to the utilitarian opinion, the end of human action, is necessarily also the standard of morality . . .' (2.10)

together with an existence that is as rich as possible in higher pleasures. But how are these two elements of the end to be weighed or compared?

Mill implicitly raises a question about comparison when he asks whose pleasures are to be considered. He follows Bentham in including 'the whole sentient creation' (2.10). Questions about comparison of quantity and quality matter if we are trying to decide how the pleasures of different sentient creatures are to be weighed. A greater quantity of pleasure might result from a policy of increasing the population of animals capable of experiencing pleasure without consuming too many natural resources; but this policy might not ensure the multiplication of higher pleasures.

Mill, therefore, seems not to see the full significance of his doctrine of quality of pleasure. It not only introduces a non-utilitarian conception of value, but also requires a non-utilitarian conception of the end to be achieved by morality.

1131. The Composition of Happiness

If this discussion of quality of pleasures were an isolated section of *Utilitarianism*, it might be an aberration from Mill's normal utilitarian position. Mill's remarks about the standard of morality might even persuade us that his doctrine of quality of pleasures does not matter much for his argument as a whole. But it does not stand alone. The view that the ultimate good consists of elements that deserve to be chosen for their value, as distinct from their quantity of pleasure, returns in Mill's discussion of the character of happiness.

Mill discusses this question in the course of his argument to prove that happiness is the ultimate end of conduct. After his argument (which we must consider later) to show that happiness is one end (4.3), he claims that it is the only end. He considers the anti-utilitarian objection that virtue is another end, since we pursue it for its own sake.[21] According to a psychological hedonist, this claim about virtue rests on an error; we misunderstand our state of mind if we think we value virtue for itself, and not only as a means to pleasure. According to a hedonist about value, we are not justified in valuing anything but pleasure for its own sake.

Mill does not offer these utilitarian replies to the anti-utilitarian objection. He believes that non-instrumental desires for objects other than happiness are both psychologically possible and rationally justifiable, even though utilitarians are right about the role of happiness. For if we desire these other objects for their own sakes, we thereby also desire them as parts of happiness.[22] Hence our only ultimate end is happiness. We can be utilitarians without

---

[21] 'They desire, for example, virtue, and the absence of vice, no less really than pleasure and the absence of pain. The desire of virtue is not as universal, but it is as authentic a fact, as the desire of happiness. And hence the opponents of the utilitarian standard deem that they have a right to infer that there are other ends of human action besides happiness, and that happiness is not the standard of approbation and disapprobation.' (4.4)

[22] 'The ingredients of happiness are very various, and each of them is desirable in itself, and not merely when considered as swelling an aggregate. The principle of utility does not mean that any given pleasure, as music for instance, or any given exemption from pain, as for example health, is to be looked upon as means to a collective something termed happiness, and to be desired on that account. They are desired and desirable in and for themselves; besides being means, they are a part of the end.' (4.5) Mill's doctrine of parts of happiness is carefully discussed, from a point of view that is unsympathetic to eudaemonism, by Skorupski, *JSM* 295–307.

degrading every ostensible end other than pleasure to the status of a purely instrumental means to pleasure. We need not abandon all the convictions of a non-utilitarian about non-instrumental value.

For the moment, we need not consider Mill's account of how we can come to desire virtue for its own sake. We need only ask whether the possibility or the correctness of such a desire conflicts with the utilitarian conception of the end. He recognizes parts of happiness that are distinct from means to happiness; means are causal and instrumental, whereas parts are constitutive. Mill therefore appeals to the difference, noticed by Aristotle and Aquinas, between different ways that things can be 'for the sake of' an end.

We have often discussed the legitimacy of the distinction that Mill relies on. It is difficult to make much sense of Aristotelian eudaemonism without the distinction. Mill has good reason to believe that the distinction is important. He has already used it in his claim that people who refuse to sacrifice their human dignity for lower pleasures have made it an 'essential part' of their happiness (2.6). He puts forward a reasonable view of happiness, and of the relation of other non-instrumental goods to happiness as the ultimate end.

1132. Hedonism v. Eudaemonism in Mill

But if we welcome Mill's conception of happiness and other non-instrumental goods, we may doubt whether it fits utilitarianism.[23] Mill does not argue that his claims about happiness are true of pleasure. The claim that we regard virtue as a part of happiness is intelligible. The claim that it is a part of pleasure is more difficult to understand, and Mill does not make it intelligible. His claim about parts of happiness supports eudaemonism, but his official position is hedonism.[24]

Mill does not reconcile hedonism with the eudaemonist view that makes virtue a constituent of happiness. He sets out to show that a holistic conception of happiness (as a whole, containing parts chosen for their own sakes) is not 'in the smallest degree, a departure from the happiness principle', which he identifies with the principle of utility (4.5). Since the principle of utility says that 'by happiness is intended pleasure' (2.2), Mill's claims about happiness do not prove the point he needs to prove about pleasure.

Grote notices the conflict that results from Mill's failure to apply his Aristotelian claims about happiness to his hedonism.[25] He suggests that Mill begins (in Chapter 2) with

---

[23] Moore, *PE* 123–4, attacks Mill's account of parts of happiness on the ground that it conflicts with his hedonism. Mill's doctrine of happiness is carefully discussed by Berger, *HJF*, ch. 2, who ascribes a non-hedonist conception of happiness to Mill.

[24] This contrast between hedonism and eudaemonism is marked by Grote, *EUP* 46. Mill and Aristotle; see Crisp, *MU* 87–8.

[25] 'It appears to me that there is an inconsistency between what Mr Mill says in his second chapter, where he follows the Epicureans in developing the idea of happiness into definite, measurable, describable pleasure, to be tested by experience, and what he says in the fourth chapter, where he is proving that happiness is the only thing which men desire, because other things, such as virtue, which they may desire, and which appear different from happiness, are really, if only men desire them, a part of their happiness. If happiness is to be kept in this latter generality, which is necessary for Mr Mill's object in the fourth chapter, it must not, as in the second, be made convertible with felt pleasure. . . . In reality, if happiness is "the desirable", then the notion of it is vague and indefinite, of great importance indeed to the guidance of action, but what cannot by any means, of itself, furnish a practical principle for this.' (Grote, *EUP* 72–3)

hedonism, but later (in Chapter 4) turns to eudaemonism. Grote agrees with Whewell's view that if we conceive happiness as a compound of goods, we need to specify the components before we can find out how to achieve it. He also agrees with Whewell's view that happiness, rightly conceived, must include moral elements. If hedonism were true, we would not need to specify the elements of happiness in this way.

Grote's contrast between the hedonism of Chapter 2 and the eudaemonism of Chapter 4 is too simple, as we can see from his account of Chapter 2. For already in that chapter Mill deserts a hedonist theory of value, through his doctrine of quality of pleasures. The non-hedonic value that he implicitly recognizes fits into a doctrine of parts of happiness; hence Mill speaks of a part of happiness in his remarks on the sense of dignity (2.6). But Grote is basically right to say that Mill's defence of hedonist utilitarianism rests on a conception of happiness that does not allow parts of happiness.

To explain why Mill does not notice this implication of his argument, we may consider his associationist account (in agreement with Gay and Hartley) of how we come to choose virtue—or anything else except pleasure—for its own sake.[26] He mentions the original instrumental connexion of each of these non-hedonic goods with pleasure, and uses Godwin's example of the miser.[27] A miser comes to care about money for its own sake because of its previous instrumental connexion with pleasure; that is how we come to care about the ends we care about for their own sakes.[28] We originally pursue fame or virtue for the sake of the pleasure resulting from its effects, not for the pleasure resulting directly from it. But later we pursue it even apart from any prospect of pleasure resulting from its effects.

In saying that we now pursue or value virtue 'for its own sake', Mill combines two points: (1) We come to enjoy being virtuous even apart from its further effects, because of its past association with pleasant further effects, just as an old married couple might enjoy hearing a tune that used to be played when they went out together before they were married. (2) We come to regard virtue itself as a part of our good, because we regard it as a non-instrumental good. Mill's associationist account may explain the first result, but it does not explain the second. The first result does not make virtue part of our happiness. If it becomes part of our happiness (our good), it does not become part of our pleasure.

In Mill's view, this objection misinterprets the utilitarian conception of happiness. But his answer does not make his conception clear. First, he endorses the eudaemonist view that happiness is composed of states and activities not confined to pleasure; these are the 'parts' of happiness. Next, however, he describes the parts of happiness as 'sources of pleasure', and so abandons a eudaemonist conception of happiness for a hedonist conception.[29] To

---

[26] Gay and Hartley; §871.   [27] Godwin; §1116.

[28] 'What was once desired as an instrument for the attainment of happiness, has come to be desired for its own sake. In being desired for its own sake it is, however, desired as part of happiness. The person is made, or thinks he would be made, happy by its mere possession; and is made unhappy by failure to obtain it. The desire of it is not a different thing from the desire of happiness, any more than the love of music, or the desire of health. They are included in happiness. They are some of the elements of which the desire of happiness is made up.' (Mill, U 4.6)

[29] 'Happiness is not an abstract idea, but a concrete whole; and these are some of its parts. And the utilitarian standard sanctions and approves their being so. Life would be a poor thing, very ill provided with sources of happiness, if there

regard something as a source of pleasure in its own right is not necessarily to regard it as non-instrumentally good; and so Mill's explanation does not explain the attitude that it sets out to explain.

We may be able to understand Mill's obscurity and apparent indecision if we recall the difficulties in his discussion of quality of pleasure. He may well suppose that his claims about pleasure explain non-instrumental goodness; for we often take pleasure in something because we judge it to be non-instrumentally good. If this is the sort of pleasure we take in virtue, our enjoyment of it depends on our belief that it is non-instrumentally good. But this way of explaining the connexion between pleasure and goodness is incompatible with Mill's hedonist conception of goodness.

One might further argue that the doctrine of parts of happiness is incompatible with Mill's hedonism because of the implications about substitution. If I think of happiness as having parts of different degrees of importance, I will not believe I can compensate for the loss of more important good by an increase in a less important good. Hence I will not believe, for instance, that I could compensate for losing my friends by increasing my enjoyment in sunbathing; for I do not think that in general an increased quantity of pleasure in x can be substituted for pleasure in y without affecting my happiness. This failure of substitution makes the holist conception of happiness incompatible with hedonism.

In answer to this objection, Mill holds that hedonism is compatible with failure of substitution. Such failure results from his doctrine of quality of pleasure. His views about parts of happiness and his views about quality of pleasure support each other. But this mutual support shows that both doctrines conflict with hedonism. The failure of substitution guaranteed by the doctrine of quality of pleasure is intelligible only if some pleasures are to be valued for some feature distinct from their pleasantness. Mill has not shown, therefore, that the failure of substitution demanded by his holist account of happiness fits a purely hedonist account of value.

These conflicts in Mill's claims about goodness are worth examining not because they refute his claims about happiness but because they show that he cannot combine these claims with hedonistic utilitarianism. Sidgwick avoids any conflict by rejecting the doctrine of quality of pleasure and the holist conception of happiness. Moore and Rashdall reject hedonistic utilitarianism to argue that the good to be maximized includes non-hedonic elements; Grote calls this position 'ideal utilitarianism'.[30] In the view of Grote and Sidgwick, ideal utilitarianism loses the theoretical advantages of utilitarianism.

---

were not this provision of nature, by which things originally indifferent, but conducive to, or otherwise associated with, the satisfaction of our primitive desires, become in themselves sources of pleasure more valuable than the primitive pleasures, both in permanency, in the space of human existence that they are capable of covering, and even in intensity.' (4.6) The first sentence requires a eudaemonist, rather than a hedonist, conception of happiness. But the third sentence returns to hedonism.

[30] See Grote, *EUP* 47: 'an aspiring and truly ideal utilitarianism, or lofty eudaemonism . . .'. Elsewhere Grote speaks of Mill's 'neo-utilitarianism'. See 25: 'Mr Mill has a better right than any one to say what the word "utilitarianism" shall be taken to apply to, since it appears he was the first to give it its philosophical application. If it is to mean what he would now have it mean, much of the old charge against disappears. But if he allows the meaning of the term as it was understood both by friends and enemies when the charges he censures were made against it, then what he now proposes must be considered a kind of neo-utilitarianism which may be in some measure sympathized with and accepted even by those who think that the old charges were deserved.' Cf. 60: 'Mr Mill's neo-utilitarianism . . .'

1133. Utilitarianism and Liberty

If Mill's claims about value conflict with his hedonistic utilitarianism, does the conflict affect the practical significance of his moral theory? His conception of value would be practically irrelevant if it were a roundabout route to claims that hedonistic utilitarians could prove more directly or easily. But if it leads to divergences from the practical recommendations favoured by hedonistic utilitarianism, these divergences give us a further reason for choosing between Mill's theory and the hedonistic utilitarian theory of value.

A hedonist utilitarian might suspect that Mill's views about value introduce unwelcome vagueness into the practical recommendations of a utilitarian theory. If we cannot settle the character of the end by simply identifying it with pleasure, but we must find components of the end by relying on judgments about non-instrumental value, will it not be difficult to know what these judgments imply in practice? Mill's conception of non-instrumental value may seem to be a retreat from the precision sought by earlier utilitarians.

But the earlier utilitarians may have no good reason to expect the precision they seek. Bentham, Godwin, and James Mill, in contrast to the older utilitarians down to Paley, believe that reference to utility allows us to criticize and to reform common-sense morality and accepted political practice. They are entitled to believe this only if they can say what is required by the utilitarian standard of morality. But empirical hedonic calculation, uninfluenced by non-utilitarian judgments of value, does not clearly prove that the reformers are right and the conservatives are wrong. And so the fact that Mill appears less precise than Bentham does not show that he is really less precise, or that his conception of the end will be less useful in practice.

Some of these questions may usefully be raised about Mill's essay *On Liberty*. The recommendations in this essay are familiar and important. Mill announces that 'the object of this essay is to assert one very simple principle ... that the sole end for which mankind are warranted, individually or collectively, in interfering with the liberty of action of any of their number is self-protection' (*OL* 1.9).[31] He defends this 'Harm Principle' in three areas: (1) Thought, including discussion, expression, and publication (ch. 2). (2) 'Individuality' in tastes and pursuits, involving the freedom to do what we like and to spend our life as we please, subject to the constraint of not harming others (ch. 3). (3) Combination, including the right to join other consenting adults in pursuits that are protected under individuality (chs. 4–5).

Mill claims that he can defend these recommendations by utilitarian argument. He forgoes 'any advantage which could be derived to my argument from the idea of abstract right as a thing independent of utility' (1.11). But he clarifies his appeal to utility, by saying that he appeals to it 'in the largest sense, grounded on the permanent interests of man as a progressive being' (1.11). The permanent interests he has in mind appear in the epigraph to the whole essay. Mill quotes from Humboldt on the importance of 'human development in its richest diversity'. A conception of human development underlies Mill's arguments for freedom of thought and for the opportunity to experiment in ways of living.

---

[31] *OL* is cited by chapter and paragraph.

The argument rests, therefore, on Mill's claim that the human good consists in the development and realization of distinctively human capacities. These capacities are realized in an environment that includes the sorts of freedom that Mill advocates. If we attributed hedonistic utilitarianism to Mill, we might question his assumptions about human development. Why is it not an empirical question whether human development leads to a larger balance of overall pleasure? If we ask this empirical question about Mill's principles for the restriction of freedom, it is not clear that we ought to favour his principles. Sidgwick notices this objection from the 'empirical hedonist' point of view that he takes to be the utilitarian method (*ME* 478).

But if Mill's claims about human development are not empirical claims about means to maximum pleasure, but are part of his interpretation of the human good, his views about freedom and its limits are more plausible. If he does not maintain a hedonist conception of the good, he need not claim that people who develop their rational capacities in rational inquiry and practical deliberation necessarily gain more pleasure and avoid more pain than those who are denied these opportunities. In his view, the development of these rational capacities is to be chosen for its own sake. He relies on his doctrine of quality of pleasure and on his holist conception of happiness. These doctrines do not at once vindicate all his claims about the extent of freedom, but they make his position stronger than it would be on an empirical hedonist basis.

1134. Aristotelian Naturalism in Mill

In *On Liberty*, Mill assumes that the development of one's rational capacities is a suitable life for a human being as a rational creature. His advice is addressed to those who would not exchange the form of existence characteristic of a human being for the existence of a non-rational animal, even one that achieved a large surplus of pleasure over pain. He therefore seems to advocate a 'life according to human nature', in one familiar sense of that expression. It is a sense that one might take him to have ruled out in his essay 'Nature', where he takes a critical and destructive attitude to claims about nature.[32] He speaks in that essay as though his objections undermine the advice of the Stoics and Butler to live in accordance with nature.[33] Butler's naturalist principle does not seem to admit of a reasonable interpretation that makes it both morally significant and morally acceptable.[34]

It is difficult, however, to explain Mill's claims about the human good in *On Liberty* without reliance on some elements of the naturalism that he professes to avoid. In comparing the pleasures of human beings with those of pigs, he appeals to the differences between human beings and pigs. When he advocates human development, he appeals to

---

[32] Mill on nature; §1393.   [33] Mill, 'Nature' = *CW* x 376.

[34] '. . . the doctrine that man ought to follow nature, or in other words, ought to make the spontaneous course of things the model of his voluntary action, is equally irrational and immoral. Irrational, because all human action whatever, consists in altering, and all useful action in improving, the spontaneous course of nature: Immoral, because the course of natural phenomena being replete with everything which when committed by human beings is most worthy of abhorrence, anyone who endeavoured in his actions to imitate the natural course of things would be universally seen and acknowledged to be the wickedest of men.' ('Nature', 402)

the capacities that belong to human nature rather than to the nature of another animal, and he takes these distinctive capacities to offer some guide to the capacities that ought to be developed.

One might use Mill's arguments against naturalism to argue against his views on self-development. Human beings have capacities for wasting their time, for pointless exercises of ingenuity, for indifference, for cruelty, and for the destruction of themselves and others. Are these not all just as natural as the capacities that Mill wants to develop? And does his naturalism not therefore require him to advocate their development?

Mill would have an answer to this objection if he distinguished the essential capacities of a human being, as a being with a rational and social nature, from all the other capacities that belong to a human being naturally. If he drew such a distinction he would support the position of Aquinas, Grotius, and Butler (among others). He seems to rely on aspects of Aristotelian naturalism that have no explicit place in his reflexions on nature.

This partial appeal to Aristotelian naturalism affects Mill's practical proposals on freedom. From a utilitarian point of view, and from Mill's point of view in his critical comments on 'a priori' moralists, non-hedonist principles introduce a dangerous vagueness and indefiniteness into moral principles and into practical prescriptions. Mill endorses Bentham's use of the principle of utility as a basis for deducing practical recommendations without reliance on any 'foreign' principles ('Whewell', 194). *On Liberty* might be regarded as an application of the principle of utility to questions of urgent practical, political, and legislative significance. But the practical implications are derived from apparently 'foreign' principles. They rely on those aspects of Mill's conception of the good that are furthest from hedonist utilitarianism. If we replace his Aristotelian claims about self-development with an appeal to the balance of pleasure and pain, it is difficult to support any definite practical conclusions.

It does not follow that the Aristotelian elements in Mill are preferable to the properly utilitarian elements. For we have not examined either the legitimacy of his derivation of practical proposals from his Aristotelian principles or the plausibility of the proposals. But if Mill's proposals are plausible and important, they do not demonstrate the practical value of utilitarian argument. On the contrary, they may suggest the practical value of the 'foreign' principle of Aristotelian naturalism.

Mill's discussion of liberty is an important part of his attempt to correct an error that he notices when he discusses Bentham's exclusive attention to moral value.[35] Bentham expects the morally enlightened person to attach value only to pleasure and pain and to the universal maximization of pleasure. Mill suggests that this is not all that matters in human life, and that morality should recognize other elements of value. His concern in *On Liberty* with the development of human capacities answers the charge, urged by Nietzsche, that the dominance of morality tends to reduce human beings to respectable mediocrity.[36] Mill argues that, on the contrary, morality tends to encourage human fulfilment in all its variety. But his argument depends on acceptance of an Aristotelian rather than a Benthamite conception of the human good.

---

[35] See 'Bentham', 112, quoted in §1114.   [36] Nietzsche on mediocrity; §1102.

1135. Utilitarianism and Common-Sense Morality

Mill's interpretation of the human good suggests an account of the end that the utilitarian seeks to promote. To see whether this is a morally appropriate end, he might try two sorts of argument: (1) If he compares utilitarian recommendations with intuitive moral judgments, and he shows that utilitarianism partly agrees with and partly improves intuitive judgments, he can legitimately argue that our intuitive judgments already support utilitarianism. (2) If he shows that the utilitarian principle is the uniquely reasonable moral first principle, he can legitimately argue that we ought to follow it even against our intuitive judgments.

Both of these arguments appeal to moral judgment. The first appeals to a large number of relatively non-theoretical and immediate judgments. The second appeals to a higher-level moral judgment about principles. The first argument appeals to 'intuitive' judgments, in the sense of immediate and spontaneous judgments. The second might be taken to appeal to moral 'intuitions', understood as ultimate claims to knowledge resting on no more fundamental principles. Sidgwick distinguishes and elaborates the two arguments in *Methods*. But Mill already presents and exploits them. He uses the first argument in Chapter 2, and the second in Chapter 4. In Chapter 5, on justice, he returns to the first argument in the light of his account of the first principle.

Mill develops the first argument to answer criticisms that he takes to rest on misinterpretations of utilitarianism.[37] Among the 'obvious and gross' misapprehensions are those that allege a significant gap between utilitarianism and common-sense morality. Mill defends the utilitarian view on the rightness of actions and the goodness of agents, on expediency and rightness, and on the moral outlook of Christianity. On all these points, he maintains the view of his earlier essays that utilitarian secondary principles coincide largely with common sense.

He introduces secondary principles into his discussion of the utilitarian calculation of consequences.[38] Common-sense principles, he argues, reflect our past experience of the consequences of actions, and so they serve as secondary principles for the utilitarian. He is right to claim that past experience informs us about some of the consequences of actions. But he assumes that the consequences we know about from our past experience are those that are relevant to utilitarianism. The assumption is true only if common-sense principles reflect our experience of the effects of actions on maximum overall pleasure. But do our common-sense principles rest on experience of hedonic consequences?

---

[37] 'It may not be superfluous to notice a few more of the common misapprehensions of utilitarian ethics, even those which are so obvious and gross that it might appear impossible for any person of candour and intelligence to fall into them; since persons, even of considerable mental endowments, often give themselves so little trouble to understand the bearings of any opinion against which they entertain a prejudice, and men are in general so little conscious of this voluntary ignorance as a defect, that the vulgarest misunderstandings of ethical doctrines are continually met with in the deliberate writings of persons of the greatest pretensions both to high principle and to philosophy.' (Mill, *U* 2.22)

[38] 'Again, defenders of utility often find themselves called upon to reply to such objections as this—that there is not time, previous to action, for calculating and weighing the effects of any line of conduct on the general happiness. . . . The answer to the objection is, that there has been ample time, namely, the whole past duration of the human species. During all that time, mankind have been learning by experience the tendencies of actions; on which experience all the prudence, as well as all the morality of life, are dependent.' (2.24)

Mill tries to show that the consequences we have learned about are hedonic.[39] He begins with the modest conditional claim that if people generally accepted utilitarianism, their common-sense rules would have embodied beliefs about utilitarian consequences. But he seems to move to the categorical claim that they have acquired such beliefs. The categorical claim is justified only if people have accepted utilitarianism. But he has not yet shown that they have accepted it.

Mill assumes, as he assumed in his arguments against Whewell, that any moral principle that considers consequences for human welfare is implicitly utilitarian. That is why he believes that utilitarians can rely provisionally on common-sense principles.[40] In his view, appeals beyond the secondary principles to a first principle will be relatively infrequent, and when they are necessary, the utilitarian principle resolves conflicts best.[41] It provides a 'common umpire' because it is independent of the conflicting secondary principles; it neither merely restates any one of the secondary principles nor merely conjoins them.

We might be inclined to accept Mill's argument if we think of the actual influence of utilitarianism on legislation—the sort of influence for which Mill praises Bentham. If, for instance, we apply a utilitarian test to laws, we can rely on some quite widely shared moral assumptions about what promotes people's interests, and we can show that a given law does or does not promote them. But if we are asked to assess the utility of an action or policy simply by its consequences in pleasure and pain, we may be puzzled. How can we know what these consequences will be? And why we should be guided by our hedonic judgments rather than by our other moral judgments?

Bentham does not separate his criticism of legislation from his hedonic theory of value. In his view, we expose the flaws in a law or institution by considering the balance of pleasure and pain it produces, in contrast to the balance of pleasure and pain that might result from a different law. But the apparent plausibility of some of Bentham's criticisms may not depend on these hedonic calculations. If we find that 19th-century Poor Laws simply increase the dependence and destitution of the poor who are forced into workhouses, we may not stop to calculate how painful they find their situation, and how pleasant other people find it, in

---

[39] 'It is truly a whimsical supposition that, if mankind were agreed in considering utility to be the test of morality, they would remain without any agreement as to what is useful, and would take no measures for having their notions on the subject taught to the young, and enforced by law and opinion. ... mankind must by this time have acquired positive beliefs as to the effects of some actions on their happiness; and the beliefs which have thus come down are the rules of morality for the multitude, and for the philosopher until he has succeeded in finding better.' (2.24)

[40] '... that mankind have still much to learn as to the effects of actions on the general happiness, I admit, or rather, earnestly maintain. ... But to consider the rules of morality as improvable, is one thing; to pass over the intermediate generalizations entirely, and endeavour to test each individual action directly by the first principle, is another. It is a strange notion that the acknowledgment of a first principle is inconsistent with the admission of secondary ones.' (2.24)

[41] 'If utility is the ultimate source of moral obligations, utility may be invoked to decide between them when their demands are incompatible. Though the application of the standard may be difficult, it is better than none at all: while in other systems, the moral laws all claiming independent authority, there is no common umpire entitled to interfere between them; their claims to precedence one over another rest on little better than sophistry, and unless determined, as they generally are, by the unacknowledged influence of considerations of utility, afford a free scope for the action of personal desires and partialities. We must remember that only in these cases of conflict between secondary principles is it requisite that first principles should be appealed to. There is no case of moral obligation in which some secondary principle is not involved; and if only one, there can seldom be any real doubt which one it is, in the mind of any person by whom the principle itself is recognized.' (2.25)

comparison with the balance of pleasure and pain that would result from more effective measures. We are probably influenced by the thought that some people suffer undeserved deprivation, and that other people display indifference or callousness.

These moral reactions, however, are irrelevant to Bentham's criticism, if they do not result from an accurate estimate of the balance of pleasure and pain. Would such an estimate not change our judgments? Indeed, one might argue that every oppressive social policy (as we might initially describe it) could be made into a desirable one, if we could only increase the pleasure of the oppressors to a high enough level to compensate for the pain falling on the victims.

Doubts about Mill's claims need not be confined to critics of utilitarianism. To see that he needs some argument for his interpretation of common sense, we might recall Godwin's views on the implications of utilitarianism.[42] Mill needs to answer Godwin on two main points: (1) Godwin suggests that the best way to promote utility is to be a direct utilitarian, applying the utilitarian test to the choice of a particular action in a particular situation. (2) He maintains that the results of utilitarian calculation depart sharply from common sense.

Agreement with Godwin on the first point makes it difficult to disagree with him on the second. Unless we think we are incapable of assessing the total hedonic consequences of particular actions, we can think of cases in which the best action, from the utilitarian point of view, would normally be recognized as immoral. Godwin is indeed rather half-hearted in his utilitarianism. If he requires us to save a benefactor of mankind rather than an ordinary, not spectacularly beneficent person, should he not also advocate the painless and secret killing of some useless people if their death would make beneficent people even more beneficent? Perhaps they would take the resources made available by the absence of the useless people, and use them for the good of humanity. The difference between failing to save and killing ought not to matter in its own right, on Godwin's principles. If we are allowed, or even required, to calculate utility in this way, we can hardly agree with common-sense moral principles.

1136. Indirect Utilitarianism and Common-Sense Morality

Some of these conflicts with common sense may disappear if we turn from direct to indirect utilitarianism. It is not clear whether Mill intends an indirect utilitarian interpretation of secondary principles. If he does, he disagrees not only with Godwin, but also with James Mill, who asserts that properly conscientious action depends on applying considerations of utility to particular actions.[43] If he intends an indirect utilitarian defence of secondary principles, Mill departs from the position of the more radical, reforming utilitarians (which

---

[42] Godwin; §1115.

[43] See James Mill, *FM* 235: 'To say, that men ought to act on most occasions without regard for the principle of utility, is merely to say, that they ought to act without good intentions, that is, without regard to the dictates of a well informed conscience; trusting entirely to some of the inferior impulses of their nature'. He offers a similar argument (242–3) against the view that we should apply the principle of utility to rules, but not to single actions. To accommodate habitual actions, he denies that they proceed entirely without reflexion, and maintains that they rest on very rapid reflexion. If they are actions of conscientious agents, they rest on rapid reflexion on the principle of utility (257).

he normally defends), and relies on a stock move of the more conservative utilitarians, such as Paley and Berkeley (whom he normally attacks).[44]

But even if Godwin or James Mill could be persuaded, on utilitarian grounds, to accept secondary principles to be followed without any calculation of utility in particular cases, why should he accept the secondary principles recognized by common sense? Mill needs to do more than assert the necessity of some secondary principles. He does not show that common-sense rules refute Godwin's views about the hedonic consequences of actions or rules. They refute Godwin only if they correctly assess hedonic consequences.

Mill would answer Godwin if he could show that Mill's secondary principles rather than Godwin's follow from the principle of utility, together with sufficient empirical information. But to support this claim, he would need extensive knowledge of the hedonic consequences of different rules. He does not show that if common sense takes promises to create obligations, the hedonic consequences of refusing to recognize such obligations must be worse than those of an alternative secondary principle.

Opponents of utilitarianism, therefore, have a better case than Mill supposes. He does not support his assumption that common sense provides a large stock of provisionally acceptable judgments about utility. Nor is he entitled to take it for granted in this particular controversy; for the assumption is rejected both by anti-utilitarians and by any utilitarian who agrees with Godwin.

Mill would overcome some of these objections if he were to affirm a non-empirical connexion between common-sense secondary principles and utility. He might take common morality as a partial interpretation of utility, not simply as an empirical estimate of the means to utility. If, for instance, we argue that the recognized virtues articulate the ideal of 'pride' or 'dignity' or 'nobility' that Mill mentions in his discussion of higher pleasures, we might defend common morality as a partially successful attempt to state the practical requirements of this ideal.

Secondary principles should offer some protection against the utilitarian fanaticism that Mill regards as an easy misinterpretation of the utilitarian principle. In his view, we misinterpret utilitarianism if we take the principle of utility to tell us what we should aim at in every action. The principle of utility gives us the 'test of conduct', but does not prescribe the 'exclusive motive' on which we are to act. Comte's enthusiasm for what he calls 'altruism' leads him to blur this distinction between test and motive.[45] Mill's protest against Comte is intended to leave room in a utilitarian framework for ends that are not essentially moral at all. But it should also leave room for motives and aims that belong to non-utilitarian morality.

But the distinction between test and motive does not seem to capture Mill's point. If we grant that utilitarianism does not expect us to be always thinking about maximizing utility,

[44] Some of Mill's reasons for rejecting unqualified direct utilitarianism and for disagreeing with the radical claims of Godwin and Bentham are explored by Skorupski, *JSM* 315–25. Crisp, *MU* 102–12, argues that Mill is not a rule utilitarian (of the type described by Urmson, 'Interpretation', and Brandt, 'Credible'). See also Mabbott, 'Interpretations'.

[45] '...we are obliged...to charge him [Comte] with making a complete mistake at the very outset of his operations—with fundamentally misconceiving the proper office of a rule of conduct. He committed the error which is often, but falsely, charged against the whole class of utilitarian moralists; he required that the test of conduct should also be the exclusive motive to it.' (Mill, 'Comte', 335, discussed by Skorupski, *JSM* 357)

and allows us to pursue other ends, he still believes that it allows us to pursue these other ends only in so far as the pursuit of them maximizes utility. But why should we believe that this test leaves the appropriate room for these aims? Once he recognizes these other worthwhile ends, it is not clear why Mill is still entitled to assume that only the principle of utility should tell us when it is appropriate to pursue them.

We might answer that the other worthwhile ends provide us with a conception of the contents of utility. If we understand utility in this way, it is the appropriate combination of all the ends that we appropriately pursue without conscious reference to utility. But this conception of utility does not fit the role that Mill assigns to the principle of utility. If he were to accept this conception, he would undermine his claim that the principle of utility does not rely on secondary principles, and therefore provides a common umpire between them. To give up this claim would be to give up the main theoretical advantage of utilitarianism, as he sees it. This gives us a further reason to believe that Mill's departures from strict hedonistic utilitarianism about the character of the good cast doubt on his attempts to defend other aspects of the utilitarian position.

1137. The Proof of Utilitarianism

Mill's second strategy defends the principle of utility as the correct first principle. He takes his main task in *Utilitarianism* to be a contribution to the proof of the principle. The main steps in his argument are these:

1. Questions about ends are questions what things are desirable.
2. The only proof that x is visible is x's being seen.
3. The only proof that x is desirable is x's being desired.
4. The only proof that the general happiness is desirable is A's desiring A's happiness.
5. Hence (a) happiness is a good; (b) A's happiness is a good to A; (c) the general happiness is a good to the aggregate of all persons.[46] This argument shows that happiness is an end. The argument that follows for the holistic conception of happiness[47] is intended to show that happiness is not only an end, but also the only end.

The first question arises from the conjunction of (1) and (2). From (2), we might infer that the sense Mill intends for 'desirable' is 'capable of being desired', which is the parallel to the sense of 'visible'. But we might readily have assumed that the sense of 'desirable' in (1) is 'worthy of desire'; for this seems to be the sense appropriate for an ultimate good that is to provide the criterion for what ought to be done. Hence Mill seems to equivocate on the sense of 'desirable'.[48]

---

[46] 'Questions about ends are, in other words, questions what things are desirable. ... The only proof capable of being given that an object is visible, is that people actually see it. ... In like manner, ... the sole evidence it is possible to produce that anything is desirable, is that people do actually desire it. ... No reason can be given why the general happiness is desirable, except that each person, so far as he believes it to be attainable, desires his own happiness. This, however, being a fact, we have not only all the proof which the case admits of, but all which it is possible to require, that happiness is a good: that each person's happiness is a good to that person, and the general happiness, therefore, a good to the aggregate of all persons' (U 4.2–3).

[47] The holistic conception of happiness; §1131.

[48] Moore, among others, charges Mill with this equivocation. See §1255.

Can Mill avoid equivocation if he appeals to the principle that 'ought' implies 'can'? If whatever ought to be desired can be desired, it follows that if only one thing can be desired, nothing else ought to be desired. But this proves only that at most one thing ought to be desired, not that exactly one thing ought to be desired. Hence, if happiness is the only thing that can be desired, it follows only that either happiness is worthy of desire or nothing is. Mill has not secured the further premiss he needs, that something is worthy of desire.

A further question arises about the connexion between being visible and being seen in Mill's step (2). Mill does not make the false claim that something is visible only if it is seen, but he seems to claim that we have evidence for its being visible only if it is seen (so that something in an empty room is visible because it is seen when people are in the room). Still, his claim is false; something is visible if it would be seen in appropriate circumstances, whether or not it is actually seen.

This doubt about (2) implies a doubt about (3), however we understand 'desirable'. Being desired does not seem to be necessary for being capable of being desired. Even if happiness were the only thing desired, it would not follow that it is the only thing that can be desired. Still less does it follow that it is the only thing worthy of desire. Being worthy of desire is connected in some way with what would be desired by the appropriate agents in appropriate circumstances, but Mill does not show that it is connected in the simple way suggested by (2) and (3).

Mill does not rely on this simple connexion. For (4) does not say—as we might expect from (3)—that the evidence of the desirability of the general happiness is the fact that people desire it. Mill makes the different claim that the general happiness is desirable because each person desires his own happiness. Hence (4) seems to contradict (3). He recognizes that it would be false to say that each person desires the general happiness; but he believes that the fact that each person desires his own happiness is a reason for concluding that the general happiness is desirable and therefore good.

He makes the explicit step from 'desirable' to 'good' in (5), where he also introduces 'the aggregate of persons'.[49] He treats the general happiness as the sum formed by adding the happiness of each individual to the happiness of every other individual. To show that happiness, so understood, is the only ultimate good, Mill defends the psychological hedonist claim that each person pursues her own pleasure as her ultimate end (4.10–12). It seems to follow that each person who pursues the general happiness pursues it only as a means to her own pleasure.

Mill's remark about the 'sum' of individual goods suggests that he may be relying on some assumption about impartiality.[50] He expects us to agree that if A's happiness, B's happiness, and so on are all goods, we have equal reason to promote the happiness of each, since it is equally good, and so we have reason to promote the aggregate happiness. From the impartial view, we have no better reason to promote one person's happiness than another's.

But this explanation of 'general happiness' as 'aggregate happiness' does not fit Mill's normal explanation. He normally refers to the 'greatest happiness', understood as the

[49] In a letter he explains what he means in (4) and (5): '. . . when I said that the general happiness is a good . . . I merely meant . . . to argue that since A's happiness is a good, B's a good, C's a good, &c, the sum of all these goods must be a good' (To Henry Jones, 13-6-68 = *CW* xvi, no. 1257).
[50] Mill's assumption about impartiality is discussed by Crisp, *MU* 78–83.

maximum total surplus of pleasure over pain. We have no reason to suppose that this coincides with everyone's happiness. If we could achieve a higher total pleasure by making some happy and others unhappy than we would achieve by making everyone happy, we ought to choose the higher total. The fact (granting that it is one) that each person's happiness is good does not seem to make the maximum total happiness good.

We may misunderstand Mill, however, if we take too seriously the difference between pleasure and happiness. We need to distinguish two conceptions of happiness: (a) The personal conception. We speak of A's happiness as the condition in which A is happy as opposed to unhappy. By this we mean (whatever our conception of happiness) that things are on the whole going well rather than badly for A. In this sense, happiness is to be distinguished from pleasure; if A has a little pleasure and a great deal of pain, A is unhappy rather than happy on the whole. In saying that happiness is our ultimate aim, we think of happiness in this sense. (b) The quantitative conception. We speak of happiness as a quantity of which we may have more or less. In this sense, happiness is identical to pleasure, so that if A has a little pleasure, A has a little happiness, however much pain may go with it. In this sense, A's having acquired happiness (i.e., some quantity of pleasure) does not imply that A is happy. Hence being happy, rather than happiness, is our ultimate aim.

Mill speaks of happiness in both ways. His holistic conception relies on the personal conception, but his official explanation relies on the quantitative conception. To understand his transition from the goodness of A's happiness to the goodness of the general happiness, we must consider both conceptions. So far we have seen that the personal conception does not warrant his transition. But if he intends the quantitative conception, his explanation says that if A's pleasure is good, B's pleasure is good, etc., any aggregate of pleasure is also good. The ownership of the pleasures by different people is irrelevant for deciding whether the pleasures are good.

Both interpretations of the argument about happiness rely on impartiality, and we might say in each case that we have no more reason for regarding one person's happiness as good than another's. But there is still an important difference between the two interpretations. We might say that the happiness of A and B is no better than the happiness of C and D, but that in both cases it is better if two people are happy than if only one is. Here we understand happiness personally, as something to be assessed by reference to the total condition of a person.

This is a reasonable claim, but it does not support Mill. His conclusion says that happiness (i.e., pleasure) is good, and it does not matter who is happy or how many are happy (i.e., better off on the whole); all that matters is the total pleasure achieved. To reach this conclusion, he relies on a questionable assumption about 'the general happiness' and 'the aggregate of persons'. The general happiness is not the condition in which everyone is happy (i.e., well off rather than badly off); and so Mill does not claim that the general happiness is good for all the people who are happy. The general happiness is the maximum surplus of pleasure; Mill claims that this is the good in relation to the persons whose pleasures and pains are being aggregated. He does not say, therefore, that the general happiness is good for all these people. His argument assumes that pleasure, however it is distributed among persons, is the only good.

This equation of pleasure with happiness is inconsistent with the holistic conception of happiness. But the holistic conception is necessary for Mill's argument that all objects of rational desire are included in happiness. This argument supports his conclusion that all we desire is happiness, and he needs this conclusion for his proof of utilitarianism. Hence his proof relies on two incompatible conceptions of happiness.

1138. Utilitarianism and Justice

Mill's second and more elaborate effort to show that utilitarianism accepts recognized secondary principles is his discussion of justice in Chapter 5. This chapter is best discussed after the attempted proof of utilitarianism; for some of the assumptions about impartiality that underlie Mill's proof also affect his views on justice.

Mill's discussion of secondary principles in Chapter 2 did not choose between a direct and an indirect utilitarian attitude towards them. We might have taken him to mean that the secondary principles are useful guides for finding the particular action that maximizes utility. But his discussion of justice takes a more explicitly indirect utilitarian attitude. He uses indirect utilitarianism to account for aspects of morality that might appear to raise difficulties for utilitarianism.[51]

We take various procedures and practices to be just—treating cases impartially, giving people what they deserve, treating equal cases equally, and so on. Mill discerns two common features in these procedures: (1) We want to punish anyone who violates these rules of justice. (2) Our social sympathies guide and confine our desire to punish to those injuries that damage the general interest. Without the second feature, the mere desire to punish would have no specifically moral character; it would be a mere desire to harm other people. Hence the basis of our sentiments about justice, fairness, and so on is utilitarian, since reference to utility makes them genuinely moral sentiments (5.17).

In this case, Mill applies the test of utility to the rule rather than to the particular action. Hence he takes Kant's formula of the categorical imperative to express indirect utilitarianism.[52] Though this is a misinterpretation of Kant, it may be (as Sidgwick suggests) a reasonable utilitarian adaptation of Kant.[53] If we adopt a rule, and observe it on particular occasions without regard to utility, we may benefit our collective interest (by maximizing utility) even if observance of the rule on each particular occasion does not maximize utility.

This indirect utilitarianism helps Mill to give an account of one central feature of justice. The different rules of justice protect the rights of individuals, not only the legal rights recognized by law, but also the moral rights that ought to be recognized. If we have a right, we have a valid claim against society to be assured of something. If we have a right to freedom of action in a particular area, we have a valid claim against society to be assured

---

[51] The indirect utilitarian elements in Mill's conception of justice are explored by Lyons, 'Morality' and 'Justice'.

[52] Kant means 'that we ought to shape our conduct by a rule which all rational beings might adopt with benefit to their collective interest' (Mill, U5.22).

[53] Sidgwick on Kant; §1185.

that no one will interfere with our freedom of action.[54] This assurance of protection by society raises a difficulty for direct utilitarianism; for if we make the assurance subject to considerations of utility in each particular case, we do not assure someone's protection very securely. Nor do we defend them in their possession of their right, whereas Mill recognizes that a right carries a valid claim to the defence of the right by society. This point is most obvious in Mill's discussion of liberty. He argues that we should be assured in the possession of certain liberties, even when a direct utilitarian calculation would favour infringing these liberties in particular cases.

To show that this aspect of rights does not conflict with utilitarianism, Mill offers an indirect utilitarian justification for ignoring utility in particular actions. The general interest is served because we live in a society where people do not always do what maximizes utility on particular occasions. The utilitarian effects of security, assurance, freedom of thought and action, and so on, make it clear why our rules of justice promote utility in so far as they assure us of our rights.[55]

We might concede Mill's claim that indirect utilitarian argument explains why we ought to be assured the protections that are recognized by rights. But why should we also agree that all rights rest on this utilitarian basis? And why should we agree in general that the moral element of rules of justice must be a utilitarian element? Here we return to the question that we raised about Mill's appeal to secondary principles. Granted that the utilitarian recognizes some secondary principles, why should these be the rules recognized by common beliefs about justice? Price challenges utilitarian accounts of the foundation of rights; he rejects the utilitarian assumption that all our rights depend on a demonstration that their recognition promotes utility.[56] Mill needs to show not only that an indirect defence of some rights can be offered, but also that this defence is the only moral basis for any rights.

In answer to this objection, Mill argues that a utilitarian account of justice explains the actual uncertainty of convictions about justice, whereas, if alternative accounts were correct, we ought not to be so uncertain. When we look at the actual disagreements about justice, we see that they can be resolved only by reaching a firmer conviction about what promotes utility.[57] The fact that utilitarianism introduces some uncertainties is not a reason for rejecting it, since other moral standards also introduce some uncertainties. On the

---

[54] 'When we call anything a person's right, we mean that he has a valid claim on society to protect him in the possession of it, either by the force of law, or by that of education and opinion. If he has what we consider a sufficient claim, on whatever account, to have something guaranteed to him by society, we say that he has a right to it. If we desire to prove that anything does not belong to him by right, we think this done as soon as it is admitted that society ought not to take measures for securing it to him, but should leave him to chance, or to his own exertions.' (5.24)

[55] 'To have a right . . . is to have something, which society ought to defend me in the possession of. If the objector goes on to ask why it ought, I can give him no other reason than general utility.' (5.25)

[56] See Price, *RPQM* 159, discussed in §822.

[57] 'If the preceding analysis, or something resembling it, be not the correct account of the notion of justice; if justice be totally independent of utility, and be a standard per se, which the mind can recognize by simple introspection of itself; it is hard to understand why that internal oracle is so ambiguous . . . We are continually informed that utility is an uncertain standard, which every different person interprets differently, and that there is no safety but in the immutable, ineffaceable, and unmistakable dictates of justice, which carry their evidence in themselves, and are independent of the fluctuations of opinion. One would suppose from this that on questions of justice there could be no controversy; that if we take that for our rule, its application to any given case could leave us in as little doubt as a mathematical demonstration. So far is this from being the fact, that there is as much difference of opinion, and as much discussion, about what is just, as about what is useful to society.' (Mill, *U* 5.26–7)

contrary, the character of the uncertainties we recognize supports a utilitarian analysis of the principles.

But Mill is not wholly fair to his opponents; for a reasonable non-utilitarian theory need not deny practical uncertainty or dispute. Even if the principle of justice is grasped by an intuition independent of our intuition of the rightness of utilitarian benevolence, the application of the principle may not be grasped by certain intuition without deliberation. Mill's attempt to turn the mere fact of practical uncertainty against non-utilitarian views does not seem to rest on an accurate representation of these views. He treats them all vaguely and dismissively as belonging to 'the intuitive school', and so he does not consider their argumentative resources. Moreover, he is probably influenced by his unreasonable view that any consideration of consequences amounts to acceptance of utilitarianism. He relies on this view in his critique of Whewell, and he would no doubt appeal to it if Price, for instance, were to argue that we need to consider the consequences if we are to find the right application of rules of justice.

For these reasons, we ought not to accept too hastily Mill's claim that only utilitarianism can explain uncertainties about justice. To see whether he is right, we need to consider where utilitarianism introduces uncertainty and to ask whether common-sense convictions about justice are uncertain at precisely the places where they ought to be uncertain if utilitarianism is right. If, for instance, utilitarian introduces uncertainty about principles in which we do not recognize uncertainty, or about questions that we do not recognize as relevant, we have some reason to doubt Mill's claim that it explains the moral element in our views about justice.

1139. Justice, Equality, and Utility

Mill introduces an appropriate example for testing his claims about uncertainty. He recognizes a basic point on which ordinary convictions about justice are not uncertain. The principle of justice that requires treatment of persons according to their deserts rests on a more general principle of justice that requires impartiality between persons. Everyone has some right to equal consideration for their welfare. Bentham expresses the utilitarian commitment to equality, by insisting that everyone is to count for one. This commitment is even part of the meaning of the principle of utility.[58] Hence the right to equal consideration of one's welfare is no more uncertain within utilitarianism than within any non-utilitarian theory.

Mill is right to say that Bentham's principle about everyone counting for one is an explanation of the principle of utility, if it is understood as Mill understands it. If amounts of happiness can be expressed numerically, one unit of your happiness counts for as much,

---

[58] 'But this great moral duty rests upon a still deeper foundation, being a direct emanation from the first principle of morals, and not a mere logical corollary from secondary or derivative doctrines. It is involved in the very meaning of utility, or the greatest happiness principle. That principle is a mere form of words without rational signification unless one person's happiness, supposed equal in degree (with the proper allowance made for kind) is counted for exactly as much as another's. These conditions being supplied, Bentham's dictum "everybody to count for one, nobody for more than one", might be written under the principle of utility as an explanatory commentary.' (5.36)

in the calculation of overall utility, as one unit of mine. No one's pleasures and pains are left out in this calculation. The utilitarian aims at the highest total net pleasure, summed over everyone. Hence utilitarianism is indifferent to the distribution of welfare. We decide what is best by adding and subtracting the happiness and unhappiness of the different people affected and finding the highest total, no matter how it is distributed.

The fact that the utilitarian considers everyone's pleasures and pains in computing the total pleasure and pain implies, according to Mill, that Bentham embodies an equal right to happiness in his first principle. Hence Spencer is wrong to argue that if utilitarians agree that everyone has an equal right to happiness, they accept a right prior to the principle of utility, so that the principle of utility is not the first principle after all. Mill answers Spencer by arguing that the 'equal right to happiness' simply means that everyone's happiness is equally desirable, which is an aspect of the principle of utility. Bentham's principle means that everyone's pleasures and pains are counted towards the total.[59]

Is Mill right to transform Spencer's claim about a right into his own claim about desirability? The transformation invites an objection that relies on Mill's analysis of a right. To say that you and I have an equal right to happiness is not simply to say that your happiness and mine are equally desirable. According to Mill's account of a right, you and I have an equal right to happiness only if society ought to defend both of us equally in the possession of happiness. But the utilitarian theory does not imply that society ought to defend everyone in the possession of happiness. Even if it says that your happiness and mine are equally desirable, it says nothing about our having a valid claim to be defended in the possession of happiness or in any amount of happiness. On the contrary, the principle of utility requires us to deprive particular people of all their happiness if that is the most effective means to an increase in the total happiness. Hence Mill ought not to have accepted Spencer's claim that a utilitarian has to recognize an equal right to happiness.

We might overlook the implications of Mill's view, if we supposed that utilitarianism requires us to deprive one person of happiness only if that will make more people happy. If we were willing to kill one healthy person to provide spare parts for life-saving surgery for five other people, we might sympathize with Mill on this point. But even if we were to agree with Mill on the sacrifice of one person's interest to many people's interest, we need not endorse his utilitarian principle of distribution. For all that concerns him is the total pleasure and pain. And so, if we could increase one person's pleasure by harming ten other people, we would be required to do it, if that would increase the total pleasure. Mill's references to 'the greatest happiness of the greatest number' do not imply that we should aim at the greatest possible number of happy sentient beings. We should aim at the greatest possible total of happiness, summed over the greatest number of sentient beings, whether or not most of them are happy or unhappy.

However formal, general, and open to dispute the right to equal consideration of one's interests may be, Bentham's distributive principle does not seem to satisfy it. Nor is it clear

---

[59] 'It may be more correctly described as supposing that equal amounts of happiness are equally desirable, whether felt by the same or different persons. This, however, is not a presupposition, not a premiss needful to support the principle of utility, but the very principle itself; for what is the principle of utility, if it be not that "happiness" and "desirable" are synonymous terms? If there is any anterior principle implied, it can be no other than this, that the truths of arithmetic are applicable to the valuation of happiness, as of all other measurable quantities.' (5.36n)

that his principle justifies the secondary principles of justice that Mill tries to defend by appeal to utility. As usual, Mill suggests that the secondary principles are secondary to 'social expediency' (5.36) or 'social good' (5.38). Even if he is right about this, we need not agree that the consequences relevant to social expediency or social good are the same as those that matter for the maximization of total pleasure. Mill blurs the difference between an appeal to consequences and the utilitarian appeal to total hedonic consequences.

Mill refers to Bentham's principle of everyone counting for one, in order to show that utilitarianism agrees with common principles of justice in so far as it demands equal consideration for everyone's interests. But if we think Mill is right to suppose that Bentham's principle expresses the utilitarian commitment to maximizing pleasure, we see more clearly that it conflicts with equal consideration for everyone's interests.

This conflict may not be obvious to Mill; for he may suppose that he is doing for justice what he tried to do for various non-instrumental goods in Chapter 4. There he argued that virtue is a part of happiness, so that we reconcile the pursuit of virtue for its own sake with the claim that happiness is our ultimate end for the sake of which we pursue everything. In Chapter 5, he suggests that a basic principle of justice is a part of any plausible conception of the utilitarian end, so that we reconcile the demands of justice and of utility. But in both cases, the reconciliation appears to succeed only if we are not clear about the content of hedonistic utilitarianism. Mill's proof of the principle of utility requires a hedonistic conception of happiness that is inconsistent with the holistic conception. His explanation of the utilitarian commitment to equality requires a maximizing principle that is inconsistent with a right to equal consideration of one's interests.

Mill believes that objections to utilitarianism collapse once we understand the utilitarian position correctly, and hence recognize that it does not conflict with the moral convictions that are normally urged against it. But the result of his argument is the reverse of the result he intends. Once we grasp the utilitarian position more clearly, the conflict with other moral convictions also becomes clearer.

1140. Mill and Ward on Utilitarianism and Theological Voluntarism

One of Mill's most acute critics argues that utilitarianism conflicts with one of Mill's firmest convictions about morality. Throughout his life Mill opposes theological voluntarism and affirms naturalism. But he also rejects the doctrine of the 'intuitive school' that some moral convictions have to be maintained apart from their implications for utility. Ward argues that Mill's rejection of the intuitive outlook conflicts with his opposition to voluntarism.

In his essay on Mill's views on the foundations of morality, Ward expresses some doubts about whether Mill consistently offers a utilitarian account of moral rightness.[60] Sometimes he seems to criticize Mill for agreeing with Bentham's view that utilitarianism gives an account of the meaning of moral terms; hence he finds passages where Mill does not seem

---

[60] Ward, 'Mill', 50–1. He attributes to Mill the mistake that he also attributes to theological voluntarists, 56. But he does not explain why this is not simply a mistake about the meaning of the relevant terms.

to take 'right' to mean the same as 'tending to promote happiness'. One might answer this objection by interpreting the utilitarian doctrine as an account of the nature of moral properties rather than of the meaning of moral terms. Sidgwick sees that we need to reject utilitarianism as an account of meaning if we are to answer the objections raised by Whewell and Ward.

Sometimes, however, Ward also casts reasonable doubt on whether Mill can consistently maintain a utilitarian account of moral properties. In his view, Mill's opposition to theological voluntarism does not fit his utilitarianism. He cites the eloquent passage in which Mill rejects Mansel's version of voluntarism. Mill is especially repelled by the idea that we might be forced to admit that God could oblige us to act in ways that we recognize as morally repugnant. He says he would rather suffer the consequences of disobedience than violate his moral convictions by obedience.[61] Ward remarks that the vehemence of Mill's refusal to violate his moral convictions to please God does not seem to be based on a utilitarian account of morality.

We can see Ward's point if we suppose that Mill and God are the only agents whose pleasure and pain need to be considered. Since Mill would (by his hypothesis) condemn himself to endless torture by his refusal to compromise his moral convictions, and since he would please God by obedience, the hedonic balance would apparently favour obedience. The pain Mill would suffer by violating his conscience would presumably be less than the endless suffering he would avoid. But we can make the case even more difficult for Mill if we suppose that an arbitrary and immoral God issues the same immoral command to everyone; for in that case Mill would not only harm himself by refusal to act immorally, but he would set an example that, if other people followed him, would cause them endless pain as well. In that case, concern for the pleasure and pain of others should apparently require him to obey God's immoral commands.[62]

This objection of Ward's does not apply only to divine commands. It is not clear why Mill should commit himself to disobedience to immoral divine commands if he refuses to commit himself to disobeying immoral human commands as well. On the contrary, his objection to obedience to God implies that God would be behaving as a tyrant whom we ought to disobey. But it is easy to see why the demands of maximum utility might seem to require obedience to a human tyrant who ordered us to act immorally.

[61] 'If, instead of the "glad tidings" that there exists a Being in whom all the excellences which the highest human mind can conceive, exist in a degree inconceivable to us, I am informed that the world is ruled by a being whose attributes are infinite, but what they are we cannot learn, nor what are the principles of his government, except that "the highest human morality which we are capable of conceiving" [Mansel] does not sanction them; convince me of it, and I will bear my fate as I may. But when I am told that I must believe this, and at the same time call this being by the names which express and affirm the highest human morality, I say in plain terms that I will not. Whatever power such a being may have over me, there is one thing which he shall not do: he shall not compel me to worship him. I will call no being good, who is not what I mean when I apply that epithet to my fellow-creatures; and if such a being can sentence me to hell for not so calling him, to hell I will go.' (Mill, *ESWHP*, ch. 7 = *CW* ix 103)

[62] Ward, 'Mill', 73–4, observes first that 'all Catholics will substantially agree with what we understand to be its doctrine [sc. the doctrine of the passage quoted from Mill]', and then remarks that Mill implicitly rejects utilitarianism: 'His professed theory—the fundamental principle of his whole moral philosophy—is that morality consists exclusively and precisely in promoting the happiness of one's fellow-creatures. Yet here he says, that in a particular case the true morality of all men would lie, in promoting, not the happiness, but the everlasting torment of all mankind . . . When a crucial case really comes before him, his better nature compels him to decide sternly, peremptorily, effusively, indignantly, against his own doctrine.'

Might we answer on Mill's behalf that if the tyrant could attach his orders to credible threats to impose undeserved suffering in the event of disobedience, it would no longer be immoral to obey him? But if Mill accepted this answer, he would also have to admit that he would worship and obey an immoral God if the balance of utility required it. This admission would undermine his claim that he would submit to endless torture rather than worship and obey an immoral God.

Ward, therefore, seems to have found a reasonable objection to Mill that exposes a limit in Mill's commitment to utilitarianism. Mill is always concerned to answer the objection that acceptance of utilitarianism will force us to endorse immorality. He argues that the utilitarian has good reason to take ordinary secondary principles quite seriously, because they embody his overriding commitment to the general happiness. But Ward's objection points out that a utilitarian's commitment to any secondary principle can always be dislodged by a sufficiently credible threat or offer attached to a command to violate that secondary principle. Mill's opposition to theological voluntarism manifests his rejection of flexibility towards such threats and offers. He does not recognize that, as Ward makes clear, utilitarianism demands such flexibility. This is just another case in which Mill's moral convictions conflict with his defence of utilitarianism.

1141. Does Mill Really Defend Utilitarianism?

Ward's objection makes especially clear a broader criticism on which many of Mill's opponents agree. Though Mill sets out to defend utilitarianism, his moral views do not allow him a convincing defence of it. John Grote, for instance, argues that Mill's defence of utilitarianism fails, because the version of utilitarianism that Mill defends against objections is not the version which was the target of the objections. By modifying utilitarianism so that it avoids the objections, Mill implicitly concedes that the objections to the unmodified version were justified; if they were not, why would the modifications be needed?

Grote's criticism is justified. Mill would have made the true character of his argument clearer if he had conceded that many of the objections he discusses are sound objections to the utilitarian position that they had in view. A concession on this point would have shown why Mill's proposals are important. They are not proposals for the more accurate or charitable interpretation of Bentham's position, but proposals for a different position. In Mill's view, this different position has as much right as Bentham's position to be called a utilitarian position. Hence he claims, quite honestly, that he defends utilitarianism against objections that do not touch its central claims.

But is the position that Mill defends really utilitarianism? This is more than a verbal question, if we take it to ask whether he maintains the theses that distinguish utilitarianism from other moral positions. In particular, we may wonder whether Mill retains hedonism as a theory of value. If he believes that the good consists not simply in pleasure, but in pleasure of the appropriate type, he seems to recognize some aspect of goodness that is distinct from pleasantness. Hence he cannot reasonably maintain that goodness consists simply in pleasantness. Hence he should abandon hedonism.[63]

Does this modification retain the point and the spirit of utilitarianism? We may be inclined to say No, if we recall that one apparent advantage of utilitarianism is its promise of escape from the uncertainties other moral outlooks. The 'intuitive school' (as Mill calls it) requires us to make judgments of value on the basis of comparisons and evaluations for which we can give no definite rules that are intelligible and applicable without reference to disputable moral principles. Mill believes that if we want to avoid disputable claims that result from efforts to apply indefinite rules, we have a good reason to accept utilitarianism.

His position is open to doubt, then, if he introduces the sorts of comparisons and evaluations that he attributes to the intuitive school. But once he introduces qualitative hedonism about value, he seems to introduce disputable comparisons and evaluations. For we need some way to identify higher pleasures. If we follow Mill, and so appeal to the experience of competent judges, we need some way to identify competent judges. Identification of them may introduce the disputable moral claims that we are supposed to avoid by accepting utilitarianism.

Similar doubts affect Mill's description of happiness and its parts, and his appeal to the secondary principles recognized in common-sense morality. If we regard happiness as a whole consisting of activities, we deny that happiness is simply a feeling of pleasure. If we appeal to common-sense morality to tell us what will maximize pleasure, we refuse to appeal directly to the hedonist criterion of goodness to criticize and to correct ordinary moral principles.

It would not be merely pedantic, then, to argue that Mill does not really defend utilitarianism, and that he abandons the main theoretical aims of utilitarianism once he abandons the claims about value that allow us to achieve those aims. If we sympathize with Bentham's theoretical aims, we ought not to confuse ourselves by supposing that we can achieve them by accepting Mill's version of utilitarianism. Mill's position may be preferable to Benthamite utilitarianism; but it should be considered as a distinct position, and not as a defence of utilitarianism.

---

[63] Green, *PE* §§162–7, criticizes Mill on quality of pleasure.

SIDGWICK: METHODS
AND SOURCES

1142. Utilitarianism and Sidgwick's Moral Philosophy

One critic describes Sidgwick's *Methods of Ethics* as 'on the whole the best treatise on moral theory that has ever been written'.[1] Whether or not we agree with this estimate, *Methods* deserves study as a sophisticated defence of the utilitarian position. It rests both on a close examination of the history of ethics and on a careful estimate of the different options in moral theory.

Sidgwick lays a foundation in meta-ethics and moral psychology for his normative argument. His discussion of meta-ethical issues takes up some of the arguments in Price that anticipate Moore's non-naturalism.[2] In contrast to earlier utilitarians, Sidgwick rejects both a hedonist theory of motivation and a sentimentalist account of moral obligation. He profits from the criticisms that Butler, Price, and Reid urge against Hutcheson and Hume. His views on these questions are close to rationalist and Kantian views, but he believes they can be used to defend a utilitarian normative theory.

His defence of utilitarianism rests partly on a detailed discussion of the morality of common sense. He intends his analysis to seem plausible even to non-utilitarians, and to convince them that utilitarianism is the most plausible theoretical development and revision of common sense. But he does not rely exclusively on the agreement of utilitarianism with common sense. He accepts Butler's and Price's claim that parts of common-sense morality are non-utilitarian, but he argues that we ought to reject these parts.

To justify his revisions of common sense, he relies on the foundationalist and intuitionist moral epistemology that he shares with Price and Reid. In his view, knowledge of the right and the good rests on intuitions that depend on no further inferential justification; these intuitions support utilitarianism. His moral psychology and epistemology support the conception of ultimate good that he takes to be essential to utilitarianism. In his view, the only defensible form of utilitarianism is hedonistic; the end promoted by right action is maximum total pleasure.

---

[1] Broad, *FTET* 143. See also the other estimates cited by Singer, introduction to Sidgwick, *EEM*, pp. xxvi–xxviii.
[2] Price's arguments; §812.

Sidgwick's statement of utilitarianism is a compulsory point of reference for later utilitarians who reflect on the theoretical foundations of their normative position. But many of them reject his foundationalist epistemology and his hedonist theory of ultimate good.[3] In their view, these are two of the less plausible aspects of his philosophical position, and we should try to emancipate the utilitarian normative position from them.

Are utilitarians right to abandon Sidgwick's version of utilitarianism for a version that rejects his fundamental doctrines? Or is he right to suppose that he has found the most defensible version? If he is right on this point, and if his critics are right to reject his foundationalist epistemology and his hedonism about ultimate good, he may have unintentionally found a powerful argument against utilitarianism.

1143. Sidgwick and Greek Ethics

Sidgwick describes his book as an examination of methods rather than as a survey of historical systems and outlooks.[4] Still, he often refers to his predecessors, and he has them in mind even more often than he explicitly refers to them. The Preface to *ME* [6] describes his philosophical development, and the influence of his predecessors.[5] The same influence is evident from a comparison of *Methods* with the *Outlines of the History of Ethics*. The right places for detailed discussion of Sidgwick's agreements and disagreements with his predecessors are the places in *Methods* where he confronts these other views. It is useful, however, to begin with a survey of some of his connexions to predecessors, since his views about them affect some of the main doctrines of *Methods*.

We have already examined parts of Sidgwick's evaluation of Aristotle.[6] Here it will be enough to consider his general assessment of Greek moral philosophy. He sums up his verdict in his remark that traditional accounts of the cardinal virtues are too indefinite to provide a criterion of the sort that he demands from a moral theory.[7] He would have a legitimate objection to Greek views if their principles were tautologous or trivially analytic, or so indefinite that we cannot even say what would violate them. If they claimed, for instance, that what we ought to do is what it is reasonable do, and that reason prescribes our doing what we ought to do, they would not help us to identify what is reasonable or what we ought to do.

---

[3] Some later utilitarians, however, are sympathetic to hedonism. See, e.g., Quinton, *UE*, Pref. After noticing that consequentialism is the aspect of utilitarianism that is most prominent in contemporary moral philosophy, Quinton mentions his 'belief that the hedonistic aspect of traditional utilitarianism, its most widely repudiated ingredient, is equally deserving of consideration'. See also Brandt, *TGR* 132–40, ch. 13.

[4] Sidgwick consciously avoids an explicitly historical and critical survey of previous systems, and in later editions he abbreviates his historical comments. An important example is the re-writing of iii 13. See §1187.

[5] This material was added by the editor, who says it was 'among the ms. material which Professor Sidgwick intended to be referred to, in preparing this edition for the press' (p. xiv).

[6] Sidgwick on Aristotle; §115.

[7] 'I am fully sensible of the peculiar interest and value of the ethical thought of ancient Greece. Indeed through a large part of the present work the influence of Plato and Aristotle on my treatment of this subject has been greater than that of any modern writer. But I am here only considering the value of the general principles for determining what ought to be done, which the ancient systems profess to supply.' (375n) This note first appears in [2].

Sidgwick may believe that Plato's or Aristotle's principles are as indefinite as this.[8] A claim such as 'Virtue is good for the agent' may seem plausible if we take it to mean either (1) that 'virtue' is to be defined as 'what is good for the agent', or (2) that 'good for the agent' is to be defined as 'virtuous'.[9] In either case, an initially striking claim turns out to be almost tautologous. If we affirm both claims, we do not even clarify either concept.

This objection points to an important feature of Plato's and Aristotle's argument. When they appear to offer definite moral advice, they sometimes set out principles that we can understand only in the light of their theory as a whole. If, for instance, they tell us that virtue lies in a mean, or that we ought to subordinate passion to rational desire, their advice is intelligible only in the light of their conception of the mean or of rational desire; these conceptions, in turn, are intelligible, only in the light of their general conception of the good.

This does not mean, however, that we are trapped within an uninformative circle. Aristotle tells us enough about the character of happiness and of rational desire to specify the character of the different virtues. We can understand why he believes that if rational desires are to guide passions correctly, we need bravery to guide fear and confidence, temperance to guide the pursuit of physical pleasure, and so on. Admittedly, Aristotle fails a test of definiteness that Sidgwick imposes on a method of ethics. In Sidgwick's view, a method must provide principles that, combined with the necessary empirical information, determinately identify, even for someone with no antecedent commitment to morality or beliefs about moral goodness or rightness, the specific course of action that is morally required. Sidgwick is right to claim that Greek moralists fail this test.

It is sometimes difficult to evaluate Sidgwick's frequent charge that other moral theories are insufficiently definite. As we will see, a comparison between the definiteness of utilitarianism and the indefiniteness of other theories is an important part of his argument for utilitarianism. But his claims about indefiniteness cover a wide range of demands, from the legitimate demand for something more than uninformative tautologies to the controversial demand that underlies his conception of a genuine method of ethics. If the principles of Greek ethics fail to meet Sidgwick's controversial demand, that may be an objection to his demand, not to Greek ethics.

Despite this general criticism of Greek ethics, Sidgwick observes that Plato and Aristotle have at some points influenced him more than any modern moralist has. He probably refers especially to the discussion of questions in moral psychology in Books I and II, and to the description of the different moral virtues in Book III. In his discussion of common-sense morality, he emphasizes his debt to Aristotle,[10] and in much of Book III, he follows what he

---

[8] '...almost all the ethical speculation of Greece (though in many respects of unsurpassed interest and value) is stricken with this incurable defect: such universal affirmations as it delivers concerning right or good conduct seem always to be propositions which can only be defended from the charge of tautology, if they are understood as definitions of the problem to be solved, and not as attempts at its solution.' ([1] 354) From [2] onwards, the remark about an 'incurable defect' is deleted.

[9] Aristotle on happiness and goodness: §§72, 78.

[10] See xix–xx, quoted in §67. After describing Aristotle's description of common sense, Sidgwick continues: 'Might I not imitate this...?...Indeed *ought* I not to do this before deciding on the question whether I had or had not a system of moral intuitions?'

takes to be Aristotle's example; he reviews common sense without trying to improve on it. But he takes his eventual aim to be quite different from Aristotle's. For he undertakes the review of common sense in order to see whether it rests on genuine intuitions, and he finds that it does not rest on them. A critical attitude to common sense appears to Sidgwick to be un-Aristotelian. In his view, Aristotle records and articulates, but does not systematize or criticize.

1144. The Failures of Greek Ethics and the Task of the Moralist

The two sides of Greek ethics, as Sidgwick conceives them, suggest two dangers for the moral theorist. The universal principles of Greek moralists are empty, and we need a theory of value to support principles that give some definite practical guidance. Aristotle's discussion of the virtues is uncritical. We should not simply report common sense, but should try to avoid its theoretical and practical failures. If we find universal affirmations that are more definite than anything the Greeks can offer, we will have some basis for the rational criticism of common sense.

Greek ethics displays a gap between universal principles and the specific descriptions of virtues. This gap helps to explain why Greek moralists are so ready to accept some claims about virtue and happiness that the modern reader finds difficult to believe. They accept the 'monism of practical reason', because they believe that virtue is good for the agent, not simply good from some impartial point of view.[11] Hence they hold an 'attractive', as opposed to an 'imperative', view of virtue.[12] But these views seem correct only because the crucial claims are less informative than they seem. Since 'virtue', 'good', and 'happiness' are defined in an uninformative circle, the crucial claims about virtue and happiness are empty. But Aristotle does not notice this, because of his uncritical attitude to common sense. He gives content to his universal claims about virtue and happiness by simply taking over common-sense views about the content of virtue and happiness. He does not see that his theory is too empty to support these views.

Aristotle's theory, therefore, illustrates a frequent temptation that faces the moral theorist. If we try to defend our general principles by treating them as a circle of definitions, we can find content for our theory only by helping ourselves to unexamined common sense. But if we do this, we fail in the primary task of the moral theorist, who should try to find which aspects of common sense are correct by connecting them with principles that meet Sidgwick's demands for definiteness. His judgment on Greek ethics helps us to identify some of the central and controversial claims in his system.

---

[11] 'Again, we have noticed that throughout the ethical debate that was carried on for centuries in the schools of ancient Greece (though no doubt the idea of Good was not clearly understood to mean happiness, as we use the latter term), the principle that each individual ought primarily to aim at his own good was always assumed. In Butler's language, the faculty of conscience was not yet distinguished from self-love. And so in the ancient world self-sacrifice, though often practised in a striking and touching manner, was not conceived as a duty clearly and under its proper notion: it was justified to moral reflexion as a kind of pursuit of one's own interest. As an honourable and noble mode of action, it was felt to be "good" for the agent.' ([1] 108) This passage was deleted from [3] onwards.

[12] The relevant passages are quoted and discussed in §456.

1145. Butler on Human Nature

Given this unfavourable estimate of Greek moral philosophy, Sidgwick's favourable estimate of Butler might surprise us, since Butler revives one central line of argument in the Greek moralists.[13] Moreover, it may seem difficult for a utilitarian to take Butler seriously. Whewell regards Butler as a useful source for exposing the errors of Paley's utilitarianism, because Butler upholds 'independent morality'.[14] This 'independent' morality claims that goodness is 'an absolute and inherent quality of actions'. Opponents of independent morality 'derived morality from the nature of man and the will of God jointly'.[15] Sidgwick acknowledges that utilitarianism is a version of dependent morality.[16] In later editions, he removes the reference to Whewell's division, but he still endorses the view that Whewell opposes to Butler's view.[17]

Whewell takes Paley and Bentham to be the most deeply mistaken defenders of dependent morality. According to Paley, we aim at maximum universal pleasure because we want our own pleasure and we believe in divine rewards and punishments. Moral facts are not facts about the goodness and badness of actions themselves, but facts about our desires and about the will of God. Bentham deletes Paley's reference to the will of God. According to Sidgwick, he assumes that each person cares most about maximizing his own pleasure, and that this fact somehow explains why morality is concerned with pleasure. Those who care about the maximum total pleasure use artificial sanctions to persuade those who care only about their own pleasure to conform to the utilitarian outlook.[18] According to Bentham, we have no sufficient reason, apart from our own preference or the sanctions imposed by others, to promote the goal of morality.

Sidgwick argues against Whewell that a utilitarian can reasonably accept some of Butler's defence of 'independent' morality. He accepts Butler's refutation of psychological hedonism and egoism, and so he disagrees with such utilitarians as Bentham and Mill. He agrees with Butler's view that self-love is a superior principle distinct from conscience.[19] He believes

---

[13] Schneewind remarks, *SEVMP* 7, that Butler 'is in fact the one thinker of the earlier eighteenth century who cannot be ignored if the moral philosophy of the nineteenth is to be understood.' Hayward, *EPS* 32–49, emphasizes connexions between Sidgwick and Butler, with insufficient attention to differences. He endorses Sidgwick's view on Butler's account of self-love and conscience; but see §708.

[14] Whewell, *LHMPE* 111. See §712.   [15] Whewell, *LHMPE* 52. Quoted more fully in §547.

[16] '...the systems of Epicurus and Bentham are essentially similar in being both *dependent* systems; that is, in prescribing actions as means to an end distinct from, and lying outside the actions; and thus both consist of rules that are not absolute, but relative, and only valid if they conduce to the end.' ([1] 66) This passage is first changed in [4]. Sidgwick mentions Whewell at 69.

[17] Sidgwick and Whewell are discussed by Schneewind, *SEVMP* 101–17, and 'Cambridge'; Donagan, 'Intuitionism', and 'Whewell'; Schultz, *HS* 133–4.

[18] 'If [Bentham] is asked . . . "But when you concern yourself about the public good, and call it the right and proper end of action, do you not recognize a principle of duty, obedience to which you prefer to your own pleasure?" he answers unhesitatingly, "No, I concern myself about the public good, because in me selfishness has taken the form of public spirit, and when I call it the proper end, I mean that I wish all other men to take it for such, with a view to its attainment, with which the attainment of my own greatest happiness is bound up."' ([1] 68) In [2] 73, the comment on Bentham is shortened. From [3] onwards it is deleted, and replaced by the note at 87–8, where Sidgwick is more disposed to attribute the position of the *Deontology* to Bentham, on the strength of parallels in Bentham's other works.

[19] 'I do not (I believe) differ materially from Butler in my view either of reasonable self-love, or—theology apart—of its relation to conscience.' (xix) This passage appears first in [2]. See §1200.

Butler marks a clear and sharp distinction between duty (conscience) and interest (self-love) where his predecessors had failed to see one.[20]

Unlike Butler, however, Sidgwick thinks hedonism is a correct theory of a person's good, though an incorrect theory of our actual motives; he accepts prudential hedonism without psychological hedonism. Butler sometimes describes the object of self-love as my pleasure and my private good, without clearly distinguishing them. Sidgwick exploits this aspect of Butler's view (93, 405). Butler's predominant view, however, is that my good consists in the fulfilment of my nature, not primarily in the pleasure that I derive from the satisfaction of particular passions.

Sidgwick rejects Butler's appeal to human nature, and especially to his conception of what 'accords with nature', as a support for claims about self-love or conscience (377–8). It is therefore surprising that he claims to agree with Butler's conception of rational self-love; for, in Butler's view, we have good reason to follow self-love, and self-love has authority, in so far as it accords with our nature. Similarly, it is surprising, given Sidgwick's doubts about Butler's appeal to nature, that he claims to agree with Butler on the relation of self-love to conscience; for the different ways in which self-love and conscience accord with nature are central elements of Butler's conception of them. Sidgwick does not discuss the apparent connexions between parts of Butler's doctrine that he claims to accept and parts that he rejects.

1146. Butler on Practical Reason

Sidgwick also disagrees with Butler on the nature and authority of conscience. Butler argues that rational benevolence is distinct from conscience. Since conscience expresses the demands of morality, the distinctness of these two principles implies that morality is distinct from benevolence. Butler supports his claim with some counter-examples to utilitarianism. Sidgwick, in contrast to Butler, identifies the requirements of conscience with those of rational benevolence.[21]

Butler recognizes a 'duality' of practical reason, as Sidgwick claims; for he treats both self-love and conscience as rational principles. Sidgwick also believes that Butler is committed to acceptance of a 'dualism' of practical reason that takes self-love and conscience to be equally authoritative. We have found that Butler does not accept a dualism; on the contrary, he affirms the supremacy of conscience over self-love.

Since Butler relies on claims about nature that Sidgwick doubts, it is not surprising that Sidgwick disagrees about the supremacy of conscience.[22] To see why Sidgwick thinks Butler is committed to a dualism of practical reason, and whether Sidgwick is right, we need to discuss his full treatment of the dualism.

Sidgwick's agreement with Butler, therefore, is selective. He passes over many points on which he disagrees with Butler, and sometimes he interprets Butler so as to minimize the

---

[20] See *OHE* 197–8, quoted in §708.

[21] On Sidgwick's attempt to trace a development in Butler's position see §698. Balguy is not a utilitarian; see §664.

[22] Moreover, Sidgwick supposes that Butler (especially in the 'cool hour' passage) allows self-love some ultimate authority. See *OHE* 196, discussed in §708. His view about Butler suffers from some of the ambiguities in his own view of 'ultimate' reasonableness.

degree of disagreement. Moreover, the disagreements are connected. The non-utilitarian character of conscience, as Butler understands it, helps to explain the supremacy of conscience. Conscience is fair to the legitimate claims of different people, and so to the legitimate claims of self-love. It claims, therefore, to incorporate the claims of self-love in a further stage of practical reasoning. If Butler had identified the point of view of conscience with the utilitarian point of view, it would not have been clear why it is more natural to act on conscience than to act on self-love. Sidgwick's identification of conscience, morality, and rational benevolence conflicts with Butler's argument for the supremacy of conscience.

1147. The Rejection of Sentimentalism

Sidgwick's attitude to Butler illustrates his general attitude to his rationalist and sentimentalist predecessors. Hutcheson and Hume are anti-realists in their metaphysics of moral properties, anti-rationalists in their moral epistemology, and utilitarians in their normative position. These views form an intelligible combination; for Hutcheson argues that moral goodness is simply what the moral sense approves of, and what the moral sense approves of is benevolence, understood as the disposition to maximize utility.

In Butler's view, the utilitarian outlook is not the whole of morality, and moral properties cannot be reduced to those that the moral sense approves of. In reply, Hume combines a utilitarian account of morality with a sentimentalist meta-ethics, by loosening the connexion between benevolence, understood as a sentimentalist understands it, and utility. Hume argues that justice consists in a set of rules that maximizes utility as a whole, though not in each particular action. This argument answers Butler's attempt to use intuitions about justice to reject utilitarianism. It anticipates Sidgwick's argument to show that common sense is unconsciously utilitarian.[23]

Still, Hume's commitment to sentimentalism makes it difficult to explain why we accept a system of justice. Given his account of the nature of moral judgment, some feeling of approval is needed to get a system of justice started, if we do not appeal to self-interest. But what feeling of approval could this be? Hume correctly argues that the feelings of approval that might move us to approve of particular other-regarding actions cannot be counted on to move us to approve of a distant goal such as long-term public interest. Hence the ultimate basis of our approval of justice is self-interest.[24]

Hume's agreement with Hobbes on this point exposes him to the argument of Hobbes's 'fool'. In Hume's view, we have no ground for expecting the moral point of view to be either psychologically or rationally overriding. His discussion of the 'sensible knave' rejects Butler's belief in the rational supremacy of conscience.[25] His analysis of justice might reasonably dissuade Sidgwick from any sentimentalist defence of utilitarianism. He abandons the meta-ethical basis of Hutcheson's and Hume's utilitarianism.

---

[23] On the utilitarian tendency of Hume's account of the virtues, see *ME* 86, 424–6. On Hutcheson's use of indirect utilitarian arguments, especially in *SMP*, see §647. In *OHE* 203–4, Sidgwick emphasizes the utilitarian character of Hutcheson's normative position, and begins his treatment of Hume with: 'An important step further in political utilitarianism was taken by Hume' (204).

[24] Hume on justice; §771.   [25] Hume and the sensible knave; §779.

1148. For and Against Rationalism

Sidgwick returns, therefore, to the rationalism of Balguy and Butler. But he regards utilitarian rational benevolence as the whole of morality. In their view, benevolence is only part of morality, and we have no reason to be utilitarians once we give up sentimentalism.

Rationalists argue against utilitarianism on these lines: (1) Sentimentalism makes utilitarianism seem plausible as an extension of benevolence. (2) But it fails, for reasons seen by Butler and Hume, to support utilitarianism. (3) Hence a utilitarian needs a rational principle of benevolence, and must defend utilitarianism on rationalist grounds. (4) But a rationalist has no reason to accept utilitarianism as the supreme principle. Eighteenth-century utilitarians are voluntarists or sentimentalists, whereas rationalists—including Clarke, Balguy, Adams, Price, and Reid—recognize rational principles that restrict the pursuit of utility.[26] (5) And so rationalist utilitarianism rests on an unstable combination of two mutually destructive lines of argument.

Sidgwick accepts the first three steps of this argument. Following the rationalists, he believes that reflexion on our moral judgments reveals self-evident first principles that commend themselves to impartial reason, not primarily to any moral sense or benevolent feelings. But he rejects the fourth step; reflexion on common sense does not lead us, in his view, to self-evident non-utilitarian axioms about justice, virtue, and so on. As the rationalists claim, common sense takes the first principles of common-sense morality to be self-evident, with no need of further justification and no room for it. Contrary to the rationalists, however, common-sense principles need further justification. In Sidgwick's view, extended rational reflexion shows that these principles are not self-evident.

We might reply in one of three ways: (a) We ought not to demand self-evidence. (b) Our moral judgments cannot be justified. (c) Something other than the principles of common-sense morality must be self-evident. Sidgwick accepts the third answer; he argues that the principle of utility meets the appropriate conditions for a self-evident principle. Hence he becomes a utilitarian 'on an intuitional basis' (p. xx).

Though Sidgwick acknowledges this debt to the rationalist intuitionists, he cites them only sporadically. His historical comment on intuitionism (103–4) distinguishes the earlier and more philosophical period that includes Cumberland and Clarke, and the later and less philosophical period represented by the 'Scottish school' (Reid and Stewart).[27] Neither *Methods* nor *Outlines* mentions Balguy, though Sidgwick must have known about him, at least through Whewell.[28] *Methods* does not mention Price, and *Outlines* mentions him only briefly; Sidgwick's silence contrasts with Whewell's enthusiasm for Price.[29] Some of Sidgwick's discussions of intuitionism would have benefited from a more explicit confrontation with Price's arguments.

---

[26] Rationalism v. utilitarianism and voluntarism; §867.   [27] Part of this comment is quoted in §650.

[28] In *LHMPE* 91–2, 95–8, 119–22, Whewell writes appreciatively of Balguy. He suggests briefly that Balguy is not a utilitarian, because he defends independent morality against the morality of consequences (121).

[29] The discussion of intuitionism in *ME* iii 13 does not mention Price. *OHE* 224–6 subordinates Price to Butler and Reid. But it notes the essential points about meta-ethics (224), the non-utilitarian aspects of Price's intuitionism (226), and the affinity between Kant and Price (271). Whewell on Price; §802.

From the rationalist point of view, the most original and controversial part of Sidgwick's utilitarianism is not the claim that we have a rational intuition that it is right to promote utility. Other rationalists, including Price, agree about that. Sidgwick's innovation is his claim that only the principle of utility is an object of rational intuition. This intuitionist doctrine supports the rationalist utilitarianism that might be derived from Cumberland.[30] Sidgwick, therefore, needs to show that the impartial application of the appropriate intuitionist criteria vindicates the principle of utility, but no other principle.

If this argument succeeds, it refutes Whewell. According to Whewell, defenders of 'independent morality' are realists rather than voluntarists in metaphysics, rationalists rather than empiricists in epistemology, and anti-utilitarians in normative ethics. Whewell believes that the metaphysical and epistemological supports for realism and rationalism undermine the utilitarianism of Paley and Bentham. Sidgwick defends utilitarianism on the basis of Whewell's metaphysical and epistemological premises.

1149. The Kantian Basis of Utilitarianism

Sidgwick's attitude to the rationalists illustrates his view that the best moral philosophers have not defended the right normative position. He believes anti-utilitarian philosophers have been generally right on questions in the metaphysics and epistemology of morals, but have failed to draw the right normative conclusions from them. Similarly, Kant is right to identify moral principles with categorical imperatives whose rational authority is independent of any desire that they may satisfy.[31] He is right to identify the categorical imperative with a principle that conforms to a universal law. He takes the point of view of a rational agent who considers the interests of rational agents without any special concern for his own interest, and simply treats himself as one among many rational agents.

Unlike Kant, however, Sidgwick regards the Kantian formulation of the categorical imperative as purely formal and procedural.[32] Reflexion on the nature of a rational agent and of a universal law does not, in his view, reveal the determinate principles that identify the right actions. To find such principles, we need to know the end that a universal law must promote. This end is identified by the reasoning that supports the principle of utility.

This description of the relation between Sidgwick and Kant does not make it clear which of two views Sidgwick takes: (1) The categorical imperative is purely formal: the only thing that we are categorically obliged to do, without reference to any further inclination, is to act on a maxim that does not undermine itself when universalized. Any more specific content of morality produces only hypothetical imperatives. According to this view, utilitarianism fits the categorical imperative, but so do many other moral principles. None of them is any more rational than another, from the Kantian point of view, as long as they all meet

---

[30] We have seen at §535 that Cumberland is not a utilitarian. At *OHE* 173, Sidgwick describes him as a 'precursor' of utilitarianism but not a utilitarian.

[31] On categorical imperatives see §1145.

[32] Rawls remarks: 'To be avoided at all costs is the idea that Kant's doctrine simply provides the general, or formal, elements for a utilitarian (or indeed for any other) theory' (*TJ* 251n, 1st edn.). Rawls cites Hare, *FR* (on whom see §1338). In the 2nd edn., 221n, Rawls begins 'Especially to be avoided is the idea . . .'. He deletes the reference to Hare, but cites Sidgwick, Bradley, and Hegel instead. Rashdall agrees with their view, *TGE*, ch. 5. Contrast Green, §1241.

the Kantian demand for consistency. (2) There is a categorical imperative that provides a supreme principle of morality, but we cannot discover it by Kant's methods. We must not simply consider the fact that rational agents prescribe universal laws for rational agents. We must also consider some further feature of a rational agent as such. Sidgwick finds this further feature in prudence, which he, in contrast to Kant, takes to represent a rational demand and not simply an inclination. According to this view, there is a categorical imperative. Kant is right to suppose that it has something to do with rational agency, but he attends to the wrong features of rational agency.

Sidgwick's position is closer to the second view. His argument is Kantian in so far as it appeals to the aims that are necessary for rational agents, and seeks to derive basic principles of morality from these aims. He turns the tables on Kant no less than on Butler and the rationalists. His opponents rely on the epistemology and metaphysics of morals to reject utilitarianism. Sidgwick argues that, on the contrary, sound metaphysics and epistemology of morals support utilitarianism.

1150. Earlier Utilitarianism

Sidgwick's development as a moral philosopher began from utilitarianism, and eventually he accepted a version of utilitarianism that he preferred to his early position. At first, he accepted the utilitarianism of Mill in opposition to the intuitionism of Whewell.[33] Utilitarianism gives a definite basis for criticizing and reforming existing morality; for if we see that observance of a particular rule actually does more harm than good, we often conclude that there is no reason to observe it as we do. This critical treatment of common sense is prominent in Book III of *Methods*.

Reflexion on utilitarianism led Sidgwick to question the extreme degree of self-sacrifice that the utilitarian principle requires. If the only criterion of right and wrong is the overall good, it seems that any particular person's good may be sacrificed for that end. We need some reason to believe that this degree of sacrifice is reasonable. An appeal to common sense does not help; for it rejects the degree of sacrifice that utilitarianism demands.

Sidgwick mostly considers the opposition between utilitarian self-sacrifice and the claims of self-interest. But one might also argue, as Butler does, that utilitarianism unjustly harms innocent people simply to benefit others. Whether the conflict is between self-interest and utility, or between justice and utility, we need some defence of the utilitarian sacrifice of some people's interests to maximum pleasure. In particular, we need some reason to override the objections of common sense. If we cannot rely on common sense, we need, in Sidgwick's view, some overriding intuition that justifies rejection of common sense. Hence it is misleading to contrast utilitarianism with intuitionism; a sound utilitarian system needs a basic intuition.[34]

---

[33] 'I found in this relief from the apparently external and arbitrary pressure of moral rules which I had been educated to obey, and which presented themselves to me as to some extent doubtful and confused; and sometimes even when clear, as merely dogmatic, unreasoned, incoherent.' (*ME* xv)

[34] 'The utilitarianism of Mill and Bentham seemed to me to want a basis: that basis could only be supplied by a fundamental intuition; on the other hand the best examination I could make of the morality of common sense showed

Sidgwick draws on the work of Bentham, Mill, and their early critics, and looks for the most defensible form of utilitarianism in the light of the criticisms provoked by the earlier versions. He does not include Godwin among the earlier utilitarians worth discussing,[35] even though Godwin's combination of rationalism, objectivism, and utilitarianism anticipates Sidgwick's view.

He does not discuss criticisms of utilitarianism systematically. Though he refers only once to John Grote's critique of Mill's utilitarianism (432n), he abandons Mill's position at many of the points that Grote criticizes.[36] He refers only a few times to Whewell, but he deals implicitly with some of Whewell's criticisms of utilitarianism.

1151. Objections to Mill

Sidgwick shares Mill's conviction that the utilitarian outlook is more reasonable than Bentham makes it appear, and that legitimate objections to Bentham do not refute a reformed utilitarianism. But he believes Mill is largely wrong about which parts of Bentham's position should be accepted or rejected.[37]

In the metaphysics, psychology, and epistemology of morals, Sidgwick finds that Mill has uncritically followed Bentham and underestimated the force of the rationalist position. In contrast to both Bentham and Mill, he rejects psychological hedonism and any 'naturalist' or 'positivist' account of moral judgments that relies on a combination of psychological hedonism and associationism. He rejects any attempt to reduce moral judgments to feelings of pleasure or to the product of such feelings. He abandons a sentimentalist account of moral motivation in favour of a rationalist account. He dismisses the confusions about desire and desirability that underlie Mill's attempted proof of utilitarianism. He recognizes a question that is blurred in Bentham and Mill, about how one's concern for one's own pleasure can be transformed into an impartial concern for the pleasure of everyone.

On the normative side of utilitarianism, Mill departs from Bentham, but, according to Sidgwick, in the wrong direction. In Mill's view, Bentham burdened the utilitarian position with an unreasonably narrow account of the ways in which pleasure could be the basis of value, since he explained value simply by quantity of pleasure. Mill believes that judgments about quality, as distinct from quantity, of pleasure support reasonable judgments of value that cannot be explained within Bentham's quantitative framework. Sidgwick rejects Mill's amendment of Bentham, and so he retains quantitative evaluative hedonism (93n1, 94, 121).

According to Sidgwick, Mill's appeal to judgments of value about qualities of pleasure destroys a central utilitarian position.[38] If Mill is right, moral (or other evaluative) judgments

me no clear and self-evident principles except such as were perfectly consistent with utilitarianism.' (xxi) On the relation of utilitarianism to intuitionism see §1199.

   [35] He mentions Godwin briefly at *OHE* 266 and 272n1 (an interesting footnote on Kant and Godwin).
   [36] Sidgwick and Grote; §1176.
   [37] Hayward, *EPS* 18–23, exaggerates the agreement between Sidgwick and Mill. He neglects Sidgwick's critical attitude to Mill's main innovations in utilitarianism. Schneewind, *SEVMP* 194, sums up more accurately: 'Sidgwick does not have a high opinion of Mill's work in ethics'.
   [38] See also Grote, §1126.

explain our hedonic judgments. Sidgwick's whole moral epistemology, however, demands that hedonic judgments should be independent and fundamental and that moral evaluation should be derived from these, not the other way round. His clarity on the epistemological issue allows him to explain why Mill's concessions to common sense are fatal to utilitarianism.

His treatment of common-sense morality takes a more cautious attitude than Mill's towards secondary principles. Since common sense is, as Mill argues, unconsciously utilitarian, conscious utilitarians should accept some of common-sense morality. But since common sense is imperfectly utilitarian, the utilitarian reformer has work to do. Sidgwick considers a possibility that Mill overlooks, that utilitarian criticism of ordinary moral rules and principles may reject many of them and replace them with rules that common sense rejects.

This possibility leads Sidgwick into further questions about how far it is expedient for a utilitarian to apply utilitarian criticism to ordinary rules and practices.[39] Questions about expediency arise because Sidgwick assumes that utilitarian criticisms may often undermine ordinary rules. Such questions would not arise for him if he agreed with Mill that utilitarianism and ordinary moral rules largely converge.

These disagreements with Mill make it difficult to say whether Sidgwick is more or less 'conservative' or 'radical' than Mill in his attitude to common-sense morality. Mill's attitude is conservative to the extent that he thinks common sense is already sympathetic to utilitarianism and its secondary maxims are on the whole a good guide to utility. But this conservative attitude makes him optimistic about the prospect of gradual utilitarian reform of common sense; for common sense can be expected to see that utilitarian principles do better what common sense already tries to do. Though Sidgwick believes that common sense is unconsciously utilitarian, he also believes that utilitarian principles may conflict more sharply with common sense than Mill supposes; to this extent his attitude is more radical than Mill's.

But for this very reason, he is less inclined to advocate gradual utilitarian reform. Sometimes he is impressed by the dangers of advocating utilitarianism, just because it might raise objections to common morality, and so subvert a stable social framework of moral principles. The conclusion from his more radical utilitarianism may be a more conservative attitude to reform than Mill adopts. Mill wrote *Utilitarianism* as a short defence, in order to benefit society by encouraging many more people to be utilitarians and to advocate utilitarian reforms. Sidgwick's more elaborate treatment of utilitarianism, however, makes him less confident than Mill that it would be good for society if many people were utilitarians.

These points of agreement and disagreement with Mill raise questions about Sidgwick's version of utilitarianism. He has a much clearer idea than Mill has of what is distinctive and important about a utilitarian position, as opposed to some general expression of sympathy for moral enlightenment and concern for human welfare. But is the resulting position more plausible than Mill's?

Mill defends utilitarianism through concessions both to evaluative judgments about pleasure and to common-sense morality. The two concessions are connected; utilitarianism

---

[39] On the expediency of utilitarian thinking see §1207.

is more likely to agree with common morality if its conception of the ultimate end is influenced by qualitative evaluations. Since Sidgwick rejects Mill's qualitative hedonism, he cannot rely on Mill's argument for the convergence of utilitarian and common-sense moral rules. He retains the two aspects of Benthamite utilitarianism that Mill finds most implausible. If Mill's judgment about plausibility is right, and Sidgwick's judgment about Mill is right, we may be inclined to conclude that Mill and Sidgwick together have made a good case against utilitarianism.

Comparison with Mill shows that Sidgwick's hedonism is central in his formulation of utilitarianism; that is why he describes utilitarianism as universalistic hedonism. Without hedonism, his position would fail the tests that, in his view, any acceptable moral theory must pass. Hence it is reasonable, though one-sided, to concentrate as Bradley does, on Sidgwick's hedonism.[40]

1152. Sidgwick and Other Historians

This survey of Sidgwick's treatment of his predecessors helps to show how his understanding of the philosophical questions he faces is connected with his understanding of the history of moral philosophy. His historical understanding is superior to Mill's,[41] and far superior to the summary treatment, from a utilitarian point of view, in Bain's *Mental and Moral Science*.[42] We have already discussed Mill's account of his predecessors. It is useful to add Bain's brief history, to see what an orthodox follower of James Mill thinks about his predecessors.

Bain gives an extensive summary of ancient ethics, on which he follows George Grote closely, including a detailed abstract of Aristotle's *Ethics*. Aquinas gets three pages (Bain, *MMS* 540–3). In mediaeval ethics, Bain's most noteworthy suggestion is that Aquinas 'wavers' between a conception of virtue as an acquired habitus and as an infused condition. He does not see that Aquinas carefully distinguishes the two kinds of virtues. Bain passes directly from Aquinas to Hobbes, who gets a full and sympathetic treatment.

He has a low opinion of Butler, because he supposes, as Hartley and Gay do, that Butler's account of conscience depends on ignoring the possibility of an account of its genesis by association.[43] Bain discusses Price more fully than Sidgwick does, but not very sympathetically. He is not impressed by Price's agreement with Butler on disinterested benevolence, or by his anti-utilitarian arguments.[44]

By contrast, writers who might be regarded as sympathetic to utilitarianism are treated sympathetically. Mandeville is discussed fully, since his views might be taken to anticipate

---

[40] See Bradley, 'Hedonism'.   [41] Mill and the history of ethics; §1109.

[42] The recent Continental writers whose views are described, without great enthusiasm, are Kant, Cousin, and Jouffroy.

[43] 'The radical defect of the whole scheme lies in its psychological basis. Because we have, as mature human beings, in civilized society, a principle of action called conscience, which we recognize as distinct from self-love and benevolence, as well as from the appetites and passions, Butler would have us believe that this is, from the first, a distinct principle of our nature. The proper reply is to analyse conscience; showing at the same time from its very great discrepancies in different minds, that it is a growth or product, corresponding to the education and the circumstances of each, although of course involving the common elements of the mind.' (Bain, *MMS* 578)

[44] At 646, Bain refers to Thomas Brown; see §881.

associationist views of the development of moral sentiments. Bain's description of Hutcheson relies on the *System of Moral Philosophy*, in which utilitarianism is prominent, and the moral sense—rejected by Bain on associationist grounds—is less prominent. Bain discusses neither Grotius nor Pufendorf; he mentions natural law in Cumberland's apparently more utilitarian version. He derives his account of Hume entirely from the *Inquiry*, and emphasizes its utilitarian elements.

Bain traces the utilitarian tradition in his contemporaries. His account of Paley is long and sympathetic (651). He regards Bentham as the successor of Hume and Paley; 'his peculiarity is to make it [sc. utilitarianism] fruitful in numerous applications both to legislation and to morals' (668). James Mill's special contribution is his associationist account of the growth of moral approbation (683). Bain's view of Austin and J. S. Mill is predictably favourable, and his account of Whewell predictably unfavourable.

Bain and Mill are inferior to Sidgwick as historians, partly because they do not understand moral epistemology as well as he does. Bain and the Mills agree that utilitarianism can be convincingly combined with an empiricist and sentimentalist account of moral judgment and moral knowledge. They regard Hartley's associationism as a vindication of Hutcheson's combination of sentimentalism with utilitarianism, freed from any dubious claims about a moral sense.

Sidgwick sees that this utilitarian history is open to serious doubt, since it is by no means clear that the growth of sympathetic and other-regarding sentiment vindicates utilitarianism. He sees that a convincing defence of utilitarianism has to rely on more elements of rationalism. He therefore sees some of the merits in the views of Clarke and Kant, who are the sources of his moral axioms.

His view of what matters in the history of ethics may usefully be compared with Whewell's view. Whewell believes that reflexion on rationalism supports non-utilitarian 'independent morality'. This belief is not entirely warranted; we have seen that Whewell seems to combine questions and doctrines that ought to be distinguished.[45] Still, he suggests a reasonable case for connecting rationalism with the rejection of utilitarianism. It is worthwhile to see how good a case for utilitarianism Sidgwick constructs on a rationalist basis.

1153. The Study of Methods

Though we have spoken of Sidgwick's use of his predecessors to defend utilitarianism, he does not emphasize the utilitarian aspects of his argument. He insists that his primary aim is not to endorse any previous system or to put forward a new one that will avoid the errors of previous theorists, but to examine different methods.[46] He claims not to advocate one method over others, because they all have a place in practical reasoning. His task is to see

---

[45] Whewell's conception of independent morality; §§520–3.

[46] 'The present book contains neither the exposition of a system nor a natural or critical history of systems. I have attempted to define and unfold not one Method of Ethics, but several: at the same time these are not here studied historically, as methods that have actually been used or proposed for the regulation of practice; but rather as alternatives between which—so far as they cannot be reconciled—the human mind seems to me necessarily forced to choose, when it attempts to frame a complete synthesis of practical maxims and to act in a perfectly consistent manner.' (*ME* 12)

how common sense falls into conflicts through its use of more than one method, and to see how far these conflicts can be avoided by a clear account of the relations between the methods. This task is different from the task of constructing an ethical system, which he claims not to undertake.[47]

These professions of impartiality and even of neutrality did not convince all the early readers of *Methods*. In the Preface to *ME* [2], Sidgwick asserts that readers, and in particular Bradley, who have taken him to advocate utilitarianism against the other methods have fundamentally misunderstood him.[48] He claims to have taken steps to remove occasions for this misunderstanding, and to make it clear that he criticizes all the three methods impartially.[49] Since readers of the last edition of *Methods* have the benefit of the revisions that Sidgwick made in response to readers' misunderstandings, the impartial and critical character of his examination of the methods ought to be clearer than it was to readers of the first edition.[50]

Despite Sidgwick's emphatic warnings, it is easy to agree with the readers who take *Methods* to be primarily a defence of utilitarianism, and so, in his view, reveal their 'fundamental misunderstanding'. To see whether these readers are right, we need to grasp the main points of Sidgwick's surprisingly complex and confusing discussion of methods.

1154. What is a Method?

To identify different methods, we should not simply compile a list of methods that have actually been used, and we should not simply imagine those that might be used. We should find those that we necessarily recognize as possible methods for systematic practical reasoning.[51] A method of ethics is 'any rational procedure by which we determine what individual human beings "ought"—or what it is "right" for them—to do, or to seek to realize by voluntary action' (1). If we ask what we ought to do, we are looking for 'whatever conduct may be shown by argument to be reasonable' (5).

---

[47] 'In order better to execute this task, I have refrained from expressly attempting any such complete and final solution of the chief ethical difficulties and controversies as would convert this exposition of various methods into the development of a harmonious system.' (13) 'In the course of this endeavour I am led to discuss the considerations which should, in my opinion, be decisive in determining the adoption of ethical first principles: but it is not my aim to establish such principles . . . I have wished to keep the reader's attention throughout directed to the processes rather than the results of ethical thought: and have therefore never stated as my own any positive practical conclusions unless by way of illustration: and have never ventured to decide dogmatically any controversial points, except when the controversy seemed to arise from want of precision or clearness in the definition of principles, or want of consistency in reasoning.' (14)

[48] He mentions Bradley (without naming him) as a critic who 'has gone to the length of a pamphlet under the impression (apparently) that the "main argument" of my treatise is a demonstration of universalistic hedonism' (x).

[49] 'I have certainly criticized [the morality of common sense] unsparingly: but I conceive myself to have exposed with equal unreserve the defects and difficulties of the hedonistic method. . . . And as regards the two hedonistic principles, I do not hold the reasonableness of aiming at happiness generally with any stronger conviction than I do that of aiming at one's own.' (x)

[50] Rashdall, 'Sidgwick' 200–1, discusses the revisions that Sidgwick made in the different editions of *ME*. Sidgwick considered Rashdall's unpublished comments on [2] in the preparation of [3], and considered Rashdall's published comments on [3] in the preparation of [4].

[51] Schneewind, *SEVMP* 194–204, discusses Sidgwick on methods sympathetically and carefully, and examines some of the difficulties about intuitionism and perfectionism (see below). See also Singer, 'Many'.

We set out, therefore, with the question 'Why should I do it?', and an answer to this question will tell us why the proposed action is reasonable. Different moralists offer different answers to this question, and these answers can also be found 'in the common practical reasoning of men generally' (6). The different methods result from the different practical principles 'which the common sense of mankind is prima facie prepared to accept as ultimate' (6).

This description of methods presupposes that we want answers that tell us what it is reasonable to do, and hence what we ought to do, in a categorical sense of 'ought'.[52] If we try to answer the 'Why?' question by saying 'You ought to do x because you want y and x is a means to y', we do not answer Sidgwick's question. He assumes that sometimes when we ask 'Why?', we do not want simply to be told that our action is reasonable in relation to a presupposed end whose reasonableness we do not consider. We want to be told what we categorically ought to do, and hence what is ultimately reasonable, without reference to any presupposed end.

1155. The Moral 'Ought'

This claim about 'ought' encourages Sidgwick to clarify his view of the basic questions and claims addressed by a method of ethics. He takes a method to give us a means of deciding what it is ultimately reasonable to do, what it is right to do, and what we ought to do; he takes these ways of describing the question addressed by a method to be closely connected.[53] Though the discussion of these questions goes beyond Sidgwick's initial aim of clarifying his conception of a method of ethics, it will be helpful to consider his meta-ethical claims. His statement of his position is brief, but his arguments anticipate 20th-century discussions.[54]

He does not believe that meta-ethical argument is neutral between different normative theories, since he does not believe that many different normative theories can equally well satisfy the relevant constraints derived from meta-ethics.[55] On the contrary, he believes that only utilitarianism actually satisfies these constraints. But he believes that meta-ethical argument is neutral in so far as we can fix the relevant constraints without having already made up our minds about the correct normative theory.

---

[52] On the categorical 'ought' see §1158 below. Sidgwick qualifies his claim by remarking that such a presupposition of categorically rational ends is not really needed for the recognition of methods of ethics: 'For if a man accepts any end as ultimate and paramount, he accepts implicitly as his "method of ethics" whatever process of reasoning enables him to determine the actions most conducive to this end' (8). If, however, we took account of all the ends that people have accepted as ultimate without regarding them as rational, we would probably have a different method corresponding to each end, and so we would have too many methods to describe. We reduce the number of methods if we confine ourselves to the ends that the common sense of mankind recognizes as rational ultimate ends (9).

[53] In [1], the chapter on these topics (i 3) is entitled 'Moral Reason'. In [2], it is expanded (see Preface, [7] vii), and the title is changed to 'Reason and feeling'. Later it is further expanded, and the title becomes 'Ethical judgment'. (This title appears first in [5].) In the earlier editions, the chapter briefly defends some of Sidgwick's claims about reason. In the later editions, it includes a summary discussion of some of the main questions in meta-ethics, pursuing the discussion between Hume, Price, Reid, and Whewell.

[54] Prior, *LBE*, ch. 4, discusses the relevance of Sidgwick to 20th-century meta-ethics. See also Moore, *PE* 69; Hurka, 'Moore'.

[55] Schneewind makes this claim about neutrality, *SEVMP* 226–9.

Preliminary meta-ethical discussion is important because utilitarianism has suffered from reliance on unsound metaphysics and epistemology. Utilitarians have tended to be sentimentalists, but Sidgwick believes that the rationalists have had the best of the argument on meta-ethical issues. Rationalists have been unsympathetic to utilitarianism, but Sidgwick argues—with increasing emphasis in different editions of *Methods*[56]—that a sound rationalist metaphysics and epistemology of morals supports utilitarianism.

The methods of ethics presuppose a categorical 'ought' applying to ultimate ends. Admittedly, some judgments about what we ought to do assume some antecedent end to which the action we ought to do is a means. But this purely hypothetical use of 'ought' is not the only use. Against the view that oughts are all relative to one's happiness, Sidgwick argues that we normally believe that one ought to care about one's happiness (7). The pursuit of happiness 'appears to be prescribed by reason "categorically", as Kant would say, i.e. without any tacit assumption of a still ulterior end' (7).[57]

Similarly, the categorical 'ought' claims that something is ultimately right and reasonable to do, so that it is a concern of reason rather than passion. Sidgwick defends this claim against Hume's claim that reason can never of itself be any motive to the will. Here he argues that it provides exciting reasons. Primarily, however, he argues that reason provides justifying reasons.[58] Ought-judgments, in his view, are not predictions about means to ends or consequences of actions.[59]

To refute predictive interpretations of ought-judgments, Sidgwick argues against an analysis of rightness as fitness to an ulterior end.[60] We might expect utilitarians to support such an analysis; indeed Sidgwick quotes Bentham's claim that his fundamental principle 'states the greatest happiness of all those whose interest is in question as being the right and proper end of human action' (26n).[61] To see what Bentham means by 'right' in this claim, we might turn to his explicit account of 'right'. According to Sidgwick, Bentham defines 'right' as 'conducive to the general happiness'.[62]

---

[56] See Schneewind, *SEVMP* 233–6.

[57] Sidgwick confuses the issue by making his opponent suggest that happiness is an optional end. This does not matter (as Kant points out) to the question about whether the relevant ought is categorical.

[58] See Hutcheson and Hume §§639 735

[59] '... ordinary moral or prudential judgments ... cannot legitimately be interpreted as judgments representing the present or future existence of human feelings or any facts of the sensible world; the fundamental notion represented by the word "ought" or "right", which such judgments contain essentially or by implication, being essentially different from all notions representing facts of physical or psychical experience.' (25)

[60] A less than clear utilitarian account of obligation is offered by Bain: 'In answering this question, we can do little else than revert to the primary ends already described, and to the axiomatic and self-evident character of those ends, in order to indicate the difference between what is right and what is not right in action. On the fact of man's existence is grounded the rightness and the duty of preserving that existence and of employing all the means of self-preservation. . . . Considering that human society is indispensable, in the first place, to individual preservation, and in the second place, to the gratification of a very large amount of human susceptibility, we claim for this axiom the rank of a first principle of human obligation.' (Bain, *MPP* 85) This suggests that Bain has an instrumental view of obligation, but he does not say clearly whether the 'axiomatic and self-evident' ends are obligatory. He accepts Paley's connexion of obligation with punishment: 'To illustrate further the nature of right, we would remark, that obligation implies punishment. Where a penalty cannot be inflicted, there is no effective obligation; and in cases where—though rules have been violated—punishment is not considered, obligation is virtually denied.' (86)

[61] Sidgwick quotes Bentham, *PML* 1.1, p. 11.

[62] 'Of an action that is conformable to the principle of utility, one may say always either that it is one that ought to be done. . . . One may say also, that it is right it should be done . . . When thus interpreted, the words *ought*, and *right* and *wrong*, and others of that stamp, have a meaning: when otherwise, they have none.' (Bentham, *PML* 1.10, p. 13).

Sidgwick also suggests, however, that Bentham does not, or at least should not, accept this as a general account of 'right' and 'ought'. For if it is substituted for 'right' in Bentham's claim about his fundamental principle, the principle says simply that 'it is conducive to general happiness to take general happiness as an end of action' (26n). This is an unsuitable formulation of an ultimate principle. When he says that the general happiness is the right end to aim at, Bentham seems to intend something more than that it is the end that promotes the general happiness. He seems to mean that the utilitarian end has some characteristic that makes it right, and that this amounts to more than its being the utilitarian end. One might make Bentham consistent by abandoning the claim that the utilitarian end is the right and proper end of action. Then we could confine 'right' to the evaluation of actions, and maintain Bentham's account of its meaning. But Sidgwick agrees with Bentham's implicit assumption that 'ought' and 'right' are properly applied to ends as well as to means, and therefore he rejects the purely instrumental analysis of 'right'.

1156. Subjectivism and Definition

Having argued against the instrumental and predictive understanding of 'right' and 'ought', Sidgwick considers views that rely on Hume's account of the moral sense, as opposed to his account of reason. Sidgwick agrees with most of Hume's earlier readers in attributing to Hume a descriptive, rather than an emotive, account of the meaning of moral judgments.[63] He rejects both Hume's first view, that ought-judgments report the subject's own feelings, and his second view, that they assert that other actual or counterfactual people do or would have certain feelings.

According to the first view, 'x ought to be done' and 'x ought not to be done' are both true, if the first judgment correctly reports A's feelings and the second correctly reports B's feelings. But it is clear, in Sidgwick's view, that the two judgments are contradictories, and therefore cannot both be true of the same action. Sidgwick takes this point to refute the Humean position.[64]

A revised subjectivist view might answer that moral judgments do not really make claims about actions; when I make a moral judgment, I am only entitled to assert that this is how I feel. Sidgwick answers that we characteristically distinguish moral sentiment from others by its connexion with the belief that the action is really right and is not just felt to be right (27). If we give up our belief that a certain kind of action is wrong, we may still feel some

---

Bentham's account of 'ought' and 'right' is offered only for actions. But he offers no other account of these terms in applications to ends, and so Sidgwick is justified in considering his formula as a general account of the terms.

[63] Hume on the meaning of moral judgments; §756. On the interpretation of Hume see §1301.

[64] 'This is so obvious that we must suppose that those who hold the view which I am combating do not really intend to deny it: but rather to maintain that this subjective fact of my approbation is all that there is any *ground* for stating, or perhaps that it is all that any reasonable person is prepared on reflexion to affirm.' (*ME* 27) Hume's comment on what we 'mean' in our ought judgments supports Sidgwick's suggestion about what a subjectivist of this type might really intend. See §756. But Sidgwick does not point out that the claim about what the subjectivist really intends is not relevant. For even if that claim is true, it does not seem to affect the question about the meaning of ought judgments. A consistent subjectivist position should concede that ought judgments do not mean the same as judgments about the speaker's feelings, and should infer that none of these judgments is true.

aversion to the action, but we no longer accept the moral judgment that it is wrong. Hence the moral judgment cannot simply consist in the feeling.

This argument shows that when we make a moral judgment, we take ourselves to be entitled to say more than how we feel. The revised view undermines itself if it says that when we make a moral judgment, we believe we are only entitled to report on our moral feelings. If we have distinctively moral feelings, we have feelings based on moral judgments, and we believe that we are entitled to make moral judgments that do more than report our feelings. In that case, the revised view must be modified, to say that moral judgments are all unjustified, since they all go beyond what we are entitled to assert. Sidgwick does not refute this modified view.[65]

Sidgwick sums up his arguments against subjectivism by returning to the claim that sentimentalist views are self-defeating.[66] Though he makes this claim rather briefly and without enough argument, it raises a serious difficulty for some subjectivist and non-cognitive views, by confronting them with a dilemma. Either these views describe the relevant sentiment or feeling in non-moral terms, or they do not. If they describe it in non-moral terms, they fail to describe moral sentiment. But if they describe it in moral terms, they describe a sentiment that relies on a moral judgment; hence they take for granted the moral judgment that they are supposed to be analysing.

These arguments against subjectivism are different from the earlier arguments that Sidgwick offers against a purely predictive and instrumental view of 'ought' and 'right'. The earlier arguments were about the meaning of these terms, and he introduces subjectivism as a thesis about meaning too. But the later arguments do not seem to be so clearly about meaning. Sidgwick does not seem say simply that my assertion 'x is right' means something different from 'I have sentiment S about x'. He seems to argue that when we make moral judgments, we assume that x's being right is distinct from my having some sentiment about x. This seems to be a presupposition of moral judgments, rather than a part of their meaning.

In an appendix to his argument against the social version of Hume's view, which appeals to the sentiments of other people, Sidgwick considers an account that identifies a moral judgment that x is right with the judgment that I will suffer sanctions and penalties for failing to do x. In opposition to this account, he identifies 'the special ethical use of the term', which allows us to recognize that we can be morally bound to an action for which we expect to suffer neither legal nor social penalties.[67]

Against the account of right that refers to social sanctions, Sidgwick offers two arguments: (1) To show that we can distinguish an appeal to social sanctions from an 'ought' judgment, he observes that it is not a tautology to say that social sanctions ought to be attached to

---

[65] Sidgwick takes his argument against the revised subjectivist view to defeat the second version of Humean subjectivism—referring to the 'sympathetic representation of similar likings or dislikings felt by other human beings' (28). In this case also, we can see the difference between this sympathetic representation and moral judgment if we consider changes in our moral beliefs.

[66] 'So far, then, from being prepared to admit that the proposition "X ought to be done" *merely* expresses the existence of a certain sentiment in myself or others, I find it strictly impossible so to regard my own moral judgments without eliminating from the concomitant sentiment the peculiar quality signified by the term "moral".' (28)

[67] Sidgwick's criticism may be applicable to Mill's remarks on moral obligation in *U* 5.14. But it is not clear whether Mill intends the reference to sanctions to be a full analysis of 'ought'; hence it is not clear whether he is open to the first criticism discussed in my next paragraph.

wrongdoing.[68] This is the argument that he offered against Bentham's possible utilitarian analysis of 'right'. (2) He appeals to a 'crucial experience' of people changing their moral beliefs in opposition to conventional views, to show that 'duty does not mean *to them* what other people will disapprove of them for not doing'. This appeal seems different from the previous argument; it seems to refer to a common conviction about right, rather than to the meaning of 'right'.

A special case of the appeal to social sanctions is the appeal to divine sanctions. Sidgwick appeals to the 'Euthyphro Argument', claiming that when we recognize God as just in punishing sinners, we do not simply mean that God punishes sinners, but we claim that God is right to punish them. This does not mean that God will be punished for failure to punish sinners (31).

1157. The Indefinability of 'Ought'

After these arguments against views that analyse 'right' and 'ought' by reference to sentiments or sanctions, Sidgwick concludes that the notion corresponding to these terms is 'too elementary to admit of any formal definition' (32).[69] He argues that 'right' cannot mean 'maximizing utility', because 'it is right to maximize utility' does not mean the same as 'it maximizes utility to maximize utility'. The latter is a tautology, but the former is not; hence, he suggests, they cannot mean the same.

This argument, however, seems to make everything indefinable. We might equally argue that 'a vixen is a female fox' does not mean the same as 'a female fox is a female fox', and that therefore 'vixen' cannot mean 'female fox'.[70] If there are any definitions, substitutions of the sort that Sidgwick mentions will make apparently non-tautologous sentences into tautologies. Since Sidgwick does not maintain that there are no definitions, his argument about substitution is open to objection.

He might avoid this objection by explaining the point of his argument differently. He might agree that there are legitimate definitions that transform apparent non-tautologies into tautologies. But in these cases, we might say, for instance, 'Of course a vixen is a female fox; that's just what the word means'. This explanation marks the difference between our discovery of the meaning and our discovery of some further fact about vixens. But Bentham cannot intend to say this about 'It is right to maximize utility'; he takes this claim to be an interesting discovery about the right, not simply a clarification of the meaning of the term. Bentham assumes that utilitarians and non-utilitarians use 'right' in the same sense. He does not suppose that utilitarians are urging non-utilitarians to attach a different meaning

---

[68] 'In such cases, indeed, it would be commonly said that social disapprobation "ought" to follow on immoral conduct; and from this very assertion it is clear that the term "ought" cannot mean that social penalties are to be feared by those who do not disapprove.' (30)

[69] '...the notion we have been examining, as it now exists in our thought, cannot be resolved into any more simple notions: it can only be made clearer by determining as precisely as possible its relation to other notions with which it is connected in ordinary thought, especially to those with which it is liable to be confounded.' (32–3)

[70] On the Paradox of Analysis see §1258. Prior, *LBE* 104–7, discusses Sidgwick's substitution argument rather uncritically. He mentions another statement of it at *EGSM* 145.

to the word; he supposes that utilitarians draw attention to important facts about actions that are right.[71] This argument to show that 'right' does not mean 'maximizing utility' might succeed against Bentham; but it is more complex than Sidgwick's argument from substitution.

Has Sidgwick shown that the notion of 'right' is 'too elementary to admit of any formal definition' (32)? His argument applies only to nominal definitions; his points about notions, meanings, and uses of words would not show that a real definition of the property of rightness is impossible. Moreover, he restricts 'formal' definitions to those that define by notions simpler than the definiendum.[72] He thinks 'right' is simpler than 'ought' (in a narrow sense of 'ought') because 'ought' implies some conflict of motives, whereas 'right' and 'reasonable' do not. Hence we might suppose that 'reasonable', 'right', and 'ought' are increasingly complex notions, and that only 'reasonable' strictly resists definition by simpler notions.

Proposed analyses of 'ought' and 'right' try to analyse these moral notions by reference to notions referring to 'matters of fact', as Hume understands them in his arguments about 'is' and 'ought'. These are facts about what I feel or what other people would feel, or about what will happen to me if I disobey. None of these involves the characteristic moral notions of 'good', 'right', and 'ought'. Since he rejects such definitions, Sidgwick may believe that evaluative or normative notions cannot be analysed by reference to non-evaluative notions alone. Some basic moral (but not exclusively moral) notions, including 'good', 'ought', 'right', and 'reasonable', may be irreducible, if they cannot be defined through notions that can be understood without reference to these definienda. If they are irreducible, attempts at reductive definition will lead to inadequate or to circular (and hence non-reductive) accounts; either we will not capture the moral notions or we will re-introduce some of them in our analyses.[73]

Sidgwick does not conclude that basic moral notions are so elementary and unanalysable that they must simply be grasped. Though we cannot find a definition into simpler elements, we can find an explication that explains one moral notion with reference to others that eventually involve some reference to it.[74]

---

[71] Sidgwick states this argument in 'Controversies', 40: 'The utilitarian, in my view, affirms that "what is right" in any particular cases is what is most conducive to the general happiness; but he does not—or ought not to—mean by the word "right" anything different from what an anti-utilitarian moralist would mean by it'.

[72] We have already found this Lockean assumption about simplicity in Hutcheson, Price, and Reid. See §845.

[73] Sidgwick discusses reductive accounts of 'ought' in 'Distinction'. It is not always clear what he thinks about the definability of 'good'. He comments on the relation of 'good' to 'desired': '... we must identify it not with the actually *desired*, but rather with the *desirable*:—meaning by "desirable" not necessarily "what *ought* to be desired" but (1) what would be desired, with strength proportioned to the degree of desirability, if it were judged attainable by voluntary action, (2) supposing the desirer to possess a perfect forecast, emotional as well as intellectual, of the state of attainment or fruition.' (110–11, reference-letters added.) It is reasonable not to identify the desirable with what ought to be desired, since Sidgwick believes that 'ought' implies some degree of reluctance, but with what would appropriately be desired. But it is not clear what exactly Sidgwick means. Since 'desirability' appears in (1), the definition is not entirely non-circular; and it is difficult to see how to eliminate the circularity. Nor is it clear what (2) means; does a perfect forecast include a correct forecast of the actual goodness or desirability of the anticipated event? It is at any rate not clear how far Sidgwick believes notions such as 'right' or 'appropriate' can be eliminated from a definition of 'good'.

[74] The notion of 'ought' can be made clearer 'by determining as precisely as possible its relation to other notions with which it is connected in ordinary thought, especially to those with which it is liable to be confused' (33).

1158. The Categorical 'Ought'

Sidgwick has now completed his argument for the elementary character of 'ought'. He adds some clarifications: (1) In the narrow ethical sense 'ought' implies 'can'. But the wider sense that refers to some standard without reference to my ability to follow it is often appropriate and 'cannot conveniently be discarded' (33). (2) Moral judgment does not allow a particularist analysis; for it implicitly treats particulars as belonging to some definable class, which is the implicit object of moral judgment (34). (3) In rational beings, 'as such' moral judgments tend to move us to action (34). 'As such' suggests that it is not part of the meaning of 'ought' that one who sincerely assents to an ought-judgment must be motivated to act on it.[75] Sidgwick suggests that we can recognize an 'ought' without being moved by it, but it is irrational to be in this condition. (4) As Kant claims, 'ought' implies some conflict of motives. A will without conflict—a Kantian holy will—can act rightly, but it cannot do what it ought to do.

After these clarifications, Sidgwick returns to his original claim that the moral 'ought' is categorical. If it were purely hypothetical, it could be analysed in instrumental and predictive terms. But if it could be analysed in such terms, perhaps referring to sentiments or sanctions, we would have no reason to say that it presents categorical reasons; it would just present facts about sentiments or sanctions. If, however, the moral 'ought' is indeed categorical, we have good reason to suppose it is also unanalysable; it is difficult to see how we could explain its sense in terms that we understand independently of our understanding of 'right', 'ought', and so on.

Sidgwick's explanation of the categorical character of 'ought' improves on Kant. He sees that categorical imperatives are not confined to deontological, as opposed to teleological, conceptions of morality, or even to morality as opposed to self-interest. Wherever we recognize an end 'at which it is ultimately reasonable to aim', we recognize a categorical imperative, even if the end is perfection, the general happiness, or one's own greatest good. Sidgwick rightly appeals to Butler to show that it is reasonable to regard one's greatest good as the object of a categorical 'ought'. Hence he rejects Kant's claim that one's greatest good is simply an object of inclination (unless we are morally required to pursue it).

He argues that a categorical 'ought' is present in the Kantian hypothetical imperative, because this imperative prescribes our taking the fittest means to our end, and that prescription is not itself relative to any end.[76] This account of the 'ought' involved in instrumental rationality corrects an omission in Kant, who does not explain what is rational about following a hypothetical imperative.[77] Contrary to Hume, Sidgwick takes it to be categorically reasonable to pursue the fittest means to one's ends. This reasonableness does

---

[75] The connexion of 'ought' with motivation is discussed further by Falk, 'Motivation'. Some of his remarks raise relevant questions about Sidgwick.

[76] 'But even if we discard the belief that my end of action is unconditionally or "categorically" prescribed by reason, the notion "ought" as above explained is not thereby eliminated from our practical reasonings: it still remains in the "hypothetical imperative" which prescribes the fittest means to any end that we may have determined to aim at.' (37) '. . . it . . . implies the unreasonableness of adopting an end and refusing to adopt the means indispensable to its attainment.' (37) Prior, *LBE* 36–43, discusses Sidgwick on the categorical 'ought'. In his Critical Notice, 119–20, Mackie defends Kant against Prior, but seems to misunderstand Prior and Sidgwick (who claim that some categorical 'oughts' are non-moral, not that prudential 'oughts' are really moral). Deigh, 'Judgment', discusses Sidgwick's view further.

[77] Kant on hypothetical imperatives; §906.

not consist simply in the fact that one will want to pursue the fittest means to one's ends if one wants to achieve one's ends.

In Sidgwick's view, we must recognize an 'ought' implied by the hypothetical imperative even if we reject a categorical 'ought' applied to ends. But perhaps he should say instead that if we recognize the 'ought' implied by the hypothetical imperative, we recognize a categorical 'ought' applied to ends. For the hypothetical imperative implies the imperative 'You ought to pursue the fittest means to your ends'. This is a categorical imperative, and it seems to prescribe an end, even if it is an end that consists in pursuing a certain type of means to non-categorical ends. We might also doubt whether we can really recognize this categorical imperative and still reject a categorical imperative directed to the pursuit of one's own good. How could it be rationally required to pursue efficiency in the pursuit of one's aims if it were not rationally required to care about one's aims as a whole over time? But the latter rational requirement seems to be a categorical imperative of reasonable self-love.

The weakest of Sidgwick's arguments against proposed analyses of 'ought' is his argument from substitution, and the least plausible of his claims is his claim that the notion of 'ought' is simple or elementary. These aspects of his position have been influential in 20th-century meta-ethics. But his arguments can be modified and adapted to make a more reasonable point about the non-reducibility of moral concepts to concepts of Humean 'matters of fact'. To endorse this point is not to claim that moral properties are not Humean matters of fact.

Sidgwick is rather less interested in this latter question than we might expect. It might seem initially plausible to express his utilitarian doctrine as saying that moral rightness is felicificity (tendency to maximize happiness), even though 'right' does not mean 'felicific'. But this is not how he puts it. Though he recognizes the questions 'What does "right" mean?' and 'What actions are right?', he does not examine the further question 'What is rightness?' or 'What property explains why right actions are right?'. This question is the Socratic question, which Suarez, Cudworth, and Butler try to answer.

It would have been better if Sidgwick had tried to answer the Socratic question; for the connexion between the property rightness and the explanation of why particular actions (rules, etc.) are right points to a significant weakness in Sidgwick's position. Simply showing that rightness and felicificity are co-extensive is not enough to show that actions are right because they are felicific. Attention to the explanatory question casts doubt on some of Sidgwick's arguments for utilitarianism. Ross recognizes this connexion between the meta-ethical and the normative issues, but it is not prominent in Sidgwick's discussion.[78]

1159. What Methods are There?

Now that Sidgwick has argued that we can appropriately ask what we ought to do in a categorical sense of 'ought', and that this sense introduces a question about what is right and ultimately reasonable, he returns to his account of methods. In his view, happiness and excellence (or perfection) are the only ends recognized as ultimately reasonable objects of pursuit. Since the happiness that we take as an end may be one's own happiness or the

---

[78] Ross; §1282.

general happiness, egoistic hedonism (egoism) and universalistic hedonism (utilitarianism) are the two methods aiming at happiness. We might expect egoistic and universalistic perfectionism to correspond to the two forms of hedonism.[79]

Not every principle that clams to be ultimately reasonable introduces an ultimate end. Sidgwick argues that modern moral theory rejects the ancient view of ethics as the study of the ultimate good.[80] The ancient view is teleological, whereas the modern view is deontological, because it takes moral principles to be unconditionally binding without reference to any further end that they promote.[81] Sidgwick calls this approach 'intuitionism'. We might try to fit it into a teleological mould by treating right action and morally good character as the ultimate end. But Sidgwick rejects this interpretation of intuitionism. Butler's example shows that we may regard happiness as distinct from morality, and take morality to be binding on us apart from considerations of happiness. A deontological conception of morality does not commit us to a strongly moralized Stoic conception of the ultimate good. We might therefore expect the two types of hedonism and two types of perfectionism to be classified as teleological methods, in contrast to deontological methods.

Sidgwick, however, recognizes only three methods: egoistic hedonism, utilitarianism, and intuitionism. The deontological method of intuitionism absorbs the teleological method of perfectionism.[82] This division blurs the fact that intuitionism says nothing about the nature of the ultimate end, but still generates a distinct method.[83] Perfectionism, in contrast to intuitionism, holds a specific conception of the ultimate end (as consisting in perfection) and a teleological view of rightness.

He also distinguishes the different methods as different 'modes of thought' (13) that 'find a response in our nature' (14). Our attraction to these different modes of thought is indicated by our tendency to agree that (1) it is reasonable to pursue one's own pleasure, that (2) we have a moral sense, that (3) we make intuitive moral judgments, and that (4) we regard

---

[79] On Sidgwick's reasons for taking hedonism to be the only form of egoism worth considering, see §1164.

[80] '. . . the conception of ethics as essentially an investigation of the "Ultimate Good" of Man and the means of attaining it is not universally applicable, without straining, to the view of Morality which we may conveniently distinguish as the Intuitional view; according to which conduct is held to be right when conformed to certain precepts or principles of Duty intuitively known to be unconditionally binding. In this view, the conception of Ultimate Good is not necessarily of fundamental importance in the determination of Right conduct except on the assumption that Right conduct itself—or the character realized and developed through Right conduct—is the sole Ultimate Good for man. But this assumption is not implied in the Intuitional view of Ethics . . .' (3) A longer description of the ancient view in [1] is quoted in §456.

[81] On the use of 'deontological', see Whewell, §1119.

[82] His explanation of his procedure in [1] is this: 'Again, the method which seeks the individual's perfection as ultimate is closely akin to that which aims at conformity to certain absolute rules; virtue being the most prominent element in our notion of human perfection. It will therefore be convenient to treat these together as two varieties of what we may call Intuitionism.' ([1] 9) In [2] and later edns., he has this (or something similar): 'And since Virtue is commonly conceived as the most valuable element of human Excellence—and an element essentially preferable to any other element that can come into competition with it as an alternative for rational choice—any method which takes Perfection or Excellence of human nature as ultimate End will prima facie coincide to a great extent with that based on what I called the Intuitional view: and I have accordingly decided to treat it as a special form of this latter.' (11)

[83] 'It is true that here we may say with Aristotle that the end is the action itself, or a certain quality of it (conformity to a rule), and not something outside of and consequent on the action: but in common language, when we speak of acting for an end, we mean something different from the action itself, some consequence of it. Again, while most moralists hold that right action is always (whether through natural laws or supernatural appointment) followed by consequences in themselves desirable), which may be regarded as in a certain sense the end of the action: still many of the school called Intuitivist or Intuitional hold that our obligation to obey moral rules is not conditional on our knowledge of the end and of its connexion with the actions prescribed.' ([1] 3) This is abbreviated in [2] and further in later editions. [2] deletes the reference to Aristotle.

general happiness as a paramount end.[84] The first and the fourth of these modes of thought introduce egoistic and universalistic hedonism, and so introduce teleological methods. The third mode introduces intuitionism without any teleological aspect; perfectionism is eliminated. The second mode may also introduce intuitionism; Sidgwick does not suggest that a moral sense introduces its own distinct method.

Once Sidgwick has claimed that the perfectionist method is a special case of the intuitionist method, he no longer tries to characterize different methods by reference to different rational ends. He assimilates the two methods because they coincide in practice. Perfectionism claims that morality itself, without reference to any external ends, gives sufficient practical guidance to show us what we should do and what sorts of characters we should form, without reference to any beliefs about the good that are derived from some non-moral source. If morality can give us this sort of practical direction, it must, as intuitionists claim, tell us what is right without reference to any external end. Sidgwick's assimilation of the two methods ignores the possibility that some versions of perfectionism recognize non-moral components of perfection that may not be subordinate to moral virtue.[85]

The three methods—two teleological and one deontological—dominate the rest of *Methods*.[86] Sidgwick considers the natural objection that his list of methods is not exhaustive because his list of 'reasons which are widely accepted as ultimate grounds of action' is not exhaustive (78). He gives some reasons for eliminating some of these grounds from his discussion. The three he mentions are the will of God, self-realization, and life according to nature. These reasons may appear to present 'deeper and more completely satisfying answers to the fundamental questions of Ethics' (79) than Sidgwick's methods present, because they

[84] 'When I am asked "Do you not consider it ultimately reasonable to seek pleasure and avoid pain for yourself?" "Have you not a moral sense?" "Do you not intuitively pronounce some actions to be right and others wrong?" "Do you not acknowledge the general happiness to be a paramount end?" I answer "yes" to all these questions. My difficulty begins when I have to choose between the different principles, or inferences drawn from them.' (14) In [1] 12, the first question is significantly different: 'When I am asked, "Are you not continually seeking pleasure and avoiding pain?" . . .' The question is changed in [6]. Perhaps Sidgwick decided that it was misleading to represent the plausibility of the first method through a psychological claim, and so he changed it to a claim about reasonableness. Answering Yes to all these different questions seems to be perfectly consistent, especially as they are formulated in [1], where the first three simply ask whether we acknowledge certain considerations. The fourth question does not necessarily introduce a rival claim; it only asks whether we regard general happiness as a paramount end, not whether we treat it as the one and only paramount end. Some question about the consistency of affirmative answers to all the questions arises with the later formulation of the first question. Here Sidgwick introduces ultimate reasonableness, but he does not explain what he means by it.

[85] If an intellectualist interpretation of Aristotle on happiness is correct, he holds such a version of perfectionism. See §82.

[86] In i 6 (which in *ME* [1] is entitled 'The methods of ethics'; but in [2] and later is entitled 'Ethical principles and methods'), Sidgwick describes the methods without any necessary reference to different rational ultimate ends defining different methods: 'The aim of Ethics is to systematize and free from error the apparent cognitions that most men have of the rightness and reasonableness of conduct, whether the conduct be conceived as right in itself, or as the means to some end commonly conceived as ultimately reasonable.' (77) 'What then do we commonly regard as valid ultimate reasons for acting or abstaining? This, as was said, is the starting-point for the discussions of the present treatise: which is not primarily concerned with proving or disproving the validity of any such reasons, but rather with the critical exposition of the different "methods"—or rational procedures for determining right conduct in any particular case—which are logically connected with the different ultimate reasons widely accepted. In the first chapter we found that such reasons were supplied by the notions of Happiness and Excellence or Perfection (including Virtue or Moral Perfection as a prominent element), regarded as ultimate ends, and Duty as prescribed by unconditional rules.' (78) At [1] 59, Sidgwick gives a longer summary of the three methods. He speaks of 'ultimate ends' (59) and 'ultimate grounds' (60), but not of what is 'ultimately reasonable'.

connect 'what ought to be' with 'what is', and so connect ethics with metaphysics.[87] This connexion, however, disqualifies them from the role that Sidgwick has in mind.[88] He does not endorse Hume's view (or the view often attributed to Hume) that we cannot rationally argue from 'is' to 'ought'.[89] But he claims that the two sorts of claims are easily confused.

Sidgwick deals briefly with the theological and the naturalistic account of ultimate reasons. He argues that the appeal to the will of God can be reduced to an appeal to happiness, or perfection, or self-realization, and so does not 'suggest any special criterion of rightness' (80). His discussion of naturalism argues that any clear conception of nature that does not already build in the ethical conclusions we want to reach will clearly lead us to false ethical conclusions. Though he does not explicitly discuss Butler's conception of nature,[90] he probably takes it to build in ethical conclusions and so to involve vicious circularity.

1160. What Makes a Distinct Method?

Sidgwick's reasons for disqualifying some prima facie methods of ethics become clearer when he explains one of his demands. He implies that a rational ultimate end generates a distinct method only if it provides a first principle that is both (1) independent—not relying on any other principle for any of its content, and (2) practically definite—capable of yielding, by itself, clear practical guidance.[91]

The second condition determines Sidgwick's classification of methods.[92] His remarks about perfectionism and intuitionism might suggest that similarity in form of reasoning is more important than difference in basic principles. Though one of these outlooks is teleological and one is deontological, they both reason in the same way to find out what should be done, since they both refer to principles that are taken to be known without reference to any external end.

On this basis, one might suppose that the two teleological outlooks, Epicureanism and utilitarianism, follow the same method. For they both claim that what is ultimately

[87] Albee, *HEU* 375–6, points out that [1] does not mention self-realization as a possible end that defines a method. He observes that Bradley's *ES* was published after [1].

[88] 'The introduction of these notions into Ethics is liable to bring with it a fundamental confusion between "what is" and "what ought to be", destructive of all clearness in ethical reasoning: and if this confusion is avoided, the strictly ethical import of such notions, when made explicit, appears always to lead us to one or other of the methods previously distinguished.' (79)

[89] Hume on 'is' and 'ought'; §752.

[90] He alludes to Butler's first two senses of 'natural' (81), but does not directly discuss the third, unless the 'more physical view of our nature' (82) is meant to refer to it.

[91] In his view, naturalism is not a method, because it is not 'capable of furnishing an independent ethical first principle' and one cannot extract from it 'a definite practical criterion of the rightness of actions' (83).

[92] 'Hence arises difficulty in the classification and comparison of ethical systems; since they often appear to have different affinities according as we consider Method or Ultimate Reason. In my treatment of the subject, difference of Method is taken as the paramount consideration; and it is on this account that I have treated the view in which Perfection is taken to be the Ultimate End as a variety of the Intuitionism which determines right conduct by reference to axioms of duty intuitively known; while I have made as marked a separation as possible between Epicureanism or Egoistic Hedonism, and the Universalistic or Benthamite Hedonism to which I propose to restrict the term Utilitarianism.' (83–4) In [1] 64, Sidgwick does not announce a preference for classification by methods. He makes the change in [4].

reasonable is determined by some end external to reasonable action, and on this point they differ from the intuitional method shared by intuitionism and perfectionism. Though Epicureanism takes the relevant external end to be one's own happiness, and utilitarianism takes it to be universal happiness, both outlooks rely on the same pattern of practical reasoning, and so they seem to share one method.

Sidgwick, however, denies that Epicureanism and utilitarianism embody the same method. He separates the two forms of hedonism by appeal to a different criterion. He claims that the practical convergence between intuitionism and utilitarianism justifies him in treating egoism and utilitarianism as distinct methods.[93] But they do not meet his normal criteria for distinct methods, since they reason in the same way; they both reason teleologically, though they aim at different ends.

We might, then, ask whether Sidgwick really means that practical convergence determines the identity of a method. In that case, one might suppose that indirect utilitarianism and intuitionism use the same method, in so far as they take account of the same considerations. Both outlooks take account of many of the same right-making characteristics (e.g., whether a promise has been made, or whether an innocent person will suffer with no significant gain to anyone else) and reach many of the same conclusions.[94] None the less, Sidgwick treats intuitionism and utilitarianism as two distinct methods because they reach their conclusions by different types of reasoning. Here—in contrast to his discussion of egoism and utilitarianism—he seems to treat the form of reasoning, as opposed to practical convergence or divergence, as the basis for identifying and distinguishing methods.

He seems to have no good reason, therefore, for recognizing all and only his three methods as distinct methods of ethics. He does not justify his treatment of teleological perfectionism and deontological intuitionism as the same method. And if we concede that they are the same method, he gives no good reason to attribute different methods to egoism and to utilitarianism. Either utilitarianism and egoistic hedonism share a method or utilitarianism, intuitionism, and perfectionism share a method.

If we dissent from Sidgwick's claim that his three methods are the methods of ethics, what else in *Methods* should we doubt? If he could show that an impartial examination of all the plausible answers to questions about ultimate reasons supports utilitarianism, he would have reached an impressive result. For he would have shown that, even if we do not set out to defend utilitarianism, we find ourselves drawn to it through an impartial examination of ultimate why-questions and possible answers to them. If, however, his three methods do not exhaust ultimate reasons, a comparison of these three methods may not reveal the best method; for one of the methods excluded from the comparison may be superior to any of the three that he compares.

---

[93] '. . . the practical affinity between Utilitarianism and Intuitionism is really much greater than that between the two forms of Hedonism' (85).

[94] Indirect utilitarians accept 'as practically valid the judgments of right and wrong which the Common Sense of mankind seems intuitively to enunciate' (85), but none the less have claimed that moral principles are right in so far as they promote the general happiness: 'On this view [sc. indirect utilitarianism], the *method* of Utilitarianism is certainly rejected: the connexion between right action and happiness is not ascertained by a process of reasoning. But we can hardly say that the Utilitarian principle is altogether rejected: rather the limitations of the human reason are supposed to prevent it from apprehending adequately the real connexion between the true principle and the right rules of conduct.' (85)

His claim to have examined all the methods of ethics affects the concluding discussion in *Methods*. Sidgwick supports his claim of impartiality by claiming to have reconciled intuitionism and utilitarianism. But we have already found reasons to doubt this claim, given his treatment of intuitionism. We will need to return to it in our discussion of Sidgwick's conclusions.[95]

1161. What is 'Ultimately Reasonable'?

The different methods of ethics include different conceptions of what is ultimately reasonable, and so answer the ultimate why-questions. By 'ultimately' reasonable, Sidgwick means at least that they involve categorical reasonableness, as distinct from reasonableness relative to some end that is desired without any question of reasonableness. All three methods are methods of 'determining right conduct' (496), and they correspond to 'different practical principles which the common sense of mankind is prima facie prepared to accept as ultimate' (6), or 'valid ultimate reasons for acting or abstaining' (78).[96]

Sidgwick takes 'reasonable' to be univocal, so that each of the three methods ascribes the same property to the actions that it asserts to be ultimately reasonable. But his introduction of the three methods does not vindicate his assumption. Even if some principles tell us what is categorically reasonable, and not just reasonable relative to an assumed end, 'reasonable' may be elliptical; what is reasonable may be reasonable from a certain point of view or relative to certain reason-giving considerations. Once the relevant considerations are explained, they may leave no further question about which considerations are more or less reasonable; for if 'reasonable' is elliptical, the expansion may re-introduce the different considerations whose reasonableness is being considered.

According to this view, it is a mistake to ask which considerations are reasonable simpliciter. To ask this would be no more sensible than to ask which climate is more suitable simpliciter. Different climates are suitable for different results (growing tomatoes, spending a summer holiday, working in an office, etc.), and it is idle to ask which of these suitable climates is more suitable simpliciter. Sidgwick believes that this sort of analysis is inapplicable to ultimate reasonableness, but he does not explain what is wrong with it.

Even if we grant that 'reasonable' is univocal, Sidgwick's claims raise a question about ultimate reasons. A reason (or end, or principle) might be ultimate in either of two ways: (1) It is non-derivative; it tells us what is rational in its own right. (2) It is a reason of last resort, and hence an overriding reason, so that the principle embodying it is practically supreme. We may mark the same division by speaking of 'an ultimate end' and 'ultimate ends' (to capture (1)) and 'the ultimate end' (to capture (2)). Only one end can be the ultimate end, but many ends may be non-derivative, and so each may be an ultimate end.

This difference between types of ultimate reasons affects Sidgwick's claims about his different methods. If they involve different non-derivative reasons, we may find a number

---

[95] Relations between the methods; §§1199–1200.

[96] This claim about ultimate reasons and ultimate reasonableness is absent from the corresponding places in [1]. Probably Sidgwick adds it to later editions in order to show how the different methods are irreducibly different.

of ultimate and non-competing principles that define different non-competing methods. In particular, we may conclude that the principle of prudence and the principle of morality are both ultimate principles, each of which tells us what is non-derivatively reasonable and what we ought to do. But we may still treat them as answers to different questions, since one tells us what we ought to do in our own interest and one tells us what we ought to do from an impartial point of view.

We may therefore doubt Sidgwick's claim that the different methods are rivals. He assumes that if two methods 'conflict', we cannot accept both as they stand.[97] But what does he mean by 'conflict'? If conflict involves two contradictory conclusions from two methods, we cannot accept both methods. But if two methods give us conflicting practical advice, we need not reject either of them. If one method tells me that it is ultimately (non-derivatively) reasonable that I prefer my interest to yours, and a second method tells me that it is ultimately reasonable that I prefer your interest to mine, the two methods do not reach contradictory conclusions; for it may be true that each course of action is non-derivatively reasonable. If two methods 'conflict' in this sense, we can still accept both.

If we recognize more non-derivatively reasonable practical principles than one, we may still ask which (if any) is most reasonable. If we answer this question, we have found a principle that overrides our other principles by being the ultimate principle among our ultimate principles. But it is not obvious that we need to answer this question, or that we can answer it. Sidgwick believes that we need to answer it, though he does not believe it is easy to answer it. His introduction of the three methods does not show that they create a rational demand to identify the overriding principle. We need to see whether his later argument fills the gaps in his initial statements. Plausible assumptions about methods and about ultimate reasonableness do not obviously raise the questions that *Methods* tries to answer.

---

[97] '. . . the philosopher seeks unity of principle, and consistency of method at the risk of paradox, the unphilosophic man is apt to hold different principles at once, and to apply different methods in more or less confused combination.' (6) 'We cannot, of course, regard as valid reasonings that lead to conflicting conclusions; and I therefore assume as a fundamental postulate of Ethics, that so far as two methods conflict, one or other of them must be modified or rejected.' (6)

SIDGWICK: THE EXAMINATION
OF METHODS

1162. Psychological Hedonism

Sidgwick's first method of ethics is hedonistic egoism. He rejects hedonism as an account of motives (psychological hedonism), but accepts it as an account of one's own interest (prudential hedonism). The version of egoism that includes prudential hedonism is a method of ethics in Sidgwick's view, because it claims that it is ultimately reasonable of me to pursue my own pleasure.

Sidgwick disagrees with utilitarians, including Mill, whose prudential hedonist doctrine rests on psychological hedonism (iv 4). He therefore rejects Green's criticism of utilitarianism, because Green combines attacks on psychological hedonism with attacks on the ethical doctrines that Sidgwick separates from it (see *EGSM* 104–5). Sidgwick recognizes that Bentham and Mill combine psychological and ethical hedonism; in his view, this combination damages the case for utilitarianism, by linking it to a psychological claim that is easily refuted.

However, the critics who argue from the falsity of psychological hedonism to the falsity of prudential hedonism may not be as confused as Sidgwick believes they are. Even though psychological and prudential hedonism are distinct positions, the considerations that make the psychological position attractive may also make the prudential doctrine seem attractive. If no other considerations commend the prudential doctrine, we may reasonably lose interest in the prudential doctrine if it is separated from the psychological doctrine. Sidgwick's arguments give us an opportunity to test this suggestion.

He accepts some of Butler's objections to psychological hedonism. He does not believe that whenever we claim to desire some object other than pleasure, we really desire only the pleasure that results from achieving the object. But he takes the hedonist thesis to be only empirically false; he rejects Butler's and Price's argument to show that it necessarily misrepresents the character of pleasure and its relation to desire. For he denies Butler's claim that taking pleasure in x presupposes some desire for x apart from the pleasure of x (45).

Butler assumes that every pleasure essentially has an object that rests on some belief, so that taking pleasure is always taking pleasure in F in the belief that we have achieved F.[1] Sidgwick concedes a point to this claim of Butler's about the belief-dependence of pleasures; he recognizes that someone's moral beliefs (for instance) may sometimes affect her pleasures and pains (40). But he does not take all pleasure to depend on belief. He is right to disagree with Butler on this point. Butler assumes that all pleasure involves taking pleasure in x qua F and desiring F for its own sake in advance of any pleasure in x; hence pleasure in x qua F depends on the belief that there is something valuable about F. Sidgwick points out that this is not true for all desires and all pleasures.

Butler's error on this point, however, does not matter much; for his case against psychological hedonism stands if some pleasures are value-dependent in the way he describes. Hence Sidgwick's disagreement with him does not affect Sidgwick's rejection of psychological hedonism.

1163. Psychological Hedonism and Prudential Hedonism

Butler's arguments against psychological hedonism suggest a possible objection to prudential hedonism as well. Hedonists might suppose that they have proved prudential hedonism if they prove that everything good for a person must also be pleasant. But they would be wrong. If the pleasure of some of these goods is value-dependent pleasure, essentially taken in some object regarded as non-instrumentally good, our taking pleasure in such an object conflicts with prudential hedonism.

Sidgwick agrees that some pleasures are belief-dependent, but he does not recognize the difficulties that they raise for prudential hedonism. If the ultimate good includes belief-dependent pleasures, and if some of these pleasures are also value-dependent, the good does not consist in pleasure alone; for some pleasures that constitute the good depend on the value that we attach to something other than pleasure. Sidgwick agrees with the critics who maintain that Mill's qualitative hedonism is a rejection rather than a defence of hedonism. But he does not point out that his objection to Mill's qualitative hedonism commits him to the rejection of ultimately value-dependent pleasures.

To counter objections to hedonism, Sidgwick discusses the alleged 'paradox of hedonism'. Sometimes we can gain most pleasure only if we do not think of gaining pleasure all the time; we enjoy what we are doing more if we absorb ourselves in the activity itself and do not always think about how much we are enjoying it. In Sidgwick's view, this 'paradox' is no objection to hedonism. He observes that sometimes we need to aim at pleasure indirectly by interesting ourselves in other things, without thinking about their yield of pleasure (48–51). He sees that this indirect pursuit of pleasure is no objection to prudential hedonism.

But Sidgwick's answer to the paradox of hedonism does not remove the whole difficulty that Butler sees. If some pleasures that we have reason to pursue are value-dependent, the reason that we should not think solely about pleasure all the time is not simply that it will spoil our enjoyment. If we are to gain all the pleasures that we value, we must gain

---

[1] Butler on pleasure; §688.

value-dependent pleasures, and we cannot gain these without valuing something other than pleasure. If some of the pleasures that constitute our good are belief-dependent, they cast doubt on prudential hedonism.

These arguments from the falsity of psychological hedonism to the falsity of prudential hedonism fail if Sidgwick shows either (a) that all our apparently value-dependent pleasures are really concerned with means to value-independent pleasures, or (b) that even if we actually pursue other ends than value-independent pleasures, we have no reason to do so. He chooses the second option; his defence of it needs to be examined.

1164. Hedonism and Eudaemonism

Sidgwick claims that prudential hedonist egoism is the only form of egoism that is clear enough to be worth discussing (i 7). If egoism is a distinct method of ethics, it is a principle of choice and action that has different practical implications from those of the intuitionist and utilitarian methods of ethics. But non-hedonistic egoism is too indefinite in its content to have any definite practical implications (95). The non-hedonistic egoism characteristic of Greek ethics identifies an agent's ultimate end with his eudaimonia, and argues that one ought above all to pursue one's own eudaimonia. According to Sidgwick, this simply amounts to saying that one ought to pursue one's own good, and this advice is not definite enough to offer the practical guidance required of a method of ethics.[2]

We might argue that the advice to pursue one's own eudaimonia is not quite as empty as Sidgwick takes it to be; since eudaimonia is happiness, Greek eudaemonism identifies one's good with one's happiness. Sidgwick answers that to translate Aristotle's term 'eudaimonia' by 'happiness' is to invite confusion between his conception of the good and a hedonist conception.[3] Similarly, he objects to Mill's view that power and fame may be 'parts' of happiness.[4] He finds it equally useless to follow Green in identifying an agent's good with self-realization.[5]

---

[2] '. . . we must discard a common account of egoism which describes its ultimate end as the "good" of the individual; for the term "good" may cover all possible views of the ultimate end of rational conduct. Indeed it may be said that egoism in this sense was assumed in the whole ethical controversy of ancient Greece; that is, it was assumed on all sides that a rational individual would make the pursuit of his own good his supreme aim; the controverted question was whether this good was rightly conceived as pleasure or virtue or any *tertium quid*.' (*ME* 91–2) Hayward, *EPS* 132, in the course of discussing egoism, remarks: '. . . the revival of the useful Aristotelian word "eudaemonism" by Professor James Seth and others is a step in the right direction, though hedonists will, no doubt, regard it as a step backwards into vagueness'.

[3] 'Aristotle's selection of *eudaimonia* to denote what he elsewhere calls "human" or "practicable" good, and still more the fact that, after all, we have no better rendering for *eudaimonia* than "happiness" or "felicity", has caused his whole system to be misunderstood: so that he is often thought to have taught a species of hedonism. We may conjecture that it was not without doing some violence to common usage that Aristotle could bring his readers to understand by *eudaimonia* that kind of well-being that consists of well-doing, and of which pleasure is not the element but the inseparable concomitant: and if the term "happiness" is used, it is almost impossible for the English reader to seize Aristotle's exact view.' ([1] 76n) This note is abbreviated in [7] 92n. Cf. *OHE* 56n2. Sidgwick's criticisms of Reid and Stewart; §836.

[4] Mill's remarks are intelligible if he conceives happiness as something like eudaimonia and understands eudaimonia in partly non-hedonist terms; but Sidgwick attributes Mill's remarks to 'a mere looseness of phraseology, venial in a treatise aiming at a popular style' (93n1). Any non-hedonist conception of happiness involves 'manifest divergence from common usage'. This criticism of Mill might be directed equally plausibly against Whewell's conception of happiness. See §1121.

[5] An appeal to self-realization introduces further vagueness, since it 'seems to be a form into which almost any ethical system may be thrown, without modifying its essential characteristics' (95). These judgments about eudaemonism agree

These claims about the emptiness of eudaemonism seem to conflict with Sidgwick's view that the Greek moralists hold an 'attractive' rather than an 'imperative' view of morality. He believes that they treat the moral virtues as aspects of an agent's own good, not as requirements that may conflict with it. But if their attractive conception rests on their eudaemonism, and their eudaemonism is empty, the difference between an attractive and an imperative conception of morality also seems to be empty, a mere difference in formulation and arrangement without substantive content. Sidgwick does not say that the division between imperative and attractive conceptions is purely verbal; but how can he avoid saying so, given his claims about eudaemonism?[6]

His position is consistent, given his reason for believing that eudaemonism is 'empty'. In contrast to the eudaemonist claim, the claim that one ought to maximize one's own pleasure has sufficient content to satisfy him. Once we add the purely empirical information that this or that identifiable course of action maximizes my pleasure, we know that this is the course of action I ought to pursue. The eudaemonist formula, however, cannot simply be combined with this empirical information to give definite practical guidance; hence eudaemonism does not provide a distinct method of ethics. In this sense it is 'empty'. But this sort of emptiness still allows eudaemonism to underlie a distinctively 'attractive' conception of morality.

We might agree with Sidgwick's claim that eudaemonism is 'empty' in his sense, but reply that it is none the worse for that. For Aristotle does not intend us to derive detailed practical guidance from the bare eudaemonist principle. We find practical guidance from the detailed specification of eudaimonia, which requires the sort of deliberation that is described in the *Ethics*; but this deliberation does not rest on purely empirical considerations. Even if the bare eudaemonist formula is too empty to define a distinct method of ethics by Sidgwick's standards, the human good may still be eudaimonia, and an account of eudaimonia may have important moral consequences. Sidgwick assumes that a method of ethics must be both independent and practically definite, so that no further ethical judgment is needed to provide practical advice (83). But perhaps we have no good reason to demand such a method.

Sidgwick would expose a more serious flaw in eudaemonism if he could show that eudaemonism cannot be worked out in sufficient detail to provide a distinctive conception of morality. To support this objection, he would have to show that a plausible non-hedonist account of a person's good cannot be found, and that even if it could be found, it would have no interesting implications for our conception of the virtues. Sidgwick believes eudaemonist views have these faults. We have already discussed his account of this aspect of Aristotle's ethics, and we will discuss his critique of Green later. His dismissal of eudaemonism in *Methods* is reasonable only if these more detailed criticisms are correct.

1165. Prudential Hedonism

Even if hedonistic egoism is the only form of egoism that is clear and definite enough to be a method of ethics, prudential hedonism may still be false; for success or failure in providing a

---

with Hegel; see §1009. See Bradley's comment on Sidgwick's claim, §1215. Aristotle's eudaemonism; §68. Albee, *HEU* 379–80, criticizes Sidgwick's understanding of self-realization.

⁶ Imperative v. attractive conceptions; §456.

distinct method of ethics does not settle truth or falsity. Sidgwick needs a proof of prudential hedonism; for he accepts the utilitarian view that the morally right maximizes the good of sentient creatures, assessed impartially and conceived as pleasure.

Sidgwick denies that Butler's arguments against psychological hedonism damage prudential hedonism. If the end includes value-dependent pleasures that rest on some conviction about the intrinsic value of their objects, a conception of the end as pleasure does not meet Sidgwick's demands; for it rests on further convictions about non-hedonic value. He therefore needs to show that the good is value-independent pleasure.

He argues that neither virtue nor virtuous action can be an end in itself, because they must be defined by reference to some right that is distinct from them. Since we cannot plausibly claim that the only thing that is right is the virtuous attempt to do what is right, virtues are valuable only as parts of a desirable conscious life.[7] But if we concede this point, we may still maintain, with Mill and with many non-utilitarians, that virtue and other non-hedonic goods are parts of the ultimate good.[8]

Sidgwick now claims (395–6) that what is to be valued for its own sake is some state of consciousness, and in particular some desirable state of consciousness. In support of this claim, he observes that a given physical movement is not good in itself apart from consciousness.[9] We might reply, however, that if we also take states of consciousness entirely out of their mental and physical context, they lose value. Sidgwick seems to show at most that some desirable consciousness is a necessary element of anything we can regard as ultimately good.[10]

He rejects as paradoxical the view of Greek philosophers that a virtuous but extremely painful life is good on the whole.[11] His rejection seems hasty. One might acknowledge, as Aristotle does, that pain is a major evil, but still claim that a virtuous person's life is on the whole good because it is better on balance than any life without virtue.

---

[7] 'And what has been said of Virtue, seems to me still more manifestly true of the other talents, gifts, and graces which make up the common notion of human excellence or Perfection. However immediately the excellent quality of such gifts and skills may be recognized and admired, reflection shows that they are only valuable on account of the good or desirable conscious life in which they are or will be actualized, or which will be somehow promoted by their exercise.' (395) Sidgwick's argument for the exclusion of virtue and virtuous action from the ultimate good is well criticized by Rashdall, 'Sidgwick', 223–5.

[8] 'Shall we then say that Ultimate Good is Good or Desirable conscious or sentient Life—of which Virtuous action is one element, but not the sole constituent? This seems in harmony with Common Sense; and the fact that particular virtues and talents and gifts are largely valued as means to ulterior good does not necessarily prevent us from regarding their exercise as also an element of Ultimate Good...' (395–6) Sidgwick regards Mill's belief in parts of happiness as inconsistent with utilitarianism (93n1). Schneewind, SEVMP 315–16, discusses the bearing of this argument on Mill's view. This passage (395–8) is discussed further in §1216.

[9] 'I cannot conceive it to be an ultimate end of rational action to secure that these complex movements should be of one kind rather than another, or that they should be continued for a longer rather than a shorter period.' (398)

[10] Bradley, CE 92–3, points out Sidgwick's exaggeration of the conclusion of his arguments involving abstraction. See §1214.

[11] 'In the same way, so far as we judge virtuous activity to be a part of Ultimate Good, it is, I conceive, because the consciousness attending it is judged to be in itself desirable for the virtuous agent; ... We may make the distinction clearer by considering whether Virtuous life would remain on the whole good for the virtuous agent, if we suppose it combined with extreme pain. The affirmative answer to this question was strongly supported in Greek philosophical discussion: but it is a paradox from which a modern thinker would recoil...' (397) In the first sentence, Sidgwick seems to assert that virtue is good only as a means to desirable consciousness, but the rest of the passage does not support this claim. In 'on the whole', he includes the views of Plato and Aristotle as well as the more obviously counter-intuitive view of the Stoics who believe that virtue is the whole of the good and pain is not an evil at all.

This claim is not an obvious paradox from which one ought to recoil. But even if a virtuous but extremely painful life has more evil than good in it, the fact that it is virtuous might still be a valuable feature of it, so that pleasure would not be the only good.

Moreover, if a virtuous but extremely painful life has no positive value, it follows only that virtue is insufficient for positive value, not that pleasure alone has positive value. If x is not good all by itself, but x and y constitute a good, it does not follow that y is good and x is not; for y may also not be good by itself.[12]

This gap in Sidgwick's argument casts doubt on his claim that knowing and willing are not parts of desirable consciousness. Since knowing the truth or wanting the good is valued not simply because of the internal features of that state of consciousness, but because of its relation to truth or goodness, he infers that the value of such states is not simply the value of states of consciousness. He supposes he has proved that the good must consist wholly in states of consciousness; hence he infers that knowing the truth and wanting the good cannot be part of the good. He is right to claim that knowing the truth and wanting the good are valuable partly because of their relation to something external to consciousness; but since his argument has proved only that states of consciousness are part of one's good, he has not shown that externally directed states cannot also be part of it.

Sidgwick now asks whether a desirable conscious life must include more than pleasure.[13] The view that certain 'ideal' goods besides happiness (understood as pleasure) are parts of the ultimate end may seem more plausible than Sidgwick's view.[14] But he replies that the purely hedonistic view is intuitively compelling, because in a cool hour we can justify only those pursuits that conduce to happiness.[15] This argument faces two objections: (1) If he is right, it shows only that goods other than happiness cannot be the sole constituents of the good. (2) Common sense does not agree with him if 'happiness' is understood in a narrowly hedonistic sense.

Even if we found Sidgwick's claim plausible, we would not have shown that it is a genuine intuition, since an intuition must be consistent with all other intuitions.[16] For his purposes, it is not enough if we agree that pleasure itself is still good in abstraction from all other alleged goods; we must also agree that any variation in other alleged goods and in their relation to pleasure is irrelevant to goodness. If, for instance, total pleasure were slightly increased as a result of the prevalence of vice, ugliness, or ignorance, it must be certain that this total situation would be better than a slightly lower, though still high, level of pleasure resulting

---

[12] Moore discusses organic unities at *PE* 144.

[13] 'Still, it may be said that . . . we may take "conscious life" in a wide sense, so as to include the objective relations of the conscious being implied in our notions of virtue, truth, beauty, freedom; and that from this point of view we may regard cognition of truth, contemplation of beauty, free or virtuous action, as in some measure preferable alternatives to pleasure or happiness—even though we admit that happiness must be indeed be included as a part of ultimate good.' (400)

[14] Moore, *PE* 144–7, objects reasonably to Sidgwick's claims.

[15] 'Admitting that we have actual experiences of . . . preferences . . . of which the ultimate object is something that is not merely consciousness: it still seems to me that when . . . we "sit down in a cool hour", we can only justify to ourselves the importance that we attach to any of these objects by considering its conduciveness, in one way or another, to the happiness of sentient beings.' (401)

[16] See §1182.

from the prevalence of virtues and goods. For if pleasure is the only ultimate good, any overall gain in pleasure, however small, must always be preferable, whatever the overall loss, however large, in other alleged goods.

Suppose, for instance, that Steve is a political prisoner, John is a prison guard who enjoys torturing Steve, and Bill enjoys watching John torture Steve. From the hedonist point of view, the total situation is better if Bill (unknown to Steve) watches John torture Steve than if John tortures Steve unobserved. Steve does not suffer any more than he would if John tortured him unobserved, and Bill gets the pleasure he would not get if John kept all the fun to himself. In this situation, there is more pleasure because there is more cruelty, and so, from the hedonist point of view, it must be better. In this situation, intuitive judgments do not support hedonism.

Sidgwick might argue that our intuitive judgments here are not helpful, because they do not abstract from irrelevant features. Perhaps, for instance, we are inappropriately influenced by the fact that Bill's cruel enjoyment of the torture will dispose him to torture people himself or to favour such policies. Even if we modify the example to rule out such instrumental badness, we are still—the hedonist may argue—influenced by it, so that we do not give a fair hearing to pleasure in abstraction from everything else.

These doubts about our intuitive judgments in these counterfactual situations are exaggerated; the adjustments that are needed to rule out bad consequences of cruelty are small. But if the doubts were justified, they would also undermine the hedonist argument by abstraction. For we might argue that we cannot abstract pleasure itself from the activities and states we take the pleasure in; our favourable judgment is directed not at pleasure alone, but at the total situation of which it is a part. Either Sidgwick's argument from abstraction is worthless, if he is sceptical about counterfactual thought-experiments, or some thought-experiments count against hedonism.[17]

One of the earliest thought-experiments used against hedonism is Plato's examination of the life of pleasure separated from rational awareness of past, present, and future rational agency. If Plato is right, hedonism is incompatible with rational concern for one's own happiness, understood as eudaimonia, and hence as including goodness in one's life as a whole life of a temporally extended rational agent.[18] Plato raises a serious difficulty for Sidgwick's position. For Sidgwick accepts an 'axiom of prudence' that prescribes equal concern for all of one's conscious life. This is consistent with a hedonist account of the good, but it is not clear why anyone who accepts it should also accept hedonism, or why a hedonist should regard it as an axiom.

Sidgwick recognizes that his arguments may not reconcile common sense to a purely hedonist account of the good. He suggests that common sense concentrates too much on gross material pleasures, which are less important (402).[19] But if we follow Sidgwick's advice, and take account of all the different states and activities that we regard as sources of pleasure, we will raise a further difficulty for hedonism. He is right to say that pleasures include many that we take to be more significant than gross material pleasures. But we take them to be more significant because they are essentially pleasures taken in objects that we take

---

[17] Cf. also Bradley's thought experiment of function v. pleasure, §1222. [18] Plato's argument; §53.
[19] He also suggests that common sense is too impressed by the paradox of hedonism. See §1163.

to be intrinsically valuable. Our discrimination among pleasures reflects our non-hedonic discrimination among the objects of pleasure.

Sidgwick, however, believes that the value of the object does not explain the value of the pleasure; for pleasures taken in different objects differ, as such, only in their instrumental value. In circumstances where gross physical pleasures provided a larger total of pleasure, he believes we ought to prefer them. It is fair, then (contrary to Sidgwick), to object to hedonism because it over-values gross material pleasures, and it fails to explain the higher value of other pleasures.[20]

1166. Hedonism and Foundationalism

Sidgwick's belief in prudential hedonism rests not only on its inherent plausibility, but also on the needs of his theory. If we reject prudential hedonism, nothing else seems available to 'systematize human activities' (406). We can ask a non-hedonist how we are to compare the value of different non-hedonic goods with each other, and how we are to compare their value with the value of happiness (construed as pleasure).[21] Neither non-hedonistic eudaemonism nor qualitative hedonism is a proper method of ethics, because neither of them provides an independent criterion of reasonable action. These two positions rely too much on intuitionism, because they rely on ethical judgments, or other judgments of value, that are not simply judgments about means to some external end.[22]

Sidgwick, therefore, prefers 'empirical hedonism'. He recognizes that we may not find it attractive. Since our capacity for the predictions and comparisons that are needed to estimate probable quantities of pleasure is imperfect, empirical hedonism offers us uncertain conclusions.[23] Nor can we easily reduce the uncertainty; neither the claim that following

[20] If Sidgwick were to rely on Mill's doctrine of higher and lower pleasures, the objection from common sense would collapse. But Mill's doctrine assumes the non-instrumental goodness of other things besides pleasure, and hence conflicts with hedonism.

[21] 'I have failed to find—and am unable to construct—any systematic answer to this question that appears to me deserving of serious consideration; and hence I am finally led to the conclusion . . . that the Intuitional method rigorously applied yields as its final result the doctrine of pure universalistic hedonism. . .' (406–7) The 'hence' here implies that the systematizing character of hedonism counts heavily in its favour. Sidgwick acknowledges that, if it were not for this consideration, he would have no answer if we were unconvinced by his attempt to undermine recalcitrant convictions. Hedonism introduces system because it answers questions about the pursuit of other goods by 'a common standard for comparing these values with that of happiness' (406), or a 'common criterion of the comparative value of the different objects of men's enthusiastic pursuits' (406). A common standard is something beyond non-hedonic goods, identical to none of them, that gives us precise answers about the appropriate extent and limits of the pursuit of each of them.

[22] 'And even when further defined as Egoistic Hedonism, [egoism] is still imperfectly distinguishable from Intuitionism if quality of pleasures is admitted as a consideration distinct from and overruling quantity. There remains then Pure or Quantitative Egoistic Hedonism, which, as a method essentially distinct from all others and widely maintained to be rational, seems to deserve a detailed examination.' (95) Non-hedonistic eudaemonism relies on some non-instrumental judgments about one's own good. Reliance on such judgments seems to fall short of intuitionism, as Sidgwick usually understands it, since it does not seem to rely on judgments about the morally right; but here he seems to conceive intuitionism in a wider sense that embraces all non-instrumental value judgments.

[23] '. . . I conclude that it would be at least highly desirable, with a view to the systematic direction of conduct, to control and supplement the results of such comparisons by the assistance of some other method: if we can find any on which we see reason to rely.' (150) In speaking of 'some other method', he probably does not mean 'some other method of ethics' in his technical sense; for if we had to rely on that, egoistic hedonism would not be a method of ethics in its own right. He means that we would like some method, apart from case-by-case predictions, of estimating

common morality maximizes pleasure nor quasi-scientific rules about sources of pleasure offer principles that we can substitute for empirical observations and comparisons (195).

Still, Sidgwick accepts egoistic empirical hedonism as a method of ethics. Even if it conflicts with our other judgments of value, the authority of rational self-love makes it reasonable to follow the empirical hedonist method.[24] If we are in doubt about whether pushpin or poetry is better, we may not be able to settle our doubt by simply consulting our intuitive view that activities involving a wider range of intellectual and aesthetic capacities are better; for our doubt about pushpin and poetry may imply a doubt about this broader intuitive view. If we appeal to the broader principle that different forms of intrinsic value realize different aspects of oneself, this principle does not help us until we agree about what is involved in self-realization. But in an appeal to pleasure no further questions about intrinsic value remain; only empirical questions are left.

These empirical questions may still be difficult to answer. It is not always easy to predict the pleasure and pain to be expected from a particular course of action, or from the cultivation of a particular pattern of action; people's expectations of pleasure and pain may be influenced by what they value. Sidgwick answers that the difficulties of applying the hedonist standard do not raise theoretical difficulties in principle. Our only difficulty is our current ignorance about the hedonic consequences of different courses of action. By contrast, non-hedonic conceptions of the good raise difficulties of principle, in so far as they may rely on moral or other evaluative judgments that do not rest on a non-evaluative foundation.

Why should it matter whether difficulties in the application of a principle are empirical rather than theoretical? A principle that raises only empirical difficulties may not be easier to apply. Our judgments of intrinsic value may lack the systematic character that they would acquire if they were subordinated to a hedonist conception, but they might still be relatively confident and clear, and might allow a definite answer. According to these judgments, we might conclude confidently that poetry is better than pushpin and that kindness is better than cruelty. But if we are asked to support our comparative judgment on strictly hedonist grounds, we may be unsure whether one activity will actually yield less pleasure than another. Hence, the mere fact that empirical hedonism removes theoretical difficulties of application and replaces them with purely empirical difficulties does not make it more readily applicable to practice.

The advantages of empirical hedonism, therefore, are epistemological rather than practical. Convictions about intrinsic value should be derived, in Sidgwick's view, from a conception that can be applied to practice without any appeal to further evaluative convictions. We

the likely quantitative yield of pleasure from different types of action. But the various methods he considers do not succeed. Common-sense rules of thumb are not reliable. Hence we look for some more general theoretical principles: 'The question then remains, whether any general theory can be attained of the causes of pleasure and pain so certain and practically applicable that we may by its aid rise above the ambiguities and inconsistencies of common or sectarian opinion, no less than the shortcomings of the empirical-reflective method, and establish the Hedonistic art of life on a thoroughly scientific basis.' (160) No such theoretical principles, however, can be found.

[24] 'The effort to examine, closely but quite neutrally, the system of Egoistic Hedonism . . . may not improbably have produced on the readers mind a certain aversion to the principle and method examined, even though (like myself) he may find it difficult not to admit the "authority" of self-love, or the "rationality" of seeking one's own individual happiness. (199) . . . A dubious guidance to an ignoble end appears to be all that the calculus of Egoistic Hedonism has to offer.' (199–200) In 'even though . . .' Sidgwick suggests that our conviction of the authority of self-love should dissuade us from rejecting egoistic hedonism, despite its unattractive features.

should not rely on convictions that rest on a less determinate general principle, such as a principle about intrinsic value and self-realization. Sidgwick's foundationalist conception of moral knowledge underlies his preference for prudential empirical hedonism as well.

But even if he is right about the superior systematizing power of a hedonist theory of the good, should that persuade us to accept such a theory? If the hedonist theory gives us an answer we are inclined to reject, the mere fact that it gives a clear answer does not give us a reason to accept hedonism. Even if system—as Sidgwick understands it—is welcome, a theoretical position that introduces system may not be preferable to every less systematic position. He introduces the appeal to system only as a concluding consideration in his argument for hedonism.

1167. Is Egoism a Method of Ethics?

Sidgwick believes that his preferred version of egoism is a plausible method of ethics.[25] It is one of the principles that claim to be ultimately reasonable. These principles 'find a response in our nature' and their 'fundamental assumptions are all such as we are disposed to accept' (14). But this case for egoism relies on Sidgwick's ambiguous notion of 'ultimate' reasonableness.[26] If we took 'ultimately reasonable' to mean 'supreme', we might not concede at the outset that egoism is ultimately reasonable, whereas we might readily agree that egoism is non-derivatively reasonable.

Sidgwick's principle of egoistic hedonism demands 'the adoption of his own greatest happiness as the ultimate end of each individual's actions' (119).[27] To support this demand, Sidgwick points to the wide acceptance of the principle 'that it is reasonable for a man to act in the manner most conducive to his own happiness' (119).[28] His principle of egoistic hedonism makes one's own happiness the ultimate end of one's actions, whereas the widely accepted principle simply says that it is a reasonable end.

Hence he does not give a good reason for treating egoism as a method of ethics, if a method of ethics fixes overriding reasons. The widely accepted egoist principle says nothing about the comparative reasonableness of pursuing one's own interest over other things; it only represents the pursuit of one's own interest as non-derivatively reasonable. This moderate egoist principle finds a response in our nature. But the egoist method that Sidgwick discusses rests on the much less obviously plausible claim that one's own interest is the ultimate end, to which everything else is subordinate.

It is easy to miss the difference between the two principles, because Sidgwick speaks both of ultimate reasonableness and of one's ultimate end, and one might readily suppose

[25] Albee, *HEU* 382–6, justly criticizes Sidgwick's reasons for treating egoism as a method of ethics, and especially questions his appeal to reasonableness.

[26] Ultimate reasonableness; §1161.

[27] This does not appear in [1] 107. In Sidgwick's view, egoism implies 'the adoption of his own greatest happiness as the ultimate end of each individual's actions', and a 'method of determining reasonable conduct' that is guided by that end. Sidgwick acknowledges that we may doubt whether this is really a method of ethics, on the ground that 'a system of morality, satisfactory to the moral consciousness of mankind in general, cannot be constructed on the basis of simple Egoism' (119). He agrees with this claim that simple egoism cannot provide a basis for morality. At 119n he refers forward to ii 3 §2 and ii 5, where he mentions ways in which egoistic hedonism does not coincide with morality.

[28] Not in [1] 109.

he is making the same point each time. But the claim that it is ultimately reasonable to pursue one's own interest is evidently plausible only if 'ultimately' means simply 'non-derivatively'. It does not follow that it is overridingly reasonable to pursue one's own interest, and hence to treat one's own interest as the ultimate, and hence overriding, end. Sidgwick's arguments to show that the claim about non-derivative reasonableness is widely accepted (119–20) do not support the claim about overriding reasonableness.

If we do not accept the claim about overriding reasonableness, we have no reason to treat egoism as a method of ethics; for it need not profess to guide all one's practical reasoning. A method that does not profess comprehensiveness cannot provide practical guidance independently of all other practical principles, as a method of ethics is supposed to do. Hence Sidgwick cannot treat egoism as a method unless he thinks of it as a claim about overriding reasonableness. If egoism is only a claim about non-derivative reasonableness, it is plausible, but it is not comprehensive enough to constitute an independent method of ethics. But if it is a claim about overriding reasonableness, it is comprehensive enough, but it is not clearly plausible.

Can more be said to show that egoism gives us overriding reasons? One might argue on Sidgwick's behalf that some moralists have accepted egoism about overriding reasons. The claim that one's own happiness is the appropriate ultimate end for a rational agent is familiar from Greek and mediaeval ethics. One might conclude, then, that this historical precedent gives Sidgwick a good reason for treating egoism as a method of ethics.

This defence of Sidgwick, however, does not fit his comments on the Greek and mediaeval tradition. For he treats eudaemonism as a version of egoism that is better avoided. In his view, claims about one's own good are too indefinite to provide a proper method of ethics until they are understood hedonistically. The only version of egoism that he thinks worth considering is quantitative hedonistic egoism. If we think egoism is supremely reasonable for eudaemonist reasons, we do not endorse Sidgwick's claim that hedonistic egoism is supremely reasonable.

Any plausible version of egoism, therefore, fails Sidgwick's demand for an independent method of determining what it is reasonable to do. Hedonism satisfies this demand (in his view), but if it is not a plausible version of egoism, it does not 'find a response in our nature' (14), and so it is not a method of ethics. Sidgwick proceeds as though we ought first to agree that egoism seems ultimately reasonable, and we ought not to retract that agreement once we see what he means by 'ultimately reasonable' and what version of egoism he intends. But his explanation of his position casts doubt on his conclusion. Our initial agreement does not commit us to agreeing that egoistic hedonism is overridingly reasonable.

1168. The Importance of Hedonism

Sidgwick's hedonism does not appeal to most of the later theorists who have called themselves utilitarians. Whereas he defines utilitarianism as a hedonist doctrine, many of his successors understand utilitarianism more broadly; they reject hedonistic utilitarianism in favour of various forms of non-hedonistic consequentialism.

We might suppose that if we abandon hedonism, the rest of Sidgwick's theory can stand more or less as it is. Where he speaks of calculating balances of pleasure, we can speak of calculations involving our preferred conception of the utilitarian end, but (on this supposition) the rest of what Sidgwick says about utilitarianism, its method, its relation to common sense, and so on, will be the same. Sidgwick does not agree with this assessment of the role of hedonism in his theory. His belief in prudential hedonism rests partly on its theoretical role as a suitable account of the good that is mentioned in moral axioms. That is why he does not think a utilitarian can easily abandon it.

It is logically possible for a utilitarian (in other respects) to abandon hedonism. Some non-hedonist view might conceivably give a clear account of the human good without presupposing any of the evaluative judgments that Sidgwick wants to eliminate from first principles. Such an account could be used to replace hedonism in Sidgwick's version of utilitarianism; we could then say that what is morally right is what promotes the good, so understood.

But though this possibility is open, it is difficult to see how any plausible account of the good will satisfy it. Moreover, objections to a hedonist theory can be adapted for use against a non-hedonist theory that tries to specify the good, and to provide a basis for choice among different goods, without reliance on further evaluative judgments. If, for instance, we replace pleasure with desire-satisfaction or preference-satisfaction, we raise many of the same objections; the satisfaction of some desires seems to be bad for us, if they have bad objects.[29]

If we try to meet these objections by describing the good as the satisfaction of appropriate desires, we cannot identify the right action without resort to further judgments about appropriateness, and then our conception of the good no longer offers the sort of criterion that Sidgwick wants.[30] He has good reason, then, to defend prudential hedonism; for the difficulties that face prudential hedonism indicate more general difficulties for a utilitarian theory that tries to meet Sidgwick's epistemological conditions.

This is not a conclusive argument for agreeing with Sidgwick about the connexion between hedonism and the rest of utilitarianism. But it is a reason for taking his claim about hedonism and utilitarianism quite seriously. The reason we have considered raises a broader question about utilitarianism and foundationalism. We have examined an argument for hedonism that rests on a foundationalist conception of moral principles and principles of intrinsic value. This argument will not apply to utilitarianism in general, if utilitarianism is defensible apart from foundationalism. To see what Sidgwick thinks, we need to examine his arguments for utilitarianism.

1169. Strategies of Argument

We might have expected Sidgwick to discuss universalistic hedonism after egoistic hedonism, so that we could compare the two hedonistic methods of ethics. But instead he

---

[29] See Brandt, *TGR* 247–53; 'Utility'; Sen, 'Welfarism', 473. Further discussion; §1207.
[30] This is the version of utilitarianism that Moore, *PE*, and Rashdall, *TGE*, defend.

discusses intuitionism, to exhibit the broad extent of agreement between intuitionism and utilitarianism. If he had turned directly from egoistic hedonism to utilitarianism, the arguments that demonstrate the empirical and uncertain character of hedonist calculations would apparently have demonstrated the same points about utilitarianism. It would not even have been clear why egoistic and universalistic hedonism are two methods, rather than the same method applied to two different ends.

Sidgwick uses his review of common-sense morality and intuitionism to argue dialectically. After an examination of common sense that does not presuppose the truth of utilitarianism or any other moral theory, he argues that utilitarianism is the best way to systematize common sense. But he also presents an 'axiomatic' argument to show that the principle of utility can be derived from principles that we can see, on reflexion, to be self-evident axioms. This argument shows that utilitarianism is credible in its own right.[31]

A critic needs to examine the two forms of argument and their application. If we accept Sidgwick's dialectical argument, but reject his axiomatic argument, we may accept utilitarianism on a purely dialectical basis. We might also—for all we have seen so far—accept the axiomatic but not the dialectical argument, and so accept utilitarianism on purely axiomatic grounds. And if we accept the dialectical strategy, but do not believe that it vindicates utilitarianism, we might apparently still be convinced of utilitarianism by axiomatic argument.[32]

1170. Deontological Morality and the Intuitional Method

Before we discuss Sidgwick's dialectical strategy, we need to say a little more about the common-sense outlook to which he applies this strategy. He calls it an 'intuitionist' outlook. He distinguishes his position from this intuitionist position. Still, the utilitarian doctrine that he reaches through his axiomatic strategy is utilitarianism 'on an intuitional basis'. He recognizes that 'intuition' and 'intuitionist' can be used in different ways, and that he uses them in different, though related, senses.

Moral philosophers often speak of moral 'intuitions' or 'intuitive judgments', just as philosophers speak of intuitions in other areas. Our intuitions are immediate because they are elicited without derivation from explicit general principles. If we accept a doctrine of a moral sense, as Reid understands it, we may regard our intuitive moral judgments as the operations of our moral sense.[33] These judgments may be about particular cases or about general principles. Moral philosophers who hold quite different epistemological positions may recognize these intuitions. When we call them intuitions, we do not imply that they need or allow no further justification. Common-sense morality is 'intuitionist' in the minimal sense that it includes many intuitions, or intuitive judgments.

---

[31] The two directions are fully examined by Schneewind, *SEVMP*, chs. 9–12, who seems to attribute more probative force to the dialectical argument than Sidgwick attributes to it. Against Schneewind, see Singer, 'Equilibrium'.

[32] We need to include 'apparently' in some of these claims; further examination of each strategy may show that they are not independent. See §1182.

[33] Reid on the moral sense; §842.

When Sidgwick speaks of an outlook as 'intuitionist', he intends this correct claim about common sense.[34] But he also intends some further claims at a higher theoretical level. These further claims sometimes make it difficult to know what position he regards as intuitionist.[35]

Sometimes he uses 'intuitionism' for a deontological conception of the right.[36] That is why he treats intuitionism as a distinct method of ethics, in contrast to the teleological method common to the two hedonistic methods. He adds that its moral principles are claimed to be 'intuitively' known to be unconditionally binding. If 'intuitively' refers to the sort of intuition that is clearly present in common-sense morality, Sidgwick claims that common-sense morality treats some basic principles deontologically, as binding independently of whether they promote some external end.

A further intuitionist doctrine holds that common-sense intuitions point to true principles grasped by intuition.[37] Sidgwick describes this outlook as a form of the 'intuitional method' (101); it is the 'dogmatic' as opposed to the merely 'perceptual' phase of intuitionism (102). In speaking of 'clear and finally valid' intuition, it claims that some common-sense rules, or modifications of them, are principles that can be known to be true without reference to any further inferential support. Such principles would count as 'scientific axioms' that would be 'available in clear and cogent demonstrations'.

We might, therefore, expect an examination of an 'intuitional method' to discuss (i) common-sense intuitive convictions, or (ii) a normative claim, constituting a deontological conception of the right, or (iii) an epistemological foundationalist claim to have found fundamental principles grasped by intuition. These three positions are logically independent. If we agree that our ordinary moral convictions are intuitive, because they are not explicitly based on an explicit theory, we still need not agree that the most faithful account of them is deontological. Nor does a deontological conception of the right imply a foundationalist claim that our basic principles of the right must be moral axioms knowable non-inferentially.

None the less, Sidgwick combines these three positions in his examination of a dogmatic intuitionist position in Book III, which discusses the morality of common sense. Some of his remarks might be taken (a) to criticize the vague or unsystematic character of our intuitive convictions, or (b) to express doubts about a deontological account of our intuitive

---

[34] '. . . the moral judgments which the present method attempts to systematize are primarily and for the most part intuitions of the rightness or goodness (or the reverse) of particular kinds of external effects of human volition . . .' (210). Sidgwick asks whether it is legitimate to take the existence of such intuitions for granted, and he asserts that it is legitimate, once we make it clear that 'intuition of p' does not imply the truth of p: 'I wish therefore to say expressly, that by calling any affirmation as to the rightness or wrongness of actions "intuitive," I do not mean to prejudge the question as to its ultimate validity, when philosophically considered: I only mean that its truth is apparently known immediately, and not as the result of reasoning. I admit the possibility that any such "intuition" may turn out to have an element of error, which subsequent reflection and comparison may enable us to correct . . .' (211)

[35] Skorupski, 'Methods', 62–7, discusses Sidgwick on intuitions.

[36] This is his first description of the intuitional method, 'according to which conduct is held to be right when conformed to certain principles or precepts of Duty, intuitively known to be unconditionally binding', without any reference to an external end (3). This is one sense he attaches to 'intuitionism': 'Meanwhile by intuitionism we are to understand a method which to a certain extent—indeed, in so far as it is clearly distinguished from hedonistic methods—prescribes certain actions to be done without regard to their consequence . . .' ([1] 82) A shorter statement appears at [7] 98.

[37] '. . . the fundamental assumption is that we can discern certain general rules with really clear and finally valid intuition. It is held that such general rules are implicit in the moral reasoning of ordinary men, who apprehend them adequately for most practical purposes, and are able to enunciate them roughly; but that to state them with proper precision requires a special habit of contemplating clearly and steadily abstract moral notions. . . . It is such a system as this . . . which will chiefly occupy us in Book III.' (101)

convictions, or (c) to express objections to a deontological account of the right, or (d) to express doubts about whether the principles emerging from a deontological account of our intuitive convictions meet the foundationalist epistemological standards for being axioms.

Sidgwick may combine these different positions because he believes they are connected aspects of the intuitional method. For he may believe that a deontological account of the right needs a foundationalist epistemology. A deontological view claims that certain kinds of actions are right 'in themselves'. One might take this to imply that if one understands the claim that (for instance) one ought not to kill innocent people, one can see, without reference to any other moral claims, that it is true. One may therefore suppose that the truth of deontological claims is to be grasped atomistically, by considering one deontological claim at a time. And so one may infer that a deontological normative doctrine rests on a foundationalist epistemology. In that case, 'intuitionism' correctly describes both the normative and the epistemological claim.

But this account of intuitionism is open to doubt. For we might maintain that some kinds of actions are right 'in themselves', without reference to an end external to right action, but we might still claim to grasp their rightness by reference to our convictions about other right actions and about goods that are distinct from right actions. If that is our view, our normative theory is deontological, but our epistemological assumptions are holist rather than foundationalist. Sidgwick believes that intuitionism is defensible only if some axioms emerge from common-sense intuitions. He is right, if foundationalism is true. But we have no reason to impose foundationalism on common sense, or on a deontological normative theory that seeks to explain common sense.

1171. Dogmatic v. Philosophical Intuitionism

Sidgwick describes the combination of deontological intuitionism with foundationalist epistemology as 'dogmatic' intuitionism. According to Price, morality rests on a plurality of principles without any definite rules of priority among them; no principle is superior to all the others. Price mentions 'heads of virtue' that rest on different self-evident principles. He agrees with Butler's rejection of the reduction of all morality to benevolence.[38] Sidgwick contrasts this dogmatic intuitionism with 'philosophical' intuitionism, which seeks a deeper basis for the dogmatic intuitionist's principles.[39] Utilitarianism is a philosophical version of intuitionism because it looks for the basic and undeniable principles from which the common rules can be deduced.[40]

---

[38] Price on benevolence; §822.

[39] '...the resulting code seems an accidental aggregate of principles, which stands in need of some rational synthesis...[A] third species or phase of Intuitionism...attempts to find for [the morality of common sense] a philosophic basis which it does not itself offer: to get one or more principles more absolutely and undeniably true and evident, from which the current rules might be deduced, either just as they are commonly received or with slight modifications and rectifications.' (102)

[40] 'The three kinds of intuitionism...might be termed respectively perceptional or instinctive, dogmatic, and rational or philosophical. The first of these, as was said, is, if taken strictly by itself, a complete negation of method, and so offers nothing to be investigated. The second method proceeds by reflexion upon common sense, and therefore can only deviate from common opinion in its results very slightly, where common opinion is manifestly confused and obscure. The third...I have presented...only as a problem, of which it is impossible to foresee how many solutions may be

Sidgwick assumes that if the common-sense view of rightness is best explicated by a deontological normative theory, it needs a foundationalist epistemology. In distinguishing dogmatic from philosophical intuitionism, he assumes that it is legitimate to examine common-sense morality to see whether its alleged axioms achieve a rational synthesis.

But his demand for rational synthesis seems to conflict with foundationalism. If we suppose that our justification for accepting p as a basic principle depends on seeing a connexion between p and our other basic principles q and r, we demand rational synthesis because we are holists about justification. But if we can know p in itself, without reference to any inferential justification, we do not need a rational synthesis that would confer inferential justification. Foundationalists may consistently claim that a rational synthesis of p, q, and r increases our justification for belief in p; but they cannot make this synthesis necessary for p or q or r to be an axiom. If this is a fair objection, Sidgwick cannot reasonably demand a rational synthesis on the basis of his foundationalism, and so he has no good reason to prefer philosophical to dogmatic intuitionism.

We might give a different reason, however, for seeking a rational synthesis. Pluralist intuitionists, such as Price and Reid, accept a number of basic principles, without any further principle to decide between them when they give conflicting directions. This possibility of unresolved conflict among basic principles is (we may hold) a practical defect in a moral system. To remove the possibility of conflict, we need just one basic principle, to order the other principles.

Sidgwick assumes that every acceptable moral theory must remove any possible conflict among basic principles, and that it must provide a principle to remove possible conflicts. But these assumptions are disputable. If he relies on them, his preference for the philosophical stage over the purely dogmatic stage of intuitionism is also disputable. The failure of intuitionists to meet his demand for rational synthesis is not a decisive objection to their position.

1172. Intuitionism and Common-Sense Morality

Sidgwick's claims about intuitionism complicate our initial contrast between the dialectical and the axiomatic strategies. We have spoken of the dialectical strategy as though it reflected the holist assumptions that we find in Aristotle and again in Rawls; but this is not Sidgwick's view. He treats the method of common-sense morality as intuitionist, and he takes intuitionism to include a deontological normative doctrine and a foundationalist epistemological doctrine. Moreover, he accepts foundationalism, while he rejects a deontological outlook; and so he accepts one aspect of the intuitionist position without the other.

His various claims about intuitionism recall some of the difficulties that we found in recognizing intuitionism as a distinct method of ethics. The distinct method comes from a deontological normative theory. This normative theory might appear to be separable from foundationalist epistemology. But this is not how it appears to Sidgwick. He examines deontological conceptions of the right from a foundationalist point of view.

attempted: but it . . . will be more satisfactorily studied after examining in detail the morality of common sense.' ([1] 89) Abbreviated at [7] 102.

A utilitarian systematization of common sense has to reject some elements of common sense. For if common sense accepts, as Sidgwick claims it does, a deontological normative position, it cannot be reconciled with the teleological position of utilitarianism. Moreover, if common sense is committed to foundationalism, it must accept as axioms some principles that the utilitarian cannot regard as axioms, since the utilitarian cannot regard any non-teleological principles of right as axioms.

It is not clear, however, that common sense, or the most plausible explication and clarification of it, accepts the epistemological standards that Sidgwick builds into his description of dogmatic and philosophical intuitionism. Nor is it clear that failure to meet these standards is a serious defect in a normative position. Even if the principles of common-sense morality are not axioms, they might still be true and rationally acceptable.

1173. The Review of Common-Sense Morality

Sidgwick's dialectical argument includes a review of common-sense morality. He models his approach on Aristotle's description of the particular virtues of character.[41] He does not suggest that Aristotle's conception of happiness guides the description of the virtues. If Aristotelian eudaemonism is empty, it does not control Aristotle's description of the virtues; hence his description simply lists the traits and behaviour approved by common sense.

Though Sidgwick gives credit to Aristotle for the method he follows in his review of common-sense morality, he takes his larger aim to be different from Aristotle's. He reviews common sense to see whether it rests on genuine intuitions, and he finds that it does not. Sometimes the principles accepted by common sense rest on controversial empirical assumption. Sometimes we cannot say what common-sense principles require in a given type of case. Sometimes common sense apparently has no advice to offer. Hence the principles implicit in common sense do not embody genuine intuitions.

Since the utilitarian principle answers these questions raised by common sense, common sense is unconsciously utilitarian. Utilitarianism, already present to some extent in common-sense moral reasoning, gives better answers, measured by principles accepted by common sense, than common sense can give from its unaided resources. This is the dialectical defence of utilitarianism. Such a defence does not show, according to Sidgwick, that the principle of utility is true or that it is a genuine ethical first principle; to show that we must apply the axiomatic strategy as well. But the dialectical strategy removes an objection that might turn us against utilitarianism, and hence might persuade us not to treat the principle of utility as an axiom.

How can Sidgwick consistently claim both (i) that common sense is unconsciously utilitarian, and (ii) that the outlook of common sense is intuitionist—that is, deontological and foundationalist? We cannot say that common sense is unconsciously utilitarian and consciously intuitionist; for both intuitionism (understood as including pluralism) and

---

[41] See xix–xx, quoted in §§67, 1143. Sidgwick on Aristotle; §115.

utilitarianism are theoretical doctrines that consider questions that the ordinary moral agent overlooks. If common sense is intuitionist, it must also be unconsciously intuitionist. How, then, can it be intuitionist rather than utilitarian, if it is unconsciously utilitarian?

Sidgwick might refer to the different ways in which both intuitionism and utilitarianism might claim to fit common sense. Pluralist intuitionism might claim to give an accurate account of the implicit attitude of common sense to its principles. But a utilitarian account of common sense does not claim that common sense implicitly recognizes a highest principle behind the plurality of principles that it treats as self-evident. It refers to a different aspect of common sense, its tendency to rely on considerations of utility in reaching practical conclusions. Practical consideration of utility does not imply recognition of the principle of utility as the single ultimate principle.[42]

But this division between an intuitionist attitude to principles and a utilitarian attitude to practice is difficult to maintain. For if common sense regularly relies on utilitarian considerations, even in cases where they conflict with the implications of non-utilitarian principles, it implicitly accepts the principle of utility; hence an intuitionist reconstruction of its attitude to moral principles is wrong. Sidgwick, therefore, ought not to describe the outlook of common sense as intuitionist. He ought to treat intuitionism and utilitarianism as two contrasting accounts of common sense, each of which recognizes, emphasizes, minimizes, and rejects different aspects of common-sense morality.

Sidgwick is less than clear on these issues, because he tends to assume that if common-sense morality is not utilitarian, it must be intuitionist. He does not consider the possibility of a deontological outlook that is not intuitionist, because his conception of intuitionism includes both a deontological normative position and a foundationalist epistemological position. The main question is whether we should accept the intuitionist pluralism of Price or Whewell, who recognize a number of principles on an equal footing, or the intuitionist monism of Sidgwick, who recognizes one supreme principle.

1174. Common Sense: Advantages of Utilitarianism

The dialectical argument (summarized in iii 11, iv 3) claims that utilitarianism displays system in common-sense morality where we might not otherwise have seen it. It does not regard common-sense morality as a mere collection of rules, maxims, and so on with no logical structure—as rules of etiquette might be in some societies at some times. Instead, it shows how different rules support one another, and why changes in one aspect of common-sense morality lead to changes in another. The utilitarian outlook displays system in common-sense morality in different ways.[43]

(1)   First, utilitarianism gives a vindicating explanation of some common-sense rules. We can explain the point of rules about promises, respect for property, etc., by appeal to

---

[42] Contrast Smith's view, discussed in §799, and cited by Sidgwick at 424. Smith denies that moral sentiments are based on considerations of utility, but he argues that the results of acting on them tend to maximize utility.

[43] These different aspects of system include the 'dependence argument' and the 'systematizing argument' discussed by Schneewind, *SEVMP* 279–85.

their utility. We often defend actions and policies by appeal to their good consequences. We show our concern for good consequences if we limit rules, or defend breaches of them, by appeal to consequences. Though common sense appears at first sight to accept a number of general, definite, and exceptionless rules, we limit the application of these rules by consideration of good consequences. The rules against lying and breaking promises illustrate a pervasive feature of common sense. Sidgwick partly endorses Mill's claim that, from a utilitarian point of view, common-sense principles are subordinate maxims—more specific ways of promoting utility in the appropriate conditions. Though utilitarians sometimes depart from common-sense maxims, they also point out the general utility of such maxims. They may even argue that it is better, from the utilitarian point of view, to follow these maxims without making exceptions, because the process of making exceptions may involve worse results than the results of failure to make exceptions.

(2) Sometimes utilitarianism gives an amplifying explanation. For many actual or conceivable situations, common-sense rules offer no definite answers, but utilitarianism offers us a definite answer in principle. We do not suppose that our rules about, say, telling the truth and keeping promises are completely without exception, but we cannot state the exceptions precisely and exhaustively. Sometimes common-sense rules do not tell us exactly what to do; sometimes they tell us exactly what to do in some cases, but leave other cases that are hard to decide. The principle of utility, however, gives us a definite guide for every situation. It also resolves difficulties that arise from a conflict between two common-sense maxims.

(3) In other cases, utilitarianism offers an undermining explanation. Perhaps some of our rules once promoted utility, but no longer promote it, so that reflexion on utility may convince us to abandon these rules. For instance, the 'double standard' about adultery condemns adultery by married women more strongly than it condemns adultery by married men. If a particular society attaches importance to inheritance, and to legitimacy as a basis for inheritance, this double standard might appear reasonable. But once any utilitarian basis has disappeared, we may see that the double standard is discredited.[44] Undermining explanations may also help to systematize common-sense morality as a whole; for if we no longer see any utility in a rule, we may be less disposed to take it seriously.

These three aspects of utilitarianism sum up Sidgwick's reasons for believing that if we think about the basis of ordinary moral convictions, we will come to accept the utilitarian principle.[45] The main weight of his argument rests on the claim that utilitarianism tends to vindicate our common-sense moral rules and maxims. If he is right on this point, he strengthens his other defences of utilitarianism.

---

[44] This appeal to errors about utility may not cover every case in which utilitarianism disagrees with common sense. If there are many cases of unexplained divergence, we may find our confidence in utilitarianism shaken. But if there are few enough of them, in comparison to the number of rules and exceptions that allow a utilitarian explanation, we may legitimately prefer the utilitarian position.

[45] Utilitarianism must draw on some intuitions: '... such abstract moral principles as we can admit to be really self-evident are not only not incompatible with a utilitarian system, but even seem required to furnish a rational basis for such a system.' (ME 494) But only the principle of utility is really self-evident.

1175. Conflicts between Common Sense and Utilitarianism

At first sight, the most plausible aspect of a utilitarian account of morality is its apparent coincidence with reflective and enlightened common sense.[46] We sometimes recognize that some rules need to be qualified, and that the appropriate qualifications must attend to consequences. The utilitarian who agrees with Mill argues that common sense is broadly right, and that utilitarianism explains why it is right.

But how far does this role of consequences in common-sense morality help the utilitarian argument? Utilitarianism does not simply claim that consequences matter. Since utilitarianism is universalistic hedonism, it claims that the morally relevant consequences are hedonic consequences. This aspect of utilitarianism casts doubt on the claim that utilitarianism, as opposed to consequentialism in general, explains common sense. Even if some rules should be violated because of their consequences, the relevant consequences may be determined by the importance of the rules that are observed or violated. This degree of consequentialism about the right is not necessarily a utilitarian position. It may not even be a purely teleological conception of the right. Perhaps the right action is the one that most accords with certain principles of duty, hierarchically ordered; it may not be the action that most tends to realize some good defined independently of the right.

Whewell raises this objection to Paley. He agrees with Paley that consequences matter, but he argues that Paley's consequentialist defences of specific moral rules do not rely on the hedonic consequences that ought to be relevant if Paley's theory of value were correct.[47] Mill's appeals to common-sense maxims and to ordinary consideration of consequences are open to the same objection. Sidgwick does not answer Whewell's objection to the utilitarian argument. To show that the connexion between the principle of utility and the right rules of conduct 'has always been to a large extent recognized by all reflective persons', Sidgwick repeats Mill's claim that even professedly non-utilitarian moralists such as Whewell appeal to utility.[48] But this attempt to enlist Whewell's appeals to consequences in support of utilitarianism is open to the objection that Whewell urges against Paley and Mill. Neither here nor in his discussion of common sense does Sidgwick show that the consequences that matter to common sense are purely hedonic.[49]

---

[46] This may be why Bain takes utilitarianism to be so obvious: 'Indeed, it is hardly possible to maintain any opposite doctrine, or to say that the greatest possible amount of happiness ought not to be attained, or that any conduct calculated to produce this maximum is other than right.' (*MPP* 88) Bain has a rather loose conception of utilitarianism; see §1176.

[47] See Whewell, §1121.

[48] 'Indeed, so clear is it that in most cases the observance of the commonly received moral rules tends to render human life tranquil and happy, that even moralists (as Whewell) who are most strongly opposed to Utilitarianism have, in attempting to exhibit the "necessity" of moral rules, been led to dwell on utilitarian considerations.' (*ME* 85–6) 'Tranquil and happy' introduces utility only if we accept (contrary to Whewell) a hedonist conception of happiness.

[49] Collini, 'Experience', 350, discusses Sidgwick's cautious attitude to political tradition and innovation. To illustrate Sidgwick's 'Burkean respect for the historically formed shape of existing institutions', he quotes Sidgwick, *EP* 14, on the tradition of respect for the verdicts of juries, even though they are, in Sidgwick's words, 'a blunt and clumsy instrument for the administration of criminal justice'. He mentions a similar defence of the House of Lords. These are examples to illustrate Sidgwick's general point that 'while it is a grave and not uncommon error to treat generalizations as to human conduct which are only approximately true as if they were universally and absolutely true, it is a no less serious mistake—and perhaps it is at the present time the more prevalent and dangerous mistake—to throw a rule aside as valueless, or treat it as having only a vague and indefinite reality, because we find it subject to important limitations and exceptions.' (*EP* 13)

Sidgwick could have found a vivid illustration of this point in Godwin's critical attitude to common-sense morality. Godwin believes that a correct understanding of the practical relevance of utility requires radical revision of common-sense rules. To see whether Sidgwick's more conservative attitude or Godwin's more radical attitude is right, we need to compare their conceptions of utility and the assumptions on which they base their practical recommendations. Sidgwick does not support his view of the implications of utilitarianism by a comparison with Godwin's view.

We might, therefore, reasonably doubt Sidgwick's defence of utilitarianism on the basis of common-sense appeals to the consequences of actions for some aspects of the welfare of some of the people affected. To see whether common-sense consequentialism supports utilitarianism, we must consider the consequences that a universalistic hedonist takes to be relevant, and see whether common sense takes these to be the only relevant consequences. Sidgwick does not show that common sense agrees on this point with utilitarianism.[50] Hence the consequentialist aspects of common sense do not prove Sidgwick's claim about the vindicating role of utilitarianism.

Moreover, consequences do not seem to be all that matters for rightness. Butler and others offer apparently non-consequentialist reasons for sometimes preferring justice over benevolence. We believe that certain kinds of distribution, and certain types and degrees of punishment, are just or unjust, for non-consequential reasons. It is not obvious, for instance, that more serious crimes should receive more severe punishments than less serious crimes, if we are thinking purely about good consequences. If we expect some degree of proportion between crime and punishment, we seem to disregard consequences.

Such examples do not straightforwardly refute the utilitarian claim to have found a vindicating explanation of common sense. For we can try to deal with them through indirect utilitarian argument; perhaps the bad effects of particular actions are outweighed by the overall effects of accepting a system of rules that in some cases prohibits the consideration of consequences. But indirect utilitarianism does not answer the basic objection to the purely hedonic consideration of consequences; even if these are considered indirectly, they may still be the wrong ones to consider, or only some of the ones that ought to be considered. It is doubtful, therefore, whether an indirect utilitarian argument could justify the aspects of common sense that reject calculation of hedonic consequences.

1176. Common Sense: Actions and Reasons

We have been considering questions about the extensional equivalence of utilitarian morality and common-sense morality. But the resort to indirect utilitarianism raises a question about whether extensional equivalence is all that matters. A mere proof of extensional equivalence between the principle of utility and common sense would not support a utilitarian account of common sense, or a utilitarian conception of morality.[51] A utilitarian explanation of

---

[50] In ME iv 3, Sidgwick makes it clearer which consequences matter to the utilitarian, and how far these match the ones that matter to common sense.

[51] The assumption that extensional equivalence is all that matters is clear in Bain's defence of utilitarianism. He argues that opposition to utilitarianism rests on a narrow view of utility that considers too few people or too short a time.

common-sense morality claims to be correct, and not merely to be a possible explanation of our approving of the actions we actually approve of. The demand for a correct explanation is the demand that Socrates presents to Euthyphro, and that Cudworth and Price urge against positivism and sentimentalism.

In asking Socrates' question, we raise a difficulty for utilitarianism.[52] For we might argue that the (presumed) agreement of common-sense principles with utilitarianism does not constitute our justification for believing them, or the principle on which we have reason to retain or revise them. According to this view, our main rational justification for acceptance of these principles would remain even if the utilitarian defences failed. If we consider some of the requirements of justice or humanity, we may decide that if they did not promote utility, we would still have good reason to accept them. We might say this, for instance, about the costs of installing ramps for access to buildings by wheelchairs. Perhaps this maximizes total utility; but that is not our main concern. Even if accessibility involved some decrease in total utility, this would not by itself decide us against accessibility.

For similar reasons, John Grote objects to the implications of utilitarian attitudes to slavery. In his view, what matters in deciding about the rightness of slavery is the human nature of slaves. Since slaves are human beings no less than other people, slavery is open to objection because it is inappropriate to hold human beings as property. If this is the basis of our objection to slavery, we do not also need to be convinced that the abolition of slavery will increase overall utility. If we were to insist on applying this utilitarian test, we might miss the morally overriding considerations.[53]

Conservative utilitarians might reply that utilitarianism gives the right account of our reasons for our actions, and that we are wrong if we suppose our reasons are not utilitarian. Utilitarians might argue, for instance, that the reasons we think we rely on are not our real reasons, because we do not actually think about actual or possible situations in the way we would think of them if we had given a true account of our reasons. They might argue that we do not take a given non-utilitarian principle as seriously as we claim to take it, or that we take a utilitarian principle more seriously than we claim to take it. This sort of argument might show that we implicitly rely on utilitarian reasons.

The prospects for such a defence of utilitarianism, however, are dim. Objections to utilitarian accounts of our reasons seem most plausible precisely when we reflect most

---

'But it does not follow that a more comprehensive utility, including the present and future interests of society at large, is insufficient as a moral end and a ground of obligation. The partisans of the right as against the useful have never yet proceeded upon this view of the useful. They have not clearly shown that, supposing everything provided for that concerns the well-being of human society, considered through its whole duration, there would still remain a class of actions demanding to be enforced in the name of morality.' (Bain, *MPP* 7) The reference to a class of actions shows that Bain thinks only of extensional equivalence.

[52] Butler on utilitarianism; §700. Cf. §1283.

[53] See Grote, *EUP* 319–26. See esp. 318–19: '. . . utility . . . is certainly at this moment the principle upon which slavery would be defended; while yet I suppose we may say that the opinion of civilized man has come to the conclusion, nearly universal, that slavery is wrong . . . Utilitarianism seems just what, in the way of argument, hinders the settlement of a question which man's moral feeling would otherwise have settled. It is said that the slaves are happier as they are than they would be if free; and the putting the question upon this issue makes it more difficult to decide, and gives more scope for persistence of opinion in the opposite direction, than almost any other. . . . Genuine utilitarianism only makes the question hopelessly discussible; there must be a reference to something besides utilitarianism . . . to give hope of settling it.' Sidgwick's reviews of Grote in 'Grote I' and 'Grote II' do not discuss this objection to utilitarianism (though Sidgwick is sympathetic to much of Grote's criticism of Mill).

carefully on actual and possible cases. Reflexion seems to show that even agreement about what to do in actual cases does not mark agreement on principles and reasons.

Conservative utilitarians might appeal to the comprehensiveness and definiteness of the principle of utility. If we want to be guided by the most comprehensive and definite principle that tells us what to do in actual cases, and we recognize that the principle of utility is the most comprehensive and definite principle, we might agree that we implicitly accept the principle of utility, and that we ought to adjust our other principles to it. But this argument seems to exaggerate the importance of comprehensiveness and definiteness, and especially of their combination. Why should these virtues in a principle—even if they are virtues—convince us to prefer a principle that conflicts with the reasons that seem to matter most to us after reflexion on actual and counterfactual cases? Even if we would like something as definite as utilitarianism claims to be, that is not a good reason for preferring utilitarianism, or for relying on this preference as a basis for a choice among moral theories.

If these are good reasons for rejecting a conservative utilitarian approach to common-sense reasons, a utilitarian might deny that a utilitarian explanation needs to capture the reasons recognized by common sense. According to a radical utilitarian approach, common sense is more likely to be correct about which actions are right, and more likely to be wrong about which reasons for doing these actions are the right reasons. We might take common sense to offer guesses about the causal origin of right actions, and we might suppose that the utilitarian replaces these guesses with more plausible causal accounts.

We might, then, take common-sense views about appropriate reasons and principles to be parallel to pre-scientific causal explanations. We expect a scientific theory to accept observations, or most of them, but we do not require it to accept pre-scientific explanations; on the contrary, we expect a scientific theory to provide a more general explanation that may be far from common sense. Similarly, then, we might suggest that common sense has found the actions that tend to promote utility, but has not grasped their explanation. We might offer a sociological argument in support of this utilitarian picture. If a society has managed to exist for some length of time, its members must have worked out some way to get on well enough to preserve their society against external attack and against internal tensions that would reduce them to a Hobbesian state of war. As circumstances change, they gradually, though often unconsciously, change their patterns of behaviour to suit the changes. A utilitarian theory explains this process and makes its goal explicit.

Such historical and sociological explanations, however, do not support a utilitarian theory. A utilitarian morality does not seem especially suitable for the preservation of a given society (if the Feudal System, or the Ancien Regime, is an example of a society); on the contrary, Benthamite utilitarianism aimed at the transformation, and hence the destruction, of existing society. Nor does it seem especially suitable for the preservation of 'society' in a broader sense (if, e.g., French society in 1760 and 1860 are understood as the same society); many different moral outlooks seem to be capable of encouraging habits and practices that prevent a collapse into a state of war. One might appeal to history and sociology to show that moral outlooks tend to adapt themselves to new circumstances if a practice that resulted in good consequences begins to result in bad consequences.

But this fact supports utilitarianism only if every sort of sensitivity to good and bad consequences amounts to utilitarianism. For these reasons, the analogy between a utilitarian theory of ordinary moral behaviour and a scientific theory that explains observations is not helpful.

In any case, this approach to common-sense morality is misguided if common-sense views about appropriate moral reasons are not causal hypotheses. We might value low blood pressure because we believe it will reduce the risk of heart attacks; if this causal hypothesis turned out to be false, we would not care about low blood pressure. But we do not seem to value the motives and aims of virtuous people simply as means to the appropriate sorts of actions. Our views about morally appropriate motives reflect our views about better and worse agents.[54] These views may be more reliable than our views about actions. If they are reliable, they may legitimately be used to evaluate a utilitarian position.

If we take account of reasons and considerations as well as of actions, we may doubt whether utilitarianism provides a vindicating or an amplifying explanation. If it achieves approximate extensional equivalence, but it does not endorse the considerations and reasons that matter, it does not explain common-sense morality. Nor does it provide an undermining explanation. Even if some common-sense rules 'outlive their usefulness', as measured by utilitarian standards, they may still be right, if they match the morally relevant reasons and considerations.

If these are reasonable objections to the utilitarian account of common sense, we might give a non-utilitarian explanation of the rough extensional equivalence of utilitarianism and common sense. Utilitarian thinking may, in proper circumstances, serve as a rule of thumb for reaching the right actions; but some other theory is needed to explain exactly what is right about the conclusions it reaches, and why it can be expected to reach the right results on the occasions when it does.

This account of utilitarian reasoning might explain why we approve of some of Bentham's or Mill's applications of the principle of utility without approving of their utilitarian premises. If their attention to consequences is tacitly constrained by non-utilitarian moral considerations, they may reach some of the right conclusions. They do not, for instance, engage in unprejudiced hedonistic calculation of the pains suffered by the oppressors who can no longer oppress, in comparison with the pleasures and pains of the former victims of the oppression; they simply assume that the benefit to the oppressed outweighs the harm to the oppressors.[55] The moral assumptions that prejudice utilitarian calculation explain why the utilitarian finds the right answer.[56] In reply to Sidgwick, one might argue that enlightened utilitarians such as Mill are unconscious intuitionists.

---

[54] See, e.g., Aristotle on the virtues; §112.

[55] A similar comparative judgment about pleasures and pains seems to underlie Singer, 'Famine', if its advocacy of famine relief is to be defended on utilitarian grounds.

[56] Bradley, CE 116, comments: 'Deduced by a man of practical good sense, the conclusions of the hedonistic art of life would never seriously conflict with common morality. There are good psychological reasons for that. But once admit the principle, and what is to happen if men with no sense nor hold on real life, but gifted with a logical faculty, begin systematically to deduce from this slippery principle? Is this not a danger, and is it a wholly imaginary danger?'

1177. Moral Theories and Definite Answers

We have now considered the aspect of Sidgwick's dialectical strategy that depends on the general agreement of utilitarianism with common sense. Another aspect of this strategy appeals not to agreement on specific moral decisions and recommendations, but to more general virtues of a utilitarian system. Common sense recognizes that these are virtues in a moral outlook, and admits, or can be persuaded to admit, that its own current outlook lacks these virtues. The failure of common sense gives us a reason to prefer the utilitarian outlook. Even if this is not by itself a decisive argument for preferring utilitarianism over common sense, it raises questions about Sidgwick's aims for moral theory, and their influence on his conception of utilitarianism.

The main question arises from Sidgwick's claim that utilitarianism gives more definite answers than common sense gives.[57] His demand for definiteness is one of his initial criteria for a genuine method of ethics. The same demand shows why Greek ethics is unhelpful for his purposes, why we ought to set aside non-hedonistic egoism and Green's claims about self-realization, and why we ought to reject intuitionist accounts of the right such as Clarke's and Price's. But is the demand for definiteness reasonable? Sometimes it may be legitimate to complain that a given theory promises practical guidance but provides only circles of definitions. But Sidgwick also requires a theory to give us principles that, if combined with appropriate empirical information, give us definite practical answers.

A theory that states a general principle applicable to every case is not good enough. The bare formula of Kant's categorical imperative is no more help than 'Always do the right thing' or 'Always act in accordance with right reason'. This general principle does not allow us to find the action that would count as acting in accordance with right reason here and now; we do not even know, without some further moral reflexion, what questions we should ask in order to find the right thing to do. Our eventual decision about what to do seems to depend on this further moral reflexion, not on the general principle about right reason; and so the general principle seems irrelevant to practice.

In contrast to these unhelpful general principles, utilitarianism is definite, because we can apply it to practical questions without further moral reflexion. Given any description of any situation that is worth thinking about in the light of the empirical facts, our moral theory, conjoined with all the relevant empirical information, ought to give an answer that is definite enough to prescribe a particular course of action.[58] Sidgwick and Mill believe that economics, social psychology, and sociology either supply or will supply this information, and that we need a moral theory to tell us how to use it.[59] Measured by this standard,

---

[57] '... the difficulties which we found in the way of determining by the Intuitional method (i.e. common sense) the limits and the relative importance of these duties are reduced in the utilitarian system, to difficulties of hedonistic comparison.' (*ME* 439)

[58] This standard is meant to set aside mere logical possibilities, since we might not think a theory has to give definite answers applying to them. We will accept this standard if we want a moral theory to assure us that when we face decisions, we will not be held back by specifically moral disagreement or uncertainty. A method of ethics, as Sidgwick conceives it, is expected to meet this standard; utilitarianism is the only plausible moral theory that meets it.

[59] Mill and Sidgwick both wrote on political economy (on Sidgwick, see Schultz, *HS* 534–9). Sidgwick expresses some doubts about the progress of sociology in 'Prophecy'. He states his view about the relevance of sociology to ethics at 'Relation of ethics', 258–9, before arguing for the essential distinctness of ethics from sociology. Sidgwick's doubts are

the Kantian categorical imperative (as Sidgwick understands it) fails. Since it does not settle moral disputes, it has not done the work that moral philosophy should have done before we use our empirical information.

Sidgwick's criticism of common-sense morality presupposes this standard of definiteness in a moral theory.[60] He often points out that some question arises that common-sense morality cannot settle, even if all the relevant empirical information is available. Utilitarianism is definite because its supreme principle of right requires the maximization of pleasure, and because quantities of pleasure and means to pleasure are empirically knowable. Nothing further needs to be said, from the moral point of view, about what counts as pleasure. To apply the theory, we need to know what it is to experience pleasure, but this knowledge does not require any further moral argument or intuition.

If utilitarianism is to be definite, not every version is acceptable.[61] If we accept a non-hedonistic version, the elements of utility may be indefinite, since we may need to make further judgments of value to identify them. A quantitative hedonist conception of the end removes these difficulties. If hedonic comparisons considered the comparative (non-quantitative) value of different pleasures resulting from a given action, utilitarianism would not give definite answers. Hence Mill's form of hedonism does not give us definite answers. The relevant form of hedonism, then, must be purely quantitative; this is the form that Sidgwick defends.

1178. Utilitarianism and Definite Answers

Sidgwick's demand for definiteness appears reasonable, because it appears reasonable to want a theory that takes us from practical uncertainty to empirical uncertainty. We cannot reasonably expect a moral theory to resolve empirical uncertainty for us; but it appears reasonable to ask a theory to resolve every uncertainty that can be attributed to our moral beliefs. Sidgwick relies on this assumption about the desirability of definite answers, just as Hegel relies on it to attack Kantian morality and to defend the Ethical outlook.[62]

The method of utilitarianism (iv 4–5) makes common-sense principles more definite by subordinating them to the principle of utility.[63] Though utilitarians recognize that common sense is on many points 'unconsciously utilitarian' (iv 3), they do not suppose that it coincides exactly with the results of utilitarian calculation. The difficulties in applying utilitarianism are not 'theoretical perplexities', but only practical questions, whereas the difficulties in common sense are theoretical perplexities. If we reduce uncertainties to empirical uncertainties, and

especially aroused by the large pretensions of Spencer's 'evolutionary' sociology. See Collini, *LS*, ch. 6; *PM* 244–7; Schultz, *HS* 249–50.

[60] Cf. Bradley's criticism, *CE* 104–6. Like many of Bradley's criticisms, this passage suggests a reasonable objection rather than stating it.

[61] See §1165.   [62] Hegel's objections to the emptiness of Kantian morality; §1021.

[63] 'No doubt, even if this synthesis of methods be completely accepted, there will remain some discrepancy in details between our particular moral sentiments and unreasoned judgments on the one hand, and the apparent results of special utilitarian calculations on the other; and we may often have some practical difficulty in balancing the latter against the more general utilitarian reasons for obeying the former: but there seems to be no longer any theoretical perplexity as to the principles for determining social duty.' (*ME* 495) Bradley discusses the method of utilitarianism at *CE* 109–10.

thereby make our theory definite, we also remove theoretical perplexities and reduce the difficulties to purely practical ones.[64]

The principles of common sense sometimes leave us in theoretical perplexity. The traditional doctrine of the just war, for instance, does not allow us to determine, without further moral reflexion, who is innocent, or how to distinguish foreseen from intended consequences, in the conditions of modern warfare. Nor do prohibitions on suicide and murder make it clear, without further moral reflexion, when the withdrawal of 'extraordinary' medical treatment counts as murder. The further reflexion that is needed to apply these principles and rules to practice may raise theoretical perplexity.

The possibility of theoretical perplexity, however, does not make these principles and rules useless; nor is a more definite theory necessarily more useful. On the contrary, if a more definite theory needs empirical information that is difficult to find, a less definite theory may be more useful. A prohibition on the torture of innocent people does not tell us precisely who is innocent; we may need further moral judgments to decide that. None the less, this prohibition is often easy to apply, since we are often confident that the potential victim is innocent. The direct utilitarian prohibition 'Don't torture anyone unless it would maximize utility' is more definite, by Sidgwick's standards, but it may be more difficult to apply to practice.

Some moral argument and judgment, therefore, are needed to apply less definite moral outlooks to practice; but we often succeed in applying them to practice by these means. Not all the applications are indisputably correct, and some of them certainly arouse disputes. But are we better off if we choose the definiteness offered by a utilitarian theory?

1179. Definite Answers and Practical Difficulties

To see whether we are better off or worse off if we accept utilitarianism, we should consider the difficulties that Sidgwick recognizes in utilitarian calculation. He does not share the view of utilitarians who might attempt 'a thorough revision' of the rules of common sense, so as to aim directly at maximum utility. He believes this attempt is unrealistic.[65] We cannot construct a plausible utilitarian code of conduct if we ignore the effects of its acceptance on people who are accustomed to the morality of common sense (468).[66] Hence the scope for utilitarian revision of ordinary moral views may be limited.[67]

---

[64] Sidgwick supposes it is a sign of progress that 'the difficulties which we found in the way of determining by the Intuitional method the limits and the relative importance of these duties are reduced in the utilitarian system, to difficulties of hedonistic comparison.' (439)

[65] 'But in thus stating the problem we are assuming that . . . we can frame with adequate precision a system of rules, constituting the true moral code for human beings as deduced from utilitarian principles. And this seems to have been commonly assumed by the school whose method we are now examining. But when we set ourselves in earnest to the construction of such a system, we find it beset with serious difficulties.' (467)

[66] 'The nature of man and the conditions of his life cannot usefully be assumed to be constant, unless we are confining our attention to the present or proximate future; while again, if we are considering them in the present or proximate future, we must take into account men's actual moral habits and sentiments, as a part of their nature not materially more modifiable than the rest.' (469) On acceptance utility, see Brandt, 'Credible' and 'Merits'.

[67] 'Now in the present rudimentary condition of sociology it does not appear to me that we have sufficient data for deducing the best rules of mutual behaviour for human communities, as they are to exist at some future period. And

Some of Sidgwick's doubts would be removed if (1) we had a reasonable prospect of reaching the utilitarian goal through some more accessible goal, or if (2) we could be sure that specific secondary maxims would lead us in the right direction. Sidgwick rejects the first suggestion, because of his doubts about the progress of sociology. He opposes the suggestions of Spencer and Stephen that we can achieve the utilitarian goal through some supposedly accessible goal such as evolutionary development or efficiency in self-preservation (470–3).[68] Against the second suggestion, he argues that Mill's principles about liberty (478) have no sound utilitarian basis.[69]

Sidgwick is doubtful about these secondary goals and principles because he believes that empirical hedonism is the only available standard. In his view, we already recognize this in deliberation about 'natural good'; for we rely on empirical hedonism in pursuing intrinsically desirable non-moral ends. The utilitarian relies on empirical hedonism in morality as well (479).[70] The egoistic empirical hedonist has no true general principles that remove the necessity of uncertain empirical predictions and comparisons. The same is true of utilitarian calculation; indeed, questions about the general happiness introduce further complications and uncertainties that encourage doubts about radical reform. If we induce people to question a common-sense code that may on the whole be felicific and may be difficult to change piecemeal, the effects may be bad. The danger of these bad effects will often discourage utilitarians from taking the risks that would be involved in changing accepted codes.

Moreover, utilitarian reformers must not simply consider rules and principles that they want everyone to accept. They must also consider the occasions on which they might think it better if some people break the rule that everyone else accepts. Sidgwick believes that such occasions may arise; the argument that violations undermine the rule loses force the more firmly most people tend to keep the rule (487–9). It may, therefore, sometimes be obligatory, on utilitarian grounds, to violate secretly a moral rule whose observance one advocates openly. One may be required to adopt an esoteric morality and to conceal the fact that one has adopted it.[71] A careful and conscientious examination of the implications of utilitarianism may result in the decision to prevent most people from learning the truth of utilitarianism.

These are not all the difficulties in applying utilitarianism to practice. Those that Sidgwick recognizes arise from the variety of the hedonic consequences that we have to predict. But we need to consider not only the likely 'spontaneous' reactions of people to a particular situation—those reactions they are likely to have apart from the efforts of others to make them react favourably. We must also consider their 'manufactured' reactions. Reformers and legislators may be able to control hedonic consequences, since human tendencies to pleasure and pain are to some degree malleable. Even if we set

therefore I should judge, from a strictly utilitarian point of view, that any attempt, such as Bentham made, to dispense with the morality of instinct and tradition, would be premature and ill-advised.' ([1] 438) This is abbreviated, and the reference to Bentham is removed, in [7] 474.

[68] These comments on Spencer and Stephen were added in [3].
[69] The comments on Mill and on Bain were added in [3].   [70] The passage is quoted in §1248.
[71] 'And thus a utilitarian may reasonably desire, on utilitarian principles, that some of his conclusions should be rejected by mankind generally; or even that the vulgar should keep aloof from his system as a whole, in so far as the inevitable indefiniteness and complexity of its calculations render it likely to lead to bad results in their hands.' (490)

aside crude devices such as drugs and surgery, we cannot set aside, from the utilitarian point of view, the prospects of changing people so as to make them prefer a particular arrangement that they would otherwise not have preferred.[72] Unless we know enough about the likely development of the capacity to manufacture reactions, we cannot measure hedonic consequences.

When we add these difficulties in applying utilitarianism to those that Sidgwick raises, we can see that these practical difficulties are also relevant to the moral theorist. They make the answers to our most important questions depend on empirical information that (i) we cannot obtain, or (ii) we ought not to obtain, or (iii) we ought to suspect in some other way.

For example: (i) Some of the utilitarian calculations that Sidgwick considers, when he discusses esoteric morality, for instance, are quite complex and uncertain, but they are not so uncertain in principle (he insists) that a utilitarian can justifiably ignore them. (ii) The best way of obtaining some of the relevant information might be by experimentation, using means that (from the common-sense point of view) are immoral. A utilitarian cannot dismiss the possibility that the information obtained would have good enough consequences to justify the means used to obtain it. (iii) The possibility of manufactured pleasures suggests that the utilitarian will often have to endorse the actions of those who are willing and able to control other people's pleasures and pains.

Egoistic hedonism, according to Sidgwick, appears to offer 'a dubious guide to an ignoble end' (200). Universalistic hedonism may not aim at an ignoble end, since it seems to demand self-sacrifice rather than concentration on one's own interest; but it seems to offer guidance that is at least as dubious as the calculus of empirical egoistic hedonism. The utilitarian theory is uninformative in practice because it is so definite. We remove theoretical indefiniteness and perplexity by an appeal to hedonic consequences, but this appeal throws all other practical principles into doubt.[73]

Common-sense principles, however, declare some empirical information to be irrelevant, and therefore avoid the possibly fruitless search for it. Killing the innocent is not normally justified by its good consequences, and therefore we need not normally calculate consequences of this or that action, or of having this specific rule. In abnormal situations, it may be clear, for instance, that some more urgent rule or permission—the duty to save many innocent people, or the permission to preserve oneself—may make a difference. But if we require it to be clear (and not just conceivable) that this higher principle applies to a situation, we do not need to inquire into every situation where we have the choice of killing or not killing the innocent, to see whether some further principle applies.

---

[72] Sidgwick considers malleability in his discussion of egoistic hedonism (147). Elster, 'Grapes', discusses some connected questions about the formation of preferences.

[73] In his review, Bain suggests that Sidgwick exaggerates the difficulties that arise for utilitarianism from the uncertainty of hedonistic calculation. He suggests that if we regard ethics as aiming at the relief of pain rather than the maximization of pleasure, we have a simpler task. 'But, as regards ethics, the greatest consideration remains; protection from pain is the chief thing sought by moral restraints and enactments. Morality does not cater for men's pleasures, it only secures them from molestation in pursuing pleasures for themselves.' (Bain, 'Methods', 185) Bain does not explain how, on strictly utilitarian grounds, these restrictions on utilitarian calculation are to be justified. He faces a dilemma: (a) A utilitarian argument may be offered, which must apparently be subject to all the uncertainties that—Bain admits—arise from calculation about maximizing pleasure. (b) Alternatively, a non-utilitarian argument may be offered, and so Bain has to reject utilitarianism. Sidgwick comments on Bain at 477–8.

Common sense, therefore, tells us something about the empirical information that matters in different cases. It does not hold our morality hostage to all the empirical questions that the utilitarian has to face. The definiteness of utilitarianism, therefore, does not give it a decisive theoretical advantage over common sense. The fact that utilitarianism requires us to postpone our moral judgments until we have completed extremely difficult (as Sidgwick believes) calculations is a theoretical flaw in utilitarianism. The fact that common-sense morality is more often insensitive to the results of such calculations is a theoretical advantage.

Utilitarians may answer that if it would be a bad idea to seek empirical information, they will refrain from seeking it, on utilitarian grounds, and they will stick to common-sense reflexion and balancing. If we are willing, as Sidgwick clearly is, to be indirect utilitarians, we can give a utilitarian reason for accepting objections to calculations of utility. But this answer casts doubt on utilitarian objections to the indefiniteness of common-sense principles. For the utilitarian must now admit that it is reasonable to live with the theoretical perplexity of common sense. If we all have to live with principles that create theoretical perplexity, the fact that principles create this perplexity is not a good reason to abandon them.

But the utilitarian may not even be entitled to this answer. Further objections arise: (1) It is not obvious why the utilitarian will see utilitarian reasons to ignore utilitarian calculation in just those cases in which common-sense morality requires us to ignore utilitarian calculation on moral grounds. The utilitarian position is still open to objection from the point of view of common-sense morality, and cannot claim to give an adequate explanation of it. (2) If utilitarians recognize the bad results of utilitarian calculation in some cases, why should they decide to fall back on common-sense morality in these cases? We need some utilitarian argument to establish an appropriate presumption in favour of common-sense morality. But this argument itself must rely on the prediction of hedonic consequences, and so it will be vulnerable to all the uncertainties that affect such arguments. Perhaps a utilitarian needs some rules of thumb, but why should they coincide with the principles of common-sense morality?

Mill's confidence that common-sense morality provides reliable secondary principles seems misplaced. A utilitarian examination of common sense shows, according to Sidgwick, that utilitarian arguments can be given for some aspects of common sense and against other aspects. To justify a bias in favour of common sense, do we not need to know whether utilitarian considerations on the whole support a bias towards common sense? But such knowledge may be beyond our capacity for utilitarian calculation.

These objections to utilitarian calculation do not show that it is never reasonable to consider hedonic consequences, or to look for the optimal action from a hedonic point of view. Some questions about pleasure are clear and restricted enough to allow a definite enough answer for practical purposes. But this does not favour utilitarianism against common sense. For no one, certainly not Sidgwick, claims that common sense never gives us clear enough answers; the utilitarian complains that it leaves a large area of obscurity because of its indefiniteness. If utilitarianism leaves an equally large area of obscurity because of practical difficulties in its application, we have no reason to prefer it over common sense.

1180. Common-Sense Objections to Quantitative Hedonism

Sidgwick's quantitative hedonism supports his claim that utilitarianism avoids the theoretical perplexities of theories that give less definite answers. And we have seen that we need a clear grasp of the implications of quantitative hedonism before we can assess the degree of coincidence between common-sense appeals to consequences and the utilitarian appeal.

Sidgwick's discussion of utilitarianism and common sense (iv 3) examines the utilitarian arguments for common-sense rules and the utilitarian explanation of exceptions and qualifications to these rules. When he discusses the duty of universal benevolence in comparison with more limited duties that appear to conflict with utilitarianism, he affirms the utilitarian position, with reference to Bentham's example of animals.[74] In his defence of Mill against Whewell, Sidgwick acknowledges that intuitionists need not deny that we have any duties to animals. He objects fairly to Whewell's explanation that refers to the duty of cultivating humane sentiments. He acknowledges more explicitly than Mill does the utilitarian concern for the greatest happiness of non-rational animals, not merely for the prevention of cruelty to them. But, like Mill, he does not answer Whewell's objections to the alleged positive duty to maximize the pleasure of non-rational animals at the price of inflicting pain on human beings. He mentions only one respect in which the utilitarian principle agrees with common sense, without mentioning its conflict with common sense.

Sidgwick argues that we have utilitarian reasons to recognize more restricted duties that limit the appeal to universal benevolence. He points out some utilitarian benefits of the restrictions, and he offers a general guide for assessing these benefits, according to the utilitarian method of 'hedonistic comparison'.[75] But he over-simplifies the utilitarian's task. For if we are to justify such duties, we must compare the hedonic consequences of acceptance of these duties with the hedonic consequences of alternatives. For instance, we might try to reduce people's ordinary non-utilitarian expectations, and weaken their natural benevolent affections, in order to cultivate 'enthusiasm for humanity'. These changes would reduce the pain of disappointment and the pleasure of satisfying such affections, and so would alter the results of hedonic calculation. Sidgwick does not ask whether institutions and practices embodying these alterations would be better than those favoured by common sense.

Though Sidgwick believes many utilitarian calculations are uncertain, he assumes that we can draw on 'a mass of traditional experience' about the effects of conduct on happiness.[76] Similarly, Mill assumes that accepted secondary maxims embody the results of

---

[74] 'Nor . . . does the comprehensive range which utilitarians give to benevolence, in stating as their ultimate end the greatest happiness of all sentient beings, seem to be really opposed to common sense; for in so far as certain intuitional moralists restrict the scope of the direct duty of benevolence to human beings and regard our duties to brute animals as merely indirect and derived "from the duty of self-culture", they rather than their utilitarian opponents appear paradoxical.' (431)

[75] '. . . each of the preceding arguments has shown us different kinds of pleasures gained and pains averted by the fulfilment of the claims in question. There are, first, those which the service claimed would directly promote or avert: secondly, there is the pain and secondary harm of disappointed expectation, if the service be not rendered: thirdly, we have to reckon the various pleasures connected with the exercise of natural benevolent affections, especially when reciprocated, including the indirect effects on the agent's character of maintaining such affections.' (439)

[76] 'The consideration of this question, therefore, from a utilitarian point of view, resolves itself into a comparison between the total amounts of pleasure and pain that may be expected to result respectively from maintaining any

experience in what tends to promote utility.[77] But traditional experience on the promotion of happiness may not always help with accumulation of pleasure. The precise quantitative utilitarian conception of happiness and pleasure differs from the common-sense conception that underlies the 'mass of traditional experience'. We cannot assume, without detailed examination from the hedonistic point of view, that traditional experience provides a utilitarian with a provisional starting point.

If we consider quantitative hedonism apart from traditional views about how to promote happiness, we seem to face some sharp conflicts with common sense. According to quantitative hedonism, we should seriously consider whether (for instance) the pain suffered by people who hate the thought of inter-racial marriages is so intense that it counts against permitting such marriages. Would it become more justifiable to prohibit such marriages if they caused more intense disgust in more people? From the hedonist point of view, it is arbitrary to stipulate that we are not to consider such pleasures and pains in deciding what is right.[78] Even if people are disgusted only because they believe that such marriages are wrong, that does not make their disgust any less genuine. From the utilitarian point of view, the source of pain or pleasure does not make it more or less appropriate to count the pleasure in calculating hedonic consequences. Common sense considers some consequences while ignoring others; but from the utilitarian point of view, selective attention to hedonic consequences is unjustifiable.

Since quantitative hedonism forbids the exclusion of any pleasures from utilitarian calculation, it confronts us with predictive difficulties. How are we to estimate the pain suffered by people who find obscene publications disgusting, in comparison with the pain suffered by people who would like to read them and are prevented? The judgments we actually make on such issues do not seem to be determined by our predictions about relative amounts of pleasure and pain. If we follow strictly hedonist criteria, it is difficult to reach an answer. Though hedonist utilitarianism gives completely definite answers, in the sense that we have defined, it raises these further difficulties.

It may seem unfair to focus on a version of utilitarianism that relies, as Sidgwick's version does, on purely quantitative hedonism. But he has good reason to prefer this version of utilitarianism.[79] Since its conception of the end can be described independently of our moral convictions, it gives us an external criterion for the resolution of moral disputes. If

given rule as at present established, and from endeavouring to introduce that which is proposed in its stead. That this comparison must generally be of a rough and uncertain kind, we have already seen; and it is highly important to bear this in mind; but yet we seem unable to find any substitute for it. It is not meant, of course, that each individual is left to his own unassisted judgment in dealing with such questions: there is a mass of traditional experience, which each individual imbibes orally or from books, as to the effects of conduct upon happiness; but the great formulae in which this experience is transmitted are, for the most part, so indefinite, the proper range of their application so uncertain, and the observation and induction on which they are founded so uncritical, that they stand in continual need of further empirical verification; especially as regards their applicability to any particular case.' (477)

[77] See Mill, §1135.

[78] The implications for utilitarianism of 'external preferences' (i.e., preferences about how other people should be treated, apart from any further impact on the satisfaction of one's other preferences) are discussed by Dworkin, 'Discrimination', 234–8.

[79] Edgworth agrees with Sidgwick on this point: 'He who accepts the form of utilitarianism stated in the *Methods of Ethics*, must be prepared to accept the dictum of Bentham, "Quantity of pleasure being equal, push-pin is as good as poetry" . . . The other species of utilitarianism which recognizes kinds of pleasure is, as Mr Sidgwick has remarked, not to be distinguished from intuitivism.' (Edgeworth, *NOME* 25–6)

we consider inter-racial marriages, we might say that from the moral point of view, we ought not to count the pleasures and pains of people who are irrationally prejudiced against these marriages. But if we say that, we must add further principles about which pleasures or pains count; then we introduce some disputable moral principles into our statement of the utilitarian criterion. Once we do this, the utilitarian criterion no longer gives us a self-sufficient basis for the evaluation of moral rules.

We may sum up our conclusions on the dialectical argument for utilitarianism: (1) Utilitarianism does not seem to give the correct vindicating explanation. (2) Once we see what quantitative hedonism implies, it is not clear that utilitarianism provides either an amplifying or an undermining explanation.[80]

---

[80] Edgeworth, *NOME*, explores and defends the implications of quantitative hedonism. He calculates the optimal pattern of distribution of resources required by utilitarianism, particularly emphasizing the importance of diminishing marginal utility. Hence he calls it an essay in 'exact' utilitarianism. He states his general view about distribution: 'With regard to the theory of distribution, there is no indication that, at any rate between classes so nearly in the same order of evolution as the modern Aryan races, a law of distribution other than equality is to be wished . . . With regard to the theory of population, there should be a limit to the number. As to the quality, it were to be wished that the quality be as high (in the scale of evolution) as possible, ceteris paribus, and as long as the number is not impaired. But if number and quality should ultimately come into competition, as seems to be not impossible, then the indefinite improvement of quality is no longer to be wished. . . . Not the most cultivated coterie, not the most numerous proletariate, but a happy middle class shall inherit the earth.' (78)

SIDGWICK: AXIOMS OF MORALITY

1181. Limitations of the Dialectical Strategy

One aspect of Sidgwick's dialectical strategy is close to the method that Rawls calls Aristotelian. According to Rawls, its aim is to achieve 'reflective equilibrium'; the principles we find by reflexion on common sense are those that make most sense of the common-sense judgments we start with, though our initial judgments may also be adjusted in the light of the theory.[1] In some cases, we may achieve equilibrium either by adjusting our initial judgments to fit the theory or by the reverse process.

This aim of mutual adjustment may not satisfy us, however, if we want to find true moral principles that really explain and justify our initial judgments. If we are to be reasonably assured that we are going in the right direction, we seem to need some reason, external to this process of mutual adjustment, for believing that some initial judgments, or some principles, are more likely to be true than others. Our beliefs on this point will then guide the process of adjustment.

Sidgwick's comparison of utilitarianism with common-sense morality aims at more than mutual adjustment. For he believes that the common-sense moral outlook is 'intuitionist' in the epistemological sense; it treats some basic principles as objects of intuition. The older intuitionists, including Price and Reid, claim that some of our intuitive judgments, both about particular cases and about general principles, are grasped by intuition.[2] If we can reasonably treat some, but not all, of our intuitive judgments as genuine intuitions, we have a reasonable starting point from which to decide about the appropriate direction of adjustment.

Sidgwick rejects this older intuitionist solution. He denies that our intuitive judgments are genuine intuitions; for they conflict, they are unspecific, and they often do not guide us in unfamiliar situations. A principle grasped by genuine intuition gives independent support to our initial convictions, and allows us to correct and to extend our initial convictions. But the alleged intuitions derived from common sense do not meet these conditions.

---

[1] See Rawls, *TJ* §9. At 51n/45n, Rawls takes Sidgwick to follow a method very close to his own.
[2] Reid's intuitionism; §845.

1182. The Axiomatic Strategy and Dialectical Argument

This negative judgment on the putative intuitions recognized by earlier intuitionists does not dissuade Sidgwick from looking for real intuitions, but he recognizes that the search for them is difficult. In his view, principles that are objects of genuine intuition are either self-evident or self-evidently derivable from self-evident principles. But it is difficult to find adequate grounds for believing that a principle is self-evident.

Sidgwick sets out four conditions for determining whether an apparently self-evident proposition has 'the highest degree of certainty obtainable' (338). These conditions do not define or constitute self-evidence. Nor do they state necessary or sufficient conditions.[3] They are tests that help us to decide whether or not we should treat a given claim as self-evidently true, and hence as knowable by intuition.

The tests are: (1) If p is self-evident, the terms in which p is stated must be clear and precise. (2) The self-evidence of p must be 'ascertained by careful reflection' (339). In some cases, we can see that the appearance of self-evidence is merely the result of positive law, upbringing, or social practice (e.g., the laws of honour or etiquette). We are entitled to be confident that p is self-evident only if we can discount the possibility of any undermining explanation of our appearance of self-evidence. (3) Every intuition must be consistent with every other intuition. (4) General consent by apparently competent judges strengthens the appearance of self-evidence, and the absence of such general consent weakens the appearance of self-evidence.

We might summarize Sidgwick's claims about self-evidence by saying that a principle p is, as far as we can tell, self-evident if and only if (i) we have considered all the reasonable objections to p that we can think of; (ii) we still believe p; and (iii) we can find no proposition (or set of propositions) q such that we believe that if we gave up believing q we ought to give up believing p. Without this third condition, we would merely have reason to believe that p is well confirmed, not that it is self-evident.[4]

The four tests do not mention the dialectical strategy, but we could hardly apply them without dialectical argument. The second and fourth tests require a critical examination of allegedly self-evident principles and a comparison of our reaction to them with the reaction of other apparently competent judges. This examination and comparison seem to require a dialectical discussion. Suppose, for instance, that a putatively self-evident axiom conflicts sharply with a basic principle that emerges from thinking about common-sense morality—for instance, with our view that we should never inflict harm on an innocent person simply for our own pleasure. In the face of such a conflict, how could we any longer reasonably believe that the putative axiom is really an axiom?

Dialectical argument, then, seems to be needed to support a claim to have found an axiom. Hence utilitarianism on an intuitional basis faces an objection if the implications of the principle of utility still seem, after careful reflexion, to conflict with basic principles accepted by common-sense morality. If the principle of utility loses in dialectical argument, Sidgwick loses one reason for treating it as an axiom.

---

[3] Crisp's helpful discussion in 'Boundaries', 70–2, speaks of the four tests as 'conditions of self-evidence', and seems to treat them as necessary and sufficient conditions. Shaver, RE 62–71, discusses Sidgwick's conception of self-evidence and the tests for it.

[4] Sidgwick does not state (iii) explicitly; but perhaps it is included in his second condition.

1183. Self-Evidence

But even if we can support a principle by dialectical argument, we have not yet shown that it is a self-evident axiom. If we find some inferential justification q for p, and we believe that we would no longer be justified in believing p if we did not believe q, we have undermined the claim that p is self-evident, even if p is true and justified. To maintain the belief that p is self-evident, we must believe that even if we thought q false, we would still think we had sufficient reason to believe p. Sidgwick needs to show that even if we can give an inferential defence of a given candidate axiom, we are justified in believing the candidate axiom without the inferential defence.

To show that we do not need an inferential defence, we might look for some principle p such that every argument for any other principle uses p; we might infer that p cannot be justified by any argument from any other principle. But this argument is unsound. For if p is used in inferences and arguments that we are inclined to accept, that fact is itself a justification of p that appeals to its consequences. Hence this basic status of p does not show that p is self-evident.

Sidgwick needs to claim, then, that the justificatory role of p helps to convince us initially that p is self-evident, but is not needed to sustain the justified belief that p is self-evident. The justificatory role of p causes us to take p seriously, but once we have come to take p seriously, we see that nothing we have discovered or could discover about its justificatory role could reasonably change our mind about the truth of p.

This is a consistent position, but it is difficult to accept. If we thought p had no important or fundamental role in moral argument, why should we regard it as self-evident? Even if p did not actually conflict with principles that seem most plausible in the light of dialectical argument, its irrelevance to such principles might reasonably lead us to doubt whether it is a moral axiom. It is difficult to believe that abstraction from inferential justification would still leave us with the conviction that a principle is true and justified in itself.

We may well doubt, then, whether we could reasonably take the attitude that supports the belief that a principle is self-evident. We may reconsider our doubts, however, when we consider the principles that Sidgwick offers as axioms. For, even though we may find it hard to conceive our treating a proposition as self-evident and ignoring the absence of inferential justification, we may find this easier to conceive when we consider the appropriate attitude to the principles that Sidgwick regards as self-evident.

1184. The Defects of Dogmatic Intuitionism

Sidgwick argues (iii 13) that his examination of common sense has turned up some ethical axioms that do not support the principles of common sense. He moves from 'dogmatic' to 'philosophical' intuitionism, which takes a more independent attitude to the principles discovered through reflexion on common sense.[5] Earlier intuitionists are dogmatic rather

---

[5] 'For we conceive it as the aim of a philosopher, as such, to do somewhat more than define and formulate the moral opinions of mankind. . . . though he is expected to establish and concatenate at least the main part of the commonly

than philosophical because they flatter common sense instead of criticizing it as they should. Sidgwick looks for 'primary intuitions of reason' that manifest themselves as reasonable in their own right, apart from their relation to common sense.

Before Sidgwick states the axioms that he believes we can find by examining common sense, he explains why many of the principles recognized by common sense and dogmatic intuitionism are not axioms.[6] Their imprecision disqualifies them from being objects of intuition. Price's 'heads of virtue', for instance, do not give precise guidance in all cases, and no distinct head of virtue is credible independently of other principles. The principle of utility, according to Price, is not 'absolute and independent', because we should limit and qualify our adherence to it by reference to the other heads of virtue. Limitations and qualification introduce a 'margin of conduct involved in obscurity and perplexity'; for it is not always clear, without a single supreme principle, how far we should follow utility in opposition to justice, or the reverse.[7]

Price's pluralism may threaten his intuitionism about individual principles. For, though Price claims that each principle is an object of intuition, one might reply that we have no non-inferential knowledge of, say, the principle of utility; we know it only as limited by, and combined with, the other heads of virtue. The appropriate limitations must be included in the principle that we really know. This account of our knowledge of each principle might push Price further than he wants to go in the direction of holism.[8]

But such objections to Price's position do not support Sidgwick's position; for they may show that Price ought to be a holist. We might doubt whether ethical principles ought to meet Sidgwick's demands on axioms. If Sidgwick's demands are mistaken, common-sense

accepted moral rules, he is not necessarily bound to take them as the basis on which his own system is constructed. Rather we should expect that the history of Moral Philosophy . . . would be a history of attempts to enunciate, in full breadth and clearness, those primary intuitions of Reason, by the scientific application of which the common moral thought of mankind may be at once systematized and corrected.' (373–4) Sidgwick suggests that philosophers have made less progress than they should have made. '. . . they have been hampered by the fear (not, as we have seen, unfounded) of losing the support given by "general assent" if they set before themselves and their reader too rigid a standard of scientific precision. [The following passage is omitted in [3] and later; see [7] 374.] And this has been especially the case since the reaction, led by Reid, against the manner of philosophizing which culminated in Hume. For there is certainly some truth in the charge commonly made against Reid and his followers, though it has been urged, perhaps, too sweepingly and superciliously: that under their auspices philosophy has abandoned its proper function of raising and developing common opinion into the higher state of knowledge, and condescended to flatter it into the belief that it is knowledge already.' ([1] 353) As usual, Sidgwick mentions Reid rather than Price, but he has equal reason to apply his criticism of dogmatic intuitionism to Price.

[6] The division of material between the 'Review of the Morality of Common Sense' (iii 11) and 'Philosophical Intuitionism' (iii 13) suggests that Sidgwick takes Price and Reid to maintain dogmatic intuitionism. Price's 'heads of virtue' are not meant to be axioms of the sort that the philosophical intuitionist seeks.

[7] 'The notions of Benevolence, Justice, . . . etc., are not necessarily emptied of significance for us, because we have found it impossible to define them with precision. The main part of the conduct prescribed under each notion is sufficiently clear: and the general rule prescribing it does not necessarily lose its force because (1) there is in each case a margin of conduct involved in obscurity and perplexity, or because (2) the rule does not on examination appear to be absolute and independent. In short, the Morality of Common Sense may still be perfectly adequate to give practical guidance to common people in common circumstances; but the attempt to elevate it into a system of Intuitional Ethics brings its inevitable imperfections into prominence without helping us to remove them.' (360–1; reference numbers added) This comment on common-sense principles also helps to clarify Sidgwick's attitude to dogmatic intuitionism and its failure to carry out the task undertaken by philosophical intuitionism. The pluralist intuitionism that contents itself with Price's 'heads of virtue' fails the two conditions that in (1) and (2) Sidgwick imposes on an axiom. Sidgwick is right to argue that Price's basic principles fail these conditions. But that does not mean he is right to reject Price's position.

[8] On intuitionism v. holism, cf. Price, §823; Ross, §1291s. See Gaut, 'Pluralism'.

morality may be theoretically superior to the system that Sidgwick seeks to construct on the basis of a principle that is 'absolute and independent'. It might be better, then, to modify dogmatic intuitionism in a less intuitionist direction than to follow Sidgwick in trying to make it more thoroughly intuitionist.

Sidgwick also (in iii 11) considers principles that, in contrast to the principles of the dogmatic intuitionists, do not seem to have exceptions and qualifications. The examples he considers are the principles of the traditional cardinal virtues, and the naturalist formula of the Stoics and Butler. These principles have no exceptions that make it necessary to qualify them by reference to other principles. Hence they seem to be 'absolute and independent'. But he does not believe they are genuine axioms.[9] In his view, the formulae of Stoic naturalism, revived by Butler, are 'sham axioms', since they are substantially tautological. This is an unjust evaluation of Butler's position.[10]

But even if Butler's naturalist formula is not a mere tautology, it fails the philosophical intuitionist's tests for being an axiom. It is not 'absolute and independent', since we cannot understand the relevant claims about nature without relying on some conception of what is reasonable, and this conception in turn is likely to introduce further claims about rightness and goodness. The same is true about the different principles derivable from the cardinal virtues. This feature of the principles does not imply that they are tautologous or trivial; but it implies that we cannot understand or interpret them correctly without reliance on further ethical principles. We may infer not that these are unsuitable first principles, but that we should not look for axioms of the sort Sidgwick has in mind.

1185. The Axioms of Equity and Benevolence

Sidgwick claims, however, that he can find genuine axioms by examining principles defended by earlier moralists.[11] These axioms include the principle of utility. His statement and defence of the axioms changes significantly in the different editions of *ME*, and some attention to this development will throw some light on the most controversial steps in his argument.

In *ME* [1], he discusses and endorses some principles and arguments of Clarke and Kant. He claims that their principles, properly understood, offer him the axiomatic foundation he needs. Even without prior commitment to utilitarianism, we can see that these widely

---

[9] 'But here a word of caution seems required . . . against a certain class of sham-axioms, which are very apt to offer themselves to the mind that is earnestly seeking for a philosophical synthesis of practical rules, and to delude the unwary with a tempting aspect of clear self-evidence. These are principles which appear certain and self-evident because they are substantially tautological.' (374–5)

[10] On this objection to Butler's naturalism see §§704, 707.

[11] 'Is there, then, any way between this Scylla and Charybdis of ethical inquiry, by which, avoiding on the one hand doctrines that merely bring us back to common opinion with all its imperfections, and on the other doctrines that lead us round in a circle, we may attain clear intuitive truths of substantial value? I believe there is such a way: though we must be careful not to exaggerate the amount of the moral knowledge to which it conducts us. And I think we may find it by following the two thinkers who in modern times have most earnestly maintained the strictly scientific character of ethical principles: viz. Clarke in England, and Kant in Germany.' ([1] 357) In later editions (see [7] 379), the first sentence is similar, but then Sidgwick proceeds to state the axioms in his own words. He does not refer to Clarke and Kant until [7] 384.

accepted principles are axioms that support utilitarianism. Sidgwick finds that Clarke affirms axioms of equity and of benevolence.[12] He finds the same two axioms in Kant, in the Formula of Universal Law and the Formula of Humanity. ([1] 360–4).[13]

The axioms will not convince someone who refuses to make ethical judgments altogether.[14] The arguments assume that we make some ethical judgments, and then show that these judgments commit us to a universal principle that we did not acknowledge before. In support of the axiom of equity, Clarke observes that if we resent the way others treat us, we implicitly accept that there is an appropriate way for one person to treat another, not because the other person is me, but simply because the treatment is applied to a person.[15] Butler and Reid rely on the sense of fairness implied in resentment, in order to defend something like Kant's Formula of Universal Law.

The axiom of benevolence expresses the universal implication of an ethical judgment we make about ourselves. It uses the first axiom together with the judgment that it is reasonable of an individual person to pursue her own good.[16] Clarke affirms, as Sidgwick does, that prudence is categorically reasonable. Kant must also—despite his views about hypothetical and categorical imperatives—suppose something like this in claiming that an individual rational agent necessarily thinks of himself as an end. Since I recognize that it is reasonable of me to pursue my own good, I acknowledge that it is reasonable of a rational agent to pursue his good, and so I acknowledge that it is reasonable of me to pursue the good of rational agents. The steps in this argument are controversial, and we have discussed the reasons that might be given to justify Kant in taking these steps.[17] Sidgwick recognizes some of the difficulties that arise for Kant, but he believes that the argument he ascribes to both Clarke and Kant is basically sound.[18]

The axioms derived from Clarke and Kant are not merely negative and procedural. The axiom of benevolence does not affirm the conditional claim that if it is reasonable to pursue anyone's good, it is reasonable to pursue everyone's good equally. It affirms the

[12] 'Whatever I judge reasonable or unreasonable that another should do for me: that by the same judgment I declare reasonable or unreasonable that I should in the like case do for him.' ([1] 358) '. . . our notion of ultimate good, at the realization of which it is evidently reasonable to aim, must include the good of every one on the same ground that it includes that of any one.' ([1] 360)

[13] Sidgwick criticizes Kant's argument for the Formula of Humanity, but endorses the formula ([1] 363). In [4] and later editions, the discussion of Kant is moved to the note at the end of iii 13; see [7] 389–90.

[14] 'It must be distinctly noted that here, as in the case of equity, we must start with some ethical judgment, in order that the rule may be proved: and, in fact, the process of reasoning is precisely similar in the two cases. There, an individual was supposed to judge that a certain kind of conduct was right and fit to be pursued by others towards him: and it was then shown that he must necessarily conceive the same conduct to be right for all other persons in precisely similar circumstances: and therefore judge it right for himself, in like case, to adopt it towards any other person.' ([1] 360)

[15] Clarke's arguments about equity; §631.

[16] 'Similarly here we are supposed to judge something intrinsically desirable—some result which it would be reasonable for each individual to seek for himself, if he considered himself alone. Let us call this the individual's good or welfare: then what Clarke urges is, that the good of any one individual cannot be more intrinsically desirable, because it is his, than the equal good of any other individual.' ([1] 360).

[17] Kant's argument for morality; §§960–2.

[18] This claim needs some qualification or explanation in the light of Sidgwick's belief in the dualism of practical reason. See §1200.

unconditional claim that it is reasonable to pursue everyone's good equally.[19] On this basis, Sidgwick concludes that the two axioms support utilitarianism.[20]

1186. Do the Axioms Support Utilitarianism?

This conclusion, however, is open to doubt. The axiom of benevolence claims that each person ought to aim at the happiness of each person equally. But it does not seem to endorse the maximizing aspect of utilitarianism; it neither requires nor allows us to make A happier than B for the sake of the total happiness.

Sidgwick, however, believes that the axiom of benevolence supports utilitarianism because we recognize that (1) I ought to aim at more rather than less happiness for myself, and (2) everyone ought to be treated equally. He infers that (3) I ought to aim at more happiness for another even at the cost of less happiness for myself, provided that the gain to the other is greater than the loss to me. But does this third claim follow from the other two?

Sidgwick seems to believe that it follows because a prudent person who recognizes that people ought to be treated equally will treat future states of other people in the way he treats future states of himself. Since he wants to achieve more rather than less happiness for himself, he will want to do the same for another person. And since he would accept some loss next week in order to secure a greater gain next year, he ought to accept some loss for himself in order to secure a greater gain for another.

Since Sidgwick reasons in this way, he takes prudence plus equality to require self-sacrifice.[21] Sometimes we may appear to accept his reasoning. If a given course of action imposes a trivial loss on me in order to satisfy some urgent need of yours, I ought to prefer it. But this admission does not commit us to Sidgwick's principle. If a connoisseur of Rembrandt would gain enormous pleasure from owning a Rembrandt which he could buy only if I sold my house and gave him the money, the mere fact that the increase of his pleasure would be greater than the decrease in my pleasure would not show that I ought to sell my house.

If we imagined ourselves pursuing our own happiness without regard to the legitimate claims of other people to have their interest considered, we would recognize that we were

---

[19] This feature of the axioms conflicts with what Schneewind calls 'the negative and formalistic reading of them' which predominates in the literature' (*SEVMP* 305), which he also 'in the main' accepts. In his view, 'the first edition presentation suggests . . . that all the axioms might be worded negatively' (301).

[20] 'But now, of these two propositions, the first is a necessary postulate of all ethical systems, being an expression of what is involved in the mere conception of objective rightness and wrongness in conduct: while the second is the fundamental principle of that particular system which (in Book I) we called utilitarianism.' ([1] 364)

[21] In 'Calderwood', published in 1876, Sidgwick speaks as though it were self-evident 'that what is right for me must be right for all persons in precisely similar circumstances' and 'that I ought to prefer the greater good of another to my own lesser good' (25). He speaks as though he were summarizing the axioms from *ME* [1]; but [1] makes no such claim about the second principle (prescribing self-sacrifice), which does not appear in iii 13. It appears only in [2] 356 (published in 1877). In 'Controversies' (1889), he maintains the same principle of sacrifice: '. . . the principle that another's greater good is to be preferred to one's own lesser good is . . . the fundamental principle of morality—the ultimate, irreducible basis to which reflection shows the commonly accepted rules of veracity, good faith, &c, to be subordinate.' (43) Sidgwick's acceptance of the principle of utility is closely connected to his commitment to 'altruism' (a term that he and his contemporaries learned from Comte). See Collini, *PM*, ch. 2, esp. 86–7.

acting wrongly, and thereby we would endorse a principle of impartiality. But Sidgwick also suggests that if we enjoyed something that others would enjoy more if it were taken from us and given to them, we would be acting wrongly. We have good reason to doubt this suggestion.

Moreover, even if Sidgwick's suggestion seemed plausible in a two-person case, it would raise doubts when more people were considered. For if A ought to make A worse off for B's greater good, A ought also to make both A and B worse off for C's greater good. Sidgwick's unrestricted principle of self-sacrifice for the greater good of another does not seem to be warranted by the principles derived from Clarke and Kant.

The reasoning that underlies the axioms even seems to oppose Sidgwick's claims about self-sacrifice. The axiom of equity seems to prescribe equal consideration for each person's happiness. It does not tell me to aim at more total happiness rather than less; it seems to tell me to aim at more happiness rather than less for each person. We might conclude that each person ought to have the maximum possible level of equal happiness (supposing that happiness is the only end that it is rational to aim at). The axiom of benevolence seems to prescribe concern for the happiness of this and that person; it treats the happiness of a person as morally crucial. This point separates the axiom based on Clarke and Kant from Sidgwick's principle of self-sacrifice.

The principle of self-sacrifice, therefore, seems neither to be an axiom in its own right nor to be derivable from axioms. It raises too many reasonable doubts to be accepted as an axiom. Sidgwick does not show that the reasonable doubts rest on any misconception. If we doubt whether the principle of self-sacrifice is an object of intuition, no dialectical argument is offered to remove our doubts.

Moreover, even if we accepted Sidgwick's principle of self-sacrifice for the sake of other people, we would not have endorsed the utilitarian principle. For utilitarianism requires not self-sacrifice to make other people happier, but self-sacrifice to increase the total happiness. We can see the difference between the two types of self-sacrifice if we consider utilitarianism and the increase of population. If a large number of badly off people results in a larger surplus of pleasure over pain than would result from a smaller number of well-off people, utilitarianism prescribes the first situation. Hence we might make many people worse off in order to achieve a larger surplus of pleasure over more people.

We can raise the same question even without thinking about increased population. If the deprivation to me makes several people worse off than I was before the deprivation and worse off than I am after the deprivation, but the total pleasure, summed over all of us, is greater than it would be if had not suffered the deprivation, the utilitarian principle still imposes the deprivation. Sidgwick states his principle of self-sacrifice by referring to the greater good of another person. He does not observe that a utilitarian principle of sacrifice fails to ensure that any other person or persons gain a great deal as a result of my loss.

And so, even if Sidgwick has a good case for the two axioms that he formulates with the help of Clarke and Kant, he does not vindicate utilitarianism. But he does not seem to recognize this gap in his argument. He notices that the axioms derived from Clarke and Kant do not justify the hedonistic aspects of utilitarianism, which he defends in his next chapter (iii 14).[22] But his chapter on the axioms never mentions the maximizing aspect of utilitarianism. He does not suggest that this aspect of utilitarianism needs a defence that goes beyond the axioms.

1187. A Revised Axiom of Prudence

The argument of this chapter received considerable discussion from early critics, and in later editions Sidgwick revises it so as to rely less on Clarke and Kant.[23] He introduces new principles that cannot be directly traced to previous moralists. They are not intended to replace the Clarkean and Kantian principles about prudence and equality, but simply to clarify them. Sidgwick maintains no less firmly that his principles can legitimately claim support from his predecessors.[24] We need to see whether he is right on this point.[25]

He now supports prudence by a claim about parts and wholes.[26] In the case of a particular individual, the notion of a whole is reached 'by comparison and integration of the different "goods" that succeed one another in the series of our conscious states' (382). Since it is

[22] 'And here when, at the end of a long and careful examination of the apparent intuitions with which common sense furnishes us, we collect the residuum of clear and definite moral knowledge which the operation has left, we find the same problem facing us. We seem to have done nothing: and in fact we have only evolved the suppression of egoism, the necessary universality of view, which is implied in the mere form of the objective judgment "that an end is good", just as it is in the judgment "that an action is right". What I judge to be good, I cannot reasonably think that it is abstractly and primarily right that I should have it more than another.' ([1] 366) This passage is deleted from later editions, which end with [7] 388–9. Perhaps Sidgwick believes that the deleted passage is repetitive, or that it underestimates the results he has achieved. Moreover, it claims to have achieved the 'suppression of egoism'. Bradley takes up this phrase in his critique (CE 98–104), and in his Preface to [2], Sidgwick protests that one of his critics 'has constructed an article on the supposition that my principal object is the "suppression of egoism" . . .' ([7] x). The chapter in [1] makes the supposition seem reasonable.

[23] In the Preface to [2], Sidgwick draws attention to the changes in this chapter: '. . . in c.13 (on "philosophical intuitionism"), which has been suggestively criticized by more than one writer, I have thought it expedient to give a more direct statement of my own opinions; instead of confining myself (as I did in the first edition) to comments on those of other moralists.' (ix)

[24] 'I should, however, rely less confidently on the conclusions set forth in the preceding section, if they did not appear to me to be in substantial agreement—in spite of superficial differences—with the doctrines of those moralists who have been most in earnest in seeking among commonly received moral rules for genuine intuitions of the Practical Reason.' (384) He then introduces Clarke and Kant.

[25] Rashdall, 'Sidgwick', 202, comments on the increased clarity and definiteness of [3] in comparison to [1] and [2]. He takes Sidgwick's two axioms to be: (1) It is reasonable to show an equal regard to all moments of the future consciousness of ourselves and others. (2) It is reasonable to regard one person's good as of equal intrinsic value to that of every other person. Rashdall is right to ascribe these two principles to Sidgwick. But he does not comment on how they fall short of utilitarianism. Albee, HEU 398–9, notices that Clarke and Kant are less prominent in Sidgwick's later version of his argument.

[26] In his revised presentation of the axioms, Sidgwick postpones his discussion of Clarke and Kant (384–6) until after his own argument. The main statement of his argument, at [7] 379–87, first appears in [2]. His discussion and formulation of the axioms of equity and benevolence are similar to [1]. But immediately after this discussion, he adds an important section on prudence. His new axiom of prudence underlies Clarke's principle that it is rational to aim at one's own good ([1] 360). He gives a new formulation. 'The principle [sc. of justice] just discussed, which seems to be more or less clearly implied in the common notion of "fairness" or "equity," is obtained by considering the similarity of the individuals that make up a Logical Whole or Genus. There are others, no less important, which emerge in the consideration of the similar parts of a Mathematical or Quantitative Whole. Such a Whole is presented in the common notion of the Good—or, as is sometimes said, "good on the whole"—of any individual human being. . . . I have already referred to this principle as that "of impartial concern for all parts of our conscious life":—we might express it concisely by saying "that Hereafter as such is to be regarded neither less nor more than Now."' (380–1) This new principle underlies the axiom of benevolence. On hedonism and prudence in Socrates and Plato, see §§23–4, 30, 54.

rational for me to aim at my good as a whole, and hence to try to make myself as well off as possible in my life as a whole, temporal considerations as such cannot be relevant; they can be relevant only in so far as they involve (for instance) different degrees of certainty.

We can now set out the revised axioms more fully:[27]

(1) Equity: treat people equally unless there is some morally relevant difference between them or in their circumstances (380, 390).
(2) Benevolence: the ultimate end that it is rational to pursue is everyone's good (382, 420).
(3) Hedonism: the ultimate good is pleasure (400–1).
(4) Prudence: it is rational for me to pursue my own good without drawing distinctions between different times in my life as such (381).
(5) Wholes: if x and y are parts of a logical whole (a genus) or a quantitative whole, different treatment of x and y must be justified by some relevant difference between x and y (380–1).

Wholes connects equity, prudence, and benevolence; it applies a principle of equity to different parts of one's life, and not only to different people. It applies to members of a species, as parts of 'logical' wholes. If two members are similar in the relevant respects, some special reason is needed for treating them differently. It also applies to parts of 'quantitative' wholes. In Sidgwick's view, 'such a whole is presented in the common notion of the good—or, as is sometimes said, "good on the whole"—of any individual human being'. He applies the demand for impartiality to both sorts of wholes.

He believes our ordinary attitudes to prudence assume Wholes. The prudent person is impartial between different times; she recognizes that it is irrational to be a proximist and to prefer a small short-term benefit over a large long-term benefit simply because the short-term benefit will come sooner.[28] Proximism and ultimism (the reverse preference) are no more rational than a purely temporal concern about what will happen to me on Tuesdays rather than on Wednesdays.

Prudence, in contrast to proximism and ultimism, corresponds to the relevant facts about persons. Since all the stages of my life belong to a single life, and since concern for myself requires concern for this single life, it is unreasonable to be especially concerned with any feature of it that does not give a reason for special concern. The mere time when something happens does not give such a reason.

But though Wholes clarifies prudence, it does not support utilitarianism. Wholes applies both to intra-personal cases (quantitative wholes) and to inter-personal cases (logical wholes), and prescribes impartiality and equity in both cases. But it does not support utilitarian maximization, or the resulting indifference to distribution.[29]

---

[27] A full list and discussion of the axioms is given by Schneewind, *SEVMP* 290–7. His list does not make it clear (though his discussion does) that the principle about wholes and parts is more fundamental even than the Kantian principle of equal treatment, and underlies the axioms of prudence, justice, and benevolence. I use initial capitals to refer to Sidgwick's principles, and small letters to refer to the principles that he seeks to capture.

[28] This is what Sidgwick means when he speaks of 'impartial concern for all parts of our conscious life'. He explains: '. . . mere difference of priority and posteriority in time is not a reasonable ground for having more regard to the consciousness of one moment than to that of another' (381).

[29] I use 'distribution' and 'distributive' in a non-maximizing sense.

1188. Prudence and Maximization

Though Wholes by itself does not support utilitarianism, Sidgwick's interpretation of it helps to explain how he reaches utilitarianism from the axioms.[30] He assumes that my good as a whole consists in a certain quantity, and that concern for my good is concern to maximize the total quantity of good in my life.[31] He may therefore accept a further principle as an axiom:

(6) Quantity: It is always ultimately rational, and rationally required, to maximize the quantity of good achievable in any quantitative or logical whole.

If we accept Quantity, we constrain the impartiality prescribed by Wholes, so that correct discrimination between different parts maximizes the total quantity of good. Prudence, therefore, maximizes the total quantity of good in one's life, irrespective of its distribution through different times.[32]

In [1], Sidgwick does not endorse Quantity. Nor does he formulate it as a distinct axiom in later editions. But in these later editions, his application of Wholes to the inter-personal case presupposes acceptance of Quantity in both the intra-personal and the inter-personal cases. His application of Wholes to inter-personal cases asserts the familiar principle of impartiality. But he qualifies impartiality with the quantitative claim that we ought to treat one person differently from another if we can achieve more good thereby. He assumes that the only relevant consideration for different treatment of different parts of the whole constituted by different persons is the different degree of total good that is likely to result.[33] This maximizing condition is legitimate if and only if Wholes rests on Quantity.

Sidgwick still defends Clarke's claims that (1) nothing about my good makes it rational for me to aim at it exclusively, and (2) it is rational to aim at the good of others as well as

---

[30] Schneewind, *SEVMP* 305–9, offers a different account of how Sidgwick introduces maximization into his argument. In Schneewind's view, (i) maximization is no part of the axioms themselves, but (ii) is added because nothing except maximizing goodness is a viable candidate (in Sidgwick's view) for being the right-making property of actions (308). Schneewind supports (i) by appeal to Sidgwick's remark: 'I have tried to show how in the principles of Justice, Prudence, and Rational Benevolence as commonly recognized there is at least a self-evident element, immediately cognisable by abstract intuition; depending in each case on the relation which individuals and their particular ends bear as parts to their wholes, and to other parts of these wholes' (*ME* 382). I do not think this remark shows that Sidgwick excludes maximization from the axioms themselves; I have mentioned the grounds for supposing that he assumes Quantity in his account of Wholes and of prudence. An appeal to (ii) would seriously weaken Sidgwick's argument. Failure to find any other universal right-making property does not show that maximizing utility is a viable candidate; perhaps we ought to conclude that we cannot find any single right-making property.

[31] Sidgwick believes that the good in question is pleasure; but he does not rely on this claim in iii 13, when he defends the axioms of prudence and benevolence.

[32] 'So far we have only been considering the "Good on the Whole" of a single individual: but just as this notion is constructed by comparison and integration of the different "goods" that succeed one another in the series of our conscious states, so we have formed the notion of Universal Good by comparison and integration of the goods of all individual human—or sentient—existences. And here again, just as in the former case, by considering the relation of the integrant parts to the whole and to each other, I obtain the self-evident principle that (a) the good of any one individual is of no more importance, from the point of view (if I may say so) of the Universe, than the good of any other; (b) unless, that is, there are special grounds for believing that more good is likely to be realized in the one case than in the other. And it is evident to me that (c) as a rational being I am bound to aim at good generally,—so far as it is attainable by my efforts,—not merely at a particular part of it.' (382; reference letters added)

[33] See 'unless, that is . . .' in (b) in the penultimate sentence of the passage in the previous note.

at my own good. These claims do not mention maximization.[34] Sidgwick's comment on Clarke asserts that we have a sufficient reason for treating two people differently whenever such treatment will result in a larger total good. Clarke's principle of benevolence includes no basis for this maximizing claim.

Sidgwick offers no further defence of his maximizing claim, beyond the argument for impartiality. He recognizes that his principle Benevolence seems to demand more than common sense immediately accepts. Common sense recognizes a less universal duty of benevolence. We can explain this attitude, however, by reference to the benefits of a secondary maxim that prescribes restricted rather than universal concern.[35] In the light of this explanation, reflective common sense agrees with the universal principle. Sidgwick now asserts that reflective common sense accepts maximizing.[36] Since he takes benevolence to assume Wholes, and since he interprets Wholes in the light of Quantity, he takes benevolence to accept the principle of utility. His failure to state Quantity may result from his assumption that Wholes incorporates Quantity. That is why he does not recognize that he adds a new principle to those derived from Clarke and Kant.[37]

1189. The Derivation of Utilitarianism

How do these new principles affect the original axioms? We might say that they are legitimate supplements to the original axioms, and that they allow us to incorporate the original axioms in an argument with a more definitely utilitarian conclusion. Is this the right way to understand the relation between the old axioms and the new ones?

[34] The suggestion that Sidgwick fails to distinguish (b) from (c) (in the passage from 382 just quoted), and hence takes Quantity to underlie Wholes, is supported by the conclusion that he draws from (a) and (c): 'From these two rational intuitions we may deduce, as a necessary inference, the maxim of Benevolence in an abstract form: viz. that (d) each one is morally bound to regard the good of any other individual as much as his own, (e) except in so far as he judges it to be less, when impartially viewed, or less certainly knowable or attainable by him' (382; reference letters added). The 'two rational intuitions' are those that Sidgwick has just introduced, (a) and (c). In (d) Sidgwick derives Clarke's principle of benevolence, but in (e) he glosses it with a quantitative condition that recalls (b).

[35] 'I before observed that the duty of Benevolence as recognized by common sense seems to fall somewhat short of this. But I think it may be fairly urged in explanation of this that practically each man, even with a view to universal Good, ought chiefly to concern himself with promoting the good of a limited number of human beings, and that generally in proportion to the closeness of their connexion with him.' (382)

[36] 'I think that a "plain man", in a modern civilized society, if his conscience were fairly brought to consider the hypothetical question, whether it would be morally right for him to seek his own happiness on any occasion if it involved a certain sacrifice of the greater happiness of some other human being,—without any counterbalancing gain to any one else,—would answer unhesitatingly in the negative.' (382) Cf. §1186 on Calderwood.

[37] The discussion of prudence in later editions of this chapter adds the maximizing claim to Clarke and Kant. In this chapter in [1], Sidgwick says nothing about maximizing. None the less, [1] takes utilitarianism to be a maximizing doctrine: 'By Utilitarianism is here meant the ethical theory, first distinctly formulated by Bentham, that the conduct which, under any given circumstances, is externally or objectively right, is that which will produce the greatest amount of happiness to all whose interests are affected: or more precisely (as under any given circumstances the interests of one or more may have to be sacrificed in order to secure the greatest happiness on the whole) the conduct which will produce "the greatest possible happiness to the greatest possible number".' ([1] 381) In [7] 411, Sidgwick has a briefer statement. After [1] he does not introduce explicitly maximizing principles. But he partly fills the gap left in [1], by introducing the maximizing aspect of utilitarianism in his conclusions. He makes room for this maximizing aspect by relying on maximizing assumptions in interpreting the premises of his argument. In particular, he relies on Quantity and Wholes to ensure that his conception of prudence provides a suitable basis for his utilitarian interpretation of benevolence and equity.

The new axioms differ from the old ones in their treatment of persons. The old axioms are personal; they consider the good of one person or many people, and the equal treatment of different stages in a person's life or the equal treatment of different people. Wholes and Quantity, however, are non-personal principles; they are not about one person or many people, but about parts and wholes quite generally. What is the relation between the personal and the non-personal principles?

Sidgwick does not derive Prudence from Quantity or Wholes; he takes it for granted that we think prudence is rational. Nonetheless, he seems to treat Quantity and Wholes as more basic than Prudence. In that case prudence is not fundamentally rational; our belief that it is rational can be further explained by our acceptance of Quantity. Temporal impartiality is a rational attitude because we accept Quantity, a still more basic principle of rationality. My conscious states form a whole, and I aim to maximize the total satisfaction in any whole of conscious states.

The derivation of Prudence from Quantity and Wholes implies that no self-regarding attitude is fundamentally rational.[38] My concern for my good is rational only because my conscious states constitute a whole that I can do something to affect, not because this particular whole belongs to me in particular, and not because this particular whole belongs to a single person. Intra-personal rationality rests fundamentally on non-personal rationality.

The principle of utility is the inter-personal parallel to Prudence, and inter-personal moral impartiality is parallel to inter-temporal prudential impartiality. In both cases, impartiality rests (according to Sidgwick's later view) on the maximizing prescribed by Wholes and Quantity. This impartiality is non-personal. In the original formulation of prudence and benevolence, we considered one person's good and the equal treatment of different people. But now the basic principle underlying prudence does not refer to any person's good. Similarly, the basic principle underlying benevolence does not refer to equal treatment of persons or to the greater or lesser good of this or that person.

The prudent person, therefore, seeks to maximize his own good because the parts of his life constitute the relevant sort of whole, and so he treats different times impartially. Similarly, the morally good person's aim is to maximize the total good, irrespective of whose good it is. He no more cares about the difference between the people involved than the prudent person cares about the difference between the times involved. Once we have accepted Wholes (interpreted in the light of Quantity), and seen that it applies to both quantitative and logical wholes, we must accept the principle of utility.

This argument develops Butler's suggestion that conscience and self-love rely on the same rational principle. It applies authority rather than mere strength to inter-personal as well as intra-personal relations. Similarly, Kant claims that the same basic principle underlies

---

[38] Hayward, *EPS*, ch. 6, comes close to seeing that Sidgwick's later principles do not defend prudence: 'The real basis of egoism is not in the least "I ought to have impartial concern for all parts of my conscious life", for it is equally obvious that, whether my concern is for my own or for others' welfare, my concern should be impartial as respects "hereafter" and "now". Prudence and egoism are not identical, and though the distinction is faintly recognized in the Methods (p. 381), where a transition from the egoistic to the rationally egoistic principle is affirmed . . . . the recognition is inadequate: nowhere does Sidgwick point out that impartial concern for all time is not necessarily egoistic.' (134) Hayward exaggerates Sidgwick's confusion. Sidgwick takes prudence to involve rational concern for one's own conscious life as a whole, not concern for conscious life as a whole. But Hayward almost makes it clear that the principle (Wholes) on which Sidgwick relies to argue for prudence is not personal at all.

both treating oneself as an end and treating others as ends. Sidgwick suggests that the basic principle underlying both prudence and morality is the non-personal principle Quantity, which supports utilitarianism.

Self-love often requires me to frustrate particular passions by denying their short-term satisfaction for the sake of my overall good. Sidgwick argues that this attitude of self-love is reasonable because my conscious states form a whole and (as Quantity says) we should aim to maximize the total satisfaction in any whole of conscious states. Once we accept this analysis of prudence, Sidgwick thinks we must also accept the principle of utility, which requires us to maximize the good summed over different people.

Sidgwick's new argument, therefore, is not simply the argument that he extracts from Clarke and Kant (in *ME* [1]). It includes extra maximizing principles. We may present it as follows:

(1)   Prudence is rational if and only if Quantity and Wholes are true.
(2)   Prudence is rational.
(3)   Therefore Quantity and Wholes are true.
(4)   The sum of pleasures and pains of different individuals is a whole to which Quantity and Wholes apply.
(5)   Therefore we should maximize pleasure over different individuals.

1190. The Development of the Argument

This argument for utilitarianism develops gradually in the first four editions of *ME*. Sidgwick takes the most important step in [2], where he introduces Wholes without reference to Clarke and Kant, and defends the two principles of prudence and equality by his own arguments. In [4] and later, he speaks of the axioms of prudence and of justice or equity (387). But [3] and [4] make some significant changes to [2].

In [3] and [4], Sidgwick does not add much to the content of the axioms set out in [2]. He adds only a short passage to explain that temporal neutrality does not preclude some reasoned preference for the short term; such a preference might be based on degrees of certainty. The claim about neutrality rules out only a purely temporal preference.[39]

When he has set out his axioms, Sidgwick maintains, in [2] and later, that they are genuine rather than merely apparent axioms. In [2], he supports this claim by appealing directly to Clarke.[40] In [3], he defends the claim independently, before he turns to Clarke.[41]

---

[39] See [3] 380–1, and cf. [2] 354–5. The passage beginning 'It is not, of course, meant . . .' appears in [7] 381.

[40] See [2] 356: 'No doubt by loose thinkers these principles are often placed side by side with other precepts to which custom and general consent have given a merely illusory air of self-evidence: but this seems to be less the case in proportion as a writer is in earnest in seeking among commonly received moral rules for genuine intuitions of the practical reason.' He proceeds to discuss Clarke as a writer of this sort.

[41] 'No doubt these principles are often placed side by side with other precepts to which custom and general consent have given a merely illusory air of self-evidence: but the distinction between the two kinds of maxims appears to me to become manifest by merely reflecting upon them. I know by direct reflection that the propositions, "I ought to speak the truth", "I ought to keep my promises"—however true they may be—are not self-evident to me; they present themselves as propositions requiring rational justification of some kind. On the other hand, the propositions, "I ought not to prefer a present lesser good to a future greater good", and "I ought not to prefer my own lesser good to the greater good of

He introduces Clarke and Kant to corroborate his claim, based on his own reflexion, to have found self-evident principles. Here he follows his procedure for testing claims to self-evidence.[42]

After his review of Clarke and Kant, Sidgwick adds a significant summary. He claims to have maintained the axiom of prudence that underlies rational egoism as well as the axiom of benevolence that underlies utilitarianism.[43] He looks forward to the last chapter of the book for a discussion of the relation between the two axioms, which he regards as 'the profoundest problem of ethics' ([3] 388n = [7] 386n). This anticipation of the dualism of practical reason suggests that Sidgwick intends his argument to be limited in scope.

In [2] and later, he deletes the claim that ends this chapter in [1], that he has achieved the 'suppression of egoism' ([1] 366). But he does not seem to have changed the substance of his position, since he still claims to have shown that utilitarianism overrules the principles of egoism and intuitionism (420, already in [1] 390).

In [4], Sidgwick relegates much of his discussion of Kant to a note at the end of the chapter (at [7] 389–90). But he adds one important new point. He notices that Kant does not treat prudence as a matter of obligation, except in so far as it is required by some more general duty to humanity. Against Kant, Sidgwick endorses Butler's view that one has a manifest obligation to pursue one's own good.[44] He reinforces his claim to have affirmed and defended the rationality of prudence.

1191. Has Sidgwick Justified Prudence?

So far, Sidgwick's argument for utilitarianism seems to assert that prudence is rational, but then shows that it is only derivatively rational, in so far as it relies on Wholes and Quantity. Prudence and Benevolence are two applications of these more basic principles.

This conclusion, however, faces further difficulties. Quantity does not seem suitable for Sidgwick's purposes. Since it speaks of 'any' whole, it supports prudence and benevolence indifferently, and it assigns no priority or superiority to benevolence. Here, then, we reach something like the dualism of practical reason by a different route from the route that Sidgwick takes.

---

another", do present themselves as self-evident; as much (e.g.) as the mathematical axiom that "if equals be added to equals the wholes are equal." ' ([3] 382 = [7] 383) The rest of §3 in [7] was also added in [3].

[42] The passage that begins §4 in [7] first appears at [3] 353. Sidgwick follows the procedure that he introduced at 211. There he mentions 'current opinions to which familiarity has given an illusory air of self-evidence'. He continues: 'But any errors of this kind, due to careless or superficial reflection, can only be cured by more careful reflection. This may indeed be much aided by communication with other minds; it may also be aided, in a subordinate way, by an inquiry into the antecedents of the apparent intuition, which may suggest to the reflective mind sources of error to which a superficial view of it is liable.'

[43] 'The axiom of Prudence, as I have given it, is a self-evident principle, implied in Rational Egoism as commonly accepted. Again, the axiom of Justice or Equity as above stated—"that similar cases ought to be treated similarly"—belongs in all its applications to Utilitarianism as much as to any system commonly called Intuitional: while the axiom of Rational Benevolence is, in my view, required as a rational basis for the Utilitarian system.' ([3] 388 = [7] 386)

[44] See [4] 386 = [7] 386: 'indeed, in his view, it can only be stated as a duty for me to seek my own happiness so far as I consider it as a part of the happiness of mankind in general. I disagree with the negative side of this statement, as I hold with Butler that "one's own happiness is a manifest obligation" independently of one's relation to other men . . .'

This is not Sidgwick's intention. He makes a comment on his argument in the very chapter in which he distinguishes the two types of egoism. In his discussion of the sort of proof that can be offered to the intuitionist, he claims to have offered a proof of utilitarianism as 'overruling' both egoism and intuitionism.[45] The argument that we have attributed to him so far does not secure this overruling role for utilitarianism.

The argument faces a further objection. The wholes that Sidgwick considers are the individual person's life and lives of all the actual or possible sentient beings affected by an action. But there seem to be many other wholes, including the lives of everyone in Oxford between 2008 and 2010, the lives of everyone in India in the same period, and so on. We reach a result contrary to Sidgwick's intention if it is equally rational to maximize the good summed over each of these wholes.

To answer this objection, we might modify Quantity to formulate another principle:

(7) Extension: It is always ultimately rational, and rationally required, to maximize the quantity of good achievable in the largest possible quantitative or logical whole.

While the idea of a 'largest possible' whole may still be obscure, this principle expresses the main point that we need in order to make benevolence overrule both prudence and non-utilitarian morality.

Extension supports the claim of utilitarian benevolence to be overriding, but it creates some difficulties for prudence. We saw earlier that Sidgwick may take Prudence to be derivatively rational, because it is an instance of the policy recommended by Wholes and Quantity. But if we replace Quantity with Extension, we do not seem to make Prudence rational. It would be rational to seek to maximize the good in my own life if the stages in my life were the only whole that I could affect. But there will be very few situations of this sort, and so prudence will normally be rejected in favour of a policy that conforms to Extension.

If this is the right account of Sidgwick's argument, he does not argue from the rationality of prudence to utilitarianism. He really argues from the apparent rationality of prudence. Reflexion on prudence helps us to see that our ultimate rational principle is Extension. We might think that this justifies prudence, until we recognize that we can affect larger wholes than our own lives. But once we recognize this, we see that prudence is not rational in most circumstances. It would be rational only in circumstances analogous to those in which preference for short-term results would be rational. If we have reason for confidence that one action would benefit us, and we have no reason for confidence that an alternative action would do more to promote the total good, we would have a reason to act for our

---

[45] '. . . it would seem that the process must be one which establishes a conclusion actually *superior* in validity to the premises from which it starts. For the Utilitarian prescriptions of duty are *prima facie* in conflict, at certain points and under certain circumstances, both with rules which the Intuitionist regards as self-evident, and with the dictates of Rational Egoism; so that Utilitarianism, if accepted at all, must be accepted as overruling Intuitionism and Egoism. At the same time, if the other principles are not throughout taken as valid, the so-called proof does not seem to be addressed to the Intuitionist or Egoist at all. How shall we deal with this dilemma? How is such a process—clearly different from ordinary proof—possible or conceivable? Yet there certainly seems to be a general demand for it. Perhaps we may say that what is needed is a line of argument which on the one hand allows the validity, to a certain extent, of the maxims already accepted, and on the other hand shows them to be not absolutely valid, but needing to be controlled and completed by some more comprehensive principle. Such a line of argument, addressed to Egoism, was given in chap. xiii. of the foregoing book.' (420)

own benefit.[46] But Sidgwick can hardly suppose that we are always or usually justified in doubting whether a self-sacrificing action would promote the total good. Hence he cannot reasonably suppose that Extension will always or usually lead us to recommend the actions that a self-interested person would choose.

Sidgwick does not believe that his new principles reject the rationality of prudence. On the contrary, he believes that he supplements and explains the principles that he derives from Clarke and Kant. He does not believe that his claims about wholes undermine the initial claims about prudence. As we have seen, he marks his disagreement with Kant on the independent rationality of prudence, and agrees with Butler.

He seems, therefore, to have misunderstood the force of his argument. Though he believes he has expounded the rationality of prudence, he has really explained only the apparent rationality of prudence. If his other principles are right, the rationality of prudence is only apparent.

But even if we use Extension to explain the apparent rationality of prudence, rather than to vindicate prudence, it is open to doubt. Our belief in the rationality of prudence does not seem to rest on our acceptance of Extension together with our abstracting from, or forgetting, the fact that we can affect larger wholes than our own lives. Even if we keep in mind the fact that we can affect larger wholes, we do not immediately conclude that it is not rational to aim at our own good in particular.

This question about prudence points to a more general question about the argument. It no longer appears to be an argument addressed to an egoist. If Extension has to be a premiss of the argument, Sidgwick seems to rely on something unhelpfully close to his utilitarian conclusion. Admittedly Extension is not the same as the principle of utility. It is a general principle that the principle of utility applies to the special case of distribution of good between persons. Perhaps some people might accept the Extension without at first realizing that it commits them to the principle of utility. But Extension does not seem so obviously plausible that it could reasonably be expected to appeal to someone who did not already accept the principle of utility.

Despite these objections, the argument we have offered Sidgwick seems to be close to the one that he eventually offers. In his view, the sacrifice of a present good for a greater future good is relevantly parallel to the sacrifice of my good for the greater good of another. The parallel is clear once we see that both cases of sacrifice rest on the acceptance of Extension. The apparent rationality of prudence and the real rationality of benevolence can both be understood once we see that they rest on the rational requirement stated in Extension.

We can now see the difference between the Clarkean and Kantian axioms and the new principles that Sidgwick adds. Contrary to Sidgwick, the new principles do not leave him in 'substantial agreement' (384) with Clarke and Kant. Nor do they state the implications of the old axioms. Nor are they more fundamental axioms that make the old axioms into subordinate principles. The new principles provide Sidgwick with an argument for utilitarianism, but they do not show that the old axioms support utilitarianism. On the contrary, they conflict with the old axioms. Since he relies on Wholes and Extension, he

---

[46] Hayward, *EPS* 119, emphasizes this concession to egoism, and suggests that most of the time, for epistemic reasons, benevolence will actually support self-interested behaviour.

rejects the rationality of prudence, and he does not compare my good with the good of this or that other person. The argument relies on non-personal principles, and implicitly rejects the personal principles of Clarke and Kant.

1192. Rawls's Objections

Rawls criticizes Sidgwick's argument by accepting Sidgwick's analysis of prudence and denying its application to distribution between persons.[47] In the prudential case, only one person's gains and losses are considered, and so the burdens I impose on myself at one time are compensated for by the benefits that I gain at another time in maximizing my own total utility. But in the inter-personal case, we may maximize the total utility by imposing burdens on one person to benefit another.[48] Rawls speaks as though we might agree with Sidgwick about prudence and object only in the inter-personal case.

Rawls does not seem to give a fair account of Sidgwick's argument. If we were right about Wholes and Extension, we can hardly accept Rawls's suggestion that we ought to agree, or might consistently agree, with Sidgwick about prudence but not about benevolence. For Sidgwick's treatment of prudence does not rely on any claim about the states of the same person; it simply relies on Wholes and Extension. These two principles both explain the apparent rationality of prudence and eliminate the difference that Rawls alleges between intra-personal and inter-personal maximization.

Sidgwick's argument for utilitarianism does not treat different people as though they were the same person. For Wholes and Extension are not confined to the intra-personal case. They are general principles about all parts and wholes, and so they do not depend on ignoring the fact that pleasures and pains can belong to different people. Sidgwick neither forgets nor denies the fact that the people involved in distribution are different. He recognizes that they are different (esp. 404), but in this case he thinks the difference is unimportant. Prudent people do not deny that next week and next year are different times, or that next week comes sooner than next year; they simply deny that these facts are relevant, in their own right, to the distribution of goods in their lives. Similarly, utilitarians do not deny that different people are different; they simply deny that the difference is relevant, in its own right, to inter-personal distribution of goods. Since Rawls does not contest Wholes and Extension, he gives no reason to disallow their application to distribution between persons.

If, then, we doubt Sidgwick's conclusion, we need to dispute Wholes or Extension or both. Perhaps Rawls intends to dispute them. For sometimes he argues that maximization

---

[47] See Rawls, *TJ* §30. Price anticipates the main point of his objection. He suggests that the utilitarian attitude results from treating questions about distribution of happiness among different people as though they were parallel to questions about distribution within a single person. See *RPQM* 160, quoted in §822. Perhaps Rawls recalls Ross, *FE* 75: 'We do not, in fact, think that persons other than ourselves are simply so many pawns in the game of producing the maximum of pleasure, or good. We think they have definite rights, or at least claims, not to be made means to the giving of pleasure to others; and claims that ought to be respected unless the net pleasure, or good, to be gained for the community by other action is very considerable.' In 'unless . . .', Ross gives a greater weight to the claims of utility than Rawls gives them. Ross in turn may be recalling Price.

[48] Hence Rawls claims that 'there is a sense in which classical utilitarianism fails to take seriously the distinction between persons' (*TJ* 163; cf. 23–4). His account of Sidgwick's argument is criticized by Shaver, *RE* 95–8.

is reasonable in the intra-personal case, but not in the inter-personal case. In Rawls's view, distribution of good across different times does not matter, because it is the same person who gets the good, whenever she gets it, and so she is compensated for her earlier or later sacrifice. But if one person sacrifices, and a second person gets the benefit resulting from this sacrifice, the first person is not compensated for her sacrifice, and so it is unreasonable to maximize.[49]

If this is Rawls's argument, he means to reject Wholes and Extension, not to deny that the conscious states of different people form a whole to which Wholes and Extension apply. He agrees with the maximizing aspect of Extension, but not with its non-personal aspect; for he assumes that the scope of maximizing is limited by the number of persons whose conscious states are considered. The principle that Rawls suggests allows prudence—my concern for my own welfare—and also allows paternalism; for it seems to imply that it would be all right for me to impose sacrifices on you to maximize your total good. The principle of compensation seems to apply as long as one person is being considered; it is not restricted to consideration by the agent of her own good.

Sidgwick and Rawls, then, offer different explanations of an alleged fact—our acceptance of a maximizing strategy in prudential reasoning. We need to ask whether the alleged fact that they seek to explain is a genuine fact, and, if it is genuine, which explanation of it is preferable.

1193. Prudence and the Self

But before we consider this question about prudence and maximization, we need to discuss a complication in Sidgwick's views. So far we have found that his attitude to prudence is basically non-personal; the apparent rationality of concern for one's own maximum good rests on the real rationality of the non-personal principles, Wholes and Extension. Sidgwick, however, does not seem to take this view. He takes the rationality of prudence to depend on claims about personal identity; but the truth of these claims should not matter if he relies on non-personal principles. Either we have misinterpreted Sidgwick or he has not fully understood his position.

He notes that he has taken prudence to be rational without any defence of its rationality. He allows the possibility of questioning the rationality of prudence. In particular, he supposes that if Hume were right to deny any persisting self, he would have undermined prudence, because it would rest on a false assumption about continuity.[50] He seems to assume, then, that we are right to take the rationality of prudence for granted if and only if we are right to believe in a persisting self that Hume denies.

---

[49] Brink discusses sacrifice and compensation in 'Rationale'.

[50] 'From the point of view, indeed, of abstract philosophy, I do not see why the Egoistic principle should pass unchallenged any more than the Universalistic. I do not see why the axiom of Prudence should not be questioned, when it conflicts with present inclination, . . . it must surely be admissible to ask the Egoist, "Why should I sacrifice a present pleasure for a greater one in the future? Why should I concern myself about my own future feelings any more than about the feelings of other persons?" . . . I do not see how the demand can be repudiated as absurd by those who adopt the views of the extreme empirical school of psychologists, . . . Grant that the Ego is merely a system of coherent phenomena, that the permanent identical "I" is not a fact but a fiction, as Hume and his followers maintain; why, then, should one part of the series of feelings into which the Ego is resolved be concerned with another part of the same series, any more than with any other series?' (418–19) Sidgwick's treatment of this question is discussed and criticized by Parfit, RP, ch. 7.

The significance that Sidgwick attaches to the choice between a non-Humean and a Humean conception of the self is puzzling. He seems to say that if we accept a Humean conception, we can ask why one part of this particular series of feelings should care about another part of the same series more than about any other series of feelings. Though he does not say that this question would not arise for non-Humeans, he seems to assume that it would not arise for them; why else would it be relevant to bring in Hume at this stage?

Why does the question arise for Humeans? Sidgwick's statement of the question might appear to show why the question need not arise for them. For even if we do not speak of a permanent and identical ego, but only of a series, we can still distinguish parts of the same series from parts of a different series. Hence we may say that one part of a series cares more about other parts of the same series it than it cares about parts of other series, precisely because they belong to the same series. Non-Humeans speak of the same ego where Humeans speak of the same series; but why does that matter? Sidgwick does not seem to show that a Humean conception of the self casts doubt on the rationality of prudence.

This objection overlooks the fact that Sidgwick takes the Humean theory to be eliminative rather than reductive. That is why he claims that Hume makes the permanent, identical 'I' a fiction rather than a fact. The fact that two conscious states belong to the same Humean series makes prudence puzzling, whereas the fact that they belong to the same self makes prudence intelligible.

We might support Sidgwick through a particular interpretation of his question about why one part of a given series should care about another part of that series more than about any other series. We might take 'any other series' to include arbitrary collections of experiences. Sidgwick may mean that a Humean series is an arbitrary collection, whereas a non-fictional self is a non-arbitrary collection, or not a collection at all. If Hume eliminates selves and replaces them with arbitrary collections, he casts doubt on prudence. For prudence involves concern for me tomorrow and me in ten years, on the assumption that these are phases of something less arbitrary than the conjunction of three arbitrary phases such as me now, the Queen tomorrow, and a farmer in China next week. Reflexion on arbitrary collections explains why it matters whether we accept a Humean conception of the self.

1194. A Puzzle about Prudence and the Self

Though this is a reasonable account of Sidgwick's view that a Humean view of the self undermines prudence, a further question arises. We found earlier that his argument for utilitarianism relies on Extension. If that is so, it does not rely on the assumption that we have non-Humean selves, because it does not rely on the rationality of prudence. It should not matter whether a self is an arbitrary series or not, because the apparent rationality of prudence does not depend on the assumption that the self is a non-arbitrary series. On the contrary, Sidgwick considers the apparent rationality of prudence only in order to uncover the ultimately rational principle Extension.

The difference between Quantity and Extension is relevant to Sidgwick's treatment of prudence. Quantity makes prudence rational, because it applies to every whole; but it fails to make benevolence overrule prudence. To avoid this result, we replaced Quantity with Extension, which makes benevolence supreme, but does not make prudence rational. Extension makes the restriction of our attention to a single self irrational. It does not matter, from this point of view, whether the self is or is not a Humean collection. Even if the ego is permanent and identical, Wholes and Extension give us no reason to suppose that concern for maximizing the good realized in the experiences of this ego is rational. Sidgwick's argument, therefore, supports an objection to his claims about the self.

Moreover, if his claims about prudence relied on a non-Humean view, they would cast doubt on utilitarianism. If prudence depends on the assumption that the self is a non-arbitrary collection, benevolence should apparently depend on the assumption that the aggregate of sentient beings is a non-arbitrary collection over which it is rational to maximize. If sacrifice of present for future good is rational because it secures the greater good of one and the same non-arbitrary collection, the sacrifice of one person's good for the universal good seems to be rational if and only if it also secures the greater good of a non-arbitrary collection. But what is this non-arbitrary collection? Whatever makes a single self a non-arbitrary collection, it is difficult to see how the aggregate of actual and possible selves affected by a particular action could have that kind of unity.

To appreciate this difficulty for Sidgwick, we may compare his argument with Hazlitt's treatment of self-love and concern for others. In his brief essay, Hazlitt argues that concern for one's own future is no more intelligible or rational than concern for others. To achieve prudent concern for myself, I have to go beyond my primitive attachment to my immediate concerns. I have to learn that this future self is the same self as the one I am concerned about now, and that its welfare will require action in the future. To achieve concern for others, I have to learn that they are persons no less than I am, and that they matter no less than I matter. In both cases, I have to learn that something to which I am not immediately attached deserves my concern. The argument is no less indispensable, and no more cogent, in the case of prudence than in the case of concern for others.[51]

Hazlitt agrees with Sidgwick in so far as he believes that prudence and concern for others are both rational, and that prudence is no more rational than concern for others. But he does not take concern for others to involve utilitarian maximizing concern. In so far as he recognizes this question, he seems to hold something closer to a principle of equity, which, as we saw, does not commit us to utilitarianism. And so he does not need to argue from prudence to utilitarianism. Sidgwick faces a peculiar difficulty because he accepts a utilitarian conception of concern for others.

---

[51] According to Hazlitt, disinterested concern for another is no more unintelligible than concern for one's future self. We love our own good because it is good; we love our own good in particular only because we know more about ourselves than about other people (Hazlitt, *EPHA* 18). 'The only reason for my preferring my future interest to that of others must arise from my anticipating it with greater warmth of present imagination. It is this greater liveliness and force with which I can enter into my future feelings, that in a manner identifies them with my present being: and this notion of identity being once formed, the mind makes use of it to strengthen its habitual propensity, by giving to personal motives a reality and absolute truth which they can never have.' (*EPHA* 74) In 'Self-love', Hazlitt endorses Butler's objections to psychological egoism. He raises some more radical questions about personal identity. Having distinguished the past, present, and future selves, he adds: '...I admit that you have a peculiar, emphatic, incommunicable, and exclusive interest or fellow-feeling in the first two of these selves; but I deny resolutely and unequivocally that you have any such natural, absolute, unavoidable, and mechanical interest in the last self, or in your future being, it being necessarily the offspring of understanding and imagination (aided by habit and circumstances), like that which you take in the welfare of others, and yet this last interest is the only one that is ever the object of rational and voluntary pursuit, or that ever comes into competition with the interests of others.' (173) Sidgwick does not show awareness of Hazlitt's essay.

We may be able to defend Sidgwick better if we consider more carefully the role of prudence in his argument for benevolence. We have seen that he does not rely on Wholes and Extension to prove that prudence is rational. He is right, since these principles imply that prudence is not rational. He sets out from the apparent rationality of prudence. He may suppose that we initially believe prudence is rational because of further implicit beliefs:

(1)   My self is not an arbitrary collection.
(2)   If Hume were right, it would be an arbitrary collection.
(3)   Hence Hume is wrong.
(4)   Prudence is rational if and only if my self is not an arbitrary collection.
(5)   Hence prudence is rational.

This account of our initial belief would justify Sidgwick in claiming that common sense takes the rationality of prudence for granted because it takes the permanence of the ego for granted.

Sidgwick relies on this belief in the rationality of prudence in order to uncover our deeper commitment to Wholes and Extension. On reflexion, we discover that it is not simply the fact that I am a permanent self that makes prudence seem justified; for we discover that we approve of maximizing our own good only because we accept Wholes and Extension. Once we understand Wholes and Extension, we see that prudence is only apparently rational. Since we no longer believe that prudence is really rational, we assume neither the truth nor the falsity of Humean views of the self.

This explanation of Sidgwick's claims about prudence and the self requires us to mark a distinction that he does not mark between (a) the presuppositions of the common-sense belief in prudence, and (b) the premises of his argument for utilitarianism. If we suppose that his argument affirms the rationality of prudence, we might also suppose that it relies on the presuppositions of the common-sense belief, and hence we might suppose that Sidgwick is committed to the falsity of Humean views of the self. But we have seen that his argument begins from the apparent rationality of prudence, and that it does not affirm, but implicitly denies, the real rationality of prudence. And so Sidgwick need not accept or reject the Humean view.

Our defence of Sidgwick's various claims raises a further question for him. We have already noticed the different roles of personal and of non-personal principles in the development of his thought. In the first edition, he tries to reach utilitarianism through personal principles; these are the old axioms derived from Clarke and Kant. In later editions, he adds claims about maximization, without making them completely explicit. These claims commit him to non-personal principles that undermine the rationality of prudence. Sidgwick, however, does not see that his argument for utilitarianism undermines prudence. If he had seen this, the revisions to his argument would have been more extensive than they actually are.

We can now see more clearly the dilemma that faces Sidgwick: (1) His earlier argument rests on the personal principles embodied in the old axioms; it relies on prudence plus equality. This argument affirms the rationality of prudence, but it does not support utilitarianism, because it does not justify maximization. (2) His later argument rests on non-personal principles about wholes and parts. This argument supports utilitarianism, but it rejects the rationality of prudence. It offers an implausible explanation of the apparent rationality of prudence.

Sidgwick does not seem to be justified, therefore, in claiming that his argument for utilitarianism ought to convince a certain kind of egoist. It ought not to convince anyone who thinks that prudence is rational in its own right. The only opponent whom it ought to convince is the one who is already committed to a strong principle of maximization. His argument does not make maximization appear any more plausible to someone who does not already accept it.

It would not be easy for Sidgwick to modify his position so that he affirms the rationality of prudence. His discussion of the Humean account of the self makes it clear where the difficulty arises for him. If he takes the rationality of prudence to depend on the non-arbitrary character of the self, and affirms the rationality of prudence, he undermines his argument from prudence to utilitarianism. This is the defect, from a utilitarian point of view, in the old axioms. Prudence and equality, as Clarke and Kant understand them, are personal principles. They affirm that facts about persons, as such, matter in prudential and moral reflexion. But if they matter, they cast doubt on Sidgwick's argument for utilitarianism. Sidgwick's non-personal principles avoid this defect in the old axioms, but they do not give him a plausible argument for utilitarianism.

1195. Persons, Wholes, and Distribution

Both Sidgwick and Rawls assume that the rational or apparently rational attitude to one's good is a maximizing attitude. But this assumption is open to doubt. Even if purely temporal discrimination is irrational, it may not be rational to aim at maximizing our total good without any regard to the times of our life over which it is distributed. Concern for whether our life ends well or badly, or undergoes steep rises and falls in well-being, is not a concern for the nearer or more distant time in its own right; hence it is not purely temporal. A reason for accepting temporal neutrality is the fact that I have multiple concerns and a longer-term interest. But this might require me to be fair to different aspects and phases of myself, not to aim at maximizing some total irrespective of its effect on each part.

Suppose, for instance, that I can choose between two sorts of lives, and that I can measure the surplus of pain over pleasure or pleasure over pain year by year. In life L1 I will have forty years at -5 (a net balance of 5 units of pain over pleasure) per year, five years at $+500$ per year, and then five years at -20 per year. The resulting happiness for life L1 is $2500 - 300 = 2200$. In life L2, I will have forty years at $+30$ followed by 10 years at $+50$. The resulting happiness for life L2 is $1200 + 500 = 1700$. Life L2 achieves a lower total of happiness, but it is more uniformly happy, and gets better as it goes along. Life L1 achieves a higher total, but is much more uneven, ends badly, and for most years is much worse than L2. It may not be clear that L1 or L2 ought to be preferred if we had the choice. But it does not seem obvious that we must prefer L1.

Sidgwick does not discuss these questions. Perhaps he thinks they do not matter because he interprets Wholes through Extension. Wholes says only that some relevant distinction is needed to justify the different treatment of different parts. If 'relevant' means only 'relevant to the aims of a rationally prudent person', it does not rule out concern for distribution throughout one's life. But since Sidgwick takes 'relevant' to mean 'relevant to maximizing the total', he takes Extension to be the basic principle that controls the interpretation of Wholes.

His maximizing principle implies a certain conception of the structure of the self, and hence of its good, over time. If we want to acquire or to produce something without internal structure, pure maximization might be reasonable. If we simply try to collect sand or petrol, we might reasonably say that we want to gather as much as possible, and that it does not matter where we put it; the best arrangement is the one that allows us to store as much as possible. This idea of accumulation involves indifference to distribution because it involves indifference to structure. If I add to a heap, or if I pour more petrol into a tank, I make the heap or the pool bigger, and it does not matter where I add it.

Some wholes, however, do not allow indifference to distribution. A statue of an animal is an organic whole; it is not simply a collection of parts, because they have to fit together in the right way in a whole.[52] If we were making a statue, we probably ought not to concentrate all our effort on the nose, in the belief that if we made it extremely beautiful, we would compensate for the ugliness of every other part of the figure, and so would maximize the total beauty in the statue. Organic wholes show why temporal neutrality does not imply indifference to distribution. If I am making a statue, I should not suppose that the part I am just about to carve is somehow the most important, no matter what part it happens to be; I should be neutral between the different times at which I have to carve the different parts. But I do not try to maximize without regard to distribution.

According to Sidgwick, a prudent person seeks pure accumulation, so that the different times do not matter as long as the largest quantity is collected. This aim suits prudential quantitative hedonism; for the fact that a state of pleasure belongs to the life of a single person does not affect its desirability. But if the structure of myself and my life makes no difference to the character of my good, one may be puzzled about why one should aim at good for oneself in particular. Sidgwick's hedonist conception of the good makes Extension seem more plausible by making prudence seem less intelligible.[53]

The introduction of hedonism at this stage is open to a further objection from Sidgwick's point of view. He intends his derivation of the axioms to be independent of any particular conception of the good, since he believes that non-hedonist moralists such as Clarke and Kant accept them. Contrary to Sidgwick, however, either quantitative hedonism or some other quantitative conception of the good seems to be needed to support Extension. Clarke's and Kant's principles neither rely on Extension nor support it.

A purely accumulative conception of prudence conflicts with an organic conception of a self. According to an organic conception, a prudent person seeks to achieve a good with some structure in which the relation of the different parts matters. Sidgwick misses one feature of Butler's picture of rational self-love. For Butler accepts Plato's political analogy;

---

[52] This is what Bradley calls an 'infinite' whole. See §1220. Albee, *HEU* 405, notices that Sidgwick's assumption about one's own good is controversial: '... the good is here assumed to be not merely a mathematical whole ... but a quasi-physical aggregate, as opposed to an organic whole. And this plainly begs the question, as against certain forms of ethical theory for which the author has no sympathy, as, for instance, self-realization.'

[53] The discussion in Parfit, *RP*, ch. 13, is relevant to these questions in Sidgwick.

in his view, we pursue rational aims that form a rational plan that gives the right place to each of my particular passions, so that none of them dominates the others. A person regards herself as an end in relation to her different desires, and does not try to maximize a total that is indifferent to distribution. Bradley explores this organic conception of a self and its good, in opposition to Sidgwick.[54]

If, however, we criticize Sidgwick's argument in this way, we may believe that there is a closer analogy than Rawls allows between prudence and morality. Rawls believes that prudence involves maximizing whereas morality forbids it; but if prudence also rejects maximizing, prudence and morality do not differ on this point. One might argue, as Plato and Butler do, that prudence and morality are analogous in ways that Sidgwick and Rawls, for different reasons, both reject. Perhaps prudence involves doing justice to one's different interests and legitimate concerns. This feature of prudence may support the claim that morality involves some sort of justice between different people's interests and concerns. In each case, we reject Sidgwick's Extension in favour of a distributive principle. It does not follow that the very same distributive principle operates in prudence and morality. But if distributive considerations are relevant to prudence, Sidgwick's idea of arguing from the principles of prudence to the principles of morality may be reasonable.

1196. Prudence and Benevolence

Sidgwick's interpretation of prudence influences his comparison between one person's good and the good of many people, and therefore his account of the parallel between prudence and benevolence (382). The notion of one's own good on the whole is formed 'by comparison and integration of the different "goods" that succeed one another in the series of our conscious states'. When he applies Wholes both to prudence and to benevolence (382), Sidgwick assumes Extension. The only relevant consideration for distinguishing different parts of the whole constituted by different persons is the different quantity of total good that is likely to result.

If we doubt Sidgwick's identification of an individual's good with maximum pleasure (or other quantity), irrespective of distribution, we should also doubt his interpretation of benevolence. In the case of benevolence, as ordinarily understood, distributive considerations matter. We might agree that one person's good matters as much as another's from the impartial 'point of view of the universe'. But we might infer, for Kantian reasons, that morality should protect each person, and should not treat one person simply as a part to be manipulated in order to maximize some total satisfaction summed over the whole.

We might draw this non-utilitarian conclusion from Clarke's and Kant's principles. Their divergence from Sidgwick's position is relevant to his argument, since he takes the agreement

---

[54] Bradley; §1218. Cf. Rashdall, *TGE* i 65n: 'We might also criticize Prof. Sidgwick's tendency to ignore the unity and the continuity of the self. No doubt the self cannot be regarded as having value when abstracted from the successive conscious states in which it manifests itself, but it is equally impossible to estimate the value of the conscious states in entire abstraction from the permanent self which is present in all of them.'

of other moralists to be important. He does not ascribe Extension to any of them. His account of benevolence supports utilitarianism only to the extent that it goes beyond the axioms derived from Clarke and Kant.

Sidgwick recognizes that his conception of benevolence differs from common sense; but he suggests that the difference lies primarily in the extended and impartial nature of benevolence, as he conceives it. He does not explain why we should endorse the conception of benevolence that aims at a total happiness summed over the aggregate of sentient beings. Like Hutcheson and (more surprisingly) Butler, he assumes that universal concern for other people, as prescribed by benevolence, is the same as concern for total good, as prescribed by utilitarianism. If his claims about benevolence are controversial, we may doubt whether his alleged axiom Benevolence is really an axiom.

1197. Utilitarianism and Equality

In Sidgwick's view, utilitarians seek to maximize total happiness rather than average happiness, and so they may advocate (for instance) any increase of population that increases the total happiness at the cost of average happiness.[55] This implication about population applies no less to dogs, vultures, or rats than to human beings; utilitarians are indifferent to distribution among all these sentient beings.[56]

Despite this basic indifference to distribution, Sidgwick also mentions circumstances in which a utilitarian will care about distribution. We need a distinct principle of distribution in order to make the utilitarian criterion as complete as possible, because the principle of utility alone does not seem to be a complete criterion. Some questions about distribution do not seem to affect total utility, but we still need to decide them. They may be practically important; for even if the distribution always affects the total quantity of happiness, we will not always know what the effect is, and so we will have to consider questions about distribution on the assumption that the total of happiness will be unaffected.[57]

Sidgwick finds a distributive principle by relying on a doubtful interpretation of Bentham's principle that everyone is to count for one. Bentham's principle seems to say that everyone's pains and pleasures should be counted equally (if they are equal in degree) when we assess total pleasure and pain resulting from a given action or policy; this principle says nothing about the distribution of happiness. Sidgwick takes this principle to claim that if total happiness is unaffected by the distribution of happiness between A and B, it should be

---

[55] 'But if we foresee as possible that an increase in numbers will be accompanied by a decrease in average happiness or vice versa, a point arises which has not only never been formally noticed, but which seems to have been substantially overlooked by many Utilitarians. For if we take Utilitarianism to prescribe, as the ultimate end of action, happiness on the whole, and not any individual's happiness, unless considered as an element of the whole, it would follow that, if the additional population enjoy on the whole positive happiness, we ought to weigh the amount of happiness gained by the extra number against the amount lost by the remainder.' (415) Broad, *FTET* 249–50, takes this to be an objection to utilitarianism. Ross, *FE* 70–1, quotes and endorses Broad's criticism. See Parfit, *RP*, ch. 17.

[56] Cf. Mill and Whewell on Bentham, §1124.

[57] 'It is evident that there may be many different ways of distributing the same quantum of happiness among the same number of persons; in order, therefore, that the utilitarian criterion of right conduct may be as complete as possible, we ought to know which of these ways is to preferred.' (416)

distributed equally to A and B.[58] He takes this to be a consequence of Kantian principles. He therefore agrees with Mill in taking Bentham's principle to express a commitment to equality.[59]

On the one hand, Sidgwick believes that (1) the principle of equal distribution makes 'the utilitarian criterion of right conduct . . . as complete as possible', so that it seems to be part of the utilitarian theory. On the other hand, (2) equal distribution seems to be added to the principle of utility, not derived from it; for it applies to cases in which the principle of utility gives no reason for distributing happiness to one person rather than another. These two claims do not seem consistent. For if utilitarianism is true, the principle of utility is a complete criterion of rightness; any other criterion must be derivable from it as a means of maximizing utility. But if some further criterion is needed, utilitarianism is false. Sidgwick, therefore, seems to imply that utilitarianism is false.

But how do we know the principle of utility is incomplete? Sidgwick says that if utility is unaffected, 'it becomes practically important to ask whether any mode of distributing a given quantum of happiness is better than any other'. He suggests that the utilitarian formula does not answer this question. But the utilitarian formula answers that no mode of distribution is better than any other. If giving equal happiness to A and B, giving more to A and less to B, and giving more to B and less to A, would have exactly the same effect on total utility, utilitarianism makes the distribution of happiness between A and B morally indifferent.

Sidgwick seems to suppose that we need a distributive principle to cover distributions in which utility is unaffected, because we know that moral questions arise in such distributions. But if that is so, utilitarianism is false; for it does not give us the basic principle from which all other true moral principles can be derived. This would be no less true even if the independent distributive principle applied only to cases in which utility is unaffected.

A utilitarian cannot consistently accept a presumption in favour of equal treatment. If the principle of utility gives the sole criterion of moral rightness, no principle can be morally right if it cannot be derived from the principle of utility. Since, therefore, the presumption of equal treatment cannot be derived from the principle of utility, a utilitarian cannot accept it as morally required. Sidgwick ought to conclude that utilitarian principles leave it morally indifferent, and up to our non-moral preferences, how we distribute the total between different people, in cases where the distribution does not affect the total.

1198. An Objection Derived from Equality

If Sidgwick admits an independent moral principle of distribution where utility is unaffected, he raises a further difficulty for utilitarianism. How do we know that the distributive principle

---

[58] 'In all such cases, therefore, it becomes practically important to ask whether any mode of distributing a given quantum of happiness is better than any other. Now the Utilitarian formula seems to supply no answer to this question: at least we have to supplement the principle of seeking the greatest happiness on the whole by some principle of Just or Right distribution of this happiness. The principle which most Utilitarians have either tacitly or expressly adopted is that of pure equality—as given in Bentham's formula, "everybody to count for one, and nobody for more than one". And this principle seems the only one which does not need a special justification; for, as we saw, it must be reasonable to treat any one man in the same way as any other, if there be no reason apparent for treating him differently.' (416–17)

[59] See Mill, §1139.

is subordinate to the principle of utility, and that it is relevant only when it does not affect utility? We do not seem to have a reliable intuition that the slightest increase in utility justifies the grossest inequality in distribution. If we recognize an independent distributive principle, we ought to treat it as a distinct head of virtue, and accept Price's pluralism about supreme principles.[60]

Sidgwick claims that a Kantian principle of equal treatment both (1) is included in the principle of rational benevolence, and (2) justifies the presumption of equal distribution. According to the first claim, the Kantian principle tells us to discriminate between people only by morally relevant features, when moral considerations are involved. From a utilitarian point of view, the only morally relevant features are those that affect the total utility. Sidgwick infers that equal distribution is required if and only if total utility is not affected. But his conclusion does not follow. The Kantian principle does not forbid unequal treatment in situations that do not involve moral considerations.

According to the utilitarian, moral considerations are those that affect total utility. If, then, distributions that do not affect total utility do not raise moral question, we are morally free to distribute happiness as we please in these cases. Neither Bentham's principle nor the Kantian principle seems to support Sidgwick's claim that the utilitarian will accept a secondary principle favouring equal distribution. Any such principle would be an unjustified addition to the principle of utility.

We can see the puzzling element in Sidgwick's treatment of equality if we look more closely at the Kantian principle he appeals to. It is not plausible to claim, on Kantian grounds or on any others, that we ought always to distribute equally unless there is a good moral reason for inequality. We are morally free to give more to our friends, or to our chosen charitable causes, at the expense of other equally deserving people. It is appropriate to demand equal distribution only in cases where we have no moral permission for unequal distribution, or (to put it another way) in cases where a question of distribution is morally significant. This condition does not make the demand for equality trivial or useless, but it cannot be applied without further moral judgment about moral significance.

The advantage of utilitarianism, according to Sidgwick, is that it gives a definite answer to this question about moral significance. It tells us that a choice between two options is morally significant if and only if it affects utility. And so, in cases where utility is not affected, our distributive choice is morally insignificant. Sidgwick, therefore, seems to abandon utilitarianism when he claims that equal distribution is required in cases where utility is not affected. For if utilitarianism is true, these are not morally significant cases; but Sidgwick assumes that they are morally significant. If his assumption is right, he has discovered an axiom that is not subordinate to the principle of utility. Moreover, this axiom has a disadvantage that Sidgwick complains of in the alleged axioms of common sense; moral judgment is needed to identify the cases that are morally significant.

If Sidgwick has to treat the presumption of equality as a distinct axiom, we may reasonably doubt whether it is subordinate to utility. Though he treats it as a simple addition to the

---

[60] Ross, *FE* 72, objects to Sidgwick's use of this principle: 'The principle of justice in the distribution of happiness can in no way be derived from the principle bidding us produce the greatest total of happiness. If it is true, as Sidgwick holds, then it is independent of the greatest happiness principle; and if it is independent of it, is capable of coming into conflict with it.'

principle of utility, it seems to raise far-reaching questions about whether he can consistently claim to endorse utilitarianism.

The presumption of equality raises a further difficulty about utilitarian maximization. For it implies that equal distribution between persons matters for its own sake, apart from its contribution to utility. This role for persons conflicts with Sidgwick's non-personal treatment of prudence and benevolence. Quantitative hedonism does not deny the reality of persons, but it attaches no distinctive or fundamental moral significance to them. The analysis of prudence is meant to show us, through Quantity and Wholes, that basic moral significance belongs to wholes of conscious states. Whether these conscious states belong to one person, or many persons, or no person, is irrelevant to their moral significance. The non-personal aspects of utilitarianism leave no room for a moral presumption in favour of equal treatment or equal distribution of happiness among persons. The presumption of equality takes the treatment of persons to matter in its own right, whereas the argument for utilitarianism takes only the conscious states of persons to matter.

Sidgwick's treatment of the presumption of equal treatment exposes a conflict in his arguments about the axioms. On the one hand, he follows Clarke and Kant; on the other hand, he seeks to derive utilitarian principles.[61] The treatment of utilitarianism and distribution shows that he does not reconcile the two sides of his argument. The principles derived from Clarke and Kant do not support utilitarianism. Reflexion on his discussion of distribution suggests that these principles actually conflict with utilitarianism.

1199. The 'Synthesis' of Utilitarianism and Intuitionism

The last chapter of *Methods* discusses the three methods that have determined the structure of the book.[62] The examination of intuitionism in Book III ends with a claim to have reconciled utilitarianism and intuitionism.[63] The last chapter reasserts this claim, and compares these two methods, now reconciled, with egoism.[64]

Is Sidgwick right to claim that he has 'reconciled' or 'synthesized' utilitarianism with intuitionism? His claim is obscure because of his complex use of 'intuitionism'. He uses the term to refer to (1) an epistemological position that relies on principles grasped by intuition; (2) a deontological attitude to moral principles;[65] (3) perfectionism. Which of these outlooks has he reconciled with utilitarianism?

---

[61] In [1] the conflict is especially obvious. Since the principles Sidgwick derives are not specifically utilitarian, they do not support his maximizing position. In later editions, the conflict is less obvious, because he interprets the axioms so that they favour maximizing utilitarianism.

[62] In [1], the last chapter is called 'The sanctions of utilitarianism'. In later editions it is called 'Concluding Chapter: the mutual relations of the three methods'. [1] does not contain the long first paragraph on intuitionism and utilitarianism at [7] 496–7.

[63] '...I am finally led to the conclusion (which at the close of the last chapter seemed to be premature) that the Intuitional method rigorously applied yields as its final result the doctrine of pure Universalistic Hedonism.' (406–7) [1] reaches the same conclusion at 375, and re-affirms it at the end of the chapter: '...I am forced to leave the ethical method which takes perfection, as distinct from happiness, to be the whole or chief part of ultimate good, in a rudimentary condition. ... we may perhaps conclude that common sense will admit, as its most certain intuition, most precisely stated, the first principle of utilitarianism.' ([1] 378)

[64] [2] adds 456–7 at the beginning of the chapter.   [65] Cf. Rawls's use of 'intuitionism', §1412.

He reconciles the first intuitionist position with utilitarianism, because (he argues) our genuine intuitions favour utilitarianism.[66] But he rejects the second position, and does not reconcile it with utilitarianism. Similarly, the version of perfectionism that values moral virtue as a non-instrumental good is the only version that might even appear to agree with deontological intuitionism. This version of perfectionism is inconsistent with Sidgwick's hedonist account of non-instrumental good.

Since he claims that he has reconciled the utilitarian with the intuitionist method, we need to recall which intuitionist attitude he has identified with a method. For this purpose the second and third uses of 'intuitionism' are relevant. The method that he calls 'intuitionist' is normally the deontological approach to morality. But that is the method he has not reconciled with utilitarianism; on the contrary, he has rejected it. Hence he has not reconciled intuitionism with utilitarianism in the sense that is relevant to comparison of methods.[67] When he speaks of an apparent opposition between utilitarianism and intuitionism, he uses 'intuitionism' for the intuitionist method—the deontological doctrine that recognizes a plurality of basic principles grasped by intuition without reference to any further justifying ultimate end.

Sidgwick's initial claim that he is a 'utilitarian on an intuitional basis' refers to his claim to have reconciled or 'synthesized' the two methods called 'utilitarianism' and 'intuitionism'.[68] But if 'intuitionism' refers to the intuitionist method, he does not synthesize it with utilitarianism. For the intuitionist method treats common-sense principles as objects of intuition. This is the position that Sidgwick discusses in his examination of common-sense morality. But this position neither agrees with nor collapses into utilitarianism.[69]

---

[66] 'We have found that the original antithesis between intuitionism and utilitarianism must be entirely discarded: since the first principle of utilitarianism has appeared as the most certain and comprehensive of intuitions, and most of the others naturally range themselves in subordination to it, and even seem to be most thoroughly understood when considered as partial applications of it unconsciously and imperfectly made.' ([1] 472) In later editions, this comparison of the methods is moved from the end to the beginning of the last chapter, and expanded: 'We have found that the common antithesis between Intuitionists and Utilitarians must be entirely discarded: since such abstract moral principles as we can admit to be really self-evident are not only not incompatible with a Utilitarian system, but even seem required to furnish a rational basis for such a system. Thus we have seen that the essence of Justice or Equity (in so far as it is clear and certain) is that different individuals are not to be treated differently, except on grounds of universal application; and that such grounds, again, are supplied by the principle of Universal Benevolence, that sets before each man the happiness of all others as an object of pursuit no less worthy than his own . . .' (496)

[67] It is not surprising, therefore, that Calderwood, 'Intuitionalism', treats Sidgwick as an opponent of intuitionism. Though his criticisms of [1] are not very discerning in detail, he sees that Sidgwick opposes the deontological aspects of the position that he and Calderwood call 'intuitionist'. In his reply, Sidgwick protests that Calderwood is wrong to treat him as an opponent of intuitionism, since he thinks philosophical intuitionism supports utilitarianism. He rests his anti-deontological argument on the claim that the intuitions he endorses in iii 13 are self-evident, but other alleged intuitions are not self-evident. This reply does not seem to meet Calderwood's point, which relies on Sidgwick's deontological sense of 'intuitionism'.

[68] '. . . the opposition between utilitarianism and intuitionism was due to a misunderstanding . . . I could find no real opposition between intuitionism and utilitarianism. The utilitarianism of Mill and Bentham seemed to me to want a basis; that basis could only be supplied by a fundamental intuition; on the other hand the best examination I could make of the morality of common sense showed me no clear and self-evident principles except such as were perfectly consistent with utilitarianism.' (xx–xxi)

[69] In [1] he claims only that utilitarianism and common sense generally coincide. In later editions he goes into more detail: '. . . while other time-honoured virtues seem to be fitly explained as special manifestations of impartial benevolence under various circumstances of human life, or else as habits and dispositions indispensable to the maintenance of prudent or beneficent behaviour under the seductive force of various non-rational impulses. And although there are other rules which our common moral sense when first interrogated seems to enunciate as absolutely binding; it has appeared that

Sidgwick's claim to have reconciled the two methods may also result from an obscurity we have noticed in his treatment of the axioms. He claims to derive his axioms from principles accepted by the intuitionist moralists Clarke and Kant. Since he does not distinguish the position of Clarke and Kant from a maximizing principle, he believes he has reconciled intuitionism with utilitarianism.[70] If he were right about Clarke and Kant, he would have a good reason to believe that basic intuitionist principles support utilitarianism. But this would not show he had reconciled utilitarianism with the intuitionist method. For, even if intuitionists are implicitly committed to acceptance of utilitarianism, they are not utilitarians; their deontological attitude is inconsistent with the teleological utilitarian doctrine.

But in any case, the axioms derived from Clarke and Kant do not support utilitarianism. Sidgwick reaches the principle of utility only by adding a maximizing principle to the axioms derived from the intuitionists. He departs from intuitionism at the very point where he advocates utilitarianism.

He ought to have concluded, therefore, that he rejects intuitionism in so far as its principles conflict with maximizing utility. We find this conflict with utilitarianism because of 'our particular moral sentiments and unreasoned judgments'.[71] If we are utilitarians, we do not listen to intuitionist principles in a case of conflict, because we do not regard them as ultimately reasonable. Bradley claims justifiably that the principal object of *Methods* is a demonstration of utilitarianism. Though Sidgwick claims to examine the possible methods impartially, his claims tend to mislead us about the real tendency of his argument.[72]

1200. Egoism and the Ultimately Reasonable

Though Sidgwick believes his argument has reconciled two of his three methods, utilitarianism and intuitionism, he believes it is more difficult to reconcile utilitarianism (or the synthesis of utilitarianism and intuitionism) with hedonistic egoism. He believes that in examining these two methods we face a 'dualism' rather than a synthesis in practical reason.

careful and systematic reflection on this very Common Sense, . . . results in exhibiting the real subordination of these rules to the fundamental principles above given. . . . No doubt, even if this synthesis of methods be completely accepted, there will remain some discrepancy in details between our particular moral sentiments and unreasoned judgments on the one hand, and the apparent results of special utilitarian calculations on the other; and we may often have some practical difficulty in balancing the latter against the more general utilitarian reasons for obeying the former: but there seems to be no longer any theoretical perplexity as to the principles for determining social duty.' (496–7) Some of the same points are more briefly stated at [1] 473, at the end of the last chapter.

[70] Bradley, *CE* 100–1, denies that Sidgwick's two principles lead to utilitarianism. But his reasons rest on such a gross misinterpretation of the principles that they do not identify the basic weakness in Sidgwick's argument.

[71] He also speaks of 'the conflict that will partially continue between what we may now call instinctive and calculative morality'. ([1] 473)

[72] Hayward, *EPS*, ch. 1, and Schneewind, *SEVMP* 192, are more inclined than I am to agree with Sidgwick's description of the aims of *ME* and with his view that critics who regard it as a defence of utilitarianism have misunderstood him. Hayward reaches this conclusion by exaggerating the place of egoism in Sidgwick's overall position. Schneewind argues that it is a mistake to treat *ME* as primarily a defence of utilitarianism, because it is primarily an exploration of methods. This judgment takes insufficient account of the ways in which Sidgwick's description and assessment of different methods are shaped by utilitarian presuppositions. Schneewind, however, also recognizes that in several places, including iii 13, iv 2, and the last chapter, Sidgwick 'seems to abandon his stance of neutrality and to argue in his own voice for utilitarianism' (263).

To understand this dualism, we may usefully compare Sidgwick's argument with Butler's discussion of self-love and conscience. In Butler, these two superior principles cover the two areas of practical reason, prudence and morality. The content of prudence is relatively free of controversy,[73] but the content of morality is more controversial. We need to decide whether morality is to be identified with the demands of utilitarian rational benevolence, or if it includes non-utilitarian principles that sometimes override utility. Once we settle this question about the content of morality, we can ask a clear question about whether morality (represented by conscience) or one's own good (represented by reasonable self-love) matters more, and hence we can ask whether conscience or self-love is supreme.

A comparison with Butler suggests that Sidgwick raises difficulties for himself by treating his three methods as though they were on the same level. It would have been better if he had treated hedonism and other forms of egoism as candidates for expressing the content of prudence, and utilitarianism and intuitionism as candidates for expressing the content of morality. Once we compare the different candidates in each area, we can pick the two finalists, to see which of them is superior to the other.

Sidgwick does not present the issue in this way for two reasons: (1) He thinks it is easier to see that egoistic hedonism is the only viable candidate on the side of prudence than to see that utilitarianism is the only viable candidate on the side of morality. (2) He wants to mark the affinity between egoistic hedonism and universalistic hedonism (utilitarianism). Hence he recognizes egoistic hedonism, utilitarianism, and intuitionism as methods, without making it clear what a distinct method is.

The character of the three methods introduces a question that Butler does not raise about self-love and conscience. Sidgwick believes that the three methods are different ways of determining what is 'ultimately reasonable'. He might mean two things by 'ultimate': (1) Non-derivative, that is, rational in its own right. (2) The reason of last resort, that is, the overriding reason, and hence 'supremely' reasonable.[74] This ambiguity infects the final stages of his argument. It is still not clear in the last chapter of *Methods* what Sidgwick means by claiming, and why he claims, that it is ultimately reasonable to take my own interest as my overriding end.[75]

The ambiguity in Sidgwick's conception of the ultimately reasonable appears in his claim that other moralists believe that egoism is ultimately reasonable.[76] He cites moralists who agree that a completely reasonable outlook will reconcile morality with self-interest. They do not all say, however, that, in case of conflict, self-interest always overrides morality; even

---

[73] Prudence is not entirely free of controversy, in Butler's view, since people disagree about whether it counsels adherence to morality.

[74] Ultimate reasonableness; §1161.

[75] Perhaps Bain suggests a solution along these lines, though his formulation is not clear enough to be very helpful. 'There clearly must be two things postulated as the foundations of human duty, each for itself and on its own merits. It is reasonable for each one to seek their own happiness; it is right, reasonable, for each to give up, if need be, their own happiness for the sake of the happiness of some other persons. The first motion being put and carried nem. con., the second becomes an independent and substantive motion, and must be put on its own distinct grounds of acceptance.' (Bain, 'Methods', 195–6). It is not clear whether Bain means only that each principle is non-derivatively reasonable, or also means that morality is supreme.

[76] He cites Butler, Clarke, and Berkeley, to support the claim that many Christian moralists believe that 'the realization of virtue is essentially an enlightened and far-seeing pursuit of Happiness for the agent' (120).

Clarke's maximum concession to self-interest does not go so far.[77] Hence they do not agree that egoism is supremely reasonable.

Sidgwick's treatment of Butler illustrates his obscurity about ultimate reasonableness. Butler recognizes self-love and conscience as two distinct superior principles, and tries to show that they agree; Sidgwick infers that Butler regards them both as ultimately reasonable. His inference is justified if he means that Butler takes both to be non-derivatively reasonable. But it is unjustified if he means that Butler takes both to be supremely reasonable. This latter claim conflicts with Butler's assertion of the supremacy of conscience. When Butler tries to harmonize self-love with conscience, he does not concede that self-love claims to be, or that it is, supremely reasonable. He simply thinks it is theoretically and practically important to show that both conscience and self-love are in accord with our nature. He tries to show this by showing that they agree.

If Sidgwick wanted better evidence to show that Christian moralists regard self-interest as supremely reasonable, he might have appealed to theological voluntarists who think morality is a waste of time unless it offers rewards in this life or the afterlife. But their strong assertion that self-love is supremely reasonable does not evidently accord with common sense. Nor does Sidgwick show how common sense supports the strong assertion rather than the weaker assertion that self-interest is non-derivatively reasonable. Against the view that self-interest is not properly a virtuous motive, he suggests that common sense regards self-interested action as prima facie reasonable.[78] 'Prima facie' suggests a moderate interpretation of 'ultimately reasonable'; reasons of self-interest are always good reasons as far as they go, whether or not they can be shown to promote any further end. Common sense implies that we need a good reason to act without reference to self-interest; but it does not imply that no such reason can be given, or that the only good reasons are those that identify instrumental means to self-interest.[79] Common sense, therefore, does not suggest that egoism is supremely reasonable.

1201. Why is There a Dualism of Practical Reason?

This ambiguity in 'ultimately reasonable' helps to explain the appearance of a 'dualism of practical reason'. According to Sidgwick, egoism tells me to pursue my own happiness above all, and utilitarianism tells me to pursue the general happiness above all. These instructions may require incompatible actions. In this respect, they generate practical conflict. If we cannot show that one of these methods is superior to the other, do we face a dualism of practical reason?[80]

---

[77] Clarke on morality and self-interest; §673.

[78] 'Indeed, it is hardly going too far to say that common sense assumes that "interested" actions, tending to promote the agent's happiness, are prima facie reasonable: and that the onus probandi lies with those who maintain that disinterested conduct, as such, is reasonable.' (120) Shaver, *RE* 154–7, examines Sidgwick's belief in the wide acceptance of egoism.

[79] The obscurity in Sidgwick's claims about ultimate reasonableness re-appears in Schneewind's account of the 'viability of egoism', *SEVMP* 353–4.

[80] On the dualism see further Scotus, §368; Butler, §708. Sidgwick speaks of a 'dualism' in [2], in the course of denying that the main aim of his book is the suppression of egoism and a demonstration of utilitarianism: 'And as regards the

In Sidgwick's view, a dualism of practical reason implies a conflict between two methods, each of which appears to embody an axiom or axioms, and this conflict gives us reason to doubt whether any of these apparent axioms is really an axiom. The doubt arises because we are justified in treating a given principle as an axiom only if we believe it is consistent with other apparent axioms. Sidgwick believes that the dualism of practical reason reveals an apparent inconsistency between apparent axioms.

Given these conditions for a dualism, egoism and utilitarianism do not create a dualism if they only state what is non-derivatively reasonable. For even if they imply practical conflict, no dualism results. Two principles that generate practical conflict may both embody axioms; for they may be consistent even if they prescribe incompatible actions. If both egoism and utilitarianism are non-derivatively reasonable, we have some reason to prefer our own happiness, and some reason to prefer universal happiness. Our principles are (for all we have shown) consistent, and so they might still be axioms. Practical conflict between non-derivatively reasonable principles is not sufficient for a dualism of practical reason, since only an apparent inconsistency between principles creates a dualism.

To show that we seem to be committed to inconsistent principles, Sidgwick must take each of the two methods to affirm that its basic principle is supremely rational.[81] He is right to claim that if we have equally good reason to affirm that both egoism and morality are supremely reasonable, practical reason is in conflict with itself, and we cannot regard either principle as an axiom, since our apparent axioms seem to be inconsistent with other apparent axioms. To reach a dualism, therefore, Sidgwick has to interpret 'ultimately reasonable' as 'supremely reasonable'.

But now it becomes doubtful whether Sidgwick has shown that his methods create a dualism. Even if we conceded that common sense regards morality as supremely reasonable, or that his axiomatic argument has shown this, he has not shown that common sense regards egoism as supremely reasonable or that we have some further convincing reason

two hedonistic principles, I do not hold the reasonableness of aiming at happiness generally with any stronger conviction than I do that of aiming at one's own. It was no part of my plan to call special attention to this "Dualism of the Practical Reason" . . . ; but I am surprised at the extent to which my view has perplexed even those of my critics who have understood it. I had imagined that they would readily trace it to the source from which I learnt it, Butler's well-known Sermons. I hold with Butler that "Reasonable Self-love and Conscience are the two chief or superior principles in the nature of man", each of which we are under a "manifest obligation" to obey: and I do not (I believe) differ materially from Butler in my view either of reasonable self-love, or—theology apart—of its relation to conscience.' ([7] xii) This passage does not make it clear whether 'dualism' refers simply to (i) the existence of two basic principles of ultimate reasonableness, or also to (ii) the conflict between these two principles. Sidgwick's arguments for a dualism, and especially his treatment of egoism, are effectively criticized by Skorupski, 'Methods'.

[81] 'Again, there are others who will say that though (a) it is undoubtedly reasonable to prefer the general happiness to one's own, when the two are presented as alternatives; still (b) it remains also clearly reasonable to take one's own greatest happiness as one's ultimate and paramount end. They will maintain that the proof offered in ch. 2 does not really convert them from egoistic to univeralistic hedonism; but only convinces them that, unless the two can be shown to coincide, practical reason is divided against itself. They will urge further that, if we are to choose between the two, egoistic hedonism has clearly a prior claim on our assent. . . . So that it becomes of fundamental importance to ascertain how far these two aims admit of being reconciled . . .' ([1] 461, reference letters added) In (a) and (b), the critics affirm that each of the two methods is supremely reasonable. Hence each of them appears, in Butler's terms, to claim to be supreme. And Sidgwick agrees that we need to see whether they can be reconciled: 'For the negation of the connexion [sc. between virtue and self-interest] must force us to admit an ultimate and fundamental contradiction in our apparent intuitions of what is Reasonable in conduct; and from this admission it would seem to follow that the apparently intuitive operation of the Practical Reason, manifested in these contradictory judgments, is after all illusory' (508).

to hold this view about egoism. To reach a dualism, he needs to endorse the claims of theological voluntarists about self-interest. But these voluntarists do not believe that morality is supremely reasonable, and so they avoid a dualism. If we reject their view, and we claim that morality is supremely reasonable, it is not clear why we ought still to maintain that egoism is supremely reasonable.

Sidgwick's previous argument for utilitarianism gives us a further reason to doubt whether both egoism and utilitarianism are supremely reasonable.[82] He takes the rationality of prudence to rest on principles that also commit us to rational benevolence.[83] Apparently it would be unreasonable to accept the rationality of prudence without also accepting the rationality of benevolence, since they are two aspects of the same principle. Hence we might take the arguments for prudence and utilitarianism to show that utilitarianism is supremely reasonable, and that egoism is not supremely reasonable. Whether we consider the common-sense attitude to egoism or the attitude that should result from Sidgwick's arguments about the axioms, we have found no reason to claim that egoism is supremely reasonable, or to recognize a dualism of practical reason.

1202. Egoism and 'Reasonable for Me'

Sidgwick, however, believes that his argument for utilitarianism does not refute every sort of egoist.[84] In his first edition, he has egoists in mind when he insists that his axioms will not appear axiomatic to those who do not agree from the start to take the ethical point of view.[85] The initial ethical judgments assert that it is right for others to treat me in a particular way, and that is 'intrinsically desirable' that I pursue my own welfare. If, then, I do not acknowledge the supremacy of the ethical point of view, Sidgwick's arguments give me no reason to acknowledge the supremacy of axioms that we reach by starting from this point of view. If I am this sort of egoist, then, in Sidgwick's terms, the arguments for the axioms give me no reason to treat morality as a real 'method of ethics', because I have no reason to agree that it tells me what is supremely reasonable. This conclusion does not seem to leave us with a contradiction in practical reason. It only seems to show that we do not know, from Sidgwick's proof of utilitarianism, whether

---

[82] Bradley expresses justified doubts about the consistency of Sidgwick's position. See *CE* 73n, 102n, and esp. 116. He suggests that Sidgwick's previous discussions of the reasonable are inconsistent with his explanation of the rationality of egocentric egoism. Appealing to Sidgwick's claim in the last sentence of iii 13 ('Whatever I judge to be good, I cannot reasonably think that it is abstractly and primarily right that I should have it more than another' ([1] 366)), Bradley comments: 'This again has been the constant theme, and the nerve of the main argument. How did we suppress the egoist but by this. And now why did we knock down the egoist at all if we meant to set him up again?'

[83] In his view, 'the axiom of Prudence, as I have given it, is a self-evident principle, implied in Rational Egoism as commonly accepted' (386). This is not in [1] 364, or in [2] 360. It is added in [3] 388. In [3] and later editions, Sidgwick also adds a note referring forward to his concluding chapter. In [3] 388, and [4] 387, but not in [5] (which says the same as [6]), he says: 'The axiom of prudence, as I have given it, is the self-evident principle on which, according to me, rational egoism is based; it makes explicit the ground on which Butler, Reid, and their followers have attributed "reasonableness" and "authority" to self-love'.

[84] All editions claim not to have refuted egoism, but different editions offer different explanations. Hayward, *EPS*, ch. 5, claims that Sidgwick becomes more favourable to egoism in later editions. He does not argue plausibly for this claim, though he is right to point out that Sidgwick tries to explain the egoist position more fully.

[85] See [1] 360, quoted in §1185.

self-interest or morality is supremely reasonable; for his proof does not address that question.

To show why the egoist has a way out, Sidgwick limits his argument to 'the point of view of the universe' (cf. 420), the strictly impartial perspective on maximizing the total good of the sentient beings affected.[86] An egoist 'who strictly confines himself to stating his conviction that he ought to take his own happiness or pleasure as his ultimate end' is not open to any argument that would require him to accept the principle of utility as an ultimate principle superior to the egoistic principle (420). For such a person, 'it cannot be proved that the difference between his own happiness and another's happiness is not *for him* all-important' (420). This insertion of 'for him'[87] is meant to indicate the space left for egoists to deny the exclusive rational supremacy of morality.

In his last chapter, Sidgwick clarifies the egoist's position.[88] He now distinguishes two egoist positions (420, 497): (1) Egocentric egoism. My happiness is most important to me: it

---

[86] '. . . the applicability of this argument depends on the manner in which the Egoistic first principle is formulated. If the Egoist strictly confines himself to stating his conviction that he ought to take his own happiness or pleasure as his ultimate end, there seems no opening for any line of reasoning to lead him to Universalistic Hedonism as a first principle; it cannot be proved that the difference between his own happiness and another's happiness is not for him all-important. [The preceding clause was added in [3].] In this case all that the Utilitarian can do is to effect as far as possible a reconciliation between the two principles, by expounding to the Egoist the sanctions of rules deduced from the Universalistic principle, . . . It is obvious that such an exposition has no tendency to make him accept the greatest happiness of the greatest number as his ultimate end; but only as a means to the end of his own happiness. It is therefore totally different from a proof (as above explained) of Universalistic Hedonism. When, however, the Egoist puts forward, implicitly or explicitly, the proposition that his happiness or pleasure is Good, not only for him but from the point of view of the Universe,—as (e.g.) by saying that "nature designed him to seek his own happiness",—it then becomes relevant to point out to him that his happiness cannot be a more important part of Good, taken universally, than the equal happiness of any other person. And thus, starting with his own principle, he may be brought to accept Universal happiness or pleasure as that which is absolutely and without qualification Good or Desirable: as an end, therefore, to which the action of a reasonable agent as such ought to be directed.' (420–1) In [1] 391, the passage from 'When, however, the Egoist . . .' continues as follows (reference letters added): 'When, however, the Egoist offers, either as a reason for his egoistic principle, or as another form of stating it, the proposition that his happiness or pleasure is (a) objectively desirable or good; he gives the ground needed for a proof. For we can then point out to him that his happiness cannot be (b) more objectively desirable or more of a good than the similar happiness of any other person: (c) the mere fact (if I may so put it) that he is he can have nothing to do with its objective desirability or goodness. Hence, starting with his own principle, he must accept the wider notion of universal happiness or pleasure as representing the real end of reason, the absolutely Good or Desirable: as the end, therefore, to which the action of a reasonable agent as such ought to be directed.' [2] 389 is similar to [1], except that at (b) it introduces the reference to 'a part of good, taken universally', in line with the appeal to Wholes in III xiii, and at (c) deletes 'the mere fact . . . goodness'. Later editions, beginning with [3] 381, add the reference to the point of view of the universe at (a), in line with [7] 382 (where [2] 355 just has 'a part of universal good' instead of 'the point of view of the universe').

[87] This is not in [1] or [2]. It is added in [3] 416.

[88] '. . . we have discussed the rational process . . . by which one who holds it reasonable to aim at his own greatest happiness may be determined to take Universal Happiness instead, as his ultimate standard of right conduct. We have seen, however, that the application of this process requires that the Egoist should affirm, implicitly or explicitly, that his own greatest happiness is not merely the rational ultimate end for himself, but a part of Universal Good: and he may avoid the proof of Utilitarianism by declining to affirm this. It would be contrary to Common Sense to deny that the distinction between any one individual and any other is real and fundamental, and that consequently "I" am concerned with the quality of my existence as an individual in a sense, fundamentally important, in which I am not concerned with the quality of the existence of other individuals: and this being so, I do not see how it can be proved that this distinction is not to be taken as fundamental in determining the ultimate end of rational action for an individual. . . . And further, even if a man admits the self-evidence of the principle of Rational Benevolence, he may still hold that his own happiness is an end which it is irrational for him to sacrifice to any other; and that therefore a harmony between the maxim of Prudence and the maxim of Rational Benevolence must be somehow demonstrated, if morality is to be made completely rational.' (497–8) This is added in [4]. As Hayward, *EPS*, ch. 5, points out, Sidgwick adds this clarification in reply to criticism by Von Gizycki. See 'Controversies', 44–5.

is rational for me to care most about my own happiness. (2) Impartial egoism. My happiness is most important 'from the point of view of the universe', so that it is rational without qualification that I care most about my own happiness.[89]

Impartial egoism can be refuted. Since it claims that prudence is rational from the impartial point of view, it is committed to Quantity and Extension, and hence to the utilitarian principle. Egocentric egoism, however, cannot be refuted by such arguments. Sidgwick's axioms capture the impartial point of view of the universe, but they do not override the egocentric point of view unless we have already agreed that the impartial point of view is supreme, and therefore overrides the egocentric point of view. We seem to have no reason to agree that the impartial view is supreme, either (i) from the egocentric point of view, which prefers itself, or (ii) from some third point of view outside both the egocentric and the impartial view—for there is no such third point of view.

In the light of these remarks, we should restrict the argument about prudence and benevolence to the impartial point of view. Quantity and Extension show why it is reasonable, from the impartial point of view, to be prudent, but they do not show why it is reasonable for me to be prudent. From the impartial point of view, we explain prudence through the two non-personal principles that also commit us to utilitarianism. But from the egocentric point of view, nothing else makes it reasonable for me to pursue my own overall interest.[90]

What does Sidgwick mean by saying that it is reasonable for me to do x?[91] We might take him to mean that it is reasonable that I do x, and hence that my doing x is reasonable. But if Sidgwick meant this, he would not be entitled to distinguish 'reasonable for me' from 'reasonable' simpliciter. Perhaps, then, he treats it as parallel to 'good for me'. We cannot validly argue that if it is good for me to do x, my doing x is good simpliciter. Similarly, in Sidgwick's view, we cannot validly argue that if it is reasonable for me to do x, my doing x is reasonable simpliciter. In that case, 'reasonable for me' seems to mean 'reasonable, relative to me', and the egocentric egoist evaluates actions by considering whether they are reasonable relative to him.

But this account of 'reasonable for me' still does not fit Sidgwick's argument; for it does not explain how both the egoist and the impartial point of view claim rational supremacy. If I claim only that pursuit of my own interest is reasonable, relative to me, I do not claim that it is either non-derivatively or supremely reasonable simpliciter, and hence I do not deny that morality is supremely reasonable.

We would deny that morality is supremely reasonable, if we denied that anything is supremely reasonable simpliciter. Perhaps 'reasonable relative to me' and 'impartially reasonable' exhaust the reasonable; everything reasonable is reasonable in one of these two respects, but nothing is reasonable in some further respect. According to this view, the question 'Is what is reasonable relative to me or what is impartially reasonable supremely

---

[89] In [1], he suggests that the mere fact that I am I as opposed to someone else cannot be a good reason for claiming that I ought to be treated differently from someone else ([1] 391). Later he suggests that this is a good argument from the impartial point of view, but not from the egocentric point of view, which considers what is most important to me.

[90] These reasons for taking Quantity and Wholes to express the impartial view raise doubts about Schneewind's attempt, *SEVMP* 361–4, to treat some of the axioms as supports for egoism. Schneewind does not treat the axioms as basically non-personal. But if they are non-personal, the attempt to restrict them to one's own good appears arbitrary.

[91] Moore and Broad on Sidgwick's argument; §1273.

reasonable?' has no interesting answer; for the last occurrence of 'reasonable' must be replaced by one of the two expansions of 'reasonable', and then we get uninteresting answers.

If this is what Sidgwick means, he has no dualism of practical reason. A dualism requires apparently contradictory claims to rational supremacy. But the claims that what is reasonable relative to me is supremely reasonable relative to me and what is impartially reasonable is impartially supremely reasonable do not contradict each other. Hence they do not create any 'ultimate and fundamental contradiction in our apparent intuitions of what is reasonable in conduct' (508); for the idea of what is supremely reasonable turns out to rest on a misunderstanding. In that case, the duality in practical reason is different from the one that Sidgwick describes, because it does not involve contradictory claims about what is reasonable all things considered.

We have still not seen, therefore, how Sidgwick's claims about the egoist point of view could justify his conclusion that two axioms of practical reason appear to be contradictory. His attempts to show that we have cogent reasons for regarding both self-interest and morality as rationally supreme are open to doubt.

1203. Agent-Relative Reasons?

Perhaps, however, Sidgwick's claims about what is most important 'for' a particular agent suggest a broader question. His argument to show that egocentric egoism is irrefutable may be applicable to more than egoism.[92] Perhaps he means that if I am concerned exclusively about what is important for me, arguments about what is most important from the universal point of view will be irrelevant to me; moreover, no principle superior to my concern for what is important to me and to the universal point of view proves that I ought to take the universal point of view. This may be true whether I take the pursuit of my own happiness to be the rational ultimate end for me or I think self-sacrifice and devotion to others is most important for me. In either case, I may be unmoved by what can be said from the universal point of view.

According to this interpretation, Sidgwick recognizes agent-relative and agent-neutral reasons.[93] An agent-relative reason for me to act depends on facts about me, and does not apply, as agent-neutral reasons do, to agents without such restrictions. My obligation to apologize is agent-relative, since it depends on whether I have given unnecessary offence,[94] whereas my obligation not to give unnecessary offence is agent-neutral, since it applies to everyone, irrespective of what they have done. Some agent-relative reasons apply to me because of who I am. Since everyone ought to take care of their own health, I am the one to whom this reason applies when my health is concerned. Hence I have reasons for me

---

[92] See Hurka, 'Moore', 611.

[93] On agent-relative reasons see Nagel, VN 153: 'If . . . the general form of a reason does include an essential reference to the person who has it, it is an agent-relative reason. For example, if it is a reason for anyone to do or want something that it would be in his interest, then that is a relative reason.' Cf. Parfit, RP 142–4.

[94] More exactly, my obligation to apologize depends on whether I or someone closely enough related to me has given the offence (to allow a British Prime Minister in the 21st century to apologize for the actions by the British government in the 19th century).

to take care of my health that are not automatically reasons for me to take care of other people's health or for others to take care of my health. On this pattern, the claim that I have a reason to promote my own good says that A has a reason to promote B's good if A = B. This reason is non-derivative in so far as it is not derived from the reasons that everyone has to promote people's good.

Perhaps, then, Sidgwick's argument to show that egocentric egoism cannot be refuted applies to agent-relative reasons 'for me'. If I am initially unwilling to take the universal agent-neutral point of view, I cannot be given a cogent reason for abandoning the agent-relative view and taking the universal view. If the reason that is offered is agent-relative, I do not abandon the agent-relative point of view; but if I am offered an agent-neutral reason, I will not be persuaded, since I have been given no reason to take such reasons seriously from an agent-relative point of view. I have no rational escape, then, from a purely agent-relative perspective.

The contrast between agent-relative and agent-neutral reasons may capture some of Sidgwick's grounds for introducing 'reasonable for him' in his account of practical reason. But the acceptance of these two types of reasons does not seem to support his position as a whole. Recognition of irreducibly agent-relative reasons is characteristic of common-sense morality and of dogmatic intuitionist pluralism. If we believe we have a duty to repay debts or to keep promises and that these duties are not simply means to fulfilling our agent-neutral duty to maximize utility, we reject utilitarianism. But if Sidgwick recognizes irreducibly agent-relative reasons that are not purely instrumental to agent-neutral utilitarian reasons, he has a good reason to believe that intuitionism conflicts with utilitarianism, so that he has not synthesized the two methods. If, then, we agree that an agent-relative egoist has no agent-relative reason to be an agent-neutral utilitarian, we should apparently also agree that an agent-relative intuitionist has no reason to be a utilitarian either.

Moreover, the introduction of agent-relativity does not explain all of Sidgwick's contrasts between egoistic and universal reason. Agent-relative reasons are impartial, and discernible from the 'point of view of the universe'. But we can see from an impartial point of view why it is reasonable that each person take care of their own health (since each person is normally in the best position to do this); these reasons 'for me' are no less reasons for everyone else in the same position as me. Nothing about agent-relative reasons casts doubt on the existence of agent-neutral reasons; and so recognition of both types of reasons does not confront us with any dualism.

Perhaps, then, we ought to look for an account of agent-relative reasons that explains why Sidgwick might suppose they rule out the recognition of ultimately reasonable agent-neutral reasons. We might take agent-relative reasons to depend not on facts about different people, but on concerns of different people. According to this view, what is reasonable for me is determined by what I care about, whereas what I care about is not subject to considerations of reasonableness in the same way. This restricted scope for appraisals of reasonableness rules out our claiming that it is reasonable for someone to act in ways that are unrelated to their antecedent concerns. Sidgwick would be right to claim that someone who recognizes only these agent-relative reasons cannot be given a reason for acting on agent-neutral reasons that are not relative to antecedent concerns.

This conception of agent-relative reasons, however, should not be welcome to Sidgwick. For his conception of practical reason throughout his book rejects the restricted notion of reasonableness that is implicit in the view that reasons are relative to concerns. The dualism of practical reason presupposes the belief in categorical reasonableness that he accepts from the beginning. Sidgwick cannot regard it as meaningless or misconceived to ask whether what is reasonable relative to my concerns is reasonable all things considered. He seems to have no good reason to affirm a dualism of practical reason.

1204. Why Does the Dualism Matter?

From his contrast between egocentric egoism and the impartial point of view of the universe, Sidgwick concludes: (i) No argument can persuade those who accept only egocentric reasons that they ought to occupy the impartial point of view or ought to recognize its supremacy. (ii) We have no reason to expect that the egocentric and the impartial points of view can be reconciled in principle. (iii) It remains an open question how far they can be expected to conflict in actual cases.

These conclusions appear to Sidgwick to undermine his whole attempt to systematize the outlook of practical reason. The egoistic principle and the utilitarian principle both appear to be axioms. But axioms cannot conflict, whereas these two principles conflict. Hence at most one of them can be an axiom, and we have no reason to regard either one as an axiom.

This estimate of the situation is puzzling, in the light of Sidgwick's discussion of axioms. When we try to find axioms, we look for principles that seem, on reflexion, to be ultimately reasonable; we do not look for principles that seem ultimately reasonable relative to a particular agent. The egocentric outlook seems ultimately reasonable only if it seems ultimately reasonable to do what is ultimately reasonable relative to an agent. But Sidgwick does not show that the egocentric principle is ultimately reasonable. He gives us, therefore, no reason to suppose that the egocentric principle defines a 'method of ethics', or that it is an apparent axiom that conflicts with the other apparent axioms.

This objection applies however we resolve the ambiguity in Sidgwick's conception of the 'ultimately' reasonable. If he is just speaking of non-derivative reasonableness, he has not shown that what is reasonable relative to an agent is non-derivatively reasonable. And even if he had shown that, he would not have shown that it is rationally supreme. Sidgwick has not shown, therefore, that we face a contradiction within practical reason. We may not be able to settle all the questions that arise about the comparative reasonableness of self-interest and morality. But the most plausible way to understand the questions does not present us with two principles that both claim rational supremacy.

Sidgwick does not seem to have identified the basis of a serious question about self-interest and morality. The question that Butler expects us to ask in a cool hour concerns the harmony of self-love and conscience; it does not assume that egoistic reasons are overriding. The assumption that egoistic reasons override moral reasons is common to Hobbes, Mandeville, and theological voluntarists, but other moralists do not accept it. One can ask reasonable questions about self-love and morality, but they do not introduce Sidgwick's dualism.[95]

---

[95] Sidgwick's reasons for accepting the dualism are discussed by Schultz, *HS* 213–47.

We do not face Sidgwick's conflict if we say simply that it is non-derivatively reasonable to follow both the egocentric and the utilitarian principle. If we recognize both the utilitarian and the egoist principle as ultimate principles that need no further justification, but we do not regard either as supreme, we do not face a contradiction, since neither principle professes to tell us what is supremely reasonable. We still face practical conflict. But practical conflict does not prove any fault in our theory. Even if we are utilitarians, we may find that on some occasions utilitarian considerations incline us in each of two conflicting directions, and that the balance of utility is not clear. In these cases, it will not be clear what our moral axiom requires. Similarly, if utilitarian and egoistic considerations sometimes incline us in different directions, it will not always be clear what it is supremely reasonable to do; but why should we expect that we will always have an answer to this question? Sidgwick does not show why practical conflicts between utilitarianism and egoism cast doubt on either principle.

1205. How Should the Dualism be Resolved?

Sidgwick believes that if we accept both the axiom of benevolence and the axiom of egoism, either we must admit that the two axioms are in conflict, and hence cannot both be axioms, or we must somehow show that they are extensionally equivalent. In support of the second option, he suggests that we may appeal to some claim about 'the moral government of the universe' (508). He leaves it an open question how far we are entitled to believe the relevant claim about the universe simply on the strength of our moral beliefs (509).

Sidgwick's solution to the conflict between the two alleged axioms does not match his presentation of the conflict. We face a conflict that threatens their axiomatic status only if we regard each of them as both ultimately reasonable and supreme, and they have contradictory implications. But if egoism and utilitarianism both claim to be supremely reasonable, and therefore conflict in principle, an appeal to cosmic order does not reconcile them.[96] If each principle claims to be ultimate and supreme, they seem to conflict, even if their practical consequences may, in some imagined circumstances, be the same. For utilitarianism requires me to take the general happiness as my ultimate end, and not to be exclusively concerned about my own happiness; egoism, however, requires me to be exclusively concerned about my own happiness. To act on one or other of these principles is to choose between two mutually exclusive views about what is ultimately and supremely reasonable; cosmic order does not change this fact.

If this is admitted, Sidgwick should not affirm that these alleged axioms are really axioms. For consistency with other axioms is a test for an axiom (341, 508). If two alleged axioms are inconsistent, at most one of them can be an axiom. Sidgwick thinks the appearance of inconsistency can be removed by appeal to cosmic order. But since the extensional equivalence ensured by cosmic order does not remove the inconsistency of the principles, the argument for their axiomatic status fails. Sidgwick argues that our attempt to frame a

---

[96] See Broad, *FTET* 253–6, Schneewind, *SEVMP* 372–4. I do not think Schneewind adequately answers all of Broad's questions about the priority of one axiom over the other.

perfect ideal of rational conduct fails unless we appeal to cosmic order.[97] He thereby suggests that an appeal to cosmic order might prevent this failure. But we have no reason to agree. We have created a dualism of practical reason as soon as we recognize two contradictory principles that claim rational supremacy, no matter what we say about their extensional equivalence.

On all these points, Sidgwick's discussion of the dualism of practical reason is puzzling. We have reason to doubt whether the difficulties he tries to solve are genuine difficulties for his position, as he has previously explained it. If they are genuine difficulties, his proposed solution does not solve them.[98]

1206. Questions about Sidgwick's Dualism

Even if Sidgwick's discussion of the egoistic and the utilitarian points of view is unsatisfactory, and even if he is wrong about the nature of the problems that it raises, some of the issues that he raises are important. For we may find it plausible to regard both morality and self-interest as non-derivatively reasonable, and we may sympathize with Butler's attempt to reconcile them. Does Sidgwick show that Butler fails?

Sidgwick makes the issues especially difficult for himself because he exaggerates the distance between the egoistic and the moral points of view. On the one hand, he identifies the moral point of view with utilitarianism, which is completely impartial and impersonal, and offers no special rights or assurances to any individual. On the other hand, he rejects any non-hedonistic form of egoism as too vague for any useful purpose. It is easy to see why actions that maximize the balance of pleasure within my own life are not likely to be those that maximize the balance of pleasure summed over all the lives of all sentient creatures.

If, however, we accept a non-hedonistic account of a person's good, we have a better prospect of showing that morality promotes it.[99] And if we accept a non-utilitarian account

---

[97] 'Hence the whole system of our beliefs as to the intrinsic reasonableness of conduct must fall, without a hypothesis unverifiable by experience reconciling the individual with the universal reason . . . If we reject this belief . . . the cosmos of duty is thus really reduced to a chaos: and the prolonged effort of the human intellect to frame a perfect ideal of rational conduct is seen to have been foredoomed to inevitable failure.' ([1] 473) In [1], this is the end of the book.

[98] Rashdall criticizes Sidgwick's dualism in *TGE* i 55. He believes that Sidgwick mistakenly separates the right from the good, since he takes the right and rational action to consist in promoting universal pleasure, but takes the good to consist in pleasure: 'Reason, we are told, requires us to act at times in a way contrary to our interest from love of the "right and reasonable as such"; yet we are to treat all other human beings but ourselves as incapable of rational desires, as beings for whom it is reasonable to desire nothing but pleasure. Moral action is rational action; and rational action consists in the gratifying of desires which, it is admitted, become irrational and immoral as soon as they collide with the general interest.' (55) Rashdall argues that the pursuit of my own pleasure can be rational for me only if does not conflict with other people's pleasure, and that a similar restriction must be imposed on each other person's pleasure that morality promotes as its end. Once this is conceded, we find that it cannot be reasonable in the same sense to pursue the egoistic and the universal end: 'If the Egoist is pronounced reasonable when he says "my pleasure is good", and the universalistic Hedonist equally reasonable when he says "the general pleasure is good", does that not show that the terms "reasonable" and "good" are really used in different senses?' (56) Rashdall argues that if 'reasonable' is applied to the egoist's end it can only refer to consistency or to purely instrumental rationality, which is not what Sidgwick intends in speaking of the reasonableness of pursuing the universal good. In reply to this objection, Sidgwick might reply that, in the first passage quoted above, Rashdall himself equivocates on 'rational'; the pursuit of my own good at the expense of the universal good is irrational only in the universal sense. But this reply gives further point to Rashdall's question about whether Sidgwick has shown that egoism and utilitarianism are rational in the same sense.

[99] Rashdall, 'Sidgwick', 221–3, develops this criticism of Sidgwick.

of morality, we have a better prospect of showing that it does not clash radically with a person's own good. Butler believes that morality includes the obligation to pursue one's own good, which is not subordinate to the demands of total utility. Kant argues that morality requires treatment of persons as ends, not merely as means. Neither Butler nor Kant accepts the utilitarian opposition to self-love within the moral point of view.

Sidgwick's arguments about the irremediable vagueness of non-hedonistic conceptions of self-interest, and about the difficulties of non-utilitarian morality, challenge the approach of Butler and Kant. But his challenge is open to objection. He makes his views of the nature of one's own good and the nature of morality more precise than the views of common sense. The difficulties that he faces show why the less precise views of common sense may be preferable.

But even if the contrast between self-love and morality is less stark than Sidgwick makes it seem, a question remains. For even a more complex conception of self-interest and a less self-sacrificing conception of morality may still leave a gap between the two points of view. Butler suggests that the two points of view can be reconciled in principle, since conscience takes the point of view of our whole nature, and morality best fulfils our whole nature. Kant defends Butler's position by arguing that morality expresses our conception of ourselves as free rational agents. Such arguments suggest that our concern for our self-interest is not fundamental, but rests on a further conception of ourselves that is fully expressed in the moral point of view.

Sidgwick does not cope with all possible defences of an agent-neutral point of view. He does not consider the possibility that once I examine the presuppositions of an agent-relative outlook, I find that it presupposes, or leads me to accept, the authority of agent-neutral reasons. Even if at first I do not see that I am committed to acceptance of agent-neutral reasons, further examination of my initial point of view may show me that I am committed to acceptance of them.

The types of argument that are available to us depend on our conception of agent-relative reasons. Reasons that are strictly relative to our concerns and desires do not exhaust good reasons for me. A rational person concerned with no one except herself still seeks to make her concerns and desires reasonable in the light of facts about herself and her situation. The reasons she appeals to in evaluating her concerns and desires are agent-relative to the extent that they appeal to facts about her. But they are not essentially confined to herself, as opposed to other agents of the same kind. If I appeal to reasons that refer to my age, sex, occupation, capacities, and so on, I appeal to reasons that refer to a person with these properties. These are reasons for this sort of person, not simply reasons for me.

Unless we have an unduly narrow conception of the reasons that an agent can appeal to in saying what is reasonable for her, we need not believe that an agent can find what is reasonable for her without finding what is reasonable simpliciter. Similarly, unless we have an unduly narrow conception of agent-relative reasons, we cannot find what is reasonable from an agent-relative point of view without finding what is reasonable from an agent-neutral point of view. Sidgwick's division between 'reasonable for me' and 'reasonable simpliciter' does not distinguish two irreducibly different types of reasons.

Butler does not see the difficulty that Sidgwick raises. Perhaps it does not arise for him. When we think about the authority of self-love, we see, according to Butler, that it is the authority of practical reason organizing our nature as a whole. It is part of our nature to accept the universal (non-egocentric) principles accepted by conscience. Self-love, we might say in Kantian terms, affirms the importance of treating oneself as an end in relation to particular passions. When we see that this is important, we can also see the importance of treating oneself as an end in relation to other people. The value that we attach to practical reason is revealed both in self-love and in morality. It is equally important for Butler that morality allows some reasonable scope for self-love. He distinguishes morality from benevolence partly to explain how morality protects my pursuit of my own interest. Even if morality does not always coincide with self-love, it does not require the suppression of self-love. For Sidgwick, no such solution is possible, since utilitarianism offers no protection to self-interest. Part of Sidgwick's difficulty, therefore, results from his conception of morality.

Can anything more be said to show that when we think about self-love more carefully we discover a reason for taking the universal point of view of morality more seriously? That would be a way to show that self-love itself leads us into the universal point of view, so that we may not face the dualism that disturbs Sidgwick. Bradley tries to answer this question.

1207. Prospects for Utilitarianism: Conservative Defences

Sidgwick shares with Mill the aim of vindicating a utilitarian theory, by showing that a defensible and recognizably utilitarian position can be separated from the questionable aspects of Benthamite utilitarianism. But he differs from Mill about the aspects of Benthamite utilitarianism that ought to be retained. Mill abandons Bentham's theory of value in order to further Bentham's aim of presenting utilitarianism as a critical and enlightened approach to moral and social reform. In Sidgwick's view, Mill really abandons utilitarianism.

In contrast to Mill, Sidgwick defends quantitative hedonism. He believes that the main fault in Benthamite utilitarianism is its acceptance of sentimentalist and voluntarist claims in meta-ethics. Contrary to previous rationalists, Sidgwick believes that rationalist meta-ethics allows a defence of quantitative hedonism. This defence, however, is costly; for it requires Sidgwick to abandon Mill's aim of defending the utilitarian approach to practical ethics. When Sidgwick explores the practical implications of quantitative universalistic hedonism, he admits that they are often obscure and uncertain, and may conflict with the views of those who would normally be recognized as morally enlightened people. In admitting all this, he admits that some criticisms of Benthamite hedonism are reasonable, and maintains, contrary to Mill, that a genuine utilitarian position remains open to such criticisms. These features of utilitarianism require caution in the application of utilitarian reasoning to practical questions, and even hesitation about the open advocacy of utilitarianism.

This part of Sidgwick's position brings him close to the 'old utilitarians' (as Grote calls them), who rely on utilitarianism to vindicate existing moral and political practices, not to criticize them. He does not go as far as to claim that utilitarianism justifies existing practices, but he concludes that it often casts doubt on attempts to criticize or to reform them.

Despite these implications of his position, Sidgwick believes it is the most defensible version of utilitarianism, and the most defensible version of any moral theory. If we agree that utilitarianism is the best hope for a moral theory, but we are also convinced by the objections to Sidgwick's version, we may conclude that our moral judgments cannot be systematized into any coherent theory. For he argues that no alternative theory is likely to find principles that meet his epistemological conditions. He seeks self-evident axioms—principles that can be understood and believed independently of prior moral convictions. Moreover, he requires these principles, together with available empirical information, to provide an effective method for resolving moral disputes and conflicts. No other theory seems likely to succeed where utilitarianism fails.

The conviction that utilitarianism is the best hope for a moral theory partly explains why some of Sidgwick's successors have tried to repair some of the faults in his argument. If we have understood the advantages as well as the disadvantages of Sidgwick's version of utilitarianism, we can more easily decide whether the later amendments really result in a more defensible version.

Sidgwick does not devote much space to the distinction between direct and indirect utilitarianism. But later utilitarians have argued that it supports Sidgwick's dialectical argument. Though particular acts that violate common-sense principles seem to be required by the principle of utility, we may promote utility better on the whole if we refuse to maximize utility in particular cases. The common-sense rules that conflict with direct utilitarianism can be given a utilitarian defence; and this defence seems to show that utilitarianism can cope with apparent counter-examples derived from common-sense principles.[100]

How much does this help? Some of the old objections still face indirect utilitarianism. If we can find an indirect utilitarian defence for a moral principle, is that the right reason for accepting the principle? This question revives the issue about utilitarianism and reasons. Moreover, if we assume quantitative hedonism, we find that some of the rules that would maximize pleasure seem likely to conflict with common-sense morality. These difficulties for indirect utilitarianism revive some of the difficulties for direct utilitarianism. To this extent, an indirect theory may not help utilitarianism.

The objections that arise from hedonism may support Mill's defence of utilitarianism without quantitative hedonism. We might try to substitute want-satisfaction or preference-satisfaction for the specifically hedonist doctrine of the good. For want-satisfaction seems to be an important element of welfare; and it may seem attractive to try to free the utilitarian commitment to maximizing human welfare from the rather narrow hedonist doctrine of what welfare consists in.

But while a conception of welfare as want-satisfaction may be useful for some purposes as a simplifying assumption, it is less useful in moral contexts. Some of people's preferences are bad for them. Sometimes we can manipulate people's preferences in circumstances where they would have been better off with different preferences. And if some preferences are bad enough, perhaps they should have no weight from the moral point of view. An appeal to preferences seems even less plausible than hedonism on some of the crucial points.

We might answer these objections by taking common-sense moral principles to be partly definitive of utility. If, for instance, we are convinced that some specified moral principles are true, and if we are also convinced that some form of utilitarianism must be true, then we might be willing to allow these moral principles to decide what maximizing utility consists

---

[100] Different versions of indirect utilitarianism are defended by Brandt, 'Credible', and Adams, 'Motive'.

in. We might exploit Mill's suggestion (though perhaps not in the sense that he intends) that secondary principles incorporate the experience of humanity in accumulating truths about utility. This move would answer the two difficulties we have raised. But it would force utilitarianism to give up the virtues that Sidgwick prizes: epistemological independence from ordinary moral convictions, and the prospect of an effective procedure for resolving conflicts. For the alternative view makes our conception of utility as clear or obscure as the relevant moral principles are.

1208. Prospects for Utilitarianism: Revisionary Defences

The introduction of indirect utilitarianism and the rejection of hedonism bring utilitarianism closer to ordinary morality, and so support the dialectical aspect of Sidgwick's argument. The other possible strategy is to argue for the rational acceptability of the crucial utilitarian principles, even if they conflict with ordinary morality. In this spirit, Parfit defends utilitarian indifference to distribution between persons. In his view, the opposition to such indifference rests on the assumption that the difference between persons is rationally significant; this is why we think it is morally significant whether a sacrifice of mine causes a greater benefit to me or to you. But are we right to think so?

If the difference between persons were rationally significant, prudential reasons would be rationally distinctive. I would therefore have a distinctive reason to prefer my more remote greater good over my closer but smaller good, but I would have no similar reason for preferring a greater good for you over a smaller good for me. According to Parfit, however, prudence is not distinctively rational. He suggests that if we prefer prudence over benevolence, we might as well prefer proximism (preferring my nearer future states over my more distant ones, simply because they are nearer) over prudence. If proximism is irrational, it is also irrational to prefer my welfare over the general welfare, just because it is mine.[101]

Parfit claims to strengthen this argument against prudence by showing that survival, rather than identity, is what matters in concern for the future; and since one person can survive in another, there is no reason to insist that there is anything special about the concern one should have for oneself. If Parfit is right, Sidgwick is wrong to suppose that there is anything especially rational about egoism, but his opponents are also wrong to suppose that utilitarianism ignores some morally significant division between persons. If this argument succeeds, it undermines an objection to utilitarianism.

The cost of accepting Parfit's argument, however, is severe. For Sidgwick's argument for benevolence rests on the rationality or apparent rationality of prudence (interpreted in Sidgwick's terms). If we reject his claims about prudence, we are left with no basis for recommending morality. If we are convinced by Parfit, we will deny that there is any rational intermediate position between proximism and benevolence; but Parfit's argument leaves us with no reason to prefer one of these extreme positions over the other. While it shows that benevolence may not be contrary to reason, it does not show why benevolence rather than proximism is rationally required.

---

[101] See Parfit, *RP*, chs. 6–9.

Parfit and Sidgwick agree on one point about prudence, that it is not ultimately and fundamentally rational. According to Sidgwick, it is apparently rational because it is an instance of Quantity and Extension, which are the fundamentally rational principles. But since it is an instance of these principles, it is more rational than proximism. That is why the apparent rationality of prudence can be used to show that we implicitly accept Extension, and therefore are committed to acceptance of utilitarianism. If Parfit were right, we would have no reason to take these crucial steps in Sidgwick's argument.

Parfit's argument, therefore, seems to warrant scepticism about morality rather than acceptance of utilitarianism. If we disagree with him, and believe that proximism is less rational than prudence, we may defend prudence by appealing to survival rather than identity. In that case, however, we may revive the objections to Sidgwick's conception of benevolence.

1209. Ideal Utilitarianism

The best defence of parts of utilitarianism may be the one that Sidgwick believes is the most hopeless. Rashdall's 'ideal utilitarianism' revives Mill's attempt to describe the utilitarian conception of the good in ways that may include aspects of value that are recognized in common morality, but excluded by quantitative hedonism. The good is constituted partly by distinctively moral values, not only by states and activities that can be recognized as good without any prior commitment to morality.[102] Though this position is not utilitarianism, as Sidgwick understands it, it contains a utilitarian element in so far as it accepts some degree of consequentialism in its conception of moral rightness.

The ideal utilitarian suggests that the objections to utilitarian arguments from consequences can be overcome once we build some moral constraints into the conception of the end that determines the sorts of consequences that we regard as desirable. This position is teleological, but it claims to have overcome the objections to consequentialism that result from a false identification of consequentialism with utilitarianism. Looked at from the other side, an ideal utilitarian tries to prevent our sympathy with consequentialism from misleading us into the belief that we must also accept strict utilitarianism.

Ideal utilitarianism cannot assert the independence and priority of the good in relation to morality. Sidgwick takes these assertions about the good to constitute a crucial theoretical advantage of utilitarianism. We may, however, question his demands for independence and priority. If an ideal utilitarian theory loses these features, that may not be a severe loss.

But does ideal utilitarianism disarm the most serious objections to consequentialism? If moral principles contain an essentially retrospective element, a purely consequentialist theory may fail to do justice to this element, no matter how many concessions it makes to moral value in its conception of desirable consequences. On the one hand, consequences

---

[102] Rashdall introduces his position as follows: 'This view of ethics, which combines the utilitarian principle that ethics must be teleological with a non-hedonistic view of the ethical end I propose to call Ideal Utilitarianism' (*TGE* i 184). Moore accepts this position in *PE* and *E*. Rashdall, however, departs further than Moore does from Sidgwick's view, in so far as Rashdall denies, and Moore affirms, that goodness is independent of rightness. Brink, *MRFE*, ch. 8, offers a brief account of a non-hedonist doctrine that he calls 'objective utilitarianism'.

seem to matter to moral rightness; to this extent defenders of ideal utilitarianism are right to claim that they defend an authentically utilitarian position. On the other hand, the line of argument that begins with Butler suggests strongly that a purely consequentialist conception of moral rightness commits the same error of reduction and over-simplification that underlies stricter forms of utilitarianism.

On this point, there is room for dispute about whether the most plausible elements of utilitarianism have been given their proper place in moral theory. But whatever we think on this question, Sidgwick's clear and detailed statement of a utilitarian theory presents a strong case against it.[103]

[103] Albee, *HEU* 417, comments on Mill and Sidgwick: '...these two eminent utilitarians...did their work so well that they helped their successors even to transcend the method of ethics for which they themselves stood'.

84

BRADLEY

1210. The British Idealists

Green and Bradley are the British idealists who most deserve the attention of a moral philosopher. From the mid-19th century to the early part of the 20th, Hegel was a significant philosophical influence in Britain, especially in Oxford and in Scotland.[1] But idealists other than Green and Bradley are either inferior or derivative[2] or less interested in moral philosophy.[3]

In contrast to Hegel, Green and Bradley treat ethics in its own right, not as a part of political theory or cultural history. Moreover, they do not rely explicitly on the rest of Hegel's philosophy. Bradley begins *Ethical Studies* from the views (he claims) of a fair-minded person reflecting on ordinary beliefs about freedom and morality; the distinctively Hegelian features of the theory emerge from the later stages of reflexion.[4]

Both Green and Bradley develop their position in dispute with the utilitarianism that they regard as the main contemporary rival. They connect utilitarianism with empiricism; this is one reason for Green's elaborate and hostile discussion of Hume. The dispute is two-sided. Sidgwick replies to Bradley's criticisms in the later editions of *Methods*, and reviews the first edition of *Ethical Studies*. Green is one of his targets in *Methods*, and, at greater length, in *Green, Spencer, and Martineau*.[5] We may hope that this debate between Sidgwick and his idealist opponents will throw some light on the main issues that bear on the plausibility of each position.

Green and Bradley argue that the most plausible alternative to utilitarianism combines the sound elements in Aristotle, Kant, and Hegel. We ought, in their view, to prefer this composite position to Kant's position, and to any development of Kant's position that rejects the teleological aspects of traditional naturalism and of Hegel.

---

[1] Quinton, 'Idealism', surveys the history of idealism in Britain.

[2] See, e.g., Bosanquet, *PIV*; Muirhead, *REM*. Bosanquet and Bradley are discussed by Sweet, 'Bosanquet'. Muirhead briefly surveys Moore, Prichard, Carritt, and Ross, from a point of view sympathetic to Green and Bradley.

[3] McTaggart, *NE*, chs. 64–8, discusses some metaphysical questions about value, but his concerns are different from those of Green and Bradley (in *ES*).

[4] Hegelian assumptions may well also influence Bradley implicitly at earlier stages in his argument.

[5] Schultz, *HS* 338–63, offers a favourable assessment of Sidgwick's critique of Green.

The idealists do not rely on the earlier English moral philosophers who oppose empiricism and utilitarianism. The rationalist moralists from Cudworth to Reid receive no attention from Bradley, and surprisingly little from Green. On this point, the idealists differ from Sidgwick, with unfortunate effects. For Sidgwick sees that Kant and utilitarianism are not the only positions worth considering, and he tries either to incorporate or to answer the arguments of his predecessors. The idealists, however, unjustly neglect most of English moral philosophy.[6]

If we recognize this neglect, we may evaluate the idealist position more accurately. If, for instance, we find that Bradley relies on points that are already familiar from Butler and the rationalists, we may be readier to take Bradley's arguments seriously. This evaluation does not treat Bradley as less Hegelian; for we have seen that some of Hegel's arguments are closer to those of some of his predecessors than they might appear in his presentation of them.

1211. The Impact of Idealism

In most English moral philosophy in the 20th-century, the prevalent view was that Kant offers the main alternative to utilitarianism. The idealist option was not found equally persuasive. Unfortunately, it was not subjected to the sort of criticism that would reveal the main reasons for rejecting it.

Why were Green and Bradley so widely neglected by their successors in moral philosophy? A partial explanation is the broader rejection of idealism in 20th-century Anglophone philosophy, beginning with Russell and Moore.[7] This is only a partial explanation, however. It is not clear that idealist ethics has to be discarded with the rest of idealism. Indeed, Green's moral and political philosophy was taken seriously even after Hegelian views had fallen out of favour in the rest of philosophy. It was still read and discussed in the 1920s and 1930s.[8] It received detailed, though selective and unsympathetic, criticism from Prichard and Plamenatz in the 1920s and 1930s.[9] Idealist views did not receive the sort of defence

---

[6] '. . . one of the unfortunate effects of the intellectual conquest of Britain by Germany has been the curious neglect of the very rich and valuable ethical literature which begins with Cumberland and Cudworth (or perhaps, taking dates of publication into account, one should say Samuel Clarke) and culminates in Richard Price. We might indeed have expected that men like Green and Bradley would have found a kindred spirit in the author of the *Sermons on Human Nature*; but in fact Bradley, as far as I can recollect, shows no knowledge of the British rationalistic moralists, and in the *Prolegomena to Ethics* Butler receives only the barest incidental mention.' (A. E. Taylor, 'Features', 273–4)

[7] See Hylton, *RIEAP*, esp. chs. 1–2 on Green and Bradley.

[8] Lamont, *IGMP* 19, remarks that he intends his book as a paraphrase and exposition of *PE*, and adds: '. . . until comparatively recently such explanations are probably all that would have been expected. Today, however, when Green's merits are apt to receive less recognition than they deserve, it may be felt that some apology is due for encouraging any tendency to retain the *Prolegomena* as a university text-book.' (19) In his defence of Green, Lamont asserts not only that 'it is undoubtedly the greatest treatise on moral philosophy produced by the British school of idealism', but also that 'there are few writings on ethics which compare with the *Prolegomena* for breadth and profundity of moral insight' (19–20). These remarks, in a book published in 1934, suggest that Lamont thought that attitudes to Green were changing. At the time, Lamont was a lecturer in Glasgow; he had an Oxford doctorate and had been a member of Balliol College, Oxford.

[9] See Prichard, 'Duty and interest' (1928) and 'Obligation' in *MODI*; Plamenatz, *CFPO*. Ross refers to Green's *PPO* at *RG* 50–2. Joseph shows more sympathy with some of Green's views in *SPE*, esp. ch. 9 (published in 1931, the year after Ross's *RG*).

that they deserved. Green died young, and Bradley withdrew almost completely from moral philosophy for fifty years, between the two editions of *Ethical Studies*.[10]

A more important and relevant reason for the comparatively slight impact of Green and Bradley on ethics is the impression they have often created of being a dead end. The reasons for this impression are different in the two cases.

The later sections of Bradley's book impose some strain on the reader who is used to Sidgwick or Mill. The chapter on 'My Station and its Duties' might be dismissed as an ultra-conservative rejection of critical moral theory.[11] The following chapters gradually lead away from morality to metaphysics and religion.

The same objections do not apply to Green. Many readers have found his tone inspiring. Others have found it disagreeably high-minded. Many have found his work thin in moral substance. The very title of *Prolegomena to Ethics* may have been discouraging, and its contents do not make it clear how we are to pass from prolegomena to ethics itself.[12] The general impression of vagueness and imprecision has suggested to some people that it is not worth-while to see whether anything further can be done with Green's principles. On this ground, Broad compares Green unfavourably with Sidgwick.[13] While probably no one now would go quite as far as Broad, the suggestion that anything true in Green is too vacuous to

---

[10] See Preface to *ES*, 2nd edn. (1927): 'Ethical Studies appeared in 1876, was soon out of print, and has never been re-published. For many years stray copies of the book have been eagerly sought for, but for students and the general public it has remained practically unobtainable.' In 1924, Bosanquet described the publication of *ES* as an 'epoch-making event' ('Life', 58). He is surprised that it has had so little influence: '. . . it still appears to me surprising that the strictly philosophical implications of this work have not produced a more complete transformation, not merely of ethical doctrine, but of the entire interpretation and stand-point from which the permanent value of Kantian ethics can and ought to be approached. It appears to me absolutely plain that by developing the conception of "law universal" into that of a concrete system, embodied in the actual whole of existing institutions, and yet furnishing through its particulars a content in which the universal end lives and grows within the individual will, a meaning is given to the Kantian ethical idea which Kant very likely would have disowned, but which really satisfies the theoretical demand which his system recognized but failed to meet.' (58) The moral that Bosanquet draws from Bradley might more easily be drawn from Green. To explain the lack of influence of *ES*, Bosanquet says: 'Partly its influence must have been diminished by the fact that it soon passed out of print and has remained inaccessible to most students ever since. One constantly observes that arguments and ideas derived from it appear unfamiliar to most writers of the day, and when reproduced by others, even if favourably received, are received as novelties. Partly too, I am convinced that the book, though brilliantly written, suffered from the excess of thought and experience which it contained. It is to most books of philosophy like Dickens or Meredith to most novels; a page of it would dilute into a hundred of any other.' (59) One might not look forward to a dilution and expansion of Meredith on this scale, but Bosanquet's remark on Bradley is apt.

[11] Rashdall's comments on Bradley throughout *TGE* are severe, acute, and often entertaining. He observes, e.g., that 'Mr Bradley (who seems rarely to touch upon practical matters without violent and obvious exaggeration) has laid it down that for a man "to wish to be better than the world is already to be on the threshold of immorality". . . It would be truer to say that the man who is content to be as moral as his neighbours has already passed considerably beyond that threshold.' (ii 158) It is not surprising that Rashdall comments in general: 'I have so frequently criticized the writings of Mr F.H. Bradley that I should like to say that, fundamentally as I dissent from his ultimate position, I believe that no one has a deeper sense than myself of personal obligation to his brilliant writings, or a deeper appreciation of the stimulus which he has given to philosophical progress . . . Unfortunately, ethics seems to me precisely the side of philosophy on which his influence has been least salutary.' (i, pp. vii–viii) This critical attitude to Bradley contrasts sharply with Rashdall's sympathy for both Sidgwick and Green. A fairer account of Bradley's ethics is offered by Wollheim, *FHB*, ch. 6.

[12] We learn from A. C. Bradley's Preface to *PE* that Green chose this title.

[13] 'Even a thoroughly second-rate thinker like T. H. Green, by diffusing a grateful and comforting aroma of ethical "uplift", has probably made far more undergraduates into prigs than Sidgwick will ever make into philosophers.' (Broad, *FTET* 144) Broad's judgment is fairly criticized by Lamont, *IGMP* 21 (just after the defence of Green quoted above): '. . . I am sure that, of Sidgwick's many distinguished disciples, past and preset, not one would endorse Dr Broad's estimate of Green'. In Lamont's view, 'That Green was a great philosopher will be admitted by all who have devoted much time to the study of his work' (20).

be helpful in thinking about morality might be widely accepted, perhaps even by those who have bothered to read what he says. On this point, they agree with one of Sidgwick's main objections.[14]

We may reasonably ask whether Green's general principles can be shown to yield reasonably definite moral implications. The difficulty here is not that Green says nothing about their moral implications; it is clear, for instance, that he favours individual freedom, and the intervention of the state in certain areas to secure the welfare of its citizens. These views are not commonplaces, from the point of view of his contemporaries or of the present. The difficulty is that he does not say much to show that his general claims about self-realization support the concrete moral views he holds.

To answer this question, we need to ask another one: what standard of definiteness should we impose on a theory like Green's? We have seen reasons for doubting Sidgwick's conditions for definiteness; utilitarianism achieves his conditions only at the cost of theoretical flaws.[15] We ought not to assume that we know, in advance of formulating or examining different moral theories, the appropriate standard of definiteness. We should be willing to adjust our expectations, if we recognize truth as a distinct property of a theory from its usefulness in answering detailed questions. Utilitarians ought to accept this distinction; they often point out that if we do not like the results of a utilitarian theory, we must recognize that the truth is not always what we would like it to be.[16] Parallel considerations suggest that a utilitarian cannot reasonably hold every theory to some pre-theoretical demand for definiteness and pragmatic usefulness.

Still, some types of indefiniteness would indeed disqualify a theory from serious consideration. If, for instance, the Idealist position left us entirely unable to make any progress on the main questions that divide different moral theories, it would be useless. This is the point of Sidgwick's objection that Green's position seems to give us no more than 'a form into which almost any ethical system may be thrown, without modifying its essential characteristics' (*ME* 95).[17] If Green and Bradley are open to this objection, their views do not contribute much to moral philosophy.

1212. Differences Between Bradley and Green

It is difficult to settle questions of temporal priority and mutual influence between Bradley's *Ethical Studies* and Green's *Prolegomena*.[18] Many of their arguments are quite similar, and both positions seem open to many of the same objections. But it is worthwhile to discuss them separately, since they emphasize different points and develop the same points differently.

---

[14] More recently Green has been ably defended by Thomas, *MPG*, and Brink, *PCG* (and his edn. of *PE*).

[15] Sidgwick and definite answers; §1177.   [16] See, e.g., Railton, cited in §1368.

[17] Sidgwick on Green; §1164.

[18] *ES* appeared in 1876; Green's *PE* was not published until 1883. *PE* was based on Green's lectures from 1877 onwards. Parts of Green's *LK* belong to lectures of 1878–9 (Nettleship's note, *CW* ii 82). Green does not refer to *ES*, though he had apparently read at least some of the essays before they were published; see *CW* v 465 (letter probably from 1876). Bradley mentions his debt to Oxford idealism (*CE* 3), but it is not clear how much he knew of the content of *PE* from his knowledge of Green's views before 1877. At *ES* 96n, he acknowledges Green's earlier work. These references do not undermine Taylor's judgment that *ES* and *PE* 'seem to be virtually independent' ('Bradley', 464).

Moreover, they differ on some important issues, and do not present a single idealist position. Bradley is much closer to Hegel than Green is. Green is more sympathetic than Bradley and Hegel are to Greek eudaemonism and to Kant. He does not treat these views as simply one-sided approaches to the truth, as Hegel does; he treats them as statements of the truth that need to be clarified.

On Greek eudaemonism, it is not easy to say how far Bradley agrees with Green. He is silent about Hegel's belief in the deep gulf fixed between the Greeks and us.[19] He believes the Greeks are right about the basic question of ethics.[20] But he does not rely explicitly, as Green does, on Greek ethics as a support for his own argument. The role that Green ascribes to Greek ethics is a distinctive feature of his theory. On Kant, the difference between Bradley and Green is much clearer. Bradley's criticism of Kant follows Hegel quite closely, whereas Green does not seem to rely on Hegel at all.

1213. Free Will, Responsibility, and the Self

Bradley begins with the vulgar notion of responsibility because it rests on a conception of the self that both the standard accounts of responsibility ignore. They are wrong to neglect this conception of the self, because it contains the outline of the truth.

Libertarian indeterminists, as Bradley understands them, believe that I am free not only to do what I choose, but also to choose what to choose and to will what to will; and they suppose that if any antecedent conditions determine my will, my will is not free. And so, if a will is free, no reason or consideration can determine it one way or the other. Bradley objects that this view makes choice and decision arbitrary; any good reason that was responsible for my deciding one way rather than another would thereby 'determine' it, and so would destroy freedom. Hegel calls this kind of freedom 'arbitrariness' (PR §15), since the rejection of any determining condition implies the rejection of any normal basis for decision.

Not all versions of a libertarian view are evidently open to these objections. Reid, for instance, believes that his version of libertarianism affirms the central role that Bradley demands for the self. Libertarians who appeal, as Reid sometimes seems to appeal, to 'agent causation' recognize the role of the self and of the agency that is distinct from a sequence of events.[21] Moreover, Bradley does not show that ordinary beliefs about the influence of character on actions presuppose deterministic causation; perhaps they assume causal tendencies that might occasionally fail.

Still, Bradley raises a plausible objection. Reid agrees that an account of free will should reject the dissolution of the self into a series of events, and should safeguard the causal role of the self in action. Why does this role require indeterminism? And why does the self lack this role if its influence is fully determined? As long as the self has real causal efficacy, does it not express our freedom, even if its choices are fully determined? The emphasis that Green and Bradley lay on the self as the subject of choice and responsibility suggests that the truth of determinism might not matter.

---

[19] See *ES* 125–6, 140–1.
[20] '. . . now for us (as it was for Hellas) the main question is: There being some end, what is that end?' (*ES* 81)
[21] Reid and agent causation; §833.

These questions about libertarian views also raise doubts about the version of determinism that Bradley and Green reject. This version removes any central role for the self in willing. It supposes that our actions can be predicted from facts and conditions about us that do not mention our self-expressing will and decision. Whether the determinists' story mentions environment, impulses, sensations, or physiological states, it leaves out (according to Bradley) will and character; and so the essential components of decision and free action are lost.

Bradley is obscure, as Green is, on whether he thinks this dissolution of the self into events follows from all determinist accounts, or only from some. In his view, prediction of our actions on the basis of our character is no threat to responsibility.[22] What, then, is the objectionable form of prediction? At first, Bradley objects to all comprehensive predictive laws.[23] But he does not seem to reject comprehensive prediction in itself. Prediction of one's character and actions does not threaten responsibility any more than prediction of one's actions on the basis of one's character would threaten it (18). The doubts arise from the dissolution of the self.[24]

But what is dissolution? Bradley mentions different relations between the self and the not-self: (1) The genesis of the self from the not-self. (2) The deduction of the self from the not-self. (3) The disappearance of the self into selfless elements. These are not the same. If we build a car, we build it out of elements that are not a car. But we might find it difficult to deduce all the behaviour of the car from our knowledge of the most elementary components that it is made from. Even if we could do this, we would not have made the car disappear into non-cars. Much of its behaviour would be explained by its being a car, not by its being a collection of non-car elements; and this would still be true even if its behaviour could all somehow 'in principle' be predicted from complete knowledge of its components and its environment.

Similar questions arise when Bradley supports common sense by denying the possibility of a predictive science of human actions (21–6). It is not clear whether he rejects (1) a predictive science of human actions as such, or (2) a science of the movements that constitute human actions. It might be reasonable to conclude that the first sort of science would abolish responsibility. If a science that makes no mention of selves and characters in its explanatory scheme could explain every genuine fact that we explain by reference to selves and characters, we might indeed conclude that our actions and characters are fictions, with no significant explanatory role. But if we are to reach this conclusion, the putative science has to explain, and not merely predict.

But if Bradley has the second sort of science in mind, why should he take it to be a plausible basis for rejection of responsibility? For even if we can predict the physical movements that constitute putatively responsible actions, it does not follow that their

---

[22] 'the prediction which is not objected to, is mere simple prediction founded on knowledge of character' (*ES* 16).

[23] '. . . the ordinary man would probably be little short of horrified to find that the whole of his history, everything which as gone to settle his character, every element in the evolution which has made him what he is, had been foretold in detail before his birth.' (17).

[24] 'But what he was horrified at was to find the qualities of his being deduced from that which is not himself. He can not bear to see the genesis of himself, or his self in becoming. (18) . . . such prediction is, in a word, the construction of himself out of what is not himself; and that, as we saw, he cannot understand. If, from given data and from universal rules, another man can work out the generation of him like a sum in arithmetic, where is his self gone? It is invaded by another, broken up into selfless elements, put together again, mastered and handled, just as a poor dead thing is mastered by man.' (20).

properties as responsible actions are not genuine properties, or that they are not parts of genuine explanations of our actions. Mere prediction is not the same as explanation.[25]

Bradley means that a predictive and explanatory science that explained everything needing explanation about human action, but did not essentially refer to the causal influence of human selves and characters, would be a reasonable basis for the denial of responsibility. A determinist thesis that does not affirm the possibility of such a science does not undermine responsibility. Bradley, then, is right to maintain that some determinist accounts fail to recognize the essential role of the self and character, and that we are justified in rejecting such accounts, since we have no reason to believe that the causal influence we attribute to the self is illusory.

Some determinist accounts are open to Bradley's objection. Hobbes and Hume try to show that questions about responsibility raise no serious difficulties for determinism, because we have a sufficient basis for attributing responsibility whenever the causal chain goes through some appropriate internal state in the agent. Hobbes suggests that any desire will do. Hume is more careful, and argues that a durable state is needed, so that character has a special role in responsible action.[26] His appeal to permanence, however, does not replace an appeal to the will and the self. Durability alone does not determine the relation of a trait to an agent. If a trait is durable, but not subject to the influence of rational reflexion, its durability does not make the agent responsible for actions that result from this trait. A compatibilist emphasis on internal causation, even on durable internal causal tendencies, does not explain ordinary views about responsibility.

Bradley concludes that neither libertarians nor determinists can justify our beliefs about moral responsibility.[27] Beliefs about responsibility depend on a conception of the self that neither libertarians nor determinists can accommodate.

This result is relevant not only to questions about responsibility, but also to more general questions of philosophical method. If we find that the current philosophical theories are inconsistent with vulgar beliefs, we might conclude that, since vulgar beliefs underlie our moral practices, we should ignore philosophy.[28] Alternatively, we might conclude that we have exposed the falsity of vulgar superstition, and that we should replace it with enlightened philosophy. Bradley's conclusions may remind us of Hume's reactions to the sceptical arguments in the *Treatise*; in some moods, Hume believes he should abandon the vulgar beliefs, but when he is out of his study he retains them, even though he recognizes that they are rationally untenable.

In Bradley's view, however, these possible reactions do not exhaust the possibilities. For perhaps a plausible philosophical position can justify vulgar beliefs.[29] His candidate is Hegel's

[25] Bradley's objections to a science of human behaviour are worth comparing with Davidson's, in 'Mental events', and 'Psychology'.

[26] Hume on responsibility; §742.

[27] 'And our conclusion must be this, that of "the two great schools" which divide our philosophy, as the one, so the other stands out of relation to vulgar morality; that for both alike responsibility (as we believe in it) is a word altogether devoid of signification and impossible of explanation.' (40–1)

[28] '. . . we also should leave these philosophers to themselves, nor concern ourselves at all with their lofty proceedings' (41).

[29] 'But there remains still left a third moral, which, as I am informed, has been drawn by others; that if we are not able to rest with the vulgar, nor to shout in the battle of our two great schools, it might then be perhaps worth our while to remember that we live in an island, and that our national mind, if we do not enlarge it, may also grow insular; that

position. He does not expect to undermine the intuitive convictions that he sets out from; the apparently less 'extravagant' empiricists and utilitarians are the people who undermine intuitive convictions. He looks for a way to justify the intuitive convictions, once they are properly understood.

The vulgar notion of responsibility introduces us to the irreducible self. It also introduces us to distinctions among different states of the self. Responsibility requires some sort of freedom from certain kinds of external and internal determination. But it does not require unlimited freedom from determination. If I could not determine my actions by states of myself, I would not be free and responsible, since I could not assert myself in action. Hence we might conclude that freedom requires the capacity to assert myself. Since my self is different from your self, we might infer that my freedom consists in my capacity to assert my particular self; 'I am free when I assert my private will, the will peculiar to me' (57).

In Bradley's view, this claim about freedom does not discriminate appropriately among states of oneself. We are still not free, in his view, if we assert our private will but we are slaves of our lusts and do not express our true selves.[30] We might suspect him of equivocation here; for the sort of freedom that is relevant to responsibility may not seem to be the sort that concerns us when we speak of someone being a 'slave' of his lusts. Surely a slave of his lusts has the freedom that makes him responsible? Bradley speaks of his vices; but if he were really quite unable to refrain from acting on his lusts, he would not be vicious, but simply the victim of irresistible desires. Bradley seems not to recognize the importance of distinguishing negative from positive freedoms (as Kant understands them).[31]

Still, though Bradley moves too quickly here, he may be right to connect the freedom of responsibility with the freedom to assert a self that is distinct from particular impulses. Responsibility matters to us because we are responsive to reasons, and treatment of us as responsible agents offers us reasons that we can respond to. In forming our actions and our character by reasons we 'realize'—by putting it into practice—the self that is guided by these reasons. In this way, we seek to realize our rational selves.

If this is how we understand 'self-realization', Bradley is right to conclude that the realization of the true self is the aim of the free will. He supposes that this conclusion raises a further question: what is my true self? But we might wonder whether there is much more to say about this question. We might say that realizing my true self is simply realizing my rational plans, whatever they may be. Bradley thinks that this is too simple an answer. A fuller answer, in his view, takes us from questions about responsibility into more central questions of moral philosophy.

not far from us there lies (they say so) a world of thought, which, with all its variety, is neither one nor the other of our two philosophies, but whose battle is the battle of philosophy itself against two undying and opposite one-sidedness; a philosophy which *thinks* what the vulgar *believe*; a philosophy, lastly, which we have all refuted, and, having so cleared our conscience, some of us at least might take steps to understand.' (41)

[30] 'Suppose I am a glutton and a drunkard; in these vices I assert my private will; am I then free so far as a glutton and a drunkard, or am I a slave—the slave of my appetites? The answer must be, "The slave of his lusts is, so far, not a free man. The man is free who realizes his *true* self." Then the whole question is, What is this true self, and can it be found apart from something like law? . . . Reflexion shows us that what we call freedom is both positive and negative. There are then two questions—What am I to be free to assert? What am I to be free from? And these are answered by the answer to one question—What is my true self?' (57)

[31] Kant on negative and positive freedom; §943.

1214. Why Should I be Moral?

After this argument from responsibility to self-realization, Bradley lets go of self-realization for the moment, and turns to morality. He does not begin with theories of morality or with description of the moral phenomena that a theory might try to capture. Instead he begins with a question—'Why should I be moral?'—that might appear to belong at a later stage of the inquiry. If I ask this question, I must apparently have some conception of what is involved in being moral. Hence we might suppose that our answer to Bradley's question requires some discussion of moral theory.

Bradley, however, rejects this order of argument. In his view, his question is the right place to start, because it tells us something important about 'the moral point of view' (58). On the one hand, morality seems to provoke his question. For we assume that it is not a waste of time, but is rationally justifiable; hence there must surely be some point to being moral, and hence there must be some answer to Bradley's question. On the other hand, morality seems to disallow the question; if we suppose that we can appropriately ask it, we show that we do not understand 'the voice of the moral consciousness' (61).

If the question 'why?' seems both obviously reasonable and obviously illegitimate, we might suppose that it is ambiguous and that we need to distinguish the reasonable from the illegitimate question. This is also Bradley's strategy.[32] Though some of his discussion might appear to reject the why-question, he eventually shows that it can be understood as a reasonable question.

Virtue and the why-question seem incompatible because we believe two things: (1) Virtue is to be chosen for its own sake 'and not as a means to something beyond' (58). (2) To ask why virtue should be chosen is to ask for some end to which it is a means, and therefore to assume that it is to be chosen as a means to something beyond. Bradley supposes that most people who ask the why-question agree with (2) and therefore reject (1).

In presenting the issue this way, Bradley primarily has utilitarianism in mind. He is right to say that utilitarians accept (2) and reject (1). One might argue for utilitarianism by suggesting that if morality is a rational practice, there must be some point in being moral, and hence something that we achieve by it; if we could give no answer to that question, it would not be rational to take morality so seriously.

Bradley points out that this argument confronts a utilitarian with a choice (59–61). If we ask why we ought to pursue the end that morality promotes, the utilitarian might give either of two answers: (a) It is not rational to pursue maximum pleasure, since there is no further end to which maximum pleasure is a means. (b) It is inherently rational to pursue maximum pleasure in its own right, not because of its promotion of any further end. The first answer reflects a Humean view that there is nothing rational about pursuing one end rather than another. This answer might appeal to sentimentalist utilitarians, who simply assert that maximum pleasure appeals to our benevolent sentiments. The second answer is Sidgwick's alternative to sentimentalist utilitarianism. He believes we have an intuition of

---

[32] 'Both virtue and the asking Why? seem rational, and yet incompatible one with the other; and the better course will be, not forthwith to reject virtue in favour of the question, but rather to inquire concerning the nature of the Why?' (58–9)

the inherent rational desirability of maximum pleasure, and that we have no such intuition about virtue.

Neither utilitarian answer shows that virtue is not desirable for its own sake. If we are sentimentalists, we will say that it is no more rational or irrational to choose virtue for its own sake than to choose pleasure. Some sentimentalists—following Hume[33]—might claim that in fact we do not choose it for its own sake, but this claim is open to question. A rationalist has to rely on some argument similar to Sidgwick's argument to show that, on reflexion, pleasure is the only thing we think deserves choice for its own sake.[34]

Bradley shows that the appropriateness of the why-question does not give us a reason to accept utilitarianism; for the impartial application of the question does not clearly support an instrumental view of morality against a non-instrumental view. This is why Bradley believes that acceptance of the why-question for virtue and not for pleasure is simply a dogmatic preference for utilitarianism.[35] If utilitarians and their opponents engage in a competition of intuitions, to see whether utility or virtue is an end in itself, utilitarians do not seem the clear winners. On this point, Bradley agrees with Price and Reid against the utilitarian view that virtue must be instrumental to some further goal.

This part of the argument might suggest that Bradley means to reject the why-question. But even if we agree that the question asks about the instrumental usefulness of morality, he has not given a sufficient reason for believing that the moral consciousness rejects it. If we value morality only instrumentally, we are in conflict, as Bradley says, with the moral consciousness. But if we believe that the instrumental value of morality gives us a reason for being moral, but we also believe that its non-instrumental value gives us a sufficient reason for choosing it, how are we in conflict with the moral consciousness? Curiously, Bradley does not consider this position, even though Aristotle, Aquinas, Butler, Reid, and many theological moralists hold it. Butler, for instance, insists that the Epicurean, instrumental outlook is not the religious or the moral outlook on life; but he does not believe it is incompatible with the moral outlook on life to ask about the instrumental benefits of morality.

If we recall Butler's position, we notice that Bradley has no sufficient reason for claiming that application of the why-question to virtue prejudices the issue in favour of utilitarianism. The confusion in his position is clear in his description of the moral consciousness.[36] He is right to claim that, according to the moral consciousness, moral goodness requires choice of the morally good for its own sake, and prohibits choice of the good for nothing but its instrumental value. But neither of these claims supports his view that it is immoral even to consider the instrumental benefits of virtue, as Butler does. Bradley attacks the theological moralists who advocate the ' "do it or be damned" theory of morals' (62n), but he does not

[33] Hume on the motive to virtue; §767.

[34] Sidgwick, *ME* iii 14. See §1165. Bradley discusses the argument carefully (more carefully than he usually discusses Sidgwick) at *CE* 90–8.

[35] 'The question itself . . . can not be put, except in a form which assumes that the utilitarian answer is the only one which can possibly be given . . . The words "Why should I" mean "What shall I get by", "What motive have I for" this or that sort of conduct?' (61) Bradley quotes from J. F. Stephen, *LEF* 276.

[36] 'That consciousness, when unwarped by selfishness and not blinded by sophistry, is convinced that (a) to ask for the Why? is simple immorality; (b) to do good for its own sake is virtue, (c) to do it for some ulterior end or object, not itself good, is never virtue; and (d) never to act but for the sake of an end, other than doing well and right, is the mark of vice.' (62, reference letters added)

say whether he opposes Butler's position, or only opposes Paley's more extreme view that rewards and punishments provide the only reason for being virtuous. He gives no reason to believe that Butler's position is in itself immoral.

But in any case, we should not agree that the why-question confines us to consideration of the instrumental value of morality. The why-question prejudices the issue in favour of utilitarianism only if we assume that the instrumental value revealed by the Why-question is the only sort of value that belongs to morality.

So far Bradley's argument has reached a conclusion quite similar to that of Prichard's discussion of similar questions.[37] Prichard believes that most moral philosophers have gone astray by allowing the why-question. To disallow it, Prichard appeals to the common moral consciousness, which he takes Kant to express. Though Prichard does not mention Bradley, his account of the common moral consciousness is quite similar to Bradley's, and contains the same confusion as Bradley's. One might expect Bradley to infer, as Prichard infers, that we ought simply to reject any attempt to answer the why-question. Sometimes, indeed, he seems to reject it.[38] Rejection of the why-question supports a deontological doctrine asserting that morality is to be followed for its own sake, and that no further explanation or reason can be given.

Bradley, however, does not draw Prichard's deontological conclusion. He argues that the instrumental interpretation of the why-question is not the only legitimate interpretation.[39] Under one legitimate interpretation, the question simply asks whether our reason for being moral is instrumental or non-instrumental. It does not necessarily give a further reason for being moral. But Bradley also suggests that the question may help us to identify some further reason for being moral beyond the bare claim that morality is choiceworthy in itself.[40] If we form some conception of 'the end for man' and show that morality satisfies this conception, we understand why morality is to be chosen for its own sake. We may understand morality by seeing how it is a part of some larger end. As a part, it may contribute to the realization of the other parts of the end.

In these ways, we can answer the why-question without assuming a purely instrumental status for morality. In saying that I should be moral because morality is the whole or a part of the end for a human being, I connect morality with some end that I recognize as valuable for reasons that are not exclusively moral.

As Bradley recognizes, this understanding of the why-question aligns him with Aristotle. (He does not remark that it also aligns him with Aquinas.) He does not argue at this

[37] See Prichard, 'Mistake?', discussed in §1400. He does not mention Bradley in this context. He mentions him briefly at 'Obligation', 87, as one of those (his other example is Butler) about whom it is difficult to be sure what questions they are asking about morality.

[38] 'It is quite true that to ask Why should I be moral? is ipso facto to take one view of morality, is to assume that virtue is a means to something not itself.' (61)

[39] 'Is it not clear that, if you have any ethics, you must have an end which is above the Why? in the sense of What for?; and that, if this is so, the question is now, as it was two thousand years ago, Granted that there is an end, *what* is this end? And the asking that question, as reason and history both tell us, is not in itself the presupposing of a hedonistic answer, or any other answer.' (61) 'Has the question, Why should I be moral? no sense then, and is no positive answer possible? No, the question has no sense at all; it is simply unmeaning, unless it is equivalent to, *Is* morality an end in itself; and, if so, how and in what way is it an end?' (64)

[40] 'Is morality the same as the end for man, so that the two are convertible; or is morality one side, or aspect, or element of some end which is larger than itself? Is it the whole end from all points of view, or is it one view of the whole?' (64)

stage against the strictly deontological conclusion that Prichard draws, and does not defend the Aristotelian teleological conclusion. But his failure to consider Prichard's conclusion is reasonable. For Prichard's conclusion is warranted only if we cannot find an Aristotelian answer to the why-question, or if the answer is so empty that it is morally insignificant. We cannot decide whether the Aristotelian inquiry is futile until we see the results it offers. Prichard rejects the Aristotelian inquiry because he believes that it attributes purely instrumental status to morality. To see whether we can give a better reason than Prichard's, we need to see what the Aristotelian inquiry achieves.

1215. Introduction of Self-Realization

Bradley has argued that the right interpretation of the why-question, in accord with the moral consciousness, treats morality as the whole or a part of the ultimate end. He postpones the question about whole and part, and for now describes the end as self-realization.[41] The self that is dissolved or ignored by the two prevalent theories of responsibility is our aim in rational action. Genuinely free action aims at the realization of ourselves as rational agents (57). We seek the realization of our rational selves rather than the expression of passions and impulses. Bradley believes that a grasp of what we try to realize in rational action will clarify the end that is partly achieved by morality.

Bradley tries to articulate an account of self-realization and to show how morality realizes the self. Sidgwick misunderstands Bradley's appeal to self-realization, because he supposes that, in Bradley's view, a correct and complete account of self-realization allows an immoral way of life to realize the self. Bradley claims that this is a misunderstanding, because he seeks an account of self-realization that makes it clear that only the moral outlook realizes the self.[42]

Despite the importance that Bradley attaches to a correct account of self-realization, or perhaps because of it, his exposition and articulation are difficult to grasp. He is similar to Hegel and different from Green in so far as he expounds his position, including his conception of self-realization, dialectically. We start from a rough conception, and consider various attempts to articulate it; these attempts are open to objections that seem plausible at the level of understanding that we have reached. Sometimes Bradley ignores possible defences of the position being rejected, or ignores objections to the position he favours. Often he ignores them deliberately, reserving the replies or objections for a later stage of the discussion.

---

[41] 'What remains is to point out the most general expression for the end in itself, the ultimate practical "why"; and that we find in the word *self-realization*.' (64)

[42] Bradley protests against misinterpretations of his view that fail to take seriously his account of self-realization. In particular, Sidgwick's criticisms, in his view, are vitiated by misunderstanding: 'The fact that when I speak of self-realization "we naturally think of the realization or development into act of each one of the potentialities constituting the definite formed character of each individual" is not surprising, until we have learnt that there are other views than those which appear in the *Methods of Ethics* (72 ff). And this we very soon do if we proceed. I have written at some length on the good and the bad selves (*ES* vii); and on p. 161 I have repudiated distinctly Mr Sidgwick's understanding of the term. I thought I had left no doubt that characters might be partly bad, and that this was *not* what I meant by self-realization as = end.' (*CE* 678) Here and in his following comments on Sidgwick's review, Bradley insists that a proper understanding of self-realization makes his claims about morality plausible.

This point applies especially to his discussion of My Station and its Duties, which is sometimes taken to represent Bradley's view of the true conception of morality. Though he thinks it is superior to the Kantian and utilitarian theories, he does not take it to be beyond objection.[43] He passes beyond the morality of my station and its duties to ideal morality (Essay vi). But even then he has not given his final account of self-realization, which has to wait until the next essay (Essay vii). For Hegelian reasons, he believes that we can reach an adequate account only if we try inadequate accounts and appreciate their inadequacy.

It will be best to follow Bradley's order. We should begin with his preliminary discussion of self-realization in Essay ii, and then turn to his discussion of different conceptions of morality, before we consider his further remarks on self-realization.

1216. Self-Realization and the Moral Outlook

Bradley recognizes that his claims about self-realization may seem obviously false. He considers the objection that some ends fall outside myself, and therefore cannot be included in self-realization, even if I realize myself—in the minimal sense just described—in achieving them.[44] Bradley argues from the moral point of view, and specifically from the fact that the morally good person chooses the right action for its own sake. Even if the right action fails to achieve the result it aims at, it is still to be chosen for itself, and to this degree 'failure may be equivalent morally to success' (65).

Bradley's statement of his view contains the exaggeration or confusion that we have already found in his discussion of the moral consciousness. He speaks as though the moral point of view attaches no value to the external result pursued by the morally good person: 'The act for me means my act, and there is no end beyond the act' (65). To say this is to make it arbitrary that we regard one action as right rather than another. But this exaggeration or confusion does not undermine Bradley's whole argument. He is right to say that in morality we attach value to our doing the action for a specific reason, not simply to the result being achieved. We value the action retrospectively—for its relation to our will, as an expression of a specific rational choice—and not only because of the action that results from our choice, as a means to achieving further results.

To make this point clear, we might compare it with Sidgwick's discussion of non-instrumental value. Sidgwick recognizes that some people regard virtuous action as either a part or the whole of the ultimate good. He answers them by distinguishing the action from the consciousness, and arguing that action without consciousness lacks intrinsic value. He then asserts that all the intrinsic value must belong to consciousness (ME 397–400). We have seen that Sidgwick's argument is illegitimate; from the fact that the action lacks intrinsic value without consciousness we cannot infer that the consciousness alone without

---

[43] 'The theory which we have just exhibited . . . and over which perhaps we have heated ourselves a little, seems to us a great advance on anything we have had before, and indeed to be in the main satisfactory . . . None the less, however, must we consider this satisfaction neither ultimate, nor all-inclusive, nor anything but precarious.' (202) Wollheim, 'Self', 4–8, discusses Bradley's strategy, and emphasizes the limitations of 'My Station and its Duties'.

[44] ' "There surely are ends", it will be said, "which are not myself, which fall outside my activity, and which, nevertheless, I do realize, and think I ought to realize." We must try to show that this objection rests upon a misunderstanding, and, as a statement of fact, brings with it insuperable difficulties.' (ES 65)

the action has all the intrinsic value. We should allow the intrinsic value to belong to the action as an expression of a state of consciousness.

Sidgwick sees that this is a possible view, and tries to answer it.[45] He argues, against Bradley, that action, understood as the expression of the rational self, should be excluded from the ultimate good. This argument, however, depends on Sidgwick's questionable attempt to isolate our consciousness from the action we are conscious of, and to attribute all non-instrumental value to the bare consciousness without the conscious action. He gives no good reason for confining all non-instrumental value to bare consciousness. The failure of Sidgwick's argument supports Bradley's view that actions have non-instrumental value in so far as they realize a rational self and its aims.

If this is the right way to relate Bradley to Sidgwick, we can answer one of Sidgwick's objections to the conception of the good as self-realization.[46] He argues that it ought to be avoided in a discussion of the methods of ethics, because of its indefiniteness, which allows almost any ethical system to be subsumed under it (ME 91, 95). But his discussion of ultimate good shows that self-realization is not entirely uninformative. For if the good is self-realization, Sidgwick is wrong to claim that it is simply pleasure; and so he has to show that the good is not self-realization. He does not suggest that the concept of self-realization is so indefinite that a hedonist can allow that the good is self-realization.

If Sidgwick were right about the nature of the good, we ought to be able to abstract all the results we achieve from the rational will that achieves them, and this abstraction ought to show that all non-instrumental value is contained in the result rather than in the actions of the rational will. If, for instance, I value my benevolent action simply as a means of increasing your welfare, I ought to be able to imagine that some natural process, independent of anyone's will, increases your welfare in exactly the same way and to the same degree. In that situation, I ought to conclude that nothing of non-instrumental value has been lost. A parallel thought-experiment should convince me that if the effects on my consciousness of my actions could be achieved by some other process, nothing of non-instrumental value would be lost. But we have no reason to agree with Sidgwick's claim that we regard our agency simply as a means that might be replaced by other means to produce the same non-instrumental value. Therefore we have a good reason to agree with Bradley that we attribute non-instrumental value to self-realization in its own right, apart from its further results.

Bradley is right, therefore, to argue that moral consciousness suggests that we attach non-instrumental value to self-realization. But he does not rest his case simply on morality. He recognizes that some people (he has Mill in mind, without naming him) take non-instrumental concern for virtue to be parallel to a miser's non-instrumental concern for money—a non-rational growth from a desire that is originally instrumental (ES 66).[47] He

---

[45] From ME [5] onwards, Sidgwick notices and discusses the sort of view that Bradley defends. See ME 396, quoted and discussed in §1165. This section (from the beginning of §3 on 396 to the middle of §4 on 398) was revised in ME [5] and the quoted passage was added. Earlier editions had also revised this chapter significantly. Some revision was reasonable, since Bradley, CE 91, justly criticizes the argument of ME [1] on this point. Sidgwick's revisions, however, do not answer Bradley's basic criticism.

[46] It is unlikely that Bradley has Sidgwick specifically in mind. ES 128 implies that at least some of ES was written before ME [1] was published in 1874.

[47] See Mill, U iv 6.

therefore tries to explain self-realization independently of morality, and to show why it is the end of rational action.

1217. Self-Realization in Rational Action

Bradley argues that in rational action we try to realize the self.[48] He cannot legitimately argue from the mere fact that I am aware that an action realizes me in a certain way to the conclusion that self-realization is what I want. For he agrees that such an argument from awareness of the prospect of pleasure to the conclusion that pleasure is the end would be misconceived (67 and Essay vii). But does he make an analogous mistake when he claims that I really aim at self-realization?

After he has set aside the error that underlies hedonism, Bradley tries to show the legitimate place for self-realization.[49] But his claims may not inspire confidence. He speaks of feeling oneself affirmed in something not oneself, but what does this mean? We may be equally puzzled by Bradley's view of volition as 'the self-realization of an idea with which the self is identified' (CE 515).[50] He argues that successful willing is partial self-realization; when I act on my will, I achieve self-realization because I perform an action that I endorse, so that I identify myself with it.[51]

To decide whether Bradley does more than express obscurely the simple fact that when I act I achieve something that I had not previously achieved, we may return to his claims about the moral consciousness. In morality it is not trivial to claim that I value the self-realization in which the action consists; for I value the action not only because of what it achieves, but because it is the result of the will to do the right action. The same point, in his view, applies to rational action in general.

This point is clearest in the interconnexion of desires and aims.[52] If I want to climb Mount Everest, I want that as part of a life that involves my caring about certain things and realizing certain aims. It would be foolish to decide to climb Everest if I just happened to feel like

---

[48] '. . . let us try to show that what we do do is, perfectly or imperfectly, to realize ourselves, and that we can not possibly do anything else; that all we can realize is (accident apart) our ends, or the objects we desire; and that all we can desire is, in a word, self.' (ES 66)

[49] 'For all objects or ends have been associated with our satisfaction, or (more correctly) have been felt in and as ourselves, or we have felt ourselves therein; and the only reason why they move us now is that, when they are presented to our minds as motives, we do now feel ourselves asserted or affirmed in them. The essence of desire for an object would thus be the feeling of our affirmation in the idea of something not ourself, felt against the feeling of oneself as, without the object, void and negated; and it is the tension of the relation which produces motion. If so, then nothing is desired except that which is identified with ourselves, and we can aim at nothing, except in so far as we aim at ourselves in it.' (68)

[50] 'There is an existing not-self together with the idea of its change, and there is my self felt as one with this idea and in opposition to existence. And there follows normally the realization of the idea, and so of my self, in the actual change of the not-self; and this process must arise from the idea itself. And the process, at least to some extent, must be experienced by my self. In volition, if I attempt to find less than all this, I find that volition has disappeared.' (CE 516)

[51] 'The existence, we may say, is changed by the idea to itself, and in the same process the self as one with the idea realizes itself in the not-self. This process of self-realization must, up to a certain point, be experienced as such by the self, and the self must become aware also, however momentarily, of the resulting harmony and peace. My world in a completed volition is not merely something which is there for me and which agrees with itself. My world has become so far the existing expression and realization of my own self.' (CE 520)

[52] Green's holism about aims; §1236.

it; before setting out to do it, I should be confident that it really matters to me. I form the aim of climbing Everest as part of being a mountain-climber, or being someone who takes on difficult and challenging projects (etc.). I want this future result (climbing Everest) as part of a future self who takes it to be significant. If I will not care at all about it when I have done it, it is probably foolish to embark on it now. I aim at climbing Everest, therefore, in so far as it is significant for myself.

To explain why action realizes a self, Bradley assumes that we do not usually approach our choices with a completely fixed set of present and future aims and attitudes. Sometimes, admittedly, I can say that my desires will be relatively fixed. I know I will want food in the future, and so on the basis of this future desire it is reasonable for me to make some provision for eating tomorrow, and for eating in five years. But in other cases, the choice I make now will partly fix my future desires, and so I cannot discover the rational choice by simply thinking about what my future desires will be. If, for instance, I do not learn to play a violin, I will not want to set aside time for my violin practice later; but if I learn to play it, I will care about time for practice. I have two different potential selves now, and I realize one self rather than the other in the future. In this sense, as Bradley claims, rational action realizes a certain sort of self; it not only carries out the plan of some self, but also alters the self in the course of carrying out the plan.

If I recognize that different plans for the future lead to different changes in myself, and therefore to different possible futures for myself, I can hardly be indifferent to this fact. Prudence presupposes some concern about my future; but the future I am concerned about is not simply the satisfaction of desires I expect to have in the future. I recognize that I would be worse off with some desires than others, however completely the inferior desires might be satisfied. Self-concern presupposes concern for the realization of some capacities rather than others, not simply for the satisfaction of desires.

This may show that some concern for self-realization is basic, because elementary forms of rational desire presuppose it. But does concern for self-realization define an ultimate end, as Bradley supposes? To see whether he is right, we should examine his claims in the light of a reasonable conception of an ultimate end. As we have seen in our discussions of eudaemonism, an ultimate end need not be the only end we care about for its own sake, and it need not make everything else instrumental to it.[53] A reasonable conception treats an ultimate end as comprehensive. If, then, self-realization is the ultimate end, it should include other ends, and these other ends should be pursued partly as forms of self-realization.

Eudaemonism is defensible partly by appeal to holism. We may reasonably try to understand our aims, ends, and principles as a mutually supporting system rather than unconnected or conflicting demands. Similarly, if we recognize that self-realization is one legitimate end in the light of which we can appraise other ends, we may reasonably try to understand other ends so that they fit into a conception of self-realization.

This conclusion is weaker than the one that Bradley reaches; for he seems to regard the inclusion of other ends in self-realization as logically inescapable rather than rationally desirable. He seems to infer that since all free action involves self-identification, it must all aim at self-realization. This inference is unwarranted. The weaker conclusion about what is

---

[53] Aristotle on the ultimate end; §77.

rationally preferable still allows some principles and ends to impose rational demands that are independent of self-realization, or even conflict with it. But it is preferable not to have to recognize such principles, because they lead to further difficulties. Lack of mutual support deprives ends and principles of one form of rational defence. Conflict is a basis for objection; if, for instance, the acceptance of moral principles requires us to reject apparently powerful non-moral reasons, we may question the reasons that introduce such conflicts.[54]

This weaker conclusion is enough for the purposes of the main idealist argument. If we can form a reasonable conception of self-realization, we have some reason to prefer an account of morality that makes morality promote self-realization. This reason is not overriding; we may find that the demands of morality cannot be subordinated, even non-instrumentally, to self-realization. But we have some reason to see whether Bradley is right to claim that morality fits into self-realization.

1218. Realizing the Self as a Whole

These features of self-realization cast doubt on Sidgwick's objection that idealist claims about self-realization in rational action make no interesting difference to the content of a moral theory.[55] Sidgwick's claim conflicts with his attitude to self-realization in his account of non-instrumental value. But he might still be right to claim that appeals to self-realization tell us nothing about the content of morality itself. If the constraints of self-realization constrain the nature of morality, we must have some idea (even if incomplete) of what they are before we consider morality. Bradley specifies them further in Essay ii.

First, he argues that concern for realizing a self involves concern for a whole. Not every conception of ourselves actually realizes us, because not every conception takes account of our self as a whole.[56] Since the sense is a genuine whole, it is more than an aggregate or sequence of states; the whole that we aim at is an organic whole, not just the sum of its parts.[57]

If the self is an organic whole, self-realization has a structure that suits the organic structure of the self. This is a significant ethical conclusion. For an end suitable to a self that is an organic whole cannot be described in purely quantitative terms.[58] Bradley, therefore, rejects any conception of the good that ignores the organic conception of the self.[59]

---

[54] On the importance of harmony, see Green, 'Freedom', §24.   [55] See Sidgwick, §1164.

[56] 'Let us take this for granted, then; but is this what we mean by self-realization? Is the conclusion that, in trying to realize we try to realize some state of ourself, all that we are driving at? No, the self we try to realize is for us a whole, it is not a mere collection of states. . . . If we may presuppose in the reader a belief in the doctrine that what is wanted is a state of self, we wish, standing upon that, to urge further that the whole self is present in its states, and that therefore the whole self is the object aimed at; and this is what we mean by self-realization.' (ES 68)

[57] 'Can you possibly succeed in regarding the self as a collection, or stream, or train, or series, or aggregate? If you cannot think of it as a mere one, can you on the other hand think of it as a mere many, as mere ones; or are you not driven, whether you wish it or not, to regard it as a one in many, or a many in one? Are we not forced to look on the self as a whole, which is not merely the sum of its parts, nor yet some other particular beside them?' (68–9)

[58] 'Self-realization, as we saw, was the object of desire; and so, as above, on the one hand is the self, which we are forced to look on as a whole which is in its parts, as a living totality, as a universal present throughout, and constituted by its particulars . . . On the other side is the mere feeling self, the series of particular satisfactions . . .' (95)

[59] 'The point to observe is the heterogeneous nature of the self to be satisfied, and of the proposed satisfaction.' (95–6)

The heterogeneity of the organic self suggests that we cannot compare different goods and ends quantitatively. If we thought our good consisted in maximizing some quantity of pleasure, irrespective of what we take pleasure in, it would be reasonable, in some conceivable circumstances, to trade the pleasure we take in the welfare of our friends for some immense or prolonged aesthetic pleasure. Mere quantity, however, is not what we care about; we try to realize different aspects of ourselves in some connexion to each other. This is the point of the organic comparison. We would not give up our ability to walk for an extraordinarily acute sense of smell; each organ has some of its value because of its relation to the other organs and to their mutual support. Hence Bradley prefers an organic over a quantitative conception of self-realization.

1219. Realizing Selves by Realizing Capacities

The organic and heterogeneous character of the self implies that not every sort of whole achieves self-realization. Some mistaken conceptions of self-realization value the sort of whole that is achieved through harmony at the expense of the differences that constitute the heterogeneity of the self.[60] According to the view that Bradley attacks, we achieve self-realization if we form some organic conception of ourselves, irrespective of its content. On this view, an organic conception matters only because it gives us some integrated plan for our lives, so that each of our smaller-scale plans tends to support, not to undermine, our other plans. If every equally integrated plan equally achieves self-realization, we ought to sacrifice other things to achieve integration. But integration is easier to achieve if we include fewer elements; hence we ought to care about very few things and make sure that they fit together well.[61]

According to Bradley, this view of one's welfare makes the mistake of people who notice that it would be easier to construct a theory if it had to explain only a few observations. Such theorists might decide not to consider too many observations, so that they can have an elegant and tidy set of coherent beliefs. But they would be wrong; a theory should fit all the facts that need to be considered, or all the relevant facts.

A similar point holds, in Bradley's view, about self-realization. A harmonious plan for our lives is misguided if it leaves out many capacities that deserve to be actualized.[62] It is arbitrary, for instance, to identify ourselves with the fulfilment of our actual desires and preferences. For we have many capacities that the fulfilment of our actual desires will leave unfulfilled. Since our selves include these capacities, we have some reason to seek to fulfil our selves by realizing these capacities, not simply by fulfilling our actual desires.

Bradley's claim about realizing capacities is difficult to spell out satisfactorily. Some capacities seem trivial, or bad, or in some other way not worth fulfilling. Realizing my capacity to do various foolish things that would get me into the *Guinness Book of Records*

---

[60] 'Is a consistent view all that we want in theory? Is an harmonious life all that we want in practice? Certainly not. A doctrine must not only hold together, but it must hold the facts together as well.' (74)

[61] This idea of integration recalls Cynic views about the adaptation of desires to circumstances. See §37.

[62] 'It is no human ideal to lead "the life of an oyster". We have no right first to find out just what we happen to be and to have, and then to contract ourselves to that limit.' (74)

seems to be a parody of self-realization. Again, the capacity for extreme cruelty is a bad capacity. If we seek to realize capacities, how can we avoid the fulfilment of trivial or bad ones?

Any attempt to answer this question seems to raise a more basic difficulty in counting capacities. Is my capacity to play poker a different capacity from my capacity to play bridge? If it is, does self-realization require the fulfilment of both capacities? Or are they both instances of some more general capacity? And is this the capacity to play cards, or is it some still more general capacity that might also be fulfilled by playing chess? It is easy to present a long list of doubts about any attempt to work out a viable conception of self-realization, understood as the realization of capacities.

We might reply that self-realization consists in the fulfilment of important or valuable capacities, not just of any old capacities. But this answer invites further questions. An appeal to self-realization is supposed to be the basis of morality, not to presuppose morality; but can we distinguish important or valuable capacities on purely non-moral grounds? If not, and if we must appeal to morality at this stage, must an account of self-realization presuppose a good deal of morality?

Perhaps these doubts do not preclude appeals to self-realization. Many allegedly different capacities involve very similar mental or physical processes; raising my arm twice involves quite similar processes to raising my arm once, whereas raising my arm involves quite different processes from those involved in thinking about calculus. Some reasonable ways to classify capacities avoid the unwelcome result that we realize a significantly different capacity in every different action.

Moreover, Bradley's position does not require a full account of self-realization to be prior to any claims about morality. Bradley need only say that some views about self-realization underlie some of our beliefs about human welfare, and that these views about self-realization explain some aspects of morality. We may agree, for instance, that if people are forced to spend all their time in the struggle for mere existence and subsistence, they are harmed. The harm does not consist simply in the fact that they do not enjoy what they are doing.[63] If they did enjoy it, they might even be worse off in a certain respect; for they would not even recognize that they have capacities that could be fulfilled and are being left unfulfilled in this sort of existence. Bradley claims, then, that self-realization requires the full development of the full range of a person's capacities; this is how he rules out the life of an oyster (74).

1220. Realizing Selves as Infinite Wholes

To explain full self-realization and the full range of a person's capacities, Bradley maintains that the self is not merely a whole, but an infinite whole, so that self-realization involves the realization of an infinite whole as infinite (74). He does not think the mind is infinite either in the ordinary sense, that it is a finite series that has been added to without limit, or in the sense that it is something quite different from anything finite (77). He takes it to be infinite

---

[63] Cf. Sidgwick on the plasticity of desire, §1179.

in the sense that it is not limited by anything outside itself. A finite straight line is limited at each end by things outside it. A circle, by contrast, has no ends to mark its limits. Similarly, the infinite whole that is required by self-realization has no limits for it set by something outside itself.

On the basis of this conception of an infinite whole, Bradley advises us to realize ourselves as infinite wholes and to be specified wholly within ourselves.[64] Specification involves the different aspects of ourselves, as determined by the different sorts of activities that we choose; but what does it mean for this specification to fall within ourselves? Bradley recognizes an objection to his advice. We are finite, and must recognize things other than ourselves that require some actions rather than others in response to them. How can it be reasonable to aim at being specified wholly by ourselves?

We specify ourselves by ourselves in so far as we fall wholly within ourselves.[65] Bradley distinguishes parts of our lives in which we feel (as we might say) 'at home' from parts in which we feel 'alienated'. If we feel alienated in a part of our lives, we may still recognize this part as fulfilling aims that we value independently of these particular circumstances; but we think the action is imposed on us in some relevant sense by external circumstances.

Suppose, for instance, that someone threatens us with death unless we agree to be his slaves, and he requires us to be coal-miners in especially dangerous and unhealthy conditions.[66] If we accept slavery, we will do what we want to do and prefer to do, in so far as this is what we think better in the circumstances facing us. None the less, it is bad for us to be in that situation and to have to make that choice. Moreover, we choose to do something to which we attach no independent value. In such a case, we might say that what we do is alien to us, and we have it forced on us from outside; it is not a choice we want to have to make, and we are alienated from the action that we choose in that situation.

We may also consider a variation on this case. I am already doing what I prefer to do; I am a painter, and this is what I care about most. Then I am enslaved, but my new owner requires me to keep on doing what I was doing already. I have lost something because I have been enslaved; but I have not been forced to do something I would not have valued apart from being forced to choose it. Since this is precisely the activity that I would have most valued even outside these circumstances, it has not been forced on me by circumstances. In this case, I am not alienated from my activity, though it is still bad for me to be denied a certain sort of freedom.

This is why Bradley says we do not want to be limited by anything external, but want to fall wholly within ourselves. We do not want our actions to be simply the result of adaptation to external conditions; we also choose our actions to realize our capacities. This is sometimes and to some extent up to us. If we have to find enough money to support

[64] 'If the reader to whom this account of the infinite is new has found it in any way intelligible, I think he will see that there is some sense in it, when we say "Realize yourself as an infinite whole"; or, in other words, "Be specified in yourself, but not specified by anything foreign to yourself".' (78)

[65] 'It is not that I want to increase the mere quantity of my true self. It is that I wish to be nothing but my true self, to be rid of all external relations, to bring them all within me, and so to fall wholly within myself.' (79)

[66] This is the situation of Hobbesian agents, in so far as they have to respond to dangers and threats by choosing situations that they would prefer not to be in. Aristotle draws a relevant contrast at *Pol.* 1332a7–27, where he distinguishes the necessary from the fine (*kalon*).

ourselves, and if no occupation we can find allows us to do anything we could value for its own sake as part of our self-realization, then this whole aspect of our lives will be alienated activity. If, however, we see something worth choosing for itself in this or that occupation, it is less alienated activity. According to Bradley, we ought to conceive self-realization in such a way that, as far as possible, we see our lives realizing ourselves, not alienated from ourselves, as far as possible.

We have two different ways to reduce alienation and to come close to the condition of an infinite whole; either we can change our actions so that they are less alienated or we can change our conception of self-realization. Bradley relies on the second method of reducing alienation. This is a reasonable method, provided that it is not too elastic. Bradley does not suggest that we ought always to talk ourselves into removing alienation, no matter what objective conditions we find ourselves in, so that, for instance, slavery or oppression will not produce alienation once we change our view of them. Bradley has already rejected the excessively elastic view of self-realization. He argues that we ought not to concentrate wholly on moulding our desires to make them more harmonious or easier to satisfy. We would be making the same mistake if we were to mould our desires so that we found less of our lives alienated and more of them falling within ourselves.

The realization of the whole nature of the self is not independent of external circumstances. But it may not depend on them as much as we sometimes suppose it does. Some features of our lives that initially seem alienating, because they are unwelcome or frustrating to us given our actual desires, may turn out to promote self-realization, once we understand ourselves better. Bradley defends this claim about the relations to other people that are imposed by morality. Once we understand these claims better, and also understand ourselves better, we see that the claims of morality are not simply restraints that we have to submit to for Hobbesian reasons; they also allow actions that realize the whole nature of the self.

1221. Errors about Self-Realization

Now that we have clarified some aspects of Bradley's initial claims about self-realization, we may seek some further clarification through his criticism of other moralists, especially utilitarians and Kant. In *Ethical Studies*, he states this criticism by exposing the errors and exaggerations of different views of self-realization.[67]

Bradley's critical discussion has different purposes. It is a diagnosis of other people's errors, a further argument for the importance of self-realization, and a partial clarification of his claims about self-realization. He argues that his opponents do not recognize that they implicitly rely on a conception of the self and of self-realization. Once we see this, we can see why some of their claims are plausible, since their conception of the self is partly right. But some of their assumptions about the self are false, and these errors infect the rest of their ethical theory. Hence Bradley tries to show how many objectionable features of utilitarian and Kantian moral theory rest on mistaken assumptions about the

---

[67] Bradley omits this line of criticism in 'Hedonism'.

self. These assumptions help to explain why a theory seems correct to adherents who do not question their presuppositions about the self and about self-realization, and why the theory seems wrong once we look more deeply into the underlying conception of the self.

Bradley's use of these claims about self-realization helps to dispel the suspicion that both the concept and his partial explication of it are too vague to be of any use. They cannot be completely empty if they have the diagnostic and critical role that Bradley claims for them; for if we see that some moral theories fail because of their errors about self-realization, we can formulate some plausible necessary conditions for self-realization. Moreover, an appeal to self-realization does not simply expose other people's errors. Bradley claims that their errors are often the results of exaggeration rather than complete failure. Both utilitarian and Kantian views capture aspects of self-realization. When we see that some aspects are recognized by other theorists, we can be more confident that a better theory of self-realization ought to incorporate these aspects.[68]

Bradley criticizes other theorists by appealing to some basic features of self-realization that he has set out in his discussion of the will. He follows Hegel (*PR* §5–11) in distinguishing the particular impulses (the desire to eat, or sleep, or write a novel) from the universal form of will, which is the agent's consciousness of herself as a continuing self choosing her various projects, and so not wholly absorbed in any one of them. The particular impulses and desires provide the content for the universal form; they give us something to will and to do, and self-realization needs them. But the realization of the self is not simply the sum of the satisfactions of all the different impulses.

Idealist claims about the universal aspect of the self agree with Butler's and Reid's claims about superior principles, in contrast to particular passions.[69] As Butler and Reid suggest, the universal aspect of the self is not confined to the moral aspect, but is also present in self-love. Self-love is concerned with the universal in so far as it is concerned with a self that is present in one's different particular impulses, persists through them, and has some structure that makes it more than a collection of them. Bradley clarifies this universal aspect of the self by referring to the elements he has distinguished in his preliminary account: temporal continuity, structure, heterogeneity, and realization of capacities. Though these clarifications do not yet yield a precise conception, they tell us enough, in his view, to refute utilitarianism and Kant.

Sidgwick is wrong, therefore, to claim that we can fit any ethical theory into the constraints of self-realization without altering its essential content. He is right to say that different theories may incorporate conceptions of self-realization; simply having some conception of self-realization or other does not ensure that we will hold the correct moral theory, or even that we will hold one sort of moral theory rather than another. It does not follow, however, that self-realization is unimportant, or that one should not try to work out a correct account of it. Bradley argues that once we reflect more explicitly on this aspect of different theories, we can identify their different mistakes and we can see how to correct them.

---

[68] Similarly, Sidgwick appeals to other theorists in support of his claim to have found moral axioms: *ME* 384.
[69] Superior principles; §§683, 828.

1222. Utilitarianism

Many of Bradley's objections to utilitarianism are open to doubt, as his second thoughts acknowledge.[70] He sometimes admits the weakness of some of his objections to the practical application of utilitarian principles; he sees that sometimes he has criticized utilitarianism because of difficulties that confront any normative theory and do not count against any one theory in particular. But his main theoretical objections deserve consideration.

Bradley claims that the self to be realized is 'a whole which is in its parts, as a living totality, as a universal present throughout, and constituted by its particulars' (95). The hedonist conception of the good mistakenly identifies the self with 'the mere feeling self, the series of particular satisfactions'. The hedonist, therefore, 'has taken the universal in the sense of all its particulars' (98).

We reach a hedonist conception of the good from a one-sided conception of the self whose good it is supposed to be. The hedonist treats the self as a collection of desires for different particular objects, and develops a strategy for maximizing the satisfaction of these particular desires. Since hedonism ignores the universal aspect of the will, it overlooks the fact that the satisfaction of the self is something beyond the total satisfaction of impulses. Hedonists make this error because they do not notice that the self finds its satisfaction partly in a specific order and structure within which its various impulses are satisfied.

The hedonist is right to believe that pleasure is closely connected with the achievement of the end. If the end is self-realization, pleasure is important, because it is 'the felt assertion of the will or self' or 'felt self-realizedness' (131). Bradley suggests that perhaps there is no exercise of function (which he takes to be a part of self-realization) apart from some pleasure.[71] Because of this connexion between self-realization and pleasure, the anticipation of self-realization also causes the anticipation of pleasure, and this anticipation causes anticipatory pleasure in the anticipated self-realization and in the pleasure associated with it.

Psychological hedonists make two mistakes. First, they suppose that the end we aim at is the pleasure resulting from the self-realization, not the self-realization itself. Further, noticing the anticipatory pleasure we take before we act (as distinct from the pleasure we look forward to), they suppose that this pleasure is the motive to action. Bradley argues that the hedonist doctrine confuses the pleasure taken before the action, in anticipating the result of the action, with the pleasure taken in the result.

If hedonists agree with Sidgwick, so that they abandon psychological for prudential hedonism, the idealists still claim to see a mistake about the character of the self whose good is to be described. Both Bradley (*CE* 87) and Green (*PE* §364) recognize that Sidgwick is not a psychological hedonist, but they still reject his hedonist conception of the good. Bradley's objections are connected with a general difficulty in Sidgwick's conception of prudence. Sidgwick has to construe this in purely maximizing terms; he must suppose that the end

---

[70] See the square-bracketed footnotes added in the second edition of *ES* (after more than forty years), on 94, 101, 105, 107, 108, 110, 114, 116, 122.
[71] 'The function brings its own pleasure, however small, though the whole state may be painful.' (132)

is something homogeneous and non-organic that we realize simply to the extent that we increase some quantity of it. Sidgwick needs this maximizing conception of prudence, to show that we accept the principles (Wholes and Extension) that underlie the utilitarian principle.[72]

Bradley argues that Sidgwick is wrong about the good because he is wrong about the nature of the self whose good is being considered. Sidgwick believes that the good is homogeneous and non-organic. But the self is heterogeneous and organic. Since the self is heterogeneous, it matters what we take pleasure in. For instance, someone who had reduced his desires to very undemanding ones, and could train himself to get a great deal of pleasure from the satisfaction of them, would not necessarily achieve his good. In saying that the self has organic structure, we claim that we care about realizing some plan for ourselves that has some rational structure; we do not achieve this simply by gaining a great deal of pleasure from realizing one part of it. This is why it is not always reasonable to sacrifice some periods of our life for greater pleasure in other periods.

A hedonist might answer that most people actually get more pleasure from the satisfaction of a variety of desires; given the nature of the self, we cannot achieve maximum pleasure unless we realize the self as a whole. This more moderate form of hedonism, however, may undermine the original reason to take hedonism seriously. We may incline to hedonism because we think we can use a purely quantitative procedure to maximize pleasure. But if we need further judgments of comparative value in order to decide what maximizes pleasure, hedonism alone does not answer the questions it is meant to answer.[73]

Since we implicitly recognize the unity and structure of the self, the end we seek is 'some definite unity, some concrete whole that we can realize in our acts and carry out in our lives' (ES 95). The hedonist answer fails to satisfy the demand for structure.[74] If the hedonist's candidate for the good consists simply in the quantity realized in a series with no necessary internal structure, it is an unsatisfactory candidate.

Structure and permanence must, from the hedonist point of view, simply be means to the end of achieving pleasure. This relegation of non-hedonic ends to a purely instrumental status implies that the hedonist cannot believe he is realized in most of his life; for most of it will be a mere means to the episodes that he values for their own sakes. Bradley's objection to the hedonist attitude to morality applies more widely.[75] A hedonist agent is alienated from most of his actions and states, in the sense that he does not find himself in most of them; it is only in his pleasures, and not in his thoughts, choices, and actions themselves, that he can find himself realized.

Bradley turns to the hedonist's reasons for believing that we recognize the self-evidence of the claim that pleasure is the end. This is Sidgwick's intuitional argument for hedonism.

---

[72] Sidgwick on Extension; §1191.

[73] Bradley presents objections to Sidgwick's idea of maximum pleasure (CE 83–8, 125–7; ES 97–9). Some of these objections are no better than Green's; see §1238. Sidgwick replies in 'Hedonism'.

[74] 'How, then, if pleasures make no system, if they are a number of perishing particulars, can the whole that is sought be found in them? It is the old question, how find the universal in mere particulars? And the answer is the old answer, In the sum. The self is to be found, happiness, is to be realized, in the sum of the moments of the feeling self.' (ES 96–7)

[75] '...his morality is nothing to him as an end, but only as a means; and the bitterness of his lot is filled up by the thought, that the means he does not care for are always with him, and the end he lusts after away from him.' (99)

In Bradley's view, Sidgwick misinterprets genuine truths about pleasure that we can better explain without accepting hedonism. The hedonist argument claims to separate elements that are logically inseparable.[76] Pleasure necessarily follows the achievement of an end, and greater pleasure necessarily follows the achievement of a more highly valued end. Still, a preference for greater pleasure is not necessarily a preference for greater pleasure in abstraction from everything else; and an admission that an end is not worthwhile without pleasure is not an admission of the truth of hedonism.

Sidgwick's intuitional argument for hedonism, therefore, is not strong enough to undermine the previous points about self-realization. Its weakness is clear even if we do not initially favour the idealist claims about self-realization as the ultimate end. If we are persuaded by these claims, the weakness in Sidgwick's position is still clearer.

Once we reject Sidgwick's hedonism, we can also question his route to the dualism of practical reason. He assumes that the egocentric view that confines itself to consideration of what is 'reasonable for me', in a strictly agent-relative sense, is irrefutable. He believes this for two reasons:[77] (1) Nothing within my commitment to reasonableness for me requires me to consider, or to be guided by, what is reasonable simpliciter. But Sidgwick's argument for benevolence relies on the reasonableness simpliciter of his principles. Hence it cannot reach me. (2) If I consider only what is reasonable for me, I have no reason to consider for its own sake the interest of anyone other than myself.

We cast doubt on the first reason if we can show that a correct conception of myself includes some commitment to be guided by what is rational simpliciter. We can show this if we can show that I think of myself as a rational agent who is guided by standards of what is rational simpliciter; these standards go beyond what is conditionally rational in relation to the concerns or aims I happen to recognize. We cast doubt on the second reason if we can show, by appeal to what is reasonable for me, that the self-confined egoist conclusion does not follow. We can show this if we can show that a proper conception of reasonable aims for me, given my implicit conception of myself, requires concern for the interests of others for their own sake.

It is not clear which of Sidgwick's two reasons is Bradley's target; perhaps he does not distinguish them. Sometimes he seems to attack the second reason and to argue that, even if I confine myself to what is reasonable for me, I discover that, given the nature of my self, I have reason to pursue the interests of others for their own sake.[78] These claims about the self do not question the exclusive attachment to what is reasonable for me.

---

[76] 'To say, Function is the end, is by no means to say, Pleasure is not good. It is to say, Pleasure is an inseparable element in the human end, and in that sense is necessarily included in the end; and higher life implies pleasure for the reason that life without pleasure is inconceivable. What we hold to against every possible modification of Hedonism is that the standard and test is in higher and lower function, not in more or less pleasure. *If* anyone can prove that higher life means less or no surplus of pleasure, *then* he can fairly ask us to face the alternative.' (*CE* 97)

[77] Sidgwick's dualism; §1206.

[78] 'No doubt there is a method of arguing with the Egoist in the sense of the man who takes his self for his end. Argument is possible as to the nature of the self; and the Egoist may be convinced, perhaps, that he has made a mistake.' (*CE* 99) '. . . if the self to be realized is not exclusive of other selves, but on the contrary is determined, characterized, made what it is by relation to others; if my self which I aim at is the realization in me of a moral world which is a system of selves, an organism in which I am a member, and in whose life I live—then I cannot aim at my own well-being without aiming at that of others.' (*ES* 116)

In the same context, however, Bradley also seems to attack Sidgwick's first reason.[79] He suggests that, in discovering the real nature of my self, I do not remain within considerations of what is reasonable for me, but I also recognize a universal. We need to consider more precisely what Bradley means by this. But at least he means that we recognize ourselves as bound by principles that are not simply what each person sees as reasonable for himself; they are principles that we can all see as reasonable simpliciter. If this is what Bradley means, he implies that we can refute both of Sidgwick's reasons for the dualism of practical reason, if we examine the real character of the self and of self-realization.

In Bradley's view, recognition of moral principles involves more than the acceptance of some principles as conditionally reasonable for each of us, given our interests and concerns. The relevant principles must also be objectively reasonable. In believing this, Bradley aligns himself with Kant. Once we see how he takes Kant to have misunderstood this universal aspect of the self, we can see more clearly how he thinks it should be understood.

1223. Criticism of Kant

The error that Bradley attributes to Kant is excessive emphasis on the purely universal aspect of the self in opposition to the particular. Utilitarians consider only the satisfaction of particular passions, as though there were no superior principles making an essential difference to our self-realization. Kant, by contrast, isolates the rational superior principles from the particular passions that give them their content. Bradley does better than Hegel (or, at least, he is clearer than Hegel) in explaining how Kant's position is one-sided.

The critique of utilitarianism makes clear the points on which Kant is right. Bradley argues that we do not regard ourselves as homogeneous collections of impulses, and therefore we do not aim at purely quantitative satisfaction. Nor do we regard ourselves as mere individuals guided by considerations of what is reasonable for us (as Sidgwick puts it), relative to our individual desires and aims. Kant sees that we also recognize principles defining what is reasonable simpliciter for rational agents.

The initial exposition of self-realization suggests the main points on which Kant is wrong. Self-realization involves the realization of the self as an infinite whole, 'fitting the facts', and therefore realizing our capacities in some harmonious order. But Kant does not aim at the realization of the whole self, and does not regard morality as a way of realizing the whole self; for, in his view, different aspects of the self are too antagonistic to allow harmonious realization. In Bradley's view, Kant is right to suppose that Kantian morality requires the rejection and suppression of one conception of the self, but he is wrong to suppose that this is a correct conception of morality or of the self. This basic error is the source of Kant's more specific errors.

---

[79] After the passage just quoted, Bradley continues: 'The others are not mere means to me, but are involved in my essence; and this essence of myself, which is not only mine but embraces and stands above both me and this man and the other man, is superior to, and gives a law to us all, in a higher sense than the organism as a whole gives a law to the members. And this concrete and real universal makes the morality, which does exist, possible in theory as well as real in fact.' (116)

To identify these specific errors, Hegel and Bradley allege two main faults in Kant. They object to the emptiness of Kantian morality, claiming that Kant's separation of the form of a maxim from its content leaves no moral principle.[80] They also object to Kant's dualism. Kant requires the rational self to repress the non-rational self, and requires duty to suppress self-interest. These dualistic aspects of Kant assume a conflict between the moral and the non-moral that distorts the character of morality.

These objections expose Kant's basic mistake (as the idealists suppose) about morality and the self. If he had seen that we aim at the realization of the self as a whole, he would also have seen that the mere form of a maxim cannot provide a basic principle of morality. The form reflects only one aspect of the self—its rational, critical approach to desires; it pays no attention to the desires that should be reconciled and not simply criticized. If we neglect most of the self that is to be realized, our principles lack definite content. In trying to follow such principles, we deny other aspects of the self any claim to realization.

Both of the main criticisms of Kant lead to the same conclusion. Since the rational will aims at self-realization, and self-realization involves the whole self, we avoid Kantian emptiness and dualism. Both the emptiness and the dualism come from a partly correct, but partly erroneous Kantian conception of the self, and therefore from a partly erroneous conception of self-realization.

1224. Emptiness

According to Bradley, Kant excludes all matter from moral principles, and leaves only the form of a maxim. He leaves himself with nothing but the general requirement that our principle must be non-contradictory. Hence morality requires nothing more than acting consistently.[81] In Bradley's view, this conception of a moral requirement has no moral content, because it says that 'whatever act is self-consistent is legal', and hence any policy that does not contradict itself is morally permissible (155).

Kant's view, so understood, results in a self-contradiction. For it implies that the test of moral worth is whether an act is done to avoid contradiction.[82] This test leads to self-contradiction, because we cannot act for the sake of being consistent and for no other reason.[83] If we are to do any specific action, we must do it for the sake of something besides avoiding self-contradiction; hence we must have some desire to realize some particular content, and we cannot act for the sake of the form alone, if the formal aspect of a maxim is mere non-contradiction.[84]

---

[80] Schopenhauer presents this objection to Kant; see §1049.

[81] 'The standard, we saw, must be formal; it must exclude all possible content, because content is diversity; and hence the residue left to us for a standard is plainly identity, the identity which excludes diversity; and of this we can say only that it is, and that it does not contradict itself. Our practical maxim, then, is, Realize non-contradiction.' (148)

[82] 'Whatever act is self-consistent and is done for the sake of realizing self-consistency, and for the sake of nothing else, is moral.' (148)

[83] 'In its simplest form the contradiction is this. "Realize non-contradiction" is the order. But "non-contradiction" = bare form; "realize" = give content to: content contradicts form without content, and so "realize non-contradiction" means "realize a contradiction".' (151)

[84] For a similar argument about non-contradiction, see Hegel, *PR* §135.

These criticisms express Hegel's and Bradley's view about the meaning of Kant's remarks about contradiction in willing. Kant is committed (in their view) to this claim about the categorical imperative, because of his previous demands on a good will. Even if he wanted to give more content to the categorical imperative than Hegel and Bradley says he gives it, he might not be entitled to do this, given the purity of a Kantian good will.

We have already considered different interpretations of 'can will' in Kant's first formulation of the categorical imperative: (1) Schopenhauer supposes that Kant is thinking of what we can will from an egoistic point of view; and so he criticizes Kant for introducing a heteronomous motive at this point in his argument. (2) Hegel and Bradley suppose that Kant avoids heteronomy, and so they take 'can will' to mean 'can consistently choose'. This corresponds to Schopenhauer's view of what Kant ought to say, in contrast to what Kant says.

Neither interpretation is correct. When Kant asks what we can consistently will, he asks what we can consistently will from the point of view of a rational agent, apart from any empirical preferences. The question that we need to answer in order to understand the categorical imperative is different from Schopenhauer's and Bradley's questions. According to Schopenhauer, the question is 'What do you want in your own interest?' According to Bradley, the question is 'What is it consistent for you to want?' Kant's real question, however, is 'What can you accept from the point of view of a rational agent, apart from any empirical preferences?'

Kant answers that a rational agent as such chooses something more definite than mere consistency in choosing. A rational agent as such chooses to treat rational agents as ends in themselves rather than simply as means. We cannot tell what the Formula of Universal Law says without reference to the Formula of Humanity. Hence the Formula of Universal Law is not simply a demand for consistency.

This answer to Hegel and Bradley provokes their deeper question. For even if the Formula of Humanity gives some content to the categorical imperative, Kant may not be entitled to it. Given what he says about the purity of the moral will, perhaps the principle of treating persons as ends must be imported from outside the rational will itself, and so must rest on some desire or preference—perhaps some sympathy with others. In that case, the Formula of Humanity cannot be used within Kant's self-imposed limits.

According to Hegel and Bradley, Kant relies on mistaken abstraction; he identifies an essential aspect of rational willing, but speaks as though this could be the whole of rational willing by itself.[85] Hegel relies on his claim that the universal side of an action is the agent's intention in 'identifying herself' with the action.[86] In rational action, I do not merely want to do what I do. I also identify myself with the action: I actually approve of acting on the desire that I act on. Such action is to be contrasted with action on, for instance, some irresistible and unwelcome compulsion or addiction.

A further universal aspect of an action is present in moral action. An important element of morally mature agents is the fact that they accept moral requirements conscientiously. They can reflect on what they are told to do, and on their desire to follow a particular

---

[85] 'Duty itself in the moral self-consciousness is the essence of the universality of that consciousness, the way in which it is inwardly related to itself alone; all that is left to it, therefore, is abstract universality, and for its determinate character it has identity without content, or the abstractly positive, the indeterminate.' (Hegel, PR §135) On Hegel, see §1021.

[86] See Hegel, PR §119.

rule or instruction; they can decide whether or not to endorse it because it seems right to them when they compare it with their general view of what is right. Hegel believes that this reflective, individual acceptance is an essential element in the right attitude to morality. It is a 'universal' element in willing because it is common to all choices, with their various different contents. Moreover, if I act conscientiously, I do not regard this as a purely private preference, but I suppose that other people can be expected to respect it; I think of moral principles as having some claim on other people's acceptance.

Kant's error, according to Hegel, is to focus on these essential elements of rational action and moral action, and to suppose that they constitute a substantive principle of morality. Kant is right to say that as a rational agent I distinguish myself from a mere series of impulses and desires; I recognize myself as having a further attitude to these desires. On this basis, we can distinguish the rational from the purely sensuous self. Kant is also right to say that as a moral agent I regard myself as acting on some principle that is both 'subjective' and 'objective'. It is subjective because I accept it for myself, and do not just regard it as imposed by arbitrary authority. It is also objective because it claims other people's acceptance. But he is wrong to suppose that these essential elements in moral willing can be, or ought to be, isolated from the other elements and made the basis of a moral law.

In Kant's view, however, this description of the moral outlook does not go far enough. He believes that the moral outlook includes not only one's identification of oneself with one's action, conscientiousness, and an appeal to other people's agreement, but also some assumptions about the kind of consideration that is relevant and the kind of agreement that we expect. These further assumptions imply, in Kant's view, that the analysis of the moral outlook tells us more than Hegel and Bradley admit. Our conception of morality assumes that some considerations give equally good reasons for all rational agents as such. Kant argues these considerations involve treating rational agents as ends. Whether he is right or wrong, he does not seem to be open to the idealists' objection. They believe that the moral point of view contains only a general attitude of conscientiousness. Kant believes that it contains a critical point of view that separates acceptable from unacceptable moral principles. This critical point of view helps us to see that moral principles have to give reasons for rational agents as such, and that such reasons must treat persons as ends.

The objection that Kant's emphasis on form without matter prevents him from appealing to anything more than mere non-contradiction rests on a misunderstanding of his contrast between form and matter. He says 'the material of a practical principle is the object of the will' (*KpV* 27); it is what we aim at in this or that particular action. Kant says that if this object is the 'determining ground of the will, the rule of the will is subject to an empirical condition'. On the other hand, 'If all material of a law, i.e., every object of the will, considered as a ground of its determination, is abstracted from it, nothing remains except the mere form of giving universal law'.

Kant does not imply that we are not moved by any empirical desire or motive at all. He requires us to abstract from it 'considered as a ground of determination of the will'. If we are acting on a moral principle, the fact that some result of the action appeals to us on non-moral grounds cannot be our reason for doing the action. If the action appeals to us because it benefits us, or because we sympathize with other people, that sort of reason is inappropriate for morality. But it may still give us one reason for doing the action.

When Kant abstracts matter, he refers to empirical grounds of determination. He does not mean that the moral principle that is left has no content at all. Hence the contrast between form and matter is not the same as the contrast between form and moral content; for the form is an essential part of the moral content. The idealists suppose that when Kant is talking about the form of a maxim, he refers to something that is absolutely constant despite all variations in what the maxim actually tells us to do. Kant need not say this. He means that the moral content of a maxim is not determined by the empirical objects of desire that might attract us to the action. On the contrary, the aspect of the maxim that gives us moral reasons for the action is an aspect that appeals to rational agents as such.

The distinctive feature of Kant's view, overlooked in Hegel's and Bradley's objections, is the claim that the removal of empirical determining grounds does not eliminate all morally relevant content. If we consider what a rational agent as such has reason to accept, we can find reasons that have enough content to support some maxims and reject others. To see whether Kant has found these reasons, we need to see whether Kant has given sufficient reason to believe that the reasons we have for treating ourselves as ends are equally reasons for treating persons in general as ends.

Idealist criticism of the emptiness of the Kantian moral will is worth comparing with other people's criticism of the idealist conception of self-realization. The two lines of criticism are quite similar. The idealists suppose that Kant has no practically useful account of what rational agents will as such, because he abstracts from all the purely empirical aims of different people and he does not take any moral constraints for granted. Critics of the idealists suppose that self-realization has no practically useful content if we abstract from all the particular desires and capacities of different people, and we do not limit it by some presuppositions about morality. In reply to criticisms of self-realization, Bradley argues, from general claims about action, responsibility, and will, that we can find a practically useful account of self-realization. Kant argues, from some quite similar claims in these areas, that we can find a practically useful account of what rational agents will as such.

It is rash of Bradley, therefore, to criticize Kant for emptiness; he answers very similar criticisms in his own account of self-realization. The similarity between the two lines of criticism, and between the two lines of reply, suggests that Kantian claims about the will and idealist claims about self-realization have even more in common than Bradley realizes. Perhaps they appeal to the same facts about rational agency, and one account needs to be completed by the other. So far, we are in no position to justify this speculation. We must return to it later in the discussion of Bradley, and especially in the discussion of Green, who makes this common element in the Kantian and the idealist positions a central part of his main argument.

1225. Dualism

Idealists object to the Kantian 'dualist' claim that morality, as Kant conceives it, involves a permanent conflict between the moral and the non-moral self.[87] In Kantian morality, this

---

[87] 'The "empirical" self, this me, is no less than the self which is a formal will, an element of the moral subject. These elements are antithetical the one to the other; and hence the realization of the form is possible only through an

antagonism is permanent. As Bradley puts it, 'The lower self in morality is not led, nor coaxed, nor consulted, but forced' (147). Antagonism is essential to Kantian morality, since morality requires us to 'negate the sensuous self', but if the sensuous self is negated, the possibility of morality disappears (155). If we obey the categorical imperative, it leads to the destruction of the conditions that it presupposes, and hence it violates the requirement of non-contradiction. Just as promise-breaking requires the existence of promises, but also undermines it, so morality requires the existence of the sensuous self, but also undermines it.[88]

Bradley is wrong to claim that Kant requires permanent conflict between the rational and the sensuous self. He relies on a mistaken interpretation of Kant's remarks about acting from duty. In his view, Kant believes that an action has moral worth only if the agent's moral motive conflicts with all other motives (cf. Hegel, PR §124). Kant, however, argues that the moral motive must be sufficient even if other motives conflict with it; he does not insist that the other motives must actually conflict with the moral motive.

Still, Bradley raises a reasonable question. For Kant requires some connexion between a person's moral will and her non-moral motives. Awareness of the moral law ought to produce some feeling of 'respect' for the law. Bradley asks whether Kant can explain how we acquire the appropriate respect. This seems difficult for Kant. For respect is a favourable attitude; when we are aware of acting on the moral law, we feel some 'inner satisfaction', not in some ordinary source of pleasure, but in living up to our conception of our personal worth. Acting on the moral law is connected not only with feelings of guilt, but also with feelings of shame and self-esteem. We may 'feel guilty' or have 'guilt feelings' if we violate some norm that we do not really accept or care about; this is the sort of feeling that the non-moral self might easily have towards the moral law. But this is not all that Kant has in mind. He believes we also feel genuine guilt, of the sort that requires acknowledgment of the legitimacy of the norm we have violated. Moreover, he also believes that we legitimately feel some sort of pride in keeping the moral law (though in another respect it strikes down all pride); we are right to feel shame in failing to keep it, because we regard it as an ideal that we accept and feel committed to.

If these attitudes to the moral law involve our feelings, they involve the non-moral self. But Kant's description of non-moral motivation does not seem to make this intelligible; the non-moral self aims at maximum pleasure, and is moved by hypothetical imperatives that rest on this aim. If Kant cannot explain why the non-moral self is impressed by the moral law, he has too narrow a conception of the non-moral self. Indeed, if we agree with Reid and Butler, much of what Kant says about reason and motivation in the moral self could also be said about the non-moral self. We have already noticed that Kant's claims about practical

---

antagonism, an opposition which has to be overcome. It is this conflict and this victory in which the essence of morality lies. Morality is the activity of the formal self forcing the sensuous self, and here first can we attach a meaning to the words "ought" and "duty".' (Bradley, ES 146)

[88] Is Bradley's objection to Kantian dualism consistent with his objection to Kantian emptiness? His point seems to be this: (a) On the one hand, Kant sets out to negate the sensuous self, since morality is defined by its opposition to empirical motivation. (b) On the other hand, when he tries to spell out what morality can say once all empirical motivation has been excluded, he has nothing left but empty formalism. (c) Bradley goes even further and suggests that even the requirement of non-contradiction cannot be satisfied, since a successful effort to suppress the sensuous self would leave no sensuous self to suppress.

laws and categorical imperatives apply to the non-moral self no less than to morality, even though Kant confines them to morality. This tendency in Kant supports Bradley's criticism that Kant gives a mistakenly crude conception of the non-moral self.

If we were to correct this tendency in Kant, we would also call into question some of Kant's excessively sharp contrasts between his position and a eudaemonist view of moral and non-moral motives. As we saw before, doubts about these contrasts would reasonably incline us to try to reconcile Kant with the traditional naturalist views that he rejects. The prospects for such reconciliation can usefully be considered when we discuss Green's reconstruction of Kant.

1226. My Station and its Duties: Reconciliation of Morality with Self-Realization?

Bradley's essay 'My Station and its Duties' has two aims: (1) It offers an account of morality that embraces the correct elements in utilitarian and Kantian views and avoids their errors. (2) It advances Bradley's argument to show that morality, correctly understood, is an essential part of self-realization, correctly understood. The errors of utilitarian and Kantian ethics result from false conceptions of the self, and especially of the relation between the particular and the universal aspects of the self. Hence accounts of morality and of self-realization should clarify each other.

The discussion of utilitarianism and Kant leaves us with a sketch of the solution we seek. The realization of the good will is the end prescribed by morality; to show that morality realizes ourselves, we must show that realization of the good will is self-realization. In Bradley's view, we show this if we identify morality with my station and its duties.[89]

But is this even a distinct conception of morality? Will not every moral theory, including utilitarian and Kantian theories, recognize that morality is articulated in stations and duties—specific social roles (farmer, cook, police officer, etc.) with specific duties attached to them? A moral theory might tell us what sorts of stations and duties are morally required and morally permissible—whether, for instance, the institutions that administer punishment should discriminate between innocent and guilty. But the mere recognition of stations and duties does not seem to be controversial.

We would take a more controversial moral position if we were to say that one's moral outlook ought to be that of the stations and duties of one's particular society,[90] and that one ought not to look outside it. To take this view is to reject utilitarianism and Kantianism

---

[89] '... the end is the realization of the good will which is superior to ourselves; and again the end is self-realization. Bringing these together, we see that the end is the realization of ourselves as the will which is above ourselves. And this will (if morality exists) we saw must be "objective", because not dependent on "subjective" liking; and "universal", because not identifiable with any particular, but standing above all actual and possible particulars. ... It is a concrete universal, because it not only is above but is within and throughout its details, and is so far only as they are.' (162)

[90] In his later thoughts (169n, 170n, 173n), Bradley recognizes that he is not clear about the nature of the social whole within which the stations and duties are assigned—whether it is one of Hegel's three (family, civil society, state), or something else.

because they are critical attitudes to morality; they criticize 'positive' morality—existing moral outlooks or practices—by reference to some principles external to it.[91]

Perhaps, then, Bradley affirms the futility of critical moral theory. Perhaps the morality of my station and its duties implies that there is nothing more to morality than positive morality, consisting in the moral practices and outlook of our particular society. If there are different societies, there are different positive moralities, but there is no true morality outside them.[92]

We might, however, take a different view about the relation of stations and duties to morality. To say that morality consists of stations and duties is to insist that it achieves its point and aim only in so far as it defines a system of moral duties specifying social roles. Bradley understands this system as a social organism. An organic self is an infinite whole because it embraces the different capacities of the self in its way of life. Similarly, then, an organic state embraces the self-realization of its members.[93]

According to this view, the demand for a morality of stations and duties sets a task for a moral theory. The correct moral theory will not specify rules for the maximizing of utility, or for the protection of specific rights and the fulfilment of specific obligations; it will specify a range of stations and duties that realize each member of the community that includes these stations and duties. The positive morality of an actual community may not include the stations and duties that realize all the individual members.

If this is Bradley's position, he seems to hold a teleological conception of morality. Instead of saying that it ought to aim at maximum utility, he seems to revive the view that it ought to aim at the common good of its members, understood as their self-realization. But this description of his position is misleading, if taken by itself. For he does not believe that the social organism is simply a means to self-realization. Nor can the demands of self-realization provide us with a list of requirements for a morally appropriate society. The view that we can assess societies by such lists of independent requirements is one of the errors that Hegel finds in a social contract theory.[94]

Since identification with the aims of the social organism is part of self-realization, the success of the social organism in achieving pre-social ends does not determine its moral legitimacy. Bradley infers this from the Aristotelian doctrine of a human being as a political animal. He also infers that a correct conception of self-realization, and hence of morality, must partly be the product of social interaction, and hence cannot be a condition of adequacy that is external to it. Bradley connects his claim about the essentially social character of

---

[91] Positive v. critical morality: §998.

[92] 'Let us now consider our point of view . . . against the common error that there is something "right in itself" for me to do, in the sense that there must be some absolute rule of morality the same for all persons without distinction of times and places . . . It is abundantly clear that the morality of our time is not that of another time, that the men considered good in one age might in another age not be thought good . . . The motive to deny it is the belief that it is fatal to morality. If what is right here is wrong there, then all morality (such is the notion) becomes chance and convention, and so ceases. But "my station and its duties" holds that *unless* morals varied, there could be no morality; that a morality which was *not* relative would be futile, and that I should have to ask for something "more relative than this".' (189)

[93] 'In the realized idea which, superior to me, and yet here and now in and by me, affirms itself in a continuous process, we have found the end, we have found self-realization, duty, and happiness in one—yes, we have found ourselves, when we have found our station and its duties, our function as an organ in the social organism.' (163) Bradley's conception of a social organism is criticized by Wright, 'Organism'.

[94] Hegel on the social contract; §1017.

self-realization with his defence of the relativity of morality and the absence of critical standards external to positive morality.[95]

But the social character of self-realization does not prove the futility of critical morality. Perhaps only some forms of society achieve the social aspect of self-realization for their members. Acceptance of one's station and its duties within the right sort of society may be an element in self-realization, not simply a means to it. But critical moral theory may identify the right sort of society and the right sorts of stations and duties.

1227. Different Roles of my Station and its Duties

These different lines of thought are sometimes difficult to separate in Bradley's discussion. Three main claims seem to be present at different places in the essay: (1) I realize myself in my current station and its duties. (2) I realize myself in some station or other and in its duties. (3) I realize myself in the station and duties that are specified by correct moral principles.

The first claim is the explicitly conservative part of Bradley's argument—though his later criticism of the morality of my station and its duties shows that he thinks its conservative aspects are open to objection.[96] According to this view, I achieve my self-realization in fulfilling the duties attached to my social role, whatever the role and duties may be. All there is to morality is the pattern of stations and duties embodied in a given society; and every pattern of positive morality, so understood, achieves self-realization. On this view, attempts to formulate a critical moral theory that examines the positive morality of one's own society are misguided.

Bradley's later argument suggests—especially in the second part of this essay (202–6)—that he rejects the first claim. The second claim is more plausible. It does not imply that every station or social role realizes the self of its occupant (so that, for instance, slaves realize themselves by occupying the role of slave). It claims only that some social roles, and the moral principles that partly define them, achieve self-realization.

This second claim rests on the plausible observation that social roles and positive morality may contribute to self-realization for many people. For self-realization includes at least the achieving of goals that we set for ourselves as the aims for our lives. If these goals include the fulfilment of social roles, self-realization includes the fulfilment of these roles. Some people see their self-realization partly in being a parent, a doctor, a musician, and so on; and the fulfilment of these roles depends on the nature of a society and its expectations. Many of these social roles involve moral rules and expectations too.

This is why Bradley believes that moral principles and practices give us different ends, and therefore a different conception of ourselves from the one we would have without morality.

---

[95] 'We hold that man is *phusei politikos*, that apart from the community he is *theos ê thêrion*, no man at all. We hold again that the true nature of man, the oneness of homogeneity and specification, is being wrought out in history . . . This realization is possible only by the individual's living as member in a higher life, and this higher life is slowly developed in a series of stages. . . . The notion that full-fledged moral ideas fell down from heaven is contrary to all the facts with which we are acquainted.' (190) The Greek phrases inexactly recall Aristotle, *Pol.* 1253a2–3, 29.

[96] Bell, 'Insufficiency', discusses the morality of my station and its duties and the transition to ideal morality.

Perhaps this need not always be so. Being a sales assistant or a company director need not make a large difference to one's conception of oneself. One might perhaps simply think of it as a way to make a living, and think of oneself as primarily aiming at what one does in one's spare time; being a volunteer firefighter, or a parent, and so on.

But social roles normally affect their occupants more deeply. Occupants characteristically take pride and pleasure, or feel guilt and shame, in certain situations apart from their instrumental benefits. They regard themselves as soldiers, police officers, teachers, parents, members of clubs, and so on. In so far as we regard ourselves as occupants of certain roles, we try to fulfil their obligations. Hence morality involves stations and duties.

Bradley believes that this aspect of morality shows what is inadequate and one-sided in a Kantian conception. He picks out two connected Kantian mistakes (174–6): (1) Kant assumes some sharp conflict between morality and self-interest. But there is no need to assume this. For the 'interest' we aim at is not simply the satisfaction of this or that non-moral desire. We aim at self-realization, which requires the realization of our capacities in some system. Morality, and particular moral relations, make us aware of new capacities, and new possibilities of fulfilment. (2) Kant identifies the moral will with the will to act on some purely formal principle independent of any specific empirical content. But this is not how we find morality in my station and its duties. When Kant supposes that the good will meets his conditions, he separates the self from the specific requirements and aims connected with a particular social role. But this conception of a self is a misguided abstraction; we cannot form any conception of ourselves outside the selves that occupy particular roles.

The morality of my station and its duties gives us an opportunity to realize ourselves in ways that would not be open if we conceived our ends non-morally. The sorts of ends and aims that are open to us if we are guided by morality in our relations to other people surpass any ends that we could conceive otherwise. For some aims are made possible by cooperative action in general. Obvious examples are those that involve a team or an orchestra or a family. If we think of these cases, the suggestion that morality extends self-realization is not surprising. In so far as we form the aims that express our social role, we open new possibilities of self-realization.

1228. Self-Realization and True Morality

These connexions between moral principles and the defining of ends and roles support Bradley's second claim, that some moral principles define activities that promote self-realization for some people. But this conclusion leaves open some questions about morality. (1) The argument has been about positive morality and moral principles, in the sense in which we might speak of the morality of the Babylonians or the Tartars. It simply involves some positive morality or other to define social roles. Different, even contradictory, moral principles might define roles appropriate to self-realization. Hence, this role for morality does not help us to distinguish true moral principles from others. Sometimes Bradley embraces this consequence, because he rejects critical morality. But since he does not consistently reject it, we seem to need some connexion between true, critical morality and self-realization. (2) So far we have argued only that social roles contribute to self-realization for some people. We have left open the possibility that some people concentrate on ends that involve social roles, and other people do not, so that morality is relevant to self-realization only for people of the first sort. In that case, what should we say about people who do not identify themselves with any sort of social role, and who try not to care about any social role? Why can they not achieve their self-realization in some other way? Is there any reason to identify ourselves with some social role rather than some other sort of end?

These questions make it reasonable to consider Bradley's third claim about self-realization, stations, and duties: one realizes oneself only in the station and duties specified by true morality. This claim implies that a social role defined by true moral principles is necessary for self-realization for everyone. It does not imply that this social role is the only sphere in which anyone achieves any self-realization; Bradley recognizes non-social aspects of self-realization, but he believes that everyone's self-realization includes activities defined by principles of true morality.[97] Why should we regard the morally good self as the only real self?

Bradley seems to overlook an obvious possibility. If we suppose that self-realization consists simply in the realization of our capacities, we might suppose we can achieve it, and so achieve a 'real' self, in all sorts of bad activities. The mere appeal to self-realization does not seem to distinguish the right from the wrong goals that an agent might aim at in the pursuit of self-realization.[98]

1229. The Good Self

Bradley answers this objection in Essay vii.[99] Here he distinguishes the good self from the bad, and tries to explain why the good self that is realized in morality is the real self (279–312).

The good self differs from the bad self in its unity and harmony. Moral development results in the discovery of unity in our aims.[100] The bad self lacks unity.[101] Nothing holds together the various objects desired by the bad self besides the fact that it desires them. It comes closest to the picture of the self that is presupposed by a hedonist doctrine of the good. The universal aspect of the self scarcely influences the choice of particular ends.

---

[97] Bradley believes I realize myself only in so far as I identify myself '. . . with the good will that I realize in the world, by my refusing to identify myself with the bad will of my private self. So far as I am one with the good will, living as a member in the moral organism, I am to consider myself real, and I am not to consider the false self real.' (182)

[98] This objection is raised by Rashdall, TGE, Bk. 2, ch. 3.

[99] Wollheim, 'Self', discusses the moral psychology of Essay vii.

[100] '. . . the good which the child thus lives itself into and lives in, is in the main harmony with itself. And hence the self, which feels itself to be one and a whole, feels in the good the answering harmony of its own true nature, and divines that what realizes it as a system realizes itself, and that the jarring and discrepant is false and untrue.' (291) 'The good self satisfies us because it answers to our real being. It is in the main a harmony, it is subordinated into a system; and thus, in taking its content into our wills and realizing that, we feel that we realize ourselves as the true infinite, in one permanent, harmonious whole.' (303)

[101] The content of the bad self '. . . has no unity in itself; it is not subordinated to a single controlling principle. It is a chance collection, united partly by interlacing of habits, partly by relative subordination to this or that bad end; but its various habits and ends are self-contradictory, e.g. lust and laziness, pride and greediness, hatred and coward-ice.' (296)

We may doubt Bradley's claims about the disunity of the bad self. Could we not form a highly unified, single-minded but evil plan for our lives? We would have adopted (as Kant puts it) an evil maxim that involves the universal aspect of the self; we would not simply live by impulse, but we would have a plan for our lives.[102] Why is the most unified plan the one that includes a concern for morality?

Bradley suggests (in his earlier discussion of the 'life of an oyster') that we could have an extremely unified life confined to a few pursuits. This possibility suggests a different sort of evil person from the one whom he primarily seems to have in mind. Apparently, I might achieve a high degree of harmony in my life by being both miserly and averse to risk; in that case, I will not endanger my hoard by risky adventures to increase it.

The possibility of this sort of evil person requires us to qualify Bradley's suggestion that an evil person suffers from mental and practical chaos. But it does not undermine his basic point that the bad self lacks rational order, because it does not thoroughly subordinate its particular aims and impulses to an explicit conception of itself as an infinite whole. Since it cannot remain a rational self without being somewhat influenced by its universal aspect, it cannot entirely lack rational order. But its degree of rational order is partial, since it does not extend to the bad person's ends; these are simply the products of his inclinations. Since his inclinations have not been formed by rational criticism, they do not display any rational order.

If we acknowledge this difference between the rationally ordered and the unordered self, we may still deny that this difference separates the morally good from the morally bad self. Why should rational order and unification result in moral goodness? From some points of view, we might suppose that this result is quite unlikely. For we might think moral goodness depends especially on the appropriate sentiments and emotions that attach us to the interests of others, irrespective of our other aims and concerns. If we train these sentiments to fit into a rational system of ends, perhaps they will not be as tenacious as they should be. If self-realization requires a rational order, it may conflict with the requirements of morality.

This anti-rationalist conception of moral goodness is no more opposed to Bradley's conception of morality as part of the rationally ordered self than to utilitarian and Kantian views about the rational character of moral goodness.[103] It raises a special difficulty, however, for Bradley. For he sometimes affirms the intuitive character of ordinary moral judgments, and argues against attempts to 'educate' these judgments through utilitarian principles. But his conception of morality and the good self shows that he has to advocate the education of ordinary moral sentiments to conform to rational judgment.

1230. Being a Whole by Joining a Whole

To grasp Bradley's reasons for believing that the unified self is the morally good self, we ought to go back to his general claims about self-realization. Once he has argued that

---

[102] Kant on the evil maxim; §§943–4.
[103] Hume's defence of this anti-rationalist conception; §782. Aristotle on vice; §§93, 110–11.

self-realization requires us to realize ourselves as infinite wholes that fall wholly within ourselves, he argues that I cannot be an infinite whole unless I am part of some larger whole (79). To fall wholly within myself, I must extend the area of my concerns that I accept as rationally choiceworthy for its own sake. I aim at 'homogeneity', some systematic unification of my ends. I also aim at 'specification', which requires a comprehensive systematic unification that does justice to the whole nature of the self. To be an infinite whole, I need a systematic and comprehensive structure that embraces a whole life that I choose for its own sake.[104]

In Bradley's view, I cannot meet these requirements for being an infinite whole without being part of a larger social whole.[105] This social whole achieves greater specification; more of my capacities are realized in moral and social interactions. It achieves greater harmony and homogeneity; for if my relations with others are based on trust and mutual confidence, I am less likely to frustrate some ends by pursuing others. It makes more of me fall 'within myself'; for if I have moral concerns for others, fewer of my activities involve unwelcome necessity that is external to what I pursue for its own sake.

To defend this last claim, Bradley considers the objection that the larger social whole constrains and restricts me, because it imposes external demands that reflect the needs and aims of the whole rather than my own needs and aims.[106] He answers that my relations to others need not be purely external. In recognizing the aims of the whole as my own aims, I recognize a common good as my good.[107]

This attitude to the social whole, however, is not necessary. I have a choice about whether I treat the social whole as 'internal' to me and my aims, or as external—simply a necessity that I have to deal with in order to pursue my private aims. Why should I look at it one way rather than the other? Bradley assumes that we must in any case recognize the ends of others in our conception of our self-realization. Why, then, should we recognize them as part of a common good? Why not recognize them instrumentally?

If we took a purely instrumental attitude to the aims of others, our concern for these aims would be alienated parts of our life. We have some reason, then, to form a conception of our self-realization that includes concern for the good of others for its own sake. Since we have to deal with other people anyhow, it is better to find non-instrumental value in relations

---

[104] 'It is not that I wish to increase the mere quantity of my true self. It is that I wish to be nothing *but* my true self, to be rid of all external relations, to bring them all within me, and so to fall wholly within myself. I am to be perfectly homogeneous; but that I can not be unless fully specified, and the question is, How can I be extended so as to take in my external relations?' (79)

[105] '[Continued from the previous quotation.] Goethe has said, "Be a whole *or* join a whole", but to that we must answer, "You cannot be a whole, unless you join a whole." The difficulty is: being limited and so not a whole, how extend myself so as to be a whole? The answer is, be a member in a whole. Here your private self, your finitude ceases as such to exist; it becomes the function of an organism. You must be, not a mere piece of, but a member in, a whole; and as this must know and will yourself.' (79)

[106] '[The objector:] "The more perfect the organism, the more is it specified, and so much the intenser becomes its homogeneity . . . The unity falls in the whole, and so outside me; and the greater specification of the whole means the making me more special, more narrowed and limited, and less developed within myself."' (79)

[107] 'The relations of the others to me are not mere external relations. I know myself as a member; that means I am aware of my own function; but it means also that I am aware of the whole as specifying itself in me . . . It is false that the homogeneity falls outside me; it is not only in me, but for me too; and apart from my life in it, my knowledge of it, and devotion to it, I am not myself.' (80)

with them. They would be alienated from us if we treated them as means, sometimes costly and unwelcome, to ends altogether distinct from the good of others.

This point does not imply that we can make ourselves find self-realization in just anything; some external circumstances may prevent self-realization. Still, we can reasonably allow external circumstances to have some influence on how we conceive our self-realization. Any realistic conception of self-realization requires some co-operation with other people; we might take a purely instrumental attitude to this co-operation, or we might try to incorporate it into our conception of self-realization. The purely instrumental attitude makes relations with other people an alienated part of our life. If we seek to avoid this sort of alienation, we incorporate morality into our self-realization. If our self-realization should extend as far as possible in our lives, it must include morality.

This argument only shows that it would be desirable to form a conception of self-realization that includes morality. We cannot form such a conception, however, if we conclude that no plausible view of our self-realization includes morality. This is the conclusion of the bad self; moral relations are no part of any rational system of ends, but simply disagreeable instrumental means that we choose to get the benefits that we seek from other people for our self-confined ends.

Bradley rejects these doubts about morality. Morality extends our aims because it allows us to identify our own aims with those of some larger whole. He speaks of an individual as an organ in a moral organism, or a 'heartbeat in its system' (163). Morality gives us a basis for non-instrumental concern for the welfare of others. It gives me broader aims than those that involve states of myself, since I come to care about other people and other aims non-instrumentally. As a moral person, I do not regard other people's ends as outside my own.[108] I come to identify my will with the will of the larger moral organism, and so I achieve more complete self-realization. Since this attitude to morality allows me to care about more aspects of my life as part of my self-realization, it extends the area of self-realization over more of my life. I no longer have to regard the moral aspects of my life as purely instrumental from the point of view of self-realization.

This is why Bradley believes that the good self, the self that identifies itself with the concerns of morality, achieves a degree of unity and comprehensiveness that the bad self lacks. I find self-realization in more of my life if I include the requirements of morality in my self-realization.

We can therefore overcome Sidgwick's dualism of practical reason. According to Sidgwick, if we take the egocentric point of view that asks 'What is reasonable for me?', we have no reason to prefer the universal point of view that asks 'What is reasonable without qualification?' Bradley appeals to self-realization to take us from the egocentric to the universal point of view. We begin from the egocentric question 'What will realize me?' But Bradley argues that we extend our concerns and interests so as to achieve self-realization only if we identify our interest with other people's interests, and only if we regard universal reasons as good reasons for acting in their own right. Responsiveness to universal reasons is characteristic of the rational self that I identify myself with and that I want to realize.

---

[108] 'I am morally realized, not until my personal self has utterly ceased to be my exclusive self, is no more a will which is outside others' wills, but finds in the world of others nothing but self.' (80)

1231. Morality and Ends

How well does Bradley defend his most controversial claim, that the correct morality is part of everyone's self-realization? A comparison between his position and Kant's suggests that each position might improve the other in some places.

Bradley argues that morality does not conflict with self-realization by including principles that require concern for the interests of other people for their own sake. On the contrary, this is a reason for supposing that the moral outlook is part of self-realization. He opposes the view that morality has a regulative role, and argues that it has a constitutive role in self-realization.[109]

Examples of purely regulative rules are those that guide the flow of traffic. They take for granted our desire to travel from one place to another by the quickest and safest route. In some cases, they regulate speed in the interest of safety, or force us to co-ordinate our actions with other people's for our mutual benefit. While it might seem more convenient for me to take the shortest and quickest route by driving through a red traffic light or driving the wrong way on a one-way street, my own safety and the safety of other people require me to stop at traffic lights and to follow one-way rules. But traffic rules are not justified by the new activities that they make possible. If they work, they allow me to do the sorts of things I wanted to do already—drive around reasonably quickly and safely. The possibility of driving in the permitted direction on a one-way street is not in itself an important opportunity that they open for me.

Other rules, however, are not merely regulative. The clearest cases of such rules are rules of a game. The rules of chess do not regulate our chess-playing activities in the way that traffic rules regulate our driving. For we can drive without one-way traffic, traffic lights, and so on, but cannot play chess without following rules of chess. A new activity is open to us if we accept rules of chess, and closed to us if we do not accept them.[110] In this case, the rules are constitutive, not purely regulative.

Part of the function of moral principles is regulative. They characteristically tell us what it is and is not all right to do in the pursuit of ends that we would pursue whether or not we cared about morality. Hence the analogy with traffic rules is initially appealing. Rules about promising, lying, cheating, etc. presuppose that we are already doing something (making agreements, communicating, trying to make a profit, etc.) that we would be doing apart from morality. One might infer that morality is simply a means for regulating non-moral pursuits and activities in ways that benefit everyone or most people. On this view, morality is to be assessed by its success in carrying out this instrumental function.

Kant rejects this strictly instrumental role for moral principles, and hence rejects this reason for regarding them as purely regulative. He argues that moral reasons are reasons for everyone irrespective of whether or not morality fulfils some non-moral aim or goal.

---

[109] On regulative and constitutive rules, see Rawls, 'Rules'; MacIntyre, *AV* 118–19.

[110] Games are perhaps a special case, since one might say that the whole idea of a game is to engage in some otherwise pointless activity with the aim of (in some cases) displaying some special sort of skill. But the idea that we must accept some rules or principles if we are to have a certain sort of end, or to be able to take part in a certain kind of activity, is not confined to games. Hence the study of activities that are partly constituted by the acceptance of certain principles is relevant to questions about self-realization.

Sometimes, however, he still speaks as though the function of morality were purely regulative, telling us whether something that we want to do on other grounds is morally acceptable or not. Kant claims that morality introduces an end in itself because it imposes a 'supreme limiting condition' on the pursuit of other ends. This makes the role of morality appear strictly regulative.

But this is not the only way to look at morality. It is also constitutive; aims and activities are open to us, once we take the moral point of view, that are not open to us otherwise. This is the feature of morality that Bradley emphasizes and that he thinks Kant neglects.

Kant does not entirely neglect this feature of morality. He recognizes ends that are also duties; they are characteristic of virtue, and they result from acceptance of the categorical imperative.[111] Still, Kant does not exploit this feature of morality as Bradley exploits it; he does not explore the possibility that the ends resulting from morality help to achieve the good that the rational agent already pursues from the non-moral point of view. In Kant's view, the moral and the non-moral components of the supreme good remain distinct and unconnected. Since he does not recognize the non-moral pursuit of one's own good as a feature of rational agency as such, he does not believe that morality gives this rational pursuit a new direction and a new content. On this point, the idealists are justified in claiming to correct Kant.

Bradley's defence of morality, however, is incomplete. If the acceptance of a given rule or principle makes an attitude or activity possible, it does not follow that the principle is acceptable. If, for instance, we hold the view that Aristotle holds of a slave, as a living implement or instrument, it becomes possible to think of ourselves as having used a slave skilfully, in the way we would use a hammer skilfully. In that case, we will not give the slave any credit, any more than we give a hammer or a paintbrush any credit. This is a possibility of self-realization that is opened to us if we think of some people as slaves. But it does not follow that the principles constituting the institution of slavery are to be recommended.

What sorts of ends, then, are made possible by morality, and to what extent can we regard these an appropriate part of self-realization? Bradley points out that a particular social role will tend to modify our conception of ourselves and of the ends in which we find our self-realization. But it does not follow that the modification is desirable, or that it really promotes self-realization.

1232. Kantian Morality and Self-Realization

To make further progress, it may be useful to begin from some Kantian principles. These will suggest ways in which the recognition of specific moral relations to other people alters our conception of ourselves and the ends we care about.

If we care about other people non-instrumentally, many activities that would not otherwise matter to us for their own sake come to matter to us. Some doctors, for instance, may

---

[111] Kant on virtue and ends; §933.

care about the welfare of their patients, while others may care about their income or their status in the profession. In the first case, they can be concerned about the patients' being well, irrespective of their further concern; they have something they recognize as realizing themselves, and not simply as a means to something that realizes them.

Morality, as Kant conceives it, does not simply involve relations of concern with restricted groups of other people—friends, patients, colleagues, and so on. It involves relations of respect with other people in general. In Bradley's view, this extended concern causes us to regard the ends of some larger system—our community—as our own ends, so that we find ourselves realized in the activities of the community. Whatever the community does I regard as an activity of mine, so that I realize more capacities in the activities of the community than I could realize if I were concerned only with what I could do as an isolated individual.

This answer does not seem sufficiently discriminating. Apparently, we could come to take the sort of attitude that Bradley describes as long as we could identify ourselves with the aims and activities of some larger community. But while this requires an outlook that is not purely selfish, it does not seem to require morality. For we could take this self-identifying attitude towards a larger whole if we could be taught to regard our own individual interests and concerns as of no value whatever, and to attach value only to the aims of the larger system. Correct morality plays no distinctive role in this process.

When Kant claims that as a rational agent I regard myself as an end, he introduces self-realization. When I aim at a particular end, I care not simply about achieving that result, but about achieving it for myself, as a part of a life that realizes my capacities as a whole. Bradley's claims about self-realization help to explain one of Kant's points about regarding myself as an end; I care about myself as something distinct from the satisfaction of my desires, since the satisfaction of my desires is insufficient for my welfare.

According to Kant, the moral point of view treats rational agents as ends; I treat them the same way I treat myself. I regard myself as an end, in so far as I give myself priority over the achievement of some particular aim or desire. Similarly, I regard other people as ends, in so far as I give them priority over the achievement of anyone's particular aims or desires. If I treat persons as ends, I do not allow them to be sacrificed simply for someone else's purposes.

If, then, I treat others as ends in the same way as I treat myself, does that make some distinctive contribution to self-realization? What distinctive aims and goals do I acquire by regarding persons as ends, and how do these goals contribute to self-realization?

We can appeal to Bradley's claims about falling wholly within myself, and not having my activities alienated. If I have a relation of mutual respect with another person, and I regard the other as an end, then my relations with the other are not wholly instrumental. The attitude of mutual respect makes me regard myself as part of a mutually respecting community, so that I come to regard the fulfilment of the ends of this community as ends that realize myself.

What is the alternative to this? If I do not adopt the point of view of mutual respect, I have to make some co-operative relations with others depend on (a) particular relations of friendship etc. that cause me to be concerned for their ends; or (b) purely instrumental co-operation, which does not contribute in its own right to my self-realization. Mutual respect, however, gives me some basis for co-operation apart from exclusive attachments to particular people.

This attitude to mutual respect appeals to the effects of my concern for others. But my conception of myself is equally affected by how I expect other people to look at me. If I take the point of view of mutual respect, I believe I deserve respect from others simply as a person, not because of some accomplishment that demands admiration, or because of some way I can be useful to other people, or because someone else happens to like me. This point of view on myself values activities of mine that are not necessarily useful to others, and do not necessarily serve their particular aims or goals. And so mutual respect prevents a certain sort of subordination to the ends of others in the ends that I value for myself.

In these ways, the principles of Kantian morality are constitutive. They make possible certain sorts of activities and outlooks that make a distinctive contribution to self-realization. Bradley's argument would be stronger, therefore, if it relied more explicitly on Kant. He needs to explain how morality gives me some reason to identify my own ends with the ends of other people; but he does not give a clear account of how morality can do this. The organic expressions he uses to explain himself are not as useful as they might appear. Kant's views on the moral outlook help to make Bradley's claims more plausible.

Kant also explains why the self that is described in 'The Vulgar Notion of Responsibility' turns out to be also the self realized by morality. For Kant believes that we are responsible agents because we are negatively free, capable of being determined by practical reason, and that the rational agency that is realized in morality is positive freedom, our being determined by this practical reason. Similarly, Bradley believes that the self that we seek to realize is the self as a rational agent, not just a collection of desires. Kantian morality claims to embody the principles appropriate for rational agents who want to be treated as rational and responsible—not just as means to be exploited—in their relations to each other. Hence the self we recognize in our convictions about responsibility is the self that is realized in morality.

This is simply a sketch of how one might try to fit Kantian morality into an account of self-realization. To make the sketch a bit more detailed, we might try to answer these questions:

1. What is involved in treating persons as ends? It requires concern for a person's welfare in its own right, as opposed to the satisfaction of any other aims or desires. But can we say more about the specific moral implications of this view?
2. Can we say more precisely what attitudes to ourselves and other people result from treating persons as ends? How does this express or affect our conception of ourselves?
3. Can we say enough about self-realization to make it seem plausible that the attitudes connected with the treatment of persons as ends promote self-realization?
4. Can we say enough about self-realization to show that the treatment of persons as ends plays a sufficiently important role in self-realization? Our answer to this question affects the sort of priority that one assigns to morality in comparison with other aims. If we believe that Kantian morality plays only a minor role in self-realization, we will not take the demands of morality very seriously. We need to show, therefore, that morality is not just a minor element in self-realization.

We can return to these questions in our discussion of Green's account of morality. We can also explore them in connexion with Rawls. In contrast to Green, Rawls does not try to defend an idealist conception of morality and self-realization. On the contrary, he tries to defend Kant without adopting an idealist view. But it is worth considering the possibility that Rawls helps us to defend a more idealist, and less purely Kantian, attitude to morality.

1233. The Scope of Morality

Not all morality is included in the morality of 'My Station and its Duties'. Bradley does not even believe that all morality is social; he argues for its development beyond the area of social morality.

He does not claim that all self-realization belongs, as such, to morality. Artistic production or scientific discovery might realize the agent's capacities, but we do not say that the agent is morally good 'just in so far as, and because, what he produced was good of its sort and desirable in itself' (214). Nor, however, does Bradley believe that morality is concerned only with the aspects of a person's conduct that affect the interests of others. Moral character cannot be assessed simply by examining that part of one's life and actions that affects others. Such assessment is inadequate, because morality is concerned with the whole of someone's life, including its non-social aspects.[112] Bradley supposes that this conception of morality implies that it has a non-social aspect.

The distinctive feature of morality lies in its relation to the will.[113] Simply engaging in artistic or scientific activity does not make it part of morality. Moral excellence 'does not lie in mere skill or mere success, but in single-mindedness and devotion to what seems best as against what we merely happen to like' (229). In his 'Concluding Remarks', Bradley argues that this attitude to morality, fully understood, leads beyond morality and into religion. This is because morality is concerned with what ought to be and is not; hence it commits us to demand something that cannot be: 'Not only is nothing good but the good will, but also nothing is to be real (so far as willed) but the good; and yet the reality is not wholly good' (313). Since morality demands the reality of the good, it demands the form of religious belief for which the good is ultimately real.

Does Bradley show any contradiction in morality? If 'nothing but the good is to be real' meant 'nothing but the good is real', the claims of morality would conflict with the fact that evil exists. If it meant 'nothing but the good will be real', morality would predict the abolition of evil. But when morality says that 'nothing but the good is to be real', it means 'nothing but the good ought to be real', which does not conflict with the reality of evil. Bradley does not show, therefore, that morality makes claims that—apart from religious beliefs—contradict what we know to be true.

---

[112] 'To be a good man in all things and everywhere, to try to do always the best, and to do one's best in it, whether in lonely work or in social relaxation to suppress the worse self and realize the good self, this and nothing short of it is the dictate of morality.' (215)

[113] 'Morality, then, will be the realization of the self as the good will. It is not self-realization from all points of view, though all self-realization can be looked at from this one point of view; for all of it involves will, and, so far as the will is good, so far is the realization moral.' (228–9)

Perhaps Bradley could defend himself by appealing to Kant's argument to show that the demands of morality assume the possibility of success in achieving the results that morality aims at. If we lack the sort of assurance that is given by religious belief, then we would have to conclude that the demands of morality are unreasonable. If Bradley has this argument in mind, he needs to show that morality is incomplete unless we can be assured of a degree of success that is assured only by religious belief.

GREEN

1234. Green and Bradley on the History of Ethics

Green's *Prolegomena to Ethics* is different from Bradley's *Ethical Studies* in its structure. It begins with a long discussion (in Book i) of metaphysics, arguing for a Hegelian conclusion, and only then (in Book ii) turns to the will and (in Book iii) to moral theory. Hegelian metaphysics forms (as Green's title for the whole book might suggest) the prolegomena to ethics. The rest of the work, however, appears, at first sight, to be less metaphysical than *Ethical Studies*. It appears to be intelligible without constant reference to the metaphysical argument, and it does not seem to be part of a cumulative metaphysical argument of the sort that Bradley develops.

Hegel pays very little attention to moral philosophy between the Greeks and Kant, and his treatment of Greek moral philosophy is influenced by his views about the fundamental difference between the Greek and the modern outlook. Green is different on this point.[1] Though he does not treat Aristotle as a contemporary, he takes himself to accept the basic Aristotelian principles as a basis for sound moral philosophy. From Hegel's point of view, Green is hopelessly insensitive to profound historical and intellectual differences.

Green's first major published work was his long introduction to Hume, in which he criticizes Hume's ethics from a Kantian point of view.[2] It is surprising that, like Bradley, he refers very little to the rationalist side of English moral philosophy before Kant. As Oxford undergraduates, Green and Bradley must both have been familiar with Butler, but Bradley refers to him not at all, and Green very little. Still, even though Green does not mention his rationalist predecessors, his arguments often agree with theirs, and a comparison with Butler is often helpful.

Green differs from both Hegel and Bradley in his attitude to Kant.[3] Bradley, following Hegel, regards Kantian morality as a one-sided position that a true moral theory must

---

[1] The references to Aristotle in Bradley are significant; see §1214. But they are not as prominent as they are in Green.

[2] Green's view that Hume's outlook needs a systematic answer, both in epistemology and in moral philosophy, agrees with Reid's assessment of him. Whewell does not give Hume such prominence.

[3] According to Taylor, 'Bradley', 464, 'in later life Bradley used to express the view that Green's close dependence on Kant had an unfortunate effect on the permanent value of his work'. Bradley would evidently have been surprised by the prominence of Kantian moral philosophy later in the 20th century.

correct. Green is not uncritical towards Kant, but he is more favourable than Bradley. In his view, Kant grasps the true account of morality, but combines it with some false assumptions; once these are pruned from his position, and the remaining elements are properly explained, the true position has been found. This at least appears different from Bradley's judgment that Kant's view is hopelessly one-sided and needs to be incorporated in a quite different view.[4]

For this reason, it is reasonable to regard Green as basically a Kantian; this is how Sidgwick interprets both his metaphysics and his ethics. Sidgwick does not mention Hegel; he often argues that difficulties confronting Kant return to confront Green as well. This would not be a reasonable approach to Bradley. Admittedly, the substantive difference between Green's and Bradley's attitudes to Kant may not turn out to be as large as this contrast would suggest; but the apparent difference is a suitable starting point for discussion.

Green's attitude to Kant and to Aristotle makes his view of the history of ethics more static than the view held by some modern philosophers, especially Hegel and Sidgwick. He is similar, on this point, to Butler, who sets out to explain and to defend the traditional naturalist position maintained by Greek moralists. Green suggests that once Kant is appropriately corrected, his position turns out to be a development of the Aristotelian position, not a radical departure from it. This conclusion would be no less unwelcome to Kant than to Hegel; but our discussion of Kant suggests that it is defensible.[5]

Though Bradley and Green differ in their emphasis, and in some of their conclusions, they clarify each other, and comparison makes the main line of argument clearer. Both of them take the end of human life to be 'self-satisfaction' or 'self-realization'; Green uses both terms (e.g., PE 175–6), while Bradley prefers the second.[6] Green agrees with Bradley that the Humean, empiricist, and utilitarian outlook gives an inadequate conception of self-realization. But he does not agree with Bradley's criticisms of Kant. He believes Kant contains the right account, together with some misconceptions.

The task of a moral theory, in Green's view, is to explain how morality achieves self-realization, and to show how it realizes the self better than we can realize it without morality. If this account informs us about the character of morality and helps us to defend morality, 'better' here cannot simply mean 'morally better'. We must rely on some conception of self-realization and its degrees that is not simply a product of our conception of morality.

Green seeks to describe self-realization, and to explain why it is the all-embracing end, to which morality itself must be somehow subordinate. The role that Green assigns to self-realization commits him to a teleological conception of morality.[7] To defend this conception, he should answer the Kantian objection that a teleological outlook cannot capture the essential character of the moral imperative.

---

[4] Brink, PCG 110–14, compares Green with Bradley (whom Brink treats rather severely).

[5] Kant and Aristotle; §§971–3.   [6] I cite Green's works by sections rather than by pages.

[7] 'And hence the differentia of the virtuous life, proceeding as it does from the same self-objectifying principle which we have just characterized as the source of the vicious life, is that it is governed by the consciousness of there being some perfection which has to be attained, some vocation which has to be fulfilled, some law which has to be obeyed, something absolutely desirable, whatever the individual may for the time desire; that it is in ministering to such an end that the agent seeks to satisfy himself.' (Green, PE 176)

1235. The Self and the Will

Green begins his account of self-realization with an account of the self to be realized. He begins Book ii of *PE* with a chapter on 'the freedom of the will' that distinguishes the freedom that concerns him from the conditions that the libertarian and the determinist recognize. He defines his position through a general account of desire and will.

Hegel distinguishes the particular from the universal element in the self, and argues that rational self-conscious subjects of desire 'put themselves into' their particular desires.[8] We might say that they acknowledge some desires as their own, or identify themselves with this or that desire. Green explores these claims about putting ourselves into a desire.

He believes that a self-conscious subject or agent cannot be a part of nature, so that its actions cannot be explained by the sorts of causal laws that explain natural processes. He relies on a Kantian argument, turned in an idealist direction. He agrees with Kant's view that our knowledge of an objective world is knowledge of how it is for self-conscious subjects; hence he accepts the Kantian case for connecting a priori knowledge with subjective states of the knowers. He draws the idealist conclusion that the objective world is how it is only for a self-conscious subject. Green claims: 'Only in virtue of self-consciousness is there for us a world to be known. In that sense, man's self-consciousness is his understanding' (120). If we emphasize 'for us' and 'to be known', this is simply a Kantian claim that we would not know about the world if we lacked self-consciousness. But Green emphasizes 'a world' as well, claiming that the very existence of the world—not simply its existence as object of knowledge—depends on self-consciousness.

The relevant self-conscious subject cannot be you or me, since the world is independent of finite subjects. Hence the relevant subject must be what Green calls an 'eternal consciousness' that reproduces itself in you and me (67). Since this consciousness is presupposed by nature, it cannot itself be a part of nature (77). Green welcomes this result, because he believes that if self-conscious agents were a part of nature, they would not be free, and would not be appropriate subjects of morality. Idealism takes Green by a shorter route to Kant's conclusion that freedom is not a property of human beings as existing in nature, space, and time, but really belongs to them as atemporal subjects.

Green's claim that freedom excludes nature agrees with Kant's incompatibilist assumptions.[9] He may have in mind two different objections to determinism: (a) The view that rational wills and selves are temporal, and hence determined by previous events in time, is incompatible with freedom. (b) The view that reference to 'self-seeking subject' can be

---

[8] Hegel on the self; §1002.

[9] 'According to what has been said, the proposition, current among "determinists" that a man's action is the joint result of his character and circumstances, is true enough in a certain sense, and, in that sense, is quite compatible with an assertion of human freedom. It is *not* so compatible, if character and circumstances are considered reducible, directly or indirectly, to combinations and sequences of natural events. It *is* so compatible, if a "free cause", consisting in a subject which is its own object, a distinguishing and self-seeking subject, is recognized as making both character and circumstances what they are.' (106)

eliminated in favour of descriptions of events that do not mention such a subject is incompatible with freedom. The second of these objections is Bradley's objection in 'The Vulgar Conception'; Bradley does not treat the first objection as part of the vulgar conception.

If Green intends the first objection, it is clear why he insists that the self-conscious subject must be atemporal, and that, as Kant says, no sequences of events can be strictly attributed to it. If he does not intend this objection, it is difficult to see why he insists on the atemporality and non-natural character of the subject.

But his concessions to determinism do not suggest that he denies temporal sequences in the subject. In his discussion of planning for the future, he seems to assume temporal and causal sequences.[10] He speaks as we normally do, in accordance with Bradley's vulgar conception, with no explicit commitment to a particular metaphysical belief in a non-temporal self; we assume that our past and present selves affect our future selves, just as the past and present states of any other stable but enduring object affect its future states. He affirms this vulgar conception against one indeterminist approach to freedom; he denies that we can secure freedom within temporality if we claim that free actions do not necessarily follow from prior conditions. Rather than denying causal connexions between temporal states of the self, he grants that actions result necessarily from character and circumstances (109).[11]

These views on freedom are consistent if Green objects not to determinism in itself, but to the version of determinism that denies any essential role for self-seeking subjects and characters in the explanation of human actions.[12] This version of determinism eliminates any reference to the self, and refers only to external circumstances and events, and to mental states that do not involve the self.[13] Bradley also rejects this version of determinism. Both idealists insist that the self is irreducible in explanation of rational and responsible action, though neither of them says precisely what versions of determinism conflict with this irreducibility.

If the versions of determinism that Green rejects are those that omit the appropriate role for the self, his demand for an atemporal subject is open to question. It does not seem to follow from his belief in the ineliminable and irreducible self. On the contrary, it seems to raise difficulties for this belief, since it undermines ordinary claims about the effects of deliberation on action. The atemporal conception of the subject would be reasonable only if Green accepted the incompatibilist claim that determination by the past excludes freedom; but he seems to reject this incompatibilist claim.

---

[10] '. . . just in so far as his future depends on his present and his past, it depends on this consciousness, depends on a direction of his inner life in which he is self-determined and his own master, because his own object . . . So far from the dependence of his future upon what he now is being a reason for passivity, . . . it would only be the absence of this dependence that could afford a reason for such passivity.' (112)

[11] This aspect of Green's argument convinces Sidgwick that Green really accepts determinism; *EGSM* 16–22. Sidgwick pays insufficient attention to identifying the doctrine that Green rejects.

[12] On determinism, see Thomas, *MPG* 122–9.

[13] Green discusses determinism and the will further in 'Freedom', 8–14, which amplifies *PE*, but does not seem to answer the questions we have raised. Lamont, *IGMP* 72–80, reproduces some of the ambiguities in Green's attitude to determinism. He is more definite in his rejection of indeterminism, and in his resistance to the reduction of the self to events. Though he does not allow that his position is consistent with determinism, it is not clear that his view about the role of the self and character is incompatible with determinism. Brink, *PCG* 23, summarizes: 'We can accept Green's claims about moral personality without endorsing his non-naturalism. We need only agree that responsibility presupposes deliberative self-government and, hence, self-consciousness, rather than indeterminism.'

1236. Self-Satisfaction and Self-Identification

If Green is primarily concerned to argue that the self-conscious subject, as such, is a necessary element in free action, what role does he ascribe to this subject? He does more than Bradley does to answer this question, and to explain why the appropriate role for the subject ensures the kind of freedom that is relevant to responsible action. In Green's view, a want or appetite moves us to a distinctively human action only if it belongs to a subject who presents the want to himself.[14] The presentation of the want introduces a 'new agency', even though the want itself is not 'intrinsically altered' (89). In any genuine act of willing, 'a self-conscious individual directs himself to the realization of some idea, as to an object in which for the time he seeks self-satisfaction' (154).

This reference to the self makes our actions imputable to us. When Esau sold his birthright for a bowl of soup, he was not moved simply by hunger.[15] He acted because he 'presented' the satisfaction of this want to himself as his greatest good in the circumstances, and presented himself having satisfied this want and achieved this good. Esau did not act without thinking, or in ignorance of the consequences of his actions; he realized he would have to pay an exorbitant price to satisfy his hunger and he was willing to pay it.[16]

Since the presentation of one's greatest good requires the presentation of the self, Green rejects accounts of free action that exclude reference to the self. We want to explain why Esau chose the soup in the face of the fact that he had to sell his birthright to get it. We do not explain this by simply citing his hunger. Simple hunger might explain the action of agents who are unaware of reasons for holding on to their birthright and going hungry for the moment; but it does not explain Esau's action.

Has Green a good enough reason for insisting on a self-conscious subject? Could we not capture the comparative aspects of Esau's choice by simply attributing some practical reasoning to him? Why should the practical reasoning involve reference to himself or to his own satisfaction?

In Green's view, self-satisfaction connects the fact that I conceive my desires as belonging to me as a subject with the fact that I deliberate about their satisfaction. When we find that we do not endorse a particular desire, we often modify that desire to fit our other desires.[17]

---

[14] 'It only becomes a motive, so far as upon the want there supervenes the presentation of the want by a self-conscious subject to himself, and with it the idea of a self-satisfaction to be attained in the filling of the want.' (89) Lamont, *IGMP* 88–94, explains Green through a contrast between (i) inclinations and (ii) desires that result from consideration of what 'fits most harmoniously into a universe of possible satisfactions'. Such consideration involves taking account of the implications of satisfying one desire for the satisfaction of other desires.

[15] See *Genesis*, 25:30–4: 'And Esau said to Jacob, "Let me eat some of that red pottage, for I am famished!"... Jacob said, "First sell me your birthright." Esau said, "I am about to die; of what use is a birthright to me?" Jacob said, "Swear to me first." So he swore to him, and sold his birthright to Jacob ... Thus Esau despised his birthright.' Green comments: 'The motive lies in the presentation of an idea of himself as enjoying the pleasure of eating the pottage, or (which comes practically to the same thing) as relieved from the pain of hunger. Plainly, but for his hunger Esau could have no such motive ... But the hunger is not the presentation of himself as the subject of pleasure, still less the presentation of that particular pleasure as under the circumstances his greatest good ...' (*PE* 96)

[16] On vice and self-satisfaction in Aristotle, see §§109–10.

[17] '... in every desire I so far detach myself from the desire as to conceive myself in possible enjoyment of the satisfaction of other desires, in other words, as a subject of happiness; and the desire itself is more or less stimulated or checked, according as its gratification in this involuntary forecast appears conducive to happiness or otherwise.' (127)

If I form a desire or aversion for a particular object, but consider the implications of getting this object for the other things I care about, I may alter my desire or aversion. Sometimes if I think about how much something matters to me, I may postpone or forgo something else that looks appealing at the moment. I may decide that it is better to overlook some slight than to start some quarrel that I will regret; for I may realize that I care more about keeping the other person's friendship than I care about expressing my anger now. Alternatively, I may endorse my current anger; for I may realize that this apparently trivial slight is really one of a sequence of slights I have ignored, and I may then decide that it is time to take a stand.

Such cases help to explain why Green attends to my conception of myself as a single subject; it determines which desires I choose to modify, frustrate, or execute.[18] The unity of the subject gives us a single set of overriding concerns. In the light of these concerns, we estimate the value of one possible object of desire by reference to other possible objects of desire and to possible outcomes that leave this desire unsatisfied. Our estimates introduce different presentations of ourselves; for they require us to think of our future selves in different ways.[19] Deliberation requires this connexion and comparison. The result of deliberation expresses the commitment of the self as a whole to a course of action that is chosen for the sake of self-satisfaction.

Even if self-identification is a necessary feature of action that realizes rational agency, we may still not be convinced that the end aimed at in self-identification is some good for me, or some state of myself, called 'self-satisfaction' or 'self-realization'. Green describes the idea of self-satisfaction as a 'desire for personal good' (91). He assumes that it is trivially true to describe the desire for personal good as a desire for good to oneself.[20]

We may object that this new description is not trivial at all, but introduces two restrictions on our conception of any possible end for rational agency: (1) If I speak of a good for me, I seem to imply that the end is essentially agent-relative,[21] so that in some way its relation to me is relevant to my having the sort of reason I have for concern about it. (2) If I speak of self-satisfaction and happiness, I seem to imply that the good must not only be related to me in some way, but must also be a state of myself, not simply a fact about something related to me. Each of these restrictions on possible ends is controversial. For we seem to recognize ends that are agent-neutral, because they rely on reasons that are not essentially related to any particular agent; and we equally seem to recognize ends that are my ends, but are not essentially states of me.

Green rejects a division between ends that belong to my good and ends that do not, because of his holistic claims about our aims and our conception of ourselves. In his view,

---

[18] 'It is thus equally important to bear in mind that there is a real unity in all a man's desires, a common ground of them all, and that this real unity or common ground is simply the man's self, as conscious of itself and consciously seeking in the satisfaction of desires the satisfaction of itself.' (129)

[19] 'The objects of a man's various desires form a system, connected by memory and anticipation, in which each is qualified by the rest; and just as the object of what we reckon a single desire derives its unity from the unity of the self-presenting consciousness in and for which alone it exists, so the system of a man's desires has its bond of union in the single subject, which always carries with it the consciousness of objects that have been and may be desired into the consciousness of the object which at present is being desired.' (128)

[20] '. . . for anything conceived as good in such a way that the agent acts for the sake of it, must be conceived as *his own* good, though he may conceive it as his own good only on account of his interest in others.' (92)

[21] On agent-relativity, see Sidgwick, §1203.

a conception of ourselves influences our attitude to the effects of one end on another. We are never so absorbed in any one desire that we ignore its effects on other desires.[22] Our conception of a whole self influences and connects our consciousness of particular desires.[23] The good that I aim at is not necessarily a state of myself, as opposed to someone else; but it reflects my conception of the appropriate combination of my different aims in so far as they realize my different capacities.[24]

1237. Degrees of Self-Identification

This reference to the whole self explains the difference between being inclined to a course of action and having decided to do it. It also helps to explain actions that seem to involve conflict, or less than whole-hearted endorsement. Once we understand the role of the self, we can correct mistaken views about a conflict between desire and will, and about the possibility of acting against one's conception of the greatest good. Green discusses the cases that Aquinas describes by introducing consent and election, and agrees quite closely with Aquinas' conclusions.[25]

According to Green, the division between desire and will rests both on the true belief that an inclination is different from a desire directed towards an object (137–8), and on the false belief that the desire directed towards an object is not a desire at all. He argues that the case in which I prefer one desire to another is not properly, or not fully, described as a case in which the stronger desire wins. Such a description suggests falsely that the only relevant difference between the desires is strength (139). The successful desire is the one that the agent identifies himself with, and this identification does not reflect a mere difference in strength.[26] The self-identification with a particular object results from a comparison of the future self with this object and the future self without it, and from a decision in favour of the first option.[27]

Green tries to explain why we say that someone acted on a desire against his will. Sometimes, he suggests, we use 'will' for one of the inclinations that does not move us.[28] That is what St Paul means in saying that 'To will is present with me, but how to perform

---

[22] 'We are never so exclusively possessed by the desire for any object as to be quite unaffected by the thought of other desired objects, of which we are conscious that the loss or gain would have a bearing on our happiness . . . Our absorption in it [sc. any particular desire] is never so complete but that the consideration of a possible happiness conditional upon the satisfaction of other desires makes a difference to it, though it may not be such a difference as makes its sign in outward conduct.' (127)

[23] 'The objects of a man's various desires form a system, connected by memory and anticipation, in which each is qualified by the rest . . . the system of a man's desires has its bond of union in the single subject, which always carries with it the consciousness of objects that have been and may be desired into the consciousness of the object which at present is being desired.' (128)

[24] Desire and personal good; Thomas, *MPG* 181–4, 198–201.   [25] Aquinas on consent; §§295–6.

[26] Green could usefully have referred to Reid's division between animal and rational strength. See §841.

[27] 'It implies . . . the presentation of an object with which the man for the time identifies himself or his good, and a consequent effort to realize this object. (140) . . . the gratification of the hatred has become what it was not . . . , an object which the man seeks to realize, one which for the time he has made his good.' (141)

[28] ' "My poverty but not my will consents", says the seller of poisons in "Romeo and Juliet". Here the consent, though said not to be of the will, might have been enough to hang for. The will is only the strong competing wish which does not suffice to determine action.' (143)

that which is good, I find not' (*Rom* 7:18 AV).[29] In these cases, the 'will' that is not acted on does not express one's identification of oneself with the action 'willed'.[30]

Sometimes, however, my deliberate choice, not under the pressure of any pressing inclination, seems to reject the course of action that I identify myself with. Sidgwick believes that such actions happen; he mentions both incontinent and self-sacrificing actions.[31] Though Sidgwick does not say so, self-sacrificing actions seem to raise a more serious difficulty for Green, as they do for eudaemonism in general. In these cases, Scotus believes we reject happiness for something higher.[32] Even if we explain incontinent action as a result of the influence of powerful emotions and non-rational impulses, no equally obvious explanation seems available for the apparently rational and reflective preference of the morally right over the action with which I identify myself.

How can Green exclude the possibility that I might sometimes choose not to act on the option that I identify myself with? He answers this question when he maintains that even impulsive or unreflectively habitual action rests on self-identification.[33] We ascribe such actions to ourselves retrospectively, when we explain, or defend, or excuse ourselves. According to Green, retrospective self-ascription of the action implies prospective self-identification with it.

This attempt to cope with apparent cases of voluntary actions that do not proceed from self-identification seems to make the appeal to self-identification trivial. Reference to self-identification is clarifying in cases where I have tried to integrate a proposed course of action with my other aims and values, so that I come to regard it as the appropriate course of action for me, taking into account all the aims that constitute me. It seems unhelpful, therefore, to appeal to this same notion of self-identification for cases in which I have apparently failed to integrate the action in this way. Sometimes it seems clear that I have acted without comparing the action with other options, and without seeing an appropriate connexion between it and the other aims and attitudes I attribute to myself. If Green claims that, simply because I have chosen the action, I must have identified myself with it, he seems to abandon those aspects of self-identification that clarify some other actions.

The suggestion that self-imputation or self-ascription implies self-identification is initially attractive, since it suggests how a prospective attitude might explain the retrospective attitude. But the suggestion now appears over-simplified. We might, however, be

---

[29] The AV, quoted by Green, translates *heuriskô*, omitted in UBS (see *Greek New Testament*) text and NRSV.

[30] Bradley discusses a topic related to incontinence, in 'Can a man sin against knowledge?' (*CE*, ch. 6). Here, however, he is discussing the question whether we can act against conscience and moral judgment; this is a question about the existence of an internal connexion between moral judgment and action. Bradley considers an argument for internalism that relies on an internal connexion between judging an action wrong and feeling it to be wrong. He agrees that there is this internal connexion, but argues that the feeling may not be so vivid, and may not be attended to so closely, that it ensures action. His rejection of this internal connexion does not commit him one way or the other on Green's claims about incontinence.

[31] 'I hold . . . that in "wilful sin" I have chosen evil known as such; on the other hand, in deliberate self-sacrifice I have preferred the "good" of others to mine—not consciously identified it with mine.' (Sidgwick, *EGSM* 27)

[32] Scotus on rejection of happiness; §363.

[33] 'In such a case the man makes the object, which the passion or habit suggests, his own, and sets himself to realize it, just as much as in the case where he contemplates alternatives. The evidence of this is his self-imputation of the act upon reflection. He may make excuses for it . . . but these very excuses witness that he is conscious of himself as other than the inducements and influences of which he pleads the strength, and conscious that it is not from them, but from himself as affected by them, that the action proceeds.' (*PE* 147)

reluctant to abandon it altogether; for the opposite view, that acting on impulse, or unreflective habit, or on incontinent desires, is simply acting on the strongest desire is equally unattractive, and, as Green implies, makes self-imputation of the action difficult to understand.

We might try to resolve this question by arguing that the appeal to self-identification is over-simplified, but not completely mistaken. Aquinas' distinction between actions that we do 'electing' and those we do 'from election' would have been useful to Green for this purpose. Aquinas introduces this distinction to explain incontinence within the Socratic assumptions that he shares with Green. In Sidgwick's view, Green's acceptance of the Socratic assumptions prevents him from agreeing with the 'modern Christian consciousness' in its recognition of deliberate sin.[34] Sidgwick does not discuss Aquinas' treatment of sin. It seems rather difficult to deny a Christian consciousness of sin to Aquinas, but his treatment of sin reflects the Socratic assumptions that Sidgwick takes to be incompatible with the 'modern' Christian conception. Aquinas believes that the distinction between electing an action and acting from election copes with the apparent counter-example arising from incontinence. If he is right, Green might appeal to this distinction without abandoning his claim that all voluntary action depends on self-identification.

Even better, Green might helpfully have used the distinction that Aquinas does not fully exploit, between consent and election (ST 1–2 q78 a4 ad 3).[35] He suggests the crucial difference when he says that the passion or habit suggests an object that the agent makes his own. This implies a lesser degree of self-identification than in cases where the suggestion comes from the agent's own reflective examination of the object in the light of his other aims and values; for the suggestion is less closely connected with the agent himself, if the agent himself is constituted by his reflective aims and values.

The fact that impulsive (and so on) action requires a lesser degree of self-identification does not show that it requires none. Aquinas believes that some connexion to the agent's conception of his final good is required; that is why he insists that the agent elects without acting from election. Though will and deliberation do not suggest this action, will consents to the suggestion coming from a passion; in Green's terms, the agent identifies himself with it.

This explanation does not reduce the idea of self-identification to triviality. We act on impulse if we thoughtlessly decide it is all right to act on it because we need not or should not bother to compare this with our reflective values; perhaps the matter is too small, or we distrust the reflective conclusion we are likely to come to in this case. We might, indeed, sometimes be justified in trusting our immediate or impulsive or habitual reactions against the conclusion we would reach from reflective deliberation on that occasion. People who act impulsively and incontinently are those who have no good reason for relying on their

---

[34] '. . . he (sc. Green) is so far under the influence of ancient Greek and especially Aristotelian modes of thought as to ignore usually, and expressly exclude sometimes, that wilful choice of wrong known to be wrong which is so essential an element in the modern Christian moral consciousness of "sin".' (Sidgwick, EGSM 25) It is not clear what Sidgwick means by 'modern' here. Perhaps he refers to the Christian consciousness formed by Scotus and his followers, or by the Reformation.

[35] Aquinas on consent; §§252, 296.

impulses, but still think it is all right to follow them in this particular case. The sort of people they are, and hence the general pattern of their self-identification, affects their tendencies to follow impulse in different situations.

Green would be well advised, then, to modify his claims about self-identification so as to recognize that its role in impulsive, incontinent, and unreflective habitual action is different from its role in deliberate action. Consideration of Aquinas' discussion of these questions would have shown Green how to complicate his position in ways that make it more plausible.

Sidgwick objects that Green's position makes the deliberate choice of a vicious course of action impossible, because, in Green's view, vicious action is always due to an intellectual mistake about how to achieve self-satisfaction. Sidgwick believes this is an unwelcome consequence of Green's position, because someone who sees where self-satisfaction lies can still reject it deliberately, either because of a vicious refusal to pursue it or because of a decision to sacrifice one's own self-satisfaction for the good of others (*EGSM* 28, 41).

Green ought to agree that his view makes vice the result of a mistake about the sources of self-satisfaction, and he ought to deny that this conception of vice is as implausible as Sidgwick supposes it is. Unless we take the unreasonably rigid view that no intellectual error can be the source of blameworthy actions or states, we need not infer that the vicious person's intellectual error frees him from blame.[36] According to Green, the vicious person is aware of the virtuous person's idea of self-satisfaction, and rejects it. To explain why the vicious person rejects this idea, Green turns to his account of the difference between the morally good and morally bad will, which we must consider later.

1238. Self-Realization and the Errors of Hedonism

If Green has given the right account of rational desire, he has also explained the connexion of freedom with self-realization. What I really want, according to Green, is the fulfilment of a general desire for self-realization or for 'the fulfilment of one's possibilities'.[37] In fulfilling these possibilities we are free; for we lack freedom if we are impeded and frustrated in fulfilling our possibilities.

This may appear too simple an argument for connecting self-realization with freedom. Green might reasonably suppose that we lack freedom if we are conscious of having frustrated possibilities. But not everyone who fails to fulfil his possibilities recognizes that he is failing to fulfil them. Does his ignorance simply remove the consciousness of lack of freedom? Or does it also remove the lack of freedom? Green presumably intends the first answer. He wants to say that in so far as some of an agent's important possibilities are unrealized, to that extent the agent is unfree whether or not he knows it.

---

[36] Aquinas and Scotus on intellectual error and blame; §§262, 366.

[37] 'Just as the consciousness of an unattainable ideal, of a law recognized as having authority but with which one's will conflicts, of wants and impulses which interfere with the fulfilment of one's possibilities, is a consciousness of impeded energy, a consciousness of oneself as for ever thwarted and held back, so the forecast of deliverance from these conditions is as naturally said to be a forecast of "freedom" as of "peace" or "blessedness"'' (Green, *LPO*, 'Freedom', 18)

Green does not mean that we are free only if we realize all the possibilities that are open to us; some of them are trivial, and in any case the choice of one course of action implies the non-realization of other possibilities. Green also speaks of 'becoming perfect'.[38] Freedom consists in acting on some conception of self-realization, which involves some conception of perfection. Green clarifies these claims about freedom and perfection through his discussion of the development of our conception of self-realization.

He traces the first stages of the development of an adequate conception of self-realization by contrasting self-realization with the hedonist conception of the ultimate end. Though his initial remarks about self-realization have not yet clarified its moral implications, Green believes they help us to see that hedonism rests on a mistaken explanation of a fact that his views about self-realization explain correctly. Self-realization characteristically results in a feeling of pleasure,[39] but the hedonist takes this result to be the aim of desire.[40]

Green argues that pleasure cannot constitute the aim of a rational agent because it is a mere 'perishing series'.[41] Sometimes he seems to mean that the hedonist's goal cannot be realized all at once, but has to be realized over time, so that it is only partly present at each time. But what is wrong with a goal of this sort? Sidgwick is right to reject Green's complaint about the intelligibility of the hedonist conception of the ultimate end (*EGSM* 107–13).

Green has a more reasonable objection. At one stage, he allows that a maximum sum of pleasures is conceivable, but he argues that it is conceivable only for agents who conceive themselves as enduring selves who care about something other than pleasure (220). He draws attention to the temporal aspect of maximizing pleasure over one's life. We can imagine how I might compare two pleasures available now (from drinking coffee and drinking tea, for instance) and might choose the greater pleasure. We might suppose that maximizing pleasure over one's whole life is a choice of the same sort. But it is different in important ways. Someone who cares about maximum pleasure over time conceives herself as a temporally extended agent, has some capacity for planning for the whole of her life, and has some interest in exercising this capacity. She compares the present with the nearer and the more distant future, and forms some strategy for her life as a whole. The sort of agent who could accept prudential hedonism is already the sort of agent who aims at self-realization.[42]

As Green recognizes, we might agree with the argument so far, but still insist that one achieves self-realization only through maximum pleasure over one's life. He answers that someone who seeks self-realization far enough even to conceive of a sum of pleasures summed over her whole life ought also to recognize that such a sum of pleasures cannot

---

[38] 'But though the natural impulses of the will are thus the work of the self-realizing principle in us, it is not in their gratification that this principle can find the satisfaction which is only to be found in the consciousness of becoming perfect, of realizing what it has it in itself to be.' (*LPO*, 'Freedom', 21)

[39] Self-realization may also involve pain in so far as it requires the frustration of other desires (*PE* 159).

[40] 'We saw that, in all such desire as can form the motive to an imputable act, the individual directs himself to the realization of some idea, as to an object in which he seeks self-satisfaction. It is the consciousness that self-satisfaction is thus sought in all enacted desire, in all desire that amounts to will, combined with the consciousness that in all self-satisfaction, if attained, there is pleasure, which leads to the false notion that pleasure is always the object of desire.' (158)

[41] Sidgwick, *EGSM*, discusses Green's claims about the perishing series in detail.

[42] Brink, *PCG* 29–40, discusses Green's criticism of hedonism.

satisfy her.[43] Such a conception of the self requires some good that is more permanent than a series of pleasures.[44]

Green relies on the cumulative character of the actions and experiences that constitute an agent's good. An agent realizes herself over time, since her developing capacities and interests work themselves out in the way of life that she chooses. She cares, therefore, about the historical sequence of development, not merely about the succession of episodes at different times. This is why the enlightened pursuit of self-realization seeks some specific state of oneself and of the people whose interest one identifies with one's own interest; the most obvious end of this sort is the well-being of one's family or one's community (PE 230). On the hedonist view, however, agents satisfy themselves only because they repeatedly satisfy a repeated desire. The relation of one satisfaction to another has no intrinsic value for a hedonist. But the hedonist is wrong; for, since there is more to ourselves than a repeated desire for pleasure, our good consists in more than the satisfaction of this desire.

This point is not as clear as it should be in Green's discussion, because he suggests that a good that realizes oneself must be permanent, in contrast to pleasure, which is transitory. Sidgwick objects that it is arbitrary of Green to connect self-satisfaction with permanence rather than with pleasure, since Sidgwick finds no good reason for distinguishing self-satisfaction from pleasure in the first place (ME 135; EGSM 103–4). Sidgwick misunderstands Green on this point; he attends too little to the connexion between self-satisfaction and self-realization, and so he does not notice the connexion between self-realization, permanence, and non-hedonic value. To realize a self is to bring into being a self with its various capacities realized in the right mutual relations. However schematic our description of this state may be, it is a state with some structure that connects different capacities and activities. The heterogeneous character of this self rules out a purely quantitative description of our end.

Since we try to realize a self with a specific structure, we value for their own sakes the states and relations that constitute this structure. Green is therefore partly justified in claiming that, according to this conception of the self, virtues are to be acquired and valued for their own sake, whereas a hedonist must always treat them as purely instrumental to pleasure (PE 363). Green has not yet argued that the relevant virtues are the recognized moral virtues. But he has argued that self-realization will be expressed in some states of a person, and hence that these states are valuable for their own sakes, not simply for their results. According to a hedonist, states of character are to be valued simply for their causal contribution to some further purely quantitative end. This attitude conflicts with our conviction that the end must be appropriate for a heterogeneous self with different capacities to be realized in different non-instrumentally valuable states.

---

[43] 'A desire to satisfy oneself, then, as distinct from desire for a feeling of pleasure, being necessary even to desire for a sum of pleasures, the question is whether it can be a contemplated possibility of satisfying oneself *with pleasures* that yields the idea of a true or highest good, with which particular gratifications of desire may be contrasted.' (PE 222)

[44] 'This idea [sc. of something good on the whole] arises from a man's thought of himself as there to be satisfied when any feeling, in the enjoyment of which he may have sought satisfaction, is over. It is the idea of something in which he may be satisfied, not for this time and turn merely, but at least *more* permanently. Could a contemplated series of pleasures, then, seem to him to offer this relatively permanent satisfaction? . . . Could he be deluded by his own faculty of summing the stages of a succession into supposing that a series of pleasures, of which only one will be in enjoyment at each stage of the series, and none at all at the end, is the more lasting good of which he is in search?' (223) Cf. Bradley, CE 85–6; ES 97–8. Sidgwick replies at ME 133–6.

Green's objection about permanence, then, misses his main point; the fact that the hedonist end cannot be realized all at once is no objection to it. He is right, however, to fasten on the connexion between the desire for a temporally extended good and the structure of a temporally extended self. The fact that we want—as Sidgwick's hedonism requires—pleasure over our whole lives shows that we are concerned about our whole lives. The character of our whole lives and of the selves whose lives they are shows that we cannot be satisfied with a purely quantitative end that lacks the structure that we demand in an end suitable to our selves.

This argument against Sidgwick adapts Plato's main argument to show that hedonism and eudaemonism are incompatible. Green implicitly suggests that the Cyrenaic position is the only consistent hedonist position about value, and that when Sidgwick rejects Cyrenaic indifference to prudence, he also presents a fatal objection to his theory of value.[45]

These claims about the conflict between self-realization and hedonism would lose some of their force against hedonism if Sidgwick were right to claim that reflexion on the character of the ultimate good reveals the truth of hedonism. He complains justly that Green misunderstands and underestimates the main argument in *Methods* for hedonism about the ultimate good (*EGSM* 123–8). Green seems to confuse Sidgwick's views on intuitionism (the approach of common sense) with his appeals to intuition (which may well differ sharply from the views of common sense). That is why he represents Sidgwick's argument for hedonism as an appeal to common sense (*PE* 365). In fact, Sidgwick offers two arguments, one of which appeals to intuition; only the second appeals to common sense (*ME* 400–2). Green passes over the first argument and considers only the second.

Green also misunderstands the connexion Sidgwick sees between pleasure and desirable consciousness. Contrary to Green, he does not take pleasure to be defined as desirable consciousness, and hence his claim that pleasure is desirable consciousness is not trivially analytic (see *PE* 366). On this point Sidgwick also rejects Bradley's interpretation, which fixes, as Green does, on Sidgwick's claims about pleasure as desirable consciousness (*CE* 90–3).

But even though both Green and Bradley misunderstand Sidgwick on this point, they have reasonable objections. Since pleasure is logically distinct from desirable consciousness, some argument is needed to show that pleasure is the only sort of consciousness that is desirable for its own sake. Sidgwick's argument on this point is weak. His various thought experiments show that we do not recognize any ultimate and complete good that does not include desirable consciousness. We may even concede that the desirable consciousness that is included must itself include pleasure. But it does not follow that the only intrinsic good is pleasure, detached from any of its circumstances, relations, or objects. On this point Sidgwick offers only a bare appeal to intuition with no further argument (*ME* 400–1).[46]

1239. Does Utilitarianism Require Hedonism?

Bradley and Green believe that if we reject the hedonist conception of the self, we will also find reasons to reject the utilitarian attempt to understand the relation between morality

---

[45] The Cyrenaics and eudaemonism; §34.   [46] Sidgwick on pleasure; §1165.

and the self. For Sidgwick, this relation raises difficulties for the justifiability of morality; indeed, it results in the 'dualism of practical reason'.

We should reject Sidgwick's dualism, according to Green, by rejecting the assumption that ' "reasonable self-love", desire for one's own true good, is equivalent to desire for a sum of pleasures' (226). But this departure from Sidgwick still allows conflicts that persuade Sidgwick of the dualism of practical reason. As Sidgwick remarks, we may face some practical conflict as soon as we admit that self-realization has different elements that may conflict, or that one person's self-realization may conflict with other people's (GSM 106). Green's account of morality may generate no less conflict than Sidgwick faces.

This does not refute Green's criticism of Sidgwick's dualism. For Sidgwick aims not only to point out the fact of practical conflict, but also to derive it from the separate and irreconcilable outlooks of self-love and morality. He maintains that we encourage the outlook of morality by encouraging the universal point of view, in contrast to the outlook of self-love. None the less, he argues that the outlook of the egoist who regards the pursuit of his own good as most reasonable for him, is irrefutable. If this is the outlook of self-love, Sidgwick believes that no point of view outside self-love and morality can show that either point of view is more reasonable than the other.[47]

Sidgwick relies on a conception of the self and on a conception of morality. He assumes that, according to a correct conception of the self, rational concern for the self does not require the sort of concern for others that is prescribed by morality. To refute Sidgwick, it would not be enough to show that rational self-concern requires some degree of concern for others; the dualism of practical reason remains if this concern for others is different from specifically moral concern.

We ought not to accept Sidgwick's conception of the moral point of view without question. He reaches the dualism of practical reason because he believes that the moral point of view is universal, impersonal, and maximizing. In his view, it values not respect for persons, or even the welfare of persons, but the maximization of good, however it may affect the welfare of persons—even if, for instance, we achieve greater overall pleasure by increasing the number of people and making everyone worse off than they would have been if there had been fewer people. We may not be convinced that this complete subordination of persons, including oneself, to maximization of good, is required by morality.

These doubts about Sidgwick's dualism show that his argument rests on doubtful assumptions about the self and morality. If we take rational self-concern to be less separate from concern for others, and if we take morality to be less separate from concern for persons, the sort of concern required by rational self-concern may be closer to moral concern than Sidgwick's picture would allow.

1240. Does Non-Hedonist Utilitarianism Answer Green?

Green and Bradley are right, therefore, to suppose that the rejection of a hedonist conception of the self casts doubt on Sidgwick's argument. If we reject Sidgwick's purely quantitative

[47] Sidgwick on egoism; §1202.

conception of the aim of self-love, we should reconsider the argument for dualism in the light of a truer conception of the self and self-concern.

The idealist conception undermines Sidgwick's proof of utilitarianism. We saw that Sidgwick's argument from prudence to benevolence rests on the assumption that rational self-love aims at pure accumulation, without any distributive constraints.[48] This assumption is reasonable only if we take the self to be homogeneous to a degree that makes quantitative comparison and accumulation appropriate. If, however, we agree with Bradley about the heterogeneity of the self, we have no reason to accept Sidgwick's assumption. We reasonably treat the self as an organic whole, both at a time and over time. In an organic whole, indifference to distribution is unreasonable. Hence, Sidgwick's account of prudence and his argument from prudence to benevolence must be rejected.

The refutation of Sidgwick's argument does not refute utilitarianism; for we may be able to find some different argument for the principle of utility, or for some non-hedonist parallel to it that would preserve the main features of a utilitarian theory. But, as Sidgwick points out, it is not easy to think of plausible arguments to fill the gap left by the failure of his argument. He believes, therefore, that utilitarians should accept his quantitative hedonist account of self-love. Green and Bradley are right to suppose that they have found a plausible objection to a central utilitarian doctrine.

How much of utilitarian normative ethics collapses if we cannot defend Sidgwick's axiom of benevolence? If we follow more recent trends in utilitarian theory, we will suppose that the crucial feature of utilitarianism is its consequentialist theory of the right, according to which the rightness of an action (or rule, or state of character, if we are indirect utilitarians) is determined by its good consequences. From this point of view, it does not seem to matter whether we take the good to consist in pleasure, or in preference-satisfaction, or in the achievement of some 'objective list' of goods that are good apart from pleasure or preference.[49] Do the idealist criticisms, as we have understood them so far, raise a difficulty for this conception of the right?

The answer depends on how we understand the relation of right and good. We retain Sidgwick's aim of finding an independent criterion of moral rightness only if we understand consequentialism to say that right actions are those that promote some good that is defined independently of the right. But if we abandon quantitative hedonism as a theory of value, it is more difficult to give a convincing account of the good to which the right is purely instrumental. If we reject the demand for independence, we give up another of Sidgwick's theoretical ambitions, but we may retain the view that rightness of actions, rules, and states of character, is simply a function of its causal consequences.

Green suggests that attention to self-realization casts doubt on this consequentialist doctrine of rightness. In his view, the moral virtues are to be understood as aspects of self-realization, not simply as means to some further result that is distinct from states of character. If he is right, we have no reason to believe that the rightness of states of character is purely instrumental. Hence we have a reason for rejecting the consequentialist doctrine of rightness.

---

[48] Sidgwick on prudence; §1195.   [49] 'Objective list' is derived from Parfit, RP 4.

We cannot assess this argument against utilitarianism until we know whether Green is right to claim that the states of character that realize the self include the moral virtues. If he is wrong, we could concede his point that self-realization consists in being a certain way and in having certain states of character, but still insist that morality is purely instrumental to such states of character, which would be the consequences of morality, and not part of morality itself. But Green is right to suggest that if self-realizing states of character include the moral virtues, consequentialism is mistaken; for these aspects of moral rightness will be good non-instrumentally, in their own right, and not simply for their causal consequences.

Should consequentialism restrict itself to causal consequences in determining rightness? A generous conception of consequences claims that if x is right because x constitutes y or is a part of y or realizes y, x is right because of its consequences. A version of consequentialism that relies on this generous conception of consequences is not refuted by Green's claims about the moral virtues. If moral virtues are right because they promote self-realization by being parts of it, self-realization is the right-making consequence of the moral virtues. According to this notion of consequences, every teleological view, including eudaemonist views, will be consequentialist, and it will be consistent to say that x is right both because of itself and solely because of its consequences, because the 'consequences' are marked by descriptions that identify x as a part of some whole.

This generous notion of consequences, however, threatens to make the consequentialist claim unhelpful. It does not quite turn all theories of the right into consequentialist theories; for it still excludes an intuitionist theory that insists that, for instance, just acts are right simply because they are just, and nothing further about justice explains why it is right. Perhaps Clarke, Price, and Ross are non-consequentialists about some aspects of the morally right, even according to this most generous version of consequentialism. However, consequentialism now includes many positions that are usually contrasted with it. Kant, for instance, becomes a consequentialist simply because he believes that just actions are right because they conform to the formula of universal law, and because they express respect for humanity as an end; these descriptions of just actions pick out consequences, according to the generous conception.

If this very broad version of consequentialism is the only tenable version, consequentialism does not vindicate utilitarianism. For acceptance of this broad consequentialism does not decide between the views of Aristotle, Butler, Kant, Mill, and Sidgwick about the nature of the right. Hence it does not help us to decide whether to be utilitarians.

If, then, the idealist conception of self-realization shows us that the only defensible version of consequentialism is the broad version, it raises a serious objection to utilitarianism. The essential elements of utilitarianism are not defensible independently of Sidgwick's hedonism; they are undermined by idealist claims about self-realization. It is doubtful, therefore, whether one ought to try, as Rashdall does, to combine utilitarianism and idealism, and to present the result as 'ideal utilitarianism'.[50] To accept the idealist argument

---

[50] Ideal utilitarianism; §1209.

is to admit that no useful version of consequentialism gives a plausible account of the right.

Rejection of consequentialism as a general theory of the right does not imply that consequences do not matter, or even that causal consequences do not matter. We might well agree with Butler and Price that sometimes they matter. If we cannot show that non-consequential principles always take precedence over consequential principles, we may have no systematic basis for deciding when consequences matter. But, as we have seen in discussing Sidgwick, the mere fact that one theory systematizes more than another does not vindicate the theory that systematizes more.

1241. Green's Defence of Kant

Green recognizes the aspects of Kant that support Bradley's accusations of emptiness and dualism, but he does not endorse these accusations. If we compare his discussion of Kant with Bradley's, after noticing how closely Bradley and Green agree in their conception of self-realization and in their objections to utilitarianism, we ought to be surprised by their disagreement about Kant. We do not know whether Green intends an implicit criticism of Hegel, or Bradley intends an implicit criticism of Green; but in any case, Bradley stays closer to Hegel than Green does.

We ought not to exaggerate the differences. On the one hand, Bradley might well agree that Green's account of Kant presents the elements in Kant that an idealist can accept. On the other hand, Bradley's dialectical and antagonistic approach emphasizes an aspect of Kant that Green sets aside for his own purposes.

Still, Green and Bradley seem to disagree on something important about Kant. Bradley implies that Kant has grasped only one side of a correct conception of the will; because he does not allow realization of the self as a whole, he cannot avoid emptiness and dualism. Green, however, believes that Kant incorporates the basic truths about self-realization. We ought to identify the categorical imperative with the self-realizing principle, and we ought also to accept the different formulations of the categorical imperative as accounts of self-realization, not simply as accounts of one side of self-realization. Kant's mistakes lie in the false beliefs that he adds to these true basic principles about self-realization.

In Green's view, the question about whether or not there is a categorical imperative comes to a question about whether all 'ought' judgments are about means to the satisfaction of antecedent desires. The Kantian view insists that not all 'ought' judgments are about means to satisfy desires, because some assert a reason to have one desire rather than another.[51]

---

[51] 'The real question, then, is . . . whether there is such a thing as a "categorical imperative" at all, or whether there are only hypothetical imperatives; in other words, whether there is an element in the formation of character and determination of conduct consisting in a consciousness of the desirable as distinct from the desired (a consciousness of an object which determines desire instead of being a result of the desire for pleasure), or whether, on the other hand, the consciousness of obligation being ultimately dependent on desire for pleasure, each obligation is conditional upon a preponderance of pleasure accruing in the result, and thus upon the susceptibilities to pleasure and pain of the individual involved.' (Green, *LK* 104)

In taking this to be the essential feature of a categorical imperative, Green implies that Kant's most general description of a categorical imperative says nothing explicitly about morality. Kant offers an account of practical laws that does not depend on his conception of morality.[52] Green tries to elucidate this account. He suggests that the moral consciousness essentially involves a rational agent's presenting an end to himself, rather than having a non-rational end imposed on him.[53]

This teleological element in Green's account may appear to conflict with Kant's exclusion of all ends from the account of the categorical imperative. He appears to move Kant still closer to idealism through his suggestion that the end is the agent himself. This allegedly Kantian claim comes close to Green's conception of the end as self-satisfaction.

Green, however, believes that his interpretation of Kant is legitimate, because his conception of self-satisfaction meets Kant's conditions for a practical law. It is not the product of an empirical inclination; it is necessary, according to Green, for being a rational agent at all. It is not a merely empirical fact about rational agents that they regard themselves as temporally extended agents with different capacities to be fulfilled in an appropriate order. To aim at self-satisfaction is to follow a practical law, even though it does not distinguish a morally good from a morally bad person.

Green considers the objection that the teleological character of his basic principle conflicts with Kant's exclusion of any purposes or objects, Since Kant excludes all matter from the categorical imperative, does he not leave the imperative with no content? Green may not have been thinking of Bradley in stating this objection; he might have derived the objection from Hegel.[54] He answers that Kant's argument does not exclude ends altogether, but excludes ends that do not support laws.[55] In Green's view, the morally important reason for the exclusion of some ends rests on Kant's separation of desire based on inclination from desire based on some obligation distinct from inclination.[56] Since obligation distinct from inclination belongs to the aim of self-satisfaction, this end cannot reasonably be excluded from a categorical imperative. Green argues that the Formula of Humanity relies on an end that involves obligation. Kant agrees that some end is needed to give content to the categorical imperative, even though he does not pursue the consequences of this

---

[52] Kant on practical laws; §903.

[53] In Green's view, the vital question raised by Kant's claims about a categorical imperative of morality originating in reason is this: 'Is the distinctive thing in the moral consciousness rightly held to be the presentation to the moral agent of an end or object consisting in his self, as determined by a self-imposed law, in virtue of its mere form as law and self-imposed?' (*LK* 106)

[54] 'Exclude from the law, as Kant requires to be done, all relation to a "matter" or "an object of which the reality is desired", and what is left of it but a word? Does not the notion of "duty for duty's sake", in short, when logically worked out, prove self-contradictory, since it reduces itself to a duty to do nothing? And is not Kant's real merit the negative one of having worked out this notion more logically than anyone else, and so made this self-destructive result apparent?' (*LK* 110)

[55] '. . . when Kant excludes all reference to an object, of which the reality is desired, from the law of which the mere idea determines the good will, he means all reference to an object other than that of which the presentation ipso facto constitutes the moral law.' (*LK* 111)

[56] 'But it is one thing first to desire an object, of which the presentation does not in itself carry with it any idea of obligation (of a claim independent of any inclination we may happen to have), but, on the contrary, is itself simply a conscious inclination. . .; it is another thing to be conscious of an object as desirable in such a way that the consciousness carries with it the idea of a law, a claim on me to make the object mine whether I am inclined to do so or no.' (*LK* 111)

agreement in his general claims about imperatives, maxims, and ends. This end is to be found in humanity as an end in itself.[57]

Green's concentration on the Formula of Humanity departs from Hegel and Bradley. Both of them, agreeing with many other critics of Kant, take the Formula of Universal Law to capture the essential character of the categorical imperative, and treat the others as variations that add nothing essential to the initial statement.[58] In taking the claims about humanity seriously, Green follows Kant's intentions. But should he take Kant's claims about ends in themselves to support his own view that a moral principle must have a teleological character? Does Kant not insist so strongly on the purely negative character of the end in itself that he removes all teleological content from objective ends?

Green tries to clarify Kant's claims about the end in itself by appeal to Green's claim that action involves self-consciousness and aims at self-satisfaction. These references to self make an agent responsible for an action.[59] The aim of self-satisfaction is necessary for responsibility; we accept responsibility for our own actions in so far as we attribute them to ourselves, and we regard others as responsible in so far as they are capable of the same self-attribution. The role of self-satisfaction in responsible action is not automatic endorsement of a desire. To endorse a desire, we have to see how it fits with the other aims that we attribute to ourselves, and so we regard ourselves as ends that are prior to any specific object of desire. Green's views about self-satisfaction make Kant's claims about rational nature as an end clearer than Kant makes them.

Green inherits from Kant the difficulty of explaining the connexion between regarding oneself as an end and regarding rational agency in general as an end. The appeal to self-satisfaction seems to increase this difficulty, by attributing an egocentric attitude to each rational agent. How is this egocentric attitude to be the basis of a moral law? One might start from the fact that responsible agency is a feature that we attribute to ourselves in common with other people. But Green tries a different approach that relies on the gradual growth of one's conception of self-satisfaction. Though it is satisfaction of ourselves, it does not exclude concern for others.[60] The development and clarification of our conception of self-satisfaction reaches a conclusion in which we regard rational agency, not just our own rational agency, as an end.

---

[57] 'That in that law, the willing obedience to which characterizes a good will, there is implied some relation to an object, and that this object moves the will in the right sort of obedience to the law, appears from his account of man as an absolute end, on which he founds the second statement of the categorical imperative.' (*LK* 111)

[58] Kant on the formulae of the categorical imperative; §§918, 920.

[59] 'In short, in order to become a spring of *moral* action (an action morally imputable, or for which the agent is accountable, an action to which praise and blame are appropriate), the animal desire or aversion must have taken a new character from self-consciousness, from the presentation of oneself as an object, so as to become a desire or aversion for a conceived state of oneself, or for an object determined by relation to oneself. It is because the moral agent is thus conscious of himself as making the motive to his act, that he imputes it to himself, recognizes himself as accountable for it, and ascribes a like accountability to other men, with whom he could not communicate unless they had a like consciousness with his own.' (*LK* 113)

[60] '... the presentation of self as an absolute end ... is not a presentation of it as an empty and abstract self, but as a determinate self, as in a certain state determined by relation to certain objects, or of those objects as determined by relation to it; and further ... the state and the objects have yet to be attained or brought into existence ... The character of the will, then, though it is always a presentation by the agent of himself as an absolute end, will vary according to the state of himself, or according to the objects, determined in thought by relation to himself, which he seeks to attain, or, as we commonly express it, according to the nature of the man's dominant interests.' (*LK* 118)

If an egocentric concern develops into a non-egocentric concern, one aspect of Kantian dualism is mistaken. In Kant's view, as Green interprets it, a psychological hedonist account is correct for all our motives and aims except the moral motive, and so only the moral motive realizes the rational self. Green remarks that Kant's division between purely hedonistic desires and the moral motive fails to explain most of the desires and projects in which people find self-satisfaction.[61] An adequate conception of the self and of self-realization need not entirely reject Kant's account of the moral motive; but it should reject Kant's identification of the moral self with the rational self to be realized.

We may suspect that here Green departs from Kant, and makes it pointless to try to reconcile their two positions. Such a suspicion would be unjustified. For we have found that he is right to claim that Kant's concept of a categorical imperative does not imply that only moral imperatives are categorical, or that every non-moral imperative is purely hypothetical and aims at the satisfaction of inclination. Green finds categorical imperatives in the aims in which we pursue our own self-realization without reference to the interests of others. He is justified in arguing from Kant's concept of a categorical imperative, to show that Kant unduly restricts the extent of categorical imperatives.

Green's account of development claims that the pursuit of self-satisfaction gradually results in a principle that recognizes rational agents as ends in themselves. The account is alien to Kant, as Green recognizes, in so far as it rejects Kant's dualism of motives. But it is not entirely alien, since it agrees with Kant's basic conception of motivation by reason.

The appropriate conclusion of the development of the aim of self-satisfaction is the acceptance of a 'universally binding law of conduct because recognized as such' (*LK* §125). We try to find a more adequate expression of self-satisfaction, and a good person recognizes an absolute good that requires 'unconditional and universal' obedience.[62] But does this conception of 'unconditional and universal' obedience meet Kant's condition? An egocentric aim that rests on a conception of some good that is not conditional on my likes and dislikes still appears to fall short of the Kantian condition. For, as Green has shown, the distinction between the desired and the desirable seems to apply no less to egocentric aims than to non-egocentric aims that require respect for certain ends of other people.

Green takes for granted a point we discussed in examining Kant's views on treating oneself and others as ends.[63] He introduces Kant's sense of 'unconditional and universal' if he means to say that in regarding an end of my own as desirable for me as a rational agent, I also take myself and my rational agency to deserve respect from myself and from others. In claiming respect for my ends as the ends of a rational agent, I am committed to according the same respect to the ends of rational agents as such. It is not clear from Green's explicit argument here that he sees he needs this further claim about self-satisfaction. We should see whether

---

[61] '. . . we are falling into a false antithesis if, having admitted (as is true) that the quest of self-satisfaction is the form of all moral activity, we allow no alternative (as Kant in effect seems to allow none) between the quest for self-satisfaction in the enjoyment of pleasure, and the quest for it in the fulfilment of a universal practical law. Ordinary motives fall neither under the one head nor the other.' (*PE* 160; cf. *LK* 119)

[62] 'The rule of conduct upon which the good man acts . . . bears an authority derived from an ideal of absolute good, of which the operation upon him transcends his powers of definite intuition and expression, and is therefore presented as having a claim upon his obedience not conditional upon his likes and dislikes, a claim in that sense unconditional and universal.' (*LK* 125)

[63] Kant on treating oneself as an end; §923.

he justifies it, explicitly or implicitly, in his account of the growth of our conception of the content of self-satisfaction.

Green suggests that the content of the categorical imperative can be understood by attention to the Formula of Humanity, understood in the light of his claims about self-satisfaction. In his view, this interpretation of Kant also supports Kant's claim that morally good agents are autonomous, because they impose the law on themselves. Green recognizes that Kant's claim is surprising and initially seems difficult to reconcile with the belief that moral principles are objective and independent of us. But he believes that the truth in Kant's view can be understood and separated from denial of objectivity, once we see the connexion of autonomy with self-satisfaction.[64] Green has a sound Kantian basis for his distinction between the claim that we impose the law on ourselves and the claim that we make it for ourselves.[65] He believes that self-imposition can be understood and vindicated by reference to self-satisfaction.

Green relies on a contrast between principles that we impose on ourselves and those that we accept from elsewhere. In one respect, any free action rests on what we impose on ourselves, since it involves our connecting the proposed action with our conception of self-satisfaction. However, not every aim is self-imposed in the same way. Indeed, Green could make his point clearer if he were to accept our suggestion (derived from Aquinas) about the different ways in which responsible actions may be connected with our conception of self-satisfaction.[66] Sometimes an aim is suggested by other people, or by some inclination independent of rational reflexion. If we simply accept this aim without examining it to see whether it fits an adequate conception of self-satisfaction, the aim is, in one important respect, externally imposed, though we freely adopt it and freely act on it. If we accept an end after the appropriate examination, it is self-imposed in a stronger sense. This is the condition that Kant describes as autonomy.

This distinction explains how we give ourselves the law, or impose the law on ourselves. Our conception of the law comes from ourselves, as rational agents; we do not simply respond to suggestions coming from elsewhere. This does not mean that we are free to make up the content of the law. Even if it is objectively true that one ought to avoid inflicting unnecessary pain, it is still open to one person to accept it because he has been told to, or because he is averse to causing pain, and open to another person to accept it as a result of rational reflexion about self-satisfaction. In the second case, it is reasonable to say that we impose the law on ourselves.

Green's exposition does not always distinguish attempts to clarify Kant from attempts to defend Kant through Green's ideas. But some of his claims illuminate Kant. Even if we do not agree with Green's positive views, he is right to claim that Kant has a relatively general

---

[64] '. . . the moral law is the product of the individualizing principle in man, that which alone enables him to say, "I am myself and not another", and to think of anything as his own. We properly enough represent this state of the case by saying that the moral law is self-imposed. This is quite compatible with saying that it is not of our own making in the sense that it is not the product of any desire or aversion . . . which any one of us or any number of us happen to have. It does not rest with you or me, in the ordinary sense of the words, or with anything which we may or may not will or do, whether there shall be such a law or no, any more than it rests with us whether we shall or shall not be rational beings.' (LK 125)

[65] Kant on the author of the obligation v. the author of the law; §987.

[66] Different relations to self-satisfaction; §1267.

conception of a categorical imperative, which does not make moral imperatives the only categorical imperative. Similarly, Green is right to attend to the Formula of Humanity, and to Kant's dualism about motives. In these cases, he presents a fairer account of Kant than the account on which Hegel and Bradley base their criticism.

His insertion of some of his own views about self-realization into his discussion of Kant is an attempt to defend Kant on the basis of claims that Kant does not make. Such a defence may be legitimate; Green does not import alien or un-Kantian elements. But to see whether it succeeds, we need to see whether the doctrines introduced to defend Kant are defensible. We should therefore look more closely at Green's positive account of morality and its relation to the development of the idea of self-satisfaction.

1242. Green's Appeal to Greek Ethics

Green may seem to offer a roundabout defence of an account of self-satisfaction that does justice to Kant. He recognizes that his account of the good may seem rather vague and lacking in practical content, and that it may seem inferior to utilitarianism on this point. In his view, such judgments are partly mistaken and partly irrelevant. He does not think a normative theory of the sort he offers can achieve the degree of practical precision that his critics want; but he does not believe his theory is as vague as the critics suppose, or that utilitarianism is really better off.

Book iii of the *Prolegomena* is about 'The moral ideal and moral progress'. In opposition to hedonism Green sets out his conception of moral good. He identifies it with attachment to a conception of the desirable in contrast to the desired.[67] Though the vicious will aims at self-realization, it takes its conception of the desirable from what 'the individual may for the time desire'. The good will, by contrast, recognizes an object that deserves to be desired; that recognition of an end provides a basis for critical reflexion on actual desires.

Green claims that this end must be realized gradually, and that we cannot claim at any time to have completed the process of realization (178). We cannot treat self-realization as an end whose composition we know determinately in advance of trying to achieve it in particular situations. In some cases, our situation may reveal ways to self-realization that would not otherwise have occurred to us; in other cases, it may close off possibilities that would have been open to us. On the one hand, I have more capacities than those I might recognize by simply reflecting in abstraction from specific situations, On the other hand, some of the possibilities that might seem open in the abstract are not open in this particular situation. The differences arise not only from facts about my natural environment, material resources, technical equipment, and so on, but also from facts about other people and the ways they conceive their self-realization.

---

[67] '. . . the differentia of the virtuous life, proceeding as it does from the same self-objectifying principle which we have just characterized as the source of the vicious life, is that it is governed by the consciousness of there being some perfection which has to be attained, some vocation which has to be fulfilled, some law which has to be obeyed, something absolutely desirable, whatever the individual may for the time desire; that it is in ministering to such an end that the agent seeks to satisfy himself.' (*PE* 176)

But even if our conception of self-realization ought to take account of our specific context and situation, why should it take account of the historical growth of this conception? Why should we not start from where we are, however we got there? Green implies that we can understand the main elements of self-realization better by seeing how they have been embodied historically. Some features of our current morality express the best we can do towards articulating self-realization, while other features may reflect mistaken attempts at self-realization. If we understand this historical development, we can understand and evaluate the different aspects of the current moral outlook that presents us with a particular conception of self-realization.

Much of Green's clarification of self-realization is occupied by 'the development of the moral ideal' (Bk iii, chs. 3–5). One chapter discusses 'the Greek and the modern conception of virtue' (iii 5), because Green believes that Greek moral philosophy embodies the correct outlook. He appeals to Greek ethics to show how the apparent conflict between duty and interest can be resolved. This apparent conflict arises from the ethical theories of Hobbes, Butler, Kant, and Sidgwick; and it appears to force us into Sidgwick's dualism of practical reason.[68] Green believes we can escape the dualism because Greek ethics helps us to remove any grounds for believing in a genuine and insoluble conflict between duty and interest.

Green argues: (1) A person's good is self-satisfaction. (2) Self-satisfaction, adequately conceived, consists in the full realization of a rational agent's capacities. (3) The full realization of our capacities requires us to will the good of other people for their own sake. Hence we avoid the dualism of practical reason if we set out a true conception of a rational agent's good.

Greek ethics tries to develop and to articulate the true conception of an agent's good. In both Plato and Aristotle, according to Green, the virtues require the expression of 'a will to be good, which has no object but its own fulfilment' (251). This is the sort of will in which Aristotle finds a person's good; and therefore he agrees with Green's view that duty (the expression of the will to be good) and interest are reconcilable.

Green believes the Greek moralists have found the right moral ideal, and therefore they and their successors have been right to reject other Greek ideals and practices. For the Greek moralists see that a person's good consists in having the will to be good; and when we understand what this sort of will pursues, we can criticize other Greek views about morality. The general principles and ideals embodied in Greek moral philosophy may not justify the specific practices and attitudes that the Greeks tried to justify by reference to the principles and ideals. The content that we can reasonably ascribe to the principles and ideals may not be the content that makes sense of the specific practices and attitudes.

We might be surprised, therefore, that Green concentrates on Aristotle rather than on Stoic principles and ideals, which seem less embedded in Greek institutions and practices. We might be still more surprised that the part of Aristotle he appeals to is the detailed account of the particular virtues of character. This may seem to be the least promising part of Aristotle's ethics for philosophers who seek to defend Aristotelian doctrines. For this part

---

[68] In Green's view, the dualism of practical reason 'is a conclusion which, once clearly faced, every inquirer would gladly escape, as repugnant both to the philosophic craving for unity, and to that ideal of "singleness of heart" which we have been accustomed to associate with the highest virtue.' (226)

of the *Ethics* appears to be the most evidently outdated and superseded part. The particular virtues often seem remote from our moral experience, because they often assume social conditions remote from our historical experience.

It is reasonable, then, for Sidgwick to take a purely historical view of the Aristotelian particular virtues. He takes Aristotle as his model for a descriptive account of common sense, but not for a critical moral theory.[69] Bradley, by contrast, seems to reject (in some parts of 'My Station and its Duties') the possibility of critical moral theory altogether. From his point of view, the allegedly uncritical character of Aristotle's account is not a reason for objecting to it.

Aquinas takes a different view of Aristotle's account of the specific virtues; he claims to extract from it a statement of principles that can help us to improve Aristotle's statement of what these Aristotelian virtues require. Green, without reference to Aquinas, takes the same view of Aristotle.[70] In his view, Aristotle reaches his conception of the virtues (i) from his conception of happiness; (ii) from some true general principles about how happiness is achieved in different virtues; and (iii) from further beliefs, true and false, about the sorts of actions that fulfil these general principles. Since the general principles are correct, and since we agree with Aristotle about them, we can use them to modify the third element in his conception.

Green believes, therefore, that a historical study of ethical reflexion should present a rational development. Moreover, its rational element should be intelligible not only retrospectively, but also from the point of view that people take at each stage. He does not mean that we can now see some true elements in Aristotle's position that Aristotle could not have seen; this might be a Hegelian retrospective view. In Green's view, we should be able to justify the later stages and correct the earlier, by arguing from principles that are acceptable, even if they are not accepted, at the earlier stage. At a later stage, the relevant principles may be clearer, but they should be accessible at the earlier stage. We should, and we can, capture Aristotle's outlook from his own point of view, and use his outlook to examine the details of his position.

Sidgwick rejects Green's appeal to Greek ethics. His objections are often legitimate, in so far as he identifies places where Green is historically loose or inaccurate. He believes it would be significant if Green were right and the Greeks could be shown to anticipate his claims about self-realization. It would be relevant to see whether Plato and Aristotle helped to explain the content of self-realization, or offered possible lines of defence.[71] Sidgwick's belief that Green fails on this point reinforces Sidgwick's view that appeals to self-realization are unhelpfully uninformative. Conversely, if Green is right, he partially vindicates appeals to self-realization against Sidgwick's objections. It is helpful, therefore, to see whether Sidgwick's criticisms are so damaging that they undermine Green's main aim of connecting self-realization with morality.

---

[69] Sidgwick on Aristotle; §1143.   [70] Aquinas on Aristotelian virtues; §§329–30.
[71] Schneewind, *SEVMP* 411, points out the connexion between historical and philosophical issues: 'Sidgwick's detailed criticism of Green's discussion of Greek morality and moral philosophy shows both the inadequacies of Green's historical vision and his failure to enrol Aristotle in a consensus in his favour . . . Green's admission of the forward-looking impotence of his principle vitiates his view as to its retrospective strength. A moral principle too vacuous to support a method of rational criticism is necessarily too weak to sustain a method of historical explanation.'

1243. Green's View of the Aristotelian Virtues

Green argues that the Greek moralists found the true principle of morality in a 'disinterested interest' in the good.[72] This statement of the general principle of morality offers no specific guidance for action. But we can find principles that guide action, if we look at Aristotle's discussion of the particular virtues.

Green sees that Aristotelian bravery may appear unpromising. Its range is much narrower than the range of courage, as we usually conceive it; for it is confined to citizen-soldiers facing death in battle for their city-state. This restricted conception of bravery separates Aristotle from Socrates, whose wider conception seems more intelligible to us. In so far as Aristotle confines bravery to the conventional tests of military valour, he may well seem rather thoughtlessly conservative.[73]

According to Green, however, Aristotle's narrow conception of the scope of bravery makes it clear that he is talking about the virtue that we also find in a Quaker philanthropist who faces all sorts of dangers and obstacles in the course of working quietly for the relief of suffering (258–9). Greek citizens and modern philanthropists share a principle of 'self-devotion to a worthy end in resistance to pain and fear' (258), or, more exactly, 'the willingness to endure even unto complete self-renunciation . . . in the service of the highest public cause which the agent can conceive' (260).

If this is the principle, Aristotle has a reason to restrict bravery to danger in war, because this is the highest public cause that he can conceive. Facing danger in war is important not because it shows that the individual is daring or reckless, but because it is needed for the safety of a particular community; the community survives only if its citizens are willing to face death in war on its behalf. Hence Aristotle's restriction of the scope of bravery has an unexpected result; it expresses the general principle of bravery more clearly. His restrictive conception of bravery supports Green's wider conception.[74] The historical context of Aristotle's theory shows how the Aristotelian virtue can be freed from these particular historical limitations.

This approach to Aristotelian bravery recalls Aquinas' approach. Aquinas acknowledges that he differs from Aristotle about the actions in which one ought to display bravery, but he believes that Aristotle's views about the 'principal' or 'special' displays of the virtues help us to find the actions that (in our non-Aristotelian situation) fully embody the same virtues.[75]

Aristotle also accepts a narrow conception of temperance. Not every sort of self-restraint or appropriate balance in the gratification of appetites involves temperance; it is confined to the pleasures of the senses, and specifically to the senses of taste and touch (EN 1118a23–b8).

---

[72] 'Once for all they conceived and expressed the conception of a free or pure morality, as resting on what we may venture to call a disinterested interest in the good; of the several virtues as so many applications of that interest to the main relations of social life; of the good itself not as anything external to the capacities virtuously exercised in its pursuit, but as their full realization.' (PE 253)

[73] On Socrates see Plato, Laches, 191c–e. Sidgwick might well seem justified in remarking that Socrates' approach to the virtues is apparently more congenial to Green's account (EGSM 60n).

[74] Hence Aristotle has a good reason for refusing to follow Socrates' view that bravery is present in every sort of situation where people face danger for some worthwhile end.

[75] Aquinas' account of the range of Aristotelian virtues; §330.

According to Green, temperance is restricted in this way because it aims at the good of the community, and the desires that it restrains are especially dangerous, in Aristotle's view, to the common good.[76] The temperate person has the right principle of virtue in so far as he is guided by the demands of the common good.[77] If we attended simply to the pleasures that Aristotle connects with temperance, and ignored their connexion with the common good, we would not see why temperance, as Aristotle conceives it, is an important virtue. But since, in Aristotle's view, these pleasures are particularly dangerous to the common good, the virtue he describes is a genuine virtue of character. Once we see the principle that Aristotle follows in his restriction of the scope of temperance, we can both accept his view that temperance is the virtue that restrains appetites that endanger the common good and question his view that the appetites he considers are in fact the most dangerous.

Bravery and temperance are the only two Aristotelian virtues that Green describes in any detail. He intends them as examples to support a general explanatory account of the Greek conception of virtue. Though Aristotle's account of the scope of different virtues at first seems strangely restricted, the restrictions reflect his views about what promotes the common good, and each virtue is a state of character that expresses the agent's identification of his own good with the common good.

To see how far Green's claims can be generalized, we need to evaluate two claims. (1) We see the point of Aristotle's description of a virtue if we look at the actions he counts as instances, or primary instances, of the virtue and ask why he counts them as instances of it. In each case, we should answer that these actions are especially connected with a common good. (2) Aristotle's general remarks about the moral motive support Green's view of the particular virtues. Green mentions the demand that the virtuous person should act for the sake of the fine (kalon), and he takes this demand to acknowledge the non-instrumental value of virtuous action. The content of a given virtue reflects Aristotle's belief that action for the common good is non-instrumentally good, and therefore fine.[78] We can see whether Green is right if we see whether Aristotle's remarks support these two main claims about virtuous action and about the fine.

Sidgwick rejects Green's claims. In his view, Green exaggerates the degree of system to be found in Aristotle's account, and is wrong to treat the common good as Aristotle's standard

---

[76] 'It must be admitted that, when Aristotle treats most methodically of sôphrosunê, he does little to specify the particular form of the interest in the kalon which he considered to be the basis of the virtue. ... But to a Greek who was told that the virtue of temperance was a mastery over certain desires, exercised tou kalou heneka [sc. for the sake of the fine], there would be no practical doubt what the motive was to be, what was to be the object in which a prevailing interest was to enable him to exercise this mastery. It could only be reverence for the divine order of the state, such a desire to fulfil his proper function in the community as might keep under the body and control the influence of overweening lust.' (PE 263).

[77] 'It was this character of the motive or interest on which it was supposed to rest, that gave to sôphrosunê an importance in the eye of the Greek moralist which, if we looked simply to the very limited range of pleasures—pleasures of the merely animal nature—in regard to which Aristotle supposes the "temperate man" to exercise self-restraint, would scarcely be intelligible. Not the mere sobriety of the appetites, but the foundation of that sobriety in a truly civil spirit, in the highest kind of rational loyalty, gave the virtue its value.' (263)

[78] After introducing the conception of a moral motive of 'purity of heart' that chooses the virtuous action for its own sake (251), Green claims that Aristotle is describing this motive when he says that acting for the sake of the kalon is the characteristic motive of the virtuous person. In 252 he quotes EN 1122b6–7 in Greek; his editor translates the passage rather inexactly. The connexion between the kalon and the common good is defended in 256 fin., 263 (partly quoted above).

of ethical approval. The details of Aristotle's accounts of the particular virtues do not fit the systematic account that Green attributes to Aristotle. Green restricts the range of bravery to Greek citizens concerned with the common good of their city; but in fact Aristotle remarks that a monarchy as well as a *polis* honours brave men (1115a31–2).[79] Nor does he confine temperance to citizens of a *polis*, as he ought to do if Green were right.[80] In these respects, Green's view is too narrow for Aristotle, but in other respects it is too broad. Aristotle does not believe that a brave person displays bravery in sickness or in a shipwreck as he does in war (1115a35–b6); but Green's view implies that Aristotle ought to have regarded these as clear examples of bravery. Similar errors undermine the rest of Green's account of the Aristotelian virtues.[81] Aristotle's appeals to the fine express his aesthetic appraisal of actions, and characters; they do not mark any special role for the common good in fixing the content of the virtues.[82]

1244. Aristotle on the Fine and the Virtues

One major disagreement between Green and Sidgwick takes us back to the difficulty that we have often encountered in understanding Aristotle's conception of the fine. In Stoics sources, the Greek '*kalon*' and its Latin equivalent '*honestum*' might reasonably be translated by 'right'; later readers of the Stoics take this term to designate moral rightness and moral value as distinct from prudential or hedonic or aesthetic value.[83] But this is by no means so obvious in Aristotle.

The contrast between Aristotle and the Stoics reappears in Aquinas and Suarez. The relatively inconspicuous role of the fine in Aristotle is reflected in Aquinas; and we may wonder whether Suarez is justified in importing the Stoic notion of the right into Aquinas' discussion of the moral good. We can ask a similar question about Green and Sidgwick. According to Green, the connexion between virtue and fineness shows that Aristotle is basically right about the nature of the moral motive and about the connexion between the agent's good and the good of others. Sidgwick, however, draws the opposite conclusion; the references to the fine show that Aristotle does not distinguish moral from aesthetic judgments, so that we cannot expect clarity from him about the nature of moral goodness.

Despite the importance of fineness in the *Ethics*, Aristotle discusses it only briefly. But our discussion of Aristotle, Aquinas, and Suarez has given some reasons for agreeing with Green on the connexion between the fine, the individual's good, and the common good. Green is right to maintain that Aristotle argues from his conception of happiness to the conception of

---

[79] '. . . even an ordinary Greek would not have denied that a mercenary of the Persian king might be as valiant as possible.' (Sidgwick, *EGSM* 92)

[80] 'The idea that *sôphrosunê* would not be laudable except in a republic—which is really what Green's phrase comes to—would have appeared to Aristotle absurd.' (Sidgwick, *EGSM* 94)

[81] On temperance, see Sidgwick, *EGSM* 93.

[82] Taylor defends Green against Sidgwick's criticism in his review of *EGSM*. Jones replies on behalf of Sidgwick in 'Green's account'. Jones stresses Aristotle's appeal to the *kalon*, taking Sidgwick's account of it for granted. If, however, Green's account of it is right, the appeal to the *kalon* supports Green's general position.

[83] On *kalon* and honestum see §§332–4 (Aquinas); 438 (Suarez); 609 (Shaftesbury); 855 (Reid).

a common good as the focus of virtuous action. He renders Aristotle's definition of happiness as 'the full expression or realization of the soul's capacities in accordance with its proper excellence' (254), and he argues that Aristotle finds the full realization of these capacities in an agent's effective concern for the good of the community.[84]

These claims rest on solid Aristotelian support; for Aristotle claims that the happiness of an individual person must include the happiness of family, friends, and fellow-citizens (*EN* 1097b8–11, 1169b16–19, 1170b14–19). This link between the agent's happiness and the common good explains why a rational agent is justified in valuing the virtues of character that require him to do the fine action for its own sake. Fine action has a justified claim on him because it aims at the common good, and he, as a rational agent aiming at his own good, also has reason to aim at the common good.

But even if Green is right about Aristotle's conception of the virtues and their relation to the fine, he might still be wrong about the particular virtues. Aristotle does not fully articulate his general conception, and does not explicitly and emphatically apply it to the particular virtues. Sidgwick suggests that Green's attempt to systematize Aristotle's account of the virtues around the fine and the common good, as Green understands them, simply reflects Green's inattention to the details of Aristotle's position.[85]

We have already considered this dispute between Sidgwick and Green in our discussion of Aristotle's description of the specific virtues. We have found that Green is right, and that the details of Aristotle's description confirm the claim that he is guided by his general claim that the virtuous person aims at the fine, understood as the common good.[86]

Some apparently minor details of Aristotle's description of bravery help to answer some of Sidgwick's specific objections.[87] When Aristotle says that the brave person does not fully display bravery in sickness or shipwreck, he refers to private journeys, rather than to naval battles; and so the circumstances do not involve the common good. In any case, Aristotle assumes that the brave person has to face sickness and shipwreck rather passively (1115b4–6), so that the circumstances do not offer the opportunity for active pursuit of the common good. If at least one of these explanations is correct, Aristotle's judgment about these cases fits Green's account. Moreover, Aristotle probably denies (contrary to Sidgwick) that the subjects of a king display the primary sort of bravery.[88] He may be thinking of such people when he mentions those who stand firm in danger under compulsion (1116a29–b3); and he clearly denies that these people are brave.

Similarly, we have seen that Aristotle is concerned with temperance and intemperance because of their effect on the common good.[89] Wanton aggression (*hubris*) is a characteristic display of intemperance against other people (1129b21), and it suggests why the fine is

---

[84] On concern for the good of the community see *PE* 206–8, 229–32, 240–5.

[85] Further discussion of Green and Aristotle; Thomas, *MPG* 308–10; Lewis, 'Content'.

[86] Aristotle on the fine and the common good; §116.

[87] The relevant Aristotelian virtues are discussed more fully in §§118–21.

[88] Aristotle is not out of step with Greek common sense and tradition. See Herodotus vii 103.4, 104.4, 210.2.

[89] As Green says: '. . . such a check should be kept on the lusts of the flesh as might prevent them from issuing in what a Greek knew as *hubris*—a kind of self-assertion, and aggression upon the rights of others in respect of person and property, for which we have not an equivalent name, but which was looked upon as the antithesis of the civil spirit' (*PE* 265).

a proper aim for the temperate person. Concern for the common good explains why some of the different aspects of intemperance should be avoided. Sidgwick suggests that Green's account forces Aristotle into the manifestly absurd conclusion that temperance is praiseworthy only in a republic (i.e., a Greek *polis*) where citizens acknowledge that the state pursues their common good (*EGSM* 94). But the conclusion is not obviously absurd. Even though other communities besides a *polis* have reason to cultivate temperance in their members, perhaps only a *polis* gives an agent reasons to regard temperance as non-instrumentally good and fine. For if virtuous people are to regard an action as fine, and hence as worth choosing for its own sake, they must agree that it promotes a common good that they value as part of their own good. Not every political system makes it reasonable to take this attitude.[90]

Sidgwick raises further objections derived from virtues that Green does not discuss, especially about liberality (*eleutheriotês*) and magnanimity. But we have seen that Aristotle is more systematically concerned with the fine and the common good than we might initially suppose from his description of these virtues; Green's silence does not show that his position is indefensible.[91]

Sidgwick is right to remark that Aristotle's description of liberality fails to distinguish self-regarding from benevolent expenditure. But this observation does not refute Green, but actually helps him. For we ought to expect Aristotle to draw a sharp distinction between self-regarding and benevolent actions only if we suppose that a person's self-regarding ends will also be predominantly selfish, and that benevolence must be added to, and will probably conflict with, his true conception of his own good. This is Sidgwick's view of the relation between self-love and benevolence; he gives Butler credit for having distinguished the two principles. Sidgwick believes they imply the dualism of practical reason. But Aristotle recognizes no such dualism; if the common good is a part of the agent's own good, self-regarding actions include benevolent actions. Aristotle's failure to draw a sharp distinction supports Green.[92]

Green argues that a Christian conscience can both accept the Aristotelian virtues and reject Aristotle's views about their extension. Sidgwick presents magnanimity as a clear counter-example to this attempted reconciliation.[93] But we have seen that the role of the fine and the common good in the magnanimous person's thoughts and actions confirms

[90] Green suggests that it is reasonable under 'the regime of equal law, the free combination of mutually respecting citizens in the enactment of a common good' (263).

[91] One of Green's copies of the *Ethics* contains this marginal note: 'Liberality really a particular form of the virtue which manifests itself in these general ways. If transformation of false egotism into true is taken as a basis of virtue, then the several virtues can all be developed from a single root. Aristotle fails to develope them because he does not clearly recognize this basis. No unity of principle either in relation of virtues to the person or to the *pathê*... The true view of virtue in relation to egotism most nearly approached by Aristotle in account of philia in 8th and 9th books' (*Ethics*, Copy A, facing p. 61).

[92] Green recognizes this point about benevolence: 'No doctrine of sympathy or disinterested benevolence in Aristotle; contrast moralists of last century. This scarcely a drawback. In these moralists taken for granted that man lives either for pleasure or at least for his own good as not consciously identified with that of others. Accordingly they essay [?] to show that there are sympathetic pleasures, in seeking which we please (not = do good to) others; or that self-love may be *balanced* by disinterested benevolence. But Aristotle's fundamental notion is that every [?] one should live for his state. No need then to dwell on benevolence as a balance of selfishness, or on sympathy as a series of pleasures of which pleasure of another is condition' (*EN*, Copy B, on *EN* viii, facing p. 150).

[93] Sidgwick, *OHE* 63, quoted in §121.

Green's general view. In this as in other cases, Aristotle does not simply describe the traits of character that common sense counts as virtuous. He modifies and moralizes common sense, in order to insist on the central role of the virtuous person's correct election (*prohairesis*). This election aims at the agent's own good, but also thereby at the fine and the common good. Aquinas presents a reasonable reconciliation of Aristotle's claims about magnanimity with Christian claims about humility. If Green had known Aquinas' treatment of the Aristotelian virtues, it would have helped him to strengthen the points on which Sidgwick criticizes him.

Green is right to claim that Aristotle's conception of happiness supports a systematic description and defence of the moral virtues. If the argument that Aristotle describes and partly executes is reasonable, it suggests that appeals to self-realization have useful moral content. Reflexion on Aristotle shows that specific virtues of character claim our attention in so far as they aim at the common good, which in turn claims our attention as part of our own good. Aristotle needs to show that concern for the common good is part of the fulfilment of a rational agent's capacities, which he identifies with happiness. To show this, Aristotle relies, above all, on his account of friendship.[94] Green sees that this part of Aristotle's theory needs explanation, and he devotes a large section of *Prolegomena* to clarifying his own views on the common good.

1245. The Self and the Common Good

Green's discussion of Aristotle on the virtues of character sets him the task of showing more precisely how self-realization leads to morality. He has argued that the principle of self-realization is a Kantian categorical imperative, because it expresses our conception of the desirable in contrast to the merely desired. If his account of Greek ethics is defensible, the Greek moralists believe that this conception of self-realization supports the moral virtues, because one's own self-realization requires concern for the good of others. If Green is to show that reflexions on the Aristotelian virtues support Kantian morality, he needs to argue for two claims: (1) Concern for my own good requires concern for a common good that includes the good of others. (2) This concern for a common good includes concern for persons as ends in themselves.[95]

We might accept the first claim without accepting the second; indeed, Aristotle seems to illustrate the distance between them.[96] Friendship, as he understands it, involves concern for the common good of myself and my friends. If it can be extended to fellow-citizens, it involves concern for their common good also. If the Stoics are right, and we can extend friendship so that we regard all human beings as fellow-citizens, self-realization involves concern for everyone.[97] But this extension of self-concern does not—at first sight at least—involve equal concern for everyone as an end; hence it seems to fall short of Kantian morality.

---

[94] Aristotle on friendship and the common good; §§122–8.
[95] On different elements in Green's argument for morality, see Thomas, *MPG* 279–87.
[96] Brink, *PCG* 44–55, defends some of Green's claims about the common good by reference to Aristotle on friendship.
[97] The Stoics on extension of self-concern; §§194–9.

Green, however, accepts Kantian morality, and so he should defend both the claims we have distinguished.

He introduces the common good at the point in his theory where Bradley introduces the self's demand to be an infinite whole by identifying itself with a whole. Bradley believes that I identify myself with a whole by identifying myself with my station and its duties, which is the way in which I contribute to, and participate in, a whole. Is Green's appeal to the common good equivalent to Bradley's claims about wholes?

Green appears to differ from Bradley on some important points: (1) Green takes the common good to secure the demands of Kantian morality, including the Formula of Humanity. Bradley does not affirm such a close connexion with Kantian morality, and he does not mention the Formula of Humanity. (2) If we speak of a common good, individuals do not seem to be submerged, as they might seem to be in Bradley's conception of the social whole. The common good of A and B is a good for A and a good for B; but if A and B are parts of some whole C, what is good for C need not be good for both A and B. If two pictures are part of a collection, and the collection is endangered by a flood or a fire, the preservation of the collection may require us to abandon one picture and save the other, but we do not do what is best for the abandoned picture.

On this point, Bradley's claims about wholes need some clarification. If my leg cannot achieve its good without the good of the rest of my body, amputation of my leg to save my life does not make the amputated leg worse off than it would be if it were not amputated.[98] This organic conception does not completely absorb the good of each part in the good of the whole, but it recognizes the connexion between the good of the part and the good of the whole. Bradley's demand for identification of oneself with the social whole might suggest that I become indifferent to, or perhaps do not even acknowledge, my own local good, but consider only the global good of the social whole, and think of my own good only as contributing to it. But this degree of indifference does not follow from an organic doctrine that acknowledges the distinct good of each part. It is not always clear whether Bradley recommends indifference to one's own good or simply argues that it depends organically on the good of the whole.[99]

Green's conception of a good that is common to, not separate from, different individual goods rejects indifference to one's own good. The conception of a common good ensures some consideration for the good of each individual involved, so that the good of the whole is also good for each of those involved in the whole. This distributive demand is somewhat weaker than the demand that seems to result from the Kantian formula of humanity, since a common good might not be equally good for everyone, and so it might—unless something further can be said to justify the inequality—violate the requirement of treating each person equally as an end. But at least we can see how Green might develop a conception of a common good that meets Kantian conditions that Bradley either rejects or neglects. Can this specific conception of a common good be justified by reference to self-realization?

---

[98] Cf. Epictetus ii 6.9–10 on the foot and the body (quoted in §164), and Aquinas on justice, §338.
[99] This issue in Hegel is discussed by Neuhouser, Review of Wood, 319–20.

1246. The Development of Concern for the Common Good

The pursuit of self-realization includes an impulse towards self-perfection (177).[100] This impulse implies the will to improve oneself and the idea 'of something, he knows not what, which he may and should become' (192), or of some 'absolutely desirable' object 'which is other than the object of any particular desire' and 'consists in the realization of capacities which can be fully known only in their ultimate realization', or 'the fulfilment of himself, of that which he has in him to be' (193). According to Green, this impulse leads us to the pursuit of a common good that involves non-instrumental relations to other people.[101] Someone who aims at a common good 'cannot contemplate himself as in a better state, or on the way to the best, without contemplating others, not merely as a means to that better state, but as sharing it with him' (199). Green claims that part of our normal development in relation to other people is the formation of this non-instrumental concern for them. As we develop our conception of our own good as something more than the gratification of our immediate desires, we recognize a common good for ourselves and others.[102]

Why should our conception of self-realization develop in this social direction? Green sometimes rejects this question, on the ground that the social aspects of my conception of my good need no special explanation. Self-realization is not to be understood as an end for abstract individuals considered apart from their actual desires and interests.[103] Actual people are interested in other people and in larger communities, and want to fulfil their social desires as well as their self-confined desires. We have to fulfil the general possibility of self-realization through opportunities that are available for people like us in our social environment.

[100] Dewey, 'Motive', criticizes Green unfairly for his claims about perfection that cannot be wholly achieved in specific forms of society. He argues that this distance between actuality and perfection makes Green's appeal to perfection empty.

[101] The relevant interests '. . . are not merely interests dependent on other persons for the means to their gratification, but interests in the good of those other persons, interests which cannot be satisfied without the consciousness that those other persons are satisfied.' (PE 199)

[102] Lamont, IGMP 212–15, attacks the egoistic aspect of Green's view of self-realization as the end. He suggests (214) that Green's mistake is analogous to the one he criticizes in hedonism. His criticism does not do justice to Green's aim of reconciling prudential and moral aims, and so of avoiding Sidgwick's dualism. Campbell, 'Intuition', 121–41, offers a more sympathetic account of Green's main argument.

[103] 'The idea, unexpressed and inexpressible, of some absolute and all-embracing end is, no doubt, the source of such devotion, but it can only take effect in the fulfilment of some particular function in which it finds but restricted utterance. It is in fact only so far as we are members of a society, with which we can conceive the common good as our own, that the idea has any practical hold on us at all, and this very membership implies confinement in our individual realization of the idea. Each has primarily to fulfil the duties of his station.' (PE 183) 'Now the self of which the man thus forecasts the fulfilment is not an abstract or empty self. It is a self already affected in the most primitive forms of human life by manifold interests, among which are interests in other persons. These are not merely interests dependent on other persons for the means to their gratification, but interests in the good of those other persons, interests which cannot be satisfied without the consciousness that those other persons are satisfied. The man cannot contemplate himself as in a better state, or on the way to the best, without contemplating others, not merely as a means to that better state, but as sharing it with him.' (199) Whether or not Green means to allude to Bradley in referring to 'the duties of his station', the phrase marks a point on which he agrees with Bradley. The first sentence of this passage should help to dispel Dewey's suggestion that Green's view entirely separates the realization of the self from concrete activity in particular situations. According to Dewey, 'In conceiving of capacity, then, not as mere possibility of an ideal or infinite self, but as the more adequate comprehension and treatment of the present activity, we are enabled to substitute a working conception of the self for a metaphysical definition of it' ('Ideal', 661). It is difficult to see why Green should accept the antithesis that Dewey implies in his claim about substitution.

This refusal to abstract human nature from the social attachments of actual human beings is reasonable, in so far as it reminds us that non-instrumental concern for others as part of one's own good is not a philosopher's construction, but a familiar, and perhaps unavoidable, part of normal mental and moral development. But this observation does not answer the question about justification. For we might still want to ask whether this attachment to others is a merely natural fact.

We can specify this question in two further questions: (1) Is it part of the self-realization only of people who happen to have acquired these other-regarding ends, so that people who do not acquire such ends can achieve self-realization in other ways? (2) Even if some attachment to others is a part of normal development, people differ in the strength of such attachments, and hence in the extent to which they care about them above other ends. Why, then, ought we, from the point of view of self-realization, to care about them to the degree prescribed by morality?

Green's reluctance to seek a justification for concern for others obscures these questions. But he offers some answers to them. One answer appeals to the permanence of the good that we seek in order to realize ourselves.[104] If I regard my well-being as including the well-being of others, my self-realization is less intermittent and imperfect than it would be if I regarded my well-being as confined to myself. The co-operation of others will help my efforts towards the end I was aiming at. If I am concerned with these others as I am with myself, I will value their self-realization in the way I value my own, and so I will make my own well-being more permanent.

1247. The Non-Competitive Common Good

A further feature of the common good makes my own good more permanent and stable by including it. Green takes a common good to be essentially non-competitive, in contrast to the goods that Aristotle calls 'contested' (*perimachêta*, EN 1168b19); any of us can possess it without leaving less of it for other people (245).[105] Since we must identify our good with the good of a larger whole, we must conceive it as non-competitive.[106]

If we took our own self-realization to conflict with that of others, it would be unstable. For any benefit to someone else would be a potential threat to me; I would always have to consider whether it is in my self-confined interest to allow this benefit to another. This is how Hobbes's contractors calculate. Hobbes implicitly admits Green's point, since he tries to prevent this sort of calculation within the moral framework of the state, and therefore

---

[104] 'Having found his pleasures and pains dependent on the pleasures and pains of others, he must be able in the contemplation of a possible satisfaction of himself to include the satisfaction of those others, and that a satisfaction of them as ends in themselves and not as means to his pleasure. He must, in short, be capable of conceiving and seeking a permanent well-being in which the permanent well-being of others is included.' (PE 201; cf. 203, 216, 229–30)

[105] 'This well-being he doubtless conceives as his own, but that he should conceive it as exclusively his own—his own in any sense in which it is not equally and coincidentally a well-being of others—would be incompatible with the fact that it is only as living in community, as sharing the life of others, as incorporated in the continuous being of a family or nation, of a state or a church, that he can sustain himself in that thought of his own permanence to which the thought of permanent well-being is correlative. His own permanent well-being he thus necessarily presents to himself as a social well-being.' (232)

[106] Spinoza on non-competitive goods; §516. Cf. Broad, *FTET* 43.

tries to silence the doubts raised by the 'fool'. Green argues that we prevent this mutually destructive calculation and the resulting instability in our well-being only if we recognize a non-competitive good.

In Green's view, this non-competitive common good satisfies the Kantian requirement that we should treat rational agents as ends, because we recognize each person as pursuing her own self-realization in the way that we pursue ours. He even suggests that human society presupposes the conception of persons as ends.[107] Mutual recognition of persons as ends is necessary for the sort of co-operation that distinguishes societies from mere alliances of self-assertive individuals.[108] Green appeals to the Aristotelian conception of citizens as 'equal and similar' in certain respects. In his view, the relevant respects involve recognition as ends. A purely Hobbesian alliance, therefore, does not produce the sort of society that we are familiar with. He would have strengthened his argument if he had remarked that Hobbes recognizes the presumption of equality as a law of nature (Lev. 15.21), but cannot defend it within his own account of the basis of the laws of nature.[109]

Green suggests a different sort of connexion between society, self, and persons as ends. He asserts that I conceive myself as a person only in a context where persons are recognized as ends in themselves.[110] The recognition of myself and the bettering of my life as an end for me requires me to recognize others as ends in themselves for me (cf. 201). This is the point where Green passes from a merely shared good to a good that satisfies the Kantian Formula of Humanity. But he does not defend the transition in any detail, and his different remarks about it are not developed far enough to constitute a detailed argument; they offer at most fragments or suggestions of arguments.

Perhaps we can defend Green if we consider the connexion between (i) self-realization in another person, (ii) a non-competitive good, and (iii) treating each other as ends. If the good that A and B both aim at is competitive, A cannot find himself realized in B's ends unless they happen to promote the self-confined ends of A. But if A cares about B for B's own sake, in the way A cares about A, the achievement of B's ends also realizes A's ends. Hence A and B must regard each other as deserving non-instrumental concern.

So far this is an Aristotelian argument; Green relies on the considerations that we have discussed in examining Aristotle's discussion of friendship. He alludes to, but does not clearly exploit, a Kantian consideration that is needed to take us from non-instrumental concern to respect for rational agents as ends. In regarding my aims as desirable, worthy of desire, as opposed to being simply desired, I also, according to Kant, take them to deserve respect, as

---

[107] 'Such society is founded on the recognition by persons of each other, and their interest in each other, as persons, i.e. as beings who are ends to themselves, who are consciously determined to action by the conception of themselves, as that for the sake of which they act. They are interested in each other as persons in so far as each, being aware that another presents his own self-satisfaction to himself as an object, finds satisfaction for himself in procuring or witnessing the self-satisfaction of the other.' (PE 190).

[108] 'The combination of men as isoi kai homoioi [equal and similar] for common ends would be impossible. Thus, except as between persons, each recognizing the other as an end in himself and having the will to treat him as such, there can be no society.' (190)

[109] Hobbes actually contrasts his presumption of equality with Aristotle's claims about natural inequality. Green's allusion to Aristotle (Pol. 1287b33–4) and Hobbes's allusion reflect two opposed attitudes to Aristotelian political theory. On Hobbes on equality, see §505.

[110] 'So human society presupposes persons in capacity—subjects capable each of conceiving himself and the bettering of his life as an end to himself—but it is only in the intercourse of men, each recognized by each as an end, not merely a means, and thus as having reciprocal claims, that the capacity is actualized and that we really live as persons.' (PE 183)

the ends of a rational agent, from other rational agents. This is the crucial step that explains how I can take my pursuit of my own good not to compete with other people's pursuit of their own good. Both my good and their good are regarded as proper objects of mutual respect.

Green's account of the development of morality consists in an account of 'the extension of the area of common good' (206–17). He argues that gradually we come to identify our good with the good of larger social groups, so that eventually we are concerned with the interests of humanity as a whole. This extension results from the recognition of wider areas of possible co-operation in a common good.[111] Green presupposes a rational impulse towards co-operation, on the reasonable assumption that co-operation in a common good is an extension of my own self-realization. This assumption gives us a reason to seek further co-operation with possible co-operators. The mere fact of 'growing means of intercourse' might simply offer the prospect of more competition or of more domination.[112] But if we already acknowledge implicitly that we have an interest in the expansion of areas of co-operation for a common good, we have a reason to look for further areas of co-operation. When we recognize that we find such areas in so far as we deal with people with whom we can communicate as 'I' and 'Thou' (cf. 216), we expand the area of co-operation and common good.

Green recognizes that this tendency to expand co-operation is not inevitably the strongest tendency in a given society; but he believes it is a reasonable and natural tendency. The task of the historian is not to explain why this tendency is effective, but to explain why it is sometimes retarded 'by those private interests which have made it inconvenient for powerful men and classes to act upon it'. He mentions the American Confederate States as an example (209).

This extension of our conception of the participants in the common good is the source of the impartiality that is central to the moral point of view. Morally sensitive people consider the interests of everyone affected before they act to benefit people near to them (212), so that no one will suffer from other people's confined loyalties or restricted imagination. This is also the source of a fully developed sense of justice, which fulfils the maxim 'ius suum cuique' (211), because it recognizes that everyone has the same rights and deserves equal respect on that account.

1248. The Common Good, Utilitarianism, and Kant

The extension of the area of the common good leads us to care about the good of humanity impartially. On this point, Green agrees with utilitarianism because it 'has

---

[111] '. . . if at the root of such obedience . . . there has been an idea of good, suggested by the consciousness of unfulfilled possibilities of the rational nature common to all men, then it is intelligible, that, as the range of this idea extends itself . . . the sense of duty which it yields . . . should become a sense of what is due to man as such . . .' (207) 'Given the idea of a common good and of self-determined participators in it, . . . the tendency of the idea in the minds of all capable of it must be to include, as participators of the good, all who have dealings with each other and who can communicate as "I" and "Thou". With growing means of intercourse and the progress of reflection the theory of a universal human fellowship is its natural outcome.' (209)

[112] Green mentions the role of trade and conquest. He is not an enthusiast for empire (216).

most definitely announced the interest of humanity . . . as the end by reference to which all claims upon obedience are ultimately to be measured' (333). Some utilitarians speak as though this general reference to the interest of humanity or the common good of human beings, without special privileges for any particular group, is all that the utilitarian position amounts to; and then they are puzzled that otherwise enlightened people reject utilitarianism.[113]

Green argues that this defence of utilitarianism does not face the basic question. He claims that his view supports the Kantian principle of treating humanity as an end in itself, and he defends the Kantian principle against the Benthamite policy of taking each person to count for one (214). The utilitarian differs from the Kantian principle because it does not assign value to persons but to their pleasures.[114]

The utilitarians' practice has been better than their theory (as Aristotle says of Eudoxus, EN 1172b15–18), because they have interpreted the utilitarian criterion through their own wishes and aspirations. Utilitarian reformers have recognized that some people's interests have been unjustifiably excluded from consideration, and they have offered the utilitarian criterion to explain why the exclusion is unjustifiable. But Green argues that it does not explain this, because it does not assign the appropriate value to persons.

He criticizes the distributive implications of the utilitarian criterion.[115] Since utilitarians aim at maximum pleasure, their criterion does not exclude the oppression of the weaker by the stronger.[116] Green concludes that if we took the utilitarian criterion seriously, we would always violate the Kantian criterion in principle, since we would not be treating persons as having an equal claim to happiness,[117] but we would always make our treatment of them depend on the total resultant pleasure. This argument equally refutes Sidgwick's suggestion that Bentham's principle implies some bias towards equal distribution, and requires equal treatment of persons when total happiness is not affected.[118]

When Green explores the implications of the utilitarian criterion, he does not allege that actual utilitarians are likely to advocate immoral policies. Many utilitarians are enlightened and humane, but this outlook results from their 'unscientific interpretation' of well-being,

---

[113] Bain offers this defence of utilitarianism; see §1125.

[114] 'The Benthamite would repudiate or pronounce unintelligible the notion of an absolute value in the individual person. It is not every person, according to him, but every pleasure, that is of value in itself; and in accordance with this view he has to qualify the formula we have been dwelling on, so as to empty it, if not of all practical significance, at any rate of the significance which we have ascribed to it, and which has been the real guide to the reforming utilitarian.' (214) 'Impartiality of reference to human well-being has been the great lesson which the utilitarian has had to teach. That "unscientific" interpretation of well-being which the men most receptive of the lesson, on the strength of their own unselfish wishes and aspirations, have been ready to supply, has made them practically independent of any further analysis of it, when once the equality of claim to it had been thoroughly recognized.' (333)

[115] 'Upon Hedonistic principles it will only be as "supposed equal in degree" that one person's happiness, i.e. his experience of pleasure, is to count for as much as another's . . . it is hard to see how the formula, thus interpreted, can afford any positive ground for that treatment of all men's happiness as entitled to equal consideration, for which Utilitarians have in practice been so laudably zealous.' (214)

[116] '. . . for the stronger being presumably capable of pleasure in higher degree, there could be nothing to show that the quantity of pleasure resulting from the gain to the stronger through the loss to the weaker was not greater than would have been the quantity resulting if the claims of each had been treated as equal.' (214)

[117] Several difficulties would arise if we were to try to be more precise about what people have an equal claim to. It would be unreasonable to claim that people have a right to be equally happy.

[118] Sidgwick on distribution; §1198.

not from a consistent application of the utilitarian criterion. Green takes utilitarianism to require the application of 'empirical hedonism' (as Sidgwick describes it) to practical questions, and he observes that if we really practise empirical hedonistic calculation, we have no compelling reason to rule out the immoral results that he describes. This is a fair observation on the method that Sidgwick regards as the only appropriate method for a consistent utilitarian.[119]

Sidgwick's preference for empirical hedonism over the 'unscientific interpretation' of well-being is justified within his theoretical assumptions. He looks for a 'common measure' because he tries to remove all moral perplexity from practical questions, and to replace it with purely empirical uncertainties that we may hope to remove through the advance of the relevant empirical sciences. He justifies his reliance on empirical hedonist calculation by claiming that this is the standard way to regulate the pursuit of non-moral goods. To abandon this method is to return to the theoretical uncertainty and indefiniteness that Sidgwick tries to remove from moral reasoning.

The demand for the replacement of moral by empirical uncertainty is not an arbitrary preference for one kind of uncertainty over another. If Sidgwick were to defend utilitarianism against Green's objection by appealing to unscientific interpretations as legitimate applications of the utilitarian criterion, he would be allowing moral assumptions to control our judgment about which pleasures and pains matter more than others. But what is the status of such moral assumptions? Either (1) they are simply derived from the utilitarian criterion, so that they are really empirical hedonist rules; or (2) they are non-utilitarian moral principles. The first answer takes us back to the questions about empirical hedonism. The second implies that utilitarianism is not a complete moral theory. For these principles that control the application of the utilitarian criterion seem to restrict the pursuit of maximum pleasure. If we admit this, and we cannot fix the order of these principles, in relation to one another and to the principle of utility, we seem to be pluralist intuitionists rather than utilitarians.

These are the difficulties that face Mill's utilitarianism and the 'ideal utilitarianism' of Rashdall and Moore. Sidgwick sees these difficulties and so he rejects the unscientific interpretations that might replace empirical hedonism. In doing so, he admits the legitimacy of Green's criticisms of the utilitarian method.

Green is right, therefore, not to be too concerned about the alleged indefiniteness of his conception of the ethical end. We might be tempted to compare it unfavourably with the definiteness of the utilitarian end. But utilitarians achieve definiteness only at the cost of allowing immoral consequences. If they draw back from these consequences by allowing

---

[119] 'And in saying that this must be the method of the utilitarian moralists, I only mean that no other can normally be applied in reducing to a common measure the diverse elements of the problem with which he has to deal . . . how far the increase of wealth or of knowledge, or even the improvement of health, should under any circumstances be subordinated to other considerations, I know no scientific method of determining other than that of empirical Hedonism. Nor, as I have said, does it seem to me that any other method has ever been applied or sought by the common sense of mankind, for regulating the pursuit of what our older moralists called "Natural Good,"—i.e. of all that is intrinsically desirable *except* Virtue or Morality, within the limits fixed by the latter; the Utilitarian here only performs somewhat more consistently and systematically than ordinary men the reasoning processes which are commonly admitted to be appropriate to the questions that this pursuit raises. His distinctive characteristic, as a Utilitarian, is that he has to apply the same method to the criticism and correction of the limiting morality itself.' (Sidgwick, *ME* 479) For discussion, see §1179.

unscientific interpretations, they introduce indefiniteness. Green does not seem to be any worse off than they are.

Green objects to the implications of utilitarianism in order to contrast it with his views on distribution. He affirms that the common good incorporates Kantian distributive principles rather than utilitarian principles. The Kantian principles specify a right of each person to the appropriate sort of equal consideration. But Green rejects a further Kantian claim about the place of such a right in a moral theory. According to the Kantian, moral principles assign rights to individuals that are prior to and independent of the pursuit of the good. In Green's view, however, rights are to be discovered by appeal to the common good.[120] He takes his claim that rights are derived from a person's end to imply that they are derived from a common end.[121] This derivation of rights from the common good does not (in Green's view) face the Kantian objection to utilitarianism, since it does not subordinate individuals to some further end. We avoid this subordination by making the common good genuinely common and non-competitive.

1249. The Composition of the Common Good

To ensure that the common good is non-competitive, Green sometimes identifies it with the attainment of the morally good will, which is the will to attain the common good.[122] This conclusion results from the reflexion that extends the area of the common good.[123] If we are interested only in the common good of a few people, we may pursue a good that is non-competitive in relation to these few, but competitive in relation to everyone else. Hence a Greek democracy based on slavery pursues the common good of the free citizens at the expense of the slaves. But as we extend the range of people to whom the common good is common, we narrow the range of people who can lose by it; when the common good is recognized as embracing everyone, no one can lose by it. And so the good that we reach at the end of the process of extension must be wholly non-competitive.

The only wholly non-competitive good is the good will or 'self-devotion to an ideal of mutual service' (244). If we do not acknowledge this, our idea of universal community will be ineffective. It will result in the granting of formal rights, but will not move us to provide the resources for using these rights beneficially. The prohibition of slavery does not by itself affect the ordering of life 'as to secure for those whom we admit that it is wrong to use as

---

[120] ' "Natural rights", so far as there are such things, are themselves relative to the moral end to which perfect law is relative. A law is not good because it enforces "natural rights", but because it contributes to the realization of a certain end. We only discover what rights are natural by considering what powers must be secured to a man in order to the attainment of this end.' (Green, LPO 20)

[121] 'In the ethical sense it means that rights are derived from the possession of personality as = a rational will (i.e. the conception which man possesses of being determined to action by the conception of such a perfection of his being as involves the perfection of a society in which he lives) . . .' (LPO 27)

[122] 'The only good in the pursuit of which there can be no competition of interests, the only good which is really common to all who may pursue it, is that which consists in the universal will to be good.' (PE 244)

[123] 'Following out that extension, . . . we found that its outcome was the intuition of the educated conscience that the true good must be good for all men, so that no one should seek to gain by another's loss, gain and loss being estimated on the same principle for each.' (240)

chattels much real opportunity of self-development' (244). If we do not ensure the beneficial use of formal rights, civil society remains essentially competitive.[124] We resolve this conflict between our pursuit of an expanding common good and the remaining competitive aspects in society only if we recognize that the true good is being good. This is what Kant sees in saying that the only unqualified good is a good will.

Green's identification of the true good with moral goodness is directly related to his reflexions on contemporary politics. He sees that aspirations to extend the area of moral and political concern conflict with the irremediably competitive framework in which we place ourselves and others with whom we claim to share a common good. His view of the true good is crucial to his theory, and to the application of his theory to practice.

When he refers to Kant, he seems to commit himself to a doctrine even more extreme than Kant's. Kant says only that the good will is the only unqualified good; by this he means that it is the only good that never needs qualification or regulation by a superior good.[125] Where Kant speaks of an unqualified good, Green speaks of the only true good. We have some reason to take this to mean 'the only good that is really good', since the moral good is the only non-competitive good and the common good we aim at must be non-competitive.

Still, the identification of the good with the morally good copes with only one part of Green's argument about the good—the demand for a common, and hence non-competitive, good. It does not cope with the prior description of the good as self-realization. Green is justified in claiming that, if his previous argument is right, achieving a good will must be part of my own good, since acting on a morally good will is acting in accordance with the requirements of practical reason, which must be part of my self-realization as a rational agent. But how could realizing a good will be the whole of self-realization? We seem to have other capacities, distinct from our capacity from morality, that need to be fulfilled if we are to achieve our good.[126]

The claim that the good is non-competitive now seems to face an objection derived from the claim that it is self-realization. These other aspects of a person's good do not all appear to be non-competitive. Even if our good has non-competitive elements, it may have competitive elements too.

Green recognizes some of these objections. He considers an apparent counter-example to his view of self-realization and to his view of Greek ethics. Aristotle is often thought to maintain that theoretical study is the whole of the good that realizes us as rational beings; in that case, he rejects any role for moral goodness in the ultimate good. But even if it is not the whole of the ultimate good, theoretical study, in Aristotle's view, is the most important part of the good. Hence Aristotle's view conflicts with Green's claim that the good will is the true good (289).[127]

---

[124] 'Civil society may be, and is, founded on the idea of their being a common good, but that idea in relation to the less favoured members of society is in effect unrealized, and it is unrealized because the good is being sought in objects which admit of being competed for.' (244)

[125] Kant on the goodness of the good will; §912.

[126] Brink, PCG 60–9, examines Green's commitment to different versions of a claim about non-competition ('moderate' v. 'extreme' harmony of interests).

[127] Green does not deal fully with this objection, but intended to return to it. See the editor's note on PE 290.

Moreover, even if the argument for identifying the true good and the moral good were not open to these objections, the consequences of the identification raise serious difficulties, clearly presented by Sidgwick.[128] If A tries to promote the good will in B, A needs some conception of the good will in B. But if the good will in B is simply the will to promote the good will in C, we still do not know what the good will in B is until we know what the good will in C is . . . and now we face a vicious regress. The same regress will result if we say that each individual's good is the will to promote the good of others; no one will be able to form any conception of what will actually promotes the good of others until we have some view of a good that does not consist entirely in promoting the good of others.

These difficulties are quite similar to those that would face the Stoics if they regarded virtue as the only reasonable object of concern; they avoid such difficulties by their doctrine of preferred indifferents, and Green also needs to show that a person's good (according to the non-Stoic conception of the good that he accepts) includes non-moral elements.[129]

He assumes that self-realization requires more than a morally good will. When he comments that negative rights do not always result in self-development for people admitted to negative rights (245), he surely does not mean that they would have achieved complete self-development if they had been both legally free and morally good. We might argue that if they had been left in the same social and economic position, they would have had the same opportunities (which, indeed, they had all along) for patience, endurance, self-sacrifice, and other aspects of moral goodness, and would have been freed from the temptations to pursue wealth and power instead. To attribute this argument to Green would be to distort his position. When he speaks of the aims of people devoted to a common good, he sometimes speaks of people who aim at such undeniably material results as the sanitation of a town.

Fortunately, Green's arguments about self-realization do not support the extreme claim that self-realization is nothing more than a morally good will. If he had been committed to the extreme claim, he would have cast serious doubt on his whole position. He should revise his exclusively moral conception of the good.[130]

Can the non-competitive character of the good be secured without the extreme claim about the good and the moral good? Some of Green's remarks suggest a less extreme claim that he may sometimes intend, without clearly distinguishing it from the extreme claim. If morality regulates the pursuit of competitive goods, self-realization may include competitive elements, but still may be non-competitive.

Green does not always take the common good to be exhausted by the will to promote the common good.[131] He also describes the ultimate end as full self-realization, which he understands as the fulfilment of human capacities (193, 197, 207). Moral traits (concerned with other people's good) are part of that development and fulfilment of human capacities (207); but he does not always suggest that they are the whole of the good to be promoted.

---

[128] See Sidgwick, *EGSM* 73.   [129] The Stoics on goods and preferred indifferents; §§183, 186–7.

[130] Lamont, *IGMP* 190–6, argues convincingly that Green's general views about the good do not commit him to his claim that the good is nothing more than the good will. He points out that the non-competitive good that the virtuous person aims at may be composed of competitive goods; it is non-competitive in so far as it is regulated by morality. Lewis, 'Content', argues that Green is more deeply committed to the extreme non-competitive view.

[131] See Sidgwick, *EGSM* 69–77.

When he discusses Aristotle on bravery, Green remarks that we now include in self-realization many faculties and dispositions that Aristotle does not include.[132] The relevant faculties and dispositions are not just the moral ones; the Greeks already recognized these. Nor do the obscure labours of love aim exclusively at making people morally better. The more comprehensive view of the capacities to be realized results from the extended view of who ought to share in self-realization, if the good is to amount to 'a full realization of the faculties of the human soul' (286).

The good will is to imply 'a whole world of beneficent social activities, which it shall sustain and co-ordinate' (288). The ultimate end is 'the perfect life itself, as resting on a devoted will' (303). When Green mentions the specific ways in which the good 'as consisting in the full realization of human capabilities' has been realized, he mentions non-moral activities—technical, scientific, and artistic—among the ways in which human beings have been civilized (337).

He need not claim, therefore, that the common good is realized entirely in activities that we share with others. His remarks are more moderate than that. Someone who cares about other people's good 'cannot contemplate himself in a better state, or on the way to the best, without contemplating others, not merely as a means to that better state, but as sharing it with him' (199). Such a person considers 'a permanent well-being in which the permanent well-being of others is included' (201), or 'an idea of absolute good common to him with them' (202), or 'an absolute and common good; a good common to the person conceiving it with others, and good for him and them' (203). This good is common in the sense that one person does not fully realize his own good unless other people realize their good; but it does not imply that we all achieve our self-realization in exactly the same activities.

If, then, the common good includes both moral and non-moral elements, how is it non-competitive? This question arises especially when we try to fit goods such as the pursuit of arts and sciences and other non-moral goods into the common good. Green is in some doubt about this (289–90, p. 312n).[133] The common good may be non-competitive (in the sense that A does not pursue A's own good to the exclusion of B's), but still not entirely free of potential conflict (if A's good requires resources that might also be needed for B's good and cannot be used for both A and B without some loss to each). In that case, the reference to the common good does not remove all distributive questions about the allocation of goods to different people who none the less all participate in the common good.[134]

The relevant non-competitive good, then, is (1) the composite composed of the good will and the non-moral competitive goods that the good will regulates, rather than (2) the good will in abstraction from the goods it regulates. Sometimes Green seems to have the first conception in mind; sometimes he seems not to distinguish it properly from the second conception. The first conception fits his other arguments better.

---

[132] 'Faculties, dispositions, occupations, persons, of which a Greek citizen would have taken no account, or taken account only to despise, are now recognized as having their place in the realization of the powers of the human soul . . . It is in consequence of this recognition that the will to endure even unto death for a worthy end has come to find worthy ends where the Greek saw nothing but ugliness and meanness, and to express itself in obscure labours of love . . .' (PE 260)

[133] See also Lamont, IGMP 190–6, 216–18.

[134] On distributive questions, see Prichard, MODI 81, who anticipates Rawls, TJ §30.

According to this first conception, the common good does not remove all distributive questions. Such questions arise, but are settled by the regulative role of the good will. They do not undermine Green's position. For if he is entitled to incorporate the Formula of Humanity in his conception of the common good, he has some basis for approaching distributive questions. The common good is the good of rational agents who all deserve respect as rational agents; this basis of respect fixes some constraints in the distribution of resources that cannot be shared by everyone. We have more reason to allow competition if it is regulated by non-competitive principles.[135] This answer does not settle every reasonable question about distribution, but it suggests that Green's theory does not face a fatal objection here.

This regulative function for morality is Kantian. Green's view is distinctive because he does not regard morality as an external limit on our pursuit of our good, but as a regulative component that imposes a limit on other components and puts them in order. Sometimes we might decide that morality requires us to restrain our pursuit of music (376–9), but this is not a sacrifice of self-realization for the sake of morality. If Green is right, it is a choice of self-realization, through the preference for a primary component over a secondary.[136]

This solution does not tell us precisely when such apparent sacrifices are needed. Nor, however, is it simply a re-description of them that pretends they involve no significant loss. Green is entitled to his claims about the regulative role of morality if he is right to say that self-realization requires the extension of my concerns and interests that commits us eventually to the moral point of view. If we believe that morality and self-realization can conflict, we overlook the primary place of the moral outlook in self-realization.

1250. Kant and Idealism

How far does Green reconcile the eudaemonist and the Kantian outlooks? Does his reconciliation achieve his aim of avoiding a dualism of practical reason? Is his total view a coherent moral position, or simply an attempt to combine irreconcilable elements?

Green and Bradley say too little about how morality allows me to recognize my ends in the ends of others. Their claim about morality needs some defence, since not every conception of morality seems to have the result that they describe. Sidgwick's conception of morality, for instance, does not seem to require the identification of my ends with the ends of others. I think of my pleasure and pain as part of the total to be maximized, and I care about maximizing the total more than maximizing my own good; but I still think of my good as distinct from, and possibly conflicting with, the good of the whole. This, indeed, is the basis of the dualism of practical reason for which Green and Bradley criticize Sidgwick.

What does a Kantian view imply on this question? According to Kant, if I take the moral attitude, I care about what happens to other people just because they are other moral agents. I care about this in so far as I regard them as ends in themselves, not subordinate to other ends of mine. If I care about them as ends, I also take a different view of myself

---

[135] Competition; §1104. [136] Cf. Bradley on elements of self-realization, §1233.

and my relation to them. I do not look at other people and my relations to them in a purely instrumental way. I look at them as other rational agents who have a certain kind of claim on me and on whom I also have the same kind of claim. If I recognize this aspect of other people, I also accept their ends as my ends (in so far as I believe they deserve the same sort of concern from me as I think my ends deserve from me, from the moral point of view). I therefore find my aims realized in them.

A Kantian conception of morality and its relation to my ends may allow us to combine an element from Kant with an element from the idealists, to explain the relation between morality and self-realization. The Kantian element is the claim that morality involves concern for people as ends, because one takes to them the attitude that one regards as appropriate to oneself. According to Kant, I regard myself as an end in so far as I recognize myself as a rational agent, not just a collection of desires with reason in an instrumental role. In thinking of myself this way, I both make demands on other people—to have myself treated non-exploitatively—and recognize obligations to them—to treat them as ends, non-exploitatively.

The idealists add that this attitude I take to others in relation to myself also affects my conception of myself, and my conception of the activities that I regard as expressing myself. It promotes my self-realization, because I can see self-realization in more activities than I could have seen it in otherwise. The content of morality makes some difference to this. For, according to a Kantian conception, morality does not prescribe the subordination of myself to some larger whole; it involves my acceptance of principles that I can see are appropriate to rational agents who deserve to be recognized as such. In so far as I regard other people as ends, I regard their ends as my ends; and since my self-realization consists in the achievement of my ends, it also consists in achieving those ends of other people that are also my ends.

According to Kant, the moral point of view consists in treating rational agents in general as ends, and hence in treating them, in one respect, as I treat myself. I regard myself as an end, in so far as I give myself priority over the achievement of some particular aim or desire. Similarly, I regard other people as ends, in so far as I give them priority over the achievement of anyone's particular aims or desires. If I treat persons as ends, I do not allow them to be sacrificed for anyone's purposes.

If I treat others as ends in the same way as I treat myself, how does that contribute to self-realization? What distinctive aims and goals do I acquire by regarding persons as ends, and how do these goals contribute to self-realization? These are questions that Green asks himself in his reflexions on Kant. The common good he describes involves concern for persons as ends in themselves. This concern involves the view that people count for something in their own right, just as rational persons and not because of some further feature that interests us about them. To consider myself this way is to adopt a particular attitude of self-respect towards myself. To consider others this way is to adopt some attitude of mutual respect.

To explain why mutual respect contributes to self-realization, Green relies on his account of a non-competitive good. The relevance of such a good to self-realization is even clearer if we take it (as we suggested earlier) not to be entirely non-competitive, but to consist of competitive elements regulated by non-competitive elements. The importance of recognizing non-competitive elements in one's good becomes clear once we accept these claims about self-realization: (1) One's own self-realization involves the fulfilment of one's capacities as a rational agent. (2) The fulfilment of these capacities involves competition with other rational agents, since it requires the use of limited resources. (3) I take my own agency to deserve respect from others. (4) If I take the agency of others to deserve respect, I recognize other people as common deliberators about the good, rather than simply as competitors.

Kant's main contribution is the third claim; Green recognizes it when he describes the common good as a good that recognizes each person as an end. He does not say enough to make it clear how the attitude of mutual respect for persons as ends creates a distinctive sort of non-competitive good. But if we try to make this point clear, we confirm his claim that this particular sort of non-competitive good promotes self-realization.

To see why this is so, we need to distinguish the non-competitive good based on mutual respect from other sorts of non-competitive good. A good might be non-competitive for some agents simply because they have no desires for any goods that might conflict with the desires of others. A monastic community, observing vows of poverty, chastity, and obedience, might meet this condition, if its members do not take a competitive view of their moral or religious achievements. But mutual respect does not require a good that has no competitive elements. If we take other people to deserve respect as ends, we bring distributive questions within the range of practical reason, and in doing so we extend our rational agency over our lives as a whole.

We can see the role of practical reasoning if we consider the alternative to a common good based on mutual respect. From the point of view of reasonable self-love, it is reasonable for me to pursue my own greatest good. But reasonable self-love has nothing to say about the relative reasonableness of my pursuit of my greatest good and your pursuit of your greatest good. If we have nothing more to say than what reasonable self-love can offer, we must leave conflicts between my pursuit of my good and your pursuit of mine to be settled by inclination and (if necessary) force, rather than by practical reason. But we do not have to accept this conclusion. For if I believe my own agency deserves respect from others, and you believe the same about yours, we can achieve mutual respect by allowing that different people's pursuit of their own ends is legitimate within the constraints of mutual respect. The practical reasoning that allows for pursuit of individual ends is not simply a means to securing this pursuit; it is also a further good that realizes the participating individuals as rational agents. Green has a good reason, therefore, to claim that it is a non-competitive common good.

86

MOORE

1251. Moore and Sidgwick

Principia Ethica is a critical essay on some of the main doctrines of Sidgwick, with a secondary focus on Kant.[1] In the course of his examination of Sidgwick's utilitarianism and Kant's 'metaphysical' system, Moore also discusses Mill, Spencer, and some neo-Hegelian doctrines (e.g., about internal relations). But his main claims in moral philosophy are all directly relevant to Sidgwick.[2]

Moore follows Sidgwick and Price in their rejection of attempts to define all basic moral concepts.[3] He agrees with their realist metaphysics of morality, and so he recognizes moral properties. He departs from Sidgwick in taking 'good', rather than 'right' and 'ought' to be the basic indefinable ethical term, but his arguments about 'good' are (as he points out) similar to those that Sidgwick uses for 'right' and 'ought'.

Moore accepts Sidgwick's moral epistemology, in so far as he endorses an intuitionist and foundationalist conception of moral knowledge. He does not rely on Sidgwick's dialectical argument; he is much readier than Sidgwick is to put forward moral claims on the basis of intuition without trying to connect them to common sense. Like Sidgwick, he is a 'utilitarian on an intuitional basis', but he does not reach this position by systematic comparison with 'intuitionism' in the sense that refers to the deontological outlook of common sense and 'dogmatic intuitionists' such as Price and Reid.

He also agrees with Sidgwick, against the dogmatic intuitionists, in his utilitarianism, but with some important differences. He does not rely on intuition for his utilitarian doctrine of rightness, since he believes that the utilitarian account of the right is conceptually true. He is not a hedonist, and so he believes that the right promotes a good that contains elements

[1] On Moore and Kant, see Baldwin, *GEM* 10–12, 67–8, 332–3.

[2] Bosanquet's review notices the influence of Sidgwick, but does not mention Moore's debt to Sidgwick's argument about definition. Some other readers show a tendency to exaggerate Moore's originality, contrary to his explicit statements. For instance, Robinson's review of Ross, *FE*, claims that Ross's books 'are not as different from *Principia Ethica* as that book is from anything that came before it' (417). See also Baldwin, *GEM* 68. Hurka, 'Moore', emphasizes the continuity between Moore and his predecessors and contemporaries.

[3] According to Raphael, *MS* 1n, Moore had never (in 1947) read Price. Price is not prominent in Sidgwick's discussion; see §1148. It would be a little surprising, however, if Moore had never read Selby-Bigge, *BM*, which contains the crucial passages from Price. Barnes, 'Price', 165–7, points out some connexions between Price and Moore.

other than pleasure. In this respect, he is an 'ideal' utilitarian. But, in contrast to Rashdall, he does not treat moral rightness or moral value as an element in the ultimate good. His defence of his normative doctrines does not rely, as Sidgwick's does, on any argument to show that they fit the reflective judgments of common sense. He is a less cautious intuitionist than Sidgwick.

Sidgwick qualifies his endorsement of utilitarianism by arguing that hedonistic egoism also appears to be ultimately reasonable, and that the apparently axiomatic status of both egoism and utilitarian forces us into a dualism of practical reason. Moore excises this element of Sidgwick's position by attacking Sidgwick's defence of egoism, and in particular Sidgwick's account of what is 'reasonable for me'.

This brief comparison suggests that Moore is closer to Sidgwick in his meta-ethics than in his moral epistemology and normative ethics. Some of his criticisms of Sidgwick are acute and helpful, but we may well doubt whether the clearer and less qualified doctrines that replace Sidgwick's careful explanations, concessions, and restrictions are more plausible.

The different parts of Moore's position have not been equally influential. His first chapter, 'The Subject-Matter of Ethics', contains a section in which Moore puts forward his views about Good.[4] This part of *Principia* has been most often studied.[5] It is by no means the only part of *Principia* that deserves study, but its importance both in Moore's argument and in 20th-century debate makes it reasonable for us to begin with it. Many of Moore's successors criticize some parts of his argument about Good, but try to maintain and to defend the insights they find in it. They do not agree about which parts are the errors and which are the insights.

1252. Compositional Definitions

Moore separates the question 'What things are good?' from the question 'How is Good to be defined?' (57).[6] We must answer the latter question to have a sound basis for answering the former.[7] The definitional question does not concern a word, and it does not ask for an answer that expresses the meaning of one word in other words. Moore wants to find 'that object or idea which . . . the word is generally used to stand for' (58).

He introduces three kinds of definitions (59–60): (1) an arbitrary verbal definition; (2) a verbal definition proper, that is, a non-arbitrary verbal definition; (3) a compositional

---

[4] I follow Moore in the Preface to *PE*, 2nd edn. (cf. Lewy, 'Moore', 135n) in using the initial capital to indicate whatever it is that Moore is considering when he criticizes the adequacy of attempted naturalistic definitions. This might be understood as the meaning of the word 'good' (or, as Moore suggests in the new Preface, one sense in which it is used), or the concept 'good', or the property of goodness. Moore, indeed, may identify these three things; but it may sometimes be useful to question this identification. Hence I will not use inverted commas in asking about definitions of Good. (Moore's practice in the use of inverted commas in talking about Good seems to vary unsystematically.)

[5] Moore wrote part of a preface to a second edition of *PE*, in which he criticizes especially his argument in Chapter 1, and tries to say what is central and defensible in his meta-ethical claims. Lewy describes the contents of the new Preface in 'Moore'. The preface itself, probably written in 1921–2, was published with the reprint of *PE* (called a 'second edition') in 1993. Moore's new Preface anticipates and accepts many of the objections raised by his critics, and tries to re-state a thesis that he still accepts. His remarks help us to understand *PE* better, but they were not available to Moore's original critics.

[6] Pages cited from 2nd edn.

[7] '. . . it is impossible that, till the answer to this question be known, any one should know *what is the evidence* for any ethical judgment whatever.' (58)

definition that analyses the definiendum into its component parts.[8] Moore allows that Good has the second kind of definition; that is why we translate the English 'good' by the French 'bon'. He denies that Good has the third kind of definition, because 'it is not composed of any parts, which we can substitute for it in our minds when we are thinking of it' (60). We can find such a definition of Horse, because we can say that 'it has four legs, a head, a heart, a liver, etc., etc., all of them arranged in definite relations to one another' (60). Good has no such definition.

The simple notion Yellow illustrates indefinability. By 'simple', Moore means that 'just as you cannot, by any manner of means, explain to anyone who does not already know it, what yellow is, so you cannot explain what good is' (59). Such explanation is impossible because Yellow has no compositional definition.[9] This sort of definition satisfies two conditions: (1) It enumerates the 'different properties and qualities' of which an object is composed (59). (2) When we have enumerated all of these, we have reached the simplest terms. Complete definition, therefore, is decomposition into the simplest parts or elements (59), If 'F is G and H' is a compositional definition, G and H are simpler than F.

Moore makes it difficult to know when we have found a compositional definition, because he offers no clear tests of simplicity. He suggests that a compositional definition of Horse reduces a horse 'to its simplest terms', which cannot be further defined. But the 'parts' he mentions in his example are four legs, a heart, a liver, etc., arranged in definite relations. Mention of these parts does not give us a compositional definition; for they are 'parts' in an organic, physical sense. They are logically as complex and definable as Horse.

Moore adds that a correct compositional definition allows us to substitute the thought of the parts for the thought of the whole to be defined, and lose nothing; substitution is functional equivalence in thought.[10] It is difficult to see how Moore's example satisfies this condition; how could we still have our thoughts about horses if we simply thought of the conjunction of equine parts and their arrangement? We might think of this as a conjunction of many conjuncts (leg, head, eye . . . and arrangement) or of two conjuncts (the list of parts as one conjunct, and the arrangement as the other). Thinking about either of these conjunctions is not the same as thinking about the whole. We might be able to think of a whole horse without being able to enumerate all the equine parts. Equally, thinking about the conjunction of the parts and their arrangement is not the same as thinking about the parts in their arrangement. I could look at all the detached parts of a horse, and think about the arrangement that would make them a horse, but I might still not think about them in this equine arrangement.[11]

Perhaps Moore does not intend the thought 'of all its parts and their arrangement' to be the thought of a mere conjunction. Perhaps he means that we can substitute thoughts about

---

[8] Moore has no special name for this sort of definition.

[9] Compositional definitions 'describe the real nature of the object or notion denoted by a word, and which do not simply tell us what the word is used to mean' (59).

[10] 'We might think just as clearly and correctly about a horse, if we thought of all its parts and their arrangement instead of thinking of the whole' (60). Hence Good is indefinable because 'it is not composed of any parts, which we can substitute for it in our minds when we are thinking of it' (60).

[11] Aristotle makes this point in his discussion of letters and syllables in *Met.* vii 17. Bosanquet, 'Critical Notice', 258–9, notices the strangeness of Moore's conception of definition: 'This is manifestly false even in Mr Moore's example of the horse. When we think of it through its parts, of course, we think of them as parts of a horse, the point of view contributed by S. It is true that roughly we may take P as a substitute for S, but strictly it would be incomplete apart from the single point of view of the whole given in S and further determined in the analysis P.' (259)

parts in their arrangement, or about parts as arranged, for our thoughts of a whole. But this claim is also open to question. Thoughts of parts as they are arranged are thoughts about the whole. Hence we cannot 'substitute' thoughts about parts as arranged for thoughts of a whole, and we cannot think of parts as arranged 'instead of' a whole; for we cannot substitute a thing for itself.

Moreover, even if we can substitute thoughts about the organic parts of a horse for thoughts of the horse, we do not understand Moore's claim about compositional definition. These organic parts are logically as complex as the whole, and that is why we can substitute the thought of them for the thought of the whole. If Moore had introduced logically simple parts rather than organic parts, we could not have substituted the thought of them for the thought of the whole.

So far, then, it is difficult to evaluate Moore's claim that Good has no compositional definition. The claim may well be true, but not because of anything distinctive about Good. Moore's demands for simplicity and substitution make it difficult to say whether anything has a compositional definition. Good and Horse seem equally indefinable by Moore's tests.

1253. Real Definitions

Moore's conception of compositional definition raises a further question about his later argument. He seeks the simplest parts of the nature and composition of a horse, not of the meaning of 'horse'. Hence he seeks a real definition, not a nominal definition. The sort of definition that he wants is not a formula that expresses one's meaning in other words (58).

The introduction of real definitions casts doubt on Moore's objection to the claim that 'good' simply means 'pleasant'. He rejects this conceptual hedonism because it rests on a false claim about the meaning of the word 'good'. To show that the claim is false, he asserts that Good is simple and indefinable, and so has no compositional definition. But even if Good is simple, the word 'good' may have a verbal definition; might the hedonist not be right about the verbal definition? The simplicity of Good counts against conceptual hedonism only if it implies that Good has no nominal definition; but Moore's concern with compositional definition does not seem to tell us anything about nominal definition.

If we are looking for a real definition, we ought not to raise questions that are relevant only to a nominal definition. In particular, a real definition may not capture the common meaning of a term; we can use 'horse' competently without knowing the real essence of a horse. Hence we do not refute a candidate real definition by showing that it does not capture analytical truths about a term or concept.

The compositional definitions that interest Moore are real definitions that introduce logically simple elements. But could there be real definitions that are not compositional? An Aristotelian definition such as 'a human being is a rational animal' or 'a good F is whatever fulfils the function of F' seems to offer an explication that introduces elements that are no less complex than the definiendum. If non-compositional real definitions are possible, an argument to show that something lacks a compositional definition does not show that it lacks a real definition.

Moreover, even if a definition must be compositional, some things that lack a compositional definition may allow 'explications' that describe their non-simple components and so give an account of their real nature. Price, for instance, argues that 'right', 'ought', and other moral ideas are indefinable, but he does not infer that they are inexplicable.[12] Sometimes Moore seems to admit that some expressions are synonymous with 'good', and that we can grasp the relevant concept by speaking of 'intrinsic value (worth)' and of what 'ought to exist'.[13]

1254. What is the Naturalistic Fallacy?

It is surprising, then, that Moore maintains that if Good has no compositional definition, it is logically simple, and hence inexplicable, as Yellow is (59). This comparison of Good to Yellow rests on the controversial assumptions that all real definition is compositional, and that anything that lacks a compositional definition is logically simple and inexplicable. Moore believes that, since Good is indefinable (58), there are no analytic truths about it, and no axioms about it can be defended by appeal to meaning.[14]

In his view, everyone who takes Good to be definable commits the 'naturalistic fallacy'. He gives the fallacy this name because naturalists commit it. Naturalists define Good as some natural property; hedonistic naturalists, for instance, identify it with pleasantness. They define the Good in this way because they confuse the property with the things that have it.[15] Naturalists argue from 'All Fs are G' to ' "F" is to be defined as "G" '. They observe (we may concede) that all good things are also pleasant and vice versa, and so they define Good as pleasantness.

Naturalists are not the only ones who commit this basic error of arguing directly from co-extensiveness to definition. Non-naturalists who try to define Good by reference to other non-natural properties also commit the naturalistic fallacy; their error is typical of 'metaphysical ethics'.[16] Hence we need not pause at the moment to clarify Moore's notion

---

[12] Price on definition and explication; §813.

[13] 'Every one does in fact understand the question "Is this good?" When he thinks of it, his state of mind is different from what it would be, were he asked "Is this pleasant, or desired, or approved?" It has a distinct meaning for him, even though he may not recognize in what respect it is distinct. Whenever he thinks of "intrinsic value" or "intrinsic worth," or says that a thing "ought to exist," he has before his mind the unique object—the unique property of things—which I mean by "good". Everybody is constantly aware of this notion, although he may never become aware at all that it is different from other notions of which he is also aware.' (PE 68)

[14] '...propositions about the good are all of them synthetic and never analytic...' 'nobody can foist upon us such an axiom as that "Pleasure is the only good" or that "The good is the desired" on the pretence that this is "the very meaning of the word" ' (58–9). Moore overstates the first conclusion. For he allows some analytic truths about Good, not only tautologies (such as 'Good is good', which he affirms, 58), but truths about connexions with other concepts, such as 'Good belongs to the goods that right actions promote'.

[15] 'It may be true that all things which are good are *also* something else, just as it is true that all things which are yellow produce a certain kind of vibration in the light. And it is a fact, that Ethics aims at discovering what are those other properties belonging to all things which are good. But far too many philosophers have thought that when they named those other properties they were actually defining good; that these properties, in fact, were simply not "other", but absolutely and entirely the same with goodness. This view I propose to call the "naturalistic fallacy".' (62)

[16] Moore explains: 'It should be observed that the fallacy, by reference to which I define "Metaphysical Ethics", is the same in kind: and I give it but one name, the naturalistic fallacy' (91). His claims are helpfully sorted out by Frankena, 'Fallacy', 6–9. I take the basic error alleged by Moore to be the last one described by Frankena, the confusion of universal synthetic propositions with definitions.

of 'natural properties', since it does not matter to this part of his argument. The naturalistic fallacy, then, is the fallacy that naturalists and others commit in trying to define Good, because, in Moore's view, any attempt to define Good confuses truths about Fs with the definition of 'F'.[17] He believes that this confusion 'is to be met with in almost every book on ethics' (65).

At first sight, Moore's last claim seems unreasonable. Perhaps some people think Good is definable because they cannot tell the difference between co-extension and definition. But might some people not be well aware of the difference, and still believe they have reasons for identifying Good with (say) pleasantness? Whether they are right or wrong, they do not seem to argue in the way Moore describes. They might argue that the proposed defining property not only belongs to all good things, but also is identical to Good. Such an argument would not commit any obvious fallacy. Perhaps the books on ethics that Moore refers to offer this non-fallacious argument about the properties that they identify with Good. Hence it does not seem clear that almost every book on ethics commits the naturalistic fallacy.

To show that those who try to define Good commit the naturalistic fallacy, Moore needs to argue as follows: (1) All attempts to define Good fail. (2) Hence all attempted definitions of Good merely present us with—at best—co-extensive properties. (3) If, in the light of (1) and (2), we were to propose a definition of Good, we would be confusing a statement of co-extensiveness with a statement of identity. (4) In confusing these two sorts of statements, we would commit the naturalistic fallacy.

We already know enough about natural properties, as Moore conceives them, to see that Moore's refutation of the naturalistic fallacy does not refute a naturalist account of Good. If Moore shows that all attempts to define Good commit a naturalistic fallacy, he refutes both naturalist and non-naturalist definitions of Good. But he does not refute naturalism. For we might avoid the naturalistic fallacy by affirming that Good is indefinable, but still accept naturalism by identifying Good with some indefinable natural property. Moore recognizes that Yellow is such a property. Why should Good not be another? The argument about definition has nothing to say on this question. To see whether Moore has some other reason for rejecting naturalism, we need to wait until we have seen what he believes about natural properties.

1255. Who Commits the Naturalistic Fallacy?

Among the books on ethics that commit the naturalistic fallacy Moore includes Mill's *Utilitarianism*.[18] To show that his objections reveal the error in naturalist theories, Moore discusses Mill's notorious argument from the (alleged) fact that only pleasure is desired to

---

[17] 'It is a very simple fallacy indeed. When we say that an orange is yellow, we do not think our statement binds us to hold that "orange" means nothing else than "yellow", or that nothing can be yellow but an orange.' (66)

[18] Relying on Sidgwick, Moore asserts that Bentham mistakenly takes his claims about pleasure, right, and good to include the claim that (roughly) 'right' means 'pleasant'. But Sidgwick regards this as an oversight of Bentham's, rather than as a considered attempt at a definition of 'right'.

the claim that only pleasure is desirable, and the conclusion that only pleasure is good.[19] Moore claims that in this argument Mill commits the naturalistic fallacy.[20]

Mill takes 'desirable' to be equivalent to 'good', since he substitutes 'each person's happiness is a good to that person' for 'each person's happiness is desirable to that person'. If 'good' means 'desirable', 'desirable' should mean 'ought to be desired', so that no fallacy is involved. But Moore alleges that Mill commits a fallacy of equivocation in claiming that the only proof that x is desirable is x's being desired, just as the only proof that x is visible is x's being seen. The fallacy lies in Mill's move between 'desirable (i.e., ought to be desired)' and 'desirable (i.e., can be desired)'. If 'desirable' is to be equivalent to 'good', it should mean 'ought to be desired' or 'good to desire', but if it is to play its intended role in Mill's argument, parallel to 'visible', it must mean 'can be desired'.[21]

Moore believes that Mill's equivocation commits the naturalistic fallacy, because he thinks Mill argues directly from the fact that everything good is desired to the conclusion that 'good' means 'desired'. But this claim about Mill does not seem justified. To show that what each person desires is good to that person Mill assumes that being desired is the only proof one can give of something's being desirable. He does not assume either that 'desirable' means 'desired' or that 'good' means 'desired'. The assumption about meaning is Moore's gift to Mill. Without it, we have no reason to suppose that Mill commits the naturalistic fallacy.

Moore makes a similar allegation about Mill on desire and pleasure.[22] Mill claims that desiring x and thinking of x as pleasant are one and the same, and it is both physically and metaphysically impossible to separate them. According to Moore, Mill observes that whatever we desire we think pleasant, and infers that 'desire' means 'think pleasant', thereby committing the naturalistic fallacy. To show that Mill makes a claim about the meaning of 'desired', Moore claims that, according to Mill, it would be evidently self-contradictory to say that I think of x as pleasant, but I do not desire x. But it is not clear that Moore is right. The psychological and metaphysical impossibility of desiring without thinking pleasant do not commit Mill to the claim that 'desire' means 'think pleasant'. The assumptions that commit Mill to a naturalistic definition of 'desire' are Moore's assumptions, with no basis in Mill. Mill is not the clearest or most careful writer, but Moore does not show that he commits the naturalistic fallacy.[23]

Moore's allegations about the naturalistic fallacy, therefore, cannot bear much argumentative weight. They will convince us only if he proves his first claim, about the failure of all attempted definitions of Good. If that first claim is correct, he proves his main point without

---

[19] Mill, *U* 4.3.

[20] 'Mill has made as naive and artless a use of the naturalistic fallacy as anybody could desire. "Good", he tells us, means "desirable", and you can only find out what is desirable by seeking to find out what is actually desired. . . . The important step for Ethics is this one just taken, the step which pretends to prove that "good" means "desired".' (118)

[21] Mill's argument; §1137.

[22] Moore quotes Mill '. . . to think of an object as desirable (unless for the sake of its consequences) and to think of it as pleasant are one and the same; and . . . to desire anything except in proportion as the idea of it is pleasant, is a physical and metaphysical impossibility' (*PE* 124, quoted from Mill, *U* 4.9.).

[23] We may spare ourselves an examination of Moore's discussion of Herbert Spencer, who is probably more confused than Mill. In the discussion of metaphysical ethics, Moore's exegesis is even more captious and disputable than in his discussion of Mill. See, e.g., the criticism of Kant, 177–80; Moore picks on Kant's use of 'imperative' and 'law' without asking what Kant means by these notions. His objections are based on misunderstanding.

reference to any naturalistic fallacy; and if the first claim is false, those who try to define Good need not commit any fallacy. How, then, does Moore refute all attempted definitions of Good?

1256. The Open Question Argument

In Moore's view, all attempted definitions of Good violate a necessary condition for a correct definition; it must not create an 'open question'.[24] A proposed definition of Good as F leaves an open question if we can significantly ask whether F is good.[25] If someone tries to define Good as what we desire to desire, we refute it by noticing that the question 'Is it good to desire to desire A?' is as intelligible as 'Is A good?' A correct definition of F as G closes the question 'Is G F?' The question is closed if it as trivial and easily answered as 'Is a bachelor an unmarried adult male?' The latter question is simply the question 'Is an unmarried adult male an unmarried adult male?', which is 'insignificant' and 'unintelligible'.

To decide whether a question is open or closed, in Moore's sense, we need to know for whom it is open or closed. The example we have just given might suggest that we have a closed question if and only if anyone who asked the question, understanding the words used to ask it, would thereby know that a negative answer is self-contradictory. If, then, the question whether F is good is closed, the answer that F is not good appears self-contradictory to anyone who grasps the meaning of the question.

We might defend Moore by arguing that alleged definitions of Good do not have the logical role of proper definitions. If 'male sibling' is the meaning of 'brother', the two sentences 'A brother is a male sibling' and 'A male sibling is a male sibling' express the same proposition, since propositions correspond to meanings. If, then, Good is defined as pleasant, 'good' and 'pleasant' mean the same; hence 'The Good is the pleasant' and 'The pleasant is the pleasant' should mean the same, and should express the same proposition. But we can see that they do not express the same proposition, because we can significantly doubt or question the first, but not the second. Hence 'pleasant' cannot be the definition of 'good'.[26]

This argument has relied on claims about the identity of propositions that claim to state definitions. But Moore's case does not depend on any claims—possibly controversial—about these propositions. We can also defend him by considering biconditionals. If 'good' and 'pleasant' mean the same, then (it might appear) (1) 'x is good iff x is pleasant' must mean the same as (2) 'x is pleasant iff x is pleasant', and must express the same proposition. Similarly, if 'brother' and 'male sibling' mean the same, it follows that (3) 'x is a brother iff x is a male sibling' expresses the same proposition as (4) 'x is a male sibling iff x is a male sibling'. To see that (3) and (4) express the same proposition, we need only notice that (4) does not

---

[24] Moore uses this phrase, 72, though not as a technical term for his argument. The phrase is used as a name for Moore's argument by Stevenson, *FV* 15; Frankena, 'Ewing's case', 27.

[25] 'The hypothesis that disagreement about the meaning of good is disagreement with regard to the correct analysis of a given whole, may be most plainly seen to be incorrect by consideration of the fact that, whatever definition be offered, it may always be asked, with significance, of the complex so defined, whether it is itself good.' (67)

[26] For this argument cf. Sidgwick, §§1156–7.

introduce an open question; hence 'male sibling' gives the meaning of 'brother'. But (1) and (2) express different propositions, since (1) introduces an open question. Hence 'pleasant' is not the meaning of 'good'. An appeal to open questions seems to separate acceptable from unacceptable definitions, by appeal to sameness and difference of propositions.[27]

If, then, a correct definition cannot create an open question, but all attempted definitions of Good create open questions, they all fail, and Good is indefinable. Hence the Open Question Argument refutes not only proposed naturalistic definitions of Good, but all proposed definitions of Good whatever, since they all create open questions.

Moreover, if the appeal to an open question is legitimate, it shows that Good is not only indefinable, but also inexplicable. Price affirms conceptual connexions between good, right, value, and obligation.[28] But these connexions create open questions; hence they cannot reveal any conceptual truths about Good. If we found genuine conceptual truths, they would not create open questions.

1257. Does the Open Question Argument Show that Good is Indefinable?

Both these arguments we have offered in support of Moore (about definitional statements and about biconditionals) assume that two sentences do not express the same proposition if only one of them creates an open question—if, in other words, we can significantly doubt or question the one but not the other. In defence of this assumption, we might observe that anyone who asked 'Is a brother a male sibling?' would show that they had not understood the question. They would not ask the question if they knew the meaning of 'brother', 'male', and 'sibling'. We could dissuade them from asking the question simply by reminding of the meanings of these terms. For someone who completely grasps the meaning of the relevant terms, no correct definition creates an open question; for a complete grasp of the meaning shows us that 'a brother is a male sibling' can be made into a tautology by substituting terms with the same meaning, and that 'a brother is not a male sibling' can be made into a contradiction by the same process.

If the Open Question Argument is understood this way, Moore is right to claim that it separates acceptable from unacceptable proposed definitions. When he says 'it may always be asked with significance', he offers a logical criterion: though G is proposed as the definition of F, it is not self-contradictory to say that G is not F (e.g., that what we desire is not good). This logical criterion provides a good test for something's being analytically true, and hence for an acceptable definition.

This understanding of the Open Question Argument, however, makes it useless for Moore's purposes. For we cannot tell whether we have a genuinely open question until we know the meaning of the relevant term. If the naturalist is right to say that 'good' means 'pleasant', someone who thinks that the question 'Are good things pleasant?' is open fails to

[27] This argument is offered by Lewy, 'Moore', 143–6. He agrees that the argument introducing the Paradox of Analysis must be rejected. He suggests that Moore later believed that 'To be a brother is to be a male sibling' and 'To be a male sibling is to be a male sibling' do not express the same proposition.

[28] Price on conceptual connexions; §813.

grasp the meaning of 'good' and 'pleasant' completely. To show that the crucial questions are open, we first have to refute the hedonist's account of the meaning of 'good'. Since the recognition of genuinely open questions depends on a grasp of the meaning, an appeal to open questions cannot be used to refute a proposed account of the meaning.

We should reach the same conclusion about the Open Question Argument, therefore, as we reached about the naturalistic fallacy. To show that some theorists commit the naturalistic fallacy, we must first show that Good is indefinable. To show this, Moore argues that all proposed definitions of Good create open questions. But his argument succeeds only if he already knows that Good is indefinable. Hence the appeal to open questions leads us back to our previous question about the meaning of Good, which Moore has not answered.

If this is the right conclusion about the Open Question Argument, the argument should not convince anyone that Good is indefinable. It leaves undone all the work that needs to be done to convince us of that claim. Only a misunderstanding of the argument could persuade anyone that it marks a significant advance in meta-ethics.

1258. When is a Question Open?

We might argue this objection misunderstands Moore's claim about open questions. Our objection has assumed that 'it may always be asked with significance' means that a negative answer to the question is not self-contradictory, so that an open question provides a logical criterion. He would avoid our objection if he understood the relevant question epistemologically, so that a question is open, and can be asked with significance, if and only if a negative answer does not appear self-contradictory. If this is what it takes for a question to be open, we can identify open questions before we have a complete account of the meaning of the relevant term; we need only ask what appears self-contradictory.

But now we have too many open questions. If a question is open whenever a negative answer appears consistent to someone, correct definitions also create open questions; for someone who does not grasp the meaning of 'F' will regard all questions about F, apart from 'Is F F?' as open. But if we rule out everyone except those who grasp the meaning of 'F', we come back to the difficulty raised by the logical criterion.

We might claim, for instance, that (1) 'x is good if and only if x is pleasant' and (2) 'x is pleasant if and only if x is pleasant' express different propositions because (1) can significantly be doubted while (2) cannot. In that case, we must apparently say the same about (3) 'x is a brother if and only if x is a male sibling' and (4) 'x is a male sibling if and only if x is a male sibling'. For if we know that brothers are male children of the same parents, but we do not know what 'sibling' means, we may significantly doubt or question (3) without doubting (4). Hence (3) and (4) do not express the same proposition. In this respect, they are parallel to (1) and (2), even though 'male sibling' is a correct definition of 'brother'. Hence some correct definitions create open questions. Hence the fact that a proposed definition creates an open question does not show that it is not a correct definition.

Alternatively, we may insist that (3) and (4) express the same proposition, even though we can significantly doubt the one while believing the other. But in that case, the fact that we can significantly doubt (1) but not (2) does not show that (1) and (2) express different propositions. Hence 'good' may (for all this argument shows) still be correctly defined as 'pleasant'. Any attempt to use the Open Question Argument to refute proposed definitions turns out to exclude too many definitions.

Perhaps, then, we should say that a question about F is open if a negative answer appears consistent to competent users of 'F'. According to this test, we need not demand explicit and complete knowledge of the whole meaning of 'F' in order to identify open questions; we need only demand the sort of understanding that we attribute to competent users, whether or not they grasp the relevant concept completely and explicitly. This is what Moore seems to have in mind in claiming to find open questions about Good. He does not think it is relevant if people who have no grasp of the concept take a question to be open. He assumes that if we can use 'good' intelligently and competently, we have reliable intuitions about what is and is not self-contradictory.

But if this is Moore's intended conception of an open question, an appeal to open questions cannot refute proposed definitions.[29] When hedonists claim to define 'good', they offer the sort of account that philosophers call a 'conceptual analysis'. Appeals to open questions do not seem to refute such an analysis. A correct analysis of knowledge as justified true belief (let us suppose) raises an open question; competent users of 'know' could significantly doubt whether they have justified true belief about p even if they believe that they know p. Since philosophical analyses often claim to tell us something informative and surprising, it would be strange if they could not be significantly doubted. They are supposed to be difficult to discover, and interesting to those who have discovered them and to those who are convinced of them. If Moore were right, an analysis could be correct only if it raised no open question; but if it raised no open question, we would not have needed to look for it, since it would not be interesting or surprising to the competent user.

If, then, the Open Question Argument gave a good reason for rejecting proposed definitions, we could never discover interesting definitions.[30] If analytic truths do not raise open questions, they include only trivial analytic equivalences. Moore's view makes it unintelligible that philosophers are sometimes puzzled about the analysis of a concept; a few simple questions should dispose of every issue that can be raised.

On this point, a variant of Moore's own argument can be used against him. He argues that if goodness is felicificity, then 'goodness is felicificity' should be trivially analytic; since it is not trivially analytic, the attempted definition is obviously to be rejected. We might reply that since Moore's view makes the utilitarian account obviously false, but the utilitarian account is not obviously false, Moore is wrong about definition. Philosophers who believe it is worth looking for the analysis of a concept have not endorsed Moore's view of conceptual truths.[31]

And so, even if we try to interpret Moore's claims about open questions sympathetically, we have a good reason to doubt whether the Open Question Argument refutes any of the

---

[29] Even simple lexical definitions may create open questions for competent users. I may be able to use 'brother' quite competently even if it has never occurred to me that brothers are male siblings, and so the question 'Is a brother a male sibling?' may be open for me.

[30] This objection to Moore raises issues about the Paradox of Analysis. See Broad, *FTET* 173–4; Langford, 'Analysis'; Frankena, 'Fallacy', 7–8; Moore, 'Reply', 665–7; Baldwin, *GEM* 208–14.

[31] On conceptions of analysis, see Langford, 'Analysis'.

definitions proposed by moralists who take Good to be definable. Any philosophers who rely on his appeal to open questions to refute proposed definitions must assume a heavy burden; for they commit themselves to the rejection of all informative philosophical conceptual analyses. Philosophers who do not want to assume this burden have a good reason to avoid reliance on the Open Question Argument. But, as we will see, many of Moore's successors accept the very aspect of the Open Question Argument that rules out the possibility of the analyses that they try to find.[32]

Moore's Open Question Argument promises to dispose of proposed definitions of Good at one stroke. But it proves too much. If it were sound, it would show not only that Good is indefinable, but also that no interesting definitions could be correct.

1259. Objections to Some Naturalist Definitions of Good

Many readers of Moore who admit the flaws in his argument believe none the less that he has discovered something, even if he does prove the completely general claim that he maintains. They may reasonably appeal to the places where Moore does not simply resort to open questions, but argues more dialectically against particular naturalist definitions. In his view, they conflict with other things that naturalists want to say about Good and make it difficult for us to understand the nature of arguments and disputes about Good. How cogent are these objections to naturalism?

Relying on Sidgwick's discussion of Bentham, Moore asks whether hedonists can consistently accept the implications of their own definitions of Good (69). They accept two claims: (1) 'Good' means 'maximizing pleasure'. (2) Maximizing pleasure is good. Moore suggests that (2) excludes (1). Moore and Sidgwick claim that, in asserting (2), we mean something different from (2a) 'Maximizing pleasure is maximizing pleasure', but if (1) were right, (2a) would mean the same as (2).

This argument, however, is too hasty. If it were accepted, it would undermine all definitions; for they all equally allow us to produce unwanted tautologies by substitution. A very similar argument would disallow all equivalences of meaning. For instance, we would not use (i) ' "Female fox" means "female fox" ' in the contexts in which we would use (ii) ' "Vixen" means "female fox" '. For (i) is tautologous and uninformative, telling us nothing new about the meaning of 'female fox', whereas (ii) is informative, telling us something new about the meaning of 'vixen'. If, however, we believe in the possibility of equivalences of meaning, we might say that while (i) and (ii) mean the same, they do not convey the same information. We might, then, try to say the same about (1) and (2), the assertions about good and maximizing pleasure.

Conceptual hedonists who accept this defence against Moore should take (2) to make the meaning of 'good' explicit, in contrast to (3) 'Keeping promises is good'. The third claim tells us something beyond what we grasp from making the meaning of 'good' explicit. But if a hedonist conceptual analysis of Good is correct, we have to take 'Pleasure is good' to say simply that these are two terms for one concept. The set of characteristics indicated

---

[32] On the use of the Open Question Argument, see §§1303–4, 1327, 1361–2, 1364–5.

by 'pleasure' is the same as the set indicated by 'good'; hence we do not ascribe any further characteristics to something in calling it 'good' beyond those we ascribe in calling it 'pleasure'. If hedonists are willing to take this position, they have an answer to Moore.

What is wrong with this conceptual hedonist account of Good? Moore suggests that it 'offers no reason at all, far less any valid reason, for any ethical principles whatever' (71), and that 'when we think we have a definition, we cannot logically defend our ethical principles in any way whatever' (72). To show that naturalists deprive themselves of reasons and arguments, Moore considers naturalists who claim that Good is not pleasure but the object of desire. What do they mean? He suggests two possibilities: (a) They define Good as 'object of desire' and deny that the object of desire is pleasant. (b) They claim that Good means 'object of desire' rather than 'pleasant' (63).

In Moore's view, neither possibility offers an attractive position. (a) The first view implies that naturalists merely maintain a psychological claim, that pleasure is not the only object of desire. 'But, if this be all, where is his Ethics?' (63). They abolish ethical argument in favour of psychological speculation or assertion. If we assume a definition of Good as 'object of desire', we cannot defend our claims about what things are good by showing that they are good; we can only show that they are desired, which is not the same as showing that they are good.[33] (b) If, as the second possibility implies, naturalists claim that Good means 'object of desire' and does not mean 'pleasant', they reduce the dispute to a relatively uninteresting verbal question. When some people claim that pleasure is good, they do not intend to answer the verbal question; they surely do not just mean that pleasure is pleasure (64).

Neither option, however, seems as bad as Moore supposes. It is reasonable for non-hedonist naturalists to argue from some claims about the meaning of Good. If Good means 'object of desire', a proof that the object of desire is not pleasure proves that Good is not pleasure. Moore would be right to reject this proof only if he had shown that 'object of desire' is not the right definition of Good. The second option does not seem so bad either. A dispute about meaning need not be a 'purely verbal' question in a sense that suggests it is not worth arguing about; we might have an important question about the conceptual analysis of Good.

Moore is none the less right to suggest that a hedonist conceptual analysis does not capture what hedonists normally mean by their claim that pleasure is good. Normally they mean that pleasure has some further feature beyond being pleasure, and this further feature constitutes its goodness. This interpretation of the hedonist claim clarifies disputes between hedonists and non-hedonists about whether pleasure is good. Hedonists claim not that non-hedonists fail to grasp the concept of Good, but that they fail to see that pleasure has all the features that are acknowledged to belong to Good.[34]

---

[33] '. . . that is one alternative which any naturalistic Ethics has to face; if good is *defined* as something else, it is then impossible either to prove that any other definition is wrong or even to deny any such definition.' (63)

[34] This defence of Moore is partly derived from Prior's defence at *LBE* 7–10. Prior, however, agrees with too many of Moore's strange claims about definition. He suggests that a conceptual hedonist must admit 'that the assertion that, say, pleasure and nothing but pleasure is good, *is* for him a mere truism' (9). Prior agrees with Moore's claim that if 'Pleasure is pleasure' is a mere truism, and 'good' means 'pleasure', then 'Pleasure is good' must also be a mere truism. Mackie, 'Critical Notice', 123–4, suggests that Moore is pointing out that it is difficult to abandon the use of 'pleasure is good' as something more than a truism. But he follows Prior in accepting Moore's claims about definition. Frankena criticizes Prior on this point in his review, 555.

This is why Plato suggests that hedonists and non-hedonists about Good introduce two competing candidates for the same role.[35] A reasonable competition depends on some prior understanding of the role that the candidates claim to fill. Disputants about whether pleasure is the good argue about the qualifications of the candidates, not about the right description of the role. Since the argument about which candidate should occupy the role seems to be intelligible and reasonable, an account of Good ought to make ethical argument appear intelligible and reasonable. Hence it ought to treat hedonism as a description of a candidate for the role, not as a description of the role; for if hedonism described the role, the argument about which candidate fulfils the role would be unintelligible. Moore argues that conceptual hedonism violates this condition of adequacy; he is right to suggest that it removes the possibility of an argument that should be open to us.

Moore has a good reason, then, to suggest that some claims about the nature of goodness are not claims about the conceptual analysis of 'good'. If we suggest that anyone who rejects these claims makes a conceptual error, we distort the character of the dispute about goodness. Hedonists, therefore, ought not to be conceptual hedonists.

Moore exaggerates this reasonable point, however, in his claim that we need to treat Good as indefinable if we are to conduct ethical argument reasonably. If we argue on the assumption that we have a definition of Good, we reject certain candidates for the role on the ground that they are ruled out by the very meaning of the word.[36] But if we assume that Good has no definition, we begin with an open mind; we do not rule out any candidates on the ground that it would be implicitly self-contradictory to call them good.[37]

This seems an exaggerated claim, since it seems to deprive us of what we need to begin an inquiry. If we interview the candidates for a position with no preconceptions about what the position requires, we start with an open mind about whether they are qualified, but our mind is too open to allow a reasonable assessment of the candidates. Does Moore not leave us with too open a mind about Good? By going to the opposite extreme from conceptual hedonism, he seems to do no better than the conceptual hedonist in making the dispute about whether the good is pleasure appear intelligible and reasonable. Since the Open Question Argument rules out all explications of Good, it leaves us with nothing to argue about.

Critics who reject the rest of Moore's position have supposed that he is on to something important in his argument about the naturalistic fallacy.[38] One might believe that some naturalistic definitions of moral concepts are implausible, not because Moore is right about open questions, but because moral concepts have a role in argument that some naturalistic definitions do not capture. If we question a naturalistic definition of 'good' as 'F', we may

---

[35] The *Philebus* on the good; §53.

[36] 'For we shall start with the conviction that good must mean so and so, and shall therefore be inclined either to misunderstand our opponent's arguments or to cut them short with the reply, "That is not an open question: the very meaning of the word decides it; no one can think otherwise except through confusion."' (72)

[37] 'If we start with the conviction that a definition of good can be found, we start with the conviction that good *can mean* nothing else than some one property of things; and our only business will then be to discover what that property is. But if we recognize that, so far as the meaning of good goes, anything whatever may be good, we start with a much more open mind.' (72)

[38] See, e.g., Darwall, 'Moore', 485; Gibbard, *WCAF* 11, discussed in §1361.

say 'I can see that x is F, but is x good?' But we may not mean that an open question (as Moore understands it) arises here. We may mean that particular identifications of goodness with natural properties are open to discussion, criticism, and revision. Whereas it does not seem reasonable to hold that the identification of brothers with male siblings is in principle open to criticism and revision, it seems reasonable to hold this about pleasure (or fulfilment of human nature, or achieving the ultimate end, or conforming to the will of God), offered as an analysis of 'good' or 'right'.[39] If it is reasonable to ask 'Is it good?' about any candidate for goodness, and we want to hold open the possibility of asking that question, we have reason not to treat our candidate as giving us the analysis of 'good'. If we treated it as an analysis, we would make disputes that seem not to be disputes about meaning into disputes about meaning.

If an account of Good has to respect these plausible constraints on ethical argument, Moore's account is open to doubt. Some of his arguments are reasonable objections against some other accounts, but they do not support his account. In particular, they do not show that Good is indefinable or inexplicable. Moore does not consider attempts at definition that introduce concepts that are no simpler than Good, concepts whose definitions may involve one another and Good in some unavoidable circle. The mutual explication of these concepts may give us a reasonable starting point for arguments about candidates that would fill the role marked by 'good'.

Moore has some reasonable objections, therefore, to some definitions that treat Good as a natural property. But if we accept these objections, we need not agree that the definitions he opposes commit any naturalistic fallacy, or that the Open Question Argument exposes their error. If Moore were right, we could do without piecemeal dialectical arguments against particular definitions, because we would know they were all mistaken. But we have good reason to prefer these piecemeal arguments to Moore's excessively general arguments.

1260. Moore's Second Thoughts

In his unfinished preface to the projected second edition of *Principia*, Moore rejects some of his previous arguments, criticizes his misunderstandings of the connexions between different theses, and defends the theses that he still accepts. He still believes that Good is not identical to any natural or metaphysical property (6).[40] He distinguishes this from the claim that Good is unanalysable (5–6), and distinguishes the latter claim from the claim that Good is inexplicable. He says he has overlooked the distinction 'between expressing a word's meaning by other words, which *contain an analysis* of its meaning, and merely expressing its

---

[39] This is an attempt to capture what Adams, *FIG*, has in mind in suggesting the 'truth behind' Moore's Open Question Argument. After rejecting the argument itself, he adds: 'In the case of evaluative and normative language, however, we have a special commitment to allow that language to be used to question or challenge the value of any human thought or action and any object of human experience. We have no other language similarly apt for evaluative and normative questions and challenges; and to treat the value of any natural object or action, or . . . the correctness of any human consensus, as immune to such criticism is a fearful abridgment of ethical possibility. In a religious perspective it is idolatry.' (78)

[40] Moore now uses 'G' to indicate the property that is picked out by the use of the word 'good' that concerns him. He takes the relevant use to pick out intrinsic goodness.

meaning by other words' (9), and that once this distinction is recognized, it is clear that we can form expressions synonymous with 'good'.[41]

Moore takes these observations about definition and synonymous expressions to be relevant to his previous claims that (1) 'Good is Good and nothing else whatever', and that (2) all propositions about Good are synthetic and not analytic. He takes the first claim, if it is not trivial, to be the claim that (as we have put it) Good is inexplicable; he says he has not argued for this strong conclusion. To explain his second claim, he asserts that by 'analytic' he meant 'tautologous'.[42] But it is not clear why he asserts this. For in *PE*, his denial of analytic propositions about Good is meant to imply that the non-tautologous 'Good maximizes pleasure' is not analytic.

Moore rejects his previous view that Good is inexplicable, but he does not discuss a conclusion that he drew from inexplicability. In *PE*, he claims that, as far as the meaning of Good goes, anything whatever may be good (72); once we recognize this, we avoid the error of beginning our investigation into goodness with the dogmatic assumption that the meaning of Good itself ensures that some specific sorts of things are good. Once he allows that Good is explicable, he gives up this allegedly salutary caution in normative inquiry.

He no longer claims that Good is unanalysable, and he acknowledges that he has not refuted an analysis that defines Good by reference to (e.g.) 'right' or 'ought' (14).[43] He abandons his previous contention that Good is the fundamental unanalysable property in ethics. Indeed, he does not even claim that some one ethical property must be part of the analysis of all others; we might find several that are equally unanalysable. He now claims simply that ethical properties are neither identical to, nor analysable into, natural or metaphysical properties.[44]

If we leave aside (as Moore does) the question about metaphysical properties, the main questions Moore now faces are these: (1) What is a natural property? (2) Why is Good not a natural property? The Preface considers only the first task.

The Preface does not discuss the Open Question Argument. But if that argument were cogent, it would show that Good is inexplicable. 'Good is what we ought to aim at' creates an open question, since it does not seem obviously self-contradictory to say that we ought to aim at x, but x is not good. The same can be said of any other proposed partial explication. If no analytical proposition about Good can leave an open question, Good is inexplicable. It is puzzling, then, that the Preface claims that *PE* takes Good to be inexplicable simply because Moore was, at that stage, confusing analysis with explication (9). The Open

---

[41] Moore's claim about what he has previously overlooked does not seem quite correct. For in *PE*, he clearly recognized the possibility of verbal definitions, and declared that these were not his concern. In the new Preface, he seems to be more explicitly concerned with meanings, and hence he is readier to suppose that the possibility of verbal definitions is relevant to his task.

[42] This leads into further detailed questions. In response to the objection that 'The Good is good' is a tautology about Good, he replies that one might take 'propositions about the good' to exclude tautologies. In that case, his previous claim said that all (non-tautologous) propositions about Good are synthetic and not analytic (i.e., tautologous), and so it was itself tautologous. Moore acknowledges this in the new Preface, 10–11.

[43] A non-naturalist definition of 'good' involving 'ought' is offered by Ewing, *DG*, chs. 3–5. At 78–9 he comments on Moore's arguments.

[44] '(1) ... G is not completely analysable in terms of natural or metaphysical properties; and ... if, therefore, it is analysable at all, it certainly involves in its analysis some unanalysable notion, which is not identical with any natural or metaphysical property. ... (2) ethical propositions do involve some unanalysable notion, which is not identical with any natural or metaphysical property.' (14)

Question Argument does not rest on this confusion. It offers a reason to believe that Good is inexplicable.

If, therefore, Moore now believes (in the Preface) he has no reason to deny that Good is explicable, he commits himself to the rejection of the Open Question Argument. But that is the only argument that *PE* offers to show that Good cannot be defined as a natural property. And so Moore's later claims about *PE* cast doubt on his case against naturalism.[45]

1261. Natural Properties and Intrinsic Properties

To see whether Moore has any reasonable objections to naturalism, we need to take up a question we have postponed. What does he mean by 'natural property'? He offers different answers to this question at different times, and his answers commit him to different claims about Good.[46]

According to his first suggestion, F is a natural property if and only if we can imagine F existing by itself in time and not merely as a property of a natural object (93). Moore claims that we can imagine this in the case of most properties of natural objects, because the universal Yellow (e.g.) can exist by itself in time without any patches, shapes, or surfaces to belong to.[47] A yellow box is simply a collection of universals (Yellow, Square, Hard, and so on); it cannot exist without them, whereas they can exist without it. The existence of a particular substance simply consists in the bundling of universals that exist independently of it.

These metaphysical intuitions are puzzling. How can Yellow exist in time and space without any shape or size to give it spatial location? If Yellow can be abstracted from shape and size and still exist in space and time, why is the same not true of Good? Perhaps goodness is supervenient, so that nothing can be good without having some other property that makes it good. But, equally, nothing can be yellow without having a yellow surface, a size, and a shape. Metaphysical intuitions about the independent existence of natural properties do not show that Good is non-natural.

In the Preface, Moore does not try to define all natural properties. He now tries to identify the subset of natural properties that matters to his argument about Good. In his view, Good depends only on the intrinsic properties of its subject, but is not itself an intrinsic property (22).[48]

This claim is puzzling, because Moore might appear to imply that goodness is an intrinsic property. For he believes that non-instrumental goodness belongs to things in isolation from any specific context or relation, and in this sense is intrinsic to them. A naturalist might argue

---

[45] Lewy, 'Moore', 140, notices that in the new Preface Moore neither comments on his previous arguments against naturalism nor offers new arguments

[46] Sturgeon, 'Naturalism', 536–41, examines some of Moore's claims about natural properties.

[47] '. . . with the greater number of properties of objects—those which I will call the natural properties—their existence does seem to me to be independent of the existence of these objects. They are, in fact, rather parts of which the object is made up than mere predicates which attach to it. If they were all taken away, no object would be left, not even a bare substance; for they are in themselves substantial, and give to the object all the substance that it has.' (93)

[48] Moore says more about intrinsic properties in 'Intrinsic value', written in 1914–17, a few years before the new Preface.

as follows: (1) Intrinsic value is a property of natural objects. (2) Intrinsic value is intrinsic to the objects it is a property of. (3) If a property is intrinsic to an object, it is an intrinsic property of that object. (4) Any intrinsic property of a natural object is a natural property. (5) Hence the intrinsic value of a natural object is a natural property.

Moore rejects the third step of this argument. In his view, Good is a property that is intrinsic to good things, because it depends only on their intrinsic properties, but it is not itself an intrinsic property. But this way of blocking the argument seems arbitrary; it is difficult to see why we should deny that a property that is intrinsic to a subject is an intrinsic property of that subject.[49]

1262. Descriptive v. Non-Descriptive Properties

Later still, Moore tries to capture natural properties through a different account of intrinsic properties. He claims that intrinsic properties of an object describe it and non-intrinsic properties do not.[50] Since 'predicates of value' do not describe objects they are predicated of, they are not intrinsic properties, and hence they are not natural properties.[51]

But how (we might ask) could Good be a property of natural objects if the predicate 'good' does not describe them? If Moore were right, we could completely describe an object without mentioning all its properties. One might try to support him by recalling Hume's claim that Euclid has fully explained all the qualities of the circle without mentioning its beauty, since beauty is not a quality of the circle.

Hume does not offer a very cogent argument, however. Reid replies quite appropriately by saying that Euclid has not fully explained all the qualities of the circle, since he has missed out its beauty. And in any case, Moore disagrees with a Humean defence of a non-descriptive view; for he claims that Good is a property of good things. He should accept Ross's and Reid's reply that a description of something intrinsically beautiful is incomplete if it leaves out the beauty that is one of its properties. In predicating beauty of it, therefore, we describe it.[52]

Might we, then, suggest, on Moore's behalf, that predicates of value do not predicate properties of objects? Broad sees that this 'non-predicative' view (as he calls it) it might plausibly be inferred from Moore's position.[53] If Moore believes that predicates of value follow from intrinsic properties, but are not descriptive, and if a property is non-natural in so far as it is non-descriptive, non-naturalism raises doubts about whether Good is a property. Hence Moore's later non-cognitivist critics conclude that Good is not a property.[54]

Moore rejects this non-cognitivist conclusion. In *Ethics*, he rejects a non-predicative view of judgments about both rightness and goodness.[55] In his later discussion with Stevenson, he declares himself to be inclined to accept a non-predicative view in its emotivist form, but also inclined to doubt Stevenson's belief in emotive meaning. He suggests plausibly that

[49] Moore, 'Reply', 581–92. Broad comments at 'Moore's doctrines', 57–67; Broad, 'Latest', 350–4.
[50] 'Reply', 585.   [51] Here he builds on a suggestion in 'Intrinsic value', 297.
[52] Hume on Euclid; §748. Reid's reply; §848. Ross's reply; *RG* 120.
[53] 'His suggested criterion, with its admitted vagueness, due to the uncertainty of the relevant sense of "describe", is surely grist to the mill of supporters of what I will call "non-predicative interpretations of moral sentences in the indicative".' (Broad, 'Latest', 438)
[54] The non-cognitivist conclusion from Moore; §1293.   [55] See Moore, *E*, chs. 3–4.

the judgments to which Stevenson ascribes emotive meaning normally imply, but do not mean, that the speaker has certain emotions.[56] The arguments for emotivism do not shake Moore's cognitivism, but it is easy to see why they appeal to him; for if he thinks predicates of value are not descriptive, he comes close to a non-cognitive view.

If this were the best clarification of Moore's claims about non-natural properties, *PE* would undermine itself. Moore sets out from a cognitivist conception of Good as a genuine property of good things. But if non-natural properties are evaluative and not descriptive, and are not genuine properties of the object at all, Good cannot be both a non-natural property and a genuine property belonging to things in their own right. To avoid this conclusion, it is best to reject Moore's suggestion that non-natural properties are not descriptive. In that case, he has given no satisfactory account of a natural property.

1263. Why is Ethics Not a Natural Science?

If it is difficult to explain Moore's claim that Good is not a natural property, does he really need it? Would it matter to his overall argument if he conceded that Good is, or may be, a natural property? He mentions two implications of naturalism: (1) Good would belong to an existing natural science that would replace ethics (92).[57] (2) Ethics would turn out to be an 'empirical or positive' science whose conclusions 'could all be established by means of empirical observation and induction' (91).[58]

According to the first claim, our recognition that Good is a natural property would involve the disappearance of ethics. Mill would replace ethics with psychology and Clifford would replace it with sociology (92). Moore assumes that all possible natural sciences already exist, and that if Good is a natural property, it is already dealt with exhaustively and exclusively by exactly one of these existing natural sciences. These assumptions are open to doubt. Even if Good were a property that already concerns some natural science, the ethical treatment of it might still require a distinct natural science of ethics.[59] (Similarly, climate might belong to several distinct sciences.) Alternatively, if Good is an indefinable natural property, it might require its own special natural science of ethics.[60]

Moore's second claim does not assert that if naturalism were true ethics would disappear, but only that ethics would turn out to be an empirical science. This result implies the disappearance of ethics only if ethics could not be an empirical science. The method of an 'empirical science' or 'natural science', according to Moore, is empirical observation and induction; it observes things and properties other than goodness, rightness, and

---

[56] 'Reply', 541.
[57] Similarly, Ewing, *DG* 36, takes naturalism to analyse ethical concepts solely in terms of the concepts of a natural science, so that it makes ethics a branch of a natural science.
[58] Moore does not distinguish these two implications.
[59] This possibility is explored by Sturgeon, 'Naturalism', 551–5.
[60] Prior, *LBE* 9–10, follows Moore in claiming that a consistent naturalism will have to abolish ethics and replace it with something else. His assumption about elimination is criticized by Mackie, 'Critical notice', 116. As Mackie points out, 'Prior has in effect identified the issue between naturalism and non-naturalism with that between reductionism and non-reductionism; he has suggested that a naturalistic view is necessarily a reductionist one, and this does not help to clarify the issue'. Mackie mentions Anderson as a defender of the view that Prior neglects; see Anderson, 'Advocacy', replying to Prior, 'Meaning'.

obligatoriness, and other predicates of value.[61] If, then, Good and other evaluative properties are non-natural, not all true conclusions about these properties can be reached by observation and induction confined to properties other than these.

To decide whether this is a plausible account of the method of natural science, we need a clearer conception of observation and induction. If they are confined to the collection of sensory data and statistical generalizations from them, they do not exhaust the method of natural sciences. To fit the method of natural sciences better, we might say that induction includes not only statistical generalizations, but also the formation of hypotheses and inferences to the best explanation. These 'inductive' methods include comparison of a given hypothesis with other apparently plausible principles, and so they seem to go beyond generalizations from observed instances. If our account of induction is complex enough to fit the method of a natural science, it becomes harder to show that a particular form of argument is distinct from observation and induction. Hence it becomes more difficult to show that the method of ethics could not be the method of a natural science.

1264. Evaluative Properties and Non-Natural Properties

We might, then, try an alternative clarification of non-natural properties. Moore identifies them with evaluative properties ('predicates of value'). Instead of looking for a positive account of natural properties, and hence a negative account of non-natural properties, we might rely on a positive account of evaluative properties and a negative account of non-evaluative properties. We might assume that evaluative properties or predicates are essentially connected with acts of evaluation, so that they are not descriptive after all. This would be another route to a non-cognitivist conclusion.

But we need not take this route. If we believe, for instance, that goodness, rightness, obligation ('oughtness'), and reasons need to be explained by reference to one another, we may claim that evaluative properties are those that need to be explained by reference to one or other of these properties. Even if we have only a list of properties, and cannot say what they have in common (apart from this fact about how they are to be explained), it may still be worthwhile to argue that true judgments about them cannot be reduced to, or replaced by, judgments that do not introduce these properties.

Moore's views might encourage us to reject analyses of evaluative concepts that replace them with non-evaluative concepts. We might understand 'naturalistic' analyses as including only non-evaluative concepts. This suggestion is not very precise until we characterize evaluative concepts more precisely. Some of Moore's successors have taken them to be essentially non-descriptive (as Moore himself sometimes does), and hence as essentially emotive or prescriptive in meaning. This account, however, is open to severe objections, as we will see. We may simply have to list concepts such as 'good', 'right', 'ought', and 'reason', and to suggest that an analysis of any one of these has to include at least one of the others, or some concept that eventually has to include one of them in its analysis. Perhaps, for instance, the right is

---

[61] Broad comments on this aspect of Moore's position in 'Some features', 62–7. He reasonably suggests an epistemological basis for the division between natural and non-natural; this basis raises further difficulties. See §1362.

what would be prescribed by any of the cardinal virtues, but an analysis of the concepts of the virtues will re-introduce 'right' or 'good', or one of the other terms we began from.

This suggestion does not support Moore's claim that Good is simple and inexplicable. If nothing satisfies his conditions for a definition or analysis, that may be because these conditions are questionable. Rather than endorse them, we would do better to say that 'good' is definable and analysable, but only through a list of concepts that may be labelled 'evaluative'. In this respect, Moore has a good case against 'naturalistic' analyses, if these are non-evaluative, in the sense just described. But even if he is right, goodness, rightness, and so on may still be natural properties. Moore supposes that the question about whether Good is a natural property matters because natural properties are those studied by natural science. We have found no reason to conclude that moral properties are not natural, since we have found no reason to conclude that evaluative properties are not natural.[62]

If the properties essentially related to goodness and to one another (the evaluative properties) cannot be explained without reference to one another, a systematic body of knowledge about these properties and things that have them cannot dispense with evaluative terms. Let us grant that such a body of knowledge is different from other natural sciences, because none of them includes such terms. It still does not follow that our ethical knowledge cannot be a natural science in its own right. Such a conclusion would follow only if we already knew that no natural science could essentially include evaluative terms. But we would know that about a natural science only if we already knew that the presence of such terms is inconsistent with a scientific method that proceeds by observation and induction. But if we avoid an unreasonably narrow conception of observation and induction, it is difficult to pronounce that the scientific method precludes the presence of evaluative terms. Hence, we might agree with Moore's view that Good is essentially an evaluative property, but we might still refuse to infer that it is not a natural property.

1265. The Open Question Argument and Real Definitions

Our discussion so far has not yet recognized the strangest feature of Moore's meta-ethical argument, including his appeal to the Open Question Argument. We have followed him in speaking of Good rather than 'good' because, as we saw, he did not take his inquiry to be about a word or a concept. His original question was not about a nominal definition or conceptual analysis. He originally asked whether Good has a compositional real definition.

Moore, however, does not seem to keep these two distinct sorts of definitions in mind. He simply says he is looking for the 'object or idea' that the word 'good' is generally used to stand for (58), and he is therefore not primarily interested in a verbal definition that simply tells us how someone chooses to use a word. He does not think of facts about the meaning of a word as simply facts about how it is used; he thinks that the meaning is the idea before our mind, and that this is the object that we should be trying to discover and describe. This object is a property, and the inquiry tries to discover what sort of property Good is.

---

[62] Jackson, 'Cognitivism', claims that the identification of moral properties with natural properties is more closely connected than I have suggested with naturalistic conceptual analyses. He relies on claims about supervenience. See also *FME*, chs. 5–6, and §1363.

It is difficult, nonetheless, to see how Moore could be so indifferent to verbal definitions and to uses of words. He is interested not in the different ideas before our mind when we use the word 'good' in its various senses (which he acknowledges), but the one idea that we have before our mind when we use the word in the sense relevant to his inquiry. We cannot know which of the various possible ideas associated with 'good' we are being asked to examine until we have convinced ourselves that we are using the word in the sense that Moore takes to be relevant.

He assumes that a property is the meaning of a term, so that if two terms are not synonymous they do not pick out the same property. Unless Moore believes this, his arguments about the naturalistic fallacy could not show that Good is not identical to any natural, metaphysical, or complex property. For these arguments purport to show that two terms or expressions do not mean the same, because they create an open question.

But if we look for a real definition, the Open Question Argument seems irrelevant; for it is difficult to see how a correct compositional definition could avoid open questions. If we assemble all the simplest elements into which we have analysed Horse, it seems significant to ask 'Are all these elements a horse?' If Moore's opponents offer compositional definitions of Good, they are not refuted by open questions.

The same point applies to all real definitions, even if they are not all compositional in the sense that Moore describes. Since real definitions do not necessarily correspond to the common concepts of their definienda, they may raise open questions. And so, even if—contrary to fact—the Open Question Argument provided a reasonable test of adequacy for some definitions, it would not provide a reasonable test for the sort of definition that interests Moore.

Why should Moore assume that if we want to find the property Good rather than the extension of 'good', we should look for the concept or meaning of Good? He has a good reason to investigate the question 'What is Good?' and to distinguish it from 'What things are good?' He agrees with Socrates and with others who have deployed the Socratic distinction to reject accounts of moral properties that offer co-extensive descriptions without proper explanatory definitions. If this is the point of Moore's inquiry, we can ask whether his conception of properties allows them the appropriate role in moral inquiry.

He may be influenced by the fact that both concepts and properties are non-extensional. If two terms have the same extension, it does not follow that they express the same concept or introduce the same property. The non-extensional character of properties makes it reasonable for Socrates to insist that an answer to his question 'What is the F?' requires more than a list of F things. Hence we might try to explain the non-extensional character of properties by identifying them with concepts.

But this is not the only possible explanation. Moore's compositional definition of Horse does not seem to be a nominal definition that defines a word or concept by giving its meaning. It might be interpreted as a real definition, telling us about the essence of horses rather than about the meaning of 'horse'. Even if there are non-obvious but correct conceptual analyses, accounts of concepts do not seem to be the same as real definitions.[63] If we also take properties to be explanatory, we may doubt whether they are the same as concepts.

---

[63] Carnap, MN 16–23, identifies concepts with properties.

An account of an explanatory property should display its explanatory character. If we suppose that there is some disease that causes certain symptoms, including red spots, high temperature, and so on, we may call this disease 'measles'. One true description of the explanatory condition is 'measles'; hence measles explains the symptoms of measles. But we have not yet shown why measles explains these symptoms if we describe it only as 'measles'; this is no better than saying that a drug puts us to sleep because it has a dormitive virtue. To show how this condition is explanatory, we have to say enough about measles to show the appropriate explanatory connexion between features of a specific internal condition and the various external symptoms. In that case, we will have found an explanatory account of the explanatory condition.

The relevant explanatory property is non-extensional. Though the hurricane in Cuba was the event mentioned in the headline of today's paper, the property of being mentioned in the headline did not explain the flooding in Cuba; its being a hurricane (let us suppose) explained the flooding. But though explanatory properties are similar to concepts in being non-extensional, they are different in allowing non-synonymous descriptions to pick out the same property. Our description of the process of discovery of an explanatory account presupposes that we can find two non-synonymous descriptions of the same explanatory condition; the second description is more complicated than the first, and it displays the explanatory character of the condition.

Similarly, then, an inquiry into goodness or rightness should look for an explanatory property that has a number of non-synonymous descriptions. We prove that goodness is identical to what maximizes pleasure if we prove that the tendency to maximize pleasure explains why things are good. If we understand the explanatory task, we have good reason to suppose that our earlier and later descriptions of the same explanatory property are not synonymous. If we find the appropriate explanation, our later description of the explanatory property will be a real definition. We have every reason to expect that such a definition will raise an open question.

If, then, we take naturalist hedonism to offer an explanatory account that provides a real definition of Good, Moore's appeal to the Open Question Argument is irrelevant. Even if he had shown that it is not a conceptual truth that goodness is a natural property, he would not have shown that goodness is not a natural property. Though the concept of goodness is not the same concept as the concept of maximum pleasure, the two concepts might still be concepts of just one property. If we want to know what property goodness is, we ought not to follow Moore's method.

1266. Does Non-Naturalism Require Intuitionism?

Moore believes that his account of Good commits him to an intuitionist account of our knowledge of Good and of other moral properties. In his view, we cannot know what moral properties are, or that things have them, by ordinary sorts of empirical or a priori argument, but must simply recognize them without any further inference or argument.

Which aspect of Moore's doctrine commits him to intuitionism? He claims that Good is (a) indefinable, (b) inexplicable, and (c) non-natural. His first two claims follow from the Open Question Argument. His third claim does not follow from the Open Question Argument, since an inexplicable property such as Yellow may still be natural. Which of these claims implies that moral properties can be known only by intuition?

Sometimes Moore suggests that if some form of conceptual naturalism were true, moral epistemology would be easy. We would define 'good' as (e.g.) 'pleasant', and so our question about what things are good would be answered simply by finding out what things produce pleasure. We can find this out, in Moore's view, by ordinary empirical knowledge. But if conceptual naturalism is false, we cannot give this account of moral knowledge in this way.

Against conceptual naturalism Moore suggests that the indefinability of Good is necessary and sufficient to show that ethics must rest on intuitions.[64] He denies that we can derive anything from the meaning of 'good' that restricts the sorts of things that can be good. If we ask 'What kinds of things ought to exist for their own sakes?', the meanings of the relevant terms do not allow us to form the appropriate empirical questions.[65] We must therefore begin with intuitions about what things are good.[66]

But it is not clear that Moore relies on the indefinability of Good. When he speaks of what we can derive from the meaning of good, he seems to imply that we need analytic truths about goodness in order to avoid appeals to intuition. But even if Good is indefinable, it may still be explicable and (as the Preface agrees) we may know analytic truths about it. To show that we must appeal to intuition, Moore needs to say that Good is inexplicable. Since the Open Question Argument shows, if it is sound, that Good is inexplicable, it seems to be the basis of Moore's intuitionism.

If this is what Moore means, it is puzzling that he connects intuitionism with non-naturalism. Non-naturalists who believed that Good is definable or explicable (including those who accept 'metaphysical ethics') would apparently not need to be intuitionists, since they could rely on analytic truths (e.g., 'good' means 'what ought to be desired', or 'what fulfils the human function', or 'what brings the universe closer to perfection'). Conversely, naturalists who believed that Good is indefinable and inexplicable would apparently need intuitions, since they would have no analytic truths to rely on. Non-naturalism does not seem to be relevant in its own right to intuitionism.

Perhaps Moore relies on his view that the Open Question Argument refutes both naturalism and the forms of non-naturalism that take Good to be explicable. And so he tends to suppose that the only position that needs to be considered is his version of non-naturalism. Perhaps that is why he connects non-naturalism with intuitionism.

Alternatively, Moore might disagree with the arguments that seem to make some naturalists into intuitionists and to give some non-naturalists a way out of intuitionism. Even if we cannot define a simple natural property, perhaps we can give the meaning of the term

[64] 'We cannot tell what is possible, by way of proof, in favour of one judgment that "This or that is good", or against another judgment "That this or that is bad", until we have recognized what the nature of such propositions must always be. In fact, it follows from the meaning of good and bad, that such propositions are all of them, in Kant's phrase, "synthetic": they must all rest in the end upon some proposition which must be simply accepted or rejected, which cannot be logically deduced from any other proposition. This result, which follows from our first investigation, may be otherwise expressed by saying that the fundamental principles of ethics must be self-evident.' (PE 193).

[65] '. . . no relevant evidence whatever can be adduced; from no other truth, except themselves alone can it be inferred that they are either true or false.' (34)

[66] 'In order to express the fact that ethical propositions of my first class are incapable of proof or disproof, I have sometimes followed Sidgwick's usage in calling them "intuitions".' (35)

empirically (perhaps ostensively), and this will be the basis for empirical knowledge without any appeal to intuition. Conversely, he might believe that a non-natural definition provides no basis for empirical knowledge, since we cannot use these non-naturalist definitions by themselves to find empirical knowledge; we lack empirical knowledge of what ought to be desired, and so on. This would be a reason for believing that non-naturalism rather than indefinability or inexplicability leads to intuitionism.

If this is what Moore means, his conception of non-natural properties puts them beyond empirical knowledge and beyond natural science. But we have found that it is difficult to form a clear conception of non-natural properties on this basis, partly because it is not clear how we are to draw the limits of empirical knowledge. He seems to mean that natural properties are those whose instances can be recognized empirically. Our knowledge about good things would be empirical if (1) we defined Good as 'pleasant', (2) we knew empirically that walking is pleasant, and so inferred that (3) walking is good. If we cannot identify Good with a property whose instances we can recognize empirically, we have no empirical knowledge of good things.

In the case of Good, we lack a definition that would give us any empirical knowledge parallel to (2). Hence Moore claims that we need fundamental synthetic propositions about good that 'must be simply accepted or rejected, which cannot be logically deduced from any other proposition' (193). We know empirically that walking is pleasant because we simply experience it (or deduce it from simple experiences of pleasure), but we do not know by experience, or by deduction from experience, that pleasure is good. This is something we must simply accept or reject.

Later critics agree with Moore that non-naturalism is committed to these fundamental synthetic propositions that are matters of intuition; they use this implication of non-naturalism to argue that non-naturalism commits us to unreasonable epistemological claims.[67] We may postpone discussion of these attacks on non-naturalism.

1267. Non-Naturalism and Holism

But even before we discuss these objections to non-naturalism, we can see at once that Moore seems to offer us false alternatives. He suggests that if basic synthetic propositions cannot be logically deduced from any other proposition, they must be simply accepted or rejected. We might doubt this suggestion. For we have some initial judgments about good things; we believe it is good to give harmless pleasure in normal conditions, that it is normally good not to get extremely angry at someone's trivial error, and so on. Our general view about what things are good might be defended as a generalization or systematization of these initial judgments.

Moore is right to claim, therefore, that we must begin by treating some synthetic judgments as credible. But these initial judgments need not be 'simply accepted or rejected'. They may be accepted provisionally, subject to revision in the light of comparison with our other views about goodness and other moral properties. This approach to moral knowledge

---

[67] See especially Strawson, 'Intuitionism', discussed at §1279.

is holist rather than intuitionist. It does not satisfy the empirical constraint that we could satisfy if we accepted a naturalist definition of Good. But intuitionism, understood as a foundationalist epistemological doctrine, is not the only alternative to empiricism.

We might avoid intuitionism, therefore, even if we agree that Good is both non-natural and indefinable. If we believe that moral properties are indefinable but explicable, they allow analytic truths, and we seem to avoid Moore's route to intuitionism. If we could give a complex and informative explication of 'good' or other moral concepts, we might find some connexions between 'good,' 'ought', 'right', 'obligation', and 'reason'.[68] This is the route that Ewing follows. In his view, a defence of this route refutes Moore's claim that Good is indefinable. But even if we agreed with Moore on this point, we might still agree with Ewing that Good is explicable. If we agree with him on this point, we do not have to begin with intuitions.

To examine a normative theory, then, we need to compare the implications of the theory with our initial judgments about what we ought to do, what we have reason to do, and so on. These initial judgments are 'intuitive' in the sense that they are not based on an explicit theory; they are the starting points for the formation of an implicit theory. But our attitude to them need not be intuitionist. We need not treat any of them as a foundation for which no further justification can be given. If we are holists, we can compare a given normative position with the intuitive beliefs that constitute our explication of moral concepts.

This criticism of Moore shows how far he relies on his extreme view that Good is inexplicable, and not simply indefinable. The more plausible parts of his case against naturalism do not support the extreme view. The Open Question Argument, however, supports it. If we reject the Open Question Argument, we will not agree with Moore about the implications of his non-naturalism.

1268. Conceptual Utilitarianism and the Open Question Argument

Moore takes it to be an advantage of his meta-ethical argument that it allows us to approach normative ethics with an open mind, once we recognize that 'as far as the meaning of good goes, anything whatever may be good' (72). On this point, he wants to deprive utilitarianism of any apparent support that it might gain from analytical utilitarianism. This apparent support would not be real support, since, as Moore argues quite plausibly, what utilitarians seem to want to say about good and maximizing pleasure does not fit well with an interpretation of their claims that treats them as conceptual analyses.[69] He infers that a normative theory should begin with an intuition, not with an appeal to the meaning of 'good'.

On this point, Moore agrees with Sidgwick, who also rejects conceptual utilitarianism. He also agrees with part of Sidgwick's utilitarian account of the right. He takes the right

---

[68] See Ewing, *DG* 41–2: 'I do not agree that goodness is simple and indefinable. All non-natural concepts need not be indefinable, provided they are definable in terms of some other non-natural concept. What I do maintain is that "goodness" cannot be defined wholly in non-ethical terms.' (45) Ewing seems to speak without distinction here of 'natural' and of 'non-ethical' terms.

[69] See Mackie, 'Critical notice', 123–4.

to consist in the promotion of independently good consequences (i.e., consequences whose goodness does not consist, wholly or partly, in their rightness).[70]

But Moore disagrees with Sidgwick's route to a utilitarian account of the right. In Sidgwick's view, 'ought' and 'right', are unanalysable, and hence he rejects a conceptual utilitarian analysis of them.[71] Moore uses Sidgwick's argument about 'ought', in order to show that 'good' is unanalysable, but he does not follow Sidgwick on 'right' and 'ought'. For these concepts (and for 'duty' and 'obligation'), he accepts the utilitarian analysis that he rejects for 'good'. Moore's reasons for this position are worth examining, even though he did not accept it for long.[72] If we see why he is a conceptual utilitarian about some concepts and not about others, we can form a clearer view of the grounds for his non-naturalism about Good.

We might be surprised by Moore's acceptance of conceptual utilitarianism for 'right', given that he rejects a conceptual utilitarian account of 'good' for the reasons that Sidgwick offers against a conceptual utilitarian account of 'right' (69). According to Sidgwick, Bentham makes two claims: (1) It is right to promote the general happiness. (2) 'Right' means 'promoting the general happiness'. Sidgwick argues that these two claims are inconsistent, because Bentham does not intend the first claim as an account of the concept 'right', but as an ethical assertion about the sorts of things that are right.[73] Since Sidgwick agrees with this ethical assertion, he believes Bentham ought to give up (2) and retain (1). This is also the form of Moore's argument against conceptual utilitarians who define 'good' as 'pleasant', but intend 'The good is the pleasant' to be an ethical claim, and not simply an account of the concept. Should he not agree with Sidgwick about Bentham?

He agrees that Bentham cannot consistently hold both of his claims, but he disagrees with Sidgwick about which one Bentham should give up. In Moore's view, (2) is correct.[74] Bentham goes wrong by adding (1), the ethical claim that it is right to pursue the general happiness.[75] Here Bentham commits the naturalistic fallacy, because he confuses what is predicated of the right (in 'It is right to pursue the general happiness') with the property of rightness itself. If Bentham had identified one sense of 'right' (the utilitarian analysis) and had confined his claims to that sense, he would have argued legitimately, because he would not have asserted (1) as an ethical claim. Hence Moore sets out to do what Bentham

---

[70] On this point, Moore agrees with Sidgwick, and disagrees with Rashdall's version of non-hedonist utilitarianism (*TGE* 59–71). See §1209.

[71] At *ME* 32, Sidgwick states his claim about '"ought", "right", and other terms expressing the same fundamental notion'. In his view, 'the notion which these terms have in common is too elementary to admit of any formal definition'. Darwall, 'Moore', 469, infers that Sidgwick takes 'normativity' to be the fundamental notion. Sidgwick does not explicitly include 'good' among the relevant terms.

[72] See Ross, §1277.   [73] Sidgwick, *ME* 26. See §1157.

[74] 'For the word "right" is very commonly appropriated to actions which lead to the attainment of what is good; which are regarded as *means* to this ideal and not as ends-in-themselves. This use of "right", as denoting what is good as a means, whether or not it be also good as an end, is indeed the use to which I shall confine the word. Had Bentham been using "right" in this sense, it might be perfectly consistent for him to *define* right as "conducive to the general happiness", *provided only* (and notice this proviso) he had already proved, or laid down as an axiom, that general happiness was *the* good, or (what is equivalent to this) that general happiness alone was good. For in that case he would have already defined *the* good as general happiness (a position perfectly consistent, as we have seen, with the contention that "good" is indefinable), and, since right was to be defined as "conducive to *the* good", it would actually *mean* "conducive to general happiness".' (*PE* 70)

[75] I take this to be the main point of Moore's criticism. He also criticizes Bentham for applying 'right' to ends, and not only to means.

should have done, using 'right' only to mean 'promoting good consequences'. If one sticks consistently to that sense, one will not affirm the ethical claim that it is right to promote the general happiness.

This defence of a utilitarian definition of 'right' suggests that we might also defend conceptual utilitarianism about 'good', by claiming that we use 'good' to mean 'maximizing pleasure'. Would we not avoid the naturalistic fallacy about 'good', as long as we did not assert 'It is good to maximize pleasure' as an ethical claim?

One might argue that this easy escape from the naturalistic fallacy fails to reckon with Moore's Open Question Argument. If the naturalistic definition of 'good' were correct, then 'what maximizes pleasure is good' would mean the same as 'what maximizes pleasure maximizes pleasure'. But they do not mean the same, because we can significantly ask whether what maximizes pleasure is good.

This appeal to the Open Question Argument, however, seems to bear equally on the utilitarian account of 'right'. In asserting that what is right is what is conducive to good, we do not mean that what is conducive to good is conducive to good. For we can agree that x is right, and still significantly ask whether x is conducive to good (and vice versa).

Moore might reject this application of the Open Question Argument to 'right'. If we use 'right' in the utilitarian sense, we do not create an open question; for we cannot agree that x is right and still significantly ask whether x promotes the good. 'What is right is what is conducive to good' can be reduced to a tautology by substituting for 'right' a synonymous expression. Hence the Open Question Argument gives a result favourable to conceptual utilitarianism, once we grasp the relevant sense of 'right'.

But it seems easy to use this argument in support of a utilitarian analysis of 'good'. If we consistently use 'good' in the utilitarian sense and avoid the ethical claim that pleasure is good, we raise no open question. Why could utilitarians not claim to be using both 'good' and 'right' in the senses that make the utilitarian analyses correct?

These defences of conceptual utilitarianism rely on our earlier observation that we cannot apply the Open Question Argument until we grasp the meaning of the relevant word, and therefore we cannot use it to refute accounts of the meaning of the word. This observation supports Moore's conceptual utilitarian account of 'right', by showing that the Open Question Argument does not touch it. Hence Moore's claims about 'right' seem to support our previous objections to the Open Question Argument, by showing that it does not touch a conceptual utilitarian account of 'good'.

1269. Conceptual Utilitarianism and Ethical Argument

We noticed, however, that Moore's most plausible objection to conceptual utilitarianism does not turn on his claim that Good is inexplicable, but on the narrower point that a utilitarian definition of the concept deprives it of its normal and legitimate use in ethical argument. Does this objection affect his definition of 'right'?

Moore seems to suggest that 'right' and 'good' should be treated differently. If both concepts were given utilitarian definitions, two basic utilitarian principles would turn out to be clarifications of the meanings of words, used in a particular sense. But then these two principles would not be ethical assertions. A utilitarian theory, however, needs some ethical assertions; its basic principles cannot simply be definitions of ethical terms. Hence Moore sometimes objects that utilitarians cannot argue for their ethical claims if they reduce them to definitions.

One might object that an appeal to a definition or meaning is sometimes a form of argument. If we can show that our opponents' view about the right conflicts with the meaning of 'right', we show they are conceptually confused, and thereby we defend our view. Hence Bentham suggests that the only clear meaning we can give to ethical terms is the meaning given by utilitarian definitions. Once we are clear about the meaning of the relevant terms, and once we use them with a clear meaning, we see that we have been unconscious utilitarians all along.

Moore believes that not all ethical argument fit this pattern. According to conceptual utilitarianism, professed non-utilitarians about right and good contradict themselves, or use the terms with no clear sense, or use them in an irrelevant sense. But if we agree with Moore's view that these options do not cover all disagreements, we have to limit conceptual utilitarianism. If utilitarians avoid conceptual utilitarianism about 'good', they allow real ethical disagreements. Their genuine ethical claims about what is good are the basis for the rest of their theory. A conceptual utilitarian account of 'right' is acceptable, therefore, if it follows an ethical claim about the good.

This argument, however, shows only that not all ethical assertions should be reduced to definitions. Why should we reject conceptual utilitarianism about 'good', rather than about 'right' or 'ought'? Moore might answer that we have real disagreements about goodness that do not simply reflect confusion or unclarity; hence the relevant sense of 'good' does not allow a conceptual utilitarian definition. If we were to use 'good' only in the utilitarian sense, what we would say would be irrelevant to actual disputes.

But this argument also applies to 'right'. If some disputes about what is right are not about what promotes the good, the relevant sense of 'right' is not the utilitarian sense. If Moore denies that there are such disputes about rightness, why should we agree that there are such disputes about goodness? These questions support Sidgwick's view that we should not offer a conceptual utilitarian account of either 'right' or 'good'. Sidgwick tries to answer the question that Moore overlooks, and so he argues for a utilitarian normative theory of rightness.

Moore does not address the normative question, because he assumes conceptual utilitarianism about 'right'. He criticizes a parallel assumption about 'good', in his attack on those who 'foist upon us such an axiom as that "Pleasure is the only good" or that "The good is the desired" on the pretence that this is "the very meaning of the word"' (59). He foists on us the axiom that the right is what conduces to the good on the pretence that this is the very meaning of 'right'.

1270. Value, Normativity, and Obligation: Frankena on Moore

Moore's treatment of goodness and rightness suggests a broader question about his view of the basic ethical concepts. Frankena argues that Moore's analysis of 'right', 'duty', 'ought', and 'obligation' by reference to promotion of good conflicts with his belief that Good is indefinable, but supports his belief that Good is not a natural property.[76] Frankena's argument is this: (1) If it is obligatory to promote the good, it is analytic that Good is such that we ought to promote the good.[77] (2) If it is analytic that Good is such that we ought to promote the good, Good is not indefinable. (3) Hence, if it is obligatory to promote the good, Good is not indefinable. Frankena infers that if Good is 'normative', it is not indefinable.[78]

The force of Frankena's argument about the right and the good depends on the relation between the intrinsic goodness that we ought to promote and the property Good that good things share. The intrinsic goodness that we find by knowing what things are good is analytically tied to 'right' and 'ought'. But Moore denies that this analytic connexion implies any analytic truth about Good itself. In his view, the connexion between Good and the obligation to promote the good is synthetic.[79]

But Frankena's argument might be used against the Open Question Argument. Suppose we are told that x, y, and z are possible objects of pursuit, and that x is good but y and z are bad, and we are asked which of x, y, and z we ought to pursue or have a reason to pursue. If we did not think we had already been given a reason to pursue x, we would show (one might argue) that we did not understand 'good'. Though Moore's question might appear to be significant, we discover on reflexion that a complete grasp of 'good' includes a grasp of its normative character. Frankena's argument casts doubt on Moore's view that Good is inexplicable.

Different conceptions of an open question allow different responses to this argument: (1) We might argue that the claim about Good and reasons does not create an open question, since we should decide whether a question is open only in the light of a complete grasp of the concept. (2) We might concede that it creates an open question, since competent users may not recognize that Good is essentially normative until they think about it; in that case, an analytic truth may create an open question. Whichever way we think of open questions, they do not support a sound objection to the claim that Good essentially gives reasons.

But even if Good is partly explicable through analytic connexions with 'ought' and 'right', it may not be definable. According to Moore, a definition must resolve something into simpler parts; but we have no reason to believe that every explication introduces simpler parts. In our present case, 'ought', 'right', and 'reason' do not appear to be simpler than 'good'; for we might explain 'right' through 'ought' and 'ought' through 'reason', but then we might also explain 'reason' through 'right' or 'ought' or 'good'. This circle of explications does not provide a compositional definition of any of the properties that are explicated.

---

[76] Frankena, 'Obligation and value', 16.

[77] Frankena recognizes that Moore might consistently hold that the connexion between goodness and obligation is synthetic, but he does not think Moore takes this view. He comments: 'Yet I cannot help feeling, as I read on, that Moore really attaches a connotation of obligatoriness to the notion of intrinsic goodness, and regards the good as somehow having a normative significance as such' ('Obligation and value', 14).

[78] '. . . anyone who regards the good as normative, or who holds it to be part of the meaning of the good that it enjoins us to take a certain attitude toward it, must reject the view that goodness is a simple intrinsic quality' (16). Frankena's 'or . . .' seems to be an explication of 'normative', not an alternative to it. In 'Reply', 567, 573–4, 604, Moore understands a normative concept as 'ought-implying', and Frankena accepts this account, at PM 210.

[79] This is Moore's answer to Frankena, in 'Reply', 575. This discussion contains both some exaggerated criticism on minor points and some cogent objections.

Hence Frankena's plausible claims about the analytic connexion between 'good' and 'ought' do not show that Good is definable.

Frankena believes that the essential normativity of Good defeats Moore's claim that Good is simple and indefinable, but supports his claim that Good is non-natural.[80] Moore has exactly one good reason, in Frankena's view, for denying that Good is a natural property: its essentially normative character. If it is essentially normative, it is definable; hence it cannot be both indefinable and non-natural. But Frankena does not say why Good must be non-natural if it is essentially normative. If essential normativity requires a conceptual connexion, a naturalist who believes that Good is essentially normative must believe that for some natural property F, it is analytic that if x is F, we ought to pursue x.

Frankena might answer such a naturalist by appeal to Moore's Open Question Argument. One might argue that the question 'I know that x has this natural property F, but ought I to pursue things that have F?' is significant. Hence (one might infer) a natural property cannot be essentially normative. But this argument proves too much for Frankena's purposes. The question 'I know that x is good, but ought I to pursue x?' also appears significant. If, then, no natural properties are essentially normative (because they all raise open questions), Good is not essentially normative either (since the claim about normativity also seems to raise an open question). Since Frankena objects, quite reasonably, to Moore's use of the Open Question Argument, he has not justified his claim that no natural property is essentially normative.[81]

Moreover, we need not suppose that essential normativity implies an analytic connexion. A naturalist who believes that Good is an essentially normative property need not even believe that 'x ought to be pursued' follows analytically from 'x has natural property F and Good is identical to F'. We might believe that the essential normativity of F is part of F's real essence, but not an analytic truth about F.

Perhaps, however, Frankena believes that by 'non-natural' Moore simply means 'normative'. In that case, it would be trivial that no normative property is natural. But Moore does not seem to intend this as a trivial truth. He wants to show that Good is not a natural property, because if it were a natural property, it would be an object of natural science; he does not seem to think it is a trivial truth that no natural science can deal with essentially normative properties. And so, even if Frankena is right to claim that Good is essentially normative, he does not give Moore any further reason to claim that it is not natural. His argument shows that if we reject the Open Question Argument, Moore has no good case against naturalism.[82]

1271. Why Utilitarianism?

Though Moore distinguishes his conceptual utilitarian account of 'right' from any ethical claim, he also accepts utilitarian ethical claims. He rejects Sidgwick's belief in a fundamental

---

[80] '. . . what makes ethical judgments seem irreducible to natural or to metaphysical judgments is their apparently normative character, that is, the fact that they seem to be saying of some agent that he ought to do something.' (Frankena, 'Obligation and value', 17) Though this is a claim about judgments, Frankena also makes the analogous claims about terms and properties.

[81] See Frankena, 'Fallacy'.   [82] Further discussion of Frankena: §§1361–2.

intuition of the truth of hedonism about the good.[83] But he agrees with Sidgwick's view that actions are right in so far as they tend to maximize non-moral good. Hence we may say (despite Sidgwick's preferred usage) that Moore is a non-hedonistic utilitarian.

Moore's reasons for accepting utilitarianism are not clear, because—despite his concern to separate conceptual from ethical judgments—they are not sharply distinct from his conceptual utilitarianism. He does not believe that a utilitarian analysis of 'right' warrants the ethical judgment that it is right to maximize the good; in fact, he criticizes Bentham for combining the ethical judgment with a utilitarian conceptual analysis. But it is difficult to see how he avoids this combination. For, in his view, all ethical judgments that include 'ought', 'right', or 'duty' require a utilitarian analysis.[84] Hence the judgment that we ought to do x, or that it is right to do x, means that x is the best means to y and y is the most intrinsic good we can get in the circumstances. Anyone who asserts that we have an absolute duty to do x asserts that x will have the best consequences.

Moore does not justify this claim. Conceptual utilitarianism (in his view) fits only one sense of 'right'. Do discussions of right action always use this sense? According to Moore, if we can significantly ask whether what conduces to intrinsic good is right, we do not use 'right' in the purely instrumental sense. Some of Moore's opponents believe that the question 'This action promotes the good, but is it right?' is significant; hence they appear not to use 'right' in the utilitarian sense. When Moore claims that a judgment that x is right 'can only mean' that x promotes the good, he seems to overlook this possibility, even though he concedes that the utilitarian sense of 'right' reflects only the use that he has decided to adopt.

His argument against Bentham suggests that he needs to recognize a different sense of right apart from the one that has the utilitarian analysis. For Moore cannot express his utilitarianism by asserting that we ought to promote the good, unless he uses 'ought' in some sense that does not make 'we ought to promote the good' synonymous with 'it promotes the good to promote the good'. Either 'right' or 'ought' or 'reason' seems to need a non-utilitarian analysis if it is to express a utilitarian ethical judgment.

Once we allow that one of these concepts has a non-utilitarian analysis, how are we to reach a utilitarian ethical judgment? Moore's moral epistemology would lead us to expect that we must rely on some intuition. But he does not follow Sidgwick's practice of comparing his apparent intuition with allegedly conflicting intuitions to see whether he can show that the rivals are not genuine intuitions. In his view, the assertion 'I am morally bound to perform this action' is identical with the assertion 'This action will produce the greatest possible amount of good in the universe' (197). He argues for this claim by arguing that the obligatory action 'must be unique in respect of value'. Since it is not plausible to maintain either that it is the only thing with intrinsic value or that it has more intrinsic value than anything else, it must be the action that results in the most intrinsic value.

---

[83] See Sidgwick, §1165.

[84] 'Ethical judgments are commonly asked in an ambiguous form. It is asked "What is a man's duty under these circumstances?" or "Is it right to act in this way?" or "What ought we to aim at securing?". But all these questions are capable of further analysis; a correct answer to any of them involves both judgments of what is good in itself and causal judgments. This is implied even by those who maintain that we have a direct and immediate judgment of absolute rights and duties. Such a judgment can only mean that the course of action in question is *the* best thing to do; that, by acting so, every good that *can* be secured will have been secured.' (76)

This argument is sound only if it is never right to choose a course of action that embodies or produces less intrinsic value than some other possible action. But a deontologist has good reason to affirm that this is sometimes right. Perhaps we have sufficient moral reasons for acting a particular way because we have made a promise, or because someone is entitled to demand it. We may grant that the action deserves to be chosen for its own sake, and in that respect is intrinsically valuable.[85] But the intrinsic value may not be the ground of the moral obligation; the grounding may go in the reverse direction. Moore's arguments, therefore, do not vindicate a utilitarian conception of obligation.

1272. Intrinsic Value

If Moore is right, normative ethical judgments are either causal judgments about which actions will result in the most intrinsic good or judgments about which things are intrinsic goods. Moral judgments about obligations and duties are causal judgments about means to maximum intrinsic good, and they are always to be revised in the light of judgments about intrinsic goods or about means to them. But the revision cannot go the other way, since the goodness of intrinsic goods is wholly non-moral.

Moore assumes that a list of intrinsic goods can be used as a guide to moral obligations. He does not consider the possibility that morality requires us to realize only those intrinsic goods that are relevant from the moral point of view. But it does not seem obvious that all judgments of intrinsic goodness immediately introduce moral obligations. We might, for instance, believe that it would be intrinsically good if there were more lakes, without believing we are morally required to create more lakes. If we allow moral restrictions on the promotion of intrinsic goods, not all judgments about moral rightness seem to be about the promotion of intrinsic goods.

Further questions arise about the moral adequacy of Moore's conception of intrinsic goods. In his view, they have three essential features: (1) They are good non-instrumentally, not simply as a causal means to some further good. (2) They are essentially good; though their goodness is not an intrinsic property, it follows from their intrinsic properties.[86] (3) They are good in isolation; their goodness comes simply from their non-relational properties, not from their context or circumstances or from any relations to other things.

Moore implies that every intrinsic good is both essentially and non-relationally good. He must therefore either (a) deny that there are any essentially relational things or (b) deny that any such things are non-instrumentally good, or (c) deny that one ought to realize this non-instrumental goodness. The third option seems unattractive; why should we try to realize only intrinsic goods and neglect other non-instrumental goods? The first option imports a controversial metaphysical thesis into ethics.[87] Probably, then, Moore accepts the second option.

---

[85] Ross, however, *RG* 132, denies that a right action, as such, has intrinsic value, even though its rightness is intrinsic to it.

[86] See *PE* 55–7, 236–8, and 'Conception of intrinsic value'.

[87] At *E* 47, Moore distinguishes 'intrinsically good' from 'good for its own sake'. But his distinction is not the one we are trying to draw. He takes what is good for its own sake to be composed wholly of parts that are intrinsically good; hence it must itself be intrinsically (i.e., non-relationally) good.

If this is his view, it conflicts with apparently plausible grounds for recognizing some essentially relational non-instrumental goods. Some goods seem to be non-instrumentally good because of their causes. A kind action, for instance, seems to be non-instrumentally good because it is an expression of kindness; its instrumental goodness may be negligible, but it seems to have some non-instrumental goodness that is distinct from the non-instrumental goodness of the kindness that produces it. If A is kind and A does an action out of kindness, we seem to refer to two non-instrumental goods, not just to one. Moore's method of isolation leaves out such candidates for intrinsic goodness.

This issue is complicated by Moore's Principle of Organic Unities (§18), according to which 'the value of a whole must not be assumed to be the same as the sum of the values of its parts' (79). Moore rejects the argument from (1) A is composed of B and C, (2) A has great intrinsic value and B has very little, to the conclusion (3) C has intrinsic value. We can begin with something that has very slight intrinsic value, add something with no intrinsic value, and end with a compound that has much greater intrinsic value than either of the parts. Moore may believe that his principle disposes of apparent counter-examples such as the expression of kindness. He discusses the view that things owe their value solely to the fact that they are realizations of the true self, and he argues plausibly that things do not owe their value solely to this. If we consider the effects in isolation, and find that they have some intrinsic value, we cannot ascribe all their value to their relation to the true self.[88]

This argument, however, does not show that the causal source of an action cannot be responsible for some, or even for all, of its non-instrumental value. Making a cup of tea might be an act of kindness. Making tea has no intrinsic value, taken in isolation; it may even have no instrumental value (if A makes tea for B, but, unknown to A, B hates tea and is unreasonably angry at A). But the act of kindness—that is to say, the action as caused by the virtue of kindness—has non-instrumental value. In this case, the non-instrumental value comes entirely from the causation of the action. Moore's claims about organic unities prohibit us from inferring immediately that the causal process itself (exercising the virtue of kindness) has intrinsic value. But they still allow us to maintain that the non-instrumental value of the act of kindness depends on its causation; hence Moore does not show that all non-instrumental value is non-relational.

If, therefore, Moore's intrinsic goods do not include all non-instrumental goods, right actions may not be right only in so far as they produce intrinsic goods. Even a utilitarian account of rightness does not support Moore's limited conception of the end to be aimed at. Why should we ignore the non-instrumental goodness that is not intrinsic? His 'method of absolute isolation' (§112) assumes that no non-instrumental goodness can be

---

[88] '. . . we may easily refute this statement, by asking whether the predicate that is meant by "realizing the true self", supposing that it could exist alone, would have any value whatever. Either the *thing*, which does "realize the true self", has intrinsic value or it has not; and if it is has, then it certainly does not owe its value solely to the fact that it realizes the true self.' (237) When Moore speaks of 'the predicate that is meant by "realizing the true self"', we might think he is speaking of the property of realizing the true self. But if this is what he means, the next sentence makes no sense; for it discusses the 'thing'—the state of affairs—that realizes the true self. Probably the 'predicate that is meant . . .' is supposed to pick out the state of affairs in question; hence, for instance, if we claim that an act of kindness realizes the true self, Moore is asking us to consider the intrinsic value of an act of kindness. He argues correctly that if an act of kindness, considered without reference to its causation, has intrinsic value, its value cannot come entirely from a causal fact about it.

relational; but that assumption conflicts with some apparently reasonable beliefs about non-instrumental goods.

1273. Intrinsic Goods and Egoism

Moore's disputable assumptions about intrinsic value underlie another aspect of his utilitarianism. Sidgwick qualifies and complicates his utilitarianism by arguing that both utilitarianism and egoism appear to be ultimately reasonable. Moore deals with Sidgwick's dualism by simply rejecting Sidgwick's argument on behalf of egoism. We have found some reason to question Sidgwick's argument to show that egoism is 'ultimately reasonable', if 'ultimately' means 'supremely'. But if 'ultimately' means simply 'non-derivatively', we might find Sidgwick's argument for egoism plausible, without agreeing that it leads to a dualism.

One might doubt whether Sidgwick's plausible claim that it is non-derivatively reasonable for me to care about my own good supports only a thesis about what is reasonable 'for me'. He seems to commit himself to a thesis of 'universal reason' (as he calls it). For it is difficult to see how I could accept the first-person formulation of the principle without also accepting the universal claim that it is reasonable for A to care about A's own good. I could equally well say that it is reasonable that I care about my good, or that I am being reasonable when I care about my good; I do not introduce some special kind of reasonableness called 'reasonableness for me'.

Still, Sidgwick is right to claim that the reasonableness of self-love is restricted in some way. If I agree that it is reasonable for you to care about your good, I do not thereby agree that it is reasonable for me to care about your good. We might express this restriction by saying that Sidgwick recognizes 'agent-relative' reasons: whether it is reasonable for you to do a specific action depends on who you are and on your relation to it. If A has a duty to compensate B for a loss A has inflicted on B, and no one who has not inflicted the loss on B has the same duty, A has an agent-relative duty. Similarly, only someone who has made a promise is obliged to keep it. Sidgwick is right, then, to say that such reasons might threaten the supreme rationality of utilitarianism. If agent-relative reasons are non-derivative, we may ask why agent-neutral reasons override them.

Moore implicitly recognizes that Sidgwick introduces agent-relative reasons. For he responds to Sidgwick's argument for egoism by denying the possibility of agent-relative reasons. He argues that my good cannot be relative to me. If I have a good coat, the good coat is mine, and the possession of the coat is mine, but the goodness of the coat cannot be mine, since the goodness belongs to the coat and not to me; therefore it makes no sense to say that the possession of the coat is my good.[89] Moore's 'therefore' marks his questionable assumption. He assumes that when egoists speak of 'my good', they mean 'my goodness'. But in fact they mean 'my benefit', 'a benefit to me' rather than 'my goodness'. And it makes perfect sense to say that my possession of this coat is a benefit to me, not a benefit to someone else. Hence my good (benefit) may be relative to me even if my goodness is not relative to me.

---

[89] See the last paragraph of PE §59: 'In both cases it is only the thing or the possession of it which is *mine* and not *the goodness of* that thing or that possession. There is no longer any meaning in attaching the "my" to our predicate, and saying: The possession of this *by me* is *my* good.'

Broad's criticism exposes the flaw in Moore's argument. He points out that Moore's relies on the truth of 'ethical neutralism' (as Broad calls it), an extreme agent-neutral doctrine that recognizes only an obligation to maximize the balance of good. Moore shows that egoism is inconsistent with this neutralism. But he does not show that egoism is inconsistent, since he does not show that egoists have to be neutralists.[90]

Just as Moore denies agent-relative goods and reasons, he denies agent-relative ends. He assumes that if something ought to be my sole end, it is the sole good.[91] He assumes, then, that non-derivative reasons for action must aim at the good, agent-neutrally; he does not allow that what I have reason to do might sometimes depend on who I am. Moore's assumption that there are only agent-neutral reasons takes a big step towards utilitarianism, since it allows him to dismiss objections that depend on whether I have made a promise to someone, whether the person involved is a friend of mine, and all the other agent-relative reasons that have been cited against utilitarianism.[92]

The neglect of agent-relative reasons reflects the assumptions about value that underlie Moore's method of isolation. Just as he does not allow the non-instrumental value of an action to depend on its cause, he does not allow the reasonableness of an action to depend on who does it. In both cases, the argument for utilitarianism depends on an assumption that a non-utilitarian should reject.

In this case as in others, Moore's utilitarianism rests on an intuitional basis, as Sidgwick's does, but, unlike Sidgwick, Moore does not seek a non-intuitional argument to confirm that the intuitions are genuine. He does not acknowledge the force of the arguments that persuade Sidgwick that he needs to answer the non-utilitarian. Moore makes some utilitarian assumptions clear, but he does not do much to defend them. His claims about intrinsic value and about agent-relative reasons show that he overlooks objections to his utilitarian position.

Moore's dogmatic acceptance of utilitarianism cannot be traced directly to his meta-ethical outlook. His rejection of naturalist accounts of Good is intended to leave room for ethical argument, and to prevent the confusion that would result from representing ethical claims as simply conceptual analyses. But Moore contributes to this confusion; for he treats his utilitarian account of the right as though it were simply a conceptual analysis of 'right'. The same is true of his account of intrinsic value and of agent-relative goodness and reasons. In all these cases, he overlooks the questions that need ethical argument, and he assumes that we only need a clearer grasp of the concepts that we use.

At first sight, it may seem incredible that Moore's book would display this basic conflict between its meta-ethical and its normative argument. But on further reflexion, it may seem

---

[90] See Broad, 'Features', 43–57. In 'Reply', 611–15, Moore agrees that he relies on neutralism, and so he concedes Broad's main point. He now says that he meant only that if neutralism is true, egoism is self-contradictory (613). Broad discusses this view in 'Latest', 455–7.

[91] 'The only reason I can have for aiming at "my own good" is that it is good absolutely that what I so call should belong to me—good absolutely that I should have something which, if I have it, others cannot have. But if it is good absolutely that I should have it, then everybody else has as much reason for aiming at my having it as I have myself. If, therefore, it is true of any single man's "interest" or "happiness" that it ought to be his sole ultimate end, this can only mean that that man's interest or happiness is the sole good, the universal good, and the only thing that anybody ought to aim at. What egoism holds, therefore, is that each man's happiness is the sole good—that a number of different things are each of them the only good thing there is—an absolute contradiction!' (§59)

[92] Agent-relative reasons; §1290.

more credible. For though Moore intends his meta-ethical argument to leave room for normative argument, his rejection of all attempts to define or to explicate Good seems to defeat his own ends. Reliance on the Open Question Argument makes it difficult to see what we might be arguing about in normative arguments about what things are good. If we cannot begin normative arguments with any partial explication of the relevant concepts or with any beliefs that might support one theory over another, it is difficult to conduct normative arguments of the sort that Sidgwick conducts in defence of utilitarianism. Moore does not share the later 20th-century reluctance to engage in normative moral philosophy. But his approach to normative argument does not inspire confidence in this aspect of moral philosophy.

This chapter on Moore has been rather negative. It has concentrated on the main difficulties in Moore's position, as he sets it out. It has not taken much account of attempts to defend some aspects of his non-naturalism and intuitionism without the doctrines that raise the most serious difficulties. This constructive use of Moore is better studied in his intuitionist successors, and especially in Ross. To form a fair conception of the merits of Moore's position, we need to see what the later intuitionists make of it.

ROSS

1274. Ross and Intuitionism

Ross is an objectivist in the metaphysics of morality, a cognitivist and descriptivist[1] in semantics, and an intuitionist in epistemology.[2] He develops his position by a close criticism of Moore. His comments often throw light on Moore and on the difficulties that his position raises. Like Moore, he discusses Sidgwick's non-naturalism, intuitionism, and utilitarianism.[3] But, in contrast to Moore, he revives the 'dogmatic intuitionism' (as Sidgwick calls it) of Price, Reid, and Whewell, and defends a non-utilitarian doctrine of the right.[4] In contrast to Sidgwick and Moore, Ross and other 20th-century intuitionists believe that appeals to intuition support a pluralist conception of moral first principles, and so they reject Sidgwick's defence of utilitarianism on an intuitional basis.[5]

Non-naturalism and intuitionism were not popular in 20th-century philosophy. If we appeal to self-evident principles grasping non-natural qualities inaccessible to ordinary empirical observation, we need to answer reasonable doubts about how we know we have found such principles. One might object that we think something is self-evident simply because we are inclined to believe it. Could not someone with opposite inclinations or prejudices, with equal reason or lack of it, take the opposite principles to be self-evident?[6]

---

[1] More exactly, Ross is a descriptivist from the point of view of emotivists such as Stevenson, and of prescriptivists such as Hare. We have seen that Moore suggests that non-natural properties, including goodness, do not describe their subjects. But he still holds what Broad calls a 'predicative' view, which is more or less what non-cognitivists call a 'descriptive' view. See §1262.

[2] RG is reviewed by H. H. Price. FE is appreciatively reviewed by Broad (who expects that students will refer to it as 'The Right and the Better') and by Robinson (who complains that it does not say enough to refute scepticism and non-cognitivism).

[3] Ross refers to Sidgwick only once in RG, but often in FE.

[4] Whewell combines elements of intuitionism and Butlerian naturalism. See §1119.

[5] Ross shares many views with Prichard, MODI, Ewing, DG, and Carritt, TM. Carritt says: 'A name which would appear frequently among the references to contemporaries given below is that of Professor H. A. Prichard, if only his book upon the subject were ready. . . . As, however, he assures me that "we seem to differ in almost every particular", I am encouraged to think that my publication may be some slight additional incentive to his own.' Carritt's hope about the incentive was unfulfilled. Despite this cautionary note, many of Carritt's views, and especially his opposition to utilitarianism and idealism, agree with Prichard and Ross (RG was published two years later than Carritt's TM).

[6] In Strawson, 'Intuitionism', the destructive argument ends: 'Well, then, suppose we agree to bury intuitionism. What have you to offer in its place?' (31). In Nowell-Smith, E, chs. 3–4, the discussion of Ross and Broad ends: 'The study of ethics seems to end in a blind alley' (61).

A defender of the intuitionists might argue that some appeal to basic intuitions is difficult to avoid.[7] Sidgwick argues against 'dogmatic intuitionism', the pluralist position of Price and Reid, which is quite similar to Ross's position. But he still appeals to intuitions to support utilitarianism. If we cannot do without intuitions, we should not dismiss either Sidgwick's monist intuitionism or the pluralist intuitionism of Price and Ross.

This question leads to a second line of defence of the intuitionists. For we may argue that they do not need their epistemology in order to defend their meta-ethical and normative doctrines. Sidgwick's intuitionism rests on indecision about the force of holistic argument. On the one hand, he claims that his dialectical case for utilitarianism falls short of a proof and that only intuitions provide a proof. On the other hand, he acknowledges that we have no reason to believe that alleged intuitions are genuine unless dialectical argument supports them.[8] We may infer that dialectical argument is more important than Sidgwick explicitly recognizes; might its support for 'intuitions' not make the appeal to intuition superfluous? We might ask the same question about Ross's intuitionism; perhaps we can replace appeals to intuition with dialectical argument. We may reasonably ask whether this revision of Ross's epistemology strengthens or weakens his moral philosophy.

Such questions arise at several points in Ross. For though he accepts Moore's non-naturalism and intuitionism, he also raises serious objections to them. Perhaps he retains more of Moore's position than he would have retained if he had seen the full force of his objections. Ross's objections to Moore may suggest a position that is more plausible than Ross's own position.

1275. Doubts about the Open Question Argument

Ross agrees with Moore that 'good' is not a concept of a natural property, and that 'good' is indefinable.[9] But though he agrees on these conclusions, he does not accept Moore's argument for them.

The Open Question Argument shows that we can always reply to any proposed definition of 'good' as 'F' by asking whether F things are good. Hence we cannot have F before our minds in using 'good'. Hence, we may infer, 'F' cannot be a definition of 'good'.[10] But this argument is open to doubt. A definition may tell us more than what is before our minds; for a good definition is a complete account of the concept, and we may have the concept before our minds without having the complete account before our minds. Hence the fact that a definition raises open questions does not show that it does not correctly define the concept before our minds.

---

[7] '... every ethical system admits intuitions at some point ... The objection that many people feel to Intuitionism can hardly be an objection to the admission of intuition; for without that no theory can get going. The objection is rather that Intuitionism admits too many intuitions, and further that it admits intuitions that in practice contradict one another.' (FE 82)

[8] Sidgwick on intuitions; §1182.

[9] '... the fact that we use the term "good" intelligently and intelligibly without having any definition of it in our minds shows that it is indefinable.' (RG 92).

[10] '... if "good" stood for any complex ..., we ought ... to have in our minds the notion of a definite relation between definite things. It seems to me clear that we have no such notion in our minds when we use the word in ordinary discourse.' (RG 92)

Ross accepts this objection. He believes that Moore's Open Question Argument wrongly presupposes that any doubt or hesitation or question about a proposed definition refutes it. Since inquiry may remove our initial hesitation about the correctness of a proposed definition, initial hesitation is not decisive.[11] Moore's Open Question Argument proves too much; and Moore recognizes this in his discussion of the 'Paradox of Analysis'.[12] We must therefore modify Moore's method. We must examine proposed definitions, to see whether or not they express what we meant by the given term all along. We can at most establish a reasonable presumption of indefinability, after a fair examination of the most plausible candidate definitions.

If we follow this approach, we do not confine ourselves to our initial intuitions about what we mean, and the initial unfamiliarity of a candidate definition will not deter us from further inquiry. Still, inquiry should eventually show us either that some proposed definition tells us what we meant all along, or that the proposed definition is incorrect.[13] We have two methods for deciding that a proposed definition is incorrect: (1) It has the wrong extension; it includes things that we intuitively judge not to be good or excludes things that we intuitively judge to be good. (2) Even though it has the right extension, we can see that it is not what we mean.[14]

The first method already takes Ross beyond Moore. Moore does not rely on our intuitive judgment that something or other is or is not good; he relies only on the judgment that we can or cannot significantly ask whether something is good. Ross seems to rely more directly on the judgments that Socrates elicits from his interlocutors about whether (e.g.) a given action or person is good. These intuitive judgments are moral judgments (if we are considering moral goodness), not simply judgments about what appears to be a significant or an insignificant question. But are we to rely on all our intuitive moral judgments? Might some of them not be mistaken? The process of testing a proposed definition may involve more mutual adjustment than Ross explicitly mentions. Hence his first method is not as simple as it looks.

His second method also raises questions. How do we see that something is not what we mean? Ross argues that, for instance, 'equiangular triangle' is not what we 'mean all along' by 'equilateral triangle', even though it has the right extension. We learn some elementary geometry by learning about the relation between the sides and the angles of a triangle, and

---

[11] '... for there seem to be cases in which we seek for the definition of a term and finally accept one as correct. The fact that we accept some definition as correct shows that the term did somehow stand for a complex of elements; yet the fact that we are for some time in doubt whether the term is analysable, and if so, what the correct analysis is, shows that this complex of elements was not distinctly present to our mind before, or during, the search for a definition.' (RG 93)

[12] Paradox of Analysis; §1256.

[13] 'The method should, I think, rather be that of attending to any proposed definition that seems at all plausible. If it is the correct definition, what should happen is that after a certain amount of attention to it we should be able to say, "yes, that is what I meant by 'good' all along, though I was not clearly conscious till now that it was what I meant". If on the other hand the result is that we feel clear that "that was not what I meant by good" the proposed definition must be rejected.' (RG 93)

[14] 'Perhaps the most obvious ground for rejection of a definition is that we are able to point to things of which the term is predicable but the definition is not, or vice versa. And any one will be able without difficulty to think of definitions of "good" that have been proposed, which come to grief on one or other of these two objections. But even when the denotations of the term and of the definition coincide (or when we cannot be sure that they do not), we can often see that a proposed definition does not express what we *mean* by the term to be defined. It would be on this ground, for example, that we should reject a definition of "equilateral triangle" as "triangle with all its angles equal". And it is on this ground that most of the proposed definitions of "good" can be rejected . . . The point is not that the proposed definition is not seen at first sight to be true, or that it needs inquiry, but that it does not survive inquiry.' (RG 93–4)

about the necessity of the relation. To learn these elementary truths, we need to begin with some understanding of a side and an angle. If 'equilateral triangle' were defined as 'equiangular triangle' and if this were what we meant all along, we would not learn more about the angles and sides of a triangle by learning that equilateral triangles must have equal angles. A similar argument might rule out some proposed definitions of 'good', because they make it appear that our learning is not really learning.

Ross, therefore, agrees with Moore's best argument against conceptual utilitarianism. Moore believes that this view misinterprets arguments about goodness as explications of the concept. Contrary to conceptual utilitarianism, arguments about whether pleasure is the good rest on a shared concept of goodness. Similarly, Ross believes that we learn something if we come to believe that pleasure is the good, so that this belief cannot be part of our initial shared concept of goodness.

This claim is more plausible if we can say something about the shared concept of goodness, to show that it provides a basis on which we might decide about whether pleasure is or is not the good. But Ross seems to make it difficult to say anything about this initial shared concept, because he agrees with Moore's denial that Good can be defined. Why does Ross follow Moore on this point?

1276. Indefinability

Ross accepts Moore's demand for definitions to be compositional, and so he assumes that in order to find a definition of Good through these properties that are analytically connected with it, we would need to understand one of these terms without reference to the others (RG 93).[15] If we think of definition as this sort of compositional definition, it is reasonable to deny that Good is definable. Moore infers that 'good' is inexplicable, but he does not seem to be justified. For perhaps 'good', 'right', 'ought', 'reason', and 'value' are explicable by reference to one another, but none is explicable by reference to some concept (or property) that is intelligible without reference to at least one of these four. Since Ross expresses reasonable doubts about Moore's use of open questions in order to refute definitions, he has no reason to agree with Moore's claim that Good is inexplicable.

Moore and Ross do not discuss how arguments about goodness and rightness can be based on more than inspection. Moore has a reason for ignoring this possibility, since the Open Question Argument rules it out by making Good inexplicable. But since Ross rejects the Open Question Argument, he has no good reason for ignoring the possibility of explication. By ignoring this possibility, Ross weakens his best argument against naturalistic definitions. As we saw, the distinction between the concepts 'equilateral triangle' and 'equiangular triangle' is easy to draw if we recognize our progress in understanding from the initial description 'triangle with three equal sides' to 'triangle with three equal angles'. It is not so easy to trace a parallel progress in understanding of 'good' if we have no initial description to express our initial grasp of the concept. Ross seems to do himself a disservice by agreeing with Moore about the inexplicability of 'good'.

---

[15] This condition is not satisfied by organs and organisms, the example that Moore begins from; see §1252.

Ross's remarks about definitions suggest, therefore, that the Open Question Argument is not a good argument against proposed definitions or explications, and that 'good' may be explicable even if it is not definable through a compositional definition. In place of Moore's brusque appeal to the Open Question Argument, Ross offers his less clear, but more plausible, search for 'what we meant all along', which relies on intuitive moral judgments and therefore (one might expect) on a more holistic argument than Moore allows.

1277. Objections to Naturalism

Ross agrees with Moore in rejecting 'naturalistic definitions'.[16] These 'claim to define an ethical term without using other ethical terms' (FE 6), or without using 'distinctively' ethical terms (42). Accounts that include 'good', 'right', and 'ought' are non-naturalistic. Naturalistic accounts involve ordinary matters of fact that can be discovered by mere observation. If such definitions could be given, ethics would not be a distinct discipline, because all its subject matter would be absorbed by some non-ethical natural science.[17]

Ross's attempt to identify ethical terms with those that are not naturalistic, in his sense, leads to odd results. If ethical terms involved only matters of fact that could be discovered by 'mere' or 'ordinary' observation, ethics would not be a distinct discipline. But equally, if all the questions that concern physics or geology or history could be answered by ordinary observation, these would not be distinct disciplines. They are distinct disciplines partly because they discuss questions that cannot be answered by ordinary observation. But since that does not make them ethical, Ross does not show that only ethical properties are non-natural. Hence ethics might be (for all he has shown) a science parallel to physics and geology.

Ross might reply that questions in physics can in fact be settled by 'ordinary' observation; physical theories tell us which observations are relevant. But equally, we might be able to settle ethical questions by 'ordinary' observation; perhaps ethical theory tells us which observations are ethically relevant. Since Ross does not pursue these questions, his conception of a natural property is too vague to be helpful. If we suppose that he rejects all proposed definitions of an ethical property that eliminate ethical terms ('right', 'good', 'ought', and an indeterminate list of related terms), we have captured the relevant part of his objections to naturalism; we should simply keep an open mind on whether ethical properties are natural.[18]

A utilitarian analysis of 'right' would be naturalistic in Ross's sense. He rejects it by using some of Moore's arguments against such an analysis of 'good'.[19] He takes Moore to have

[16] As we have seen, the rejection of such definitions does not ensure that Good is not a natural property, since Moore allows indefinable natural properties.

[17] 'For all naturalist theories amount to saying that all the statements in which we use either the predicate "right" or the predicate "good" and think that in doing so we are dealing with a very special kind of attribute, are really statements of ordinary matters of fact which can be discovered by mere observation. Whether a certain kind of act is commanded by society, or whether it produces more pleasure than any other possible act would, is a thing to be discovered (if at all) by ordinary observation; if that is all that "ought" means, there is no need and no place for a special branch of study called ethics; for there are no ineradicably ethical terms.' (FE 7–8)

[18] Ross does not mention 'thick' ethical terms ('brave', 'temperate', 'just', 'proper function', etc.), but probably he assumes that their definitions include 'right', or 'good', or another of his ethical terms.

[19] Contrast Moore: '... to assert that a certain line of conduct is, at a given time, absolutely right or obligatory is obviously to assert that more good or less evil will exist in the world if it be adopted than if anything else be done instead' (PE 77). See §1268.

shown that 'good' and 'pleasant' stand for distinct, even if co-extensive, properties. If one treats the utilitarian claim as an analytic truth, one cannot give an account of the role of this claim in arguments and disputes about goodness. If we recognize a distinct class of analytic truths, we cannot plausibly fit the utilitarian claim into this class. One can imagine a consistent position that would treat the utilitarian claim as an analytic truth; but that position would not give the utilitarian claim the role that utilitarians give it in defences of their position.[20]

This argument, according to Ross, refutes a utilitarian analysis not only of 'good', but also of 'right'. If it avoids his objection to Moore's Open Question Argument, it should not rely on claims about what is before our minds when we use a word; for these claims do not decide whether the concept is analysable.[21] In Ross's view, we should ask not whether the proposed definition tells us what is before our minds, but whether it tells us what we meant all along. This test, imprecise though it is, tries to discount reactions to an unfamiliar or unexamined definition, and to identify the relevant reactions—those that result from having examined the definition.

Ross argues that a utilitarian account of what we mean by 'right' is incorrect, even if utilitarianism is true, because utilitarians and non-utilitarians can reasonably dispute about whether right actions maximize utility; non-utilitarians do not seem to be making the sort of mistake that we would be making if we wanted to dispute about whether vixens are female foxes. We can agree about some features that must belong to a right action, and we try to decide whether actions that maximize utility have these features or not. These features that we use to decide disputes about rightness seen to express what we mean by 'right'; we presuppose them in disputes in normative ethics. This argument gives a reason for rejecting conceptual utilitarianism about 'right' and 'good'. But it does not refute all proposed naturalistic definitions, or all proposed definitions, let alone all proposed explications that do not purport to offer an analysis.

1278. Explications

In Ross's view, we cannot give a non-naturalistic definition of rightness;[22] we can offer only synonyms. He agrees with Price's objection to accounts of 'right' and 'obligation' that eventually re-introduce the definiendum.[23] But he accepts some explications of 'right' that fail to provide definitions. If, for instance, we have an obligation to do either x or y, but no obligation to do x rather than y or y rather than x, then both x and y are right.[24] Such

[20] 'If this were not so, it would not be intelligible that the proposition "the good is just the pleasant" should have been maintained, on the one hand, and denied on the other, with so much fervour; for we do not fight for or against analytic propositions; we take them for granted.' (*RG* 8)

[21] 'Must not the same claim be made about the statement "being right means being an act productive of the greatest good producible in the circumstances"? Is it not plain on reflection that this is not what we *mean* by right, even if it is a true statement about what *is* right? It seems clear for instance that when the ordinary man says it is right to fulfil promises he is not in the least thinking of the total consequences of such an act, about which he knows and cares little or nothing.' (*RG* 8–9)

[22] A non-naturalistic definition 'includes a reference to some distinctively ethical term other than "right"' (*FE* 42).

[23] 'when one attempts to define it, one will either name something plainly different from it, or use a term which is a mere synonym of it' (*FE* 43). Price on synonymy; §812.

[24] 'Right' means 'very nearly, but not quite, the same as "obligatory" or "what is my duty"' (43).

explications do not provide a definition of 'right', because they do not provide an analysis into simpler elements. But they are none the less important. A single equivalence of this sort may be too trivial and truistic to clarify very much. But if we could collect all the plausible partial explications, the results might not be trivial; for they might show us previously unnoticed implications of equivalences that we readily accept.[25]

Ross and Broad consider some of these possibilities of non-trivial explication. Broad agrees with some of Clarke's claims about rightness as fitness. He suggests that the right action is right in a situation, and that its rightness consists in appropriateness to the situation. He mentions such examples as 'Love is the right emotion to feel to one's parents', and 'Pity and help are the right kinds of emotion and action in the presence of undeserved suffering' (FTET 165).[26] This is not an analysis of 'right'.[27] Even if we can explicate rightness by reference to appropriateness, not every sort of appropriateness or fitness will do. But if we try to capture the specific sort appropriate for moral rightness, we may need to reintroduce moral terms ('ought' or 'good'). And so we have not given a definition, even a non-naturalistic definition.

Ross also explicates rightness by reference to fitness, and rejects further analysis of the relevant sort of fitness.[28] Aesthetic suitability is similar to moral suitability 'in the way in which a situation calls for a certain act, and the way in which one part of a beautiful whole calls for the other parts' (54); that is why Greek uses 'kalon' for both aesthetic and moral properties. This form of suitability is to be contrasted with suitability to an extraneous purpose. Though one element in moral rightness is this form of suitability, we cannot completely describe the differentia of moral suitability; we can only say that it is the kind of suitability that is moral rightness (55).

Ross gives up the search for explications too soon. The further things we say about suitability do not give us a compositional definition, but they take us some way towards explication. Aesthetic suitability is not the only sort that cannot be explained by reference to extraneous ends. In speaking of health as appropriate for an organism, we are not necessarily referring to some extraneous end that the organism might achieve; perhaps we are referring to the normal state for the organism. Normality may not be explicable through merely statistical regularities; it may refer to the health, or proper functions, of the organism. Even if we cannot reduce the explicating concepts to natural concepts (as Ross understands them), we may fix the connexions between 'good', 'right', 'ought', 'appropriate', 'healthy', and 'proper function'. Even this short series of explications may tell us something non-trivial about ethical concepts.

[25] Cf. Smith, MP 29–30, on truisms and platitudes.   [26] Broad discusses fittingness further at FTET 219–21.

[27] 'What I have just asserted is not, and does not pretend to be, an analytical *definition* of "right" and "wrong". It does bring out their relational character, and it correlates them with several other notions. But the kind of appropriateness and inappropriateness which is implied in the notions of "right" and "wrong" is, so far as I can see, specific and unanalysable.' (FTET 165) Broad has not explained himself fully here. The fact that 'appropriate' in the relevant sense is unanalysable does not show that 'right' is unanalysable; for if 'right' is analysable, it should be composed of unanalysable elements. If, then, 'right' means 'appropriate for the situation', and if 'situation' (or its elements) and 'appropriate' are unanalysable, we ought to conclude, as far as this argument goes, that 'right' is analysable.

Broad seems to have a different point in mind in saying that the relevant notion of appropriateness is 'specific'. If he means 'specific to moral situations' or 'specific to moral evaluation', he may mean that it cannot be explicated without reference to rightness. 'Right' is not part of the analysis of 'appropriate' (since Broad says the relevant kind of appropriateness is unanalysable), but it is part of the explication, so that each notion must be explicated with reference to the other.

[28] He rejects an explication of fittingness as, e.g., fittingness to some purpose, 52–4. He refers approvingly to Clarke and Price, but he does not discuss the conception of fittingness defended by Butler.

This part of Ross's discussion connects his views with earlier rationalist views about rightness and fitness. If we abandon Moore's demand for compositional definition and for necessary and sufficient conditions, the sorts of explications that Ross and Broad sketch all too briefly may help us to understand how we can use moral concepts in argument, discussion, and deliberation without compositional definitions. The different roles that they play in these activities help us to find the necessary explications; and when we find the explications, we can understand and modify their use in these activities.

If, then, we attend to Ross's acceptance of explications of moral concepts, his claim that they are indefinable is less significant than it may initially have appeared. It does not imply that we must simply see that an action has a specific non-natural characteristic; for, even though rightness is non-natural and indefinable, we can argue about whether an action is right, because we agree on the features that help to explicate the concept. This implication of Ross's position takes him further away from Moore's use of the Open Question Argument. Moore disallows all non-obvious analytic truths about Good on the ground that they all create open questions. Ross's and Broad's partial explications create open questions, because they lead us to see non-obvious analytic implications of analytic truths about moral properties; hence Ross and Broad should not accept the Open Question Argument.

1279. Objections to Non-Natural Properties

If we recognize that non-natural properties need not be inexplicable, have we a reasonable basis for claiming that we can know whether an action or person has one? Some critics believe that non-natural properties are separated from ordinary observation in a way that makes them cognitively mysterious.[29] The non-naturalist wants to say that if you pay someone what you have borrowed, you do the right thing; but what is the connexion between the observable property of your action and its rightness? According to the non-naturalist, the rightness itself is not observable; nor is it definable wholly by reference to observable properties. The observable properties give us evidence for the presence of the non-natural property. According to the non-naturalist, this is neither unusual nor illegitimate; it is analogous to 'This is a salt because it is a compound of basic and acid radicals'. The various observable properties are criteria for being a salt. Similarly, we may treat the observable properties of an action as evidence or criteria on the basis of which we ascribe the non-natural moral property.

Strawson, however, argues against the non-naturalist's use of this analogy.[30] In the example of a salt (he claims), the 'because' introduces an analytic truth, and in general any

---

[29] For the sake of brevity, the following discussion moves carelessly between talk of concepts and talk of properties (following Ross and Strawson). A more careful separation of concepts from properties would still support the main conclusion.

[30] 'When the jury brings in a verdict of guilty on a charge of murder, they do so because the facts adduced in evidence are of the kind covered by the definition of "murder". When the chemical analyst concludes that the material submitted for analysis is a salt, he does so because it exhibits the defining properties of a salt. The evidence is the sort of thing that is meant by "murder", by "salt". But the fundamental moral word, or words, you say, cannot be defined; their concepts are unanalysable. So it cannot be in this way that the "because" clause of your ethical sentence functions as evidence.' (Strawson, 'Intuitionism', 26)

'because' that introduces an evidential relation must either be, or ultimately depend on, an analytic connexion between the concept in question and some empirical concept that signifies a report of sensory experience. Hence non-naturalists face a grave difficulty if they cannot ground all their evidential claims in analytic truths involving empirical concepts.

To see whether Strawson has found a grave difficulty for non-naturalists, we should consider his claim about evidential relations. He assumes that if non-natural properties are genuine properties of objects for which we can have empirical evidence, the properties must be analytically connected to the empirical concepts that are supposed to provide evidence for them. How plausible is this assumption?

It seems quite implausible in some simple and familiar cases. We take facts about our sensory states as evidence for judgments about physical objects; hence we say 'This is a doorknob because it feels hard, round etc.'. Should we say, then, that 'doorknob' is to be defined in sense-datum terms? Strawson's assumption about evidence and analytic connexions requires him to accept such definitions, if he thinks sensory states provide evidence for judgments about physical objects. But he argues quite convincingly that such phenomenalist definitions will fail (32).[31]

Statements about the external world are not the only case that raises doubts about Strawson's views on evidence. For a gap between evidence and conclusion is not uncommon. Nor does it seem to show a judgment is not factual. We sometimes make judgments about a compound (e.g., 'There is a table in front of me') and about its constituents (e.g., 'These elementary particles are moving around in these patterns'). The statements about the constituents provide evidence for the statements about the compound, but they do not mean the same. The statements about the constituents need not be epistemologically simpler or more basic (in this example, the reverse is true). Still, they are theoretically basic; they explain how our statements about the compound can be connected with our more general views about material reality. Statements about tables—about their functional properties or their conditions for persistence, for instance—cannot be translated into statements about their constituent particles, but they are still factual statements.

These examples suggest reasons for doubting Strawson's argument against intuitionism, in so far as it rests on a demand for evidential relations based on analytic connexions. If the cases we have mentioned involve relations sufficiently similar to the evidential relation of facts about (say) suffering to judgments about moral wrongness, we have no reason to deny that moral judgments are about objective properties, even if they are about non-natural properties. Non-natural properties do not seem to be exposed to justified suspicion on the basis of claims about evidential relations.

1280. Non-Natural Properties, Facts, and Values

The issue raised by Strawson deserves further exploration, because it is relevant to some broader questions about facts and values. Those who believe that value judgments are not

---

[31] Strawson's reasons are similar to those that Chisholm presents in his discussion of Lewis's phenomenalism. See §1319.

statements of fact often rely on an argument similar to Strawson's; for they argue that since the alleged evidence for evaluative judgments is not connected with their truth by analytic connexions, values are not facts. To see whether this is a good argument, we need to ask how plausible it is to demand analytic connexions.

We may doubt whether analytic connexions can reasonably be demanded, if we consider the relation between lower-order and higher-order actions. Statements about this relation illustrate a gap between evidence and conclusion, and between statements about constituents and about the thing constituted. We may truly say both that A is making marks on a slip of paper (or, at a lower level, that A is moving her fingers) and that A is buying a new car. Though the two statements do not mean the same, making these marks is sufficient for buying the car. Similarly we might say that deliberate infliction of pain on an innocent person constitutes a wrong action; nothing further is needed to make the action wrong, and that is what its wrongness consists in. In such a case, Hume is puzzled about where the wrongness is to be found. But his puzzle seems no more reasonable than it would be if he wondered how A could have bought a car simply by making a few marks on a bit of paper.[32]

Defenders of the non-factual character of evaluative judgments might concede that the gap between evidence and conclusions does not by itself show that moral judgments are non-factual. They might try a different test to show whether or not a judgment is factual. In clearly factual cases, we can connect evidence and conclusion with the appropriate sorts of factual bridge premises (e.g., 'If appearances are this way, it is reasonable to believe that there are real objects in front of us', etc.). Once these are added, we can legitimately pass from factual evidence to factual conclusion. Just the same point is available, however, in defence of the factual status of value judgments. For if we include bridge premises such as 'If you show no consideration for the feelings of others, that is wrong', we can draw the evaluative conclusion. By this test, moral judgments still appear to be factual.

One might object that we cannot find enough bridge premises of this sort to support the factual character of moral judgments. If the alleged bridge premises are non-evaluative, they seem to have exceptions. The bridge premiss we have just introduced, for instance, seems not to fit all cases. For instance, if A wants me to deceive B and B will not know about the deception, it would not be wrong of me to take no account of the fact that A will be pleased if I deceive B; perhaps indeed it would be positively wrong of me to take account of A's feeling. We might respond to this objection by modifying the antecedent of our initial bridge premiss to 'If you fail to show due consideration . . .'. Alternatively, we might say that the premiss is defeasible. It describes an action that is prima facie wrong and that becomes wrong all things considered if no special conditions obtain; but special conditions obtain in the situation we have mentioned.[33] But one might argue that both of these treatments of the bridge premiss make it no longer genuinely factual, so that the moral conclusion cannot after all be factual.

---

[32] Anscombe discusses such cases at 'Facts', 22. She considers the move from (a) I asked for the potatoes and (b) the grocer delivered them, to (c) I owe money to the grocer. She asks whether (c) consists in any facts beyond (a) and (b), and she answers: '. . . we must say, not: It consists in these-facts-holding-in-the-context-of-our-institutions, but: It consists in these facts—in the context of our institutions, or: In the context of our institutions it consists in the holding of these facts'. This point is also relevant to Hume; see §748.

[33] The legal concept of defeasibility is explained and adapted by Hart, 'Ascription', 175–9.

But this argument shows that moral judgments are not factual only if it points out a relevant difference from the bridge premises that support (for instance) conclusions about the external world. In fact, however, these bridge premises seem quite similar to those that lead to moral conclusions. In saying what appearances entitle us to conclude, that a physical object is in front of us, we sometimes have to include conditions that mention physical objects, or else we have to restrict ourselves to a claim about prima facie reasons or about what is true in normal conditions. If, for instance, I believe I am looking at a solid building rather than a deceptive appearance of a façade of a building, I believe that if I walk round the building, I will see three other sides of it. But I cannot replace this prediction with a prediction about appearances; for the latter prediction might be false even when the former prediction is true.[34]

Though this example is over-simplified, it supports the general point that the relation between value judgments and the factual evidence for them is not obviously different from the relation between factual judgments and the evidence for them. Hence we cannot appeal to a gap between factual evidence and value judgments to show that value judgments are not factual judgments. Defenders of a distinction between facts and values have not found any distinctive gap between non-evaluative factual judgments and evaluative judgments. Any gap they have found is no wider than a gap between some factual judgments and others. In that case, the existence of the gap gives no good reason for denying that moral judgments are statements of fact.

1281. A Defence of Non-Natural Properties

Our exploration of Strawson's argument against non-naturalism has suggested that, if Strawson wants to refute non-naturalism through his claim about evidence, he should also deny that moral judgments are factual and deny that there are any physical objects if phenomenalist definitions fail. But this is not the conclusion he accepts, and it is useful to consider the solution he prefers.

Strawson rejects phenomenalism about physical objects; for he denies the possibility of finding a logical connexion between statements about the sensory evidence for physical objects and statements about physical objects. But this lack of a logical connexion does not suggest to him that we should be nihilists or sceptics about physical objects. Nor does he believe we should replace concepts of physical objects with purely phenomenal concepts about appearances of chairs and tables. He prefers the position of 'the careful phenomenalist' who does not reject the ordinary belief in tables and chairs, but does not claim that they are really—metaphysically speaking—anything over and above the phenomenal evidence for them.[35]

For similar reasons, he rejects reductive non-cognitive translations of moral judgments. Nor does he affirm non-cognitivism, nihilism, or scepticism about moral judgments or

---

[34] Cf. Shoemaker, 'Causality', 207–19.
[35] '. . . who, for all his emphasis on sense-experience, neither denies that there is a table in the dining-room, nor claims to be able to assert this without using such words as "dining-room" and "table".' (33).

properties. Following a certain Wittgensteinian tendency, he suggests that the philosopher is right to point out that we make moral judgments in circumstances where we try to commend or to influence, but he believes that the philosopher should not presume to make further metaphysical claims. We should neither accept the inflated metaphysics of the non-naturalist intuitionist nor turn to the deflated metaphysics of the non-cognitivist. Each of these metaphysical positions distorts the character of ordinary moral judgment.[36] Strawson suggests, then, that it might be reasonable to go on speaking as intuitionists speak, since they do not reject, as non-cognitivists do, the apparently factual character of ordinary moral judgments. But we should not also accept the intuitionist's belief that facts and properties really correspond to intuitionist claims.

But if we see how widespread Strawson's problem really is, we may be inclined to respond less cautiously than Strawson does. If non-naturalism has so many 'companions in guilt', we may not think it is guilty of anything.[37] Both non-naturalism about moral properties and ordinary realism about physical objects are called into question by the assumption that evidence must rest on analytic truths involving empirical concepts. But if rigorous adhesion to this assumption casts doubt on the claim that sense-data can be evidence for judgments about physical objects, perhaps we should question the assumption rather than doubting whether sense-data give us evidence for judgments about physical objects. Nor is it clear why we should be as metaphysically circumspect as Strawson recommends. The fact that his recommendation requires such extreme, and apparently excessive, circumspection in so many areas might reasonably cast doubt on his recommendation.

Strawson's attack, therefore, has the unintended result of making ethical non-naturalism seem more plausible. The main fault he sees in non-naturalism is a feature that it shares with ordinary beliefs about physical objects and with the other beliefs we have discussed. According to the non-naturalist, the connexion between paying what one owes and acting rightly is synthetic. In order to use moral concepts, we have to learn some of the right synthetic connexions, since we cannot translate moral claims wholly into claims that include only observational concepts. But this fact about moral concepts need not embarrass the non-naturalist.

If Ross and Moore lack a satisfactory account of a natural property, their claim that moral properties are non-natural is difficult to evaluate. But if we take natural properties to be those that are analytically connected to observable properties, non-naturalism looks better rather than worse. For this account of a natural property makes the ordinary properties of physical objects non-natural as well; and in that case, non-natural properties do not seem to be the invention of misguided moral philosophers. If we prefer to say that the properties of physical objects are natural properties and that we observe them, we have no reason to deny that moral properties are natural in the same sense. Ross's position, therefore, might be understood as a form of non-naturalism or as a form of naturalism (if we allow the expanded conception of the natural). But in either case, it does not seem to make moral properties unknowable, and it does not seem to raise special difficulties about how we can have empirical evidence for the moral properties of people and actions.

---

[36] Some of these moves are also recognizable in Strawson's more famous paper 'Freedom'.

[37] As Mackie remarks, '. . . the best move for the moral objectivist is not to evade this issue, but to look for companions in guilt' (E 39).

1282. The Property of Rightness v. the Right-Making Property

Ross agrees with Moore in rejecting a utilitarian definition of Good. But he rejects Moore's utilitarian definition of the right as what promotes the good. He agrees with Moore's acknowledgment that a refutation of conceptual utilitarianism on these points does not refute utilitarian normative theory. Even if he has refuted a conceptual utilitarian definition of the concept 'right', a utilitarian doctrine of what right things have in common and what makes them right may still be correct.[38]

Since the utilitarian doctrine offers to say what makes right actions right, and to say that right actions are right because they have some specific property, it does not simply tell us what things are right (as Moore puts it). In Ross's view, utilitarianism is the correct moral theory if it is not only extensionally correct, but also gives the correct account of what makes things right. We might suppose that such an account gives us a real definition of rightness.

But this is not how Ross looks at it. On the contrary, he takes it to be obvious that the answer to the question 'What makes right acts right?' does not tell us what rightness is. He argues that when Moore looks for 'the reason why an action is right', he cannot be looking for rightness itself.[39] The right-making property underlies and accounts for the rightness of right actions; hence it cannot be rightness itself.

Ross assumes that these two sentences are equivalent: (a) F explains why a right act is right. (b) F explains the rightness of a right action. These two sentences seem to be parallel to: (c) F explains why the tree fell. (d) F explains the falling of the tree. Since Ross takes the explanans and the explanandum to be different, he rejects (e) rightness explains the rightness of a right action. Hence he infers that (f) the right-making property is not rightness.

This argument, however, is open to objection. It is sound if and only 'rightness' has the same sense throughout. But it may not have the same sense. As (c) and (d) show, 'rightness' in (b) is simply used to transform a why-question (as in (a) and (c)) into a description of a state of affairs (as in (b) and (d)). In that case, we need not draw Ross's conclusion. For we need not take (e) to say that rightness explains itself; we may take (e) to be parallel to (c), so that (e) says that the property of rightness explains why a right action is right, or the fact that an action is right. Since (e) does not say that something explains itself, we can accept (e), and therefore reject (f). Ross has not shown, therefore, that rightness is not the right-making property.

Ross's argument, therefore, is cogent only if 'rightness' in 'the right-making property explains the rightness of right actions' picks out the property of rightness. But it may not introduce a property at all. Perhaps we should simply understand it as the abstract noun that we often use in transforming a why-question into a question about a fact or a state of affairs. In that case, it is plausible, and not self-contradictory, to say that rightness (the property) explains the rightness of right actions (i.e., the fact that they are right).

---

[38] ' "Ideal utilitarianism" is, it would appear, plausible only when it is understood not as an analysis or definition of the notion of "right" but as a statement that all acts that are right, and only these, possess the further characteristic of being productive of the best possible consequences, and are right because they possess this other characteristic.' (*RG* 9)

[39] ' "Can we discover any single reason, applicable to all right actions, equally, which is, in every case, *the* reason why an action is right, when it is right?" [Ross quotes from Moore, *E* 9.] This is the question which Professor Moore in fact sets himself to answer. But the *reason* for an action's being right is evidently not the same thing as its *rightness*, and Professor Moore seems already to have passed to the view that productivity of maximum good is not the definition of "right", but another characteristic which underlies and accounts for the rightness of right actions.' (*RG* 10)

Ross offers a second argument: (1) Moore's search for the reason why right action is right is a search for a criterion of rightness. (2) A criterion is a test by means of which we can recognize rightness. (3) To apply such a test, we must already distinguish the criterial property from the property we are testing for. (4) Hence the criterion of rightness cannot be rightness itself.[40]

This argument turns on the use of 'criterion'. Ross uses it in an epistemological sense, to refer to a feature by recognizing which we can come to know the presence of a distinct feature. If that is the relevant sense, Ross is right to say that a criterion of rightness is not rightness itself. But a purely epistemological criterion does not explain why right actions are right; it is a symptom rather than an explanatory property. Hence the fact that rightness itself is not an epistemological criterion does not show that it is not what makes right actions right. We may also, however, use 'criterion' in a metaphysical sense, for the property that determines whether things are right. If that is the relevant sense, a criterion of rightness (i.e., what determines that right actions are right) explains why things are right; but Ross has not shown that this criterion is not rightness itself.

We have good reason, therefore, despite Ross, to believe that an inquiry into the ground of rightness inquires into rightness itself. Ross sees that it is different from an inquiry into the concept 'right', but he describes this difference wrongly. Hence he supposes that the question about what makes right actions right is about the 'ground of rightness' or the 'right-making property', not about the property of rightness itself.

1283. The Relevance of Properties to Moral Inquiry

To understand the questions that Ross faces about rightness and the right-making property, it is useful to place Moore's and Ross's inquiries in a historical context. In claiming that the question 'What is Good?' is different from the question 'What things are good?', Moore accepts Socrates' claim that a proper answer to the 'What is F?' question cannot simply get the extension of F right. Socrates defends this claim by arguing that a property that is merely co-extensive with F does not answer the questions 'What is it that makes F things F?', 'What is the F by which F things are F?', or 'What is the cause of F things' being F?'[41]

When Moore claims that an account of some property shared by good things is not necessarily an account of the property of goodness, he alludes to Plato's *Philebus* (20–1).[42] Following Plato, he concedes that pleasure and intelligence are both good. He even concedes that some proposition of the form 'intelligence is good and intelligence alone is good' would have the right form to be a definition of the good (as opposed to Good) (61). But he denies that such a proposition could be a definition of Good; for Good is some further property possessed by intelligence besides its being intelligence. In the *Philebus*, Plato tries to find the

---

[40] '. . . his [sc. Moore's] theory also seems to be essentially an answer to this question, i.e. not to the question what is rightness, but to the question what is the universal accompaniment and, as he is careful to add, the necessitating ground of rightness. Again, he describes hedonistic utilitarianism as giving us "a criterion, or test, or standard by which we could discern with regard to any action whether it is right or wrong". And similarly, I suppose, he regards his own theory as offering a different criterion of rightness. But obviously a criterion of rightness is not rightness itself.' (RG 10)

[41] Socrates' questions: §11.   [42] Moore and Plato; §1259.

further property of goodness that must be present in the good, before he tries to decide whether pleasure or intelligence manifests it more fully. This further property explains why (e.g.) intelligence rather than pleasure is the only thing that is good. That is why a purely extensional account of the things that are good does not answer our question about the definition of Good.

Theological naturalists about morality accept this demand for a non-extensional account of moral properties, in their arguments against theological voluntarism. Rationalists accept it in their arguments against the moral sense theory. Suarez believes that voluntarists are correct about which actions are right, but wrong about what makes them right, and hence about the nature of rightness. Cudworth, Balguy, and Price argue similarly that voluntarists, positivists, and sentimentalists offer inadequate accounts of moral properties, because they do not tell us what makes right actions right. To answer the explanatory question we need a non-extensional account.

In order to show that a co-extensive property G-ness is not the explanatory property F-ness we are looking for, it is reasonable to point out that in some circumstances we would doubt whether G things are F, and hence G-ness cannot be what makes F things F. If we concede that G-ness and F-ness are co-extensive, these cannot be actual or expected circumstances. Suarez, for instance, argues that if God were to command injustice and cruelty, and nothing else about persons and their circumstances were changed, God would be commanding something wrong, and hence being commanded by God cannot be what makes right actions right; hence it cannot be rightness. The voluntarist account leaves an open moral question about whether God's commands would be right in counterfactual circumstances, and does not settle that question for us.[43]

Butler's discussion of utilitarianism suggests that even if a utilitarian theory gives an extensionally correct account of what is right, it does not answer the explanatory question.[44] If we agree that all right actions are also felicific, we may argue that this is the result of a general coincidence between rightness and utility. We can see that felicificity is not necessary for rightness if we consider actions that have the other features we attribute to rightness, but are not felicific—if, for instance, some people's preferences change so that they become utility monsters or sadists or masochists. Similarly, if we were to grant that the observance of justice maximizes utility, we might point out that if people's tendencies to pleasure and pain changed enough, what maximizes utility would be unjust, so that maximizing utility does not make just actions just.

To see how rightness and utility come apart in counterfactual cases is a reasonable step towards showing that rightness is not the same property as felicificity. Our moral judgments do not align utility with rightness in cases where we modify ordinary empirical assumptions; and so the felicific tendency of actual right actions does not explain why they are right. The property of rightness explains why right actions are right, and explanations are expected to sustain counterfactuals. Mere extensional equivalence, therefore, does not show that we have identified rightness. If we leave an open moral question about whether F actions are right in counterfactual conditions, we have not shown that F-ness is rightness.

---

[43] Moral open questions; §549 (Cudworth); §661 (Balguy); §815 (Price).
[44] Butler on God as a utilitarian; §700.

To justify all the assumptions and claims about properties, counterfactuals, and explanations that underlie these forms of argument about merely co-extensive properties would be a difficult task. To speak of properties is not very precise, if we have not specified the relevant notion of a property; but it does not seem unreasonable or unfamiliar to say that the arguments about rightness and God's commands, or about rightness, goodness, and utility involve properties. Whatever properties are, they should answer an apparently legitimate question about explanation. Hence it seems reasonable to look for accounts of moral properties that are not merely extensionally adequate, but also offer the right explanations. Moore is right, therefore, to suppose that moral inquiry ought to answer the question 'What is goodness?' and that this answer should tell us more than what things are good.

1284. Ross v. Socrates on Explanatory Properties

Ross, however, seems to overlook this aspect of the Socratic question. He does not ask whether Socrates might be right to believe that the property making things F is F-ness itself. He sees that the explanatory question is not a question about meaning, but he does not separate properties from meanings.[45] For he seems to argue that since 'what maximizes good' is not an acceptable definition of the word 'right', the property rightness cannot be the property of maximizing goodness. This is why he infers that the property that makes right acts right cannot be rightness itself, but can only be the property that accounts for rightness, or 'the ground of rightness'.[46]

Ross assumes that a true statement of identity about a property must include only a term and the nominal essence corresponding to it. Since 'good' and 'right' have no naturalistic nominal essence, goodness and rightness cannot, in his view, be natural properties. These claims overlook the possibility of discovering real essences underlying nominal essences.[47] Though the doctrine of real essences is initially applied to kinds rather than to properties, it suggests an analogous claim about properties.

The claim about properties supports Socrates' and Plato's search for definitions. When Socrates looks for the pious or the just, he asks for that because of which all pious or just things are pious or just. The answer to his question will give an account of what piety or justice is. This Socratic question is the source of Aristotle's views on definition and essence, summarized in his doctrine of real definition.[48] It is also the source of Cudworth's and Balguy's conception of the 'immutable' nature of moral properties.[49] Their appeal to the Euthyphro argument may appear quite similar to Moore's use of the Open Question Argument, but they do not use the Euthyphro argument in the way Moore uses the Open Question Argument. Moore uses the Open Question Argument to refute attempted nominal

---

[45] In this respect, Ross's position is similar to that of Carnap—not an obvious philosophical ally of his. See §1265.

[46] 'Thus, answering to each of the psychological theories as to the *essence* of rightness, there will be a view as to the *ground* of rightness' (*FE* 28).

[47] Joseph, *IL* 96–106, offers a qualified defence of a doctrine of real essences. Since this must have been familiar to Ross, and since Ross in any case hardly needed instruction in Aristotelian conceptions of definition, it is strange that his discussion of Moore does not consider such conceptions.

[48] Aristotle expects a correct real definition to express the 'why' as well as the 'that'; see §67.

[49] See the references above to Cudworth, Balguy, and Price.

definitions, whereas Cudworth and Balguy look for real essences that answer the explanatory question.[50]

Hence, the explanatory question that Socrates believes is the right question for finding a correct description of the relevant property is the very question that Ross believes is the wrong question for finding this description. Ross takes it to be obvious that if we discover the right-making characteristic, we do not discover the property of rightness. If he were right, the Socratic approach would rest on a misconception about the nature of properties. But it may be Ross who misconceives the relation of properties to concepts.

It is remarkable that Ross, of all people, does not discuss the Socratic question. We cannot explain his omission by ignorance; for he was the leading Anglophone Aristotelian scholar of the 20th century, and he was especially well acquainted with Aristotle's views on nominal and real definition.[51] The task of applying some of Aristotle's doctrine to questions about the definition of moral properties seems worthwhile and potentially illuminating. It is hard to think of anyone who would have been better qualified for this task than Ross was.

1285. Ross v. Moore on Properties

Ross's concern with the difference between rightness and the right-making property leads him to raise a useful question about Moore. He claims that Moore changes his position between *Principia Ethica* and the later *Ethics*. In the earlier book, Moore seems to recognize only two questions: 'What properties are common to all good things?' and 'What is the property of goodness itself?' The Naturalistic Fallacy consists in confusing a property of the first sort with the property of goodness itself. In Moore's view, hedonism gives a clearly wrong answer to the second question, but further argument is needed to show that it gives the wrong answer to the first question. Conceptual utilitarianism, however, according to *Principia*, gives the right answer to the second question about rightness. Ross notes that, in *Ethics*, Moore uses an Open Question Argument to show that 'duty' and 'expediency' do not mean the same (*RG* 10–11), contrary to the conceptual utilitarian account of 'right' in *Principia*. This is a good reason for believing that Moore holds different views about the meaning of 'right' in *Ethics* from those that he holds in *Principia*.

According to Ross, however, Moore changes his mind on another point too, so that in *Ethics*, as opposed to *Principia*, he believes that an inquiry into the reason why right actions are right is not an inquiry into the property of rightness. Ross attributes this change of mind to Moore because he supposes Moore cannot identify what makes right actions right, or the criterion of rightness, with rightness itself. But it is not clear that Moore shares Ross's controversial assumptions on these points. In *Ethics*, Moore defends a utilitarian view about what makes right actions right. He does not regard this view as giving the meaning of 'right'. Nor, however, does he suppose it is simply a description of a co-extensive property. He describes his question about what makes things right very similarly to the way in which

---

[50] As we have seen (§1253), Moore is sometimes interested in real definitions too.

[51] He discusses Aristotle on nominal and real definition, briefly in *Aristotle*, 49–54 (first published in 1923), and at length in *APPA* (1949).

Socrates describes his question in the *Euthyphro*. He might, therefore, still take himself to be investigating the property of rightness itself.

This question about Ross's understanding of Moore draws our attention to the ways in which each of them overlooks the possible relevance of real definitions. Moore does not ignore them altogether; the compositional definitions that he speaks of are plausibly understood as real definitions. But he takes no account of the difference between nominal and real definitions in his use of the Open Question Argument to show that Good is indefinable. The Open Question Argument is relevant (at best) to nominal definitions, but Moore does not notice this limited scope of his conclusion. We might suppose that Moore's inquiry into what makes right actions right looks for the real definition of rightness, as opposed to the nominal definition of the concept. Ross, however, rejects this way of understanding Moore, because (he believes) the right-making property cannot be rightness itself. Neither Moore nor Ross learns as much as he might have learned from Socratic inquiry.

Our discussion of Ross, however, also suggests a more positive conclusion. He rejects the Socratic view that the right-making property is rightness itself, and so he abandons the search for a real definition of rightness. But his arguments offer some prospect of progress towards an answer to Socratic questions. For if the right-making property is in fact (despite Ross) rightness itself, Ross's discussion of the right-making property may help us to find the real definition of rightness. Ross's inquiries have more in common with Socrates, Aristotle, Cudworth, and others who look for real definitions, than his discussion might suggest.

1286. Arguments about the Right-Making Property

Ross's discussion of the right-making property introduces his normative ethics. Non-naturalism about the right refutes conceptual utilitarianism, but, as Sidgwick and Moore agree, utilitarians ought not to treat their view as an account of the concept 'right' (the property of rightness, as Ross conceives it). They ought to argue that utility is what makes right actions right, and hence they ought to defend a utilitarian account of the right-making property, as Ross conceives it. Whereas Moore is a conceptual utilitarian about 'right', Ross sees that Moore's arguments against a conceptual utilitarian account of 'good' apply to 'right' as well. He also disagrees with Moore's and Sidgwick's utilitarian account of the right-making property.

What is the right way to argue about the right-making property? Ross suggests that a utilitarian account might be represented as an item of a priori knowledge, either intuitive or deductive, or as an item of empirical knowledge, established by induction (RG 34). Neither of these lines of argument, however, seems to capture disputes between Price and Sidgwick, for instance, about utilitarianism. These disputes turn on 'intuitions' in the sense that applies to intuitive judgments that this or that type of action is right or wrong. These intuitive judgments do not necessarily claim to be self-evident. Nor do they appear to be empirical generalizations that might be empirically tested. Empirical testing relies on some reasonably definite account of rightness, but argument from intuitive judgments seeks an account of rightness. Ross's epistemology seems too rigid to capture the dialectical argument that Sidgwick and many others use in support of a normative theory. Fortunately, his rigid theory does not always affect his practice; some of his arguments are recognizably dialectical, even though he has no official place for them in his epistemology.[52]

Ross considers two cases that raise questions about the ground of rightness: (1) I ought (e.g.) to keep a promise, and I have no conflicting obligation. (2) I face a 'case of conscience', in which it seems that I ought to keep a promise, but I also ought to do something else that conflicts with it. He believes that the first case gives no support to utilitarianism. Only the case of conscience might suggest that utility is the ground of rightness.[53]

To understand the questions that arise in these two cases, Ross introduces two aspects of duty: (a) I have a prima facie duty in cases where there is something morally to be said for (e.g.) keeping my promise. (b) I have a duty 'sans phrase' or a 'duty proper' to do whatever there is most to be said for doing, the action that I have the overriding prima facie duty to do.[54] If, then, utility is the only ground of prima facie duty, it is the only moral consideration. If it is always the basis of duty proper, it is always the overriding moral consideration.

Ross believes that in simple cases, where we face no conflict, we clearly have prima-facie duties that do not depend on utility. The utilitarian might say that in such cases we take it for granted that keeping our promise promotes utility, and we do not stop to ask whether this is so. Alternatively, utilitarians might grant Ross's claim that we do not take an implicitly utilitarian attitude to all our prima facie duties, and so they might restrict the utilitarian claim so that it refers only to duties proper, and makes utility the only ground of overriding obligation.

Neither Sidgwick nor Moore takes this second line; they both take prima facie duties to rest on utility. They have good reason to prefer this view. For if there are non-utilitarian grounds of prima facie duty, and if in some cases we have just one prima facie duty, in these cases rightness is fixed independently of utility. Hence non-utilitarian considerations also matter, in their own right, in the cases where prima facie duties conflict. But if utility is not the only thing that matters, why should it always override? We need some further intuition that supports utility against all possible combinations of non-utilitarian grounds of prima facie duty. The utilitarian might reasonably prefer to avoid this controversial claim about intuition, and to defend a utilitarian account of prima facie duties.

Ross argues that utility is neither the sole ground of prima facie duty nor the sole ground of duty all things considered, and hence is not the ground of rightness. Since we have prima facie duties independent of utility, utilitarian considerations are not the only ones that bear on the rightness of an action, all things considered. Nor do they always outweigh other

---

[52] At FE 1–3, Ross recognizes the dialectical character of moral philosophy (though not in so many words), with reference to Aristotle and to Kant.

[53] 'When a plain man fulfils a promise because he thinks he ought to do so, it seems clear that he does so with no thought of its total consequences, still less with any opinion that these are likely to be the best possible. He thinks in fact much more of the past than of the future . . . That his act will produce the best possible consequences is not his reason for calling it right. What lends colour to the [utilitarian] theory . . . is . . . the exceptional cases in which the consequences of fulfilling a promise (for instance) would be so disastrous to others that we judge it right not to do so.' (RG 17–18)

[54] Ross explains 'prima facie duty': '. . . the characteristic (quite distinct from that of being a duty proper) which an act has, in virtue of being of a certain kind (e.g., the keeping of a promise), of being an act which would be a duty proper if it were not at the same time of another kind which is morally significant.' (RG 19; cf. FE 84–5) Ross acknowledges that his term may be misleading (RG 20), and notes in particular that 'prima facie' does not mean that it simply appears to matter. A prima-facie duty is always morally significant, but the action we have a prima-facie duty to do becomes our duty only if no superior prima-facie duty requires us to do something else.

considerations in decisions about what is right all things considered. We can conceive actions that are right, all things considered, even though they conflict with utility (*RG* 34–5). We do not think it is self-evident, or that it follows from anything self-evident, that conflicts of prima facie duties should be resolved by appeal to utility.

Ross, therefore, returns to the position of Price and defends it against Sidgwick. He believes we have no reason to agree with Sidgwick's view that common sense is unconsciously utilitarian. He agrees that prima facie duties are not duties proper, and that if we try to use them to formulate definite rules about duties proper, we will have to recognize all sorts of exceptions. Ross concentrates on promises not because he believes that promises always create especially stringent obligations, but because he believes that utilitarians misunderstand the exceptions to rules about keeping promises.[55] They suppose that if we recognize exceptions to these rules, and we admit that some of the exceptions depend on the consequences of keeping promises, we concede the main point to utilitarians. In Ross's view, we concede no such thing. We simply recognize that different prima facie duties, of which some require us to promote good and some do not, need to be considered in order to find our all-things-considered obligation.

Though Ross's distinction between prima facie duty and duty proper appears to be simply a clarification of the issue, rather than a defence of one particular account of the right-making property, it really contains the basis of his answer to utilitarianism and to other monistic theories. In one way, it is neutral between monistic and pluralistic theories, since a monist can consistently concede that we have prima facie duties of the sort that Ross describes. But if we agree with Ross that the obligation to keep a promise, for instance, is a prima facie duty rather than a duty proper, we need not acknowledge that it has 'exceptions' that might bring in utilitarian considerations. The alleged exceptions are not instances in which the prima facie duty lapses; the prima facie duty remains even in cases where we ought not, all things considered, to keep a promise.[56] Once we see this, we can recognize the possibility that cases that seem to help Sidgwick's dialectical defence of utilitarianism can be explained better by reference to competing prima facie obligations.

1287. How Does Ross Argue Against Utilitarianism?

Ross's arguments against a utilitarian account of the ground of rightness are brief, but clear and forceful. But his account of what he is doing in these arguments is obscure. He takes them to show that the utilitarian principle cannot be known a priori. But he does not take them to refute the utilitarian principle altogether. He still leaves open the possibility that it could be established inductively, and hence known a posteriori (*RG* 36). The claim that has

---

[55] 'The space I have given to discussing the duty of fulfilling promises might lay me open to the suspicion that I attach an undue importance to this duty . . . I do not suppose that I take, in fact, a more rigorous view of this duty than a utilitarian is likely to do . . . My object is not to suggest that the duty is more binding than a utilitarian thinks it is, but to suggest that it is binding on quite a different ground.' (*FE* 113)

[56] To speak more exactly, not all the 'exceptions', and in particular not all those that seem to help the utilitarian, are cases where the prima-facie duty lapses. There may be cases where we have no prima-facie obligation to keep a promise (e.g., if it was made under coercion or false pretences), but these are not the ones that concern Ross and utilitarians.

been refuted, according to Ross, is the claim that this co-extensiveness can be known a priori (34). But the refutation of this claim does not refute the further claim that the right and the optimific can be known empirically to be co-extensive (36).

These claims about co-extensiveness, however, are not the claims that Ross initially set out to discuss. He set out (16) to discuss Moore's claim that the right-making characteristic of right actions is their being optimific. If a characteristic is right-making, it must be, as Moore says, '*the* reason why an action is right, when it is right' (10). Ross's observations that we do not take all our prima facie duties to aim at maximum utility, and that utility is not always what we aim at in settling on our duty all things considered, show that we do not take utility (or, strictly speaking, being optimific) to be the right-making characteristic either. But it is difficult to decide where Ross stands on co-extensiveness. Would he agree, for instance, that if co-extensiveness were necessary, or could be known a priori,[57] utility would be the right-making characteristic? He has not explained why we should agree to that.

Ross now asks whether we have empirical knowledge of the co-extensiveness of 'right' and 'optimific'. He does not take the truth or falsity of this empirical claim to have been settled by his observations about prima facie duties and our resolution of conflicts between them. Perhaps this is because his examples were not counter-examples known empirically, but possibilities introduced to show that the connexion between rightness and utility is not self-evident. At any rate, he does not presume that he knows the answer to an empirical inquiry about the coincidence of rightness and utility. But he observes that the utilitarian does not know the answer either.[58]

The answer to this question, however, does not seem to answer the question about the ground of rightness (the right-making characteristic). If utility and rightness are not co-extensive, utility is not the ground of rightness; but if they are co-extensive, it does not follow that utility is the ground of rightness. If we are looking for the right-making characteristic, and F-ness is proposed as the right-making characteristic, we might apparently try to decide whether F-ness is right-making by asking whether right actions are right because they are F. Ross considers a related question. In considering whether maximizing utility is the right-making characteristic, he asks whether (a) we ought to do right actions because they are right or (b) we ought to do optimific actions because they are optimific. He claims first that this question is 'really unmeaning', but then asserts that the first answer is right and the second is wrong.[59]

---

[57] Ross does not distinguish these two claims. But we will want to distinguish them, if we are willing to recognize necessary truths known a posteriori. On the relevance of such truths see, e.g., Adams, 'Modified'.

[58] 'The advocates of utilitarian systems have been so much persuaded either of the identity or of the self-evident connexion of the attributes "right" and "optimific" (or "felicific") that they have not attempted even such an inductive inquiry as is possible. And in view of the enormous complexity of the task and the inevitable inconclusiveness of the result, it is worth no one's while to make the attempt.' (*RG* 37)

[59] 'What, after all, would be gained by it [sc. the attempt just mentioned]? If, as I have tried to show, for an act to be right and to be optimific are not the same thing, and an act's being optimific is not even the ground of its being right, then if we could ask ourselves (though the question is really unmeaning) which we ought to do, right acts because they are right or optimific acts because they are optimific, our answer must be "the former". If they are optimific as well as right, that is interesting but not morally important; if not, we still ought to do them (which is only another way of saying that they *are* the right acts), and the question whether they are optimific has no importance for moral theory.' (*RG* 37) *FE* 69 has no corresponding remark.

Why is the question 'really unmeaning'? And if it is unmeaning, how can Ross give such a confident answer to it? The right-making characteristic seems to be the one because of which right actions are right. To find it, we ought to be able to say whether right actions are right because they are optimific and whether optimific actions are right because they are optimific. Ross seems to suppose that we ought to do right actions because they are right, and that if we find the right-making characteristic, we ought to be able to substitute its name or description for 'right' in 'because they are right'. If being optimific were the right-making characteristic, actions would be right because they are optimific.

Sometimes Ross suggests that utility is not the right-making characteristic because it is not self-evident that right actions are optimific, whereas it is self-evident that we have prima facie duties distinct from utility. When we understand the relevant proposition, we need no further argument or proof in order to see that it is true.[60] He does not say whether it is self-evident, in this sense, that utility is not the ground of duties all things considered. He says only that it is not self-evident that we ought to break a promise whenever the breaking of it would maximize utility (36). He does not say whether it is self-evident that we sometimes ought to keep a promise even at some cost to utility.

Ross implies, however, that in some circumstances we ought to keep a promise, or fulfil some other prima facie duty not grounded on utility, even if our doing so is not optimific. He takes it to be clear that utility alone does not give a sufficient reason to override our obligation to keep a promise.[61] Anyone who thinks a gain in utility automatically makes it our duty, all things considered, to break a promise 'may be suspected of not having reflected on what a promise is' (39).

From this objection, Ross concludes that we do not know that maximizing utility is the 'foundation' of right.[62] This conclusion seems too modest. He has argued not only that we do not know that utility is the right-making characteristic, but also that we know, or at least have good reason to believe, that it is not. He appeals to 'what we really think' in order to show that it is not self-evident that utility is the right-making characteristic.[63] But his account of our convictions suggests that they also imply that the utilitarian claim is false. For he attributes to us the view that promise-keeping is binding without reference to utility, and that this binding character is not always overridden by utility. Hence he

---

[60] 'That an act, qua fulfilling a promise . . . [etc.] is prima facie right, is self-evident; not in the sense that it is evident from the beginning of our lives, or as soon as we attend to the proposition for the first time, but in the sense that when we have reached sufficient mental maturity and have given sufficient attention to the proposition it is evident without any need of proof, or of evidence beyond itself. It is self-evident just as a mathematical axiom, or the validity of a form of inference, is evident.' (RG 29)

[61] 'Then its *net* good effects are . . . greater than those of the fulfilment of the promise; and the utilitarian is bound to say forthwith that the promise should be broken. Now, we may ask whether that is really the way we think about promises? Do we really think that the production of the slightest balance of good, no matter who will enjoy it, by the breach of a promise frees us from the obligation to keep our promise?' (38)

[62] 'I conclude that the attributes "right" and "optimific" are not identical, and that we do not know either by intuition, by deduction, or by induction that they coincide in their application, still less that the latter is the foundation of the former.' (39)

[63] 'But if we are told, for instance, that we should give up our view that there is a special obligatoriness attaching to the keeping of promises because it is self-evident that the only duty is to produce as much good as possible, we have to ask ourselves whether we really, when we reflect, *are* convinced that this is self-evident, and whether we really *can* get rid of our view that promise-keeping has a bindingness independent of productiveness of maximum good. In my own experience, I find that I cannot, in spite of a very genuine attempt to do so . . .' (40)

concludes that it is the fact that an act is (e.g.) the keeping of a promise that makes it right.[64]

This less modest description of the objections to utilitarianism is more prominent in *Foundations of Ethics*, where Ross takes the issue about the ground of rightness to be decisive for the truth or falsity of the utilitarian position, not just for whether or not we know it to be true.[65] He endorses some of Butler's claims about conscience and utility (*FE* 78–9). Butler concedes, for the sake of argument, that God is a utilitarian who arranges everything so as to maximize utility, but he argues that, even if this were true of God, it should make no difference to conscience or to its approval of other things besides optimific action.[66] Ross endorses Butler's argument as an account of 'what we really think' about rightness. Similarly, he attacks utilitarianism on the basis of convictions about justice and distribution. He does not simply claim that these convictions show utilitarianism not to be self-evident; he also asserts that they show it to be false. He accepts Butler's objections to utilitarianism, and concludes that utilitarianism is an over-simplified conception of the ground of rightness (79).

1288. Utilitarianism and Self-Evidence

Attention to these claims exposes a weakness in one of Ross's arguments, and reveals a better argument. His most frequent argument assumes that the utilitarians prove that utility is the right-making characteristic only if they prove that the connexion between rightness and utility is self-evident or can be deduced from some self-evident connexion. Given this view of what the utilitarian ought to prove, Ross answers by claiming that the crucial utilitarian claims are not self-evident.

Is Ross right to require a utilitarian to show that the connexion between rightness and utility is self-evident or deducible from a self-evident connexion? To prove that utility is the right-making characteristic, we need to prove that it is that because of which right actions are right, or the property that explains (in the relevant sense, whatever that is) why they are right. Ross does not prove that an explanatory connexion must be self-evident or deduced from something self-evident.

A defence of his claims might go as follows: (1) An explanatory connexion is a necessary connexion. (2) Any necessary connexion can be known a priori. (3) Whatever can be known a priori is either self-evident or deducible from something self-evident. If Ross relies on these assumptions, it is easier to see why he tries to prove that utilitarian claims are not self-evidently true.

But, even if Ross accepts these three assumptions, they do not make his case more plausible, since they are disputable. We might accept (1), for some sense of 'necessary

---

[64] '. . . my act is right qua being an ensuring of one of the particular states of affairs of which it is an ensuring, viz., in the case we have taken, of my friend's receiving the book I have promised to return to him.' (*RG* 46) Ross goes on to quality this formulation.

[65] 'The test I would prefer to impose is a different one, viz. this: when we reflect, do we really come to the conclusion that such an act as promise-keeping owes its rightness to its tendency to produce maximum good, *or* to its being an act of promise-keeping? It seems clear that utilitarianism has not established inductively that being optimific is always the ground of rightness, and as a rule utilitarians have not attempted to do so.' (*FE* 69)

[66] Butler on utilitarianism; §700.

connexion'. But we might resist (2); and even if we accept (2), we might resist (3). If we distinguish the ontological claims about necessity from the epistemological claims about the a priori, we may doubt whether all necessity is knowable a priori. The connexion between being known a priori and being self-evident is still less obvious. If we agree with Kant's claim that some principles can be shown to be known a priori by being shown to be presupposed by the possibility of experience, we may not know they are true until we see that they are related to experience in this way; at any rate, we need not agree that they are self-evident. If, then, Ross's arguments against a utilitarian account of the right-making characteristic all depended on these specific claims about the necessary, the a priori, and the self-evident, they would rest on doubtful assumptions.

But he does not merely argue that the utilitarian claim is not self-evident; he also argues that it is false. If utility were the right-making characteristic, every other apparent right-making characteristic would be either derived from utility or a ground of prima facie duty that always gives way to utility as the only ground for duty all things considered. Ross's examples show that some of our convictions count against the utilitarian position.

Ross's appeals to 'what we really think' do not suggest that ordinary convictions are relevant only to questions about what is or is not self-evident. If his defence is sound, we can also rely on them to answer questions about what makes right actions right. Ross makes a good case for the claim that we take some actions to be right apart from utility. He assumes that our convictions tell us not only that certain actions are right, but also why they are right, and why certain changes in the situation would not make the actions cease to be right.[67] One might doubt whether appeals to particular ordinary convictions are decisive, and Ross recognizes the possibility of explaining them within a utilitarian framework (FE 69); but he argues plausibly that utilitarians have no reason to override the convictions that count against utilitarianism.

Perhaps we can emancipate Ross's argument from his disputable claims about self-evidence. Part of the difficulty lies in his claim that our convictions about prima facie duties are matters of intuition, and hence known as self-evident or as having an 'axiomatic character' (FE 84). He opposes this to the utilitarian claim that these convictions state 'intermediate axioms' (as Mill supposes) that we take to be self-evident only because they are reliable means of promoting utility (FE 69). But one may doubt whether Ross's claims about self-evidence really fit the status that in practice he ascribes to ordinary convictions. These convictions are 'intuitive' in the broad sense that they do not explicitly rely on any theory. Moreover, we have to allow that they are initially credible if we are to engage in constructive normative ethics at all. But it does not follow that our intuitive beliefs are objects of the sort of 'intuition' that requires a foundationalist epistemology. Sidgwick recognizes these intuitive beliefs, but does not treat them as intuitions in this latter sense. If Ross were simply to insist that they are intuitions, and hence known as self-evident apart from any inferential justification, he would be assuming dogmatically that Sidgwick is wrong.

In fact, however, his attitude to intuitive beliefs is less dogmatic than it may appear. He does not believe we refute utilitarianism by simply insisting that our intuitive judgments are self-evident. He invites us to ask whether we conclude after reflexion that utility is or is not

---

[67] On explanatory claims, see Sidgwick, §1174.

the only ground of rightness.[68] He claims that he is unable to give up his convictions about promises, 'in spite of a very genuine attempt to do so' (40). How does he make this very genuine attempt?

We might suppose that it is something like an effort of will or mental concentration. But that is not the best way to attempt to give up a belief. To make a genuine attempt to give it up, we should consider the reasons against it, the reasons for believing something incompatible with it, and the effects of belief and disbelief for the rest of our beliefs. This process could not reasonably be confined to one belief in isolation from the rest. It would have to involve reflexion on the character of our beliefs with and without the belief we are attempting to give up.

Ross does not endorse this holist conception of the process involved in testing a belief for rejection or retention. But since he has in mind a process that involves a genuine attempt to get rid of the belief, he should require more than mere inspection or concentration confined to a single belief. The genuine attempt should include a systematic and holistic examination of our beliefs—however far this may be from Ross's intentions.

1289. Should Ross Reject Intuitionism?

In fact, this degree of holism is quite far from Ross's intentions. He agrees with Moore's view that a non-naturalist must be an intuitionist. But, as we saw in discussing Moore, we can move from non-naturalism to intuitionism only with the help of some quite questionable assumptions. Ross should be inclined to question these assumptions. For he does not agree with Moore's view that goodness is inexplicable, and so he ought not to deny that we can rely on analytic truths about it. And since Ross engages in some normative argument about the truth of utilitarianism, instead of simply taking it for granted as Moore does, he makes it clear that he relies on shared beliefs about right actions. These beliefs cannot be justified by a shared naturalistic definition of right; they are 'intuitive' beliefs in the sense that we have to regard them as initially credible before we have found any normative theory. But if we accept them as only provisionally credible, and as open to revision in the light of reflexion, we do not have to treat them as intuitions that are beyond the reach of argument.

This way of understanding non-naturalist normative argument forgoes any appeal to the foundationalist aspects of intuitionism. But Ross accepts foundationalism, even apart from non-naturalism; he does not think we have any real choice about relying on intuitions (*FE* 82).[69] But this does not necessarily imply the rejection of all dialectical argument; a foundationalist epistemology does not imply that ethical principles are beyond argument and must be simply accepted or rejected. Even if we concede to Ross that some of our intuitive beliefs about moral properties are knowledge that does not depend on any inferential justification, some reflexion and argument is needed, as Ross agrees, to decide which of our intuitive beliefs have this status. We have to make 'a very genuine attempt' (as Ross puts

---

[68] '. . . when we reflect, do we really come to the conclusion that such an act as promise-keeping owes its rightness to its tendency to produce maximum good, *or* to its being an act of promise-keeping?' (*FE* 69)

[69] Quoted in §1274.

it) to trace the consequences of abandoning a given intuitive belief. If we see that this belief conflicts with other intuitive beliefs that we are less willing to abandon on reflexion, we may conclude that this particular intuitive belief cannot be grasped by intuition (in the sense of 'intuition' that implies knowledge independent of inferential justification).

For these reasons, we might reasonably hesitate to draw the extreme epistemological conclusions that Moore draws from non-naturalism and indefinability. Though Ross does not dissent from Moore's epistemology, his arguments show that he need not have agreed with Moore. This is a criticism of Moore and Ross, but it is also a defence. For we might reject non-naturalism if we take Moore's intuitionism at face value. For we might assume that this intuitionism undermines the possibility of normative argument, and forces us to rely on some mysterious faculty of intuition. Even if non-naturalists are committed to intuitionist foundationalism, this assumption would be false; if we endorse foundationalism for Ross's reasons (for instance), we do not introduce anything mysterious, and we do not make normative argument impossible. Ross's foundationalism may be open to question, but it is not so unreasonable that it casts doubt on his whole position. Non-naturalists need not be too worried if they are committed to this version of intuitionism.

1290. Intuitionism v. Holism

Still, even if Ross's foundationalism does not have wholly unreasonable implications, we may doubt whether he needs it. If we reflect (as Ross likes to say) on Ross's normative arguments, ought we to agree with him that they demand an intuitionist and foundationalist epistemology?

Some of his arguments may be better understood within a more holist position. It is not an accident that he appeals to promises as a source of duties that cannot be wholly explained by appeal to utility. For they illustrate two connected features of some moral principles and requirements: (1) They involve relations to particular people, and thereby reflect the 'highly personal character of duty' (RG 22). (2) They are retrospective; what we are required to do depends on what has happened, not on what we expect will happen. This does not mean that consequences are irrelevant to fulfilment of the demands that rest on retrospective considerations. If I am required to compensate you for something wrong that I did to you, I am required to act in such a way that you will not lose as much as you would otherwise have lost by my action. But the considerations that fix the relevance of these consequences are retrospective.

Ross agrees with Butler's objections to utilitarianism, which rely on these same two features of non-utilitarian obligations. Utilitarianism, by contrast, generates obligations that are not tied to particular people; I do not ultimately owe anything to my friends, my family, people who have helped me, or people I have harmed, but these obligations are only means towards maximizing the welfare of persons in general.

Does it matter that our non-utilitarian convictions have these patterns? If we could not see any patterns in them, we might have some reason to agree with Sidgwick, and conclude that, if they are not unconsciously utilitarian, they are merely a non-utilitarian residue that the rational moral agent can discard. Or again, if we could convince ourselves that we should attach less rational weight to personal and retrospective principles than to impersonal and prospective principles, we might conclude that the utilitarian principle should override principles of (for instance) loyalty, justice, and fidelity. But if the principle of utility does not win on these points, we ought not to discard the personal and retrospective principles.

These objections to utilitarianism lead us back to Sidgwick's search for a rational basis for the principle of utility. His arguments lend some indirect support to Butler and Ross. Though Sidgwick argues (from questionable premises) that the principle of utility is ultimately rational, he admits that the egoistic principle also seems to be ultimately rational. But if we look closely at the 'egoistic' principle, we see that it does not really concern egoism, in the sense that requires indifference to the interests of others for their own sake. In speaking of what is reasonable 'for me', Sidgwick seems to be thinking of agent-relative reasons. These are reasons that depend on something about me and my situation. If I have ultimate (i.e., non-derivative) reasons to benefit my own family, to keep promises to people I have made promises to, and so on, I am guided by what is reasonable 'for me', in Sidgwick's sense (or in one of the senses in which he uses the expression).

Egoistic reasons are examples of agent-relative reasons, if they are non-derivative; the claim that I have a reason to promote my own good says that A has a reason to promote B's good if A is identical to B. To say that this is a non-derivative reason is to say that this reason is not derived from the reasons that everyone has to promote people's good. But egoistic reasons are not the only agent-relative reasons. Ross's arguments about the personal character of duty suggest that important moral obligations are agent-relative. Hence (from Sidgwick's point of view) they are not derivative from the principle of utility, and we have no good reason to claim that they are subordinate to it.

Sidgwick, therefore, commits himself to the existence of agent-relative reasons. He takes the conflict between what is reasonable for me and what is reasonable simpliciter to be a conflict between self-interest and morality; but it seems to be equally a conflict between agent-relative and agent-neutral morality. Since Sidgwick believes that the moral point of view is ultimately utilitarian, which is agent-neutral, he believes that morality cannot appear on the agent-relative side. Moore goes further, by trying to rule out agent-relative reasons altogether.[70] Ross does not directly address Moore's and Sidgwick's arguments; but he implicitly rejects them by arguing that some aspects of morality rely on agent-relative reasons, and that we ought not to subordinate these reasons to the agent-neutral reasons of utilitarianism. Sidgwick the utilitarian offers us strong reasons for accepting these non-utilitarian reasons.

1291. An Argument for Holism

If non-utilitarian aspects of morality express a retrospective, personal, and agent-relative outlook, this feature of them tends to support Ross's view that utility is not the right-making characteristic. But this support involves some holist thinking, since we support one conviction by connecting it to others that form a pattern in our moral thinking. This

---

[70] Moore on agent-relative reasons; §1273.

holist defence is compatible with Ross's claim that the principles we defend are grasped by intuition. We may take intuitionism to be a form of foundationalism asserting that some moral principles have a non-inferential justification that is sufficient to make them knowledge. This non-inferential justification does not exclude the addition of an inferential justification.[71]

We should reject intuitionism, however, if we are persuaded that we know principles only if they rest on inferential justification.[72] If our non-utilitarian convictions were simply things we found ourselves inclined to believe, and if we knew that they had no inferential justification relating them to a retrospective, personal, and agent-relative view, then—one might argue—we would have good reason to dismiss them.[73] Ross's defence of non-utilitarian principles implicitly relies on the intelligibility and plausibility of a personal and retrospective outlook; the principles do not seem to be known to be true independently of what we may believe about such an outlook.

Ross does not concede this point to holism. He discusses a passage in Joseph that, in his view, seems to adopt, though rather half-heartedly, a 'coherence view of truth' (FE 144).[74] But his dispute with Joseph seems to concern only a coherence view of knowledge and justification. In arguing against Joseph's view, Ross seems to over-estimate, as we noticed earlier, the cognitive status that we need to ascribe to our intuitive beliefs about (e.g.) prima facie duties. He insists, plausibly, that moral inquiry must set out from reasonable confidence in some moral claims, even without a general account of the right-making property. But he also assumes that this reasonable confidence must be knowledge that is independent of the relation of any one claim to others. In claiming that we cannot get more knowledge unless we begin with knowledge, he seems to take foundationalism for granted. If we do not concede this to him, we may look for a holist justification that will vindicate our

---

[71] See Sidgwick, §1169, on intuitional and dialectical argument. The possibility of defending intuitively known prima-facie duties by appeal to coherence is explored by Ewing, DG 203–12: 'They form a system in the sense that the different ultimate prima facie duties are so connected that to fulfil any one harmonizes with and forwards in general and on principle the fulfilment of others. . . . But if the different prima facie duties play into each other's hands in this way, that may well serve as a confirmation that we are on the right lines in admitting them, so that we are not wholly dependent on intuition, but have also this "coherence" test.' (203–4). He observes that the systematic argument is actually supported by some facts about conflicts between prima-facie duties. Many of these conflicts arise because some prima-facie duty has been violated. 'We need not therefore confine ourselves to saying that the ultimate prima facie duties are known intuitively; we can add that our intuitions of them are confirmed by the fact that to further one on the whole furthers others and to violate one tends to involve sooner or later violating others. There is thus a kind of coherence test available after all to supplement intuition.' (206–7)

[72] For further discussion, see Audi's helpful 'Prospects'. If one doubts the close connexion I have assumed between knowledge and justification, one might say that we cannot rationally believe them without an inferential justification.

[73] This is not to say that if we have not actually found any inferential justification, we ought to dismiss them. That would depend on whether we have reason to think they might be justifiable, even if not yet justified.

[74] See Joseph, SPE 107–8: 'True judgments about right and wrong must somehow connect with one another . . . as each helping to articulate the nature of that system of life or lives to which all actions with which moral judgment is concerned belong . . . Nevertheless, we confidently make many moral judgments without going so far; sometimes we claim to know that they are true. Even so, they need not be really independent. The facts of good and evil apprehended separately may yet be connected.' Ross replies: '. . . both in mathematics and in ethics we have certain crystal-clear intuitions from which we build up all that we can know about the nature of numbers and the nature of duty. And, to return to our proper subject, we do not read off our knowledge of particular branches of duty from a single ideal of the good life, but build up our ideal of the good life from intuitions into particular branches of duty. In the course of our thinking we come to know more, but we should never come to know more if we did not *know* what we start with.' (FE 144–5)

initial convictions. This is a reason to doubt the aspect of Ross's intuitionism that assumes foundationalism.

1292. Intuitionism as Pluralism

This objection to foundationalism does not refute every 'intuitionist' doctrine that Sidgwick rejects. He uses this term to refer to pluralism about ultimate moral principles, and to the denial that any one principle is prior to the others. Ross follows Price in accepting this pluralist view. He does not say, for instance, that justice always takes priority over benevolence. In his view, we cannot know by intuition—that is, certain non-inferential knowledge—that we should follow one principle rather than the other here and now. We can only rely on 'intuition' in the distinct sense of 'intuitive conviction'. Hence he cites Aristotle's remark that the decision lies with 'perception' (RG 42).

Sidgwick's argument supports pluralist intuitionism on two points: (1) He accepts a principle of justice that requires equal distribution in cases where utility does not require a particular distribution of goods. This principle does not aim at maximizing utility. Sidgwick assumes that it is subordinate to the principle of utility, but it is not clear why we should accept this assumption. As Ross remarks, Sidgwick's claim about subordination 'is a half-way house at which we cannot stop' (FE 72). (2) We can see this from Sidgwick's later argument for the dualism of practical reason. Here he allows that it is reasonable 'for me' to follow agent-relative reasons, and that they are not necessarily subordinate to agent-neutral utilitarian reasons. If we recognize agent-relative moral reasons, we allow pluralist intuitionism about morality.

Ross's appeal to perception, however, may mislead us about what pluralism implies. We need not agree that perception decides whether we ought to avoid a trivial breach of friendship in order to observe a requirement of justice that has a serious impact on the well-being or rights of other people. As Bradley remarks, intuitive judgments involve some 'intuitive subsumption' (ES 196) under principles that connect one judgment with other judgments about related cases. These connexions reveal the system in our judgments.[75] If we treat observances or breaches of rules as 'trivial' or 'serious', we rely on some further judgments about the relative importance of the aims of different types of actions and obligations. If we recognize 'aims', we do not necessarily take utilitarian or consequentialist considerations as primary, but we rely on some ranking of the importance of the results of different actions. Since our ranking may not be complete, Ross may be right to say that in some cases we must simply rely on perception. But we need not rely on it in every case. Pluralist intuitionism about principles is not committed to an irrational rejection of arguments and principles.

In this case as elsewhere, attention to the implications of some of Ross's arguments may encourage us to revise some aspects of his position. We saw that his views about

---

[75] '...these judgments are not mere isolated impressions, but stand in an intimate and vital relation to a certain system, which is their basis.' (Bradley, ES 195) This holist aspect of Bradley's position is emphasized by Muirhead, who uses it against Ross. Muirhead speaks of 'implicit reference' where Bradley speaks of 'intuitive subsumption'. He argues that it may 'enable us to see an organic connexion between rule and end' (REM 46–7).

the indefinability of moral properties need to be qualified by his remarks about their explicability. His appeal to intuition against utilitarianism does not do justice to the fact that his anti-utilitarian convictions fit together in a conception of the personal and retrospective character of some moral obligations. This conception of obligations treats persons and their responsible agency as primary sources of moral obligations and rights. In tracing Ross's intuitions to their sources, we introduce a holist form of argument that defends general principles and specific convictions by appeal to each other. This holist form of argument casts doubt not only on Sidgwick's utilitarianism, but also on Ross's foundationalism.

These implications of some of Ross's arguments give us a different picture of moral argument and moral theory from the one we would derive from considering Ross's explicit position without his arguments. While his explicit position is a non-utilitarian version of Moore's non-naturalism and intuitionism, his arguments support a position that is much closer to Sidgwick's dialectical method. His objections to utilitarianism anticipate later efforts, particularly by Rawls, to defend a systematic and holistic anti-utilitarian moral theory.[76] His defence of pluralism about basic principles also suggests that it may be reasonable to revise his position in a holist direction without admitting a single supreme principle or rule of priority.[77]

---

[76] See Rawls, §1412.   [77] See Feinberg on Rawls and intuitionism, §1413.

88

LOGICAL EMPIRICISM
AND EMOTIVISM

1293. Moore and Non-Cognitivism

Moore believes that his arguments against naturalism support an intuitionist account of our knowledge of moral properties. Ross agrees with him on this point, and tries to develop an intuitionist conception of moral judgment. But we may find it difficult to believe in simple, non-natural properties that are grasped by some (allegedly) mysterious form of intuition. Our other knowledge of objective facts does not seem to require these (allegedly) strange properties and this strange cognitive condition. If, then, we believe that Moore's argument from non-naturalism and objectivism to intuitionism is valid, but we do not accept his conclusion, we may reasonably re-examine his premises. If we accept the premises that support non-naturalism, we may question his acceptance of cognitivism and objectivism.

This response to Moore suggests an argument for non-cognitivism: (1) Cognitivism supports objectivism. (2) Non-naturalism and objectivism require intuitionism. (3) But intuitionism is false. (4) Non-naturalism is true. (5) Therefore cognitivism is false. Indeed, Moore later recognizes that *Principia* does not argue against a non-cognitivist alternative to his conclusion.[1] Those who find the intuitionist conclusion unacceptable, and yet inescapable for a cognitivist, try to convert the intuitionist's modus ponens into a non-cognitivist modus tollens.[2]

Moore takes some steps in this direction with his later conception of non-natural properties. When he suggests that all and only natural predicates describe the subject that they are properties of, he might be taken to mean that non-natural predicates are non-descriptive, and therefore do not ascribe properties to their subjects at all. This is not Moore's view, but, as Broad remarks, one might prefer this view of non-natural predicates over Moore's view that some predicates ascribe properties to their subjects but do not describe the subjects.[3]

This evaluation of Moore underlies different versions of non-cognitivism, from Stevenson's emotivism to Hare's prescriptivism and Gibbard's and Blackburn's expressivism These

---

[1] See Stevenson, *EL 272*, and §1306.
[2] Welchman, 'Revolution', underestimates the significance for non-cognitivism of Moore's arguments.
[3] Moore on non-descriptive predicates; §1262.

non-cognitivists agree that Moore refutes naturalism and implicitly refutes his own non-naturalist objectivism; hence they agree on what moral judgments are not. They disagree, however, about what moral judgments are. Later non-cognitivists agree that emotivism is unsatisfactory, and they try to formulate a non-cognitivist position that will avoid these unsatisfactory features.

1294. The Logical Empiricist Ideal of Scientific Knowledge

So far we have described non-cognitivism as the result of reflexions on Moore. But we should also consider broader philosophical influences. The philosophical background for some aspects of 20th-century meta-ethics is a version of empiricism, revised to meet some of the objections raised against the 18th-century version. The 20th-century version—called 'logical empiricism' or 'logical positivism'—claims that knowledge rests on experience not in a genetic or psychological sense, but in an analytical sense. Empiricists abandon the claim that knowledge must be psychologically derived from some identifiable episodes of sense-experience. Instead, they argue that any acceptable claim to knowledge must be capable of being verified by experience. In its simplest form, this empiricist doctrine is combined with an empiricist and verificationist theory of meaning. On this view, the sentences of a true scientific theory have their meaning determined by the empirical tests that could be performed to verify them; when we perform the relevant tests we find that they are indeed true. A theory is false, but genuinely scientific, if its sentences turn out to be false when we perform the tests needed to verify them. A theory is non-scientific if its sentences allow no empirical verification or falsification. The verificationist theory of meaning implies that these sentences are cognitively meaningless, and the empiricist theory of knowledge implies that they cannot be part of any genuine knowledge.

This conception of meaning and knowledge requires a particular conception of a priori knowledge. If the meaning of a sentence is given by its method of empirical verification, and empirical knowledge is the product of empirical verification, our knowledge of the meaning of a sentence apparently cannot be itself a matter of empirical knowledge. For every item of empirical knowledge results from an attempt to verify a sentence. But we cannot verify a sentence unless we know the appropriate method of verification; and we cannot know the method of verification without knowing the meaning that establishes the method of verification. Hence it seems that all empirical knowledge presupposes knowledge of meaning, so that this knowledge of meaning must be non-empirical, and hence a priori. Hence the logical empiricist conception of knowledge requires a conception of a priori knowledge as knowledge of analytic or conceptual truths.

Logical empiricism, in contrast to Humean empiricism, normally treats empirical science non-sceptically. Hume's analysis of causation and external existence leads him to doubt whether either ordinary or scientific claims about the external world meet empiricist criteria. These doubts influence logical empiricism, since they underlie debates about the nature of causal statements, laws, and their verification. In fact, logical empiricism runs into difficulties when it tries to explain how scientific laws meet empiricist criteria for meaning and verifiability.[4]

A resolute logical empiricist might agree that empiricist criteria cannot justify ordinary scientific theories; anyone who did that would rather be a sceptic than give up logical empiricism. In fact, however, logical empiricists in the 20th century assume that logical empiricism would be refuted if it could not explain how scientific theories are significant and verifiable. On this basic question, logical empiricists are non-sceptical.[5]

Logical empiricists not only seek to justify empirical science on empiricist grounds, but also want to distinguish genuine science from pretenders to knowledge. Here they follow Hume; for Hume's scepticism about common sense and science does not prevent him from attacking the claims of religious and metaphysical beliefs when they go beyond the area of experience.[6] The logical empiricists see three main pretenders to knowledge whose pretensions ought to be unmasked: dogmatic religion and theology, political and historical ideologies, and metaphysical theories. The empiricist criterion of meaning is supposed to demolish Christianity, Marxism, and Kantian or Hegelian idealism all at once. Their common failing is their metaphysical element; their crucial claims consist of sentences for which we cannot find any method of empirical verification, and hence their crucial claims are cognitively meaningless. This criticism of metaphysics is reminiscent of Hume and Kant; but since it relies more precisely on a claim about meaning, and since it seeks to draw a sharp contrast between metaphysical and scientific discourse, the logical empiricist position is easier to understand and to evaluate.

The critical aspects of logical empiricism cannot easily stand without the attempted vindication of empirical science. For if we discover that a strongly empiricist criterion of meaning counts sentences of a scientific theory as meaningless, we may resort to a weaker criterion; but then it is difficult to see how the weaker criterion excludes metaphysical sentences. Logical empiricists face difficulties if they find that scientific sentences and metaphysical sentences appear to have the same relation to particular procedures of empirical verification.

1295. Strict v. Moderate Empiricism

These particular empiricist claims about meaning do not exhaust the empiricist approach. From an empiricist point of view, it may seem obvious that physics is legitimate and theology is not, and that we ought to be able to tell that this is so independently of our believing

---

[4] Questions about verifiability preoccupy Hempel (*ASE*, ch. 4, a defence of a modified version of a verificationist account of cognitive significance) and Popper (*LSD*, ch. 4; he argues for falsifiability rather than verifiability as a test of cognitive significance).

[5] Schlick, 'Positivism', 95–107, offers brisk verificationist arguments against sceptical hypotheses.

[6] Hume concludes *IHU* 12 with a remark that foreshadows positivism: 'When we run over libraries, persuaded of these principles, what havoc must we make? If we take in our hand any volume; of divinity or school metaphysics, for instance; let us ask, *Does it contain any abstract reasoning concerning quantity or number?* No. *Does it contain any experimental reasoning concerning matter of fact and existence?* No. Commit it then to the flames: For it can contain nothing but sophistry and illusion.' But, in contrast to logical positivists, Hume does not include books on morals among those to be committed to the flames. Hume on scepticism and morality; §§722–3.

that physics is true and theology is not true. For an empiricist, the difference between the legitimate and the illegitimate theories depends on the relation of a theory to experience; and so, on this view, we ought to be able to show, whether or not we accept particular conclusions of a theory, that a theory does or does not rest on the right relation to experience. This empiricist assumption or aspiration is more attractive than any more precise criteria of meaning have turned out to be. One may suppose that there must be something in the empiricist assumption even if no one has succeeded in stating any precise and defensible version of it.

It is not necessarily wrong to cling to something like an empiricist assumption even if we abandon the more precise empiricist criteria. For we might reasonably be reluctant to abandon a distinction that we seem to draw fairly consistently and systematically, even if we cannot formulate it precisely. A theory that makes no difference to experience, that is compatible with all possible experience and recognizes no possible experience as counting for or against it, does not explain very much for us; for it does not lead us to expect any one situation any more than its opposite. This is a reasonable test to apply to a theory; and even if it does not work as precisely as logical empiricists might have hoped, it may support reasonable objections to some theories.

We give up something important, however, if we rest empiricism on this looser demand for empirical relevance. For we can connect most theories with experience, if we include both the right empirical assumptions and principles that connect experience with theory. We can make astrological predictions if we combine astrological theory with appropriate principles to yield to empirical predictions. The difficulty is that in the astrological case, the relevant principles and assumptions are implausible. To see whether a theory is reasonable or not, we must see what happens when it is combined with otherwise plausible theories and assumptions.

This assumption about initial plausibility introduces a holistic element into justification that is absent from stricter forms of empiricism. Instead of confronting one theory with experience, we must combine it with other theories we accept and see what results.[7] This holism also implies that we must take more for granted than a strict empiricist would. If we could confront one sentence, or even one theory, with a particular range of experience, we would not need to form any further judgments about what is true or plausible outside this particular situation. But if we need to form these judgments, the empiricist test cannot do as much as we might have thought it could. It can perhaps discriminate between some theories and others, by reference to our initial (and revisable) judgments about plausibility; but it cannot all by itself challenge all our initial judgments about plausibility at once, since the empiricist test always relies on further judgments about plausibility.

1296. Empiricism and Ethics

This logical empiricist outlook influences 20th-century non-cognitivists. Stevenson and Ayer often rely on logical empiricist assumptions without even stating them. But it is not

---

[7] Quine, 'Dogmas', 42–6, presents an influential holist attack on positivist views of verification.

obvious that non-cognitivism is the most plausible meta-ethical position for someone who accepts logical empiricist assumptions about knowledge. Logical empiricism shares some assumptions with 19th-century positivism. Bentham's cognitivist meta-ethics and utilitarian normative ethics seem to fit easily into a logical empiricist position. When Bentham says that 'ought' means something if it refers to pleasure and pain, and otherwise means nothing, he relies on a conception of meaning that suits logical empiricism.[8] If he is right, ethics becomes an empirical science.

One might expect logical empiricists to welcome Bentham's conceptual hedonism, since it seems to show how moral judgments meet empiricist conditions for meaning. Conceptual hedonism suggests a version of 'optimistic empiricism' about ethics. It fits a conception of ethics as a branch of social science, applying the results of social psychology, economics, and sociology. Conceptual utilitarianism provides the 'logic' of the relevant applied social science, by defining the relevant concepts so as to identify the empirical conclusions that answer ethical questions; then the social scientist looks for the answers.[9]

This optimistic empiricism, however, is not the most popular position among logical empiricists. Many of them accept a more pessimistic empiricist view that refuses to incorporate ethics into the logical empiricist framework of natural and social science. This pessimistic empiricism appeals to the apparent prevalence and persistence of moral dispute and disagreement. If greater knowledge of what promotes pleasure and removes pain does not produce moral consensus, perhaps optimistic empiricism about ethics is too simple, and moral judgments do not express empirical factual knowledge. Logical empiricists, therefore, might doubt whether they can be ordinary objective factual judgments.

1297. Facts and Values: Weber

One might respond to these pessimistic views about moral judgments by observing (as positivists often do) that common sense often disagrees with empirical science because common sense is attached to pre-scientific notions and uses terms with no clear cognitive significance. The logical empiricist answer is to point out the confusions of common sense and to proceed with the scientific reconstruction of the confused notions. This is Bentham's answer to doubts about utilitarianism.

Logical empiricists do not usually rely on this diagnosis of tendencies to resist conceptual hedonism, because they are influenced by a further doubt about whether ethics can be an empirical science. A division between facts and values affects many aspects of 20th-century intellectual life, and has especially affected views on the nature and functions of the social sciences.[10] In Max Weber's view, for instance, a sharp distinction between questions of fact

---

[8] Bentham; §§1113, 1156, 1259.

[9] This empiricist spirit is evident in Schlick's PE. In reply to the objection that he makes ethics a part of psychology because he treats it as a causal inquiry into the explanation of moral behaviour, he says: '. . . one might say, "In such case there would be no ethics at all; what is called ethics would be nothing but a part of psychology!" I answer, "Why shouldn't ethics be a part of psychology?"' (29) He denies that the consequence that Moore derives from naturalism is an objection to naturalism.

[10] Prior, LBE 43, traces the division between fact and value back to Keynes, SMPE, ch. 2. At 34–5, Keynes distinguishes a positive science concerned with 'what is' from a normative science concerned with 'what ought to be, and concerned

and questions of value is a prerequisite for intellectual honesty in the conduct and teaching of social science.[11] The investigator and the teacher should not represent their own evaluative judgments as the unquestionable implications of empirical inquiry. Even if one wants to put forward one's own evaluations, one should make it clear that they are different from factual assertions.[12]

One might incline, therefore, to accept a non-factual view of moral judgments because Weber associates it with several claims that one might find quite plausible. Perhaps the teacher ought to distinguish moral judgments from the specific conclusions of economics, psychology, or sociology, so that the student can see which of the teacher's assertions are empirical conclusions that all investigators need to accept, irrespective of their moral views, and which assertions need specifically moral arguments. Insistence on the separation of moral judgments may help to prevent the use of economics or social psychology, for instance, as an instrument of political control.

But even if Weber is right to separate moral judgments from the conclusions of empirical social sciences, we need not accept any sharp division between facts and values. We might simply say that we should distinguish inquiry into the facts referred to in moral judgments from inquiry into the facts proper to economics or sociology. Weber, however, goes beyond this advice to the further claim that moral judgments are judgments of value and therefore not factual judgments at all.

Since he constantly takes it for granted that moral judgments are not factual, it is not easy to see exactly why he believes it. Perhaps he believes that if we admitted moral facts as well as the proper facts of sociology or economics, we might be asked why they are not also the subject of an empirical science. Weber assumes that we cannot offer a credible description of an empirical science of morality. He is influenced by the assumption that any a priori discipline is purely formal, not about any objective facts, and that an empirical science must proceed by observation and relatively simple induction.

To explain why he rejects any conception of a science of morality, Weber attacks one view about how moral facts might be studied scientifically. He argues that a survey of trends cannot by itself justify moral conclusions. We cannot infer from the fact that theft has become more prevalent that theft is right, and we cannot infer from the fact that trade unions are less popular that trade unions are bad.[13] This objection seems to ignore Bentham's

---

therefore with the ideal as distinguished from the actual'. It is not clear, however, that Keynes intends to deny the reality of moral facts. Prior also cites Huxley, *EE*, who argues that evolutionary biology cannot derive ethical principles from biological facts. Huxley speaks of a 'fallacy' pervading the ethics of evolution: 'because, on the whole animals and plants have advanced in perfection of organization by means of the struggle for existence and the consequent "survival of the fittest"; therefore men in society, men as ethical beings, must look to the same process to help them towards perfection' (*EE* 80).

[11] Olafson, *ETCT* 54–64, discusses the context and significance of Weber's subjectivism about morality briefly and well.

[12] '... the teacher sets as his unconditional duty, in every single case, even to the point where it involves the danger of making his lectures less lively or attractive, to make relentlessly clear to his audience, and especially to himself, which of his statements are statements of logically deduced or empirically observed facts and which are statements of practical evaluations. Once one has acknowledged the logical disjunction between the two spheres, it seems to me that the assumption of this attitude is an imperative requirement of intellectual honesty; in this case it is the absolutely minimal requirement.' (Weber, *MSS* 2; first published in 1917)

[13] 'The belief is still widespread that one should, and must, or at any rate, can derive value judgments from factual assertions about "trends". But even from the most unambiguous "trends", unambiguous norms can be derived only

programme. Empirical moral science might be expected to consider the impact of different policies and institutions on pleasure and pain (or some other empirical conception of welfare and harm). Weber's examples do not show why these empirical inquiries might not lead to moral conclusions.

But perhaps Weber rejects a factual conception of morality because he believes that such a conception confuses theory with practice. He assumes some form of internalism, so that if we make a value judgment, we thereby adopt a policy and commit ourselves to action. According to this internalist view, a teacher who expressed a value judgment would thereby be advocating a particular policy. According to Weber, however, the role of the teacher should be separated from the role of the advocate, and teachers should not use their official role in order to advocate a policy. Here he relies on the connexion between his doctrine of facts and values and his institutional and political views. He believes it is important to distinguish those who collect and present the empirical facts from those who decide what to do about them. The first task belongs to the social scientist and the civil servant. The second belongs to citizens and to politicians acting with their mandate. We would blur this important division if we allowed social scientists, civil servants, teachers, or other officials, to express moral judgments in their official role; but since their official role is to present the facts, we could not reasonably prohibit them from making moral judgments if moral judgments were factual.

If this is Weber's position, however, his sharp division between facts and values rests ultimately on a value judgment—his judgment that the roles of the official and of the citizen or politician should be separated. In so far as he relies on this judgment, he presumably speaks as a citizen rather than an official or a teacher. Equally, it would be open to other citizens to oppose this judgment without risk of being wrong about any of the relevant facts. Weber would be unwise, then, to make this argument about internalism his main argument for the separation of facts from values. But his other arguments do not seem strong enough to bear the weight they would have to bear if they were separated from the argument about internalism.

1298. Facts and Standards: Popper

The moral and political side of Weber's position is especially prominent in Popper's case against a factual view of moral judgments. Popper speaks without distinction of a dualism of 'facts and decisions', a dualism of 'facts and norms' (*OSE* i 64–5), and a dualism of 'facts and standards' (ii 392).[14] The dualism expresses the doctrine of the 'autonomy of ethics, first advocated by Protagoras and Socrates' (67). Popper takes this dualism to be 'one of the bases of the liberal tradition' (ii 392).

Some of Popper's explications of his division do not seem relevant to the issue. It is difficult, for instance, to see why anyone would deny that a fact is different from a decision

with regard to the prospectively most appropriate means—and then only when the irreducible evaluation is already given. The evaluations themselves cannot be derived from these "tendencies" '. (*MSS* 22)

[14] This is the formula that he eventually prefers: '... it would have been clearer had I spoken of a *dualism of facts and policies*, or of a *dualism of facts and standards*, rather than of a dualism of facts and decisions' (Popper, *OSE* ii 383).

made in response to the fact; no one who believes in moral facts is committed to saying that they are the same as moral decisions. It seems confused to identify the difference between facts and decisions with the difference between facts and values.

But perhaps the indiscriminate use of 'values', 'norms', and 'standards' helps Popper's formulation of the distinction. We may speak of norms in two different ways: (1) Moral judgments express moral norms; the norms are what these judgments are about. Similarly, moral judgments express standards, and correct moral judgments express the correct standards. (2) If we speak of a person's or a society's values, or of social norms or standards, we may think of a norm as a decision or policy of a person or society. If we do not distinguish these two ways of speaking of norms, we may easily pass from the commonplace claim that moral standards (i.e., rightness and wrongness) are the subject-matter of moral judgments to the more controversial conclusion that norms just are moral judgments. If we think of norms in this way, it is difficult to distinguish value judgments from the values they are about.

We may also reach Popper's formulation if we rely on internalism. If we believe moral judgment is internally connected to motivation, and we believe that no judgment about facts could be internally connected with motivation, we infer that no moral judgments are judgments about facts. Internalist assumptions make it easy to pass from speaking of moral judgments to speaking of proposals and decisions.

When Popper says that the dualism he describes is one of the bases of liberalism, he means that a liberal rejects the view that facts or alleged facts about society and history make it unreasonable or futile to think about ways of changing society. Since ways of changing society involve the adoption of different norms or standards, we cannot take norms or standards to be wholly determined by general laws about how societies have been in the past or how they always necessarily are. If these laws are the only facts that could conceivably determine moral norms, and these do not determine them, no facts determine moral norms. Hence, if moral judgments are about moral norms, they are not about facts.

Weber and Popper illustrate the widespread view that the dualism of facts and values is obvious, and that enlightened social science and political action depend on the recognition of it. Moreover, they illustrate how easily some equivocations on 'value', 'standard', and 'norm' can make this meta-ethical doctrine seem inescapable.

It would be unwelcome, however, to Weber and Popper if their arguments against factual views of moral judgment rested wholly on their moral and political objections to the practical consequences of such views. For one might reply that even if moral and political grounds give us a reason to hope that moral judgments are not factual, they do not settle the question; we should not settle this theoretical question in meta-ethics on the strength of our hopes. We might also hope that cancer can easily be cured, but it does not follow that it can easily be cured. Unless we already know that meta-ethical questions are to be settled by moral and political aims and hopes, we need some further reason to believe that moral judgments are not factual.

Moore's argument now becomes relevant. Though he does not mention Weber's and Popper's political reasons for rejecting a factual conception of moral judgments, he agrees with their denial that ethics is a natural science. If naturalism were true, there would, in Moore's view, be no such thing as ethics, or ethics would be absorbed in an existing natural science. His arguments seem to support Weber's and Popper's main claims. If we believe that Moore's argument does not require strange non-natural facts, but refutes a factual view altogether, we can use Moore to dismiss all claims to have found a science—empirical or non-empirical—of morality. Logical empiricists who share Weber's and Popper's moral and political objections to moral science have a good reason to welcome part of Moore's argument.[15] If they reject naturalism, and reject Moore's non-natural facts, they can reach a non-cognitivist conclusion that supports the division between facts and values.

1299. Moore, Hume, and Non-Cognitivism

Non-cognitivism takes moral judgment to be essentially connected with motivation and action, both our own and other people's. Hence it helps to explain why the division between theory and practice is relevant to the division between factual and moral judgments. Moore and Ross pay no special attention to the practical aspect of moral judgments. One might indeed argue that their account goes wrong because they ignore this difference between moral judgments and purely theoretical judgments. In so far as non-cognitivists emphasize the practical character of moral judgments, they agree with Hume; some regard him as their predecessor.[16] A comparison with Hume will help us to identify some useful questions about non-cognitivism.

Hume offers a 'metaphysical' argument, claiming that no facts 'in the object' imply any moral judgment.[17] This argument is very similar to Moore's Open Question Argument. Hume assumes that the facts 'in the object' involve the properties that Moore regards as natural. When he claims that none of these facts is the moral rightness or wrongness of an action, he seems to be making a point about logical possibility that could be expressed through Moore's appeal to an open question. To show that the wrongness of a murder does not consist in its being the deliberate killing of an innocent person, we need only observe that (as Moore puts it) we can significantly ask whether such deliberate killing is wrong.

Hume also offers a 'practical argument' resting on the premiss that 'morals have an influence on the actions and affections'.[18] This feature of moral judgments shows that they cannot be judgments of reason, and that they cannot be about objective facts. Judgments of reason about objective facts could not influence action in the way moral judgments influence it. Hume faces two questions: (1) How do moral judgments influence action? (2) Why can 'objective judgments' (i.e., judgments of reason about what is in the object) not influence action in this way? In answer to these questions, he maintains that (1) it is logically impossible to make a moral judgment and not to be moved to act in accordance with it, whereas (2) it is logically possible to make an objective judgment and to be unmoved by it.

Though the practical and the metaphysical argument are distinct, the practical argument may seem to vindicate the metaphysical argument. If we grant the intuitions about logical

---

[15] Hare, 'Broad', 571–2, suggests plausibly that if Ayer had not been so impressed by Moore's arguments, he would probably have been a naturalist about ethics.

[16] On connexions between Moore and Hume, see Laird, SMT 17–18, 95 ('the essential point is the irreducibility of values to non-values'); Hare, LM 29–30. Sidgwick also speaks of the difference between 'is' and 'ought to be' (though without specific reference to Hume); see, e.g., ME 79. Stevenson treats Hume as a subjectivist; see EL 273–6.

[17] Hume's metaphysical argument; §§747–9.   [18] Hume, T iii 1 6. See §§744–6.

possibility that underlie the metaphysical argument, we may still wonder whether they are trustworthy, and why we have such intuitions about moral properties. But Hume's internalism answers our questions. Since moral judgments essentially influence action, and judgments about objective facts do not essentially influence action, we can see why these judgments about objective facts are not moral judgments. Our intuitions about what is and is not in the object are confirmed by recognition of the practical character of moral judgments.

This reflexion on Hume suggests a similar reflexion on Moore's argument against naturalism. From a Humean point of view, Moore's Open Question Argument refutes all naturalist definitions because they are about objective facts that do not imply any motivation. Naturalism fails, on this view, because internalism is correct.[19] But since Moore does not see that this is why naturalism fails, he infers that moral judgments are about a strange kind of objective fact, a non-natural fact. We should conclude that his refutation of naturalism rests on the falsity of objectivism.

Hume's two arguments, however, also cast doubt on each other, because they seem to rely on different standards of logical possibility. The internalism that supports the practical argument relies on claims about logical impossibility that conflict with the standards of logical possibility used in the metaphysical argument. A comparison with Moore makes this objection to Hume even clearer. The metaphysical argument relies on the test of logical possibility that supports the Open Question Argument; but the internalist claim seems to create an open question, and so cannot express a logical necessity.

This objection to Hume may also be relevant to non-cognitivism. For non-cognitivists follow Hume in accepting internalism, but they also believe that open questions imply logical possibility. If they agree with Moore's argument against naturalism, they agree that open questions indicate logical possibility. But if internalism creates open questions, they cannot consistently maintain internalism. It is worth seeing whether non-cognitivists have a good reply to this objection to the consistency of their position.

1300. Stevenson's Analysis[20]

Stevenson's case for non-cognitivism about 'good' helps us to see the role of Hume's arguments and Moore's arguments.[21] He believes that an analysis of the 'typical' sense

---

[19] This is similar to Hare's account of the success of Moore's argument. But Hare's position is more complicated. See §1327.

[20] The fullest presentation of an emotive theory is Stevenson's *EL*. It is stronger in working out the details than in telling us why we ought to take the theory seriously in the first place. He addresses this more basic question, however, in his earlier paper 'Meaning'.

[21] Stevenson never cites Hume's internalism. He mentions only Hume's subjectivist cognitivism, *EL* 273–6, and his partial recognition of disagreement in attitude, 11. But he also remarks: 'Of all traditional philosophers, Hume has most clearly asked the questions that here concern us, and has most nearly reached a conclusion that the present writer can accept' (273). Ayer does not mention Hume's internalism either. At *LTL* 107, he does not argue for the emotive component of his analysis. But perhaps his remarks on normative and descriptive ethical symbols (106) suggest the argument he has in mind.

of 'good' should satisfy three conditions:[22] (1) An analysis must show how A and B can intelligently disagree if A claims that x is good and B claims that x is bad in the same respect. Subjectivism does not show this, since A and B do not disagree about x if A asserts that A likes x and B asserts that B dislikes x. Subjectivism implies that A and B are asserting different things, not that they disagree. (2) An analysis must display an internal connexion between the judgment that an action is good and motivation to do the action.[23] (3) An analysis must avoid naturalism, since Moore has refuted it through the Open Question Argument.[24] Natural properties, as Moore understands them, are scientifically knowable properties, and therefore knowable by the existing empirical sciences.[25] Since Moore is right, 'good' cannot be defined through any scientifically knowable properties.

The first and third of Stevenson's conditions are easily understood from Moore. The third simply agrees with Moore's rejection of naturalism, without clarifying it. The first mentions one of the considerations that turn Moore and others against subjectivism. The second condition, however, is Stevenson's addition to Moore. It includes the uncontroversial claim that morality belongs to practical philosophy, but adds the more controversial claim, in agreement with Hume, that the practical character of morality determines the meaning of moral terms and moral judgments.

Stevenson's view is emotivist because he claims that the practical character of moral judgments is their dynamic use for influencing behaviour. To explain this dynamic use, he argues that they essentially convey a favourable attitude in the judge. In telling you that x is good or right or that you ought to do x, I express my favourable attitude to doing x, and thereby influence you towards doing x. Emotivists rely on the undoubted fact that we often use moral judgments to influence other people's behaviour. According to the emotivist, this fact about moral judgments expresses their essential character.[26]

Not all these three conditions are neutral conditions of adequacy that we might accept at the beginning of a discussion of naturalism and cognitivism. A naturalist would not accept Stevenson's third condition, since it simply asserts that naturalism is false. The first two conditions need to be examined more closely, to see whether Stevenson makes a good case for them, and whether his analysis satisfies them.

[22] '(1) goodness must be a topic for intelligent disagreement; (2) it must be "magnetic"; and (3) it must not be discoverable solely through the scientific method.' (FV 15)

[23] 'A person who recognizes X to be "good" must ipso facto acquire a stronger tendency to act in its favour than he otherwise would have had.' (FV 13)

[24] 'No matter what set of scientifically knowable properties a thing may have (says Moore, in effect), you will find, on careful introspection, that it is an open question to ask whether anything having these properties is good. It is difficult to believe that this recurrent question is a totally confused one, or that it seems open only because of the ambiguity of "good". Rather, we must be using some sense of "good" which is not definable, relevantly, in terms of anything scientifically knowable.' (FV 15)

[25] Hence Stevenson's third condition is illustrated by the claim that 'ethics must not be psychology' (FV 13).

[26] Stevenson develops a suggestion by Ogden and Richards, MM 227–8: 'But another use of the word [sc. "good"] is often asserted to occur . . . where "good" is alleged to stand for a unique unanalysable concept. This concept, it is said, is the subject matter of ethics. [A footnote cites Moore.] This peculiar ethical use of "good" is, we suggest, a purely emotive use. When so used, the word stands for nothing whatever . . . it serves only as an emotive sign expressing our attitude . . . , and perhaps evoking similar attitudes in other persons, or inciting them to actions of one kind or another.' In ch. 7, they offer a similar account of beauty. Stevenson cites them as a source of his views at 'Meaning', 21. He quotes the passage above in one of the epigraphs to EL.

1301. Intelligent Disagreement

The first condition seems to be neutral, since it records a feature of moral judgments that we might expect any plausible analysis to recognize. To explain its importance for Stevenson, we should return to Hume.

Hume does not draw a clearly non-cognitivist conclusion from his arguments against objectivism. He seems to endorse subjectivism. He believes that we make the judgment with the appropriate internal relation to motivation when we assert that we have the appropriate sentiment. If he takes this view, he rejects objectivism, but retains a descriptive and cognitive conception of moral judgments. Stevenson, therefore, needs to explain why we should not follow Hume in drawing this subjectivist conclusion from internalism.

Price, Reid, and Moore explain why subjectivism is unwelcome. They all point out against Hume that moral judgments do not appear to be reports on our feelings and reactions. If they were, we could not understand moral disagreement as we do. If you feel attracted to an action and I feel repelled by it, it is not self-contradictory to say that you have this reaction and I have that one. Hence if the action's being right or wrong is simply someone's being attracted or repelled, my assertion that the action is right does not contradict your assertion that it is wrong; I do not assert that what you say is false. It seems, clear, however, that if I say that an action is right and you say that the very same action is wrong, our two assertions contradict each other. A cognitivist, therefore, has reason to favour objectivism over sentimentalism.[27]

Stevenson accepts this argument. He believes that subjectivism does not explain the possibility of intelligent disagreement, and that a correct analysis should explain it. In his view, emotivism meets this condition. For the emotivist does not claim that when I make a moral judgment that is ostensibly about the rightness of some external action, I describe some feeling of mine. I describe nothing, but I express my attitude to the action.

Emotivism, therefore, is not open to the specific objection that faces the subjectivist. But it does not follow that it explains the possibility of intelligent disagreement. Stevenson, however, believes that it does explain this. In many cases, we disagree about the facts that are the cause of our attitude; in other cases, we disagree in attitude, in so far as we react differently to the agreed facts. Once we recognize these disagreements, we can explain why moral judgments allow intelligent disagreement.

This account of moral disagreement is open to question. We may plausibly object to Hume's subjectivism by observing that 'Torturing innocent people is wrong' and 'Torturing innocent people is not wrong' are contradictory. But that observation gives us no reason to prefer non-cognitivism over subjectivism; for only statements can be contradictory (since contradiction involves truth and falsehood), but non-cognitivists do not grant that moral judgments are statements. Hence neither subjectivists nor non-cognitivists explain the fact that moral judgments can be contradictory.[28]

---

[27] Adam Smith attempts to improve a sentimentalist account by introducing the reactions of other people or of hypothetical people; see §791. But it is difficult to explain the character of moral judgments by these substitutes for objectivity.

[28] Ewing, *DG* 6n, comments on Stevenson's discussion of 'how argument can be relevant to ethical disagreements on a subjectivist view'. Ewing remarks justly: 'It does not show it [sc. argument] to be relevant in the sense in which we really see it to be relevant, but in some other sense'.

Stevenson, however, denies that he needs to explain how moral judgments can be contradictory. He admits only that we can intelligently disagree in our moral judgments. He claims that disagreement in attitude is sufficient for intelligent disagreement. If I favour doing x and you are against doing x, we 'disagree' in the sense that he takes to be relevant. And if we take these attitudes in response to features of x, our disagreement is intelligent enough to satisfy the relevant condition of adequacy. He does not say, however, why we should substitute intelligent disagreement for contradiction.

But if we concede to Stevenson that moral judgments only express disagreement in attitude and do not contradict each other, why should subjectivists not exploit his concession? Though my favouring x is consistent with your aversion to x, it is opposed to your aversion, since it will move me to pursue x and your aversion will lead you to avoid x. Hence I may indicate opposition to your aversion if I say that I favour x. Hence subjectivism seems to allow the sort of opposition that Stevenson regards as 'intelligent' disagreement.[29]

If, therefore, we believe that moral judgments can be contradictory, we should reject both subjectivism and emotivism. But if we believe only that they allow 'intelligent' disagreement in attitude, we have no reason to favour emotivism over subjectivism. Stevenson does not allow us to preserve some plausible conception of moral disagreement that subjectivism cannot preserve. Both of these anti-realist views seem to do equally well or badly in explaining the disagreement in attitude that they allow and the disagreement through contradiction that they reject.

The argument about disagreement helps to explain why anti-realists tend to prefer non-cognitivism to subjectivism. But the preference is difficult to justify. For the premises of the argument from disagreement to non-cognitivism appeal only to non-cognitivists.

1302. Stevenson's Conditions for Adequate Definition

So far we have assumed that Stevenson's analysis ought to match the intuitive conditions for adequacy that we might try to agree on before we formulate an analysis. But Stevenson's conditions for an adequate definition are more complicated than we have so far recognized.

He imposes two conditions on definitions: (1) A correct analysis of the question 'Is x good?' should substitute for it a question that is 'free from ambiguity and confusion' (FV 10). The new, substituted question need not be the very same question as the old one, since the old one may have suffered from ambiguity and confusion.[30] Since an analysis improves the original question in these ways, we can understand why an analysis may be more informative than a tautology or a trivial equivalence would be. (2) Though the analysans and the analysandum need not be identical, the analysans must none the less be 'relevant'

---

[29] Stevenson rejects this defence of subjectivism by insisting that disagreement requires an expression of opposition, rather than an assertion that indicates opposition. But it is difficult to see why we should agree. Opposition seems no less clear if I make a statement that implies it than if I express it without stating anything.

[30] '... we must not expect the substituted question to be strictly "identical" with the original one. The original question may embody hypostatization, anthropomorphism, vagueness, and all the other ills to which our ordinary discourse is subject ... The questions will be identical only in the sense that a child is identical with the man he later becomes. Hence we must not demand that the substitution strike us, on immediate introspection, as making no change in meaning.' (FV 11)

to the analysandum. It is relevant if it is functionally equivalent, so that we can use the analysans without any need to resort to the analysandum.[31]

Are these two conditions consistent? To show that they are, Stevenson might argue for either of two claims: (1) The elements of ordinary discourse that need elimination are idle; they make no difference to the functions for which (even before we are enlightened by the analysis that eliminates these ills) we use the word. (2) Though they make some difference to the functions of the word in our benighted days, our understanding of the proposed analysis eliminates our desire to use the word for these functions.

But Stevenson defends neither of these two claims, and neither is plausible. The first claim is false if, for instance, an analysis shows that 'F' has several senses, but we previously took it to be univocal. We may have used 'F' to reflect on the common property that we attributed to all Fs, but we can no longer use it for that function if we find that it is not univocal. Might not we suffer some parallel loss from an analysis of 'good' if we discover that it does not stand for any objective property?

The second claim is also open to question. It is not obvious that our understanding of an analysis will remove our benighted inclinations. If a proposed analysis finds different senses for 'F', which we supposed to be univocal, we may reject the analysis on the benighted ground that we can no longer use 'F' for its previous function. Might we not have equally benighted reactions to an analysis of 'good'? Might we not still want to say things that presuppose the ills that have been removed?[32] Intuitionists may argue that the emotivist analysis fails the condition of functional equivalence. If we take 'good' to have the sense Stevenson attributes it, we cannot (according to the intuitionist) use it, as we actually do, to refer to the truths, other than those belonging to empirical science, in the light of which we can guide our attitudes and aims.[33] This is a reasonable objection, similar to some of Ross's objections to emotivism.[34] We might also express it by saying that, from the intuitionist point of view, Stevenson's analysis creates an open question. His condition of functional equivalence implies that an appeal to open questions is a relevant objection.

He seems to answer this objection by appeal to his first claim about definitions—that they need not preserve 'strict' identity, and that they may 'remove ills' by eliminative revision. His analysis may fail to represent everything that we want to say with the ordinary concept of goodness; but since the residue that his analysis omits is not worth saying, and we would be confused if we even tried to say it, it does not count against his analysis. An account of 'good' that would assert both some synthetic a priori connexion to other concepts and the

---

[31] 'A defined meaning will be called "relevant" to the original meaning under these circumstances: Those who have understood the definition must be able to say all that they then want to say by using the term in the defined way. They must never have occasion to use the term in the old, unclear sense. (If a person did have to go on using the word in the old sense, then to this extent his meaning would not be clarified and the philosophical task would not be completed.)' (*FV* 11)

[32] This possibility is exploited by Mackie and Robinson in their defence of an 'error theory'. See §1372.

[33] 'When we ask "is X good?" we don't want mere influence, mere advice . . . The answer to our question will, of course, modify our interests. But this is only because a unique sort of truth will be revealed to us—a truth that must be apprehended a priori . . . To substitute for this special truth mere emotive meaning and mere factual truth is to conceal from us the very object of our search.' (*FV* 30)

[34] See Ross, *FE* 32–40, discussed in §1326.

power of influence would involve a confusion; the power of influence is the only intelligible part.[35]

Stevenson's conception of relevance requires us, having understood the definition, to be able to say all that we then want to say by using the term in the defined way (*FV* 11). But his treatment of 'good' suggests that he cannot easily satisfy this condition for relevance. Perhaps, then, we might substitute 'all that we then can reasonably (or intelligibly) want to say'. We might call this a demand for 'regimented functional equivalence'. Stevenson's comments on his analysis suggest that he claims the right to discard some of what we might still want to say but cannot say with his analysis; he discards it either because it is confused or because it rests on unacceptable metaphysical or epistemological assumptions. (He does not sharply distinguish these two possibilities.)

This account of the connexion between Stevenson's analysis and the analysandum makes his aim more similar to the positivist aim of 'explication'. Carnap adopts this aim in response to the objection that positivist analyses do not give us the content of the concepts they purport to analyse, since the analysanda include non-positivist assumptions that positivists want to eliminate from their analyses.[36] An appeal to explication helps to solve the paradox of analysis; for the explicatum (i.e., the result of a successful explication) and the explicandum express the same proposition, but differ in meaning, because their intensional structure is different.[37]

Carnap's conception of explication still includes functional equivalence, since he insists it must be possible to use the explicatum in the same way as the explicans. Hence the objections to Stevenson's analysis of 'good' still apply to an explication purporting to meet Carnap's test. To answer the objections, we might reply that an explication aims only at regimented functional equivalence; perhaps this is what Carnap intends.

1303. Can Stevenson Accept the Open Question Argument?

Let us suppose, then, that Stevenson looks for an analysis that provides an explication (in the sense just described). Even if the conditions for an explication are not completely clear, it is clear at least that the Open Question Argument is not relevant to them. Moore's argument applies (at most) to proposed accounts of meaning, and does not affect proposed explications; the fact that a proposed explication creates an open question is only to be expected, since explications seek to be informative. If, then, Stevenson's analyses aim at regimented functional equivalence in his analyses, he is justified in rejecting any objection that relies on the Open Question Argument. That is why an intuitionist cannot legitimately appeal to the Open Question Argument against an emotivist analysis.

---

[35] 'I find no indefinable property nor do I know what to look for. And the "self-evident" deliverances of reason, which so many philosophers have mentioned, seem on examination to be deliverances of their respective reasons only (if of anyone's) and not of mine.' (*FV* 31)

[36] '. . . this earlier concept, or sometimes the term used for it, is called the explicandum; and the new concept, or its term, is called an explicatum of the old one . . . Generally speaking, it is not required that an explicatum have, as nearly as possible, the same meaning as the explicandum; it should, however, correspond to the explicandum in such a way that it can be used instead of the latter.' (Carnap, *MN* 8)

[37] Carnap, *MN* 64–5. He refers to Langford, 'Analysis'.

But this conception of analysis makes it difficult to see why Stevenson rejects naturalism. He believes Moore has refuted naturalism by the use of the Open Question Argument; but the Open Question Argument is irrelevant, in Stevenson's view, to any analysis that offers an explication rather than strict identity of meaning. Moore rejects a conceptual utilitarian account of 'good' because it raises an open question; but if utilitarians represent it as an explication that allows some reform in our use of the term, it may be no worse off than Stevenson's explication. We might adapt some of Mill's remarks about justice to sketch the general form of a utilitarian explication. Mill admits (we might say) that utility is not the whole of our pre-theoretical idea of justice, but he argues that it is the genuinely moral element in it.[38] Hence a utilitarian explication of justice might be offered as a reasonable replacement for the pre-theoretical meaning. Once we understand that the moral element is purely utilitarian, we are ready to use 'justice' in a utilitarian sense. This explication may be open to cogent objections; but the fact that it raises an open question is irrelevant.

Similarly, the conception of analysis as explication casts further doubt on Stevenson's preference for non-cognitivism over subjectivism. If he offers an explicative analysis of moral judgments, it does not matter—he might have argued—that it violates our intuitive sense that moral judgments can be contradictory; for explications do not try to respect our intuitive beliefs. But this answer is equally open to a subjectivist who offers an explication.

Stevenson's conception of analysis, therefore, seems to present him with a dilemma. On the one hand, he needs it to answer the cognitivist's objection that emotivism does not capture the meaning of moral terms. On the other hand, it undermines his arguments against objectivist naturalism (which he rejects by appeal to the Open Question Argument) and against subjectivist naturalism (which he rejects by appeal to contradiction). The conception of analysis that answers objections to non-cognitivism also undermines arguments for non-cognitivism.

1304. Can Stevenson Do Without Moore?

If Stevenson's conditions for an acceptable analysis conflict with his acceptance of Moore's Open Question Argument, how should he make his position consistent? It might seem difficult for him to do without Moore's argument; for he takes it so seriously that he incorporates it among his conditions of adequacy for an analysis.[39] But does he accept more of Moore than he needs to? He cites Moore's argument to show that ethics cannot be an empirical science and that ethical questions cannot be wholly settled by the methods of empirical sciences. If he abandons this as a condition of adequacy, he is left with the first two conditions: the possibility of disagreement, and 'magnetism'.

We have seen that emotivism does no better than subjectivism in explaining disagreement, and it clearly does less well than objectivism. Hence Stevenson would apparently be well advised not to rest his case for emotivism on his first condition of adequacy, and would

---

[38] See Mill, *U* 5.17: 'I conceive that the sentiment itself does not arise from anything which would commonly, or correctly, be termed an idea of expediency; but that though the sentiment does not, whatever is moral in it does'.

[39] See also *EL* 272 on Moore.

apparently lose nothing by abandoning the first condition. Should he, then, rely exclusively on the second condition?

He argues that he can deal with the demand for magnetism better than any cognitivist accounts do. Hence he does not seem to need his third (anti-naturalist) condition in order to defend his analysis. Moreover, if emotivism satisfies the second condition, it will satisfy the third also, without any obvious appeal to Moore's Open Question Argument. For, in his view, the magnetism condition by itself implies that ethics cannot be an empirical science. Since moral judgments have their distinctive emotive meaning, they do not follow from, and are not inductively supported by, the factual judgments that could belong to an empirical science.[40]

If Stevenson's position is revised in this way, it avoids any appeal to arguments—such as the Open Question Argument—that are irrelevant to the correctness of an explication. He holds a consistent position if he relies exclusively on his second condition of adequacy, requiring us to explain the 'magnetism' of moral judgments. He rests his case on Hume's claim about the practical character of moral judgments; but he revises Hume by drawing a non-cognitivist rather than a subjectivist conclusion. How, then, does he explain his demand for magnetism, and how does he think emotivism satisfies it?

1305. The 'Magnetism' of Moral Judgments

The demand for magnetism involves a connexion between one's making a moral judgment and one's own motivation.[41] The connexion is not an empirical tendency for one's views about whether this or that action is good to affect one's tendency to favour or to reject the action. Stevenson accepts Hume's internalist claim that it is part of the meaning of moral judgments that they influence the agent towards action. But elsewhere he changes the metaphor that expresses his internalism. Instead of speaking of the 'magnetism' of 'goodness', he speaks of 'contagion'; moral judgments tend to move other people, as well as oneself, to favour an action.[42]

Here Stevenson accepts a different internalist claim from Hume's. Hume thinks primarily of the influence of my moral judgments on my actions, and so identifies them with reports of my feelings, which directly influence my action. Stevenson, however, accepts an internal connexion between my judgments and your motivation. He asks how A's telling B 'Your action will cause suffering to innocent people' differs from A's telling B 'Since your action will cause suffering to innocent people, it is wrong'. His questions about moral judgments are about utterances of them in specific communicative contexts.[43]

---

[40] '...empirical grounds are not inductive grounds from which the ethical judgment problematically follows. (This is what traditional interest theories imply.) If someone said "close the door", and added the reason "we'll catch cold", the latter would scarcely be called an inductive ground of the former. Now imperatives are related to the reasons which support them in the same way that ethical judgments are related to reasons.' (FV 28)

[41] 'A person who recognizes X to be "good" must ipso facto acquire a stronger tendency to act in its favour than he otherwise would have had.' (FV 13) A lot depends on 'ipso facto' here.

[42] '...the *contagion* of warmly expressed approval, the interaction of attitudes that makes each man's favourable evaluation strengthen and invigorate the other's.' (EL 22)

[43] See EL, ch. 3.

If Stevenson took the contagion of moral judgments to be an empirical feature of them, analyses that he rejects might account for it. Objectivists may appeal to the content of moral judgments to explain why we normally take our own moral judgments seriously and want other people to share them. Subjectivists may point out that my report of my favourable feeling towards an action often, in the right circumstances, encourages other people to share it. If we take moral judgments to report the reactions of ideal observers, we can try to explain why we tend to be affected by the reactions of such imaginary people. If Stevenson rejects these proposed explanations of contagion, he should not take contagion to be an empirical characteristic of moral judgments. He must be an internalist on this point too. If internalism is correct, we can reject all theories that imply that it is logically possible for a genuine moral judgment not to be contagious.

He does not argue at length for internalism about contagion. He considers this case: (1) We tell A that what he did was wrong. (2) A says he agrees it was wrong. (3) A adds that because it was wrong he will do it again.[44] Stevenson suggests that one way to make sense of (2) is to suppose that by 'wrong' A means 'conventionally but erroneously thought wrong'. But even under this interpretation of (2), we would (in his view) reject A's claim to be agreeing with us, since we were trying to secure agreement in attitude to the action.

Stevenson agrees that we can use factual judgments as means of changing attitudes. Though we use them for this purpose, they still state a fact; a tendency to change attitudes is no part of their meaning. We can see this by noticing that they still mean the same even when they are not used to change attitudes. If the sign, 'It rains every day in Manchester' appears in the window of an umbrella shop in Manchester, it might be used to persuade people to buy umbrellas. But a meteorologist who said this in answer to a question about the weather in Manchester would not be trying to persuade anyone. Still, the sign in the umbrella shop and the meteorologist would mean the very same thing. By contrast, if Stevenson is right to say that moral judgments are internally related to contagion, their persuasive use is inseparable from their meaning.

To see whether the emotivist is right, we should ask two questions: (1) Can we use moral terms without an actual or intended persuasive effect? (2) Have they a different meaning in these cases? Stevenson answers Yes to both questions. In some cases, 'the ethical terms are practically devoid of any emotive *effects*' (*EL* 83), but we are not using the ethical terms in their normal sense.[45] We may treat 'good' (for instance) as having the same use as 'usually approved' or 'approved in some society' (as in 'Infanticide was good in Sparta') (84).[46] Cases of cancellation such as 'I approve of this, but it is bad', may sometimes be interpreted as 'I approve of this, but my elders abuse me for doing so' (96).

---

[44] 'Suppose that we are trying to convince a man that something he did was wrong. He replies: "I fully agree that it was, and for that very reason I am all the more in favour of doing it over again." Temporarily puzzled to understand him, we shall be likely to conclude, "This is his paradoxical way of abusing what he considers our outworn moral conventions..." But whatever we may make of his meaning... we shall scarcely take seriously his protestations of agreement. Were we not trying all along to make him disapprove of his action? Would not his ethical agreement with us require that he share our disfavour—that he agree with us in *attitude*?' (*EL* 16–17)

[45] Cf. Ayer, *LTL* 105–6.

[46] Here ethical terms 'are used in contexts that are not emotionally active' and 'such contexts require no further attention' (84).

Whenever such interpretations are not plausible, Stevenson believes that the judgment that includes the cancelling clause is self-contradictory.[47] If we deny that it is self-contradictory, we must be thinking of a different sense of the ethical terms. Since moral judgments change their meaning when they are not used in persuasive contexts, but ordinary factual judgments keep their meaning, the persuasive use of moral judgments is part of their meaning.

Stevenson's use of 'approve' here may complicate the question. We might take approval to involve something more than a favourable attitude; we might take it to include the belief that something deserves to be favoured. In that case, our claiming to approve of x while rejecting the included belief would be self-contradictory. But Stevenson understands 'approval', so that it simply refers to a favourable attitude. When we keep this in mind, it is not at all obvious that 'x is bad, but I approve of x' is self-contradictory.[48]

1306. Moore's Criticism of Stevenson

Moore raises some helpful questions about magnetism, in his reply to Stevenson's discussion of Moore's non-naturalism. Moore considers the version of emotivism that analyses 'It was right of Brutus to stab Caesar' as 'I approve of Brutus's action: do approve of it too!', so that it is partly autobiographical.[49] He suggests that the autobiographical element in the analysis confuses the meaning of what we say with what we imply in saying it. If we say 'It's raining', we imply that we believe that it is raining, but we do not assert that we believe it. The fact that we can normally infer that you believe that p from your asserting that p reflects the proper relation of belief and assertion; you should assert what you believe, and believe what you take to be true. If I accept this norm about assertion and belief, and I believe that you believe I accept it, I imply that I believe it is raining when I assert that it is raining, but I do not assert that I believe it is raining. Similarly, one ought to desire what one thinks good; hence we can normally assume that if you think something good you desire it, since we assume that you are rational and desire what you ought to desire. For corresponding reasons, I may imply that I desire something when I say that it is good. Still, I do not say that I desire it, and my statement does not mean that I desire it. If, then, I say that what Brutus did was right, I imply that I approve it, but I do not say so.

Moore's comparison with assertion and belief makes his claim about approval even more plausible than he takes it to be. One might say that belief is internally connected to asserting to be true, so that it would be contradictory to say 'I know that it isn't true, but I can't help believing it'. In such cases, I might have a powerful illusion or appearance; 'I know it isn't true, but I can't help its looking that way' is quite intelligible. Desire, however, is not internally connected to thinking good in the same way (pace Socrates), since not all desire is rational. Hence 'I know it's bad, but I want to do it none the less' is parallel not to 'I know

[47] 'But if his tone of voice permits no such interpretation, we shall, no doubt be bewildered at the man's deliberate efforts to contradict himself . . . [He] has affirmed both his unqualified approval and his unqualified disapproval of the same measure. It can be of no service to ethics to insist that "I approve of X and X is bad" is *always* a contradiction—as the alternative interpretations above will show; but it lends itself to that interpretation unless explanatory remarks are made.' (*EL* 97) By 'alternative interpretations' Stevenson means 'usually approved', and so on.

[48] Ewing, *DG* 9; Pitcher, 'On approval', 210–11, notice the ambiguity in 'approval'.　　　[49] Moore, 'Reply', 542–3.

it isn't true, but I still believe it', but to 'I know it's harmless but it still looks dangerous'. Reflexion on Moore's example suggests that the connexion between goodness and approval is only typical, rather than universal, and that we can use 'good' in exactly the same sense without conveying approval.

Stevenson accepts Moore's objection to the autobiographical element in the emotivist analysis, and abandons it, retaining only the imperative element (*FV* 210–14). In Moore's view, the version of emotivism that includes only the imperative element and eliminates the autobiographical element is more plausible than the version that includes both elements. He is inclined to believe—though also inclined to reject—the purely imperative version ('Reply', 554).

1307. Hare's Criticism of Stevenson

Moore's restraint in criticizing Stevenson may be historically significant, since it may have encouraged others to agree with Stevenson's view that emotivism meets Moore's objection by simply dropping the autobiographical element in the analysis. Moore does not dispute Stevenson's account of the non-autobiographical element. Stevenson speaks of magnetism, persuasion, and influence. Moore follows him in treating all these as equivalent to an imperative analysis. To see some of the questions that arise about this element of the analysis, it is useful to introduce Hare's objections.

Stevenson treats imperatives as devices for changing other people's attitudes; he does not distinguish the view that moral judgments are imperative from the view that they have emotive meaning.[50] According to Hare, Stevenson wrongly assimilates the activity of prescribing or commending to the activity of persuading.[51] They are different activities; to issue an imperative is to tell someone to do something, but it need not lead to an attempt to get him to do it.

To express this difference between imperatives and attempts to persuade, Hare introduces Austin's distinction between locutionary, illocutionary, and perlocutionary acts. Roughly, the locutionary act is what we say, the illocutionary act is what we do in saying it, and the perlocutionary act is what we achieve as a result of saying it.[52] An illocutionary act is performed simply by saying the right thing in the right context, irrespective of any effect we produce in other people, whereas the perlocutionary act is performed only when our saying something has the relevant effect.

Commands are illocutionary acts, whereas persuasion secures compliance with a command, and is a perlocutionary act. Imperatives are connected with action, in so far as compliance with an imperative is an action. But an imperative may be issued even if no one

---

[50] 'It is easy to see, therefore, why the so called "imperative theory" of moral judgments raised the protests that it did. Because based on a misconception of the function, not only of moral judgments but also of the commands to which they were being assimilated, it seemed to impugn the rationality of moral discourse.' (Hare, *LM* 15)

[51] 'The processes of *telling* someone to do something, and *getting* him to do it, are quite distinct, logically, from each other . . . we must first tell someone what to do, and then, if he is not disposed to do what we say, we may start on the wholly different task of trying to get him to do it.' (*LM* 13–14)

[52] Austin introduces these distinctions in *HDTW* 94–104. See Hare, *SOE* 50–1, 109–10. Hare, 'Austin's distinction', raises doubts about some of Austin's claims.

complies with it, and even if we do not try to make anyone comply with it. We succeed in commanding if we say the right thing in the right conditions; 'right thing' and 'right conditions' are defined without reference to an attempt to secure compliance or success in securing compliance. Whether or not we use the command in any attempt to secure compliance, and whether or not we succeed in any attempt, we may perform the act of commanding.

If, then, moral judgments are imperatives, they are illocutionary acts that we perform by saying the right thing in the right context. But if they are essentially attempts to persuade, they try to produce a particular effect in the hearer, so that they require more than our saying the right thing in the right context. If they are persuasive devices, they consist in perlocutionary acts or attempts at them.

Hare observes that many ordinary and intelligible moral judgments cannot be construed as attempts to persuade. Suppose that Albert has been conscripted into the army, but has pacifist tendencies. Albert asks Bill, 'Ought I to serve in the army?', and Bill answers, 'Yes, you ought'. Bill need not be trying to get Albert to change his mind, and Albert need not take Bill to be trying to do this. As Hare understands the case, Albert 'asked for advice, not influence or inducement' (Hare, *SOE* 113), and Bill may give advice without attempting to influence Albert to take the advice. In this case, the frequent persuasive use of moral judgments is cancelled; hence the persuasive use is not essential to their being moral judgments.

1308. Implications of Moore's and Hare's Objections

It is useful to consider Moore and Hare together, since their arguments suggest that they might reasonably have gone further than they actually go in their criticisms. Why, for instance, does Moore not think his objection to the autobiographical clause of Stevenson's analysis applies equally to the other clause? Perhaps he thinks that the first-person element in Stevenson's analysis is a statement, and so can be studied by considering another case where a statement (I believe it's raining) can be implied, though not meant when we make another statement (it's raining). If Moore takes the point to apply strictly to statements, perhaps he does not think it can be extended to the second-person element, which is strictly non-cognitive.

Hare's argument, however, suggests a plausible extension of Moore's argument. For though Hare introduces Austin's distinctions to state his objection, his basic point repeats Moore's distinction between what my utterance means, and what it may imply, or may be used to convey. Given the first-person connexion between thinking good and rationally wanting, it is easy to see how we can convey that we want something by saying it is good. We convey or imply an attitude, not some further belief or judgment or statement. To suppose that you are conveying your wants through your judgments about what is good, I need to assume that you think of yourself as rational. Similarly, if I think you regard me as rational, I will assume (in the right circumstances) that when you tell me that x is good, you are trying to get me to choose x, and you are conveying to me your own favourable attitude to x. This is no reason to say that your attitude or the persuasive effect of your utterance is somehow part of its meaning.

Similarly, we can explain how, when the relevant assumptions do not hold, my judging x good may not express a favourable attitude and may not involve my trying to persuade you. If I believe you do not care about what is good, I will not say that x is good in order to persuade you to favour x. If I believe that you disagree with me so much about what is good that my belief that x is good is likely to turn you against x, I may say that x is good in order to dissuade you from choosing x. If this is so, the way in which the judgment that x is good may be persuasive is similar to the ways in which other factual judgments may be persuasive. We need not attach different senses to 'good' in these different cases.

Moore's and Hare's criticisms suggest that we can explain the persuasive use of moral judgments and still reject Stevenson's claim that they have persuasive meaning, and therefore are not factual judgments. If we believe that A will be killed if he walks through a minefield, our normal reason for telling him he will be killed if he walks through it is to discourage him from walking through it. If A agreed that he would be killed, and for that very reason wanted to walk through the minefield, A would be suicidal. If A agreed that he would be killed, and none the less wanted to walk through the minefield, A would be indifferent to his safety. In the normal case, we tell A he will be killed because we are trying to make A disapprove of walking through the minefield. But we are trying to do this by securing A's agreement in belief about whether he will be killed; we hope that the change in attitude will follow the agreement in belief. If, however, we know that A does not care about his safety, but A asks us whether he will be killed if he walks through the minefield, and we answer that he will be, he will (if he believes us) agree with us in belief, but not in attitude.

Why, then, should we not say the same about telling A that it would be bad for him to walk through a minefield? If he is indifferent to his safety, he will not take its being bad for him as any reason to avoid walking through the minefield; if he is suicidal, he will taking its being bad for him as a positive reason to do it. But in each case, he seems to agree with our judgment that it is bad for him.

If this argument is plausible, Moore's objection to one part of Stevenson's analysis can be extended, contrary to Moore's intention, to the rest of the analysis. Moreover, when we see the connexion between Moore's argument and Hare's argument, we can see the possibility of extending Hare's argument too. Though Hare intends to attack Stevenson's claim that moral judgments are essentially persuasive, by distinguishing persuading from commanding, his argument seems to cast doubt on an imperative analysis as well. We will need to return to this question in a discussion of Hare.[53]

1309. Emotivism and Meaning

We might reply on Stevenson's behalf that in these cases where the persuasive aspect of an ostensible moral judgment is separable from its meaning, we are using the terms in a non-moral sense; the moral sense of the terms is the essentially persuasive sense. If it seems to us that we use the terms in the same sense whether or not they are used to persuade, we

---

[53] On Hare see §1326.

are wrong. We see we are wrong once we grasp the emotive character of genuine moral judgments.

This would be a legitimate reply, if we had some independent support for an emotivist analysis. This support should not rely on arguments that introduce an emotive sense to explain the persuasive use of moral judgments; for we have found that we do not need a distinct sense to explain this use. If an emotivist analysis rests on no independent support, the claim that the moral sense of terms is essentially persuasive seems to be an arbitrary stipulation about the sense of 'moral'.

Stevenson, however, believes he has independent support for an emotive theory. Our arguments against his treatment of 'non-standard' cases (those in which he assumes a change of sense) have appealed to cases where we can point to a descriptive meaning (as in 'It's going to rain'). Stevenson might agree that if we could also find an appropriate descriptive meaning for 'good', we could hold that this descriptive meaning is common to persuasive and non-persuasive contexts of utterance. But he claims that we cannot find a common descriptive meaning for 'good'. Moore showed (according to Stevenson) that we cannot give its meaning in naturalistic terms. If we agree with Moore and we still believe that 'good' has a descriptive meaning, we have to be non-naturalist intuitionists, and so commit ourselves to an unacceptable epistemology and metaphysics. Since we cannot plausibly recognize a common descriptive meaning, we must accept the emotivist analysis that postulates different senses of 'good' in persuasive and non-persuasive contexts. Even if this appeal to different senses seems initially implausible, it is preferable to either of the positions—naturalism and intuitionism—that we are forced into if we look for a common descriptive meaning.

We can now see more clearly why Stevenson cannot do without Moore's Open Question Argument. We wondered whether he might rely entirely on his first two conditions of adequacy: possibility of contradiction, and magnetism (including contagion). But he does not vindicate his claims about magnetism and contagion; he does not show that these belong to the meaning of moral judgments, because he does not argue effectively for the internal connexions that he asserts. To answer this objection, Stevenson has to argue that the Open Question Argument rules out the cognitivist alternatives to emotivism.[54] If we have an argument, relying on Moore and independent of internalism, for an emotive analysis of 'good', we have a reason for accepting internalism, and for treating apparent counter-examples as peripheral cases that do not undermine the emotivist's claim about the central meaning of 'good'. Stevenson does not rely on magnetism and contagion to provide an independent argument for emotivism; he relies on them simply as the best explanation of the success of the Open Question Argument.

---

[54] According to Stevenson, Moore sees that all naturalistic analyses of 'good' fail because they do not capture 'an added factor which the purely scientific analyses of ethics are accustomed to ignore' (EL 272). This factor is the emotive meaning, which Moore 'has intellectualized . . . into an indefinable *quality*' (272). We can sum up Stevenson's argument as follows: (1) Moore's Open Question Argument proves that goodness cannot be a natural property. (2) But (contrary to Moore) there are no non-natural properties. (3) Therefore Moore proves that goodness is not a property. (4) Therefore 'good' cannot have purely cognitive meaning. (5) If its meaning is not purely cognitive, it must be emotive. (6) Hence the meaning of 'good' is emotive. This argument needs to be formulated in different ways, to take account of Stevenson's different views about whether the meaning of 'good' is partly autobiographical (and therefore partly cognitive).

1310. The Inadequacy of an Emotivist Analysis

To see how far Stevenson needs to rely on the Open Question Argument, we may consider a further objection to his account of moral judgments as persuasive devices. So far we have considered reasons for believing that persuasion (or intent to persuade) is not necessary for a moral judgment. But even if we conceded that it is necessary, we might still doubt whether it is sufficient. If the expression and communication of emotion is necessary and sufficient for moral judgments, this emotive element is all that moral judgments add to the factual statements on the basis of which the emotion is expressed. But if we compare moral judgments with conventionally accepted signs of expressing emotion—tones of voice, exclamations, exclamatory words ('Boo!'), and so on, they seem to include something that the mere exclamation itself leaves out.

If, then, we say that my moral judgment simply indicates that I have a favourable or unfavourable feeling about the action, we have not distinguished moral judgments from other means of expressing emotion. For I might express an unfavourable attitude to your stealing because it is dangerous for you and for some reason I care about your interests, or because it is inconvenient for me, or because I have some snobbish disdain for the practice of stealing small sums of money. Again I might express an unfavourable reaction to killing simply because the sight of blood (as a result of killing or surgery) makes me feel sick. If I state a fact and express favourable or unfavourable feelings about it, I do not necessarily say anything about the nature of the feelings.

A moral judgment, however, seems to imply something about the specific character of my feelings. If I simply found your theft inconvenient to me, or I simply felt queasy at the sight of the blood resulting from someone's being killed, I would not thereby have made any moral judgment. Hume sees this point clearly when he seeks to identify the specific sentiment that is characteristic of the moral point of view.[55] Similarly, Ayer does not say that a moral judgment serves to express just any favourable or unfavourable feeling. He argues that the judgment evinces my 'moral disapproval', and that it is equivalent to 'a peculiar tone of horror', or to the addition of 'special exclamation marks'; it shows that the utterance of the sentence is accompanied by 'certain feelings' in the speaker.[56] He may mean that moral judgments essentially express a special, and specifically moral, type of approval, not just any old approval.

What is special about the moral kind of approval? An emotive theory cannot easily answer this question.[57] For if the expressive function of moral judgments is only one essential aspect of them, and if the moral judgment asserts or implies that our reaction rests on some further basis, the theorist needs to describe the further basis. Since the emotive theorist does not describe it, emotivism does not capture the nature of moral judgments. Though we

---

[55] Hume on moral sentiment; §§761–2.

[56] 'Thus if I say to someone, "You acted wrongly in stealing that money", I am not stating anything more than if I had simply said, "You stole that money". In adding that this action is wrong I am not making any further statement about it, I am simply evincing my moral disapproval of it. It is as if I had said, "You stole that money", in a particular tone of horror, or written it with the addition of some special exclamation marks. The tone, or the exclamation marks, adds nothing to the literal meaning of the expression. It merely serves to show that the expression of it is attended by certain feelings in the speaker.' (Ayer, *LTL* 107)

[57] This objection is clearly presented by Ross, *FE* 34. It is developed by Hare; see §1326.

might have thought that acceptance of an emotive element in moral judgment undermines cognitivism, the opposite seems to be true; for in order to say what is special about moral emotion, we need to appeal to some underlying claim about the sorts of facts that make the emotion appropriate.

Stevenson has an answer ready for this objection. He might legitimately point out that it rests on our pre-analytic concept of a moral judgment. Since he offers an analysis that does not necessarily accept the pre-analytic concept, we should not be surprised if it seems to deprive moral judgments of some feature that we confusedly thought they had. We were confused in thinking that some moral fact gave us a reason for our emotion, because the Open Question Argument assures us that there are no moral facts. Our sense of the inadequacy of the emotive analysis rests on our failure to see the implications of Moore's refutation of cognitivism. Though Moore thought he was only refuting naturalism, the faults in non-naturalist cognitivism rule out all cognitivist accounts.

1311. Emotivism and Analytic Truth

But if Stevenson defends his emotivism in this way by appeal to the Open Question Argument, he faces the difficulty that we raised earlier. For his conception of analysis seems to be inconsistent with reliance on the Open Question Argument, since the Open Question Argument is irrelevant to proposed analyses. An example of this difficulty appears in his defence of internalism and emotive meaning. He claims that it is analytically true that moral judgments are attempts to persuade. But this claim about analytic truth seems to create an open question, since it does not seem contradictory to affirm that we have made a moral judgment and to deny that we have any desire to act on it or to persuade others to act on it. To show that the Open Question Argument is inapplicable, Stevenson must assume that there are non-obvious analytic truths; if there are such truths, the fact that an alleged analytic truth creates an open question does not show that it is not an analytic truth.

It is not only Stevenson who seems to endorse both the Open Question Argument and a conception of analytic truth that rules out reliance on the Open Question Argument. Ayer's discussion of analytic truth makes it clear that the emotivist faces a difficult choice. On the one hand, Ayer goes even further than Moore in his use of the Open Question Argument. On the other hand, he seems to argue implicitly against appeals to the Open Question Argument.

Ayer claims that Moore's argument refutes a utilitarian theory of moral properties. He assumes, therefore, that one ought to argue against an account of a property by appealing to intuitions about what is self-contradictory.[58] Since he thinks it is clear without argument

---

[58] 'We cannot agree that to call an action right is to say that of all the actions possible in the circumstances it would cause, or be likely to cause, the greatest happiness, or the greatest balance of pleasure over pain, or the greatest balance of satisfied over unsatisfied desire, because we find that it is not self-contradictory to say that it is sometimes wrong to perform the action which would actually or probably cause the greatest happiness, or the greatest balance of pleasure over pain, or of satisfied over unsatisfied desires . . . And to every other variant of utilitarianism with which I am acquainted the same objection can be made. And therefore we should, I think, conclude that the validity of ethical judgments is not determined by the felicific tendencies of actions, . . . but that it must be regarded as "absolute" or "intrinsic", and not empirically calculable.' (Ayer, *LTL* 104–5)

that the rejection of conceptual utilitarianism is not self-contradictory, he follows Moore in believing that the relevant intuitions are immediate intuitions, recording our initial impression of obvious contradiction.

Ayer goes further than Moore in his claims about what the Open Question Argument can establish. He suggests that it refutes utilitarianism, considered as a theory of the 'validity' of ethical judgments. Moore is careful not to suggest this; for he recognizes that Sidgwick is not a conceptual utilitarian, and that the truth of utilitarianism does not depend on the truth of conceptual utilitarianism. To refute utilitarianism, we need to show not merely that it is not self-contradictory for a non-optimific action to be right, but that some such actions are right; hence we need to rely on intuitive moral judgments. Moore believes that these judgments support utilitarianism. Ayer relies only on immediate judgments about what is self-contradictory.[59] These do not seem to refute utilitarianism; for a cautious utilitarian, such as Sidgwick, does not claim that utilitarianism cannot be denied without self-contradiction.

But even if Ayer attacks only conceptual utilitarianism, his argument is open to question. Utilitarians might maintain that it is indeed self-contradictory to claim that an action is right but does not maximize utility, but we do not see this if we rely on our uninstructed intuitive judgments about what is self-contradictory. If the utilitarian is allowed this reply, Ayer's argument collapses. If further reflexion about the concept of right or good is allowed before we decide what is or is not consistent, it might or might not favour utilitarianism. But its mere possibility would undermine Ayer's claim to have refuted utilitarianism. He answers this objection only if he admits immediate judgments about analyticity as decisive evidence in arguments about the nature of a given concept.[60]

In fact, however, Ayer endorses a wider conception of analytic truth. He introduces this wider conception in answering Ewing's attack on the logical empiricist claim that all a priori truths are analytic.[61] Ewing argues that in some cases 'p entails q' is true a priori even though 'q' is not part of the meaning of 'p'. Ayer replies that Ewing has no genuine counter-examples, because he conceives meaning too narrowly. In Ayer's view of the 'meaning' of a sentence, it is analytic that what the sentence entails is part of its meaning.[62] Since not all entailments are obvious, not all truths of meaning are obvious.[63]

This wide conception of analytic truth and conceptual truth allows an emotivist a possible defence of the claim that moral judgments have emotive meaning. For the mere fact that it seems consistent to make a moral judgment while cancelling its emotive use does not

[59] Moral judgments are already open to suspicion, from the logical empiricist point of view; and so arguments that assume the reliability of some moral judgments inherit the suspicions attached to moral judgments in the first place.

[60] This objection to Ayer is presented clearly by Smith, *MP* 36–9. He does not discuss Ayer's broader conception of analytic truth.

[61] Ayer, *LTL* 17–18. Ayer responds to Ewing, 'Linguistic theory', esp. 221–8.

[62] 'If you say . . . that *q* is not part of the meaning of *p* if it is possible to understand *p* without thinking of *q*, then clearly one proposition can entail another without containing it as part of its meaning; for it can hardly be maintained that anyone who considers a given set of propositions must be immediately conscious of all that they entail. This is, however, to make a point with which I do not think that any upholder of the analytic view of entailment would wish to disagree . . . The answer is that they are using a criterion of meaning, . . . from which it follows that when one proposition entails another the meaning of the second is contained in that of the first.' (*LTL* 18)

[63] Bennett appeals at length to unobviously analytic truths in order to reject candidates for synthetic a priori truths. See *KA* 4–12.

show—according to the wider conception of analytic truth—that it is consistent. The emotivist might try to show that it is unobviously analytic that moral judgments are magnetic and contagious.

But Ayer does not explain how he can both affirm this wide conception of analytic truth and accept the Open Question Argument, which presupposes a narrower conception. If entailment determines meaning, not all analytic truths are trivial and obvious. But now utilitarians are free to claim—for all Moore and Ayer show—that it is non-obviously analytic that whatever is right maximizes utility. Ewing is right to argue that Ayer does not always accept the wide conception of analytic truth.

The emotive theory, therefore, faces a dilemma. If emotivists accept a narrow conception of analytic truth (so that its denial is obviously self-contradictory), they cannot show that it is part of the meaning of moral judgments that they express emotions; for it is not obviously self-contradictory to speak of a moral judgment separated from any expression of emotion. If, however, they accept a wide enough conception of analyticity to disarm this first objection, they cannot accept Moore's argument against naturalism, and so they have no reason to accept an emotive rather than a cognitive conception of moral judgments.

This internal conflict in the emotivist position would not matter if we could defend emotivism from internalism alone, without appeal to non-naturalism. But we have found that the case for internalism is too weak to bear the weight of non-cognitivism. Emotivism needs support from Moore's Open Question Argument. But Moore's argument relies on a conception of definition that is implausible in itself and inconsistent with the views of analytic truth that support internalism.

1312. Does Emotivism Discredit Morality?

Now that we have seen what emotivists are committed to, we can try to understand the objection that emotivism tends to 'discredit ethics'.[64] Stevenson and Ayer believe that the objection is unfair. To see whether they are right, we need to consider different ways in which one might 'discredit' ethics. For the objection they answer may not be the one that their opponents intend.

We might say that a practice has been discredited if people engage in it less often than they used to. In that case, we can decide whether someone has discredited the practice if we examine the behaviour of the appropriate people. If this is all there is to discrediting, an emotivist need only show that emotivists behave in roughly the same way as non-emotivists do. Stevenson may have this behavioural test in mind when he discusses the claim that emotivism discredits ethics. He argues that his views do not require us to value morality less than we otherwise would; for the acceptance of emotivism is consistent with taking moral rightness seriously in certain ways.[65] Someone may consistently accept emotivism

---

[64] Ross makes this remark at *FE* 38, where he describes Stevenson's emotivism as 'the latest attempt to discredit ethics'.

[65] 'The criticisms that have been levelled against these [sc. emotivist] views have shown more impatience than understanding. They have usually assumed that an emotive analysis represents an effort to "discredit ethics"—and

and try to avoid cruelty, greed, or cowardice. These observations show that an emotivist can consistently value moral rightness and the moral virtues.

But this answer does not settle all the relevant questions. For emotivists may stick to their old moral behaviour simply through force of habit or irrational attachment. If that is the explanation, their behaviour does not show that emotivism does not discredit ethics. For we can discredit something without changing our own or anyone else's behaviour, if we show that what we took to be a good reason for accepting it is really not a good reason. We might, then, discredit morality without holding a theoretical view that logically excludes any favourable attitude to morally right behaviour. If we undermine reasons that we thought we had for caring about morality, we may discredit it without being hostile to it.

If, therefore, we think we have a good reason to care about morality because we think moral considerations about actions give us good objective reasons, based on the features of the actions themselves, for avoiding some actions and doing others, emotivism deprives us of the good reason that we think we have, and to this extent discredits morality. If we think moral considerations have something more to be said for them than mere expressions of emotion would have, a theory that reduces moral judgments to expressions of emotion discredits morality. Stevenson does not answer this objection.

He might fairly point out that he does not maintain that ethical judgments ought to be made capriciously. If he believes they ought not to be made capriciously, he will (on his view) try to influence people not to make them capriciously. But it is not clear how far he can capture the relevant idea of a non-capricious judgment. We might think that a non-capricious judgment should be taken more seriously because we form it after a full review of the facts; emotivism allows non-capricious moral judgments of this sort. But 'after a full review' does not quite capture what we take to be important about reflective judgments. Suppose I review all the facts about sitting and standing now, and I find the only difference between them is that my standing will make no difference to anyone, whereas my sitting will cause my death and yours. If I now judge that I ought to sit down, my judgment results from this full review of the facts, and so it meets Stevenson's condition for being non-capricious. But we may still find it capricious; for we believe that non-capricious judgments are based on the relevant facts, Hence we cannot identify a non-capricious judgment until we identify the relevant facts and we recognize the reasons that they give for our moral judgment.

This assumption about a rational basis for non-capricious judgment has no place in the purely temporal and causal sequences that Stevenson recognizes. Since our intuitive views about moral reasons have no place in Stevenson's analysis, it is not as unfair as he claims it is to conclude that emotivism removes the reasons we thought we had for making moral judgments, and therefore undermines a reason that we thought we had for taking morality seriously.

---

indeed that very phrase was used even by so astute a critic as W. D. Ross . . . To compare ethical judgments to imperatives is not to deny that imperatives have an important use. To say that ethical judgments express feelings is not to imply that all feelings are to be inhibited. To say that ethical judgments are "neither true nor false" is not to maintain . . . that they are to be made capriciously, in ignorance of one's self, or the nature and consequences of the object judged.' (*EL* 266)

1313. Does it Matter if Emotivism Discredits Morality?

Stevenson does not say whether he thinks it would matter if emotivist meta-ethics really did tend to discredit morality. Would this be a reason for rejecting emotivism? Stevenson does not answer this question. His defence of emotivism might suggest that he agrees with his opponents' view that if emotivism discredited morality, it ought to be rejected. But he might not agree with their view. He might simply want to rebut this charge that would be embarrassing if true. It need not imply that immoral consequences are relevant to the assessment of emotivism.

Hume considers the objection that Stevenson considers, but he takes a more definite position. He argues that it is always wrong to assess the truth of a philosophical theory by considering its implications for morality.[66] Ayer takes a similar view about emotivism. He considers the empirical question about whether people who accept emotivism are in fact more likely to act immorally. His answer to the empirical question is No, but he denies that the question is even relevant to judgments about the truth of emotivism.[67]

Neither Hume nor Ayer answers the more interesting question about discrediting, since they consider only the behavioural consequences of accepting a philosophical theory. We might ask them: would it matter if emotivism undermined our reasons for taking morality seriously? They seem to answer No. For they do not try to rebut the suggestion that emotivism would undermine these reasons, and they do not suggest that their failure to rebut the suggestion counts against the truth of emotivism. We may fairly presume that they take all such considerations to be irrelevant to the truth of emotivism.

Hume and Ayer seem to go too far. They would be right to argue that the undermining effect of emotivism on morality is not a sufficient reason for rejecting emotivism. But why should we infer that this effect is entirely irrelevant? If we test a theory by comparing its implications with the other convictions that we take to be reasonable, it seems arbitrary to isolate a meta-ethical theory from comparison with our reasonable moral convictions.

This holist attitude to justification may be unwelcome to logical empiricists. Perhaps moral judgments are suspect until they can be shown to meet empiricist conditions for significance. If they cannot meet these conditions, we should not assume their truth or rationality when we assess a philosophical analysis. And so, if emotivism has immoral implications, they cannot rationally matter to emotivists who are also logical empiricists. They might feel some emotional regret, as moral agents, but they have no philosophical grounds for taking any rational account of that regret.

Willingness to suspend judgment about intuitive moral beliefs contrasts with the non-sceptical attitude of logical empiricists to the truths of common sense and natural science about the physical world. If logical empiricists are convinced that their principle of significance implies that all the statements of common sense and science about material objects are

---

[66] See Hume, T ii 3.2.3, quoted and discussed in §783.

[67] 'If it could be shown, as I believe it could not, that the general acceptance of the sort of analysis of moral judgments that I have been putting forward would have unhappy social consequences, the conclusion drawn by illiberal persons might be that the doctrine ought to be kept secret. For my part I think that I should dispute this conclusion on moral grounds, but this is a question which I am not now concerned to discuss. What I have tried to show is not that the theory I am defending is expedient, but that it is true.' (Ayer, 'Analysis', 249).

purely metaphysical and therefore meaningless, they normally take that to be a reason for trying to revise their principle of significance.[68] They do not take their initial formulation of a principle of significance as an axiom to be maintained at all costs; they are willing to expose it to some kinds of holist arguments. But they are unwilling to argue in the same way about ethics. Hence their application of empiricist criteria to natural science and to ethics is controlled by an initial presumption against ethics and in favour of natural science.

Why should we suspend belief in all our moral judgments while we examine the emotivists' arguments? If we are told that the general plausibility of logical empiricism justifies a sceptical attitude to ethics, we may wonder why it is fair to claim to have established the general plausibility of logical empiricism without thinking about ethics. For if ethics provides a striking counter-example to the plausibility of logical empiricism, a favourable presumption of sufficient generality has not been established. Hence we have no reason to accept Hume's maxim or to apply it to emotivism; it is fair to consider the consequences of a theory for morality in considering whether to accept the theory.

Meta-ethical theories do not necessarily leave moral beliefs unaffected. Equally, moral implications of a meta-ethical theory may be relevant to questions about its truth or plausibility. We need not begin from blind acceptance of all our initial moral beliefs; we might reasonably revise our first impressions about what is morally right, and about how a meta-ethical theory might affect our intuitive moral beliefs. Such caution is similar to the caution that is appropriate in testing scientific theories against our initial intuitive convictions. Some of our convictions may be mistaken and open to revision; even whole classes of them may be open to justified suspicion. But we have no reason to believe that our intuitive moral beliefs as a whole are so unreliable or irrelevant that we ought to ignore them in examining a meta-ethical theory.

1314. Emotivism, Scepticism, and Nihilism

We have understood emotivism, as Stevenson and Ayer understand it, as an account of the meaning of moral terms and judgments. As an account of meaning, it is an attempt to answer the question that Moore answered in his account of goodness. Measured by this standard, it is open to objection. We have noticed, however, that Stevenson sometimes suggests a different conception of his task. He implies that an analysis might fail his test of functional equivalence because the analysandum presupposes the truth of some indefensible cognitivist and realist assumptions. He does not infer that emotivism may be an incorrect analysis of moral concepts and judgments; hence he does not ask whether emotivism might be defended on other grounds even if it must be rejected as an account of meaning.

The question that Stevenson implicitly raises recalls the choice that Hume sometimes faces between a reductive conclusion and a sceptical or nihilist conclusion. A reductive conclusion on causation says that there are causes and effects and they are simply constant

---

[68] See, e.g., Hempel, *ASE*, ch. 2. When Hempel points out that a proposed criterion of significance would rule out a certain type of sentence, he continues: 'And since sentences of this type constitute an integral part of scientific theories, the verifiability requirement must be regarded as overly restricted in this respect' (105). A similar criterion is presupposed at 110–11, 121.

conjunctions; since we are right to believe in constant conjunctions, we are right to believe in causation. A sceptical conclusion says that causation is something more than constant conjunction, and that, since we do not know whether there is anything more than constant conjunction, we do not know whether there is causation, so that our ordinary belief is unjustified. A nihilist conclusion says that causation is more than constant conjunction, and that, since there is nothing more than constant conjunction, there is no causation.

Hume seems to face a similar choice between different conclusions that he might draw from his account of moral judgments. He says that when you pronounce an action or character to be vicious, 'you mean nothing but' that you have some sentiment towards it (T iii 1.1.26).[69] This might be a reductive account of what a moral judgment is. But it might be a sceptical claim that all we are really doing in making a moral judgment is expressing a feeling; since moral judgments purport to do more than express feelings, and we do not know whether they do anything beyond expressing feelings, our moral judgments are unjustified. Or it might be a nihilist claim that, since there is nothing more for moral judgments to do beyond expressing feelings, they are not true. Hume normally treats his account of moral judgments as non-sceptical and non-nihilist, and hence as a reductive view. But one might argue that he sometimes takes a sceptical or nihilist view of his account of causation. Might one take such a view of his account of morality?

These tendencies in Hume suggest a sceptical or nihilist defence of emotivism. We might say that moral judgments include a cognitive element that rests on an unjustified (according to the sceptic) or plainly false (according to the nihilist) belief in moral reality and moral truth. They also include an emotive element, described by an emotive theory. Understood this way, emotivism might be taken as an 'error theory', exposing an error in moral judgments (by rejecting their first element) and describing what is left (in the second element) once the error is recognized.[70]

We might express this version of emotivism as a claim about what moral judgments 'really are' or (to adapt Hume's phrase) 'all that we mean' or 'all that we are talking about' in making moral judgments. Though we may suppose pre-analytically that we are appealing to factual considerations (other than the 'scientific' ones that Stevenson mentions) that give reasons for our attempts to influence other people, we are only trying to influence other people (and perhaps ourselves).

This revised version of emotivism commits its defenders to abandoning Stevenson's and Ayer's claim to be neutral on substantive moral issues. The revised version avowedly rejects some convictions that underlie the ordinary use of moral judgments, and hence it discredits ethics, as the critics of emotivism allege.[71] But it dismisses the objection that emotivism does not fit our moral concepts and judgments; such an objection is irrelevant to a sceptical or nihilist position. Even if emotivism does not capture what we mean, its revised version may capture all that we are entitled to say.

---

[69] Hume on 'meaning'; §§756–7.

[70] The possibility of combining a non-naturalist objectivist conceptual analysis of moral judgments with a sceptical view of their truth is noticed by Ewing, DG 37–8, and by Robinson, 'Emotive theory'. (Ewing 40n mentions Robinson.) Ayer also seems to endorse this view in 'Freedom', 31–3 (he mentions Mackie, but not Robinson). See also MacIntyre, AV 12–13; his alternative interpretation of emotivism is not exactly the same as mine.

[71] For further discussion of discrediting see §1380.

The revision of emotivism does not remove the main defects that provoke criticisms of its adequacy as conceptual analysis. Even if it is not claiming to be conceptual analysis, the revised version is open to adapted versions of the criticisms. Once we understand why it is not plausible to claim that the emotive or persuasive use of moral judgments is part of their meaning, we can also see why it is not plausible to claim that their primary function is emotive or persuasive. In different contexts, moral judgments may have different functions, and if we want to combine a nihilist or a sceptical position with some account of what we do with them, we have no reason to favour the emotivist account.

Revised emotivism retains the original weakness of emotivism; it gives no good reason to concentrate on the communicative contexts that involve attempts to persuade. Stevenson defends this concentration either by appeal to his interpretation of the Open Question Argument or by appeal to internalism about motivation. Both defences rely on conceptual claims of the sort that revised emotivism tries to avoid. Since the relevant conceptual claims are both implausible in themselves and difficult to reconcile with other emotivist claims about analytic truths, they do not help revised emotivism either.

We do not significantly strengthen emotivism, therefore, if we treat it as part of an error theory rather than as reductive conceptual analysis. Sceptics or nihilists who add emotivism as an account of the residue of moral judgments that remains after we set aside indefensible factual claims do not make their position any more plausible. The same basic difficulties face revised emotivism.

Though error theorists have no good reason to be emotivists, it is intelligible that the combination might seem attractive. The view that moral judgments are persuasive devices that we use to influence the feelings and actions of others captures one use of moral judgments. To say that this is all that they do may appear to be a hard-headed, empirical, disillusioned, somewhat cynical view that appeals to people who are afraid of being taken in by high-sounding but empty ideals and slogans. Such people may also insinuate that opponents of emotivism are nostalgic, obscurantist, lacking in analytical clarity, or unscientific, unwilling to face the unvarnished facts. Since these motives may make emotivism seem attractive apart from its intrinsic merits, it is all the more appropriate to recognize the difficulties that confront it.

LEWIS

1315. Lewis as a Naturalist

Lewis is a systematic philosopher. He defends his views in ethics by appeal to the principles that underlie his views in logic, epistemology, and metaphysics. He is an empiricist both about meaning and knowledge. He believes that judgments about objective states of affairs in the world are 'non-terminating judgments'. They must eventually be explained by reference to 'terminating judgments' that are to be understood as predictions of possible experience. The relevant experience consists in apprehensions of what is given in experience. Apprehensions of the given are purely 'expressive'; they do not constitute knowledge, because they are not subject to any possible error (*AKV* 183–4). Statements about them can be false only if one lies about them. They cannot be false because one honestly mis-describes them.

Lewis also holds a characteristically empiricist doctrine about a priori knowledge. He rejects any belief in synthetic a priori truths. But he attaches great importance to analytic truths (379). He denies that they are simply reports of linguistic conventions, and he takes them to be the main objects of philosophical analysis.

These empiricist doctrines underlie Lewis's approach to ethics. He opposes 'naturalism' to 'transcendentalism'. He denies the possibility of synthetic a priori moral truths. In his view, objective moral judgments about the goodness and badness of actions or events or people are non-terminating judgments. They are explicable through terminating judgments that refer to direct experience of value.

Lewis's naturalism agrees with Mill's view that the sole evidence of desirability in a thing is its being actually desired (378). Judgments of value are ultimately predictions about what will be immediately and infallibly recognized as valuable.[1] Lewis regards this as a naturalist or 'humanist' conception of value because it identifies value with what human beings in fact find immediately valuable. A transcendentalist view rejects this predictive view of judgments

---

[1] 'All those who would define value in a way which it brings it home in the end to a quality directly disclosed or disclosable in experience, and a quality which *when* disclosed is unmistakeable, represent the same generic type of conception which is here put forward.' (*AKV* 398)

about value, and hence rejects the immediate experience of value as the ultimate arbiter of intrinsic value.[2]

What is this immediate experience of value that Lewis refers to? It is supposed to be the evaluative analogue to immediate experience of the given; hence it is immune to honest error through misidentification. One might take Lewis to refer to a feeling of pleasure. This gives some idea of what he has in mind, though he regards 'pleasure' as a rather restrictive term for the relevant valued quality. The experience of value that he has in mind covers all the forms of liking, satisfaction, and feeling good.[3] If we accept a naturalistic view of value, we claim that judgments of value are predictive judgments that refer ultimately to immediate experiences of liking.

Synthetic judgments about value all have this form of indirect prediction of immediate experiences of liking; hence they are all empirical judgments. When Lewis comes across judgments about value that do not seem to him to be empirical judgments, he infers, consistently with his general empiricist position, that they are analytic judgments, so that if they are true, they are analytically true. Among these judgments he includes statements of different theories about goodness. Analytic judgments, therefore, include these apparently unpromising candidates: 'Pleasure is the good'; 'Goodness is a simple, unanalysable quality'; 'A thing is constituted good by being the object of an interest'; and 'Nothing is unqualifiedly good but a good will' (378). These seem unpromising candidates because they do not seem to be accounts of the meaning of the different terms; nor do the supporters of these claims seem to have intended them as accounts of meaning. In some cases, indeed, they have denied that they are accounts of meaning.

Lewis's claim introduces us to his conception of analytic truth. When he maintains that these are all analytic judgments, he does not mean that they are all linguistic stipulations. He does not, for instance, believe that they represent different people's recommendations about how to use the term 'good'. They are attempted 'explications of one intension by another and more familiar or more lucid meaning' (379). That is why philosophical analysis is a serious and informative undertaking.

This conception of the status of a hedonist account of goodness conflicts with Moore's view. According to Moore, who follows Sidgwick, hedonists are misguided if they treat their claim as an analytic judgment about the concept 'good'. Despite Bentham's occasional aberration, hedonists normally suppose they correct our views about the sort of thing that is good, not our views about what 'good' means. As Ross puts it, they are arguing about good-making properties, not about the concept or property of goodness itself.

---

[2] 'Every such view might be called a naturalistic or humanistic conception of values; since it holds the natural bent of the natural man stands in no need of correction in order validly to be the touchstone of *intrinsic* value. It repudiates the conception that with respect to intrinsic values we are natively incompetent, or born in sin, and can discern them justly only by some insight thaumaturgically acquired, or through some intimation of a proper vocation of man which runs athwart his natural bent.' (398)

[3] 'We can only rely upon the improbability that what is so generally exhibited in the experience of everyone, and is so universally of interest, and hence so commonly remarked, could fail to be correctly identified by reference to the multiplicity of occasions on which all of us use adjectives of prizing and disprizing. The immediately good is what you like and what you want in the way of experience; the immediately bad is what you dislike and do not want.' (404)

Lewis does not explain why he disagrees with this conception of hedonism as a synthetic claim about goodness. But his general view of judgments of value makes it clear why he regards all these judgments as analytic. He denies, for good reason, that hedonists are making an empirical prediction about the character of things that everyone, or most people, find good; for they do not seem willing to consider the possibility of counter-examples drawn from some people's judgments about goodness. On this point, Moore and Ross agree. Ross, for instance, recognizes that, as Lewis claims, arguments about the good-making property or properties are not empirical arguments of the ordinary sort. In Ross's view, this recognition of the non-empirical character of the arguments is quite consistent with his claim that hedonists are not telling us about the concept of goodness; for Ross allows synthetic a priori judgments. But this option is not open to Lewis.

Is this a serious objection to Lewis's view? We might argue that if he fails to allow the possibility of synthetic and a priori claims about goodness, he is guided by his empiricist doctrine of the a priori rather than by a plausible conception of what hedonism claims. For, as Sidgwick argues, the hedonist position is more plausible if it rests on some agreement about the meaning of 'good' and the concept of goodness; Sidgwick does not take himself to argue that non-hedonists do not understand what they mean by 'good' and 'pleasant'.

Lewis, however, rejects this argument. He answers that Sidgwick, Moore, and Ross have too narrow a conception of the analytic. Even if hedonists rely on some agreement about the concept of goodness, they may none the less be taken to offer a fuller explication of the concept. This fuller explication will introduce further analytic truths, but they will not be obviously analytic. The unobviously analytic truths (or falsehoods) that constitute these explications will include many of the judgments that we would otherwise be tempted to treat as synthetic and a priori.

If Lewis resorts to claims such as these to defend the claim that apparently synthetic judgments are really analytic, is it worth his while to maintain the empiricist doctrine that all a priori truths are analytic? The class of unobviously analytic truths is difficult to identify. How, we might wonder, are we to tell whether a given a priori truth is synthetic or unobviously analytic? To answer this question, we need a reasonably clear notion of the meaning or intension of a term or concept. But we might wonder whether any such notion will allow as many truths to be analytic as Lewis allows.

We might also attack Lewis's claim about hedonism from the opposite direction. If we doubt whether the hedonist thesis is analytic, we might question his claim that it is a priori rather than empirical. He believes it is not empirical because it does not seem to be properly related to terminating judgments and immediate experiences of value. But we might suggest that it is offered not as a mere generalization about these judgments, but as an explanation of them. A hedonist might argue that we make these terminating judgments about value because hedonism is true. Explanatory judgments do not seem to meet Lewis's conditions for objective empirical judgments; but should we infer that they are not empirical but a priori? He may be as unreasonably rigid in his conception of empirical judgment as he is in his rejection of synthetic a priori judgments.

1316. The Error in Non-Cognitivism

Lewis combines his empiricism and naturalism with opposition to non-cognitivism. He sets out to show that evaluative judgments can be statements of empirical knowledge, and that in these circumstances they can state objective truths. He regards subjectivism and non-cognitivism as errors that simply need to be stated to be shown to be untenable.[4] Though he never names Stevenson or any other emotivist, he believes that their position is unreasonable enough to deserve nothing more than brief refutation.

His attempted refutation consists in his version of the claim that non-cognitivism discredits ethics. This version revives the Stoic argument that Scepticism about goodness leads to 'inaction' (*apraxia*).[5] Lewis agrees with the Stoics in distinguishing rational action from simple behaviour. His version of the inaction argument, in agreement with the Stoic version, considers the necessary conditions for rational—or, as Lewis puts it, 'sensible' action. In his view, sensible action essentially aims at achieving or avoiding something to which we ascribe positive or negative value.[6] In his view, to ascribe value to something is to believe that the thing has some property that makes it valuable; and hence it is to hold some factual belief about the thing we want to get.[7]

A non-cognitivist might answer this argument by agreeing that sensible action requires us to ascribe value to the object we want to achieve, but adding that the ascription of value requires only a favourable attitude; it does not require us to believe that the object has some property. I need to believe that something I can do will achieve this object, but my attitude to the object itself need only be desire. Lewis seems to assume illegitimately that a factual belief is needed.

Lewis does not consider this defence of a non-cognitivist conception of sensible action. Perhaps he ignores it because he does not believe it meets his objection. He suggests that action becomes pointless 'unless there can be some measure of assurance of a valuable result which it may realize' (366). Some degree of assurance that we will get something we favour may not seem adequate. For if I favour something, but believe that my getting it will achieve nothing valuable because my want is foolish, I do not act sensibly if I try to get it. My favouring an object gives me a reason to try to get it only if I believe that my favour is correctly directed, because the object is really valuable. This reply is equally effective if we introduce higher-order attitudes; even if I favour my favouring x, it does not follow that I have any reason to try to get x unless my highest-order favouring picks out some object that is worth having. According to this argument, favourable attitudes warrant us in acting on

---

[4] 'But this is one of the strangest aberrations ever to visit the mind of man. The denial to value-apprehensions in general of the character of truth or falsity would imply both moral and practical cynicism. It would invalidate all action; because action becomes pointless unless there can be some measure of assurance of a valuable result which it may realize.' (366)

[5] The Stoics on inaction; §139.

[6] 'Action—at least action of the sort called rational and sensible—is for the sake of realizing something to which positive value is ascribed, or of avoiding something to which disvalue is ascribed.' (366)

[7] '... no intention or purpose could be serious, and no action could be practically justifiable or attain success, if it were not that there are value-predicates which represent empirical cognitions, and are predictive and hence capable of confirmation or disconfirmation.' (371–2) These predicates belong to 'value-judgments which are true; judgments which predict the accrual of value-quality as a consequence of action, and which are positively verifiable by adoption of the mode of action in question' (373).

them only if we have some reason to believe that what they favour is really valuable. This last belief cannot be given a non-cognitive analysis if is to give us a genuine reason.

If this is what Lewis has in mind in his distinction between behaviour and sensible action, he revives something close to Butler's argument about superior principles, and applies it to non-cognitivism. Butler asserts that nothing would be a greater absurdity than our failing to approve of one action more than another; we could not act rationally if we simply acted on the strongest desire without consideration of the merits of different possible actions.[8] Non-cognitivists satisfy the letter of Butler's position, since they claim to approve one action over another. But Lewis suggests that non-cognitivists do not really agree with Butler because they do not agree that we can form rational judgments on the merits of different actions. Though we may prefer one action to another as a result of thinking about some of its non-evaluative properties, these properties do not give us a reason to prefer one action unless they make the action better than the alternative. Our belief that it is better than the alternative is the basis for our favouring the action. The belief would not give us a reason to favour the action unless it were distinct from our favouring the action.

Lewis's argument, therefore, may exploit Butler's argument for superior principles to show what is wrong with non-cognitivism about judgments of value. It is less powerful than it might be because he neither considers nor refutes possible non-cognitivist replies. Nor is it decisive against non-cognitivism, any more than Butler's argument is decisive against someone who denies that we act on superior principles. Both Butler and Lewis assume that we have a reason to favour the actions we favour, and that this reason reflects some fact about the actions that is distinct from the fact that we favour them. They may be right that we commonly agree about this assumption, once we are clear about it. But non-cognitivists may reply that this assumption rests on an illusion, and that we can expose the illusion by seeing why evaluative judgments cannot be about facts distinct from our favourable attitudes.

But though this reply is open to a non-cognitivist, it carries a price. Stevenson and Ayer profess to offer an analysis of evaluative judgments, not a demonstration of their impossibility. They reject the charge that they discredit ethics. If Lewis is right, however, they not only discredit ethics, but also deny that we ever act on the sorts of reasons that we think we act on. If we believe that we act on reasons that are distinct from our favourable attitudes, the grounds for accepting non-cognitivism have to be stronger than our grounds for believing that we act on such reasons. This is a heavy burden of proof for the non-cognitivist to have to assume, and Lewis gives us some reason to doubt whether we ought to find non-cognitivism plausible in the face of such an objection. Though his objection is brief, it deserves some attention.

1317. Objectivity

Lewis rejects both non-cognitivism and subjectivism on the ground that they do not allow sensible action. The argument that we have considered may also be used against

---

[8] Butler on absurdity; §685.

subjectivism. If my favouring an action does not give me a reason to favour it, my believing that I favour it does not seem to give me a reason either. If I favour it for some reason, the reason is expressed by my belief that it has some evaluative property that grounds my favour, and this property cannot simply repeat the fact that I favour the action. For these reasons, Lewis rejects non-cognitivism and subjectivism, and maintains the position that he calls 'objectivism'.

His objectivism, however, is restricted. He denies that judgments about the goodness of objects are simply judgments about the feelings of the judge, and therefore he avoids one form of subjectivism. When I say that Picasso's paintings are good and you say they are not, we are genuinely disagreeing with each other because only one of our judgments can be true. Lewis explains how these judgments can be true or false by taking them to be empirical judgments. They are predictions about most people's immediate experiences of liking, or about the experiences of people who have become accustomed to viewing a certain range of paintings; hence they are capable of being true or false and are in principle verifiable.

About immediate experience of liking, however, Lewis is a subjectivist. If I say that it is good to be lying in the sun now, or that it is good to be looking at this Picasso now, I may be reporting my immediate experience of liking. If that is what I am doing, I cannot be wrong through honest error. If you are in the same situation and say that it is bad, also reporting your immediate experience, you cannot be wrong through honest error. We may appear to contradict each other, to a hearer who does not understand that each of us is reporting an immediate experience. But we do not really contradict each other; for my immediate experience of liking is consistent with your immediate experience of disliking.

Lewis, therefore, accepts one aspect of subjectivism that critics regard as a weakness. They argue that subjectivism gives the wrong result, failing to recognize contradictions where we intuitively recognize them. Non-cognitivists believe that they do better here, not because they recognize genuine statements that are genuinely contradictory, but because they do more to explain the appearance of contradiction, by appealing to disagreement in attitude. Lewis answers that genuinely contradictory evaluative judgments are confined to objective judgments that predict experiences of immediate liking. But reports of these experiences of immediate liking do not allow the same possibility of contradiction. The evaluative judgment that I will have such an experience is a terminating judgment, and, since it makes a definite prediction that can be verified or falsified by an immediate liking, it can be decisively and completely verified or falsified (375). Objective judgments are non-terminating; they make claims about the truth of terminating judgments, but not about any definite set of them, and so they cannot be decisively verified. But they have empirical meaning, and they allow partial empirical verification.

Lewis, therefore, maintains that sometimes when we affirm that x is good, we simply report our experience of immediate liking, and so we do not really contradict someone who affirms that x is bad, and uses 'good' in the same sense. He therefore takes a more complicated view of the possibility of contradiction than he would take if he were a thorough objectivist or if he were a non-cognitivist. A thorough objectivist might deny that 'good' has the purely reporting sense that Lewis ascribes to it, and so might affirm that its use always allows genuine contradictions. A non-cognitivist denies that evaluative judgments can ever be genuinely contradictory, and affirms that all apparent contradictions are really differences in attitude. Over a wide range of moral judgments, Lewis keeps closer to the phenomena of moral judgment and closer to objectivism, since he allows real disagreement based on real contradiction. But for the reporting use of 'good', he takes the subjectivist view that there is no contradiction.

1318. What are Evaluative Judgments About?

Even though Lewis affirms objectivism to the degree just described, he restricts the scope of objective evaluative judgments to predictions about immediate experiences of liking. Why should we agree that evaluative judgments have such a restricted scope? We can extend the scope by including counterfactual predictions about informed judges or impartial spectators, but these extensions still do not seem to yield the content that we normally ascribe to evaluative judgments. For we normally take it to be logically possible that people's immediate experiences are mistaken; and we suppose that if they were mistaken, that need not affect the truth of the relevant judgments.

Why, then, should we accept Lewis's claim about the content of evaluative judgments? In his view, it is the only option if we reject both transcendentalism and non-cognitivism. His reasons for rejecting non-cognitivism are fairly clear. But it is not so obvious why he rejects transcendentalism, or even what he is rejecting. Since his description of transcendentalism is vague, it is not clear how many positions display the faults—whatever they are—that he tries to avoid.

One view that he rejects seems to say that human beings are radically wrong about the sorts of things that are valuable, and that they need to discover some 'vocation of man' that is altogether disconnected from their natural desires and aims. We can perhaps see why such a radically revisionary view would be open to objection. But it is puzzling that Lewis seems to treat Kant as a transcendentalist moralist of this extreme sort. Though Kant does not take moral principles to be hypothetical imperatives based on the actual desires of a particular human being, or even of all or most human beings, he neither says nor implies that ordinary human inclinations are irrelevant to questions about what is morally right or valuable. If Kant counts as a transcendentalist for Lewis, perhaps transcendentalism includes views that are less extreme and more plausible than they might appear from Lewis's description.

Transcendentalists, then, may include those who deny that all evaluative judgments are non-terminating judgments, because they deny that their whole meaning is expressed by terminating judgments (376).[9] To support his conception of evaluative judgments, Lewis seems to rely on his empiricist doctrine of significance. In his view, we have to introduce some set—even if it is not clearly defined—of terminating judgments, if we are to understand the practical implications of value judgments. Any acceptable account of value judgments

---

[9] 'Any particular confirmation of such a judgment comes by way of finding true some terminating judgment which is a consequence of it. And while there is no limit to the number of such terminating judgments, truth of which follows from the objective judgment of value, still there is nothing contained in the meaning of it which is not expressible by some terminating judgment or other. If, beyond what is thus expressible as some possible confirmation of it, the objective value-judgment should be supposed to have a further and different component of its significance, we should be unable to say or even to think to ourselves what this further component signified, or what conceivable difference the holding or not holding of it in fact would make to anybody under any thinkable circumstances.' (376)

must give them the practical significance that they can have only if they have the purely predictive character that Lewis ascribes to them.

We might reasonably dispute Lewis's doctrine of significance. But we might concede some of it and still question his meta-ethical inferences. Let us grant that an account of value judgments must imply some terminating judgments about immediate experiences of liking. Let us even grant that value judgments would be irrelevant to human choice and action unless we could connect them to some terminating judgments. Still, we may not be convinced that Lewis is right about the nature of the appropriate connexion. We might, for instance, say that what is good must tend to promote feelings of liking, pleasure, or satisfaction in a properly constituted subject. We may explain what a properly constituted subject is by saying that such subjects take pleasure in the appropriate things, or that their capacities for taking pleasure have been well trained or rightly directed.

This account falls short of Lewis's demands in so far as it does not take the meaning of value judgments to be exhausted by terminating judgments. Nor does it provide the sort of terminating judgment that Lewis expects. For we cannot identify the subjects whose immediate experiences of liking are to be considered without reference to some of our evaluative judgments, about what it takes for a subject to be properly constituted, well trained, and so on. From Lewis's point of view, an account that relies on further evaluative judgments about subjects of experience is unsatisfactory. It cannot give our initial evaluative judgments about goodness any genuine cognitive content; for we do not know what to apply our initial judgments to until we understand the further evaluative judgments. If the further evaluative judgments must be explained by still further evaluative judgments, we seem to face either an infinite regress or a vicious circle.

1319. Terminating Judgments and Objective Judgments

Should we be disturbed by this threat of a regress or a circle? To see what we should think about Lewis's position on judgments about goodness, we may usefully look at a different application of his doctrine about meaning and terminating judgments. He applies the same doctrine to beliefs about physical objects. These beliefs are not the same as terminating judgments, since tables and chairs are external objects about which we may be in error.[10] We may not have purely expressive terms readily available, but we can create them from our ordinary physical-object terms. Instead of saying that I am opening the door, I can say that I am having a door-opening experience, where 'door-opening' does not commit me to the existence of any door or any act of opening, but refers only to the sensations that we normally associate with our belief that we are opening a door.

According to Lewis, then, if physical objects are knowable, they are knowable through the experiences captured in terminating judgments. For these experiences are all that we directly know, and any significant claims about other things are significant only in so far

---

[10] '[Terminating judgments] are phrased in terms of direct experience, not of the objective facts which such experience may signalize or confirm; and for this reason they are statable only in expressive language, the terms of which denote appearances as such.' (203)

as they refer to experiences.[11] Alleged facts about physical objects that cannot be known wholly by immediate experiences are not knowable at all. To grasp the content of factual judgments in so far as they are knowable, we have to express them in terminating judgments predicting the occurrence of immediate experiences.

The relevant terminating judgments, however, have to be conditional; we have no reasonable prospect of translating categorical objective judgments into categorical predictions about experiences.[12] Hence the judgment that the wall in front of me is brown may be understood as a conditional prediction: 'If I have the appearance of looking in front of me and if . . . (etc.), then I will probably have the appearance of seeing brown'. In each case, the 'of . . .' following 'appearance' does not identify the cause of the appearance (looking, seeing brown), but simply indicates the character of the appearance; it is the sort of appearance that I have when I suppose I am looking in front of me or seeing brown.

The predictions about appearances give us the cognitive meaning of the objective judgment about the wall. We must be able to make these predictions if we are to be in a position to form a reasonable belief that the objective judgment is true. Hence, Lewis assumes, the predictions about appearances must follow analytically from the objective judgment (249). Though the set of predictions giving the meaning of objective judgments will be long and complex, we must assume such a set if we are to attach a meaning to the objective judgment.

This demand for analytic connexions between objective judgments and predictions that are wholly about appearances (call these 'phenomenal predictions') confronts Lewis with a difficulty that Chisholm exposes.[13] We may think Lewis is right, because we often seem to make phenomenal predictions when we make objective judgments. But these predictions depend on some assumption about normality or standard conditions. If objective judgments are to be analytically connected to phenomenal predictions, these assumptions about standard conditions must also be expressed in phenomenal terms. But it is difficult to see how we could express them in such terms. We cannot say that if there is a doorknob in front of me, then if I have the appearance of putting out my hand, I will probably have the appearance of holding something round and solid. This prediction is probable only in standard conditions. If something is wrong with my hand, the appearance of putting out my hand will not result in the normal appearance; and if the doorknob has some peculiar paint on the surface, it may not feel solid.

The difficulty that faces Lewis here does not consist in the fact that the phenomenal predictions we make on the basis of objective judgments are not universally true; he recognizes that they are only probable. The difficulty is that the conditions that make them probable seem to be objective conditions. If I try to replace 'Nothing is wrong with

---

[11] 'The existence of a thing, the occurrence of an objective event, or any other objective state of affairs, is knowable only as it is verifiable or confirmable. And such objective facts can be verified, or confirmed as probable, only by presentations of sense. Thus all empirical knowledge is vested, ultimately, in the awareness of what is given and the prediction of certain passages of further experience as something which will be given or could be given.' (203).

[12] 'The main reason why such predictions must be thus conditional, instead of categorical, is the simple one that, broadly speaking, there is nothing in the way of human experience which is predictable entirely without reference to conditions which action supplies and may alter.' (205) 'The sense meaning of any verifiable statement of objective fact is exhibitable in some set of terminating judgments each of which is hypothetical in form; it is a judgment that a certain empirical eventuation will ensue if a certain mode of action be adopted.' (211)

[13] Chisholm, 'Problem'.

my hand' with 'I have the usual appearances of my hand', that will not work, since the appearances of my hand may be misleading about the condition of my hand. My appearances of my hand are reliable only on the assumption that I have them in normal conditions, as specified by objective judgments. Whenever we try to express a clause about normal conditions in phenomenal terms, the resulting phenomenal clause can replace the original clause only if the phenomenal clause itself is said to hold only in normal conditions; and then we have introduced a second mention of normal conditions, raising the same question about its expression in phenomenal terms. Our attempt to replace objective judgments with phenomenal predictions seems to force us into a vicious regress, since we cannot get rid of the reference to normal conditions.

Lewis rejects Chisholm's criticism of attempted translations into phenomenal predictions. In his view, Chisholm overlooks two things: (1) We do not need to look outside phenomenal features of situations to identify the objective circumstances that affect these features. (2) The phenomenal predictions are probabilistic.[14] How effective are these answers?

The first answer relies on the claim that the phenomenal features of situations often make us aware of their non-standard character. If, for instance, we look at a square from an angle, we have a non-square appearance, but we also have some phenomenal indication that we are looking at the square from an angle (357). But this point does not help Lewis. We take our appearance to indicate that we are looking at the square from an angle only if we assume that the circumstances are normal, so that no strange mirrors are distorting the appearances. Our interpretation of the appearances appeals to objective circumstances.

Lewis's second answer invites a similar objection. Even our probabilistic predictions rely on assumptions about normal conditions. If we change these assumptions, predictions that were probable cease to be probable. And these assumptions about normal conditions are expressed in objective terms. The relevant probabilistic judgments do not seem to follow analytically from the objective judgments; they are warranted only on the basis of assumptions about standard conditions. Hence terminating judgments do not exhaust the meaning of objective judgments.

It is difficult, therefore, to avoid the force of Chisholm's objection to Lewis's claims about the relation between terminating judgments and objective beliefs. But Lewis believes that we must reject Chisholm's conclusion that objective beliefs are not analytically connected to terminating judgments. In his view, the only alternative to Lewis's views about objective beliefs and terminating judgments is a coherence theory of empirical truth, which soon leads to scepticism. Since Chisholm is committed to an unacceptable coherence theory of truth, his conclusion cannot be accepted.[15]

Why does Lewis suppose that his opponents are committed to a coherence theory of truth? It is fairly easy to see why he thinks they are committed to some coherentist claims about empirical knowledge. For if we can justifiably treat sensory experience as evidence for objective judgments, we must (if Lewis is wrong) presuppose the justifiability of some

---

[14] See Lewis, 'Chisholm', 360.

[15] 'And the suggestion will be that some kind of coherence-theory of empirical truth should be considered instead . . .' ('Chisholm', 356) 'My own belief is that if Professor Chisholm's point can be made good, then there will be nothing left for us but scepticism; because I am convinced that any coherence-theory will have defects which are fatal.' ('Chisholm', 357)

objective judgments about normal conditions, which can themselves be justified only if some further assumptions about sensory experience and objective conditions are justified. If, then, we are to justify any one objective judgment on the basis of terminating judgments, we must appeal to its place in the whole body of our objective beliefs and terminating judgments; we cannot set out from any immediate sensory experiences as our foundation. This conception of knowledge appeals to coherence as a basis for justification, and rejects any justification independent of coherence.

Further argument is needed, however, to show that this conception of justification and knowledge commits us to the view that truth also consists in coherence among our judgments, as opposed to correspondence between our judgments and independent facts. One might argue that if justification consists in coherence, our justified beliefs give us no reason to believe that they correspond to any independent reality, and so a conception of justification as coherence commits us to scepticism about independent reality. But this is a rather hasty attack on coherence about justification. It is not so clear that such a view gives us no basis to believe in truth as correspondence.

In any case, one might wonder whether Lewis's rejection of coherentism saves him from scepticism about the truth of objective judgments. If he is a phenomenalist about objective judgments, he avoids scepticism only by (apparently) conceding the sceptic's basic point, that we cannot know any reality beyond our sensory experiences. One might argue that coherentism about truth concedes the sceptic's basic point, by reducing our expectations about truth; but if that is a fair objection against coherentism about truth, it seems an equally fair objection against phenomenalism. In any case, it is not obvious that Lewis's objections about coherence theories of truth and about scepticism provide decisive reasons for rejecting coherence theories of justification and knowledge about objective beliefs.

Chisholm observes that Lewis sometimes seems more inclined to treat coherence as a source of justification. Lewis asks how we can use immediate experiences as a basis for terminating judgments that predict immediate experiences. He notices that we must presume the general reliability of memory if we are to have any basis for prediction.[16] But if we tried to establish the reliability of memory by appeal to immediate experiences, this attempt would itself have to presuppose the reliability of memory. Hence we seem to proceed in a circle, if we appeal to experience to justify memory and we appeal to memory to support appeals to experience. But Lewis does not treat this circle as vicious. Instead he responds with an appeal to coherence. He relies on two claims: (1) An assumption that we need in order to avoid complete scepticism is legitimate. (2) We can confirm the legitimacy of our assumption by showing that it results in a coherent ('congruent') set of beliefs.[17]

In the light of these claims, it is difficult to see why Lewis is so alarmed by Chisholm's conclusions about terminating judgments and objective beliefs. If these conclusions lead to scepticism, Lewis's empiricism leads to scepticism. But if Lewis can fairly avoid scepticism by assuming that memory is prima facie credible, Chisholm can apparently avoid it by

---

[16] The argument he gives on 332 presupposes a verificationist conception of meaning.

[17] 'First; whatever is remembered . . . is prima facie credible because so remembered. And second; when the whole range of empirical beliefs is taken into account, all of them more or less dependent on memorial knowledge, we find that those which are most credible can be assured by their mutual support, or as we shall put it, by their congruence.' (334)

assuming that some objective beliefs are prima facie credible. And if it is fair for Lewis to support his assumption about memory by appeal to the coherence of the resulting set of beliefs, it seems equally fair for Chisholm to appeal to coherence to support an assumption about objective beliefs. Lewis appeals to coherence as part of an answer to scepticism; he does not mention his charge that coherence plunges us into scepticism.

Lewis's claims about memory, therefore, seem to speak against his views about objective beliefs and terminating judgments. He defends his empiricism about objective beliefs on the ground that the alternative view appeals to coherence and eventually forces us into scepticism. But he agrees that his own empiricism leads to scepticism unless we introduce a non-sceptical assumption and support it by appeal to coherence. Not only is his empiricism about objective beliefs open to objections, but his defence against these objections rests on assumptions that he abandons when he sees that he needs to assume the prima facie credibility of memory.

1320. Empiricism and Ethics

This brief consideration of Lewis's views on beliefs about physical objects is worth our while if it helps us to evaluate his phenomenalist claims about judgments of value. He defends his phenomenalism about the relation of objective value judgments to experiences of value on the ground that the 'transcendentalist' alternative takes human inclinations and preferences to be irrelevant to real value. We can now see that if transcendentalism is simply the denial of Lewis's empiricism, it is not so bad, and need not dismiss human inclinations in the way that Lewis alleges. Moreover, Lewis's naturalist alternative is unattractive, in so far as it relies on his phenomenalism.

Lewis's defence of naturalism against transcendentalism about value relies on the assumptions that underlie his defence of phenomenalism about objective beliefs and terminating judgments. But his defence of phenomenalism is unsuccessful, for the reasons set out by Chisholm. And in any case Lewis is not a complete phenomenalist; for he recognizes that if his phenomenalism is not to lead to complete scepticism, it must rest on some non-phenomenalist presupposition about the prima facie credibility of memory.

Once we notice these breaches in Lewis's empiricism about objective judgments, why should we be reluctant to allow analogous breaches in his empiricism about judgments of value? His view about the meaning of objective judgments of value implies that their meaning is given by terminating judgments that predict experiences of immediate liking. This view is open to question; for it seems consistent to judge that something is good and that people will not like it or its consequences. If something is good for human beings, it should promote their welfare, and welfare should include experiences of immediate liking directed to the appropriate objects in people whose likings are appropriate.

This introduction of 'appropriate objects' and 'appropriate likings' violates Lewis's conditions for terminating judgments; for we can explicate appropriateness only through further non-terminating objective judgments. If we take people's immediate likings as prima facie relevant to value, we presuppose that they have roughly appropriate likings. This presupposition is parallel to the presupposition that we need if we are to take terminating judgments as evidence for objective beliefs. In both cases—judgments of value and objective beliefs about physical objects—the analytic connexions demanded by Lewis's empiricism cannot be found.

Lewis's attempt to adhere steadfastly to his empiricist principles is therefore quite instructive. He cannot reasonably adhere to them in judgments about the physical world; for good reasons he introduces non-empiricist presuppositions in order to avoid scepticism. We have equally good reasons to reject his empiricist analysis of value judgments. If we agree, as we should, that judgments about goodness cannot be translated wholly into terminating judgments, and we reject unreduced judgments of value, we have to be sceptics. But we have no better reason to reject these unreduced judgments of value than we have to reject unreduced objective beliefs about the physical world.

It is equally instructive to notice the different reactions to different aspects of Lewis's position. His empiricism about objective beliefs about the physical world has been generally rejected, and probably rather few people would defend his phenomenalism. Moral philosophers are less disposed to reject his empiricism about judgments of value. But it is not clear why the two aspects of his empiricism should be treated differently.

1321. Norms and Rationality

Lewis rejects subjectivism and non-cognitivism on the ground that they do not allow sensible action. We understood his conception of sensible action to include the demand that we act on the basis of some belief about the merits of an action which gives us a reason to choose it. He is equally confident that sensible action requires recognition of norms and acceptance of imperatives. Norms and imperatives constrain us to look beyond immediate pleasure and pain to some future condition that may give us a reason to act differently from how we would act if we were absorbed in our present pleasures and pains.[18] Here again Lewis exploits Butler's claim that any recognizable human life needs adherence to superior principles.

Though Lewis recognizes that norms matter to human life, he does not offer a clear conception of what is required for following a norm. He speaks as though following a norm only requires the 'finding of a constraint'. But unless we know more about the relevant sort of constraint, we do not yet seem to have found a norm. We might, for instance, find ourselves reluctant or unable to ignore our fear of future unwelcome results. But this attitude seems to fall short of the acceptance of a norm; for we might recognize fear of future suffering as a merely psychological fact about us, and we might not see any reason to prefer this attitude to a more careless attitude to the future.

Lewis combines this purely psychological account of the normative with a purely psychological account of the rational. He suggests that in rational action we do not find the

---

[18] 'To act, to live, in human terms, is necessarily to be subject to imperatives; to recognize norms. Because to be subject to an imperative means simply the finding of a constraint of action in some concern for that which is not immediate; is not a present enjoyment or a present suffering. To repudiate normative significances and imperatives in general, would be to dissolve away all seriousness of action and intent, leaving only an undirected floating down the stream of time; and as a consequence, to dissolve all significance of thought and discourse into universal blah.' (481)

appropriate interpretation of 'rational' by turning to inference and logical validity. Rational agents are those who are capable of being constrained by the thought of unwelcome consequences.[19] This practical rationality is not derived from logical consistency, but is the source of it. Consistency is simply refusal to accept now what I will later be unwilling to accept (480). This purely causal account of rationality seems inadequate because it relies on a purely causal account of constraint. The mere fact that the thought of future pain results in aversion does not make me rational; a rational aversion should rely at least on some comparative judgment about the badness of the future pain in relation to any good results that I might achieve from the action that causes the pain. It is difficult, then, to see how rationality can be analysed as mere susceptibility to future regret for our actions.

Lewis believes that if we are rational, we accept a categorical imperative. He gives two accounts of this imperative: (1) It prescribes consistency in thought and action. (2) It prescribes concern for oneself in the future and on the whole.[20] These two accounts seem quite different. The first speaks only of consistency, which apparently requires no particular concern for the future; but the second prescribes concern for myself in the future and on the whole. But Lewis thinks the two formulations are equivalent. In his view, we could recognize no imperative of consistency in the absence of any concern for our future state; and so some concern for our future is needed to explain why we should care about being consistent.

It is less clear, however, why Lewis believes that concern for our future requires concern for oneself 'on the whole'. In 'on the whole', he implies that I should be equally concerned for all parts of my future, as such. Here he agrees with Sidgwick's principle of impartiality between different times, against the proximist view that cares more about the nearer time simply because it is nearer.[21] He admits, as Sidgwick does, that ignorance or uncertainty may justify less concern for some parts of my future over others; but he believes that the bare fact that one part of my future is more distant than another is no reason for less concern about it.

Lewis defends this impartial view of self-concern in his discussion of Bentham's claims about propinquity. He notices that when Bentham advises us to prefer the nearer pleasure to the more distant, it is not clear whether the advice is based on epistemic considerations, or is independent of them. If the considerations are merely epistemic, Bentham has no need to pick out propinquity as a distinct ground of preference, since it has already been covered in the advice to prefer the more certain over the less certain. Perhaps, then, Bentham advocates a proximist preference for nearer pleasures in their own right. Lewis describes this proximism as 'fractional prudence'.[22] Lewis recognizes that many people act on this 'anomalous' attitude of fractional prudence rather than on rational grounds. To act on

---

[19] 'To be rational, instead of foolish or perverse, means to be capable of constraint by prevision of some future good or ill; to be amenable to the consideration, "You will be sorry if you don't", or "if you do".' (480)

[20] 'The final and universal imperative, "Be consistent, in valuation and in thought and action"; "Be concerned about yourself in future and on the whole"; is one which is categorical. It requires no reason; being itself the expression of that which is the root of all reason; that in the absence of which there could be no reason of any sort or for anything.' (481)

[21] See Sidgwick, §1187.

[22] 'It is to be feared that what he [Bentham] intends is the anomalous conception that, although we should rationally be concerned about the future, we should be less concerned about it according as it is more remote—and this quite independently of the greater doubt which attaches to the more remote in general. This might be called the principle of fractional prudence or of prudence mitigated by impulse.' (493)

rational grounds, we have to observe the 'rational principle that concern for the good in a whole life should rule our conduct' (493). Lewis acknowledges that this rational principle is a categorical imperative that cannot be further argued for; but he maintains that anyone who acts on the principle of fractional prudence in cases where it diverges from the principle of prudence will have a less good life on the whole.

It is puzzling that Lewis treats the principle of prudence as a categorical imperative. He believes that a categorical imperative applies to us if we are rational at all; and to be rational is simply to be subject to normative guidance, and hence (according to Lewis's account of the normative) to be subject to regret for what we have done. But proximists do not abandon normative guidance; they are influenced by thoughts of future good and evil, but by a narrower range of consequences than those that affect impartially prudent people. If proximists are guided by norms, why should we suppose that only the principle of prudence is the genuine principle of reason?

Lewis might reasonably argue that proximists are incompletely rational, because they are influenced by a consideration (temporal propinquity) that ought not to influence them. He would be justified if he argued that, from the point of view of practical reason, the mere fact that I care less about x than about y is not by itself a reason for caring less about x than about y, if I have otherwise better reason for caring more about x than about y. This argument, however, presupposes a conception of practical reason that includes the recognition of considerations favouring an action apart from my inclination for or against it. This rationalistic conception of practical reason was not included in Lewis's psychological reduction of reason to the causal influence of thoughts about future pain and pleasure.

His appeal to practical reason, therefore, presupposes a non-reductive account that conflicts with his explicit account. The choice between the principle of prudence and the principle of fractional prudence relies on a rationalistic account of practical reason that cannot be captured within his purely psychological account. His attempt to explicate practical rationality in purely psychological terms exposes the difficulty of capturing practical rationality within these limits.

A rationalistic treatment of prudence and practical reason underlies Lewis's fuller attempt to express the basic principle of rationality, which he formulates as the Law of Objectivity.[23] This law tells us to attend to our conception of the facts rather than to our feelings about the facts that we recognize. In Lewis's view, this law justifies our acceptance of the principle of prudence, on the ground that proximism distorts our conception of the facts through our bias towards propinquity. If we try to act on the facts, we will give no less inherent weight to the more distant than to the less distant future, because the difference that propinquity causes in our perception of the facts corresponds to no difference in the facts.[24] Fractional prudence, therefore, prevents us from giving the appropriate weight to our view of the facts.

---

[23] 'So conduct and determine your activities of thinking and of doing, as to conform any decision of them to the objective actualities, as cognitively signified to you in your representational apprehension of them, and not according to any impulsion or solicitation exercised by the affective quality of your present experience as immediate feeling merely.' (GNR 89)

[24] 'Conduct yourself, with reference to these future eventualities which cognition advises you that your activity may affect, as you would if these predictable effects of it were to be realized, at this moment of decision, with the poignancy of the here and now, instead of the less poignant feeling which representation of the future and possible may automatically arouse.' (GNR 89)

We prefer prudence to fractional prudence not only because we are afraid of having to be sorry for what we have done, but because we recognize the requirement to face the facts as we think they are, not as they are distorted by our inclinations.

If we follow Lewis's advice to face the facts and to avoid distortion by inclination, we should not necessarily confine ourselves to the distorting effects of temporal propinquity. We might also ask whether our non-rational desires and inclinations may not sometimes distort our comparative judgments of value. Lewis's empiricism connects the meaning of value judgments with terminating judgments, but we may wonder whether his view allows sufficient influence to the relevant facts. His empiricism about value judgments seems to obstruct the proper consideration of facts about the overall good.

1322. Synthetic Intuitions about Value

How, then, are we to form the all-important judgment of value about 'the good in a whole life'? Lewis tries an answer that stays within the constraints of his empiricism about value. First, he considers an over-simple empiricist suggestion. We might consider each immediate experience of liking or disliking—the experience mentioned in a terminating judgment—in order to see how they all add up when we consider all the experiences at all the relevant times. Once we have seen this, we have found all the relevant value. We may call this an aggregative conception of overall value in a whole life.[25]

Lewis, however, rejects this purely aggregative conception for a good reason. He points out that the relations between the experiences sometimes affect the value of the whole that is composed of the experiences. Here we need a 'synthetic intuition' (506). Since the value of the whole is not simply the aggregate of the value of the parts taken in isolation, we cannot grasp it simply by surveying each part in isolation.[26]

Non-aggregative value appears in several familiar and important situations: (1) We may value a result of our effort because it results from our efforts, whereas we would not value it in the same way if it did not result from those efforts. If I climb a hill, I may want to look at the view, so that I would be disappointed if mist obscured the view; but I would not value being able to see the view in the same way if I had not climbed the hill first. (2) In listening to a symphony, I do not simply value the individual passages, even the best ones. The value of each passage depends partly on its context, and so we cannot discover the total value of the symphony by aggregating the value of the individual passages taken in isolation. This is what Lewis means by claiming that we have to grasp the total value through synthetic intuition.[27]

[25] '. . . if this whole is constituted by experiences A, B, and C together, then the value of it will be simply the values found in A, B, and C, with no addition or diminution by reason of the relation of these experiences to one another . . . if you find a certain value in experience having such and such a character, and another value in experience of another sort, then the value you *should* find in the whole constituted by two such experiences together, is simply the aggregate of these two values without reference to any further fact.' (*AKV* 494)

[26] 'And because the character of it which we wish to apprehend is affected by the manner of its internal organization, the kind of synthesis which is called for cannot be accomplished by treatment of it as an aggregate.' (506)

[27] 'One could not, for example, by selecting from among Beethoven's symphonies the three movements which are rated highest, and juxtaposing these, create a better symphony than Beethoven ever wrote.' (496)

Lewis's defence of synthetic intuition is plausible in its own right, and also relevant to his conception of prudence. He argues that prudence is the rationally required attitude because it involves concern for one's life as a whole, not simply for particular episodes of it that happen to appeal to us more (e.g., the nearer future). If he is right about the non-aggregative value of wholes, he has a good reason for saying that prudence is aware of value that fractional prudence is likely to overlook. If one's life, or significant aspects of one's life have non-aggregative value because they are wholes, one needs to recognize them as wholes in order to have the appropriate synthetic intuition of their value. Parents try to bring up their children well; they have to think about the whole of their children's upbringing, and they will lose sight of what they are trying to do if they focus on some parts of the upbringing to the exclusion of others that are equally important. Scientists try to carry out research programmes, and they will be distracted from the value in their projects if they focus irrationally on some aspects rather than others. A selective focus on the future that leaves out some aspects that are no less significant than the ones we focus on will distort our conception of the value to be realized, not only because we will miss some valuable episodes, but also because we will miss some of the contextual value of the episodes that we focus on.

In this way, Lewis's arguments about prudence and about synthetic intuition of value support each other. But when we take them together and consider their implications, they seem to raise a difficulty for his views about immediate experiences of liking. He treats these experiences as parallel to the awareness of what is given in sense-perception; they are episodes about which we can be mistaken only if we lie, not because we fail to recognize what we are aware of. How are we to apply this parallel to experiences of value, if we keep in mind Lewis's claims about synthetic intuition? If I am listening to a symphony with enjoyment, I am having immediate experiences of liking. But do I necessarily recognize them for what they are? If I do not recognize that my enjoyment of the parts of the symphony rests partly on synthetic intuition, I may suppose that I am enjoying this part of the symphony in isolation; I may infer that I would enjoy it no less if I heard it all by itself. In that case, I fail to recognize what I am enjoying, and hence fail to recognize part of the character of my experience of liking. Hence my experience is not immune to honest error.

If this is true, some experiences of value must be more complex than Lewis supposes they are, and he fails in his aim of grounding judgments about value in simple, immediate experiences. He might perhaps distinguish (a) the immediate experience of liking from (b) the judgment about its source or basis. Then he might claim that synthetic intuition enters only in judgments about the source. But this does not seem satisfactory. If, as Lewis correctly claims, I enjoy a result of my effort as such, my judgment about the source of my enjoyment is not separate from the character of the enjoyment itself; it is part of what I enjoy, and I have not correctly described my enjoyment unless I include this feature of it.

Even if we were to allow Lewis to separate the immediate enjoyment from the judgment about its source, we would not protect his position from objections. For now we might legitimately doubt whether objective judgments of value imply terminating judgments about immediate liking. They seem to imply judgments about liking with a certain character, which depends on a judgment about the source. This objection presents another obstacle to Lewis's empiricism about judgments of value.

Lewis's claims about prudence and the synthetic intuition of value are reasonable. They show that if we are to take account of the relevant facts about value, we have to avoid both distortion and blindness. Proximism introduces distortion, because it does not allow us to count all of our future with its proper weight. An aggregative conception of value blinds us to the value that we recognize through synthetic intuition. Lewis rightly argues that immediate experience of particular isolated episodes should not be given complete authority in fixing value. But he does not consider the implications of this argument for his empiricism about value judgments. It is difficult to see how the value judgments that recognize all the relevant facts, including those about the future as a whole and about non-aggregative value, can be given their whole meaning by terminating judgments about immediate experiences of liking. His empiricism about value judgments is open to question even apart from questions about prudence and synthetic intuition. Once we raise these questions, we seem to have good reason, on the basis of his views, to question his empiricism about values.

1323. The Moral Point of View

Lewis does not say much in *AKV* about the basis of the particular form of evaluative judgment that involves moral judgment. But he seems to think that the basic moral principle is no more arguable than the basic principle of prudence. He makes two claims about it: (1) A Kantian principle of universalizability (as Sidgwick and Hare understand it) is part of the concept of 'morally right'. If we make judgments about the right, we must, unless we are confused, make universal judgments. (2) We need a moral sense in order to acknowledge a distinction between right and wrong. Without this moral sense, we could not be argued into any principle of action.[28]

The remarks do not seem to fit each other, because the recognition of conceptual truths about 'right' or 'morally right' does not seem to require a moral sense; it only seems to require a grasp of the concept 'right'. A moral sense is perhaps needed if we are to grasp that this or that action is right, if (that is to say) we are to make synthetic moral judgments. But why do we need synthetic moral judgments in order to recognize conceptual truths?

Perhaps we can see why Lewis introduces a moral sense if we notice how his treatment of moral principles is different from his treatment of prudential principles. He claims that the basic principle of prudence is analytically true, but that does not settle the question of whether anyone should be prudent. In answer to this question, Lewis argues that prudence constitutes a categorical imperative, because it is part of consistency and reasonableness in action, and if we give that up we are not rational thinkers at all and are not open to

---

[28] '. . . the fundamental dictum of justice, "No rule of action is right except one which is right in all instances, and therefore right for everyone", is likewise not a principle acceptance of which either requires to be or could be inculcated by argument where natively the recognition of it should be absent. Logically considered, it is a tautology; it merely expresses a formal character of the correct or justified, implicit recognition of which is contained in acknowledgement of the distinction between right and wrong. Given this moral sense, recognition of the principle is mere self-clarification; and where the moral sense should be lacking, argument for this or any other principle of action would be pointless.' (482)

argument. He seems to give no similar argument for the categorical status of any principle of morality.

But though this is true in *AKV*, Lewis, in *GNR*, tries to connect morality with the basic Law of Objectivity that requires us to decide in the light of our view of the facts. He suggests that the moral counterpart to the prudent person's recognition of the equal reality of the future is the moral person's recognition of the equal reality of other people and their mental states. If we accept their equal reality, we are committed to two principles. One prescribes compassion for creatures whose suffering is as poignant as our own. The other prescribes respect for creatures that are capable of acting on rational principles, including the principle that requires us to proceed on the basis of our apprehension of the facts rather than on our inclinations.[29]

Lewis does not explain why the recognition of other people as similar to me in the relevant ways requires either compassion or respect for them. If I were concerned about myself and my experiences simply because I am one creature with these experiences, pleasures, and pains, the recognition that others are like me in the relevant ways would indeed give me a reason for concern about them. But if I am concerned about myself because I am myself, it is not clear why recognition of others who are similar to myself but are not me should require me to treat them as I treat myself. Sidgwick distinguishes these two types of self-concern in his discussion of the type of egoism that leads to a dualism of practical reason.[30] Lewis assumes that he need only consider the 'universal' type of self-concern that does not rest on an essentially first-personal attitude. But he does not show that everyone has to have this universal type of concern. If he could show that some of my attitudes to myself treat me simply as one agent capable of pleasure, pain, and rational action, he would have an argument to show that the law of objectivity requires similar treatment for others.[31]

How do we discover the relevant treatment for others? Lewis answers this question when he discusses the determination of 'impersonal' value, 'to be gauged by reference to all those who might be affected by the existence of it' (545). These questions, in his view, can be settled only through the exercise of 'empathetic imagination'.[32] We try to imagine another person's experience of value; A considers not what A would experience as valuable in B's situation, but what A would experience if A were B. This exercise of empathy can establish something about impersonal value, but it is not enough by itself. How are we to decide if one action seems to offer more satisfaction to a few people and an alternative action offers a lower level of satisfaction to more people? To answer this question we have to imagine ourselves living the lives of all the people affected in turn, to imagine their different

---

[29] '... the dictate to govern one's activities affecting other persons, as one would if these effects of them were to be realized with the poignancy of the immediate—hence in one's own person. The dictate is to respect other persons as the realities we representationally recognize them to be—as creatures whose gratifications and griefs have the same poignant factuality as our own; and as creatures who, like ourselves, find it imperative to govern themselves in the light of the cognitive apprehensions vouchsafed to them, by decisions which they themselves reach, and by reference to values discoverable to them.' (*GNR* 91)

[30] Sidgwick on types of egoism; §1200.   [31] See Kant, §962.

[32] 'We have to "put ourself in the place of" the other person ... and gauge value as realized by him on the supposition of whatever fundamental likeness to ourself seems justified by the evidence of his behaviour and other pertinent circumstances.' (*AKV* 545)

experiences of value. The preference that we form as a result of the relevant process of empathetic imagination settles the impersonal value.[33]

To form this preference is not the same as to act on it. Lewis does not—as Hare does—describe this process as a means to forming the moral judgment that the action I would (in these circumstances) prefer is the one I ought to do. Lewis recognizes that the determination of impersonal value does not answer the ethical question about how I should weigh impersonal value.[34] If we imagine everyone's direct experiences of value, according to Bentham's maxim of everyone's pleasure counting equally, we have a rule for the determination of impersonal value. But once we have reached our judgment of impersonal value, a further question arises about whether we ought to be guided by impersonal value, or by our own interest, or by some non-egoist principle that does not seek to maximize impersonal value, as Lewis understands it. This, at any rate, is the view that we seem to find in *AKV*. In *GNR*, however, Lewis argues that if we follow a rational principle based on objectivity, we have to follow Bentham's maxim.

To see what is involved in Lewis's empathy-based preference, we need to recall some of what he has already said about the sources of value, and especially about the importance of synthetic intuitions. What is involved in my living the life of each affected person seriatim? If I think of each person's life as part of my own life, then surely I need to consider the non-aggregative value of the whole life I imagine myself leading in this way. But how do I do this? If I consider a situation in which A is very happy and B is very miserable against an alternative in which both are in an intermediate condition, I might prefer a life that starts with B's life and then improves to A's life over the intermediate life, but prefer the intermediate life over the one that begins with A's life and ends with B's. Hence my preference will be affected by the order in which I consider the lives. In that case, my preference will give no clear answer about impersonal values.

Could we solve this problem by stipulating that the order in which I imagine myself living A's and B's life is unknown? But that stipulation seems to make the problem worse; for if I do not know the order, I do not know the non-aggregative value of any given life that combines different lives, and so I do not know which combination I would prefer. If I am a risk-taker, I may prefer to give myself the chance of ending with A's life and accept the risk of ending with B's life; but if I am averse to risk, I may prefer the intermediate life. In that case, the impersonal value will depend on apparently irrelevant facts about me.

But is it unfair to suppose that Lewis asks me to imagine other people's lives as part of my own life? Perhaps I should imagine myself not as a single Methuselah, but as having a series of lives that do not form a single life, so that they lack the non-aggregative value

---

[33] 'Supposing that you have envisaged the experiences of all these persons involved, as accurately and adequately as you are able to do, which of these two objects would you prefer if the experiences of all these persons were to be your own; as, for example, if you had to live the lives of each of them seriatim?' (547)

[34] 'We should not confuse the problem of assessing the value of an object . . . with the ethical question, "What manner of giving weight to the value-experience of others, in comparison with our own, is morally imperative in determining our own conduct?" . . . this ethical question is distinct from any question of evaluation—which last is always a question of empirical facts of some kind. Probably we should not quarrel with the ethical dictum, "Each to count for one, and none for more than one". But whether or not we recognize this ethical command to be concerned about the value-experience of others as if it were our own, at least such giving of equal weight to the experience of each person is involved in the intent of the whole class of value-judgments commonly made in that manner which we here speak of as "impersonal".' (545–6)

that belongs to a single life. This will not answer the question about non-aggregative value, if a series of lives can form a whole with non-aggregative value. And apparently they can form such a whole. If A makes some progress towards discovering the cure for cancer, and then B builds on A's work to discover the cure, A's life gains non-aggregative value from its contribution to B's life. It still seems, then, that the order is not irrelevant. Should we, then, simply stipulate that a series of lives cannot have non-aggregative value? This stipulation would be unrealistic, and hence the method for determining impersonal value would be open to objection.

We might try to keep the spirit of Lewis's imagination-based preference by imagining that I live all these people's lives simultaneously, rather than successively, to eliminate the non-aggregative value that results from order. But if the lives are all part of a single life, a problem of non-aggregative value enters again, if I imagine myself 'multi-tasking'. If I live the life of someone who suffers terribly, this may distract me from the life of someone who is discovering the cure for cancer; but if I can discover the cure for cancer despite these distractions, that may actually increase the value to me of discovering the cure for cancer. But this value that would be present in a single life is not present in the same way in two different people's lives. Here the first-person imagination seems to introduce an element that is irrelevant to the situation being considered.

Perhaps, then, I should imagine myself living several lives at once, not as a single person multi-tasking, but as several unconnected lives, each of which is my life. The first-person imagination is needed so that I understand what each person suffers and enjoys, but it does not collect the lives of all these people into one life. The difficulty with this imaginative experiment is that we cannot easily see what, on Lewis's grounds, we would prefer. We may think we know what we would prefer because we think we would prefer the highest net satisfaction, summed over this series of lives that we regard as our own lives; but we have no rational basis for thinking we would prefer this. If we are thinking about a single life, Lewis gives us reasons to act on a principle of prudence that is equally concerned for all the parts of our whole life; but this is a principle that precisely does not apply to simultaneous lives that are not to be considered part of a single life. Hence we have no reason to believe, on Lewis's grounds, that I will prefer to maximize over different lives that I regard as mine, but not as part of a single life.

This argument suggests something may be more deeply wrong with Lewis's appeal to preferences based on imagination. If I imagine different people's 'experiences of value' (550) as simultaneous and as all mine, but not part of a single life, I seem to leave out the actual relations between the different people involved, including the fact that one of them is me, another is a friend of mine, another is unrelated to me, and so on. In concentrating on their experiences of value, I seem to leave out the origins and sources of these experiences. But Lewis tells us that relational properties of experiences are sometimes relevant to their value; that is why their value cannot be wholly aggregative. If we follow his instructions about how to assess impersonal value, we seem to leave out some aspects of value that he has drawn to our attention. Since these are genuine aspects of value, we should agree with him about them, and reject his account of impersonal value.

We have a further reason for doing this if we recall the second rational imperative that Lewis introduces in *GNR*. This imperative prescribes respect for other rational agents as such. He sees that this principle is distinct from the law of compassion, but he does not consider the possibility that it may conflict with the law of compassion, as he presents it. Why should we suppose that we accord equal respect to other people if we simply count the strength of each person's desire together with other people's? It seems that A's aims and interests can be overridden by B's desires, however foolish they may be, provided only that B's desires are stronger, or that B would suffer more from having them frustrated. If we doubt whether this is a plausible result, we may reasonably doubt whether Lewis's maximizing conception of impersonal value fits the requirement of respect for other rational agents. The utilitarian and the Kantian elements seem to conflict in Lewis's position, just as they do in Sidgwick's. The Kantian elements refer to the rights and obligations of persons, but persons get lost in the assessment of value that utilitarians rely on for practical guidance.

This conclusion marks a basic conflict in Lewis's attempt to work out a systematic analysis of knowledge and valuation. It is systematic in so far as it offers a reductive empiricist analysis of value judgments that takes their meaning to be exhausted by terminating judgments. This analysis follows the pattern of Lewis's analysis of judgments about physical objects, and it is open to the same criticisms. Similarly, his account of rationality, prudence, and inter-personal value sticks to his empiricist constraints, and raises the same doubts.

Lewis deserves discussion, however, not only because he exposes some of the objections that face systematic empiricism about value, but also because he sets out some of the basic principles that are especially difficult to reconcile with systematic empiricism. He affirms that value judgments are about objective facts, that there is a categorical imperative of practical reason, and that the value of a whole cannot be reduced to the aggregative value of its parts. His arguments for these claims are plausible and important in their own right, and they give us an especially clear view of some aspects of value and practical reason that make an empiricist analysis especially implausible. Lewis not only defends empiricism, but clearly sets out some of the reasons that make empiricism about value difficult to believe. His clear analysis, and his clear formulation of the principles that cast doubt on his analysis, are helpful for discussion of attempts to revive empiricist analyses. It is often useful to ask whether the objections that face Lewis's position can be used or adapted to cast doubt on less resolute versions of empiricism.

90

HARE: A DEFENCE
OF NON-COGNITIVISM

1324. Hare's Aims

One might regard Hare as a successor to emotivism who offers an improved version of non-cognitivism, in opposition to both naturalism and the non-naturalist cognitivism of Moore and Ross. A critic may ask whether and in what ways Hare's prescriptivism improves on emotivism, and whether the improvements allow Hare to answer the objections to emotivism without raising further objections.

Though this approach to Hare captures part of his position, it does not do justice to his main aims. In particular, it overlooks some differences between his attitude and Stevenson's attitude to the task of the moral philosopher. Stevenson tries to fit moral judgment into positivist preconceptions about meaning and knowledge. If we accept emotivism, we get rid of mysterious moral facts, and so we are not puzzled about how we can know anything about them. Stevenson argues that this account of moral judgment is less destructive to morality than we might suppose, but he does not suggest that his analysis will encourage us to take morality more seriously than we would take it if we were cognitivists. Nor does he suggest that if emotivism were more harmful to morality than he believes it is, that would be a reason for doubting it.

Hare, by contrast, believes that prescriptivism does justice to morality and encourages us to take morality seriously. He does not say that prescriptivism does as well as cognitivism in showing why we should take morality seriously. He claims that prescriptivism does better. If cognitivism were right, moral judgment would be a purely theoretical enterprise, and it would not be clear to us why we legitimately expect our moral judgments to guide our actions. But if we are prescriptivists, we can see why morality matters.[1]

---

[1] A typical passage is the beginning of the preface to *MT*: 'I offer this book to the public now rather than later . . . because of a sense of urgency—a feeling that if these ideas were understood, philosophers might do more to help resolve important practical issues. These are issues over which people are prepared to fight and kill one another; and it may be that unless some way is found of talking about them rationally and with hope of agreement, violence will finally engulf the world. Philosophers have in recent years become increasingly aware of the role that they might have in preventing this; but they have lacked any clear idea of what constitutes a good argument on practical questions. Often they are content with

In Hare's view, a sound meta-ethical theory helps us to reach a sound position in normative ethics. Stevenson's meta-ethics makes it difficult to see any room for normative moral philosophy. If Moore is right to claim that every attempt to identify moral properties with natural properties involves the naturalistic fallacy, morality cannot be an object of natural science. If Stevenson is right, only an object of natural science can be an object of knowledge. Since the combination of ethical non-naturalism with empiricism seems plausible to many 20th-century philosophers, normative moral knowledge is ruled out. Philosophers influenced by logical empiricism often believe that the only a priori truths are analytic, true by virtue of the meaning of terms. Hence many believe that the moral philosopher can only analyse moral concepts and judgments. Since normative ethics cannot be reduced to conceptual analysis, normative ethics seems to fall outside philosophy.

This conception of the philosopher's task leaves no room for the normative moral theorist. Normative theorists describe the general principles underlying our moral judgments, and put forward normative theories to correct ordinary judgments. Sidgwick is perhaps the most self-conscious about the presence of both elements in his argument. But from a characteristically 20th-century point of view, this conception of the moral philosopher's task rests on a confusion of two different inquiries, neither of which is the proper business of a philosopher. The descriptive inquiry belongs to a sociologist, psychologist, or anthropologist, who has the necessary skills in the empirical description and analysis of moral beliefs and practices. The normative inquiry does not belong to any expert; philosophers have no special right to pronounce on normative moral questions. Hence some 20th-century moral philosophers follow Stevenson and disclaim special competence in normative ethics. They often insist that their meta-ethical arguments are neutral on normative questions.[2]

It is easier to give up normative moral philosophy if we believe that no progress has been made in normative inquiry. We might support such a belief from a pessimistic survey of normative ethics between Sidgwick and Ross. Ross's objections to utilitarianism lead him to a plurality of irreducibly distinct principles with no systematic method for arranging them in any hierarchy. In cases of conflict, we just have to see, on this account, that one or the other principle is to be followed. Though this form of intuitionism allows objective moral knowledge, it may encourage scepticism. For the more we appeal to things that we 'just have to see' and the less argument we can give for seeing them one way rather than another, the more doubts we arouse about whether anything is there to be seen. Intuitionism is a non-sceptical position, but it may encourage those who recognize no philosophical knowledge beyond conceptual analysis. Even if we do not follow Stevenson into emotivism, we may want to confine moral philosophy within the narrow limits of his conceptual inquiry.

appeals to their own and others' intuitions and prejudices; and since it is these prejudices which fuelled the violence in the first place, this is not going to help.'

[2] See Ayer, 'Foreword' to Nowell-Smith, *Ethics*: 'There is a distinction, which is not always sufficiently marked, between the activity of a moralist, who sets out to elaborate a moral code, or to encourage its observance, and that of a moral philosopher, whose concern is not primarily to make moral judgments, but to analyse their nature. Mr Nowell-Smith writes as a moral philosopher. He shows how ethical statements are related to, and how they differ from, statements of other types, and what are the criteria which are appropriate to them.' Nowell-Smith does not in fact confine himself to the tasks that Ayer allows to the moral philosopher. He defends, for instance, a rule-utilitarian position against Ross's intuitionism, by quite familiar normative arguments.

Hare accepts the logical empiricist reasons for separating moral philosophy from normative ethics, as Sidgwick conceives it. But he believes that none the less the moral philosopher can give strong reasons for a normative position. Though a correct account of morality does not imply any normative conclusions, we can reach normative conclusions if we combine prescriptivism with plausible non-moral assumptions about normal human motivation. Prescriptivism vindicates utilitarianism, but without the normative premises that Sidgwick uses. Hare rejects both a dialectical argument from common-sense morality and an axiomatic argument from intuitions. If he is right, the combination of prescriptivist meta-ethics with reasonable psychological assumptions eliminates weaknesses in earlier defences of utilitarianism.

One part of Hare's argument addresses readers who already reject cognitivism; it aims to make them prescriptivists rather than emotivists. Another part is directed to cognitivists (or 'descriptivists', as Hare calls them); it aims to make them non-cognitivists. The two parts of the argument are connected; non-cognitivism will seem more plausible once we recognize that non-cognitivists need not be emotivists.

The main points of agreement and disagreement between Hare and emotivism will appear from this summary of his view: (1) Moral judgments are not imperatives, but they are similar to imperatives in being essentially prescriptive. They entail imperatives, and so have a characteristically prescriptive force; in saying that x is good, I thereby prescribe or commend it. This force is part of the meaning of moral judgments. (2) Moral terms are not always used with a prescriptive sense.[3] Other uses involve non-prescriptive 'inverted commas' senses of the moral terms. (3) Moral judgments have both descriptive and prescriptive meaning. (4) Moral judgments are not only prescriptive but also universalizable and overriding.

Since the first two features constitute Hare's prescriptivism, we may usefully examine them before we consider his other views. The third and fourth features are especially relevant to the normative implications of his theory; they should show us how far his other views depend on his prescriptivism.

1325. Conditions of Adequacy

In his late work *Sorting Out Ethics*, Hare sets out some intuitive convictions about morality, in order to compile a list of six conditions of adequacy for a theory (42).[4] These conditions are neutrality, practicality, incompatibility, logicality, arguability, and conciliation. In contrast to Stevenson, Hare tries to formulate these as neutral criteria that a cognitivist can accept in advance. Practicality and incompatibility correspond approximately to two of Stevenson's requirements ('magnetism' and 'intelligent disagreement'); but Hare states practicality in terms that do not assume the truth of internalism.[5] Logicality and arguability mark the

---

[3] The prescriptive use gives the central 'evaluative' sense that marks 'the essential purpose of moral language' (*LM* 171).

[4] These are 'the features of moral language and its logic, as we have them, which a theory must do justice to if it is to be tenable' (*SOE* 118).

[5] On practicality, see *SOE* 119 (on the 'So what?' reaction, discussed at §1330 below).

main ways in which emotivism fails. Neutrality and practicality mark the main failures of cognitivism.[6] Hare believes that only his prescriptivist position meets all six requirements.

These conditions of adequacy suggest some questions: (1) How are we to decide whether these are the right conditions? (2) Is Hare right to claim that all and only these conditions are relevant in assessing meta-ethical theories? (3) Is he right to claim that his theory satisfies them all, and other theories do not? We can clarify the different conditions in discussing Hare's argument.

Hare treats these six conditions as conditions of adequacy, but he does not treat any intuitive moral beliefs in the same way; for he takes his six conditions to be conceptual truths, and believes that none of them commits us to any definite normative claims. To see whether something is a conceptual truth, we ought to appeal only to linguistic data, and specifically to the recognition of utterances as deviant.[7]

Since our recognition of contradictions or their absence is not supposed to depend on moral intuitions (which Hare refuses to rely on), moral intuitions should not influence our acceptance of Hare's six conditions of adequacy.[8] One familiar method of argument in normative ethics relies on considered moral judgments that capture (as Ross puts it) 'what we really think' about moral questions. These beliefs are intuitive in the sense that they are not explicitly derived from any general normative theory. Ross is an intuitionist in so far as he treats these intuitive beliefs as an acceptable starting point for theory; Rawls agrees with him. Hare believes that this method, which he calls 'argument from received opinion', is the wrong method for normative ethics, because it imposes a basically conservative attitude to the conventional moral views of our time and place. In Hare's view, we have a better method than dialectical argument from intuitive moral beliefs. The arguments to show that moral judgments are prescriptive and universalizable are strictly conceptual arguments; but if we agree that moral judgments have these features, we must—according to Hare's argument—accept utilitarianism as well.[9]

Hare offers further conditions of adequacy in his claim that a correct account of morality should resolve the apparent conflict between freedom and reason in our moral beliefs. Two convictions appear to conflict: (1) I am free to make my own mind up on moral questions. (2) I ought to make my mind up on some rational basis.[10] Though these convictions appear to conflict, both should be respected. But other meta-ethical views cannot reconcile them (Hare believes); descriptivism[11] violates the conviction about freedom, whereas emotivism violates the conviction about reason. Only prescriptivism respects both convictions. Hare

---

[6] See *SOE* 118–19.

[7] 'Among the kinds of deviance that especially interest the moral philosopher in his capacity of logician are self-contradictions. Thus, if it is alleged that a moral word has a certain meaning, and we find ordinary people perfectly ready to accept as not self-contradictory what would, according to the proposed meaning, be self-contradictory statements, that will be a reason for abandoning the proposal as a proposal about what people *do* mean by their words. . . .' (*MT* 13)

[8] See 'Received opinion', 120–8; *MT* 12–13.

[9] 'Utilitarianism' is Hare's strongest statement about the purely conceptual character of his argument for utilitarianism.

[10] 'Against this conviction, which every adult has, that he is free to form his own opinion about moral questions, we have to set another characteristic of those questions which seems to contradict it. This is, that the answering of moral questions is, or ought to be a rational activity. Although most of us think that we are free to form our own opinions about moral questions, we do not feel that it does not matter what we think about them . . . We feel, rather, that it matters very much what answer we give, and that the finding of an answer is a task that should engage our rational powers to the limit of their capacity.' (*FR* 2–3)

[11] Hare prefers to use 'descriptivism' where others use 'cognitivism'.

represents these as intuitive convictions of thoughtful people, not as views that reflect some particular meta-ethical theory.

But do these intuitive convictions even appear to conflict?[12] Though it is up to me to form my moral convictions, I seem no less free if I believe I ought to form them rationally. Nor does the combination of freedom and reason seem to be peculiar to morality. Scientists who recognize that they ought to be guided by the evidence thereby recognize that they ought to be guided by reason. But they inquire no less freely. Are moral inquiry and decision any different?

Hare thinks they are different, because he interprets the conviction about freedom as implying freedom from any decisive influence of the relevant facts. In some areas, facts can in principle require us to reach specific conclusions on pain of being inconsistent or misusing language; but there are no such facts about morality.[13] This conviction expresses a view about autonomy that some have ascribed to Kant.[14] Hare agrees with the 'modern Kantians' who believe that morality expresses our autonomy because it allows us to make our own law without being constrained by any facts about right and wrong that are prior to the exercise of our will.

Hare has a reasonable basis for his claim that morality presupposes freedom; we can be fairly held responsible for our moral convictions, and so must be free to form them. Perhaps he believes this is not true about factual convictions, since these can be honestly mistaken if we are unaware of the relevant facts. But this is not enough to show that morality is independent of facts. If the relevant facts are accessible enough to us, we might be fairly held responsible for our moral beliefs even if true moral beliefs depend on antecedent moral facts.

This reflexion on Hare's claims about freedom suggests some of the difficulties in his claim to rely strictly on a purely conceptual and non-normative basis for his meta-ethical arguments. For his initial assumption about freedom seems to rely on a controversial claim about independence of moral facts. This controversial claim does not seem to be part of the concept of morality. Hence Hare's actual starting point seems to be less austere than he takes it to be. One might wonder why it is legitimate to start from his assumption about freedom, but illegitimate to start from moral convictions that seem less controversial than this assumption.

1326. Prescriptivism v. Emotivism

Hare agrees with most, though not all, of Stevenson's reasons for rejecting both naturalism and intuitionism, and for taking non-cognitivism to be the only plausible option. But he argues that emotivism fails to explain the rationality of moral judgment, because it treats

---

[12] These questions are forcefully raised in Taylor, 'Critical notice', 47–8.

[13] 'For if I say that the world is flat, we can in principle be shown certain facts such that, once we have admitted them, we cannot go on saying that the world is flat without being guilty either of self-contradiction or of a misuse of language. That nothing of this sort can be done in morals is a thesis which must have the support of all those who reject naturalism.' (FR 2)

[14] Kant and autonomy; §986.

moral judgments as expressions of emotion and attempts at persuasion.[15] Since emotivism give us an implausible account of moral judgments, we would have some reason (in Hare's view) to be meta-ethical sceptics if emotivism were the only possible non-cognitivist position. But Hare defends non-cognitivism through an analysis that substitutes commendation and prescription for the emotivists' references to expression of emotion.

We can see what is distinctive about Hare's position if we recall Ross's criticism of non-cognitivism (*FE* 32–40).[16] Ross argues that moral judgment is neither the expression of emotion nor the issuing of a command. First, he argues that an expression of emotion is not sufficient by itself for a moral judgment. If an expression of emotion is distinctively moral, it has a distinctively moral basis. I might have many reasons for favouring or rejecting an action, but I have a moral reaction only if my favour or rejection rests on a moral judgment. Hence the moral judgment cannot simply be an expression of emotion. For similar reasons, it cannot be simply the issuing of a command.[17]

We might concede to Ross that emotions and commands are not sufficient for moral judgment. But we might still argue that they are necessary; perhaps moral judgments are not simply commands or expressions of feeling, but they must include this non-cognitive element in addition to the judgment that is its basis. Ross answers that emotions and commands are not necessary for moral judgment: (1) First-person and third-person moral judgments, and moral judgments about the past, do not contain any imperative or persuasive element. The non-cognitivist rashly generalizes from second-person judgments. (2) Even when we use a moral judgment to command or to persuade, the imperative or emotive element can be separated from the moral judgment itself.[18]

In Hare's view, Ross goes too far in supposing that a refutation of emotivism refutes a non-cognitivist view. Both Stevenson and Ross are wrong to assimilate imperatives to attempts to persuade. Because of this mistake Ross assumes that if moral judgments are not essentially persuasive, they are not essentially imperative either. Hare believes he has a better reason than Ross has for rejecting Stevenson's claim that the emotive use of moral judgments is primary. He believes that moral judgments are 'magnetic' not because they are persuasive devices, but because they are prescriptive.

Hare's case depends on how we understand the internalist claim that underlies Stevenson's assumptions about magnetism and contagion. If a sincere moral judgment that I ought to do x is internally connected to a favourable emotion towards doing x, Hare's explanation fails. But if the relevant connexion links a sincere judgment that I ought to do x with an order (addressed to myself or to someone else) to do x, Hare's account satisfies the internalist constraint.

On these questions, Hare stands between Stevenson and Ross. He answers Ross's first objection (to show that emotions are insufficient) by arguing that moral judgments have an imperative character that rests on the right basis; the basis, in Hare's view, need not be

---

[15] See *LM* 12–16; Warnock, *CMP* 30–2.

[16] Hare does not mention Ross's criticism, though he must have been aware of it. Moore's objection to Stevenson (published later than Ross's *FE*) is similar; see §1306.

[17] Cf. Kant's criticism of the sentimentalist account of the moral feeling, §927.

[18] 'The attempt to induce the person addressed to behave in a particular way is a separable accompaniment of the thought that the action is right, and cannot for a moment be accepted as the meaning of the words "you ought to do so-and-so".' (Ross, *FE* 34)

a distinct moral judgment. In answer to the second objection (to show that emotions are unnecessary), he concedes that we can make moral judgments without trying to persuade, but he denies that we can make non-imperative moral judgments. In his view, an accurate account of imperatives answers Ross's objection (cf. Hare, SOE 113–14). Ross believes that, since we can cancel the normal persuasive use of moral judgments, this use is no part of their meaning. Hare agrees. But Ross also believes that, since we can cancel the normal prescriptive use of moral judgments, this use is no part of their meaning. Here Hare disagrees.

Hare argues that we can use moral terms without prescriptive force only in 'inverted commas' uses where the terms lack their standard meaning. He recognizes fewer 'inverted commas' or 'non-standard' uses than Stevenson recognizes, but more than Ross recognizes. Unlike Stevenson, he thinks moral judgments keep their standard sense in non-persuasive contexts. Unlike Ross, he believes they do not keep their standard sense in non-prescriptive contexts. Why should we agree with Hare instead of going all the way with Ross?

Hare believes he has a cogent answer to non-naturalist cognitivists such as Ross. Ross is a non-naturalist because he accepts Moore's Open Question Argument. But Hare believes that the only plausible explanation of the success of Moore's argument relies on prescriptivism. If he vindicates this claim, he has a good reason to claim that Ross's refutation of emotivism fails to refute non-cognitivism.

1327. Hare's Reconstruction of Moore

Hare believes—with qualifications to be considered—that Moore's Open Question Argument shows that 'good' has no naturalistic definition, and he agrees with Stevenson's view that it shows more than Moore recognizes. Stevenson rejects the non-naturalist cognitivism of Moore and Ross because it introduces 'mysterious' non-natural facts. Hare has a more interesting and potentially more effective argument. In his view, once we grasp why Moore's argument is sound, we can also see that it rules out non-naturalist cognitivism. The argument is sound because the function of moral terms is to commend. Given this function, the meaning of moral terms is essentially prescriptive.[19]

Hare's argument is open to two familiar objections: (1) The Open Question Argument seems to rule out all informative definitions whatever. Hence it does not seem to be sound. Hence it does not seem to be a suitable premiss in an argument against opponents who deny that moral judgments essentially have prescriptive meaning. (2) Even if Moore refutes naturalism, non-cognitivism does not seem to be the only option; we might prefer non-naturalist cognitivism.

---

[19] 'Thus it is this fact, that in some of its uses "ought" is used evaluatively (i.e. as entailing át least one imperative) that makes a naturalistic analysis impossible ... A logician who neglects these uses will make his task easy, but at the cost of missing the essential purpose of moral language ... For all the words discussed in Parts II and III have it as their distinctive function either to commend or in some other way to guide choices or actions; and it is this essential feature which defies any analysis in purely factual terms. But to guide choices or actions, a moral judgment has to be such that if a person assents to it, he must assent to some imperative sentence derivable from it; in other words, if a person does not assent to some such imperative sentence, that is knock-down evidence that he does not assent to the moral judgment in an evaluative sense—though of course he may assent to it in some other sense (e.g. one of those I have mentioned). This is true by my definition of the word evaluative.' (LM 171–2)

Hare tries to answer these objections. He acknowledges that Moore goes too far, because the Open Question Argument would, as critics complain, rule out perfectly acceptable definitions. He illustrates this point with 'Whatever is a young dog (the proposed definition of "puppy") is a puppy'. We would certainly find the latter sentence informative in situations where we would not find 'Whatever is a young dog is a young dog' informative, and so, if we followed Moore, we would have to deny that 'young dog' is a definition of 'puppy'. Hare agrees that we ought not to follow Moore.

But he thinks a revised version of the Open Question Argument refutes a naturalistic definition of 'good'.[20] He compares 'Whatever is C (the proposed naturalistic definition of "good") is good' with 'Whatever is a young dog is a puppy'. We can see what Moore was getting at if we consider an acceptable paraphrase of the claim about puppies: 'The sentence "A young dog is a puppy" is analytic'. This is an acceptable paraphrase because it does not prevent us from saying anything we want to say in saying that a young dog is a puppy. But if we consider an analogous paraphrase of 'Whatever is C is good' as 'The sentence "C is good" is analytic', we do not respond in the same way. Since we want to use the sentence 'Whatever is C is good' to commend C things, we will not treat our statement as analytic; for if it were analytic, it could not be used to commend C things.[21]

Suppose, for instance, that we claim that goodness in knives is sharpness, and propose 'sharp' as a definition of 'good' in 'good knife'. Since we can use 'whatever is a sharp knife is a good knife' to commend sharp knives, and since we could not use it this way if it meant the same as 'whatever is a sharp knife is a sharp knife', 'sharp' cannot be a definition of 'good' in 'good knife'. Any term, therefore, that can be defined in naturalistic terms cannot also have the function of commending. Hence we can never accept a naturalistic analysis of a term that is used to commend.

This argument is preferable to one that simply asserts or assumes the soundness of Moore's Open Question Argument. It neither asserts nor presupposes the point to be proved, that moral judgments have prescriptive meaning. Hare argues as follows: (1) Moral terms have a commendatory function. (2) Since they have this function, no naturalistic analysis is possible. (3) Hence their meaning is not purely descriptive, but partly prescriptive. Still, the argument as it stands is open to doubt. The inference from (2) to (3) rests on the assumption that naturalism and non-descriptivism are the only possibilities. But they are not: one might either accept a non-naturalist descriptive analysis or affirm that moral concepts are unanalysable, and still be a descriptivist. Hare, however, as we will see, believes he has good reasons for ignoring these two possibilities. Hence we may, for the moment, grant his inference from (2) to (3).

---

[20] '... Moore's argument ... rests, albeit insecurely, upon a secure foundation; there is indeed something about the way in which, and the purposes for which, we use the word "good" which makes it impossible to hold the sort of position which Moore was attacking, although Moore did not see clearly what this something was. Let us, therefore, try to restate Moore's argument ...' (LM 83–4)

[21] 'Thus it is not true to say that the means used to upset naturalistic definitions of value-terms could be used equally to upset any definition. Value-terms have a special function in language, that of commending; and so they plainly cannot be defined in terms of other words which themselves do not perform this function; for if this is done, we are deprived of a means of performing this function. But with words like "puppy" this does not apply; one may define "puppy" in terms of any other words which will do the same job.' (LM 91)

Hare intends the same argument when he claims that the 'action-guiding' character of moral judgments precludes our validly inferring a moral judgment from a statement of fact. It is the function of moral judgments (Hare claims) to guide action; they can perform this function if and only if they entail imperatives; but if they entail imperatives, they have prescriptive, and not merely descriptive, meaning. Hence Moore's argument re-states the fundamental point made by Hume, Plato, Aristotle, and Kant (*LM* 29).[22] Hare assumes that moral judgments have a commendatory or action-guiding function if and only if (as Moore believes) moral terms have no naturalistic analysis and (as Hume believes) no moral judgments follow from purely factual judgments. He takes Moore's view to be true if and only if Hume's view is true, because if moral terms had a naturalistic analysis, moral judgments would follow from factual judgments.

1328. Commendatory Function

Hare's argument turns on the inference from the commendatory function of moral terms to the conclusion that they have no naturalistic analysis. The inference depends on the meaning of the claim that a term 'is used to commend' or that 'its function is to commend'. If this does not beg any question against a cognitivist, it should simply mean that we can use moral terms to commend, or that their appropriate use is commendation. Hare takes commendation to introduce an imperative. Hence A uses a term 'F' to commend doing x to B if and only if A intends B to understand A to be telling B 'Do x' in saying that x is F. Hare does not assume that 'F' has prescriptive meaning. The claim that 'Do x' is part of the meaning of 'x is F' is his conclusion, but it is not a premiss.

Hare believes that 'good' retains this commendatory function even in statements that, according to the naturalist, ought to be analytic. Hence the judgment 'Pleasant things are good' can be used to commend pleasant things. In that case, it is synthetic rather than analytic. And so 'pleasant' is not the definition of 'good'.[23]

In this argument, Hare assumes that analytic statements cannot be used to commend. But why does he assume this? 'Pleasant things are good' may be used to commend pleasant things to someone who cares about pleasure; it will commend them by reminding him that this is what 'good' means. Hare may argue that from the premises that (1) 'Pleasant things are good' means the same (according to the conceptual hedonist) as 'Pleasant things are pleasant'; and (2) we cannot use a tautology to commend. But even if both of these premises are true, they do not show that we cannot use a statement synonymous with a tautology to commend.

Hare argues against this conclusion by appeal to a different example. If 'good' in 'good strawberry' meant 'sweet and ripe', we could not, he argues, use 'Sweet and ripe strawberries

---

[22] In Hare's view, 'No imperative conclusion can be validly drawn from a set of premisses which does not contain at least one imperative' (*LM* 28). Hare believes that this principle applies directly to moral judgments: 'If we admit . . . that it must be part of the function of a moral judgment to prescribe or guide choices, that is to say, to entail an answer to some question of the form, "What shall I do?"—then it is clear . . . that no moral judgment can be a pure statement of fact' (*LM* 29).

[23] On 'painful', cf. Hare, 'Pain'.

are good' to commend them; but since we use it commend them, this cannot be the right definition. Hare seems to argue: (1) The sentence (1a) 'Sweet and ripe strawberries are good' means the same (according to the naturalist definition) as (b) 'Sweet and ripe strawberries are sweet and ripe'. (2) But we do not use (b) to commend sweet and ripe strawberries. (3) But we use (a) to commend them. (4) If (a) and (b) meant the same, we could not use (a) but not (b) to commend. (5) Hence (a) and (b) do not mean the same.

The fourth step in this argument is the most doubtful. Hare agrees that though (c) 'A puppy is a young dog' and (d) 'A young dog is a young dog' mean the same, we can use (c), but not (d) to explain what 'puppy' means. A parallel point seems to apply to (a) and (b). We would not normally use a tautology such as (b) for commending things; but it does not follow that we cannot use (a) for commending, even though it means the same as a tautology. In the right circumstances, with the appropriate assumptions about the interest of our hearer in strawberries, we could use a sentence such as (a) for commendation even if it is also definitional.

On this basis, it is easy to see how 'good' can be used to commend if it means 'pleasant'. The commendatory use is not too puzzling if we suppose that we are normally interested in pleasure. If we believe that 'good' means 'pleasant', 'x is good' normally gives us a reason for choosing x. If A believes that B is interested in pleasure, and that B accepts the hedonist analysis of 'good', A can use 'x is good' as a way to commend doing x to B, by communicating to B A's belief that x is pleasant. However implausible a conceptual hedonist account of 'good' may be, it seems to explain the commendatory function of 'good'.

If, then, we attribute to Hare only the plausible premiss that 'good' is used to commend, he has neither a cogent defence of Moore's argument against a naturalistic definition of 'good' nor a cogent alternative route to Moore's conclusion. His argument would prove too much; for many terms, in the right conditions, can be used to commend, and—on the pattern we have described—retain their commendatory use even in analytic truths. Suppose that the Department of Agriculture defines 'prime' beef as 'containing at least 10% fat'. Even so, we can use 'This prime beef has at least 10??% fat' to commend it to a buyer with the appropriate tastes in beef. Hence Hare's argument faces one of the objections to Moore's argument, that it rules out apparently acceptable definitions.

1329. Evaluative Use Without Prescriptive Meaning?

Hare would have a stronger argument, therefore, if he could show that the commendatory aspect of 'good' and other moral terms is not simply a feature of their use on the right occasions with the right audience, but a part of their meaning. He considers the objection that moral judgments are no more action-guiding than ordinary factual judgments may be in appropriate contexts (*LM* 163). The objector points out that 'The train is about to leave' may be action-guiding, if it is addressed to someone who wants to catch the train, but this action-guiding force is not part of its meaning. Similarly (the objector suggests), 'ought' may be used with action-guiding force in the right context, but this force is not part of its meaning. Hare sees that this objection 'strikes at the root of my whole argument' (*LM* 163).

He concedes that sometimes 'ought' (for instance) can be used in a non-prescriptive sense. But on these occasions (he claims), 'ought' occurs in inverted commas. The proper paraphrase of 'I ought to do x, but I don't commit myself to doing it' is (for instance[24]) 'It is generally believed that one ought to do x'. But in this paraphrase, the embedded 'ought' still has a prescriptive sense; for one cannot give a purely 'naturalistic' analysis of it (*LM* 171). We cannot give an adequate paraphrase that does not contain an embedded 'ought'; hence we cannot give a naturalistic analysis; hence the embedded 'ought' cannot have purely descriptive meaning. The prescriptive sense of 'ought' has to be invoked even to explain uses of 'ought' that are non-prescriptive.

Hence Hare's main claim is that 'ought' has one sense in which its commendatory force is part of its meaning.[25] We find this sense in the 'ought' that is embedded in the analysis of the non-prescriptive senses of 'ought' (as in the example just given). But how are we to decide whether this embedded 'ought' has a prescriptive meaning? An alternative view might treat this alleged meaning as a use of utterances of 'ought' in appropriate contexts. Perhaps, then, commending is an illocutionary act that we perform on the right occasions by saying something with the appropriate meaning. If I believe you want to avoid being bitten by a guard dog, I may warn or advise you not to go on to the building site by telling you it is patrolled by guard dogs. Similarly, I may commend an action to you by telling you it is good or that you ought to do it, if I believe you are concerned to do what you ought to do or what it is good to do.

We might try to test the suggestion that 'ought' has prescriptive meaning by considering whether we can cancel the commendatory force of an ought-judgment without changing the meaning. Suppose that A tells B it is dangerous to walk through the field full of landmines. A intends this information as advice to B. If A discovers that B is indifferent to the danger, A no longer intends this information as advice. But A still believes the same thing and gives B the same information. The sense of 'dangerous' does not change when it is no longer used to give advice. Similarly, if A discovers that B does not care about doing what ought to be done, A may no longer intend ought-judgments as advice or commendation to B, but A still seems to believe the same ought-judgments. It seems arbitrary to claim in this case that 'ought' must have changed its sense, and that A to could not truly claim to believe just the same ought-judgments. Apparently A can cancel the commendatory force of the ought-judgments without changing their meaning.

Hare's argument, therefore, does not justify the crucial step from commendatory function to prescriptive meaning. His argument about definition and commendation does not show that we cannot give naturalistic definitions of terms that have a commendatory function. He is right, therefore, to assert that if the commendatory use of 'good' can be assimilated to the commendatory use of descriptive terms, he faces an objection that 'strikes at the root' of his whole argument. His answer to the objection is not conclusive.

1330. Moral Judgments, Reasons, and Prescriptions

Sometimes Hare defends prescriptivism by appeal to internalism about moral judgments and reasons for action.[26] The internalist about reasons says that we do not understand the

---

[24] *LM* 170 mentions other possibilities.   [25] This over-simplifies Hare's position. See *FR* 75–6.

[26] When he claims that moral judgments entail imperatives, Hare adds, as though he were repeating himself: 'A judgment is not moral if it does not provide, without further imperative premisses, a reason for doing something' (*LM* 31).

judgment that x is wrong if we do not believe that the wrongness of x gives a reason against doing x. Hare believes that acceptance of this internalist claim commits us to prescriptivism.[27] He expresses the same view about reasons in his claim about the necessary 'practicality' of moral judgments. If A convinces B that it is right to do x, B cannot answer 'So what?'[28] Any 'So what?' reaction would show that B did not understand that they had reached agreement on a moral question. In Hare's view, only the recognition of prescriptive meaning allows us to conclude, as we should, that a 'So what?' reaction is logically ruled out. If we recognize that moral judgments give reasons, we cannot react with 'So what?' If we cannot recognize that moral judgments give reasons unless we treat them as having prescriptive meaning, we exclude a 'So what?' reaction if and only if we treat moral judgments as having prescriptive meaning.

If Hare is right about this, he has a plausible argument for prescriptivism. For we may incline to accept internalism about reasons even if we have not yet accepted prescriptivism. If we believe that the rightness of an action counts not at all in favour of doing it, we might well be understood as simply reporting other people's moral judgments, but not really affirming that the action is right. If Hare can show that acceptance of this internalism about reasons commits us to prescriptivism, he has an argument that addresses someone who is not convinced in advance of prescriptivism.

It is not clear, however, that reasons imply imperatives, so that acceptance of a reason implies assent to some corresponding imperative. An internalist claim about moral judgment and reasons seems plausible if we consider justifying reasons. Hence we might agree with Hare, if he asserts no more than an internal connexion between morality and justifying reasons. But this internal connexion does not support prescriptivism; if I simply recognize a reason for doing x, I may not commend it to myself or to anyone else, and I may not intend any imperatives.

Even if we take a rather implausible view of justifying reasons, so that we connect them directly with desires, we need not agree with Hare. We might claim, for instance, that I have a justifying reason to do x if and only if x would promote the satisfaction of some desire of mine. In that case, I recognize a reason for doing x just in case I recognize that doing x would promote the satisfaction of my desire for y. But I still need not assent to any imperative requiring me to do x. For though I might notice that I have some desire for y, I might not care very much about y just now, or I might care much less about y than about z, which x does not promote. If we can take this attitude to moral principles, the reasons that they provide do not entail imperatives.

---

[27] '. . . moral words have . . . (1) a commendatory or condemnatory or in general prescriptive force which ordinary descriptive words lack. [Here Hare refers to *LM* §5.4, the section in which he explains where Moore was right (the example of "puppy" and "young dog").] The person who thinks that (2) the fact that an act would be wrong is no reason at all for not doing it shows thereby that he has not fully grasped the meaning of the word. He may have grasped its descriptive meaning, so that he is able to apply it infallibly to the right actions, according to the current moral conventions; but there is another part of its meaning, (3) the prescriptive or evaluative, which he has not grasped.' (*MT* 71; reference numbers added)

[28] '. . . if, at the end of a moral argument, one of the disputants is forced to agree to a moral conclusion, but can then say "Yes, it would be wrong to do that; but so what?", then the system of moral argument is a fraud.' (*SOE* 119; cf. *MT* 71) Cf. 'Relevance', 112–14.

A more plausible view of justifying reasons conceives them as facts, or presumed facts, in the light of which it would be reasonable to act. If the fact that exercise promotes my health is a reason for taking exercise, I may recognize that I have this reason to exercise, but I may still not want to exercise; hence I do not assent to any imperative about taking exercise. If I accept an internal connexion between making a moral judgment and recognizing a justifying reason of this sort, I may still have no motive for doing the relevant action; in that case, I accept no imperative.

Internalism about moral judgments and reasons brings us closer to prescriptivism if we believe that the reasons implied by moral judgments are motivating reasons, and not simply justifying reasons. But this strong claim is difficult to accept. We may often take people's failure to act, or even to be motivated to act, on their moral judgments as evidence of their insincerity in making the supposed moral judgments. Our attitude, however, does not necessarily support internalism. We may simply assume that most people care about morality. If you say you are sure it will not rain, but you look carefully for your bulky umbrella before you go out, we may reasonably suspect that you are after all not sure that it will not rain; but we do not assume an internal connexion between meteorological judgments and motivation.

Hare's belief in internalism about motivation is open to question for the reasons that led to doubt about his argument from commendatory use to prescriptive meaning. His argument requires the connexion between moral judgment and motivation to be analytic, part of the meaning of a moral judgment. But an apparently more plausible explanation treats the connexion as synthetic, resulting from our normal assumptions about how moral judgments, given their descriptive meaning, are related to people's concerns. The facts about moral judgment and motivation that Hare cites are important; but their importance does not clearly support a prescriptivist claim about meaning.

Even if we accept internalism about moral judgments and motivating reasons, we do not commit ourselves to prescriptivism. For we might concede to Hare that recognition of a reason is not compatible with complete indifference to the action for which we believe we have a reason. But it is compatible with refusal to engage in the action; for I might recognize that I have a slight reason to do x, but not a very strong one, and that I have stronger reasons to do y. If I allow that moral judgments imply some reason, and hence some motivation, they may still not move me to prescribe the action. Hare's conclusion follows only if we recognize an internal connexion between moral judgments and recognition of overriding motivating reasons, and hence of overriding desires. But this internalist thesis is too controversial to provide a suitable premiss for Hare's argument. It reflects Hare's view that moral judgments are not only prescriptive but also overriding. We need to consider his claims about the overriding character of moral judgments later. For the moment, we need only notice that it does not follow from internalism about reasons.[29]

Hare does not show, therefore, that to avoid the 'So what?' reaction to moral judgments we must accept prescriptivism. We avoid the 'So what?' reaction if we recognize some

---

[29] He also seems to blur the distinction between motivation and prescription in his argument for utilitarianism. See §1341.

internal connexion between morality and justifying reasons. But the most plausible views of justifying reasons do not commit us to prescriptivism.

1331. Is Hare's Position Consistent?

We may now return to our earlier question about Stevenson, Ross, and Hare. Is Hare right to claim, against Ross, that the objections to an emotive theory do not spread to an imperative theory? We have found that his argument from commendatory use to prescriptive meaning provokes the objection that he uses against Stevenson. To refute Stevenson, Hare seems to assume a principle about meaning, use, and cancellation: (1) If we can cancel a standard force of moral judgments, either by context or by an explicit act of cancellation, and still make a consistent moral judgment, the standard force is no part of the meaning of the moral judgment. Stevenson, on the contrary, maintains some internal connexion between meaning and force: (2) It is self-contradictory to make a sincere moral judgment without the appropriate connexion to action. Since he believes (2), he takes non-emotive uses of moral terms to involve different senses of the terms.

Hare's position appears to be unstable, because he seems to accept both the principle of cancellation in (1) when he argues against Stevenson, and the internalist principle in (2) when he argues against Ross. His observation that we can sometimes use moral terms to give advice without any attempt to persuade seems to rely on cancellation; but cancellation also seems to show that we can use moral terms without giving advice (or commanding, prescribing, commending). Emotivism fails because it identifies the meaning of moral judgments with aspects of their use that can be cancelled.[30] Hare's theory seems to be open to the same objection.

Hare argues against Stevenson by reference to a case in which someone makes a moral judgment but does not try to persuade anyone. We have seen that if the pacifist-inclined Albert says to Bill, 'I suppose you think I ought to serve in the army, don't you?', and Bill answers, 'Yes, you ought to serve'. Albert is not asking Bill for persuasion, and Bill is not trying to persuade Albert. The question simply recognizes the difference of opinion between himself and Bill, and Bill acknowledges this difference of opinion. In the right context, 'You ought to serve' could have been part of an attempt to persuade, but in the present context it is not used for that purpose.[31]

---

[30] '...we must not step from the true explanation of the meaning of imperatives (namely that an imperative is the kind of speech act, the complaisant or accordant response to which is to do, or become disposed to do, the thing specified) to the false notion that an imperative sentence is, essentially, an attempt to get something to do the thing specified, and that this is an explanation of its meaning. Usually it is an attempt to get the thing done, but not essentially.' (SOE 112)

[31] On Albert and Bill, see §1307. In his early paper 'Will', Hare makes the relevant point clearly. He appeals to the possibility of disavowing any persuasive aim as a reason for denying that moral judgments are essentially persuasive. He argues that even when persuasion is acknowledged to be impossible, moral judgments do not cease to be true and relevant. 'If it were an essential purpose of moral judgments to persuade, they would become inappropriate in all cases where we knew that persuasion would be ineffective. But this is not the case. If a man is a very hardened offender, and if therefore the addressing of moral judgments to him will not alter his behaviour (whatever you say he is bound to go on doing it), we do not on that account stop saying that he ought not to act as he does.' (213) This argument about persuading seems to apply no less to commending and prescribing. Can we not explicitly and truthfully disavow them also?

We can apparently adapt this example to cast doubt on Hare's claim about prescriptive meaning. The same dialogue in the same circumstances gives us reason to doubt whether Bill is advising Albert to serve in the army. If Albert has made his mind up, he is not asking Bill for advice, and if Bill realizes Albert has made his mind up, Bill is not wasting his time by giving Albert orders or advice that Bill realizes would be pointless. But when Albert asks Bill what Bill believes, Bill truthfully declares his moral belief. Admittedly, if Albert had asked Bill, 'What do you advise me to do?', and Bill had answered 'You ought to serve', Bill would have given Albert advice. Similarly, if Albert had expected Bill to command him, and had asked 'What are your orders?', Bill's reply 'You ought to serve' would have been an order issued in response to Albert's request. Moral judgments may have, in the right context, the illocutionary force of prescribing, commanding, or advising, but this force can be cancelled; it is not part of their meaning.[32]

A similar appeal to cancellation raises doubts about Hare's claim that 'ought' has a distinct 'inverted commas' sense in cases where it is not used prescriptively. He suggests (as Stevenson does) that in 'inverted commas' cases 'ought' means (for instance) 'it is generally supposed that you ought'. This may sometimes be suggested by non-prescriptive uses of 'ought', but it can hardly be the meaning, since the suggestion can be cancelled. In the circumstances we have described, where Bill is neither trying to persuade, nor prescribing, nor advising, Bill might clarify his statement of his moral belief by saying 'It isn't generally supposed that you ought to serve, but still you ought to'.[33] Bill does not seem to contradict himself in saying this, even though he uses 'ought' non-prescriptively; hence he does not seem to use 'ought' in Hare's inverted commas sense.

One might argue that though Bill does not seem to contradict himself, he really contradicts himself none the less. But it is difficult for Hare, no less than for Stevenson, to defend this claim. Hare rejects Stevenson's claim that we contradict ourselves in cancelling the emotive force of moral judgments (in cases where the emotivist paraphrases do not work). It seems arbitrary of Hare, therefore, to resort to claims about self-contradiction in cases where we cancel the prescriptive force of a moral judgment. Should we not say that in both sorts of cases the judgment is consistent, and the moral term has a descriptive meaning?

Comparison of Hare's argument against Stevenson with a descriptivist's argument against Hare suggests that Hare's basic argument for non-cognitivism is open to the objection that he uses against Stevenson. Moore's and Ross's objections to emotivism apply to prescriptivism as well.

1332. Non-Naturalism and Intuitionism

In this discussion of Hare's arguments for prescriptivism, we have conceded that the position he opposes may be described indifferently as 'naturalism' or 'descriptivism'. But we may

---

[32] Austin's terminology may be used to express this objection to both Stevenson and Hare. But the objections of Moore and Ross show that the basic point does not depend on Austin.

[33] The same point applies to Hare's other suggestions at *LM* 169–71.

want to question this concession. Moore and Ross maintain non-naturalist descriptivism.[34] How does Hare argue against them?

In *LM*, he holds a confusingly broad conception of natural properties. He goes beyond Moore's view of natural properties as those that are the subject-matter of natural sciences. Moore's description is vague enough to raise many difficulties, but at least Moore does not suggest moral properties are the only non-natural properties. In Moore's view, those who identify moral properties with metaphysical properties are not naturalists, though they commit the naturalistic fallacy. Hare, however, assumes that all definitions of moral terms in descriptive terms are naturalistic. When he summarizes his argument against naturalism (*LM* 171), he says that 'good' defies any analysis in purely factual terms. He implies, then, that the same argument defeats non-naturalistic factual analyses. But it is not clear what he includes among such analyses. He insists that a purely 'factual' judgment must exclude all 'covertly evaluative' expressions.[35] But he claims that all definitions that exclude covertly evaluative expressions are naturalistic definitions. Hence he seems to deny the possibility of any 'factual' or 'descriptive' accounts that are not naturalistic.

Hare's assumptions about covertly evaluative expressions are controversial. He claims that these include such terms as 'normal', 'healthy', and 'promoting human flourishing'. But these terms do not seem to be evaluative in Hare's technical sense, since they do not seem to entail imperatives. They are related to norms, reasons, and to concepts such as 'appropriate' and 'ought'. But it does not follow that they are entail imperatives, unless 'ought' and so on entail imperatives. But we should not concede this about 'ought' and so on unless we are convinced that no factual account of them is possible. But we will be convinced of this only if we are already convinced of the truth of non-cognitivism. We cannot simply reject descriptive accounts that include evaluative expressions on the ground that descriptive accounts of evaluative expressions are impossible. Hare does not seem to give a completely fair hearing to non-naturalist factual analyses of moral concepts.

The difference between Moore and Hare suggests some further questions for Hare: (1) Why does he believe that only moral properties are non-natural? If, on the one hand, he uses 'natural' simply as a synonym for 'non-moral', his account of the natural is different from Moore's. If, on the other hand, his claim that all non-moral properties are natural is synthetic, how is it to be justified? (2) Why should we suppose that all definitions of moral concepts that introduce non-natural properties thereby introduce moral properties?

In *SOE*, in contrast to *LM*, Hare recognizes non-naturalist descriptivism as a distinct possibility. He takes it to claim that moral concepts can be defined only in moral terms.[36] He

---

[34] Moore expresses some doubts about whether moral predicates 'describe'. See Broad's doubts about Moore's doubts, §1262.

[35] 'Let us suppose that someone claims that he can deduce a moral or other evaluative judgment from a set of purely factual or descriptive premises, relying on some definition to the effect that V (a value-word) means the same as C (a conjunction of descriptive predicates). We first have to ask him to be sure that C contains no expression that is covertly evaluative (for example "natural" or "normal" or "satisfying" or "fundamental human needs"). Nearly all so-called "naturalistic definitions" will break down under this test—for to be genuinely naturalistic a definition must contain no expression for whose applicability there is not a definite criterion which does not involve the making of a value-judgment.' (*LM* 92)

[36] 'But an intuitionist, at any rate, has to think that there are these sui generis properties like goodness and wrongness. The only definition that can be given of them is negative; . . . an intuitionist is someone who thinks that in order to give the truth conditions of these statements we have to use specifically moral terms.' (*SOE* 64)

seems to assume, therefore, that all non-moral concepts introduce natural properties. But if there are non-natural non-moral properties, non-naturalists need not confine themselves to moral terms in their definitions of moral concepts. We may believe that concepts such as 'ought', 'appropriate', and 'reason' are not naturalistically definable, but we do not thereby assume that they are exclusively moral. If we can define moral terms by reference to these concepts, we may have defined moral terms through non-moral terms, though not through natural terms. Hare's account of non-naturalist descriptivism blurs two distinct questions.

Hare objects to non-naturalist descriptivism on the ground that it is committed to intuitionism. Descriptivists try to specify the meaning of moral terms with reference to their truth conditions (*SOE* 82). Naturalist descriptivists fail, according to Hare, because people can apparently apply moral terms to different natural properties with the same meaning; but at least the naturalist can specify the natural properties that are relevant to determining the meaning of moral terms. Non-naturalist descriptivists are worse off, because they cannot appeal to observable properties to justify or to explain moral claims. They claim that moral properties are objects of non-observational knowledge that rests on no further justification or evidence.[37] Intuitionists, as Hare understands them, claim that (e.g.) the judgment that killing the innocent is wrong allows neither further justification nor further explication of what constitutes its wrongness.

Why should non-naturalist descriptivists (whom Hare calls 'intuitionists') accept the particular intuitionist epistemology that Hare attacks? If they reject naturalism, they claim that moral terms cannot be defined exclusively by reference to natural properties. If 'ought', 'reason', and so on are non-natural concepts, but not exclusively moral concepts, we may claim to define moral terms in non-natural but non-moral terms. If we are to understand moral terms, the circle that we have to break into is not the (supposedly) narrow circle of moral concepts, but the broader circle of non-natural terms. If an action's being wrong consists in its violating principles about what is owed to people, or about what is appropriate to a given situation, we cannot identify the relevant property without relying on assumptions about what is owed or appropriate in a given situation. Similarly, one might say that the right food for plants is what is appropriate for the plant's situation; what is appropriate is what the plant needs, and what it needs is what promotes its healthy or flourishing condition. If we also believe that it is healthy and flourishing when it tends not to wither and die, we might form some views about the food that the plant needs. We have not given a wholly non-evaluative definition of 'right food for plants'. The judgment that they are better off if they do not shrivel and die is a synthetic judgment about when they are better off. If we say all this, we are 'intuitionists', in Hare's view, about the right food for plants.

Perhaps, then, the mark of Hare's 'intuitionist' is reliance on synthetic judgments connecting empirical conditions with rightness. Hare seems to mean this when he suggests that an intuitionist must claim some capacity to recognize right action; any given natural

---

[37] 'It seems that, since he is not allowed to appeal to the observable non-moral properties of objects, there is nothing he can do except to say that the researcher just can recognize the class of actions that people call wrong. How is he to recognize them? Only, it would seem, by having the ability or capacity to recognize them . . . it should be clear by now that an intuitionist . . . cannot do without a faculty [of intuition]. For unless a linguistic researcher possessed such a faculty, the class of actions that people called wrong would be quite indeterminate, and so his research would be quite inconclusive; the truth conditions of moral statements might be almost anything.' (*SOE* 83)

property will bear on something's rightness only on the assumption that this is, say, appropriate in the situation. But it is not clear that this sort of 'intuitionism' (if we use Hare's label) commits us to the strong intuitionist claim that moral properties are not subject to explication or argument, and must be recognized by some faculty that cannot be further analysed.

Hare argues, in agreement with Strawson, that if non-naturalist cognitivists allow only synthetic rather than analytic connexions between empirical evidence and moral judgments, their position is open to epistemological suspicion.[38] But our earlier reflexions on Strawson cast doubt on this objection. If non-naturalist descriptivism is true, we cannot master moral concepts by grasping the appropriate definitions and simply applying our empirical knowledge (assumed to be knowledge that includes no evaluative concepts). Mastery of moral concepts also requires the capacity to make synthetic judgments relating natural and evaluative concepts. This is because the evaluative concepts are defined through one another, and so none of them can be defined wholly with reference to non-evaluative concepts.

This circle does not seem vicious. Hare agrees that the example of the modalities shows that some circles of definitions are all right (64). Modal terms are definable with reference to one another, and are not definable non-modally, but we need no faculty of modal intuition. If, similarly, 'good', 'right', 'ought', 'appropriate', 'reason', 'norm', and so on are inter-definable, and some of these (allegedly) moral terms always appear in a definition of each moral term, we can recognize that someone uses a moral term by recognizing that it stands in the appropriate definitional and inferential relations with these other moral terms. An observer who tried to understand our use of moral terms could not understand any one of them without grasping at least one other moral term. But this sort of circle is neither peculiar to moral terms nor obviously vicious.

Hare is right, therefore, to say that if non-naturalist descriptivism is true, we cannot reach moral knowledge by empirical knowledge (as he understands it) together with knowledge of the relevant definitions. Moral knowledge about particular actions or types of action depends on some initial grasp of some synthetic moral truths, if all evaluative concepts are moral. But is this a defect in non-naturalist descriptivism?

1333. Argument from the Neutrality of Moral Language to Prescriptivism

Hare's main case for prescriptivism depends on his arguments from commendatory function and from internalism. But these are not his only arguments. He also claims that familiar features of moral judgment and argument do not fit descriptivism. He has good reason to claim that these are indeed familiar features of moral judgment; if we can see whether or not they allow a descriptivist account, we will see how much a descriptivist account can explain.

Hare argues that moral concepts are not only practical but also 'neutral', and that only a non-descriptivist analysis captures their neutrality. By this he means that an adequate analysis

---

[38] On Strawson see §1279.

must be acceptable to both sides in any moral argument.[39] He sums up this condition in the slogan 'No substantial disagreement without verbal agreement', which he says is fatal to naturalism and to most other kinds of descriptivism (*MT* 69). He relies on a reasonable objection to (for instance) a conceptual utilitarian account of 'right'. If a normative utilitarian claims that it is right to maximize happiness, and a deontologist claims that it is not always right to maximize happiness, the conceptual utilitarian must say one of two things: (a) The normative utilitarian is simply reminding us of the meaning of 'right', and the deontologist simply displays ignorance of the meaning. (b) If the deontologist is not simply contradicting herself, she is using 'right' in a different sense from the normative utilitarian; hence she is using a different concept from the one the utilitarian uses, and their two claims do not really contradict each other. Neither of these answers captures our sense that deontologists and utilitarians can have a genuine dispute in which neither side is conceptually confused and both sides are using the relevant term in the same sense.[40]

These are unwelcome results of using a normative theory such as utilitarianism as a means of conceptual analysis. Moore sees that these results are unwelcome; that is why he argues that conceptual naturalism about 'good' commits a fallacy (though he accepts conceptual utilitarianism for 'right'). He tries to make clear the error that leads to these unwelcome results in our effort to understand moral arguments. We may well agree that Moore has exposed a genuine difficulty in conceptual naturalism, even if we do not agree with his further moves.

The appeal to neutrality is closely connected to Hare's argument that objective naturalism leads to relativism because it cannot explain disagreement. He argues that since different parties (individuals or societies) will (according to the objective naturalist) define 'right' with reference to different objective properties, each party will have a different concept of 'right'. And so, if each of the societies S1 and S2 has internally consistent beliefs, we will have no room to say 'What society S1 thinks is right is right, and what S2 thinks is right is wrong'. If our concept of right is different from those of S1 and S2, we can only record the fact that what they think is right (in their sense of 'right') is not right (in our sense).[41] If an objective naturalist analysis were right, we would have to say that when Homer uses 'agathos', it means 'brave (well-born, etc.)' and that when Plato uses it, it means 'just, temperate (etc.)', so that when Plato says 'Homer's heroes are not *agathoi*' he is not disagreeing with Homer's judgment that they are *agathoi*. For similar reasons we would have to deny that '*agathos*' (as used by Homer) is properly translated by 'good'.[42] All these implications of a naturalistic analysis are to be rejected.

A conceptual naturalist, however, need not embrace relativism. A conceptual utilitarian naturalist has to say that if another society lacks a concept of F such that it is analytically true that if an action is F it promotes utility, that other society lacks the concept of rightness (even if it has a word 'right'). But we need not infer that what they call 'right' is right for

---

[39] '. . . it is always fatal to try to smuggle moral opinions of substance into one's ethical theory in the guise of mere definitions or explanations of meaning, as in effect the objectivistic naturalists do.' (*SOE* 118)

[40] Lewis, *AKV* 378 denies this assumption, claiming that the disputed thesis is analytic. See §1315.   [41] See *SOE* 69.

[42] Adkins, *MR*, offers a good example of the approach favoured by Hare. His treatment of *agathos* and related terms as 'the most powerful words of commendation' in Homer and later Greek (30) presupposes an account such as Stevenson's and Hare's. Adkins relies on Stevenson's conception of a persuasive definition (38–40).

them, as a relativist claims; what they call 'right' may be (for instance) pleasing to the gods, or suitable for keeping the ruling class in power, but this does not make it really right.

The threat of relativism, therefore, seems to be illusory. Hare's argument about different societies seems to be simply a version of his argument about disagreement. He believes we can see that Homer, Plato, and we have three different views about a good person; we distort the facts if we suggest that the alleged disagreement involves three different concepts, only the third of which (ours) is the concept 'good'. According to Hare, whatever objective natural property we mention in a proposed analysis of 'good' or 'right', someone might deny that such things are good. Such a denial does not involve the introduction of a different sense of the word; it introduces a substantive dispute. Hare illustrates this point by considering other properties that might be mentioned in a naturalistic analysis: the satisfaction of needs, or the promotion of human flourishing, or the satisfaction of preferences (SOE 73–8).

Why should we say that disputants in such cases use 'good' or 'right' in the same sense, so that there is a genuine dispute between them? Hare suggests that the replacement of apparent disagreement by mere equivocation would be all right if descriptivism were true; for if moral judgments simply describe features of agents and actions, we ought not to be surprised if people who ascribe different descriptive properties use the terms in different senses, and so do not disagree substantively.[43] But (in Hare's view) we believe that Homer and Plato genuinely disagree just because one commends and the other condemns the same type of action. The univocity of the moral terms they use consists entirely in their shared commendatory function. Hence we must recognize that their shared meaning is prescriptive meaning.

In this argument, Hare does not simply assume that the commendatory force of a moral word must be part of its meaning. He argues: (1) In these disagreements, the moral words must be used with the same meaning. (2) But all that they have in common is their prescriptive force. (3) Hence their common meaning must consist in their prescriptive force. He now has an argument for identifying prescriptive force with the meaning of moral words.

1334. Disagreement, Argument, and Reform

The same connexion between recognition of disagreement and recognition of prescriptive meaning emerges from Hare's treatment of moral reform. If a reformer claims that it is wrong not to love our enemies, he uses 'wrong' in the sense in which his contemporaries use it. But if descriptivism is right, we can look at the actions and properties to which 'wrong' refers. If these do not include failure to love one's enemies, the reformer misuses 'wrong' (SOE 72–3). Hence the descriptivist view makes it 'by definition impossible to preach moral reform' (73). Hare replies that reformers can preach moral reform because they and their

---

[43] 'There would be no harm in all this if all they were doing were *describing* the act of fighting. They would just be attributing various descriptive properties to the act of fighting. The trouble starts when we begin using "wrong" for the purpose for which it actually *is* used in language, namely for *condemning* acts. . . . it is very natural . . . to think that the people in the two cultures are, respectively, condemning and refusing to condemn the act of fighting. Then they *are* contradicting each other.' (69)

contemporaries use 'wrong' with the same prescriptive meaning. Those who say that slavery is wrong condemn it, and those who say it is not wrong refuse to condemn it. Their genuine disagreement consists simply in disagreement in attitude (as Stevenson puts it).[44]

Hare's argument is over-simplified. Let us suppose that 'wrong' means 'tending to reduce social cohesion'. Reformers might argue that slavery is wrong, even though it is not currently recognized as wrong, because it reduces social cohesion, even though most people do not yet recognize this. Hare's thesis about the possibility of preaching moral reform must go further than the cases that a conceptual naturalist can easily explain. In his view, if we take 'F' to include all the natural properties that, according to the naturalist, are mentioned in the concept of 'wrong', it is possible for reformers to claim that slavery is wrong, even though it is not F, and to be genuinely disagreeing with their contemporaries. In that case, according to Hare, only prescriptive meaning is left to constitute the meaning that reformers share with their contemporaries.

But is shared prescriptive meaning necessary and sufficient to account for our sense of genuine moral disagreement? If we make the prescriptive meaning explicit, we can imagine the reformers saying 'We condemn slavery', and contemporaries saying 'We don't condemn slavery'. That does not seem enough to suggest genuine moral disagreement. If one side says 'We condemn slavery, because it is wrong', and the other says 'We don't condemn it, because it is not wrong', we may now suspect that they have a genuine moral disagreement. But if that is so, the added clause 'because it is wrong' cannot simply repeat the act of condemnation, but should give some specific ground for it. If people disagree about rightness or wrongness, we expect that they will say contradictory things about the same action. Hare, following Stevenson, believes that the appearance of contradiction in such cases can be explained by divergence in attitude.[45] But if we try to understand the disagreement between reformers and their contemporaries, we find that divergent attitudes do not explain the appearance of disagreement.

What, then, is needed for a real disagreement? It does not seem enough to say 'I condemn it because it is wrong'. We might also reasonably expect 'because it is wrong' to introduce some relevant reasons. Let us consider two examples: (1) The reformers say 'We condemn slavery because it increases the pleasure of the slaves and of everyone else in society, and for no other reason', and the contemporaries say 'We do not condemn slavery, because it increases ... (etc.)'. (2) The reformers say 'We condemn slavery, because it inflicts undeserved harm on innocent victims' and contemporaries say 'We do not condemn slavery, precisely because it inflicts ... (etc.)'.

In either of these cases, it would be difficult to find a genuine disagreement about the morality of slavery. We might be more inclined to say, in the first case, that the reformers have a strange attitude to a right-making characteristic, and, in the second case, that contemporaries have a strange attitude to a wrong-making characteristic. It is certainly not obvious (without further information) that the mere fact that one side condemns and the other commends the same practice shows that they have a genuine disagreement about the moral rightness or wrongness of the practice. We might be more inclined to say they express different attitudes to morality.

---

[44] Hare often praises Stevenson's discussion of Moore; see §1300.   [45] Stevenson on disagreement, §1301.

Reflexion on the preaching of moral reform suggests, therefore, that Hare is right to consider disagreement as a test of a meta-ethical theory, and that his theory fails his test. Even if his objections raise difficulties for naturalist descriptivism, non-naturalist descriptivism may do better. According to the non-naturalist descriptivist, moral disagreement involves the use of concepts such as 'ought', 'reason', and so on, suitably linked to one another; the use of these concepts and the appropriate inferences marks out their disagreement as moral. Suppose that the reformers and their contemporaries attach moral terms to different natural properties (being a slave, having one's freedom restricted), but connect them with the same non-natural properties (violating rights, unjustified harm). We can then understand why they disagree on moral grounds, and do not merely commend different courses of action.

Hare might reply that this non-naturalist view is not really descriptivist. For, in his view, the common feature of the concepts we have mentioned is prescriptive, rather than purely descriptive, meaning. If the circle of concepts has to include 'ought' or 'reason', Hare might regard this as equivalent to his own claim that the shared meaning of moral terms is prescriptive. But why should we agree about this? In order to agree, we would also have to agree that the meaning of 'ought' etc. is prescriptive; but we have no reason to agree about this in advance of the argument from disagreement and reform. For this argument is meant to show that the meaning of 'ought', etc. is prescriptive; but if a premiss of the argument says that their meaning is prescriptive, the argument is viciously circular.

Non-naturalist descriptivism, therefore, still seems viable. If we are unconvinced by Hare's arguments from commendatory function to prescriptive meaning, we may prefer non-naturalist descriptivism over prescriptivism. We might reach a different conclusion if we agreed with Hare that non-naturalist descriptivism is committed to the epistemological views that he attributes to intuitionism; but his argument for this claim is open to doubt.

1335. Further Options for Cognitivism

Hare's account of disagreement raises a more general question about his outlook. We may agree with him that genuine disagreement on moral questions presupposes something in common between the disputants. Hare assumes that what they have in common is a shared meaning. Since he argues that the shared meaning cannot be descriptive meaning (which gives too few genuine disagreements), he concludes that it must be purely prescriptive meaning. But his conclusion is open to doubt, since it does not allow genuine disagreements.

If Hare's conclusion is false, which of his premisses should be rejected? Perhaps he should not deny the possibility of shared concepts and descriptive meanings. Alternatively, we might object to his claim that genuine disagreement requires shared concepts that include shared analytic truths. This objection questions Hare's assumptions about meanings, concepts, and beliefs. He believes that concepts correspond to meanings and analytic truths, and that they are revealed by conceptual analysis. We might doubt this general view in philosophy of language. In defending non-naturalist descriptivism against Hare's criticisms, we have taken for granted the background assumptions in philosophy of language, especially in the theory of meaning, that Hare shares with earlier 20th-century non-naturalists. We have assumed that two speakers share the same concept and disagree about its application if and only if they acknowledge the same analytic truths as necessary and sufficient for specifying the concept and the property corresponding to it, and for giving the meaning of the word of which the concept is the sense.

For reasons outside moral philosophy, we might doubt these assumptions. We may doubt whether the distinction between analytic and synthetic truths is tenable. If we explain analytic truth by reference to meanings, and meanings and concepts by reference to analytic truths, we may conclude that we are being given too small a circle of explanation, and that the belief in a sharp distinction ought to be abandoned.[46] Even if we do not deny that there are analytic truths, we may doubt whether all and only the analytic truths connected with a concept are known a priori and held in common by any two speakers possessing the concept. If, for instance, one speaker rejects some of the truths previously regarded as analytic, but retains the most basic synthetic truths, it might be arbitrary to deny that the two speakers share the concept, or that they can disagree without equivocation.

This general possibility seems especially plausible in cases of change and disagreement in the history of science. Here it is sometimes plausible to claim that earlier and later scientists have the same concept, even though they may disagree about the fundamental theoretical truths connected to it. Their possession of the same concept consists in, for instance, its being connected with the same observations, playing a similar role in answering the same questions, but not necessarily in the acceptance of a particular set of analytic truths.[47]

Though the reasons supporting any of these doubts about concepts and meanings are complex and disputable, the doubts are relevant to Hare's argument about disagreement, and, more generally, to his main questions and aims. If he is wrong about the connexion between concepts, meanings, analytic truths, a priori knowledge, and agreement or disagreement, his search for an analysis of the relevant moral concepts may be misguided, not because moral concepts are especially intractable, but because this is the wrong approach to all or most concepts.

An approach to moral concepts that recognizes these doubts about conceptual analysis might use some elements of naturalistic and non-naturalistic descriptivism, without offering conceptual analyses.[48] Perhaps we can use moral judgments in disputes and arguments without equivocation, to the extent that we accept some of the same specific judgments about particular cases or types of cases and some of the same inferences involving moral concepts. If, for instance, we thought that morality had nothing to do with human interests, or if we thought that unprovoked violent attack on our friends and neighbours needed no excuse, or if we saw no connexion between what it is right to do, what we ought to do, and what we have reason to do, perhaps we would not be using moral concepts or making moral judgments. But it does not follow that some specific set of judgments or inferences is necessary and sufficient for us to share moral concepts. A, B, and C might all make moral

---

[46] Hare alludes to these questions at *MT* 77–83. He does not comment on the fact that the sceptical argument against analytic truth—that the circle of explanation is too small—is similar to his objection to non-naturalist descriptivism.

[47] On concepts and disagreement, see §1382.

[48] Hare remarks (*MT* 77–8) that if we doubt the distinction between analytic and synthetic, we cannot use his way of distinguishing naturalist from non-naturalist descriptivism.

judgments, because the overlaps between A and B and between B and C in judgments and inferences are quite large, even though the overlap between A and C is smaller.[49]

We might, then, agree in part with naturalism, if we suppose that we must accept some of the same content if we are to share moral concepts. But we might also agree in part with non-naturalism, if we suppose that the inferential connexions between moral concepts cannot be wholly replaced by connexions between concepts that do not include 'reason', 'ought', and so on. Such a view would commit us neither to analytical naturalism nor to an intuitionist epistemology.

This account of moral concepts conflicts with Hare's claim that moral judgments are necessarily practical. If someone did not recognize moral considerations as reasons for action, we might have some reason to doubt whether they grasped moral concepts. But someone might agree that moral considerations are offered as reasons, but still deny that they actually are reasons. If grasp of the same concept requires overlapping judgments and inferences, rather than the acknowledgment of just the same set of analytic truths, someone might deny that moral considerations are reasons, but still retain enough other judgments and inferences to convince us that they are speaking non-equivocally of morality. A Nietzschean immoralist, or a 'sensible knave' amoralist, still attaches the normal senses to moral terms.

If we replace shared analytic truths with overlapping central beliefs, we will take Hare's conditions for adequacy of an analysis as suggestions about the central beliefs and assumptions that we share in using moral concepts. But we will not expect these suggestions to give us a set of necessary and sufficient conditions for having the same concepts.

If, therefore, we believe in the possibility of conceptual analysis, as Hare understands it, we have good reason to prefer a descriptivist analysis over his prescriptivist analysis. But if we do not believe in conceptual analysis, we have even stronger reasons to deny that moral judgments necessarily have prescriptive meaning.

1336. Universalizability

Hare's prescriptivism is his distinctive contribution to the debate begun by Sidgwick and Moore, since it is his version of non-cognitivism. But it is not all that he has to say about the meaning of moral judgments. For all sorts of commands can be issued on many different sorts of basis. Some are arbitrary; some rest on power or authority; some rest on shared preferences. Not every basis for a command seems to be a sufficient basis for a moral judgment. We noticed earlier that if alleged moral reformers simply condemn slavery without giving any further grounds, it is not clear that they really make a moral judgment about it. Something more seems to be needed for moral judgments.

Hare believes that moral judgments are universalizable. He exploits Kant's suggestion that a genuine moral imperative can be prescribed as a universal law, and his interpretation of Kant is similar to Sidgwick's.[50] Sidgwick, however, treats the formula of universal law

---

[49] For such a view of moral judgments, see Smith, *MP* 29–32 on 'platitudes'. See also §1264.

[50] Hare does not mention Sidgwick in this connexion. Indeed the paucity of references to Sidgwick in Hare's books is remarkable. (See, e.g., *MT* vi.) Even the essay 'Could Kant have been a utilitarian?' in *SOE* never mentions Sidgwick's rather similar argument for a rather similar conclusion.

as an axiom, a synthetic moral principle, whereas Hare treats it as a conceptual truth. He claims that if a principle is my moral principle, I must be willing to prescribe it as a universal law that holds not only in the present situation, but in all situations that are like it in the relevant respects. When I judge that I ought to . . . because . . . , the 'because' clause states the situation to which the prescription applies, and therefore the respects in which the prescription is universalizable (*LM* 176). The judgment that you ought not to smoke here because there are children here tells you that you ought not to smoke where there are children. Hence the reason for the particular judgment reveals the universal principle that we commit ourselves to.

This form of universalizability follows from the basic fact that a moral prescription rests on some reason. We can illustrate this point equally with 'good'. If some particular thing is good, it has some good-making feature, and so if something else has the same good-making features, it is also, to that extent, good. A moral judgment, then, is not only prescriptive, but universally prescriptive. The character of the universal prescription depends on the descriptive aspect of the moral judgment; and this is revealed by the principle that I cite in explaining and justifying a moral imperative.

Hare's appeal to universality answers objections that would arise if he simply took moral judgments to have prescriptive meaning. Commands can be based on taste, momentary preferences, self-interest, and many other things; hence a merely prescriptive theory of moral judgments allows moral judgments to have any of these characteristics, even though we normally suppose that moral judgments cannot have them. Hare's theory, however, is not merely prescriptive; he rules out these unsuitable foundations for moral judgments by appeal to universalizability.[51]

What Hare has said so far is not trivial, since it distinguishes moral principles from imperatives that do not demand reasons in the same way. But it still leaves a lot open. We do not yet know, for instance, what kinds of properties are to be included. Can we include historical and demonstrative features or definite descriptions that are designed to pick out just one person or time or place? We might rule these out on the ground that they are not genuine respects of similarity for this purpose. But we seem to need some guidance to find the relevant respects.

1337. Are Moral Principles Overriding?

Prescriptivity and universalizability by themselves do not capture the range of moral judgments. Aesthetic judgments, for instance, might satisfy both conditions without thereby being moral. We might take this point to favour descriptivism. Aesthetic judgments, we might argue, are not connected with human good and harm, and do not take this good and harm to be the basis of the relevant sorts of reasons. Morality differs because it gives a central role to good and harm.

Hare rejects this concession to descriptivism on the ground that it violates his demands for neutrality and practicality. In his view, we can still have a moral disagreement with

---

[51] On universalizability, cf. Hare, *MT*, ch. 6, discussing Mackie, *E*, ch. 4.

people who declare that human welfare and harm do not matter; they are not putting something else in place of morality, but affirming a moral position of their own. Nazis, for instance, have a moral outlook, even though they do not agree with other people about what matters in morality. Their moral views are not their views about human welfare and harm, but their overriding views. This is why aesthetic judgments are not moral. We allow aesthetic judgments to be overridden by moral ones; we do not qualify aesthetic judgments by exceptions that refer to moral considerations, but we recognize that in cases of conflict they must give way to moral considerations (FR 168–9). Moral principles, however, do not give way to any higher considerations; they are necessarily overriding.[52]

This condition on moral principles has the disadvantage of making Butler's questions about the relation of self-love and conscience, and Sidgwick's questions about the relation between egoistic and universal reason, logically impossible, on the usual understanding of them.[53] Both Butler and Sidgwick are usually taken to ask whether purely prudential or moral considerations are overriding. They do not seem to intend to ask whether self-love or conscience constitutes morality; they presuppose that conscience constitutes morality, and frame their question on that basis. It does not seem self-contradictory or even especially odd to wonder whether moral considerations are overriding, or to claim that morality is all right in its place, but it should be subordinate to other considerations.

Hare might be right to suppose that moral considerations are related to questions about authority and supremacy. One might argue that moral principles claim to be overriding, and that the moral point of view claims to assess other points of view by reference to considerations that are taken to override them. But agreement on this point does not support Hare's claim that anyone who holds, or even to some extent acts on, moral principles must accept the claim of morality to supremacy.

Hare might also be right to argue that Nazis held (or could have held) moral views. The fact that they were indifferent or hostile to the interests of most human beings might not by itself prove that they did not hold moral views. But we need not explain why their views were moral by adding the further (allegedly) analytical truth that moral judgments are overriding. We might simply point out that they had a lot to say about the virtues, and about the perfection and welfare of some people, and that they explained their lack of concern for other people's welfare by arguing that these people were (in important respects) sub-human. This explanation for indifference to some people's welfare makes the Nazi position intelligible as morality; if they had thought that Jews and Slavs were no less human than Aryans, their position would have been more difficult to understand as a moral position.[54]

The addition of overridingness to Hare's conditions for moral judgments, therefore, seems to raise more difficulties for Hare than it solves. If he had given strong reasons for

---

[52] 'There is a sense of the word "moral" (perhaps the most important one) in which it is characteristic of moral principles that they cannot be overridden in this way, but only altered or qualified to admit of some exception. This characteristic of theirs is connected with the fact that moral principles are, in a way that needs elucidation, superior to or more authoritative than any other kind of principle. A man's moral principles, in this sense, are those which, in the end, he accepts to guide his life by . . .' (FR 169) Later Hare qualifies this claim by restricting it to one's supreme moral principles (MT 60–1).

[53] Does Butler treat the supremacy of conscience as true by definition? See §697.

[54] Warnock, CMP 58–9, takes a possibly more restrictive attitude to Nazis. See Hare, MT 187.

rejecting a cognitive account of moral judgments, we might be willing to agree about which principles count as moral principles. But if we are not convinced by his arguments against cognitivism, we may reasonably wonder whether his claims about overridingness do not suggest a reason for preferring cognitivism over prescriptivism. Some opponents[55] have argued that his prescriptivism fails to take account of important constraints on the content of moral principles. Even if prescriptivity, universalizability, and overridingness are necessary conditions for moral judgments, they may not be sufficient. In Hare's view, anyone who maintains any set of judgments that meet his formal conditions, no matter what their content, argues from a moral point of view and accepts moral principles. A consistent amoralist must reject such principles altogether.[56] But one may doubt this account of amoralism.

Hare's view seems open to objection because it allows judgments to count as moral that do not seem to have anything to do with morality. If someone is prepared to prescribe universally that some principle should be followed that has nothing at all to do, in his view or anyone else's, with the interests, rights, or welfare of human beings, he seems as clear a case of an amoralist as we can find. Hare agrees that we should not count someone's overriding aims as constituting the agent's moral outlook simply because they are overriding; he believes that they are moral principles if and only if they are also universalizable and prescriptive. But these further features do not seem to distinguish the moral from the non-moral. If the principles that meet all Hare's conditions are purely self-concerned, or have no recognizable connexion with human interests, they seem to be indifferent to morality. Moral principles need some further content.

We might express this further demand in either of two ways: (1) A moral outlook consists of principles expressing concern for human interests. (2) A moral outlook includes principles that have some intelligible connexion with considerations about human interests. The first condition is open to one of Hare's objections. He observes that if we insist on too much shared content we might have to say that Homer, for instance, makes no moral judgments (or that his characters make none) and that therefore we can have no moral dispute with them (MT 53–64, 187). For Homeric values (let us suppose) do not include any clearly defined set of principles that are concerned with human welfare; and so if morality requires principles focussed on human welfare, Homer has no morality. But the view that Homer has no morality misses something important about Homer. Though he does not assign the same place to human welfare that other outlooks assign to it, he has views about how considerations of human welfare are connected with other aims. These views are appropriately treated as an expression of Homeric morality. The second condition explains how Homer has a moral outlook.

This second condition shows that not all attempts to define moral principles by their content are open to Hare's most plausible objections about the narrowing of the scope of moral disputes. The second condition leaves open the possibility of border-line or indeterminate cases. But it should not be criticized on this ground; for we might well find outlooks that in some ways seem to be moral outlooks and in some ways do not. Considerations of content do not seem irrelevant to determining the extent of moral principles.

---

[55] An early statement of this objection to Hare is Foot, 'Moral beliefs'.   [56] On the amoralist, see MT 183.

1338. Prescriptivism and Utilitarianism

The combination of prescriptivity and universalizability helps Hare to pass from meta-ethics to normative ethics without appeal to any intuitive judgments.[57] He argues that if moral judgment is prescriptive and universal, normal people have reason to accept utilitarianism. Suppose A is a creditor, B has failed to repay a debt, and A then judges 'I ought to have B put in prison' (or 'B ought to be put in prison'). If A accepts this ought-judgment on the ground that one party is a creditor and the other a debtor, A accepts the universal principle that whenever people cannot pay their debts, their creditors ought to have them put in prison. When A considers the application of this universal principle, A sees that it applies to A in the counterfactual situation where A is the debtor and B is the creditor; but A does not accept this application of the general principle. Hence A withdraws the original ought-judgment (*FR* 91).

Hare might appear to rely on a familiar type of moral argument. Someone may use the question 'How would you like it if that happened to you?' to show us that we do not really accept a particular principle that we thought we accepted. When we think about it happening to us, we see that a principle is unfair; we recognize the unfairness when we think of ourselves as victims. If, then, we are concerned about fairness, we may use the thought of ourselves as victims of a principle to see whether we really think it is fair.

But this familiar pattern of argument is not Hare's argument; for it does not consist simply in generalizing from the thought of ourselves as victims, but requires some prior judgment about what is fair. As Kant points out, the judge imposing a penalty on a guilty defendant might also reflect that she would not like it if she had to suffer the same penalty if she were found guilty. This reaction does not show that the punishment is unjust. On the contrary; it would scarcely be a punishment at all if the victim did not mind suffering it. To make this 'How would you like it . . . ?' argument give reasonable results, we must rely on further intuitive moral judgments, contrary to Hare's instructions.

Hare avoids appeal to moral judgment by making the judge imagine the reactions of everyone who is affected by the principle in question.[58] Whatever features of the situation I recognize as reasons for treating one person in a particular way must be equally good reasons in all relevantly similar situations. I discover whether I recognize something as a reason by seeing how I react to it when I imagine everyone in the relevant situation. I am to count each person's reaction equally in reaching my overall attitude to the universal principle.

Hare interprets the utilitarian principle of equality in more strictly formal terms than other utilitarians use. As Bentham and Mill understand the principle, it requires every person's pleasure to count for as much as everyone else's, and insists that any different treatment of different people must be justified by appeal to maximizing total utility; since this determines

---

[57] For present purposes, we can take overridingness for granted without explicit mention.

[58] 'The principle often accepted by utilitarians, "Everybody to count for one, nobody to count for more than one", can both be justified by the appeal to the demand for universalizability, and be used to provide an answer to our present question. For what this principle means is that everyone is entitled to equal consideration, and that if it is said that two people ought to be treated differently, some difference must be cited as the ground for these different moral judgments. And this is a corollary of the requirement of universalizability.' (*FR* 118) Cf. Sidgwick's treatment of the utilitarian principle of equality, §1198.

moral relevance, they insist that every difference in treatment must be justified by a morally relevant difference between individuals. Hare, however, does not appeal to any antecedent notion of moral relevance, which would give moral judgments a descriptive element that he rejects. Hence his principle of equality does not preclude discrimination against people with red hair here and now, provided that I am willing to have the rule applied to red-haired people in general.

Instead of importing some principle of moral relevance to restrict the permissible universal principles, Hare relies on normal human motives. He claims that in ordinary people who care more about avoiding harm to themselves than about harming others, recognition of the implications of a universalized prescription will alter the initial vindictive judgment about imprisoning debtors. Hence people with the normal inclinations to avoid pain and advance their own interests will respond to the requirement of universalizability by rejecting the principles that a utilitarian theory rejects.[59]

Hare's argument from universal prescriptivism to utilitarianism unifies two apparently contrasting outlooks in normative ethics. Those who take Kant seriously often reject utilitarianism. Utilitarians tend to suggest that anything true in Kant's categorical imperative must be subordinate to the principle of utility. Hare argues, following Sidgwick, that the appearance of a conflict between these two normative outlooks is misleading, because they do not and cannot answer the same questions.

From one point of view, Kant's categorical imperative is a higher principle than the principle of utility; for it belongs to meta-ethics, stating a necessary condition for any genuine moral principle. As Kant puts it, the categorical imperative is purely formal; given Hare's conception of the purely formal, the categorical imperative is part of the concept of morality. In that case, it is satisfied by utilitarian and non-utilitarian moral theories, and Kant is mistaken to suppose that the categorical imperative itself, understood as a purely formal principle, could justify non-utilitarian moral principles.

Hare's interpretation of the categorical imperative is a recognizable descendant of Hegel's. Hare, however, does not use it to attack Kant. In his view, Kant anticipates one of Hare's insights into meta-ethics. Kantian meta-ethics supports utilitarianism, once we make some weak and plausible assumptions about normal human capacities and desires. These assumptions tell us what we 'can will' to be a universal law, and therefore tell us the conclusions that people like us are committed to when we accept the categorical imperative.

Despite the neutrality of meta-ethics, this argument vindicates utilitarianism. Though conceptual utilitarianism gives the wrong answer to Hare's question 'What is morality?', understood as a purely formal meta-ethical question, utilitarianism is the most appropriate normative moral theory for normal human beings. For, once we recognize the formal and conceptual constraints involved in moral thinking, we can resist utilitarianism only by a fanatical commitment to ideals that do not recommend themselves to most people. Utilitarians cannot defend their position even to all those people who (as Sidgwick puts it) are willing to look at practical questions from the point of view of the universe; but they can defend it to normal, non-fanatical people.

[59] The substance of the moral judgments of a utilitarian comes from a consideration of the substantial inclinations and interests that people actually have, together with the formal requirement that the prescriptions which they prompt have to be universalizable before moral judgments can be made out of them. (*FR* 118)

The fact that Hare's theory has these implications for normative ethics is a point in its favour. Emotivism makes it difficult to understand what all the fuss is about in normative ethics, and especially why the fuss sometimes resembles rational argument. Hare's universal prescriptivism explains the soundness of Moore's argument; it safeguards the truth of non-cognitivism; but it maintains the rationality of moral thinking, and explains why both the Kantian and the utilitarian outlooks are defensible, in their proper places. The systematic explanatory power of the theory is a reason for taking it seriously.

It is worthwhile, then, to examine Hare's argument for utilitarianism, both to see whether it is plausible, and to see whether it is a purely conceptual argument that does not rely on any intuitive moral beliefs. Two questions arise: (1) Can he prove his utilitarian conclusion a priori? Do the same sorts of considerations that show that moral judgments are prescriptive and universal also show that they have to be utilitarian? If Hare succeeds, it is apparently a complicated analytic truth that moral judgments are utilitarian. In that case, his argument for the utilitarian conclusion has to be entirely conceptual; each of the steps must be a conceptual truth or follow analytically from one. (2) Can Hare begin with his universal prescriptivism, and add something plausible to lead him to a utilitarian conclusion? If the relevant truths are not all analytic, some may be either (a) empirical generalizations, or (b) substantive moral judgments. In the first case, Hare would derive moral conclusions out of non-moral premises. In the second case, Hare would have to revise his objections to reliance on intuitive moral judgments. But he might still have an argument that would convince someone who is less reluctant than he is to argue dialectically.

1339. Utilitarianism Derived from Preferences

Hare's argument for utilitarianism depends on the motives of 'ordinary' people who do not care so much about their ideals that they are prepared to pursue them entirely without regard to their interests; they are guided by a normal degree of prudence in considering how much they care about any one of their aims.[60] Hare argues that these ordinary people who prescribe universally will be moved by 'golden rule' arguments. For when they realize that they would not like it if they were the victims of the course of action that they advocate, they will withdraw their prescription. Reflexion on their 'then-for-then' preferences in imagined situations alters their 'now-for-then' preferences and hence their prescriptions. Hare argues that I cannot prescribe that I torture you to get information from you, once I fully represent all the situations implied by the universal principle I presuppose; for among these situations is your torturing me to get information from me. Since I would not prefer then that you torture me, I do not prefer now that you torture me then, and so I cannot prescribe the principle that allows you to torture me then.

This complex argument may be represented as follows: (1) Suppose I affirm that I ought to torture you. (2) My reason (since this is an ought-judgment) is that I want information from you. (3) And so the universal judgment is U (Whenever A wants information from B, A ought to torture B). (4) I can affirm this universal judgment if and only if I prescribe T (that

---

[60] Prudence is discussed further at *MT* 99–106.

you torture me if you want information from me). (5) To find out whether I can prescribe T, I must ask whether I prefer to be tortured in situation S (where you want information from me, and I have the preferences that you now have when I want information from you). (6) To find whether I prefer not to be tortured in S, I must fully represent S. (7) If I were in S, I would prefer not to be tortured. (8) If I fully represent myself being tortured in S, I now prefer not to be tortured in S. (9) Since I prefer not to be tortured in S, I cannot prescribe T. (10) Since I cannot prescribe T, I cannot prescribe U. (11) Hence I cannot prescribe that I ought to torture you.[61]

In Hare's view, ordinary people's preferences allow us to predict the universal prescriptions they will accept once they see the implications of these prescriptions in actual and counterfactual cases. If I incline to a certain principle, and I recognize that it has to be universalized, I will, if I am clear-headed, want to see what I am committed to. To see this, I must imagine the consequences, whether they are probable or merely logically possible, of acting on my principle. To imagine these consequences, I have to imagine myself having the preferences of each person who is affected by the principle.[62]

If, then, I find pain unwelcome, and I notice that someone else is suffering pain, I find the sufferer's situation unwelcome because it is painful, whether or not the sufferer's pain affects my own interests. If, then, I am influenced by my reaction to the sufferer's pain, I will not assent to a principle that requires the infliction of pain on this victim. The preferences that I form about the imagined situations become a prescription that may disagree with the principle I was initially inclined to accept.

We might object that, even if I understood how a victim of torture is suffering and that I would suffer in his situation, I might be indifferent now to what I would suffer then. I may agree with Hare about my 'then-for-then' preferences—what I would prefer to happen in S. But I need not infer anything about my 'now-for-then' preferences—what I now prefer about what would happen in S. If I am not very interested in what would happen to me in counterfactual conditions, representation of my then-for-then preferences does not affect my now-for-then preferences. Hare disallows this objection by defining 'full representation' so that it includes the formation of the relevant now-for-then preference.[63] Hare does not affirm a psychological thesis, that if I do not form the relevant now-for-then preference I must have missed some discoverable feature of your suffering; he tells us that the meaning of 'full representation' includes the preference.[64] But if that is so, we may ask why the formation of my now-for-then preference should require 'full representation', in the special sense defined

---

[61] This summary is derived from *MT*, chs. 5–6 and from the summary in *SOE* 133–4. The argument is carefully discussed by Gibbard, 'Hare's analysis'.

[62] '...he may very much want not to have done to him what I am saying I ought to do to him (which involves prescribing that I do it). But we have seen that if I fully represent to myself his situation, including his motivations, I shall myself acquire a corresponding motivation, which would be expressed in the prescription that the same thing *not* be done to me, were I to be forthwith in just that situation. But this prescription is inconsistent with my original "ought"-statement, if that was, as we have been assuming, prescriptive.' (*MT* 109)

[63] '...having an aversion to *my* forthwith suffering like that is a condition of full representation' (*MT* 99). Similarly, '...I cannot know the extent and quality of others' sufferings and, in general, motivations and preferences without having equal motivations with regard to what should happen to me, were I in their places, with their motivations and preferences.' (*MT* 99)

[64] Hence step (8) of Hare's argument becomes analytically true. But if we accept (8) on this basis, we may then raise a question about (6).

by Hare. Apparently, I could survey all the facts without 'full representation', and then, being indifferent to my fate in counterfactual circumstances, prefer that I be tortured.

Hare adds a further argument to support his claims about full representation. He suggests that 'I' is not a wholly descriptive word, but partly prescriptive. If, then, I think of myself as the one who suffers, I must 'identify' myself with his suffering. But I cannot identify myself with him unless I take on his preference not to suffer; I do not really think of myself as being him unless I take on his preferences. (MT 97) This claim of Hare's is difficult to accept. If I think of myself as suffering what you suffer, I have to think of myself as taking on the preferences that you have when you suffer. But these seem to be then-for-then preferences rather than now-for-then preferences. Perhaps there is a sense of 'identification' in which Hare's claim is analytic. Sometimes we might say you have not really identified yourself with a sufferer unless the suffering causes you to form a now-for-then preference not to suffer it. But if we accept that, a question arises about whether Hare's special kind of identification is needed for relevant factual knowledge of another person's sufferings. If we may grant that it is needed for 'full' representation in Hare's special sense, we may still doubt whether full representation is needed for the formation of the relevant sort of now-for-then preference.

In Hare's view, however, my eventual prescription expresses the now-for-then preference that results from the then-for-then preferences directed to the different situations I imagine. Since I prefer less pain to more pain, my various then-for-then preferences will result in the utilitarian prescription.

1340. Preferences and Probabilities

Let us agree that in the circumstances described by Hare we form a now-for-then preference not to be tortured. But how do we form the prescription that no one be tortured in the relevant situation? In Hare's view, all prescriptions imply preferences.[65] Since prescriptions are action-guiding and entail imperatives, they express some preference for one action over another. A moral prescription, being overriding, expresses my overall preference. I might say, when I think about going to the supermarket, that I have some preference for not standing in queues, spending money, etc., but none the less I prefer to go to the supermarket, because my overall preference is to buy food. But Hare also assumes that every now-for-then preference implies a prescription,[66] so that I will always refuse to prescribe in accordance with any principle that allows a hypothetical situation that I do not prefer. He implies that talk of prescriptions rather than preferences or motivations is simply a verbal change.[67] Is he right?

Hare's procedure forms my now-for-then preference without considering the probability of each situation. But normally, as Hare recognizes, we form our overall preferences or

---

[65] 'these prescriptions are all the expressions of preferences' (MT 179).

[66] See MT 109, quoted above. See also 178: 'If the first of these preferences outweighs the second, the doctor will accept the [first] universal prescription . . . For the second of these prescriptions goes against the balance of the doctor's own preferences.'

[67] 'It will be convenient if we continue sometimes to speak, not in terms of motivational states, nor even of preferences, but in terms of the prescriptions which are their expressions in language.' (MT 107)

prescriptions by considering probability as well as desirability.[68] If I am about to mow the lawn, it might strike me that if the lawn-mower were to explode without warning, I would be injured. But if I think the mower is unlikely to explode, my preference about that unlikely situation does not give me a predominant preference not to use the lawn-mower. I have a much stronger now-for-then preference for not being injured by an exploding mower than I have for mowing the lawn; but if the possibility being considered is unrealistic, it does not affect my overall now-for-now desire to use the lawn-mower.

It is not clear, then, why preferences about unlikely situations must lead me to reject a general principle that allows those situations.[69] Perhaps we begin by doing what Hare tells us to do; we consider all the relevant situations to discover our now-for-then preferences about them. But we then add our beliefs about the probability of the different situations, and adjust our preferences to suit them. We reach our prescription about what to do only after we consider probability. Hence I might prefer, all things considered, to torture you, if I think it is very unlikely that I will be the victim of torture.

A Kantian might protest that someone who reasons in this way is not taking the moral point of view. The point of putting myself in the place of the victim of torture is not to think about how likely this is to happen to me, but to think about how bad this is for the victim, by making clear to me how he feels about being tortured. This moral comment, however, does not help Hare. If he has to rely on some initial conception of the moral point of these imaginative experiments, and in particular of the irrelevance of probability, he takes for granted the main point that his experiments are meant to establish. An appeal to a moral demand for impartiality would be an appeal to 'received opinion' of the sort that Hare rejects.

1341. Preferences v. Prescriptions

So far we have not questioned Hare's assumption that a prescription simply corresponds to our strongest preference, no matter what the source or the basis of the preference. This assumption is doubtful, however; for we might think that moral prescriptions are based on rational principles that may not reflect mere preferences. Not every preference we form, even a strong preference, becomes a rational prescription. Before we decide to commit ourselves to a principle, we may ask whether a strong preference deserves attention, and especially whether it deserves a degree of attention proportional to its strength.[70]

Hare almost recognizes this point in FR. He acknowledges that universal prescriptivism combined with attention to everyone affected by a principle does not result in utilitarian principles.[71] People who stick to their original prescription no matter what it costs them in any counterfactual situation are 'fanatics' who care more about 'ideals' than about 'interests'.

---

[68] See MT 47.   [69] Cf. Rawls on maximin, §1423.

[70] In saying this, I mean to concede Hare's internalist claim that if I judge I ought to do something, I commit myself to doing it and I form a preference for doing it. Even if this true, it does not follow that our strongest preference automatically becomes our prescription.

[71] At SOE 133, Hare says that MT, ch. 5 (on the effect of thinking about another person's suffering) depends on prescriptivity, whereas ch. 6 depends on universalizability.

If A is a fanatic, A may stick to A's original judgment that B ought to be put in prison for debt, even when A considers the implications of the principle for everyone else affected. When A thinks of A being imprisoned for debt, A forms a then-for-then preference for not being imprisoned, but does not form the 'normal' now-for-then preference for not being imprisoned if A were to be a debtor; A's fanatical attachment to imprisonment for debt inhibits the 'normal' formation of preferences.[72]

This is Hare's position in *FR*. But it is unsatisfactory. If a fanatic is capable of not forming the relevant now-for-then preferences, how do ordinary people form them? In *FR*, Hare appeals to 'substantial inclinations and interests'. He might have in mind (1) concern for avoidance of pain rather than adherence to some ideal, or (2) sympathy for people's sufferings rather than adherence to an ideal. The first inclination would not be enough for Hare's purposes; it runs into our previous objection about probability. Even if I care more about avoiding pain than about carrying out my ideals, the improbability of my suffering pain might lead me not to count it for much in comparison with my other views. But if Hare has to rely on the second inclination—the claim that 'normal' people care more about other people's sufferings than about any other moral consideration—he makes a controversial moral demand that might leave us with rather few 'normal' people.

In *MT*, however, Hare no longer relies on this appeal to normality. He believes that his conception of full representation removes most of the space for fanaticism (*MT* 170–82). Since full representation of the prisoner's suffering as my own requires me to form his preferences for that situation, it requires the now-for-then preference not to be tortured. I can be a fanatic only if my fanatical desires are so strong that I would suffer more pain from their frustration than everyone else would suffer if I carried them out. Whereas *FR* left room for fanatics who do not move from then-for-then to the appropriate now-for-then preference, *MT* closes this gap.

This solution rests on a questionable account of the fanatic. The possibility of fanatics, as conceived in *FR*, might be explained by the fact that a preference need not result in the corresponding prescription. Even if I agree with Hare about my now-for-then preference, I may deny that this preference has the appropriate rational standing for me to endorse it as my prescription. We can see this point in an artificial case. Suppose that everyone watches a 'reality television' show that is broadcast throughout the world. And suppose nearly all the viewers, apart from a few with scruples, would get great pleasure from watching a Manxman (chosen by lot) killed on television. If their pleasure is greater than the discomfort of the few scrupulous people, and if the victim does not mind very much, then—following Hare's procedure—I will form the now-for-then preference that I be killed on television if I am the unlucky Manxman.

This is the kind of example that Hare often attacks as irrelevant because it is unrealistic. But it points to a logical gap between a now-for-then preference and a prescription. If I think about the kind of preference that these viewers of reality television form, I might intelligibly decide that it should not count for much in deciding what to prescribe. If this decision is logically possible in the face of a now-for-then preference formed by Hare's method, not

---

[72] 'The substance of the moral judgments of a utilitarian comes from a consideration of the substantial inclinations and interests that people actually have, together with the formal requirement that the prescriptions which they prompt have to be universalizable before moral judgments can be made out of them.' (*FR* 118)

all now-for-then preferences result in the corresponding prescription. Why, then, ought we to prescribe on the basis of our now-for-then preferences resulting from a survey of the then-for-then preferences of people in the relevant situations? An answer to this question would have to come from a normative moral theory that vindicates preference-based utilitarianism. Hare's argument for a utilitarian conclusion rests on a utilitarian normative assumption that supports the move from now-for-then preferences to prescriptions.

Hare's controversial assumptions about preferences underlie his argument against fanaticism. He considers a fanatical doctor who refuses to withhold intensive care from a patient because he insists on doing all he can to preserve her life. If he knows that the patient will suffer severe pain from intensive care, he will form a preference that he not suffer in that way if he were to be the patient. To decide what to do, he has to consider which of his two preferences—for keeping the patient alive and for not suffering what the patient will suffer if she is kept alive—is stronger. If the doctor replies that his preference for keeping the patient alive rests on a moral conviction, not on a mere preference, Hare rejects the answer. He insists that a moral prescription is simply the preference that one is willing to universalize.[73]

Hare is right to claim that if a moral prescription is simply a universalizable preference, the fanatical doctor's reply is illegitimate. But he has not proved the relevant point about prescriptions. His assimilation of prescriptions to preferences even obscures the basic difference between his prescriptivism and Stevenson's emotivism. Hare complains legitimately that Stevenson's position fails to recognize the rational aspects of moral judgments. But one might make the same complaint about Hare's account of how prescriptions emerge from preferences.

In the light of his view about prescriptions, Hare suggests that the fanatical doctor can maintain his position only if his preference is so much stronger than the patient's that he would suffer greater pain if she were not given intensive care than she would suffer if she were given intensive care. Though Hare regards this balance of preferences as unlikely, he believes that it would justify our prescribing that the patient receive intensive care to save the doctor from the suffering he would undergo.[74]

This is an even stranger position than the refusal to treat the doctor's purported moral conviction as anything more than a preference. Hare seems to license the argument that any sort of harm to another is justified as long as the agent enjoys it enough or would suffer severe enough pain if he were prohibited; we need only show that the pain or pleasure of the agent would be great enough to outweigh the pain of the victim.

Hare suggests that this does not matter. In his view, even if it is logically possible that the rapist would suffer greater pain if he were prevented than his victim suffers, that is such

---

[73] 'If the doctor wishes to avoid this consequence . . . he can do it only by somehow boosting his own preference for keeping the patient alive. It will be suggested at this point that he can do this by claiming that, after all, his is not just a mere *preference* like that of the patient not to suffer; it is a *moral conviction*.' (*MT* 178) 'These prescriptions are all the expressions of preferences . . . The only advantage given to moral prescriptions over others is that the prescription finally chosen has to be universal or universalizable . . . If the doctor says "My initial preference is based on moral conviction, so it has to prevail", he is taking the argument in the wrong order; it is an argument whose purpose is to *arrive at* a moral conviction by critical thought.' (179)

[74] 'In that case even critical thinking will say that the suffering of the two taken together will be minimized by putting the patient under intensive care. The case is now beginning to look a bit far-fetched.' (*MT* 180)

a fantastic case that it does not matter if Hare's method prescribes allowing the rapist to commit the rape (*MT* 182). But this dismissal of unlikely cases as irrelevant is too simple. For if Hare is right, the allegedly fantastic case displays the considerations that actually matter to us in ordinary cases. In his view, our confidence in prohibiting rape must rest on a judgment about the comparative pleasure and pain of rapists and victims (and potential rapists and victims), and we must withdraw our prohibition if we come to believe that the rapist's pleasure is probably greater than the victim's pain (if they are the only people affected). We might reasonably doubt whether moral prescriptions are entirely based on such considerations.

If these are consequences of Hare's reduction of prescriptions to preferences, his treatment of fanaticism not only fails to support his reductive view, but casts some doubt on it. The doubt suggests a further doubt about his attempts to free meta-ethical argument from any appeal to moral intuitions. If we accept the reduction of prescriptions to preferences, we must apparently accept the normative implications that Hare recognizes (in his utilitarian judgment about the fanatical preferences of the doctor). If we reject these normative implications, we have a reason to reject Hare's reductive treatment of prescriptions. It is difficult to see how we can reasonably decide the meta-ethical question without relying on our normative views.

This would not be an impressive argument against Hare if he had offered a sound conceptual argument for his utilitarian conclusion. But since his argument is not purely conceptual, it is relevant to consider his normative assumptions. The assumptions about preferences and prescriptions rely on the utilitarian position that is supposed to result from Hare's argument. Hence his argument offers no support to utilitarianism if we are not already convinced that utilitarianism is true.

1342. The Gap Between Prescriptivism and Utilitarianism

If these objections to Hare are reasonable, we do not reach utilitarianism from the formal features of moral judgments together with the attitudes of normal non-fanatical people. We reach it only with the help of some initial moral principles. If Hare has to take the truth of these principles for granted, he seems to rely on a starting point that he calls 'intuitionist'.

In that case, he fails to derive a utilitarian conclusion from the starting points that he allows himself. His failure is not surprising, given his sympathy for a particular interpretation of one of Kant's formulae of the categorical imperative. Kant requires us to act on a maxim that we 'can will' to be the maxim of a universal law. Hare believes we ought to understand 'can will' in a purely formal and logical sense, so that it refers to simple consistency. He agrees with the critics of Kant who argue that this requirement is too weak to lead to anything like morality if 'can will' means simply 'can assent to without self-contradiction'. All sorts of intolerable maxims are consistent. Hare sees that mere consistency is not enough to reach any definite moral conclusion. But he thinks we can reach a moral conclusion if we supplement consistency with some assumptions about the motives of the normal person. He supposes that an appeal to what we are willing to put up with will give more definite results.[75] But if we assume ordinary prudence, the resulting prescriptions do not get us close to utilitarian morality. If we assume more than that, the results we get depend on the motives we assume.

If Hare's argument from universal prescriptivism to utilitarianism were sound, it would be important. It would show that a purely meta-ethical analysis of moral concepts, combined with some weak assumptions about ordinary people's motives and concerns, supports a utilitarian normative theory over a deontological theory. It would turn out that, for ordinary people, the correct meta-ethical theory rules out a deontological normative theory. Since Hare believes this conclusion, he believes he has a strong argument against a deontological normative theory. His arguments clarify our moral thinking because they show us that normal people engaging in moral discourse will accept utilitarian ethics if they understand what they are doing. Our deontological intuitions are to be explained by indirect utilitarianism.[76] If we resist utilitarian resolutions of conflicts between prima facie duties, Hare believes we have failed to grasp the character of moral argument for normal people. Once we see this, we can see how to resolve moral disputes that some people treat as conflicts between irreconcilable intuitions.[77] Hare agrees with Sidgwick in believing that the philosopher's task is done when the only unresolved questions are empirical—however intractable these questions may be.[78]

But if Hare's argument is unsound, his account of the nature of moral judgment as essentially universal and prescriptive does not support utilitarianism or any other normative theory. Hare's defence of a 'two-level' version of utilitarianism needs to be examined on its own merits, apart from the support that he seeks to derive from meta-ethics.

Is this a loss to prescriptivism? We might think so, if we accepted two-level utilitarianism. For we might look more favourably on prescriptivist meta-ethics if it led to a normative theory that we find independently plausible. But if we are not utilitarians, the discovery that prescriptivism leads to utilitarianism might raise doubts about prescriptivism. If we are satisfied that Hare's argument from prescriptivism to utilitarianism is unsound, we remove one ground for doubt about prescriptivism.

Prescriptivism has been considerably elaborated since its initial formulation. Suitable elaborations may say something to cope with the apparent fact that moral judgments and concepts have descriptive meaning, that reasons can be given for them, that they can stand in logical relations, and can have the other properties that descriptivists present as objections to non-cognitive analyses.

A full and just evaluation of prescriptivism, or of some other form of non-cognitivism that has been similarly elaborated, should certainly consider these elaborated versions. But they may also divert attention from one of the basic questions. It is not enough to show that prescriptivism can do quite a lot to accommodate the phenomena of moral judgment. It is worth seeing whether it can do this only if we are initially persuaded to take it seriously.

---

[75] See *SOE* 160–3. Hare discusses the significance of Kant's division between will and simple preference.

[76] *MT* 44–5 distinguishes the 'critical' level of the 'archangel' from the 'intuitive' level of the 'prole'. Hare criticizes deontological views: '. . . we cannot all of us, all the time, behave like proles (as the intuitionists would have us do) if there is to be a system of prima facie principles at all. For the selection of prima facie principles, and for the resolution of conflicts between them, critical thinking is necessary.' (45) Hare takes critical thinking to be utilitarian.

[77] See the passage quoted in §1324, from the preface to *MT*.

[78] Sidgwick on moral and empirical uncertainty; §1177.

We ought to be persuaded if and only if we are impressed by the positive arguments for prescriptivism. These positive arguments are those that bring us back to the disputes that arise from reflexion on Moore. Though one may build an impressive superstructure on non-cognitivist foundations, it does not vindicate the theory unless the foundations are sound. The foundations are open to question.

EXISTENTIALISM

1343. Ethical Relevance

In 1946, Sartre published a short essay, 'The humanism of existentialism' (literally, 'Existentialism is a humanism'). He mentions three reasons for writing it: (1) 'Existentialism' was widely used, but little understood. (2) The philosophical position referred to with this term was widely believed to have distinctive implications for morality. (3) These implications were widely believed to be hostile to morality.[1] In Sartre's view, an accurate understanding of existentialism shows that the second popular belief is true, and the third is partly false. He admits that existentialism supports the rejection of some traditional conceptions of morality, both theistic and non-theistic; but he insists that existentialism is not hostile to morality as such, but in fact supports a distinctive outlook on morality.

Since Sartre believes that existentialism conflicts with some traditional moral outlooks, he cannot claim without qualification that its outlook will be intuitively acceptable. But he claims, none the less, that it has some intuitive support. More specifically, those who take human freedom and human dignity to constitute the basic and supreme moral values will find that the existentialist agrees with them. This is part of what he means by claiming that existentialism is a humanism ('Humanism', 61–2).

Sartre's essay was part of a movement that provoked Heidegger's 'Letter on Humanism', published in 1947. Heidegger's response to the 'humanistic' interpretation of existentialism is complex and unfriendly. His correspondent asks, 'How should one restore meaning to the word "humanism"?' Heidegger answers that one should not restore meaning to it, but discard it.[2] But he does not make it clear exactly what he objects to. (1) He might mean that the substance of Sartre's version of humanism is correct, but Sartre ought not to use the traditional term 'humanism' to describe it. (2) He might mean that

---

[1] According to critics of existentialism, '. . . if we reject God's commandments and the eternal verities, there no longer remains anything but pure caprice, with everyone permitted to do as he pleases and incapable, from his own point of view of condemning the points of view and acts of others' (Sartre, 'Humanism', 32).

[2] 'This question proceeds from your intention to retain the word "humanism". I wonder whether that is necessary. Or is the damage caused by all such terms still not sufficiently obvious? True, "-isms" have for a long time now been suspect. But the market of public opinion continually demands new ones. We are always prepared to supply the demand. Even such names as "logic", "ethics", and "physics" begin to flourish only when original thinking comes to an end.' (Heidegger, 'Letter', 195)

in associating himself with traditional humanist aspirations, Sartre misses the point of existentialism.

The letter as a whole suggests that Heidegger has the second point in mind. He believes that his fundamental inquiries into being and existence undermine attempts to formulate any set of claims about human beings that could support moral claims. Though Sartre rejects traditional ways of connecting claims about human beings with moral claims, he still believes in a connexion. This is why, according to Heidegger, he does not really emancipate himself from the presuppositions of traditional metaphysics, however much he rejects the conclusions that traditional moralists have drawn.

If this is the right way to understand Heidegger's letter, he implicitly accuses Sartre of failing to take the existentialist argument to its logical conclusion. Sartre does not see that his arguments against traditional moral outlooks undermine his own outlook as well. He must be wrong, therefore, in his answer to common views about existentialism; for he is not entitled to claim that it supports a distinctive moral position that deserves respect from those who accept some traditional humanist values.

But if Sartre gives the wrong answer to the questions about existentialism, what is the right answer? Should he have said that existentialism has no moral implications at all? Or should he have said that its moral implications are more destructive than he admits, and that they undermine even the aspects of traditional humanism that he accepts? These questions are difficult to answer from what Heidegger says, since he has very little to say about ethics that is directly relevant. To answer them on his behalf, we need some idea of the relevant aspects of his general philosophical outlook, so that we can see the ethical implications.

Whatever the purely philosophical significance of existentialism may be, its broader impact has been extensive. In this respect, it is similar to logical positivism. In both cases, certain claims believed to be characteristic of a philosophical view have appeared to support attitudes to values in general, and to moral values in particular, that have become current outside philosophical circles. Sartre believes that the popular view of existentialism is mistaken; we need to ask whether his clarification of the existentialist position refutes the popular view.

In the case of Heidegger, a special issue arises. For he took a conspicuous role in public life as a supporter of National Socialism. Though he spent only a short time as a university official carrying out the Nazi programme in his university, his attitude to the Nazi regime and the Nazi outlook during the twelve years of the Third Reich fell well short of unqualified disapproval.[3]

These aspects of Heidegger's show something about his character, but one might argue that they are philosophically irrelevant. If Einstein had sympathized with the Nazis, he would not have thereby discredited his physics. If Frege had lived long enough, he might have sympathized with the aims of National Socialism,[4] but he would not thereby have discredited his work in logic and philosophy of language. Sometimes, however, the political outlook of scientists is relevant to the status of their scientific work. Nazi racial theories

---

[3] See 'Self-assertion' and 'Overcoming metaphysics'.

[4] See Dummett, *FPL* xii, who remarks that Frege was 'at least at the end of his life, a virulent racist, specifically an anti-semite'.

and some Soviet genetics involve bad science corrupted by political ends. Some interpreters claim to have found something similar in Heidegger.[5] This approach to Heidegger would be more credible if it could fasten on an explicit moral and political theory. But he presents no explicit theory of this sort.

Heidegger's inexplicitness on this point, however, does not make his political stands irrelevant to a study of his philosophy. We might agree that his philosophy is compatible with opposition to National Socialism. It still remains to ask whether his philosophy gives him any reason to oppose National Socialism. It would be foolish to ask this question about Frege's philosophy, which does not touch on moral and political questions. Heidegger's philosophical outlook is not detached from morals and politics to this degree. It offers an account of human beings and their situation in the world that, in Heidegger's view, supports conclusions about the character of human action, and about deluded and enlightened ways of understanding oneself in relation to other people and to one's social environment. According to one line of argument, beliefs on these questions are the basis of views about human freedom, rights, and dignity that are incompatible with, for instance, the outlook of National Socialism. If the effect of Heidegger's general outlook is to undermine these 'liberal' beliefs and to suggest that they rest on illusions, he makes it easier to support a political position that rejects individual freedom, equal treatment, and respect for human dignity as a basis for political action. If Heidegger argues against the theoretical foundations of liberalism, he is not necessarily a philosophical apologist for National Socialism, but his philosophical views may deprive him of some grounds for opposition to his political outlook.

This line of criticism is controversial. For some defenders of the liberal assumptions that conflict with Fascism and National Socialism argue that these assumptions neither need nor allow theoretical foundations, so that we should not be disturbed by an argument that explodes any alleged theoretical foundations.[6] Defenders of political commitment without theoretical foundations agree with Sartre on one important aspect of his polemic against traditional moral philosophy. If they are right on this issue, Heidegger is not open to justified criticism for undermining the alleged foundations of liberalism. If, however, they are wrong, he may be open to justified criticism.

1344. Motivation for Existentialism

Heidegger shares with other 20th-century philosophers a preoccupation with the relation of philosophy to the natural sciences. He rejects the positivist view, derived from Kant, that philosophy deals with the a priori, and hence (given the positivist conception of the a priori) the purely conceptual and formal aspect of knowledge. He also rejects the position of the later Wittgenstein, that philosophy is concerned with 'grammar', with the elucidation of everyday concepts and linguistic practices in ways that avoid philosophical errors. Still, he shares with these other philosophers the general view that philosophy is neither an

---

[5] Two brief statements among the numerous (and often highly polemical) discussions of this question: Habermas, 'Heidegger', esp. 195–6; Olafson, *HGE* 13–14.

[6] An extreme version of this view is maintained by Rorty, *CIS*, chs. 1–3.

empirical natural science nor a non-empirical science that can claim to discover truths about an objective world that are not available to ordinary empirical sciences. In rejecting these views about philosophy, he takes himself to reject the main tradition of philosophy that goes back to Plato and Aristotle.

Heidegger's diagnosis of the errors of the tradition is significantly similar to the diagnosis offered by German-speaking philosophers who have strongly influenced Anglophone philosophy. He believes that the tradition goes astray by claiming to provide the sort of knowledge that only the natural sciences can provide. Aristotelian metaphysics offers to tell us the truth about entities in the natural world; it does not tell us the truths of physics or chemistry, but truths, discovered by a priori argument, about entities that are studied by physics or chemistry. Heidegger agrees with Carnap and with the later Wittgenstein that there are no truths of this sort to be discovered about the world studied by the empirical sciences; these sciences are the only ones capable of telling us the truths about the world so described. Philosophy, as he conceives it, should not be a competitor or colleague of the empirical sciences. It should focus on the questions that are prior to a conception of the world as an object of empirical science.

1345. The Starting Point

In the Introduction to *Being and Time*, Heidegger argues that traditional metaphysics has concealed and obscured the questions that it ought to have clarified, and that therefore we must go back past its origins to see the initial questions that have been concealed. Why does he suppose that traditional metaphysics has gone astray, and why does he believe he can do better?

His first objection to traditional metaphysics is that it has reached the conclusion that we need not investigate the meaning of Being, because Being is taken to be clear.[7] In his preliminary (and, he insists, incomplete) statement of the reasons for the neglect of the question about Being, Heidegger mentions three standard claims about the concept of Being: that it is the most universal concept, that it is indefinable because it is universal, and that it is self-evident (g3–4/mr22–3).

These standard claims raise a doubt about Heidegger's assertion that questions about Being are neglected. If these claims about the concept of Being are right, they do not make it unnecessary to inquire into Being itself—into whatever the concept of Being is a concept of. If the concept of Being has the broad extension that Heidegger describes, an inquiry into Being itself should be an inquiry into things in general, and into what they are.

If this is what it means to inquire into Being, philosophers seem to inquire into Being in so far as they inquire into things in general. Dualism and materialism about minds and bodies, theism and atheism about God, idealism, phenomenalism, and realism about

---

[7] 'On the basis of the Greeks' initial contributions towards an Interpretation of Being, a dogma has developed which not only declares the question about the meaning of Being to be superfluous, but sanctions its complete neglect . . . That which the ancient philosophers found continually disturbing as something obscure and hidden has taken on a clarity and self-evidence such that if anyone continues to ask about it he is charged with an error of method.' (*BT* g2/mr21) I cite *BT* by the pages of the German edn. (g) and of Macquarrie and Robinson's trans. (mr).

external objects—these are all metaphysical doctrines about the sorts of things there are, and hence they seem to be doctrines about Being. Few philosophers regard the answers to all these questions as self-evident; and hence they do not neglect questions about Being, understood as embracing questions about the sorts of things there are.

This answer, however, does not satisfy Heidegger. In fact it seems to him to support his claim that philosophers neglect inquiry into Being. In his view, this approach to the task of philosophy regards something as self-evident that it should regard as open to question. Philosophers work within some presupposition that ought to be made explicit and subjected to discussion. The presupposition that they have neglected concerns the character of the inquirer who considers Being. Hence inquiry into Being begins from the proper starting point if and only if it begins with questions about the inquirer into Being.[8] Traditional philosophy, therefore, has neglected an inquiry that might be expected to clarify some of the presuppositions of an inquiry into Being. An inquiry into the inquirer into Being ought to reveal some of the concerns and assumptions that guide the inquirer's inquiries into Being.

It may seem surprising that Heidegger suggests that traditional philosophy has ignored his question about the inquirer. For the advice to consider the inquirer before we start the inquiry that the inquirer conducts seems familiar. It seems to recall Aristotle's initial arguments in *Metaphysics*, iv about the requirements of significant thought and speech, or Locke's and Kant's advice to consider our own cognitive capacities before we make ambitious claims to knowledge of various things. Traditional philosophy has not ignored the character of the inquirers into being; on the contrary, it has regularly taken their character to be relevant to the questions that we can reasonably ask, or the knowledge that we can reasonably expect to find, about the subject we inquire into.

Perhaps, then, Heidegger believes that these references to the inquirer do not go far enough, and that if we examined the character of the inquirer more thoroughly, we would find that it permeates the inquiry more completely than traditional metaphysics has supposed. Since we begin with human beings as inquirers, we might expect to find that the inquiry is more anthropocentric than traditional philosophy has supposed.

According to Heidegger, this focus on the presuppositions of metaphysics is an example of a more widespread contemporary tendency of different disciplines to question their initial assumptions. The mere accumulation of information, and the prosecution of inquiries within fixed assumptions and presuppositions, is unsatisfying, and when we are unsatisfied we turn to more fundamental questions.[9] We try, therefore, to find new foundations for

---

[8] 'Looking at something, understanding it and conceiving it, choosing, access to it—all these ways of behaving are constitutive for our inquiry, and therefore are modes of Being for those particular entities which we, the inquirers are ourselves. Thus to work out the question of Being adequately, we must make an entity—the inquirer—transparent in his own Being. The very asking of this question is an entity's mode of *Being*; and as such it gets its essential character from what is inquired about—namely, Being. This entity which each of us is himself and which includes inquiring as one of the possibilities of its Being, we shall denote by the term "Dasein". If we are to formulate our question explicitly and transparently, we must first give a proper explication of an entity (Dasein), with regard to its Being.' (g7/mr26–7).

[9] 'The level which a science has reached is determined by how far it is *capable* of a crisis in its basic concepts. In such immanent crises the very relationship between positively investigative inquiry and those things themselves that are under interrogation comes to a point where it begins to totter. Among the various disciplines everywhere today there are freshly awakened tendencies to put research on new foundations.' (g9/mr29)

our inquiries. We might try to express Heidegger's point in terms borrowed from Kuhn. Perhaps he means to contrast 'normal science', which operates within a shared 'paradigm', with the times of crisis and revolution, in which inquirers eventually shift their paradigms. The paradigm fixes the criteria and assumptions that determine whether a hypothesis is worth taking seriously and how one ought to try to confirm or to refute it. But when a crisis arises, these criteria and assumptions are called into question; they have to be examined by some method that does not already assume their soundness.[10]

In order to 'put research on new foundations', Heidegger believes he faces 'the task of destroying the history of ontology' (g19/mr41). It needs to be destroyed because it causes us to misunderstand our relation to Being. We approach Being through a particular tradition that claims to be the uniquely correct way to understand Being. By its assumption of unique correctness, a particular tradition tends to conceal the fact that it is simply one possible tradition, and hence historical, and hence contingent.[11]

Heidegger illustrates his claim by commenting on the later treatment of Greek ontology. When Greek ontological claims were detached from their historical origins, they came to be treated as self-evident and independent of any historical origin.[12] Though later philosophy has modified what it received from the Greeks, it has modified it without reference to its historical origin, and hence has taken over some of its basic content without examination or criticism.

This search for historical understanding explains what Heidegger means when he speaks of 'destroying' traditional ontology. He destroys it as a body of fixed doctrine detached from any historical origin, because it has no right to claim this non-historical fixity. Instead he looks at it in close relation to the circumstances in which it came into being.[13] This search for the 'birth certificate' of our basic ontological concepts is not meant to result in cynicism or relativism about the traditional ontology, but in a clearer appreciation of its 'positive possibilities'.

A naive reader of Heidegger's call for historical understanding might undertake the historical study of philosophy, as philosophers have often understood it. We might suppose we could read Aristotle's treatises and examine his arguments, and conclude that his doctrine of substance, say, is broadly correct, though mistaken in this or that detail. In that case, we would have a point of view from which we could criticize the later history of metaphysical inquiry. We might conclude, for instance, that Aquinas is wrong in his treatment of matter, but right in his use of a doctrine of substantial form in his account of the soul, that Descartes,

---

[10] Kuhn, *SSR*, ch. 5, argues that paradigms are prior to rules. In ch. 9, he discusses how changes in paradigms change 'the criteria determining the legitimacy both of problems and of proposed solutions' (109).

[11] 'When tradition thus becomes master, it does so in such a way that what it "transmits" is made so inaccessible, proximally and for the most part, that it rather becomes concealed. Tradition takes what has come down to us and delivers it over to self-evidence; it blocks our access to those primordial "sources" from which the categories and concepts handed down to us have in part quite genuinely drawn. Indeed it makes us forget that they have had such an origin, and makes us suppose that the necessity of going back to these sources is something which we need not even understand.' (g21 = mr43)

[12] 'In the Middle Ages this uprooted Greek ontology became a fixed body of doctrine.' (g22/mr43)

[13] 'If the question of Being is to have its own history made transparent, then this hardened tradition must be loosened up, and the concealments which it has brought about must be dissolved. We understand this task as one in which by taking *the question of Being as our clue*, we are to *destroy* the traditional content of ancient ontology until we arrive at those primordial experiences in which we achieved our first ways of determining the nature of Being—the ways which have guided us ever since.' (g22/mr44)

Locke, and Spinoza are wrong to abandon the Aristotelian doctrine of substantial form, and that Leibniz is right, in certain respects, in wanting to revive it.

This is the sort of historical inquiry that Heidegger rejects. He believes it misunderstands his argument, because it assumes that the right approach to Aristotle's works is the approach sanctioned by the metaphysical tradition. Such an approach treats Aristotle's questions and arguments as accessible from a non-historical point of view, and open to evaluation by the standards that we might apply to any philosopher of any age. Hence this approach to the history of the metaphysical tradition is itself the product of that tradition, and so (Heidegger infers) it cannot be used to understand the historical conditions of the tradition. To accept such an approach is to overlook what Heidegger is looking for in his search for a birth certificate.

Heidegger, therefore, does not expect his historical inquiry to conclude that Aristotle or Aquinas or Descartes was right in some respects and wrong in others. He suggests that the search for such conclusions reflects a tradition-bound approach to metaphysics that will be open to objection in the light of historical understanding.

We already gather that Heidegger's historical inquiry is anthropocentric in some distinctive way, because it attends to the human being as the inquirer. It is also supposed to be 'phenomenological'. In his view, the *phainomenon* is what primarily 'shows itself'. He connects *logos* with 'discourse', which he connects with *apophainesthai* (usually translated 'express'), which he associates with *phainesthai*, and renders 'reveal'. Hence 'phenomenology' is 'to let that which shows itself be seen from itself in the very way in which it shows itself from itself' (g34/mr58).

If we set aside any objections to Heidegger's excursions into Greek, we may understand his phenomenological inquiry to rest on two assumptions: (1) It is concerned with what shows itself and is in that respect evident. It is therefore not concerned with discovering some reality behind appearances that is represented in, or imperfectly indicated by, appearances. It does not rely on any distinction between appearance and reality, and does not pursue reality in opposition to appearance. (2) Though we are not concerned with any reality underlying appearances, we do not assume that we are always in a position to see what shows itself as it shows itself. What is evident when we look at it correctly may none the less be covered by something that we have to remove in order to see what is evident.

A rough analogy may convey Heidegger's main point. Suppose a bright light is being projected on to a screen, but the screen is dirty. Once we clean the screen, we can see the light clearly. We reach a phenomenological understanding once we remove the distortions and concealments that result from the dirty screen. But we are concerned simply with the phenomenon; we need not examine the nature of light, from a physicist's point of view, and we need not speculate about where the light is coming from or how it is produced by its source. The questions about what 'lies behind' the phenomenal light are irrelevant from the phenomenological point of view.

Why must the method used in finding the birth certificate of ontological concepts be phenomenological? Heidegger seems to assume that it is both possible and necessary to uncover an 'everyday' understanding of Being from the point of view of human beings, and that this everyday understanding provides a point of departure for the metaphysical schemes that cover and conceal it. Because we are familiar with these metaphysical schemes, we do not notice, until we attend to it, the everyday understanding that lies behind them; instead we take the schemes themselves to be the only way of understanding reality.

This phenomenological approach may be reasonable. A defender of Platonic or Aristotelian metaphysics, for instance, ought to agree that these metaphysical schemes do not simply report the explicit conceptual scheme of common sense. Ordinary Greeks, no less than ordinary people of other ages, recognize tables, parents, trees, right and wrong actions, pain, pleasure, and so on, but they do not explicitly recognize Platonic Forms or Aristotelian substantial forms and actualities. Plato and Aristotle believe things about their favoured metaphysical entities that are not precisely what common sense explicitly believes about any of the items that it recognizes. To see the difference between metaphysics and common sense, we should begin with a perspicuous account of common sense.

The disagreement between the Platonic or Aristotelian metaphysician and Heidegger arises at the next stage. For the metaphysicians claim that their metaphysical schemes give the best account of those elements in the common-sense outlook that are rationally defensible. If Heidegger agreed with this, he would have shown that traditional metaphysics passes the test he imposes on it when he looks for its birth certificate. It would turn out to be correct and legitimate, and we would have no reason to turn away from it to some other metaphysical scheme or to abandon metaphysics.

If, then, traditional metaphysics is mistaken, he must believe that a phenomenological inquiry will expose something illegitimate in the assumptions of traditional metaphysics. The illegitimacy cannot consist simply in the fact that the metaphysical scheme is not exactly the same as the explicit common-sense outlook. To see what Heidegger takes to be illegitimate or questionable in traditional metaphysics, we need to see what we discover by phenomenological inquiry.

1346. Human Beings and the World

Since our starting point is anthropocentric, we begin by considering the outlook of human beings as those beings for whom the question of Being arises. Heidegger believes that this fact about human beings determines our approach to their outlook and to their relation to the world.

First, he infers that, since Being is an issue for every human being, the essence of a human being must consist in his existence (g42/mr67). This means that we must take the essence of a human being to consist in his being open to possibilities.[14] Though human beings are essentially open to different possibilities, they may not recognize that they are open to them. The ones who recognize their essential openness to different possibilities are the ones who live authentically (g42–3/mr68), but many human beings live inauthentically without being any less open to possibilities in fact.

From this essential openness to possibilities, Heidegger believes he can infer that one standard conception of the pre-theoretical outlook of human beings must be mistaken.

---

[14] 'Furthermore, in each case Dasein is mine to be in one way or another. Dasein has always made some sort of decision as to the way in which it is in each case mine. That entity which in its Being has this very Being as an issue, comports itself towards its Being as its ownmost possibility.' (g42/mr68)

We might think of human beings as merely 'present-at-hand', but this conception of them would ignore their openness to possibilities.[15] To treat human beings as things merely present-at-hand would be to suppose that we could describe them as mere objects of theoretical study, as items with fixed characters that they possess in their own right. But we should not look at them in this way; we should look at them in their essential openness to possibilities.

This inference is open to question. Does not Heidegger himself treat human beings as having a fixed nature and character—their being essentially open to possibilities? If we grasp this fact about them, and consider what it implies, can we not find other essential properties of human beings? We might ask, for instance, whether we could be open to possibilities, in the specific way that Heidegger has in mind, if we lacked consciousness or if we lacked reason. If the answer to these questions is No, we may reasonably infer that human beings are essentially rational animals. But Heidegger rejects this account of human beings, on the ground that it ascribes a 'fixed' nature to human beings and does not clarify the ontological question at issue (g48/mr74).

Perhaps Heidegger believes that this attempt to argue from his conception to a traditional conception of human beings departs from the phenomenological method, since it tries to discern something lying behind the phenomenon that he is trying to make manifest. In looking for the phenomenon itself, we should not (in his view) confuse this search with a search for presuppositions or foundations.

If this is Heidegger's position, his reliance on a phenomenological method is controversial. If it forbids us to raise questions that seem reasonable, why should we engage in an inquiry that excludes these questions, rather than an inquiry that allows us to go beyond the phenomena, narrowly construed? We can return to this question once we have seen where we get with the phenomenological method.

If we agree to study human beings as essentially open to possibilities that they may or may not recognize, we should start with them in their everydayness.[16] We ought not to begin with any 'concrete possible idea of existence', because any such idea would prejudice the inquiry in favour of some particular conception of human beings. A bias towards some particular conception would be incompatible with phenomenological method. We might, for instance, assume at the outset that all human beings desire to know, or that all human action aims at the good, as Aristotle seems to assume at the start of the *Metaphysics* and the *Nicomachean Ethics*. If we assume that, we already assume that we can legitimately inquire into knowledge or rational action, abstracted from the rest of the human context.

One might ask whether starting with 'everydayness' does not also amount to beginning with 'some concrete possible idea of existence'. Does this starting point not also prejudice the

---

[15] 'Dasein does not have the kind of Being which belongs to something merely present-at-hand within the world, nor does it ever have it. So neither is it to be presented thematically as something we come across in the same way as we come across what is present-at-hand.' (g43/mr68–9)

[16] 'But this tells us that if we are to Interpret this entity *ontologically*, the problematic of its Being must be developed from the existentiality of its existence. This cannot mean, however, that "Dasein" is to be construed in terms of some concrete possible idea of existence. At the outset of our analysis it is particularly important that Dasein should not be Interpreted with the differentiated character of some definite way of existing, but that it should be uncovered in the undifferentiated character which it has proximally and for the most part. This undifferentiated character of Dasein's everydayness is *not nothing*, but a positive phenomenal characteristic of this entity.' (g43/mr69)

inquiry against those approaches that reject some aspects of the everyday conception of the world? An answer to this question depends on how far Heidegger requires the metaphysician to remain within the everyday outlook.

Still, even the most revisionary metaphysics must somehow take account of the everyday outlook. Since that is the outlook that, according to the revisionary metaphysician, needs to be revised, we ought to begin by understanding what it is that the metaphysician seeks to revise. Understanding the everyday outlook may show us that some of the metaphysician's criticisms rest on misunderstanding.

On this point, one might well sympathize with Heidegger's advice to begin the everyday outlook. We might take him to be saying what Austin says when he remarks that ordinary language does not have the last word, but it has the first word.[17] If, however, the study of the everyday outlook has only the first word, can it be used to refute metaphysicians who claim that it does not have the last word?

1347. Being in the World

The everyday condition must be understood, according to Heidegger, as 'being-in-the-world' (g53/mr78). He uses this hyphenated expression because he insists that 'it stands for a *unitary* phenomenon' (g53/mr78). He wants to deny that it has two separable elements, the human being who has this being and the world in which he has this being. But he does not deny that there are different elements to be understood: the human being, the character of his being, and the world in which he has his being (g53/mr78–9). Once we understand these different elements, we can see the difference between the everyday condition and the starting point of traditional metaphysics.

It is particularly important, according to Heidegger, not to concede that the relation between a human being and the world is the relation between subject and object (g60 = mr87). If we conceded that, we would concede the initial assumption of traditional ontology, which recognizes both a subject and an object confronting it. Once we concede this initial assumption, we inevitably find ourselves asking how the subject makes contact with this object 'outside' it, and we raise all the problems of traditional metaphysics and epistemology (g60–1/mr87).

But how can Heidegger refuse to recognize a division between subject and object, if he is not an idealist? He does not affirm that human minds create the world simply by thinking about it, or that the world is simply a mode of human experience. Must he not, therefore, recognize human subjects and objects independent of them?

Heidegger's answer to this objection explains why he treats 'being-in-the-world' as a unitary phenomenon. For though the human being and his world are two distinct aspects of this phenomenon, and though we fail to understand the phenomenon as a whole unless we grasp both aspects, they are not identifiable or intelligible independently of each other. On the one hand, human beings are essentially oriented towards the world. On the other hand, the everyday world is essentially a world of significance for human beings.

---

[17] Austin, 'Excuses', 185: 'Certainly, then, ordinary language is *not* the last word: in principle it can everywhere be supplemented and improved upon and superseded. Only remember, it *is* the *first* word.'

To capture the claim about essential connexion, we might deny that human beings are 'in' the world in a purely physical or spatial sense. Such a sense might suggest that they are in the world in the way in which apples might be in a basket; the nature of each apple is independent of its specific position in the basket, and of its being in the basket at all. The essential properties of human beings, by contrast, include their being in the world. This world that is essential to them, moreover, is not some purely physical space, but an anthropocentric environment that Heidegger describes in more detail. As he explains: 'Ontologically, "world" is not a way of characterizing those entities which Dasein essentially is *not*; it is rather a characterization of Dasein itself' (g64/mr92).

1348. Equipment and Environment

The phenomenological analysis of everydayness begins with the things that belong to the everyday anthropocentric world.[18] Our interaction with these things is not purely theoretical or observational. We are actively related to them in so far as we manipulate them. These items that we manipulate are not mere 'things' (*res* or *pragmata*; see g68/mr96–7), but 'equipment'. Their status in the world is not merely existing, but being 'ready-to-hand' (zuhanden; g69/mr98).

In regarding things as equipment, we regard them teleologically, with reference to specific purposes that they might be used for.[19] We think of things teleologically, in relation to ourselves, in relation to other people, and in relation to other pieces of equipment. Even if we do not travel on aeroplanes, we can think of a strip of tarmac as a runway that is part of an airport that allows planes to take off and land, to transport passengers, to carry out the aims that require travel.

Not all the things that we regard as equipment need to be artifacts that have been produced, as hammers and saws (Heidegger's favourite examples) have been, to carry out some goal-directed task. We may also look at non-artifacts from a teleological point of view. We may look at a field as suitable for cultivation, or at the weather as suitable for agriculture or recreation, and we may look at a river as a barrier to communication (needing to be bridged or avoided) or as a means of communication (needing to be navigated).

These previous examples suggest that when we look at non-artifacts from a teleological point of view, we do not only look at them as suitable for carrying out some purpose, but we also look at them as unsuitable. These things are not ready-to-hand, but simply 'present-at-hand' (vorhanden), and this is how we understand them. But our understanding of them does not lift them out of a teleological, anthropocentric context altogether. Heidegger

---

[18] 'The Being of those entities which we encounter as closest to us can be exhibited phenomenologically if we take as our clue our everyday Being-in-the-world, which we also call our *"dealings"* with the world and with entities within-the-world. Such dealings have already dispersed themselves into manifold ways of concern. The kind of dealing which is closest to us is, as we have shown, not a bare perceptual cognition, but rather that kind of concern which manipulates things and puts them to use; and this has its own kind of "knowledge".' (g66–7/mr95)

[19] 'A totality of equipment is constituted by various ways of the "in-order-to", such as serviceability, conduciveness, usability, manipulability.' (g68/mr97)

illustrates this point by considering a broken and unusable artifact.[20] We take the same view of a non-artifact that 'stands in the way' of our concern (g73/mr103). When we look at it this way, we understand it in a teleological context in which it presents an obstacle.

This analysis is meant to show that readiness-to-hand is not a property that we attribute to some things partly on the basis of some prior recognition of their non-teleological, merely present-at-hand character. We should not take ourselves to recognize a physical object as having a certain shape and colour, then recognizing it as made of iron and wood, and then inferring that it will be useful for hammering nails. When we recognize something in our environment as ready-to-hand, it is not because we recognize it as something present-at-hand 'upon which equipment ready-to-hand is somehow founded' (g75/mr105). On the contrary, we grasp something as present-at-hand on the basis of a prior grasp of things as equipment. When something fails to fit appropriately into a system of things as equipment, and we see that it does not fit, we recognize it as simply present-at-hand. In recognizing that it does not fit, we still take the anthropocentric view from which we classify things by considering how well they serve as equipment.

From this conception of things as equipment for our aims, or as unsuitable for serving as equipment, or as obstacles to our aims, we can understand the conception of the world that is inseparably linked to being-in-the-world. Since human beings are not 'in' the world in a merely spatial or local sense, the world they are in is not simply a big place. To grasp the world is to grasp equipment for our purposes, and obstacles to these purposes, in their systematic connexions.

Some grasp of systematic connexions is presupposed in any conception of things as equipment. In thinking of hammers as equipment, we also have to think of the teleological role of nails, wood, beams, frames, walls, houses, suburbs, cities, and so on. We introduce a larger system if we consider a piece of the navigational equipment of an aeroplane that is used for inter-continental flights. Though we may not always recognize this system, sometimes it is 'lit up' for us, when we think more fully about what is ready-to-hand and about the present-at-hand things that constitute obstacles for us.[21] We do not reach a conception of the world by inference from our smaller-scale beliefs about equipment. We always presuppose it, but only some situations make it clear to us that we always presuppose it.[22]

These features of everydayness help to explain why Heidegger refuses to separate the subject from things in the world. Human beings essentially regard themselves as being-in-the-world, as concerned with things in relation to their purposes. Moreover, they regard things in the world, and the world presupposed by concern with these things, as essentially connected with their concerns. The teleological, anthropocentric, conception of the world explains why the subject and the world essentially involve each other.

---

[20] 'This presence-at-hand of something that cannot be used is still not devoid of all readiness-to-hand whatsoever; equipment which is present-at-hand *in this way* is still not just a Thing which occurs somewhere. The damage to the equipment is still not a mere alteration of a Thing—not a change of properties which just occurs in something present-at-hand.' (g73/mr103)

[21] 'Whenever we encounter anything, the world has already been previously discovered, though not thematically. But it can also be lit up in certain ways of dealing with our environment. The world is that in terms of which the ready-to-hand is ready-to-hand.' (g83/mr114)

[22] The worldhood of the world is 'the Being of that ontical condition which makes it possible for entities within-the-world to be discovered at all' (g88/mr121).

1349. Objections to Descartes

This outline of everydayness is the basis for some of Heidegger's criticisms of Descartes's starting point. In his view, Descartes's conception of the world as an 'extended thing' (res extensa) rests on his conception of substance (g92/mr125). Substances include both the independent substance (God) and finite substance, both thinking and extended. But we can understand the concept of substance that is applied to finite and infinite substance only if we 'clarify the meaning of Being which is *"common"* to the three kinds of substance, one of them infinite, the others both finite' (g93/mr126). But Descartes fails to do this; he follows the mediaevals in recognizing the 'analogical' signification of 'Being', but he does not clarify this signification even as much as the mediaevals do; 'the meaning remains unclarified because it is held to be "self-evident"'' (g93/mr126).

Descartes recognizes a world of extended substance that is spatially external to think-ing substance, and confronts thinking substance as an object to be known. But this is not a self-evident starting point, as Descartes supposed. He has failed to pursue Heidegger's inquiry into the kind of being that belongs to things in the world, as an essential and inseparable constituent of being-in-the-world. He assumes that being is simply present-at-hand, and takes presence-at-hand to be intelligible independently of its relation to readiness-to-hand. Hence he does not recognize that the conception of the world as a set of objects separable from the knowing subject rests on an abstraction from the teleologically ordered everyday world. Descartes looks at the world in math-ematical terms, but his mathematical interests are not the foundation of his intellectual outlook. They are the result of a prior assumption that things are purely present-at-hand.[23]

Though Descartes moves from traditional ontology to modern mathematical physics and its foundations, he follows traditional ontology in his assumptions about knowledge. He assumes that knowledge consists in a direct view or 'beholding' of the objects of knowledge without any distortion.[24] That is why Descartes rejects the senses; they do not give us a direct 'beholding' of the objects themselves, but only of apparent or superficial properties of the objects. Some non-sensory condition is needed to meet Descartes's conditions for genuine knowledge.

According to Heidegger's description, the Cartesian takes a non-anthropocentric view, and treats the world as an object of inquiry in abstraction from the aims and purposes of the subject. This is why Heidegger questions the traditional division between subject and

---

[23] 'Instead he [sc. Descartes] prescribes for the world its "real" Being, as it were, on the basis of an idea of Being whose source has not been unveiled and which has not been demonstrated in its own right—an idea in which Being is equated with constant presence-at-hand. Thus his ontology of the world is not primar-ily determined by his leaning towards mathematics, a science which he chances to esteem very highly, but rather by his ontological orientation in principle towards Being as constant presence-at-hand, which mathemat-ical knowledge is especially well suited to grasp. In this way Descartes explicitly switches over philosophically from the development of traditional ontology to modern mathematical physics and its transcendental foundations.' (g96/mr129)

[24] 'The problem of how to get appropriate access to entities-within-the-world is one which Descartes feels no need to raise. Under the unbroken ascendance of the traditional ontology, the way to get a genuine grasp of what really is has been decided in advance: it lies in *noein*—"beholding" in the widest sense; *dianoein* or "thinking" is just a more fully achieved form of *noein* and is founded upon it.' (g96/mr129)

object. He regards this division as a misleading abstraction from being-in-the-world.[25] The study of being-in-the-world clarifies the 'ontological necessity' and 'ontological meaning' of the presupposition about subject and object. We should treat the conception of things as present-at-hand as a development from the conception of things as equipment, and not as a fundamental and unquestionable conception of things.

One might, then, reasonably take Heidegger to mean that the study of this ontological background reveals the basically anthropocentric character of the conception of being-in-the-world from which we abstract the world as something merely present-at-hand. When we think of the world as something independent and objective, confronting the subject as inquirer, we think we have found something non-anthropocentric, but really we have only focussed on one aspect of being-in-the-world. It is therefore a mistake to think of the point of view of 'pure inquiry' as a means of access to some conception of the world as it is in itself, apart from any anthropocentric interest of ours.[26] We think of the point of view of pure inquiry in this way only because we ignore the context from which we have abstracted it.

Heidegger himself does not speak of 'abstraction'; but it is difficult to avoid using this term if we are to grasp what he takes to be questionable in traditional ontology and especially in the standard view of subject and object. For he does not mean to deny the distinction between subject and object on the strength of idealism or neutral monism or some other doctrine that takes a position within traditional metaphysics. In his view, the distinction is all right in its place, but traditional metaphysics takes it out of its place and thereby misunderstands it.

Some abstractions result in misunderstanding if we do not recognize that they are abstractions. If, for instance, we think of individuals as simply 'economic agents', moved only by considerations of profit, loss, and maximizing individual preference-satisfaction, but we do not recognize that our conception is a simplifying abstraction, we will be surprised that actual people do not behave that way. If, however, we recognize that it is an abstraction from the motives of actual people, we can use the economic model appropriately. Perhaps Heidegger intends this judgment on traditional metaphysics. Perhaps he believes that it does not properly grasp the partial and purpose-relative character of its starting point, and so falsely concludes that it inquires into how things really are in their own right, apart from any human purpose or aim.

According to Heidegger, therefore, Descartes takes for granted as a starting point something that he ought to have examined from more basic principles. He treats things

---

[25] 'But because this structure of Being remains ontologically inaccessible, yet is experienced ontically as a "relationship" between one entity (the world) and another (the soul), and because one proximally understands Being by taking entities as entities-within-the-world for one's ontological foothold, one tries to conceive the relationship between world and soul as grounded in these two entities themselves and in the meaning of their Being—namely, to conceive it as Being present-at-hand. And even though Being-in-the-world is something of which one has pre-phenomenological experience and acquaintance, it becomes *invisible* if one interprets it in a way which is ontologically inappropriate . . . So in this way it becomes the "evident" point of departure for problems of epistemology or the "metaphysics of knowledge". For what is more obvious than that a "subject" is related to an "Object" and vice versa? This "subject-Object-relationship" must be presupposed. But while this presupposition is unimpeachable in its facticity, this makes it indeed a baleful one, if its ontological necessity and especially its ontological meaning are left in the dark.' (g59/mr85–6)

[26] This idea of pure inquiry is developed by Williams in (appropriately) his discussion of Descartes. See esp. his description of the 'absolute' conception, *DPPE* 64–7, 210–12, 244–9.

as present-at-hand without recognizing that this treatment of them is the result of an abstraction from their character as equipment. To regard things as present-at-hand is not the single compulsory starting point for inquiry, and so it should not be taken for granted as our fundamental point of view on things as they really are in their own right. It is a later stage than the primary conception of being-in-the-world that regards things as ready-to-hand. Similarly, a conception of things as extended objects making up a world of extended objects is not a basic, self-evident starting point. It is also an abstraction from our conception of a world that exists in its various properties and relations for a human being who sees its parts in their significance as equipment.

If, then, Heidegger's claims about being-in-the-world are correct, and if he describes Descartes's position correctly, he has identified an error in Descartes. In treating something as fundamental that is really derivative, Descartes mis-describes his starting point.

1350. A Voluntarist Objection to Descartes

We may well wonder, however, whether Heidegger's criticism of Descartes matters, even if it is correct. Even if we grant that Descartes has omitted a basic conception of being-in-the-world from which the conception of 'mere' confrontation between subjects and external objects is an abstraction, might it not be reasonable, for Descartes's purposes to omit this first stage and pass on to the abstraction? One might argue that it is irrelevant to Descartes's inquiry to begin with the fact that we encounter hammers, lorries, and power stations; the differences between these physical objects is irrelevant to (for instance) the fact that we can raise just the same sorts of sceptical doubts about their existence.

This reply would be mistaken if Heidegger had shown that the abstraction involved in Descartes's starting point rests on some mistake. If, for instance, the conception of things as merely present-at-hand rests on some false belief whose falsity could be shown by appeal to Heidegger's account of being-in-the-world, Descartes picks the wrong starting point. But the considerations Heidegger has offered do not show that Descartes's abstraction involves any mistake. Even if our everyday thought of present-at-hand things treats them as gaps or failures in a general pattern of ready-to-hand things, it does not follow that we make any mistake in regarding them as merely present-at-hand, without reference to any place they may have or fail to have among ready-to-hand things. Moreover, Heidegger does not argue that we make any mistake on this point.

But even if Descartes's starting point does not rest on any false beliefs, he might none the less be wrong about its status. He treats it as a compulsory starting point for any inquiry that can be expected to lead to knowledge of the world. We might infer from Heidegger's examination of everydayness that the Cartesian starting point is not compulsory, but optional. We might grant that, from Heidegger's point of view, no mistake is involved in treating things as simply present-at-hand, but then we might add that we do not have to treat them this way. While Descartes's abstraction may be useful for some purposes, it is unhelpful for other purposes. We have no reason to believe that it is somehow the unique way to a grasp of reality as it fundamentally is, or that conceptions of the world that refrain from this abstraction are necessarily superficial or mistaken.

If this is Heidegger's point, his criticism of traditional metaphysics rests on a claim that is more familiar in disputes about the sources of value. One voluntarist claim about the source of value rests on assumptions about the freedom and sovereignty of God; another rests on assumptions about the freedom of the human will. From these points of view, any evaluative truths are true only in relation to some prior choice that is not itself open to assessment by further evaluative truths.

If Heidegger intends to appeal to this voluntarist outlook, and to apply it to the foundations of metaphysics, he believes that the conception of the world as consisting of extended present-at-hand objects reflects a choice that cannot be assessed by appeal to standards of truth and falsehood. If this is what he means, it is reasonable for him to infer that the conclusions reached from this choice-based standpoint do not uniquely correspond to any set of facts that must be recognized in advance of the various possible choices that we might make.

If this anti-Cartesian argument is to be non-trivial, it cannot affirm that the adoption of a metaphysical outlook is a choice in the sense that one could refuse to be rational enough to adopt it. If refusal to choose this outlook is a failure to be rational, the possibility of such a refusal does not refute the claim that the outlook is uniquely rational. To present a stronger objection to Descartes, Heidegger must argue that other choices besides the Cartesian choice are equally rational, either because they all meet criteria of rationality to the same positive (non-zero) degree, or because criteria of rationality are equally inapplicable to them all. If he successfully argues for this claim about equal rationality, Heidegger will show that the Cartesian starting point is merely optional.

1351. Questions about Heidegger's Objections to Descartes

Has Heidegger has found a cogent argument for the merely optional character of the Cartesian starting point? The weakness in his argument is clear from a comparison with Aristotle. Heidegger agrees with Aristotle in so far as he takes the everyday conception of being-in-the-world to be teleological, but he differs from Aristotle in giving priority (as Aristotle would put it) to craft (*technê*) over nature (*phusis*). Aristotle mentions both aspects of teleological order, and remarks that in looking at things as objects of craft, we come to recognize their natural character; as objects of craft they have no 'internal principle of change', but such a principle belongs to them as natural objects (*Phys.* 192b16–32). In Aristotle's view, the outlook based on craft reveals the more basic character of the natures of things.

This Aristotelian point affects Heidegger's claims about equipment. For when we consider things as equipment, one of the first things that strike us is the fact that the things that we use or would like to use as equipment are not wholly plastic to our purposes and preferences. It is easier to cut grass than to cut trees; hence it would suit us if we could use piles of grass as tables and chairs, instead of having to cut trees. But grass cuttings, however we might like to use them, are not suitable for use as tables and chairs. In dealing with things as ready-to-hand, as suitable or unsuitable equipment for a particular purpose, we have to adapt ourselves to the character of the things; we have to select some things and not others as suitable for use. It is difficult to understand what we are doing in using objects for our purposes unless we face the fact that objects have inherent characteristics independently of our purposes.[27]

Heidegger does not examine the ways in which the everyday outlook depends on recognition of independent objects. Objects appear as independent, because we cannot adapt them at will to our purposes; we recognize them as distinct pieces of equipment for different ends, and we do not regard every object as all-purpose equipment. If we did not recognize independence, we could not deal with ready-to-hand things in the everyday way.

Recognition of independence is prior, therefore, even to the distinct recognition of things as present-at-hand. Even if all the things we encountered were precisely the sort of equipment we expected them to be, we would have to recognize their independent character. Once we recognize their independent character, we have to acknowledge that the proper use of them as equipment requires some knowledge of their independent character. Such knowledge is not simply knowledge of what we want to use them for or can use them for; it must also be knowledge of what they are like in their own right, since this knowledge is a precondition for intelligent use.

If, then, a sensible view of things as equipment requires a view of them as independent objects with characteristics that they have in their own right, this latter view is not a mere abstraction. The 'objective' point of view is not the only point of view that we can take; to that extent it may be called an abstraction. But it is not a misleading abstraction; it is a basic presupposition of the everyday point of view itself, as we can see once we examine our attitude to things as equipment.

In that case, Heidegger's advice to begin with being-in-the-world, and hence with an anthropocentric conception of our environment, does not support his conclusions. If we begin with the anthropocentric view of the world as consisting of things in significant relations to human purposes, we must suppose it consists of things that we deal with intelligently, so as to advance our purposes. We cannot deal with them intelligently unless we recognize that they have natures independent of our purposes. Even things that are produced by our intentional action have to be dealt with in ways that recognize that they are not infinitely adaptable to our purposes; that is why we maintain and repair them. Hence the everyday point of view presupposes the legitimacy of the conception of the world as containing things with distinct and independent natures. Hence it presupposes the legitimacy of the point of view of traditional metaphysics.

This argument may be too hasty. Perhaps the conception of the world that we reach by reflexion on the presuppositions of everydayness is just an 'ordinary' or 'common-sense' picture of an objective world of independent things. Traditional metaphysics may need a 'point of view of pure inquiry' that is further from the ordinary picture of an objective world. But Heidegger has not justified any such claim. The outlook that he attributes to

---

[27] Ryle presents a related objection to Heidegger: '... the attempt to derive our knowledge of "things" from our practical attitude towards tools breaks down; for to use a tool involves knowledge of what it is, what can be done with it, and what wants doing' (Review, 369). One might try to help Heidegger by appeal to the distinction that Ryle draws between knowing how and knowing that (see Ryle, CM, ch. 2, published 20 years after his review). But such an appeal would not answer Ryle's basic objection.

traditional metaphysics can be defended from the everyday outlook that emerges from his own account of being-in-the-world. If we recognize that things have inherent characters, independent of the purposes we might want to use them for, and that we need to know their inherent characters, we accept the elements of the traditional metaphysical outlook, as Heidegger understands it. At least, if this is not the traditional metaphysical outlook, we need some clearer account of how the metaphysical outlook departs from the everyday point of view.

This defence of the objective metaphysical outlook suggests an answer to voluntarist claims. If the everyday outlook presupposes things with independent natures, belief in such things is not merely optional. We would not be justified, therefore, in taking voluntarism about values to apply to the choice of the basic outlook of traditional metaphysics. Since intelligent action requires interaction with things in the world and adaptation of them to our purposes, and since any intelligent adaptation of them requires us to recognize their independent natures, recognition of independent natures is not a mere option on which equally rational agents might make different choices. The outlook of traditional metaphysics does not rest on a merely optional attitude to the relation of human beings to their world.

For these reasons, traditional metaphysicians need not reject Heidegger's account of everydayness. They should simply argue that it is incomplete, since it leaves out the crucial role of our conception of independent reality. He has not raised a serious objection to the starting point of traditional metaphysics, but has vindicated this starting point.

1352. Self and Others

Heidegger attacks both sides of Descartes's division between subject and object. Since Descartes takes them to be independent, he not only recognizes objects that are merely present-at-hand, but also finds it difficult to say how we can know them. This is because he recognizes an independent subject. He relies on a solipsistic method that tries to work out from an ego that we can understand separately from the world that it occupies along with other things. In Heidegger's view, this conception of the subject conflicts with what we know about ourselves in the world. Phenomenological analysis reveals the primacy of our being in a world of other significant, ready-to-hand things. We should not begin from an isolated subject that can doubt the existence of anything else, but from subjects who necessarily recognize themselves in relation to other things in the everyday world. Cartesian solipsism also asserts the logical and epistemological priority of myself over other selves; hence Descartes's inquiry suspends judgment about other minds as well as about external material objects. Heidegger believes that phenomenological analysis reveals the error in this part of the Cartesian starting point as well. He exposes this error in Division One, Part IV on 'being with' and on the 'They'.

On the one hand, he takes the individual to be (roughly speaking) essentially constituted by relations to others. On the other hand, he seems to suggest that the others, in the form of the 'They' (or the 'One'; das Man), exercise a bad influence on the self. These two claims about the role of others may conflict. If others exercise a bad influence, we seem to be able to distinguish the self from what others make it. If their influence is constitutive of us, what makes it a bad influence? We can hardly say it is bad for the self in question, since the sense would not be what it is without this constitutive influence. To see whether Heidegger faces a genuine conflict here, we need to look more closely at the different roles of others.

The essential relation of selves to other selves follows from our view of things around us as ready-to-hand. If we regard them as equipment, we refer them to some work to be carried out by someone, or to some use for someone's purposes.[28] The position of others is different from that of equipment, since we do not regard them as objects to be used. Nor are they simply present-at-hand, since they are not related to equipment in the way present-at-hand things are related to it. I recognize them as being related to equipment in the way I am myself related to it; hence they have the sort of being that Dasein has (g118/mr154).

This way of describing others might suggest that I first recognize myself and my relation to equipment, and then recognize others by analogy with myself. But Heidegger believes that this is a back-to-front account of my relation to others; I do not distinguish myself from others whom I recognize as having the same relation to equipment.[29] His claim is puzzling. How I can regard myself as being among a number of people unless I distinguish myself from them? If I were not different from them, I would not be among this number of people.

But perhaps Heidegger means something less extreme than literal absence of distinction between myself and others. He may mean that I do not identify myself independently of my relation to others, because I regard it as essential to myself that I am one among others. I would not regard myself as a being for whom things have significance as equipment unless I regarded myself as one among a group of people for whom things have this significance.

Heidegger suggests this point when he draws his conclusion from the observations about our sameness of being. I essentially regard myself as one among a number of people who have concern, because we all find significance in ready-to-hand things.[30] Hence 'Dasein is essentially Being-with' (g120/mr156). This is not the empirical 'ontic' claim that in fact there are many people or that an individual is never alone. Even being alone contains an essential reference to others, because one is a being for whom others are missing.[31] Similarly, a given key is essentially for opening a specific lock, and this remains true even if the lock has been destroyed and the key survives. The particular shape and size of the key are explained by its

---

[28] '... along with the equipment to be found when one is at work, those Others for whom the "work" is destined are "encountered too". If this is ready-to-hand, then there lies in the kind of Being which belongs to it (that is, in its involvement) an essential assignment or reference to possible wearers, for instance, for whom it should be "cut to the figure".' (g117/mr153)

[29] 'By "Others" we do not mean everyone else but me—those over against whom the "I" stands out. They are rather those from whom, for the most part, one does *not* distinguish oneself—those among whom one is too. This Being-there-too with them does not have the ontological character of a Being-present-at-hand-along-"with" them within a world. This "with" is something of the character of Dasein; the "too" means a sameness of Being as circumspectively concernful Being-in-the-world.' (g118/mr154)

[30] 'By reason of this *with-like* Being-in-the-world, the world is always the one I share with Others. The world of Dasein is a *with-world*. Being-in is *Being-with* Others. Their Being-in-themselves within-the-world is *Dasein-with*.' (g118/mr154-5)

[31] 'Even Dasein's Being-alone is Being-with in the world. The Other can be *missing* only *in* and *for* a Being-with. Being-alone is a deficient mode of Being-with; its very possibility is a proof of this.' (g120/mr156-7)

relation to the lock, whether or not the lock exists; in that respect, it is a key for which the appropriate lock is missing.

Has Heidegger given a good reason to believe that this analogy holds for human beings? He does not argue that selves are constituted partly by being recognized as such.[32] He does not mention how others look at me, but only how I necessarily look at or think about others. He does not explain why I necessarily see myself as 'being with' others, and hence in relation to others.

We might defend his conclusion by considering the way we find significance in things. Perhaps I cannot regard ready-to-hand things as equipment for myself alone. If I want to fix a bracket to a wall, I might see nails and a hammer as equipment for me, whether or not I believe that others see them as equipment. But if I understand that they are equipment for me, I must also see them as equipment for anyone who wants to fix brackets on walls or to carry out any other task for which hammer and nails would be suitable. My conception of myself as a user of equipment must include, therefore, some implicit reference to users generally. One might try to support Heidegger by saying that my conception of equipment includes my 'being-with' other potential users.

This conclusion, however, does not seem to exclude the relevant form of solipsism. For even if my conception of myself as a user essentially refers to other logically possible users, it does not imply that anyone else exists or that it is necessary for someone else to exist, or that I recognize myself only in relation to them. I do not seem to see myself in the sort of essential relation to others that the analogy of the key and the lock would suggest.

This difference between what Heidegger seems to claim and what he is entitled to claim may matter. We need to see whether any of his further moral or evaluative claims rest on our attributing to others a place that is not warranted by his arguments about being-with. It is not immediately clear, however, what further claims he rests on his anti-solipsist arguments.

1353. Care

In recognizing our being with others, we also take a distinctive attitude towards them. This is different from the attitude of concern that we take towards equipment.[33] 'Care' or 'solicitude' for other people does not imply that I will actually (or, as Heidegger says, 'factically') pursue the good of others or pay attention to their concerns and desires. Even indifference to other people is a mode of solicitude. Whether or not we 'care' about them in the ordinary sense, we take Heidegger's attitude of care towards them.[34]

What is the point of calling indifference to others a mode of care? Heidegger seems to mean that it is different from the attitude of 'concern' that we might have to ready-at-hand

---

[32] On recognition see §960 (on Fichte).

[33] 'Concern is a character-of-Being which Being-with cannot have as its own, even though Being-with, like concern, is a *Being towards* entities encountered within-the-world. But those entities toward which Dasein as Being-with comports itself do not have the kind of Being which belongs to equipment ready-to-hand; they are themselves Dasein. These entities are not objects of concern, but rather of *solicitude*.' (g121/mr157)

[34] '...Dasein maintains itself proximally and for the most part in the deficient modes of solicitude. Being for, against, or without one another, passing one another by, not "mattering" to one another—these are possible ways of solicitude.' (g121/mr158)

things, and from the sort of indifference that we might have towards present-at-hand things. If we regard other people as necessarily being subjects for whom things are significant, and not simply as things that are significant for me, we recognize them as like ourselves and as different from equipment.

Perhaps these subjects are necessarily possible objects of care. If equipment is significant for me, I can think of myself as using it for some purpose. My purposes are derived from my ends and interests. If my ends and interests affect how I act, I must care about my ends and interests. Hence I recognize myself as an actual object of care to myself. If I think there are other people for whom equipment is significant, I must think of them as caring about their ends and interests. Hence I must think of them as actual objects of care to themselves.

If I recognize myself and others as actual objects of care to someone, must I also recognize them as possible objects of care to me? It is difficult to deny this possibility. If things are significant for them, they try to fulfil their purposes. Since I know what it is like to fulfil my purposes, and their purposes are similar to mine, I know what it is like to fulfil their purposes. Nothing more seems to be needed to make it possible for me to fulfil their purposes. In this respect, other people differ from equipment and from present-at-hand things. I have no choice about whether to be indifferent to the purposes of equipment, since it has no purposes; it does not operate for its own purposes, but for the purposes of agents.[35] I have a choice, however, about whether to be indifferent to the purposes of other human beings. Hence my indifference to them includes the refusal of an acknowledged possibility of care for their purposes.

These facts about the possibility of care may underlie Heidegger's general statement about the character of being-with. He claims that Dasein is essentially for the sake of others (g123/mr160). He explains this claim by emphasizing that he is not talking about the actual care of one person for another, but about the essential possibility of care.[36] But from this claim about the possibility of care he seems to infer that each of us is also for the sake of others.[37] It is not easy to see the basis for this inference.

Does Heidegger mean that the purposes of others essentially guide my purposes, so that I adjust my ends so as to fulfil theirs? He does not seem to have proved anything as strong as this. Being for the sake of others seems to involve co-operation, but Heidegger does not suggest that our relations with others are necessarily co-operative. Perhaps, then, all the forms of care (in the sense that includes indifference and hostility) count, in Heidegger's view, as being for the sake of others, just in so far as they take account of others as agents with purposes.

Heidegger recognizes different modes of care for others, and expresses some preferences among them. Sometimes we 'leap in' for another (g122/mr158) and dominate him; in this

[35] Cf. Aristotle's remark that we cannot really want something for the sake of a bottle of wine, since it has no 'sake'. Things with 'sakes' are possible objects of care. They seem to include other agents than human beings, since non-human animals seem to have purposes.

[36] '...because Dasein's Being is Being-with, its understanding of Being already implies the understanding of Others. This understanding, like any understanding, is not an acquaintance derived from knowledge about them, but a primordially existential kind of Being, which, more than anything else, makes such knowledge and acquaintance possible. Knowing oneself is grounded in Being-with, which understands primordially.' (g123–4/mr161)

[37] 'Even if the particular factical Dasein does *not* turn to Others, and supposes that it has no need of them or manages to get along without them, it *is* in the way of Being-with. In Being-with, as the existential "for the sake of" Others, these have already been disclosed in their Dasein.' (g123/mr160)

case, we treat the other as something ready-to-hand, subordinated to our own purposes. Heidegger takes a preferable form of care to be the one that does not leap in for the other, but 'leaps ahead' of him, in such a way as not to take away his care, but 'to give it back to him authentically as such for the first time' (g122/mr158–9). In this case we allow the other to become 'transparent' to himself and thereby free for his care for himself (g122/mr159). Heidegger prefers this liberating care over the dominating care of those who leap in for the other. Still, he recognizes that both are possible forms of care, and that indifference is a third form of care.

The best form of care frees the other, because it allows him to act on the recognition of his own concerns. Heidegger does not explain why this results in our being 'authentically bound together' (g122/mr159). It is not even clear whether he assumes that we ought to be able to see, on the basis of what he has told us, that the authentic relation is better than the other forms of care.

One might argue on his behalf that the authentic relation is best because it recognizes the facts about human subjects. In so far as I recognize myself as a subject for whom equipment is significant, I also recognize that it is significant for any subject with purposes similar to mine. I acknowledge that such a subject would be another for whom equipment is significant because he has distinct purposes; this is what distinguishes him from equipment and from present-at-hand things. In the form of care that frees the other, we recognize that he has his own concerns, and we allow them to determine what he does. In the inferior forms of care, we do not acknowledge the distinct purposes that make the other a subject distinct from oneself.

This defence of the authentic relation between people is open to two objections: (1) The inferior forms of care do not seem to deny the facts about being-with. I can recognize that you have distinct purposes from mine, but I may still not want them to determine your actions. The fact that you have distinct purposes makes you more useful to me if I want to manipulate you, since I may be able to induce you to respond more flexibly than a mere piece of equipment would. Persuasion, threats, intimidation, deception all seem to recognize the relevant facts about being-with. It is not clear how the liberating form of care recognizes any facts that these other forms of care overlook. (2) If Heidegger had an argument in favour of the liberating form of care, he would apparently contradict his objections to the 'humanistic' outlook. In his view, humanists mistakenly attempt to rest evaluative claims on facts about the human condition. His claims about authenticity seem to make the mistake that he criticizes in others.

We might have a better defence of some of Heidegger's claims if we understood being-with differently. According to his description, one thinks of oneself as something other than equipment in so far as one recognizes in oneself the purposes that make equipment significant for oneself. But if I value these purposes, must I not also believe that I deserve to have my purposes respected by others who have purposes? If I am committed to this belief, I also have a reason to respect others who are like me in being subjects of purposes.

This Kantian argument needs some explanation and defence. Since it reaches the conclusion that Heidegger seems to intend in some of his remarks about authenticity, we might suppose he intends it. But it is difficult to defend this supposition. The most difficult part of the Kantian argument depends on the sense and the plausibility of claims about value and desert. But Heidegger does not introduce these claims into his argument. Hence he does not provide materials for a Kantian argument, even though we might try to derive the relevant materials from his remarks about significance.

We might find another starting point for a Kantian argument in Heidegger's contrast between persons and equipment. This contrast might suggest that while we regard equipment as instrumental to the purposes of agents, we do not regard these agents themselves as equipment; hence (we might infer) we regard them as ends in themselves. But though this is a suggestive point that we might derive from Heidegger, he does not affirm it.

His remarks about authenticity, therefore, still present us with a puzzle. Any attempted argument for his conclusions seems to go beyond his premises, explicit and implicit. In one way, this is not surprising, since the relevant sort of argument would be open to his objections against 'humanism'. But in another way, it is surprising, since his claims about authenticity seem to be left without support, if no 'humanist' argument supports them.

1354. The 'They'

So far, Heidegger's attitude towards others has been favourable. He has suggested that we must refer to others if we recognize ourselves as distinct from equipment. He describes care as an essential element in being-with. He infers that (for reasons he has not so far made clear) respect for others is the appropriate response to our recognition of their relation to us. But when he goes into more detail on the role of others, he seems less favourable to them.

If we distinguish ourselves from others, we recognize some degree of 'distantiality' (g126/mr164). But this difference between myself and others does not appear to me simply as the difference between me and this person, that person, and every other particular individual. It appears to me as a difference between myself and the anonymous 'They' (das Man).[38] Though the They consists of individuals, this is not how it strikes us. It appears as an undifferentiated collection to which the individual is subordinated, and which exercises a 'dictatorship' (g126/mr164) over one's beliefs, tastes, and preferences.

As Heidegger notes, we encounter the They innocuously in our dealings with equipment. If we travel on a train or read a newspaper, we know that others maintain the railway or produce the newspaper, but we do not look on them as particular individuals; they are just the mass of individuals who work for the railway or the newspaper. In these ways, contact with the They is an inevitable part of everyday life.

But the influence of the They extends further than these contacts with unspecified other individuals. It also forms the outlook of the individual, through a process of 'levelling down of all possibilities of Being' (g127/mr165). Since the They takes the average point of view, it

[38] 'But this distantiality which belongs to Being-with, is such that Dasein, as everyday Being-with-one-another, stands in *subjection* to Others. It itself *is* not; its Being has been taken away by the Others. Dasein's everyday possibilities of Being are for the Others to dispose of as they please. These Others, moreover, are not *definite* Others. On the contrary, any Other can represent them. What is decisive is just that inconspicuous domination by Others which has already been taken over unawares from Dasein as Being-with . . . The "who" is not this one, not that one, not oneself, not some people, and not the sum of them all. The "who" is the neuter, the *"they"*.' (g126/mr164)

'keeps watch over everything exceptional' and tends to erase it through its levelling outlook. Since we cannot trace the outlook of the They to anyone in particular, it does not seem to be the result of anyone's choice; no one seems to be responsible for it. Hence we may readily look on it as an inevitable feature of our environment.

Since we take the outlook of the They to be inevitable and independent of our choice, we incorporate the assumptions and presuppositions of the They into our own outlook. In our conception of ourselves, we include not only a relation to others and their purposes, but also their outlook in our outlook.[39] A particular self first thinks of itself as the They-self, and does not distinguish itself from the outlook of the They. It takes some special attention to identify the distinct self that can live authentically as something more than a reflexion of the They.

Two sides of Heidegger's description of the They have provoked dispute among interpreters. On the one hand, he seems to represent the influence of the They as an inevitable element in any genuine subject. It is simply part of his anti-Cartesian account of the first-person outlook. On the other hand, he suggests that the influence of the They is to be regretted, because it tends to interfere with the expression of the authentic self.[40]

How does the They interfere with authenticity? If the authentic self takes hold of itself in its own way, the They must prevent it from doing that. Perhaps it does so by concealing the extent to which the apparently inevitable constraints imposed by the They are really not inevitable, but alterable by choice. We might compare Greek arguments about nature and convention. While we might have supposed that burial is the only decent way to dispose of dead bodies, we may be shaken from that view by discovering that some peoples practice cremation with no sense that it is any less decent. Once we realize that the views of the They around us are not compulsory for everyone, we see that things that we previously took to be independent of our will are open to our choice. The authentic self does not necessarily disagree with the outlook of the They, but it recognizes that it is up to itself to choose to agree or to disagree with the They.

We may therefore take Heidegger's claims about the They to reinforce the voluntarism that we attributed to him in discussing his objections to Descartes. If the everyday world of equipment presents itself to us as suitable or unsuitable to our purposes, we may infer that it is a mistake to try to form a conception of a world 'in itself' separated from the uses that we choose to find in it. The pressure of the They may conceal this role for choice from us, because it represents the 'levelled down' choices of the average person as the only way to conceive the world. But once we understand that the pervasive assumptions of the They are not inevitable, we see that the apparently basic assumptions of our view of the world

[39] 'The self of everyday Dasein is the *they-self*, which we distinguish from the *authentic Self* —that is from the Self which has been taken hold of in its own way. As the they-self, the particular Dasein has been *dispersed* into the "they", and must first find itself. . . . If Dasein is familiar with itself as the they-self, this means at the same time that the "they" itself prescribes that way of interpreting the world and Being-in-the-world which lies closest. Dasein is for the sake of the "they" in an everyday manner . . .' (g129/mr167)

[40] See Olafson's account of the They, in *HGE* 38–9. To follow the They, in his view, is to do things because they are the done thing, as opposed to doing them for one's own reasons. One need not be eccentric or 'individual' to get away from the They. When we acquire skill in driving, we first just do it because we are told to, but then we modify the patterns we have learnt, by exercising our own skill and understanding. Dreyfus, *BW*, ch. 8, presents a contrasting view of the They. Olafson discusses Dreyfus's view in 'Coping', 54–63. Dreyfus replies in 'Interpreting'.

are open to choice. The task of ontology is to uncover this role of choice by exposing the influence of the They, and therefore by removing a false assumption of inevitability.

1355. Moods, Affects, and Being-In

In Part V, 'Being-in as Such', Heidegger says more about the influence of the They on one's conception of oneself and of one's choices. He discusses the sense in which we are 'in' the world, and explains how the They constitutes the world that we belong to. He continues his attack on the individualist view that we recognize ourselves as subjects separate from a world of objects that are primarily objects of contemplative knowledge. He has already said that we know ourselves primarily in relation to objects recognized as equipment for our purposes, and in relation to others. He now raises a question about the way in which we find ourselves in the world.

According to the view that Heidegger rejects, we can distinguish the case in which we simply see things as they are from the various cases in which we see things in a certain light. We tend to distinguish the times when everything 'looks black' because we are in a bad mood, or when we look at things through rose-tinted spectacles because we are in a good mood, from the times when we simply see things as they are because we are free from the influence of a particular way of looking at things.

Heidegger agrees with this view to some extent. He believes that moods cause as to 'see things in a certain light'. But he disagrees with it in so far as he denies that the way to see things as they are is to be free of moods. To look for a way of seeing things independently of moods is to regard things as purely present-at-hand and to suppose that we have to regard them in this way if we are to know them as they are. Heidegger is not satisfied with this 'rationalist' conception of purely theoretical cognition. But he does not believe that the right answer to rationalism is a defence of the irrational influence of moods. On the contrary, if we admit that moods are irrational, distorting features of our awareness, we have already conceded too much to rationalism, because we have conceded that reason is confined to the awareness of things as present-at-hand.[41]

To see what is wrong with the rationalist view, we ought to notice that the purely contemplative attitude is itself a mood, in so far as it abstracts from certain features of other moods, and looks at things with its own particular emphasis.[42] While it may be legitimate to look at things through this mood, it is still one mood among others, and we have no reason to affirm that all other moods necessarily distort the way things actually are.

For this reason, Heidegger rejects the view that the study of the emotions—such as we find in Aristotle's *Rhetoric*—is secondary to a study of our knowledge of the world. The

---

[41] 'From the existential-ontological point of view, there is not the slightest justification for minimizing what is "evident" in states-of-mind, by measuring it against the apodictic certainty of a theoretical cognition of something which is purely present-at-hand. However the phenomena are no less falsified when they are banished to the sanctuary of the irrational. When irrationalism, as the counterplay of rationalism, talks about the things to which rationalism is blind, it does so only with a squint.' (g136/mr175)

[42] 'Yet even the purest *theôria* has not left all moods behind it; even when we look theoretically at what is just present-at-hand, it does not show itself purely as it looks unless this *theôria* lets it come towards it in a *tranquil* tarrying alongside.' (g138/mr177)

emotions that the orator appeals to are not additions to the everyday world that we initially experience; they are the way the world presents itself to us in common. In recognizing the public world of the They, we recognize a world of (for instance) friends and enemies, of dangerous and praiseworthy things.[43] The They does not represent these attitudes as optional or eliminable or subjective features added to a shared knowledge of an objective world; the features that these attitudes reveal are part of the objective world itself. For similar reasons, Heidegger does not believe that we first recognize a future evil and then fear it. The fearfulness of the future is part of what we initially recognize in it.[44]

The presence in the public world of features recognized by emotions is closely connected with the ready-to-hand character of things. We recognize them as suitable or unsuitable for our purposes; part of this recognition is our awareness of them as threatening or welcome. Recognition includes not only our recognition of the relation of things to our purposes, but also our recognition of ourselves as bearers of possibilities in relation to things. We do not first identify ourselves as some centre of consciousness, and then notice the ways in which we are capable of interaction with things and with other people. The self we identify consists of these possible ways of interaction.[45]

In our ascription of possibilities to ourselves, we also recognize some sort of freedom. Our attribution of alternative possibilities to ourselves may be a partial basis for the belief in metaphysical liberty of indifference, but Heidegger argues that it is an insufficient basis. Though we recognize that things leave different possibilities open to us, in so far as they may interact in different ways with our various purposes, it does not follow that nothing determines us to interact in one way rather than another.[46]

This attribution of possibilities to ourselves in relation to the world introduces the possibility of inauthenticity and authenticity. We may take our cue either from the possibilities that the They attributes to us, or from our own reflexion on the world and our relation to us.[47] The They presents us with a conception of ourselves in our various roles and in our relation to things and people. Since it does not present this conception as a social construct or as the result of influence by others, it does not urge that we need to choose to accept it, or even that we need to consider. It appears to us as the only possible way to look at ourselves in relation to other things and people. Hence we never even think about whether these are the roles and relations we want; for it does not appear to us that our choices and wants are relevant.

---

[43] 'Contrary to the traditional orientation, according to which rhetoric is conceived as the kind of thing we "learn in school", this work of Aristotle must be taken as the first systematic hermeneutic of the everydayness of Being with one another. Publicness, as the kind of Being which belongs to the "they", not only has in general its own way of having a mood, but needs moods and "makes" them for itself.' (g138/mr178)

[44] 'We do not first ascertain a future evil (*malum futurum*) and then fear it. But neither does fearing first take note of what is drawing close; it discovers it beforehand in its fearsomeness.' (g141/mr180)

[45] 'The kind of Being which Dasein has, as potentiality-for-Being, lies existentially in understanding. Dasein is not something present-at-hand which possesses its competence for something by way of an extra; it is primarily Being-possible. Dasein is in every case what it can be, and the way in which it is its possibility.' (g143/mr189)

[46] 'Possibility, as an *existentiale*, does not signify a free-floating potentiality-for-Being in the sense of the "liberty of indifference". In every case Dasein, as essentially having a state-of-mind, has already put itself into definite possibilities.' (g144/mr183)

[47] 'Understanding is either authentic, arising out of one's own Self as such, or inauthentic. The "in-" of "inauthentic" does not mean that Dasein cuts itself off from its Self and understands "only" the world. The world belongs to Being-one's-Self as Being-in-the-World.' (g146/mr186)

The sort of understanding is prior to elementary cognition of the world, and is not constructed from it.[48] Pure intuition—a view of things as present-at-hand—is not prior epistemically, and we should not accept the mistaken conception of knowledge that begins from it.[49] Once we recognize that the elementary conception of the world conceives things as ready-to-hand and not as purely present-at-hand, we can see what is wrong with an account of elementary knowledge as pure intuition, without any of the everyday understanding of myself as a user of equipment. Our elementary conceptions pervade our sensory cognition. Just as we do not primarily see pure visual qualities, we do not hear pure sounds; we hear sounds as of cars and motor-cycles, and only gradually learn to hear sounds as mere sound (g164/mr207).

The same point applies to language and logic. Heidegger denies that the basic categories are those imposed by formal ontology and logic; the task is to 'liberate' grammar from logic (209), by tracing it back to its origins in the everyday understanding of the world. To be in the everyday world is to be partly constituted by the moods and expectations determined by the They, and we cannot completely escape the influence of the They and of the everyday world. We are 'in' this world not in a purely physical sense, but because we essentially belong to the network of assumptions, concerns, and moods that form both the world, as we experience it, and ourselves, as we recognize our place in it.

1356. The They and its Idle Talk

Our everyday understanding involves the world as formed by the outlook of the They, which expresses itself in 'idle talk' (g167/mr211). Heidegger's description of idle talk clarifies some of his previous remarks about the influence of the They. In speaking of idle talk he does not intend to disparage it; nor does he intend any 'moralizing critique' of the everyday life that is dominated by the influence of the They (g167/mr211).

Perhaps we can grasp the sense in which idle talk is idle, or 'mere' talk, if we contrast it with a stereotype of assertion. We may think the basic linguistic act is the act of assertion in which A conveys to B A's belief that things are a certain way, with the intention of causing B to share A's belief that this is how things are. Idle talk is not purposeful in this sense. Since the They engages in it, no particular subject expresses his individual belief and no one intends any particular subject to share his belief. The idle talk of the They involves 'gossiping and passing the word along'.[50] If I take part in this idle talk, I simply report what 'they said' or 'what is said'. I do not state my own belief, and I do not attribute the relevant belief to

---

[48] 'By showing how all sight is grounded primarily in understanding (the circumspection of concern is understanding *as common sense*), we have deprived pure intuition of its priority, which corresponds noetically to the priority of the present-at-hand in traditional ontology. "Intuition" and "thinking" are both derivatives of understanding, and already rather remote ones.' (g147/mr187)

[49] 'This grasping which is free of the "as", is a privation of the kind of seeing in which one *merely* understands. It is not more primordial than that kind of seeing, but is derived from it. If the "as" is ontically unexpressed, this must not seduce us into overlooking it as a constitutive state for understanding, existential and a priori.' (g149/mr190)

[50] 'What is said-in-the-talk as such, spreads in wider circles and takes on an authoritative character. Things are so because one says so. Idle talk is constituted by just such gossiping and passing the word along—a process by which its initial lack of grounds to stand on becomes aggravated to complete groundlessness.' (g168/mr212)

anyone; nor do I vouch for its truth. None the less, the talk that I pass on affects both me and other people. It influences our beliefs and attitudes, even though we do not expressly assent to it.

The influence of idle talk is intelligible in the light of Heidegger's previous remarks about moods. Even if I do not think about gossip, and even if I do not assent to what it says, it may affect the way I look at future situations.[51] Perhaps I hear the gossip that says Smith and Jones have quarrelled. Even if I do not believe the gossip, I may interpret Smith's and Jones's behaviour when they are together differently from how I would have if I had not heard this gossip. The idle talk that has gone the rounds has affected my mood and attitude, and thereby has affected my view of the relevant situations.

This influence of the They tends to prevent individuals from seeing that apparently inevitable features of their environment are not really inevitable. Heidegger believes that when I conform to the outlook expressed in idle talk, my understanding has been 'uprooted'.[52] Perhaps he means that my understanding has been uprooted from myself and transferred to the outlook I absorb from the They. I do not keep my understanding rooted in myself, because I do not recognize that it is up to me to decide whether or not to conform to the outlook of the They. I do not have to see the world through the various roles and purposes that the They suggests to me. It is up to me to choose the significance that things will have for me. Once I realize that, I may still choose to conform to the outlook of the They, but now I conform authentically because I see that I have a choice.

Such an interpretation of authentic understanding may appear more individualistic than Heidegger intends. Indeed, it may seem to commit the individualistic error that he warns us against in his general description of being in the world. But it is difficult to see what roots the They uproots us from if we do not suppose that it uproots us from the possibility of understanding and choosing things for ourselves.

If this is the right way to understand the contrast between authentic being and the uprooted condition in which the They dominates us, we may take Heidegger's general aim to be the defence of the voluntarist outlook that we have previously claimed to find in him. Attention to the elementary structure of being in the world shows us that the features of the everyday world depend on our purposes, and therefore on our choice; but it also shows us that the influence of the They tends to conceal this freedom.

The same contrast between freedom and blind conformity—blind because it does not realize that it has a choice about whether to conform—appears in Heidegger's comments on the ways in which the They controls and represses curiosity. Since the They presents various things as familiar, and indeed as compulsory, not subject to inquiry, it discourages questions about things that the They takes for granted.[53] Fashions and trends illustrate

---

[51] 'The dominance of the public way in which things have been interpreted has already been decisive even for the possibilities of having a mood—that is, for the basic way in which Dasein lets the world "matter" to it. The "they" prescribes one's state-of-mind, and determines what and how one "sees".' (g169–70/mr213)

[52] 'Idle talk, which closes things off in the way we have designated, is the kind of Being which belongs to Dasein's understanding when that understanding has been uprooted . . . Ontologically this means that when Dasein maintains itself in idle talk, it is—as Being-in-the-world—cut off from its primary and primordially genuine relationships-of-Being towards the world, towards Dasein-with, and towards its very Being-in.' (g170/mr214)

[53] 'Idle talk controls even the ways in which one may be curious. It says what one "must" have read and seen. In being everywhere and nowhere, curiosity is delivered over to idle talk . . . Curiosity, for which nothing is closed off, and

Heidegger's point. When a particular style of clothes is in fashion, that is what 'everyone is wearing this year', and when it is out of fashion, 'no one wears that any longer'. When something is 'not done', or 'over', the They inhibits questions about whether it should be done any more.

Since our experience of others is also mediated by the influence of the They, idle talk changes the character of our being with others. The They creates certain expectations about other people, so that we interpret them in the light of these expectations.[54] Heidegger also suggests that these expectations put us against one another; but it is not clear why he thinks so. It is true that we watch one another to see how the expectations we have acquired from the They are or are not fulfilled. But these expectations may be favourable, and so, if the other fulfils them, they do not seem to put us against one another. Perhaps Heidegger means not that the expectations created by idle talk are must be unfavourable, but that since they often are unfavourable, they tend to introduce an element of suspicion and opposition into our interactions with others that would have been absent if we were not influenced by idle talk.

1357. Falling and Authenticity

Heidegger summarizes this discussion of the influence of the They and of idle talk by describing the condition of people who are subject to these influences as 'falling'; this is what happens to us when we find ourselves in this everyday mode of being (g175/mr219). But as soon as he has said this, he warns against a misunderstanding. We might take him to contrast some initial condition of persons in which they are better off and from which they decline into the world of the They. But this is not what he means; he does not try to reconstruct the unfallen form of existence from which the fallen is a decline.[55] Fallenness is not a bad and deplorable condition that we may hope to be rid of (g176/mr220); nor does it happen to us 'from outside' (g177/mr221). It is part of our most basic and ineliminable condition.

None the less, it seems to be a condition that we can alter and have reason to alter. It seems to convey a false but avoidable impression that authenticity is unnecessary.[56]

---

idle talk, for which there is nothing that is not understood, provide themselves . . . with the guarantee of a "life" which, supposedly, is genuinely "lively".' (g173/mr217)

[54] 'The Other is proximally "there" in terms of what "they" have heard about him, what "they" say in their talk about him, and what "they" know about him. Into primordial Being-with-one-another, idle talk at first slips itself in between. Everyone keeps his eye on the Other first and next, watching to see how he will comport himself and what he will say in reply. Being-with-one-another in the "they" is by no means an indifferent side-by-side-ness in which everything has been settled, but rather an intent, ambiguous watching of one another, a secret and reciprocal listening-in. Under the mask of "for-one-another", an "against-one-another" is in play.' (g175/mr219)

[55] 'This term [sc. "falling"] does not express any negative evaluation, but is used to signify that Dasein is proximally and for the most part *alongside* the "world" of its concern. This "absorption in" has mostly the character of Being-lost in the publicness of the "they". Dasein has, in the first instance, fallen away from itself as an authentic potentiality for Being its Self, and has fallen into the "world".' (g175/mr220)

[56] 'Idle talk and ambiguity, having seen everything, having understood everything, develop the supposition that Dasein's disclosedness, which is so available and so prevalent, can guarantee to Dasein that all the possibilities of its Being will be secure, genuine, and full. Through the self-certainty and decidedness of the "they" it gets spread abroad increasingly that there is no need of authentic understanding or the state-of-mind that goes with it.' (g177/mr222)

Heidegger does not intend any claim about the 'corruption of human nature'; instead, he intends to describe the prior condition that is presupposed by any assertions about corruption (g179f/mr224). Still, he implies that the They suggests something false. It suggests that authenticity is unnecessary, because we should be perfectly satisfied as we are. Since the status quo appears inevitable, it would be idle to think about changing it.

Contrary to the impression given by the They, authenticity is possible, because it is up to us to recognize the influence of idle talk on our outlook and to make up our minds about whether we want to accept this influence. Indeed, one might suppose that Heidegger exposes the influence of idle talk in order to show us that we can take a more independent attitude to the They than we would take if we did not recognize that we have a choice. One might reasonably infer that Heidegger approves of this more independent attitude, and that he intends us to endorse and to acquire a more authentic form of existence. If he did not intend this, what would be the point of calling this form of existence 'authentic', or of uncovering the possibility of authenticity beneath the surface of the everyday world?

These inferences have no explicit warrant in Heidegger. He might reply that they reflect a 'humanist' misunderstanding of his position. But this reply would not be totally convincing. His discussion of the influence of the They and of the possibilities of authenticity marks a division between blind conformity and some form of autonomy and self-direction. Even when we take account of all his warnings against individualist misunderstandings, he holds out the prospect of some form of self-direction that fits human beings better than thoughtless conformity fits them. He does not suggest that the prospect of authenticity is an individualist illusion. On the contrary, he suggests that we gain a clearer view of this prospect through the study of everyday being in its subjection to the They. Study of subjection seems to help us to avoid it.

1358. Anxiety

The impression that Heidegger advocates the development of authenticity is strengthened by his discussion of anxiety. This attitude reflects some distance from what the They tells us. We start off with the They-self that is formed by the assumptions and expectations of the They. Still, our potentiality for being is an issue for us.[57] The They-self is not all that we recognize in ourselves. If we were completely absorbed in the They-self, which makes things seem compulsory and inevitable, we could hardly regard our own potentiality for being as an issue.

The recognition of this issue, and hence the recognition of the distance between the They-self and one's own potentiality for being, is expressed in anxiety. One response to recognition of this distance is to 'flee in the face of oneself' so as to be absorbed in the

---

[57] 'The Self, however, is proximally and for the most part inauthentic, the they-self. Being-in-the-world is always fallen. Accordingly Dasein's "average everydayness" can be defined as Being-in-the-world which is falling and disclosed, thrown and projecting, and for which its ownmost potentiality-for-Being is an issue, both in its Being alongside the "world" and in its Being-with Others.' (g181/mr225)

outlook of the They.[58] One flees in the face of oneself because of anxiety.[59] If we are capable of this anxiety, we recognize ourselves as distinct from the attitudes and assumptions of the They. Anxiety is a proper attitude towards things that can be otherwise, not towards the present and inevitable.

Heidegger confirms that this anxiety results from awareness of alternatives. The character of the world, and the fact that it is not inevitable, are first disclosed by anxiety.[60] If we are anxious, we do not take the world presented to us by the They as the only possibility.[61] If we went along with the outlook of the They, we would also find the tranquillity that comes from absorption in the everyday world. Anxiety prevents tranquil absorption. The familiar and public would make us tranquil, unless we were somehow aware that the familiar outlook is not the only possible one. If we took the outlook of the They completely at face value, we would not notice any basis for anxiety. Since we are anxious, even if we are not sure what we are anxious about, we must be aware of an alternative possibility. If we regard our being as an issue for us, we see that we need not accept the publicly interpreted world.

This discussion of anxiety, therefore, makes it clear that we have an alternative to the acceptance of the outlook of the They. It does not make it clear, however, what the alternative is. Heidegger's description of the outlook of the They seems to contrast it with some sort of autonomy or self-direction—though Heidegger does not express it in this way. If we see that we have an alternative to mere conformity to what the They tells us, we also see that it is up to us to decide whether to conform to it. Heidegger does not tell us that we ought to exercise this freedom to decide. But he connects this freedom with authenticity, and hence with living in accordance with one's own capacities. He might be taken to claim that freedom and the possibility of authenticity belong to the human essence. He rejects humanist arguments that rely on claims about the human essence; but we might wonder how he avoids such an argument here.

We might draw different conclusions from Heidegger's claims about anxiety and authenticity: (1) Instead of following the views of others about how things are, I ought to try to find out how they really are, since I can see that the views of the They do not carry any legitimate authority; they are simply passed along. (2) Instead of supposing that I am a passive believer, I ought to recognize the primacy of my will and choice.

[58] 'Dasein's absorption in the "they" and its absorption in the "world" of its concern, make manifest something like a *fleeing* of Dasein in the face of itself—of itself as an authentic potentiality-for-Being-its-Self. This phenomenon of Dasein's fleeing *in the face of itself* and in the face of its authenticity, seems at least a suitable phenomenal basis for the following investigation.' (g184/mr229)

[59] 'The turning-away of falling is grounded rather in anxiety, which in turn is what first makes fear possible. . . . That in the face of which one has anxiety is Being-in-the-world as such.' (g186/mr230)

[60] 'Being-anxious discloses, primordially and directly, the world as world; . . . the world as world is disclosed first and foremost by anxiety, as a mode of state-of-mind.' (g187/mr232)

[61] 'Anxiety thus takes away from Dasein the possibility of understanding itself, as it falls, in terms of the "world" and the way things have been publicly interpreted. Anxiety throws Dasein back upon that which it is anxious about—its authentic potentiality-for-Being-in-the-world, which as something that understands, projects itself essentially upon possibilities.' (g187/mr232) 'Being-familiar with . . . This character of Being-in was then brought to view more concretely through the everyday publicness of the "they", which brings tranquillized self-assurance—"Being-at-home", with all its obviousness—into the average everydayness of Dasein.' (g188–9/mr233) '. . . Dasein, which for the most part remains concealed from itself in its authenticity because of the way in which things have been publicly interpreted by the "they", becomes disclosable in a primordial sense in this basic state-of-mind.' (g190/mr235)

These two conclusions imply different attitudes towards voluntarism. The first concedes nothing to voluntarism. I exercise my choice to find out how things are, as opposed to how they are said to be on the dubious authority of the They. The second conclusion, however, favours voluntarism. According to this conclusion, if I reject the authority of the They who present things as compulsory, I reject the idea of things being compulsory or independent of my will, and I affirm choice as the basis of cognition as well as action. Heidegger does not say which conclusion we should draw.

1359. Authenticity and the Errors of Traditional Ontology

He returns to some of these questions, however. At the end of his discussion of care and anxiety he attacks traditional assumptions about knowledge, truth, and reality (§§43–4). This attack supports a voluntarist interpretation of claims about authenticity.

He objects to the conception of truth as correspondence of judgments or assertions to independent facts. In his view, this conception assumes the fundamental character of a conception of the world as a collection of present-at-hand things constituting an independent reality that confronts a bare subject who is independent of it. Such a conception of the world and the subject underlies the problem of scepticism and the various attempts to answer it.

Heidegger believes that if we incline to take scepticism seriously, whether we accept it or try to refute it, we have misunderstood its basis.[62] For in order to take the sceptical doubt seriously, I have to suppose that I understand its initial assumption. Hence I have to understand the assumption that I know that I, as subject, exist, but I do not know whether things external to me exist. Both Descartes and Kant begin with this supposition.[63] Since Kant concedes this much to Descartes, he accepts the mistaken Cartesian assumption, and does not see that it is unintelligible.[64] The Cartesian mistake rests on the assumption that the world is to be treated as something present-at-hand.

To avoid the mistake, therefore, we need to recognize that the world is not primarily present-at-hand, but ready-to-hand, as an expression of our purposes. Similarly, we are essentially concerned to express our purposes, which we define primarily with reference to things that we treat as equipment. Since we know ourselves primarily as agents with purposes towards things we recognize as equipment, we cannot separate ourselves as subjects, essentially independent of objects for our use, from objects that are essentially independent of users.

One might express Heidegger's claim by saying that the character of the external world is determined by our choice to use things in a particular way. This would be a one-sided

---

[62] 'The question of whether there is a world at all and whether its Being can be proved, makes no sense if it is raised by Dasein as Being-in-the-world; and who else would raise it?' (g202/mr246–7)

[63] 'It seems at first as if Kant has given up the Cartesian approach of positing a subject one can come across in isolation. But only in semblance. That Kant demands any proof at all for the "Dasein of things outside of me" shows already that he takes the subject—the "in me"—as the starting-point for this problematic.' (g204/mr248)

[64] 'The "scandal of philosophy" is not that this proof has yet to be given, but that such proofs are expected and attempted again and again. Such expectations, aims, and demands arise from an ontologically inadequate way of starting with something of such a character that independently of it and "outside" of it a "world" is to be proved as present-at-hand.' (g205/mr249)

way of expressing his position; for it is equally true that our character is determined by the character of things we find as objects of our purposes. Once we grasp this inter-dependence of subject and equipment, we see that both the pursuit of objective truth and the sceptical doubts about it rest on the same illusion.

We have some reason, therefore, to draw a voluntarist conclusion from Heidegger's remarks about anxiety and authenticity. If we take the authentic outlook to involve a search for the true outlook, in contrast to the outlook communicated by the They, we suffer from the illusion that we can discover something about a world of purely present-at-hand things. If we avoid the effects of this illusion, we reject the outlook of the They in order to affirm our own choices in opposition to the apparent inevitability of the choices imposed by the They.[65]

1360. Authenticity, Facts, and Values

If Heidegger accepts these conclusions about authenticity and truth, he offers us a reason to agree with Sartre's claim that morality is essentially left open by objective truths about the world. Sartre opposes an Aristotelian view that facts about the essence of human beings support evaluative conclusions about how we ought to act. Heidegger agrees with Sartre in so far as he rejects any attempt to rest conclusions about value on objective truths about the world or human nature. The belief that we could justify our choices by appeal to independent reality rests on the illusion that underlies both scepticism and objectivism.

We might be tempted to interpret this anti-objectivist view as an affirmation of the separation of facts and values. Such an interpretation suggests a connexion between Heidegger and Sartre, on the one hand, and positivism and non-cognitivism, on the other. We might regard both outlooks as descendants of Kant's contrast between nature and freedom, and as more remote descendants of mediaeval voluntarism.

While it is reasonable and in some ways illuminating to point to this connexion, it is also misleading. For Heidegger does not endorse the contrast between nature and freedom, or between fact and value. On the contrary, he tries to undermine the contrast, since he casts doubt on assumptions about nature and objectivity. While choice has a basic constitutive role in a practical outlook, it has a no less basic role in a theoretical outlook. We do not conceive, and cannot coherently conceive, the world as merely present-at-hand; and so (Heidegger infers) we cannot recognize facts that common sense or scientific inquiry seeks to discover about a world that is independent of our choice and will. Our aims, purposes, and choices constitute facts no less than they constitute values; and so it is an illusion to contrast facts that are independent of our choice with values that depend on our choice.

From the point of view of a positivist critic of the belief in moral facts, Heidegger is one of those who look for companions in guilt.[66] Scepticism or nihilism about objective

---

[65] Guignon, 'Authenticity', 278–84, offers a more favourable assessment of Heidegger's claims about authenticity.
[66] On companions in guilt see Mackie, E 39, and §1281.

moral facts is usually intended to show that moral judgments need a different treatment from the treatment that is appropriate for ordinary factual judgment; hence it affirms local scepticism or nihilism within a global non-sceptical and realist position. Heidegger's account of being-in-the-world rejects the contrast that underlies positivism. If we fastened on his voluntarism about values, but overlooked his rejection of objectivism about (supposed) facts, we would miss one point of his critique of traditional metaphysics.[67] We might state his position loosely: since facts about the world turn out to be more like values than like facts (as positivists conceive them), we cannot maintain that values are less objective than facts.

On this point, then, Heidegger exploits a tendency that we noticed in Nietzsche's criticism of morality.[68] Sometimes Nietzsche criticizes morality (or slave morality, or modern morality) as a misinterpretation. At other times, he rejects any conception of truths and facts that are independent of a perspective. His more radical claim about facts and perspectives makes it more difficult to say what it is that morality misinterprets. It does not seem to misinterpret the facts as viewed from its own perspective; and if we say that it does not recognize facts viewed from other perspectives, the same is true of every other perspective. Nietzsche may want to say that some perspective is superior to others, but it is difficult to understand that claim as more than a claim made from a particular perspective.

Heidegger's ethical claims are not specific enough to show that his position contains a conflict. But it seems to contain an unresolved tension. On the one hand, his remarks about authenticity might be used to support a moral position that values the assertion of independent choice that does not simply conform to the outlook of the They.[69] On the other hand, his voluntarism about the constitution of the world makes it difficult to see any basis for this moral position. The claims about authenticity may be defended on the basis of a view about the nature of human beings as essentially free and capable of rational choice. But this sort of essentialism seems to reflect a conception of the world that Heidegger tries to undermine through his account of being-in-the-world.

It is difficult to reach an unequivocal judgment, therefore, about the dispute between Heidegger and Sartre over existentialism and humanism. It is not unreasonable of Sartre to emphasize Heidegger's remarks about freedom and authenticity as the basis of a moral outlook. Nor, however, is it unreasonable of Heidegger to reject this attempt to draw a humanist conclusion from his position. Some acquaintance with Heidegger's view tends to support an initial objection to Sartre's claims. According to Sartre, human beings have no essence, and are therefore free to choose for themselves how to live; he infers that they

---

[67] Reiner, DI 146–67, identifies and criticizes Heidegger's rejection of any objective conception of values. He mentions Heidegger's aim of eliminating the subject–object dichotomy, and some of the errors that resulted from the way he executed this aim (163–5).

[68] On Nietzsche see §1103. Heidegger discusses some of the relevant aspects of Nietzsche in his lectures. See N iii, ch. 5, on the 'estimation of value as the essence of "truth"'. According to Heidegger, Nietzsche means 'that the essence of correctness will by no means find its explanation and basis by saying how man, with the representations occurring in his subjective consciousness, can conform to objects that are at hand out of his soul, how the gap between the subject and the object can be bridged, so that something like a "conforming to" becomes possible. With the characterization of truth as estimation of value, the essential definition of truth is rather turned in a *completely different direction*.' (37)

[69] On this tension in Heidegger, and especially on the different roles of voluntarism, see Olafson, PP 70–7. He mentions connexions between Nietzsche and Heidegger at 71n.

ought to choose freely and authentically. It is difficult to distinguish this position from the claim that human beings are essentially free; in other words, Sartre seems to revert to the essentialism that he professes to reject. Heideggers's attack on humanism implicitly points out this incoherence in Sartre's position, but Heidegger does not avoid the claims about authenticity that lead Sartre into incoherence.

REVIVALS OF NON-COGNITIVISM

1361. Should the Open Question Argument be Revived?

We have now examined the main statements of non-cognitivism. This chapter mentions some re-statements and defences that try to answer objections to Stevenson's and Hare's arguments. After a period of declining interest, the study of meta-ethical questions revived in the last quarter of the twentieth century, and a short treatment can hardly do justice to the complex and sophisticated work that has already appeared. Some of the most important work has emerged from fruitful reflexion on meta-ethical questions in relation to contemporary epistemology, metaphysics, philosophy of science, and philosophy of language. It would be a long task to cover this whole area in enough detail to make its philosophical context and significance clear. But it may be useful to pick up a few questions that we have already discussed in Moore and his successors, to see whether recent discussion throws new light on these questions. This principle of selection does not imply that these are the only questions worth discussing.

Recent non-cognitivists rely on Moore's Open Question Argument.[1] Blackburn, for instance, takes it to be 'reasonably secure' that some moral judgments do not follow from any 'naturalistic facts'.[2] Conceptual naturalism collapses in the face of the Open Question Argument, because evaluation is different from description.[3], [4] Similarly, Gibbard endorses Moore's argument and applies it to the concept of rationality. He argues against definitions or analyses of 'rational' on the basis of 'reasons of the very kind that Moore put forth in his attacks on various "naturalistic" definitions of "good" '.[5] He uses Moore's method for deciding when an analysis fails, and appeals to an open question.

---

[1] Darwall, Gibbard, and Railton, 'Fin de siècle', 116, recognize the objections to Mooore's views about meaning and definition, but none the less believe that 'it seems impossible to deny that Moore was on to something'.

[2] Blackburn considers the claim: 'There are some moral propositions that are true, but whose truth is not entailed by any naturalistic facts about their subject' (EQR 120). Blackburn's conviction that this claim is 'reasonably secure' (121) rests on the arguments that lead Moore to reject analytical utilitarianism.

[3] 'If the realist claims identity of conceptual content between "is good" and "creates happiness", . . . the open question argument strikes. In a nutshell, evaluating things is different from describing them. One could describe something as creating happiness with a perfectly clinical detachment, or even with regret.' (RP 317)

[4] Moore sometimes says that only natural properties are descriptive; §1262. But he does not agree with non-cognitivists in supposing that if they are not descriptive, they simply express attitudes.

[5] Gibbard, WCAF 11. He discusses Moore in more detail in THL, ch. 2.

This optimistic attitude to the Open Question Argument relies on three assumptions: (1) The Open Question Argument is cogent. (2) It is cogent because it reveals the essentially 'normative' character of moral terms and judgments. (3) No cognitivist account can capture this essentially normative character.

The relation between the first assumption and the second is not completely clear. Recent defenders of the normativity of moral judgments have sometimes appealed to Frankena's assessment of Moore. According to Frankena, Moore is right to reject naturalism because he implicitly grasps the normative character of moral judgments.[6] By this Frankena means that moral judgments essentially include oughts and reasons, which Frankena takes to be essentially non-natural. But he does not explain why he thinks they are non-natural. In his defence, we might argue that any proposed definition of them in naturalistic terms commits the naturalistic fallacy, because it is subject to the Open Question Argument. But Frankena cannot offer this defence, since he denies that the Open Question Argument is cogent. If we are to treat the essential normativity of moral judgments as a sign of the cogency of the Open Question Argument, we need to answer objections to the Open Question Argument.[7]

1362. Moore and Normativity

If Frankena is right to claim that Moore proves the essential normativity of moral concepts or judgments, does he help non-cognitivism? We might agree with Frankena if he simply means that we cannot give an account of moral concepts without introducing other normative concepts. A plausible account of 'good' might explicate it as 'meeting the appropriate standards' or 'what would be rationally desired', or 'what we have good reason to aim at in the appropriate area'. An account of any of these concepts will re-introduce a reference to 'good' or 'ought'. In speaking of these as 'normative' concepts we mean that they refer to reasons for choosing or acting, and we explain 'reasons' by concepts that introduce appropriateness or something related to it. Neither 'norm' nor 'reason' nor 'ought' nor 'appropriate' appears to be the basic concept.

But even if Moore's arguments suggest that normative concepts cannot be reduced to non-normative concepts, his specific arguments may not be cogent. In particular, the Open

---

[6] Frankena on Moore; §1259. Darwall, 'Frankena', 691–5, discusses Frankena's views on normativity in 'Obligation and value'.

[7] Darwall, 'Moore', 485, seems to combine Frankena's views about essential normativity with endorsement of the Open Question Argument. He believes that Moore indicates a basic point about normativity and freedom: 'We can step back from any perspective given us even by our most critically informed desires and sensibly ask whether what we have best reason to do just is to promote valuable states . . . And we can assert without contradiction or conceptual confusion, that this is not so, that there are other, agent-relative reasons.' Darwall represent this as 'a form of the open question argument' (483). Perhaps Darwall means that if one applies Moore's tests for an open question, one finds that it is not conceptually confused or self-contradictory to deny that one has best reason to promote valuable states. But this is not a very strong argument to show that this denial is not conceptually confused, unless Moore's tests are good tests for lack of conceptual confusion. But they would not be good tests for this unless they were good tests for self-contradiction. But—as many agree—they are not good tests for self-contradiction, since they identify only statements that are not obviously self-contradictory, which may still be self-contradictory. Alternatively, Darwall may mean that Moore is right to use facts about what is self-contradictory or conceptually confused to establish whether it is true that we have best reason to promote valuable states. In that case, he should agree that Moore's arguments give us no reason to agree with Darwall about what is not conceptually confused or contradictory.

Question Argument may not give us a good reason to believe that normative concepts are irreducible. We may rely on different grounds that ought not to be confused with the Open Question Argument. If, for instance, someone tries to explain what we ought to choose by appeal to what an informed agent would choose, we can find counter-examples in which informed agents with warped desires would not choose what they ought to. To deal with such counter-examples, we need to add that the informed agent has appropriate desires. If we consider examples of this sort, we may claim to see a systematic and predictable failure of eliminative accounts of normative concepts. Such an argument does not rely on considering whether we can significantly ask whether informed agents choose what they ought to. It relies on the traditional method of looking for counter-examples that seem plausible on reflexion. This method relies on moral judgments, not merely on judgments about what seems significant or what is self-contradictory.

The irreducibility of normative concepts refutes naturalism only if normative concepts are not natural. Moore hardly gives us a good reason to believe this about normative concepts, since he has no satisfactory account of the natural. We might suppose he has in mind a concept of the natural that makes natural properties those that can be grasped by the senses or defined by reference to properties graspable by the senses.[8] If we can make this test clear enough, we may well conclude that normative concepts are not natural in this sense.

But this sense of 'natural' does not capture Moore's main reason for wanting to deny that goodness is a natural property. He wants natural properties to include all the properties that are mentioned in a natural science; for he wants to make sure that ethics cannot be a natural science. The irreducibility of the normative to the non-normative does not ensure this result; for natural sciences (taken to include social sciences) may deal with normative properties. Hence the fact that a concept or a property is normative leaves open the possibility that it is natural in one sense that is important to Moore.

Even if we agreed that moral concepts are not natural, we would not have agreed that they are non-factual. If by 'values' or 'evaluative concepts' we simply mean 'normative concepts', we may agree that they are irreducible to non-evaluative concepts. But it does not follow that they are non-factual. If I ask you to give me a reason to take an umbrella, you give me a reason by mentioning the fact that I will get wet. Perhaps this fact is a reason for me because of the further fact that I do not want to get wet. In citing reasons, we introduce facts. The essential connexion between normative concepts and reasons does not show that these concepts are not factual. If we are to agree with Hare's view that Moore's argument requires moral judgments to have essentially prescriptive meaning, we have to accept the questionable claim that reasons include or imply motives.

---

[8] Broad, 'Features', 62, suggests this account of what Moore has in mind in speaking of natural properties: 'any characteristic which either (a) we become aware of by inspecting our sense-data or introspecting our experiences, or (b) is definable wholly in terms of characteristics of the former kind together with the notions of cause and substance'. See also §1264.

1363. Supervenience and Objectivist Non-Naturalism

To show that the essential normativity of moral concepts supports non-cognitivism, we may argue that objectivist non-naturalist descriptivism is not a plausible alternative. Strawson and Hare argue that non-naturalist descriptivism accepts an incredible account of the relation of empirical evidence to moral judgments about particular situations. Similarly, Blackburn argues that non-naturalist descriptivism conflicts with plausible views about the supervenience of moral facts on natural facts. Though non-naturalists claim that natural facts do not entail moral facts,[9] they believe (according to Blackburn) that moral properties supervene on natural properties: a subject cannot possess a given moral property without also possessing a relevant natural property, and it cannot lose the moral property without also losing the relevant natural property.[10]

Non-entailment and supervenience imply that (1) no truth about x's moral properties follows from any truths about x's natural properties; (2) necessarily, if x and y have the same natural properties, they have the same moral properties; and (3) if x changes in respect of all its natural properties, it changes in respect of its moral properties as well.[11]

The first and second judgments seem to commit a realist to arbitrary discriminations. If x and y have all the same natural properties, we have no possible ground for regarding x (say) as good and y as bad;[12] but how can we agree to that while rejecting entailment? If realists reject entailment, they are not entitled to help themselves to supervenience without explaining why it is true. But if they reject supervenience, they make moral truths unimportant.[13]

Must a non-naturalist objectivist accept supervenience? It is reasonable to accept some necessary connexions between a given moral property and other properties. If, for instance, we claimed that x is good and y is not good, but x and y differ in no other respect besides goodness, we would recognize no properties in which something's goodness consists.[14]

We might claim that this connexion between goodness and other properties is a feature of the meaning of 'good'; perhaps something is good just in so far as its other properties meet certain standards of appropriateness or suitability. If those other properties meet the relevant standards, anything with the same properties must meet those standards.[15] Hence some properties other than goodness entail that whatever has them is good. But supervenience,

---

[9] Blackburn, EQR 120.   [10] EQR 115.

[11] '. . . we are asked to make intelligible the notion of a state of affairs subject to the constraint that its existence does not follow from the naturalistic facts *being* as they are, but its continued existence follows from the natural facts *staying* as they are. Now, while I cannot see an inconsistency in holding this belief, it is not philosophically very inviting.' (EQR 119)

[12] EQR 122. Blackburn takes this to be a special difficulty for a realist who recognizes moral states of affairs independent of our beliefs, attitudes, or purposes. A non-realist might say that it would be arbitrary to refuse to take the same attitude to two things with the same natural properties; but since realists do not think that moral judgments simply express attitudes, they need to explain why reality could not require us to make the judgments that might appear to involve arbitrariness.

[13] EQR 121. Blackburn claims that 'in the case of ethics, supervenience seems to be built into the discourse—it is analytic . . .' (RP 315). He takes it to be obvious: 'I doubt very much whether anyone would feel entirely happy about disputing it, so even if there is no very good argument for it that a realist need accept, it may be quite proper to accept it as an axiom of meta-ethics' (EQR 121).

[14] This is Hare's explanation of supervenience at LM 80–1.

[15] Blackburn agrees with this: 'One thing, then, that must be established in defending this part of the argument is that if somebody claimed, say, that an action was absolutely identical in every respect with another, except that it was much

as Blackburn understands it, implies two further claims: (1) It applies to all moral properties, not just to goodness. (2) It says not only that every moral property depends on some other property, but also that it supervenes on some natural property. These two claims make the thesis more controversial.

The first claim is plausible; it implies that if courage were to change from being more to being less valuable, this change would consist in something other than simply becoming less valuable. The second claim is more or less plausible according to the range of natural properties. We might take moral properties to supervene on some non-moral properties, introduced by such predicates as 'ought', 'right', 'healthy', 'appropriate', 'suitable', 'beneficial'. These are not exclusively moral predicates, and the normative properties they pick out are not simply moral properties. Moral properties supervene on non-moral properties if they supervene on these normative properties; perhaps some of these non-moral normative properties even entail moral properties.

Blackburn, however, denies that these normative properties are natural properties.[16] For he takes natural facts to exclude all normative facts, since he takes the issue about entailment to be about whether 'is' entails 'ought'.[17] Natural facts include only 'is' facts without any 'ought'. Hence he demands a logical connexion between supervenient moral properties and non-normative properties. But this claim about supervenience is open to question. A non-naturalist objectivist may fairly deny that moral facts are entailed by natural facts, so understood, and so may reject Blackburn's claim about supervenience.

The objectivist, therefore, may reasonably reject Blackburn's second component of supervenience ('Necessarily, if x and y have the same natural properties, they have the same moral properties'). Suppose that saying something you believe to be false with intent to deceive is telling a lie (so that 'lie' picks out a natural property). It is possible that, though x and y are both lies, x is right and y is wrong, since (we may assume) lying is sometimes right and sometimes wrong. Hence the same natural properties do not ensure the same moral properties.

We may defend Blackburn's claim about supervenience by trying to expand our description of the natural properties of x and y so that they specify the precise circumstances that make x right and y wrong. Hence we might describe x more fully as 'telling a lie when we are trying to prevent an attempted murder'.[18] But this natural property may not ensure that x is right and y is wrong; perhaps we ought not to tell a lie to prevent an attempted murder if the prospective victim is a cruel tyrant, or . . . etc. Do we know a priori that all the features that would make it wrong to lie in one case and right in another can be captured in the natural properties of the two actions? If we do not know it a priori, we do not know a priori that two actions that have all the same natural properties have the same moral properties as well.[19] If we do not know these things a priori, we have no reason to agree that the supervenience of the moral on the natural is a conceptual truth about moral concepts.

---

worse; or that a feature of character like courage had changed in no way in its nature, relations, consequences, yet was of much less value than formerly; it would be a logical and not merely a moral mistake that had been made.' (EQR 116)

[16] Here I speak loosely about properties and predicates. See §1382.   [17] EQR 120.

[18] For this purpose we assume that 'murder' is a natural concept ('intentional homicide'), and does not imply that the homicide is unjustified.

[19] Blackburn perhaps alludes to this possibility at RP 317, commenting on particularism. But I do not believe that the possibility I have envisaged commits us to particularism.

Non-naturalist objectivists ought to agree that if moral properties had no connexion with non-moral properties, we would have reason to wonder why we take them seriously. They ought also to agree that some truths about moral properties, including goodness, seem to imply some analytic truths about supervenience. But these admissions do not support Blackburn's claims about supervenience.[20]

These objections to Blackburn's second claim do not undermine his third claim ('If x changes in respect of all its natural properties, it changes in respect of its moral properties as well'). The difference between the two claims reflects the difference between properties and property-instances. If normative properties depend on or are constituted by non-normative properties, some changes in non-normative property-instances in x will change normative properties in x too. Similarly, if x changes in its normative properties, it seems to do this by changing in some of its non-normative properties; these changes are the basis for the change in normative properties. But it does not follow that the instances of the same natural properties in y will constitute just the same normative properties in y.

Still, the third thesis is open to doubt. Consider a variant on the story of Job: Job is honest and rich; he has a loving, successful, and flourishing family, good health etc. But he loses all these things except his honesty. He no longer displays it in any of the same actions. He never used to be tempted to steal a loaf of bread, but now he is tempted to do this. His honesty shows itself in entirely different actions and in different mental states and tendencies. If he can remain the same person while differing in all his natural properties, apparently he can retain the same moral properties; they are still constituted by natural properties, but by different ones. Non-naturalism does not seem to violate obvious truths about the supervenience of the moral on the natural.

1364. Gibbard's Argument for Non-Cognitivism

If the arguments against naturalist and non-naturalist objectivism are not convincing enough to rule out cognitivist accounts of moral judgment, the case for non-cognitivism has to rest on the strength of the positive arguments for non-cognitivism. Gibbard tries to construct a positive case. As we saw, he claims to rely on the considerations that underlie Moore's Open Question Argument. If these were all he relied on, his case would be open to the objections that apply to Moore's argument.

In practice, however, Gibbard does not confine himself to an appeal to Moore's open questions. He considers both an account that identifies rationality with instrumental rationality and an account that identifies it with the choices made after exposure to full information.[21] He argues that some apparent cases of rational behaviour do not fit these accounts, and some apparent cases of irrational behaviour fit them. He also points out that if we deny that behaviour fitting one or another of these accounts is rational, we do not seem to be using the term in a different sense; we seem to be denying precisely what the account asserts.

This is similar to Moore's argument against conceptual utilitarianism. Moore does not merely claim that it appears to be consistent to ask whether a given proposed definition

---

[20] Further discussion of supervenience: Jackson, 'Cognitivism', and *FME*, ch. 5.
[21] See Brandt, *TGR*, discussed at §1434.

is false. He also argues that people seem to have an intelligent argument that would not be so clearly intelligent if they were simply using the relevant terms in different senses. This is a reasonable, though non-conclusive, objection to conceptual utilitarianism. It does not simply appeal to open questions. The same can be said of Gibbard's argument about rationality. Though he speaks as though it were simply an instance of Moore's Open Question Argument, it appeals to intuitive beliefs that go beyond the bare appearance of consistency.

Moore does not recognize the difference between his plausible argument against conceptual utilitarianism and his appeal to the Open Question Argument. Hence it is not surprising that Gibbard seems not to distinguish reliance on the Open Question Argument from reliance on intuitively plausible counter-examples and objections. The difference between the two forms of argument is none the less important. While it is easy to see that 'It is right to maximize utility' creates an open question, it is more complicated to show that we have a plausible counter-example.

We need to bear this difference in mind in considering Gibbard's conclusions about descriptive accounts of rationality. If he relies on the Open Question Argument, his argument may be this: (1) Some descriptive analyses of rationality create an open question. (2) We can reasonably expect that all other descriptive analyses will also create an open question. (3) We ought to reject analyses that create an open question. (4) Hence we ought to reject all descriptive analyses. The first two steps are quite plausible, and the argument is valid. But the third step relies on the least defensible aspect of the Open Question Argument; if we accept it, we seem to rule out all non-obvious analyses of any concept.

If, however, Gibbard relies on intuitive beliefs about rationality that go beyond beliefs about consistency, his argument may be this: (1a) Some descriptive analyses are open to reasonable objection. (2a) We may justifiably expect that the same will be true of all other descriptive analyses. (3a) We ought to reject analyses that are open to reasonable objection. (4) Hence we ought to reject all descriptive analyses. (3a) is more plausible than (3), partly because 'reasonable objection' is vague; its vagueness indicates that it is difficult to capture the considerations relevant to a philosophical analysis. But now (2a) seems a reckless generalization from (1a). Some more trial and error than Gibbard allows seems a prerequisite for a general case against descriptivism.

Gibbard does not discuss possible analyses that include a normative concept (e.g., 'desires appropriately modified'). Since he has not yet proved that no normative concepts are descriptive concepts, he cannot fairly assume that analyses that include normative concepts are non-descriptive. They may create open questions, and may be open to objections, but further argument is needed to decide how reasonable the objections are. Moore rejects such analyses of Good because he expects an analysis to introduce simpler elements. But unless Gibbard accepts this particularly questionable doctrine of Moore's, he has no reason to reject such analyses.

Perhaps, however, he relies less heavily on arguments against descriptive analyses because he believes that a survey of these unsuccessful analyses reveals the meaning of 'rational.' He agrees with Hare in generalizing from disagreements about descriptive analyses to the conclusion that the common meaning is not descriptive, but prescriptive or (as Gibbard puts it) expressive.[22] In his view, if we reject a 'full information' account of rationality because we believe that the exposure of our desires to a vivid confrontation with full information might leave us with irrational desires, we thereby endorse the desires we have rather than those we would eventually reach (22).

Gibbard's argument is similar to Hare's argument from the commendatory function of moral terms to their prescriptive meaning. His conclusion seems to capture the standard illocutionary force of statements about rationality; for we may agree that usually our calling something rational is a way of endorsing it. But Gibbard also claims that the endorsement gives the meaning of 'rational'; this is the element that descriptive analyses leave out.

1365. Objections to Gibbard's Account

Even if we question Gibbard's argument for his account of rationality, the account might none the less be plausible. Since his argument and conclusion are quite similar to Hare's, we may ask whether he overcomes the main objections to Hare's version of non-cognitivism.

He agrees with Hare's argument from the possibility of intelligent dispute to the conclusion that the missing element in descriptive analyses is prescriptive meaning.[23] But though Hare argues that descriptivism cannot explain intelligent disagreement, his analysis seems no better off. If one person commends an action and another refuses to commend it, they may not have an intelligent disagreement. Similarly, Gibbard rejects some descriptive analyses of rationality by appeal to the possibility of intelligent non-confused disagreement about different accounts of rationality. But then he suggests that the possibility of such disagreement rests on a shared meaning that consists simply in our endorsing whatever actions or attitudes we count as reasonable. How does my endorsing x and your endorsing not-x or refusing to endorse x allow intelligent disagreement about x? We seem to be simply recording opposed attitudes. If the disagreement is intelligent, our endorsement should rely on some ground that could be argued to be relevant. To find the concept of rationality we should look for the relevant sort of ground. Hence endorsement does not seem to be sufficient for an account of rationality.

Nor does it seem to be necessary; for an objection to Hare's position also applies to Gibbard. I normally endorse behaviour or beliefs or attitudes that I take to be rational all things considered, and hence my calling something rational regularly has an endorsing force. But this force can be cancelled without an apparent change of meaning. Perhaps I can envisage a process of changing my outlook by exposure to facts and logic, and by appropriate guidance by these facts and logic. Suppose I believe that this would be a rational process, and that if I went through this process, the outcome would be a more rational outlook than I have now. I also believe it would be rational for me to acquire this outlook. But since I find that outlook utterly repugnant, I do not endorse that outlook, and I do not endorse going through the process that leads to it. Such cases seem not only possible but also sometimes

---

[22] 'What we should note . . . is that the funny cases—the cases where Brandt's account labels crazy acts rational—have a systematic import. The word "rational", in the sense we are after, has an automatically recommending force.' (Gibbard, WCAF 20)

[23] See Hare, SOE 72–3, discussed in §1334.

actual. Some people who regard the death penalty as an appropriate means of vengeance might agree that they could form a more rational attitude to it; but since they hate the thought of having this more rational attitude, they do not endorse the attitude or the process leading to it.

This example is parallel to those that cast doubt on a prescriptivist account of moral judgments. The non-cognitivist, as usual, has two possible replies: (1) The supposition that appears coherent is not coherent. We contradict ourselves if we think we can regard something as rational without endorsing it (or vice versa). (2) The supposition is coherent because it uses 'rational' in a different sense from the non-cognitivist's sense. We should treat such cases as 'non-standard' or 'inverted commas' uses.[24]

Gibbard's arguments against other analyses cast doubt on these replies. The first reply seems equally open to descriptivists about rationality. They might say that the appearance of an intelligent disagreement is misleading, and we are confused if we reject the descriptivist analysis. Gibbard might reasonably reply that one ought not to dismiss a disagreement that seems quite intelligent. But in that case, one ought not to dismiss as confused the view that we can regard something as rational without endorsing it. Gibbard's second reply also allows descriptivists to answer his initial objection. Defenders of the 'full information' account, for instance, might say that they are analysing only one sense of 'rational' and that apparent dissenters from their analysis use the term in a different sense. Gibbard might reasonably reply that it is arbitrary for descriptivists to multiply senses in cases where their opponents appear to deny exactly what they assert. But it seems equally arbitrary of him to protect expressivism by resort to different senses.

These objections might be expressed differently in accordance with different interpretations of Gibbard's initial arguments. If he relies, as he suggests, on the claim that descriptive analyses create open questions, his analysis seems to violate his standards; for we only need to show that it appears significant to ask whether we endorse what we regard as rational. If he relies on the claim that descriptive analyses are subject to reasonable objections, it is not so easy to show that his analysis violates his standards; we must also be satisfied that the intuitive beliefs about rationality that we rely on are reasonable beliefs. But in order to evaluate Gibbard's case, we can ask an easier question: Is it any less reasonable to believe that we can count something as rational without endorsing it than it is to believe that we can deny that a desire resulting from full information is rational? The first belief seems as reasonable as the second. But if Gibbard refuses to rely on intuitive beliefs about rationality, he denies himself the most plausible objection that he raises to some descriptive accounts.

For these reasons, his position is internally unstable. A fair and impartial application of the standards underlying his criticisms of descriptivism casts doubt on his expressivism.

1366. An Evolutionary Argument for Non-Cognitivism

These arguments for non-cognitivism have relied on conceptual and a priori arguments to show that moral judgments are essentially prescriptive or expressive. Blackburn supports

---

[24] See Gibbard, *WCAF* 48–50.

a non-cognitivist conclusion by a different sort of argument. In contrast to Stevenson and Hare, he does not appeal directly to a conviction about the necessary magnetism or commendatory function of moral language. He relies on a developmental story about the origin and growth of moral practices and judgments.[25] If Blackburn is right, Sidgwick should not have been reluctant to inquire into the 'origins of the moral faculty'.[26] Attention to the origins favours the internalist position that takes values to be 'intrinsically motivating'. The evolutionary advantage of morality seems to come from helping those who help us, not simply from thinking about helping them. Hence morality is intrinsically connected with motivation and action; hence it is a set of attitudes.[27]

We may concede that morality would probably not have promoted survival if creatures who had it did not act on it. But does that concession support non-cognitivism? A similar argument seems to apply to some cognitive states. Deer who recognized wolves and did nothing about it would probably not last long; nor would human beings who believed a snowstorm was coming and set out on a long journey anyhow. But we would hardly infer from this that their belief that a snowstorm was coming was not a belief.

Blackburn's argument actually suggests a plausible way of understanding morality as consisting partly in moral beliefs. If earlier human beings held beliefs about how to achieve their aims, if these beliefs were roughly correct, and if achieving their aims helped them to survive, we can see why human beings with such beliefs tended to survive and to reproduce. We could say the same about beliefs about their interest or their welfare. Admittedly, it is logically possible that these beliefs were true but the environment was so unfavourable to their achieving their good that they did not survive; but equally it is logically possible that co-operative creatures might have faced such an unfavourable environment that they did not survive. Whether we understand morality as including moral beliefs or as consisting primarily in attitudes, we can see why creatures with a morality would be more likely to survive and reproduce.

It is not clear, then, how Blackburn's evolutionary speculations support non-cognitivism. A cognitivist who wants to accommodate these speculations has to ascribe an appropriate content to moral beliefs; but it is easy to meet this condition. The evolutionary advantages of moral judgments do not require intrinsically motivating states; it is enough if we can explain why human beings act regularly on moral beliefs.

But even if moral judgments were once beneficial because they were intrinsically motivating, it does not follow that they are now intrinsically motivating. Even if intrinsically

---

[25] Blackburn agrees with Mackie on this general point: 'In Mackie's terms, morality is an invention that is successful because it enables things to go well among people with a natural inheritance of needs and desires that they must together fulfil. Moral thought becomes a practice with a purpose.' (EQR 164) Unlike Mackie, however, he believes that a developmental account of morality supports emotivism: 'The point is that the state of mind starts theoretical life as something else [than a belief]—a stance, or conative state or pressure on choice and action. Such pressures need to exist if human beings are to meet their competing needs for a social co-operative setting. The stance may be called an attitude, although it would not matter if the word fitted only inexactly; its function is to mediate the move from features of a situation to a reaction, which in the appropriate circumstances will mean choice.' (EQR 168)

[26] See Sidgwick, ME, p. v: 'I have avoided the inquiry into the origin of the moral faculty—which has perhaps occupied a disproportionate amount of the attention of modern moralists . . .'. See also 4–5, 212–14.

[27] 'Evolutionary success may attend the animal that helps those that have helped it, but it would not attend any allegedly possible animal that thinks it ought to help but does not. In the competition for survival, it is what the animal *does* that matters. This is important, for it shows that only if values are intrinsically motivating is a natural story of their emergence possible.' (EQR 168–9)

motivating moral judgments helped our ancestors to survive and to reproduce, moral judgments might now have changed their character so that they are more cognitive than they used to be. This would be easy to understand, if human beings have stopped simply reacting to situations that provoked a certain kind of feeling, and have tried to control their reactions in the light of some judgments about the nature of the situations; the relevant moral terms might gradually come to convey the judgments about the situation, detached from the reactions themselves.

One might imagine (truly or falsely) that something like this is true of children. Their moral judgments might at first function as attitudes, but they might gradually learn to form their attitudes in the light of judgments about objective properties of actions and people. Even if moral judgments grow out of attitudes, they may not be attitudes; their growth may have transformed them from intrinsically motivating attitudes to judgments that are less directly connected to motivation. Blackburn's speculations about the origin of the moral faculty do not refute Sidgwick's doubts about whether such speculations help meta-ethical inquiry.[28]

1367. The Appeal of Quasi-Realism

Even if we are not convinced by the specific arguments for non-cognitivism that rely on Moore, we may still believe that non-cognitivism offers us a clear and intelligible account of the place of moral judgments in an account of the natural world. Objectivism commits us to moral facts and properties that create new metaphysical and epistemological difficulties for us if we try to fit them into a plausible account of the natural world. This aspect of objectivism makes it unwelcome to philosophers who are sympathetic to positivism. Even those who are not positivists about natural science may hesitate to admit new facts and properties that the natural sciences do not recognize. Blackburn's argument about supervenience raises doubts about the metaphysics and epistemology of objectivism. Even if his argument fails, we might prefer an account of moral judgments to avoid the potentially controversial facts and properties that are specific to morality.

To counter this argument against moral facts and properties, we might appeal to the apparently objectivist character of our moral thought and judgments. We may incline towards objectivism if we think we need objective moral facts to do justice to the character of our moral judgments and the importance we attach to moral thought and action. Hence we seem to see a case for objectivism in the manifest character of moral judgment. We use moral judgments in arguments that require the truth of the premisses, and in conditionals that seem to require a descriptive analysis. Our arguments include moral premisses as though they were just as factual and descriptive as the other premisses that we use. Similarly,

[28] Blackburn argues that Putnam's observations on the division of linguistic labour support non-cognitivism. See *EQR* 200–1. But if these observations apply to moral judgment, they seem equally available to a cognitivist, to explain how someone could use a moral term without the normal descriptive meaning. Division of labour explains the possibility of 'inverted commas' uses (as Hare calls them) without resort to a different sense of the term. But it does not tell us whether the purely non-cognitive or the purely cognitive use is the 'inverted commas' use. On division of labour, cf. Sturgeon, 'Contents', 26.

we use conditionals including a moral antecedent and a non-moral consequent (or the reverse) without supposing that we need to treat them differently from entirely non-moral conditionals.

According to this cognitivist argument, therefore, non-cognitivism appears to work only if we confine ourselves to such simple utterances as 'You ought to keep this promise that you made'. Non-cognitivism more obviously fails for non-assertive uses of moral concepts, such as 'If it is right to keep promises you have made, and you have made this promise, you ought to keep this promise'.[29]

Blackburn tries to answer this argument for a cognitivist analysis of moral concepts.[30] His theory is quasi-realist because it allows us, on the one hand, to make the moral judgments that have been taken to support a realist conceptual analysis, but, on the other hand, to reject realism as conceptual analysis and as metaphysical theory. Quasi-realists distinguish the 'ostensibly realist' data from the genuinely realist interpretation, and they argue that we can retain the ostensibly realist data without the interpretation that introduces realist metaphysics. The ostensibly realist data include our tendency to treat moral judgments as though they were simply statements capable of truth and falsity, rather than expressions of attitude that are neither true nor false. The cognitivist takes these data to show that moral judgments are really true and false, and that therefore (since subjectivist cognitivism is implausible) they correspond to some independent facts, which require a realist understanding. Blackburn answers that the ostensibly realist data of moral judgment do not require an objectivist analysis.[31]

His non-cognitivist position is 'projectivism'. We recognize that we are simply expressing our attitudes, but we project these attitudes on the world, as though the world really had some property in its own right that corresponds to our attitude to it. If you are welcome to our house, you do not acquire some property of welcomeness, or some relation of welcomeness to our house; though we speak as though your being welcome were a property of yours, we recognize that we simply express an attitude to you. Projectivism about moral judgments seeks to show that we can account for judgments about right and wrong in the same way as we account for judgments about being welcome.

Projectivists, therefore, can mimic cognitivists, in Blackburn's view, because they can describe a use for the utterances that cognitivists interpret as assertions about facts. First, they interpret a conditional such as 'If you ought not to cause pain to any sentient beings, you ought not to cause pain to rats' truth-functionally, so that it is equivalent to the negated conjunction 'Not [(you ought not to cause pain to any sentient beings) and (you are permitted to cause pain to rats)]'. Then they replace both the whole judgment and the constituent ought-judgments with expressions of attitudes, so that the whole conditional

---

[29] Ewing, *DG* 13, points out that some apparent features of moral judgments—e.g., their use in reasoning—seem to presuppose descriptivism. Geach, 'Ascriptivism', develops Ewing's point. He remarks on the general difficulty that arises in applying a non-descriptive account of moral judgments to contexts in which the relevant judgment is not asserted but (e.g.) is a part of a conditional. '. . . condemning a thing by calling it "bad" has to be explained through the more general notion of predicating "bad" of a thing, and such predication may be done without any condemnation . . . It is therefore hopeless to try to explain the use of the term "bad" in terms of non-descriptive acts of condemnation' (253)

[30] Here Blackburn disagrees with Mackie. See esp. *EQR*, ch. 8.

[31] Some of the relevant assumptions favour descriptivism in general, rather than objectivist descriptivism in particular. They favour objectivism only on the assumption that we can safely reject subjectivist descriptivism—a point on which Moore, Stevenson, Hare, Blackburn, and others agree against Hume.

expresses an attitude towards the concurrent holding of two other attitudes. Our acceptance of the conditional is our expression of a favourable attitude towards the concurrent holding of an unfavourable attitude to causing pain to any sentient beings and an unfavourable attitude to causing pain to rats. Similarly, we might interpret other conditionals as involving an attitude, favourable or unfavourable, to some other combination of attitudes.[32] Let us use 'Yes!' for the relevant positive attitude and 'No!' for the relevant negative one and 'OK!' for the relevant neutral one signifying that something is neither prescribed nor prohibited. Then we will explain 'If x is wrong, y is wrong', truth-functionally, as equivalent to Not (x is wrong and y is permissible), which is analysed as No! [No!(x) and OK!(y)]. We express attitudes to certain combinations of attitudes and failures to combine attitudes.

1368. Quasi-Realism on Conditionals

To see whether quasi-realism analyses answer the argument for realism that appeals to the ostensible realism of moral judgments, we may consider the proposed analysis of conditionals. Perhaps non-cognitivists can attach some sense to these conditionals, but is it the sense we normally attach to them?

We might doubt a truth-functional analysis of the conditional as a negated conjunction. Non-cognitivists assume that 'if p, then q' is captured by 'not (p and not-q)'; that is why they analyse a conditional moral judgment as an attitude that rejects the conjunction of two attitudes. But we have reason to claim that 'if p, then q' is not a negated conjunction; it presents p as connected to q in a way that makes the truth of p a reason for believing q.[33] An attitude to a conjunction of attitudes does not capture the reason-giving force of the antecedent.

But even if a conditional is simply a negated conjunction, we can assent to a conditional with a moral component even if we reject the non-cognitivist's attitude to a conjunction. If we accept the conditional about causing pain to sentient creatures and to rats, we believe: Not (we ought not to cause pain to sentient creatures and it is permissible to cause pain to rats). The quasi-realist paraphrases: No! [No! (cause pain to sentient creatures) and OK! (cause pain to rats)]. But we might loathe rats so much that we cannot bring ourselves to disfavour willingness to cause pain to rats. I may assent to the conditional without overcoming my loathing for rats; hence I may not disfavour the combination of the two attitudes. This objection reflects the fact that combinations of attitudes do not seem to behave as combinations of assertions do. If 'if p, then q' is true, 'p and not-q' is false. But we may consistently accept the conditional 'if you ought to do x, you ought to do y' and the combination of attitudes in Yes! (x) and No! (y).

This objection to a quasi-realist account of conditionals repeats the main point underlying the earlier objection to Gibbard's account of judgments of rationality as acts of endorsement. Judgments of rationality seem to have a role that may diverge from the role of endorsements. Similarly, moral judgments seem to have a role that may diverge from the attitudes that non-cognitivists introduce in their analysis.

---

[32] See *EQR* 187, a reply to Schueler, 'Modus Ponens'.
[33] A non-Philonic view of 'if . . . then' is defended by Strawson, *ILT* 82–90, and rejected by Grice, *SWW*, ch. 4, briefly answered by Strawson and Wiggins, 'Grice', 523–5.

These divergences between judgments and attitudes are not confined to cases where (as in the example about rats) the endorsement lags irrationally behind the moral judgment. It might also appear rational to separate the moral judgment from the endorsement. I might, for instance, believe that if abortion is permissible, infanticide is sometimes permissible. Hence I accept: Not (abortion is permissible, and infanticide is impermissible). But it does not follow that my attitude is: No! [(OK! (abortion) and No! (infanticide)]. My attitude might be Yes! [OK! (abortion) and No! (infanticide)]. Perhaps I take this combination of attitudes on consequentialist grounds; if I believe that people who think infanticide is permissible in some cases will come to be less reluctant about it than they should be, a 'slippery slope' argument may persuade me to favour the attitude that opposes infanticide, even though I do not believe infanticide is wrong.

In these examples, the attitudes I favour are not those that I think are warranted by the facts or by what is really right and wrong. I might have other grounds, rational or non-rational, for favouring some attitudes over others.[34] Sidgwick, for instance, does not assume that the true moral position is also the position that we ought to encourage people to accept or to act on. In his view, we might believe utilitarianism, but favour non-utilitarian attitudes. If that is a position worth considering, the separation of endorsing attitudes from beliefs is not simply a logical possibility. It reflects a morally significant question about how, or how far, we should represent our moral beliefs in the attitudes that we hold or favour. If a quasi-realist analysis ignores this question, it does not capture the ostensible character of our moral judgments.

Non-cognitivists might try two replies to such objections:[35] (1) The objections rest on a confusion; they are really self-contradictory, even though this is not obvious. (2) They rely on using the crucial terms in a non-standard sense, but the standard sense is given by the non-cognitive analysis. Does either of these replies deal plausibly with the apparent separation between beliefs and attitudes?

We might maintain that Sidgwick really prescribes or endorses utilitarianism; he simply decides not to advocate it in some circumstances. To show that he really endorses it, we may point to the fact that his ground for advocating some non-utilitarian rules is itself utilitarian. But if we take this view, the sense of 'endorse' that applies to his attitude to utilitarianism is difficult to explain without reliance on belief. In that case, 'endorsement' does not support a non-cognitivist analysis.

The reverse of this difficulty arises for Sidgwick's advocacy of non-utilitarian rules. Must we not say that he believes these rules, if we accept the non-cognitivist analysis of belief as endorsement? But if we say this, we seem to overlook the difference between his view of utilitarianism and his view of the non-utilitarian rules.

Non-cognitivists, therefore, cannot easily show that it is inconsistent to believe one thing and endorse something incompatible with it. It is equally difficult to show that Sidgwick believes utilitarianism only in some non-standard sense of 'believe'. Non-cognitivists might

---

[34] See Sturgeon, 'What difference?' The difference between truth-conditions and acceptance-conditions is clearly marked by Railton, 'Alienation', 167–8.

[35] In *EQR* 190, Blackburn argues that we can make sense of a notion of inconsistency in desires that is appropriately parallel to inconsistency in belief. He does not show that desiring that not-p is inconsistent with believing that p is right; but he would need to show that in order to show how he could translate conditionals into combinations of attitudes.

claim that if Sidgwick does not favour utilitarianism, he does not really believe it, but only believes that it would be right to maximize utility if circumstances were ideal. But this treatment of his position ignores the difference between people who advocate non-utilitarian rules because they believe it is right to follow them and people who advocate them because they believe it is too dangerous to advocate doing the right thing in these circumstances. As Moore, Hare, and Gibbard all argue, we should be reluctant to transform apparently intelligible disagreements into equivocations. Hare and Gibbard use this point against descriptivism, but it seems to undermine their position.

A quasi-realist account of conditionals faces one of the main objections to prescriptivism, which Moore raises against Stevenson. Though we often make moral judgments with prescriptive force, we can sometimes cancel this force without a change in meaning. Similarly, our assent to a conditional often conveys, but need not always convey, our prescription about a certain combination of attitudes. We can assent to a conditional without favouring the combination of attitudes that we would normally be taken to favour in assenting to the conditional. Prescriptions differ from beliefs because they may be adopted in response to the consideration of practical consequences, whereas our beliefs about right and wrong are not normally adopted on this basis.[36] Moreover, our beliefs rationally commit us to other beliefs, but prescriptions do not commit us to other prescriptions without consideration of consequences; we saw this in the example about abortion and infanticide. We may recognize the implications of our moral beliefs without prescribing the conduct that is implied. Since prescribing is an act that has consequences, we may consider the consequences of prescribing before we make up our minds about whether or not to prescribe. If our prescriptions follow our assessment of the consequences of prescribing, they may come apart from our assent to conditionals. The quasi-realist, projectivist, non-cognitivist analysis does not give the sense of the conditionals as we normally use them.

1369. Quasi-Realism on Counterfactuals and Independence

An especially important part of the projectivist attempt to mimic realism concerns its analysis of judgments that seem to assert or to imply the independence of moral truths and facts from our attitudes and judgments. A familiar theological naturalist objection to theological voluntarism argues that it is not someone's willing or commanding x that makes x right, and that x would not change from being right to being wrong simply as a result of someone's willing or commanding differently. Similarly, Balguy rejects sentimentalism on the ground that if our sentiments were to change, that would not change moral rightness and wrongness. Similarly, our sentiments might improve so that they become more correct than they are now; hence correctness cannot be determined by our sentiments.

Blackburn does not argue against the truth of the naturalist claims. In his view, non-cognitivists need not agree with voluntarists and sentimentalists. From a non-cognitivist

---

[36] We strengthen this contrast if we can show that we never adopt a belief on the basis of expected consequences, because a belief is not the sort of thing that can be deliberately adopted. But even if some beliefs could be adopted, we have no reason to agree that all moral beliefs are adopted.

point of view, we can disfavour the ceasing to disfavour cruelty if people become less prone to disfavour it; hence we need not accept the sentimentalist view that provoked Balguy's objections. Blackburn considers the counterfactual: 'Even if we had approved of it or enjoyed it or desired to do it, bear-baiting would still have been wrong'. He explains it as expressing disapproval of forming our approval or disapproval of bear-baiting by consideration of the attitudes of spectators or judges.[37]

Similarly, non-cognitivists can allow moral improvement, if they approve of the formation of attitudes by mechanisms they approve of, even though they do not now approve of those attitudes.[38] Since one takes attitudes not only to actions but also to attitudes and to the processes that form attitudes, one can conceive improvements in one's attitudes, because one can approve of particular ways of testing, developing, or modifying them.

These arguments show that projectivists can allow fallibility and possible improvement, and that they can conceive a correct point of view that is (in one respect) outside their present sentiments. But do they recognize the possibilities that we normally recognize? If we claim that the moral facts are external to our point of view, beliefs, or sentiments, we suppose it is logically possible for the facts to be what they are even if our beliefs and sentiments are mistaken. Quasi-realists, however, cannot agree. They can only allow that I might at present favour a process of developing attitudes that would produce attitudes that I would eventually prefer to the attitudes that I at present favour. The sense to be attached to 'improvement' is fixed by two higher-order attitudes: the one I take at present to a specific process of forming attitudes, and the one I will take in the future to the attitudes that I will have formed by this process.

Hence, the projectivist interpretation of claims about the fallibility of one's attitudes admits only that we may disapprove of some attitudes by reference to other attitudes. This is not how we normally understand the fallibility of attitudes. Even if we did not favour the process that forms certain moral judgments and even if we would not accept the judgments that would result from that process, those judgments might still be true. Moreover, even if we favour the process that forms these judgments, and even if we would accept the resulting judgments, the judgments might still be false. If we allow these possibilities, we separate the truth from our attitudes; but the projectivist does not separate it. Though projectivists can attach a sense to the claims that cognitivists rely on, they cannot attach the normal sense to them. The normal sense allows possibilities that projectivists do not allow.

The projectivist interpretation, therefore, is another attempt to represent the rational criticism of attitudes by appealing to higher-order attitudes.[39] But the multiplication of attitudes does not capture the possibility of the criticism or evaluation of attitudes; it always leaves some attitude beyond criticism that apparently ought not to be beyond criticism.

---

[37] '... on the construal of indirect contexts that I offer, it comes out as a perfectly sensible first-order commitment to the effect that it is not our enjoyments or approvals to which you should look in discovering whether bear-baiting is wrong (it is at least mainly the effect on the bear).' (EQR 153)

[38] 'A simple example would be the worry that a certain attitude, or the way in which one holds a certain attitude, is not so much the outcome of a proper use of imagination and sympathy, which one admires, but is the outcome, say, of various traditions which one does not ... So the quasi-realist can certainly possess the concept of an improved standpoint from which some attitude of his appears inept.' (EQR 20)

[39] On higher-order attitudes, see §1068, on Kierkegaard's aesthetic agent.

1370. What Should We Expect from Quasi-Realism?

Non-cognitivist analyses of conditionals and counterfactuals show that the ostensible realism of moral judgments does not force non-cognitivists to admit a gap in their analysis. If the point of mentioning conditionals, inferences, counterfactuals, and so on, were to show that non-cognitivism has something to say about these uses of moral concepts, the non-cognitivist analyses we have discussed would vindicate the non-cognitivist position.

But one might object that this is too easy a test for non-cognitivism; the mere fact that it can imitate ordinary moral judgments may seem to be irrelevant. Perhaps we can make a synthetic diamond that no one can tell apart from a real diamond by inspection, and that one can even use for all the industrial uses of real diamonds. Even so, it is not a real diamond; for it has been deliberately made to imitate the features of a real diamond, whereas a real diamond has not been made for this purpose. Similarly, a copy of a painting by Vermeer, however well executed, is not a Vermeer; the features of the Vermeer explain the features of the copy, but the reverse is not true. Similarly, then, if a non-cognitivist can imitate the cognitivist's moral judgments without accepting cognitivism, it does not follow that non-cognitivism is the right account of moral judgments. For the explanation and justification of the different combinations of attitudes that appear in a non-cognitivist analysis may require a cognitivist interpretation of moral judgments. If, for instance, we endorse or express certain attitudes when we do, that may be because we believe the underlying moral judgments are true. If the success of non-cognitivism theory depends on imitation of distinctions drawn by the cognitivist, the non-cognitivist implicitly acknowledges that cognitivism is correct.

Hence the non-cognitivist analysis answers the cognitivist interpretation of moral judgments only if it is independent of any cognitivist basis; it cannot depend on judgments taken to be true or false as the basis of the relevant attitudes. But if we take the non-cognitivist analyses to be independent in this way, do they remain plausible? We have seen that they attach some sense to (e.g.) counterfactuals, but they do not attach the normal sense to them. Since, according to the cognitivist, the normal sense of moral judgments requires a cognitivist interpretation, it gives us an argument against non-cognitivism.

Does this objection demand too much from projectivism? If projectivists have a use for ordinary moral judgments, should they be expected to prove that they use them in just the way that cognitivists use them? One might defend non-cognitivist quasi-realists by arguing that appeals to the normal sense of various claims are illegitimate. If we reject quasi-realist interpretations that involve higher-order attitudes, do we insist dogmatically on a realist interpretation? Should we not simply say that there is no normal sense that can be cited in favour of either realism or anti-realism?[40]

---

[40] This might rest on a Quinean view that there is 'no fact of the matter' about what we normally mean. See Quine, *OR* 38: 'It is indeterminate in principle; there is no fact of the matter'. We can be 'translated' in a number of ways that are all equally accurate, if they all capture our tendencies to respond favourably or unfavourably to this or that situation. One might argue that we have no determinate tendency to respond one way or the other to a rather complex question such as 'Is it possible that I favour the process leading to favouring x and that I favour favouring x as a result of that process, but x is wrong?' But if this sceptical view were right, Blackburn's interpretations would be pointless attempts to answer a misguided question.

To see what standards we might fairly impose on a quasi-realist analysis, we should ask what the analysis is meant to show. We might give it an antecedent or a consequent role in the argument. It has an antecedent role if it is meant to show that the ostensible features of moral judgment do not support cognitivism. If we can show this, we may argue that cognitivism introduces unnecessary facts and properties. A quasi-realist analysis has a consequent role if it is meant to support independently cogent arguments for non-cognitivism, by showing that the implications of non-cognitivism are not as radical as we might have supposed.

An antecedent role for quasi-realist analyses imposes higher standards of adequacy than a purely consequent role would demand. For the antecedent role implies that those who are not yet disposed to accept non-cognitivism will lose nothing if they are non-cognitivists. For this purpose, it is relevant to ask whether the sense that quasi-realist analyses attach to moral judgments is the normal sense. If it is not the normal sense, we have reason to favour realism, and quasi-realist analyses do not make non-cognitivism more plausible.

A lower standard might reasonably be imposed if the quasi-realist analyses follow a cogent argument for non-cognitivism. For in this case they are not intended to persuade us to take non-cognitivism seriously; they are only intended to show that we need not reconsider our acceptance of the independent argument for non-cognitivism. If we already have good reason to accept non-cognitivism, we may argue that it can retain ordinary moral judgments, suitably re-interpreted. But if this is the function of non-cognitivist analyses, they do not provide the main argument for non-cognitivism; they help only if we incline to non-cognitivism for some other reason.

What role do Gibbard and Blackburn intend for non-cognitivist analyses? Neither of them rests the whole argument for non-cognitivism on the correctness of these analyses, and so we may suppose that they intend them to have only a consequent role in their position. It might not matter, then, if their analyses do not give the normal sense of moral judgments. But if they dismiss cognitivist objections on this ground, positive support for non-cognitivism relies on the Open Question Argument and the other arguments we have considered. If these arguments are open to doubt, the possibility of quasi-realist analyses does not answer all reasonable doubts about non-cognitivism.

1371. Non-Cognitivism v. Nihilism

If we accept these objections to quasi-realist analyses, we might still agree with non-cognitivism on one central issue. Even if moral judgments require a cognitivist and objectivist interpretation to capture their normal sense, we need not infer that there are objective moral facts and properties. We might conclude instead that moral judgments rest on metaphysical errors. Perhaps a non-cognitivist ought to point this out, and therefore ought to refuse to take on the burden of offering a non-cognitivist analysis that captures the normal sense of moral judgments.

This sympathetic but selective attitude to non-cognitivism departs from Hare and Blackburn on a central point. They both deny that moral discourse, in its normal sense, supports cognitivism and objectivism, and therefore they do not agree that they reject ordinary judgments. The selective attitude is closer to Stevenson's suggestion that his explications try to 'remove the ills' of ordinary judgments but do not capture their meaning exactly. We might, therefore, treat the quasi-realist analyses as revisions and replacements of ordinary moral judgments rather than as accounts of their normal sense.

According to this selective treatment of non-cognitivism, we should defend nihilism or scepticism about moral properties as a preliminary to a non-cognitivist replacement for them. For if moral judgments rest on metaphysical assumptions that warrant a sceptical or nihilist response, we should replace them with judgments that avoid the unwarranted assumptions.

This revised version of non-cognitivism needs to explain what is wrong with moral judgments in their normal sense, and why non-cognitive attitudes are the best replacement of them. One argument for non-cognitivism is a conceptual argument relying on internalism. But this argument is inappropriate for a replacement. If we are willing to abandon the realist metaphysics underlying moral judgments and to replace them with something else, why not abandon their (allegedly) internal connexion to motivation as well? If we try to replace, and not to analyse, moral judgments, we need to consider the different replacements that might be offered.

If, then, we take the central insight of non-cognitivism to be its rejection of the argument from the ostensible realism of moral judgments to a cognitivist and objectivist account of moral properties, we need to reconsider the case that might be made for scepticism and nihilism. Mackie's statement of this case will help us to explore some of the further questions that arise about quasi-realism and nihilism.

OBJECTIVITY AND ITS CRITICS

1372. Further Attacks on Objectivism

Non-cognitivism has seemed appealing partly because the other options have seemed unappealing. If we agree that Moore has refuted naturalism, and we do not accept the non-naturalist realism of Moore and Ross, non-cognitivism may appear to be the only option. But some reasonable alternatives to non-cognitivism and non-naturalist realism have been defended. In this chapter we will confine ourselves to a survey of some of these positions, and indicate their connexion to earlier debates in meta-ethics.

Moore is not clear about what he is trying to describe or analyse in his discussion of goodness. Most of the time, he seems to be asking about some feature of the world, and he looks for the feature that good things actually have in common. But he also speaks as though he is asking about the meaning of the word 'good'. We might take different views of his arguments if we think of them as raising these distinct questions. If his arguments showed that our concept of goodness is a concept of a simple non-natural property, it would not follow that there is any simple non-natural property corresponding to this concept.

This option of agreeing with Moore about our moral concepts and disagreeing with him about the metaphysics of morality seems attractive to Mackie and Robinson.[1] Robinson agrees with Ross's view about the moral concepts, but infers that nothing has the properties that moral concepts attribute to things.[2] Ross does not consider this possibility about moral concepts, but, as Robinson notices, he considers it about aesthetic concepts. We speak as though beauty were an objective property of things, but (in Ross's view) reflexion shows us that it is not. Robinson suggests that the same is true of moral concepts. The moral goodness and badness of things is not an objective feature of them, but simply a feature of our attitude

[1] Robinson, 'Emotive', cites Mackie, 'Refutation'. Hare mentions Mackie and Robinson together, at *MT* 78. See §1314. Ewing, *STMP* 23, remarks that an error theory of the sort defended by Mackie and Robinson is the only reasonable position for a 'subjectivist' (by which he means roughly 'non-cognitivist'). Mackie, 'Refutation', anticipates his fuller argument in *E* on many points. He mentions objections from queerness and relativity (78). He offers an error theory (81–2), which he illustrates by reference to Hume on the idea of necessary connexion.

[2] See Robinson, 'Emotive', 83: 'The descriptive function of the ethical words is more or less as elucidated by . . . Ross . . . That is to say, they name unanalysable qualities belonging to certain acts or objects in complete independence of all human feelings and thoughts . . . In this descriptive use the ethical words involve an error, because nothing has such an unanalysable independent attribute as they name.'

to them. Emotivism, therefore, gives the true account of the real moral properties, but it does not give the true account of our ordinary use of moral terms; for the ordinary use includes an error.

Since Robinson denies that he rejects morality, he disapproves of the title of Mackie's paper 'A Refutation of Morals' on the ground that Mackie should not have claimed to refute morality. Since Robinson believes that nothing has the features that moral judgments ascribe to things, his reluctance to admit that he rejects morality is difficult to understand. Someone who believes that no moral judgment is true appears to reject morality.[3]

Robinson rejects this view of his position, on the ground that he does not reject the actions that morality favours. If morality tells us that we ought to keep promises or that consideration for other people is right, Robinson agrees to the extent that he favours promise-keeping and consideration for others, just as we normally do when we make the relevant moral judgments. But it does not follow that he accepts morality. For when we judge that these actions are right, we do not simply favour them; we also judge that they deserve to be favoured because of their rightness. Since Robinson agrees that this is the sense of moral judgments, he rejects them. Morality consists in more than simply favouring the actions that morality favours; we might favour these actions for non-moral reasons or for no reason. Moral reasons rest on the relevant moral facts. Since Robinson believes there are no such facts, he rejects morality.

He proposes none the less to continue to make moral judgments and to assent to judgments made by non-emotivists. He will therefore say things that he takes to be false or meaningless, in order to convey his favourable attitude towards the actions (etc.) that are said to be right or good. He has a reason to do this if he thinks his attitudes are more likely to be taken seriously if they are conveyed in moral terms. Other people will not recognize that he is simply conveying his attitudes; they will suppose that he favours things because he believes they are right. If everyone agreed with Robinson, and knew that everyone else agreed with him too, no one would gain this advantage from the use of moral judgments.

Robinson believes that moral judgments are false or meaningless because they assume that there are objective moral properties, when in fact there are none. But he does not say why he thinks there are no objective moral properties. Mackie presents a fuller case against morality, in his early paper and in the book published 30 years later. In his view, cognitivist and objectivist accounts of moral properties give the right account of the meaning of moral terms. But objectivism and common sense are mistaken because no real properties match the descriptions that are embodied in our moral judgments. Statements about witches or ghosts are factual statements; people once took them to describe facts about the objective world, but they were empirically mistaken. Similarly, believers in objective properties are victims of empirical error, not of conceptual confusion.[4]

---

[3] Paton points this out in his discussion of Robinson in 'Emotive'.

[4] See Mackie, 'Refutation', 81: 'Moral terms do mean objective qualities, and everyone who uses them does so because he believes in objective moral facts. But if the very terms of common speech may include errors and confusions within themselves, so that they cannot be used at all without falsity, if, we may add, philosophy may be permitted to enquire into these errors by observing a few facts for itself and founding inductive conclusions on them, the moral sceptic need not be so soon disheartened.'

Objectivism, however, does not rest on a simple empirical error that is straightforwardly corrigible by further empirical information. An example of a relatively simple error might be the belief that the sun is smaller than the earth and rotates around it. A more complex error is the tendency to suppose that features of our attitudes to the world are really features of the world itself. According to Hume, we tend to associate events so that we regard A as a sign that B will happen. As a result of this tendency, we believe in an objective connexion between A and B.[5] If we take an objective connexion to be necessary for causation, and we find there are no objective connexions, we will conclude that there are no causal relations either. Our belief in causal relations corresponds to a fact about us—our tendency to associate one event with another—but not to the objective fact that is necessary for causal relations.

We might rely on Hume's account of moral judgments to draw a similar conclusion (not Hume's) about the error involved in ordinary moral judgments.[6] We discover that moral judgments do not correspond to any moral properties 'in the object'; since our ordinary moral beliefs assume objective moral properties, we conclude that our ordinary beliefs are all false. They do not correspond to nothing; but since they correspond to facts about our sentiments, not to the objective facts that would make them true, they are all false. Here again we tend to treat something as objective that is really the product of our subjective view.[7]

Mackie offers two main arguments to show that an objectivist makes this mistake, and that therefore our ordinary beliefs are mistaken: the Argument from Relativity and the Argument from Queerness. It is useful to take them in reverse order.

1373. What Difference Does Objectivity Make?

If moral judgments were objectively true, they would describe things with moral properties. But, according to Mackie, no plausible scientific view of the world has any room for such properties; that is what makes them 'queer'. Hence we have a compelling reason to doubt their existence.

Mackie believes that real moral properties would be queer because they would have to be 'objectively prescriptive'.[8] A property F is objectively prescriptive for some agent A if and only if: (1) F is an objective property of some action x (i.e., 'F' does not refer to A's state of mind, as, e.g., 'pleasant' would); and (2) if A believes that some action x is F, then A has a motive to do x. A has the relevant motive not because A already desires something F, but simply because A believes that x is F.[9] This feature of moral properties makes them queer,

---

[5] "Tis a common observation, that the mind has a great propensity to spread itself on external objects, and to conjoin with them any internal impressions, which they occasion, and which always make their appearance at the same time that these objects discover themselves to the senses.' (Hume, *T* i 3.14) Blackburn appeals to this passage at *SW* 210. In contrast to Mackie, he takes Hume to be a projectivist.

[6] Mackie believes that his acceptance of an error theory follows Hume. See Hume, §§756–7.

[7] The comparison between values and secondary qualities is discussed by McDowell, 'Values', and by Dancy, 'Two conceptions'.

[8] In 'Refutation', Mackie does not give this reason for believing that moral properties are queer. He gives it in *E*.

[9] Sometimes Mackie speaks as though the mere existence of the property, irrespective of anyone's beliefs, were sufficient to motivate. But probably he does not intend this extreme form of queerness.

because we cannot understand how anything of the sort we recognize in a scientific view of the world could have this particular property of motivating us all by itself.

Mackie's argument requires him to show that (1) moral judgments are objective; (2) they are prescriptive; and (3) the combination of objectivity and prescriptivity makes them queer. His first two claims should not be understood as reports of explicit judgments. It does not matter, then, for his purposes whether or not we often say 'This is objectively right', or 'You ought to do this whether or not anyone thinks so'. He means that we implicitly treat our moral judgments as objectively correct, corresponding to objective moral facts, so that if there are no such facts, they are false.

To show that moral judgments are objective, Mackie distinguishes the relevant sort of objectivity from the objectivity that is relative to the choice of a standard.[10] If we want to appoint a qualified accountant, it is an objective fact that this candidate does or does not meet our standard, but Mackie denies that this sort of objectivity is sufficient for the objectivity of morality. To identify the relevant type of objectivity, he appeals, following Kant, to the categorical character of moral imperatives.[11] Whether or not we want the effects of justice, justice is still right and injustice wrong.

Mackie sees that the assertion that moral judgments claim objectivity needs some defence (20). Since he does not assert that we often use 'objective' and similar terms in our moral judgments, he needs some other argument to show that we implicitly claim objectivity. Hare disputes Mackie's assertion, on the ground that there is no real issue about whether there are objective moral properties. Hare considers a world in which people care about all the things they care about in the actual world, but the things they care about have no objective value. In his view, the moral 'states of affairs' in the world without objective value would be the same as those in the actual world. Hence, even if things in the actual world have objective value, it is irrelevant to the moral states of affairs (21).

Mackie compares Hare's view with Berkeley's view about external objects. Since people might have all the same experiences in a world without external objects as they have in the supposed world with them, it cannot make any difference, according to Berkeley, whether there are objects or not. Berkeley infers that there is no room for scepticism, because there is nothing more to the existence of objects than the existence of the relevant experiences. In Mackie's view, Berkeley does not refute scepticism, and does not show that sceptical questions cannot arise. For we believe we are talking about external objects and that we have the experiences we have because we are aware of these objects. Berkeley's view is incompatible with our conception of the world, not just with a philosophical interpretation of our conception. We do not regularly affirm the reality of external objects, but our understanding of our experiences and their causes would be different if we did not believe in external objects.

To show that Hare makes Berkeley's mistake, Mackie points out that Hare overlooks the effect of a belief in objective moral values. If there are objective values, our subjective concerns may be correct if they have the appropriate sort of support and origin. If we believe

---

[10] 'Something may be called good simply in so far as it satisfies or is such as to satisfy a certain desire; but the objectivity of such relations of satisfaction does not constitute in our sense an objective value.' (E 27)

[11] Williams, 'Fabric', 205–6, criticizes Mackie for appealing to Kant in support of the sort of objectivity that Mackie intends.

our concerns may have this sort of support in facts external to our concerns, we believe in objective values.[12] The actual wrongness of theft warrants my prescribing that one should not steal. If there are no objective values, nothing outside my prescriptions warrants my prescribing one thing rather than another. But in making judgments about physical objects we regard the features of the object itself as providing our criteria, independently of our choice or attitudes. In moral judgment, similarly, we count the rightness of the object as a feature that warrants a specific judgment.

Moreover, a belief in objectivity may influence not only our views about the basis of our concerns, but also the kinds of concerns that we form. Mackie notices that Hare ignores this possibility in his stipulation of two worlds in which people have the same concerns. Hare considers people's concerns at a time, but does not consider how their concerns might arise or develop. If we think we are guided by objective facts, we might expect our attitudes to develop and change in ways in which they would not develop if our concerns were purely subjective. We might reasonably be concerned, for instance, to find out the relevant facts, and to modify our later concerns in the light of what we think we have discovered. If we do not believe in objective facts, we lack these concerns about the ways in which our concerns might develop.

These are good reasons to believe that it matters whether we take moral properties and facts to be objective or not. We have a different reason for taking an action seriously if the action itself—not the way we react to it—is the basis for warranted moral judgments about it. Once we see what difference it makes whether we believe in objective values or not, we have a good reason to agree with Mackie's view that our moral judgments assume objective values; for our thought about the basis of our concern reflects belief in objective values. We assume that the features of an action itself in its circumstances make it right or wrong; what we think about it does not decide its rightness or wrongness.

The first part of Mackie's case against morality, therefore, is plausible. He shows that our moral judgments rely on the assumption of objective values. If there are no objective values, our judgments that actions are right or wrong are not true, because reality lacks the features that are needed to make our judgments true. This part of Mackie's argument is useful not only for his case against morality, but also for a case in favour of objectivism; it shows that a belief in objective values makes a difference to our other moral judgments.

The rest of his case against morality is also worth exploring in some detail. Even though Mackie states it quite briefly, he introduces arguments that also influence other people. A discussion of some of his arguments will give an idea of a case for moral nihilism.

1374. Are Moral Judgments Essentially Prescriptive?

According to Mackie, objective moral requirements are essentially prescriptive because they are intrinsically imperative and action-guiding (*E* 29). Non-naturalism about moral

---

[12] 'In the one [world] there is something that backs up and validates some of the subjective concern which people have for things, in the other there is not.' (22)

properties captures this essentially action-guiding feature of moral judgments.[13] A purely naturalist view leaves out the categorical character of moral requirements, because it makes requirements relative to choices and desires. But a purely non-cognitive view leaves out the objectivity of moral requirements.[14] Plato's conception of the Form of the Good includes both the objective and the prescriptive elements required by our ordinary conception of morality.[15]

Mackie's conception of prescriptivity combines two claims: (1) Moral judgments state categorical requirements, because the reasons that they express do not depend on an agent's antecedent desires or preferences.[16] (2) Moral judgments are essentially prescriptive in Hare's sense, because they entail imperatives and one cannot accept them without being motivated to act on them.[17] If we accept this second claim about prescriptivity, we are internalists about moral judgments and motivation.

Since Mackie claims support from Moore, he agrees with Hare that Moore's argument reveals the essential prescriptivity of moral judgments. Some naturalist analyses of 'good', 'ought', and related concepts try to define them wholly through non-normative concepts (concepts other than 'reason', 'rational', 'appropriate', etc.). These non-normative naturalist analyses leave out the fact that moral concepts are essentially reason-giving. If a non-normative naturalist analysis were correct, moral concepts would be only contingently reason-giving. This argument supports non-naturalism, if nothing normative can be natural. One might argue that this defence of non-naturalism supports Mackie's first claim about prescriptivity. But it does not support the second, unless we add internalism about motivation.[18]

If we see the difference between internalism about reasons and internalism about motivation, we may doubt the examples Mackie offers to show that belief in objective prescriptivity is well entrenched in the history of ethics. He mentions Plato's Forms and Clarke's relations of fitness as examples of such a belief. But they are plausible examples of internalism about reasons, not about motives.[19]

To see that Mackie combines different claims about objectivity, we may consider his treatment of Kant. To show that moral judgments are prescriptive in the first sense, by being categorical, Mackie relies on Kant's conception of categorical imperatives, on the assumption that Kant has grasped a genuine feature of moral requirements. A categorical

[13] 'No doubt it was an extravagance for Moore to say that "good" is the name of a non-natural quality, but it would not be so far wrong to say that in moral contexts it is used as if it were the name of a supposed non-natural quality, where the description "non-natural" leaves room for the peculiar evaluative, prescriptive, intrinsically action-guiding aspects of this supposed quality.' (E 31–2)

[14] 'In fact both naturalist and non-cognitive analyses leave out the apparent authority of ethics, the one by excluding the categorically imperative aspect, the other the claim to objective validity or truth.' (E 33)

[15] 'The Form of the Good is such that knowledge of it provides the knower with both a direction and an overriding motive; something's being good both tells the person who knows this to pursue it and makes him pursue it.' (E 40)

[16] 'A categorical imperative, then, would express a reason for acting which was unconditional in the sense of not being contingent upon any present desire of the agent to whose satisfaction the recommended action would contribute as a means . . .' (E 29)

[17] 'not purely descriptive, certainly not inert, but something that involves a call for action . . . and one that is absolute . . .' (E 33)

[18] Some of Mackie's (and other people's) assumptions about reasons and motives are appropriately questioned by Parfit, 'Normativity'.

[19] For discussion of Mackie's historical claims, see §745.

imperative rests on a reason that is independent of any desire of the agent that would be satisfied by acting on the imperative.[20] Mackie takes the denial of objectively prescriptive entities or truths to be the denial of categorical imperatives.[21]

These Kantian categorical imperatives, however, need not be prescriptive in Hare's sense. In Kant's use of the term, the moral law is an imperative only in an agent who has motives that actually or potentially oppose the law. A law is a principle about what is necessary or required; Kant does not suggest that its meaning is essentially prescriptive. Kant believes in categorical requirements and reasons; moral judgments give us reasons that do not depend on our having specific aims or desires antecedent to the acceptance of such reasons. Hypothetical requirements give reasons that depend on antecedent aims and desires, and so would cease to be reasons if we lacked the relevant aims and desires.

Mackie has good grounds for taking moral requirements to be categorical in this sense. We do not believe we can escape them by altering our desires. On the contrary, if we altered our desires in order to avoid caring about the aims of morality, we would be more, and not less, open to moral criticism. If we are indifferent to moral considerations, we ought to change so that we are no longer indifferent to them. This 'ought' does not depend on our having the relevant sorts of inclinations.

We have a short route from categorical requirements to prescriptivity if we believe that categorical requirements state objective reasons, and all reasons either are or include motives. In that case, a judgment gives us a reason only if it elicits a motive in us. Hare takes the connexion between moral judgments and reasons to imply the prescriptive character of moral judgments. From the second-person point of view, he claims that if I say you have a reason to do x, I am ordering you to do x.

But we need not accept these claims about the connexion between reasons, motives, and commands. We might reply that there are reasons for us to do x if it would be good or appropriate if we were to do x, whether or not we care about doing x. If this is the right conception of reasons, I might recognize that you have misguided desires and that you are not likely to listen to any advice, but I still might say that you have a reason to do x.

Perhaps prescriptivists about reasons are misled by the fact that statements about what you have reason to do often serve as advice. But this imperative character of moral judgments is a feature of how tokens of them are used in certain contexts, not a feature that belongs to them in their own right. If Mackie is to defend objective prescriptivity, he has to endorse some of Hare's questionable claims about prescriptive meaning, and their questionable implications about 'inverted commas' senses. We have no reason to agree that moral judgments are objectively prescriptive in Mackie's second sense. Knowing that x has a moral property may not motivate someone to act; the practical character of tokens of a judgment depends on other features of the agent and the audience.

---

[20] 'A categorical imperative, then, would express a reason for acting which was unconditional in the sense of not being contingent upon any present desire of the agent to whose satisfaction the recommended action would contribute as a means—or more directly. . . .' (Mackie, *E* 29)

[21] 'So far as ethics is concerned, my thesis that there are no objective values is specifically the denial that any such categorically imperative element is objectively valid. The objective values which I am denying would be action-directing absolutely, not contingently . . . upon the agent's desires and inclinations.' (29)

1375. What is Wrong with Objective Prescriptivity?

Our discussion of the different elements in Mackie's conception of objective prescriptivity may clarify his argument to show that objectively prescriptive facts and properties are unacceptably queer, because they do not fit into a plausible scientifically informed view of the world. To see what Mackie hopes to prove, it is useful to compare his view with Hare's.[22] Mackie argues: (1) Moral judgments are inherently prescriptive. (2) Moral judgments are about objective facts. (3) Hence, all acceptable moral judgments are objectively prescriptive. (4) But no judgments are objectively prescriptive. (5) Hence no moral judgment is true.

Mackie argues plausibly against Hare that (2) is part of the ordinary concept of morality, and that it supports an objectivist conceptual analysis of morality. He agrees with Hare, however, in accepting (1) and (4). His objection to morality rests on his argument to show that the conjunction of (1) and (2) does not fit any reasonable world-view. Hare does not offer this objection; instead he rejects (2) and infers that moral judgments are not factual statements. Though Mackie agrees with Hare on (4), he rejects Hare's account of it. In his view, it is logically possible for judgments to be objectively prescriptive. In saying that such judgments do not fit into any reasonable world-view, he takes himself to present an empirical objection. Hare, however, believes both that objectively prescriptive judgments are logically impossible, and that this is really Mackie's view.[23]

Hare's case is plausible, if we combine objectivity with the second element in Mackie's conception of prescriptivity. If a property F is both objective and prescriptive, it is true and knowable a priori that necessarily, anyone who believes x has F is inclined towards x. We might be in a position to know this a priori if we also knew further facts about the believer; but Mackie insists that objective prescriptivity is independent of any further facts.

In the face of a claim that something is objectively prescriptive in this sense, we might reply that we have been given too little to fix a necessary connexion that can be known a priori. On the contrary, we might reasonably claim to know a priori that nothing is objectively prescriptive in this sense.[24] But this reason for rejecting objectively prescriptive properties is not about queerness as Mackie understands it, since it is an a priori argument. If it were about queerness, it would be an empirical argument.

To show that his argument against objective prescriptivity is empirical, Mackie maintains that it is logically possible for moral properties to be objectively prescriptive, and that we know only empirically that this logically possible situation does not obtain. He suggests that the truth of theism would justify belief in objective prescriptivity. If God were the source of authoritative moral requirements, some moral judgments would be objectively prescriptive (E 48). If theism is contingently false and its falsity is known only empirically, the same is true of objective prescriptivity.

---

[22] Hare discusses Mackie in 'Ontology'.

[23] '. . . I think it incoherent to posit such properties (simply because the words, or the properties, would have to be descriptive and prescriptive at once, which nobody who understood these expressions could suppose them to be) . . .' (Hare, MT 85)

[24] This point does not endorse of Hare's attack on objective prescriptivity. One might defend internalism while rejecting scepticism and non-cognitivism. Wedgwood, NN, defends such a view.

We have already discussed Mackie's view of divine commands, and found reasons to deny that theism vindicates objective prescriptivity. Divine commands ensure neither categorical imperatives nor essentially motivating moral properties; nor, therefore, do they secure objectively prescriptive principles. If theistic ethics is logically possible, it does not follow that objectively prescriptive principles or properties, as Mackie conceives them, are logically possible.[25]

If Mackie does not show that it is only contingently false that no moral properties are objectively prescriptive, we have some reason to agree with Hare's claim that the real basis of Mackie's objection is a priori. He has a reasonable a priori objection to objective prescriptivity, if it is taken to include motivation. But it is not clear that this objection casts doubt on the existence of moral facts and properties, since Mackie has not shown that we conceive them as objectively prescriptive in the sense that he needs for his argument.

1376. Supervenience

Mackie's other criticism of objective prescriptivity applies to non-naturalist objectivism even without any claim about motivation. He questions the supervenience of objectively prescriptive properties on ordinary properties. The 'natural' fact that A deliberately causes extreme pain to B, an unwilling victim, purely for A's amusement does not entail, by any logical or semantic necessity, that A is doing anything wrong. But, according to the non-naturalist, the natural fact is evidence that what A is doing is wrong; indeed it constitutes the wrongness of A's action. The non-naturalist believes that the wrongness 'supervenes', despite the lack of logical or semantic necessity, on the natural properties. But Mackie doubts whether this relation between the ordinary properties of the action and its wrongness is intelligible within a plausible account of the world.[26] He believes that supervenience involves queerness, and that therefore we know empirically that moral properties do not supervene on natural properties. Hare, however, suggests that this argument is really a priori and conceptual, rather than empirical.[27]

Mackie's puzzle about supervenience is similar to Hume's puzzle about how anything 'in the object' can be the basis of the apparently new relation that is referred to by 'ought'. It seems to be no more intractable than Hume's problem. If we understand the principles that assert some connexion between rightness and the promotion of human interests, we can see why cruelty is wrong. The relevant principles include moral principles, if conceptual naturalism is mistaken and moral and evaluative concepts cannot be eliminated in favour of non-evaluative concepts. But we do not seem to rely on anything mysterious.

Perhaps Mackie denies this last claim because he agrees with Strawson's objection that non-naturalist objectivism does not allow an analytic connexion between the evidence, provided by the non-moral properties, and the conclusion, introducing the moral property.[28]

---

[25] Mackie on divine commands; §606.

[26] 'The wrongness must somehow be "consequential" or "supervenient"; it is wrong because it is a piece of deliberate cruelty. But just what *in the world* is signified by this "because"?' (*E* 41)

[27] Hare, *MT* 82–3.   [28] Strawson; §1279. See also Blackburn, §1363.

But Strawson's objection to non-naturalism rests on an a priori claim about evidence, not on an empirical objection. In this case also, then, we have some reason to agree with Hare's claim that Mackie really relies on a priori rather than empirical argument. The a priori argument seems to revive Strawson's arguments against intuitionism. Mackie does not seem to rely on queerness, as he understands it.

In any case, neither Strawson's argument nor Blackburn's revival of it refutes non-naturalist objectivism. If the failure of analytic connexions is a reason for doubt about non-natural properties, the doubt seems to spread to areas in which many non-sceptical philosophers reject it. The dispute between Chisholm and Lewis suggests that the difficulty raised for non-natural properties also arises for judgments about appearances and objects; for the relevant connexions are synthetic rather than analytic. Since Mackie is not a phenomenalist, he accepts Chisholm's claims about physical objects. Some concessions to realism about ordinary physical objects seem to be necessary for understanding empirical science.[29] To learn concepts of physical objects, we need to learn the relevant evidential connexions, even though the meanings cannot be wholly given through these connexions. Moral concepts do not seem to be different in principle; like concepts of physical objects, they cannot be learned through isolated definitions specifying their non-moral evidence.

1377. What is Wrong with Queerness?

Let us lay aside these doubts about whether Mackie's arguments against moral properties are as empirical as he takes them to be. Let us suppose that moral properties are not open to a priori objections, but none the less are not part of a scientific account of the world.[30] Does that matter?

What is a 'scientific' account of the world? If such an account can tell us what sorts of properties are acceptable, and what sorts are unacceptably queer, it should embrace all real objects, events, and properties. If, then, moral properties are part of the world, moral theory is part of science, and any account of the world that leaves out moral properties is incomplete. We cannot decide, therefore, whether we have found a scientific account of the world until we have decided whether moral properties are part of the world. In that case, the claim that a scientific account does not include moral properties cannot be used to show that there are no real moral properties; the argument needs to proceed in the reverse order.

Perhaps, then, the scientific point of view should be described more narrowly, so as to cover only the properties (objects, events, etc.) recognized by physical science (on the assumption that we know what this is). If physical science does not mention moral properties, perhaps that is what makes them queer. But physical science tells us the properties of physical reality,

---

[29] See E 39, partly quoted in §1281.

[30] Mackie does not speak explicitly of a scientific account of the world. He speaks of 'value features of quite a different order from anything else with which we are acquainted' (40). Instead of such features, 'How much simpler and more comprehensible the situation would be if we could replace the moral quality with some sort of subjective response which could be causally related to the detection of the natural features on which the supposed quality is said to be consequential' (41). If simplicity and comprehensibility were measured by uneducated, unscientific common sense, we would have to rule out many scientific theories as introducing queer entities. It would be more plausible to understand Mackie as measuring these things by the standards of scientific theory.

which is only a proper part of reality. Physical science does not mention the properties that interest economists, sociologists, and historians any more than it mentions moral properties. All these properties are queer, from the point of view of physical science, but this sort of queerness does not justify suspicion.

Does this defence of queer properties miss the point? Physical science, we might argue, tells us about the ultimate constitution of things and properties. Though it does not tell us directly how many properties there are, it tells us that all genuine properties have a physical basis or constitution. Economic cycles, wars, and social classes have a physical basis, and are therefore parts of reality, even though physics does not mention them. This thesis about the ultimately physical constitution of reality is sometimes called 'naturalism'.[31] Does it give us a useful test for deciding whether moral properties are unacceptably queer?

The demand for physical constitution might be applied in either of two ways: (1) Since we do not know the physical constitution of moral properties, we have good reason to doubt the reality of moral properties. (2) Since we have good reason to affirm the reality of moral properties, we have good reason to believe that they have a physical constitution, even if we do not know what it is. We will prefer the second argument if we are disposed to believe in the reality of moral properties. To undermine the second argument, we need to undermine belief in real moral properties. If it is difficult to see, then, how the appeal to physical constitution could be used to undermine this belief.

Do non-naturalist objectivists believe in queer properties? If physical science does not include any moral knowledge, the conceptual knowledge that grasps moral concepts goes beyond the conceptual knowledge we need for physical science. But this sort of queerness is neither objectionable nor the sort that Mackie probably has in mind. To disallow queer properties of this sort, we would have to claim that natural science (in the narrow sense just mentioned) already includes all the properties and concepts that we need for theory and practice; but we have no reason to believe this about natural science. Moreover, naturalism, understood as the claim that all real properties have a physical basis, allows non-naturalism, as Moore and Ross understand it. Though their accounts of natural properties are unsatisfactory, they do not imply that non-natural properties have no physical basis.

Mackie's claim that queer properties are open to suspicion does not mean simply that they are not included in empirical science. He believes that the world-view of physical science has no room for them and should dispose us to reject them. The property of being bewitched, for instance, requires us to allow causal inferences that we have good reason to reject. If moral properties were queer in this sense, we would have a reason to reject them. But a non-naturalist objectivist account of moral concepts and properties does not seem to involve this objectionable kind of queerness. It involves non-analytic evidential relations; but in that respect it demands no cognitive capacities that go beyond those we need to grasp concepts of physical objects.

We could establish a presumption against moral properties if we could show that they require (for instance) causal mechanisms of a sort that appear to be impossible in the light of what we know about causation. But the mere observation that physical theories do not

---

[31] See §1383.

explicitly mention moral properties, as such, does not support moral scepticism. No doubt these properties are different from those recognized by physical science; but many properties recognized by one science might appear queer from the perspective of another, and this need not be an objection to them.

1378. Objective Prescriptivity and Categorical Requirements

Some of Mackie's case to show that moral properties are queer assumes that they are 'objectively prescriptive' in the sense that implies internalism about moral judgments and motives or non-analytic supervenience of moral on non-moral properties. But he also rejects objective prescriptivity in the sense that implies categorical requirements independent of the agent's desires. Are these unacceptably queer?

He mentions categorical requirements in his discussion of Aristotelian eudaemonism, claiming that it equivocates between descriptive claims about what human beings aim at and evaluative claims about what they ought to aim at (E 47). In making these evaluative claims, it claims to present categorical requirements. Mackie suggests that his objections to objective prescriptivity refute any claims about categorical requirements.[32]

But if we accept categorical requirements as claims about reasons, and we understand reasons as external reasons, we need not accept internalism about moral judgments and motivation. Hence Mackie's previous attack on objective prescriptivity, understood as including internalism, does not affect the belief in categorical requirements. Against these requirements, he suggests that the variety of human aims and desires casts doubt on any claim about a single human good. Whatever we offer as objective reasons, he suggests, different people with different aims may not be interested in these reasons.

This appeal to variety of desires and aims suggests a sceptical argument against objective reasons. But the argument is open to question. For if reasons are independent of desires, the variety of desires may simply show that some people's desires mislead them about what they have reason to do. This is not simply a point about morality. If prudence as well as morality presents categorical imperatives, they answer Mackie's doubts. Though the step from objective reasons to objective moral reasons is still controversial, the variety of actual aims does not defeat objectivism.

1379. Relativity and Disagreement

Mackie's other argument against objectivism appeals to 'relativity', and specifically to variation and disagreement between moral views and moral outlooks. Though he attaches less importance to it than to the argument from queerness (E 38), it probably influences more people. Many who observe the variations of moral beliefs and practices between different cultures cannot see how any moral principles could describe objective facts about the world.

---

[32] 'But if it is claimed that something is objectively the right or proper goal of human life, then this is tantamount to the assertion of something that is objectively categorically imperative, and comes fairly within the scope of our previous arguments.' (E 47)

If moral disagreement is to cast reasonable doubt on the objectivity of moral judgments, we should not be able to explain it in the ways we might explain disagreements about scientific judgments.[33] In Mackie's view, the distinctive feature of moral disagreement is its apparent causal origin. In the case of scientific disagreements, it is plausible to assume that there is some objective matter of fact that people are disagreeing about. In the case of moral disagreement, Mackie suggests, it is not plausible to assume this; moral disagreements reflect preferences for alternative ways of life.[34]

This argument rests on the assumption that no disagreement reflecting adherence to different ways of life is about a matter of fact. But the assumption is false. Supporters of the Nazi regime developed theories of race in support of racist policies. They probably could not have been convinced that they were wrong. People who deny any causal link between smoking and lung cancer may be difficult to convince that they are wrong. Their resistance to evidence and argument may result from their preference for smoking, or from their attachment to the industry that depends on people's desire to smoke. But they hold false beliefs on a matter of fact. The fact that their beliefs reflect their extra-scientific preferences does not persuade us that there is no question with an objectively correct answer. We have reasonable beliefs about the objective facts, and we can explain why these people's dissent does not cast reasonable doubt on our beliefs. We might say that people have some bias or vested interest or prejudice in favour of one answer that leads them to resist the weight of evidence and argument.

Why should we not explain disagreements about ethics in the same way? The same prejudices and vested interests support the strange biological theories and the strange ethical views of the Nazis. The causal origin of their biological views does not persuade us that they were not wrong about the objective facts. So why should the causal origin of their ethical views persuade us of this?

We would be wrong to dismiss the Nazis in this way if we were not entitled to rely confidently on the moral judgments that they rejected. But the particular beliefs that the Nazis rejected seem to be quite reliable; in the light of these apparently reliable beliefs, we can explain why the Nazis made the errors they made. This is how we might explain the errors made by biologists supporting Nazi theories about race. The error that we attribute in the moral case does not seem to be basically different from the sort we attribute in the scientific case; and so we might question the disanalogy suggested by Mackie. He would have a strong case for the disanalogy if we were already convinced that moral judgments are not about objective facts. But since the argument from disagreement should persuade us into that conviction, and should not presuppose it, it does not help him.

The comparison between scientific agreement and moral disagreement raises a more general question about what constitutes a fair comparison between scientific and ethical judgments.[35] Mackie's argument is most plausible if we compare well-entrenched scientific

---

[33] On this point see further Gewirth, 'Positive'. For the contrast between positive and normative cf. and contrast Keynes, quoted in §1297.

[34] '. . . scientific disagreement results from speculative inferences or explanatory hypotheses based on inadequate evidence, and it is hardly plausible to interpret moral disagreement in the same way. Disagreement about moral codes seems to reflect people's adherence to and participation in different ways of life. The causal connexion seems to be basically that way round . . .' (Mackie, E 36)

[35] This argument is derived from Gewirth, 'Positive', 325.

or common-sense beliefs about the physical world with areas of moral controversy. But a fair comparison ought to compare the well-entrenched with the well-entrenched, and the controversial with the controversial. Such a comparison should show whether moral and scientific beliefs differ on the point that Mackie mentions.

We might suppose that this objection is beside the point, because there are no well-entrenched moral beliefs. Are they are not all essentially controversial, because we can always find some society or group or individual to controvert them?[36] But this reply to the objection involves a further unfair comparison, resting on a 'normative' attitude to science and a 'positive' attitude to ethics. If we say that there can be insoluble 'ethical' disagreement over fundamentals, we take a positive attitude, since we count as 'ethical' anything that might constitute the morality of a society or a person. This is why the anthropological examples, examples derived from the Nazis, and so on, seem relevant. But if we consider 'scientific' agreement and disagreement, we take a normative attitude. We tend not to consider everyone's beliefs about the world. If we think some views—astrology, parapsychology, pre-Copernican astronomy, for instance—are not to be taken seriously now, we do not take them to mark significant disagreements. Unless we are sceptics about scientific knowledge, we take the normative attitude to scientific disagreement.

Why, then, should we not also take a normative attitude to moral disagreement? If we do, we need to identify judgments that are properly regarded as basic and reliable, so that we can rule out moral views that conflict with them. One basic principle might be this: The interests of every person affected by an action count for something in determining whether the action should be done. This principle does not say how much people's interests should count, but it rules out moral views that say the interests of some people affected count for nothing. Not everyone has always followed this principle, just as not everyone has always followed basic norms of scientific practice. But it is widely accepted; views that ignore it have tended to be rejected; we would not seriously consider moral views that explicitly rejected it. Why is this not a normative constraint on the ethical theories that deserve to be taken seriously?

This appeal to normative constraints counters the claim that the history of ethics lacks the progress and convergence typical of the history of scientific inquiry. Disagreement with any ethical position is always possible, but it may not always be reasonable. If we take convergence in science to support the view that theories are talking about some objective reality, we can say the same about ethics. We try to decide, for instance, how much the interests of different people should count, and which actions are required by the appropriate degree of consideration for their interests. The difficulty of this task does not undermine the view that when we formulate moral theories and try to apply them in practice, we discover or approach some objective truth.

Our estimate of the degree of convergence and progress to be found in the history of ethics should consider not only the history of moral institutions and practices in different societies, but also the development of moral theory. Variation in moral practice does not necessarily prove variation in moral beliefs. For different external conditions may warrant

---

[36] For instance, Toulmin, *EPRE* 165n, remarks: 'I recall a conversation with Bertrand Russell in which he remarked, as an objection to the present account of ethics, that it would not have convinced Hitler'.

different practices, characters, and training.[37] Moreover, members of different societies are sometimes conscious of compromising, or adapting, or violating, their moral views in order to cope with their circumstances. Practice does not give unequivocal evidence for moral outlooks.

The history of moral theory can also help us to identify the extent of convergence or disagreement. We have found, for instance, that the grounds for supposing that the concerns of ancient and mediaeval moralists are alien to our own, or to those of modern moralists, are quite weak. On some issues, the views of 'pre-modern' moralists correct those of some modern moralists. If we examine the arguments and assumptions underlying different moral theories, we see that the area of disagreement is much smaller than it might appear if we took expressed disagreements at face value. If, for instance, we compare the defensible statements of Aristotle's, Kant's, and Hegel's positions with their own statements of them, we find that they disagree much less than their own statements of their views might suggest. Intelligent exegesis, sympathetic understanding, and rational criticism influence one another, and an accurate critical history may support a particular view of the nature of morality and moral judgment.[38]

If this is true, the anti-objectivist argument that rests on the failure of convergence in ethics is open to question. If we compare ethical progress fairly with scientific progress, the variation and disagreement displayed by moral beliefs do not seem sharply different from what we ought to expect if true moral judgments describe objective facts. Moreover, the study of ethics may reveal to us an extent of agreement that we would not otherwise have expected.

1380. A Place for Morality Without Objectivity

The failure of Mackie's arguments does not vindicate objectivism. He might still be able to show that no plausible account of the character of objective moral facts is available, and that the only justified beliefs underlying our moral judgments are beliefs about something other than objective facts. He tries to show this by arguing that our use of moral judgments does not rely on any justified beliefs about objective moral facts.

Mackie describes himself as a moral 'sceptic', because he does not affirm objective values. His argument, however, presents a case for rejecting objective values, not merely for suspending judgment about them. Hence he seems to be a moral nihilist who holds that nothing satisfies our moral concepts. But he does not advocate either the abandonment of morality or indifference to it. He describes his position as a 'second-order' view, about

---

[37] Some of these sources of variation are discussed sensibly by Lecky, *HEM* i 92–110. In his view, '. . . in every age virtue has consisted in the cultivation of the same feelings, though the standards of excellence attained have been different' (109).

[38] This point may be offered as an illustration of one of Gadamer's claims about interpretation: '. . . application is neither a subsequent nor a merely occasional part of the phenomenon of understanding, but co-determines it as a whole from the beginning . . . the interpreter seeks no more than to understand . . . what this piece of tradition says, what constitutes the meaning and importance of the text. In order to understand that, he must not want to disregard himself and his particular hermeneutical situation. He must relate the text to this situation, if he wants to understand it at all.' (*TM* 289 = *WM* 307)

morality, not a 'first-order' view that takes a particular position on moral questions.[39] His rejection of objective values implies that it is not wrong to commit murder, but he neither advocates nor permits murder. Second-order scepticism does not dictate a particular first-order moral outlook.

Moral nihilists leave themselves room for first-order moral commitment. Moreover, they ought (in Mackie's view) to commit themselves to morality, and they ought to observe its requirements. For although no moral judgments are true, we do something useful by making them and acting on them.[40] Morality, as normally conceived, secures the sorts of benefits for us that Hobbes and Hume recognize; it secures the means of 'peaceful and commodious living' for people with limited sympathies who can form conventions and agreements. Morality has an 'object' or a 'point' (E 107) that we care about, and it tends to achieves this point. We have good reason, therefore, given what we care about, to practise and to advocate morality. Hobbesian and Humean explanations of morality give us hypothetical imperatives; it is worth behaving justly, keeping promises, and so on, if and only if we share the goals that make morality worthwhile for us. But since neither the acceptance nor the rejection of these goals is right or wrong, the actions, and practices that promote them are not right or wrong either. If they were right or wrong, they would rest on categorical requirements.

We might wonder why the success of morality in achieving goals that we accept is a reason for making moral judgments that are not true. An alternative would be to affirm the hypothetical imperatives that we can defend in the light of Hobbesian or Humean goals. Perhaps Mackie could reply that 'enlightened' hypothetical imperatives are less useful for achieving Hobbesian and Humean goals than 'unenlightened' moral judgments would be. If we pretend that our principles are categorical requirements and therefore non-optional, we may encourage observance of them by people who do not, or do not always, share our goals. Perhaps, then, we should retain moral judgments because they are useful, even though they are not true.

We might defend this attitude to morality by recalling Mackie's arguments against Hare to show that there is a real issue about objective values and that our ordinary moral judgments presuppose objectivity. The fact that we take moral judgments to have objective grounds gives them a force and importance that they would not have otherwise. The implications of objectivity give Mackie a reason to retain moral judgments and to advocate their retention. The very fact that they say more than he thinks we are entitled to say may make them more effective means to the ends that give morality its point. Hume's analysis of causation offers a parallel. Hume thinks one essential element in causation is objective necessary connexion, and he believes there is no such thing. But he does not recommend that we give up speaking of objective causation.[41] Similarly, Mackie thinks moral judgments involve

---

[39] '... what I am discussing is a second order view, a view about the status of moral values and the nature of moral valuing, about where and how they fit into the world. These first and second order views are not merely distinct but completely independent: one could be a second order moral sceptic without being a first order one, or again the other way round.' (Mackie, E 16)

[40] It is not clear whether Mackie believes that moral judgments are all false (because they rest on the implicit belief in objective values), or that they lack truth value (because they rest on a false presupposition that is needed for them to be either true or false). In either case, he is not merely sceptical about them.

[41] Hume on scepticism and causation; §722.

an illegitimate objectification of our subjective concerns, but he does not recommend that we replace moral judgments with ones that reveal their purely subjective basis more transparently.

But under what circumstances is it useful to retain moral judgments, once we recognize that they lack the basis that would make them true? We need to consider (1) the case in which the agents who act on the moral judgments have not recognized that they are false, and (2) the case in which they have recognized this.

In the first case, we might suppose that moral nihilists behave as though moral judgments were true, allow other people to persist in their belief in the objective basis of morality, and, if they can, encourage this belief. When Plato introduces the myth of the metals into the ideal state, he intends the people who are guided by it to believe it is true.[42] If this is the role that Mackie intends for moral judgments, he advocates 'esoteric' moral philosophy, for the reasons envisaged by Sidgwick. He tries to convince moral philosophers that moral judgments are not true, but he also ought to warn them not to tell anyone else.[43]

The second case, however, is more difficult. If we all believe that no moral judgments are true, what do we gain from using them? It might be better to get used to Hobbesian and Humean hypothetical imperatives than to risk confusing ourselves by making moral judgments. Those who follow moral judgments more often than they would follow hypothetical imperatives are those who do not recall that moral judgments are not true. If we keep in mind that they are not true, we may even be less likely to observe them than we would be if we looked at them as hypothetical imperatives. If people believe that moral principles, understood as categorical requirements, are not true, we may be better off if they are taught to share the goals that the hypothetical imperatives advance than if they are encouraged to follow moral principles that they take not to be true.

But perhaps this is not a decisive argument against the retention of morality by people who recognize that it is not true. We might treat it as a myth that is useful even though we do not believe it. Perhaps some tendencies to racism would be reduced if we spoke as though all human beings were descended from a single Asian couple called Adam and Eve and so all constituted one extended family, even though we did not believe this story. Moral judgments might do something similar for us; with appropriate training we might act as though they were true, even though we do not believe them, because we have been trained to suspend disbelief.

It is difficult to be sure, however, how useful moral judgments would be in these circumstances. It might be dangerous to suggest that the rejection of racism rests on some myth that no one believes; someone who reminds us that the myth is not true may persuade us that racism is all right. Similarly, someone who reminds us that the myth of morality is not true may easily persuade us that we have been deceived in taking morality seriously.

But whether Mackie intends the 'esoteric' or the 'mythical' account of moral judgments and moral theory, he seems to advocate revision of attitudes to morality. We do not normally believe that morality is a myth, or that its mythical status should be recognized by

---

[42] See Plato, *Rep.* 414b–415d.   [43] Sidgwick on esoteric morality; §1179.

some and concealed from others. It is surprising, then, that Mackie does not suggest that the conclusions of his philosophical arguments are especially dangerous to moral practice. His arguments seems to require us to choose between an esoteric and a mythical account of moral judgments. These two accounts have different practical implications, which are different from the practical implications of objectivism. An esoteric or a mythical view of moral judgments would explain why we might disbelieve all moral judgments without abandoning them. But, whichever of these views explains our retention of morality without objectivity, the meta-ethical argument about objectivity seems to require some revision of our attitude to actual moral judgments.[44]

This conclusion suggests that the division between 'first-order' and 'second-order' inquiries is not very helpful in this case, and that it does not support Mackie's main point. We can mark a simple division by saying that in second-order inquiry into morality we do not assert anything of the form 'F is wrong', but confine ourselves to assertions such as 'The judgment "F is wrong" is a statement (prescription, objectively true, etc.)'. The first-order judgments are those that are mentioned, but not asserted, in the second-order inquiries. This simple division, however, does not divide moral judgments from judgments about morality in the way that Mackie intends. The judgments 'Murder is wrong even if no one thinks so' and 'What you did was wrong, because society disapproved of it' are first-order judgments, according to the simple division, but they are judgments about the metaphysical ground of moral rightness and wrongness. A meta-ethical inquiry may affect our estimate of such first-order judgments.

We might, then, declare that these are second-order judgments simply because they have metaphysical implications, so that we make it trivially true that metaphysical inquiry does not affect first-order judgments. But this is not the position that Mackie defends. His division is meant to support his view that ordinary moral thought and action is logically independent of inquiry into the objectivity of values. But study of his argument shows us that his view is open to question.

1381. How Should We Replace Morality?

If we agree with Mackie's rejection of morality, but we are not convinced by his reasons for retaining moral judgments, under a fictional or an esoteric interpretation, we might consider the replacement of moral judgments with 'post-moral' judgments that do some of the same work. In that case, we no longer represent practical judgments as stating categorical requirements. If we accept Mackie's view of the useful practice that might replace morality, the relevant judgments will state hypothetical imperatives.

These judgments will not be objectively prescriptive, and so will not be internally connected with motivation. They will contribute to motivation for people who accept the ends that we promote if we act on our post-moral judgments. This is quite similar to the position that we might ascribe to Hobbes and to Hume if, despite their professions, we take them to offer a replacement for morality. They have different views about what the relevant

---

[44] See Sturgeon, 'What difference', n.8 on Mackie.

ends and the relevant hypothetical imperatives are, but they take the same view about the status of post-moral judgments. Our account of these judgments will be straightforwardly cognitivist and factual.

An alternative process of replacement might follow Robinson's suggestion that we retain the emotive element in moral judgment (as he believes) and abandon the descriptive element. We might adapt Blackburn's quasi-realist projectivism for this purpose, but instead of treating it as an account of moral judgment, we might treat it as a replacement. We might regard Blackburn's quasi-realist interpretations as indicating the sense that ought to be attached to post-moral judgments by speakers who have rejected the realist assumptions underlying moral judgments.

What reasons might be given for preferring the replacement of morality by post-moral expressions of attitude (as the revision of Blackburn's position would require) over the use of post-moral factual judgments (as the revision of Mackie would require)? Post-moral factual judgments might be preferred on the ground that they overlap significantly with moral judgments. Even if moral judgments do not state categorical requirements, post-moral judgments may state hypothetical imperatives directed to ends that most people share. In that case, we will be right to believe that post-moral judgments state objective facts closely connected to the facts that moral judgments were supposed to state. If, however, we try to replace moral judgments with post-moral expressions of attitude, we do not display the connexion between morality and the post-moral system directed to Hobbesian and Humean ends.

If we replace morality with post-moral factual judgments, we abandon any internal connexion between moral judgment and motivation. Post-moral expressions of attitude retain this internal connexion. But if we believe (contrary to Mackie and to Blackburn) that externalism is the right account of moral judgments, we will not suppose that the truth of internalism about post-moral judgments is a point in their favour. We do not need internalism to make the connexion between moral judgment and motivation intelligible. If the ends promoted by post-moral hypothetical imperatives are widely shared, post-moral judgments will tend to be connected with motivation and action.

If, then, we are convinced by nihilist argument against morality, we have good reason to prefer Hobbesian post-morality to an expressivist alternative. We might even infer, as Hobbes does, that post-morality is really morality, and that Mackie's claim to have refuted morality is mistaken. But Mackie has good reasons for rejecting this inference. Though he has insufficient reasons for taking moral judgments to be objectively prescriptive in his sense, he has good reasons for taking them to present categorical requirements, and hence he has good reason to present his eventual position as a substitute for morality rather than morality itself.

We should not, however, accept Mackie's argument against morality. His grounds for rejecting the possibility of categorical moral requirements are weak. His reasons for believing that internalism must be true of moral judgments rest on a failure to distinguish motives from reasons. Once we see the weaknesses in his case against morality, we need not embrace his nihilist conclusion. If morality does not need to be replaced, it is not so urgent to decide what should replace it.

1382. Are Moral Concepts Natural?

If the different arguments for non-cognitivism and against objectivism are open to question, some form of objectivism may appear attractive. But what form is most plausible? Doubts about objectivism arise if each of the apparent options is unappealing. Moore's Open Question Argument casts doubt on naturalism; but non-naturalist objectivism raises metaphysical and epistemological doubts. Which of these doubts should we try to remove if we are inclined towards objectivist cognitivism? Some of the questions that arise about Moore suggest more plausible versions of objectivism.

His question whether Good is a natural property is ambiguous on some relevant points. Is he speaking of the concept 'good' or the property of goodness? And what does he mean by 'natural'? We might use 'property' so that properties match concepts, meanings, and nominal definitions, or we might use it so that properties match real definitions, but may not match nominal definitions. Ross approximately captures this distinction in speaking of the property of goodness itself (found by a nominal definition of 'good') versus the good-making property (not revealed by a nominal definition of 'good').[45] Since Moore often professes a lack of interest in the use of words, we might suppose he is asking about a real definition of goodness. But his arguments usually seem to be about the concept of goodness and the meaning of 'good'.

Moore's arguments suggest that utilitarians ought not to offer a utilitarian account of the concept of moral rightness.[46] For they have intelligent disputes with non-utilitarians about whether rightness is what maximizes utility; the parties to the dispute argue about the same thing and rely on the same initial beliefs about it. Their dispute is not about the analysis of a concept or the meaning of a term. That is why utilitarian normative arguments should not confine themselves to what competent users of the term understand, or to the logical consequences of what they understand. They take the concept and the meaning as an agreed starting point. Utilitarians and non-utilitarians share the same concept of rightness and mean the same thing by 'right'. In Ross's terms, they agree about the property of rightness, but they disagree about the right-making characteristic.

We might support this description of the dispute by a comparison with scientific discoveries. When we discover the specific gravity of gold, we can claim to have discovered its real essence. But we have not formed a new concept of gold; nor do we use the word with a new meaning. The concept and meaning are given by the 'nominal essence'. If two theories disagree about the nature of heat or light, they use the terms with the same meaning.[47] These analogies suggest that a utilitarian or Kantian theory should begin from a concept of rightness that allows a starting point for the defence of the theory.

Moore is right, then, to reject conceptual utilitarianism about of goodness. Contrary to Moore (in *Principia*), the same can be said about a utilitarian account of the concept of rightness. But if we reject these suggested accounts of the concept, should we go further

---

[45] Ross on properties and definitions; §1282.
[46] This is not Moore's view, given his conceptual utilitarian account of rightness. See §1268.
[47] This account of change in theory and change in meaning is over-simplified. But plausible modifications or complications would still secure the point that discoveries about the property are different from discoveries about the concept or meaning (as Moore conceives it). Some of the issues are discussed by Field, 'Theory change', esp. 477.

with Moore and agree that 'good' is not a concept of a natural property at all? An answer to this question is difficult to find, given Moore's hopelessly obscure conception of a natural property. But if we suppose that natural concepts are those that are definable without any normative terms, we might reasonably decide that 'good' is not a natural concept. We will simply mean that 'good', 'ought', 'right', 'appropriate', and so on, are definable in terms of one another.

If we say this, we may still accept Moore's claim that 'good' is simple and indefinable, in one sense that he intends. Since he regards definition as analysis into simpler elements, he believes that 'good' is indefinable. He is right to claim that we cannot find any simpler concepts that provide a complete analysis of moral concepts. But 'good' may not be altogether indefinable. Failure of analysis does not mean that the concept must simply be grasped by intuition, or that it is indescribable or inexplicable.

It seems arbitrary of Moore, therefore, to insist that the only definitions are those that meet his conditions for an analysis into simpler terms. If Moore's criteria make moral concepts indefinable, we should infer not that they are indefinable, but that Moore's criteria are mistaken. Without resort to Moore's Open Question Argument, we might reasonably infer that 'good' and other moral concepts are definable, but non-natural.

So far we have not questioned the assumption that an account of a concept 'F' should provide necessary and sufficient conditions for being F, and that one grasps the concept by grasping these necessary and sufficient conditions. But such conditions do not seem to be needed for different people to share the concept of F or to use 'F' with the same meaning. If we consider historical developments leading to discoveries, or we consider disputes between contemporaries, we find that they need to share some beliefs about F, to agree about some examples of F, to assign a similar explanatory role to Fs, and so on. But though their beliefs may need to overlap in some of these ways, they may have the same concept even if they do not share any definite subset of beliefs.

We might, then, come closer to Moore's position if we deny that a correct account of 'good' or another moral concept provides necessary and sufficient conditions, and conclude that—in this sense—the concept is indefinable. But this conclusion may not show anything about moral concepts in particular. If many concepts elude definition through necessary and sufficient conditions, this sort of indefinability is not peculiar to moral concepts. Nor does it imply simplicity or inexplicability.

1383. Are Moral Properties Natural?

We have reason, then, to agree with some of Moore's conclusions, though not with all of his arguments for them. But these conclusions do not fix the character of moral properties. A scientific theory may tell us the nature of heat or the real essence of gold. In telling us this, it describes a property that is distinct from the nominal essence of 'gold'. We might grasp the nominal essence without knowing what gold really is. The same may be true of moral properties.

Moore rightly distinguishes questions about the property of goodness from questions about what things are good. He sees that discovery of the extension of 'F' is not the same as discovery of the nature of F-ness. Properties are non-extensional; for the property provides the explanation of the characteristics that belong to members of the class, and so allows us to make claims about counterfactual conditions. If, for instance, the same physical condition that we have discovered in measles occurred without the normal symptoms, it would still be measles, and if the normal symptoms occurred without the same underlying physical condition, the condition underlying them would not be measles. But our grasp of the property that people suffering from measles have in common is different from our grasp of the concept of measles.

Moore assumes without good reason that discovery of the real character of a property is discovery of a nominal definition; if he did not assume this, his Open Question Argument would be irrelevant to proposed definitions. He assumes that if we are looking for something not purely extensional that is common to all genuine Fs, we must be looking for the concept of F.

If, however, we take properties to be explanatory, we may reasonably interpret the utilitarian theory as an attempt to describe the property of rightness, rather than the concept of rightness. It is irrelevant to object that this theory does not tell us what we usually mean when we say an action is right. But it is relevant to object that it does not explain what makes right actions right. Even if all or most of the actions we initially judge to be right tend to maximize utility, this tendency may not be their right-making property.

If inquiry into concepts is different from inquiry into properties, we can still ask whether moral properties are natural, even if moral concepts are non-natural. If our grasp of moral concepts does not tell us whether the corresponding properties—if there are any—are natural, moral concepts are not concepts of natural properties, and to that extent Moore is right. But moral properties may still be natural properties.

To decide whether they are natural properties, we have to resolve some of Moore's obscurity about what counts as natural. If (as he sometimes suggests) natural properties are those that are recognized by a natural science, we need to know what natural sciences there are. If the only natural sciences were physics, chemistry, and biology, economics and psychology would not deal with natural properties. But if social and behavioural sciences, including history, are natural sciences, any discipline that gives us knowledge of objective features of the world seems to be a natural science.[48] If, then, moral theory gives us knowledge of objective moral facts, it seems to be a natural science. In that case, naturalism follows from belief in objective moral properties.

This conclusion conflicts with the views of Moore and Ross; for they believe both that moral theory gives us knowledge of objective moral facts and that moral facts are not the subject-matter of any natural science. But the sense of their belief remains obscure, given their obscurity about natural science. If they simply mean that moral facts are not the subject-matter of physics, their non-naturalism is correct, but not distinctive of ethics. If they have a broader conception of a natural science, they do not say why it is not broad enough to include moral theory.

Perhaps they do not take this possibility seriously because they assume that the method of natural science is empirical, and the method of moral theory is a priori. But a clear

---

[48] Ethics v. natural science; §1263.

formulation of this division of methods is no easier to find than a clear account of a natural science; and it is not clear that any accurate and plausible account of 'empirical' and 'a priori' methods will exclude ethics from natural science.

Sometimes Moore seems to mean that moral properties are non-natural because they are not descriptive; perhaps he means by this that they are not purely descriptive, but also normative. But this division does not fit his view that natural properties are those recognized by a natural science; for some natural sciences appear to recognize normative properties. Medicine, social psychology, sociology, and history are natural sciences (according to the broader conception), but they recognize normative properties; hence the fact that moral properties are normative does not show that they are not natural.

Let us, then discard Moore's claims about natural properties and natural science, and assume that natural properties are simply defined as those that are non-normative, so that it is not essential to them that they give reasons or present what we ought to do.[49] Even so, the fact that moral concepts are non-natural does not show that moral properties could not be natural. If hedonistic or preferential utilitarianism were correct, and if one assumed that an action's giving pleasure is not essentially normative, one might argue that moral properties are not essentially normative. If utility can be understood in purely psychological terms, we may say that rightness—the right-making property—is a natural property, because it is a property recognized by non-normative psychology. Moore rejects this naturalist claim about goodness.

The best argument for Moore's conclusion is not Moore's argument. The explanatory property that right actions have in common should appear to us on reflexion to be the property that needs to stay the same or to change in actions that remain right or change from being right to being wrong. This is the sort of property that Cudworth looks for when he argues against Hobbes's account of moral properties.[50] Ross offers a similar argument against utilitarianism.[51]

If naturalism, in the narrow sense just mentioned, were right, it would offer a vindicating reduction of moral properties to non-moral properties. But this reductive ambition may be as unrealistic as some other reductive ambitions that have been widely abandoned. Biology may not be reducible to physics, or psychology to physiology, or sociology to individual psychology. But irreducibility does not imply that moral properties are mysterious or open to justified suspicion, still less that they are simple and unanalysable. And so, even if we discover that naturalism, in the narrow sense, fails when it is applied to properties as well as to concepts, we need not revert to Moore's conception of the nature of moral properties.

If this is right, we can accept some of Moore's arguments about naturalism. We may even agree that moral properties are simple and unanalysable, in his restrictive sense; but we will not infer that they are indefinable, according to more appropriate criteria for definability. Nor need we accept the most extreme version of intuitionism that Moore and Ross maintain. Non-naturalism requires us to accept the position that Strawson calls 'intuitionism', in so far as it requires us to deny that connexions between non-moral evidence and moral conclusions are analytic. But this denial of analytic connexions is not a legitimate ground for suspicion. It

---

[49] See Frankena, §1270. [50] Cudworth on immutability; §§547–9. [51] Ross and utilitarianism; §1287.

does not commit us to a strongly foundationalist epistemology that would be open to cogent objections. Moore's and Ross's version of intuitionism is not the only form of objectivism that does justice to Moore's arguments. If we allow other forms of objectivism to be live possibilities, we will not take doubts about extreme intuitionism to be a good reason to accept non-cognitivism. And so we ought not to agree with the non-cognitivist view that Moore's arguments have undermined objectivism.

1384. Varieties of Objectivism

Different versions of objectivism reflect different strategies of defence; for objectivists disagree on questions about how much they ought to concede to their opponents about the character of any possible moral knowledge of objective facts. We need some idea of the appropriate dialectical context.

Where should the burden of proof lie? Should the anti-objectivist be expected to refute objectivism, and should we take the failure of anti-objectivist arguments to support object-ivism? We might argue that the failure of anti-objectivism simply shows that objectivists can account for facts about prescriptivity, facts and values, descriptive meaning, disagreement, and so on. This might not seem a good reason to accept objectivism. We have a better reason if we can also show that objectivism accounts for these features of moral judgment better than subjectivist and non-cognitivist theories account for them. This is why it is worth discussing non-cognitivist attempts to capture the different features of moral judgment without taking its apparently cognitive and objective character at face value.

Opponents of objectivism usually agree that in rejecting an objectivist account of moral properties and facts they reject the tendency of common sense. A non-cognitivist claims that the appearance of objectivism is a misleading feature of moral language, but that we do not really believe in objective moral facts. A nihilist supposes that objectivist convictions are false beliefs presupposed by common-sense views of morality.[52]

In both cases, the opponents of objectivism accept the burden of proof, since they concede that objectivism is closer to common sense. Much of our practice of moral argument and moral discovery assumes that what is morally right and wrong is independent of our tastes, preferences, and ways of life. Despite the advice of anti-objectivist moralists and (especially) social scientists, we think about morality in these ways, and we have no reason to suppose we ought to follow their advice. Objectivists may reasonably seek to expound the objectivism implicit (as Mackie argues) in common sense and to defend it against attacks.

What sort of defence is needed, and what sorts of attacks need answers? Many critics of the objectivity of morality characteristically compare morality with some recognized source of objective truths, typically a physical science.[53] They object to morality on two main

---

[52] See §1373 on the dispute between Hare and Mackie.

[53] This sort of comparison is clear in Mackie, and in Williams's discussion of the 'absolute' conception. See §1349; *ELP*, ch. 8. One might suppose that Nietzsche's argument is different, since it explores the psychological roots of morality without any explicit comparison with genuine sciences or with an ideal of objectivity (which Nietzsche questions in any case). But the difference may not be so great. For Nietzsche suggests that the subjective origins of morality undermine the claim of moral judgments to truth and objectivity. If morality has the sources that Nietzsche mentions, but this fact does not undermine claims to truth and objectivity, he does not discredit morality. See §§1102–3.

points: (1) Morality cannot meet the standards of progress and rational convergence that apply to a scientific discipline. (2) The facts and properties recognized by morality do not fit into the account of the world developed by scientific disciplines. These two objections correspond to Mackie's arguments from relativity and from queerness.

Defenders of moral objectivity might accept the challenge offered by the critics; we might call this position 'moderate' objectivism. Alternatively they might dispute the terms in which the challenge is expressed, and argue that the standards for objectivity need to be modified when morality is considered; we might call this 'radical' objectivism.[54]

The radical strategy argues that the physical sciences do not provide the relevant standard of objectivity, and that it is premature to assume that every discipline claiming objective truth must be readily integrated with the existing body of scientific theory. If the moral point of view requires us to recognize properties that do not seem to be constituted by any properties recognized by other scientific disciplines, and if moral properties are accessible and detectable only to those who already accept some moral judgments, that is not necessarily a reason for suspicion. It will arouse suspicion only in those who do not recognize the integrity and distinctiveness of the moral outlook. We ought to question narrow scientific criteria for objectivity, not the claims of morality.

In so far as the moderate strategy tries to ground the properties recognized by one discipline in the properties recognized by another, it assumes that current fundamental scientific theories are complete and unified on the essential points. But we will believe this about them only if we already believe that they embrace the whole of reality; and we will not believe that they do this if we are not convinced that they embrace moral reality. The appeal to scientific standards of objectivity seems to be parallel to the argument for materialism in philosophy of mind that rests on the success of materialist assumptions in other areas. In both cases, it is difficult to present the argument in a form that avoids begging the crucial question; for opponents will argue that they have found a counter-example to the claim that the scientific point of view captures the whole of reality. From their point of view, defences of the scientific point of view seem to collapse into dogmatic confidence in the correctness of contemporary natural science.

Objections to over-confident scientism are reasonable, but they do not necessarily support a radical rather than a moderate defence of objectivism. Radical objectivism relies on two claims: (1) A demand for scientific objectivity implies a Procrustean view of moral objectivity. (2) We ought not to impose this Procrustean view on moral objectivity.

A moderate objectivist rejects one or the other of these claims. If we accept the radical objectivist's characterization of scientific objectivity, we must accept the first claim and deny the second. We agree that scientific objectivity imposes 'Procrustean' demands, in the sense that it presents epistemological and metaphysical demands that can be understood independently of our understanding of particular sciences. Objective moral truths, on this

---

[54] The labels are not meant to suggest that 'moderates' are committed to a weaker form of objectivism than 'radicals' accept, but only that they are more moderate in their attitude to the criteria of objectivity presupposed by natural sciences. One might also describe the two positions as 'naturalist' and 'anti-naturalist'. Some of these different realist views are defended in Brink, *MRFE*, esp. ch. 2, 6; Sayre-McCord, ed., *EMR* (including Boyd, 'Moral realist'; Sturgeon, 'Explanations'; Platts, 'Moral Reality'); McNaughton, *MV*; Nagel, *VN*.

view, must fit these demands, and hence ordinary views about morality may need to be bent and modified to suit the appropriate ideal of scientific objectivity.

But an alternative defence of a moderate strategy might accept the radical's second claim and reject the first. The radical takes for granted some relatively clear criteria for scientific objectivity, and argues that they are not generous enough to let morality in on their terms. To concede this much, however, may be to accept a misleading picture of scientific objectivity and ontology.

The choice that faces the moderate objectivist may be clearer if we consider the Procrustean demands of logical empiricism. If we admit that morality cannot meet the standards of scientific knowledge imposed by logical empiricism, we ought not to infer that it cannot meet the proper standards of scientific objectivity. On the contrary, the logical empiricist standards are implausible for any science; the failure of morality to meet them does not exclude it from being a science.

A similar approach is worth considering when other contrasts between science and morality are alleged. We have seen that attempts to contrast scientific convergence with moral disagreement do not rest on a fair comparison; if we compare natural science and morality fairly, the differences are not as sharp as they initially seemed. This point is still clearer if we compare morality not with physical sciences, but with economics or psychology or sociology or history. If standards for scientific knowledge exclude all these disciplines, the failure of morality to meet them does not support scepticism about morality. For whatever one thinks about the specific achievements of one or another social science, scientific inquiry and discovery seem to be possible in these areas. If these disciplines do not match our standards, the fault lies in the standards, not in the disciplines. But these disciplines display considerable disagreement about relevant evidence, and unresolved dispute between competing theories. They do not seem to make it insuperably difficult for morality to be a scientific discipline.

These reasons for rejecting a Procrustean account of 'scientific standards' make the division between a moderate and a radical defence of objectivism appear less sharp than it might otherwise appear. If we assume that scientific standards are to be derived from physics, or rather from a philosopher's idealization of it, the task of fitting morality into a scientific world-view may appear to require some Procrustean treatment of it.[55] But if we take a broader view of scientific standards, it is not clear that they impose any exacting constraint on an account of morality.

Perhaps, then, defenders of moral objectivism ought not to commit themselves unreservedly to a moderate or to a radical strategy. It is hard to find a convincing argument to show that objectivist claims for morality are defensible only if they can be shown to meet standards that are derived from empirical science. On the other hand, the outright rejection of such standards may result in acceptance of a false dichotomy that the moderate strategy can avoid.

This conclusion about defences of objectivism may be criticized for excessive attention to epistemological issues, as though the integration of morality into a scientific world-view

---

[55] This objection might be appropriate if Williams's 'absolute conception' captured the relevant conception of a scientific world-view.

required it to follow certain principles of method. This conception of the issue may be too influenced by a positivist conception of the 'logic of science' that would allow us to determine a priori whether a given discipline has the character of a genuine science. One might argue that the most important question is not logical or epistemological, but ontological: does morality describe features of the real world, as the scientific world-view conceives it?

One approach to this question relies on a version of naturalism, not in the senses relevant to Butler or Moore, but in a sense that opposes naturalism to supernaturalism. The naturalist claims that the whole of reality is exhausted by things made of the things recognized by natural science, and more specifically by basic physical science. This naturalist position does not insist that all real properties must be properties recognized by basic physical science; it only insists that every event involving these properties must be identical to, or constituted of, events recognized by basic physical science. Even if physics does not recognize tables, tables are part of a naturalistic world-view if every event that involves tables consists wholly of events that involve elementary physical particles. Similarly, minds and mental events are part of a naturalistic world-view if they are also made of physical events. Further specification of the crucial relations of being 'made of' or 'constituted' raises further complications; but for present purposes we may take this formulation of naturalism to be clear enough.

If this is the right way to formulate the ontological constraint imposed by naturalism, moral properties might satisfy it. Even if they are essentially normative, so that nothing can be a moral property without including some reason for rational agents to act in a certain way, they may still be natural properties in the sense required by naturalism. We have no reason to believe that events with normative properties cannot be composed ultimately of purely physical events. Since the naturalist constraint is quite weak, it is difficult to see how a plausible objectivist account of moral properties would violate it. We might reasonably keep an open mind on the truth of the naturalist constraint and on whether moral properties violate it.

1385. Objectivism and Justification

A further argument for a moderate strategy in defence of objectivism relies on a global conception of justification. If the same sorts of considerations that reasonably persuade us to recognize natural and social sciences as rational disciplines ought also to persuade us to recognize the claims of morality, the cost of rejecting morality is raised. The difficulties of a foundationalist conception of moral knowledge may incline us to accept a global conception of justification within moral theory; and if we go this far, it is reasonable to take global considerations seriously in considering the relation between moral knowledge and other sorts of knowledge. And so, if we accept global justification within morality, we have a good reason to accept it outside morality too.

If we accept a global view of justification, we have a further reason to suppose that a dialectical approach to moral beliefs and moral theory can yield objective truths. We might wonder how the beliefs emerging from critical examination of common-sense morality bring us closer to objective truths.[56] We can answer these doubts if the conclusions of our examination of common moral beliefs fit the beliefs that seem justified in other areas.[57] But if we rely on this sort of defence, we ought to be open to global arguments more generally, and so we ought to take the moderate strategy seriously in defences of objectivism.

If on the other hand, we adopt the radical strategy on the assumption that the moderate strategy is bound to fail, we may leave more room for moral scepticism.[58] If we say that morality reveals an area of objective truth, but reveals it only to those who are willing to accept the moral point of view as a self-sufficient arbiter of reality and objectivity, we have to face further questions. Why in particular should we take the outlook of the moral point of view seriously?[59] Defenders of astrology or witchcraft look at things from their point of view and claim to reveal a distinct type of reality. Why should we take one point of view more seriously than another? If we seek some rational method of deciding, we cannot avoid some global considerations. We will accept one outlook as a genuine source of objective knowledge and reject another, partly because of connexions, or lack of connexions, with other apparent sources of knowledge of objective truths. An attempt to answer apparently reasonable questions leads us to take the moderate strategy seriously.

1386. Implications for Normative Ethics?

If attacks on objectivism are not decisive, moral judgments may express knowledge of objective facts just as much as any other judgments do. Is this a purely theoretical question, or does it have any practical implications?

If we face disputes or disagreements, and if we are influenced by anti-objectivist views of morality, then we will tend to suppose that some issues are factual disputes, and that others are moral disputes that cannot be settled by discovery of further facts, and are not open to rational argument and resolution in the way that ordinary factual disputes are. That is why anti-objectivists claim that moral disagreements and disputes are either disputes about non-moral facts or else conflicts of value judgments. If, however, the anti-objectivist case fails, moral judgments may be no less factual and objectively correct than any other sort of judgment. Hence, we might reasonably expect moral judgments to be open to rational argument, leading to resolutions, or possible resolutions, or moral disputes.

Common-sense attitudes to morality may not unequivocally support either objectivism or anti-objectivism. The apparent difficulty of settling moral disagreements has been cited as a source of support for anti-objectivist views. But the existence of these disagreements may support objectivism; for we do not take them to be simply differences in attitude. We

---

[56] Method and justification; §§1182–4, 1407.   [57] See Daniels, 'Equilibrium'.

[58] The fact that the radical strategy leaves room for moral scepticism does not seem to everyone to be an objection to it. See McDowell, 'Hypothetical', 78, who maintains that moral imperatives are categorical, but still believes that 'one need not manifest irrationality; in failing to see that one has reason to act as morality requires'.

[59] One might argue that this question is itself misguided. Such an argument might rest on a claim about the incommensurability of different forms of life. This claim might be attributed to Winch, ISS, ch. 4, and 'Primitive', 11–13. It is discussed by MacIntyre, 'Idea', 227–8. Winch draws some of the implications for ethics in 'Good man' and 'Integrity'. The issues are related to some of those raised by Prichard; see §1400.

normally suppose that it is possible to change our moral views for the better. Moreover, we suppose that we do this not simply by reflecting on our preferences, but by changing our preferences in the light of what we take to be the morally correct answers. We believe we ought to be ready to examine our moral views and to change them in the light of reflexion, for reasons that seem to apply equally to any other area of rational inquiry.

If moral inquiry is a search for objective facts, it is reasonable to take this attitude to morality. But if there are no objective facts to be discovered, why should the attitude we would take to a factual inquiry fit a moral inquiry? Anti-objectivists may offer an account of the procedures that seem like inquiries into objective facts, but they cannot entirely accept objectivist assumptions about moral inquiry. Why, for instance, should we compare different moral views or theories to see what can be said for each of them? Why should we not instead try to confirm our previous moral beliefs by persuading ourselves of the error of every other view? An anti-objectivist view need not endorse the sort of dogmatism that would be rejected in any inquiry into objective facts; but it does not explain what would be wrong with such an attitude in morality.[60]

These questions in meta-ethics are connected to some questions in normative morality. Anti-objectivism does not require us to accept or reject any specific normative views, but it casts doubt on some normative assumptions and practices that are justifiable if an objectivist explanation of them is accepted.

1387. Objectivism and Dogmatism

We may clarify some of these issues if we consider a moral argument against objectivism. It is sometimes supposed that the rejection of any claim to objective truth is the best support for an appropriately tolerant, non-dogmatic attitude to other people's moral beliefs and outlooks, and that objectivism is liable to lead to a misguided desire to impose our beliefs on other people.[61] One might refer to the example of religious toleration. One might suppose, for instance, that as long as believers were convinced of the objective truth of their beliefs, they wanted to impose them on other people, and that they became tolerant only when they became more sceptical. Similarly (one might argue), belief in objective moral truths leads to dogmatism, so that we become unreasonably confident about the truth of our own particular moral judgments, and become too eager to force other people to conform to our practices.

To show that objectivism need not result in dogmatism, we need to see the difference between the belief that there are objective moral facts and the belief that we know all of

---

[60] Related questions are discussed by Sturgeon, 'What difference', and 'Contents', and by Blackburn, 'Causes', and 'Reply'.

[61] Westermarck, *ER* 58, argues that the practical implications of subjectivism are irrelevant to its truth: 'It is needless to say that a scientific theory is not invalidated by the mere fact that it is likely to cause mischief. The unfortunate circumstance that there do exist dangerous things in the world, proves that something may be dangerous and yet true.' He continues: ' . . . I think that ethical writers are often inclined to overrate the influence of moral theory upon moral practice, but if there is any such influence at all, it seems to me that ethical subjectivism, instead of being a danger, is more likely to be an advantage to morality. Could it be brought home to people that there is no absolute standard in morality, they would perhaps be on the one hand more tolerant and on the other hand more critical in their judgments.' (59).

them. The parallel with scientific inquiry shows that the first objectivist belief need not result in the second. If we believe that there are objective moral facts to be discovered, and that we have made progress towards their discovery, we may still reasonably believe that there is further progress to be made.

Indeed, one might go further, and say that objectivism makes it easier to see why we should often be modest and tentative, as we are in many scientific cases, about claiming to know the final truth of the matter. Scientific disciplines try to discover objective facts, and these are often difficult to discover; that is why we ought to be modest in our claims. If the same is true about morality, we ought to be modest here also.

If, on the other hand, we do not think morality is about objective facts, why should we be tentative and undogmatic in our attitude to moral controversies? Anti-objectivists may take an open-minded and undogmatic attitude to moral controversies, but why should they suppose that this is the appropriate attitude? If they are not looking for objective facts, the methods of argument, dispute, comparison, and discussion that are often used for inquiry into objective facts are not directly relevant to moral inquiry.

Anti-objectivists may give consequentialist reasons for taking an undogmatic attitude. Perhaps they will prefer the results of undogmatic consideration of facts on which different people's attitudes rest; flexibility in one's attitudes may result in an adjustment of attitudes that everyone prefers to their previous attitudes. But this is a hazardous claim about the consequences of inquiry. We might reasonably be reluctant to make our defence of undogmatic moral inquiry rest on these uncertain predictions; indeed we might be reluctant to make it rest on consequentialist argument at all. Anti-objectivists seem to offer a questionable defence of the undogmatic and open-minded outlook that they take to be threatened by objectivism.

A moral objectivist cannot be expected to be undogmatic and open-minded about everything; if we believe some real progress has been made, there are some moral beliefs that we will suppose we are entitled to hold confidently and firmly. It does not follow, however, that we will necessarily be intolerant of disagreement, or eager to coerce those who do not act on the same convictions. That depends on what the beliefs are, and what harms result from imposing or failing to impose conformity. These questions raise further moral questions; and we have good reason to suppose that among the beliefs we hold confidently will be some belief in the benefits of freedom and the prima facie wrongness of coercion.

Opponents of objectivism are not clearly better off. Anti-objectivism by itself does not imply tolerance. If all an anti-objectivist's moral beliefs were tentative, the belief in tolerance would have to be tentative also. To protect tolerance, anti-objectivists must have some confident beliefs. And so they cannot argue that the confidence resulting from objectivism is necessarily a threat to tolerance.

This discussion is rather too simple. For no one believes that toleration of everything is a good thing, or that one ought never to force other people to conform to any specific set of moral principles; further moral and political argument is needed to fix the appropriate area of toleration. But the present arguments are perhaps enough to show that objectivism is not open to any simple and clearly justified objection derived from the value of open-mindedness and toleration.

1388. Implications for Moral Theory?

If meta-ethical issues are connected to some normative questions, do they suggest reasons for preferring one normative theory to another?

It is easiest to see how an objectivist theory could be true if we think of a theory that defines moral properties (as opposed to the meanings of moral terms) as recognizable non-moral properties. Quantitative hedonism about the good and hedonistic utilitarianism about the right provide the right sort of theory for an objectivist defence. But if we have described some of the appropriate sorts of arguments for an objectivist position, a definition mentioning only non-moral properties is not the only account of moral properties that ought to seem plausible on objectivist grounds.

The range of defensible theories is wider if we recognize that accounts of moral properties need not be reductive. A reductive account would allow us to replace statements about moral properties with statements about non-moral properties, without loss of truth or explanatory content. But it is not in general reasonable to insist that if a theory is to be accepted into a body of theories, its statements must be replaceable by statements of some other theory. The demand for replacement cannot be fulfilled between psychology and its physiological basis, or between sociology and its psychological basis. If a similar demand for reduction is inappropriate in morality, a true moral theory may include ineliminably moral properties. If, for instance, we identify the good with human welfare, and the right with the promotion of welfare, the presence of some clearly evaluative, and perhaps strictly moral, term such as 'welfare' may be legitimate, and a theory that eliminates such terms may not be preferable.

If we see this point, we may look more sympathetically on a range of theories that would otherwise be regarded with suspicion. Sidgwick, for instance, objects to all theories of the good except quantitative hedonism on the ground that the properties introduced in the definition are not readily understood in non-moral or non-evaluative terms. But the restriction he imposes is unreasonable. Admittedly, we need some identifiable non-moral basis for identifying instances of these properties; but if this basis falls short of providing an account of the moral property itself, the property need not be mysterious. We gain this benefit from the moderate objectivist strategy. Since Sidgwick's demand is unreasonable in non-moral cases, we should not impose it on morality.

Meta-ethical theory, then, does not answer all the questions that have been answered differently by different normative moral theories. But it makes some difference; for it shows that we ought not to rule out non-reductive accounts of the good and the right. We ought not to suppose, then, that hedonistic utilitarianism, for instance, has some clear theoretical advantage over theories that fail to meet utilitarian standards of intelligibility. Meta-ethical inquiry suggests that these standards of intelligibility have no sound epistemological or metaphysical basis. An examination of different normative moral theories should not be constrained by unwarranted restrictions on their character.

VERSIONS OF NATURALISM

1389. Attitudes to Naturalism

Conceptions of morality that appeal to facts about human nature have held a central place in the sequence of theories that we have considered in this book. It is fairly easy to see why they have a central place in a discussion of ancient moral theories; for Plato, Aristotle, Epicureans, and Stoics all support their moral conclusion by explicit claims to facts about the essential characteristics of human beings. It may be less obvious that this emphasis on appeals to nature is appropriate in a discussion of mediaeval theories; for one might argue that the theological starting points of these theories make claims about human nature relatively unimportant, or at least secondary. But we have found that this is not a good reason to deny that mediaeval theories are naturalistic. We may reasonably understand Aquinas' outlook as a defence of Aristotelian naturalism. We have found that in his defence of an Aristotelian outlook Aquinas also describes that outlook more fully; and so we should rely on him both for a full statement and for a defence of Aristotelian naturalism.

We ought not to suppose, however, that Aquinas is all there is to mediaeval moral theory. One good reason to consider Scotus and Ockham is their presentation of an alternative to naturalism. Scotus' division between nature and freedom supports his claim that basic principles of morality depend on the exercise of freedom and choice rather than on the understanding of facts about nature. Since this contrast between nature and freedom has sometimes been taken to be a distinctive feature of a modern outlook, it is worth our while to notice that it develops within mediaeval moral argument, in conscious opposition to Aristotelian naturalism.

A discussion of Hobbes and his successors cannot reasonably ignore the different appeals to nature that we find in 17th and 18th-century moralists. In these debates, we have tried to distinguish the 'Aristotelian' or 'normative' naturalism defended by Suarez, Cudworth, and Butler, from the role of nature in Hobbes, Hutcheson, and Hume. Butler's naturalism provides an appropriate point of comparison with Kant. We have found reasons to question the arguments that have convinced many people, including Kant, that Kantian ethics marks a sharp point of departure from Aristotelian naturalism. The most plausible parts of Kant can be reconciled with the most plausible naturalist claims. To this extent we have reason to agree with Green's attempt to harmonize Kant with an Aristotelian outlook, even though Green's case for harmony needs to be improved.

But when we come to the 20th century, do we perhaps find more decisive reasons to reject Aristotelian naturalism? The weight of meta-ethical argument in the past century may appear to support anti-naturalism. On the one hand, we may suppose that this is a grain of truth in the attack on naturalism that begins with Moore. On the other hand, the modern outlook that is often called 'naturalism' may well seem to differ from its Aristotelian homonym on just the points that seem to matter for an Aristotelian moral theory.

Not everyone has drawn these conclusions. Foot has defended a version of naturalism that is quite close to Aristotle's, in opposition both to 20th-century meta-ethical objections and to Kantian outlooks. It is worth considering whether this defence succeeds, and whether the contrast with Kantian views is justified. We have already found reasons to agree with Green's rejection of this contrast, and we should ask whether later arguments give us good reasons to change our mind on this point.

Discussion of these questions is, from one point of view, preliminary to a more detailed discussion of Aristotle, since we might hold that we need to answer them before we can decide how seriously we ought to take Aristotle. That is why we have already considered them to some degree in the chapters on Aristotle. But a full consideration of them at that point would have been difficult, because some of the main objections to Aristotelian naturalism arise from 20th-century debates. One may doubt whether these debates have presented any new and serious difficulties for Aristotelian naturalism; but it is difficult to decide that question without considering them in their theoretical context. A detailed answer on behalf of Aristotle or Aquinas or Butler or Green would require attention to details of their position. But in this chapter we will simply have to recall some aspects of the views that we have already considered at greater length. On the one hand, this chapter may throw some retrospective light that will help us to reconsider those naturalist theories. On the other hand, we may find that those theories are not out of place in contemporary discussion, if neither older nor newer objections cast serious doubt on them.

1390. Naturalism Without the Naturalistic Fallacy

Many critics believe that Aristotle's naturalism makes his ethical theory unacceptable as a whole, even if parts of it are defensible.[1] Some objections rely on meta-ethical doctrines. Hume's arguments about 'is' and 'ought' are often taken to initiate this line of criticism. But Moore's criticism of naturalism is sometimes taken to set anti-naturalist meta-ethics on a firm basis. To see whether this is so, we should return to some conclusions from our discussion of Moore.

---

[1] Olafson, PP, ch. 1, gives a clear summary of naturalism, as often ascribed to Aristotle, and of objections to it. Falk, 'Nature', discusses some naturalist claims sympathetically, from the point of view of someone who accepts an internal connexion between moral judgment and motivation. A persuasive defence of some aspects of naturalism is offered by Foot, NG.

Some critics of naturalism claim that Moore has refuted it by showing that it commits the naturalistic fallacy.[2] The argument is this: (1) The meaning of moral terms is not given by definitions that mention natural properties, such as being in accordance with human nature. (2) Meanings correspond to properties. (3) Therefore, moral properties cannot be identical to natural properties.

We have found reasons to doubt the first premiss of this argument. Moore's main reason for claiming that naturalism commits a fallacy is his Open Question Argument. But this argument rests on unreasonable conditions for definitions, and so it does not show that any fallacy is involved in naturalistic definitions. Even if Moore had a clear account of what natural properties or naturalistic definitions are, he would not have shown that they raise any special difficulties.

We might, however, grant that Moore's objection to naturalistic definitions contains the grain of truth that underlies his objection to conceptual utilitarianism. He suggests correctly that moral argument requires some initial grasp of moral concepts that does not incorporate the conclusions of the theory that we seek to defend through moral argument. Even if we reject the Open Question Argument, we may accept this objection to any version of naturalism that tries to incorporate the theory into our initial understanding of such concepts as 'good', 'right', 'ought', and so on.

But this objection to naturalistic definitions does not affect Aristotelian naturalism. For the meta-ethical naturalism that Aristotle endorses is not a claim about meanings or concepts, but about properties.[3] This aspect of the Aristotelian position is obscure to a critic who fails, as Moore and Ross fail, to distinguish concepts from properties, and hence fails to distinguish nominal from real definitions. Once we draw the relevant distinctions, however, we can see how to interpret Aristotle's arguments for naturalist claims. He does not claim that the concepts or meanings of 'good', 'happiness', 'virtue', and so on are to be identified with the concepts of function, agreement with nature. He claims instead that moral terms refer to natural properties. According to Aristotle, 'the human good' and 'activity of the soul in accord with virtue' refer to the same condition of a person; but he does not suggest that we discover this by noticing that the two concepts are the same.

If, therefore, we disagree with Aristotle, we must refute his claim that welfare, goodness, virtue, and so on are to be identified with aspects of the fulfilment of human nature. General meta-ethical arguments about the nature of moral concepts do not refute his claims about the identity of moral and natural properties.

1391. Morality and Motivation

This reply to objections that rely on Moore also disposes of one of Hume's arguments about 'is' and 'ought'. His claim that moral properties cannot be 'in the object' assumes (in

---

[2] Moore; §§1255–6. The relation between Aristotle's claims and Moore's arguments is complex. It depends on, e.g., (i) Moore's conception of a natural property; (ii) whether Aristotelian claims about nature involve only the properties that Moore counts as 'natural' (or those he counts as 'metaphysical'; see his comments on Stoic claims about nature, PE §67).

[3] Moore and Ross on properties; §§1265, 1283–4.

Moore's terms) that there should be no open question about whether an alleged definition is correct; but this condition for definition raises the same doubt that Moore's argument raises.

Hume's other argument rests on the assumption that moral concepts are internally connected to motivation. The internalist argument, defended by Hutcheson and Hume, is this:[4] (1) If we judge sincerely that we ought to do x, we are motivated to choose x. (2) But we could consistently judge something to be required by human nature and still be indifferent to it. (3) Therefore, this cannot be the right account of what we ought to do.

The first premiss of this argument is dubious, since the case for internalism is not compelling. But even if this and the second premiss were both true, the conclusion would not follow. For the first premiss at most tells us the character of moral concepts and moral judgments; it does not tell us anything about the nature of the properties that they refer to. Hence it does not tell us that a naturalist account of these properties is false. If internalism about ought-judgments is right, it tells us that we cannot sincerely judge that we ought to follow nature until we are motivated to follow nature. But it does not tell us that we cannot have reason to be motivated to follow nature. It is still open to the naturalist to convince us that facts about human nature are the ones that we have reason to consider in deciding what we ought to do.

1392. Naturalism, Facts, and Values

Some criticize naturalism because it claims to derive values from facts, or an 'ought' from an 'is', and we have reasons (derived from Hume) for rejecting any such derivation.[5] Even if we reject Moore's argument against naturalism, we may be convinced by arguments to show that no judgments about values are conceptually connected with truths about facts. But even if we grant that no conceptual connexion can be found, we have not necessarily found a powerful objection to naturalism.

We have seen that the absence of conceptual connexions is not a good reason for denying the possibility of legitimate inferences. Truths about physical objects, for instance, are not conceptually connected to truths about sensory impressions; nor are truths about unobservables conceptually connected to truths about observables. But we do not take the absence of conceptual connexions to be a good reason to reject all arguments from impressions to physical objects or from observables to unobservables. Hence, the argument from lack of conceptual connexion does not show that we cannot have legitimate arguments from facts about human nature to moral conclusions.

Alternatively, the objection about facts and values might be taken to claim that we cannot find any legitimate argument, deductive or non-deductive, from natural facts to moral conclusions. If this objection is correct, it raises a difficulty for naturalism. But we can hardly show it is correct without considering specific arguments one by one. The naturalist

---

[4] Hutcheson and Hume; §§642, 744–5.   [5] Hume on is and ought; §752. Facts and values; §1297.

872

argument is one of the specific arguments that need to be considered; we do not know in advance that it cannot be legitimate.

If, then, we recall the general meta-ethical arguments about naturalism, we do not find a powerful case against Aristotelian naturalism. Even if we give anti-naturalist arguments more credit than they deserve, they do not cast doubt on an Aristotelian position, once it is properly understood.

1393. Naturalism and Conceptions of Nature

We might grant, then, that Aristotelian naturalism is free of conceptual error, but we might still take a sceptical attitude to it. According to the sceptic, claims about natural properties give no sufficient reason for drawing moral conclusions, even though they give sufficient reasons for drawing other conclusions about natural properties.

Naturalist claims about morality are evidently open to sceptical objection, if we suppose that claims about human nature tell us what everyone, or almost everyone, is like and what everyone does.[6] We may grant that these claims pick out the agents to whom moral principles apply. Moral principles, however, as Aristotle agrees, tell us to act in ways in which we are not naturally determined to act (EN 1103a18–b2). Facts about human nature seem unsuitable for moral claims.[7]

Mill's essay 'Nature' is a clear statement of this argument against naturalism. It is directed against the claim that following nature is a true and important moral principle.[8] Mill mentions the prominence of appeals to nature in ancient ethics ('Nature', 376), but he suggests—rather strangely, and without offering any historical support—that Christianity has tended to inhibit the tendency to appeal to natural law. He welcomes the decline in appeals to natural law, because he takes these appeals to rest on the untenable assumption that what is generally true of people, apart from training or education or society, is what they ought to do.

Mill's argument rests on the assumption that 'nature' refers without distinction to all the natural, as opposed to the acquired, aspects of human motives and tendencies.[9] Most of his essay is devoted to the relatively easy task of arguing that natural processes without human intervention are not a good guide to the right. Mill conjectures (382) that human reluctance to interfere with nature arises from the conception of nature as a divine order that human beings ought not to disrupt. We are irrationally influenced by this superstitious reluctance, even though it is inconsistent with our view that we ought to improve our natural conditions

---

[6] Moore discusses naturalism, so understood, in *PE*, ch. 2. He discusses a metaphysical conception of nature in ch. 4.

[7] Hume (quoted in §728) argues that none of the senses of 'natural' that he considers marks out a distinctive sense in which virtue is natural and vice unnatural. He presents an objection that Butler also acknowledges as one that he has to answer: '...there were not wanting persons, who manifestly mistook the whole thing...' (*Sermons*, P 13, quoted in §678).

[8] 'It is proposed to inquire into the truth of the doctrines which make Nature a test of right and wrong, good and evil, or which in any mode or degree attach merit or approval to following, imitating, or obeying nature.' (Mill, 'Nature', 377).

[9] '...those parts of our mental and moral constitution which are supposed to be innate, in contradistinction to those which are acquired' ('Nature', 399).

and develop our characters (393). Not surprisingly, Mill concludes that the advice to follow nature is both irrational and immoral.[10]

Mill, however, ignores the difference between the claim that human beings have natural traits and characteristics and the claim that they have a nature. This distinction underlies Butler's normative naturalism, and since Mill ignores it, his objections have no force against Butler, and hence have no force against Aristotelian naturalism.

According to Butler, mere facts about natural traits are not enough to support moral claims. The relevant facts are about human nature as a system, which are distinct from facts about what human beings naturally do. Though human beings naturally tend to fall ill, illness is not part of the nature of human beings, but actually tends to undermine their natural constitution.

If, then, critics of naturalism are to undermine the naturalism of Aristotle and Butler, they need to attack the Aristotelian normative conception of nature as a system. Two sorts of criticism would be relevant to this conception of nature: (1) We might argue that the distinction between the normative conception of nature and mere facts about what people naturally do cannot be plausibly maintained. (2) We might accept the distinction, but argue that it does not support the moral conclusions that naturalists try to derive from it. We have seen that Nietzsche sometimes seems to favour one line of criticism, sometimes the other.[11]

With these questions in mind, it is useful to examine criticisms of naturalism that have been presented by Williams and MacIntyre. Though they do not explicitly distinguish the two lines of criticism that we have noticed, their discussion of appeals to nature helps us to see how one might state the relevant criticisms and how one might answer them.

1394. Naturalism as Metaphysical Biology

Williams notices that if Aristotle takes happiness to be distinct from pleasure or satisfaction of desire, he relies on some conception of a person's real interest. According to such a conception, S's real interests may not be reflected in her actual or counterfactual desires (if these counterfactual desires are non-circularly specified, so that the counterfactual conditions do not include 'if S were aware of her real interests').

According to Williams, Aristotle explains the relevant notion of a real interest by appeal to a nature.[12] According to Aristotelian teleology, human nature includes an 'inner nisus' characteristic of the human species. The earth has a natural and intrinsic tendency to move towards the centre of the universe, some plants have an intrinsic tendency to grow towards the sunlight, and animals have an intrinsic tendency to seek food when they are hungry. If

---

[10] Mill, 'Nature', 402, quoted in §1134.   [11] Nietzsche and nature; §§1103–4.

[12] 'Aristotle himself held a very strong theory of general teleology: each kind of thing had an ideal form of functioning, which fitted together with that of other things. He believed that all the excellences of character had to fit together into a harmonious self.' (Williams, *ELP* 43) 'In Aristotle's teleological universe, every human being (or at least every nondefective male who is not a natural slave) has a kind of inner nisus toward a life of at least civic virtue, and Aristotle does not say enough about how this is frustrated by poor upbringing, to make it clear exactly how, after that upbringing, it is still in this man's real interest to be other than he is.' (44).

we could discover a parallel intrinsic tendency in a human being, we could (according to Williams's account of Aristotle) claim to have found the human good.[13]

Aristotle's position, therefore, belongs to a discredited biological theory, and indeed to a discredited world-view. Williams infers that if Aristotle's discredited metaphysical biology[14] cannot support a plausible account of real interests, no credible substitute for Aristotelian biology can support such an account.[15] An evolutionary concept of fitness cannot determine the good of a person in a plausible way. Psychological theory might support ethical conclusions of the sort we need for an account of real interests, but only if it already relies on ethical premises (*ELP* 45).

Williams's argument expresses the first sort of criticism of normative naturalism. He denies that anything fits Aristotle's or Butler's conception of human nature as a system. If Aristotelian biology were true, it would support the conception of human nature that the normative naturalist needs. But since Aristotelian biology is false, nothing supports normative naturalism.

1395. Does Naturalism Need Metaphysical Biology?

Do we need anything quite as demanding and controversial as Aristotelian metaphysical biology in order to support normative naturalism? Butler does not suppose that he commits himself to so much of the Aristotelian outlook on the world; he seems to believe that he can support normative naturalism on a slimmer metaphysical basis. To see why one might suppose that Butler is mistaken, it is useful to consider MacIntyre's argument to show that metaphysical biology has an important role in Aristotle's views on flourishing and well-being.

According to MacIntyre, we can see why Aristotle needs metaphysical biology if we consider a superficially attractive attempt to do without it. Part of the point of naturalism is to find some point of view outside different ideals supported by different cultures, societies, and ways of life. An appeal to nature seems to offer the prospect of deciding which of these ideals really fit the human beings to whom they are presented as ideals. We might, try, then, to form some conception of well-being that is neutral between different ideals, in the hope of arguing from that conception that we need some specific virtues.

And so we might disagree about (for instance) whether we should spend most of our time on accumulating wealth, or thinking about quantum physics, or watching baseball. But we might none the less agree that we need the executive virtues that will allow us to pursue our main aims (whatever they are) without being distracted by attractions that we will later wish we had avoided. On this basis, we might agree that we need something like courage and

---

[13] The Aristotelian argument, then, is this: (1) If x is of kind K, then the fulfilment of the inner nisus of Ks is x's real good. (2) If x is a normal human being, x has an inner nisus towards the virtuous life. (3) Therefore, if x is a human being, the virtuous life is x's real good.

[14] 'Metaphysical biology' is MacIntyre's phrase (see below), but it captures Williams's estimate of Aristotle's doctrine.

[15] 'If Aristotle, with his strong assumption about the nisus of each natural kind of thing toward its perfection, cannot firmly deliver this result, there is not much reason to think that we can.' (Williams, *ELP* 44).

temperance.[16] Would this be a naturalist argument that avoids any appeal to controversial metaphysical claims about nature?

In MacIntyre's view, this strategy is not promising. He argues that an account of the virtues cannot reasonably ignore the conflicts between different conceptions of well-being.[17] The difference between these conceptions defeats any attempt to defend Aristotelian naturalism on the basis of economical metaphysics. At this point, Aristotelian metaphysical biology becomes relevant. For it allows us to appeal to something outside the conflicting conceptions of well-being that have arisen in our cultural history. Since a teleological theorist needs to appeal to something outside these conflicting conceptions, metaphysical biology plays an important role in a teleological theory.[18] Without metaphysical biology, we have no credible appeals to nature. Since metaphysical biology is not credible, no appeal to nature is credible.

MacIntyre's criticism of appeals to well-being without metaphysical biology seems to introduce different objections: (1) We cannot form any general conception of well-being that is not simply an expression of one of the conflicting cultural ideals, unless we appeal to metaphysical biology. (2) We can form such a conception, but it will be too general to give us any definite account of any virtues; such an account must rely on one of the conflicting cultural ideals. (3) The general conception, independently of any conflicting cultural ideals, gives us an account of some virtues, but not of all the virtues that a moral theory should describe.

The most serious criticism of a non-biological and 'non-cultural' conception of well-being (i.e., a conception that does not rest on any of the conflicting cultural ideals) is the first. The second implies that the ethical use of such a conception is too limited to let us carry out any of the major tasks of ethical theory. The third criticism implies that some tasks of moral theory cannot be carried out if we rely wholly on a general conception of well-being; but the general conception may still be useful.

MacIntyre's criticism of a general conception of well-being is rather similar to Williams's criticism of attempts to rely on claims about well-being as a foundation for ethical claims. Williams argues that, if we abandon metaphysical biology, we cannot find a non-ethical basis in well-being for ethical claims; we will find an appropriate conception of well-being only if we illegitimately help ourselves to ethical claims. Similarly, MacIntyre alleges that any claims about well-being that are specific enough to support any interesting claims about the

---

[16] 'It has been argued that all we need to provide in order to justify an account of the virtues and vices is some very general account of what human flourishing and well-being consists in. The virtues can then be adequately characterized as those qualities necessary to promote such flourishing and well-being, because, whatever our disagreements in detail on *that* subject, we ought to be able to agree rationally on what is a virtue and what a vice.' (MacIntyre, *AV* 52).

[17] 'This view ignores the place in our cultural history of deep conflicts over what human flourishing and well-being do consist in and the way in which rival and incompatible beliefs on that topic beget rival and incompatible tables of the virtues. Aristotle and Nietzsche, Hume and the New Testament are names which represent polar opposites on these matters. Hence any adequate teleological account must provide us with some clear and defensible account of the *telos*; and any adequate generally Aristotelian account must supply a teleological account which can replace Aristotle's metaphysical biology.' (*AV* 52).

[18] In his later work, MacIntyre perhaps modifies this claim, because of his heavier reliance on appeal to tradition. See *WJWR*, chs. 6–8, on Aristotle, where metaphysical biology is not prominent (though cf. 192–3, 205, on Aristotle and Aquinas).

virtues must already rely on some of the disputed cultural ideals that a general conception of well-being is supposed to by-pass.

Both of these critics, then, maintain that metaphysical biology plays an important part in any ethical theory that seeks foundations in well-being, and indeed that any theory based on well-being is fatally flawed if it does not appeal to metaphysical biology. They do not say this to show that we ought to take metaphysical biology seriously. On the contrary, they suppose that metaphysical biology has been discredited, and that, since it has been discredited, appeals to well-being do not provide a foundation for ethical theory.

1396. Naturalism and Teleology

These criticisms of Aristotelian naturalism draw our attention to Aristotle's use of a teleological doctrine of nature. His account of human nature expresses his views about the function and the ends of human beings. These teleological views belong to his biology. Certainly, some of his beliefs about the natural world, including the living parts of it, have been discredited. But how much of his natural teleology belongs among these discredited beliefs? We should not assume that if Aristotle introduces some of his natural philosophy into his ethics, he must be building his ethical theory on a basis that we cannot take seriously. We have seen that Hobbes tends to assume that if we are not Aristotelians about the natural world as a whole, we should not accept Aristotle's views about human nature and the human good. But, as Leibniz points out, not all aspects of the Aristotelian view are equally open to criticism.

We have seen that Aristotle's conception of the human function does not rely on a teleological doctrine that has been refuted by modern science.[19] His claims about nature, essence, and function are not evolutionary claims, because they offer static rather than genetic explanations. Even if we know nothing about the theory of evolution, or about the evolution of the organs of animals, we may have good reason to believe that the function of the heart is pumping blood. Similarly, Aristotle's claims about the human function do not seem to depend on pre-modern scientific theories.

In his view, a human being's nature and essence consists in living in accord with practical reason. Rational plans and aims explain the character of the rest of the system that constitutes human nature. This does not mean that every function of every organ is controlled by rational planning (as Aristotle notes at EN 1102a32–b12). It means only that rational planning gives system to human life as a whole.[20]

Do these claims about essence and function belong to metaphysical biology? We may say that they do, if we mean only that claims about essence are part of Aristotle's metaphysics, and that claims about function are part of his natural philosophy, especially his account of living creatures. But if this is all we mean, we have no reason to reject metaphysical biology. Aristotle's claims are reasonable in their own right, apart from any questionable doctrines about the nature of the universe or natural processes.

---

[19] Aristotelian teleology; §75.   [20] Aristotle's naturalism: §§74–7.

1397. Objections to Naturalism Without Metaphysical Biology

We have now found reasons to believe that Aristotle's naturalism is neither meta-ethically untenable nor scientifically incredible. It does not rest on evidently implausible claims about the grounding of ethics in wholly non-evaluative truths about biology. If Williams and MacIntyre are right, the naturalist position that Aristotle actually holds should turn out to be ethically useless, in so far as it does without discredited metaphysical biology. Are they right to reject it on this basis?

Williams believes that the rejection of metaphysical biology casts serious doubt on any effort to treat an account of well-being as a foundation for an ethical theory.[21] In Williams's view, either metaphysical biology or Darwinian evolutionary theory would provide the right sort of premisses for a theory of well-being, since each theory would rely on clearly non-ethical premisses. But neither of these theories—for different reasons—provides premisses that are both ethically plausible and non-ethically warranted.

Williams considers the possibility of turning to psychology rather than to Aristotelian or Darwinian biology. He rejects some psychological theories (his examples are psycho-analytic theories) because they already involve recognizably ethical thought, and are therefore too close to the ethical conclusions we want to justify.[22] If we do not rely on a covertly moral theory, we may resort to a non-ethical theory of human nature; but such a theory will tell us that it is quite possible for some people to be ethically bad but happy, and ethically good, but unhappy (ELP 45–6).[23]

Williams offers two different views of how a theory may be 'too close' to an ethical conclusion: (1) If a psychological theory is, or includes, an ethical theory, it cannot supply an account of well-being that supports an ethical life. (2) If a psychological theory includes any ethical thought, it cannot supply an account of well-being that supports an ethical life. Since not every ethical thought amounts to a whole ethical theory, these two objections apply to different positions. The first objection seems to apply only to a limited range of psychological theories, whereas the second objection seems to apply to a wider range of positions.

The first objection seems plausible. For we might indeed wonder how a theory of well-being that already incorporates a whole ethical theory could support an ethical life. Such a theory would be a strongly moralistic version of naturalism; apparently, it must have already presupposed a conception of an ethical life in the ethical theory that is incorporated at the beginning. If so, it is not clear how it could offer any further support to an ethical life.

But this objection does not seem to apply to every version of naturalism. Even if some evaluative claims about nature are ethical thoughts, the acceptance of these ethical thoughts does not seem to presuppose acceptance of a whole ethical life. The presence

---

[21] Williams clarifies his views on Aristotelian naturalism in 'Replies', 194–204 (esp. 203–4), in reply to Nussbaum's argument in 'Nature' that Aristotle is not a naturalist.

[22] '...this does disqualify them from giving an independent account of well-being, and so providing a foundation for ethical life' (Williams, ELP 45).

[23] '...it is hard to believe that an account of human nature—if it is not already an ethical theory itself—will adequately determine one kind of ethical life as against others.' (52).

of an ethical thought in a theory need not make the theory into an ethical theory that presupposes the ethical life that is to be justified. Hence, some versions of naturalism avoids Williams's dilemma.

This attempt to distinguish Williams's two objections would fail, however, if all ethical thoughts required acceptance of an ethical theory and of ethical life. It is difficult to see whether Williams maintains this strong claim about ethical thoughts. According to his initial remarks about the ethical, we recognize an ethical consideration, and make an ethical judgment, if we make some judgment about our lives in relation to the lives of other people.[24] But sometimes he suggests a more demanding conception. We refute (we may grant) a sceptic about material objects if we can produce one material object. But it is not so clear (in Williams's view) that we refute a sceptic about ethical truths by producing one ethical truth. It would not be enough, for instance, if we could gain the sceptic's assent to the truth that 'given the choice, one should not surgically operate on a child without anaesthetic' (25). In Williams's view, such an example counts as an example of the ethical only to someone who already recognizes the ethical.[25] Even if sceptics accept an obvious ethical truth, it does not follow that they accept it qua ethical. To accept it qua ethical, they must accept the network of considerations that belong to an ethical life; they must agree, for instance, that other people's interests count for something. Acting on one benevolent impulse might be regarded as no different from acting on any other whim or impulse; and those who regard it in this way do not, in Williams's view, recognize the ethical.

These questions about the requirements for ethical thought may help to explain why Williams might not agree to separate his two objections (presupposing an ethical theory v. presupposing an ethical thought) to any theory that includes an ethical thought in an attempt to support the ethical life. Still, even the more demanding view about the requirements for ethical thought does not require us to agree that acceptance of an ethical thought presupposes acceptance of an ethical theory or an ethical life. Perhaps Williams is right to suggest that we cannot intelligibly accept just one ethical thought, entirely unrelated to a network of ethical considerations. But even if we agree with this suggestion, an ethical thought need not depend on an ethical theory or an ethical life.

If, then, we distinguish theories that include (or presuppose) some ethical thought from those that include an ethical theory, we may usefully apply the distinction to some questions about Aristotle. His claims about well-being, and the underlying claims about human nature, may include some ethical thoughts; but in conceding this (for the sake of argument), we would not necessarily agree that they incorporate an ethical theory. If claims about well-being incorporated an ethical theory, they would not provide a suitable basis or support for an ethical theory. But if they simply include some ethical thoughts, they may still provide a suitable basis for ethical theory.

---

[24] '...we have a conception of the ethical that understandably relates to us and our actions the demands, needs, claims, desires, and, generally, the lives of other people, and it is helpful to preserve this conception in what we are prepared to call an ethical consideration.' (12) Williams does not even explicitly require an ethical thought to involve a favourable attitude to the demands (etc.) of other people—though the context suggests that he may intend this.

[25] 'A limited benevolent or altruistic sentiment may move almost anyone to think he should act in a certain way on a certain occasion, but that fact does not present him with the ethical . . . The ethical involves a whole network of considerations, and the ethical sceptic could have a life that ignored such considerations altogether.' (25).

For similar reasons we may reject the dilemma that MacIntyre presents for Aristotelian naturalism. According to MacIntyre, either we rely on metaphysical biology or we fail to escape the influence of contested cultural ideals. It is not clear that these options exhaust the possibilities. Claims about well-being may not be entirely non-controversial or non-contested, but they may be only minimally contested; if that is so, they may support one ideal over another without already presupposing the ideal that they support.

These arguments mark some logical space for an Aristotelian theory. We still need to decide whether such a theory includes any ethical judgments; whether it stops short of relying on a whole ethical theory; and whether it provides support for an ethical theory and an ethical life. If the answer to all these questions is Yes, Aristotle maintains a version of naturalism.

1398. Naturalism and Real Interests

To see what questions a naturalist theory may be able to answer, it is useful to discuss some of Williams's remarks about well-being and interests. He considers whether we can properly appeal to the real interest of a person in order to explain how victims of brainwashing are harmed, even though they do not mind what has happened to them. We might plausibly claim that the release from brainwashing was in the victim's real interest, even if the victim did not want it at the time, because it removed some more general incapacity that we can identify through some further 'normative conception of human functioning' (*ELP* 43).[26] Release from brainwashing is in A's interest, even if A does not want to be released when he has been brainwashed, because it brings A closer to human functioning.

Williams's reply to this suggestion is puzzling. He observes that not everything that is in one's interest is something that one needs in order to function better.[27] It follows that an appeal to function does not provide a necessary condition for something being in an agent's interest. But we might concede this point, and still maintain that function is sufficient for for interest. Hence we might well concede that in some cases it is in A's interest to do or have specific things because A wants them, and that in general getting what one wants is (with some qualifications) one of the things in one's interest. It is still open to us to argue that some of my interests transcend my wants because they are connected with my human functions, and that these connexions between interest and functions also explain why it is in my interest to get various things that do not directly promote my human functions. We might argue, for instance, that a human being is the sort of creature whose

---

[26] 'If an agent does not now acknowledge that a certain change would be in his interest and if, as a result of the change, he comes to acknowledge that it was in his interest, this will show that the change really was in his interest only on condition that the alteration in his outlook is explained in terms of some more *general incapacity* from which he suffered in his original state, and which has been removed or alleviated by the change.' (42–3).

[27] Williams considers this suggestion: 'Why not just say that a change is in someone's real interest if the result of that change would be to bring him closer to normal human functioning? The answer is that not everything in someone's interests is necessary to his human functioning, or is something that he *needs*.' (43) Williams's opponent suggests that (1) F is in A's interest if F brings A closer to human functioning. This suggestion states a sufficient condition for F's being in A's interest. Williams's reply assumes that (2) If F brings A closer to human functioning, A needs F. He claims that (3) It is not the case that if F is in A's interest, A needs F. Hence he is entitled to conclude that (4) It is not the case that if F is in A's interest, F brings A closer to human functioning. But (4) does not refute (1).

good consists in a certain kind of function and activity that requires (with qualifications) having one's desires satisfied, and that this is why desire-satisfaction is normally in my interest.

If a normative theory of functions discovers sufficient conditions for real interests, it supports ethical life. If we find that such a theory supports an ethical life, we have a reason to believe that it is in a person's interest to live an ethical life. Whether it is in a person's overriding interest depends on the character of the interests that the functional theory does not cover.

To cast doubt on the prospects of such a theory, Williams mentions 'everyday facts' (45), such as the fact that some people who try to practise the ethical virtues are miserable, and the fact that some horrible people are not miserable at all. These everyday facts are certainly relevant, and need to be explained. But they do not obviously present an insuperable difficulty.

Admittedly, virtue is not necessary for certain kinds of pleasure, enjoyment, satisfaction with one's situation and so on. We may concede for present purposes that such results may be open to vicious people as well. But we should not be content with such conceptions of well-being. We have reasons (suggested by the example of brainwashing) to take seriously a normative conception of human functions. If we take such a conception seriously, we need not be immediately persuaded by the 'everyday facts' that Williams mentions.[28]

1399. The Connexion Between Nature and Well-Being

If we believe that some belief in human functions supports a reasonable conception of real interests, why should we suppose that naturalism is the appropriate basis for plausible claims about functions? To see what naturalism can contribute, we may usefully recall some aspects of Aristotle's position that we have discussed in more detail.

If human nature essentially involves a certain sort of guidance by practical reason, people fail to fulfil their nature if they lack rational guidance. This would be similar to saying that people cannot fulfil their nature if they are entirely unable to exercise their senses or coordinate their bodily movements to any significant degree at all. But a normal human being has not got especially acute or well-developed senses. So why should we be concerned for anything above the normal level in guidance by practical reason? The normal human being is not especially virtuous, but Aristotle wants us to be especially virtuous.

To see how Aristotle answers this question, we ought to consider the intended connexion between the human good and eudaimonia. The concept of the human good defines the sort of agency that is characteristic of a rational agent, trying to arrange all the agent's ends in a rational structure. This partly specifies what is involved in being a rational agent and performing the human function. The concept of eudaimonia, by contrast, defines the goal of the aspirations of actual human beings. This is supposed to be something that we recognizably care about and that shapes our various activities. It is, or at least seems, logically possible that the eudaemonic judgments we make have nothing much to do with

---

[28] Foot, *NG*, ch. 4, discusses some relevant questions.

the judgments we make about the human good. This would be the case, if, for instance, we agreed with the views of eudaimonia that Aristotle rejects from the start (in *EN* i 5).

This is clear in the case of the life of mere gratification, since Aristotle says it involves preference for the life of beasts. But it is also true of the life devoted to the pursuit of honour. If all we cared about was what other people think of us, we would not be connecting our good with activity at all, let alone with the activity that is distinctive of human beings as opposed to other agents. The same is true, if less obviously so, of virtue; for exclusive focus on it would imply that we were not concerned with fully developed and successful rational agency in one's life as a whole. The fact that we reject these conceptions of eudaimonia shows, in Aristotle's view, that we connect happiness with the full exercise of those capacities whose partial exercise is characteristic of the normal human being.

Aristotle expresses this claim rather unobtrusively. He asserts that a human being is naturally political, and that a self-sufficient life must be sufficient for a human being, understood as having such a nature. And he says that we take happiness to be self-sufficient (*EN* 1097b6–11). This is not the relatively uncontroversial claim that happy people have what they want; it also imposes a condition on what they must want if they are to have a correct conception of happiness.

These judgments about happiness and nature display a two-way connexion. (1) The claims about nature explain these judgments; that is why the Function Argument comes after the claims about happiness and the final good. The claims about nature show that our judgments about happiness are not arbitrary, but rest on an understanding of the sorts of agents that we are, and on a conception of our good that is parallel to our conception of the good of other organisms. (2) The judgments about happiness extend our judgments about nature. Our conception of the normal agent guides us in forming a conception of the ideal agent, but the two conceptions are not identical. Normal agents may still be incompletely rational. Our views about happiness show how we can develop this incomplete rationality in ways that are not constrained by the limitations of the normal human being.

To see whether these claims produce any interesting theoretical results, we may recollect Aristotle's position schematically: (1) Human nature consists in rational agency, that is, in exercising the capacity to guide behaviour by practical reason. (2) The human good consists in the full actualization of this capacity in fulfilling our other capacities. (3) The virtues are the different ways of actualizing this capacity.

The first of these claims is the basis for Aristotle's account of the good. But it would not help him without some defence of the second claim. If we were convinced that there is nothing more to happiness than desire-satisfaction, Aristotle would be wrong. Nor is the third claim trivial. If there were no especially close connexion between the different virtues and the different ways of actualizing the capacity to be guided by practical reason, Aristotle's third claim would be false.

It would be especially clear that the third claim is false if we could not find the relevant connexion between guidance by practical reason and the other-regarding virtues of justice and friendship. One might try to explain the character and rational basis of justice without appeal to practical reason. Perhaps we could trace it to the sorts of insecurity that lead to the instrumental desire for cooperation, as Hume does. Or perhaps we could understand it as an expression of sympathetic feelings towards the sufferings of others; this is an explanation that Hume rejects. In either case, we would have a strong argument against Aristotelian naturalism.

Aristotle, therefore, appears to hold a naturalist position that is neither ethically empty nor open to the general objections we have considered. He seems to rest some non-trivial claims on his conception of nature. These include the claims that happiness has to embrace the good of others besides the agent, that self-love requires concern for the good of others, and that friendship with virtuous people is a necessary component of individual happiness. We have seen that Aristotle defends these claims, and that later naturalists offer further support for them.

1400. Moral Objections to Naturalism

But even if Aristotelian naturalism supports reasonable judgments about human welfare, we may still reject it as a basis for morality, on the ground that we ought not to ask for the sort of foundation of morality that we would derive from Aristotelian naturalism. This is the objection that Prichard expresses in his question 'Does moral philosophy rest on a mistake?' We have discussed some relevant questions in connexion with Kant. Since Prichard presents a Kantian or quasi-Kantian objection in extreme terms, it is worth seeing whether he adds any cogent arguments to those we have found in Kant.

Prichard's answer to his question, understood one way, is Yes. We might suppose that the task of moral philosophy is to explain, understand, and justify moral obligation, by showing that we have good reasons to recognize some things as morally obligatory. If we assume that the relevant sort of explanation, understanding, and justification must connect moral obligation with something that can be recognized as rational by someone who does not yet accept morality as obligatory, we have missed the whole point of moral obligation, as Prichard understands it. That is why he believes that '. . . the subject [sc. moral philosophy], at any rate as usually understood, consists in the attempt to answer an improper question'.[29] In the light of this basic objection, Prichard attempts to explain what he calls 'the extreme sense of dissatisfaction produced by a close reading of Aristotle's ethics'.[30] Though Aristotelian naturalism is not the only position that incurs Prichard's disapproval, it is certainly one of them. Hence he accuses Butler and Green of making the same mistake about what a moral philosopher should try to do.

Prichard's objection might be expressed by saying that morality has its own distinctive reasons that are essentially inexplicable by reference to anything else. We might call this the 'separateness' of morality.[31] Prichard thinks it is a way of capturing what Kant means in speaking of the autonomy of morality. In Prichard's view, asking a question about the basis

---

[29] Prichard, *MODI* 1. Part of Bradley's discussion of 'Why should I be moral?' anticipates Prichard's objection; see §1214.

[30] His explanation is this: 'Why is the Ethics so disappointing? Not, I think, because it really answers two radically different questions as if they were one: (1) "What is the happy life?" (2) "What is the virtuous life?" It is, rather, because Aristotle does not do what we as moral philosophers want him to do, viz. to convince us that we really ought to do what in our non-reflective consciousness we have hitherto believed we ought to do . . . Now, if what I have just been contending is true, a systematic account of the virtuous character cannot possibly satisfy this demand.' (*MODI* 13).

[31] Winch defends some similar claims; §1385.

of moral obligation is asking the wrong question.[32] McDowell sympathizes with Prichard's objection.[33] Prichard appears to believe that the separateness of morality is something we know a priori; we discover it by reflexion on the failure of every attempt to find a basis or explanation for moral obligation. This thesis of separateness is stronger than a thesis about independence; we might say that moral obligation rests on reasons that we would have whether or not we could find a naturalistic basis for them. This claim about independence does not imply that no such basis is possible; it simply says that such a basis would not capture the nature of moral reasons. Prichard does not explain why his claim about separateness is to be preferred over the claim about independence.

According to the alleged mistake that Prichard rejects, scepticism about moral obligation is at least logically possible. If we find that claims about moral obligation have no justification outside further claims about moral obligation, we have some reason to conclude that such claims are unjustified. Prichard, however, maintains that this sort of scepticism is logically impossible; for if we look for any external justification of moral obligation, we show that we misunderstand its character. Since naturalism looks for some external explanation and justification of morality in a conception of human nature, it makes the mistake that Prichard attacks.

The cogency of Prichard's objection to the 'mistaken' conception of moral philosophy rests on the plausibility of his assumption about the separateness of morality. It is not obvious that we have mistaken the character of morality if we deny the assumption about separateness. Since the assumption is not obviously true, it needs some defence.

To see what sort of defence the assumption of separateness needs, we must distinguish this assumption from a Kantian claim that might easily be confused with it. Kant insists on the non-instrumental character of morality; it is not simply a device for finding means to ends that we already care about, but, on the contrary, acceptance of morality gives us a particular conception of what ends are worth caring about.

The difference between this Kantian thesis and the assumption of separateness is especially important for the discussion of naturalism. Separateness is incompatible with a naturalist account of morality; but the Kantian thesis may be compatible with it. For if morality consists partly in the discovery of the ends whose achievement constitutes the fulfilment of human nature, morality gives us a different conception of the end; it does not simply give us a way of finding means to achieve a conception of the end that we already care about. If the crucial point in the Kantian thesis is the rejection of any purely instrumental conception of morality, it need not raise any difficulty for naturalism.

We have discussed the Aristotelian treatment of the non-instrumental aspects of morality in our account of the relation of non-instrumental non-final goods to happiness. If we say we choose them for the sake of happiness, we do not mean that we think of them as having products distinct from themselves that promote happiness (as justice, say, promotes security, which allows us to engage in more theoretical study). We also claim that we

---

[32] Prichard takes the same view about knowledge. See *MODI* 14–16; *KP* 86–98.

[33] See McDowell, 'Role', 15; someone engaged in a naturalist project 'risks being accused of missing the point of moral thought; that the demand is a mistake is a well-known doctrine of H. A. Prichard'. McDowell interprets Aristotle's views so that they do not violate Prichard's doctrine. His attitude to the doctrine in 'Naturalism' is more complex.

choose them as parts of happiness. When we choose them in this way, we have a different conception of happiness from the conception of someone who attributes different parts to happiness.[34]

This distinction between purely productive or instrumental means and components or constituents explains how morality is not purely instrumental. If we think the grain of truth in Prichard's objection is its claim about the non-instrumental character of morality, we cannot assume that naturalism conflicts with a proper appreciation of the role of morality. We have taken one step towards answering the objection that naturalism cannot attribute the proper status to morality.

If this is an adequate defence of naturalism, we ought not to agree with Prichard's view that moral philosophy rests on a mistake if it tries to defend moral obligation by appeal to rational principles that are external to morality. While some external principles reduce morality to an instrumental status, not all external principles do this, and, in particular, naturalist principles do not do this.

This defence of naturalism, however, is no help against Prichard if he relies on the thesis of separateness. Is this thesis reasonable?

It is difficult to see how Prichard's arguments support the thesis of separateness in particular. He is right to maintain that someone who is always asking why he ought to do this or that action that he is morally required to do is missing the point about moral obligation. Someone who understands morality also understands that it requires us to observe its demands without waiting to see what we will gain by doing it. But we might accept all this and still see nothing wrong with Butler's procedure of sitting down in a cool hour and thinking about the point of morality. Butler does not advise us to think about this every time we face a moral demand.

Prichard's attempt to prohibit thoughts about the point of morality seems to be reasonable only if we confuse the outlook of the agent who faces a particular moral demand and the outlook of the reflective agent who thinks about why she ought to take the attitude she takes when she faces a particular moral demand. Once the two outlooks are distinguished, it does not seem reasonable to insist that the second outlook must accept the assumption of separateness.

We might try to explain Prichard's mistake by a comparison with a similar mistake that Ross might make in his defence of intuitionism. Ross argues convincingly that if we consider whether to keep this particular promise, it is irrelevant to consider the balance of utility that would result from keeping it or breaking it. His objection to indirect utilitarianism is less convincing. He seems to believe that we can also see immediately that it is wrong to break promises, without reference to utility or to any other general principle. But he also mentions the 'personal' character of duties; they are retrospectively concerned with what individual people have done, not prospectively concerned with utility or other good consequences.[35] Here he implicitly acknowledges that we can say something more about what makes right actions right. Our answer to this question does not necessarily affect what we think about

---

[34] Prichard discusses questions relevant to non-instrumental non-final goods at *MODI* 5–6. He assumes without warrant that only motives, and not actions, can be non-instrumentally good.

[35] Ross on duties; §1290.

when we face a particular choice about what to do, but it may affect our views about what we should look for in facing particular situations.

Both Ross and Prichard, therefore, seem not to distinguish the right attitude for the agent who faces a choice from the right attitude for the agent who reflects on how to face choices. Once we distinguish the two attitudes, we may reasonably be less inclined to accept Prichard's assumption about the separateness of morality from any external justification. And if we do not accept this assumption, we need not agree that naturalism is part of the moral philosophy that rests on a mistake.

1401. Moral Arguments for Naturalism

If we have found that naturalism does not rest on any mistake about the nature of morality or of moral philosophy, can we go further and show that it captures something important about the nature of morality? If some argument of this sort is plausible, naturalism may not be not only worth considering as an account of morality, but actually indispensable for any plausible account.

We may return to our discussion of Williams's objections to naturalism. To answer these objections, we relied on some claims about a person's real interest that seem both initially plausible and favourable to naturalism. It may be helpful to make some of these claims more explicit, by giving a few cases in which one might be inclined to believe that some naturalist claim is relevant and plausible. Some of the moral claims that a naturalist appeals to are quite simple and elementary.

Naturalist claims about a person's (or other organism's) interests, good, or welfare seem to be plausible rivals to accounts that refer to the person's wants or desires. The naturalist claim asserts that A's good is determined by what A is, by A's actual characteristics, rather than by what A wants. Purely subjective desire-based theories face the obvious objection that we can want what is bad for us.

If we try to modify a subjective theory to meet this obvious objection, we need to introduce hypothetical wants. We may refer to what we would want in idealized circumstances, or to what the idealized agent would want.[36] But these modifications of a subjective theory face a dilemma: (a) Suppose that we define the hypothetical wants non-circularly, without any reference to the desires of agents who know what is good for them. In that case, we still face plausible counter-examples of people who want what is clearly bad for them. (b) We avoid these counter-examples by introducing some unreduced reference to the agent's good.

If subjectivists accept the second horn of the dilemma, they admit defeat. If they choose the first horn, they need to dismiss the intuitive objections to the results of hypothetical desire. But we are entitled to dismiss these objections only if we are satisfied that no sense can be made of the assumptions underlying them. Naturalism suggests a way to understand and to defend a reasonable alternative to a subjective conception of welfare. It suggests that a person's interest is determined by what the person is, by her actual traits and characteristics.

---

[36] See the discussion of Brandt, §1434.

This objective conception of welfare presupposes Butler's view of a nature as a system rather than a collection of traits and desires. If we reject a subjectivist account of interests, we recognize that sometimes we desire F even though not-F is better for us. But satisfaction of our desire for F fulfils some aspect of our nature, since the desire rests on some natural basis. Hence its being against our nature must consist in its being contrary to some system or hierarchy distinct from a collection of desires or traits. We do not refute this naturalist conception of welfare by arguments that treat something's nature simply as a collection of natural traits.

A naturalist conception of welfare clarifies the basis of some duties. In particular, it helps to explain those duties towards people that require us to shape their desires in particular ways. If, for instance, we are responsible for the welfare of a child, we have not necessarily discharged our responsibility if we simply ensure that the child can reliably satisfy the desires she has acquired in growing up.

Aristotle accepts this naturalist point in his remark that no one would reasonably choose to retain the outlook of a child even if one could completely satisfy childish desires (*EN* 1174a1). He suggests that if we are capable of something more than the childish level of thought, we are being harmed if we are prevented from developing beyond it. For similar reasons, Bradley argues that the 'life of an oyster' is no life for a human being, even though it causes no distress to someone who is unaware of anything better.[37] Even if we do not miss what we lack, we may still be harmed, and other people may not have fulfilled their duty towards us.

This claim about duty also seems to presuppose some conception of nature as system. For it would be absurdly demanding to say that if it is possible for A to have developed so as to have been F, A has been wronged if A has not been allowed to be F. When we consider the traits or characteristics that A ought to be allowed to develop, we seem to rely on some idea of those that are basic or especially important in A.

These considerations might lead in different directions. Some traits, such as rationality, seem to be basic and common to human beings. Other relevant traits might be distinctive capacities of A as opposed to other people. We sometimes, and in some circumstances, believe that people have been wronged if the development of their distinctive capacities has been stunted or impeded. But we are also selective in our view of which distinctive capacities really matter for this purpose. We seem to rely on some conception of how different capacities fit together in a human being.

Some of the questions that arise in duties that require the formation of other people's also arise in a political context, in reflexions on oppression and liberation. One might say that freeing people from oppression is valuable only because it allows them to do certain things that they wanted to do and were prevented from doing. But this is an inadequate answer, because oppression can sometimes shape people so that they actually prefer their present condition to the condition they would be in if they were not oppressed.

Liberation, therefore, consists partly in opening opportunities that people ought to have even if they do not regret the lack of them, and perhaps do not initially want them even when they have them. Claims about the badness of oppression and the value of liberation

---

[37] Bradley on the life of an oyster; §1219.

rest on claims about characteristics of the oppressed or liberated people that are not limited to what they want.

Moreover, if we try to identify the sorts of opportunities that should be opened, and which ones matter more than others, we seem to assume that people have natures, rather than simply desires or capacities. For some opportunities seem more urgent or important. These are the ones that matter more in judgments about the badness of oppression, or the goodness of liberation, that are not simply derived from what the people involved actually want.

These applications of naturalism are connected to, but distinct from, the application that is most immediately relevant to Aristotle. He believes not only that claims about nature are the basis of principles about the treatment of others, but also that they are the basis for the virtues of character. The virtues, in his view, are not simply intelligible in the light of demands resting on the nature of other people; they are also perfections of the agent's own nature.

To affirm this connexion between nature and virtue is to maintain that moral virtues are not simply a device for restraining one's own natural tendencies for other people's benefit (as Hobbes believes), or even for deforming one's natural tendencies. People who think of moral virtues as simply a restraint on a person's nature thereby reject naturalism. The naturalist claim is initially plausible; we do not normally think of morality simply as a device to make us fit in with other people. We also tend to think of a morally better person as a better person simpliciter, on the assumption that moral perfections are a part of human perfection.

This sketch of considerations favouring naturalism has introduced two distinct appeals to nature: (1) Nature provides the basis for claims about the good for, or the good of, or the welfare of, a person. (2) It also provides the basis for claims about the goodness, excellence, or perfection of a person. Claims about nature, therefore, belong both to Aristotle's account of happiness and to his account of the virtues. The two kinds of claims must be systematically connected, since he believes that the virtues that perfect a person's nature also achieve the good of a person with this nature. The *Ethics* supports this systematic connexion. Later works in the Aristotelian tradition, including those of Aquinas, Butler, and Green, offer further support.

1402. Moral and Non-Moral Aspects of Naturalism

This moral argument for naturalism presupposes that claims about human nature can support moral claims. The familiar examples we have offered show that this is not a surprising presupposition, and that we accept it in many arguments that we take to be cogent. But we still need to say how the natural facts are morally relevant. Once we reject general attacks on the possibility of deriving values from facts, we will no longer take the sceptical attack on naturalism to be obviously correct. But we still need to explain what sort of support natural facts provide for moral conclusions.

To ask some of the right questions about Aristotle, it is useful to notice different possible views about the relation between claims about nature and ethical claims. Then we can look for reasons to attribute one or another view of their relation to Aristotle.[38]

First, we might take a 'strongly foundational' view, holding that claims about nature are (a) independent of any moral claims; (b) non-normative; and therefore (c) capable of providing an independent foundation for moral claims. According to this view, the claims about nature are claims in biology that provide an independent foundation for claims about welfare. This is the position of some 'scientific' moralists in the 19th and 20th centuries who have tried to 'found' morality on evolutionary biology.[39] We might suppose Aristotle is offering a similar theory with pre-modern biology as its foundation. If we treat this as a substantive thesis about what makes things right and wrong, or about constitutive properties, we will take the sceptical objection to apply.

A second possible view is a 'strongly moralized' view of claims about nature. It treats claims about nature as a part of moral theory, not an independent basis for it. According to this view, a properly moral conception of human nature is part of a moral theory, and is not borrowed from biology. This view of naturalism underlies Nietzsche's attack on Stoic naturalism. He complains that when the Stoics claim to identify the life according to Stoic virtue with the life according to nature, they are really trying to make nature conform to Stoic virtue.[40] Nietzsche believes that this is a misguided anthropomorphizing projection on to nature.

But we might accept Nietzsche's conception of naturalism and also defend the Stoics in principle. Their projection of Stoic values would be illegitimate (we may agree) if they relied on it for theoretical knowledge of nature. But from the moral point of view, it is legitimate to pick out certain aspects of human beings as primarily important, and to formulate our practice of picking out such aspects as a conception of human nature. Hence this strongly moralized version of naturalism appears in several recent writers who are sympathetic to Aristotle or the Stoics, but are impressed by the force of objections to the strongly foundational position.[41]

From this point of view, many common objections to naturalism may be irrelevant. If moral claims do not compete with scientific claims as accounts of the world that we study from the point of view of theoretical knowledge, it may be inappropriate to attack them as bad science. And if claims about nature are claims within moral theory, they may not involve any of the illegitimate transitions attacked by different forms of meta-ethical anti-naturalism. Similarly, if the relevant conception of nature is strongly

---

[38] See also the discussion of Hegel on eudaemonism, §§1009–10.

[39] The first large-scale example of this attempt to exploit evolutionary biology is the work of Herbert Spencer, fairly criticized by Sidgwick in *EGSM* and by Moore in *PE*.

[40] 'Your pride wants to impose your morality, your ideal, on nature—even on nature—and incorporate them in her; you demand that she should be nature "according to the Stoa", and you would like all existence to exist only after your own image . . . For all your love of truth, you have forced yourselves . . . to see nature the wrong way round, namely Stoically . . .' (Nietzsche, *BGE* 9).

[41] The strongly foundational version is criticized by Annas, *MH*, chs. 3–4, 9; McDowell, 'Naturalism'; Nussbaum, 'Nature'. They do not consider any third possibility besides the strongly foundational and the strongly moralized views.

moralized, it may not be open to Prichard's charge of making moral philosophy rest on a mistake.

One might suspect, however, that strongly moralized naturalism concedes too much to anti-naturalist arguments that we have found to be less than cogent. If we do not see anything wrong in principle in the attempt to derive moral conclusions from non-moral premises, and if we do not believe that attempts to justify morality by non-moral considerations reflect a mistake about morality, we may not be eager to show that naturalism avoids these alleged mistakes. Moreover, the cost of avoidance is severe. For naturalism is attractive partly because it affirms that morality is not a closed circle, but engages directly with facts about human beings that we can see to be important apart from any commitment to the moral point of view.

A strongly moralized version of naturalism is open to objection to the extent that it abandons this justificatory role for claims about nature. We may express the objection through a possibly misleading, but possibly pertinent metaphor. If claims about nature are really a branch rather than a root of moral theory, do we leave moral theory rootless in some rather damaging ways?

Our description of the strongly foundational and the strongly moralized versions of naturalism leaves some logical space for a third version. A strongly foundational view claims to rest on a non-normative natural foundation. A strongly moralized view treats claims about nature as being not only normative, but also expressions of a moral theory. These different interpretations of naturalist claims suggest the possibility of a holist view that differs both from a strongly foundational view (proceeding from the bottom up) and from a strongly moralized view (proceeding from the top down). It assumes that one ought to look for some sort of mutual support between claims about nature and moral claims.

One version of holist naturalism takes claims about nature to be partly normative, but non-moral.[42] This possibility may appear more plausible once we recognize that the natural need not be identified with the purely biological. Many claims we make about physical objects are not claims within physics; similarly, many claims about living organisms are not claims within biology. We interact with them in ways that make it appropriate to attribute properties to them that are different from those attributed to them by biology.

One should not assume, therefore, that natural properties are explicitly recognized by one's favoured empirical science.[43] Even though Aristotle, Chrysippus, and Aquinas (e.g.) make some claims about nature that belong to pseudo-science or outdated science, their whole conception of nature, in so far as it bears on moral theory, need not be discredited by these errors; for the conception of nature relevant to ethics need not vary in accordance with scientific variation.

We can support the view that naturalist claims are evaluative but non-moral if we consider Aristotle's claims about nature. Claims about something's natural, or normal, or healthy

---

[42] In saying that they are normative, I mean that they rely on claims about health, welfare, normal conditions, and goodness. I do not mean to claim that normative concepts or properties can be characterized by anything more informative than enumeration.

[43] This conception of natural properties should be contrasted with Moore's conception of them as those that are the concern of empirical sciences. See §§1261–3. I do not mean that genuine natural properties could be incompatible with those recognized by empirical science.

condition seem to be evaluative but not moral. Claims about the nature of a watch (e.g.) depend on beliefs about what a watch in normal working order is like, and these depend on what is good for a watch. Some evaluative or normative beliefs have to be presupposed. The same is true about a human being; beliefs about what makes human beings the unified systems they are also depend on beliefs about normality and about what makes us better or worse off. But these beliefs do not seem to depend on the sorts of moral beliefs that we argue about in discussions of the moral virtues. Though Aristotle's naturalist arguments do not derive the evaluative from the non-evaluative, they seem to derive the moral from the non-moral.

This version of naturalism is holist in so far as it neither tries to derive evaluative principles from a wholly non-evaluative basis nor takes moral norms to be the basis of all normative claims about nature. It looks for mutual support between moral principles and the normative non-moral principles about human nature. Since claims about nature are not simply claims within physical or biological sciences, we need not assume that they are entirely unaffected by other normative views, including moral views. It would be difficult to argue that, for instance, normative claims about health and illness are entirely uninfluenced by morality, but they do not seem to be mere consequences of a specific moral theory. This example offers us a plausible conception of the way in which the normative assumptions underlying claims about nature are non-moral.

But we can defend holist naturalism even if we do not agree that these normative foundations of claims about nature are non-moral. Even if we conceded that some of them are actually moral assumptions, we need not endorse the strongly moralized version of naturalism. For, as we saw in our discussion of Williams, naturalist claims may be relatively weak moral claims. But they may help to support relatively stronger claims. Instead of claiming that we rely on a non-moral but normative conception of nature to support normative moral claims, we might claim that we rely on weak moral claims about nature to support stronger moral claims. In that case, the naturalist offers an appropriate basis for explanation and justification.

We have no good reason, therefore, to dismiss Aristotelian naturalism from consideration. We saw that it was a mistake to dismiss it on the false assumption that 17th-century science had discredited it. It would equally be a mistake to dismiss it on the false assumption that 20th-century meta-ethics or metaphysics has discredited it. If we review Aristotelian naturalism in the light of the arguments discussed in this chapter, we find good reasons to take it seriously. It deserves to be regarded as a viable participant in the prolonged dialectical argument that Socrates began.

RAWLS: THE JUST, THE FAIR, AND THE RIGHT

1403. Rawls and his Predecessors

In the previous three chapters, we have pursued some questions in the moral philosophy of the present or the recent past, in order to discuss some of the developments in 20th-century meta-ethics (in Chs. 92–3) and their relevance to Aristotelian naturalism (in Ch. 94). In this chapter and the next, we take a step back chronologically, to Rawls's *Theory of Justice*, published in 1971. Though this book is by no means the most recent contribution to normative moral theory, it is none the less a suitable focus for some further discussion of the questions that have arisen in the previous few chapters.

Rawls's book is a major work that bears comparison with Sidgwick's *Methods*, and a comparison is useful on several points. Rawls rejects Sidgwick's utilitarianism and his foundationalism, and so it is worth asking whether he answers Sidgwick's main objections to non-utilitarian moral theory and to holist epistemology. Rawls seeks to defend the social contract tradition against the idealist criticisms expressed by Hegel and the British idealists. He defends a Kantian position, interpreted so as to conflict with utilitarianism, but, in contrast to Green, he does not believe that Kant needs to be defended by means of partial assimilation to an idealist version of Aristotle. These aspects of Rawls's position also mark his opposition to Aristotelian naturalism, in so far as the aspects of Kant he defends are those that tend to separate him from naturalism.

None the less, Rawls is sympathetic in certain respects both to Aristotle and to the idealists. His account of the good tries to show how some Aristotelian and idealist views can be reconciled with a firmly Kantian view that gives strict priority to the right. A discussion of this aspect of his position may help us to decide whether Green may not be right after all in his views about the connexions between Kantian and Aristotelian views. If Rawls's account of the relation between these two positions is open to doubt, we may look more sympathetically on Green's more syncretistic views.

A discussion of Rawls also gives us an opportunity to reconsider some of the meta-ethical questions that we have discussed. Since his views on some questions about justification, truth, and objectivity are obscure or perhaps inconstant, we can usefully consider how one or another metaphysical or epistemological position on these questions might affect our understanding of his moral conclusions. Here also the right conclusion to draw from reflexion on Rawls may not be Rawls's conclusion. He tries to separate his normative argument from most of these meta-ethical questions, but we may be less inclined to allow them to be separated.

Rawls's work is important not only because of its conclusions, but also because of how he reaches them. His work, no less than Sidgwick's work, reflects his prolonged reflexion on the history of moral philosophy. It is therefore useful to examine his work in order to pursue further the reflexions that have occupied us in previous chapters.

1404. A Systematic Alternative to Utilitarianism

Rawls defends a non-utilitarian conception of justice that develops and supports the attitude to moral principles that he finds in Kant. In his view, some form of utilitarianism has been the dominant systematic view in much of modern moral philosophy (*TJ* vii/xvii; cf. *PL* xvi). The comprehensive and systematic character of utilitarianism helps to explain its persistent appeal despite the criticisms it has received. The major utilitarians embed their moral theory in a broader economic and social theory; Adam Smith and John Stuart Mill, for instance, carry on the Scottish tradition of presenting moral philosophy as an introduction to jurisprudence, social and political theory, and economics. But their critics, including Grote, Bradley, and Ross, generally confine themselves to arguing that utilitarian moral theory conflicts with our intuitive convictions about right and wrong; hence they cannot offer an alternative that gives better answers to all the questions that utilitarian moral theory answered.[1]

This judgment is not true of all critics of utilitarianism. Green and Bradley argue that it is based on a false metaphysical outlook, and in particular on a mistaken view about the nature of individuals and their relations to others. This fundamental criticism, in their view, requires a re-evaluation of basic utilitarian moral assumptions. It would not be fair, then, to suggest that all critics of utilitarianism rely on a narrow range of objections based on moral intuitions.

The idealists, however, do not offer the sort of 'systematic' theory that Rawls has in mind. He is not thinking of systematic philosophical theories that connect moral philosophy with metaphysics. He is thinking of theories that develop social and economic implications. Idealist critics do not try to replace the social and economic theories that form part of the major utilitarian systems.

Are the critics wrong on this point? We might find the systematic ambitions of the major utilitarians excessive. Though their speculations may have been stimulating and progressive, might it not be better to proceed piecemeal? Moreover, though utilitarian assumptions

---

[1] 'During much of modern moral philosophy the predominant systematic theory has been some form of utilitarianism...We sometimes forget that the great utilitarians...were social theorists and economists of the first rank; and the moral doctrine they worked out was framed to meet the needs of their wider interests and to fit into a comprehensive scheme. Those who criticized them often did so on a much narrower front. They pointed out the obscurities of the principle of utility and noted the apparent incongruities between many of its implications and our moral sentiments. But they failed, I believe, to construct a workable and systematic moral conception to oppose it.' (*TJ* vii–viii/xvii–xviii) References are given to pages of the first and second edns. of *TJ* (in the form 'xx/xx') or to one edition alone (in the form 'xx/' or '/xx').

might be fruitful in economics, that does not necessarily vindicate them in ethics. It seems unreasonable to refuse to accept fundamental criticisms unless the critics can replace the whole intellectual structure that includes the utilitarian errors in ethics. The mere fact that the theory being criticized is more systematic than the criticisms does not justify retention of the theory.

Perhaps Rawls disagrees with the assumptions that underlie this defence of piecemeal criticism. It might be too simple to suppose that utilitarianism as a moral theory is basic, and should be assessed independently of the rest of (for instance) Mill's system of ideas. Perhaps the systematic character of utilitarianism is itself a reason for taking the moral aspects seriously, and hence a legitimate ground for being reluctant to accept anti-utilitarian arguments.

This would be a fair point in favour of a holist attitude to assessment of moral theories, if utilitarianism were not only systematic, but also systematically plausible. But the mere fact that a position is comprehensive and systematic does not show that we have any reason to believe it. We need to consider whether the attacks of Grote or Bradley or Ross on the moral foundations—as they understand them—of utilitarianism do or do not affect the plausibility of broader utilitarian views.

We might illustrate some of these issues from the utilitarian contribution to reform of the criminal law. The utilitarian critique of English common law was salutary, if (e.g.) it reduced the number of capital offences. But this does not show that utilitarianism is plausible, for three reasons: (1) We can also give non-utilitarian reasons for this reform. (2) A thoroughly utilitarian theory may not actually justify this reform. Utilitarians may advocate it because their claims about utility are in fact influenced by their non-utilitarian moral sentiments. (3) A thoroughly utilitarian theory freed from the influence of non-utilitarian sentiments may support repugnant social policies.

Mill recognizes that these reasons might make us hesitate to give utilitarianism the credit for the recommendations of particular utilitarians. He argues that Bentham's enlightened views on social policy should not lead us to accept his simple hedonistic utilitarianism.[2] We ought to be no less cautious in our attitude to Mill's utilitarianism; it may not deserve credit for the enlightened attitudes that he claims to derive from it. Perhaps, therefore, Rawls exaggerates the importance of the systematic character of utilitarianism.

He mentions the broad scope of utilitarianism, and the piecemeal character of anti-utilitarian arguments, because he sets out to do better than the piecemeal critics. He looks for 'an alternative systematic account of justice' (TJ viii/xviii). It is systematic not because it covers all of moral, economic, and social theory, but because the moral arguments about justice are not confined to intuitive objections to utilitarianism. They are the starting point for a description of the basic structure of a society that conforms to the requirements of justice.[3] We will think better of his views about justice if we see that they also support plausible constraints on the structure and institutions of society.

Rawls's aims are narrower than those of utilitarian moral theory, since he offers only a theory of justice, not a theory of morality as a whole. Since he does not discuss other

---

[2] Mill on Bentham; §1113.

[3] Once we understand the implications of justice for the basic structure of society, we see that Rawls's theory 'constitutes the most appropriate moral basis for a democratic society' (TJ viii/xviii).

areas of morality, he leaves open the possibility that some aspects of utilitarianism might fit these other areas. But the restricted scope of his theory may still warrant the rejection of utilitarianism as a general theory of the grounds of moral judgment. Since justice is the first virtue of social institutions, unjust laws and institutions must be abolished, no matter what other goods they secure.[4]

The point of view of justice, therefore, is prior to other aspects of morality. Hence a non-utilitarian theory of justice requires a non-utilitarian theory of morality in general. If Rawls expounds the implications of this claim about justice in a general account of the basic structure of society, he offers a systematic alternative to utilitarianism.

1405. The Social Contract Tradition

To find the right alternative to utilitarianism, Rawls appeals to the social contract tradition derived from Hobbes. The representatives of this tradition whom he mentions are Locke, Rousseau, and Kant (/xviii). A social contract doctrine derives the basic principles that govern society and the powers of the state from some initial situation of choice that involves an agreement. Rawls agrees with this procedure, and tries to display it in accordance with his convictions about system.[5]

Social contract theories give different reasons for appealing to an agreement, in their answers to various doubts and questions. (1) Does the account of an agreement describe the historical beginning of society, or of a political society? Hobbes and Locke think so. Kant does not think so. Rousseau is not entirely clear. (2) What are the characteristics of people making the agreement? Are they similar enough to us so that an argument that appeals to them also appeals to us? Hobbes and Locke think so, but Kant and Rousseau do not agree. (3) What is the moral relevance of an agreement? Hume criticizes the social contract doctrine because it tries to derive obligation from a promise. He argues that the derivation presupposes that, before we make any promise, we are obliged to keep promises; hence its attempt to derive obligation presupposes obligation, and so cannot really derive it from something else. A revival of a social contract theory needs to show that it does not make the mistake exposed by Hume.

These questions about the social contract suggest Rawls's strategy. His defence of a social contract theory is meant to answer all these questions, and to show that they do not undermine a social contract doctrine. He introduces 'simplifying devices' through the 'Original Position', the situation in which the contractors make the relevant agreement. The content of the agreement depends on the nature and situation of the contractors. If it is arbitrary to postulate these contractors, the whole device of a social contract is also arbitrary. But Rawls tries to show that the different features of the Original Position are all reasonable and non-arbitrary, from the moral point of view, and that they give the appropriate moral weight to the agreements made in the Original Position.

---

[4] Similarly, 'each person possesses an inviolability founded on justice that even the welfare of society as a whole cannot override' (§1, 3/3).

[5] He tries 'to organize them [sc. the leading ideas of the social contract tradition] into a general framework by using certain simplifying devices so that their full force can be appreciated' (/xviii). Different forms of contractarian argument and their aims are discussed by Scanlon, 'Contractualism' and WWOEO, ch. 5.

This description sketches the position that Rawls defends in *A Theory of Justice*. This book is the result of a period of reflexion extending over at least twenty years. It reconsiders and reformulates Rawls's position in ways that seek to answer objections to his earlier essays. This process of reconsideration continues in Rawls's later work, and we have to refer to this later work to see whether it revises or defends his views in ways that require us to alter a judgment we might be inclined to reach on the basis of *TJ*.[6] With this qualification, however, we ought to take *TJ* as the primary statement of Rawls's contribution to moral philosophy.[7]

1406. A Defence of Kant

Rawls intends his systematic alternative to utilitarianism to provide a systematic defence of Kant. He defends Kantian ethics against the charge that the categorical imperative is empty and 'purely formal', in some sense that prevents it from giving specific moral guidance. He argues that the categorical imperative has specific moral content, by showing that it supports one theory of justice against another. Specifically, he takes it to support a non-utilitarian theory, derived from the Original Position.[8]

A utilitarian theory claims that the tendency to maximize utility makes a principle right; the interests of particular individuals should be sacrificed for increased total utility. Rawls claims, on the contrary, that principles of justice constrain the pursuit of utility on non-utilitarian grounds. Correct principles of justice guarantee maximum equal liberty for each person, and restrict inequalities to those that benefit the worst-off.[9] Justice requires us to stick to these principles even if their observance does not maximize welfare.

Rawls argues that the Kantian requirement of treating persons as ends in themselves precludes the sacrifice of individual persons to make other people happier. He sets out principles that give content to the categorical imperative by telling us what is required by treating persons as ends in themselves (§29, esp. 179/156–7). He argues that the non-utilitarian principles chosen in the Original Position satisfy Kantian constraints better than utilitarian principles would. They connect Kant's statement of principles with specific moral instructions. Rawls argues, therefore, that we find certain aspects of the Kantian position attractive because we implicitly take the point of view of the Original Position.

The main argument for the two principles of justice proceeds without any explicit appeal to Kantian principles. Rawls claims not to rely on Kantian theory in his anti-utilitarian argument. Hence our acceptance of the starting point of the Original Position does not require prior acceptance of the principle of treating persons as ends. None the less, treating persons in the way they would choose in the Original Position is a reasonable interpretation of what it means to treat persons as ends (179–80/156–7).

---

[6] Some corrections and revisions are embodied in the second edition of *TJ* (see/xii).

[7] On the conception of 'political philosophy' that Rawls uses to describe his later work, see §1442.

[8] For this contrast with utilitarianism, see *TJ* §§5, 30.

[9] These are the 'two principles of justice' introduced in *TJ* §11. Rawls states the two principles fully at *PL* 291 (with changes, which he explains, from *TJ*). The first principle refers to 'a fully adequate system of equal basic liberties which is compatible with a similar scheme of liberties for all'. The second allows inequalities that are 'to the greatest benefit of the least advantaged members of society', and attached to positions that are 'open to all under conditions of fair equality of opportunity'. *PL* 291–4 explains the provision about liberties.

This seems to be a major difference between Kant and Rawls. For when Kant argues that persons are to be treated as ends, he means that this principle tells us something important about the metaphysical and moral status of persons; because persons are ends in themselves, the relevant judgments about fairness are to be taken seriously. According to Rawls, however, we need not believe any of this Kantian theory in order to accept the argument defining the Original Position, and we need not accept Kantian principles in order to believe that the Original Position has the moral force that Rawls ascribes to it.

Since Rawls's argument is independent of Kantian principles, it avoids reliance on dubious or controversial metaphysical aspects of Kant. Kant sometimes suggests that we can justify the moral law by appeal to freedom, and that somehow the appropriateness of the moral law for us depends on our being free agents. Rawls believes a defence of the principles of right need not invoke these aspects of Kant's theory of freedom. It is worth asking, however, whether the connexion with Kant is closer than Rawls supposes, and whether his claims about the Original Position rely on Kantian claims.

1407. Method and Justification

The role of the Original Position reflects Rawls's view of the right method in moral philosophy. His emphasis on the systematic character both of utilitarianism and of his alternative theory suggests correctly that he accepts holism rather than foundationalism in moral epistemology and method. We seek mutual adjustment between our considered judgments and the various theoretical principles that seem plausible to us, until we achieve 'reflective equilibrium' between them.[10]

Rawls does not argue at length for his method. In contrast to Sidgwick, he does not emphasize meta-ethical questions. Sidgwick defends a cognitivist and realist semantics and metaphysics, and a combination of a dialectical and intuitional approach to ethical method. He defends utilitarianism as the theory that best fits the standards that he has set out. Rawls wrote *TJ* towards the end of a period in which moral philosophers concentrated on meta-ethics, with relatively slight emphasis on normative ethics. His book tries to redress the balance by laying emphasis on normative ethics. He suggests that we can make progress in normative ethics if we stay aloof from meta-ethical controversy.

Still, his single-minded acceptance of a dialectical method commits him to some epistemological claims. Sidgwick uses this method for only one of his defences of utilitarianism. Rawls rejects Sidgwick's other method, because it appeals to allegedly self-evident principles.[11] He abandons Sidgwick's foundationalism, and so takes the method of moral philosophy to be

[10] 'By going back and forth, sometimes altering the conditions of the contractual circumstances, at others withdrawing our judgments and conforming them to principles, I assume that eventually we shall find a description of the initial situation that both expresses reasonable conditions and yields principles which match our considered judgments duly pruned and adjusted. This state of affairs I refer to as reflective equilibrium.' (*TJ* 20/18)

[11] 'The aim throughout was to show that the theory proposed matches the fixed points of our considered convictions better than other familiar doctrines, and that it leads us to revise and extrapolate our judgments in what seems [sic] on reflection to be more satisfactory ways.' (579/507) At 51n/45n Rawls underestimates the role of appeals to self-evidence in Sidgwick's moral epistemology. The picture of Sidgwick he accepts makes Sidgwick look more like Rawls than Sidgwick really is.

entirely dialectical. But he does not argue at length on more general philosophical grounds that this is the right method for moral theory. He defends the method in practice, by showing how it produces important results. Here he applies his holism to itself. We cannot settle the appropriate method, in Rawls's view, without examining the results achieved by a given method; such a question is not to be settled by purely epistemological non-moral judgments. The fact that a certain method gives morally plausible results is the best argument for using that method.[12]

This holist attitude to justification raises a question about Rawls's conclusions. Sidgwick accepts foundationalism partly because he is an objectivist about moral knowledge. In his view, a true moral theory is true not simply because it matches our moral convictions but because it expresses facts about moral rightness and goodness that are not entirely constituted by our convictions. Where does Rawls stand on this question?

A holist might answer in different ways: (1) Sidgwick is right to be an objectivist, but holism can satisfy his demands. The appropriate sort of coherence warrants a claim to objective truth. (2) Sidgwick is right to be an objectivist, and holism cannot satisfy his demands. Since the method of moral philosophy is holist, moral philosophy does not support a claim to describe objective facts about right and wrong. (3) Sidgwick is wrong to be an objectivist; moral philosophy cannot fulfil objectivist demands, but its failure does not matter.

Rawls rejects a foundationalist method and epistemology, but he does not reject object-ivism. Nor does he say whether his method fails to meet a legitimate requirement on justification. He acknowledges that a holist justification 'is open to the general complaint that it appeals to the mere fact of agreement' (580/508). He answers that 'justification is argument addressed to those who disagree with us, or to ourselves when we are of two minds' (580/508). Hence the argument for Rawls's theory of justice rests explicitly on agreement about the relevant starting points and about the relevant conceptions of justice to be considered.

But this claim about the character of justification seems not to answer all the relevant questions. Admittedly, we can justify a belief or theory to the satisfaction of particular interlocutors only if they agree with the starting points of our argument. But to satisfy particular interlocutors is not to justify. For if they are too easily satisfied, they may accept something that is not a genuine justification. If they are unreasonably stubborn, they may reject a genuine justification. Someone who is ignorant about mathematical proof, say, might make both kinds of mistake. Arguments from agreed premises will justify only if the premises are appropriate. A foundationalist believes that the appropriate starting points of moral argument are self-evident principles. If we reject this appeal to self-evidence, we must say what makes the starting points appropriate for justification.

Simple agreement might answer this question for a conventionalist who believes that a principle offers genuine justification if the parties to some argument agree on it. Though we might suppose that there is some difference between being agreed and being appropriately agreed, the conventionalist answers either that there is no difference or that the difference can be captured by appeal to further conventions and agreements.

---

[12] On reflective equilibrium see §1385, and Daniels, 'Equilibrium'. Questions about the aims of moral theory are pursued further by Scanlon, 'Aims'.

Rawls's over-simple contrast between appeals to self-evidence and appeals to agreement might allude to the difference between foundationalism and holism. Alternatively, it might express a conventionalist view about the nature of justification. But even if he holds a conventionalist view, it is reasonable to see how much of his argument justifies his principles according to a different conception of justification.

1408. Considered Judgments

Though some of Rawls's remarks on justification might suggest that he holds a purely conventionalist view of justification, such a view does not fit his early essay, 'Outline', where he introduces the different features of a considered judgment and discusses the relation between principles and considered judgments. The features of a competent moral judge include (1) intelligence; (2) normal factual knowledge of the world; (3) a reasonable, logical, and open mind; (4) sympathetic knowledge of the relevant human interests that conflict in such a way as to require a moral decision.[13]

These features of the considered moral judgments reached by such a judge are either the same as, or analogous to, those we would impose on any factual judgments that we would treat as plausible sources of information about the world.[14] When we seek judges who do not judge hastily, or on the basis of antecedent interests or biases, or because they are unreasonably wedded to some theory, we look for the characteristics of a reliable observer of external reality. If we treated moral reflexion simply as a means of self-knowledge, rather than knowledge of some external reality, why should we expect the judge to know about (e.g.) the different interests that occasion the disputes needing moral decision?[15] Our criteria suggest that we seek the sort of impartiality that we seek in reliable observations of the world.

This objectivist explanation of Rawls's criteria for considered judgments is not the only one worth considering. We might suggest instead that we want people whose judgments we can rely on for settling disputes or securing consensus. This suggestion, however, does not explain why considered judgments should rest on careful inquiry into the facts and on attention to the views of those affected by a moral decision.[16] For inquiry into facts may make it more difficult to secure consensus, if a case turns out to be more complicated than it seemed. If we simply wanted to find out about our own views or preferences, or about shared assumptions that are not truth-oriented, we would not need considered judgments that rest on careful inquiry into the facts. On this point, an objectivist explanation is more plausible.

---

[13] This list of features summarizes 'Outline', §2.3.

[14] '. . . one should note the kind of characteristics which have been used to define a competent moral judge: namely, those characteristics which, in the light of experience, show themselves as necessary conditions for the reasonable expectation that a given person may come to know something . . . Thus, the defining characteristics of a competent judge have not been selected arbitrarily, but in each case there is a reason for choosing them which accords with the purpose of coming to know.' ('Outline', 4–5)

[15] '. . . a sympathetic knowledge of those human interests which, by conflicting in particular cases, give rise to the need to make a moral decision.' ('Outline', 3)

[16] 'It is required that the judgment be one which has been preceded by careful inquiry into the facts of the question at issue, and by a fair opportunity for all concerned to state their side of the case. This requirement is justified on the ground that it is only by chance that a just decision can be made without a knowledge of the relevant facts.' ('Outline', 6)

This is not a conclusive argument for an objectivist interpretation of Rawls's conditions for considered judgments. But at least his conditions admit an objectivist interpretation, and it is not easy to explain why a non-objectivist must accept the same conditions.

1409. Moral Theory and Linguistic Theory

Though Rawls's early account of considered judgments suggests an objectivivst interpretation of his views, some of his later remarks may incline us in a more conventionalist direction. He offers an analogy to illustrate, though only provisionally, his conception of moral theory. He compares the linguistic theorist's task of 'describing the sense of grammaticalness that we have for the sentences of our native language' (47/41) with the moral theorist's task of describing our 'moral capacity', or, in this case, our 'sense of justice'. In the case of linguistics, we begin with the native speaker's intuitive sense that one sentence is grammatical and another is deviant, and we try to formulate the rules that underlie our intuitive discriminations.

This process goes in two directions; (1) Often we reject a proposed rule if it implies some result that conflicts with our grammatical sense about particular examples. (2) But sometimes we may decide that the rule is so well confirmed over such a wide range of cases, fits so well with other rules, and so on, that it is better to reject some of our particular judgments as erroneous, and to conclude that, say, a particular sort of utterance is really ungrammatical though it did not seem deviant. We formulate principles, and compare them with our theories in these two directions. If at some stage we are content with the result of mutual comparison between intuitive judgments and theories, we have reached reflective equilibrium (48/42).

Moral reflexion begins with considered judgments about moral questions—the rules, general features of morality, and judgments about particular cases, that seem to us to be most plausible at the outset. We try to formulate a theory that leads us to reflective equilibrium. Rawls's theory of justice, and in particular his formulation of his two principles of justice,[17] is meant to lead, after suitable reflexion and comparison, to reflective equilibrium.

Rawls's notion of reflective equilibrium explains why he emphasizes the systematic character of utilitarianism, and why he looks for a systematic alternative. We might find that, though utilitarianism conflicts with many considered judgments about particular cases of injustice, it organizes and explains our convictions about social policy more generally. In that case, we might decide to reject the considered judgments about injustice in order to achieve reflective equilibrium.

To answer this defence of utilitarianism, Rawls argues that his account of justice leads to reflective equilibrium in relation to all the relevant considered judgments. To see that this is so, we need a systematic argument about justice that is not confined to the discussion of a few intuitive convictions, however certain they may appear. On this ground, one might fault the anti-utilitarian arguments of, say, Price or Ross; for they reject utilitarianism on

---

[17] For the two principles see n9 above.

the basis of intuitive convictions, but they refrain—indeed they refuse on principle—to present the systematic alternative that we need to counter the systematic argument for utilitarianism. Rawls tries to show that we can find systematic, and not merely intuitive, reasons for preferring a non-utilitarian theory.

Since this is Rawls's conception of reflective equilibrium, we cannot reach it unless we have formulated some principles, and adjusted our considered judgments to them, by the appropriate reciprocal process. It is puzzling, therefore, that he advises us to use our considered judgments in reflective equilibrium to test theoretical principles.[18] This advice implies that we can reach reflective equilibrium without having made up our mind about the theoretical principles we accept. But Rawls's account of reflective equilibrium implies that we cannot do this; we reach reflective equilibrium only by mutual adjustment of our considered judgments and our theory. Any attempt to test our theory against considered judgments in reflective equilibrium is bound to support our theory; for we would not be in reflective equilibrium unless the result of the test supported the theory. In that case, the alleged test seems idle; for the fact that we are in reflective equilibrium guarantees that a comparison with our considered judgments supports the theory, and no further testing is needed.

It would be equally misleading to suggest that after accepting theory T1, we should check a second theory, T2, by comparing it with the considered judgments we accept in the reflective equilibrium created by acceptance of T1. If T1 has really brought us to reflective equilibrium, the considered judgments we accept will be those that fit T1. If T2 is incompatible with T1, the attempt to test T2 will result in rejection of T2. If, for instance, convinced utilitarians were to check Rawls's theory against their considered judgments, as adjusted to utilitarian principles, they would always reject his theory.

We ought, therefore, to compare a second theory not with the considered judgments we accept in the light of our present theory, but with the considered judgments we would be strongly inclined to accept in abstraction from our present theory. Sidgwick believes that some of our intuitive convictions can be explained as residues that have outlived their utilitarian function and ought therefore to be rejected. But we ought to consider these convictions in assessing a non-utilitarian theory of justice; for we regard them as errors only if we accept the utilitarian theory that is being called into question.

Apparently, therefore, we should revise Rawls's advice to check theories by appeal to considered judgments in reflective equilibrium; we should delete the reference to reflective equilibrium. This revision gives a clearer picture of the method that he actually follows, and fits better with his account of reflective equilibrium.

1410. Ought We to Pursue Reflective Equilibrium?

Rawls's discussion of methods suggests that we ought to test a theory by seeing how far it permits us to reach reflective equilibrium. But is this a useful suggestion? Perhaps almost

---

[18] 'There is a definite, if limited, class of facts against which conjectured principles can be checked, namely our considered judgments in reflective equilibrium.' (51/44) At 121/105, 432/379, Rawls suggests again that appeal to considered judgments in reflective equilibrium provides a test of a theory.

any moral theory could result in reflective equilibrium if we discarded our initial considered judgments ruthlessly enough. But this does not seem to be the sort of process that Rawls intends. He does not seem to use 'reflective equilibrium' so broadly that anyone who accepts a theory and judges in accordance with it has thereby achieved reflective equilibrium. He seems to regard ruthless surgery not as a possible method of reaching reflective equilibrium, but as an assertion of inability to reach reflective equilibrium.

An assertion of inability is reasonable, if we discover that our considered judgments are too chaotic or too misguided to be worth preserving, even in a modified form, within an enlightened theory. Perhaps, for instance, some of Nietzsche's views (interpreted as first-order moral claims) clash so violently and frequently with our initial considered judgments that we could not reasonably take them to give an account of our 'moral capacity' or 'moral sentiments'. If, then, we agree with Nietzsche's views, we should acknowledge that we cannot reach reflective equilibrium as a result of reflexion on our initial considered judgments.

Rawls suggests that this Nietzschean reaction is to be avoided. He believes that we should favour a theory in so far as it we can use it to reach reflective equilibrium. We should find a way to adjust principles and considered judgments to each other without radical surgery.

Why is this a reasonable test? We may agree that the method of mutual adjustment, directed to reflective equilibrium, is appropriate for Rawls's example of linguistics. This is the right method because the task of linguistics is, as Rawls says, to describe our sense of what is grammatical. However much we may legitimately revise intuitive judgments in particular cases, these are what the linguist tries to describe. Linguists do not claim to be describing something that is grammatical in itself, independently of the judgments of native speakers.[19]

But the same may not be true in moral theory. For some moral theorists claim that they are trying to find not merely our conception of what is right, but what is really right. Hence, they may not accept a condition of adequacy that relies as heavily as Rawls does on initial considered judgments. Rawls's condition of adequacy seems to be controversial.

This question may affect our choice among moral theories. For some utilitarians might not share Sidgwick's confidence in the dialectical argument for utilitarianism. They might agree that if they accepted Rawls's conception of moral theory, a non-utilitarian theory might be the best, or as good as any other theory. While common sense contains some utilitarian elements, it also contains non-utilitarian elements; fidelity to our considered judgments may not support a preference for the utilitarian elements. But—such utilitarians might argue—a cogent argument for utilitarianism rests on appeal to the self-evidence of the principles underlying the principle of utility. Hence we should accept utilitarianism even though it fails to achieve reflective equilibrium.

Rawls seems to rule out this utilitarian theory on the ground that it requires extensive revisions to common sense. A less utilitarian theory might accommodate common sense with fewer revisions. But a utilitarian might reasonably protest that this criterion of adequacy discriminates unfairly against revisionary utilitarianism. The pursuit of reflective

---

[19] At least, for the sake of comparison, we may assume, as Rawls does, that this is true. His use of the analogy with linguistics is criticized by Nagel, 'Rawls', 2n.

equilibrium seems to be too conservative an aim, therefore, if it prohibits radical revision of our considered judgments.[20]

This may not be a fatal objection to Rawls's method. For we might not count all considered judgments as equally worthy of consideration in the pursuit of reflective equilibrium. Indeed, if we compare the appeal to linguistics with Rawls's earlier criteria for considered judgments, we may suspect that the analogy with linguistics is defective at a vital point. For considered moral judgments, as Rawls conceives them, should result from careful inquiry into the relevant facts, not simply into what people generally think about the relevant facts. The linguistic analogy suggests a more conventionalist view; our data in this case are what people say and think, not some further facts beyond what they say and think.[21]

This point of disanalogy shows why we ought not to take linguistic inquiry to be exactly parallel with moral inquiry. Some considered moral judgments seem especially reliable for the same reason that makes some considered factual judgments especially reliable. They result from especially careful inquiry into the relevant facts and the interests of the people affected, and therefore they give us a reasonable starting point. A good theory, then, reaches reflective equilibrium by reconciling other judgments with these. We need not say that the favoured subset of initial considered judgments are self-evident, but we need some reason for being especially confident in them, and for adjusting our other beliefs to them.

Rawls follows this procedure. He begins with a favoured subset of considered judgments and develops a theory from them, in order to use it for the derivation of other considered judgments. This is a reasonable procedure only if it is reasonable to choose one favoured subset rather than another as our initial set of considered judgments. We need to see what Rawls can say in defence of his choice of starting point.

But if we take Rawls to be selective in this way in his attitude to considered judgments, we have to add something to his description of the method that results in reflective equilibrium. We might be tempted to suppose that linguistic inquiry aims at the sort of reflective equilibrium that we also aim at in moral theory; but we would be wrong to suppose so. For in moral theory, we look for mutual adjustment between theoretical principles and the considered judgments that result from appropriately careful inquiry into the relevant facts, and not simply into people's beliefs. Linguistics does not start from considered judgments of this sort, since it does not inquire into the facts themselves apart from what people say.

If, then, we take the analogy with linguistics to offer an adequate account of moral inquiry, we may well ascribe to Rawls an implicitly conventionalist view of justification. But if we believe that we should limit the application of this analogy by reference to Rawls's criteria for reliable considered judgments, we will not suppose that he endorses a conventionalist view.

---

[20] Singer criticizes Rawls's approach: 'The reflective equilibrium conception of moral philosophy . . . is liable to mislead in two ways: first, it slides easily into the view that moral theories are to be tested against the moral judgments made by some group or consensus . . . second, even when the "reflective equilibrium" method says no more than that one cannot consistently accept a moral theory while holding particular moral judgments incompatible with it, it puts this truth in a way that tends to give excessive weight to our particular moral judgments.' ('Equilibrium', 517). Singer prefers Sidgwick's appeal to moral axioms.

[21] Singer argues that, on one reasonable interpretation, Rawls is a subjectivist about the truth of moral theories. He asks 'is the fact that a moral theory matches a set of considered moral judgments in reflective equilibrium, to be regarded merely as *evidence* of the validity of the moral theory, or is it then valid *by definition* . . .?' ('Equilibrium', 493) He argues that Rawls commits himself to the second alternative. Hare, 'Rawls', 82 takes the same view.

1411. Is the Pursuit of Reflective Equilibrium Consistent with Objectivism?

So far we have found that Rawls's pursuit of reflective equilibrium allows an objectivist interpretation, and that his account of considered judgments may even favour objectivism. We should therefore consider Dworkin's argument to show that Rawls's method excludes objectivism. Reflective equilibrium, in Dworkin's view, cannot be expected to tell us about a moral reality independent of our beliefs, because this is not the right method for discovery of independent moral facts. We should take Rawls's method to articulate a shared moral outlook, not to discover anything that is true independently of this outlook.

Dworkin observes that, according to Rawls, we ought to adjust our considered judgments and our principles to each other, so that we are ready to reject some of our considered judgments if they fail to fit the principles that seem most plausible.[22] Dworkin considers two models that might try to explain this process of mutual adjustment: (1) A 'natural' model treats considered judgments as parallel to observations, and argues that since our theory explains these observations, it gives a true account of reality. (2) A 'constructive' model treats mutual adjustment as a demand of 'political morality' that requires decisions and rulings by judges and officials to be based on general principles that can be shown to apply to this or that particular case.

Dworkin's legal analogy (or explanation, if it is not meant as a mere analogy) agrees with Rawls's linguistic analogy, if we do not limit that analogy by reference to Rawls's criteria for considered judgments. According to Dworkin, we try to achieve equilibrium between intuitive judgments and general principles, but we do not ask ourselves whether the resulting principles and judgments fit the facts. The question about fitting the facts is appropriate only within the natural model, which does not apply to moral inquiry.

The natural model is inapplicable, according to Dworkin, because it cannot explain why we are allowed, and indeed required, to discount considered moral judgments that do not fit our principles. If the natural model were correct (he argues), anyone who discounted considered judgments would illegitimately ignore inconvenient evidence that did not fit a given theory. But the constructive model supports the rejection of considered judgments; for a judicial or administrative system is just only if officials make decisions on principle and ignore their intuitive judgment that this or that particular decision is wrong.[23] These 'independent reasons of political morality' (31) require coherence between theory and particular judgments, but they do not concern themselves about whether such coherence fits the facts.

We might object that this contrast overlooks a legitimate role for mutual adjustment within the natural model. In empirical science, we sometimes reject our observations as being misleading, because we suppose it is overwhelmingly unlikely, in the light of our other observations and theories, that these particular observations are correct. Hence the fact that moral theory practises mutual adjustment does not refute an objectivist interpretation.

---

[22] See Dworkin, 'Position', 29.

[23] 'It [sc. the constructive model] demands that decisions taken in the name of justice must never outstrip an official's ability to account for these decisions in a theory of justice, even when such a theory must compromise some of his intuitions.' (Dworkin, 'Position', 30)

In answer to this objection, Dworkin warns us not to be misled by 'false sophistication about science' (32). In empirical science, we do not simply ignore recalcitrant observations (or ostensible observations) on the ground that they do not fit our theory; we also try to explain them by pointing out that a red light shining on the white wall makes us think we see a red wall, or that the test-tube was probably dirty, and so on. But in moral theory we have no parallel obligation to explain away recalcitrant considered judgments; we are allowed to ignore them.[24] Moral theory differs from empirical scientific theory, then, not merely because it rejects some considered judgments, but because it rejects them without trying to explain them. Hence the constructive model fits moral theory, but the natural model does not.

But does moral theory ignore recalcitrant considered judgments, and ought it to ignore them? Moralists often seem to accept an obligation to explain considered judgments. Sidgwick, for instance, argues that some non-utilitarian convictions used to promote utility but no longer promote it; this is how one might explain the double standard for male and female chastity. Whether or not utilitarians are right to appeal to outworn utilitarian tendencies, they argue appropriately, if they are trying to explain recalcitrant considered judgments rather than ignore them. To this extent, they seem to follow the natural model.

Moreover, if such attempted explanations failed, and we were confident that we faced some plausible but recalcitrant considered moral judgments, we might reasonably suppose that we had some reason to be less confident in our moral theory. Questions that arise about the moral difference between doing and allowing, and about the significance of the principle of double effect, may suggest examples of considered judgments that many moralists are unwilling to accept outright, but also unwilling to dismiss without explanation. Some, in fact, believe that the recalcitrance of these considered judgments is a pervasive feature of moral thinking that casts doubt on the possibility of a unified theory.[25] Whether or not these doubts are justified, they suggest that Dworkin's account of the treatment of recalcitrant considered judgments is open to question.

Our treatment of recalcitrant considered moral judgments, therefore, does not seem to discredit the natural model. On the contrary, we seem to acknowledge the very obligation that Dworkin denies and that fits the natural model. If we find a conflict between a plausible theory and firm considered judgments that we cannot plausibly explain away, we may be uncertain about what is right, and we may find it unduly dogmatic to ignore the considered judgments as though they should not affect our attitude to our theory. Since these responses to considered judgments fit the natural model better than they fit the constructive model, they give us a non-conclusive reason to accept an objectivist interpretation of the pursuit of reflective equilibrium.

Dworkin disagrees partly because he believes that the natural model does not fit the outlook of judges and officials. He begins with the moralist who examines considered moral judgments and theories in pursuit of a theory that achieves reflective equilibrium. But then

---

[24] '. . . this procedure (sc. reflective equilibrium) argues not simply that alternative structures of principle are available to explain the same phenomena, but that some of the phenomena, in the form of moral convictions, may simply be ignored the better to serve some particular theory.' (Dworkin, 'Position', 33)

[25] This treatment of recalcitrant judgments is characteristic of Nagel's position. See, e.g., 'Luck', 'War', and 'Fragmentation'.

he introduces someone with different aims. A judge or official has the urgent task of settling particular questions about what justice requires. Attention to this official seems to divert Dworkin's attention from the moralist.

The moralist's task and the official's task are connected, but they are not the same. Dworkin is right (let us grant) to claim that officials ought to make decisions on principle. They need principles that are clear enough and reliable enough to allow an answer to practical questions; and we would not want them to hesitate, or to issue obscure instructions, because they could not explain away all their recalcitrant intuitions. For the sake of demonstrable fairness in decisions, they need (we may suppose) to rely on a definite and relatively clear principle rather than relying on moral intuitions that they cannot connect systematically to plausible principles that they can apply to other cases. Moralists, however, are not constrained by the preoccupations of officials, and they are not required to present conclusions that officials can immediately apply.

We seem to recognize this difference between morality and the constraints on officials. For sometimes we might suspect that officials have reached the wrong decision, if their principle violates some considered judgments that we have not been able to explain away. We might suspect this even if we recognize the legitimacy of the decision that they have reached on the basis of the most plausible available principle. The legitimate moral demands on officials are not overriding constraints on moral theory. Hence they cannot be used, as Dworkin uses them, to discredit an objectivist interpretation of Rawls's method in moral theory. In *TJ*, Rawls does not commit himself to constructivism. Nor does constructivism offer the best interpretation of the method he endorses.[26]

1412. The Rejection of Intuitionism

So far Rawls's aim of arguing dialectically for an alternative to utilitarianism does not distinguish his view from the anti-utilitarian outlooks of Price, Grote, and Ross. These critics of utilitarianism argue that our considered moral judgments do not support the principle of utility as a supreme principle, and that the utilitarian position overlooks other important aspects of our moral thinking. Their position is pluralist, since it recognizes a number of basic moral principles, including principles of justice, fidelity, and benevolence, none of which is always prior to the others. This is the position that Rawls calls 'intuitionism'.

The name is somewhat misleading (as Rawls acknowledges, / 30–1).[27] For the theorists Rawls has in mind need not claim that the basic principles are known by intuition to be self-evident. One might accept Rawls's method of mutual adjustment, but argue that it supports a pluralist conception of basic principles, so that no highest principle settles

---

[26] On Rawls's later views on constructivism, see §1442.

[27] 'I shall think of intuitionism in a more general way than is customary; namely, as the doctrine that there is an irreducible family of first principles which have to be weighed against one another by asking ourselves which balance, in our considered judgment, is the most just.' (*TJ* 34/30). 'Perhaps it would be better if we were to speak of intuitionism in this broad sense as pluralism. Still a conception of justice can be pluralistic without requiring us to weigh its principles by intuition. It may contain the requisite priority rules.' (35/31). Rawls's use of 'intuitionism' is somewhat similar to Sidgwick's use of the term for the morality of common sense. See §§1159–60, 1199. I will use 'intuitionism' for the pluralist position that Rawls describes. For further discussion see Williams, 'Intuitionism'; Urmson, 'Defence'.

questions of priority among principles. The reasoning that we use in settling questions about the relative importance of justice or generosity or benevolence or loyalty in particular cases is not derived from a primary principle, but it relies directly on considered judgments.[28]

Rawls rejects this pluralism about ultimate principles, because he believes it offers us no systematic alternative to utilitarianism. In his view, we should not only point out that utilitarianism fails to fit our considered judgments, but we should also present principles that settle questions of priority. In Rawls's view, no single principle settles all these questions, but we should recognize a lexical order of principles; we satisfy the claims of principle A first, then go on to B, and so on. Since the order in which we satisfy the claims of these principles is invariant, we reject pluralism.

Rawls's preference is reasonable if it is defeasible. Price or Ross might reasonably admit that it would be theoretically and practically desirable if we could find a non-utilitarian supreme principle. But they argue that we cannot find such a principle if we follow the method of moral philosophy that attends to our considered judgments. If Rawls follows a dialectical method, he cannot reasonably insist that all monist accounts of the principles of morality are to be preferred to all pluralist accounts; for even the most plausible monist account will be less plausible than a pluralist account if it fits our considered judgments less well. An absolute preference for a monist account would be reasonable only if we could rely on some principle of rationality that demands monism. Rawls's preference for monism, therefore, is not an absolute constraint on a theory. Though we might initially prefer a monist theory, we ought not to persist in this preference if we find that the appropriate dialectical examination does not sustain it.[29]

1413. What Should Rawls Prove about Justice?

Rawls proposes to refute utilitarianism and intuitionism through an argument about justice. To see whether he succeeds, we need to see what questions need to be answered, and what the answers would show about rival views.[30]

He might argue against utilitarianism as a theory of justice in particular. He refutes it if he shows that the best explanation of considered judgments about justice is non-utilitarian. In that case, justice is a source of prima facie duties (in Ross's terms) that are not fixed by purely utilitarian considerations. But refutation of a utilitarian theory of justice does not refute utilitarianism unless a utilitarian has to agree that if utilitarianism does not fit justice, it does not fit morality as a whole. One might agree to this if one believed that considerations of justice override all other moral considerations in case of conflict. Mill may believe this, but Sidgwick does not, and it does not follow from acceptance of utilitarianism.

And so, even if our considered judgments about justice do not fit the principle of utility, utilitarianism might still give the correct account of what we ought to do in cases of conflict

[28] Feinberg defends this form of intuitionism in 'Rawls'.

[29] This seems to be Rawls's view: 'Now there is nothing irrational about the intuitionist doctrine. Indeed, it may be true. We cannot take for granted that there must be a complete derivation of our judgments of social justice from recognizably ethical principles.' (39/34–5)

[30] These questions are clearly distinguished and helpfully discussed by Feinberg, 'Rawls'. He argues plausibly that Rawls's answer to the first question is more plausible than his answer to the second.

between justice and other moral principles, and in cases where questions of justice do not arise. Acceptance of a non-utilitarian conception of justice still leaves the main points of the utilitarian outlook standing. The same questions arise about intuitionism. Rawls might find principles of justice that do not require us to resort to the intuitive judgments favoured by pluralism. But conflicts between justice and other parts of morality might require resort to intuitive judgments.

If, then, Rawls is to refute utilitarianism and intuitionism, he needs to appeal to different considered judgments at different stages of his argument. He needs to discuss considered judgments within the scope of justice, about whether this or that policy or practice would be just; then we can see whether we give utilitarian answers to the relevant questions. But he also needs to consider considered judgments about what is right all things considered, not simply about what is just. We need to see whether we always accord the sort of primacy to justice that would rule out both a utilitarian and an intuitionist view about the relation of justice to the rest of morality.

Rawls says he is offering only a theory of justice and not a general theory of the right; hence we might expect that he will only reject utilitarianism and intuitionism about justice, and leave their general views of the right unanswered. But he intends his theory of justice to replace general utilitarian and intuitionist views of the right. For he claims that justice is primary in morality;[31] hence he believes that once we vindicate a non-utilitarian and non-intuitionist account of justice, we rule out utilitarianism and intuitionism about the right. He claims to defend a deontological theory; for he defines the right without a prior definition of the good (26/21–2), and he claims that the right, so understood, is prior to the good. This is a claim not only about justice, but also about the right in general.

To understand Rawls's position, therefore, we need to find his arguments for the broader claim about the right. It is easy to find the arguments for a non-utilitarian and non-intuitionist account of justice, but it is more difficult to find his case for the primacy of justice and for a deontological (and hence non-utilitarian) and monist (and hence non-intuitionist) account of the right.

1414. Why the Original Position?

The desire for a systematic and non-intuitionist alternative to utilitarianism helps to explain a distinctive feature of Rawls's use of dialectical argument. He does not argue against the principle of utility by comparing it directly with considered judgments about justice. He postpones any such comparison until after the construction of an Original Position. The device of the Original Position is his contribution both to dialectical argument and to the interpretation of the social contract tradition. Through the Original Position the social contract tradition makes dialectical argument systematic.

Acceptance of the Original Position does not ensure that the resulting principles of justice have a monist rather than a pluralist structure. But it increases our chance of reaching such principles. For the Original Position rests on a subset of our considered judgments—those

---

[31] See, e.g., the first paragraph of *TJ* §1, which Rawls sums up with 'These propositions seem to express our intuitive conviction of the primacy of justice' (4/4).

about the fairness of conditions in which we make agreements relevant to justice. If we agree to regard the Original Position as a constraint on acceptable principles of justice, we take the demands of fairness to be primary among the demands of justice. Hence we reject any intuitionist balancing of fairness against other aspects of justice. While we may still discover pluralism within our judgments about fairness, we treat judgments about fairness as prior to other considered judgments.

Similarly, if we agree to treat the Original Position as a constraint on our conception of the right, we make it more difficult to argue for intuitionism about the right. For if all principles of right conform to the Original Position, they all acknowledge the primacy of fairness; hence we do not rely on intuition to balance the claims of fairness and justice against other aspects of rightness. Since acceptance of the primacy of fairness in rightness is more controversial than acceptance of its primacy in justice, it is correspondingly more difficult to establish the starting point of Rawls's argument.

Many of Rawls's distinctive claims, about both the content and the method of his theory, depend on the role of the Original Position and the conclusions derived from it. Rawls discusses the reasoning within the Original Position in some detail. He has less to say about the reasons for taking the point of view of the Original Position.

1415. Justice, Fairness, and the Original Position

We construct the Original Position instead of merely relying on considered judgments. We do not draw on all our considered judgments about justice in looking for principles to explain them. Instead we introduce justice as fairness. An appeal to fairness explains why we construct the Original Position; each of its features can be justified by appeal to fairness.[32]

Rawls calls his doctrine 'justice as fairness' because 'it conveys the idea that the principles of justice are agreed to in an initial situation that is fair' (12/11). Let us call this the Fairness Principle. Principles of justice are for the basic structure of institutions and policies in the 'circumstances of justice' (§22). The appropriate conditions for choosing principles of justice in these external circumstances are fair conditions.

The dialectical strategy requires the considered judgments about fairness to be undisputed. If it were obvious that the Fairness Principle is inconsistent with utilitarianism, it would be a waste of time for Rawls to construct an argument against utilitarianism from the Fairness Principle. And if a utilitarian accepts the Fairness Principle, but disputes the different claims about fairness that support the features of the Original Position, the dispute needs to be resolved before we can construct the Original Position.

And so the assumptions about justice and fairness that we build into the Original Position must not be so precise that they explicitly reject utilitarianism. For it should still be an open question for us, when we look at the Original Position, whether utilitarian or non-utilitarian principles will come out of it. The conditions that specify the Original Position should not embody an explicit commitment to non-utilitarian views about justice.

---

[32] 'It is natural to ask why, if this agreement is never actually entered into, we should take any interest in these principles, moral or otherwise.' 'These constraints express what we are prepared to regard as limits on fair terms of social cooperation.' (21/19)

But if Rawls's argument is sound, the initial judgments about fairness cannot be neutral between different theories of justice, and so we cannot consistently accept both these judgments and utilitarianism. He argues that utilitarian principles would not be chosen in the Original Position. Since the Original Position is a legitimate device only in so far as it incorporates our initial considered judgments about fairness, these initial considered judgments must rule out a utilitarian conception of justice.

The Original Position, therefore, must rest on principles that are strong enough to rule out utilitarianism. Since it is designed so that it rules out only what fair initial conditions rule out, judgments that define fair conditions must somewhere be inconsistent with utilitarianism. The apparent neutrality of the initial judgments makes them suitable for a dialectical argument, in which opponents come to see that assumptions they took to be compatible with their position really are not compatible with it.

Rawls does not assume from the start that the Fairness Principle is an axiom. We need only think of it as one aspect of justice, or a sufficient condition for one sort of justice. Rawls suggests that if we try to treat it as an underlying principle of justice, we find that we can generate other principles of justice from it. That is why the argument from the Fairness Principle is interesting and complex, and we cannot predict the outcome in advance.

1416. Arguments for Fairness

Rawls connects the Fairness Principle with the general idea of regarding principles of justice as the outcome of a certain kind of rational choice.[33] We might give this remark a Kantian interpretation: if rational agents understand what is implied in positive freedom and rationality, they understand that it requires the acceptance of some specific moral principles. This interpretation, however, is useless to Rawls; if it were correct, the relevant conception of rational persons and what they know includes a great deal of disputable Kantian argument about the nature of practical reason and freedom. Rawls seeks to rely on something less disputable.

His main idea may be clarified through his remarks about pure procedural justice.[34] Suppose that people agree voluntarily to bet money in a game; no one rigs the odds, and so on. In that case, any outcome of a series of fair bets is just. We have an idea of pure procedural justice in cases where we have no prior conception of the fair outcome, but we have a clear enough idea of the fair and just procedure. In these cases, we say that whatever results from this procedure will be just. According to a conception of justice as fairness, we can describe fair conditions of agreement that ensure that whatever is agreed in those conditions is just.

If, however, we appeal to pure procedural justice to explain why an outcome is just, the procedure must actually have been followed. The mere fact that a certain pattern of

[33] According to a contract doctrine, '. . . principles of justice may be conceived as principles that would be chosen by rational persons, and . . . in this way conceptions of justice may be explained and justified' (16/14).

[34] '. . . pure procedural justice obtains when there is no independent criterion for the right result: instead there is a correct or fair procedure such that the outcome is likewise correct or fair, whatever it is, provided that the procedure has been properly followed.' (86/75)

distribution could have been reached by fair bets does not show that it is just if it has not in fact been reached this way.[35] In the case of principles of justice, however, we only seek to show that the principles could have been reached by the procedure that Rawls describes. Why does the fact that they could have been reached this way tend to justify them?

The answer depends on Rawls's discussion of fairness as a source of obligations and duties (114/99, 342/301). If some institution is just and we voluntarily accept the benefits that result from other people's bearing the burdens imposed by the institution, then it is fair to expect us to bear our share of the burdens also, whether or not we have actually agreed to the institution itself. We can support this claim about fairness by seeing that an arrangement could have arisen in fair conditions, whether or not it actually did. Even if it arose by force, or habit, or Humean convention, its fairness can be settled by considering whether it could have arisen in fair conditions.[36]

We identify fair conditions by identifying the various features that would create unfairness in the situation where we have to choose principles of justice. Then we design the Original Position so that it excludes these sources of unfairness; the result should be a description that includes everything relevant to justice and nothing irrelevant. Hence the considered judgments we need at the start are judgments about unfairness; these are supposed to determine the design of the Original Position.[37]

The Fairness Principle provides an acceptable basis for the construction of the Original Position only if all considerations relevant to justice are visible to agents making agreements in fair conditions. But people may have interests that are not visible when agreements are made, or interests whose importance is not visible when agreements are made.

Different partial analogies may make such cases clearer: (1) Joan foresees that she will become too fond of whisky if she is allowed free access to it; so she agrees with her friend Sarah that for part of each day Sarah will take the key of the cupboard with the whisky. (2) Before Joan has a child, she agrees to pay Sarah to look after the child for part of each day. But after she has the child, she becomes so attached to him that she does not want to part with him.

In both cases, Joan makes an agreement to constrain her future behaviour. In the first case, she may want to violate the agreement when she finds herself without the key of the cupboard. But her desire would be irrational. If she foresaw this desire and foresaw that it would be irrational, she would be right to make the agreement with Sarah. But in the second case, a desire to violate the agreement may not be irrational. Her desire to stay with her son is not (let us suppose) irrational; and she may not have foreseen how much she would want to stay with him. In this case, she might reasonably regret having made the agreement with Sarah, and

---

[35] Rawls emphasizes this point about pure procedural justice, 86/75.

[36] 'When a number of persons engage in a mutually advantageous cooperative venture according to rules, and thus restrict their liberty in ways necessary to yield advantages for all, those who have submitted to these restrictions have a right to a similar acquiescence on the part of those who have benefited from their submission. We are not to gain from the cooperative labours of others without doing our fair share.' (112/96) Rawls cites Hart, 'Natural rights'. Hart says: '. . . when a number of persons conduct any joint enterprise according to rules and thus restrict their liberty, those who have submitted to these restrictions when required have a right to a similar submission from those who have benefited by their submission' ('Natural rights', 185). Hart notes that a utilitarian explanation of this right and obligation is inadequate.

[37] Hence Rawls describes the principles of justice as 'those which rational persons concerned to advance their interests would consent to as equals when none are known to be advantaged or disadvantaged by social and natural contingencies' (19/17).

might reasonably try to be released from it.[38] In both cases, Joan seems to make an agreement in fair conditions, but it does not seem equally reasonable to carry it out in each case.

Where should we place the choices involved in a social contract, in relation to these examples? Fair initial conditions do not seem to be enough. To avoid cases where (as in our second example) it seems reasonable to seek to be released from an agreement, we might stipulate that the contractors know all the aims and aspirations of people in society and assign them their appropriate rational weight, and are appropriately moved to act on this basis. In that case, we might grant that the outcomes of the agreements that contractors make in fair conditions will be just.

But this is not a very helpful appeal to agreement. For if we are to specify the knowledge and motives of the contractors, we must already know the true interests of members of society. We appeal to an agreement so that we can answer questions about the justice of a society by reference to initial conditions that are easier to specify. But if the initial conditions do not include the rather stringent demands on knowledge and motivation that we have mentioned, they do not seem to ensure just outcomes.

The Fairness Principle, therefore, does not seem to provide a suitable starting point for the construction of the Original Position. The relevant notion of fair conditions must be simpler than the notion of a just social structure that we want to explain. But if it is simpler, it does not seem to capture all the relevant considerations.

If it is reasonable to doubt whether the Fairness Principle gives us the right point of view for examining questions about justice, it seems even more reasonable to doubt whether it has this role in questions about rightness as a whole. We may legitimately suspend judgment about whether this is a suitable foundation for a theory of the right.

These initial doubts about the Fairness Principle, however, have relied on examples in which we assume that the conditions are fair before we consider the nature and the correctness of the beliefs and desires of the contractors; that is why fair conditions themselves do not seem to ensure a reasonable outcome. Rawls argues that a more accurate account of fair conditions will include some conditions about the beliefs and desires of the contractors, and that these conditions ensure that agreements made in these conditions are just.

Once we accept the Fairness Principle, Rawls proceeds as follows: (1) We describe fair conditions. (2) We show that the Original Position embodies the correct interpretation of fair conditions. (3) We see what principles people would choose in the Original Position. (4) We compare these principles with our considered moral judgments.

1417. The Point of the Original Position

Rawls defends a social contract theory. He tries to describe the principles that people would accept in some situation in which they make an agreement, and he identifies these principles with the principles of justice. To this extent, his method is similar to Hobbes's. But his contract does not justify in the same way as Hobbes's does.

---

[38] Care, 'Criticism', 91, mentions the possibility of reviewing any agreement made in the Original Position. He suggests that a utilitarian procedure might commit us 'to such standards only for agreed-upon periods of time, . . . followed by systematic review of their adequacy'.

For Hobbes, the psychological description of the parties to the covenant is also meant to be a realistic description of us, even if it is not a full description. Hence, if it is rational for the parties to accept the original covenant, it is also rational for us to accept it. The appeal to a social contract is meant to explain why we, as rational egoists concerned with our own power and safety, have good reasons to accept rules of justice that secure peace and non-aggression.

In contrast to Hobbes, Rawls does not intend his description of the parties to the social contract to describe us.[39] Hence, the fact that the people in the Original Position would accept certain principles does not show that we have reason to accept them also. The contractarian claim and the Original Position have no justificatory force of their own; the mere fact that certain principles can be derived from them does not show that they are principles of justice.[40] The contract and the Original Position are subordinate to the Fairness Principle. When Rawls introduces the idea of the social contract, he identifies this idea of justice with justice as fairness (/10). The social contract is worth considering because it expresses the conception of justice as fairness; hence it rests on the Fairness Principle.[41]

The features of the people in the Original Position are not meant to be rationally appealing in their own right. In this respect, the Original Position differs from the social contract as Hobbes and Locke conceive it. In their view, the contractors capture what matters, rationally and morally, to us. But this is not true of the people in the Original Position; for they are completely amoral, lack benevolence, and differ from us in morally important ways. These people matter to us only because they embody the demands of fairness. Hence every feature that is ascribed to them must either be required directly by the demands of fairness or follow from these requirements.

The Original Position presents people who are unlike us, so that we can see what principles they accept.[42] It thereby represents a point of view that we can adopt if we choose to. When we see the basis of the Original Position, we see that we have reason to adopt this point of view. Since the Original Position presents a morally appropriate point of view, we will want to adopt that point of view, if we want to see what is morally appropriate.

To show that the Original Position represents a morally appropriate point of view, we ask what sorts of information and desires should guide moral decisions about the basic structure of society. We then design an artificial situation in which people have appropriate information and desires. We now have reason to accept the decisions that people in the artificial situation—the Original Position—will make.

---

[39] Rawls's view is perhaps closer to Hobbes's in 'Fairness'. Rawls usually compares his contractarian conception with Locke, Rousseau, and Kant, rather than with Hobbes; but the same basic contrast that I draw between Rawls and Hobbes applies to these other contractarian views as well. In contrast to Rawls, they take the contract to have some justifying force that is not derived simply from fairness.

[40] Lyons, 'Arguments', argues that the contract and the Original Position have some justifying role of their own.

[41] In §3, Rawls comments on the relation of justice as fairness to the contract tradition: 'My aim is to present a conception of justice which generalizes and carries to a higher level of abstraction the familiar theory of the social contract . . . This way of regarding the principles of justice I shall call justice as fairness.' (TJ 11/10) 'In justice as fairness the original position of equality corresponds to the state of nature in the traditional theory of the social contract . . . The original position is, one might say, the appropriate initial status quo, and the fundamental agreements reached in it are fair. This explains the propriety of the name "justice as fairness": it conveys the idea that the principles of justice are agreed to in an initial situation that is fair.' (12/11)

[42] 'The conception of the original position is not intended to explain human conduct except insofar as it tries to account for our moral judgments and helps to explain our having a sense of justice.' (120/104)

1418. The Strategy of Argument

The description of the Original Position should embody the requirements of fairness. Deductive reasoning from the nature of the Original Position should demonstrate that the parties choose Rawls's non-utilitarian principles of justice. This conclusion already favours his principles, because our initial considered judgments about justice and fairness suggest that these principles chosen in the Original Position will be just. But that is not decisive; we must also compare Rawls's principles with the rest of our considered judgments about justice, to confirm that our initial judgments fit our judgments about justice as a whole. This is how we reach reflective equilibrium about justice.

Rawls relies on the Fairness Principle to construct the Original Position, for three reasons: (1) We can accept the Fairness Principle even if we disagree on other issues about justice. (2) We can agree on a description of fair conditions even if we disagree on other issues about justice. (3) When our description of fair conditions is embodied in the Original Position, it provides an effective method for reaching specific conclusions, without appeal to further moral assumptions.

If this all works, then we get an answer to our original questions about justice, without having to assume any of the claims that are in dispute at the beginning. The first and second steps require moral judgment. According to Rawls, however, they do not require any appeal to moral principles that are in dispute among the different theories of justice.

The Original Position does its work only if it provides an effective method. We might be able to agree on a description of fair conditions, but find that this gives us too little information to tell us what people would choose. If Rawls had to build further conditions into the Original Position besides those that could be supported by the Fairness Principle, conclusions from the Original Position might not tell us anything about justice. Conditions that cannot be justified by appeal to fairness should not be needed to get results out of the Original Position.

Rawls ought not, therefore, to add any further feature to the description of the Original Position on the ground that we need it in order to reach a definite conclusion. For we should not assume in advance that the constraints of fairness warrant any definite conclusion. If we have to add a further condition that is not warranted by fairness, our conclusion tells us nothing about the requirements of justice as fairness.

People in the Original Position do not rely on moral principles. They do not, for instance, use their sense of fairness or justice to choose principles. If the description of the Original Position said that the people in it have to be fair, or that they have to be concerned to show proper regard to the interests of everyone else, or that they have to treat persons as ends, it would not be clear what sorts of decisions are required by these concerns. If this is a matter of dispute, the results of the Original Position will also be in dispute. Rawls's description of the Original Position should make it unnecessary, and indeed inappropriate, to attribute moral principles to people in the Original Position. We can grasp the considerations essential to moral reasoning by studying the considerations that enter into non-moral reasoning in the Original Position.

We find a somewhat analogous account of the free market in Adam Smith and others.[43] Each individual economic agent pursues his own interest, and the result of the conjunction of their individual actions—in the appropriate conditions—is the maximum benefit to all. Similarly, if we can design a machine to perform some complicated task, no part of the machine needs to have the whole task in mind; every part of it is relatively 'stupid', capable of performing only its own sub-task, and the complex result emerges from the appropriate combination of their sub-tasks.

These analogies help to explain Rawls's aim. Each of the individuals in the Original Position is indifferent to moral considerations; but the design of the Original Position should ensure that their agreement embodies the appropriate moral conditions. In our second example, we build the machine in accordance with our initial views about the sub-tasks involved in carrying out the initial task. Our initial views are vindicated when we find that the machine carries out the task it was built for. In the case of the Original Position, our views about fairness guide us in designing the 'machine', and our later considered judgments about justice show that it has produced principles of justice.

1419. Moral Constraints on the Original Position

The initial conditions that determine the design of the Original Position are meant to be 'widely accepted but weak' (18/16). But their weakness does not imply that they lack moral force, or that they are self-evident (585/512).[44] They are weak in the sense that they do not make controversial moral claims that defenders of rival moral theories should reject. The design of the Original Position conforms to 'the formal constraints of the concept of right' (130/112), since these constraints 'hold for the choice of all ethical principles' (130/112), and therefore for the choice of principles of justice too.[45]

Talk of choice may seem inappropriate. For it is not our choice that makes principles into morally right or just principles.[46] But Rawls does not mean that the choice by people in the Original Position determines moral rightness. On the contrary, if we reflect on the nature of the Original Position and the principles chosen there, we see that these are indeed principles of justice.

The formal constraints of the concept of right are meant to rule out none of the various competing conceptions of justice. Principles of right must be general; hence they rule out

---

[43] On Smith see §799.

[44] '. . . the conditions embodied in the description of this situation are ones that we do in fact accept . . . Thus what we are doing is to combine into one conception the totality of conditions that we are ready upon due reflection to recognize as reasonable in our conduct with regard to one another.' (587/514) The relevant choices 'conform to principles that he himself [i.e. a critic] would choose under conditions that he would concede are fair and undistorted by fortune and happenstance' (515/451).

[45] '. . . a conception of right is a set of principles, general in form and universal in application, that is to be publicly recognized as a final court of appeal for ordering the conflicting claims of moral persons.' (135/117)

[46] Moral principles are the outcome of choice if some non-realist and non-cognitivist meta-ethical views are true. But the truth of such meta-ethical views is hardly uncontroversial enough that it could reasonably be taken for granted in constructing a normative theory; and Rawls does not assert any such view. It is harder to decide how far he is actually committed to the acceptance of some such meta-ethical view. See §1442.

egoism (since they preclude mention of any particular agent). They must be public; Rawls defends this demand by appeal to Kant's view of the categorical imperative, which envisages the kingdom of ends as an 'ethical commonwealth, as it were, which has such moral principles for its public charter' (133/115). They must be the final principles that we appeal to in resolving conflicts; hence principles of moral rightness are supreme over self-interest and other non-moral ideals. These conditions do not preclude a utilitarian conception of justice, but they have some clear moral force; the demand for publicity, for instance, rules out some forms of argument for utilitarianism.[47]

The specific moral constraints that are derived from fairness are not purely procedural in any narrow sense. If, for instance, we imagined the principles of justice as those that are chosen by majority vote after an election in which everyone who is to be governed by them has a vote, we might say that this is a fair procedure, and that no one has a right to complain about the result or to disobey any principles chosen by such a process. But we do not think that following the procedure will by itself guarantee a fair or just outcome. If, for instance, some of the voters have more access to means of persuasion than others, or it is much easier for some to vote than for others, and so on, we might think the result lacks the moral force that we might otherwise attach to it. Rawls intends to include these sorts of conditions within the scope of fairness; the constraints of fairness extend beyond the choice of procedure for agreeing on principles of justice, to the conditions in which the procedure operates.

Judgments about fairness must be fair between people because they eliminate advantages or disadvantages that result from social and natural contingencies (19/17). We want to rule out the possibility of proposing a principle that one would propose only if one knew things that are irrelevant from the standpoint of justice. If, for instance, I know, but you do not, that a particular arrangement would benefit me and harm you, I might propose it without telling you what I know, since I expect that you would reject it if you knew what I know. In this case, I would be taking unfair advantage of you.

The principles, however, should not simply be fair between people; they should also be fair to each of the people involved.[48] If both A and B want to play music, a rule that forbids A to play music and allows B to play it is unfair to A in relation to B (if the other circumstances are the same). But if they both want to play music, and a rule forbids them both, it is unfair to them both (if there is no sufficient justification) in so far as it neglects the fact that both have an interest in playing music. Considerations of fairness do not arise only in deciding questions about discrimination between people; they also arise in determining whether the treatment of a person is appropriate to her nature, interests, and needs.

Hence Rawls takes principles of justice to involve rational persons concerned to advance their interests (19/17). When he says they are rational, he means simply that they follow a plan that embodies a coherent set of preferences, and that they are free from envy.[49]

---

[47] The publicity condition needs to be examined more carefully to see how far it precludes the sort of policy that is contemplated by Sidgwick in ME 489.

[48] Rawls notices a related point about justice, TJ 59/51.

[49] 'The concept of rationality invoked here, with the exception of one essential feature, is the standard one familiar in social theory. Thus, in the usual way, a rational person is thought to have a coherent set of preferences between the options open to him . . . The special assumption I make is that a rational individual does not suffer from envy.' (143/123–4)

If we did not assume this about them, a simple policy of non-discrimination would not ensure fair conditions, since one person might take unfair advantage of other people's relative indifference to their own interest. If the principles of justice are those that would be chosen in fair initial conditions, the fairness of the initial conditions must include fairness to the interests of each of the individuals involved, not simply fairness between individuals.

But do we satisfy the demands of fairness to people if we simply assume that they are rational and concerned to advance their interests? They might still have a mistaken conception of their interests.[50] If the principles suited their erroneous conception of their interests, would they be fair to the individuals involved?

We have two options: (a) We might say that they are still fair, even though the supposed rights they seek to protect and the supposed interests they promote are not genuine rights or interests. (b) We might say that a principle is not fair to these individuals if it does not actually rest on a true conception of their interests.

If we choose the first option, it is doubtful whether the principles chosen in fair initial conditions are just; the demand for fairness seems too weak to isolate just principles from others. If we choose the second option, Rawls's summary of the implications of fairness for the Original Position is incomplete. It will not be enough for people to be concerned to advance their interest, if that means 'concerned to advance what they take to be their interest'; they must also have true views about their real interests. Does Rawls's elaboration of the Original Position include the element that is omitted from his summary?

1420. Knowledge and Motivation in the Original Position

The Original Position articulates some more basic judgments about justice and fairness. In appealing to what we would agree to in circumstances that are fair, Rawls is appealing to the considered judgment that we would expect people to stick to agreements made in these circumstances. But when we speak of fair 'circumstances', we include features of the agents as well as their external environment. It is easy to see that an agreement is not binding if I make it because someone threatens me, or because I will starve if I do not make it. But it is equally true that if someone made an agreement because he was deceived, or especially altruistic, or indifferent to his interests, we would not suppose that the agreement had the same sort of moral force. We regard an agreement as just if it is entered into by fair-minded persons in conditions that are fair.

This judgment by itself does not help us to discover principles of justice; we still need to know what fair-minded persons are like. Here Rawls takes the Original Position to be useful. We insist that parties to agreements must be fair-minded because we want them not to take advantage of certain kinds of knowledge (about other people's ignorance, for instance, or about a particular circumstance that will be favourable to them), and we want them to restrain the motives that might prompt us to pursue our own interests at the expense of other people. Rawls seeks to construct a description of people who lack the sort of knowledge and the sorts of motives that move people to act unfairly for their own advantage.

---

[50] This possibility is not ruled out by the assumption of rationality, given the narrow interpretation Rawls intends for this (14/12, amplified at 142–3/123–4).

Once we have constructed this description, we need not assume in addition that people are fair-minded; for we have eliminated the things that make a fair-minded outlook necessary. In this case, we can simply say that the just outcome is what self-interested people free of the elements that tempt us to unfairness will agree to. The description of people who lack the temptations to unfairness is a description of the Original Position.

Why is it better to remove temptations to unfairness from the people in the Original Position than to rely on their fair-mindedness? This would be a bad practical strategy, since the temptations to unfairness are widespread and come along with practically indispensable knowledge and motivation. But for analytical purposes it is helpful. If we want to know what fair-minded people would agree on, we ought to remove all the temptations to unfairness, and then see what choice results.

We should not, therefore, attribute any moral beliefs to the people in the Original Position; hence we should not attribute to them the moral virtues that would prevent a person in the Original Position from trying to organize society to suit herself. To do the work that the virtues do in ordinary life, we assume ignorance; we deprive the people in the Original Position of the knowledge that would cause them to be tempted to act unfairly.[51] Once we have made the appropriate assumptions, we can appeal to pure procedural justice. If we eliminate all the tendencies to unfairness in the people in the Original Position, whatever they choose will be just.[52]

Rawls gives some reasons for the restrictions on knowledge that he incorporates in the 'veil of ignorance'. Knowledge of the place one occupies in society and of one's own conception of the good introduces unfairness, if it allows some people to take advantage of the ignorance of others. But is a veil of ignorance the best antidote to the distorting effect of knowledge? Admittedly, if we are both ignorant, I cannot use my knowledge to take advantage of your ignorance. But one might think that an agreement might be unfair to me because of my ignorance. If A induces B and C to agree that B will rake leaves from January to June and C will rake them from July to December, and A tells neither B nor C that almost all the leaves need to be raked in November, C might reasonably complain about A's failure to inform them; had they known, they would have made a different agreement. Similarly, if A induces B and C to agree to pay D $5 per hour to rake leaves between January and June and $10 per hour between July and December, they might both reasonably complain about A's failure to inform them that they were making an expensive arrangement.

In such cases, we might argue that we are treated unfairly if we make an agreement in ignorance of facts that, if we knew them, would have warranted some reconsideration of the agreement. Since Rawls assumes that the people in the Original Position are concerned to advance their own interest, knowledge of the bearing of an agreement on their own interest would warrant reconsideration. Hence it seems unfair to deny them this knowledge. Fairness seems to require that they all have all the relevant knowledge.

---

[51] The need for ignorance is well illustrated by the example at 134–5n/116n.

[52] As Rawls explains, 'the aim is to use the notion of pure procedural justice as a basis of theory' (136/118). He does not mean that in fact we have no way of checking the results of this procedure; we can appeal directly to our considered judgments about justice. His point is that if we define the Original Position correctly, we also have a basis for claiming that we have set up a mechanism for pure procedural justice.

Rawls might reply that if we all have this knowledge, we will be unable to reach any just agreement. If I know that I am rich, I will reject taxation that soaks the rich, but if I know that I am poor, I will be eager to soak the rich. But this is not an argument against the claim that fairness requires this knowledge. For we have no initial assurance that an account of fair conditions ensures an agreement on principles of justice.

But we might not agree in any case that complete knowledge precludes a just agreement. Could we not combine complete knowledge with the appropriate benevolence or respect for others? Rawls argues that this combination is unsuitable for the Original Position. He prefers the combination of ignorance with 'mutual disinterest'. Here we find some of the more controversial aspects of the Original Position.

1421. Mutual Disinterest

The people in the Original Position are 'mutually disinterested'. By this, Rawls means that they are self-confined egoists; they take no interest in the interests of other people for the other people's own sake. He excludes benevolence from the Original Position, for four reasons (e.g. 148–9/128–9): (1) Knowledge combined with benevolence would make it too difficult to reach any conclusion (140–1/121–2). (2) We need to know the relative strength of benevolent and other desires. (3) The veil of ignorance makes it unnecessary to add benevolence. (4) It 'would defeat the purpose of grounding the theory of justice on weak stipulations, as well as being incongruous with the circumstances of justice' (149).[53]

Rawls's fourth objection is not persuasive. He makes strong idealizing assumptions about the extent of people's knowledge of general facts and about their instrumental rationality, since he assumes that they are free of envy. The assumption of benevolence is no 'stronger' if 'stronger' refers to the degree of idealization.

The third objection is no more persuasive. If benevolence were included in the Original Position, Rawls's main reason for denying that people would choose utilitarian principles would disappear. Moreover, we could argue that the assumption of mutual disinterest is also 'unnecessary'. For the veil of ignorance is the not only way of preventing the distorting effect of knowledge. Benevolence seems to do the same work. To this extent, mutual disinterest and benevolence seem equally 'unnecessary'. If both are allowed, we seem to have different legitimate versions of the Original Position that lead to different conclusions.

Moreover, one might argue that benevolence is necessary to avoid unfairness. For we have seen why one might believe that the veil of ignorance is unfair, in forcing a choice in ignorance of one's own interests. If fairness requires knowledge, we need benevolence to ensure that knowledge does not prevent just agreements.

Rawls's most plausible objection to benevolence is the second, on which the first depends. We might try to answer the question about relative strength by assuming that people accept Sidgwick's principle of benevolence (they want to maximize the total good summed over everyone), and that this is their overriding motive (they care about other things too, but

---

[53] This and the previous sentence are omitted from the 2nd edn. (129, end of para 1).

always subordinate them to these concerns of benevolence). We could then apparently argue that people in the Original Position choose the Principle of Utility.

Rawls might object that this stipulation about the Original Position simply builds in utilitarianism, and that it is only one way of explaining the place of benevolence. Another way might be the stipulation that people count everyone's interest, rather than the total good, for more than their own interest. This would give us a different account of justice in our conclusion from the Original Position.

If we allow these different ways of filling in the Original Position, we might say that they are arbitrary from the point of view of fairness, and that therefore the point of view of fairness cannot generate principles of justice. We might then agree with Rawls that mutual disinterest is 'necessary', if we simply mean that, given the other features of the Original Position, we need it if we are to find a definite answer about what people will choose. If we do not assume ignorance and mutual disinterest, we cannot say how much people in the Original Position will be concerned about other people's good for its own sake.

But appeals to this sort of 'necessity' are unwarranted. For we cannot legitimately assume that the conditions imposed by judgments about fairness tell us what people in the Original Position will choose; we do not know in advance how much we can derive from fairness. Rawls has not shown that the initial judgments about fairness justify the demand for mutual disinterest.

1422. The Good v. Primary Goods

If, despite these doubts, we assume mutual disinterest plus ignorance, how thick should the veil of ignorance be? Rawls assumes ignorance of particular facts about myself and my position in society. He also assumes ignorance of facts about the good, including both (i) the good for myself, and (ii) the good for a human being.[54]

Why are both sorts of facts about the good excluded? We might agree that facts about my good are 'particular' facts that interfere with the unbiased perspective of people in the Original Position. But facts about the human good seem to be quite general, and so they should apparently be included under the general facts about human beings and society that are used in the Original Position. But Rawls does not use these facts in the reasoning of people in the Original Position. Since they might make a difference if they were used, we need some reason for not using them.

We might argue that the reasons justifying exclusion of moral beliefs also justify exclusion of facts about the good. We exclude moral beliefs from the Original Position because our task is to find the right moral beliefs and it is controversial which beliefs are right. We would defeat our purpose, therefore, if we included this controversial element in the Original Position. Similarly, if a true conception of the human good depends on correct moral beliefs, any appeal to claims about the good would apparently introduce unwelcome controversial elements.

This is a good reason for not including all facts about the human good in the Original Position. But if some facts about it can be settled without appeal to morality, should these

---

[54] Rawls does not always keep (i) and (ii) clearly apart, but his later remarks about the good imply that the Original Position excludes both.

not be included? Aristotle's account of the human good as activity of the soul in accordance with complete virtue does not include any moral elements.[55] Moral arguments are needed to decide which activities are activities 'in accord with complete virtue', but the general claim that the human good consists in the fulfilment of human rational capacities does not rest on moral argument. If this general claim fixes a fact about the human good, should that not be included in the reasoning of the Original Position?

Rawls's decision to exclude such facts about the good is easy to explain if he relies on a subjectivist account of the good as simply the fulfilment of rational desire. As we will see later, this account makes the good of different people depend on the different desires that they actually have, and not on any facts about them that are external to their desires. Hence there are no further facts about the good that need to be included in the Original Position. If Rawls did not believe this about the good, his exclusion of the relevant facts from the Original Position would be unwarranted. The exclusion, therefore, depends on further argument about the good.

Rawls does not take the people in the Original Position to hold a subjectivist conception of the good. They have no view on whether there are objective facts, external to a particular person's desires, about the human good. But Rawls sees that if I have no view about what is good for me, I cannot reason effectively in the Original Position. For we reach principles of justice by thinking of ways to advance our individual interests (within the constraints imposed by the veil of ignorance). If we have no views about our interest, we have no basis for choosing principles.

To avoid this result, Rawls allows people a 'thin theory of the good' without a 'full theory' (396/348). The thin theory tells them enough to convince them of the primary status of the 'primary social goods' (see 62/54, 92/79, 142–3/123–4). Primary goods are those that it is rational for each person to want no matter what else he wants. On this basis, people who are ignorant of their individual conceptions of good choose the two principles of justice that secure the primary goods for everyone. The first principle guarantees equal liberty to everyone. The second allows inequality in other goods provided that it benefits the worst off.

The first principle of justice is prior to the second, because the demands of equal liberty must be respected before we consider distribution of resources to secure other benefits. If we did not care about the primary goods, we would not choose these two principles in this order.

We might understand a 'thin' versus a 'full' theory of the good in different ways: (1) Though we may not be confident in saying what all the elements of the human good are, we may be confident that it includes some specific elements that either include the primary goods or require them as means. (2) Though we may believe (even confidently) that some elements of the good vary from person to person, we may hold that some indispensable elements are common to everyone, and that these common elements require the primary goods. (3) We may adopt a particular conception of the good that includes elements requiring the primary goods. (4) Without adopting any specific conception of good, we may observe that, given the variety of conceptions of the good, some resources are always or usually useful for pursuing a particular conception.

---

[55] On Aristotle's account of the good, see §77.

In the first edition of *TJ*, Rawls takes the fourth view. He defends the primary goods as resources or preconditions for executing a conception of my good.[56] They include freedom to pursue my good, the material resources needed for it, and the self-respect (better described as self-esteem) that I need if I am to think it is worthwhile to bother pursuing my conception of my good at all. To discover that these things are worth wanting no matter what else I want, I need not have any views about the objective character of the good. I need only know something about conceptions of one's good; in particular, I need to know that different people have different conceptions, and that many of them require material resources. My thin theory of the good treats the good as the satisfaction of rational desire (§63).

This thin theory, combined with some empirical information about the variety of people's rational desires and the normal means of satisfying them, shows us that the primary goods are goods because they are useful resources or preconditions for the satisfaction of rational desires. It is prudent to protect my supply of primary goods if I do not know what my conception of the good will be. Not all conceptions of the good require many primary goods, but since many require some primary goods it is a safe bet to provide for them.

Rawls, however, argues not only that the institutions of a just society assure a basic supply of primary goods, but also that they assure priority to primary goods (and among these to liberty) in relation to other aspects of people's conception of the good. For the principles of justice safeguard primary goods; and these principles take priority over any other social arrangements.[57]

The primacy of the primary goods helps to secure the priority of the right over the good.[58] The doctrine of primary goods has a vital place, therefore, in the design of the Original Position. Without it, the veil of ignorance would be too thick. If we do not appeal to primary goods, we cannot explain how self-interested people think of their interest in ways that support the principles of justice.[59]

The most serious questions about primary goods arise from doubts about Rawls's subjectivist account of the good. We will turn to these doubts later.[60] If we accept, for the moment, his account of the good, we may still question his use of the primary goods. We may grant that these goods are generally useful resources, but we seem to have no reason

---

[56] In his later discussions of primary goods, Rawls significantly modifies this claim about them. He seems to adopt the third view. See §1438.

[57] This is true once the minimum conditions necessary for the application of the principles of justice have been reached. Rawls does not believe that liberty takes priority even when limiting liberty is necessary, e.g., to avoid starvation. See 152/132, 247/217, 542/475. Though Rawls does not spell out this condition in detail (and it may not be easy to spell out), it answers some misplaced objections to his claims.

[58] '. . . in justice as fairness the concept of the right is prior to that of the good. In contrast with teleological theories, something is good only if it fits into ways of life consistent with the principles of right already on hand. But to establish these principles it is necessary to rely on some notion of goodness, for we need assumptions about the parties' motives in the original position. Since these assumptions must not jeopardize the prior place of the concept of right, the theory of the good used in arguing for the principles of justice is restricted to bare essentials.' (396/347–8) The last sentence might suggest that we somehow know, before we examine the Original Position, that the right is prior to the good. But we surely do not know this; if Rawls supposed that we know it, he would not be setting out from 'weak and widely shared' assumptions.

[59] Rawls presents a very limited veil of ignorance without any mention of primary goods in 'Fairness', 53–4: '. . . each person will propose principles of a general kind which will, to a large degree, gain their sense from the various applications to be made of them, the particular circumstances of which being yet unknown'. He added the doctrine of primary goods in response to objections by Gibbard; *TJ* x/xix.

[60] Subjectivism about the good; §§1434–5.

to grant that they are so universally important that they should always be prior to any other good.

If, for instance, we came to believe that our good consists in pleasure and contentment, it is not clear that we would still have reason to insist on guaranteed liberty; for we might be able to secure pleasure without liberty. I might be compelled to adopt other people's preferred means of securing pleasure; but if they secure pleasure for me too, why should I object to being compelled?

Moreover, once I go beyond knowledge of the thin theory of the good to knowledge of my own good, I may find that my conception of the good is an ascetic form of life. Or I may prefer to belong to a hierarchical community in which people all know their place and are contented with it, according to a nostalgic conception of the feudal system. In Rawls's view, one cannot reject these as a mistaken conception of my good.

But if people in the Original Position know that such conceptions of the good are possible, they should apparently qualify their commitment to the primary goods. They should treat them as assets that are generally useful, but not always needed. Such assets may be given up in circumstances where they are no longer useful, because, for some people, they interfere with the achievement of the good to which they are supposed to be means.

If this is the right way to treat the primary goods, they do not ensure that the right is prior to the good. If the people in the Original Position do not know that the primary goods might sometimes interfere with the achievement of one's good, they seem to suffer from an unfair gap in their knowledge. It seems unfair to them to keep them in ignorance of this relevant fact about the good. The implications of this weakness in Rawls's argument become clearer when we move on to his claims about aversion to risk.

1423. Aversion to Risk

These assumptions about the knowledge and motivation of people in the Original Position are enough, according to Rawls, to derive his two non-utilitarian principles of justice. But to see that this is so, we need to recognize a further aspect of the outlook of the contractors. They are averse to risk, and so they reason in accordance with the maximin principle; hence they try to ensure the best of the worst outcomes.

Choice guided by a maximin principle may be reasonable or unreasonable, depending on the desirability and probability of the different possible results. It is better to have my house undamaged by fire and to save the cost of insurance premia than to have it undamaged and pay the premia; but it is better to pay the premia and have the house burnt down than to pay no premia and have it burnt down. Having it burnt down is worse than having it undamaged, but if I want the better outcome in the worse situation, I will pay for insurance. It is also better (we may assume) to travel by aeroplane to Australia than to stay at home, but it is better to stay at home than to be killed in an aeroplane crash; hence the maximin principle in this case would tell me to stay at home. Since we insure our houses, but do not always avoid air travel, we follow a maximin principle sometimes but not always.

Rawls needs to show that people in the Original Position follow a maximin principle, because otherwise they may gamble on profiting from a society that assigns unequal rights and duties. Suppose I know that 90% of the people in my society will have a conception of the good that would be greatly advanced by having resources above the bare minimum, and that under utilitarianism 90% will be above the bare minimum. Why, in that case, should I not gamble on my being among the 90% above the bare minimum and among the 90% who have the appropriate conception of the good? If I am willing to gamble, I should accept utilitarian distributive principles.

Rawls believes that people in the Original Position are averse to such risks in choices that affect the basic structure of society. He does not advocate general adherence to the maximin principle, but he argues that these people will be averse to risk in the specific conditions of the Original Position.[61] Aversion to risk is not a further stipulation about the Original Position, parallel to the assumptions about knowledge and motivation that we have discussed. Hence it is not derived directly from the demands of fairness. It is supposed to follow from the facts about knowledge and motivation that are derived from the demands of fairness.

Two features of the Original Position are especially relevant: (1) The veil of ignorance about particular facts includes ignorance about the relative probability of different patterns of distribution and their effect on the welfare of different people. I do not know whether our society has a small 'aristocracy' of well-off people who also have an appropriate conception of their good, or has a small 'underclass' of people who have only the bare minimum needed to pursue their conception of their good. Hence I lack the knowledge of probabilities that normally allows me to be less averse to risk. If I did not know the probability of an aeroplane's crashing, it would not be so clear that it is reasonable to travel by air to go on holiday for a week. (2) Ignorance of one's conception of the good affects one's attitude to the goods that one might gain by gambling. Rawls claims that people will care so much about the primary goods, and so little (comparatively) about what they might get above the basic level of primary goods, that the thought of doing better as a result of gambling does not appeal strongly to them. In their ignorance, they will not gamble on finding that their society shares their own conception of the good. If they want some protection against being coerced to follow other people's conception of the good, they will affirm the priority of liberty, to protect their rights in the worst circumstances.

If we grant that aversion to risk follows from the veil of ignorance, so understood, we may still wonder whether the demands of fairness require aversion to risk. For we may ask whether the veil of ignorance should be so thick that it requires aversion to risk and acceptance of the maximin principle. Why not suppose instead that everyone has equal access to the relevant probabilities, and to relevant information about their conception of the good? Then it might seem reasonable for people to choose different principles of distribution according to different probabilities of specific outcomes.

In Rawls's defence, we might observe that this alternative to the thick veil of ignorance makes it impossible or very difficult to get a definite decision in the light of our description of the Original Position. The observation may be true, but it does not help Rawls. For we are not entitled to add features to the Original Position that we need in order to reach a definite decision. We should not take it for granted that relatively uncontroversial judgments about fairness, all by themselves, allow people in the Original Position to reach a definite decision.

---

[61] See 'Maximin', 226.

If aversion to risk, in the context of the Original Position, implies unfairness to the parties involved, we have a reason to reconsider the judgments about fairness that we used to construct the Original Position.

For these reasons, Rawls's arguments to and from the Original Position do not meet his conditions for success. He requires us to rely only on considered judgments about fairness in our construction of the Original Position. But judgments about fairness are open to dispute. One might argue against Rawls that the thickness of the veil of ignorance introduces unfairness, because it deprives people of knowledge about the good that would make a difference to their decisions. Even if this argument is not decisive against Rawls, he seems to lack a decisive reply. Considerations about fairness, then, seem to be at best (from Rawls's point of view) indecisive.

But even if we allow that fair conditions include the basis for aversion to risk, we may be puzzled, as we were in the discussion of primary goods, about why the contractors should include principles of justice in the basic structure of society. Since the principles they accept seem the best in the light of their ignorance of important facts about their society, should they not accept them provisionally, subject to possible modification when the veil of ignorance is lifted?

Such provisional acceptance makes the Original Position unable to do what Rawls expects it to do. For if we think it is possible that, when the veil of ignorance is lifted, utilitarianism would leave most of us well placed to pursue our conception of our good, should we not be prepared to accept utilitarianism in those circumstances? If we can consider that possibility when we are still behind the veil of ignorance, should we not take account of it when we formulate our principles of justice and the degree of our commitment to them?

We might answer, in Rawls's defence, that this objection wrongly treats the Original Position as though it were a real situation involving real people whose later lives are relevant. If it is simply an analytical device to express the demands of fairness, it may appear misplaced to consider what happens to the principles of justice when 'the same' people reconsider them in the light of further information. For 'the same' people with fuller information are simply ourselves, equipped with a sense of justice that disregards the fuller information that is irrelevant from the point of view of justice.

This defence of Rawls, however, does not overcome the main objection. We may grant that, according to our sense of justice, it would be wrong for me to try to modify the basic principles of justice simply because I will benefit from a modification. But to say this is to defend the Original Position by appeal to the considered judgments about justice that we use to assess the principles reached in the Original Position. According to Rawls's method, the Original Position does not need this defence, because it relies only on our prior judgments about fairness. But the constraints of fairness do not explain why we should regard principles of justice as primary, and hence as immune to revision when the veil of ignorance is lifted. If the people in the Original Position know general facts about society, they must know that they are ignorant of some facts that, if they knew them, would affect their self-interested deliberation. We might expect that, when they choose principles under the veil of ignorance, they will also provide for the possibility of coming to know these facts.

The demands of fairness, therefore, do not seem to require or to explain the fundamental status that Rawls wants to claim for the two principles of justice. From the point of view of our considered judgments about justice, we can see why he wants the two principles to be fundamental. I would undermine their whole point if I took myself to be free to revise them in the light of further knowledge. But this point of view cannot be captured within the demands of fairness, as Rawls interprets them in his exposition of the Original Position.

Rawls is open to this criticism because he tries to represent the priority of justice, and, more generally, the priority of the right over the good, through choices made under the veil of ignorance. In his view, the people in the Original Position do not need the motives of just people in order to affirm the priority of justice, because their combination of self-interest and ignorance leads them to affirm its priority. If Rawls were right about this, and he were right to say that fairness demands this combination of self-interest and ignorance in the Original Position, he would be right to say that the priority of justice can be vindicated by appeal to the demands of fairness. But the conditions of the Original Position seem to require only a conditional commitment to the principles of justice, not the unconditional commitment that would affirm their priority. Hence appeal to the Original Position does not vindicate deontological claims about the priority of justice or the priority of the right.

This criticism matters because the argument from the Original Position seeks to defend a deontological conception of justice and the right against a utilitarian conception. The defence is ineffective if we have to import deontological convictions, expressed in our considered judgments about justice, into our account of the Original Position in order to get deontological conclusions out of it. If we need to defend the Original Position by appeal to these considered judgments, we might as well appeal directly to our considered judgments about justice without a detour through the Original Position.

Rawls offers a distinctive argument against the utilitarian, because he appeals only to considered judgments about fairness that utilitarians do not initially dispute. In his view, the Original Position embodies the demands of fairness, and thereby vindicates the priority of justice against utilitarianism. But if the Original Position justifies only a conditional commitment to the principles of justice, subject to modification in the light of further information, it does not explain why utilitarianism would not be the right outlook for better-informed agents. In that case, the Original Position does not support a deontological conception of justice and the right against utilitarianism.

This conclusion does not imply that Rawls's two principles of justice are not correct, or that the Original Position does not provide a good argument for them or for his deontological outlook. We have found only that the Original Position, understood as embodying the demands of fairness, does not provide a good argument.

1424. Utilitarian Objections to the Original Position

After this discussion of Rawls's arguments for and about the Original Position, we may usefully sum up possible lines of reply that are open to the utilitarian, in order to see how Rawls might meet them. He takes his starting point in fairness not to be explicitly opposed to utilitarianism, but he argues from this starting point to two non-utilitarian principles of justice. The argument through the Original Position is meant to present the implications of fairness.

If Rawls is right, therefore, the initial conception of fairness must be implicitly, though not explicitly, inconsistent with utilitarianism. The utilitarian might reply by questioning either some of the initial claims about fairness, or the design of the Original Position, or the derivation of the principles of justice from the Original Position.

First, one might dispute Rawls's claim that the initial judgments about fairness are so weak and widely shared that a utilitarian has no good reason to reject them from the outset. The design of the Original Position assumes equal rights for each person, regardless of other considerations. If this feature of its design comes from the demands of fairness, as it should, fairness requires some unqualified respect for equal rights of different individuals. But if we really take this respect to be unqualified, and hence unaffected by considerations of utility, we have apparently ruled out a utilitarian position from the outset.

Perhaps this conclusion is premature. Indirect utilitarians might argue that they can give an adequate account of the importance to be attached to equal rights. But if we are not convinced by this indirect utilitarian argument, we will regard our initial judgments as good reasons for ruling out utilitarianism. Equally, the utilitarian might challenge these initial judgments, on the ground that they assume what Rawls seeks to prove.

If utilitarians are willing to accept the initial judgments about fairness, they may still doubt whether these judgments justify the features of the Original Position that eventually lead to the rejection of utilitarianism. Perhaps, for instance, the demands of fairness do not require ignorance plus mutual disinterest any more than they require complete knowledge plus benevolence. Both arrangements seem equally compatible with the demands of fairness.

Perhaps, alternatively, some demands of fairness conflict with Rawls's description of the Original Position. Perhaps it is unfair, for instance, to exclude consideration of our conception of our good or of the true conception of the good. If people in the Original Position should be allowed to attach some importance to the pursuit of some specific conception of the good, they may be willing to accept some greater risk in order to be able to pursue it and so they may be less averse to risk than Rawls supposes they are.

Even if Rawls correctly describes our judgments about fairness and correctly connects them to the Original Position, he may be wrong about the weight to be attached to these judgments about fairness. Our questions about an unconditional commitment to the two principles of justice help a utilitarian. For if the Original Position supports no more than a provisional commitment to non-utilitarian principles, utilitarian principles may be the right ones for better-informed agents.

1425. Doubts about Rawls's Strategy

This objection brings us back to our earlier and more basic question about what Rawls's argument from fairness might prove. Let us suppose: (1) Utilitarians accept all the reasoning in the Original Position. (2) They agree that the principles generated by the Original Position are non-utilitarian principles that cannot be understood within an indirect utilitarian framework. (3) Hence they agree that justice is a non-utilitarian element in morality. In Ross's terms, they agree that there are prima facie duties not grounded on utility. Even these generous concessions to Rawls do not refute utilitarianism. For they do not ensure that justice is prior to utility. Why should utility not override justice?

The argument in the Original Position affirms the primacy of justice, but does it justify this affirmation? The two principles take precedence over other considerations about practices and policies, because of the conditions about knowledge and motivation that are built into the Original Position. But these conditions rest on the requirements of fairness, and the Fairness Principle simply expresses our initial conception of justice as fairness. If Rawls's arguments are all cogent, our conception of justice as fairness takes justice to contain requirements that conflict with maximizing utility.

Still we need not infer that justice overrides utility. We would have to infer this only if we had initially agreed that rightness requires fairness, so that nothing could be right that would not be agreed to in fair initial conditions. In that case, a demonstration through the Original Position that fair initial conditions commit us to non-utilitarian principles would refute utilitarianism. But this is not the initial agreement about fairness that Rawls secures from us; nor would a clear-headed utilitarian allow this agreement.

Rawls's argument, therefore, does not answer the main utilitarian contention.[62] For all he shows, it could be right, even though it is not just, to pursue utility at the expense of justice. Similarly, his argument does not refute an intuitionist view that sees possible conflicts between justice and other virtues or principles, with no hierarchy of principles for resolution of the conflicts. His argument tells us why our conception of justice takes justice to be primary, but it does not tell us why we should believe our conception of justice should take precedence over other aspects of our conception of the right.

This objection to Rawls assumes that the considered judgments we are trying to explain do not include explicitly anti-utilitarian judgments. On that assumption, the objector points out that the main question about the principle of utility has not been answered.

We might, however, interpret or revise his argument so that it proceeds in this way: (1) He takes it for granted that we have non-utilitarian considered judgments that include judgments about justice. They do not simply express our conception of justice; they also express our belief—from the point of view of morality, not simply from the point of view of justice—that justice limits appeals to utility. (2) A utilitarian must either dismiss these anti-utilitarian judgments or subordinate them to indirect utilitarianism. (3) But, according to Rawls's non-utilitarian explanation, we hold our anti-utilitarian considered judgments because (a) they express the demands of fairness, and (b) we accept the primacy of the demands of fairness. (4) This explanation is superior to the utilitarian explanation.

This defence of Rawls goes beyond him in so far as it distinguishes the non-utilitarian character of justice from its primacy in rightness as a whole. It is a plausible defence only if one can support the fourth step, and vindicate the non-utilitarian against the utilitarian explanation of the relevant considered judgments.

Rawls believes that his non-utilitarian explanation based on fairness accounts for more of our considered judgments and that it is preferable for this reason. His argument is quite similar to an argument of Ross's. The utilitarian claims that we give an adequate account of non-utilitarian convictions if we give an indirect utilitarian reason for not always thinking

---

[62] See Feinberg, 'Rawls', 113–16.

about utility. Ross protests that utilitarians represent as relevant or decisive considerations that in fact are not relevant or not decisive. If they are right, we ought to advocate observance of a given rule without regard to utility only if we are satisfied we thereby maximize utility. But we can see that the calculations that matter decisively to a utilitarian are not morally decisive, however they turn out.

Rawls illustrates this point by reference to slavery (§26). He does not introduce this 'utilitarian nightmare' to suggest that utilitarian calculation supports it in the actual world. According to utilitarians, the nightmares depend on our ignoring facts about the actual world; and so opponents who appeal to nightmares rely on a futile demand for moral principles that fit all logically possible worlds. But Rawls's objection does not rely on any such demand. He argues that it matters decisively to a utilitarian how the balance of utility turns out for slavery, but this is not what matters decisively to us. This objection draws, as Ross does, on Butler's distinction between the effects of our moral outlook and the aspects of it that matter to us. Butler, Ross, and Rawls use that distinction to reject utilitarianism.

Rawls perhaps sometimes underestimates the significance of this argument. He suggests that rejection of a utilitarian basis for our convictions is a desirable optional extra or 'advantage' in his argument, rather than an essential part of it.[63] But if our considered judgments were not indifferent (in the respect just described) to utilitarian considerations, they would allow an indirect utilitarian explanation. Hence the 'advantage' that Rawls mentions seems to be essential to his argument. It explains why he does not rely on the claim that utilitarians cannot justify principles that are extensionally equivalent to his own. In his view, utilitarian principles do not capture our considered judgments, because our considered judgments contain not only judgments about which actions, practices, etc. are morally right or wrong, but also judgments about what should determine our answers to such questions.

A utilitarian might try various replies to Rawls's argument: (1) Rawls attributes too much to our considered judgments. Their alleged indifference to utilitarian calculation is really the effect of a moral theory (which should not be included among considered judgments). (2) He is right about the character of some considered judgments, but we can discount them; they simply reflect our failure to grasp the implications of utilitarianism. (3) We are entitled to reject this feature of our considered judgments, even though it rests on a plausible principle, because the principle of utility is more plausible.

Against the first reply, Rawls has a good reason to include views about relevant considerations among our considered judgments. In non-moral cases, we would not consider people very competent judges if they had no idea of what mattered to the correctness of their judgments. We do not treat them as machines that simply give responses without reasons. We have equally good reason to expect a competent moral judge to grasp the relevant reasons.

Against the second reply, Rawls might argue that his derivation of justice from fairness shows that our considered judgments about relevant considerations reflect the point of view of fairness and so are not merely a non-utilitarian residue. This argument is doubtful,

---

[63] See 161/139: '. . . there is a real advantage in persons' announcing to one another once and for all that even though theoretical computations of utility always happen to favour the equal liberties . . . they do not wish things had been different'.

however, once we distinguish judgments about justice from judgments about overall rightness. Why should we suppose that fairness supports convictions that take utility to be irrelevant to what is right all things considered?

Against the third reply, Rawls needs some argument, not confined to justice and fairness, against the principle of utility. For if we thought that utilitarianism is extremely plausible despite its failure to explain all our considered judgments, we might recognize this failure and still be utilitarians. To see what kind of argument Rawls can offer, we should turn to the Kantian side of his position.

RAWLS: THE RIGHT
AND THE GOOD

1426. The Kantian Interpretation of Justice as Fairness

We have seen why Rawls's defence of his description of the Original Position is open to objection. The appeal to judgments about fairness, regulated by the formal constraints of the concept of right, does not seem adequate for his purposes. We may be able to find a successful defence, however, if we consider what the various conditions of the Original Position seek to achieve, and we do not restrict ourselves to judgments about fairness in defending these conditions.

The provisions of the veil of ignorance seem to rely on an assumption that might be defended from a Kantian point of view. An assumption about equality underlies the rejection of any agreement in which one person takes unfair advantage of another person's ignorance. If I can take advantage of your ignorance, the agreement we make is designed to advance my interests against yours. If we reject this unfairness, we presuppose that people have equal rights, and hence that their needs and interests deserve equal concern and equal treatment apart from any further social aims or goals that may be pursued.[1]

Rawls recognizes a connexion with Kant; he takes the veil of ignorance to be implicit in Kant's formula of universal law (/118n).[2] He means that the veil of ignorance excludes information that might encourage me to make an exception in favour of myself. If I lack this information, I cannot avoid taking the attitude that the categorical imperative requires. But one might equally argue that the second formula of the categorical imperative, requiring the treatment of persons as ends in themselves, already underlies the judgments about fairness that explain the veil of ignorance.[3]

---

[1] Rawls's reliance on some right of this sort is explained by Dworkin, 'Position', 50. I do not mean to endorse Dworkin's view that Rawls's theory has to be a 'rights-based' theory in the stricter sense that Dworkin discusses, according to which some claims about rights are taken to be the absolutely fundamental elements in moral theory. Rawls comments on Dworkin at 'Political', 400n.

[2] The reference to Kant was added in the 2nd edn.

[3] Though Rawls devotes a section (§40) to the Kantian interpretation of justice as fairness, he does not mention this crucial role of a Kantian assumption. Similarly, at *LHMP* 181–3, he explains Kant's second formula by reference to the first. He does not treat the second as more fundamental.

The same concern for equal protection of different people's interests supports the exclusion of benevolence. No one is required to give up their interest simply because people have a certain sort of feeling or sentiment. If most people feel more benevolent than I feel, that is not a good reason for requiring me to give up my own interests in cases where a benevolent person would give it up. An individual is guaranteed protection of her interests irrespective of the prevalence of benevolent sentiments that might seek to maximize well-being in general.

Aversion to risk may be explained in the same way. The Original Position is meant to guarantee to each person a certain minimum protection, so that one person's interest will not be sacrificed simply in order to advance the interests of other people. Each person's interests are considered in their own right, and not simply for the sake of some further end they promote. This non-teleological commitment to the protection of individual interests helps to justify the thickness of the veil of ignorance, and hence supports aversion to risk. But such a commitment needs some support beyond the judgments about fairness that underlie the Original Position.

We endorse principles that guarantee protection of individual interests, if we regard ourselves as counting for something in our own right, independently of the goals and aims of other people. This is the attitude expressed in the Kantian view of persons as ends in themselves. Hence, we will accept Rawls's aims if we accept the Kantian formula of humanity.

Rawls claims that the theory expressed in the Original Position and in the principles of justice derived from it expresses the main points in Kant's moral theory (§40). His claims indicate some of the historical sources of Rawls's own views. They also express a view worth considering about the proper interpretation of Kant. But are they also relevant to the defence of Rawls's view? Have we any better reason for us to believe that Rawls's theory is true, if we think it captures the main points in Kant?

This question is worth asking because of an apparent difference in method between Kant and Rawls. Kant begins from what Rawls calls 'considered judgments', in so far as he argues from the 'ordinary rational knowledge of morality' (the title of Chapter 1 of *Groundwork*). But he argues from this to the metaphysics of morals and eventually to the critique of practical reason (titles of Chapters 2 and 3). He claims that while morality is the way we come to know freedom, freedom is the ultimate metaphysical ground of morality.[4] Metaphysical claims about freedom seem to be the basis of claims about morality; moral claims are objectively true in so far as they correspond to objective facts about free agents.

This attempt to rest moral theory on metaphysics seems to be alien to Rawls's method of moral argument, and to his claims about the nature of moral theory. Rawls speaks as though considered moral judgments are the ultimate court of appeal, and conformity to these considered judgments is the ultimate standard of adequacy and truth for a moral theory. This moral epistemology seems to make Kantian metaphysics superfluous. Rawls draws this conclusion in his claim that moral theory is independent of broader metaphysical theses.[5]

---

[4] See *KpV* 4; the moral law is the ratio cognoscendi of freedom, and freedom is the ratio essendi of the moral law. See §939.

[5] Rawls states his position most fully in 'Independence'. 'Political' defends a different claim about independence.

The questions about independence help to reveal similarities and differences between Rawls and Kant. If we affirm the dependence of moral theory on metaphysics, we might mean that moral theory must confine itself to metaphysical views that are settled in metaphysics independently of any contribution by moral philosophy. In that case, the dependence of moral philosophy on metaphysics would be entirely asymmetrical. Kant and Rawls agree in rejecting this asymmetrical dependence. They agree on this point because they also agree in part of their moral epistemology; they both start from considered moral judgments to seek reflective equilibrium. The adequacy of a theory is to be decided by seeing how well it fits the considered judgments that it begins from and tries to explain. Moral theory, therefore, should not rely entirely on conditions for adequacy that are imported from some other area of philosophy.

Agreement on this point about independence does not, however, imply agreement about the total independence of moral theory from metaphysics. If Kant believed in asymmetrical dependence, he would have to deny any role for God, freedom, and immortality in moral theory, since he believes that our knowledge of the physical world leaves us with no sufficient ground for these claims about reality. But he believes that morality warrants us in accepting these claims, within appropriate limits. Moreover, he believes that we must explain how these claims based on morality are consistent with our other theories about the nature of reality.

Even if we do not agree with Kant about which metaphysical claims a true moral theory commits us to, we may still agree with him that we are committed to some metaphysical claims. If we accept Kant's and Rawls's views about the method of moral philosophy, we cannot rule out the possibility of commitment to metaphysical claims.

To see how much this question matters, it is useful to see the ways in which Kantian views support some of Rawls's claims about the Original Position. We can then try to decide whether these views commit us to interesting or controversial metaphysical doctrines.

1427. Freedom and Equality

We may use Rawls's claims about freedom and equality to test his claims about the relation of Kant's views to his own. He believes that Kantian support is unnecessary. He treats Kantian doctrine as an 'interpretation' of justice as fairness, because he believes that the different features of fairness, supporting the features of the Original Position, correspond to Kantian claims. But Kant provides only an interpretation, not a substitute or a supplement or a revision, because all the moral implications of Kantian doctrine are already present in the demands of fairness.

Rawls makes three claims: (1) The provisions of the Original Position satisfy Kantian requirements. (2) These provisions are warranted by the demands of fairness. Hence (3) The demands of fairness already satisfy Kantian requirements. If Rawls's first claim is true, and his second claim false, he is right to say that the Original Position captures Kant, but wrong to say that justice as fairness captures Kant.

Since we have found some reasons to doubt Rawls's second claim, we need to examine the relation between Kantian doctrines and the demands of fairness. If Rawls is right, Kantian doctrines are unnecessary for the support of the Original Position and the principles of justice that emerge from it, even though they connect judgments about fairness with wider issues in moral philosophy. Is he right, then, to claim that Kant's doctrines support no moral requirements that we cannot already support by appeal to fairness?

The people in the Original Position act as 'free and equal rational persons, knowing only that those circumstances obtain which give rise to the need for principles of justice' (252/222). Rawls claims that the Original Position expresses the point of view from which free and equal persons who want to express their nature as free and equal look at the circumstances in which we choose principles of justice. The demand for equality explains the exclusion of any knowledge that might give anyone a special advantage. The demand for freedom explains the requirement of mutual disinterest (see esp. 253–4/223–4), which allows 'freedom in the choice of a system of final ends'.

Are these Kantian demands implicit in the intuitive conditions about fairness that underlie the Original Position?[6] These conditions do not justify all the limitations on knowledge that are imposed in the Original Position. We saw that ignorance of probabilities is not justified by the weak claims about fairness underlying the Original Position. For we might say that we are treated as equals in the Original Position if we all have an equal chance to benefit from the distributive principles that we agree on. If it is simply hard luck that I lose in an arrangement that makes most people better off than a more egalitarian principle would, then, in one sense, I am treated as an equal. Why is this not the sense relevant to Rawls's argument?

We might insist that the relevant sort of equality is a moral status that we want to protect against external chances and hazards. On this view, I want equal status not in so far as I want to have an equal chance, but in so far as I want to be an equal beneficiary of the system. I want to be an end for the principles of justice along with everyone else. I want the system, therefore, to aim at my benefit, as one moral agent, and hence to aim at the benefit of each agent equally, and not to aim at some total that overrides the benefit of each agent.

Commitment to this sort of equality explains why gambling is prohibited in the Original Position. Willingness to gamble implies acceptance of reduced prospects for some people, perhaps including oneself, to benefit other people; one gambles in the hope of not being among the losers. A more definite commitment to equality insists that no one should be exposed to these sorts of hazards simply for the benefits that other people gain. In this way, people's conception of themselves as equal in certain ways is prior to other aims that actual people might adopt.

This demand for equality implies a demand for equal rights and for some protection against harm. But this demand cannot be justified from the requirements of fairness. These requirements are supposed to be neutral between utilitarian and other views; but the demand for equality already rejects utilitarianism. The commitment to equality that precludes gambling expresses a Kantian demand that is legitimate if people have the sort of moral status that Kant attributes to them.

This would be true even if a utilitarian theory, making certain assumptions about what maximizes utility, were to endorse the principles that one would endorse on Kantian

---

[6] Rawls defends his claim about equality further in 'Kantian conception'.

grounds. Even if equal treatment and equal protection of rights maximized total utility, it would not follow that utilitarianism is the right theory. Rawls argues that his contractarian theory would be preferable even if utilitarianism led to the same principles.[7] He embeds convictions about justice in first principles. If he is right on this point, the Kantian convictions about equality and the protection of rights should be embedded in the principles that underlie the Original Position.

But if the features of the Original Position depend on a Kantian understanding of equality, the design of the Original Position cannot rely wholly on weak and widely shared principles. On the contrary, the relevant principles must be strong and Kantian. We must accept these principles at the start in order to see that the Original Position has been properly set up. Even if the Original Position leads to Kantian conclusions, it does not provide an independent argument for these Kantian conclusions.

1428. Why Accept a Kantian Doctrine of Equality?

Why, then, should we insist on the Kantian interpretation of equality that leads to the demand for protection of equal rights against any other distributive considerations? Some of Kant's argument relies on connexions between the self that we discover in claims about responsibility and the self that we discover in morality.[8] For reasons that we have discussed, some of these connexions are clearer if we consider Butler's and Bradley's view, rather than Kant's view, of the non-moral self, and then consider the Kantian moral implications.[9]

According to Butler, I think of myself as a self, not as a collection of particular passions. The self I recognize is something that is capable of guiding its choices by superior principles, by assessing the comparative weight of reasons rather than the strength of desires. Bradley claims that responsibility involves the expression of this self, and, more specifically, of the character that reflects my superior principles. If this determines how I am treated, my choices, rather than other people's choices for me, determine my treatment. The nature and extent of other people's intervention is determined by the choices I make that express myself.

Butler and Bradley explain why my view of myself in relation to my particular passions should influence my view of other people in relation to myself. Both points of view reflect my intention to express the same thing—my self, guided by superior principles. We recognize here the sort of freedom that we attribute to ourselves in recognizing ourselves as rational, responsible agents. If this argument is plausible, it establishes some connexion between self-love and the attitudes surrounding responsibility; the same attitude to oneself is expressed in each case.

Why should the attitudes attached to responsibility be relevant to further questions about moral equality? As we noticed in the discussion of Kant, we can apparently treat people as

---

[7] '...while in general an ethical theory can certainly invoke natural facts, there may nevertheless be good reasons for embedding convictions of justice more directly into first principles than a theoretically complete grasp of the contingencies of the world may require.' (TJ 161/139; cf. 262–3/232)

[8] Kant on responsibility and morality; §913.

[9] Rawls offers a further argument against utilitarianism in his remarks about the 'separateness of persons' in TJ §§29–30. For discussion see §1192 on Sidgwick.

responsible agents while treating them badly in other ways.[10] Still, responsibility is relevant. If I think you should be punished for what you intended to do, rather than for results that you could not be expected to foresee, I allow what happens to you to be determined partly by retrospective considerations. What you are like expresses itself in what you have done. In general, if we are to express rational agency, we must be treated as responsible agents, in the light of retrospective considerations. Retrospective consideration is connected with respect.

This retrospective condition might reasonably lead us to consider the impact of other social arrangements on the connexions between our decisions and choices and our actions. In this area, too, we expect what happens to us to be determined by what we choose and what we do, rather than by what would be convenient or suitable for some other end. This is why we ought to have rights guaranteed to us, without reference to their tendency to promote utility. Rights to be left alone mark out an area in which other people respect my decisions. Concern to have my decision respected will result, therefore, in my caring about negative rights. These rights are included in what Rawls says about liberty.

Kantian principles would be of limited use, however, if they could only explain why we might demand negative rights. For this would imply that principles of justice need not say anything about any positive contributions to my welfare; here we might think that some appeal to utilitarian considerations is needed. We need not draw this conclusion, however. If I have reason to want my rational plans to be effective, I have reason to want resources to carry them out. If I have reason to want these resources, I also have reason to want them to be guaranteed to me, so that I can count on them. If my access to resources is insecure, I have very limited scope for acting on my rational decisions; but my access to them is insecure if their allocation to me depends on something independent of me—for instance, on how far their allocation to me maximizes the total good. I have reason to want prospective considerations to be kept out of the principles that determine the allocation of resources to me.

Rawls sees this reason for demanding guarantees. The Kantian argument adds the connexion between the demand for guaranteed material resources and the general demand for being treated in accordance with retrospective considerations. The general demand to be assessed on retrospective grounds can be connected with the still more general and abstract demand to be treated with respect, and also with the more specific demands for certain kinds of rights and guarantees.

We should, therefore, dispute Rawls's claim that the description of the Original Position can be justified by 'weak and widely shared' assumptions about fairness. The concomitant claim that the Original Position does most of the work of refuting utilitarianism is also doubtful. Rawls suggests that—dialectically speaking—we can go into the Original Position without having rejected utilitarianism, and that then we notice, from what people in the Original Position decide, that utilitarianism has to be rejected. We have seen that, on the contrary, we can accept Rawls's description of the Original Position only if we accept at the start some strong conditions about the protection of equal rights. These conditions

---

[10] Kant on concern for other responsible agents: §§925, 965.

already reject utilitarianism. The Original Position works out the consequences of these strong conditions.

Rawls's argument may, none the less, be defensible, if we can defend the strong Kantian assumptions that it relies on. The anti-utilitarian demand for equal rights and equal guarantees can be defended from the more general preference for retrospective evaluation as a condition of respect for rational agency.

1429. Are the Principles of Justice Categorical Imperatives?

Similar questions arise about Rawls's claim that the principles accepted in the Original Position meet Kant's conditions for being categorical imperatives. The claim is doubtful if we confine ourselves to what we know about these principles from Rawls's derivation of them. It is more plausible if we accept a Kantian basis, going beyond intuitive judgments about fairness, for the provisions of the Original Position.

Rawls believes that the principles of justice are categorical imperatives because they do not rest on desires or inclinations peculiar to some people as opposed to others.[11] This is one necessary condition for a categorical imperative. But the issue is more complicated.[12] The people in the Original Position choose the principles of justice because they want the primary goods; hence the principles seem to be Kantian hypothetical imperatives. Kant's counsels of prudence rest on desires that are common to all human beings, and Rawls's principles seem to fall under this head. If Rawls accepts Kant's criterion for an acceptable moral principle, he seems not to have shown that the principles he favours are acceptable.[13]

To see whether we might modify Rawls's claim, we need to distinguish two features of the primary goods: (1) We want them because we want the resources and background conditions necessary for having the right sort of freedom of choice about our conception of the good. (2) We see that in the conditions of human life these particular resources, opportunities, etc. help to secure the right sort of freedom of choice about our conception of the good.

The second feature of primary goods relies on information that does not support a categorical imperative; for it refers especially to the specific contingencies of the human condition, not to circumstances facing all rational beings as such. This is not so clear, however, about the first feature of primary goods. If it is rational for every rational being as such to want to be free to choose her conception of her own good and to execute this conception, it is rational for every rational being to want to secure the resources and conditions for the relevant choice and opportunity, whatever they may be in the particular circumstances.

Rawls sometimes emphasizes this aspect of his argument for primary goods; it does not depend on empirical claims about the general usefulness of the resources that he mentions.[14]

---

[11] In the 1st edn., Rawls claims (253) that the principles of justice are Kantian categorical imperatives. In the 2nd edn., he says that they are analogous to categorical imperatives (222).

[12] For further discussion see Nagel, 'Rawls'.   [13] Rawls discusses Kant further in 'Themes'.

[14] This is part of Rawls's later argument for primary goods, discussed at §1438.

In material circumstances where external resources were abundant, there might be no need to insist on any particular conditions about the distribution of material goods. Still, the general principle suggested in the first feature of primary goods explains why it is reasonable to insist on the provision of material resources in the conditions that Rawls specifies for the Original Position.

If this argument is sound, the principles of justice conform to the categorical imperative, even though they are not themselves categorical imperatives. They conform to the categorical imperative in the same way that the attempt to feed a starving person conforms to it. We cannot infer from the categorical imperative itself that human beings need food; but if we know that they do, we can reasonably argue that respect for them as ends in themselves requires us to feed starving people.[15] The same sort of argument can be used to defend the principles of justice from the standpoint of the categorical imperative.

In his continuous discussion of Kant (§40), Rawls does not mention the Formula of Humanity, requiring the treatment of persons as ends in themselves. But he claims elsewhere that justice as fairness captures this feature of Kant's theory.[16] He relies on this Kantian condition in the construction of the Original Position. For if the initial conditions underlying the Original Position did not recognize that people have equal rights protecting them against damage to their interests simply to benefit other people or to promote total utility, the initial conditions would be too weak to rule out utilitarianism.

But if some demand for equal rights that are not to be sacrificed to other goals is built into the Original Position, the initial conditions are not as weak and uncontroversial as Rawls wants them to be. They seem to reflect a prior commitment to a Kantian theory. If we rely on considered judgments, we must show that they are sufficiently Kantian to support an account of the Original Position that precludes the choice of utilitarian principles.

But if this is true of our considered judgments, a more general question about method seems to arise. For it seems open to utilitarians to object to argument from considered judgments. Perhaps the utilitarian should concede that Rawls is right about considered judgments; perhaps they are as Kantian as they need to be to support Rawls's design of the Original Position. But this may simply show that considered judgments are an unreliable basis for a moral theory that seeks the truth.

Rawls might reply that moral theory does not seek, or claim to find, the truth, if the truth is something not wholly constituted by some rational reconstruction of considered judgments. If a theory seeks reflective equilibrium and nothing more, then no objection arises from the fact that it relies on Kantian considered judgments in order to support Kantian moral principles. On this view, Rawls claims to have shown nothing more than that utilitarianism fails to match our considered judgments.

But such a reply leaves room for the utilitarian rejoinder that plausible principles independent of considered judgments support the principle of utility. If this is true, the

---

[15] This distinction suggests a possible answer to the doubts that Rawls raises at 257/226.

[16] 'On the contract interpretation treating men as ends in themselves implies at the very least treating them in accordance with the principles to which they would consent in an original position of equality. For in this situation men have equal representation as moral persons who regard themselves as ends and the principles they accept will be rationally designed to protect the claims of their person. The contract view as such defines a sense in which men are to be treated as ends and not as means only.' (180/156–7)

utilitarian theory might be true, or better justified than Rawls's theory, even if Rawls's theory matches our considered moral judgments better. Sidgwick believes that his defence of utilitarianism justifies the rejection of considered judgments.

1430. The Significance of the Kantian Interpretation

To see how Rawls might answer this utilitarian objection, we should see why it matters that his principles of justice can be defended on Kantian grounds. Does a Kantian defence give a further reason to believe that these are the true principles of justice?

Rawls suggests that the Kantian defence is relevant because it describes something about the motives and desires of the parties in the Original Position.[17] If their nature as free and equal rational agents determines the content of their choices, they must care more about themselves as free and equal rational agents than about other aspects of themselves. Normally, however, Rawls excludes these evaluative commitments from the Original Position. He violates his normal rule in claiming that people in the Original Position accept this particular commitment to freedom and equality.

We might suggest a different view from Rawls's (or, alternatively, suggest this as a less literal interpretation of Rawls), that the people in the Original Position represent or model the outlook of people who want to express their nature as free and equal rational agents. They 'represent' or 'model' this outlook in the way that they represent or model a fair attitude to each other's claims, even though they do not explicitly care about fairness. Actual people who care about fairness can adopt the outlook of the artificial people in the Original Position, and (in Rawls's view) can expect to reach fair conclusions. Similarly, then, we might argue that if we (actual people) want to express ourselves as free and equal rational agents, we can confidently adopt the outlook of the people in the Original Position. The relevant sort of freedom is guaranteed by the stipulation of mutual disinterest and the priority of liberty; for these two conditions leave us free to choose our conception of our final good, and to act on it as we see fit (within the appropriate limits set by the principles of right).

This interpretation or modification of Rawls's claim suggests that the Kantian interpretation of justice as fairness appeals to us if we want to express ourselves as free and equal rational agents. Rawls confirms this suggestion in some of his later works. He attributes to moral agents two moral powers: the capacity for an effective sense of justice, and the capacity to form, revise, and rationally to pursue a conception of the good. He also attributes to moral agents, and to citizens in a well-ordered society, two highest-order interests in realizing and exercising these powers ('Constructivism', 312; cf. PL 74). They have effective desires to pursue these interests and to express these powers (PL 86).

The Kantian view deserves to be taken seriously, therefore, because of some fact about our desires. But what sort of fact? If we had no desire to express ourselves as free and equal,

---

[17] He claims that the parties in the Original Position 'have a desire to express their nature as rational and equal members of the intelligible realm' (255/225). The 'intelligible realm' consists of noumenal (i.e., intelligible) selves, who look at themselves from the point of view of rational agents as such, without reference to their inclinations and sensuous motives. This interpretation of the noumenal self is closest to the view that Kant expresses in the *Religion*.

would the Kantian interpretation be irrelevant, and would we have no reason to take it seriously? If so, Rawls's account of why we should take the Kantian interpretation seriously seems similar to his view of the good as the satisfaction of rational desire. On that view, x is good for me if I desire y, which is an end that x promotes; no facts determine, independently of my desires, what is actually good for me. Similarly, no facts independent of my desires determine whether I have reason to express myself as free and equal. I have reason to act in ways that express myself as free and equal only if I have the relevant desire; there is no further reason why I should have the relevant desire.

This is a subjectivist answer to questions about why we should take the moral point of view seriously. It makes morality rest on a hypothetical imperative. The reason for taking the moral attitude (in Rawls's theory, for taking the outlook of the Original Position seriously) arises from a desire resting on no further reason—the sort of thing that Hutcheson regards as the basis of a justifying reason.

Rawls objects to this suggestion that his account of the motivation of moral agents basically relies on desires. In his view, the autonomy of moral agents is secured by the fact that their desires are 'conception-dependent'.[18] They do not simply feel attracted to the principles of justice; they also conceive these principles as embodying their conception of themselves as free and equal. But if we agree with Rawls on this point, we may still ask about the attitude of moral agents to this conception; why do they want to act in accordance with it? We might answer that (1) they simply find it appealing, irrespective of any questions about its truth or that (2) they believe it is true.

If Rawls intends the first answer, Kantian claims are relevant only because they help to explain how moral agents view themselves. This answer does not face Sidgwick's question about whether their view is correct. Sidgwick tries to answer that question by arguing for the truth of the utilitarian principle. If Rawls intends the second answer, he admits the legitimacy of Sidgwick's question. Kant tries to answer it by arguing that the conception of ourselves as free and equal is correct, because it reflects the fact that we are free and equal; these facts about us give us reasons to express ourselves as such.

Once we admit the relevance of the question about whether the highest-order desires of moral agents rest on true or false beliefs, some metaphysical argument is relevant, in order to decide whether these are genuine facts about us. Moreover, a theory of objective reasons is needed to show that the facts can give us reasons independent of our actual desires. Kant provides some of the necessary argument, and some idea of how some of the rest of the argument might go. Rawls needs the same sort of argument, if he does not intend a subjectivist account of the Kantian interpretation. If such an argument can be given, a subjectivist claim is not all that can be offered on behalf of the Kantian interpretation.

If, however, we consider this metaphysical defence of the Kantian interpretation, we can revise some of Rawls's moral epistemology. For we will now consider the possibility of saying that we trust our Kantian considered judgments because they reflect facts about

---

[18] '. . . an effective sense of justice, the desire to act from the principles of justice, is not a desire on the same footing with natural inclinations; it is an executive and regulative highest-order desire to act from certain principles of justice in view of their connexion with a conception of the person as free and equal. And this desire is not heteronomous; for whether a desire is heteronomous is settled by its mode of origin and role within the self and by what it is a desire for.' ('Constructivism', 320) On conception-dependent desires, cf. PL 82–6.

us as free and rational agents, and that we reject a utilitarian revision of these considered judgments because it conflicts with the same facts.[19] In order to allow the appropriate sort of force to Rawls's appeal to the Kantian interpretation, we might take a different view of the status of the considered judgments explained by this interpretation.

1431. Self-Respect v. Self-Esteem

Kantian moral principles require some guaranteed status for rational agents apart from their contribution to other people's good; they thereby express respect for rational agents. Kant takes respect to be appropriate to oneself as well as to others; in regarding oneself as an end, one avoids the vice of servility.[20] In respecting myself, I recognize my own independent value, not subordinate to anyone else's ends. In respecting others, I recognize their independent value in the same way.

Rawls agrees with Kant that the treatment of persons as ends implies a certain kind of self-respect.[21] He claims that the two principles of justice satisfy the demands of self-respect, whereas the principle of utility does not. Hence the respect that is due to persons as ends requires acceptance of the two principles and the rejection of utilitarianism.

But Rawls does not mean what Kant means by self-respect. In *TJ*, he identifies self-respect with self-esteem, detached from any particular conception of one's moral value.[22] We have self-esteem if we think our life is worthwhile and it is worth the effort to act on our conception of our good. Rawls's remarks about 'self-respect' and 'self-esteem' do not refer to one's view that one deserves something from the moral point of view. Non-moral self-respect matters to people in the Original Position. Since the arguments for the two principles of justice appeal to self-respect, the relevant conception of self-respect should not rely on controversial claims about the independent value of individual persons.

The importance of self-respect for pursuing one's conception of one's good explains why it is a primary good recognized in the Original Position.[23] I will not pursue any conception of my good with any vigour unless I care enough about myself to take the trouble to do something. I must have enough interest in what happens to me, if I am to see some point in acting on my conception of my good. The two principles support my self-esteem, because they do not require me to sacrifice my prospects in life for the sake of maximizing the total or average good. They assure me that I count for something in relation to other people's interests.

---

[19] Rawls rejects this sort of view, in 'Independence'.   [20] Kant on servility; §§924–5.

[21] 'The contract view as such defines a sense in which men are to be treated as ends and not as means only. But the question arises whether there are substantive principles which convey this idea. If the parties wish to express this notion visibly in the basic structure of society in order to secure each man's rational interest in his self-respect, which principles should they choose?' (180/157)

[22] 'We may define self-respect (or self-esteem) as having two aspects. First . . . , it includes a person's sense of his own value, his secure conviction that his conception of his good, his plan of life, is worth carrying out. And second, self-respect implies a confidence in one's ability, so far as it is within one's power, to fulfil one's intentions.' (440/386) At 'Kantian conception', 260, Rawls denies that self-respect and self-esteem are the same.

[23] At *PL* 319 and *JFR* 60, Rawls maintains that it is not self-respect itself, but the social bases of self-respect that are a primary good.

Does this distinguish the two principles from the principle of utility? Rawls acknowledges that if I am a utilitarian and my society follows utilitarian principles, the sacrifices it demands from me need not undermine my self-esteem. Even if I come out worse and others come out better, it does not follow that anyone discriminated in favour of these others and against me, or that I was treated as having no value. None the less, Rawls believes self-esteem will suffer if utilitarian principles are followed.[24]

It is not clear, however, why utilitarianism should undermine self-esteem. If self-esteem consists simply in a sufficiently positive self-image to make me care about pursuing my good, I preserve it if I am assured that my relative deprivation does not reflect badly on me. Rawls assumes that such assurance preserves self-esteem. For he relies on this assurance to show that the arrangement he favours does not undermine self-esteem. The distributive element in the second principle of justice—the difference principle—is a means of ensuring self-esteem for the less fortunate.[25] But we might ask why it does not tend to weaken the positive self-image of the better off, if they feel that the rewards of their talents are being taken away from them for other people's benefit. Rawls answers, quite reasonably, that this pattern of distribution does not imply that we regard the more talented people as being worth less. The arguments from social policy do not reflect any judgments on the worth of the more talented people.

But a utilitarian can apparently say the same thing. Sacrificing one person's interests for the sake of the overall good does not reflect adversely on the worth of the victim, since the social policy requiring this sacrifice is not a statement about people's worth, but about the good that people can achieve. Within Rawls's two principles, the fact that a talented person's rewards are limited for the sake of the less well-off does not make it seem futile for talented people to pursue their plan for their lives. Equally, then, it is not clear why people whose rewards may be limited for the sake of the total good should lose their confidence in pursuing their plan for their lives.

If a utilitarian system can support self-esteem no less than Rawls's system can support it, each system seems to protect self-respect equally well, and non-utilitarian principles seem to have no special role in protecting self-respect. The demand for treatment as ends may be one support for self-esteem. But, since it is simply one support, people in the Original Position have no reason to insist on being treated as ends. Since other moral principles, including the principle of utility, can also protect self-esteem, people in the Original Position have no reason to reject utilitarianism because of concerns about self-respect.

One might argue that this defence of utilitarianism lets it off too lightly. Even if it does not undermine self-respect, does it not undermine equal respect for each person? One might

---

[24] 'The principle of utility presumably requires some to forgo greater life prospects for the sake of others. To be sure, it is not necessary that those having to make such sacrifices rationalize this demand by having a lesser appreciation of their own worth. It does not follow from the utilitarian doctrine that it is because their aims are trivial or unimportant that some individuals' expectations are less. Yet this may often be the case, and there is a sense, as we have seen, in which utilitarianism does not regard persons as ends in themselves.' (180/157). The 2nd edn. omits the last sentence. In 'there is a sense . . . ,' Rawls refers to his previous claim that the two principles treat persons as ends. But that claim was explained with reference to one's rational interest in one's self-respect, which utilitarianism does not necessarily threaten (if self-respect is self-esteem).

[25] '[The two principles] are equivalent . . . to an undertaking to regard the distribution of natural abilities as a collective asset so that the more fortunate are to benefit only in ways that help those who have lost out.' (179/156)

answer this objection in two ways: (1) It does not undermine equal respect. Everyone 'counts for one', since each person's happiness, supposed equal in degree, counts equally towards the total. (2) Equal respect is unnecessary for self-esteem. Self-esteem demands a positive attitude to oneself and one's aims in life. One may have this attitude without thinking one is as valuable as everyone else. A positive attitude to oneself does not seem to depend on a conviction that one matters as much as everyone else.[26] Rawls, therefore, does not show that the demands of self-esteem favour non-utilitarian over utilitarian principles of justice.

These defences of utilitarianism collapse, however, if we understand self-respect as Kant understands it, so that it requires respect for persons as having value in their own right, independent of their role in promoting a total good. If the Original Position is required to safeguard this conception of respect for persons, it is easier to see why it rules out the choice of utilitarian principles. But to impose this condition on the Original Position, we must already have shown that persons are ends in themselves, not simply that people want to think of themselves in this way.

1432. How Kant Might Support Rawls

Kant, therefore, does not provide 'the Kantian interpretation of justice as fairness' (title of §40). The distinctive idea of justice as fairness is the explication of justice through considered judgments about fairness. Rawls argues that the features of the Original Position can be defended through judgments about fairness that do not take any position on the questions disputed between Kantians, utilitarians, and pluralists.

An appeal to Kant does not vindicate this claim about the relation between justice and fairness, or about the relation between judgments about fairness and the design of the Original Position. Rawls really suggests a Kantian defence of the Original Position, rather than a Kantian interpretation of justice as fairness. For the Kantian premises that support different features of the Original Position are more explicitly controversial than the considered judgments about fairness that Rawls relies on.

Rejection of Rawls's account of the basis of the Original Position makes a difference to his account of the argument leading to reflective equilibrium. In his view, the two principles of justice can be supported from two different directions: (1) from our initial judgments about fairness, and (2) from our considered judgments about justice as a whole. We take the second step only after we have seen that the two principles emerge from the Original Position, and hence from considered judgments about fairness. If, contrary to Rawls, judgments about fairness do not support the design of the Original Position, these two stages are more difficult to distinguish. In order to show that people are ends in themselves and therefore deserve guarantees against being used to maximize a total good, we have to appeal to more than our judgments about fairness.

Kant's argument indicates the range of considered judgments that contribute to a plausible argument. To show that common moral judgments eventually lead us to accept the Formula

---

[26] This consideration may weaken the force of Rawls's appeal to 'the general facts of moral psychology' (181/157).

of Humanity, Kant has to appeal to the rational character of moral judgments and to the status that they presuppose for rational agents. This argument relies on a broader range of moral judgments than those that Rawls uses to defend the Original Position.

A more Kantian argument might include two stages, different from those that Rawls distinguishes. (1) We might argue that persons are ends in themselves, and therefore free and equal. (2) We might then argue that this conception of persons matches our considered judgments about justice as a whole. These stages are worth distinguishing, since we may not rely on all our considered judgments about justice when we defend the first claim, but may appeal to a subset of them, as Kant does in his argument from the common rational knowledge of morality (G, ch. 1).

The main difference between this argument and Rawls's argument comes at the first stage. This stage of the argument requires a defence of the truth of Kantian claims about the idea of personality, about freedom, and about the formula of humanity. We might have been inclined to welcome Rawls's argument because it held out the prospect of supporting Kantian conclusions without the burden of arguing for controversial Kantian premises. But this prospect is illusory. To reach Kantian conclusions, the Original Position must be designed in the light of Kantian principles. The difference between the intended role and the actual role of Kantian doctrine is the difference between a Kantian interpretation of justice as fairness and a Kantian foundation for the Original Position.

A Kantian foundation supports Rawls's views against utilitarianism. Does it also support his views against pluralist intuitionism? On the one hand, it supports his view that moral judgments do not rely on a mere collection of principles that share no higher principles. If Ross's reference to the personal character of some obligations supports a Kantian explanation that goes beyond Ross's unreduced plurality of first principles, it supports Rawls against intuitionism.[27] On the other hand, it is less clear that a Kantian foundation supports Rawls's claim that justice is prior to other obligations. Even if one agrees with a basic principle of treating persons as ends, it is not obvious that this principle always gives priority to obligations of justice. We may still have to rely on judgments that do not rely on higher principles in order to resolve apparent conflicts of obligations. This aspect of pluralist intuitionism may remain within a Kantian position.

The recognition of a Kantian foundation does not require rejection of a holist method, aiming at reflective equilibrium, in favour of a method resting on foundationalist assumptions. If holism is the right method, a defence of a Kantian foundation should rest on an appeal to considered judgments. But it should also undertake the task that Rawls does not undertake, of showing that the principles defining the Kantian foundation for justice are true.

1433. The Priority of the Right over the Good

Rawls's appeal to the Original Position is intended to support a further defence of Kant. Kant speaks as though we can see the authority of the moral law apart from any views we may

---

[27] Ross on the personal character of duties; §1290.

have formed about our good in general. Indeed, his views about the non-moral element of the human good make it an unsuitable basis for morality; for he often takes a hedonist view of the desires and aims that Butler attributes to rational self-love. Rawls agrees with Kant in maintaining the priority of the right over the good. He believes we can defend the principles of justice, and their fundamental role in the structure of society, without a full account of the good for persons.[28]

If an account of the right depended on an account of the good, Rawls's conception of the good would raise difficulties for his claims about the right. For, in his view, a person's good is constituted in a certain way by the individual person's preferences. Different people with different preferences can be expected to have different conceptions of the good. Like Kant, Rawls believes there is something inevitably subjective in conceptions of the good, but this does not affect our views of the morally right. If our justification of morality required us to show that it is a dominant part of every person's good, our task would be difficult; for apparently one person would have a reason to care about morality and another would not. But we do not face this task, because we can justify acceptance of principles of the right that are prior to any conception of the good.

Here Rawls tries to solve Sidgwick's dualism of practical reason, and also to respond to the questions that Bradley raises about the relation between the morality of 'my station and its duties' and the further social and non-social aspects of moral ideals. He rejects idealist criticisms of Kant's sharp separation of morality from other aspects of self-realization.[29] The idealists claim that morality is an aspect of self-realization, and that an acceptable account of morality depends on a full account of self-realization. Rawls replies to such arguments by asserting the priority of the right to the good.[30] But he does not neglect the questions that Bradley discusses under the head of self-realization. The whole of Part III of *TJ* is devoted to them. The discussion allows us to clarify some of Bradley's claims.

1434. A Subjectivist Conception of the Good

Rawls's conception of a person's good is subjectivist, in so far as he believes that the good is the satisfaction of rational desire, or, more generally, the fulfilment of a rational plan of life.[31] Rationality is to be understood in the narrow sense that was assumed in the description of the Original Position; it is to be assessed relatively to the agent's actual desires.[32] Actual desires for ends in themselves are ultimately beyond criticism from the point of view of rationality.

The claim that desires for ends cannot be criticized for being irrational in themselves does not mean that they are beyond all criticism. Deliberation in the light of our current desires can also affect the desires we will have later (415/364). Moreover, reflexion on how we have formed certain desires may sometimes cause us to modify them; and so the original desires may not survive as permanent features of our conception of our good (419–20/368–9).

---

[28] See his contrasts between the right and the good, §68.
[29] He answers some idealist objections to contract theory at *PL* 285–8.
[30] He states this first at 43/38, and explains it further at 449–50/394–5.
[31] At 'Political', 414, Rawls comments on the account of the good in *TJ*.
[32] See 143/123–4, quoted in §1419.

A German born in 1930 and growing up in the Third Reich might come to realize that his aversion to dark-haired Jewish-looking people and his admiration for blond-haired people are simply products of his upbringing. When he compares these attitudes with his later experience of dark-haired and blond-haired people, his aversion for the one and his admiration for the other may go away.[33]

But though this may be the result of reflexion on the formation of our desires, it need not be. If a preference or an aversion is sufficiently ingrained in us, it determines part of our good. A desire that survives exposure to the relevant facts about its origin thereby becomes a rational desire.

This subjectivist account of the good revives a question about Kant. Since he recognizes moral categorical imperatives, he recognizes reasons independent of desires. If there are categorical imperatives, A has a reason for doing x, independently of A's desires; and so, even if A has no desire for x, and has no desire for anything to which x is a means, A has some reason to acquire the relevant desires. The desires in the light of which A chooses what to do are open to further evaluation that does not simply evaluate desires in the light of other desires.

Kant recognizes categorical imperatives only in morality. In every other case, he assumes that our having a reason to do x depends on a previous desire for y, to which we regard x as a means.[34] Rawls agrees with Kant in rejecting non-moral categorical imperatives. Kant's view that all reasons other than moral reasons depend on desires makes it harder to believe that moral reasons are independent of any desire. Does Rawls face a similar objection?

1435. Doubts about Rawls's Subjectivist Account of the Good

Rawls's desire-relative account of the good is open to Bradley's objection (*ES* 74) to a conception of the good that makes the 'life of an oyster' good for a human being. For Rawls allows that if some people have only a few desires, their good consists in acting so as to satisfy those few desires. If we reject this claim about the good, we might incline to Bradley's account of the good as self-realization, understood as the realization of one's capacities.

Rawls recognizes some truth in the view of the good as self-realization. He introduces the 'Aristotelian Principle' (414/364; §65), which appears similar to a principle of self-realization (as Rawls mentions, 431/378). It says that 'other things equal, human beings enjoy the exercise of their realized capacities'. Rawls, therefore, makes self-realization relevant to the good, but because it is a source of enjoyment, not because it is part of our good apart from our preferences. The claim about enjoyment is intended as a psychological generalization, not as a normative claim about the good. If some people do not enjoy the exercise of their realized capacities, self-realization is not good for them. Someone who has formed a

---

[33] Rawls cites Brandt, who develops his conception of rational desire in *TGR*, chs. 1–6. Brandt takes a desire to be rational 'if and only if it is what it would have been had the person undergone cognitive psychotherapy', which consists of, roughly speaking, exposure to the relevant facts and logic. Brandt's views on this and related questions are convincingly criticized by Velleman, 'Good', and Sturgeon, 'Empiricism'.

[34] Kant is even more restrictive than this; he believes that every reason apart from a moral reason depends on our having some antecedent desire for our own pleasure. See §904.

non-instrumental preference for counting blades of grass has not made a mistake about his good (432/379–80). The Aristotelian Principle tells us not what is good for a person, but what most people enjoy.

This Aristotelian Principle does not capture much of Aristotle. It does not explain why we might think someone is better off if he comes to change his conception of the good from a narrow one (such as counting blades of grass) to a broader one, or why we might want to encourage people, in their own interest, to develop one sort of conception rather than another. A subjectivist account, therefore, conflicts with those considered judgments about welfare that regard some people as badly off, even if they fulfil all their rational desires (as Rawls understands rational desires). In some cases, a person's desires may be so distorted that they fail to give her a clear conception of her good.

These judgments about people's objective good influence our views about oppression.[35] Sometimes people may be oppressed by suffering the frustration of their actual desires; slaves who wanted to be free, or to live somewhere else, or to live in permanent families, were prevented. Sometimes, however, oppression does not consist in the frustration of actual desires. Oppressed groups lose the desire to do the things they are prevented from doing; they need no restraint, since their upbringing and training have eliminated the relevant desires. Slaves who have lost the desire to live in families, or who fear the loss of dependence, or who are pleased to be in a subordinate status, would not choose anything different from what they have, even if they were free to choose.

We usually regard the second aspect of slavery, as well as the first, as an oppressive aspect of it. But how can we recognize this oppression if we hold a desire-relative conception of the good? We might say that people 'really' have desires that are not obvious, so that some desires even of apparently willing slaves are being frustrated. But this reply raises difficulties for a desire-relative theory. Why should we believe that they 'really' have the un-obvious desires, if we do not already believe that it would be good for them to be treated as though these desires were being satisfied?

If we reject this appeal to un-obvious desires, and still accept a desire-relative conception of the good, we must admit that it is good for the contented slaves—given the desires they actually have—to be slaves. This kind of slavery, therefore, does not harm its victims. Perhaps the system has harmed their parents, say, in enforcing slavery; but once people have come to accept it, it no longer harms them. Defenders of a desire-relative conception of the good may still say that there is something bad about an oppressive system even if its victims accept it. But they cannot say that it is bad for the victims, that it actually harms them.

This is an unwelcome conclusion; for oppressive systems that restrict the growth of people's aims and aspirations seem to harm them in ways that seriously damage their prospect of achieving their good. We are ready to admit this in individual cases, if we are responsible for the welfare of another, or for advising them about their welfare. We do not agree that someone's welfare has been completely achieved if they are living according to a plan of life that fully satisfies their rational plans, but their rational plans are those of a contented slave. If we were charged with looking after the interests of another person,

---

[35] On oppression see also §1401.

we would not have done our work very well if we left them in the condition of the contented slave.

The desire-relative conception of the good, therefore, is unattractive. It does not allow our desires to be criticized as harmful to us apart from any conflict between these desires and other desires. The criticism of desires is a familiar and important aspect of moral and social criticism that cannot be explained within a desire-relative theory. These considered judgments do not fit Rawls's conception of the good.

Rawls's reference to the Aristotelian Principle suggests where one ought to turn for a more plausible conception of the good. If we follow Green and Bradley and identify one's good with the realization of one's capacities as a rational agent, we can follow Rawls in accepting the Aristotelian Principle, but we need not treat it as a mere psychological generalization. Though it is difficult to spell out in detail what is needed for the realization of one's capacities, Rawls gives us reasons for supposing that we have a clear enough grasp of this notion to use it in forming judgments about a person's good.

1436. The Diversity of Goods

Our examination of Rawls's conception of the good suggests that he ought to endorse an objective account of the good as self-realization, in preference to the subjective account that he endorses. Such a change might be unwelcome to him, since it might deprive him of one of his leading contrasts between the right and the good. In his view, 'it is in general a good thing that individuals' conception of their good should differ in significant ways, whereas this is not so for conceptions of right' (/393). The variety in conceptions of the good makes an account of the good unsuitable as a basis for principles of right that will be common to different individuals.

Rawls assumes, then, that conceptions of the good would not differ in desirable ways unless a person's good consisted in the satisfaction of one's desires, and not in some objective condition. But his argument to show why differing conceptions of the good are desirable refers to the fact that different people have different capacities, and that a particular individual cannot realize all his capacities, but can find some of them realized in other people.[36] This sort of difference fits an objective conception of the good as consisting in the realization of human capacities. In one way, different people's conception of the good will be the same, if they all grasp the true conception. But in another way their conceptions will be different; for the single true conception of the good will allow, and indeed require, the different activities that result from the differences in people's capacities.

An objective conception of the good, therefore, provides for the desirable differences that Rawls mentions. A subjective conception, however, does not seem to guarantee provision for them. If you think your good consists in the satisfaction of your very few desires, and I think my good consists in the satisfaction of my very few desires, our developed inclinations

---

[36] 'Human beings have various talents and abilities, the totality of which is unrealizable by any one person or group of persons. Thus we not only benefit from the complementary nature of our developed inclinations, but we take pleasure in one another's activities. It is as if others were bringing forth a part of ourselves that we have not been able to cultivate.' (448/393–4)

are not complementary, and I have no reason to take pleasure in your realizing human capacities that I do not realize. If we share a subjective conception of the good, we may have no reason to welcome differences in people's different views about how to achieve it, and if a subjective conception is true, we are not missing anything if we have rather uniform desires and satisfy them. Rawls's claim about differences assumes that people pursue the realization of their capacities, and identify this with their good. But, according to his view of the good, this is not necessary for achieving one's good.

Rawls's remarks about desirable variations in conceptions of the good, therefore, cast doubt on his conclusion. For variations are desirable because a specific objective conception of the good is plausible, not because a subjective conception is correct. Hence, claims about desirable variation do not support a conception of the good that is too subjective to provide a basis for the right. As far as these questions about the good are concerned, Rawls has not shown that the good could not be a basis for the right.

1437. Primary Goods and the Priority of the Right

An objective conception of the good is unwelcome to Rawls, because it seems to conflict with the priority of the right. Is he correct in supposing that his subjectivist views of the good fit the priority of the right better than objectivist views would fit it?

The priority of the right over the good consists in the fact that we adopt the principles chosen in the Original Position behind the veil of ignorance, before we know what our conception of our good is going to be. This structural feature of Rawls's theory secures the priority of the right. It is not an argument for the priority of the right; for we need some argument for preferring a theory with this structure over a theory with a different structure. According to Rawls, the Original Position is justified from the point of view of fairness. But according to our previous argument, it really rests on further Kantian considerations about the right. Why should these considerations be prior to the good?

Rawls's argument partly depends on the fact that the Original Position is not completely oblivious to questions about the good. For it relies on the 'thin' theory of the good, which identifies the primary goods as resources that it is rational for us to want for the sake of our good, even if we do not know our specific conception of the good. Since most conceptions of the good require some material resources, we are well advised to secure some of them. We are still free to give them up if we find that we want to be ascetics; for the assurance of liberty leaves us free to act on any ascetic preferences we may acquire.

We might argue, then, that even if Rawls's conception of the good is mistaken, this does not matter, because the theory of justice needs only the thin theory of the good that specifies the primary goods (§§15, 60.) To reach the list of primary goods, we assume that the people in the Original Position do not know their individual conceptions of the good, but they know (a) what conceptions of the good are like, including such psychological facts as those underlying the Aristotelian Principle; (b) what is needed to ensure the pursuit of one's conception of the good.

At first sight, the subjectivity of the good appears to help the argument from the primacy of the primary goods to the priority of the right over the good. We recognize that they are useful resources for pursuing different conceptions of the good. But if we were assured at the beginning that one conception of the good is correct, we would lack a reason for wanting resources that are useful within many different conceptions.

But a subjective conception does not ensure the primacy of the primary goods. On the contrary, variety in conceptions of the good threatens the priority of principles that secure the primary goods. Once we find out what our conception of the good is, why should we regard the right as prior to it? Why should I not prefer to trade the guarantees of the Original Position for a form of society that encouraged this sort of outlook more than the society favoured by Rawls would encourage it?

We might reply that, since we have accepted the principles laid down in the Original Position as forming the basic structure of society, we have constrained the choice of possible conceptions of the good. But why is this rational in the light of facts about our conception of the good, once we know what it is? We may grant that the primary goods are the best bet for people in the Original Position. People might turn out not to need, for instance, the material resources that they are guaranteed by the principles of justice, but they will not be forced to use them. If they come to accept some conception of the good quite different from the one generally accepted in their society, the principles of justice ensure that they are not forced to follow the prevalent conception.

But have we good reason to ensure that the protection of this freedom must always take first place? By accepting the point of view of the Original Position, we ensure the protection of the primary goods against other social arrangements that might be more flexible. Why should we do this? We return by another route to the question we raised before, about why the conditions defining the Original Position are fair.

Further difficulties arise if an objective account of the good is correct. We might argue that in some cases liberty will interfere with people's achieving their good, because it will allow them to pursue their own false conception, when they would be better off if coercion were applied to them. Hence we might be unwilling to accord the sort of priority to liberty that Rawls accords to it. Even if the primary goods have a place in a correct conception of the good, perhaps they are not absolutely primary. Perhaps some other good is as important as Rawls's primary goods, even though it would not advance all or most conceptions of the good.

A possible example is a good that Rawls discusses later. If we are right to attach special value to cooperation and identification with the interests of others, and we believe that some tendency to equality encourages such relations, we might not accept all the inequalities allowed by Rawls's Difference Principle, which requires every inequality to make the worst-off better off to some degree. This principle of justice is satisfied if, for instance, we allow policies that make the best-off much better off and make the worst-off only a little better off (where the 'trickle-down' effect is comparatively very small). If one saw reasons for valuing equality more highly, one might think the Difference Principle is too permissive.

One might none the less defend the priority of the primary goods. Against the objections to the priority of liberty, we might appeal to the special good of freely choosing to follow one's conception of the good. If we could show that it is always better to be left free to choose than to be forced to follow even a correct conception of one's good, then the argument against the priority of liberty would be defeated. But this defence assumes that the correct theory of a person's good assigns primacy to free choice of one's goals; hence it rests on an objective conception of the good. Since the people in the Original Position do not rely on an objective conception of the good, and since Rawls rejects such a conception, a convincing defence of the primacy of the primary goods seems to depend on premises that conflict both with the character of the Original Position and with Rawls's other views.

And so, whether we adopt a subjective or an objective account of the good, we seem to have no adequate defence of Rawls's attempt to fix the primacy of the primary goods within the constraints of the Original Position. The degree of ignorance of the good that is imposed on the people in the Original Position cannot be justified by appeal to fairness, and it undermines Rawls's claim to establish the primacy of the primary goods. It would be better to allow people in the Original Position to know the relevant facts about the good. If these facts fit a subjectivist conception, as Rawls believes, we cannot establish the unqualified primacy of the primary goods. An adequate defence of the primary goods seems to need an objective conception of the good; but we do not know, before we form such a conception, whether it will establish more primary goods than those that Rawls recognizes.

1438. Primary Goods, Freedom, and Equality

These doubts about the argument for the priority of the right assume an empirical conception of the primary goods; preference for them rests on the observation that they are often useful resources for pursuing one's conception of the good. This is how Rawls explains their primacy in the first edition of *TJ*.

The second edition, however, abandons this empirical conception. We recognize that the primary goods are resources for affirming our freedom and equality in the choice of ways of life. Since we want to affirm our freedom and equality, we want to secure the primary goods. Since we want to make our freedom and equality prior to the achievement of any specific conception of the good, we accept the priority of the right. In that case, we need not be concerned about conceptions of the good that allow us to dispense with primary goods; for we have already ruled out our acceptance of these conceptions, by affirming the priority of freedom and equality.[37]

Questions about the good allow us to return to some of our previous questions about the affirmation of one's freedom and equality. If the priority of the right rests on our wanting to affirm ourselves as free and equal, Rawls defends the priority of the right only to people who have the relevant sort of desire to affirm themselves as free and equal. People who have a different conception of their good seem to have no reason to recognize the priority of the right. The subjectivity of the good seems to undermine the defence of the priority of the right that relies on Rawls's revised account of primary goods.

Rawls avoids this objection if he takes a more Kantian position, claiming that protection of freedom and equality is relevant because we are free and equal, and not because we want to express ourselves as free and equal. According to this view, we have reason to express

---

[37] Rawls discusses liberty in *PL*, ch. 7, responding to Hart's criticism of *TJ* in 'Rawls'.

ourselves as free and equal whether or not we want to. People who lack the appropriate sorts of desires do not undermine the priority of the right.

But it is difficult to see how we could appeal to the fact that people are free and equal, and therefore ends in themselves, without implicit claims about the good. The rational grounds for expressing ourselves as free and equal rational agents also affect the content of the good. We seem to assert that people really are free and equal, so that if they safeguard their freedom and equality they express their real nature, whereas they would not express it if they were to choose arrangements that did not give priority to freedom and equality. In that case, the correct conception of the good includes freedom and equality. This claim conflicts not only with Rawls's views about the desire-relativity of the good, but also with his attempt to avoid appeals to controversial metaphysical premisses in support of his moral arguments.

Two questions need to be answered in order to assert the priority of the right: (1) We must prove that we are free and equal in the relevant senses. (2) We must prove that this fact about ourselves is important enough to justify the assertion of the priority of the right, on the ground that principles of right express our freedom and equality. The second claim seems to commit us to a specific conception of the good. For if we agreed that we are free and equal, but we took this fact to be comparatively unimportant in comparison with other aspects of our good, we would have no ground for affirming the priority of the right.

To connect claims about freedom and equality with other aspects of our good, Rawls needs an argument that connects the good with self-realization, and connects self-realization with the expression of oneself as free and equal. Neither Rawls nor Kant can do without some account of a person's good as self-realization, or without some account of the place of moral commitments in self-realization. The relevant parts of Rawls's argument appear in the last two chapters (leading up to §86 on 'the good of the sense of justice'). He seeks to show that 'it is rational (as defined by the thin theory of the good) for those in a well-ordered society to affirm their sense of justice as regulative of their plan of life' (567/497).

Rawls discusses the relation between moral and 'natural' attitudes (§74). He identifies attitudes that we cannot take towards other people unless we have some conception of justice. He mentions friendship, affection, and mutual trust, and also resentment and indignation. Rawls concludes: 'one who lacks a sense of justice lacks certain fundamental attitudes and capacities included under the notion of humanity' (488/428). If this argument is sound, certain basic attitudes and outlooks that we would not want to give up depend on our acceptance of morality.

We may agree with Rawls's claim that we cannot really be resentful or indignant if we have no moral attitudes or beliefs at all—if, for instance, we do not believe that someone acted wrongly, or that something is owed to us. Such an argument, however, does not take us far towards proving the truth of any specific moral theory. It is not clear why we need a sense of justice of the precise sort that Rawls has in mind—the sort that demands guarantees that protect us against the pursuit of maximum utility. Could a utilitarian not have the sorts of feelings that Rawls has in mind?

Moreover, even if these natural attitudes presuppose some degree of moral sensitivity, they need not be prior to other values in the way that is required by Rawls's theory. We might have attitudes that include resentment, indignation, and so on, but we might not take them to matter much, and so we might not suppose that they make morality very important. Further, if we are doubtful about morality, we might claim that sentiments that include moral concerns ought to wither away. To answer this doubt, we need to show that the relevant sentiments could not reasonably be rejected or weakened.

Kant claims that each rational agent regards herself as an end. In his view, if I regard something as an objective end in itself, I regard it as a limiting condition on the pursuit of my subjective ends, and therefore I regard it as having dignity and deserving respect. Kant claims that each person takes herself and her rational agency to impose a limit on the pursuit of subjective ends. He might simply mean that morality requires us to take this attitude to ourselves as well as other people; in that case, we cannot take such an attitude to ourselves without having accepted the moral outlook of the categorical imperative. Alternatively, he might mean that we can understand and accept this attitude to ourselves before we accept the outlook of the categorical imperative; even if in some way it also requires acceptance of the categorical imperative, we may not need to see this requirement in order to regard ourselves as ends.

1439. Self-Realization and Treating Oneself as an End

Kant's views may be clarified by reference to Green's and Bradley's views on self-realization. According to them, one's good involves realization of one's capacities and not simply the satisfaction of one's desires. When we think about our future and ourselves, we see that it would be arbitrary to limit our consideration to the desires that we actually have and expect to have in the future. Similarly, we see that a person's welfare cannot be confined to satisfaction of desires. But self-realization must include some special role for myself and my rational plans. Since we care about realizing a self, we care about making our rational choices effective in the right way, so that our future conditions are determined by our rational choices.

If other people's views about how to treat us were guided simply by what they wanted us to be like in the future, then there would be no special role for our past agency in determining other people's treatment of us. Inter-personal attitudes such as gratitude, or resentment, or anger, are characteristically expressed towards what we have done and chosen to do. If we discovered that someone had done something inadvertently or had been forced to do it, we would not regard what they have done as a proper object of such attitudes.

Apparently we might give up these attitudes. If, for instance, we expect to have no further need for benefits from someone, we might decide not to bother thanking them for what they have done. A similar expression of a purely prospective attitude on a larger, social scale would be a system of punishment or sanctions that is guided entirely by considerations of future benefit. If two people have done the same thing for the same reasons, we might, none the less, decide to treat them differently because it will be more beneficial for some other purpose to treat them differently.

Such an attitude raises the issue about utilitarianism that Rawls discusses. Utilitarianism claims that moral rules and principles rest ultimately on considerations about what will result in the best consequences. This is the aspect of utilitarianism that Rawls wants to avoid. He wants to defend a system of justice that gives certain kinds of guarantees to individuals. These guarantees are intended to protect them from treatment that fails to take account of their agency.

Kant, Bradley, and Rawls all connect the conditions for responsible rational agency with a particular view of morality. In Kant, the connexion depends on positive freedom—the recognition that we are responsible agents because we do not simply act on desires in pursuing our ends, but can also make some rational choice about the ends we pursue. In Bradley, the connexion emerges from the 'vulgar notion of responsibility'. In wanting to realize ourselves, we want to realize our rational agency, and in doing that we reject the sort of treatment that looks at us simply as possible sources of good consequences.

In Rawls, the relevant connexion appears first in the assumption that we are concerned with questions of justice because we want certain kinds of guarantees against treatment that simply expresses other people's preferences. Later he mentions the importance of the sense of justice for attitudes such as resentment, indignation, and gratitude. Our demand for guarantees and our desire to be objects of these inter-personal attitudes are expressions of the same attitude towards ourselves as agents. Someone who refused to show any gratitude to us for what we did unless it suited their own purposes would treat us unfairly. Punishment that is not guided by what people have done is unfair. The intuitive judgments about fairness that go into the construction of the Original Position reflect the same view that other people's preferences should not determine how a particular person is treated.

The character of self-realization, then, gives us reason to want to be treated with respect by other people. If they respect us, they give the proper weight to our rational choices and plans in determining what happens to us, and therefore they protect us from the preferences and aims of other people or of ourselves. We can therefore connect an aspect of self-realization with an aspect of morality. But do these arguments give us equally good reasons for taking the same attitude to others? Why should I not prefer other people to treat me as deserving respect in my own right, without having to treat other people the same way?

We want other people to treat us with respect because we are rational agents, not because we are these particular rational agents; if we did not want our rational agency to be protected, we would not be protecting what we value most. But we could not reasonably expect such respect from others without committing ourselves to respecting their rational agency. I ask them to act on some principle that they can also recognize as ensuring respect for them as rational agents. We can all recognize this principle as reasonable for us as rational agents, irrespective of our other desires and aims. If I see that it is foolish to expect other people simply to feel like treating rational agents as ends, I can see some point in our all committing ourselves to treat rational agents as ends; this is something we can all regard as expressing our rational agency. If we accept this principle, we agree to deliberate in ways that express our rational agency in the adjustment and reconciliation of our aims. This reconciliation does not depend on 'empirical' desires that are independent of our rational agency; we reconcile our aims on the basis of our being rational agents.

According to Bradley, the expansion of my ends so that they include ends that involve non-instrumental relations to other people promotes my self-realization. In so far as I can adopt ends that share the ends of others, or the ends defined for me by some social context,

I open for myself possibilities of self-realization that would not be open to me otherwise. Hence, the right conception of oneself, and especially the conception of oneself as a rational agent, requires acceptance of the ends of other rational agents.

1440. Self-Realization and Morality

So far we have explained Kant and Rawls by appeal to a conception of self-realization. If it is part of our good to realize ourselves as rational agents, we have reason to accept principles that respect people as rational agents, and so protect them against being subordinated to other people's aims. A correct conception of the self imposes a limit on what other people can do. As Kant says, the end-in-itself is a limiting condition on the pursuit of other ends.

This argument seems to impose limits on the appropriate connexion between other people's ends and mine. It seems to involve some degree of individualism, some respect for me and my ends in opposition to the ends that I might form as a result of other people's action on me. This sort of individualism seems to underlie Rawls's demand that individuals be given the sort of freedom and resources that will leave them capable of pursuing their various conceptions of their good.

Bradley, however, argues that the incorporation of socially determined ends in my own ends promotes my self-realization. This argument seems to lead, and Bradley believes it leads, to rejection of constraints that Rawls places on interference by others. The view that the moral point of view should reflect the demands of individuals for some guarantees against interference by others seems to Bradley to reflect an atomistic conception of persons. For if we realize that our conception of ourselves and our good is strongly influenced by socially determined stations and duties, the 'self' whose freedom and opportunity is being protected seems to be an unreal abstraction, not a recognizable kind of self.

If this is so, arguments from self-realization seem to support two sharply opposed conceptions of morality. This result helps to explain how both conceptions can claim some support in a reasonable conception of the self. We might conclude, however, that appeals to self-realization are less useful than we might have hoped, if they lead us in such opposed directions.

Perhaps, however, these two directions can be reconciled, if they are suitably corrected. Bradley's use of the idea of self-realization in connexion with morality fails to take account of something that Rawls learns from Kant. When Bradley recognizes that the self-realization we are looking for is self-realization as rational agents, he ought to recognize that this requires some specific constraints on our treatment by others. Hence Bradley provides some basis for the Kantian principles that he rejects.

Equally, however, a Kantian view ought to learn something from Bradley's conception of self-realization. For if Bradley is right, we cannot defend a plausible account of the basis of morality while rejecting an objective conception of the good. For this reason, Rawls's account of the right would be more convincing if he were to appeal to something like an idealist account of the good. To this extent, then, idealist criticisms of Kant are successful; they cast doubt on Kant's views about how an account of the good should fit an account of morality. But these criticisms should not turn us against a Kantian conception of morality;

on the contrary, idealist arguments allow a better defence of Kant than a purely Kantian theory can provide.

1441. Idealism and Holism

This argument has not departed far from the material provided by Rawls's discussion of moral and natural attitudes, but it has departed from the assumptions that guide his discussion. Rawls argues within a subjectivist theory of the good in order to show that the sense of justice is good for those people who have the relevant desires. He believes that the subjectivity of the good does not damage this argument, because the argument depends on the thin theory of the good that secures the goodness of the primary goods.

We have seen that it is not so easy for Rawls to affirm the universal priority of the right together with the variability of the good between individuals. For even if the priority of right, and the good of the sense of justice, depend only on acceptance of the primary goods, the primacy of the primary goods seems to be affected by different conceptions of the good. Only those who want to affirm themselves as free and equal appear to have sufficient reason to accept the priority of the right.

If we replace Rawls's subjectivist account of the good with the idealist conception of the good of self-realization, we do not necessarily undermine the priority of the right over the good. We may agree with Kant's claim that the recognition of ourselves as ends is a rational demand distinct from our conception of our good. But the cogency and importance of this rational demand is not entirely independent of our beliefs about the good. If we had to agree with Sidgwick in seeing a dualism in practical reason, we would have to acknowledge some doubts about the priority of the right, since we would have to acknowledge other apparently rational convictions that conflict with it. If, however, we agree with the idealist conception of the good, and we find that freedom and equality are primary within that conception, we have further reason to affirm the priority of the right.

This form of argument is simply an instance of Rawls's favoured holistic method. It would be contrary to the spirit of that method if we were to insist that our convictions about the morally right must be accepted independently of our conception of the good. Rawls gives us good reason to reject any such independence, since he makes the priority of the right depend on the thin theory of the good. Further examination of his views about the primary goods, freedom and equality, and the good in general, supports two conclusions: (1) We have better reason for affirming an objectivist conception of the good, and in particular a conception that connects the good with self-realization, than we have for accepting Rawls's subjectivist conception. (2) Acceptance of an objectivist conception strengthens Rawls's Kantian claims about morality, and removes some of the weaknesses that his subjectivist conception introduces into his argument.

1442. Constructivism in Moral and Political Philosophy

This revision of Rawls's position throws some light on his reasons for believing that a Kantian theory of the right should be a constructivist rather than an objectivist theory. He does not affirm this belief in *TJ*, where he is deliberately silent on metaphysical issues. But he affirms it in his essay on 'Kantian constructivism', which he regards as both Kantian and correct.

To understand Rawls's claims about constructivism, we need to consider some of the developments in his views after *TJ*. The title of his second book, *Political Liberalism*, marks a change of subject from moral philosophy to 'political' philosophy.[38] Whereas moral philosophy embraces comprehensive philosophical and moral doctrines, a purely political conception makes more restricted claims.[39] Rawls takes *TJ* to present a statement of social contract theory as a contribution to moral philosophy, and in particular as a viable alternative to utilitarianism.

We need to bear Rawls's statement in mind in reading *Justice as Fairness: A Restatement*, published only two years after the second edition of *TJ*. It is not an outline or summary of *TJ*, but a presentation of its account of justice within the constraints of a purely political conception. Given the warning in *PL* about the differences between comprehensive moral philosophy and purely political philosophy, differences between *TJ* and *JFR* may not represent a change of mind on questions in moral philosophy; they may simply represent the changes needed to transform arguments in moral philosophy into arguments in purely political philosophy.[40] We may, admittedly, find that some parts of the restatement allow a correction or modification of *TJ*; but we must be cautious in claiming this, and examine each possible modification on its own merits, to see whether it does or does not depend on considerations specific to purely political philosophy.

What is the difference between purely political constructivism and moral constructivism? When Rawls represents justice as fairness as being 'political, not metaphysical', he does not reject the idea of moral philosophy that is not merely political. He tends to speak of this as 'comprehensive moral philosophy', of which he takes utilitarianism to be an example. Though he speaks in different ways in later works of what he was doing in *TJ*, he seems to hold that it contains two things: (1) The beginnings, at least, of a comprehensive moral

---

[38] 'The aims of these lectures [sc. *PL*] are quite different. Note that in my summary of the aims of *Theory*, the social contract tradition is seen as part of moral philosophy and no distinction is drawn between moral and political philosophy. In *Theory* a moral doctrine of justice general in scope is not distinguished from a strictly political conception of justice. Nothing is made of the contrast between comprehensive philosophical and moral doctrines and conceptions limited to the domain of the political. In the lectures in this volume, however, these distinctions and related ideas are fundamental.' (*PL* xv) A similar statement of the 'fundamental difference' between *TJ* and *PL* appears in 'Public' (published 1997) = *CP* 614. For a comparison between Rawls on comprehensive moral philosophy with an 'Augustinian' view (not Augustine's), see §§228, 421.

[39] I will use 'purely political' to correspond to Rawls's special use of 'political', in order to avoid the appearance of agreeing with his view that political philosophy—understood as the subject discussed by Plato, Aristotle, Hobbes, Rousseau, and so on, observes the restrictions that Rawls imposes on 'political' conceptions.

[40] In contrast to *PL*, which says that *TJ* was engaged in comprehensive moral philosophy, rather than purely political philosophy, *JFR* says that *TJ* was ambiguous on that point: '*Theory* never discusses whether justice as fairness is a comprehensive moral doctrine or a political conception of justice . . . the reader can reasonably conclude that justice as fairness was set out as part of a comprehensive moral doctrine that might be developed later should success encourage the attempt. This restatement removes that ambiguity: justice as fairness is now presented as a political conception of justice.' (xvii). The editor of *JFR* is more definite than Rawls himself; she says that *TJ* 'presented justice as fairness as part of a comprehensive liberal outlook' (xii). Her judgment seems to agree with Rawls's judgment in *PL*. 'Political', by contrast, seems to suggest that *TJ* was really an argument in purely political philosophy, though not clearly presented as such. See 'Political', 389: 'One thing I failed to say in *A Theory of Justice*, or failed to stress sufficiently, is that justice as fairness is intended as a political conception of justice'.

philosophy that is superior to utilitarianism and intuitionism. (2) The materials from which one could construct a 'political conception of justice' ('Political', 389).

A purely political conception differs from comprehensive moral philosophy in these ways: (1) The considered judgments we start with are a proper subset of those we consider in moral philosophy, because they are about the justice of institutions (e.g., slavery and toleration). (2) The sources we draw on for finding principles belong to our public political culture. (3) Hence we set aside moral principles that seem plausible to us, and are part of the tradition of moral philosophy, but have not entered our public political culture. (4) Hence political philosophy does not do all that moral philosophy might do to achieve reflective equilibrium. The equilibrium that we seek in moral philosophy is in principle wider than what we seek in purely political philosophy.⁴¹

Even if this is true, we might in fact have no more to draw on in moral philosophy than we have in political philosophy. For we might discover that all our considered moral judgments are already operative in our judgments about political institutions and policies, and that our public political culture already contains all the moral principles that are worth considering. But to show that political philosophy has all these resources that moral philosophy might use, we would need to offer much more argument than Rawls offers. Hence we may assume that the differences between political and moral philosophy mark actual differences in our conduct of the two sorts of inquiry.

This account of the division between comprehensive moral philosophy and purely political philosophy may over-simplify the relation between Rawls's earlier and later discussions of the same subjects. But it should at least warn us that a difference of view in the later work may not imply retraction of a position taken in *TJ*; it may simply signal the difference between moral and purely political argument. Rawls does not suggest that the comprehensive moral philosophy of *TJ* rested on any mistake, or that he should not have presented it as comprehensive moral philosophy. In the preface to the second edition of *TJ*, Rawls says; '. . . I still accept its main outlines and defend its central doctrines' (/ xi).⁴²

What does it mean to defend the central doctrines of *TJ*? In some places Rawls suggests that the defence might consist in a modification that fits them into purely political philosophy.⁴³ Such a defence would suggest that *TJ* did not try to do purely political philosophy, and

---

⁴¹ 'We can regard these convictions as provisional fixed points which any conception of justice must account for if it is to be reasonable for us. We look, then, to our public political culture itself, including its main institutions and the historical traditions of our interpretation, as the shared fund of implicitly recognized basic ideas and principles. The hope is that these ideas and principles can be formulated clearly enough to be combined into a conception of political justice congenial to our most firmly held convictions. We express this by saying that a political conception of justice, to be acceptable, must be in accordance with our considered convictions at all levels of generality, on due reflection (or in what I have called "reflective equilibrium").' ('Political', 393)

⁴² This preface is dated 1990, but it was not published until 1999. The same remark appears in the preface (1987) to the French translation; see CP 415.

⁴³ He comments on the theory of goodness as rationality in *TJ*, ch. 7: '. . . there are several ways in which I would now revise the presentation of goodness as rationality. Perhaps the most important would be to make sure that it is understood as part of a political conception of justice as a form of political liberalism, and not as part of a comprehensive moral doctrine. As such a doctrine both it and the full theory are inadequate, but this does not make them unsuitable for their role in a political conception. The distinction between a comprehensive doctrine and a political conception is unfortunately absent from [*TJ*] and while I believe nearly all the structure and substantive content of justice as fairness (including goodness as rationality) goes over unchanged into that conception as a political one, the understanding of the view as a whole is significantly shifted.' (PL 176n)

that some of its doctrines are open to criticisms that would not apply to the modified doctrines that would adapt *TJ* to the constraints of purely political philosophy.[44] Still, Rawls acknowledges that the central doctrines of *TJ* are doctrines in comprehensive moral philosophy; if he defended only the versions of them that fit purely political philosophy, he would not defend the doctrines of *TJ*. Extensive changes from *TJ* are needed, according to Rawls, if we are to formulate justice as fairness within a purely political conception. He could not legitimately claim to accept the central doctrines of *TJ* if he did not accept its comprehensive moral philosophy.

1443. Political v. Moral Constructivism

Constructivism enters the discussion of Rawls with Dworkin's argument for a constructivist account of Rawls's position. Rawls does not mention this issue in *TJ*, but he introduces it later in two forms: (1) Political constructivism is a doctrine about the status of political philosophy, as Rawls conceives it. We do not represent the principles of political philosophy as capturing any independent reality. Nor do we deny that they capture it. Political constructivism is neutral; it does not reject realism, but it sets aside the question about realism. (2) Moral constructivism maintains that we can define an ideal procedure for the construction of moral principles apart from any convictions about their truth; true principles are true because they emerge from this constructive procedure. A realist position claims that the constructive procedure is the right one because it generates principles whose truth is grounded in something independent of this procedure. Hence constructivism rejects Socrates' answer to the Euthyphro question.

Political constructivism is the view that underlies *Political Liberalism*. It is the method of political philosophy. If Rawls is only a political constructivist, he is neutral on Dworkin's conclusion, since political constructivism says nothing about moral philosophy. Dworkin's arguments about the needs of officials might be especially relevant to political philosophy, but they could not be directly transferred to moral philosophy.

In *TJ* Rawls is neutral about moral constructivism. This neutral attitude, however, might have different implications for the soundness of Dworkin's argument: (1) Rawls might hold that it does not matter to moral philosophy whether we interpret the method as a realist or as a non-realist would. This claim neither endorses nor rejects Dworkin's argument. (2) He might hold that Dworkin is wrong, because the method of moral philosophy could be given either a realist or an anti-realist interpretation, whereas Dworkin argues that it must be given the anti-realist interpretation. Since it is not clear which sort of neutral position Rawls holds, we should keep an open mind in the discussion of *TJ*.

In 'Kantian constructivism', however, Rawls also defends constructivism as a doctrine in comprehensive moral philosophy, not simply as part of a purely political interpretation of

---

[44] At *PL* 177n, Rawls cites Larmore, *PMC* 118–30. Larmore briefly states a political conception of Rawls's main idea: 'Since modern, pluralistic societies cannot expect general agreement about the nature of the good life, the veil of ignorance will serve not as a basis for arriving at the truth about the good, but rather as a means for devising principles of political cooperation that are neutral with respect to the conflicting conceptions of the good.' (124) Larmore calls this the 'modus vivendi' perspective (125), which he takes to be present in *TJ* beside a more strongly Kantian perspective.

justice. His explicit discussions of Kant also ascribe to Kant the essential parts of 'Kantian' constructivism, as Rawls understands it.[45]

1444. 'Kantian' Constructivism v. Objectivism

Sometimes, then, Rawls supports Kantian constructivism in moral philosophy. But when he distinguishes political philosophy from comprehensive moral philosophy, he thereby distinguishes political constructivism from moral constructivism; he no longer asserts moral constructivism, though he does not reject it either.

Rawls's description of purely political philosophy suggests why we also need comprehensive moral philosophy. Purely political philosophy does not try to justify its principles from the moral point of view by appeal to all the available resources for reaching moral reflective equilibrium. But it is a legitimate moral question whether the principles of political philosophy can be justified from the moral point of view. Hence, we need moral philosophy in order to answer this question.

But if we admit this role for moral philosophy in justification, we can also argue that moral constructivism is not the right epistemology for moral philosophy. The argument is this: (1) Moral philosophy has the task of answering certain questions about justification. (2) Constructivism cannot answer these questions. (3) Hence moral philosophy is not constructivist. This argument needs to be explained.

Rawls argues for constructivism on the basis of claims about autonomy.[46] To grasp his claims, we need to distinguish two versions of a Kantian position: (1) Moral principles depend on facts about rational wills (as opposed to facts about human nature, sentiments, other features of the universe). (2) They depend on how we decide to look at ourselves. Only the second version meets Rawls's conditions for constructivism. He regards the first view as a form of rationalist objectivism, and believes that Kant rejects it. But we have found that Kant holds the first view rather than the second.

We have also found that Kant has quite strong reasons for rejecting constructivism, on the ground that it would make moral principles 'positive and arbitrary'. To avoid this result, we need non-positive principles, and hence principles that are not constructed. Similarly, if political philosophy has to be constructivist for the reasons Rawls gives, Kant can argue that, since every positive law has to rest on at least one natural law, political philosophy has to rest on non-constructivist moral philosophy.[47]

We can express Kant's point in Rawls's terms by saying that justificatory questions that arise about a purely political conception cannot be answered by resort to moral constructivism. Justifications, therefore, cannot be constructivist 'all the way down'. If we

---

[45] Rawls comments on 'Constructivism' in 'Political', 388–9. He suggests there that he does not mean to attribute the doctrine to Kant, and that it would be better called 'Kantian constructivism in political philosophy'. This is the essay in which Rawls is most inclined to regard *TJ* as an ambiguous and unclear statement of a political conception. In later works, especially *PL* and *JFR*, he is more inclined to treat *TJ* as an essay in comprehensive moral philosophy. In *PL* 99–100, he ascribes constructivism in moral philosophy to Kant. This ascription is confirmed by the discussion of Kant in 'Themes' and in *LHMP* 237–47.

[46] See *PL* 99; *LHMP* 72, 229, 236, 242; 'Constructivism', 345; 'Themes', 512. Some of these passages are quoted in §993.

[47] A possible historical illustration of this point; Nietzsche, §1099.

consider the 'activities' and 'conceptions' that Rawls mentions as the source of the moral law, we can raise a Kantian question: Have we some reason to pursue these activities beyond the fact that we choose to go in for them? A Kantian approach to morality denies that such choices can be the ultimate source of justification. They provide justification only if they are guided by the appropriate reasons; hence the reasons are not simply matters of choice. If our choices are genuinely autonomous and rational, they respond to the genuine reasons, and so we need to find these reasons. The Kantian doctrine, therefore, cannot be absorbed into constructivism; for constructivism leaves us with some genuine questions that Kant tries to answer.

Rawls believes that a Kantian position ought to be constructivist rather than objectivist in metaphysics, because only constructivism fixes an appropriately close connexion between moral principles and rational agency.[48] An objectivist conception, in Rawls's view, makes it a contingent fact that moral principles are appropriate for rational agents.

This criticism of objectivism applies only to the rational intuitionism that is Rawls's primary target. It does not apply to the Aristotelian naturalism of Aquinas, Suarez, and Butler. We found it difficult to defend Kant without reliance on aspects of a traditional naturalist doctrine of the human good. Examination of Rawls's views confirms that conclusion about Kant. Though Rawls presents his theory of justice as an alternative to idealist views, we have found it difficult to defend his main claims about the right without appeal to an idealist conception of the good as self-realization. In so far as this idealist conception is a revival of the traditional naturalist conception of the human good, Rawls's position is best defended within that traditional naturalist conception.

We should therefore conclude that Rawls is committed more than he believes he is to acceptance of two positions that he tends to contrast with Kantian constructivism. In so far as his claims about the right fit best with a conception of the good as the fulfilment of the capacities of rational agents, they are best defended within a naturalist outlook. And in so far as this naturalist outlook is objectivist, claiming to rely on facts about human nature and rational agency, the most plausible defence of Rawls's Kantian views should incline us not to constructivism, but to the objectivist view that the right is what is fitting to rational nature.

---

[48] Rawls on Kant; §§993–4. A kind of objectivity is preserved within a constructivist view; *LHMP* 243–7.

BIBLIOGRAPHY[1]

Abercrombie, N. J., *The Origins of Jansenism*. OUP, 1936.

Ackrill, J. L., 'Aristotle on *eudaimonia*', in *Essays on Plato and Aristotle*. OUP, 1997, ch. 11. From *PBA* 60 (1974), 339–59.

Ackroyd, P. R., and Evans, C. F., eds., *The Cambridge History of the Bible*, i. CUP, 1970.

Adam, J., ed., *The Republic of Plato*, 2 vols. CUP, 1902.

Adams, M. M., 'Is the existence of God a "hard" fact?', in Fischer, ed., *GFF*, ch. 3. From *PR* 76 (1967), 492–503.

Adams, M. M., 'Ockham on will, nature, and morality', in Spade, ed., *CCO*, ch. 11.

⸺ 'Scotus and Ockham on the connection of the virtues', in L. Honnefelder, R. Wood, and M. Dreyer, eds., *John Dunn Scotus: Metaphysics and Ethics*. Leiden: Brill, 1996, 499–522.

⸺ 'The structure of Ockham's moral theory', *FS* 46 (1986), 1–35.

⸺ *William Ockham*, 2 vols. Notre Dame, lnd.: UNDP, 1987.

⸺ 'William Ockham: voluntarist or naturalist?', in J. F. Wippel, ed., *Studies in Medieval Philosophy*. CUAP, 1987, ch. 10.

Adams, R. M., 'A modified divine command theory of ethical wrongness', in *The Virtue of Faith and Other Essays in Philosophical Theology*. OUP, 1987, ch. 7.

⸺ *Finite and Infinite Goods*. OUP, 1999.

Adams, William, *The Nature and Obligation of Virtue*, 3rd edn. Shrewsbury, 1776 (1st edn., 1754).

Adkins, A. W. H., *Merit and Responsibility*. OUP, 1960.

Albee, E., *A History of English Utilitarianism*. London: Swan, Sonnenschein, 1902.

⸺ Review of Selby-Bigge, *BM. PR* 7 (1898), 82–6.

Alberigo, J., et al., eds., *Conciliorum Oecumenicorum Decreta, 3rd edn*. Bologna: Instituto per le Scienze Religiose, 1973.

Albertus Magnus, *De bono in genere, De iustitia, De prudentia*, and *De temperantia*, in *Opera Omnia*, xxviii.

⸺ *Opera Omnia*. Münster: Aschendorff, 1951–.

⸺ *Super Ethica*, in *Opera Omnia*, xiv.

Alcinous, *Didascalicus. Alcinoos: Enseignement des doctrines de Platon*, tr. P. Louis, ed. J. Whittaker. Paris: Les Belles Lettres, 1990.

Alexander of Aphrodisias, *De Anima* = *CAG* Supp. ii 1.

⸺ *De Anima Mantissa* = *CAG* Supp. ii 1.

⸺ *De Fato* = *CAG* Supp. ii 2. Tr. and ed. R. W. Sharples. London: Duckworth, 1983.

⸺ *Dubia et Solutiones* = *CAG* Supp. ii 2.

⸺ *in Aristotelis Topica* = *CAG* ii.

⸺ *Quaestiones* = *CAG* Supp. ii 2.

Algra, K., et al., eds., *The Cambridge History of Hellenistic Philosophy*. CUP, 1999.

Allison, H. E., *Kant's Theory of Freedom*. CUP, 1990.

⸺ *Kant's Transcendental Idealism*, 2nd edn. New Haven: Yale UP, 2004 (1st edn., 1983).

Alphonsus Liguori, *Theologia Moralis*, 2 vols. Turin: Marietti, 1847 (repr. of 9th edn., 1785).

---

[1] To Volumes i–iii.

Altham, J. E. J., and Harrison, R., eds., *World, Mind, and Ethics: Essays on the Ethical Philosophy of Bernard Williams*. CUP, 1995.

Ambrose, A., and Lazerowitz, M., eds., *G. E. Moore: Essays in Retrospect*. London: Allen and Unwin, 1970.

Ambrose, *De Officiis*, 2 vols., ed. I. J. Davidson. OUP, 2001.

Ambrosiaster, *Commentarius in Epistulas Paulinas*, ed. H. J. Vogels. Vienna: Hoelder-Pichler-Tempsky, 1966 (= *CSEL* 81.1)

Ameriks, K., *Interpreting Kant's Critiques*. OUP, 2003.

——— *Kant and the Fate of Autonomy*. CUP, 2000.

——— 'The practical foundation of philosophy in Kant, Fichte, and after', in Sedgwick, ed., *RKCP*, ch. 5.

Anderson, G. W., 'Canonical and non-canonical', in Ackroyd and Evans, *CHB* i, ch. 6.

Anderson, J., 'Ethics and advocacy', *AJP* 22 (1944), 174–87.

Andrew of Neufchateau, *Questions on an Ethics of Divine Commands*, ed. J. M. Idziak. Notre Dame, lnd.: UND Press, 1997.

Annas, J., *An Introduction to Plato's Republic*. OUP, 1981.

——— 'Doing without objective values', in Everson, *ECAT,* ch. 8.

——— *Hellenistic Philosophy of Mind*. UCP, 1992.

——— *Platonic Ethics, Old and New*. Ithaca, NY: Cornell UP, 1999.

——— 'Prudence and morality in ancient and modern ethics', *E* 105 (1995), 241–57.

——— 'The Hellenistic versions of Aristotle's ethics', *Monist*, 73 (1990), 80–96.

——— *The Morality of Happiness*. OUP, 1993.

Anon. [Richard Allestree?] *The Whole Duty of Man*. London: Garthwait, 1658.

Anon., *A letter to Mr John Clarke . . . wherein it is showed that he hath treated the learned Dr Clarke very unfairly, that he hath carried the principle of self-love much too far. And that his heavy charge against the author of Beauty and Virtue, may, with more reason, be retorted upon himself.* London: Roberts, 1727.

Anon., Review of Hume, *Treatise* Book III, in J. Fieser, ed., *Early Responses to Hume, i* (Bristol: Thoemmes, 2004), 1–14. From *Bibliothèque Raisonnée* 26.2 (1741), 411–27.

Anonymus, *in Platonis Theaetetum*; in *Corpus dei Papiri*, Part 3.

Anscombe, G. E. M., *Collected Philosophical Papers, iii: Ethics, Religion, and Politics*. Minneapolis: University of Minnesota Press, 1981.

——— *Intention, 2nd edn*. Oxford: Blackwell, 1963 (1st edn., 1957).

——— 'Modern Moral Philosophy', in *Papers, iii*, ch. 4. From *Phil.* 33 (1958), 1–19.

——— 'On brute facts', in *Papers, iii*, ch. 3. From *Analysis* 18 (1958), 69–72.

——— 'Thought and action in Aristotle', in *Papers, i*, ch. 7.

——— 'War and murder', in *Papers, iii*, ch. 6. From *Nuclear Weapons: A Catholic Response*, ed. W. Stein. London: Burnes and Oates, 1961.

Anselm, *Opera Omnia, i*, ed. F. S. Schmitt. Seckau, 1938. Includes *De Casu Diaboli, De Veritate, Proslogion*.

——— *The Major Works*, ed. B. Davies and G. R. Evans (various translators). OUP, 1998.

Aquinas, *Compendium Theologiae*, in *Opuscula Theologica*, ed. R. A. Verardo. Turin: Marietti, 1954.

——— *De Caritate,* in *QD*.

——— *De Divinis Nominibus*, in *P* xv.

——— *De Malo*, in *QD*.

——— *De Potentia*, in *QD*.

——— *De Regimine Principum, 2nd edn.*, ed. J. Mathis. Marietti: Turin, 1948.

——— *De spe*, in *QD*

——— *De Veritate* (Cited as *Ver*), in *QD*.

——— *De Virtutibus Cardinalibus*, in *QD*.

——— *De Virtutibus in Communi*, in *QD*.

Aquinas, *Expositio et Lectura super Epistulas Pauli Apostoli, 8th edn.*, 2 vols., ed. R. Cai. Turin: Marietti, 1953.

_____ *in Aristotelis De Anima*, ed. A. M. Pirotta. Turin: Marietti, 1936.

_____ *in Aristotelis De Caelo*, in P xix.

_____ *in Aristotelis Metaphysica*, ed. M. R. Cathala and R. M. Spiazzi. Turin: Marietti, 1950.

_____ *in Aristotelis Perihermeneias*, in P xviii.

_____ *in Decem Libros Ethicorum Aristotelis ad Nicomachum Expositio*, 3rd edn., ed. R. M. Spiazzi. Turin: Marietti, 1964.

_____ *In Epistulam ad Romanos*, in *Expositio*, ed. Cai.

_____ *In Evangelium Ioannis*, in P x.

_____ *in Iob*, P xiv.

_____ *in Primam Epistulam ad Timotheum,* in *Expositio*, ed. Cai.

_____ *In Secundam Epistulam ad Corinthos*, in *Expositio*, ed. Cai.

_____ *Opera Omnia*, 25 vols. Parma: Fiaccadori, 1852–68.

_____ *Opera Omnia*, editio Leonina. Rome: Typographia Polyglotta, 1882– (incomplete).

_____ *Quaestiones Disputatae*, 2 vols., ed. R. Spiazzi et al. Turin: Marietti, 1949.

_____ *Quaestiones Quodlibetales*, in P ix.

_____ *Scriptum super Sententiis*, in P vi–vii.

_____ *Sententia Libri Ethicorum*, Leonine edn. xlvii–xlviii., ed. R.-A. Gauthier. 1969.

_____ *Summa contra Gentiles*, 3 vols., ed. P. Marc et al. Turin: Maretti, 1967.

_____ *Summa Theologiae*, 3 vols., ed. P. Caramello. Turin: Marietti, 1952.

_____ *Summa Theologiae*, Blackfriars edn., 60 vols., T. Gilby and T. C. O'Brian (general eds.). London: Eyre and Spottiswoode, 1964–73. Vols. cited: xix (E. D'Arcy, ed.); xxii (A. J. P. Kenny, ed.); xxiii (W. D. Hughes, ed.); xxv (J. Fearon, ed.); xxxviii (M. Lefébure, ed.); xlii (P. G. Walsh, ed.).

Ardal, P. S., *Passion and Value in Hume's Treatise*. Edinburgh: EUP, 1966.

Aristotle, *Analytica Posteriora*. OCT.

_____ *De Anima*. OCT.

_____ *De Caelo*. OCT.

_____ *De Interpretatione*. OCT.

_____ *De Partibus Animalium*. Loeb.

_____ *Ethica Eudemia*. OCT.

_____ *Ethica Nicomachea*. OCT.

_____ *Magna Moralia*. BT.

_____ *Metaphysics*. OCT.

_____ *Physics*. OCT.

_____ *Politics*. OCT.

_____ *Rhetoric*. OCT.

_____ *Topics*. OCT.

Arpaly, N., *Unprincipled Virtue*. OUP, 2003.

Aspasius, *in Ethica Nicomachea, CAG* xix.

Athenaeus, *Deipnosophistae*. BT.

Atkinson, R. F., 'Hume on is and ought: a reply to Mr MacIntyre', in Chappell, ed., *Hume*, 265–77. From *PR* 70 (1961), 231–8.

Atwell, J. E., *Schopenhauer: The Human Character*. Philadelphia: Temple UP, 1990.

Audi, R., 'Prospects for a value-based intuitionism', in Stratton-Lake, ed., *Intuitionism*, ch. 1.

Augsburg Confession, in Schaff, *CC* iii.

Augustine, *Confessiones*. OO i.

_____ *Contra Academicos*. OO i.

_____ *Contra duas Epistulas Pelagianorum*. OO x.

_____ *Contra Faustum Manichaeum*. OO viii.

_____ *Contra Iulianum*. OO x.

_____ *Contra Secundinum Manichaeum*. OO viii.

_____ *De 83 Diversis Quaestionibus*. OO vi.

_____ *De Beata Vita*. OO i.

_____ *De Civitate Dei*, 2 vols., ed. J. E. C. Welldon. London: SPCK, 1924.

_____ *De continentia*. OO vi.

_____ *De Doctrina Christiana*. OO iii.

_____ *De duabus Animis*. OO viii.

_____ *De Libero Arbitrio*. OO i.

_____ *De Moribus Ecclesiae Catholicae et de Moribus Manichaeorum*. OO i.

_____ *De nuptiis et concupiscentia*. OO x.

_____ *De Spiritu et Littera*. OO x.

_____ *De Trinitate*. OO viii.

_____ *De Vera Religione*. OO i.

_____ *Enarrationes in Psalmos*. OO iv.

_____ *Epistulae*. OO ii.

_____ *Expositio 84 Propositionum ex Epistula ad Romanos*. OO iii.

_____ *In Evangelium Ioannis*. OO iii.

_____ *Opera Omnia*, Benedictine edn., 11 vols. Paris: Gaume, 1836–9.

_____ *Retractationes*. OO i.

_____ *Sermones*. OO v.

Aulus Gellius, *Noctes Atticae*. OCT.

Austin, J. L., 'A plea for excuses', in *Philosophical Papers*, ed. J. O. Urmson and G. J. Warnock, 2nd edn. OUP, 1970, ch. 8. From *PAS* 57 (1956–7), 1–30.

_____ *How to Do Things with Words*, 2nd edn. OUP, 1975 (1st edn., 1962).

Ayer, A. J., 'Freedom and morality', in *Freedom and Morality and Other Essays*. OUP, 1984, ch. 1.

_____ *Language, Truth, and Logic*, 2nd edn. London: Gollancz, 1946 (1st edn., 1936).

_____ 'On the analysis of moral judgments', in *PE*, ch. 10. From *Horizon*, 20 (1949), 171–84.

_____ *Philosophical Essays*. London: Macmillan, 1954.

_____ 'Philosophy and language', in *The Concept of a Person and Other Essays*. London: Macmillan, 1963, ch. 1.

Backus, I., 'The Fathers in Calvinist orthodoxy: Patristic scholarship', in Backus, ed., *RCFW*, ch. 21.

_____ ed., *The Reception of the Church Fathers in the West*, 2 vols. Leyden: Brill, 1997.

Baier, A. C., *A Progress of Sentiments: Reflections on Hume's Treatise*. HUP, 1991.

Baier, K., 'Moral obligation', *APQ* 3 (1966), 210–26.

_____ *The Moral Point of View: A Rational Basis of Ethics*. Ithaca, NY: Cornell UP, 1958.

_____ *The Rational and the Moral Order*. Chicago: Open Court, 1995.

Bailey: *see* Epicurus.

Bain, A., *Mental and Moral Science*, 2nd edn., 2 vols. London: Longmans, 1868.

_____ 'Mr Sidgwick's Methods of Ethics', *M* 1 (1876), 179–97.

_____ ed., *The Moral Philosophy of Paley*. Edinburgh: Chambers, 1852.

Baius, M., *De Virtutibus Impiorum*, in *Michaeli Baii Opera*. Cologne: Egmont, 1696.

Baldwin, T., *G. E. Moore*. RKP, 1990.

Balfour, J., *A Delineation of the Nature and Obligation of Morality, 2nd edn*. Edinburgh: Hamilton and Balfour, 1763.

Balguy, J., *A Collection of Tracts Moral and Theological*. London: Pemberton, 1734.

Balguy, J., *Divine Rectitude: Or a Brief Inquiry concerning the Moral Perfections of the Deity*. London: Pemberton, 1730. Repr. in *TMT*.

——— *The Foundation of Moral Goodness*, Part 1 (1st edn., 1728) and Part 2 (1st edn., 1729). Repr. in *TMT*.

Banez, D., *Scholastica Commentaria in Primam Partem Summae Theologicae S. Thomae Aquinatis i*, ed. L. Urbano. Madrid: Editorial FEDA, 1934.

Barbeyrac, J., 'Historical and critical account of the science of morality, and the progress it has made in the world, from the earliest times down to the publication of this work', preface to Pufendorf, *JNG*, tr. B. Kennett, 5th edn. London: Bonwicke et al., 1749.

Barker, E., *Political Thought of Plato and Aristotle*. London: Methuen, 1906.

Barnes, J., 'The beliefs of a Pyrrhonist', in Burnyeat and Frede, *OS*, ch. 3.

——— *The Toils of Scepticism*. CUP, 1990.

——— Burnyeat, M., and Schofield, M., eds., *Doubt and Dogmatism*. OUP, 1980.

Barnes, W. H. F., 'Richard Price: a neglected eighteenth century moralist', *Phil.* 17 (1942), 159–73.

Barr, J., *Biblical Faith and Natural Theology*. OUP, 1993.

Barrow, I., *Works*, ed. J. Tillotson, 5th edn., 3 vols. London: Millar, 1741.

Barry, B. M., 'Warrender and his critics', in Cranston and Peters, eds., *HR*, 37–65. From *Phil.* 43 (1968), 117–37.

Barth, K., *The Theology of John Calvin*, tr. G. W. Bromiley. Grand Rapids, Mich.: Eerdmans, 1995.

Barton, J., *Ethics and the Old Testament*, 2nd edn. London: SCM Press, 2002.

Bayes, Thomas, *Divine Benevolence: Or an Attempt to Prove that the Principal End of the Divine Providence and Government is the Happiness of his Creatures*. London: J. Noon, 1731.

Bayle, P., *Historical and Critical Dictionary: Selections*, tr. R. H. Popkin Indianapolis: Bobbs-Merrill, 1965.

Beattie, James, *An Essay on the Nature and Immutability of Truth, in Opposition to Sophistry and Scepticism*, 9th edn. London: Mawman, 1820 (1st edn., 1770).

Beck, L. W., *Commentary on Kant's Critique of Practical Reason*. Chicago: University of Chicago Press, 1960.

——— *Early German Philosophy*. HUP, 1969.

——— ' "Was-must be" and "is-ought" in Hume', *PhS* 26 (1974), 219–28.

Beiser, F. C., *The Fate of Reason*. HUP, 1987.

——— *The Sovereignty of Reason*. PUP, 1996.

Bell, D., 'The insufficiency of ethics', in Manser and Stock, eds., *PFHB*, ch. 3.

Bennett, J. F., *A Study of Spinoza's Ethics*. Indianapolis: Hackett, 1984.

——— *Kant's Analytic*. CUP, 1966

——— *Locke, Berkeley, Hume: Central Themes*. OUP, 1971.

——— 'The Conscience of Huckleberry Finn', *Phil.* 49 (1974), 123–34.

Benson, H.H., ed., *Essays on the Philosophy of Socrates*. OUP, 1992.

Bentham, J., *An Introduction to the Principles of Morals and Legislation*, ed. J. H. Burns and H. L. A. Hart. London: Athlone Press, 1970.

——— *Deontology*, ed. A. Goldworth. OUP, 1983.

——— *Deontology: or the Science of Morality*, ed. J. Bowring, 2 vols. Edinburgh: Tait, 1834.

——— *Rationale of Reward*, in *Works* ii.

——— *Works*, ed. J. Bowring, 11 vols. Edinburgh: Tait, 1838–43.

Berger, F. R., *Happiness, Justice, and Freedom: The Moral and Political Philosophy of John Stuart Mill*. UCP, 1984.

Berkeley, G., *Alciphron*, in *Works*, iii.

——— 'Passive Obedience', in *Works*, vi 1–50.

——— *Works*, 9 vols., ed. A. A. Luce and T. E. Jessup. London: Nelson, 1948–64.

Berlin, I., 'The originality of Machiavelli', in H. Hardy, ed., *Against the Current*. OUP, 1981, 25–79.

Berman, D., ed., *Alciphron in Focus*. RKP, 1993.

Bett, R., *Pyrrho, his Antecedents, and his Legacy*. OUP, 2000.

———— tr. and ed., *Sextus Empiricus Against the Ethicists*. OUP, 1997.

Bible, 'Authorized Version'. *The Holy Bible . . . Translated out of the Original Tongues and with the Former Translations Diligently Compared and Revised by His Majesty's Special Command*. London: 1611.

———— *Biblia Sacra iuxta Vulgatam Versionem, 3rd edn.*, ed. R. Weber et al. Stuttgart: Deutsche Bibelgeschellschaft, 1983.

———— *Septuaginta, id est Vetus Testamentum Graece iuxta LXX interpretes*, ed. A. Rahlfs. Stuttgart: Deutsche Bibelgeschellschaft, 1979.

———— *The Holy Bible: Translated from the Latin Vulgate and Diligently Compared with Other Editions in Divers Languages*. Rheims, 1582 (NT); Douai, 1609 (OT).

———— *The Holy Bible, . . . with the Apocryphal/Deuterocanonical Books, New Revised Standard Version*. OUP, 1989.

Biel, G., *Canonis missae expositio*, 4 vols., ed. H. A. Oberman and W. J. Courtenay. Wiesbaden: Steiner, 1963.

———— *Collectorium circa quattuor libros Sententiarum*, 4 vols., ed. W. Werbeck and U. Hoffman. Tübingen: Mohr, 1979.

Blackburn, S. W., *Essays in Quasi-Realism*. OUP, 1993.

———— 'Just Causes', *PhS* 61 (1991), 1–17.

———— 'Reply to Sturgeon', *PhS* 61 (1991), 39–42.

———— *Ruling Passions: A Theory of Practical Reasoning*. OUP, 1998.

———— *Spreading the Word*. OUP, 1984.

Blair, H., 'Hutcheson's moral philosophy', *Edinburgh Review*, 1 (1755), 9–23.

Blum, L. A., *Friendship, Altruism, and Morality*. RKP, 1980.

Bobonich, C. J., *Plato's Utopia Recast: His Later Ethics and Politics*. OUP, 2002.

Bobzien, S., *Determinism, Fate, and Stoic Philosophy*. OUP, 1998.

Boethius, *Commentaria in Aristotelis De Interpretatione*. BT.

Bogue, D., and Bennett, J., *History of Dissenters*. London: 1809.

Boler, J., 'Aquinas on exceptions in natural law', in MacDonald and Stump, eds., *AMT* 161–92.

———— 'The moral psychology of Duns Scotus: some preliminary questions', *FS* 50 (1990), 31–56.

———— 'Transcending the natural: Duns Scotus on the two affections of the will', *ACPQ* 67 (1993), 109–26.

Bolton, M. B., 'Universals, essences, and abstract entities', in Garber and Ayers, eds., *CHSCP*, ch. 8.

Bonansea, B. M., 'Duns Scotus' voluntarism', in J. K. Ryan, ed., *John Duns Scotus 1265–1965*. CUAP, 1965, ch. 5.

Bonar, J., *The Moral Sense*. London: Allen and Unwin, 1930.

Bonaventure, *Opera Omnia*, 10 vols. Quaracchi: Collegium S. Bonaventurae, 1882–1902.

Bonhöffer, D., *Letters and Papers from Prison: Enlarged Edition*, ed. E. Bethge. London: SCM Press, 1971.

Bonitz, H., *Index Aristotelicus*. Berlin: Reimer, 1870 (= *Aristotelis Opera*, ed. I. Bekker, vol. 5).

Book of Common Prayer and Administration of the Sacraments and Other Rites and Ceremonies of the Church according to the Use of the Church of England (1662).

Boonin-Vail, D., *Thomas Hobbes and the Science of Moral Virtue*. CUP, 1994.

Bosanquet, B., *A Companion to Plato's Republic, 2nd edn.* London: Rivingtons, 1906.

———— Critical Notice of Moore, *Principia Ethica*. *M* 13 (1904), 254–61.

———— 'Life and philosophy', in *Contemporary British Philosophy, First Series*, ed. J. H. Muirhead. London: Allen and Unwin, 1924, 49–74.

———— *The Principle of Individuality and Value*. London: Macmillan, 1912.

Bossuet, J-B., 'Instruction sur les états d'oraison', selections in *Bossuet: oeuvres choisies*, ed. J. Calvet. Paris: Hatier, 1917.

Boswell, J., *Boswell's Life of Johnson: Together with Boswell's Journal of a Tour to the Hebrides*, ed. G. B. Hill and rev. L. F. Powell, 6 vols. OUP, 1950.

Bourke, V. J., 'The *Nicomachean Ethics* and Thomas Aquinas', in A. A. Maurer et al., eds., *Thomas Aquinas 1274–1974: Commemorative Studies*, 2 vols. Toronto: Pontifical Institute of Mediaeval Studies, 1974, i 239–59.

Bourke, V. J., *Will in Western Thought*. New York: Sheed and Ward, 1964.

Bowle, J. W., *Hobbes and his Critics: A Study in Eighteenth-Century Constitutionalism*. London: Cape, 1951.

Boyd, R., 'How to be a moral realist', in Sayre-McCord, ed., *EMR*, ch. 9.

Boyle, R., *A Free Enquiry into the Vulgarly Received Notion of Nature*, ed. E. B. Davis and M. Hunter. CUP, 1996 (orig. pub. 1686.)

_____ *The Christian Virtuoso, showing that by being Addicted to Experimental Philosophy a Man is rather Assisted than Indisposed to be a Good Christian*. London: James, 1690.

Bradley, D. J. M., *Aquinas on the Twofold Human Good*. CUAP, 1997.

Bradley, F. H., *Collected Essays*, 2 vols. OUP, 1935.

_____ *Ethical Studies*, 2nd edn., OUP, 1927 (1st edn., 1876.)

_____ 'Mr Sidgwick's hedonism', in *CE*, i, ch. 2 (orig. pub. 1877).

Bramhall, J., *A Defence of True Liberty*. Selections in Hobbes, *LN*, ed. Chappell. From *Works*, iv.

_____ *Castigations of Mr Hobbes*, in *Works*, iv.

_____ *Discourse of Liberty and Necessity*. Selections in Hobbes, *LN*, ed. Chappell. From *Works*, iv.

_____ *The Catching of Leviathan or The Great Whale*, in *Works*, iv.

_____ *Works*, 5 vols. Oxford: Parker, 1842–5.

Brandt, R. B., *A Theory of the Good and the Right*. OUP, 1979.

_____ *Morality, Utilitarianism, and Rights*. CUP, 1992.

_____ 'Some merits of one form of rule-utilitarianism', in *MUR*, ch. 7.

_____ 'The concepts of obligation and duty', *M* 73 (1964), 374–93.

_____ 'Towards a credible form of utilitarianism', in H.-N. Castaneda and G. Nakhnikian, eds., *Morality and the Language of Conduct*. Detroit: Wayne State UP, 1963, ch. 4.

_____ 'Two concepts of utility', in *MUR*, ch. 9. From H. B. Miller and W. H. Williams, eds., *The Limits of Utilitarianism* (Minneapolis: U of Minnesota Press, 1982), 169–85.

Brender, N., and Krasnoff, L., eds., *New Essays on the History of Autonomy: A Collection Honoring J. B. Schneewind*. CUP, 2004.

Brink, D. O., *Moral Realism and the Foundations of Ethics*. CUP, 1989.

_____ *Perfectionism and the Common Good: Themes in the Philosophy of T. H. Green*. OUP, 2003.

_____ 'Rational egoism, self, and others', in O. Flanagan and A. O. Rorty, eds., *Identity, Character, and Morality*. Cambridge, Mass.: MIT Press, 1990, ch. 15.

_____ 'Sidgwick and the rationale for rational egoism', in Schultz, ed., *EHS*, ch. 7.

Brissenden, R. F., ' "Sentiment": some uses of the word in the writings of David Hume', in *Studies in the Eighteenth Century*, ed. R. F. Brissenden, vol. i. Canberra: ANU Press, 1968, 89–107.

Brittain, C. F., 'Attention deficit in Plotinus and Augustine: psychological problems in Christian and Platonist theories of the grades of virtue', *PBACAP* 18 (2003) 223–63.

Broad, C. D., 'Berkeley's theory of morals', *RIP* 7 (1953), 72–86.

_____ 'Certain features in Moore's ethical doctrines', in Schilpp, ed., *PGEM*, ch. 1.

_____ *Critical Essays in Moral Philosophy*, ed. D. R. Cheney. London: Allen and Unwin, 1971.

_____ Critical Notice of Ross, *Foundations of Ethics*. *M* 49 (1940), 228–39.

_____ 'Egoism as a theory of human motives', in *CEMP*, ch. 11.

_____ *Five Types of Ethical Theory*. London: Kegan Paul, 1930.

_____ 'G. E. Moore's latest published views on ethics', *M* 70 (1961), 435–57. Repr. in Ambrose and Lazerowitz, eds., *MER*, 350–73, and in Broad, *CEMP*, ch. 15.

_____ 'Some reflexions on moral-sense theories in ethics', *PAS* 45 (1944–5), 131–66.

Broadie, S. W., *Ethics with Aristotle*. OUP, 1991.

Brobjer, T. H., 'Nietzsche's disinterest and ambivalence toward the Greek Sophists', *International Studies in Philosophy*, 33 (2001), 5–23.

Brochard, V., *Les Sceptiques Grecs*. Paris: Vrin, 1887.

Brown, C., 'Is Hume an internalist?', *JHP* 26 (1988), 69–87.

Brown, John, *Essays on the Characteristics of Lord Shaftesbury*. Dublin: Faulkner, 1752.

Brown, K. C., ed., *Hobbes Studies*. Oxford: Basil Blackwell, 1965.

Brown, Thomas, *Lectures on Ethics*. Edinburgh: Tait, 1846.

Brunschwig, J., 'On a book title by Chrysippus', *OSAP* supp. (1991), 81–95.

_____ 'The conjunctive model', in *Papers in Hellenistic Philosophy*. CUP, 1994, ch. 5.

_____ 'The cradle argument in Epicureanism and Stoicism', in Schofield and Striker, eds., *NN*, ch. 5.

Buckle, S., *Natural Law and the Theory of Property*. OUP, 1991.

_____ 'Voluntarism, morality, and practical reason', in Haakonssen and Thiel, eds., *RWN* 98–123.

Burke, E., *Reflections on the Revolution in France*, ed. L.G. Mitchell. OUP, 1993 (orig. pub. 1790).

Burlamaqui, J. J., *Principles of Natural Law*, tr. T. Nugent. London: Nourse, 1748.

Burnaby, J., *Amor Dei: A Study of the Religion of St Augustine*. London: Hodder & Stoughton, 1938.

Burnyeat, M., 'Can the sceptic live his scepticism?', in Burnyeat and Frede, *OS*, ch. 2. From M. Schofield, M. Burnyeat, and J. Barnes, eds., *Doubt and Dogmatism*. OUP, 1980, 20–53.

_____ 'The sceptic in his place and time', in Burnyeat and Frede, *OS*, ch. 4. From R. Rorty, J. B. Schneewind, and Q. Skinner, eds., *Philosophy in History: Essays on the Historiography of Philosophy*. CUP, 1984, ch. 10.

_____ and Frede, M., eds., *The Original Sceptics: A Controversy*. Indianapolis: Hackett, 1997.

Butler, J., *The Analogy and Fifteen Sermons*, ed. J. Angus. London: Religious Tract Society, 1855.

_____ *The Works of Bishop Butler*, ed. J. H. Bernard 2 vols. London: Macmillan, 1900.

_____ *The Works of Joseph Butler*, ed. W. E. Gladstone, 2 vols. OUP, 1896.

Butler, M., *Jane Austen and the War of Ideas*, 2nd edn. OUP, 1987 (1st edn., 1975).

Buttrick, G. A., et al., eds., *The Interpreter's Bible*, 12 vols. Nashville: Abingdon-Cokesbury, 1952.

Byrne, B., *Romans*. Collegeville, Penn.: Liturgical Press, 1996.

Cajetan (Tomasso de Vio), Commentary on Aquinas, *Summae Theologiae*, printed in Aquinas, *Opera Omnia*, editio Leonina.

Calderwood, H., 'Mr Sidgwick on intuitionalism', *M* 1 (1876), 197–206.

Calvin, J., *Commentarius in Epistolam Pauli ad Romanos*, ed. T. H. L. Parker. Leiden: Brill, 1981.

_____ *Commentary on Romans*. tr. H. Beveridge. Edinburgh: Calvin Translation Society, 1844.

_____ *Institutes of the Christian Religion*, 2 vols., tr. F. L. Battles, ed. J. T. McNeill. London: SCM, 1960.

_____ *Institutes of the Christian Religion*, tr. H. Beveridge. Edinburgh: Calvin Translation Society, 1845.

_____ *Ioannis Calvini Opera Selecta*, 5 vols., ed. P. Barth and W. Niessel. Munich: Kaiser, 1952–9.

Campbell, C. A., 'Moral intuition and the principle of self-realization', in *In Defence of Free Will and Other Philosophical Essays*. London: Allen and Unwin, 1967, ch. 5. From *PBA* 34 (1948), 23–56.

Capreolus, Johannes, *Defensiones Theologiae Divi Thomae Aquinatis*, ed. C. Paban and T. Pègues, 7 vols. Tours: Cattier, 1900 (repr. Frankfurt: Minerva, 1967).

_____ *On the Virtues*, tr. K. White and R. Cessario. CUA Press, 2001 (From *DTTA* vol. v.)

Care, N. S., 'Contractualism and moral criticism', *RM* 23 (1969), 85–101.

Carmichael, Gershom, *Pufendorfi De Officio Hominis . . . auxit et illustravit*. Edinburgh: Mossman, 1724. ET in *Natural Rights on the Threshold of the Scottish Enlightenment: The Writings of Gershom Carmichael*, ed. J. Moore and M. Silverthorne. Indianapolis: Liberty Fund, 2002.

Carnap, R., *Meaning and Necessity, 2nd edn*. Chicago: U of Chicago Press (1st edn., 1947).

Carone, G. R., 'Plato's Stoic view of motivation', in *MSEAT*, ed. Salles, ch. 14.

Carritt, E. F., 'Hegel's Sittlichkeit', *PAS* 36 (1935–6), 223–36.

_____ *The Theory of Morals: An Introduction to Ethical Philosophy*. OUP, 1928.

Carruthers, P., *The Animals Issue*. CUP, 1992.

Cartwright, D. E., 'Schopenhauer's narrower sense of morality', in C. Janaway, ed., *Cambridge Companion to Schopenhauer*. CUP, 1999, ch. 8.

Cassirer, E., 'Kant and Rousseau', in *Rousseau, Kant, Goethe*. PUP, 1945.

_____ *The Platonic Renaissance in England*. London: Nelson, 1953.

Cathrein, V., *Philosophia Moralis in usum Scholarum*. Freiburg: Herder, 1915.

Chappell, V. C., ed., *Hume: A collection of critical essays*. London: Macmillan, 1968.

Charles, D., 'Aristotle on well-being and intellectual contemplation', *SPAS* 73 (1999), 205–23.

_____ 'Aristotle: ontology and moral reasoning', *OSAP* 4 (1986), 119–44.

_____ *Aristotle's Philosophy of Action*. London: Duckworth, 1984.

Charlesworth, J. H., ed., *The Old Testament Pseudepigrapha*, 2 vols. Garden City, NY: Doubleday, 1985.

Chemnitz, M., *Examination of the Council of Trent*, 2 vols., tr. F. Kramer. St Louis: Concordia, 1971.

Chenu, M. D., *Toward Understanding St Thomas*. Chicago: Regnery, 1964.

Cherniss, H. F., tr., *Plutarch's Moralia*, xiii 2. Loeb. HUP, 1976.

_____ 'The sources of evil according to Plato', in Vlastos, *Plato ii*, ch. 16. From *Proceedings of the American Philosophical Society* 98 (1954), 23–30.

Chiesara, M. L., *Aristocles of Messene*. OUP, 2001.

Chignell, A. C., 'Belief in Kant'. *PR* 116 (2007), 323–60.

Chilton, John, *Positive Institutions Not to be Compared with or Preferred before Moral Virtues*. London: Roberts, 1730.

Chisholm, R. M., 'The problem of empiricism', in Swartz, ed., *PSK*, 347–54. From *JP* 45 (1948), 512–17.

Chroust, A.-H., 'Hugo Grotius and the Scholastic natural law tradition'. *New Scholasticism*, 17 (1943), 101–33.

Chrysostom, John, *Commentaria in Epistulam ad Romanos*, in *PG* lx.

Chubb, Thomas, *The Comparative Excellence and Obligation of Moral and Positive Duties . . .* London: Roberts, 1730.

Cicero, *Academica*. BT.

_____ *Brutus*. BT.

_____ *De Amicitia*. BT.

_____ *De Fato*. BT.

_____ *De Finibus Bonorum et Malorum*. OCT.

_____ *De Inventione*. BT.

_____ *De Legibus*. BT.

_____ *De Natura Deorum*. BT.

_____ *De Officiis*. OCT.

_____ *De Oratore*. OCT.

_____ *De Republica*. OCT.

_____ *Epistulae ad Familiares*. OCT.

_____ *Paradoxa Stoicorum*. BT.

_____ *Pro Murena*. OCT.

_____ *Tusulanae Disputationes*. BT.

Clark, D. W., 'Voluntarism and rationalism in the ethics of William of Ockham', *FS* 31 (1971), 72–87.

_____ 'William of Ockham on right reason', *Speculum*, 48 (1973), 13–36.

Clark, M., 'Nietzsche's immoralism and the concept of morality', in Schacht, ed., *NGM*, ch. 2.

Clarke, J., *Foundation of Morality in Theory and Practice*. York: Gent, 1726.

Clarke, S., *A Demonstration of the Being and Attributes of God* (= *DBAG*) in *Works*, ed. Hoadly, ii.

_____ *A Discourse concerning the Obligations of Natural Religion, and the Truth and Certainty of the Christian Revelation* (= *DNR*) in *Works*, ed. Hoadly, ii.

_____ *The Works of Samuel Clarke*, 4 vols., ed. B. Hoadly. London: Knapton, 1738 (repr. Bristol: Thoemmes, 2002). Cited as H.

Clement of Alexandria, *Stromata*, 2nd edn., ed. O. Stählin et al. Berlin: Akademie Verlag, 1970 (repr. 1985).

Clement, *Quis Dives Salvetur?*, ed. G. W. Butterworth (Loeb). HUP, 1919.

Bibliography

Cockburn (Trotter), C., 'Remarks on Mr Seed's Sermon on moral virtue', in *Works*, ii.

_____ *Remarks upon . . . Dr Rutherforth's Essay . . .* (1747), in *Works*, i 7–107.

_____ *Remarks upon some Writers in the Controversy concerning the Foundation of Moral Virtue . . .*, in *Works*, i, 381–455.

_____ *Works*, 2 vols. London: Knapton, 1751 (repr. Bristol: Thoemmes, 1992).

Cohen, S. M., 'Socrates on the definition of piety', in G. Vlastos, ed., *The Philosophy of Socrates*, Garden City, NY: Anchor Books, 1971, ch. 8. From *JHP* 9 (1971), 1–13.

Coleridge, S. T., *Collected Letters*, 6 vols., ed. E.L. Griggs. OUP, 1956–71.

_____ *Marginalia*, ii, ed. G. Whalley. RKP, 1984.

Colish, M. L., 'Cicero and Machiavelli', *Sixteenth Century Journal*, 9 (1978), 81–93.

_____ *The Stoic Tradition From Antiquity to the Early Middle Ages*, 2 vols. Leiden: Brill, 1985.

Colley, Linda, *Britons: Forging the Nation, 1707–1837*. London: Pimlico, 2003.

Collini, S., *Liberalism and Sociology*. CUP, 1979.

_____ *Public Moralists; Political Thought and Intellectual Life in Britain*. OUP, 1991.

_____ 'The ordinary experience of everyday life', in Schultz, ed., *EHS*, ch. 12.

Collins, S., *Selfless Persons : Imagery and Thought in Theravada Buddhism*. CUP, 1982.

Colman, J., *John Locke's Moral Philosophy*. Edinburgh: Edinburgh UP, 1983.

Commentaria in Aristotelem Graeca, 23 vols. + *Supplementum Aristotelicum*, 3 vols. Berlin: Reimer, 1882–1907.

Cooper, J. M., 'Eudaemonism, the appeal to nature, and "moral duty" in Stoicism', in *RE*, ch. 20. From Engstrom and Whiting, eds., *RDH*, ch. 9.

_____ 'Friendship and the good in Aristotle', in *RE*, ch. 15. From *PR* 86 (1977), 290–315.

_____ 'Greek philosophers on euthanasia and suicide', in *RE*, ch. 23. From B. A. Brody, ed., *Suicide and Euthanasia*. Dordrecht: Kluwer Academic, 1989, 9–38.

_____ 'Justus Lipsius and the revival of Stoicism in late sixteenth-century Europe', in Brender and Krasnoff, eds., *NEHA*, ch. 1.

_____ 'Pleasure and desire in Epicurus', in *RE*, ch. 22.

_____ 'Poseidonius on emotions', in *RE*, ch. 21.

_____ 'Political animals and civic friendship', in *RE*, ch. 16.

_____ *Reason and Emotion*. PUP, 1999.

_____ *Reason and the Human Good in Aristotle*. HUP, 1975.

_____ 'Reason, moral virtue, and moral value', in *RE*, ch. 11. From M. Frede and G. Striker, eds., *Rationality in Greek Thought*. OUP, 1996, ch. 3.

Corpus dei Papiri Filosofici Greci e Latini. Florence: Olschki. Part 1, vol. 1(1), 1989. Part 1, vol. 1(2), 1992. Part 3, 1995.

Council of Trent; see Denziger and Schönmetzer, *ES*.

Cranfield, C. E. B., *Romans*. Edinburgh: T&T Clark, 1975.

Cranston, M., and Peters, R. S., eds., *Hobbes and Rousseau*. Garden City, NY: Doubleday, 1972.

Crisp, R. S., *Mill on Utilitarianism*. RKP, 1997.

_____ 'Sidgwick and the boundaries of intuitionism', in Stratton-Lake, ed., *EI*, ch. 2.

Cronin, M., *The Science of Ethics*, 2nd edn., 2 vols. Dublin: Gill, 1920.

Cronin, T. J., *Objective Being in Descartes and Suarez* (Analecta Gregoriana 154). Rome: Gregorian UP, 1966.

Cross, R., *Duns Scotus*. OUP, 1999.

Crowe, M. B., *The Changing Profile of the Natural Law*. The Hague: Nijhoff, 1977.

Cudworth, R., *A Treatise concerning Eternal and Immutable Morality, with a Treatise of Freewill*, ed. S. Hutton. CUP, 1996.

_____ *A Treatise of Freewill*, ed. J. Allen. London: Parker, 1838 (reprinted (together with Scott, *ICTEIM*), Bristol: Thoemmes, 1992).

_____ *A Treatise of Freewill*. Included in *EIM*, ed. Hutton.

Cudworth, R., *The True Intellectual System of the Universe*, 3 vols., ed. J. Harrison. Notes by J. Mosheim. London: Tegg, 1845 (repr. Bristol: Thoemmes, 1995).

Cullity, G., and Gaut., B., eds., *Ethics and Practical Reason*. OUP 1997.

Culverwell, N., *An Elegant and Learned Discourse of the Light of Nature*, ed. R. A. Greene and H. MacCallum. Toronto: University of Toronto Press, 1971 (repr. Indianapolis: Liberty Fund, 2001; orig. pub. London, 1652). Cited as *LN*.

Cumberland, R., *De Legibus Naturae*. London: Nathanael Hooke, 1672. ET in *A Treatise of the Laws of Nature*, tr. J. Maxwell. London: J. Knapton, 1727 (repr. ed. J. Parkin, Indianapolis: Liberty Fund, 2005).

Cummins, R., 'Functional explanation', *JP* 72 (1975), 741–65.

Cuneo, T., 'Reid's moral philosophy', in *The Cambridge Companion to Thomas Reid*, ed. T. Cuneo and R. van Woudenberg. CUP, 2004, ch. 10

Cunliffe, C., ed., *Joseph Butler's Moral and Religious Thought*. OUP, 1992.

Curley, E. M., *Behind the Geometrical Method*. PUP, 1988.

Dahl, N. O., 'Plato's defence of justice', in Fine, ed., *Plato*, ii, ch 8. From *PPR* 51 (1991), 809–34.

―――― *Practical Reason, Aristotle, and Weakness of the Will*. Minneapolis: U of Minnesota Press, 1984.

Damascenus, Ioannes, *Expositio Fidei*, ed. B. Kotter. Berlin: De Gruyter, 1973.

Dancy, J. W. P., 'Two conceptions of moral realism', in Rachels, ed., *ET*, ch. 13. From *SPAS* 60 (1986), 167–87.

Daniels, N., ed., *Reading Rawls*. Oxford: Blackwell, 1975.

―――― 'Wide reflective equilibrium and theory acceptance in ethics', *JP* 76 (1979), 256–82.

Darwall, S. L., 'Autonomy in modern natural law', in Brender and Krasnoff, eds., *NEHA*, ch. 5.

―――― 'Learning from Frankena: a philosophical remembrance', *E* 107 (1997), 685–705.

―――― 'Moore, normativity, and intrinsic value', *E* 113 (2003), 469–89.

―――― *The British Moralists and the Internal 'Ought'*. CUP, 1995.

―――― Gibbard, A., and Railton, P., 'Toward fin-de-siècle ethics', *PR* 101 (1992), 115–89.

Davidson, D., 'Actions, reasons, and causes', in *EAE*, ch. 1. From *JP* 60 (1963), 685–700.

―――― *Essays on Actions and Events*. OUP, 1980.

―――― 'Mental events', in *EAE*, ch. 11.

―――― 'Psychology as philosophy', in *EAE*, ch. 12.

Davies, W. D., and Allison, D. C., *The Gospel according to St Matthew*, 3 vols. Edinburgh: T&T Clark, 1988–97.

Davis, H., *Moral and Pastoral Theology*, 5th edn., 4 vols. London: Sheed and Ward, 1946.

De Scorraille, R., *François Suarez*, 2 vols. Paris: Lethielleux, 1913.

De Sousa, R. B., *The Rationality of Emotion*. Cambridge, Mass.: MIT Press, 1987.

Deigh, J., 'Sidgwick on ethical judgment', in Schultz, ed., *EHS*, ch. 8.

Delahaye, P., 'Quelques aspects de la morale de Saint Anselme', in *Spicilegium Beccense*. Paris: Vrin, 1959, 401–22.

Denifle, H., and Chatelain, E., eds., *Chartularium Universitatis Parisinensis*. Paris: Delalain, 1896.

Dent, N. J. H., *Rousseau: An Introduction to his Psychological, Social, and Political Theory*. Oxford: Blackwell, 1988.

Denziger, H., and Schönmetzer, A., eds., *Enchiridion Symbolorum*, 36th edn. Freiburg: Herder, 1976. Cited as 'Denz.' or 'D'.

Derathé, R., *Rousseau et la science politique de son temps*, 2nd edn. Paris: Vrin 1970 (1st edn., 1950).

Descartes, R., *Oeuvres de Descartes*, 11 vols., ed. C. Adam and P. Tannery, Paris: Cerf, 1894–1913.

Dewey, J., 'Green's theory of the moral motive', *PR* 1 (1892), 593–612.

―――― 'Self-realization as the moral ideal', *PR* 2 (1893), 652–64.

Dictionnaire de Théologie Catholique, 15 vols., ed. A. Vacant et al. Paris: Letouzey et Ané, 1903–46.

Diels, H., and Kranz, W., eds., *Fragmente der Vorsokratiker*, 6th edn., 3 vols. Berlin: Weidmann, 1952.

Dillon, J. M., *The Middle Platonists*. London: Duckworth, 1977.

Dillon, R. S., ed., *Dignity, Character, and Self-Respect*. RKP, 1995.

Dio Chrysostom, *Orationes*. BT.

Diodorus Siculus, *Bibliotheca Historica*. BT.

Diogenes Laertius, *Vitae Philosophorum*. OCT.

Doddridge, P., *A Course of Lectures on the Principal Subjects in Pneumatology, Ethics, and Divinity*, 2nd edn., ed. S. Clarke. London: Buckland, 1776 (1st edn., 1763).

—— *Correspondence and Diary*, ed. J. D. Humphreys. London: Colbourn and Bentley, 1829–31.

Dodds, E. R., ed., *Plato: Gorgias*. OUP, 1959.

Doig, J. C., *Aquinas' Philosophical Commentary on the Ethics*. Dordrecht: Kluwer, 2001.

Donagan, A., 'Sidgwick and Whewellian intuitionism', in Schultz, ed., *EHS*, ch. 3. From *CJP* 7 (1977), 447–65.

—— *Theory of Morality*. Chicago: U of Chicago Press, 1977.

—— 'Thomas Aquinas on human action', in Kretzmann et al., eds., *CHLMP*, ch. 33.

—— 'Whewell's Elements of Morality', *JP* 71 (1974), 724–36.

Dreyfus, H. L., *Being-in-the-World: A Commentary on Heidegger's Being and Time, Division I*. Cambridge, Mass.: MIT Press, 1991.

—— 'Interpreting Heidegger on *Das Man*', *Inquiry*, 38 (1995), 423–30.

Driver, S. R., *Deuteronomy*. Edinburgh: T&T Clark, 1895.

Dudden, F. H., *Henry Fielding, his Life, Works, and Times*, 2 vols. OUP, 1952.

Duffy, E., 'Wesley and the Counter-Reformation', in J. Garnett and C. Matthew, eds., *Revival and Religion since 1700*. London: Hambledon, 1993, ch. 1.

Dummett, M., *Frege: Philosophy of Language*. London: Duckworth, 1973.

Dunbabin, J., 'The Two Commentaries of Albertus Magnus on the *Nicomachean Ethics*', *RTAM* 30 (1963), 232–50.

Duncan, E. H., and Baird, R. M., 'Thomas Reid on Adam Smith's theory of morals', *JHI* 38 (1977), 509–22.

Du Plessis d'Argentré, C., ed., *Collectio Judiciorum de Novis Erroribus qui . . . in Ecclesia Proscripti sunt et Notati*, 3 vols. Paris: Cailleau, 1728–36.

Düsing, K., 'Das Problem des höchsten Gutes in Kants praktischen Philosophie', *KS* 62 (1971), 5–42.

Dworkin, R. M., 'Hard cases', in *TRS*, ch. 4.

—— 'Reverse discrimination', in *TRS*, ch. 9.

—— *Taking Rights Seriously*. HUP, 1977.

—— 'The Original Position', in Daniels, ed., *RR*, ch. 2. Repr. as 'Justice and rights', in *TRS*, ch. 6.

Dybikowski, J. C., 'Is Aristotelian *eudaimonia* happiness?' *Dialogue* 20 (1981), 185–200.

Edgeworth, F. Y., *New and Old Methods of Ethics*. Oxford: Parker, 1877. Reprinted in *F. Y. Edgeworth: Mathematical Psychics and Further Papers on Political Economy*, ed. P. Newman. OUP, 2003.

Edwards, John, *The Eternal and Intrinsic Reasons of Good and Evil*. CUP, 1699.

Edwards, R. B., *Pleasures and Pains: A Theory of Qualitative Hedonism*. Ithaca, NY: Cornell UP, 1979.

Eliot, G., *Middlemarch*, ed. B. G. Hornback. New York: Norton, 1977 (1st pub. 1872).

Elster, J., 'Sour grapes: utilitarianism and the genesis of wants', in Sen and Williams, eds., *UB*, ch. 11.

Empson, W., *The Structure of Complex Words*, 3rd edn. London: Chatto and Windus, 1977.

Engberg-Pederson, T., *Aristotle's Theory of Moral Insight*. OUP, 1983.

—— 'Discovering the good', in Schofield and Striker, eds., *NN*, ch. 6.

English Articles, in *BCP* and Schaff, *CC* iii. Cited as 'Articles'.

Engstrom, S., 'Happiness and the highest good in Aristotle and Kant', in Engstrom and Whiting, eds., *RDH*, ch. 4.

—— 'The concept of the highest good in Kant's moral theory', *PPR* 52 (1992), 747–80.

—— and Whiting, J., eds., *Rethinking Duty and Happiness: Aristotle, Kant, and the Stoics*. CUP, 1996.

Epictetus, *Dissertationes* and *Enchiridion*. BT.

Epicurus, *Epicuro: Opere,* 2nd edn, ed. G. Arrighetti. Turin: Einaudi, 1973. Includes *On Nature; Sententiae Vaticanae: Kuriai Doxai.*

———— *The Extant Remains,* ed. and tr. C. Bailey. OUP, 1926.

Eusebius, *Praeparatio Evangelica,* 2nd edn., 2 vols., ed. K. Mras. Berlin: Akademie, 1982.

Eustratius, in *EN, CAG* xx.

Everson, S. E., ed., *Ethics: Companions to Ancient Thought.* CUP, 1998.

———— 'Introduction: virtue and morality', in *ECAT*, 1–26.

Ewing, A. C., *Second Thoughts in Moral Philosophy.* London: RKP, 1959.

———— *The Definition of Good.* London: RKP, 1947.

———— 'The linguistic theory of a priori propositions', *PAS* 40 (1939–40), 207–44.

Falk, W. D., 'Morality and nature', in *ORM*, ch. 9. From *AJP* 28 (1950), 69–92.

———— ' "Ought" and motivation', in *ORM*, ch. 1. From *PAS* 48 (1947–8), 492–510.

———— *Ought, Reasons, and Morality.* Ithaca, NY: Cornell UP, 1986.

Farrell, W., *The Natural Law according to St Thomas and Suarez.* Ditchling: St Dominic's Press, 1930.

Farrelly, M. J., *Predestination, Grace, and Free Will.* London: Burns & Oates, 1964.

Feinberg, J., 'Rawls and intuitionism', in Daniels, ed., *RR*, ch. 5.

Fichte, J. G., *Foundations of Natural Right,* tr. M. Baur. CUP, 2000.

———— *The System of Ethics,* tr. D. Breazeale and G. Zöller. CUP, 2005.

Fiddes, R., *A General Treatise of Morality, formed upon the Principles of Natural Reason only.* London: Billingsley, 1724.

Field, H., 'Theory change and the indeterminacy of reference', *JP* 70 (1973), 462–81.

Fieser, J., ed., *Early Responses to Hume, i.* Bristol: Thoemmes, 2004.

Fine, G., ed., *Plato, ii.* OUP, 1999.

———— 'Sceptical dogmata; *Outlines of Pyrrhonism* I 13', *Methexis* 13 (2000), 81–105.

Finnis, J. M., *Aquinas: Moral, Political, and Legal Theory.* OUP, 1998.

———— *Natural Law and Natural Rights.* OUP, 1980.

Firth, R., 'Ethical absolutism and the ideal observer', *PPR* 12 (1952), 317–45.

Fischer, J. M., 'Freedom and foreknowledge', in Fischer, ed., *GFF*, ch. 4. From *PR* 92 (1983), 67–79.

———— ed., *God, Foreknowledge, and Freedom.* Stanford, Calif.: Stanford UP, 1989.

Flanagan, O., *Varieties of Moral Personality.* HUP, 1991.

Flew, A. G. N., ' "Not proven"—at most', in Chappell, ed., *Hume,* 291–4.

———— 'On the interpretation of Hume', in Chappell, ed., *Hume,* 278–86. From *Phil.* 38 (1963) 178–81.

Foot, P. R., 'Moral beliefs', in *VV*, ch. 8. From *PAS* 59 (1958–9), 83–104.

———— *Moral Dilemmas.* OUP, 2002.

———— 'Morality as a system of hypothetical imperatives', in *VV*, ch. 11. From *PR* 81 (1972) 305–16.

———— 'Moral realism and moral dilemma', in *MD*, ch. 3. From *JP* 80 (1983), 379–98.

———— *Natural Goodness.* OUP, 2001.

———— 'Nietzsche's immoralism', in R. Schacht, ed., *NGM*, ch. 1

———— *Virtues and Vices.* Oxford: Blackwell, 1978.

Förster, E., ed., *Kant's Transcendental Deductions.* Stanford, Calif.: Stanford UP, 1989.

Foster, M. B., 'A mistake of Plato's in the *Republic*', *M* 46 (1937), 386–93.

———— 'Some implications of a passage in Plato's *Republic*', *Phil.* 11 (1936), 301–8.

———— *The Political Philosophies of Plato and Hegel.* OUP, 1935.

Fowler, T., *Shaftesbury and Hutcheson.* London: Sampson Low, 1882.

Frankena, W. K., 'Concepts of rational action in the history of ethics', *Social Theory and Practice,* 9 (1983), 165–97.

———— 'Ewing's case against naturalistic theories of value', in *PM*, ch. 3. From *PR* 57 (1948), 481–92.

_____ 'Hutcheson's moral sense theory', *JHI* 16 (1955), 359–75.

_____ 'Obligation and motivation in recent moral philosophy', in *PM*, ch 6. From Melden, ed., *EMP* 40–81.

_____ 'Obligation and value in the ethics of G. E. Moore', in *PM*, ch. 2. From Schilpp, ed., *PGEM*, ch. 3.

_____ *Perspectives on Morality*, ed. K. E. Goodpaster. Notre Dame, Ind.: UND Press, 1976.

_____ Review of Prior, *LBE*. *PR* 59 (1950), 554–6.

_____ 'Sidgwick and the history of ethical dualism', in Schultz., ed. *EHS*, ch. 6.

_____ 'The concept of morality', in Wallace and Walker, eds., *DM*, ch. 9. Later version repr. in Frankena, *PM*, ch. 10.

_____ 'The naturalistic fallacy', in *PM*, ch. 1. From *M* 48 (1939), 464–77.

Frankfurt, H. G., 'Freedom of the will and the concept of a person', in *IWWCA*, ch. 2. From *JP* 68 (1971), 5–20.

_____ 'Identification and wholeheartedness', in *IWWCA*, ch. 12. From *Responsibility, Character, and the Emotions*, ed. F. D. Schoeman. CUP, 1987.

_____ *The Importance of What We Care About*. CUP, 1988.

Frassen, C., *Scotus Academicus, seu Universa Doctoris Subtilis Theologica Dogmata*, 12 vols. Rome: Bernabo, 1721.

Frede, M., 'On the original notion of cause', in Barnes et al., eds., *DD*, ch. 9.

_____ 'On the Stoic conception of the good', in K. Ierodiakonou, ed., *Topics in Stoic Philosophy*. OUP, 1999, ch. 3.

_____ 'The Stoic doctrine of the affections of the soul', in Schofield and Striker, *NN*, ch. 5.

Freppert, L., *The Basis of Morality according to William of Ockham*. Chicago: Franciscan Herald Press, 1988.

Frey, R. G., 'Butler on self-love and benevolence', in Cunliffe, ed., *JBMRT*, ch. 12.

Furley, D. J., 'Nothing to us?', in Schofield and Striker, eds., *NN*, ch. 3.

_____ *Two Studies in the Greek Atomists*. PUP, 1967.

Fussenberger, G., ed., 'Definitiones capitulae generalis Argentinae', *Archivum Franciscanum Historicum*, 26 (1933), 127–40.

Gadamer, H.-G., *Truth and Method*. New York: Continuum, 1975. ET of *Wahrheit und Methode*, 2nd edn. Tübingen: Mohr, 1965.

Galen, *De Placitis Hippocratis et Platonis*, 3 vols., ed. P. H. De Lacy. Berlin: Akademie-Verlag, 1978–81.

Gallagher, D., 'Thomas Aquinas on the will as rational appetite', *JHP* 29 (1991), 559–84.

Garber, D. E., and Ayers, M. R., eds., *The Cambridge History of Seventeenth-Century Philosophy*, 2 vols. CUP, 1998.

Garnett, J., 'Bishop Butler and the Zeitgeist: Butler and the development of Christian moral philosophy in Victorian Britain', in Cunliffe, ed., *JBMRT*, ch. 4.

Garnsey, P., 'Introduction: the Hellenistic and Roman periods', in Rowe and Schofield, eds., *CHGRPT*, ch. 20.

Garrett, D., ed., *Cambridge Companion to Spinoza*. CUP, 1996.

_____ *Cognition and Commitment in Hume's Philosophy*. OUP, 1997.

_____ 'Spinoza's ethical theory', in Garrett, ed., *CCS*, ch. 6.

Garrigou-Lagrange, R., *Beatitude*. St Louis: Herder, 1956.

_____ *The One God*. St Louis: Herder, 1943.

Gascoigne, J., *Cambridge in the Age of the Enlightenment: Science, Religion and Politics from the Restoration to the French Revolution*. CUP, 1989.

Gaudium et Spes (De ecclesia in mundo huius temporis). Second Vatican Council. In Alberigo et al., eds., *Decreta*.

Gaut, B., 'Justifying moral pluralism', in Stratton-Lake (ed.), *EI*, 137–60.

Gauthier, D. P., 'David Hume: contractarian', in *MD*, ch. 3. From *PR* 88 (1979), 3–38.

_____ *Moral Dealing: Contract, Ethics, and Reason*. Ithaca, NY: Cornell UP, 1990.

_____ 'Morality and advantage', *PR* 76 (1967), 460–75.

Gauthier, D. P., *Morals by Agreement*. OUP, 1986.

_____ Review of Skinner, *RRPH*, *JP* 94 (1997), 94–7.

_____ 'Taming Leviathan', *PPA* 16 (1987), 280–95.

_____ *The Logic of Leviathan: The Moral and Political Theory of Thomas Hobbes*. OUP, 1969.

_____ 'Thomas Hobbes: moral theorist', in *MD*, ch. 1. From *JP* 76 (1979), 547–59.

_____ 'Three against justice: the foole, the sensible knave, and the Lydian shepherd', in *MD*, ch. 6. From *Midwest Studies in Philosophy*, 7 (1982), 11–29.

Gauthier, R.-A., 'Saint Maxime le Confesseur et la psychologie de l'acte humain', *RTAM* 21 (1954), 51–100.

_____ 'Trois commentaires "averroistes" sur l'Ethique à Nicomaque', *Archives d'histoire doctrinale et litteraire du Moyen Age*, 22–3 (1947–8), 187–336.

_____ and Jolif, J.-Y., eds., *Aristote: L'Ethique à Nicomaque, 2nd edn.*, 4 vols. Louvain: Publications universitaires de Louvain, 1970.

Gauthier, *SLE; see* Aquinas.

Gay, J., *A Dissertation concerning the Fundamental Principle and Immediate Criterion of Virtue, as also the Obligation to and Approbation of It, with some Account of the Origin of the Passions and Affections*, in King, *OE*, tr. E. Law.

Geach, P. T., 'Ascriptivism', in *Logic Matters*. Oxford: Blackwell, 1972, 250–4. From *PR* 69 (1960), 221–5.

_____ *The Virtues*. CUP, 1977.

Gemmeke, E., *Die Metaphysik des sittlich Guten bei Franz Suarez*. Freiburg: Herder, 1965.

George, R. P., ed., *Natural Law, Liberalism, and Morality*. OUP, 1996.

Gerson, L. P., *Aristotle and other Platonists*. Ithaca, NY: Cornell UP, 2005.

_____ *Plotinus*. RKP, 1994.

Gert, B., 'Hobbes and psychological egoism', *JHI* 28 (1967), 503–20.

_____ 'Hobbes, mechanism, and egoism', *PQ* 15 (1965), 341–9.

_____ 'Hobbes's psychology', in Sorell, ed., *CCH*, ch. 7.

Geuss, R., *Morality, Culture, and History*. CUP, 1999.

_____ 'Nietzsche and genealogy', in *MCH*, ch. 1.

_____ 'Nietzsche and morality', in *MCH*, ch. 7

Gewirth, A., 'Positive "ethics" and normative "science" ', *PR* 69 (1960), 311–30.

Giannantoni, G., *I Cirenaici*. Florence: Sansoni, 1958.

_____ ed., *Socraticorum Reliquiae*, 4 vols. Naples: Ateneo, 1983.

Gibbard, A., 'Hare's analysis of "ought" and its implications', in D. Seanor and N. Fotion, eds., *Hare and Critics: Essays on Moral Thinking*. OUP, 1988, ch. 5.

_____ *Thinking How to Live*. HUP, 2003.

_____ *Wise Choices, Apt Feelings*. HUP, 1990.

Gladstone, W. E., *Studies Subsidiary to the Work of Bishop Butler*. OUP, 1896.

Glorieux, P., ed., *Le correctorium corruptorii 'Quare'*, Bibliothèque Thomiste, 9 (1927).

Godfrey of Fontaines, *Les Quodlibet*, 5 vols., ed. M. de Wulf et al. Louvain: Institut Superieure de Philosophie, 1904–37.

Godwin, W., *Enquiry concerning Political Justice*, 3 vols., ed. F. E. L. Priestly. Toronto: U. of Toronto Press, 1946 (orig. pub. London, 1793; 2nd edn., 1796; 3rd edn., 1798).

Gonet, J. B., *Manuale Thomistarum, seu Totius Theologiae Brevis Cursus*. Antwerp, 1745.

Gosling, J. C. B., *Plato's Philebus*. OUP, 1975.

_____ and Taylor, C. C. W., *The Greeks on Pleasure*. OUP, 1982.

Goulet-Cazé, M.-O., *L'Ascèse Cynique*, Paris: Vrin, 1996.

Graf, T., *De subiecto psychico gratiae et virtutum, pars prima: de subjecto virtutum cardinalium*, 2 vols. Rome: Herder, 1934.

Grant, A., *The Ethics of Aristotle*, 4th edn., 2 vols. London: Longmans, 1885.

Grave, S. A., 'The foundations of Butler's ethics', *AJP* 30 (1952), 73–89.

Greek New Testament, 3rd edn., corrected, ed. K. Aland et al. United Bible Societies, 1983.

Green, R. M., ' "Developing" *Fear and Trembling*', in Hannay and Marino, eds., *CCK*, ch. 10.

Green, T. H., *Complete Works*, 5 vols. (incl. 2 additional vols.), ed. P. Nicholson. Bristol: Thoemmes, 1997. 3 vols., repr. from *Works*, ed. R. L. Nettleship. London: Longmans, Green, and Co., 1885–8.

—— copies of Aristotle's *Ethics*, in the library of Balliol College, Oxford.

—— *Introductions to Hume's Treatise of Human Nature*, in *Works*, i, 1–371.

—— *Lectures on Political Obligation and Other Writings*, ed. P. Harris and J. Morrow. CUP, 1986.

—— 'Lectures on the philosophy of Kant', in *Works*, ii, 1–155.

—— 'On the different senses of "freedom" as applied to will and to the moral progress of man', in *Works*, ii, 308–33.

—— *Prolegomena to Ethics*, ed. Brink, D. O. OUP, 2003 (orig. OUP, 1883. Repr. in *Works*, iv).

Green, Thomas, *An Examination of the Leading Principle of the New System of Morals as that Principle is Stated and Applied in Mr Godwin's Enquiry concerning Political Justice*. London: Longman, 1798.

Greenwood, L. H. G., ed., *Aristotle, Nicomachean Ethics Book Six*. CUP, 1909.

Gregory of Rimini, *Gregorii Ariminensis OESA Lectura super primum et secundum Sententiarum*, 7 vols., ed. A. D. Trapp and V. Marcolino. Berlin: De Gruyter, 1981–7.

Grice, H. P., *Studies in the Way of Words*. HUP, 1989.

Griffin, J., *Homer on Life and Death*. OUP, 1980.

Grisez, G. G., 'Natural law, God, religion, and human fulfillment', *American Journal of Jurisprudence*, 46 (2001), 3–36.

—— 'The first principle of practical reason', in A. J. P. Kenny, ed., *Aquinas: A Collection of Critical Essays*, Garden City, NY: Doubleday, 1970, 340–82.

—— *The Way of the Lord Jesus*, i. Chicago: Franciscan Herald Press, 1983.

Griswold, C. L., *Adam Smith and the Virtues of Enlightenment*. CUP, 1999.

Grote, G., *Fragments on ethical subjects*. London: Murray, 1876.

—— *History of Greece*, 2nd edn., 10 vols. London: John Murray, 1851.

—— *Plato and the other Companions of Sokrates*, 2nd edn., 4 vols. London: Murray, 1888 (1st edn., 1865).

Grote, J., *An Examination of the Utilitarian Philosophy*. Cambridge: Deighton Bell, 1870.

Grotius, H., *Briefwisseling van Hugo Grotius*, 16 vols. 's-Gravenhage: Nijhoff, 1928–96.

—— *De iure belli et pacis*, 3 vols., tr. W. Whewell. CUP, 1853 (orig. pub. 1625).

—— *De iure praedae*, tr. G. L. Williams and W. H. Zeydel. OUP 1950 (orig pub. 1604).

Grove, H., *System of Moral Philosophy*, 2nd edn., ed. T. Amory. London: Waugh, 1749.

—— *Wisdom the First Spring of Action in the Deity*, 2nd edn. London: Fenner, 1742.

Gueroult, M., *Spinoza*, 2 vols. Paris: Aubier-Montaigne, 1968.

Guignon, C. B., 'Authenticity, moral values, and psychotherapy', in Guignon, C. B., ed., *Cambridge Companion to Heidegger*, 2nd edn. CUP, 2006, ch. 10.

Guthrie, W. K. C., *History of Greek Philosophy*, 6 vols. CUP, 1962–81.

Haakonssen, K., 'Hugo Grotius and the history of political thought', *Political Theory*, 13 (1985), 239–65.

—— *Natural Law and Moral Philosophy*. CUP, 1996.

—— 'Protestant natural law theory', in Brender and Krasnoff, eds., *NEHA*, ch. 4.

—— and Thiel, U., eds., *Reason, Will, and Nature* (*History of Philosophy Yearbook* 1). Canberra, 1993.

Habermas, J., 'Martin Heidegger: on the publication of the lectures of 1935', in Wolin, ed., *HC*, ch. 11.

Hall, P. M., *Narrative and the Natural Law*. Notre Dame, Ind.: UND Press, 1994.

Hamilton, B., *Political Theory in Sixteenth-Century Spain*. OUP, 1963.

Hampshire, S. N., *Spinoza*, rev. edn. Harmondsworth: Penguin, 1987 (1st pub. 1951).

—— *Two Theories of Morality*. OUP, 1977.

Hampton, J., 'Hobbes and ethical naturalism', *Philosophical Perspectives*, 6 (1992), 333–53.

Hampton, J., *Hobbes and the Social Contract Tradition*. CUP, 1986.

Hannay, A., *Kierkegaard*. RKP, 1982.

_____ and Marino, G. D., eds., *Cambridge Companion to Kierkegaard*. CUP, 1998.

Hare, J. E., *The Moral Gap: Kantian Ethics, Human Limits, and God's Assistance*. OUP, 1996.

Hare, R. M., 'Austin's distinction between locutionary and illocutionary acts', in *Practical Inferences*. London: Macmillan, 1971, ch. 6.

_____ 'Broad's approach to moral philosophy', in P. A. Schilpp, ed., *The Philosophy of C. D. Broad*. New York: Tudor, 1959, ch. 18.

_____ 'Could Kant have been a utilitarian?' in *SOE*, ch. 8.

_____ *Essays on Philosophical Method*. London: Macmillan, 1971.

_____ *Freedom and Reason*. OUP, 1963.

_____ 'Freedom of the will', *SPAS* 25 (1951), 202–16.

_____ *Moral Thinking*. OUP, 1981.

_____ 'Ontology in ethics', in Honderich, ed., *MO*, ch. 3.

_____ 'Pain and evil', in *Essays on the Moral Concepts*. London: Macmillan, 1972, ch. 6. From *SPAS* 38 (1964), 91–106.

_____ 'Rawls' theory of justice', in Daniels, ed., *RR*, ch 4. From *PQ* 23 (1973), 144–55 and 241–51.

_____ *Sorting Out Ethics*. OUP, 1997.

_____ 'The argument from received opinion', in *EPM*, ch. 7.

_____ *The Language of Morals*. OUP, 1952.

_____ 'The practical relevance of philosophy', in *EPM*, ch. 6.

Harris, J. A., *Of Liberty and Necessity: The Free-Will Debate in Eighteenth-Century British Philosophy*. OUP, 2005.

Harrison, B., *Henry Fielding's Tom Jones: The Novelist as Moral Philosopher*. London: Chatto and Windus, 1975.

Harrison, J., *Hume's Moral Epistemology*. OUP, 1976.

_____ *Hume's Theory of Justice*. OUP, 1981.

Harrison, R., *Bentham*. RKP, 1983.

Hart, H. L. A., 'Are there any natural rights?', *PR* 64 (1955), 175–91.

_____ 'Legal and moral obligation', in Melden, ed., *EMP* 82–107.

_____ *Punishment and Responsibility*. OUP, 1968.

_____ 'Rawls on liberty and its priority', in Daniels, ed., *RR*, ch. 10. From *University of Chicago Law Review*, 40 (1973), 534–55.

_____ 'The Ascription of Responsibility and Rights', *PAS* 49 (1948–9), 171–94.

_____ *The Concept of Law*. OUP, 1961.

_____ and Hampshire, S. N., 'Decision, intention, and certainty', *M* 67 (1958), 1–12.

_____ and Honoré, A. M., *Causation in the Law*. OUP, 1959.

Hartley, D., *Observations on Man, Part 1*, 2nd edn. London: Johnson, 1791 (1st edn., 1749).

Hawkins, J., 'The Life of Johnson', in *The Works of Samuel Johnson*, 11 vols., ed. Hawkins. London: Buckland et al., 1787, vol. i.

Hayward, F. H., *The Ethical Philosophy of Sidgwick*. London: Swan Sonnenschein, 1901.

Hazlitt, W., *Complete Works*, 21 vols., ed. P. P. Howe. London: Dent, 1951.

_____ *Essays on the Principles of Human Action*. London: Miller, 1835 (1st pub. 1805).

_____ 'On reason and imagination', *CW* xii 44–53.

_____ 'Self-love and benevolence', *CW* xx 160–86.

_____ 'The new school of reform', *CW* xii 179–95.

_____ *The Spirit of the Age*. OUP, 1954 (orig. pub. 1825).

Hegel, G. W. F., *Enzyklopädie der philosophischen Wissenschaften im Grundrisse* = *Werke*, viii–x.

_____ *Lectures on the History of Philosophy, 1825–6. Volume II: Greek Philosophy*, tr. R. F. Brown et al. OUP, 2006.

———*Lectures on the History of Philosophy*, 3 vols., tr. E. S. Haldane and F. H. Simson. RKP, 1892. ET of *Vorlesungen über die Geschichte der Philosophie* = *Werke*, xviii–xx.

———*Logic*, 3rd edn., tr. W. Wallace. OUP, 1975 (1st edn., 1873). ET of *Werke*, viii.

———*Phenomenology of Spirit*, tr. A. V. Miller. OUP, 1977. ET of *Phänomenologie des Geistes* = *Werke*, iii.

———*Philosophy of Mind*, tr. W. Wallace and A. V. Miller, rev. and ed. M. J. Inwood. OUP, 2007. ET of *Werke*, x.

———*Philosophy of Right*, tr. H. B. Nisbet, ed. A. W. Wood. CUP, 1991. ET of *Grundlinien der Philosophie des Rechts* = *Werke*, vii.

———*Philosophy of Right*, tr. T. M. Knox. OUP, 1942.

———*Science of Logic*, tr. A. V. Miller. London: Allen and Unwin, 1969. ET of *Wissenschaft der Logik* = *Werke*, v–vi.

———*Werke*, 20 vols. Frankfurt: Suhrkamp, 1969–71.

Heidegger, M., *Basic Writings*, tr. D. F. Krell. New York: Harper and Row, 1977.

———*Being and Time*, tr. J. Macquarrie and E. Robinson. New York: Harper and Row, 1962. ET of *Sein und Zeit*. Tübingen: Niemeyer, 1929.

———'Letter on humanism', in *Basic Writings*, D. F. Krell tr. (New York: Harper and Row, 1977), Ch. 5.

———*Nietzsche* (ET), 4 vols., ed. D. F. Krell. San Francisco: Harper and Row, 1978–87.

———'Overcoming metaphysics', in Wolin, ed., *HC*, ch. 4.

———'The self-assertion of the German university', in Wolin, ed., *HC*, ch. 1.

Heinaman, R. E., ed., *Aristotle and Moral Realism*. London: UCL Press, 1995.

———'Rationality, eudaimonia, and kakodaimonia in Aristotle', *Phr.* 38 (1993), 31–56.

Heliodorus, *in EN.* CAG xix.

Hempel, C. G. *Aspects of Scientific Explanation*. New York: Free Press, 1965.

Henrich, D., 'Hutcheson und Kant', *KS* 49 (1957–8), 49–69.

———'Ueber Kants frühste Ethik', *KS* 54 (1963), 404–31.

Henry of Ghent, *Quodlibet I*, ed. R. Macken. Leuven: Leuven UP, 1979.

———*Quodlibet IX*, ed. R. Macken. Leuven: Leuven UP, 1983.

———*Quodlibetal Questions on Free Will*, tr. R. J. Teske. Milwaukee: Marquette UP, 1993.

———*Summa (Quaestiones Ordinariae), art. xxxv–xl*, ed. G. A. Wilson. Leuven: Leuven UP, 1994.

Henson, R. G., 'What Kant might have said: moral worth and the overdetermination of dutiful action', *PR* 88 (1979), 39–54.

Herman, B., 'On the value of acting from the motive of duty', in *PMJ*, ch. 1. From *PR* 90 (1981), 359–82.

———*The Practice of Moral Judgment*. HUP, 1993.

———'Training to autonomy: Kant and the question of moral education', in A. O. Rorty, ed., *Philosophers on Education*. RKP, 1998, ch. 19.

Herodotus, *Historiae*. OCT.

Hill, T. E., *Autonomy and Self-Respect*. CUP, 1991.

———*Dignity and Practical Reason*. Ithaca, NY: Cornell UP, 1992.

———'Self-respect reconsidered', in *ASR*, ch. 2. Also in Dillon, ed., *DCSR*, ch. 7. From *Tulane Studies in Philosophy*, 31 (19850, 129–37.

———'Servility and self-respect', in *ASR*, ch. 1. From *Monist*, 57 (1973), 87–104.

———'The hypothetical imperative', in *DPR*, ch. 1. From *PR* 82 (1973), 429–50.

Hissette, R., *Enquête sur les 219 articles condamnés à Paris le 7 mars 1277*. Louvain: Publications Universitaires, 1977.

Hobbes, T., *Body, Man, and Citizen: Selections from Thomas Hobbes*, ed. R. S. Peters. New York: Collier Books, 1962.

———*De Cive* (Latin and English), 2 vols., ed. H. Warrender OUP, 1983 (orig. pub. Latin 1642; English 1651).

Hobbes, T., *De Cive*, tr. M. Silverthorne. CUP, 1998.

_____ *De Cive*. ed. S. P. Lamprecht. New York: Appleton-Century-Crofts, 1949.

_____ *De Homine = OL* ii. Excerpt in Hobbes, *MC*, ed. Gert.

_____ *English Works*, 11 vols., ed. W. Molesworth London: Bohn, 1839–45.

_____ *Hobbes and Bramhall on Liberty and Necessity*, ed. V. C. Chappell. CUP, 1999.

_____ *Leviathan*, ed. E. M. Curley. Indianapolis: Hackett, 1994 (orig. pub. London, 1651).

_____ *Leviathan*, tr. F. Tricaud. Paris: Sirey, 1971.

_____ *Man and Citizen*, ed. B. Gert. Garden City, NY: Doubleday, 1972.

_____ *Opera Latina*, 5 vols., ed. W. Molesworth. London: Bohn, 1839–45.

_____ *The Elements of Law: Human Nature and De Corpore Politico*, ed. J. C. A. Gaskin. OUP, 1994. Cited as *EL*.

Hochstrasser, T. J., 'Conscience and reason; the natural law theory of Barbeyrac', *HJ* 36 (1993), 289–308.

_____ *Natural Law Theories in the Early Enlightenment*. CUP, 2000.

Hoffman, J., and Rosenkrantz, G., 'Hard and soft facts', in Fischer, ed., *GFF*, ch. 7. From *PR* 93 (1984), 419–34.

Hoistad, R., *Cynic Hero and Cynic King*. Lund: Bloms, 1948.

Holden, H. A., ed., *Cicero: De Officiis, 6th edn*. CUP, 1886.

Holopainen, T. M., *William Ockham's Theory of the Foundations of Ethics*. Helsinki: Luther-Agricola-Society, 1991.

Homer, *Odyssey*. OCT.

Honderich, T., ed., *Morality and Objectivity*. London: RKP, 1985.

Hooker, R., *Of the Laws of Ecclesiastical Polity*, in *The Works of Richard Hooker*, 7th edn., 3 vols., ed. J. Keble. OUP, 1888.

_____ *Of the Laws of Ecclesiastical Polity*, in *The Works of Richard Hooker*, 6 vols. ed. W. S. Hill Binghamton: Center for Mediaeval and Renaissance Texts and Studies, 1993.

Hope, V., ed., *Philosophers of the Scottish Enlightenment*. Edinburgh: Edinburgh UP, 1984.

Hopkins, J., and Richardson, H., trs., [Anselm] *Truth, Freedom, and Evil: Three Philosophical Dialogues*. New York: Harper & Row, 1967.

Hudson, S. D., *Human Character and Morality*. RKP, 1986.

Hudson, W. D., *Reason and Right*. London: Macmillan, 1970.

Hume, D., *A Letter from a Gentleman to his Friend in Edinburgh*, ed. E. C. Mossner and J. V. Price. Edinburgh: Edinburgh UP, 1967.

_____ *A Treatise of Human Nature*, ed. D. F. Norton and M. J. Norton. OUP, 2000.

_____ *Dialogues concerning Natural Religion*, ed. N. Kemp Smith. Edinburgh: Nelson, 1947.

_____ *Essays, Moral, Political, and Literary*. OUP, 1903.

_____ *Inquiry concerning Human Understanding*, ed. C. W. Hendel. Indianapolis: Bobbs-Merrill, 1955.

_____ *Inquiry concerning Human Understanding*, ed. T. L. Beauchamp. OUP, 1999.

_____ *Inquiry concerning Human Understanding* and *Inquiry concerning the Principles of Morals*, 2nd edn., ed. L. A. Selby-Bigge. OUP, 1902.

_____ *Inquiry concerning the Principles of Morals*, ed. T. L. Beauchamp. OUP, 1998.

_____ *New Letters of David Hume*, ed. R. Klibansky and E. C. Mossner OUP, 1954.

_____ *The Letters of David Hume*, 2 vols., ed. Greig, J. Y. T. OUP, 1932.

Hunter, G., 'Reply to Professor Flew', in Chappell, ed., *Hume*, 287–90. From *Phil.* 38 (1963), 182–4.

Hurka, T., 'Moore in the middle', *E* 113 (2003), 599–628.

Hursthouse, R., *On Virtue Ethics*. OUP, 1999.

_____ 'The virtuous agent's reasons: a reply to Bernard Williams', in Heinaman, ed., *AMR*, 24–33.

Hutcheson, F., *An Essay on the Nature and Conduct of the Passions and Affections. With Illustrations on the Moral Sense*, ed. A. Garrett. Indianapolis: Liberty Fund, 2002 (reprint of 1st edn. (1728), with later variants).

_____ *A Short Introduction to Moral Philosophy*, 2nd edn. Glasgow: Foulis, 1753 (1st edn., 1747). ET of *MPIC*.

_____ *A System of Moral Philosophy*, 2 vols. Glasgow: Foulis, 1755.

_____ *An Inquiry into Moral Good and Evil*, in *Inquiry into the Original of our Ideas of Beauty and Virtue*, ed. W. Leidhold. Indianapolis: Liberty Fund, 2004 (repr. of 2nd edn. (1726) with later variants).

_____ *An Inquiry into Moral Good and Evil*, in *Inquiry into the Original of our Ideas of Beauty and Virtue, 5th edn.* London: Ware, 1753 (1st edn., 1725).

_____ *Illustrations on the Moral Sense*, ed. B. Peach. HUP, 1971. From *An Essay on the Nature and Conduct of the Passions and Affections. With Illustrations on the Moral Sense*, 3rd edn. London: A. Ward et al., 1742 (1st edn., 1728).

_____ *Moralis Philosophiae Institutio Compendiaria*, 2nd edn. Dublin: McKenzie, 1787 (1st edn., 1742).

_____ *On Human Nature* (= *Reflections on our common systems of morality* and the *Inaugural Lecture on the social nature of man*), ed. T. Mautner. CUP, 1993.

_____ *Thoughts on Laughter, and Observations on the Fable of the Bees in Six Letters*. Repr. Bristol: Thoemmes, 1989. Orig. Glasgow: Foulis, 1758.

Huxley, T. H., *Evolution and Ethics*. London: Macmillan, 1894.

Hylton, P. W., *Russell, Idealism, and the Emergence of Analytic Philosophy*. OUP, 1990.

Ignatius Loyola, *Spritiual Exercises: Rules for Thinking with the Church*, in G. E. Ganss, ed., *Ignatius of Loyola: The Spiritual Exercises and Selected Works*. NY: Paulist, 1991.

Ingham, M. E., 'Scotus and the moral order', *ACPQ* 67 (1993), 127–50.

Inwood, B., *Ethics and Human Action in Early Stoicism*. OUP, 1985.

_____ 'Goal and target in Stoicism', *JP* 83 (1986), 547–56.

_____ 'Hierocles: theory and argument', *OSAP* 2 (1984), 151–83.

_____ *Reading Seneca*. OUP, 2005.

_____ 'Seneca and psychological dualism', in *RS*, ch. 2. From J. Brunschwig and M. Nussbaum, eds., *Passions and Perceptions*. CUP, 1993, ch. 6.

Inwood, M. J., 'Hegel, Plato, and Greek "Sittlichkeit"', in Z. A. Pelczynski, ed., *The State and Civil Society: Studies in Hegel's Political Philosophy*. CUP, 1984, 40–54.

Irwin, T. H., ed., *Aristotle: Nicomachean Ethics, 2nd edn.* Indianapolis: Hackett, 1999.

_____ *Aristotle's First Principles*. OUP, 1988.

_____ 'Ethics as an inexact science: Aristotle's ambitions for moral theory', in B. Hooker and M. Little, eds., *Moral Particularism*. OUP, 2000, ch. 5.

_____ *Plato's Ethics*. OUP, 1995.

_____ 'Stoic and Aristotelian conceptions of happiness', in Schofield and Striker, *NN*, ch. 8.

Jackson, F., 'Cognitivism, a priori deduction, and Moore', *E* 113 (2003), 557–75.

_____ *From Metaphysics to Ethics*. OUP, 1998.

Jackson, R., 'Bishop Butler's Refutation of Psychological Hedonism', *Phil.* 18. (1943), 114–39.

Jaffa, H. V., *Thomism and Aristotelianism*. Chicago: U of Chicago Press, 1952.

James VI and I, *Political Writings*, ed. J. P. Sommerville. CUP, 1994.

James, S., *Passion and Action*. OUP, 1997.

Janaway, C., *Beyond Selflessness: Reading Nietzsche's Genealogy*. OUP, 2007.

_____ *Self and World in Schopenhauer's Philosophy*. OUP, 1989.

Jansen, C., *Augustinus, seu doctrina Sancti Augustini de humanae naturae sanitate, aegritudine, medicina . . .* Rouen: Berthelin, 1652.

Jerome, *Commentaria in Ezechielem*, in *PL* xxv.

Johnson, T., *An Essay on Moral Obligation: With a View towards Settling the Controversy concerning Moral and Positive Duties*. London: Knapton, 1731.

Johnston, M., 'Dispositional theories of value', *SPAS* 63 (1989), 139–74.

Jones, A. H. M., 'The Hellenistic age', *Past and Present*, 27 (1964), 3–22.

Jones, E. E. C., 'Green's account of Aristotle's ethics', *Hibbert Journal*, 1 (1903), 302–5.

Jones, P., *Hume's Sentiments*. Edinburgh: Edinburgh UP, 1982.

Jonsen, A. R., and Toulmin, S. E., *The Abuse of Casuistry: A History of Moral Reasoning*. UCP, 1988.

Jordan, G. J., *The Reunion of the Churches; a Study of G. W. Leibniz and his Great Attempt*. London: Constable, 1927.

Jordan, M. D., 'Ideals of scientia moralis', in MacDonald and Stump, eds., *AMT* 79–97.

Joseph, H. W. B., *Introduction to Logic, 2nd edn*. OUP, 1916.

——— *Some Problems in Ethics*. OUP, 1931.

Josephus, *Antiquitates Judaicae*. Loeb.

Justin Martyr, *First Apology*, in *PG* vi.

Kames, Lord (Henry Home), *Essays on the Principles of Morality and Natural Religion*, 3rd edn., ed. M. C. Moran. Indianapolis: Liberty Fund, 2005. Orig. pub. Edinburgh: John Bell, 1779 (1st edn., 1751; 2nd edn., 1758).

Kamm, F. M., *Intricate Ethics: Rights, Responsibilities and Permissible Harms*. OUP, 2007.

Kant, I., *Critique of Practical Reason*, 3rd edn., tr. L. W. Beck. New York: Macmillan, 1993.

——— *Critique of Practical Reason* (cited as *KpV*), in Kant, *PP*.

——— *Critique of Pure Reason*, tr. P. Guyer and A. Wood. CUP, 1997.

——— *Critique of the Power of Judgment*, tr. P. Guyer and E. Matthews. CUP, 2000.

——— *Foundations of the Metaphysics of Morals*, tr. L.W. Beck. Indianapolis: Bobs-Merrill, 1959.

——— *Gesammelte Schriften*. Berlin: Reimer (later vols. De Gruyter), 1902–.

——— *Groundwork of the Metaphysics of Morals* (cited as *G*), in Kant, *PP*.

——— *Grundlegung zur Metaphysik der Sitten*, ed. K. Vorländer. Hamburg: Meiner, 1965.

——— 'Idea for a universal history from a cosmopolitan point of view', in L.W. Beck, ed., *Kant: On History*. Indianapolis: Bobbs-Merrill, 1963.

——— *Kritik der praktischen Vernunft*, ed. K. Vorländer. Hamburg: Meiner, 1906.

——— *Kritik der reinen Vernunft*, ed. R. Schmidt. Hamburg: Meiner, 1956.

——— *Kritik der Urteilskraft*, 7th edn., ed. K. Vorländer. Hamburg: Meiner, 1990.

——— *Lectures on Ethics*, tr. P. L. Heath. CUP, 1997.

——— *Metaphysics of Morals* (cited as *MdS*), in Kant, *PP*.

——— *Metaphysik der Sitten*, ed. K. Vorländer. Hamburg: Meiner, 1922.

——— 'On a supposed right to lie from philanthropy', in Kant, *PP*.

——— *Practical Philosophy*, tr. M. J. Gregor. CUP, 1996.

——— *Prolegomena to any Future Metaphysics*, ed. L. W. Beck. Indianapolis: Bobbs-Merrill, 1950.

——— *Religion and Rational Theology*, tr. A. W. Wood and G. di Giovanni. CUP, 1996.

——— 'What is enlightenment?', in Kant, *PP* 17–22.

Kautsky, K., *Ethics and the Materialist Conception of History*, 4th edn. ET. Chicago: Kerr, 1913.

Kavka, G. S., *Hobbesian Moral and Political Theory*. PUP, 1986.

Kemp Smith, N., *The Philosophy of David Hume*. London: Macmillan, 1941.

Kenny, A. J. P., *Action, Emotion, and Will*. RKP, 1963.

——— 'Aquinas on Aristotelian happiness', in MacDonald and Stump, eds., *AMT* 15–27.

——— *Aristotle on the Perfect Life*. OUP, 1992.

——— ed., *Aquinas: A Collection of Critical Essays*. London: Macmillan, 1970.

——— *The Aristotelian Ethics*. OUP, 1978.

Kent, B. D., 'Transitory vice', *JHP* 27 (1989), 199–223.

——— *Virtues of the Will*. CUAP, 1995.

Keynes, J. N., *The Scope and Method of Political Economy*, 4th edn. London: Macmillan, 1917 (1st edn., 1891).

Kidd, I. G., 'Poseidonius on emotion', in A. A. Long, ed., *Problems in Stoicism*. London: Athlone, 1971, ch. 9.

Kierkegaard, S., *Either/Or*, tr. H. V. Hong and E. H. Hong. PUP, 1987.

———— *Fear and Trembling; Repetition*, tr. H. V. Hong and E. H. Hong. PUP, 1983.

———— *The Works of Love*, tr. H. V. Hong and E. H. Hong. PUP, 1995.

Kilcullen, J., 'Natural law and will in Ockham', in K. Haakonssen and U. Thiel, eds., *Reason, Will, and Nature (History of Philosophy Yearbook* 1). Canberra, 1993, 1–25.

Kindstrand, J. F., ed., *Bion of Borysthenes*. Uppsala: Almquist and Wiksell, 1976.

King, P., 'Aquinas on the passions', in MacDonald and Stump, eds., *AMT* 101–32.

———— 'Ockham's ethical theory', in Spade, ed., *CCO*, ch. 10.

King, W., *An Essay on the Origin of Evil*, 3rd edn., tr. E. Law, with essay by J. Gay. Cambridge: Thurlbourn, 1739 (1st edn., 1731).

Kirk, K. E., *Conscience and its Problems*. London: Longmans, 1927.

———— *Some Principles of Moral Theology*. London: Longmans, 1920.

———— *The Vision of God*, 2nd edn. London: Longmans, 1932.

Kirk, L., *Richard Cumberland and Natural Law*. Cambridge: James Clarke and Co., 1987.

Kirwan, C. A., tr., ed., *Aristotle: Metaphysics IV, V, VI*, 2nd edn. OUP, 1992.

Kittel, G., ed., *Theological Dictionary of the New Testament*, 10 vols. Grand Rapids, Mich.: Eerdmans, 1965–76.

Kivy, P., *The Seventh Sense: Francis Hutcheson and Eighteenth-Century British Aesthetics*, 2nd edn. OUP, 2003.

Klibansky, R., and Mossner, E. C., eds., *New Letters of David Hume*. OUP, 1954.

Knox, R. A., *Enthusiasm*. OUP, 1950.

Knuuttila, S., *Emotions in Ancient and Mediaeval Philosophy*. OUP, 2004.

Korkman, P., *Barbeyrac and Natural Law*, doctoral thesis. Helsinki, 2001.

Korolec, J. B., 'Free will and free choice', in Kretzmann et al., eds., *CHLMP*, ch. 32.

Korsgaard, C. M., *Creating the Kingdom of Ends*. CUP, 1996.

———— 'From duty and for the sake of the noble', in Engstrom and Whiting, ed., *RDH*, ch. 7.

———— 'Kant's Formula of Humanity', in *CKE*, ch. 4. From *KS* 77 (1986), 183–202.

———— 'Morality as freedom', in *CKE*, ch. 6. From Y. Yovel, ed., *Kant's Practical Philosophy Reconsidered*. Dordrecht: Kluwer, 1989, 23–48.

———— 'The normativity of instrumental reason', in Cullity and Gaut, eds., *EPR*, ch. 8.

———— *The Sources of Normativity*. CUP, 1996.

Kosch, M., *Freedom and Reason in Kant, Schelling, and Kierkegaard*. OUP, 2006.

Kraut, R., *Aristotle on the Human Good*. PUP, 1989.

———— 'In defence of the grand end', *E* 103 (1993), 361–74.

———— 'Reason and justice in the *Republic*', in E. N. Lee, A. P. D.Mourelatos, and R. M. Rorty, eds., *Exegesis and Argument*. Assen: Van Gorcum, 1973, ch. 11.

———— 'Return to the cave', in Fine, ed., *Plato, ii*, ch. 9.

———— 'Two conceptions of happiness', *PR* 88 (1979), 167–97.

Kraye, J., ed., *Cambridge Translations of Renaissance Philosophical Texts*, 2 vols. CUP, 1997.

Kretzmann, N., 'A general problem of creation', in MacDonald, ed., *BG*, ch. 8.

———— 'A particular problem of creation', in MacDonald, ed., *BG*, ch. 9.

———— 'Goodness, knowledge, and indeterminacy in the philosophy of Thomas Aquinas', *JP* 80 (1983), 631–49.

———— *The Metaphysics of Creation*. OUP, 1999.

———— *The Metaphysics of Theism*. OUP, 1997.

———— Kenny, A., and Pinborg, J., eds., *Cambridge History of Later Mediaeval Philosophy*. CUP, 1982.

———— and Stump. E. S., 'Being and Goodness', in MacDonald, ed., *BG*, ch. 4.

Kuhn, T. S. *The Structure of Scientific Revolutions*, 2nd edn. Chicago: U. of Chicago Press, 1970.

983

Kusakawa, S., *The Transformation of Natural Philosophy: The Case of Philip Melanchthon*. CUP, 1995.

Laboucheix, H., *Richard Price as Moral Philosopher and Political Theorist*. Oxford: Voltaire Foundation, 1982.

La Bruyère, J., *Les Caractères*, ed. R. Garapon. Paris: Garnier, 1962 (orig. pub. 1688).

Lactantius, *Divinae Institutiones*, ed. S. Brandt. Vienna: Tempsky, 1890 (= *CSEL* xix 1).

Laird, J., *A Study in Moral Theory*. London: Allen & Unwin, 1926.

―――― *Hobbes*. London: Benn, 1934.

―――― 'Hobbes on Aristotle's *Politics*', *PAS* 43 (1942–3), 1–20.

―――― *Hume's Philosophy of Human Nature*. London: Methuen, 1932.

Lambinus, D., tr., *Ethica Nicomachea*, in *Aristotelis Opera, iii*, ed. I. Bekker. Berlin: Reimer, 1870.

Lamont, W. D., *Introduction to Green's Moral Philosophy*. London: Allen & Unwin, 1934.

Lampe, G. W. H., ed., *A Patristic Greek Lexicon*. OUP, 1961.

Langford, C. H., 'The notion of analysis in Moore's philosophy', in Schilpp, ed., *PGEM*, ch. 12.

Langton, R., *Kantian Humility: Our Ignorance of Things in Themselves*. OUP, 1998.

Larmore, C. E., *Patterns of Moral Complexity*. CUP, 1987.

―――― *The Morals of Modernity*. CUP, 1996.

Law, Edmund: *see* King.

Lawrence, G. L., 'Aristotle on the ideal life', *PR* 102 (1993), 1–34.

Lear, G. R., *Happy Lives and the Highest Good*. PUP, 2004.

Lear, J. D., *Aristotle: The Desire to Understand*. CUP, 1988.

Lecky, W. E. H., *History of European Morals from Augustus to Charlemagne*, 2 vols. London: Longmans, 1920 (orig. pub. 1869).

Le Mahieu, D. L., *The Mind of William Paley*. Lincoln, Nebr.: U of Nebraska Press, 1976.

Leff, G., *Gregory of Rimini*. Manchester: Manchester UP, 1961.

Lehrer, K., *Thomas Reid*. RKP, 1989.

Leibniz, G. W., *Die philosophischen Schriften*, 7 vols., ed. C. I. Gerhardt. 2nd edn. Berlin: Weidmann, 1875–90.

―――― *New Essays on Human Understanding*, tr. P. Remnant and J. Bennet. CUP, 1996.

―――― *Oeuvres*, 7 vols., ed. L. A. Foucher de Careil. 2nd edn. Paris: Didot, 1867–75.

―――― 'On nature itself', in *PLP*, 498–508.

―――― *Opera Omnia*, 6 vols., ed. L. Dutens. Geneva: De Tournes, 1768.

―――― 'Opinion on the Principles of Pufendorf', in Dutens, *00* iv 275–84. Tr. in Riley, *PW* 64–75.

―――― *Philosophical Letters and Papers*, 2nd edn., tr. L. E. Loemker. Dordrecht: Reidel, 1969.

―――― *Political Writings, 2nd edn.*, tr. P. Riley, 2nd edn. CUP, 1988.

―――― *Textes Inédits*, ed. G. Grua. Paris: Presses Universitaires de France, 1948.

―――― *Theodicy*, tr. E. M. Huggard. RKP, 1951.

Leiter, B., 'Nietzsche and the morality critics', *E* 107 (1997), 250–85.

―――― *Nietzsche on Morality*. RKP, 2002.

―――― 'Perspectivism in Nietzsche's *Genealogy of Morals*', in Schacht, ed., *NGM*, ch. 19.

Lesses, G., 'Virtue and fortune in Stoic moral theory', *OSAP* 7 (1989), 95–127.

Lewis, C. I., *An Analysis of Knowledge and Valuation*. La Salle, Ill.: Open Court, 1946.

―――― 'Chisholm and empiricism', in Swartz, ed., *PSK* 354–63. From *JP* 45 (1948), 517–24.

―――― *The Ground and Nature of the Right*. NY: Columbia UP, 1955.

Lewis, D., 'Dispositional theories of value', *SPAS* 63 (1989), 113–37.

Lewis, H. D., 'Does the good will define its own content? A Study of Green's *Prolegomena*', *E* 58 (1948), 157–79.

Lewy, C., 'G. E. Moore on the naturalistic fallacy', in Strawson, ed., *SPTA*, 134–46. Also in Ambrose and Lazerowitz, eds., *GEMER* 292–303. From *PBA* 50 (1964), 251–62.

Lightfoot, J. B., *St Paul's Epistle to the Philippians, 6th edn*. CUP, 1881.

Lilla, S. R. C., *Clement of Alexandria*. OUP, 1971.

Lincoln, A., *Some Political and Social Ideas of English Dissent, 1763–1800*. CUP, 1938.

Lind, J., *Three Letters to Dr Price, containing Remarks on his Observations on the Nature of Civil Liberty . . . , by a Member of Lincoln's Inn*. London: Payne, Sewell, and Elmsley, 1776.

Lipsius, J., *De Constantia*. Antwerp: Plantin, 1515 (repr. Hildesheim: Olms, 2002; also repr. in *Opera Omnia*, v).

_____ *Manuductio ad Stoicam Philosophiam, 2nd edn*. Antwerp: Plantin, 1510 (repr. in *Opera Omnia*, v).

_____ *Opera Omnia*, 7 vols. Antwerp: Plantin, 1614.

Lloyd-Jones, H., *The Justice of Zeus*, 2nd edn. UCP, 1983.

Locke, D., *A Fantasy of Reason: The Life and Thought of William Godwin*. RKP, 1980.

Locke, J., *An Essay concerning Human Understanding*, ed. A. C. Fraser. OUP, 1894.

_____ *An Essay concerning Human Understanding*, 4th edn., ed. P. H. Nidditch. OUP, 1975 (orig. pub. 1700).

_____ *Essays on the Law of Nature*, ed. W. von Leyden. OUP, 1954 (3rd imp. 1988).

_____ *The Correspondence of John Locke*, 8 vols., ed. E. S. de Beer. OUP, 1976–89.

Loeb, L. E., *From Descartes to Hume*. Ithaca, NY: Cornell UP, 1981.

Lombard, Peter, *Sententiae*, 3rd edn., 2 vols., ed. Collegium S. Bonaventurae. Grottaferrata: Editiones Collegii S Bonaventurae ad Claras Aquas, 1971.

Long, A. A., *Epictetus: A Stoic and Socratic guide to life*. OUP, 2002.

_____ 'Morals and values in Homer', *Journal of Hellenic Studies*, 90 (1970), 121–39.

_____ ed., *Problems in Stoicism*. London: Athlone, 1971.

_____ 'Socrates and Hellenistic philosophy', in *SS*, ch. 1. From *CQ* 38 (1988), 150–71.

_____ 'Stoic eudaimonism', in *SS*, ch. 8. From *PBACAP* 4 (1989), 77–101.

_____ 'Stoic psychology', in Algra et al., eds., *CHHP*, ch. 17.

_____ *Stoic Studies*. CUP, 1996.

_____ 'The Socratic legacy', in Algra et al., eds., *CHHP*, ch. 19.

_____ and Sedley, D. N., *The Hellenistic Philosophers*, 2 vols. CUP, 1987.

Lottin, O., *Etudes de Morale*. Gembloux: Duculot, 1961.

_____ *Psychologie et morale aux XIIe et XIIIe siècles*, 6 vols. Louvain and Gembloux, 1942–60.

Lucretius, *De Rerum Natura*. OCT.

Luther, M., *De Servo Arbitrio*, in *Luthers Werke in Auswahl*, iii. ET: *The Bondage of the Will*, tr. J. I. Packer and O. R. Johnson. London: James Clarke, 1957.

_____ *Lectures on Romans*, tr. W. Pauck. London: SCM Press, 1961.

_____ *Luthers Werke in Auswahl, 6th edn.*, 8 vols., ed. O. Clemen. Berlin: De Gruyter, 1966. Cited as 'C'.

_____ *Luther's Works*, 56 vols., ed. J. Pelikan and H. T. Lehmann. St Louis: Concordia, 1955–76. Cited as *Works*.

_____ *Selections*, ed. J. Dillenberger. Garden City, NY: Doubleday, 1961.

Lyons, D., *In the Interest of the Governed: A Study in Bentham's Philosophy of Utility and Law*. OUP, 1973.

_____ 'Mill's theory of justice', in *RWMMT*, ch. 3. From A. I. Goldman and J., Kim, eds., *Values and Morals*. Dordrecht: Reidel, 1978, 1–20.

_____ 'Mill's theory of morality', in *RWMMT*, ch. 2. From *Nous*, 10 (1976), 101–20.

_____ 'Nature and soundness of the contract and coherence arguments', in Daniels, ed., *RR*, ch. 7.

_____ *Rights, Welfare, and Mill's Moral Theory*. OUP, 1994.

Lyons, W., *Emotion*. CUP, 1980.

Mabbott, J. D., 'Interpretations of Mill's *Utilitarianism*', in Schneewind, ed., *Mill*, 190–8. From *PQ* 6 (1956), 115–20.

_____ 'Is Plato's *Republic* utilitarian?' in Vlastos, ed., *Plato*, ii, ch. 4.

McAdoo H. R., *The Spirit of Anglicanism: A Survey of Anglican Theological Method in the Seventeenth Century*. London: Black, 1965.

McAdoo H. R., *The Structure of Caroline Moral Theology*. London: Longmans, 1949.

Macbeath, A., *Experiments in Living: A Study of the Nature and Foundation of Ethics or Morals in the Light of Recent Work in Social Anthropology*. London: Macmillan, 1951.

McCabe, M. M., 'Extend or identify: two Stoic accounts of altruism', in Salles, ed., *MSEAT*, ch. 16.

MacDonald, S. C., 'Aquinas' libertarian account of free will', *RIP* 52 (1998), 309–28.

—— 'Aquinas' ultimate ends: a reply to Grisez', *American Journal of Jurisprudence*, 46 (2001), 39–48.

—— ed., *Being and Goodness*. Ithaca, NY: Cornell UP, 1991.

—— 'The relation between being and goodness', in MacDonald, ed., *BG* 1–28.

MacDonald, S. C., 'Ultimate ends in practical reasoning: Aquinas' Aristotelian moral psychology and Anscombe's fallacy', *PR* 100 (1991), 31–66.

—— and Stump, E. S., eds., *Aquinas' Moral Theory*. Ithaca, NY: Cornell UP, 1999.

McDowell, J. H., 'Are moral requirements hypothetical imperatives?', in *MVR*, ch. 4. From *SPAS* 52 (1978), 15–29.

—— 'Comments on "Some rational aspects of incontinence"', *SJP* 27 (1989), supp. 89–102.

—— 'Might there be external reasons?', in *MVR*, ch. 5. From Altham and Harrison, eds., *WME*, ch. 5.

—— *Mind, Value, and Reality*. HUP, 1998.

—— 'Some issues in Aristotle's moral psychology', in *MVR*, ch. 3. From *Monist*, 62 (1979), 331–50.

—— 'The role of eudaimonia in Aristotle's Ethics', in *MVR*, ch. 1. From *Proceedings of the African Classical Associations*, 15 (1980), 1–14.

—— 'Two sorts of naturalism', in *MVR*, ch. 9. From R. Hursthouse, G. Lawrence, and W. Quinn, eds., *Virtues and Reason: Philippa Foot and Moral Theory*. OUP, 1995, ch. 6.

—— 'Values and secondary qualities', in *MVR*, ch. 7. From Honderich, ed., *MO*, ch. 6.

Mace, C. A., 'Emotions and the category of passivity', *PAS* 62 (1961–2), 135–42.

McGrade, A. S., 'Natural law and moral omnipotence', in Spade, ed., *CCO*, ch. 12.

—— *The Political Thought of William Ockham*. CUP, 1974.

McGrath, A. E., *Iustitia Dei*, 2nd edn. CUP, 1998.

McGuire, J. E., 'Boyle's conception of nature', *JHI* 33 (1972), 523–42.

Machiavelli, N., *Discourses*, 2 vols., tr. L. J. Walker. RKP, 1950.

—— *Il Principe*, ed. L. A. Burd. OUP, 1891.

—— *Opere*,vols. 1–2, ed. R. Rinaldi. Turin: Unione Tipografico-Editrice Torinese, 1999.

—— *The Prince*, ed. J. B. Atkinson. Indianapolis: Bobbs-Merrill, 1976.

McHugh, J. H., and Callan, C. J., *Moral Theology: A Complete Course*, 2 vols. New York: Wagner, 1929.

MacIntyre, A. C., *After Virtue*. London: Duckworth, 1981.

—— *Dependent Rational Animals*. Chicago: Open Court Press, 1999.

—— 'Hume on is and ought', in Chappell, ed., *Hume*, 240–64. From *PR* 68 (1959), 451–68.

—— 'Once more on Kierkegaard', in J. J. Davenport and A. Rudd, eds., *Kierkegaard after MacIntyre*. Chicago: Open Court, 2001, ch. 14.

—— 'The idea of a social science', in *Against the Self-Images of the Age*. London: Duckworth, 1971, ch. 19. From *SPAS* 41 (1967), 95–114.

—— *Whose Justice? Which Rationality?* London: Duckworth, 1988.

Mackie, J. L., 'A refutation of morals', *AJP* 24 (1946), 77–90.

—— Critical Notice of Prior, *LBE*, *AJP* 28 (1950), 114–24.

—— *Ethics: Inventing Right and Wrong*. Harmondsworth: Penguin, 1977.

—— *Hume's Moral Theory*. RKP, 1980

Mackintosh, J., *Dissertation on the Progress of Ethical Philosophy: Chiefly During the Seventeenth and Eighteenth centuries*, 4th edn., with preface by W. Whewell. Edinburgh: Black, 1872 (1st pub. 1836).

McNaughton, D. A., 'Butler on benevolence', in Cunliffe, ed., *JBMRT*, ch. 13.

_____ *Moral Vision: An Introduction to Ethics*. Oxford: Blackwell, 1988.

McNeill, J. T., 'Natural law in the theology of the Reformers', *Journal of Religion*, 26 (1946), 168–82.

_____ 'Natural law in the thought of Luther', *Church History*, 10 (1941), 211–27.

McNeilly, F. S., 'Egoism in Hobbes', *PQ* 16 (1966), 193–206.

McPherson, T. H., 'The development of Bishop Butler's ethics', *Phil.* 23 (1948), 317–31, and 24 (1949), 1–22.

McTaggart, J. M. E., *The Nature of Existence*, 2 vols. CUP, 1921–7.

McTighe, K., 'Socrates on desire for the good and the involuntariness of wrongdoing', in Benson, ed., *EPS*, ch. 15. From *Phr.* 29 (1984), 193–236.

Mahoney, J., *The Making of Moral Theology*. OUP, 1987.

Mandeville, Bernard, *The Fable of the Bees*, ed. F. B. Kaye. OUP, 1924.

Mannebach, E., *Aristippi et Cyrenaicorum Fragmenta*. Leiden: Brill, 1961.

Manser, A., and Stock, G., eds., *The Philosophy of F. H. Bradley*. OUP, 1984.

Marcus Aurelius, *Meditations*, 2 vols., ed. A. S. L. Farquharson. OUP, 1944.

Martens, J. W., 'Romans 2:14–16: a Stoic reading', *New Testament Studies*, 40 (1994), 55–67.

Martens, P., ' "You shall love": Kant, Kierkegaard, and the interpetation of Matthew 22:39', in R. L. Perkins, ed., *International Kierkegaard Commentary: Works of Love*. Macon, GA: Mercer UP, 1999, ch. 3.

Martineau, J., *Essays, Reviews, and Addresses*, iii. London: Longmans, 1891.

_____ *Types of Ethical Theory*, 2nd edn. OUP, 1886 (1st edn., 1885).

Martinich, A. P., *The Two Gods of Leviathan*. CUP, 1992.

Marx, K., 'Critique of Hegel's philosophy of the state', selections in *WYM* 151–202.

_____ 'Economic and philosophical manuscripts', in *WYM* 283–337.

_____ 'On the Jewish question', in *WYM* 216–48.

_____ *Writings of the Young Marx on Philosophy and Society*, ed. L. D. Easton and K. H. Guddat. Garden City, NY: Doubleday, 1967.

_____ and Engels, F., *The German Ideology*, ed. C. J. Arthur. New York: International Publishers, 1970.

Mates, B., *Stoic Logic, 2nd edn.* UCP, 1961.

Mather, C., *Manuductio ad Ministerium*. Republished by J. Ryland. London: Dilly, 1781.

Maurer, A. A., et al., eds., *Thomas Aquinas 1274–1974: Commemorative Studies*, 2 vols. Toronto: Pontifical Institute of Mediaeval Studies, 1974.

Maurer, W., *Historical Commentary on the Augsburg Confession*. ET. Philadelphia: Fortress, 1986.

Mausbach, J., *Die Ethik des Hl. Augustins*, 2 vols. Freiburg: Herder, 1909.

Mautner, T., see Hutcheson.

Maximus Confessor, *PG* xci.

Maxwell, J., 'A Treatise concerning the Obligation, Promulgation, and Observance of the Law of Nature'. Appendix to his translation of Cumberland.

_____ 'Concerning the City, or Kingdom, of God in the Rational World, and the Defects in Heathen Deism' and 'Concerning the Imperfectness of the Heathen Morality'. Two introductory essays bound with his translation of Cumberland.

Meijering, E. P., 'The Fathers in Calvinist orthodoxy: systematic theology', in Backus, ed., *RCFW*, ch. 22.

Melanchthon, P., *Apology for the Augsburg Confession*, in *Die Symbolischen Bücher der Evangelisch-Lutherischen Kirche*, ed. J. F. Müller. Gütersloh: Bertelsmann, 1876. Tr. in T. G. Tappert, ed., *The Book of Concord*. Philadelphia: Fortress Press, 1959.

_____ *Loci Communes* (1521), in *MWA* ii 1. Tr. W. Pauck, in *Melanchthon and Bucer*. London: SCM Press, 1969.

_____ *Melanchthons Werke in Auswahl*, 7 vols., ed. R. Stupperich. Gütersloh: Bertelsmann, 1951–75.

_____ *Philosophiae moralis epitome* (1546), in *MWA* iii.

Melden, A. I., ed., *Essays in Moral Philosophy*. Seattle: University of Washington Press, 1958.

Mercer, C., 'Leibniz, Aristotle, and ethical knowledge', in R. Pozzo, ed., *The Impact of Aristotelianism on Modern Philosophy*. CUAP, 2004, ch. 5.

Mercken, H. P. F., *The Greek Commentaries on the Nicomachean Ethics of Aristotle, i.* Leiden: Brill, 1973.

Meyer, S. S., *Aristotle on Moral Responsibility.* Oxford: Blackwell, 1993.

_____ 'Aristotle, teleology, and reduction', *PR* 101 (1992), 791–825.

_____ 'Moral responsibility: Aristotle and after', in Everson, ed., *ECAT*, ch. 9.

Mill, J. S., *An Examination of Sir William Hamilton's Philosophy*, in *CW* ix.

_____ *Autobiography*, in *CW* i.

_____ 'Bentham', in *CW* x.

_____ 'Blakey's History of Moral Science', in *CW* x.

_____ *Collected Works*, 33 vols., J. M. Robson, gen. ed. Toronto: U of Toronto Press, 1963–91.

_____ *Dissertations and Discussions: Political, Philosophical, and Historical*, 4 vols. London: Parker, 1859–1875. (Vols. iii–iv published by Longmans.)

_____ 'Nature', in *CW* x.

_____ *On Liberty*, in *CW* xviii.

_____ 'Remarks on Bentham's Philosophy', in *CW* x.

_____ 'Sedgwick's Discourse' in *CW* x.

_____ 'The later speculations of M. Comte', in *CW* x.

_____ *Utilitarianism*, in *CW* x.

_____ 'Whewell on moral philosophy', in *CW* x.

Mill, James, *Fragment on Mackintosh*. London: Baldwin and Craddock, 1835.

Millar, A., 'Butler on God and human nature', in Cunliffe, ed., *JBMRT*, ch. 14.

_____ 'Following nature', *PQ* 38 (1988), 165–85.

Miller, J., and Inwood, B., eds., *Hellenistic and Modern Philosophy*. CUP, 2003.

Miller, P. N., *Defining the Common Good: Empire, Religion, and Philosophy in Eighteenth-Century Britain.* CUP, 1994.

Millican, P., ed., *Reading Hume on Human Understanding*. OUP, 2002.

Mintz, S. I., *The Hunting of Leviathan*. CUP, 1962.

Mitsis, P. T., *Epicurus' Ethical Theory*. Ithaca, NY: Cornell UP, 1988.

_____ 'Epicurus on death and the duration of life', *PBACAP* 4 (1989), 303–22.

Molhuysen, P. C., 'The first edition of Grotius' *De Iure Belli ac Pacis*', *Bibliotheca Visseriana*, 5 (1925), 101–49.

Molina, Luis de, *Liberi Arbitrii cum Gratia . . . Concordia*, ed. J. Rabeneck. Madrid, 1953.

_____ *On Divine Foreknowledge: Part IV of the Concordia*, tr. A. J. Freddoso. Ithaca, NY: Cornell UP, 1988.

Monro, D. H., *Godwin's Moral Philosophy*. OUP, 1953.

Montaigne, M., *Essais*, 3 vols., ed. M. Rat. Paris: Garnier, 1952.

Moo, D. J., *Romans*. Grand Rapids, Mich.: Eerdmanns, 1996.

Moore, G. E., 'A reply to my critics', in Schilpp, ed., *PGEM* 535–677.

_____ *Ethics*. London: Williams and Norgate, 1912 (repr., OUP, 1912).

_____ *Principia Ethica*, 2nd edn., ed. T. W. Baldwin. CUP, 1993 (1st edn., 1903).

_____ 'The conception of intrinsic value', in *PE* 280–98. From *Philosophical Studies*. RKP, 1922, ch. 8.

Moore, J., 'Hume and Hutcheson', in Stewart and Wright, eds., *HHC*, ch. 2.

_____ and Silverthorne, M., 'Natural sociability and natural rights in the moral philosophy of Gerschom Carmichael', in Hope, ed., *PSE*, ch. 1.

Moore, M. S., 'Good without God', in George ed., *NLLM*, ch. 12.

Moran, R. A., *Authority and Estrangement*. PUP, 2001.

More, H., *Enchiridion Ethicum*. ET. New York: Facsimile text society, 1930 (orig. pub. 1690.)

Moreau, J., *La Construction de L'idéalisme Platonicien*. Paris: Boivin & Cie., 1939.

Mossner, E. C., *The Life of David Hume*, 2nd edn. OUP, 1980.

——— and Ross, I. S., eds., *Correspondence of Adam Smith*. OUP, 1977.

Muirhead, J. H., *Rule and End in Morals*. OUP, 1932.

Murphy, N. R., *The Interpretation of Plato's Republic*. OUP, 1951.

Nagel, T., 'Hobbes's Concept of Obligation', *PR* 68(1959), 68–83.

——— 'Moral luck', in *MQ*, ch. 3. From *SPAS* 50 (1976), 137–51.

——— *Mortal Questions*. CUP, 1979.

——— 'Rawls on justice', in N. Daniels, ed., *RR*, ch. 1. From *PR* 82 (1973), 220–34.

——— 'The fragmentation of value', in *MQ*, ch. 9. From H. T. Engelhardt and D. Callahan, eds., *Knowledge, Value, and Belief*. Hastings-on-Hudson, NY: Hastings Institute, 1977, 279–94.

——— *The Possibility of Altruism*. OUP, 1970.

——— *The View from Nowhere*. OUP, 1986.

——— 'War and massacre', in *MQ*, ch. 5. From *PPA* 1 (1972), 123–44.

Nehamas, A., *Nietzsche: Life as Literature*. HUP, 1985.

Nemesius, *De Natura Hominis*. BT.

Nestle, W., 'Friedrich Nietzsche und die griechische Philosophie', *Neue Jahrbücher für das Klassische Altertum*, 29 (1912), 554–84.

Neuhouser, F. W., *Fichte's Theory of Subjectivity*. CUP, 1990.

——— *Foundations of Hegel's Social Theory*. HUP, 2000.

——— Review of Wood, *HET*, *JP* 89 (1992), 316–20.

Nicholas, B., *Introduction to Roman Law*. OUP, 1962.

Nietzsche, F., *Beyond Good and Evil*, tr. W. Kaufmann. New York: Vintage, 1966.

——— *Birth of Tragedy, and the Case of Wagner*, tr. W. Kaufmann. New York Vintage, 1967.

——— 'Die vorplatonischen Philosophen', in *Gesammelte Werke* (Musarionausgabe, Musarion Verlag München, 1921), iv.

——— *Human, All Too Human*, tr. R. J. Hollingdale. CUP, 1996.

——— *On the Advantage and Disadvantage of History for Life*, tr. P. Preuss. Indianapolis: Hackett, 1980.

——— *On the Genealogy of Morality*, tr. C. Diethe. CUP, 1994.

——— *On the Genealogy of Morals and Ecce Homo*, tr. W. Kaufmann. New York: Vintage, 1969.

——— *Philosophy in the Tragic Age of the Greeks*, tr. M. Cowan. Chicago: Regenry, 1962.

——— *The Portable Nietzsche*, tr. W. Kaufmann. New York: Viking, 1954.

——— *The Will To Power*, tr. W. Kaufmann and R. J. Hollingdale. New York: Vintage, 1968.

——— *Twilight of the Idols*, in Kaufmann, tr., *PN* 463–564.

——— *Werke*, 3 vols., ed. K. Schlechta. 9th edn. Munich: Hanser, 1981–2.

Norton, D. F., *David Hume: Common-Sense Moralist, Sceptical Metaphysician*. PUP, 1982.

——— and Stewart-Robertson, J. C., 'Thomas Reid on Adam Smith's theory of morals', *JHI* 41 (1980), 381–98; 45 (1984), 309–21.

Nowell-Smith, P. H., *Ethics*. Harmondsworth: Penguin, 1954.

Nussbaum, M. C., 'Aristotle on human nature and the foundations of ethics', in Altham and Harrison, eds., *WME*, ch. 6.

——— 'Pity and mercy: Nietzsche's Stoicism', in Schacht, ed., *NGM*, ch. 9.

——— *The Therapy of Desire*. PUP, 1994.

O'Donovan, O. M. T, *The Problem of Self-Love in Saint Augustine*. New Haven: Yale UP, 1980.

——— 'Usus and fruitio in Augustine, *De Doctrina Christiana* I'. *Journal of Theological Studies*, 33 (1982), 361–97.

Oakeshott, M. B., 'Introduction', in *Hobbes: Leviathan*, ed. M. Oakeshott. Oxford: Blackwell, 1946. Repr. in Oakeshott, *RP*.

——— *Rationalism in Politics and Other Essays*, expanded edn. Indianapolis: Liberty Press, 1991.

Oakley, F., 'Mediaeval theories of natural law: William of Ockham and the significance of the voluntarist tradition', in *Natural Law, Conciliarism, and Consent*. London: Variorum, 1984, ch. 15. From *Natural Law Forum*, 6 (1961), 65–83.

—— 'The absolute and ordained power of God in sixteenth-and seventeenth-century theology', *JHI* 59 (1998), 437–61.

Obbink, D., *Philodemus on Piety, Part 1*. OUP, 1996.

Oberman, H. A., 'Duns Scotus, nominalism, and the Council of Trent', in *DR*, ch. 9. From J. Ryan and B. M. Bonansea, eds., *Scotus 1265–1965*. CUAP, 1965, 311–44.

—— *The Dawn of the Reformation*. Edinburgh: T&T Clark, 1986.

—— *The Harvest of Medieval Theology: Gabriel Biel and the Late Medieval Nominalism*. HUP, 1963.

Ockham, W., *A Letter to the Friars Minor and Other Writings*, tr. J. Kilcullern, ed. J. Killcullen and A. S. McGrade. CUP, 1995.

—— *Dialogus*, ed. J. Kilcullen et al. British Academy, forthcoming (draft at <http://www.britac.ac.uk>).

—— *Opera Theologica et Philosophica*, 17 vols. St Bonaventure: Franciscan Institute, 1974–88.

—— *Quodlibetal Questions*, 2 vols., tr. A. J. Freddoso and F. E. Kelly. New Haven: Yale UP, 1991.

Offler, H.S., 'Three modes of natural law in Ockham', *FS* 37 (1977), 207–18.

Ogden, C. K., and Richards, I. A., *The Meaning of Meaning: A Study of the Influence of Language upon Thought and of the Science of Symbolism*. London: Kegan Paul, 1923.

Olafson, F. A., *Ethics and Twentieth Century Thought*. Englewood Cliffs, NJ: Prentice-Hall, 1973.

—— 'Heidegger à la Wittgenstein, or "Coping" with Professor Dreyfus', *Inquiry*, 37 (1994), 45–64.

—— *Heidegger and the Ground of Ethics: A Study of Mitsein*. CUP, 1998.

—— *Principles and Persons: An Ethical Interpretation of Existentialism*. Baltimore: Johns Hopkins UP, 1967.

Olivi, Petrus Johannes, *Quaestiones in Secundum Librum Sententiarum*, 3 vols., ed. B. Jansen. Quaracchi: Coll. S. Bonaventurae, 1924.

O'Neill, O., *Constructions of Reason*. CUP, 1989.

Opie, Amelia, *Adeline Mowbray*. Poole: Woodstock Books, 1995 (repr. of 1805 edn.).

Origen, *Commentaria in Evangelium secundum Matthaeum*. PG xiii.

—— *Contra Celsum*, 5 vols., ed. M. Bonnet. Paris: Cerf, 1967.

—— *De Principiis*, 5 vols., ed. H. Crouzel and M. Simonetti. Paris: Cerf, 1978.

Osler, M. J., ed., *Atoms, Pneuma, and Tranquillity*. CUP, 1991.

Oxford Dictionary of National Biography, 61 vols., ed. H. G. C. Matthews and B. Harrison. OUP, 2004.

Oxford Latin Dictionary, ed. P. G. W. Glare. OUP, 1982.

Pagden, A., ed., *The Languages of Political Theory in Early-Modern Europe*. CUP, 1987.

Paley, W., *Principles of Moral and Political Philosophy*, ed. D. L. Le Mahieu. Indianapolis: Liberty Fund, 2002 (orig. pub. 1785).

Palladini, F., *Discussioni seicentesche su Samuel Pufendorf*. Bologna: Il Mulino, 1978.

—— *Samuel Pufendorf, Discepolo di Hobbes*. Bologna: Il Mulino, 1990.

Palmer, R. R., *Catholics and Unbelievers in Eighteenth Century France*. PUP, 1939.

Parfit, D. A., 'Normativity', in *Oxford Studies in Metaethics*, 1 (2006), 325–80.

—— *Reasons and Persons*. OUP, 1984.

Park, R., *Hazlitt and the Spirit of the Age*. OUP, 1971.

Parker, S., *A Demonstration of the Divine Authority of the Law of Nature and of the Christian Religion*. London: Royston, 1681. Cited as *DA*.

Parkin, J., *Science, Religion, and Politics in Restoration England*. Woodbridge: Boydell Press, 1999.

Pasnau, R. A., *Thomas Aquinas on Human Nature*. CUP, 2002.

Passmore, J. A., *Hume's Intentions*, 2nd edn. London: Duckworth, 1968.

—— *Ralph Cudworth: An Interpretation*. CUP, 1951.

—— 'The moral philosophy of Hobbes', *AJP* 19 (1941), 31–43.

Paton, H. J., *The Categorical Imperative*, 5th edn. London: Hutchinson, 1965 (1st edn., 1947).

—— 'The emotive theory of ethics', *SPAS* 22 (1948) 107–26.

Patrick, S. [?], *A Brief Account of the New Sect of the Latitude-Men*. Augustan Reprint Society no. 100. Los Angeles, 1963 (orig. pub. 1662).

Patrides, C. A., ed.., *The Cambridge Platonists*. HUP, 1970.

Patrologiae Graecae Cursus Completus, 161 vols., ed. J.-P. Migne. Paris: Migne, 1857–66.

Patrologiae Latinae Cursus Completus, 221 vols., ed. J.-P. Migne. Paris: Migne, 1844–55.

Pattison, M., 'Religious thought in England', in *Essays*, 2 vols., ed. H. Nettleship. OUP, 1889, vol. ii, ch. 13.

Pegis, A. C., 'Necessity and liberty: an historical note on St Thomas Aquinas', *New Scholasticism*, 15 (1941), 18–45.

Penelhum, T., *Butler*. RKP, 1985.

—— *Hume*. London: Macmillan, 1975.

—— *Themes in Hume*. OUP, 2000.

Penner, T., 'Desire and power in Socrates', *Aperion*, 24 (1991), 147–201.

—— 'Thought and desire in Plato', in Vlastos, ed., *Plato, ii*, ch. 6.

Perry, J. 'The importance of being identical', in A. O. Rorty, ed., *The Identities of Persons*. UCP, 1976, ch. 3.

Peters, R. S., 'Emotions and the category of passivity', *PAS* 62 (1961–2), 117–34.

Philo, *Works*, tr. F. H. Colson and G. H. Whitaker. Loeb. Works cited: *De Posteritate Cain* (vol. ii); *De Cherubim* (ii); *De Ebrietate* (iii); *Quis Rerum Divinarum Heres* (iv); *Legum Allegoriae* (i); *De Plantatione* (iii).

Philp, M., *Godwin's Political Justice*. London: Duckworth, 1986.

Photius, *Bibliotheca*, 9 vols., ed. R. Henry. Paris: Les Belles Lettres, 1959–91.

Piché, D., *La condamnation parisienne de 1277*. Paris: Vrin, 1999.

Pinkard, T., *German Philosophy 1760–1860: The Idealist Tradition*. CUP, 2002.

Pippin, R. B., *Kant's Theory of Form*. New Haven: Yale UP, 1982.

Pitcher, G. W., 'On approval', *PR* 67 (1958) 195–211.

Plamenatz, J. P., *Consent, Freedom, and Political Obligation*. OUP, 1938.

—— 'In search of Machiavellian Virtù', in A. Parel, ed., *The Political Calculus: Essays on Machiavelli's Philosophy*. Toronto: U of Toronto Press, 1972, ch. 7.

—— *Karl Marx's Philosophy of Man*. OUP, 1977.

—— 'Mr Warrender's Hobbes', in Brown, ed., *HS*, ch. 4 (1). From *PS* 51(1957), 295–308.

Plato, OCT. Works cited: *Apology; Charmides; Clitopho; Crito; Euthydemus; Euthyphro; Gorgias; Hippias Major; Laches; Laws; Meno; Phaedo; Phaedrus; Philebus; Protagoras; Republic; Symposium; Theaetetus; Timaeus*.

Platts, M., 'Moral Reality', in Sayre-McCord, ed., *EMR*, ch. 12. From *Ways of Meaning*. RKP, 1979, ch. 10.

Plotinus, *Enneades*. OCT.

Plutarch, *Moralia*. Loeb. Works cited: *Adversus Colotem* (vol. xiv); *De Communibus Notitiis* (xiii); *Non Posse Suaviter Vivere secundum Epicurum* (xiv); *De Sera Numinis Vindicta* (vii); *De Stoicorum Repugnantiis* (xiii); *De Tranquillitate Animi* (vi); *De Virtute Morali* (vi).

Polybius, *Historiae*. BT.

Poncius, Joannes, *Philosophiae ad mentem Scoti cursus integer*. Lyons: Huguetan & Barbier, 1722.

Popper, K. R., *The Logic of Scientific Discovery*. London: Hutchinson, 1968 (1st German edn., 1934).

—— *The Open Society and its Enemies*, 5th edn., 2 vols. RKP, 1966 (1st edn., 1945).

Porphyry, *De Abstinentia*, 3 vols., tr. J. Bouffartigue et al. Paris: Les Belles Lettres, 1977–95.

Poseidonius, *Fragments*, 4 vols., ed. L. Edelstein, and I. G. Kidd. CUP, 1972–99. Cited as EK.

Potts, T. C., *Conscience in Mediaeval Philosophy*. CUP, 1980.

Prentice, R., 'The contingent element governing the natural law on the last seven precepts of the Decalogue, according to Duns Scotus', *Antonianum*, 42 (1967), 259–92.

Price, A. W., *Love and Friendship in Plato and Aristotle*. OUP, 1989.

Price, H. H., Critical Notice of Ross, *RG*, *M* 40 (1931), 341–54.

———*Perception,* 2nd edn. London: Methuen, 1950.

Price, R., 'A discourse on the love of our country', in D. O. Thomas, ed., *Political Writings*, CUP, 1991, 176–96.

———*A Review of the Principal Questions in Morals, corrected and enlarged 3rd edn.*, ed. D. D. Raphael. OUP, 1974 (orig. 3rd edn., 1787; 1st edn., 1758).

———and Priestley, J., *A Free Discussion of the Doctrines of Materialism and Philosophical Necessity, in a Correspondence between Dr Price and Dr Priestley.* London: J. Johnson and T. Cadell, 1778.

Prichard, H. A., 'Does moral philosophy rest on a mistake', in *MODI*, ch. 1. From *M* 21 (1912), 21–37.

———'Duty and ignorance of fact', in *MODI*, ch. 2. From *PBA* 18 (1932), 67–92.

———'Duty and interest', in *MODI*.

———*Knowledge and Perception*. OUP, 1950.

———'Moral obligation', in *MODI*, ch. 5.

———*Moral Obligation and Duty and Interest*. OUP, 1968 (*Moral Obligation*, orig. 1949; *Duty and Interest*, orig. 1928).

Priestley, F. E. L., 'Introduction', in edn. of Godwin, *EPJ*, iii 1–114.

Prior, A. N., 'Eighteenth-century writers on twentieth-century subjects', *AJP* 24 (1946), 168–82.

———*Logic and the Basis of Ethics*. OUP, 1949.

———'The meaning of good', *AJP* 22 (1944), 170–4.

Pufendorf, S., *De iure naturae et gentium*, tr. C. H. Oldfather and W. A. Oldfather. OUP, 1934.

———*De iure naturae et gentium*. Amsterdam: Hoogenhuysen, 1688 (1st edn., Lund, 1672).

———*De iure naturae et gentium*. ET: *Of the Law of Nature and Nations*, tr. B. Kennett. London: Walthoe, 4th edn., 1729.

———*De officio hominis et civis juxta legem naturalem*. Lund, 1682. Repr. OUP, 1927. ET: *On the Duty of Man and Citizen according to Natural Law*, ed. J. Tully, tr. M. Silverthorne. CUP, 1991.

———*Elementa jurisprudentiae universalis*, tr. W. A. Oldfather. OUP, 1931 (orig. pub. Cambridge, 1672).

———*Eris Scandica*, in *GW* v.

———*Gesammelte Werke*, 5 vols., ed. W. Schmidt-Biggemann. Berlin: Akademie-Verlag, 1996–.

———*Les Devoirs de l'Homme et du Cityoen*, 4th edn., tr. J. Barbeyrac. Amsterdam: Pierre de Coup, 1718.

———*Specimen Controversiarum*, in *GW* v.

Quasten, J., et al., *Patrology*, ET, 4 vols. Westminster, Md.: Christian Classics, 1986 (1st pub. 1950–78).

Quine, W. V., *Ontological Relativity and Other Essays*. New York: Columbia UP, 1969.

———'Two dogmas of empiricism', in *From a Logical Point of View*, 2nd edn. New York: Harper and Row, 1963, ch. 2.

Quinn, P. L., 'Kierkegaard's Christian ethics', in Hannay and Marino, eds., *CCK*, ch. 14.

Quinton, A. M., 'Absolute idealism', in *Thoughts and Thinkers*. London: Duckworth, 1982, ch. 18. From *PBA* 57 (1971), 303–29.

———*Utilitarian Ethics*. London: Macmillan, 1973.

Rachels, J., ed., *Ethical Theory*. OUP, 1998.

Radcliffe, E. S., 'Hutcheson's perceptual and moral subjectivism', *HPQ* 3 (1986), 407–21.

Rae, J., *Life of Adam Smith*. Repr., with introd. by J. Viner. New York: Kelly, 1965 (1st pub. 1895).

Railton, P., 'Alienation, consequentialism, and the demands of morality', in *Facts, Values, and Norms*. CUP, 2003, ch. 6. From *PPA* 13 (1984), 134–71.

Rankin, O. S., 'Ecclesiastes', in Buttrick et al., eds., *IB* v.

Raphael, D. D., 'Bishop Butler's view of conscience', *Phil.* 24 (1949), 219–38.

———ed., *British Moralists, 1650–1800*, 2 vols. OUP, 1969.

—— 'Hume's critique of ethical rationalism', in W. B. Todd, ed., *Hume and the Enlightenment*. Edinburgh: Edinburgh UP, 1974, 14–29.

—— 'Obligations and rights in Hobbes', *Phil.* 37 (1962), 345–52.

—— 'The impartial spectator', in Skinner and Wilson, eds., *EAS*, ch. 4.

—— *The Impartial Spectator*. OUP, 2007.

—— *The Moral Sense*. OUP, 1947.

Rashdall, H., 'Professor Sidgwick's utilitarianism', *M* 10 (1885), 200–26.

—— *Theory of Good and Evil*, 2 vols., 2nd edn. OUP, 1924 (1st edn., 1907).

Rawls, J., 'A Kantian conception of equality', in *CP*, ch. 13. From *Cambridge Review*, 96 (1975), 94–9.

—— *A Theory of Justice, 2nd edn*. HUP, 1999 (1st edn., 1971).

—— *Collected Papers*, ed. S. Freeman. HUP, 1999.

—— 'Justice as fairness', in *CP*, ch. 3. From *PR* 67 (1958), 164–94.

—— *Justice as Fairness: A Restatement*, ed. E. Kelly. HUP, 2001.

—— 'Justice as fairness: political, not metaphysical', in *CP*, ch. 18. From *PPA* 14 (1985), 223–52.

—— 'Kantian constructivism in moral theory', in *CP*, ch. 16. From *JP* 77 (1980), 515–72.

—— *Lectures on the History of Moral Philosophy*. HUP, 2000.

—— 'Outline of a decision procedure for ethics', in *CP*, ch. 1. From *PR* 60 (1951), 177–97.

—— *Political Liberalism*, 2nd edn. New York: Columbia UP, 1996 (1st edn., 1993).

—— 'Some reasons for the maximin criterion', in *CP*, ch. 11. From *American Economic Review*, 64 (1974), 141–6.

—— 'The idea of public reason revisited', in *CP*, ch. 26. From *University of Chicago Law Review*, 64 (1997), 765–807.

—— 'The independence of moral theory', in *CP*, ch. 15. From *Proceedings and Addresses of the American Philosophical Association*, 48 (1975), 5–22.

—— 'Themes in Kant's moral philosophy', in *CP*, ch. 23. From Förster, ed., *KTD*, 81–113.

—— 'Two concepts of rules', in *CP*, ch. 2. From *PR* 64 (1955), 3–32.

Raz, J., ed., *Practical Reasoning*. OUP, 1978.

Reath, A., 'Hedonism, heteronomy, and Kant's principle of happiness', *Pacific Philosophical Quarterly* 70 (1989), 42–72.

—— 'Legislating for a realm of ends', in Reath et al., eds., *RHE*, 214–39.

—— 'Legislating the moral law', *Nous*, 28 (1994), 435–64.

—— Herman, B., and Korsgaard, C., eds., *Reclaiming the History of Ethics*. CUP, 1997.

Reeder, J., ed., *On Moral Sentiments: Contemporary Responses to Adam Smith*. Bristol: Thoemmes, 1997.

Regan, T., *The Case for Animal Rights*. UCP, 1983.

Reginaldus, Valerius, *Praxis fori pœnitentialis ad directionem confessarii in usu sacri sui muneris*, 2nd edn., 2 vols. Mainz, 1617.

Reich, K., 'Kant and Greek ethics', *M* 48 (1939), 338–54 and 446–63.

Reichert, B. M., ed., *Monumenta Ordinis Fratrum Praedicatorum*, iii. Rome: Generalità, 1898.

Reid, T., 'A Sketch of Dr Smith's Theory of Morals', in Reeder, ed., *MS* 69–88.

—— *Essays on the Active Powers of the Human Mind*, in *Works*, ii.

—— *Works*, 2 vols., ed. W. Hamilton. 6th edn. Edinburgh: Maclachlan and Stewart, 1863.

Reiner, H., *Duty and Inclination: The Fundamentals of Morality Discussed and Redefined with Special Regard to Kant and Schiller*. ET. The Hague: Nijhoff, 1983.

Rickaby, J., *Moral Philosophy*, 4th edn. London: Longmans, 1918.

Rist, J. M., *Epicurus: An Introduction*. CUP, 1972.

Rivers, I., *Reason, Grace, and Sentiment*, 2 vols. CUP, 1991 (vol. 1), 2000 (vol. 2).

Robinson, R., Review of Ross, *Foundations of Ethics*, PR 51 (1942), 417–20.

Robinson, R., 'The emotive theory of ethics', *SPAS* 22 (1948), 79–106.

Rogers, K., 'Aristotle's conception of *to kalon*', *AP* 13 (1993), 355–71.

Roman Missal = *Missale Romanum ex Decreto Sacrosancti Concilii Tridentini*. Rome, 1570.

Rorty, R., *Contingency, Irony, and Solidarity*. CUP, 1989.

Ross, I. S., 'Hutcheson on Hume's Treatise: an unnoticed letter', *JHP* 4 (1966), 69–72.

——— *The Life of Adam Smith*. OUP, 1995.

Ross, W. D., *Aristotle*, 5th edn. London: Methuen, 1949 (1st edn., 1923).

——— *Aristotle's Prior and Posterior Analytics*. OUP, 1949.

——— *Foundations of Ethics*. OUP, 1939.

——— *Plato's Theory of Ideas*. OUP, 1951.

——— *The Right and the Good*. OUP, 1930.

——— 'The Socratic Problem', *Proceedings of the Classical Association*, 30 (1933), 7–24. Repr. in Patzer, A., ed., *Der historische Sokrates*. Darmstadt: Wissenschaftliche Buchgesellschaft, 1987, 225–39.

Rousseau, J.-J., *Basic Political Writings*, tr. D. A. Cress. Indianapolis: Hackett, 1987.

——— *Discourse on the Origin of Inequality*, in *BPW*, tr. Cress.

——— Emile, tr. B. Foxley. London: Dent, 1911.

——— Emile, tr. A. Bloom. New York: Basic Books, 1979 (orig. pub. 1762).

——— *Oeuvres Complètes*, iii–iv, ed. B. Gagnebin and M. Raymond. Paris: Gallimard, 1964, 1969.

——— *Social Contract*, ed. R. Grimsley. OUP, 1972 (orig pub. 1762).

Rowe, C. J., and Schofield, M., eds., *The Cambridge History of Greek and Roman Political Thought*. CUP, 2000.

Rowe, W. L., *Thomas Reid on Freedom and Morality*. Ithaca, NY: Cornell UP, 1991.

Rudd, A., *Kierkegaard and the Limits of the Ethical*. OUP, 1993.

Rupp, E. G., ed., *Luther and Erasmus: Free Will and Salvation*. London: SCM, 1969.

——— *The Righteousness of God: Luther Studies*. London: Hodder & Stoughton, 1953.

Russell, C., 'Divine right in the early seventeenth century', in J. Morrill, P. Slack, and D. Woolf, eds., *Public Duty and Private Conscience in Seventeenth-Century England*. OUP, 1993, ch. 7.

Russell, P., 'A Hobbist Tory: Johnson on Hume', *HS* 16 (1990), 75–9.

——— ' "Atheism" and the title page of Hume's *Treatise*', *HS* 14 (1988), 408–23.

——— *Freedom and Moral Sentiment: Hume's Way of Naturalizing Responsibility*. OUP, 1995.

——— 'Hume's *Treatise* and Hobbes's *Elements of Law*', *JHI* 46 (1985), 51–63.

——— 'Scepticism and natural religion in Hume's *Treatise*', *JHI* 49 (1988), 247–65.

Rutherforth, T., *An Essay on the Nature and Obligation of Virtue*. Cambridge: Thurlbourn, 1744.

Rylaarsdam, J. C., 'Exodus', in Buttrick et al., eds., *IB*, i.

Ryle, G., Review of Heidegger, *Sein und Zeit*, *M* 38 (1929), 355–70.

——— *The Concept of Mind*. London: Hutchinson, 1949.

S.P. *See* Patrick, S.

Saarinen, R., *Weakness of the Will in Mediaeval Thought*. Leiden: Brill, 1994.

Saastamoinen, K., *The Morality of the Fallen Man: Samuel Pufendorf on Natural Law*. Helsinki: SHS, 1995.

Sachs, D., 'A fallacy in Plato's *Republic*?', in Vlastos, ed., *Plato*, ii, ch. 2.

Salisbury, John of, *Metalogicon*, ed. C. C. J. Webb. OUP, 1929.

Salles, R., ed., *Metaphysics, Soul, and Ethics in Ancient Thought*. OUP, 2005.

Sanday, W., and Headlam, A. C., *The Epistle to the Romans*, 3rd edn. Edinburgh: T&T Clark, 1897.

Sanderson, Robert, *De Obligatione Conscientiae*, tr. and ed. W. Whewell. CUP, 1851 (orig. 1647).

——— *Sermons*, 2 vols., ed. R. Montgomery. London: Ball, Arnold, 1841.

Santas, G., *Socrates: Philosophy in Plato's Early Dialogues*. RKP, 1979.

Sartre, J. P., 'The humanism of existentialism', in *Essays in Existentialism*, tr. W. Baskin. New York: Citadel, 1970, 31–62.

Saxenhouse, A. W., 'Hobbes and the beginnings of modern political thought', in N. B. Reynolds and A. W. Saxenhouse, eds., *Hobbes: Three Discourses*. Chicago: U. of Chicago Press, 1995, Part 3.

Sayre-McCord, G., ed., *Essays on Moral Realism*. Ithaca, NY: Cornell UP, 1988.

Scanlon, T. M., 'Contractualism and moral criticism', in Rachels, ed., *ET,* ch. 19. From Sen and Williams, eds., *UB*, 103–28.

—— 'The aims and authority of moral theory', *Oxford Journal of Legal Studies*, 12 (1992), 1–23.

—— *What We Owe to Each Other*. HUP, 1998.

Schacht, R., *Nietzsche*. RKP, 1983.

—— ed., *Nietzsche, Genealogy and Morality*. UCP, 1994.

Schaff, P., *The Creeds of Christendom,* 6th edn., 3 vols. New York: Harper & Row, 1931.

Schilpp, P. A., *Kant's Pre-Critical Ethics*, 2nd edn. Evanston, Ill.: Northwestern UP, 1960 (1st edn., 1938).

—— ed., *The Philosophy of G. E. Moore*. Evanston, Ill.: Northwestern UP, 1942.

Schlick, M., 'Positivism and realism', in A.J. Ayer, ed., *Logical Positivism*, New York: Free Press, 1959, ch. 4 (German orig. in *Erkenntnis*, 3 (1932–3)).

—— *Problems of Ethics*. New York: Prentice-Hall, 1939. ET of *Fragen der Ethik* (1930).

Schmitt, C. B., and Skinner, Q., eds., *The Cambridge History of Renaissance Philosophy*. CUP, 1988.

Schmucker, J., *Die Ursprünge der Ethik Kants*. Meisenheim: Hain, 1961.

Schneewind, J. B., 'Autonomy, obligation, and virtue', in P. Guyer, ed., *Cambridge Companion to Kant*. CUP, 1992, ch. 10.

—— 'Barbeyrac and Leibniz on Pufendorf', in F. Palladini and G. Hartung, eds., *Samuel Pufendorf und die europäische Frühaufklärung*. Berlin: Akademie Verlag, 1996, 181–9.

—— 'Kant and natural law ethics', *E* 104 (1993), 53–74.

—— 'Locke's moral philosophy', in V. C. Chappell, ed., *The Cambridge Companion to Locke*. CUP, 1994, ch. 8.

—— ed., *Mill*, Garden City, NY: Doubleday, 1968.

—— ed., *Moral Philosophy from Montaigne to Kant*, 2nd edn. CUP, 2003.

—— 'Pufendorf's place in the history of ethics', *Synthese*, 72 (1987), 123–55.

—— 'Sidgwick and the Cambridge moralists', in Schultz, ed., *EHS*, ch. 2.

—— *Sidgwick's Ethics and Victorian Moral Philosophy*. OUP, 1977.

—— *The Invention of Autonomy*. CUP, 1997.

—— 'The misfortunes of virtue', *E* 101 (1990), 42–63.

—— 'The use of autonomy in ethical theory', in T. C. Heller, M. Sosna, and D. E. Wellbery eds., *Reconstructing Individualism* (Stanford, Calif.: Stanford UP, 1986), 64–75.

—— 'Voluntarism and the origins of utilitarianism', *Utilitas*, 7 (1995), 87–96.

—— 'Whewell's ethics', *APQ Monograph Series*, 1 (1968), 108–41.

Schofield, M., *Saving the City*. RKP, 1999.

—— 'Social and political thought', in Algra et al., *CHHP*, ch. 22.

—— *The Stoic Idea of the City*. CUP, 1991.

—— 'The syllogisms of Zeno of Citium', *Phr.* 28 (1983), 31–58.

—— 'Who were *hoi duschereis* in Plato, *Philebus* 44a ff?' *Museum Helveticum*, 28 (1971), 2–20, 181.

Schofield, M., and Striker, G., eds., *The Norms of Nature: Studies in Hellenistic Ethics*. CUP, 1986.

Schopenhauer, A., *On the Basis of Morality*, tr. E. F. J. Payne. Indianapolis: Bobbs-Merrill, 1965.

—— *Parerga and Paralipomena*, 2 vols., tr. E. F. J. Payne. OUP, 1974.

—— *Prize Essay on the Freedom of the Will*, tr. E. F. J. Payne. CUP, 1999.

—— *The Will as World and Representation*, 2 vols., tr. E. F. J. Payne. New York: Dover, 1966.

Schrader, G. A., 'Kant and Kierkegaard on duty and inclination', in J. Thompson, ed., *Kierkegaard*. Garden City, NY: Doubleday, 1972, 324–41. From *JP* 65 (1968), 688–701.

Schueler, G. F., 'Modus ponens and moral realism', *E* 98 (1988), 492–500.

Schultz, B., ed., *Essays on Henry Sidgwick*. CUP, 1992.

———— *Henry Sidgwick: The Eye of the Universe*. CUP, 2004.

Scott, D. J., 'Aristotle on well-being and intellectual contemplation', *SPAS* 73 (1999), 225–42.

Scott, J. B., 'Introduction', in *Suarez: Selections from Three Works*, ii. OUP, 1944, 3a–38a.

Scott, R. B. Y., tr. and ed., *Proverbs and Ecclesiastes*. Garden City, NY: Doubleday, 1965.

Scott, W. R., *An Introduction to Cudworth's Treatise concerning Eternal and Immutable Morality*. London: Longmans, 1891. Reprinted in Cudworth, *FW*.

Scott, W. R., *Francis Hutcheson*. CUP, 1900.

Scotus, Duns, *Duns Scotus on the Will and Morality*, tr. A. B. Wolter. CUAP, 1986. Cited as W.

———— *Opera Omnia*, 12 vols., ed. L. Wadding. Lyons: Durand, 1639 (repr. Hildesheim: Olms, 1968). Cited as OO.

———— *Opera Omnia*, ed. C. Balic. Civitas Vaticana: Typis Polyglottis Vaticanis, 1950–. Cited as V.

———— *Opera Philosophica*, 4 vols. St Bonaventure: Franciscan Institute, 1997–2004. Cited as OP.

———— *Quaestiones subtilissimae in Metaphysica Aristotelis* = OP iii–iv. Cited as QM.

Sedgwick, S. S., 'Hegel's critique of the subjective idealism of Kant's ethics', *JHP* 26 (1988), 89–105.

———— 'Metaphysics and morality in Kant and Hegel', in Sedgwick, ed., *RKCP*, ch. 14.

———— 'On the relation of pure reason to content: a reply to Hegel's critique of formalism in Kant's ethics', *PPR* 49 (1988), 59–80.

———— ed., *The Reception of Kant's Critical Philosophy*. CUP, 2000.

Sedley, D. N., 'The ideal of godlikeness', in Fine, ed., *Plato ii*, ch. 14.

Segvic, H., 'No one errs willingly: the meaning of Socratic intellectualism', *OSAP* 19 (2000), 1–45.

Selby-Bigge, L. A., ed., *British Moralists*, 2 vols. OUP, 1897.

Selden, J., *De iure naturali & gentium, iuxta disciplinam Ebraeorum*. London: Bishop, 1640.

———— *Table Talk of John Selden*, ed. F. Pollock. London: Quaritch, 1927.

Sen, A., 'Utilitarianism and welfarism', *JP* 76 (1979), 463–89.

———— and Williams, B.A.O., eds., *Utilitarianism and Beyond*. CUP, 1982.

Seneca, *Dialogi*. OCT. Cited: *De Beata Vita; De Benficiis; De Clementia; De Ira; De Otio*.

———— *Epistulae Morales*. OCT.

Sextus Empiricus, *Adversus Mathematicos*. BT. Cited as M.

———— *Pyrrhoneae Hypotyposes*. BT. Cited as P.

Shaftesbury, Earl of, *Characteristics of Men, Manners, Opinions, Times*, ed. L. E. Klein. CUP, 1999 (orig. pub. 1714).

———— *Characteristics*, 2nd edn., 3 vols. London, 1714.

———— *Inquiry concering virtue or merit*, ed. D. E. Walford. Manchester: Manchester UP, 1977.

———— *Letters to a Student in the University*. London, 1790.

———— Preface to Whichcote, *Select Sermons*. London: 1698.

———— *The Life, Unpublished Letters, and Philosophical Regimen of Anthony, Earl of Shaftesbury*, ed. B. Rand. London: Swan Sonnenschein and Co., 1900. Cited as PR.

———— *The Moralists: A Philosophical Rhapsody*, in *Characteristics*, ed. Klein (orig. pub. London: Wyat, 1709).

Shakespeare, William, *Hamlet*, ed. H. Jenkins. London: Methuen, 1982.

———— *Othello*, ed. M. R. Ridley. London: Methuen, 1962.

Shanley, B. J., 'Aquinas on pagan virtue', *Thomist*, 63 (1999), 553–77.

Sharp, F. C., 'Hume's ethical theory and its critics', *M* 30 (1921), 40–56, 151–71.

———— 'The ethical system of Richard Cumberland and its place in the history of British ethics', *M* 21 (1912), 371–98.

Sharp, T., Letters to Catharine Cockburn, in Cockburn, *Works*, ii.

Sharrock, R., *Hupothesis Ethike*. Oxford: Typis Lichfieldianis, 1660.

Sharvy, R., 'Euthyphro 9d–11b: analysis and definition in Plato and others', *Nous*, 6 (1972), 119–37.

Shaver, R. W., 'Grotius on scepticism and self-interest', *AGP* 78 (1996), 27–47.

_____ *Rational Egoism: A Selective and Critical History*. CUP, 1999.

Sher, R. B., *Church and University in the Scottish Enlightenment*. PUP, 1985.

Sherman, N., *Making a Necessity of Virtue*. CUP, 1997.

_____ *The Fabric of Character: Aristotle's Theory of Virtue*. OUP, 1989.

Shklar, J. N., *Ordinary Vices*. HUP, 1984.

Shoemaker, S., *Identity, Cause, and Mind,* 2nd edn., OUP, 2003.

_____ 'Identity, properties, and causality', in *ICM*, ch. 11. From *Midwest Studies in Philosophy*, 4 (1979), 321–42.

_____ 'Realization and mental causation', in *ICM*, ch. 19. From C. Gillett and B. Loewer, eds., *Physicalism and its Discontents*. CUP, 2001, 74–98.

Shorey, P., 'Plato's ethics', in Vlastos, ed., *Plato, ii*, ch. 1.

_____ *Platonism, Ancient and Modern*. UCP, 1938.

Sidgwick, H., *Essays on Ethics and Method*, ed. M. G. Singer. OUP, 2000.

_____ 'Grote on utilitarianism, I', in *EEM*, ch. 19. From *Cambridge University Reporter*, 8 Feb., 1871, 182–3.

_____ 'Grote on utilitarianism, II', in *EEM*, ch. 20. From *Academy*, 1 Apr., 1871, 197–8.

_____ 'Hedonism and ultimate good', in *EEM*, ch. 11. From *M* 2 (1877), 27–38.

_____ *Miscellaneous Essays and Addresses*. London: Macmillan, 1904.

_____ *Outlines of the History of Ethics*, 3rd edn. London: Macmillan, 1892.

_____ 'Political prophecy and sociology', in *MEA*, ch. 9.

_____ 'Professor Calderwood on intuitionism in morals', in *EEM*, ch. 3. From *M* 1 (1876), 563–6.

_____ Review of Bradley, *Ethical Studies, M* 1 (1876), 545–9. Repr. in *EEM*, ch. 22.

_____ 'Some fundamental ethical controversies', in *EEM*, ch. 6. From *M* 14 (1889), 473–87.

_____ 'The distinction between "is" and "ought"', in *EEM*, ch. 8. From *PAS* 2 (1892), 88–92.

_____ *The Elements of Politics*, 3rd edn. London: Macmillan, 1908.

_____ *The Ethics of Green, Spencer, and Martineau*. London: Macmillan, 1902.

_____ *The Methods of Ethics*, 7th edn. London: Macmillan, 1907 (1st edn., 1874; earlier edns. cited as [1], [2]. etc.).

_____ 'The relation of ethics to sociology', in *MEA*, ch. 11.

Silber, J. R., 'The ethical significance of Kant's Religion', in Kant, *Religion within the Limits of Reason Alone*, ed. T. M. Green, and H. H. Hudson. 2nd edn. New York: Harper & Row, 1960, pp. lxxix–cxxxiv.

_____ 'The importance of the highest good in Kant's Ethics', *E* 73 (1963), 179–97.

Silk, M. S., and Stern, J. P., *Nietzsche on Tragedy*. CUP, 1981.

Silvester, Tipping, *Moral and Christian Benevolence*. London, 1734.

Simons, W., Introduction to Pufendorf, *JNG*, tr. Oldfather.

Simplicius, *in Aristotelis Categorias*. CAG viii.

_____ *in Epicteti Enchiridion*, ed. I. Hadot. Leiden: Brill, 1996.

Singer, M. G., *Generalization in Ethics*. New York: Knopf, 1961.

_____ 'The many methods of Sidgwick's ethics', *Monist*, 58 (1974), 420–48.

Singer, P., *Animal Liberation*. New York: New York Review Books, 1975.

_____ 'Famine, affluence, and morality', *PPA* 1 (1972), 229–43.

_____ 'Sidgwick and reflective equilibrium', *Monist*, 58 (1974), 490–517.

Skinner, A. S., and Wilson, T., eds., *Essays on Adam Smith*. OUP, 1975.

Skinner, Q. R. D., *Machiavelli*. OUP, 1981.

_____ 'Machiavelli on virtù and liberty', in *VP, ii*, ch. 6.

_____ *Reason and Rhetoric in the Philosophy of Hobbes*. CUP, 1996.

_____ *The Foundations of Modern Political Theory*, 2 vols. CUP, 1978.

Skinner, Q. R. D., *Visions of Politics*, 3 vols. CUP, 2002.

Skorupski, J. M. A., *John Stuart Mill*. RKP, 1989.

—— 'Three methods and a dualism', *PBA* 109 (2001), 61–81.

Sleigh, R., Chappell, V., and Della Rocca, M., 'Determinism and human freedom', in Garber and Ayers, eds., *CHSCP*, ch. 33.

Slings, S. R., *Critical Notes on Plato's Politeia*. Leiden: Brill, 2005.

Smith, A., *An Inquiry into the Nature and Causes of the Wealth of Nations*, ed. E. Cannan. London: Methuen, 1925 (1st edn., orig. pub. 1776).

—— *Correspondence of Adam Smith*, ed. E. C. Mossner and I. S. Ross. OUP, 1977.

—— *The Theory of Moral Sentiments*, 6th edn., ed. D. D. Raphael and A. L. Macfie. OUP, 1976 (1st pub. 1790; 1st edn., 1759). (This edn. cited as RM.)

Smith, M., 'Dispositional theories of value', *SPAS* 63 (1989), 89–111.

—— *The Moral Problem*. Oxford: Blackwell, 1994.

Sommerville, J. P., 'From Suarez to Filmer', *HJ* 25 (1982), 525–40.

—— 'John Selden, the law of nature, and the origins of government', *HJ* 27 (1984) 437–47.

Sorabji, R. R. K., *Animal Minds & Human Morals: The Origin of the Western Debate*. London: Duckworth, 1993.

—— 'Aristotle on the role of intellect in virtue', in A. O. Rorty, ed., *Essays on Aristotle's Ethics*. UCP, 1980, ch. 12. From *SPAS* 74 (1973–4), 107–29.

—— *Emotion and Peace of Mind*. OUP, 2000.

Sorell, T., ed., *Cambridge Companion to Hobbes*. CUP, 1996.

Spade, P. V., ed., *Cambridge Companion to Ockham*. CUP, 1999.

Sparks, H. F. D., 'Jerome as biblical scholar', in Ackroyd and Evans, eds., *CHB, i*, 510–41.

Spectator, 5 vols., ed. D. F. Bond. OUP, 1965.

Spinoza, B., *Benedicti de Spinoza Opera*, 4 vols., ed. J. van Vloten and J. P. N. Land. 3rd edn. The Hague: Nijhoff, 1914.

—— *Collected works of Spinoza, i*, tr. E. M. Curley. PUP, 1985.

—— Complete Works, tr. S. Shirley. Indianapolis: Hackett, 2002.

—— *Ethics*, in Spinoza, *CWS*, tr. Curley and *CW*, tr. Shirley.

—— *Tractatus Theologico-Politicus*, in Spinoza, *CW*, tr. Shirley.

St Leger, J., *The 'Etiamsi Daremus' of Hugo Grotius*. Rome, 1962.

Stadter, E., *Psychologie und Metaphysik der menschlichen Freiheit*. Munich: F. Schöningh, 1971.

Stamm, J. J., and Andrew, M. E., *The Ten Commandments in Recent Research*. London: SCM Press, 1967.

Steel, C., 'Thomas Aquinas on preferential love', in T. A. F. Kelly and P. W. Rosemann, eds., *Amor Amicitiae*. Leuven: Peeters, 2004, 437–58.

Stephen, J. F., *Liberty, Equality, Fraternity*, 2nd edn., ed. R. J. White. CUP, 1967 (orig. 1874).

Stephen, L., *History of English Thought in the Eighteenth Century*, 2 vols. London: Smith, Elder, 1876.

—— *The English Utilitarians*, 3 vols. London: Duckworth, 1900.

Stevenson, C. L., *Ethics and Language*. New Haven: Yale UP, 1944.

—— 'The emotive meaning of ethical terms', in *Facts and Values: Studies in Ethical Analysis*. New Haven: Yale UP, 1963, ch. 2. From *M* 46 (1937), 14–31.

Stewart, D., *Dissertation on the Progress of Metaphysical, Ethical, and Political Philosophy*, in *Works, i*.

—— *Outlines of Moral Philosophy*, ed. J. McCosh. London: Allan, 1864.

—— *Philosophy of the Active and Moral Powers*, in *Works, vi*.

—— *Works*, 11 vols., ed. W. Hamilton. Edinburgh: Constable, 1855–60.

Stewart, J., *Kierkegaard's Relations to Hegel Reconsidered*. CUP, 2003.

Stewart, M. A., 'An early critic of Alciphron', *Berkeley Newsletter*, 6 (1982–3), 5–9.

—— *The Kirk and the Infidel*. Inaugural Lecture. Lancaster: Lancaster University, 1995.

_____ 'The Stoic legacy in the early Scottish enlightenment', in Osler, ed., *APT*, ch. 14.

_____ 'Two species of philosophy', in Millican, ed., *RHHU*, ch. 2.

_____ and Wright, J. P., eds., *Hume and Hume's Connexions*. University Park, PA: Penn State UP, 1995.

Stewart, Z., 'Democritus and the Cynics', *Harvard Studies in Classical Philology*, 63 (1958), 179–91.

Stobaeus, *Anthologia*, 5 vols., ed. C. Wachsmuth and O. Hense. Berlin: Weidmann, 1884–1912.

_____ *Eclogae,* in *Anthologia.*

Stone, M. W. F., 'Henry of Ghent on freedom and human action', in G. Guldentops and C. Steel, eds., *Henry of Ghent and the Transformation of Scholastic Thought.* Leuven: Leuven UP, 2003, 201–25.

Stratton-Lake, P., ed., *Ethical Intuitionism: Re-evaluations.* OUP, 2002.

Strawson, G., *Freedom and Belief.* OUP, 1986.

Strawson, P. F., 'Ethical intuitionism', *Phil.* 24 (1949), 23–33.

_____ 'Freedom and resentment', in *FR*, ch. 1. From *PBA* 48 (1962), 187–211.

_____ *Freedom and Resentment and Other Essays.* London: Methuen, 1974.

_____ *Introduction to Logical Theory.* London: Methuen, 1952.

_____ 'On referring', *M* 59 (1950), 320–44.

_____ 'Social morality and individual ideal', in *FR,* ch. 2. From *Philosophy,* 36 (1961), 1–17.

_____ ed., *Studies in the Philosophy of Thought and Action: British Academy Lectures.* OUP, 1968.

_____ and Wiggins, D. R. P., 'Herbert Paul Grice', *PBA* 111 (2000), 515–28.

Striker, G., 'Antipater, or the art of living', in *EHEE*, ch. 14. From Schofield and Striker, eds., *NN*, ch. 7.

_____ 'Ataraxia: happiness as tranquillity', in *EHEE*, ch. 9. From *Monist*, 73 (1989), 97–110.

_____ *Essays on Hellenistic Epistemology and Ethics.* CUP, 1996.

_____ 'Following nature: a study in Stoic ethics', in *EHEE*, ch. 12. From *OSAP* 9 (1991), 1–73.

_____ 'Origins of the concept of natural law', in *EHEE*, ch. 11. From *PBACAP* 2 (1987), 79–94.

_____ 'Plato's Socrates and the Stoics', in *EHEE*, ch. 15. From Vander Waerdt, ed., *SM*, ch. 9.

_____ 'The role of *oikeiôsis* in Stoic ethics', in *EHEE*, ch. 13. From *OSAP* 1 (1983), 145–67.

Stroud, B., *Hume.* RKP, 1977.

Stump, E. S., *Aquinas.* RKP, 2003.

_____ 'Sanctification, hardening of the heart, and Frankfurt's concept of free will', *JP* 85 (1988), 395–420.

Sturgeon, N. L., 'Brandt's moral empiricism', *PR* 91 (1982), 389–422.

_____ 'Contents and causes: a reply to Blackburn', *PhS* 61 (1991), 19–37.

_____ 'Hume on Reason and Passion', in D. Ainslie, ed., *Hume's Treatise: A Critical Guide.* CUP, forthcoming.

_____ 'Moore on ethical naturalism', *E* 113 (2003), 528–56.

_____ 'Moral explanations', in G. Sayre-McCord, ed., *EMR*, ch.10.

_____ 'Moral scepticism and moral naturalism in Hume's Treatise', *HS* 27 (2001), 3–83.

_____ 'Nature and conscience in Butler's ethics', *PR* 85 (1976), 316–56.

_____ 'What difference does it make whether moral realism is true?' *SJP* 24, suppl. (1986), 115–41.

Suarez, F., *De Bello*, in *OO* xii.

_____ *De Bonitate*, in *OO* iv.

_____ *Defensio Fidei Catholicae*, in *OO* xxiv.

_____ *On the Essence of Finite Being* (*DM* xxxi), tr. N J. Wells. Milwaukee: Marquette UP, 1983.

_____ *Opera Omnia*, 28 vols., ed. C. Berton. Paris: Vivès, 1866.

_____ *Selections from Three Works*, 2 vols. (vol. i, text; vol. ii, G. L. Williams et al., trs.). OUP, 1944.

_____ *The Metaphysics of Good and Evil according to Suarez*, tr. J. J. E. Gracia and D. Davis. Munich: Philosophia Verlag, 1989.

_____ *Tractatus de Legibus ac Deo Legislatore*, 8 vols., ed. L. Perena et al. Madrid: Consejo Superior de Investigaciones Cientificas, 1971–81.

Sullivan, R. J., *Immanuel Kant's Moral Theory.* CUP, 1989.

Swartz, R. J., ed., *Perceiving, Sensing, and Knowing*. Garden City, NY: Doubleday, 1965.

Sweet, W., 'F. H. Bradley and Bosanquet', in J. Bradley, ed., *Philosophy after F. H. Bradley*. Bristol: Thoemmes, 1996, ch. 2.

Tappert, T. G., ed., *The Book of Concord*. Philadelphia: Fortress, 1959.

Tarrant, H., 'The Hippias Major and Socratic theories of pleasure', in Vander Waerdt, ed., *SM*, ch. 4.

Taylor, A. E., *A Commentary on Plato's Timaeus*. OUP, 1928.

—— 'Francis Herbert Bradley', *PBA* 11 (1924–5), 458–68.

—— Review of Sidgwick, *EGSM, Hibbert Journal*, 1 (1903), 595–9.

—— 'Some features of Butler's ethics', in Taylor, *Philosophical Studies*. London: Macmillan, 1934, ch. 8 From *M* 35 (1926), 273–300.

—— 'The ethical doctrine of Hobbes', in Brown, ed., *HS*, ch. 2 (2). From *Phil.* 13 (1938), 406–24.

Taylor, C. C. W., Critical notice of Hare, *Freedom and Reason*. In Wallace and Walker, eds., *DM*, ch. 4. From *M* 74 (1965), 280–98.

—— 'Hellenistic ethics' (review of Schofield and Striker, eds., *NN*), *OSAP* 5 (1987), 235–45.

—— tr. and ed., *Plato's Protagoras*, rev. edn. OUP, 1991.

—— 'Pleasure, knowledge, and sensation in Democritus', *Phr.* 12 (1967), 6–27.

—— *The Atomists Leucippus and Democritus: Fragments*. Toronto: University of Toronto Press, 1999.

Taylor, C. M., *Hegel*. CUP, 1975.

—— *Sources of the Self*. HUP, 1989.

—— 'What is human agency?', in *Human Agency and Language*, i. CUP, 1985, ch. 1. From T. Mischel, *ed., The Self*. Oxford: Blackwell, 1977, 103–35.

Taylor, J., *Ductor Dubitantium*, in R. Heber, ed., *The Whole Works*, 15 vols. London: Ogle, Duncan, 1822, vol. xi.

Taylor, R., *Good and Evil: A New Direction*. New York: Macmillan, 1970.

TDNT

Te Selle, E., *Augustine the Theologian*. New York: Herder, 1970.

Tertullian, *Adversus Marcionem, PL* ii.

Thomas, D. O., *The Honest Mind: The Thought and Work of Richard Price*. OUP, 1977.

Thomas, G., *The Moral Philosophy of T. H. Green*. OUP, 1987.

Thomas, R., *Richard Price, Philosopher and Apostle of Liberty*. OUP, 1924.

Tierney, B., *The Idea of Natural Rights*. Atlanta: Scholars Press, 1997.

Tillotson, J. *Works*, 12 vols. London: Ware et al., 1742–4.

Tindal, M., *Christianity as Old as the Creation: or, the Gospel, a Republication of the Religion of* Nature. London, 1731.

Toland, J., *Christianity Not Mysterious: or a Treatise Showing that there is Nothing in the Gospel Contrary to Reason, nor Above it, and that No Christian Doctrine can be Properly Called a Mystery*, 2nd edn. London: Buckley, 1696 (repr. Bristol: Thoemmes, 1995).

Torrell, J. P., *Saint Thomas Aquinas, i (The Person and his Work)*. CUAP, 1996.

Toulmin, S. E., *An Examination of the Place of Reason in Ethics*. CUP, 1950.

Treloar, J. L., 'Moral virtue and the demise of prudence in the thought of Francis Suarez', *ACPQ* 65 (1991), 387–405.

Trinkaus, C. E., *In Our Image and Likeness: Humanity and Divinity in Italian Humanist Thought*. Chicago: U of Chicago Press, 1970.

Trollope, A., *The Warden*. London: Longman, 1855.

Trotsky, L., 'Their morals and ours', in *Their Morals and Ours: Marxist versus Liberal Views on Morality. Four Essays, by Leon Trotsky, John Dewey, George Novack*. New York: Merit Publishers, 1966.

Tsouna-McKirahan, V., 'Is there an exception to Greek eudaemonism?', in M. Canto-Sperber and P. Pellegrin, eds., *Le style de la pensée*. Paris: Les belles letters, 2002, 464–89.

_____ 'Socratic origins of Cynics and Cyrenaics', in Vander Waerdt, ed., *SM*, ch. 14.

_____ *The Epistemology of the Cyrenaic School*. CUP, 1998.

Tuck, R., 'Hobbes's moral philosophy', in Sorell, ed., *CCH*, ch. 8.

_____ *Natural Rights Theories: Their Origin and Development*. CUP, 1979.

_____ *Philosophy and Government, 1572–1651*. CUP, 1993.

_____ 'The "modern" theory of natural law', in A. Pagden, ed., *The Languages of Political Theory in Early-Modern Europe*. CUP, 1987, ch. 5.

Tucker, A. ('Edward Search'), *The Light of Nature Pursued*, 5 vols. London: Payne, 1768. Abridged by W. Hazlitt. London: Johnson, 1807.

Tulloch, J., *Rational Theology and Christian Philosophy*, 2 vols. 2nd edn. Edinburgh: Blackwood, 1874.

Turnbull, G., *The Principles of Moral Philosophy*. London: Millar, 1740.

Turner, F. M., *The Greek Heritage in Victorian Britain*. New Haven: Yale UP, 1981.

Tyrrell, J., *A Brief Disquisition of the Law of Nature*. London: Baldwin, 1692.

Urban, L. W., 'A revolution in Anglican moral theology', *Anglican Theological Review*, 53 (1971), 5–20.

Urmson, J. O., 'A defence of intuitionism', *PAS* 75, 1974–5, 111–19.

_____ 'The interpretation of the moral philosophy of J. S. Mill', in Schneewind, ed., *Mill*, 179–89. From *PQ* 3 (1953), 33–9.

Usener, H., *Epicurea*. Leipzig: Teubner, 1887. Cited as U.

Van Cleve, J., *Problems from Kant*. OUP, 1999.

Vander Waerdt, P. A., ed., *The Socratic Movement*. Ithaca, NY: Cornell UP, 1994.

Vasquez, G., *Commentaria ac Disputationes in Primam Secundae Sancti Thomae*, 2 vols. Ingolstadt, 1606.

Velleman, J. D., 'Brandt's definition of "good" ', *PR* 97 (1988), 353–71.

_____ 'Love as a moral emotion', *E* 109 (1999), 338–74.

Versenyi, L. G., *Socratic Humanism*. New Haven: Yale UP, 1963.

Villey, M., *La formation de la pensée juridique moderne*. Paris: Montchrestien, 1968.

Visser, S., and Williams, T., 'Anselm's account of freedom', *CJP* 31 (2001), 221–44.

Vivenza, G., *Adam Smith and the Classics*. OUP, 2002.

Vlastos, G., 'Justice and happiness in the *Republic*', in *PS*, ch. 5. From *Plato, ii*, ch. 5.

_____ ed., *Plato, ii*. Garden City, NY: Doubleday, 1971.

_____ *Platonic Studies*. PUP, 1981.

_____ *Socrates: Ironist and Moral Philosopher*. Ithaca: Cornell UP, 1991.

_____ 'Socrates on acrasia', in D. W. Graham, ed., *Studies in Greek Philosophy*, 2 vols. PUP, 1993–1995, ii, ch. 5. From *Phoenix*, 23 (1969), 71–88.

_____ *Socratic Studies*. CUP, 1994.

_____ 'The unity of the virtues in the *Protagoras*', in *PS*, ch. 4. From *RM* 25 (1972), 415–58.

Von Arnim, H., ed., *Stoicorum Veterum Fragmenta*, 4 vols. Leipzig: Teubner, 1903–24. Cited as SVF.

Von Wright, G. H., *The Varieties of Goodness*. RKP, 1963.

Vos., A., et al., eds., *Duns Scotus on Divine Love*. Aldershot: Ashgate, 2003.

Vulgate = Biblia Sacra Vulgata.

Wainewright, L., *A Vindication of Dr Paley's Theory of Morals*. London: Hatchard, 1830.

Wallace, G., and Walker, A. D. M., eds., *The Definition of Morality*. London: Methuen, 1970.

Wallace, R. J., 'How to argue about practical reason', *M* 99 (1990), 355–85.

Wallace, R. M., *Hegel's Philosophy of Reality, Freedom, and God*. CUP, 2005.

Walsh, J., 'Buridan on the connexion of the virtues', *JHP* 24 (1986), 453–82.

Walton, 'Life of Sanderson', in Sanderson, *Sermons*, i.

Wang Tch'ang-tche, J., *Saint Augustin et les vertus des paiens*. Paris: Beauchesne, 1938.

Warburton, W., *The Divine Legation of Moses Demonstrated*, 2nd edn., 4 vols. London: Fletcher Gyles, 1738.

Ward, K., *The Development of Kant's View of Ethics*. Oxford: Blackwell, 1972.

Ward, W. G., 'Mr Mill on the foundations of morality', *Dublin Review*, 18 (1872), 44–76.

—— *On Nature and Grace*. London: Burns and Lambert, 1860.

Warda, A. *Immanuel Kants Bücher*. Berlin: Breslauer, 1922.

Warner, M., 'Love, self, and Plato's *Symposium*', *PQ* 29 (1979), 329–39.

Warnock, G. J., *Contemporary Moral Philosophy*. London: Macmillan, 1967.

—— *The Object of Morality*. London: Methuen, 1971.

Warrender, H., 'The place of God in Hobbes's philosophy: a reply to Mr Plamenatz', in Brown, ed., *HS*, ch. 4 (2). From *PS* 8 (1960), 48–57.

Waterland, D., 'A supplement to . . . the nature, obligation, and efficacy . . .', in *Works*, iv 105–48 (orig. pub. 1730).

—— 'On self-love'. Sermon 3 in Sermons collected 1741–2, in *Works*, v 446–62.

—— 'Remarks upon Dr Clarke's exposition of the Church Catechism', in *Works*, iv 1–50.

—— 'The nature, obligation, and efficacy of the Christian sacraments considered', in *Works*, iv 53–104 (orig. pub. 1730).

—— 'The duty of loving our neighbour as ourselves explained', in *Works*, v 436–45.

—— *Works*, 6 vols., ed. W. van Mildert. OUP, 1856.

Watkins, J. W. N., *Hobbes's System of Ideas: A Study in the Political Significance of Philosophical Theories*. London: Hutchinson, 1965.

Watson, G. L., 'Free agency', in G. L. Watson ed., *Free Will*. OUP, 1982, ch. 7. From *JP* 72 (1975), 202–20.

Weber, M., *Methodology of the Social Sciences*, ed. E. A. Shils and H. A. Finch. New York: Free Press, 1949.

Wedgwood, R. N., *The Nature of Normativity*. OUP, 2007.

Weinfeld, M., *Deuteronomy 1–11*. New York: Doubleday, 1991.

Welchman, J., 'G. E. Moore and the revolution in ethics', *HPQ* 6 (1989), 317–29.

Wendel, F., *Calvin: Origin and Development of his Religious Thought*. London: Collins, 1963.

Wesley, J., *Sermons*, in *The Works of John Wesley*, i, ed. A. C. Outler. OUP, 1984.

Westberg, D., *Right Practical Reason: Aristotle, Action, and Prudence in Aquinas*. OUP, 1994.

Westermarck, E., *Ethical Relativity*. London: Kegan Paul, 1932.

—— *The Origin and Development of the Moral Ideas*, 2 vols., 2nd edn. London: Macmillan, 1912 (vol. i), 1917 (vol. ii).

Westminster Confession, in Schaff, *CC iii*.

Westphal, K., 'The basic context and structure of Hegel's *Philosophy of Right*', in F. C. Beiser, ed., *The Cambridge Companion to Hegel*. CUP, 1993, ch. 8.

Wetzel, J., *Augustine and the Limits of Virtue*. CUP, 1992.

Whately, R., *Introductory Lessons on Morals*. London: Parker, 1855.

—— *Paley's Moral Philosophy, with annotations*. London: Parker, 1859.

Whewell, W., ed., *Butler's Three Sermons on Human Nature*. Cambridge: Deighton, 1848.

—— *Elements of Morality*, 4th edn. Cambridge: Deighton, Bell, 1864 (1st edn., 1845).

—— *Lectures on Systematic Morality*. London: Parker, 1846.

—— *Lectures on the History of Moral Philosophy in England*. London: Parker, 1852.

—— *On the Foundations of Morals, Four Sermons* (1837), 2nd edn. London: Parker 1839.

—— Preface to Mackintosh, *DPEP*.

—— *The Platonic Dialogues for English Readers*, 3 vols. London: Macmillan, 1859–61.

Whichcote, B., *Moral and Religious Aphorisms*, ed. J. Jeffery and S. Salter. London: Payne, 1753.

—— *Select Sermons*. London: 1698.

White, A. R., 'Conscience and self-love in Butler's Sermons', *Phil.* 27 (1952), 329–44.

White, N. P., *A Companion to Plato's Republic*. Indianapolis: Hackett, 1979.

____ *Individual and Conflict in Greek Ethics*. OUP, 2002.

____ 'Rational prudence in Plato's *Gorgias*', in D. J. O'Meara, ed., *Platonic Investigations*. CUAP, 1985, ch. 6.

____ 'Stoic values', *Monist*, 73 (1990), 42–58.

____ 'The basis of Stoic ethics', *Harvard Studies in Classical Philology*, 83 (1979), 143–78.

Whiteley, C. H., 'On duties', *PAS* 52, (1952–3), 95–104.

Whitfield, J. H., *Discourses on Machiavelli*. Cambridge: Heffer, 1969.

Whiting, J. E., 'Aristotle's function argument: a defence', *AP* 8 (1988), 33–48.

____ 'Friends and future selves', *PR* 95 (1986), 547–80.

____ 'The Nicomachean account of friendship', in R. Kraut, ed., *The Blackwell Guide to Aristotle's Ethics*. Oxford: Blackwell, 2006, ch. 13.

Whittaker, J. *See* Alcinous.

Wieland, G., 'Aristotle's *Ethics*: reception and interpretation', in Kretzmann et al., eds., *CHLMP*, ch. 34.

____ 'Happiness: the perfection of man', in Kretzmann et al., eds., *CHLMP*, ch. 35.

Wiggins, D. R. P., 'Deliberation and practical reason', in *NVT*, ch. 6. From *PAS* 76 (1975–6), 29–51.

____ *Needs, Values, Truth*. Oxford: Blackwell, 1987.

____ 'Weakness of will, commensurability, and the objects of deliberation and desire', in *NVT*, ch. 7. From *PAS* 79 (1978), 251–77.

Wiles, M. F., *Archetypal Heresy: Arianism through the Centuries*. OUP, 1996.

Williams, B. A. O., 'Acting as the virtuous person acts', in Heinaman, ed., *AMR* 13–23.

____ *Descartes: The Project of Pure Enquiry*. Harmondsworth: Penguin, 1978.

____ 'Ethics and the fabric of the world', in Honderich, ed., *MO*, ch. 9. Repr. in Williams, *MSH*, ch. 14.

____ *Ethics and the Limits of Philosophy*. HUP, 1985.

____ 'Internal and external reasons', in *ML*, ch. 8.

____ *Making Sense of Humanity*. CUP, 1995.

____ *Moral Luck*. CUP, 1981.

____ 'Moral luck' in *ML*, ch. 2.

____ 'Persons, character, and morality', in *ML*, ch. 1.

____ 'Replies', in Altham and Harrison, eds., *WME*, ch. 10.

____ *Shame and Necessity*. UCP, 1993.

____ 'Voluntary acts and responsible agents', in *MSH*, ch. 2.

____ 'What does intuitionism imply?', in *MSH*, ch. 15. From J. Moravcsik and C. C. W. Taylor, eds., *Human Agency: Language, Duty, and Value*, Stanford, Calif.: Stanford UP, 1988.

Williams, N. P., *The Ideas of the Fall and of Original Sin*. London: Longmans, Green, 1927.

Williams, T., ed., *Cambridge Companion to Duns Scotus*. CUP, 2003.

____ 'How Scotus separates morality from happiness', *ACPA* 69 (1995), 425–45.

____ *The Moral Philosophy of John Duns Scotus*. Doctoral Dissertation, U. Notre Dame, 1994.

Wilson, J. M., and Fowler, T., *Principles of Morals*. OUP, 1886.

Winch, P. G., 'Can a good man be harmed?', in *EA*, ch. 10. From *PAS* 66 (1965–6), 55–70.

____ *Ethics in Action*. RKP, 1972.

____ 'Moral integrity', in *EA*, ch. 9.

____ *The Idea of a Social Science and its Relation to Philosophy*. RKP, 1958.

____ 'Understanding a primitive society', in *EA*, ch. 2. From *APQ* 1 (1964), 307–24.

Winkler, K. P., 'Hutcheson's alleged realism', *JHP* 23 (1985), 179–94.

Wippel, J. F., 'Thomas Aquinas and the condemnation of 1277', *Modern Schoolman*, 72 (1994–5), 233–72.

Wishart, W., *A Vindication of the Reverend D—B—from the scandalous imputation of being the author of a late book, intitled Alciphron or the Minute Philosopher*. Edinburgh: Wilford, 1734.

Witherspoon, J., *Ecclesiastical Characteristics, or the Arcana of Church Polity, being an Humble Attempt to Open Up the Mystery of Moderation . . .*, 2nd edn. Glasgow, 1754.

Wittgenstein, L., *The Blue and Brown Books*. Oxford: Blackwell, 1958.

Wittmann, M., *Die Ethik des hl. Thomas von Aquin*. Munich: Hüber, 1933.

Wizenmann, T., 'An Herrn Kant von der Verfasser der Resultate der Jacobisher und Mendelsohnischer Philosophie', in Hausius K. G., ed., *Materialen zur Geschichte der kritischen Philosophie*, 3 vols. in 1. Düsseldorf: Stern-Verlag Janssen & co, 1969, ii 103–44 (orig. pub. 1793).

Wolf, S., 'Self-interest and interest in selves', *E* 96 (1986), 704–20.

Wolff, R. P., *The Autonomy of Reason: A Commentary on Kant's Groundwork of the Metaphysics of Morals*. New York: Harper and Row, 1973.

Wolfson, H. A., *The Philosophy of Spinoza: Unfolding the Latent Process of his Reasoning*, 2 vols. in 1. HUP, 1948 (1st pub. 1934).

Wolin, R., ed., *The Heidegger Controversy: A Critical Reader*. Cambridge, Mass.: MIT Press, 1993.

Wollheim, R. A., *F. H. Bradley*, rev. edn. Harmondsworth: Penguin, 1969.

—— 'The good self and the bad self: the moral psychology of British idealism and the English school of psychoanalysis compared', *PBA* 61 (1975), 373–98.

Wolter, A. B., tr. and ed., *Duns Scotus on the Will and Morality*. CUAP, 1986.

—— 'Duns Scotus on the will as rational potency', in *PTJDS*, ch. 8.

—— 'Native freedom of the will as a key to the ethics of Scotus', in *PTJDS*, ch. 7.

—— *The Philosophical Theology of John Duns Scotus*. Ithaca, NY: Cornell UP, 1990.

Wood, A. W., 'Fichte's Philosophy of Right and Ethics', in G. Zöller, ed., *The Cambridge Companion to Fichte*. CUP, forthcoming.

—— *Hegel's Ethical Thought*. CUP, 1990.

—— Introduction to Kant, *PP*, tr. Gregor.

—— *Kant's Ethical Theory*. CUP, 1999.

—— *Kant's Moral Religion*. Ithaca, NY: Cornell UP, 1970.

—— *Karl Marx*. RKP, 1981.

—— 'The "I" as principle of practical philosophy', in Sedgwick, ed., *RKCP*, ch. 4.

Wood, R., *Ockham on the Virtues*. West Lafayette, Ind.: Purdue UP, 1997.

Wright, C., 'Moral values, projection, and secondary qualities', *SPAS* 72 (1988), 1–26.

—— 'The moral organism', in Manser and Stock, eds., *PFHB*, ch. 4.

Xenophon, Loeb, vol. 7. Cited: [Xenophon] *Athenaiôn Politeia*, ed. and tr. G. W. Bowersock.

—— OCT. Cited: *Memorabilia; Symposium*.

Yaffe, G., *Manifest Activity: Thomas Reid's Theory of Action*. OUP, 2004.

Zagorin, P., *Ways of Lying*. HUP, 1990.

Zeller, E., *Die Philosophie der Griechen in ihrer geschichtliche Entwicklung*, 5th edn., 6 vols. Leipzig: Reisland, 1920–3.

INDEX

The numbers refer to sections, not to pages.